America Votes 31

SAGE was founded in 1965 by Sara Miller McCune to support the dissemination of usable knowledge by publishing innovative and high-quality research and teaching content. Today, we publish more than 850 journals, including those of more than 300 learned societies, more than 800 new books per year, and a growing range of library products including archives, data, case studies, reports, and video. SAGE remains majority-owned by our founder, and after Sara's lifetime will become owned by a charitable trust that secures our continued independence.

Los Angeles | London | New Delhi | Singapore | Washington DC

America Votes 31

ELECTION RETURNS BY STATE

RHODES COOK

2013–2014

Los Angeles | London | New Delhi
Singapore | Washington DC

Los Angeles | London | New Delhi
Singapore | Washington DC

FOR INFORMATION:

CQ Press
An Imprint of SAGE Publications, Inc.
2455 Teller Road
Thousand Oaks, California 91320
E-mail: order@sagepub.com

SAGE Publications Ltd.
1 Oliver's Yard
55 City Road
London, EC1Y 1SP
United Kingdom

SAGE Publications India Pvt. Ltd.
B 1/I 1 Mohan Cooperative Industrial Area
Mathura Road, New Delhi 110 044
India

SAGE Publications Asia-Pacific Pte. Ltd.
3 Church Street
#10–04 Samsung Hub
Singapore 049483

Acquisitions Editor: Andrew Boney
Editorial Assistance: Jordan Enobakhare
Researcher: John Engelken
Database Lead: Roylene Kulesza
Database Team: Sal Hewavita, Troy King, and Andre Messier
Production Editor: David C. Felts
Typesetter: Hurix Systems Pvt. Ltd., India
Proofreader: Lawrence W. Baker
Cover Designer: Michael Dubowe
Marketing Managers: Carmel Schrire, Teri Williams

Printed in the United States of America.

ISSN: 0065-678X
ISBN: 978-1-4833-8303-3

SFI Certified Sourcing
www.sfiprogram.org
SFI-00453

This book is printed on acid-free paper.

15 16 17 18 19 10 9 8 7 6 5 4 3 2 1

Contents

List of Maps

Introduction

In recent years, presidential and midterm elections have produced distinctly different outcomes. The former, with their larger turnouts of minority and young voters, have been more favorable to the Democrats. The party has won four of the last six presidential elections and the popular vote in a fifth.

Without the excitement of a presidential race, midterm elections generate much lower turnouts that tend to be older, whiter, and more favorable to the Republicans. That was the case in 2014, as the GOP came out of the November election holding the Senate, the House of Representatives, a vast majority of the nation's governorships, and an even larger share of state legislatures.

In the process, Republicans have built up impressive majorities at virtually every level of government below the presidency, that with the exception of the Senate, Democrats could find difficult to undo any time soon.

Republicans finished the 2014 election with 54 of 100 Senate seats (54% of the total), 247 out of 435 House seats (57%), 31 of 50 governorships (62%), and 68 of 98 state legislative chambers (69%). (Nebraska has an officially non-partisan, unicameral legislature.)

Altogether, Republicans in 2014 registered a net gain of nine Senate seats, 13 House seats, two governorships, and nine state legislative chambers (all based on a comparison with its numbers on election eve). That brought the GOP control of the Senate for the first time in six years and increased their advantage in the House and the states.

Along the way, Republicans made history. They elected their largest number of senators since 2004; their highest total of governors since 1998; their greatest number of House members since 1928; and according to the National Conference of State Legislatures, their highest total of state legislative seats since 1920 (roughly 4,100 out of 7,400).

The one fly in the ointment for Republicans was that their 2014 success was achieved against the backdrop of an unusually low turnout. More than eight million fewer votes were cast for the House in 2014 than was the case four years earlier, when the "Tea Party" was fresh and new.

Still, Republicans succeeded grandly in 2014 by dominating their home turf, a large sector of the country that has sometimes been referred to as the Republican "L."

2014: GOP Romps

Recent midterm elections have been very kind to the Republican Party. The GOP won the House of Representatives in 2010 and gained control of the Senate in 2014. In addition, the 2014 balloting increased the Republican majority in the House, as well as the party's already significant advantage over the Democrats in the states, both in terms of governorships and state legislatures held. Partisan totals in each category are from immediately before and immediately after the November 2014 election. The preelection House totals include Democratic vacancies in New Jersey and North Carolina, which are credited to the Democrats, and a Republican vacancy in Virginia, which is credited to the GOP. Two independent senators who caucused with the Democrats, Angus King of Maine and Bernard Sanders of Vermont, are listed in the "Other" column. There was one independent governor elected in 2014, Bill Walker of Alaska.

	Preelection			Postelection		
	Rep.	Dem.	Other	Rep.	Dem.	Other
Governor	29	21	0	31	18	1
Senate	45	53	2	54	44	2
House	234	201	0	247	188	0

The cornerstone of the "L" is the South (the 11 states of the old Confederacy plus Kentucky and Oklahoma). It also includes the Plains states (Kansas, Nebraska, North and South Dakota) and the Mountain West (which includes Alaska). Altogether, 26 states comprise the "L."

The new Republican Senate was crafted in this swath of the country. Of the nine Senate seats that the GOP gained in 2014, three were in the Mountain West (Alaska, Colorado, and Montana), three more were in the South (Arkansas, Louisiana, and North Carolina), and one was in the Plains (South Dakota). The two other GOP Senate pick-ups were in Iowa, a battleground state in the agricultural Midwest, and West Virginia, geographically joined to the Democratic Northeast but more similar to the Republican South in its recent voting habits.

Of the 23 Senate races held last fall within the "L," Democrats won only two—reelecting Tom Udall in New Mexico and Mark Warner in Virginia. The latter won a second term by less than 20,000 votes out of nearly 2.2 million cast, a margin of less than 1 percentage point. Warner ultimately prevailed by rolling up the vote in the populous suburbs of Northern Virginia, a region of the state more akin to the Northeast than the South.

Warner's close call was one of several races in 2014 that forecasters largely missed. His was not considered a contest to watch, even though he trailed his Republican challenger, Ed Gillespie, on Election Night until the vote from Northern Virginia began to pour in late in the evening.

Across the Potomac River in Maryland, Republican Larry Hogan was elected governor in an outright upset. The assumption throughout the fall was that the Democratic lieutenant governor, Anthony Brown, was cruising to the governorship in bright blue Maryland. But in a complete surprise, voters elected Hogan, only the second Republican to win the Annapolis state house since Spiro Agnew in 1966.

2014: Close House Races

The number of highly competitive House races in 2014 continued their steady downward trend. In 2010, 55 members won with less than 52 percent of the total vote. Two years later, the number was down to 33. And in 2014, the total of sub–52 percent House winners was 27. The majority of close House winners were Democrats, most of whom were incumbents. In contrast, virtually all of the Republican House winners who were elected in 2014 with less than 52 percent were challengers or open-seat candidates. An asterisk (*) indicates an incumbent.

Republicans (13)	2014 Winning Percentage	Democrats (14)	2014 Winning Percentage
Bruce Poliquin, ME. 2	47.0%	Rick Nolan, MN. 8*	48.5%
Alex Mooney, WV. 2	47.1%	Brad Ashford, NE. 2	48.9%
Cresent Hardy, NV. 4	48.5%	John Delaney, MD. 6*	49.7%
Will Hurd, TX. 23	49.8%	Sean Patrick Maloney, NY. 18*	49.7%
Martha McSally, AZ. 2	50.0%	Louise Slaughter, NY. 25*	50.2%
Mia Love, UT. 4	50.9%	Ami Bera, CA. 7*	50.4%
Don Young, AK. AL*	51.0%	Gwen Graham, FL. 2	50.5%
Rod Blum, IA. 1	51.1%	Jim Costa, CA. 16*	50.7%
Robert Dold, IL. 10	51.3%	Julia Brownley, CA. 26*	51.3%
Carlos Curbelo, FL. 26	51.5%	Emanuel Cleaver, MO. 5*	51.6%
Frank Guinta, NH. 1	51.7%	Scott Peters, CA. 52*	51.6%
French Hill, AR. 2	51.9%	Pete Aguilar, CA. 31	51.7%
Mike Coffman, CO. 6*	51.9%	Lois Capps, CA. 24*	51.9%
		Mark Takai, HI. 1	51.9%

Meanwhile, in Democratic Vermont, two-term governor Peter Shumlin was taken to overtime by Republican businessman Scott Milne. Shumlin, the head of the Democratic Governors Association, was widely expected to win a comfortable reelection victory. Instead, he finished ahead in the balloting by less than 2,500 votes out of nearly 200,000 cast and fell short of the majority required by state law to win the election outright. The contest was decided in Shumlin's favor by the Democratic legislature in January.

Exit polling showed major reasons for the Democratic travails in 2014. Two years earlier, President Barack Obama won more than 90% of the African-American vote, and better than 70% of both the Hispanic and Asian vote. Without Obama on the ballot in 2014, the Democratic share of the African-American vote fell short of 90%, the closely watched (and gradually expanding) Hispanic vote was barely 60% Democratic, and the party's share of the Asian vote less than 50%. Meanwhile, the 18-to-29 year-old vote, which went 60% for Obama in 2012, was less than 55% Democratic in 2014.

Obama has played a significant role in recent elections. In presidential election years, his presence on the ballot has boosted the entire Democratic ticket. His party enlarged its congressional majorities in 2008 and fended off the Republicans to hold the Senate in 2012.

However, midterm elections during the Obama presidency have been little short of a disaster for Democrats. They lost the House in 2010, and the Senate in 2014, as well as losing considerable ground in the states in both years. For Democrats, it was as though they took one step forward in years that Obama was on the ballot and two steps backward when he was not.

A Look at the House

Obama's approval rating has stayed below 50% for much of his presidency, but it has been much lower than that for Congress. There are a number of words used nowadays to describe the acrimony on Capitol Hill, many of which are not very complimentary. "Partisan," "polarized," and "dysfunctional," are just a few that are regularly used. But while sharp ideological differences are often fingered as a source of the problem, a contributing factor could be geography.

When it comes to the House of Representatives, neither party is truly a national force. Republicans have the most congressional seats in the South and the Midwest. Democrats have the upper hand in the Northeast and the West.

The House Since 1990: A Political Weathervane

After a 40-year drought, Republicans gained control of the House of Representatives in 1994 and have stayed in control all but four years since. In the 2014 election, they reached a post–World War II high of 247 seats. The cornerstone of the GOP congressional majority is the South, where they hold nearly three-quarters of the 149 House seats, by far the most seats in any region of the country. Republicans also have a decided advantage in the Midwest. Democrats still control a majority of House seats in the East and the West. Regions are defined below. An "I" indicates independent, although there has been no independent House member elected since 2004.

	South				West			Midwest			East				Total House			
	R	D	I		R	D		R	D		R	D	I		R	D	I	
1990	44	85	0	D	37	48	D	45	68	D	41	66	1	D	167	267	1	D
1992	52	85	0	D	38	55	D	44	61	D	42	57	1	D	176	258	1	D
1994	73	64	0	R	53	40	R	59	46	R	45	54	1	D	230	204	1	R
1996	82	55	0	R	51	42	R	55	50	R	39	60	1	D	227	207	1	R
1998	82	55	0	R	49	44	R	54	51	R	38	61	1	D	223	211	1	R
2000	81	55	1	R	43	50	D	57	48	R	40	59	1	D	221	212	2	R
2002	85	57	0	R	46	52	D	61	39	R	37	57	1	D	229	205	1	R
2004	91	51	0	R	45	53	D	60	40	R	36	58	1	D	232	202	1	R
2006	85	57	0	R	41	57	D	51	49	R	25	70	0	D	202	233	0	D
2008	80	62	0	R	35	63	D	45	55	D	18	77	0	D	178	257	0	D
2010	102	40	0	R	43	55	D	65	35	R	32	63	0	D	242	193	0	R
2012	108	41	0	R	39	63	D	59	35	R	28	62	0	D	234	201	0	R
2014	111	38	0	R	41	61	D	61	33	R	34	56	0	D	247	188	0	R
Net Change in GOP Seats, 1994–2012	+ 38				− 12			+ 2			− 11				+ 17			

EAST - Connecticut, Delaware, Maine, Maryland, Massachusetts, New Hampshire, New Jersey, New York, Pennsylvania, Rhode Island, Vermont, West Virginia.

MIDWEST - Illinois, Indiana, Iowa, Kansas, Michigan, Minnesota, Missouri, Nebraska, North Dakota, Ohio, South Dakota, Wisconsin.

SOUTH - Alabama, Arkansas, Florida, Georgia, Kentucky, Louisiana, Mississippi, North Carolina, Oklahoma, South Carolina, Tennessee, Texas, Virginia.

WEST - Alaska, Arizona, California, Colorado, Hawaii, Idaho, Montana, Nevada, New Mexico, Oregon, Utah, Washington, Wyoming.

It has not always been this way. On the eve of the 1994 election, when the curtain was coming down on the Democrats' 40-year House reign, the party controlled a clear majority of House seats in all four regions of the country. When Republicans took control in 1994, the GOP had an advantage over the Democrats in three regions (all but the Northeast). The current GOP House dominates only two regions. And it can arguably be said that the Republican majority in the 114th Congress is based on overwhelming dominance in just one of them, the South.

There, the Republican advantage in House seats has swelled to the point that it is a virtual monopoly. The GOP had a 9-seat Southern edge coming out of the 1994 election by 2010, the margin was up to 62. And following the 2014 voting, the tally of House seats in the South stood at Republicans 111, Democrats 38 – a 73-seat advantage for the GOP in a region that a generation or two ago was solidly Democratic.

In seven Southern states, Democrats won no more than a single House seat in 2014. And across the Deep South from the Atlantic Ocean to the Texas border, the eight Democrats elected last time were all African American. Southern white Democrats—who once not only ruled the region, but often the Democratic congressional leadership as well—have become an endangered species.

Take away the South and the Democrats enjoyed a 14-seat edge in the rest of the country. But to be fair, removing the liberal kingpins of California and New York, where Democrats had a combined 34-seat advantage after the 2014 election, and the "loyal opposition" had a huge deficit of 93 seats in the remaining 48 states (224 to 131).

As it is, Republicans finished the 2014 election with 247 House seats, their highest number since the 1920s, compared to 188 seats for the Democrats. It could have been worse for the latter. Toward midnight on Election

2014: Defeated Incumbents

A disproportionate number of members of Congress who lost their seats in 2014 were Democrats, not surprising given the Republican nature of the year. Yet the most high-profile member to be defeated was a Republican, House Majority Leader Eric Cantor, who was upset in a GOP primary in his central Virginia district by a political unknown, Randolph-Macon economics professor Dave Brat. No one saw the lightning strike coming, including Cantor. Meanwhile, elements of the "Tea Party" mounted aggressive primary challenges in 2014 to six veteran Republican senators, but failed to net a single scalp. The senator who drew the most serious challenge, Thad Cochran of Mississippi, lost the GOP primary to his more conservative challenger, state Sen. Chris McDaniel. But since none of the candidates achieved a majority of the primary vote, a runoff was held in which Cochran prevailed.

The table below lists the gubernatorial, Senate, and House incumbents defeated in the 2014 primaries and general election, the number of full terms in office they were completing at the time of their loss in 2014, the percentage of the vote they received in the previous general election (2008 for senators, 2010 for governors, and 2012 for House members), and their percentage of the total vote in the 2014 general election (for those who were not sidelined in the primaries).

	Number of Terms	Previous General Election Percentage	2014 General Election Percentage
GOVERNORS (4)			
Primaries (1)			
(1 Democrat)			
Neil Abercrombie, D-Hawaii	1	58.2%	31.5%
General Election (3)			
(2 Republicans, 1 Democrat)			
Tom Corbett, R-Pa.	1	54.5%	41.5%
Sean Parnell, R-Alaska	1	59.1%	48.8%
Pat Quinn, D-Ill.	1	46.8%	46.3%
SENATORS (5)			
Primaries (0)			
General Election (5)			
(5 Democrats)			
Mark Begich, D-Alaska	1	47.8%	45.8%
Kay Hagan, D-N.C.	1	52.7%	47.3%
Mary Landrieu, D-La.*	3	52.1%	44.1%
Mark Pryor, D-Ark.	2	79.5%	39.4%
Mark Udall, D-Colo.	1	52.8%	46.3%
REPRESENTATIVES (18)			
Primaries (4)			
(3 Republicans, 1 Democrat)			
Kerry Bentivolio, R-Mich. 11)	1	50.8%	—
Eric Cantor, R-Va. 7	7	58.4%	—
Ralph Hall, R-Texas 4#	17	73.0%	—
John Tierney, D-Mass. 6	9	48.3%	—

General Election (14)
(11 Democrats, 3 Republicans)

Ron Barber, D-Ariz. 2	1	50.4%	49.9%
John Barrow, D-Ga. 12	5	53.7%	45.2%
Tim Bishop, D-N.Y. 1	6	52.5%	45.5%
Bill Enyart, D-Ill. 12	1	51.7%	41.9%
Pete Gallego, D-Texas 23	1	50.3%	47.7%
Joe Garcia, D-Fla. 26	1	53.6%	48.5%
Steven Horsford, D-Nev. 4	1	50.1%	45.8%
Dan Maffei, D-N.Y. 24	2	48.8%	40.3%
Vance McAllister, R-La. 5	@	—	11.1%
Nick Rahall, D-W.V. 3	19	54.0%	44.6%
Brad Schneider, D- Ill. 10	1	50.6%	48.7%
Carol Shea-Porter, D-N.H. 1	3	49.8%	48.1%
Steve Southerland, R-Fla. 2	2	52.7%	49.3%
Lee Terry, R-Neb. 2	8	50.8%	45.6%

Note: An asterisk (*) denotes that the 2014 percentage for Sen. Mary Landrieu (D-La.) was based on a December 2014 runoff election. The icon "@" indicates that Vance McAllister (R-La. 5) was elected in a special election in 2013 and had not served a full term at the time he was defeated.

Night, it looked as though Republican House gains might approach 20. But when all the ballots had been tallied, the GOP net gain in the House stood at 13. The reason: Democratic candidates played great defense in California. Of the 11 seats decided in the Golden State with less than 55% of the total vote, Democrats took 10 of them, including all eight that were determined by less than five percentage points.

The Methodology

The thirty-first edition of *America Votes* follows the same format of recent editions in this series. The introductory text and a variety of summary tables that accompany it seek to tie together basic aspects of the 2014 election cycle. The section that follows presents national tables of voter turnout as well as the aggregate vote for gubernatorial, Senate, and House elections by state in 2014.

The turnout table uses voter registration and "citizen" voting-age population figures compiled by the Census Bureau. In the latter, the millions and millions of noncitizens in the United States age 18 years and older are not included, giving a truer sense of the voter turnout rate than if all persons of voting age were included.

The overview material also features a summary of special elections held between the general elections of 2012 and 2014 that filled vacancies in the 113th Congress. There is also a list of changes in the congressional membership in the 114th Congress that occurred between the

2014 general election and September 15, 2015. The heart of the volume, 50 chapters—one for each state—follows the introductory material.

Each state chapter begins with a list of the current governor, senators, and representatives, followed by tables with the statewide vote for president, governor, and senator from the end of World War II (1945) to the present. A map of the state shows its counties, major population centers, and congressional districts for members of the House in the 114th Congress. Other maps are included in states with one or more particularly large population center that features a number of congressional districts. County-by-county tables of gubernatorial and Senate elections follow the maps. All these tables are from the 2014 general election, with the exception of gubernatorial contests in New Jersey and Virginia and special Senate elections in Massachusetts and New Jersey, all of which were held in 2013.

In most cases, the county tables for gubernatorial and Senate elections feature three columns of votes (Republican, Democratic, and Other). Exceptions occur where an independent or third-party candidate has received at least 10% of the statewide vote, in which case a column for his or her vote is also included. All the county tables include 2010 population figures from the Census Bureau.

A listing of votes cast for the House of Representatives is arranged by congressional district. The implementation of the 2010 Census for redistricting purposes led to changes before the 2012 election in district boundaries in all states with more than one House member. House results for elections before 2012 are not included for any state except those with a single House seat.

The conclusion of each state chapter consists of two parts. The first is a notes section containing a breakdown of votes cast in the general election for third party, independent, and write-in candidates. The total of scattered write-in votes is listed in states where they were included in the official returns. For those major party candidates who also ran on a third party ballot line, most notably the case in New York, votes are aggregated as Democratic or Republican.

The second part deals with primary elections. It opens with an explanation of who could vote in the state's primary in 2014 as well as voter registration totals at the time of the primary election. The latter is broken down by party in the 30 or so states in which voters register by party. This material is followed by Democratic and Republican primary results for governor, senator, and House held in the 2014 election cycle, as well as the results for runoff elections in states, mainly in the South, that held them.

In the six New England states, tables list the vote for governor and senator by larger cities and towns as well as by counties. In Rhode Island, the results are listed for all cities and towns.

The *America Votes* series is compiled from official results obtained from election authorities in each state. Although complete accuracy is always the goal, it can sometimes prove elusive in a work such as this. On occasion, states may belatedly report changes in their vote totals that occur after publication of this volume. And human nature being what it is, there is always an example or two (or three) of self-inflicted errors. The goal is always to keep these to a minimum. In light of the desire to make these reference volumes as useful as possible to readers and researchers, corrections of data are always welcome as are suggestions for new material.

The creation of each edition in this series has always taken a small army. Andrew Boney, the Acquisitions Editor at CQ Press, efficiently spearheaded this edition with patience and expertise. He was ably assisted by John Engelken, who worked tirelessly to help database election returns, verify election results, and provide other valuable assistance during the creation of this book. A tip of the cap is also in order to Roylene Kulesza and her team of technical experts, Sal Hewavita, Troy King, and Andrew Messier, for their database expertise and heroic work in creating the framework for the tables that you see in this book. And no list of acknowledgments is complete without mention of the book's production editor, David C. Felts, who was instrumental in turning this mass of tables and data into a book that readers will hopefully find quite usable.

Rhodes Cook
September 2015

Errata

America Votes 30

The following corrections should be made in the previous edition of *America Votes 30*, covering the 2011–2012 election cycle.

Page 60. In the Alabama 7th District Republican primary, the asterisk (*) should be deleted from next to the name of Don Chamberlain. He was not the incumbent.

Page 73. In the Arizona 6th District Republican primary, an asterisk (*) should have been placed next to the name of Ben Quayle to indicate that he was an incumbent.

Page 89. California had party registration in 2012, although all registered voters were permitted to vote in the state's primary.

Page 192. In the Louisiana gubernatorial results table, the name of the 2003 Democratic candidate was "Blanco, Kathleen Babineaux."

Page 211. In the Maryland party registration table, the Republican and Democratic numbers were basically reversed. There were roughly twice as many Democrats in Maryland as Republicans.

Page 231. In the Michigan 3rd District Republican primary, Steven Butler was a write-in candidate. That was not designated.

Page 306. In the New Mexico party registration table, the Republican and Democratic totals were reversed. They should read: Democratic, 576,456; Republican, 381,053.

Page 384. In the South Dakota party registration table, the number of active registered voters should read: Republican 235,620; Democratic, 185,844; Other, 1,927; Independent, 87,812; Total, 511,203. In addition, there were 54,689 inactive registered voters at the time of the 2012 primary.

UNITED STATES
VOTER TURNOUT 2014

State	2014 Est. Total Voting-Age Citizen Population	2014 Est. Total Registered Voters	Est. Percent of Registered Voting-Age Citizens	House Vote	Senate Vote	Governor Vote	High Race	High Race Vote	High Race Vote as Percentage of Est. Voting-Age Citizen Population	House Vote as Percentage of Est. Voting-Age Citizen Population
ALABAMA	3,519,000	2,366,000	67.2	1,080,880	818,090	1,180,413	G	1,180,413	33.5	30.7
ALASKA	503,000	336,000	66.8	279,741	282,400	279,958	S	282,400	56.1	55.6
ARIZONA	4,397,000	2,738,000	62.3	1,467,601		1,506,416	G	1,506,416	34.3	33.4
ARKANSAS	2,057,000	1,292,000	62.8	830,652	847,505	848,592	G	848,592	41.3	40.4
CALIFORNIA	24,455,000	14,113,000	57.7	7,132,641		7,317,581	G	7,317,581	29.9	29.2
COLORADO	3,732,000	2,654,000	71.1	2,000,525	2,041,058	2,041,607	G	2,041,607	54.7	53.6
CONNECTICUT	2,560,000	1,668,000	65.1	1,067,857		1,092,773	G	1,092,773	42.7	41.7
DELAWARE	661,000	442,000	66.8	231,617	234,038		S	234,038	35.4	35.0
FLORIDA	13,879,000	8,691,000	62.6	4,998,555		5,951,561	G	5,951,561	42.9	36.0
GEORGIA	6,759,000	4,306,000	63.7	2,305,665	2,567,805	2,550,648	S	2,567,805	38.0	34.1
HAWAII	956,000	490,000	51.3	360,177	353,774	366,210	G	366,210	38.3	37.7
IDAHO	1,105,000	671,000	60.7	435,157	437,170	439,830	G	439,830	39.8	39.4
ILLINOIS	8,951,000	5,716,000	63.9	3,568,002	3,603,519	3,627,690	G	3,627,690	40.5	39.9
INDIANA	4,693,000	3,048,000	64.9	1,340,814			H	1,340,814	28.6	28.6
IOWA	2,275,000	1,584,000	69.6	1,120,334	1,129,700	1,129,057	S	1,129,700	49.7	49.2
KANSAS	1,993,000	1,353,000	67.9	862,077	866,191	869,502	G	869,502	43.6	43.3
KENTUCKY	3,207,000	2,298,000	71.6	1,397,626	1,435,868		S	1,435,868	44.8	43.6
LOUISIANA	3,342,000	2,398,000	71.7	1,342,373	1,273,589		H	1,342,373	40.2	40.2
MAINE	1,045,000	799,000	76.5	592,346	604,008	611,227	G	611,227	58.5	56.7
MARYLAND	4,148,000	2,995,000	72.2	1,703,037		1,733,177	G	1,733,177	41.8	41.1
MASSACHUSETTS	4,815,000	3,250,000	67.5	1,813,816	2,084,972	2,158,326	G	2,158,326	44.8	37.7
MICHIGAN	7,246,000	5,159,000	71.2	3,089,477	3,121,775	3,156,531	G	3,156,531	43.6	42.6
MINNESOTA	3,933,000	2,822,000	71.8	1,963,539	1,981,528	1,975,406	S	1,981,528	50.4	49.9
MISSISSIPPI	2,142,000	1,628,000	76.0	626,279	631,858		S	631,858	29.5	29.2
MISSOURI	4,429,000	3,194,000	72.1	1,426,303			H	1,426,303	32.2	32.2
MONTANA	782,000	506,000	64.8	367,963	369,826		S	369,826	47.3	47.1
NEBRASKA	1,306,000	873,000	66.9	535,530	540,337	540,202	S	540,337	41.4	41.0
NEVADA	1,858,000	1,088,000	58.5	543,009		547,349	G	547,349	29.5	29.2
NEW HAMPSHIRE	1,015,000	694,000	68.3	480,920	488,159	486,183	S	488,159	48.1	47.4
NEW JERSEY	5,909,000	3,919,000	66.3	1,821,365	1,869,535		S	1,869,535	31.6	30.8
NEW MEXICO	1,417,000	919,000	64.9	511,885	515,506	512,805	S	515,506	36.4	36.1
NEW YORK	13,611,000	8,078,000	59.4	3,651,707		3,819,086	G	3,819,086	28.1	26.8
NORTH CAROLINA	6,857,000	4,779,000	69.7	2,807,998	2,915,281		S	2,915,281	42.5	41.0
NORTH DAKOTA	547,000	363,000	66.4	248,670			H	248,670	45.5	45.5
OHIO	8,509,000	5,657,000	66.5	3,000,161		3,055,913	G	3,055,913	35.9	35.3
OKLAHOMA*	2,690,000	1,644,000	61.1	653,413	820,890	824,831	G	824,831	30.7	24.3
OREGON	2,870,000	2,008,000	70.0	1,450,702	1,461,618	1,469,717	G	1,469,717	51.2	50.5
PENNSYLVANIA	9,511,000	6,121,000	64.4	3,323,533		3,495,866	G	3,495,866	36.8	34.9
RHODE ISLAND	765,000	486,000	63.6	316,257	316,898	324,055	G	324,055	42.4	41.3
SOUTH CAROLINA*	3,569,000	2,458,000	68.9	1,155,782	1,240,075	1,246,301	G	1,246,301	34.9	32.4
SOUTH DAKOTA	618,000	401,000	64.9	276,319	279,412	277,403	S	279,412	45.2	44.7
TENNESSEE	4,815,000	3,088,000	64.1	1,371,161	1,366,628	1,353,728	H	1,371,161	28.5	28.5
TEXAS	16,844,000	9,946,000	59.1	4,453,499	4,648,358	4,718,268	G	4,718,268	28.0	26.4
UTAH	1,924,000	1,101,000	57.2	565,970			H	565,970	29.4	29.4
VERMONT	482,000	324,000	67.2	191,504		193,087	G	193,087	40.1	39.7
VIRGINIA	5,888,000	3,924,000	66.6	2,135,313	2,184,473		S	2,184,473	37.1	36.3
WASHINGTON	4,776,000	3,281,000	68.7	2,029,600			H	2,029,600	42.5	42.5
WEST VIRGINIA	1,440,000	896,000	62.2	439,239	453,659		S	453,659	31.5	30.5
WISCONSIN	4,232,000	3,005,000	71.0	2,355,580		2,410,314	G	2,410,314	57.0	55.7
WYOMING	427,000	241,000	56.5	165,100	168,390	167,877	S	168,390	40.1	40.1
UNITED STATES TOTAL	*219,464,000*	*141,811,000*	*64.6*	*77,889,271*	*43,953,893*	*64,279,490*		*81,378,889*	*37.7*	*36.1*

*Oklahoma and South Carolina each held two Senate races on November 4, 2015. Only the highest totals are counted here (including Oklahoma's special election and South Carolina's general election). The other Senate races totaled 820,733 votes in Oklahoma and 1,238,982 in South Carolina.

Notes: The table does not include elections for non-voting members of the House (such as the 177,377 votes cast for House delegate in the District of Columbia).

Source: Population figures are based on U.S. Census Bureau estimates in November 2014. "Voting-Age Citizen Population" includes all U.S. citizens 18 years or older. Population estimates from "Table 4a. Reported Voting and Registration of the Citizen Voting-Age Population, for States: November 2014." U.S. Census Bureau, Current Population Survey, November 2014, http://www.census.gov/popest.

GUBERNATORIAL ELECTIONS 2013 AND 2014

State	Total Vote	Republican Vote	Republican Candidate	Democratic Vote	Democratic Candidate	Other Vote	Rep.-Dem. Plurality	Total Vote Rep.	Total Vote Dem.	Major Vote Rep.	Major Vote Dem.
Alabama	1,180,413	750,231	Bentley, Robert	427,787	Griffith, Parker	2,395	322,444 R	63.6%	36.2%	63.7%	36.3%
Alaska	279,958	128,435	Parnell, Sean R.			151,523	6,223 I	45.9%	0.0%	100.0%	0.0%
Arizona	1,506,416	805,062	Ducey, Doug	626,921	Duval, Fred	74,433	178,141 R	53.4%	41.6%	56.2%	43.8%
Arkansas	848,592	470,429	Hutchinson, Asa	352,115	Ross, Mike	26,048	118,314 R	55.4%	41.5%	57.2%	42.8%
California	7,317,581	2,929,213	Kashkari, Neel	4,388,368	Edmund G. Brown Jr.	—	1,459,155 D	40.0%	60.0%	40.0%	60.0%
Colorado	2,041,607	938,195	Beauprez, Bob	1,006,433	Hickenlooper, John	96,979	68,238 D	46.0%	49.3%	48.2%	51.8%
Connecticut	1,092,773	526,295	Foley, Tom C.	554,314	Malloy, Dan	12,164	28,019 D	48.2%	50.7%	48.7%	51.3%
Florida	5,951,561	2,865,343	Scott, Rick	2,801,198	Crist, Charlie	285,020	64,145 R	48.1%	47.1%	50.6%	49.4%
Georgia	2,550,648	1,345,237	Deal, Nathan	1,144,794	Carter, Jason J.	60,617	200,443 R	52.7%	44.9%	54.0%	46.0%
Hawaii	366,210	135,775	Aiona, Duke	181,106	Ige, David Yutaka	49,329	45,331 D	37.1%	49.5%	42.8%	57.2%
Idaho	439,830	235,405	Otter, C. L. "Butch"	169,556	Balukoff, A.J.	34,869	65,849 R	53.5%	38.6%	58.1%	41.9%
Illinois	3,627,690	1,823,627	Rauner, Bruce	1,681,343	Quinn, Pat	122,720	142,284 R	50.3%	46.3%	52.0%	48.0%
Iowa	1,129,057	666,032	Branstad, Terry E.	420,787	Hatch, Jack	42,238	245,245 R	59.0%	37.3%	61.3%	38.7%
Kansas	869,502	433,196	Brownback, Sam	401,100	Davis, Paul	35,206	32,096 R	49.8%	46.1%	51.9%	48.1%
Maine	611,227	294,519	LePage, Paul R.	265,114	Michaud, Michael H.	51,594	29,405 R	48.2%	43.4%	52.6%	47.4%
Maryland	1,733,177	884,400	Hogan, Larry	818,890	Brown, Anthony G.	29,887	65,510 R	51.0%	47.2%	51.9%	48.1%
Massachusetts	2,158,326	1,044,573	Baker, Charles D.	1,004,408	Coakley, Martha	109,345	40,165 R	48.4%	46.5%	51.0%	49.0%
Michigan	3,156,531	1,607,399	Snyder, Rick	1,479,057	Schauer, Mark H.	70,075	128,342 R	50.9%	46.9%	52.1%	47.9%
Minnesota	1,975,406	879,257	Johnson, Jeff	989,113	Dayton, Mark	107,036	109,856 D	44.5%	50.1%	47.1%	52.9%
Nebraska	540,202	308,751	Ricketts, Pete	211,905	Hassebrook, Chuck	19,546	96,846 R	57.2%	39.2%	59.3%	40.7%
Nevada	547,349	386,340	Sandoval, Brian	130,722	Goodman, Robert "Bob"	30,287	255,618 R	70.6%	23.9%	74.7%	25.3%
New Hampshire	486,183	230,610	Havenstein, Walter "Walt"	254,666	Hassan, Maggie	907	24,056 D	47.4%	52.4%	47.5%	52.5%
New Jersey *	2,120,866	1,278,932	Christie, Chris	809,978	Buono, Barbara	31,956	468,954 R	60.3%	38.2%	61.2%	38.8%
New Mexico	512,805	293,443	Martinez, Susana	219,362	King, Gary K.	—	74,081 R	57.2%	42.8%	57.2%	42.8%
New York	3,819,086	1,537,077	Astorino, Rob	2,069,480	Cuomo, Andrew M.	212,529	532,403 D	40.2%	54.2%	42.6%	57.4%
Ohio	3,055,913	1,944,848	Kasich, John R.	1,009,359	FitzGerald, Ed	101,706	935,489 R	63.6%	33.0%	65.8%	34.2%
Oklahoma	824,831	460,298	Fallin, Mary	338,239	Dorman, Joe	26,294	122,059 R	55.8%	41.0%	57.6%	42.4%
Oregon	1,469,717	648,542	Richardson, Dennis	733,230	Kitzhaber, John	87,945	84,688 D	44.1%	49.9%	46.9%	53.1%
Pennsylvania	3,495,866	1,575,511	Corbett, Tom	1,920,355	Wolf, Thomas W.	—	344,844 D	45.1%	54.9%	45.1%	54.9%
Rhode Island	324,055	117,428	Fung, Allan	131,899	Raimondo, Gina	74,728	14,471 D	36.2%	40.7%	47.1%	52.9%
South Carolina	1,246,301	696,645	Haley, Nikki R.	516,166	Sheheen, Vincent A.	33,490	180,479 R	55.9%	41.4%	57.4%	42.6%
South Dakota	277,403	195,477	Daugaard, Dennis	70,549	Wismer, Susan	11,377	124928 R	70.5%	25.4%	73.5%	26.5%
Tennessee	1,353,728	951,796	Haslam, Bill	309,237	Brown, Charles V. "Charlie"	92,695	642,559 R	70.3%	22.8%	75.5%	24.5%
Texas	4,718,268	2,796,547	Abbott, Greg	1,835,596	Davis, Wendy R.	86,125	960,951 R	59.3%	38.9%	60.4%	39.6%
Vermont	193,087	87,075	Milne, Scott	89,509	Shumlin, Peter	16,503	2,434 D	45.1%	46.4%	49.3%	50.7%
Virginia *	2,241,071	1,013,354	Cuccinelli, Ken	1,069,789	McAuliffe, Terry R.	157,928	56,435 D	45.2%	47.7%	48.6%	51.4%
Wisconsin	2,410,314	1,259,706	Walker, Scott	1,122,913	Burke, Mary	27,695	136,793 R	52.3%	46.6%	52.9%	47.1%
Wyoming	167,877	99,700	Mead, Matt	45,752	Gosar, Peter	22,425	53,948 R	59.4%	27.3%	68.5%	31.5%
TOTALS 2013	4,361,937	2,292,286		1,879,767		189,884	412,519 R	52.6%	43.1%	54.9%	45.1%
TOTALS 2014	64,279,490	32,352,417		29,721,343		2,205,730	2,631,074 R	50.3%	46.2%	52.1%	47.9%

Note: * indicated that gubernatorial elections were held in 2013. In Alaska, Independent Bill Walker was elected with 134,658 votes (48.1% of the total vote).

SENATE ELECTIONS 2013 AND 2014

State	Total Vote	Republican Vote	Republican Candidate	Democratic Vote	Democratic Candidate	Other Vote	Rep.-Dem. Plurality	Total Vote Rep.	Total Vote Dem.	Major Vote Rep.	Major Vote Dem.
Alabama	818,090	795,606	Sessions, Jeff			22,484	795,606 R	97.3%	0.0%	100.0%	0.0%
Alaska	282,400	135,445	Sullivan, Dan S.	129,431	Begich, Mark	17,524	6,014 R	48.0%	45.8%	51.1%	48.9%
Arkansas	847,505	478,819	Cotton, Tom	334,174	Pryor, Mark	34,512	144,645 R	56.5%	39.4%	58.9%	41.1%
Colorado	2,041,058	983,891	Gardner, Cory	944,203	Udall, Mark	112,964	39,688 R	48.2%	46.3%	51.0%	49.0%
Delaware	234,038	98,823	Wade, Kevin	130,655	Coons, Christopher A.	4,560	31,832 D	42.2%	55.8%	43.1%	56.9%
Georgia	2,567,805	1,358,088	Perdue, David A.	1,160,811	Nunn, Michelle	48,906	197,277 R	52.9%	45.2%	53.9%	46.1%
Hawaii	353,774	98,006	Cavasso, Cam	246,827	Schatz, Brian	8,941	148,821 D	27.7%	69.8%	28.4%	71.6%
Idaho	437,170	285,596	Risch, Jim	151,574	Mitchell, Nels	—	134,022 R	65.3%	34.7%	65.3%	34.7%
Illinois	3,603,519	1,538,522	Oberweis, James D.	1,929,637	Durbin, Richard J.	135,360	391,115 D	42.7%	53.5%	44.4%	55.6%
Iowa	1,129,700	588,575	Ernst, Joni	494,370	Braley, Bruce	46,755	94,205 R	52.1%	43.8%	54.3%	45.7%
Kansas	866,191	460,350	Roberts, Pat			405,841	91,978 R	53.1%	0.0%	100.0%	0.0%
Kentucky	1,435,868	806,787	McConnell, Mitch	584,698	Grimes, Alison Lundergan	44,383	222,089 R	56.2%	40.7%	58.0%	42.0%
Louisiana**	1,273,589	712,379	Cassidy, Bill	561,210	Landrieu, Mary L.	—	151,169 R	55.9%	44.1%	55.9%	44.1%
Maine	604,008	413,495	Collins, Susan M.	190,244	Bellows, Shenna	269	223,251 R	68.5%	31.5%	68.5%	31.5%
Massachusetts (S)*	1,177,790	525,307	Gomez, Gabriel E.	645,429	Markey, Edward J.	7,054	120,122 D	44.6%	54.8%	44.9%	55.1%
Massachusetts	2,084,972	791,950	Herr, Brian J.	1,289,944	Markey, Edward J.	3,078	497,994 D	38.0%	61.9%	38.0%	62.0%
Michigan	3,121,775	1,290,199	Land, Terri Lynn	1,704,936	Peters, Gary C.	126,640	414,737 D	41.3%	54.6%	43.1%	56.9%
Minnesota	1,981,528	850,227	McFadden, Mike	1,053,205	Franken, Al	78,096	202,978 D	42.9%	53.2%	44.7%	55.3%
Mississippi	631,858	378,481	Cochran, Thad	239,439	Childers, Travis	13,938	139,042 R	59.9%	37.9%	61.3%	38.7%
Montana	369,826	213,709	Daines, Steve	148,184	Curtis, Amanda	7,933	65,525 R	57.8%	40.1%	59.1%	40.9%
Nebraska	540,337	347,636	Sasse, Ben	170,127	Domina, David A.	22,574	177,509 R	64.3%	31.5%	67.1%	32.9%
New Hampshire	488,159	235,347	Brown, Scott P.	251,184	Shaheen, Jeanne	1,628	15,837 D	48.2%	51.5%	48.4%	51.6%
New Jersey (S)*	1,348,659	593,684	Lonegan, Steven M.	740,742	Booker, Cory	14,233	147,058 D	44.0%	54.9%	44.5%	55.5%
New Jersey	1,869,535	791,297	Bell, Jeffrey	1,043,866	Booker, Cory	34,372	252,569 D	42.3%	55.8%	43.1%	56.9%
New Mexico	515,506	229,097	Weh, Allen	286,409	Udall, Tom	—	57,312 D	44.4%	55.6%	44.4%	55.6%
North Carolina	2,915,281	1,423,259	Tillis, Thom	1,377,651	Hagan, Kay	114,371	45,608 R	48.8%	47.3%	50.8%	49.2%
Oklahoma	820,733	558,166	Inhofe, James M.	234,307	Silverstein, Matt	28,260	323,859 R	68.0%	28.5%	70.4%	29.6%
Oklahoma (S)	820,890	557,002	Lankford, James	237,923	Johnson, Connie	25,965	319,079 R	67.9%	29.0%	70.1%	29.9%
Oregon	1,461,618	538,847	Wehby, Monica	814,537	Merkley, Jeff	108,234	275,690 D	36.9%	55.7%	39.8%	60.2%
Rhode Island	316,898	92,684	Zaccaria, Mark S.	223,675	Reed, Jack	539	130,991 D	29.2%	70.6%	29.3%	70.7%
South Carolina	1,240,075	672,941	Graham, Lindsey	480,933	Hutto, C. Bradley "Brad"	86,201	192,008 R	54.3%	38.8%	58.3%	41.7%
South Carolina (S)	1,238,982	757,215	Scott, Tim	459,583	Dickerson, Joyce	22,184	297,632 R	61.1%	37.1%	62.2%	37.8%
South Dakota	279,412	140,741	Rounds, Mike	82,456	Weiland, Rick	56,215	58,285 R	50.4%	29.5%	63.1%	36.9%
Tennessee	1,366,628	850,087	Alexander, Lamar	437,848	Ball, Gordon	78,693	412,239 R	62.2%	32.0%	66.0%	34.0%
Texas	4,648,358	2,861,531	Cornyn, John	1,597,387	Alameel, David	189,440	1,264,144 R	61.6%	34.4%	64.2%	35.8%
Virginia	2,184,473	1,055,940	Gillespie, Edward W. "Ed"	1,073,667	Warner, Mark	54,866	17,727 D	48.3%	49.1%	49.6%	50.4%
West Virginia	453,659	281,820	Capito, Shelley Moore	156,360	Tennant, Natalie E.	15,479	125,460 R	62.1%	34.5%	64.3%	35.7%
Wyoming	168,390	121,554	Enzi, Michael B.	29,377	Hardy, Charles E. "Charlie"	17,459	92,177 R	72.2%	17.4%	80.5%	19.5%
TOTALS 2013	*2,526,449*	*1,118,991*		*1,386,171*		*21,287*	*267,180 D*	*44.3%*	*54.9%*	*44.7%*	*55.3%*
TOTALS 2014	*46,013,608*	*23,794,112*		*20,250,832*		*1,968,664*	*3,543,280 R*	*51.7%*	*44.0%*	*54.0%*	*46.0%*

Note: **Results listed are from the December runoff election. (S)* indicated election was a special election for a short term to fill a vacancy. In Kansas, the plurality reflects the margin of victory of Republican Pat Roberts over Independent Greg Orman, who finished second with 368,372 votes.

HOUSE OF REPRESENTATIVES ELECTIONS 2014

State	Seats Won Republican	Seats Won Democratic	Total Vote	Republican	Democratic	Other	Rep.-Dem. Plurality	Percentage Total Vote Rep.	Percentage Total Vote Dem.	Percentage Major Vote Rep.	Percentage Major Vote Dem.
Alabama	6	1	1,080,880	704,533	331,764	44,583	372,769 R	65.2%	30.7%	68.0%	32.0%
Alaska	1	0	279,741	142,572	114,602	22,567	27,970 R	51.0%	41.0%	55.4%	44.6%
Arizona	5	4	1,467,601	817,168	577,943	72,490	239,225 R	55.7%	39.4%	58.6%	41.4%
Arkansas	4	0	830,652	509,631	254,774	66,247	254,857 R	61.4%	30.7%	66.7%	33.3%
California	14	39	7,132,641	2,950,679	4,067,957	114,005	1,117,278 D	41.4%	57.0%	42.0%	58.0%
Colorado	4	3	2,000,525	1,000,197	936,417	63,911	63,780 R	50.0%	46.8%	51.6%	48.4%
Connecticut	0	5	1,067,857	418,589	638,695	10,573	220,106 D	39.2%	59.8%	39.6%	60.4%
Delaware	0	1	231,617	85,146	137,251	9,220	52,105 D	36.8%	59.3%	38.3%	61.7%
Florida	17	10	4,998,555	2,713,451	2,130,626	154,478	582,825 R	54.3%	42.6%	56.0%	44.0%
Georgia	10	4	2,305,665	1,349,076	956,361	228	392,715 R	58.5%	41.5%	58.5%	41.5%
Hawaii	0	2	360,177	120,084	235,400	4,693	115,316 D	33.3%	65.4%	33.8%	66.2%
Idaho	2	0	435,157	275,072	160,078	7	114,994 R	63.2%	36.8%	63.2%	36.8%
Illinois	8	10	3,568,002	1,721,865	1,822,779	23,358	100,914 D	48.3%	51.1%	48.6%	51.4%
Indiana	7	2	1,340,814	793,759	502,104	44,951	291,655 R	59.2%	37.4%	61.3%	38.7%
Iowa	3	1	1,120,334	595,865	509,189	15,280	86,676 R	53.2%	45.4%	53.9%	46.1%
Kansas	4	0	862,077	540,756	311,530	9,791	229,226 R	62.7%	36.1%	63.4%	36.6%
Kentucky	5	1	1,397,626	887,157	508,151	2,318	379,006 R	63.5%	36.4%	63.6%	36.4%
Louisiana	5	1	1,342,373	823,684	394,840	123,849	428,844 R	61.4%	29.4%	67.6%	32.4%
Maine	1	1	592,346	228,059	305,230	59,057	77,171 D	38.5%	51.5%	42.8%	57.2%
Maryland	1	7	1,703,037	704,400	978,267	20,370	273,867 D	41.4%	57.4%	41.9%	58.1%
Massachusetts	0	9	1,813,816	308,598	1,475,442	29,776	1,166,844 D	17.0%	81.3%	17.3%	82.7%
Michigan	9	5	3,089,477	1,466,749	1,519,030	103,698	52,281 D	47.5%	49.2%	49.1%	50.9%
Minnesota	3	5	1,963,539	913,539	985,760	64,240	72,221 D	46.5%	50.2%	48.1%	51.9%
Mississippi	3	1	626,279	329,169	230,014	67,096	99,155 R	52.6%	36.7%	58.9%	41.1%
Missouri	6	2	1,426,303	838,283	513,600	74,420	324,683 R	58.8%	36.0%	62.0%	38.0%
Montana	1	0	367,963	203,871	148,690	15,402	55,181 R	55.4%	40.4%	57.8%	42.2%
Nebraska	2	1	535,530	340,816	185,234	9,480	155,582 R	63.6%	34.6%	64.8%	35.2%
Nevada	3	1	543,009	304,809	210,147	28,053	94,662 R	56.1%	38.7%	59.2%	40.8%
New Hampshire	1	1	480,920	232,379	247,469	1,072	15,090 D	48.3%	51.5%	48.4%	51.6%
New Jersey	6	6	1,821,365	877,265	914,172	29,928	36,907 D	48.2%	50.2%	49.0%	51.0%
New Mexico	1	2	511,885	240,542	271,222	121	30,680 D	47.0%	53.0%	47.0%	53.0%
New York	9	18	3,651,707	1,554,274	2,009,444	87,989	455,170 D	42.6%	55.0%	43.6%	56.4%
North Carolina	10	3	2,807,998	1,555,364	1,234,027	18,607	321,337 R	55.4%	43.9%	55.8%	44.2%
North Dakota	1	0	248,670	138,100	95,678	14,892	42,422 R	55.5%	38.5%	59.1%	40.9%
Ohio	12	4	3,000,161	1,770,923	1,179,587	49,651	591,336 R	59.0%	39.3%	60.0%	40.0%
Oklahoma	5	0	653,413	457,613	174,022	21,778	283,591 R	70.0%	26.6%	72.4%	27.6%
Oregon	1	4	1,450,702	582,909	778,139	89,654	195,230 D	40.2%	53.6%	42.8%	57.2%
Pennsylvania	13	5	3,323,533	1,833,205	1,467,594	22,734	365,611 R	55.2%	44.2%	55.5%	44.5%
Rhode Island	0	2	316,257	122,721	192,776	760	70,055 D	38.8%	61.0%	38.9%	61.1%
South Carolina	6	1	1,155,782	734,456	382,208	39,118	352,248 R	63.5%	33.1%	65.8%	34.2%
South Dakota	1	0	276,319	183,834	92,485		91,349 R	66.5%	33.5%	66.5%	33.5%
Tennessee	7	2	1,371,161	848,846	448,421	73,894	400,425 R	61.9%	32.7%	65.4%	34.6%
Texas	25	11	4,453,499	2,684,592	1,476,476	292,431	1,208,116 R	60.3%	33.2%	64.5%	35.5%
Utah	4	0	565,970	351,034	183,491	31,445	167,543 R	62.0%	32.4%	65.7%	34.3%
Vermont	0	1	191,504	59,432	123,349	8,723	63,917 D	31.0%	64.4%	32.5%	67.5%
Virginia	8	3	2,135,313	1,143,747	845,939	145,627	297,808 R	53.6%	39.6%	57.5%	42.5%
Washington	4	6	2,029,600	981,853	1,047,747		65,894 D	48.4%	51.6%	48.4%	51.6%
West Virginia	3	0	439,239	242,823	182,484	13,932	60,339 R	55.3%	41.5%	57.1%	42.9%
Wisconsin	5	3	2,355,580	1,233,336	1,102,581	19,663	130,755 R	52.4%	46.8%	52.8%	47.2%
Wyoming	1	0	165,100	37,803	113,038	14,259	75,235 R	22.9%	68.5%	74.9%	25.1%
Total	247	188	77,889,271	40,029,863	35,628,989	2,230,419	4,400,874 R	51.4%	45.7%	52.9%	47.1%

Note: In Louisiana, the vote is based on results from the decisive round of voting in each district. In districts 1 through 4, that was the November 4 general election. In districts 5 and 6, it was the December 6 runoff.

UNITED STATES
HOUSE SPECIAL ELECTIONS 2013 TO 2014: A SUMMARY

SENATORS

REPRESENTATIVES

District	Former Member	New Member	Date Elected	Winning Percentage	Voter Turnout
Alabama 1st	Jo Bonner (R)	Bradley Byrne (R)	December 17, 2013	70%	51,406
Florida 13th	C. W. Bill Young (R)	David Jolly (R)	March 11, 2014	49%	183,772
Florida 19th	Trey Radel (R)	Curt Clawson (R)	June 24, 2014	67%	99,989
Illinois 2nd	Jesse Jackson Jr. (D)	Robin Kelly (D)	April 9, 2013	71%	83,193
Louisiana 5th	Rodney Alexander (R)	Vance McAllister (R)	November 16, 2013	60%	91,290
Massachusetts 5th	Ed Markey (D)	Katherine Clark (D)	December 10, 2013	66%	61,079
Missouri 8th	Jo Ann Emerson (R)	Jason Smith (R)	June 4, 2013	67%	62,766
New Jersey 1st	Rob Andrews (D)	Donald Norcross (D)	November 4, 2014	58%	161,275
North Carolina 12th	Melvin Watt (D)	Alma Adams (D)	November 4, 2014	75%	169,246
South Carolina 1st	Tim Scott (R)	Mark Sanford (R)	May 7, 2013	54%	143,635
Virginia 7th	Eric Cantor (R)	David Brat (R)	November 4, 2014	62%	241,313

SPECIAL ELECTIONS TO THE 113th CONGRESS

From the beginning of 2013 through the general election of 2014, 11 special House elections were held to fill vacancies in the 113th Congress. Eight were free-standing contests; the other three were held in conjunction with the November 2014 general election. In addition, there were five special Senate elections held in 2013-14. Two were free-standing elections; three were held in conjunction with the November 2014 general election. None of the House or Senate special elections held during the 113th Congress resulted in a change of party hands.

SENATOR(S)

HAWAII

Daniel Inouye (D) died on December 17, 2012. Brian Schatz was appointed to fill the vacancy and was sworn in December 27, 2012. Schatz won a special election in November 2014 to fill the last two years of Inouye's term.

August 9, 2014 Special Democratic Primary

115,445 Brian Schatz; 113,663 Colleen W. Hanabusa; 4,842 Brian Evans.

August 9, 2014 Special Democratic Primary

25,874 Cam Cavasso; 4,425 John P. Roco; 3,477 Harry J. Friel Jr.; 2,033 Eddie Pirkowski.

November 4, 2014 Special General Election

246,827 Brian Schatz (D); 98,006 Cam Cavasso (R); 8,941 Michael Kokoski (L).

MASSACHUSETTS

John Kerry (D) resigned February 1, 2013, to become secretary of state. After a five-month interim period in which William "Mo" Cowan (D) held the seat on an interim basis until Ed Markey (D) was elected in June 2013 to complete the last 18 months of Kerry's term.

April 30, 2013 Special Democratic Primary

311,219 Ed Markey; 230,335 Stephen Lynch.

April 30, 2013 Special Republican Primary

96,057 Gabriel Gomez; 67,946 Mike Sullivan; 24,662 Daniel Winslow.

June 25, 2013 Special General Election

645,429 Ed Markey (D); 525,307 Gabriel Gomez (R); 4,550 Richard Heos (Twelve Visions Party).

NEW JERSEY

Frank Lautenberg (D) died June 3, 2013. After Jeffrey S. Chiesa (R) held the seat on an interim basis until Cory Booker (D) won a special election in October 2013 to fill the last 15 months of Lautenberg's term.

UNITED STATES
HOUSE SPECIAL ELECTIONS 2013 TO 2014: A SUMMARY

August 13, 2013 Special Democratic Primary

216,936 Cory Booker; 72,584 Frank Pallone; 61,463 Rush Holt; 15,656 Sheila Y. Oliver.

August 13, 2013 Special Republican Primary

103,280 Steven M. Lonegan; 25,669 Alieta Eck.

October 16, 2013 Special General Election

740,742 Cory Booker (D); 593,684 Steven M. Lonegan (R); 5,138 Edward C. Stackhouse Jr. (Ed the Barber); 3,137 Robert De-Pasquale (I); 2,051 Stewart D. Meissner (Alimony Reform Now); 1,530 Pablo Olivera (Unity Is Strength); 1,336 Antonio N. Sabas (Freedom of Choice); 1,041 Eugene M. LaVergne (D-R Party).

OKLAHOMA

Facing lingering cancer concerns, Tom Coburn resigned his seat at the end of the 113th Congress. James Lankford (R) won a special election in November 2014 to fill the last two years of Coburn's term.

June 24, 2014 Special Democratic Primary

71,462 Connie Johnson; 57,598 Jim Rogers; 33,943 Patrick M. Hayes.

June 24, 2014 Special Republican Primary

152,749 James Lankford; 91,854 T. W. Shannon; 12,934 Randy Brogdon; 2,828 Kevin Crow; 2,427 Andy Craig; 2,272 Eric C. McCray; 1,794 Jason Weger.

August 26, 2014 Special Democratic Primary Run-Off

54,762 Connie Johnson; 39,664 Jim Rogers.

November 4, 2014 Special General Election

557,002 James Lankford (R); 237,923 Connie Johnson (D); 25,965 Mark Beard (I).

SOUTH CAROLINA

Jim DeMint (R) resigned January 1, 2013, to become president of the Heritage Foundation. Tim Scott (R) was sworn in January 3, 2013, to fill the vacancy and was elected in a special election in November 2014 to fill the final two years of DeMint's term.

June 10, 2014 Special Democratic Primary

72,874 Joyce Dickerson; 26,310 Sidney Moore; 12,253 Harry Pavilack.

June 10, 2014 Special Republican Primary

276,147 Tim Scott; 30,741 Randall Young.

November 4, 2014 Special General Election

757,215 Tim Scott (R); 459,583 Joyce Dickerson (D); 21,652 Jill Bossi (American Party of South Carolina); 532 Write-In Candidate (Unaffiliated).

REPRESENTATIVES

ALABAMA 1st CD

Jo Bonner (R) resigned August 2, 2013, to become vice chancellor of government relations and economic development in the University of Alabama System. Bradley Byrne (R) won a special election in December 2013 to fill the vacancy.

September 24, 2013 Special Democratic Primary

3,129 Burton LeFlore; 1,328 Lula Albert-Kaigler.

UNITED STATES
HOUSE SPECIAL ELECTIONS 2013 TO 2014: A SUMMARY

September 24, 2013 Special Republican Primary

18,090 Bradley Byrne; 12,011 Dean Young; 8,177 Chad Fincher; 7,260 Quin Hillyer; 5,758 Wells Griffith; 391 Daniel Dyas; 391 Jessica James; 184 Sharon Power; 72 David Thornton.

November 5, 2013 Special Republican Primary Runoff

38,150 Bradley Byrne; 34,534 Dean Young.

December 17, 2013 Special General Election

36,071 Bradley Byrne (R); 14,985 Burton LeFlore (D); 350 Write-In (Unaffiliated).

FLORIDA 13th CD

C. W. Bill Young (R) died October 18, 2013. Under Florida law, Governor Rick Scott (R) possessed no authority to name a replacement. Thus, a special election was held on March 11, 2014. David Jolly (R) won a special election in March 2014 to fill the vacancy. There was no Democratic primary.

FLORIDA 19th CD

Trey Radel (R) resigned January 27, 2014, in wake of his guilty plea on a misdemeanor charge of cocaine possession. Curt Clawson (R) won a special election in June 2014 to fill the vacancy. There was no Democratic primary.

January 14, 2014 Special Democratic Primary

0 Alex Sink (No official results reported—this was an uncontested race).

January 14, 2014 Special Republican Primary

20,493 David Jolly; 14,234 Kathleen Peters; 11,242 Mark Bircher.

March 11, 2014 Special General Election

89,167 David Jolly (R); 85,673 Alex Sink (D); 8,919 Lucas Overby (L); 13 Michael Levinson (Write-In).
As a result of Trey Radel's (R) resignation on January 27, 2014, a second special election was held in Florida. This election took place on June 24, 2014. Curt Clawson (R) won the election and has since been reelected.

April 22, 2014 Special Democratic Primary

0 April Freeman (No official results reported—this was an uncontested race).

April 22, 2014 Special Republican Primary

26,897 Curt Clawson; 18,052 Lizbeth Benacquisto; 17,789 Paige Kreegel; 7,564 Michael J. Dreikorn.

June 24, 2014 Special General Election

66,922 Curt Clawson (R); 29,314 April Freeman (D); 3,729 Ray Netherwood (L); 24 Timothy J. Rossano (Write-In).

ILLINOIS 2nd CD

Jesse Jackson Jr. (D) resigned in the shadow of an ethics investigation and health concerns. Robin Kelly (D) won a special election in April 2013 to fill the vacancy.

February 26, 2013 Special Democratic Primary

31,079 Robin Kelly; 14,650 Debbie Halvorson; 6,457 Anthony Beale; 2,563 Joyce Washington; 1,545 Ernest Fenton; 641 Anthony Williams; 459 Mel Reynolds; 207 Clifford Eagleton; 194 Fatimah Muhammad; 144 Gregory Haynes; 127 Larry Pickens; 104 John Blyth; 91 Victor Jonathan; 74 Charles Rayburn; 4 Denise Anita Hill.

February 26, 2013 Special Republican Primary

963 Paul McKinley; 939 Eric Wallace; 894 Lenny McAllister; 523 Beverly Reid.

April 9, 2013 Special General Election

58,834 Robin Kelly (D); 18,387 Paul McKinley (R); 2,525 Elizabeth Pahlke (I); 1,531 LeAlan Jones (G); 1,359 Marcus Lewis (I); 548 Curtis Bey (I); 9 Steve Piekarczyk (Write-In).

UNITED STATES
HOUSE SPECIAL ELECTIONS 2013 TO 2014: A SUMMARY

LOUISIANA 5th CD

Rodney Alexander (R) resigned September 27, 2013, to become secretary of the Louisiana Department of Veterans Affairs. Vance McAllister (R) won a special election in November 2013 to fill the vacancy.

October 19, 2013 Special Open Primary

33,045 Neil Riser (R); **18,389 Vance McAllister (R)**; 15,318 Jamie Mayo (D); 11,250 Clyde C. Holloway (R); 9,971 Robert Johnson (D); 7,083 Jay Morris (R); 3,088 Marcus Hunter (D); 2,554 Weldon Russell (D); 886 Henry Herford Jr. (L); 517 Philip "Blake" Weatherly (R); 492 Eliot S. Barron (G); 335 Peter Williams (I); 324 Tom Gibbs (I); 192 S. B. A. Zaitoon (L).

November 16, 2013 Special Open General Election

54,450 Vance McAllister (R); 36,840 Neil Riser (R).

MASSACHUSETTS 5th CD

Ed Markey (D) resigned July 15, 2013, after winning a special election to fill the remainder of John Kerry's Senate term. Katherine Clark (D) won a special election in December 2013 to fill the House vacancy.

October 15, 2013 Special Democratic Primary

21,983 Katherine Clark; 15,303 Peter J. Koutoujian; 11,160 Carl M. Sciortino Jr.; 10,163 William N. Brownsberger; 9,088 Karen E. Spilka; 1,520 Paul John Maisano; 398 Martin Long.

October 15, 2013 Special Republican Primary

4,760 Frank Addivinola Jr.; 2,478 Michael P. Stopa; 2,457 Tom Tierney.

December 10, 2013 Special General Election

40,303 Katherine Clark (D); 19,328 Frank Addivinola Jr. (R); 996 James V. Aulenti (I); 452 Jim Hall (Justice, Peace, Security).

MISSOURI 8th CD

Jo Ann Emerson (R) resigned January 22, 2013, to become president and CEO of the National Rural Electric Cooperative Association. Jason Smith (R) won a special election in June 2013 to fill the vacancy. No primaries were held by either party.

February 16, 2013 Special Democratic Primary
0 Steve Hodges (No official results recorded—candidate chosen by convention committee).
February 8, 2013 Special Republican Primary
0 Jason Smith (No official results recorded—candidate chosen by convention committee).

June 4, 2013 Special General Election

42,141 Jason Smith (R); 17,207 Steve Hodges (D); 2,265 Doug Enyart (Constitution); 968 Bill Slantz (L); 85 Thomas Brown (Write-In); 75 Robert George (Write-In); 25 Wayne Byington (Write-In); 0 Theo Brown Sr. (Write-In).

NEW JERSEY 1st CD

Rob Andrews (D) resigned February 18, 2014, in order to join a Philadelphia law firm. Donald Norcross (D) won a special election in November 2014 to fill the remaining weeks of Andrews' term. Donald Norcross (D) won both the special and general election.

June 3, 2014 Special Election Primary

17,921 Donald Norcross (D); 3,919 Frank C. Broomell Jr. (D); 3,247 Frank W. Minor (D); 359 Garry Cobb (R).

November 4, 2014 Special General Election

92,786 Donald Norcross (D); 63,727 Garry Cobb (R); 2,373 Scot John Tomaszewski (We Deserve Better); 1,647 Robert Shapiro (Stop Boss Politics); 742 Donald E. Letton (D-R Party).

UNITED STATES
HOUSE SPECIAL ELECTIONS 2013 TO 2014: A SUMMARY

NORTH CAROLINA 12th CD

Melvin Watt (D) resigned January 6, 2014, to become the director of the Federal Housing Finance Agency. A special election was held November 4, 2014, concurrent with the general election to find a candidate to complete the remainder of Watt's term. Alma Adams (D) won a special election in November 2014 to fill the remaining weeks of Watts' term.

May 6, 2014 Special Democratic Primary

14,967 Alma Adams; 7,495 Malcolm Graham; 4,431 George Battle; 2,984 Marcus Brandon; 2,034 James "Smuggie" Mitchell; 1,939 Curtis C. Osborne.
Special Republican Primary (No date provided)
0 Vince Coakley (No primary results provided)

November 4, 2014 Special General Election

127,668 Alma Adams (D); 41,578 Vince Coakley (R).

SOUTH CAROLINA 1st CD

Tim Scott (R) resigned January 2, 2013, upon his appointment to fill the Senate seat vacated by Jim DeMint (R). Mark Sanford (R) won a special election in May 2013 to fill the House vacancy.

March 19, 2013 Special Democratic Primary

15,802 Elizabeth Colbert-Busch; 682 Ben Frasier.

March 19, 2013 Special Republican Primary

19,854 Mark Sanford; 7,168 Curtis Bostic; 6,673 Larry Grooms; 4,252 Teddy Turner; 3,783 Andy Patrick; 3,479 John Kuhn; 3,279 Chip Limehouse; 2,508 Ray Nash; 867 Peter McCoy; 530 Elizabeth Moffly; 393 Tim Larkin; 360 Jonathan Hoffman; 211 Jeff King; 195 Keith Blandford; 154 Shawn Pinkston; 87 Ric Bryant.

April 2, 2013 Special Republican Primary Run-Off

26,127 Mark Sanford; 20,044 Curtis Bostic.

May 7, 2014 Special General Election

77,600 Mark Sanford (R); 64,961 Elizabeth Colbert-Busch (D); 690 Eugene Platt (Green); 384 Scattered Write-Ins (Unaffiliated).

VIRGINIA 7th CD

Upon losing in his bid for reelection, Eric Cantor (R) resigned August 18, 2014, in the wake of his primary loss to David Brat (R) in June. Brat won a special election in November 2014 to fill the remaining weeks of Cantor's term. No primaries were held for the special election.

November 4, 2014 Special General Election

148,841 David Brat (R); 91,236 Jack Trammell (D); 1,236 Write-Ins (Unaffiliated).

UNITED STATES
SPECIAL ELECTIONS TO THE 114TH CONGRESS

CHANGES FOLLOWING THE 2014 ELECTION

Following the 2014 general election, and through September 15, 2015, the following changes took place in the membership of the 114th Congress.

REPRESENTATIVES

New York 11th District—Michael Grimm resigned January 5, 2014, in light of his indictment on charges of felony tax evasion. Daniel Donovan won a special election May 5, 2014, to fill the vacancy.

Mississippi 1st District—Alan Nunnelee (R) died February 6, 2015, following his long battle with brain cancer. A special election was called for May 12, 2015, and 13 candidates campaigned for the seat. Since no candidate received a majority of the vote, a special election runoff was held June, 2, 2015, in which Trent Kelly (R) was elected to complete Nunnelee's term.

Illinois 18th District—Aaron Schock (R) resigned March 31, 2015, in light of increasing criticism surrounding his potential misuse of campaign funds. Darin LaHood (R) won a special election September 10, 2015, to fill the vacancy.

UNITED STATES

POPULAR VOTE FOR PRESIDENT 1920 TO 2012

Year	Total Vote	Republican Vote	Republican Candidate	Democratic Vote	Democratic Candidate	Other Vote	Rep.-Dem. Plurality	Percentage Total Vote Rep.	Dem.	Major Vote Rep.	Dem.
2012	129,085,474	60,933,500	Romney, W. Mitt	65,915,796	Obama, Barack	2,236,178	4,982,296 D	47.2%	51.1%	48.0%	52.0%
2008	131,313,820	59,948,323	McCain, John S. III	69,498,516	Obama, Barack	1,866,981	9,550,193 D	45.7%	52.9%	46.3%	53.7%
2004	122,295,345	62,040,610	Bush, George W.	59,028,439	Kerry, John	1,226,296	3,012,171 R	50.7%	48.3%	51.2%	48.8%
2000	105,396,627	50,455,156	Bush, George W.	50,992,335	Gore, Albert Jr.	3,949,136	537,179 D	47.9%	48.4%	49.7%	50.3%
1996	96,277,872	39,198,755	Dole, Bob	47,402,357	Clinton, Bill	9,676,760	8,203,602 D	40.7%	49.2%	45.3%	54.7%
1992	104,425,014	39,103,882	Bush, George H.	44,909,326	Clinton, Bill	20,411,806	5,805,444 D	37.4%	43.0%	46.5%	53.5%
1988	91,597,809	48,886,097	Bush, George H.	41,812,075	Dukakis, Michael S.	899,637	7,074,022 R	53.4%	45.6%	53.9%	46.1%
1984	92,652,842	54,455,075	Reagan, Ronald	37,577,185	Mondale, Walter F.	620,582	16,877,890 R	58.8%	40.6%	59.2%	40.8%
1980	86,515,221	43,904,153	Reagan, Ronald	35,483,883	Carter, Jimmy	7,127,185	8,420,270 R	50.7%	41.0%	55.3%	44.7%
1976	81,554,989	39,141,091	Ford, Gerald R.	40,829,763	Carter, Jimmy	1,584,135	1,688,672 D	48.0%	50.1%	48.9%	51.1%
1972	77,718,554	47,169,911	Nixon, Richard M.	29,170,383	McGovern, George S.	1,378,260	17,999,528 R	60.7%	37.5%	61.8%	38.2%
1968	73,211,875	31,785,480	Nixon, Richard M.	31,275,166	Humphrey, Hubert H.	10,151,229	510,314 R	43.4%	42.7%	50.4%	49.6%
1964	70,644,592	27,178,188	Goldwater, Barry M.	43,129,566	Johnson, Lyndon B.	336,838	15,951,378 D	38.5%	61.1%	38.7%	61.3%
1960	68,838,219	34,108,157	Nixon, Richard M.	34,226,731	Kennedy, John F.	503,331	118,574 D	49.5%	49.7%	49.9%	50.1%
1956	62,026,908	35,590,472	Eisenhower, Dwight D.	26,022,752	Stevenson, Adlai E.	413,684	9,567,720 R	57.4%	42.0%	57.8%	42.2%
1952	61,550,918	33,936,234	Eisenhower, Dwight D.	27,314,992	Stevenson, Adlai E.	299,692	6,621,242 R	55.1%	44.4%	55.4%	44.6%
1948	48,793,826	21,991,291	Dewey, Thomas E.	24,179,345	Truman, Harry S.	2,623,190	2,188,054 D	45.1%	49.6%	47.6%	52.4%
1944	47,976,670	22,017,617	Dewey, Thomas E.	25,612,610	Roosevelt, Franklin D.	346,443	3,594,993 D	45.9%	53.4%	46.2%	53.8%
1940	49,900,774	22,348,836	Willkie, Wendell	27,313,041	Roosevelt, Franklin D.	238,897	4,964,205 D	44.8%	54.7%	45.0%	55.0%
1936	45,654,763	16,684,231	Landon, Alfred M.	27,757,333	Roosevelt, Franklin D.	1,213,199	11,073,102 D	36.5%	60.8%	37.5%	62.5%
1932	39,761,034	15,760,684	Hoover, Herbert C.	22,829,501	Roosevelt, Franklin D.	1,170,849	7,068,817 D	39.6%	57.4%	40.8%	59.2%
1928	36,805,951	21,437,277	Hoover, Herbert C.	15,007,698	Smith, Alfred E.	360,976	6,429,579 R	58.2%	40.8%	58.8%	41.2%
1924	29,095,023	15,719,921	Coolidge, Calvin	8,386,704	Davis, John W.	4,988,398	7,333,217 R	54.0%	28.8%	65.2%	34.8%
1920	26,768,150	16,153,115	Harding, Warren G.	9,133,092	Cox, James M.	1,481,943	7,020,023 R	60.3%	34.1%	63.9%	36.1%

Republican George W. Bush lost the popular vote in 2000, but won the electoral vote and was elected president. In past elections, the other vote included: 2000 - 2,882,738 Green (Ralph Nader); 1996 - 8,085,402 Reform (Ross Perot); 1992 - 19,741,657 Independent (Ross Perot); 1980 - 5,720,060 Independent (John Anderson); 1968 - 9,906,473 American Independent (George Wallace); 1948 - 1,176,125 States' Rights (Strom Thurmond); 1948 - 1,157,326 Progressive (Henry Wallace); 1924 - 4,832,532 Progressive (Robert LaFollette).

ELECTORAL COLLEGE VOTE 1920 TO 2012

Year	Total	Republican	Democratic	Other	Other Candidate	Other Party
2012	538	206	332	0		
2008	538	173	365	0		
2004	538	286	251	1	John Edwards*	Democrat
2000	538	271	266	1	Abstained*	
1996	538	159	379	0		
1992	538	168	370	0		
1988	538	426	111	1	Lloyd Bentsen*	Democrat
1984	538	525	13	0		
1980	538	489	49	0		
1976	538	240	297	1	Ronald Reagan*	Republican
1972	538	520	17	1	John Hospers*	Libertarian
1968	538	301	191	46	George Wallace	American Independent
1964	538	52	486	0		
1960	537	219	303	15	Harry Byrd	Democrat
1956	531	457	73	1	Walter Jones*	Democrat
1952	531	442	89	0		
1948	531	189	303	39	Strom Thurmond	States' Rights
1944	531	99	432	0		
1940	531	82	449	0		
1936	531	8	523	0		
1932	531	59	472	0		
1928	531	444	87	0		
1924	531	382	136	13	Robert M. La Follette	Progressive
1920	531	404	127	0		

Asterisks indicate "faithless" electors who did not vote for the presidential candidates to which they were pledged. One of the electoral votes for Strom Thurmond in 1948, Harry Byrd in 1960, and George Wallace in 1968 was cast by a faithless elector. The rest of Byrd's support in 1960 came from unpledged electors.

12

ALABAMA

Congressional districts first established for elections held in 2012

7 members

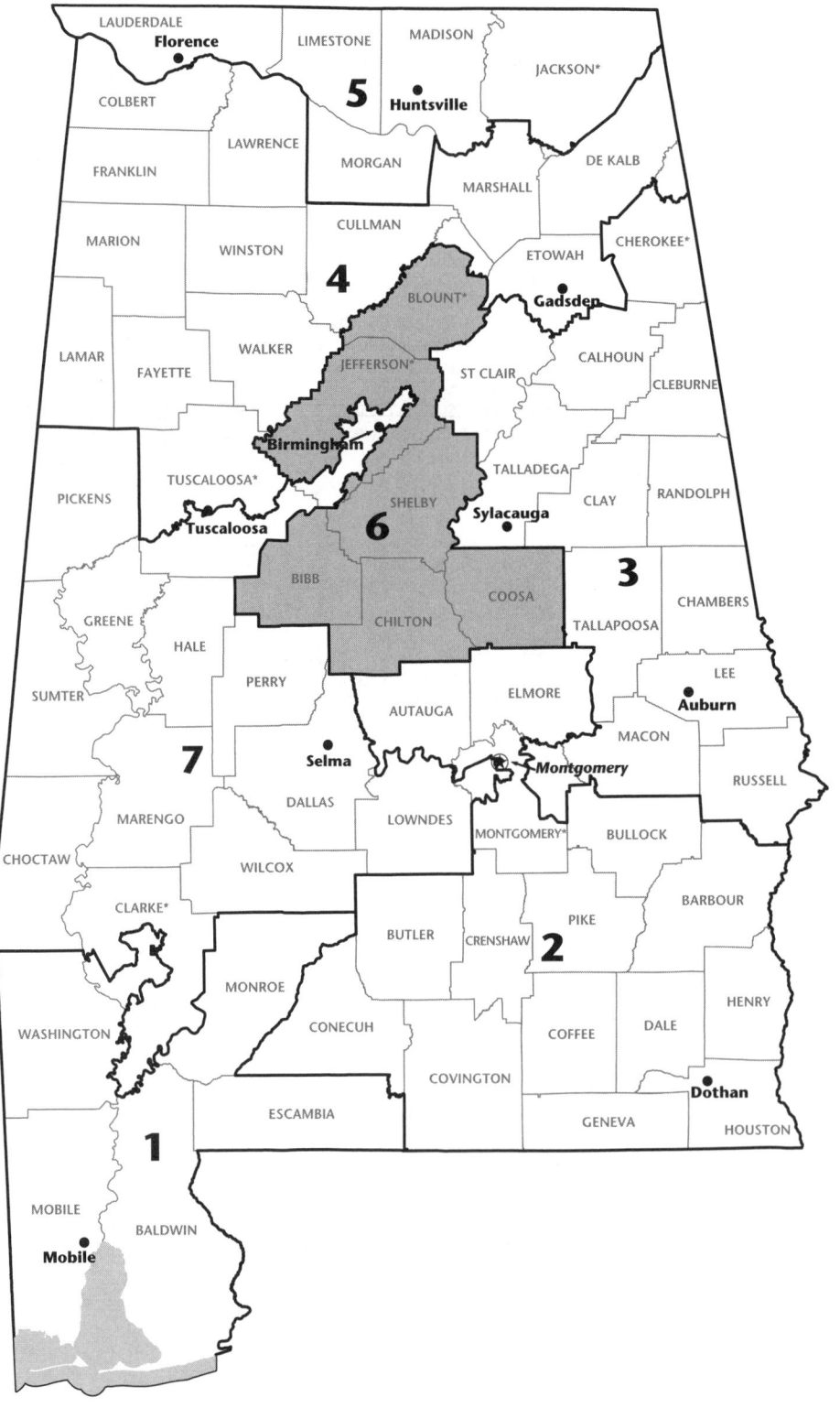

* Asterisk indicates a county whose boundaries include parts of two or more congressional districts.

ALABAMA

GOVERNOR

Robert Bentley (R). Reelected 2014 to a four-year term. Previously elected 2010.

SENATORS (2 Republicans)

Jeff Sessions (R). Reelected 2014 to a six-year term. Previously elected 2008, 2002, 1996.

Richard C. Shelby (R). Reelected 2010 to a six-year term. Previously elected 2004, 1998, 1992, 1986. Changed party affiliation from Democratic to Republican in November 1994.

REPRESENTATIVES (6 Republicans, 1 Democrat)

1. Bradley Byrne (R)
2. Martha Roby (R)
3. Mike Rogers (R)
4. Robert B. Aderholt (R)
5. Mo Brooks (R)
6. Gary J. Palmer (R)
7. Terri A. Sewell (D)

POSTWAR VOTE FOR PRESIDENT

| | | Republican | | Democratic | | Other Vote | Rep.-Dem. Plurality | Percentage | | | |
| | | | | | | | | Total Vote | | Major Vote | |
Year	Total Vote	Vote	Candidate	Vote	Candidate			Rep.	Dem.	Rep.	Dem.
2012	2,074,338	1,255,925	Romney, W. Mitt	795,696	Obama, Barack H.*	22,717	460,229 R	60.5%	38.4%	61.2%	38.8%
2008	2,099,819	1,266,546	McCain, John S. III	813,479	Obama, Barack H.	19,794	453,067 R	60.3%	38.7%	60.9%	39.1%
2004	1,883,449	1,176,394	Bush, George W.*	693,933	Kerry, John F.	13,122	482,461 R	62.5%	36.8%	62.9%	37.1%
2000**	1,666,272	941,173	Bush, George W.	692,611	Gore, Albert Jr.	32,488	248,562 R	56.5%	41.6%	57.6%	42.4%
1996**	1,534,349	769,044	Dole, Robert "Bob"	662,165	Clinton, Bill*	103,140	106,879 R	50.1%	43.2%	53.7%	46.3%
1992**	1,688,060	804,283	Bush, George H.*	690,080	Clinton, Bill	193,697	114,203 R	47.6%	40.9%	53.8%	46.2%
1988	1,378,476	815,576	Bush, George H.	549,506	Dukakis, Michael S.	13,394	266,070 R	59.2%	39.9%	59.7%	40.3%
1984	1,441,713	872,849	Reagan, Ronald*	551,899	Mondale, Walter F.	16,965	320,950 R	60.5%	38.3%	61.3%	38.7%
1980**	1,341,929	654,192	Reagan, Ronald	636,730	Carter, Jimmy*	51,007	17,462 R	48.8%	47.4%	50.7%	49.3%
1976	1,182,850	504,070	Ford, Gerald R.*	659,170	Carter, Jimmy	19,610	155,100 D	42.6%	55.7%	43.3%	56.7%
1972	1,006,111	728,701	Nixon, Richard M.*	256,923	McGovern, George S.	20,487	471,778 R	72.4%	25.5%	73.9%	26.1%
1968**	1,049,922	146,923	Nixon, Richard M.	196,579	Humphrey, Hubert Horatio Jr.	706,420	49,656 D#	14.0%	18.7%	42.8%	57.2%
1964**	689,818	479,085	Goldwater, Barry M. Sr.		Johnson, Lyndon B.*	210,733	479,085 R	69.5%		100.0%	
1960	570,225	237,981	Nixon, Richard M.	324,050	Kennedy, John F.	8,194	86,069 D	41.7%	56.8%	42.3%	57.7%
1956	496,861	195,694	Eisenhower, Dwight D.*	280,844	Stevenson, Adlai E. II	20,323	85,150 D	39.4%	56.5%	41.1%	58.9%
1952	426,120	149,231	Eisenhower, Dwight D.	275,075	Stevenson, Adlai E. II	1,814	125,844 D	35.0%	64.6%	35.2%	64.8%
1948**	214,980	40,930	Dewey, Thomas E.		Truman, Harry S.*	174,050	40,930 R	19.0%		100.0%	

Note: An asterisk (*) denotes incumbent. A pound sign (#) indicates that the state was carried by a third party candidate or independent electoral slate. **In past elections, the other vote included: 2000 - 18,323 Green (Ralph Nader); 1996 - 92,149 Reform (Ross Perot); 1992 - 183,109 Independent (Perot); 1980 - 16,481 Independent (John Anderson); 1968 - 691,425 American Independent (George Wallace); 1964 - 210,732 Unpledged Democratic; 1948 - 171,443 States' Rights (Strom Thurmond). In 1964 and 1948, the Democratic presidential candidates were not listed on the ballot. Wallace carried Alabama in 1968 with 65.9 percent of the total vote. Thurmond won the state in 1948 with 79.7 percent.

ALABAMA

POSTWAR VOTE FOR GOVERNOR

Year	Total Vote	Republican		Democratic		Other Vote	Rep.-Dem. Plurality	Percentage			
								Total Vote		Major Vote	
		Vote	Candidate	Vote	Candidate			Rep.	Dem.	Rep.	Dem.
2014	1,180,413	750,231	Bentley, Robert*	427,787	Griffith, Parker	2,395	322,444 R	63.6%	36.2%	63.7%	36.3%
2010	1,494,273	860,472	Bentley, Robert	625,710	Sparks, Ron	8,091	234,762 R	57.6%	41.9%	57.9%	42.1%
2006	1,250,401	718,327	Riley, Robert*	519,827	Baxley, Lucy	12,247	198,500 R	57.4%	41.6%	58.0%	42.0%
2002	1,367,053	672,225	Riley, Robert	669,105	Siegelman, Don*	25,723	3,120 R	49.2%	48.9%	50.1%	49.9%
1998	1,317,842	554,746	James, Forrest H. "Fob" Jr.*	760,155	Siegelman, Don	2,941	205,409 D	42.1%	57.7%	42.2%	57.8%
1994	1,201,969	604,926	James, Forrest H. "Fob" Jr.	594,169	Folsom, James E. Jr.*	2,874	10,757 R	50.3%	49.4%	50.4%	49.6%
1990	1,216,250	633,519	Hunt, Guy*	582,106	Hubbert, Paul R.	625	51,413 R	52.1%	47.9%	52.1%	47.9%
1986	1,236,230	696,203	Hunt, Guy	537,163	Baxley, Bill	2,864	159,040 R	56.3%	43.5%	56.4%	43.6%
1982	1,128,725	440,815	Folmar, Emory	650,538	Wallace, George C.	37,372	209,723 D	39.1%	57.6%	40.4%	59.6%
1978	760,474	196,963	Hunt, Guy	551,886	James, Forrest H. "Fob" Jr.	11,625	354,923 D	25.9%	72.6%	26.3%	73.7%
1974	598,305	88,381	McCary, Elvin	497,574	Wallace, George C.*	12,350	409,193 D	14.8%	83.2%	15.1%	84.9%
1970**	854,952			637,046	Wallace, George C.	217,906	637,046 D		74.5%		100.0%
1966	848,101	262,943	Martin, James D.	537,505	Wallace, Lurleen B.	47,653	274,562 D	31.0%	63.4%	32.8%	67.2%
1962	315,776			303,987	Wallace, George C.	11,789	303,987 D		96.3%		100.0%
1958	270,952	30,415	Longshore, William L. Jr.	239,633	Patterson, John	904	209,218 D	11.2%	88.4%	11.3%	88.7%
1954	333,090	88,688	Abernethy, Tom	244,401	Folsom, James E.	1	155,713 D	26.6%	73.4%	26.6%	73.4%
1950	170,591	15,177	Crowder, John S.	155,414	Persons, Gordon		140,237 D	8.9%	91.1%	8.9%	91.1%
1946	197,321	22,362	Ward, Lyman	174,959	Folsom, James E.		152,597 D	11.3%	88.7%	11.3%	88.7%

Note: An asterisk (*) denotes incumbent. **In past elections, the other vote included: 1970 - 125,491 National Democratic Party of Alabama (John Logan Cashin), who finished second. The Republican Party did not run a candidate in the 1962 and 1970 gubernatorial elections.

POSTWAR VOTE FOR SENATOR

Year	Total Vote	Republican		Democratic		Other Vote	Rep.-Dem. Plurality	Percentage			
								Total Vote		Major Vote	
		Vote	Candidate	Vote	Candidate			Rep.	Dem.	Rep.	Dem.
2014	818,090	795,606	Sessions, Jeff*			22,484	795,606 R	97.3%		100.0%	
2010	1,485,499	968,181	Shelby, Richard C.*	515,619	Barnes, William G.	1,699	452,562 R	65.2%	34.7%	65.3%	34.7%
2008	2,060,191	1,305,383	Sessions, Jeff*	752,391	Figures, Vivian Davis	2,417	552,992 R	63.4%	36.5%	63.4%	36.6%
2004	1,839,066	1,242,200	Shelby, Richard C.*	595,018	Sowell, Wayne	1,848	647,182 R	67.5%	32.4%	67.6%	32.4%
2002	1,353,023	792,561	Sessions, Jeff*	538,878	Parker, Susan	21,584	253,683 R	58.6%	39.8%	59.5%	40.5%
1998	1,293,405	817,973	Shelby, Richard C.*	474,568	Suddith, Clayton	864	343,405 R	63.2%	36.7%	63.3%	36.7%
1996	1,499,393	786,436	Sessions, Jeff	681,651	Bedford, Roger	31,306	104,785 R	52.5%	45.5%	53.6%	46.4%
1992	1,577,899	522,015	Sellers, Richard	1,022,698	Shelby, Richard C.	33,186	500,683 D	33.1%	64.8%	33.8%	66.2%
1990	1,185,563	467,190	Cabaniss, Bill	717,814	Heflin, Howell*	559	250,624 D	39.4%	60.5%	39.4%	60.6%
1986	1,211,953	602,537	Denton, Jeremiah*	609,360	Shelby, Richard C.	56	6,823 D	49.7%	50.3%	49.7%	50.3%
1984	1,371,238	498,508	Smith, Albert Lee Jr.	860,535	Heflin, Howell*	12,195	362,027 D	36.4%	62.8%	36.7%	63.3%
1980	1,296,757	650,362	Denton, Jeremiah	610,175	Folsom, James E. Jr.	36,220	40,187 R	50.2%	47.1%	51.6%	48.4%
1978	582,025			547,054	Heflin, Howell	34,971	547,054 D		94.0%		100.0%
1978S	731,610	316,170	Martin, James D.	401,852	Stewart, Donald W.	13,588	85,682 D	43.2%	54.9%	44.0%	56.0%
1974	523,290			501,541	Allen, James B.*	21,749	501,541 D		95.8%		100.0%
1972	1,051,099	347,523	Blount, Winton M.	654,491	Sparkman, Richard D.*	49,085	306,968 D	33.1%	62.3%	34.7%	65.3%
1968	912,708	201,227	Hooper, Perry	638,774	Allen, James B.	72,707	437,547 D	22.0%	70.0%	24.0%	76.0%
1966	802,608	313,018	Grenier, John	482,138	Sparkman, John J.*	7,452	169,120 D	39.0%	60.1%	39.4%	60.6%
1962	397,079	195,134	Martin, James D.	201,937	Hill, Lister*	8	6,803 D	49.1%	50.9%	49.1%	50.9%
1960	554,081	164,868	Elgin, Julian	389,196	Sparkman, John J.*	17	224,328 D	29.8%	70.2%	29.8%	70.2%
1956	330,191			330,182	Hill, Lister*	9	330,182 D		100.0%		100.0%
1954	314,459	55,110	Guin, J. Foy Jr.	259,348	Sparkman, John J.*	1	204,238 D	17.5%	82.5%	17.5%	82.5%
1950	164,011			125,534	Hill, Lister*	38,477	125,534 D		76.5%		100.0%
1948	220,875	35,341	Parsons, Paul G.	185,534	Sparkman, John J.*		150,193 D	16.0%	84.0%	16.0%	84.0%
1946S	163,217			163,217	Sparkman, John J.*		163,217 D		100.0%		100.0%

Note: An asterisk (*) denotes incumbent. **The 1946 election and one of the 1978 elections were for short terms to fill vacancies. The Republican Party did not run a candidate in Senate elections in 1946, 1950, 1956, 1974, and 1978. The Democratic Party did not run a candidate in the Senate election in 2014.

ALABAMA
GOVERNOR 2014

2010 Census Population	County	Total Vote	Republican (Bentley)	Democratic (Griffith)	Other	Rep.-Dem. Plurality	Percentage Total Vote Rep.	Dem.	Major Vote Rep.	Dem.
54,571	AUTAUGA	13,122	9,449	3,646	27	5,803 R	72.0%	27.8%	72.2%	27.8%
182,265	BALDWIN	46,299	37,783	8,452	64	29,331 R	81.6%	18.3%	81.7%	18.3%
27,457	BARBOUR	6,774	3,114	3,657	3	543 D	46.0%	54.0%	46.0%	54.0%
22,915	BIBB	4,900	3,525	1,368	7	2,157 R	71.9%	27.9%	72.0%	28.0%
57,322	BLOUNT	14,287	12,081	2,179	27	9,902 R	84.6%	15.3%	84.7%	15.3%
10,914	BULLOCK	3,193	747	2,444	2	1,697 D	23.4%	76.5%	23.4%	76.6%
20,947	BUTLER	5,912	3,155	2,750	7	405 R	53.4%	46.5%	53.4%	46.6%
118,572	CALHOUN	26,829	17,702	9,095	32	8,607 R	66.0%	33.9%	66.1%	33.9%
34,215	CHAMBERS	8,251	4,605	3,640	6	965 R	55.8%	44.1%	55.9%	44.1%
25,989	CHEROKEE	6,883	5,010	1,869	4	3,141 R	72.8%	27.2%	72.8%	27.2%
43,643	CHILTON	11,476	9,036	2,424	16	6,612 R	78.7%	21.1%	78.8%	21.2%
13,859	CHOCTAW	4,332	2,381	1,949	2	432 R	55.0%	45.0%	55.0%	45.0%
25,833	CLARKE	8,530	5,000	3,530	0	1,470 R	58.6%	41.4%	58.6%	41.4%
13,932	CLAY	4,440	3,214	1,223	3	1,991 R	72.4%	27.5%	72.4%	27.6%
14,972	CLEBURNE	3,850	3,129	717	4	2,412 R	81.3%	18.6%	81.4%	18.6%
49,948	COFFEE	10,970	8,555	2,405	10	6,150 R	78.0%	21.9%	78.1%	21.9%
54,428	COLBERT	15,711	9,551	6,119	41	3,432 R	60.8%	38.9%	61.0%	39.0%
13,228	CONECUH	4,719	2,373	2,344	2	29 R	50.3%	49.7%	50.3%	49.7%
11,539	COOSA	3,841	2,260	1,579	2	681 R	58.8%	41.1%	58.9%	41.1%
37,765	COVINGTON	7,937	6,155	1,777	5	4,378 R	77.5%	22.4%	77.6%	22.4%
13,906	CRENSHAW	4,729	2,956	1,767	6	1,189 R	62.5%	37.4%	62.6%	37.4%
80,406	CULLMAN	20,337	16,606	3,698	33	12,908 R	81.7%	18.2%	81.8%	18.2%
50,251	DALE	10,970	8,171	2,794	5	5,377 R	74.5%	25.5%	74.5%	25.5%
43,820	DALLAS	12,590	4,116	8,456	18	4,340 D	32.7%	67.2%	32.7%	67.3%
71,109	DEKALB	16,301	12,593	3,682	26	8,911 R	77.3%	22.6%	77.4%	22.6%
79,303	ELMORE	20,815	15,215	5,561	39	9,654 R	73.1%	26.7%	73.2%	26.8%
38,319	ESCAMBIA	9,054	6,013	3,032	9	2,981 R	66.4%	33.5%	66.5%	33.5%
104,430	ETOWAH	26,471	17,539	8,909	23	8,630 R	66.3%	33.7%	66.3%	33.7%
17,241	FAYETTE	6,824	4,849	1,966	9	2,883 R	71.1%	28.8%	71.2%	28.8%
31,704	FRANKLIN	7,579	4,950	2,617	12	2,333 R	65.3%	34.5%	65.4%	34.6%
26,790	GENEVA	7,343	6,119	1,219	5	4,900 R	83.3%	16.6%	83.4%	16.6%
9,045	GREENE	3,395	538	2,857	0	2,319 D	15.8%	84.2%	15.8%	84.2%
15,760	HALE	5,172	2,002	3,168	2	1,166 D	38.7%	61.3%	38.7%	61.3%
17,302	HENRY	5,116	3,333	1,780	3	1,553 R	65.1%	34.8%	65.2%	34.8%
101,547	HOUSTON	23,590	17,302	6,257	31	11,045 R	73.3%	26.5%	73.4%	26.6%
53,227	JACKSON	11,526	8,258	3,234	34	5,024 R	71.6%	28.1%	71.9%	28.1%
658,466	JEFFERSON	166,271	83,147	82,865	259	282 R	50.0%	49.8%	50.1%	49.9%
14,564	LAMAR	4,408	3,157	1,249	2	1,908 R	71.6%	28.3%	71.7%	28.3%
92,709	LAUDERDALE	23,302	15,782	7,431	89	8,351 R	67.7%	31.9%	68.0%	32.0%
34,339	LAWRENCE	9,192	5,867	3,300	25	2,567 R	63.8%	35.9%	64.0%	36.0%
140,247	LEE	26,503	16,315	10,139	49	6,176 R	61.6%	38.3%	61.7%	38.3%
82,782	LIMESTONE	23,027	17,581	5,379	67	12,202 R	76.3%	23.4%	76.6%	23.4%
11,299	LOWNDES	4,307	1,174	3,127	6	1,953 D	27.3%	72.6%	27.3%	72.7%
21,452	MACON	5,662	829	4,830	3	4,001 D	14.6%	85.3%	14.6%	85.4%
334,811	MADISON	87,094	60,277	26,097	720	34,180 R	69.2%	30.0%	69.8%	30.2%
21,027	MARENGO	6,918	3,152	3,762	4	610 D	45.6%	54.4%	45.6%	54.4%
30,776	MARION	8,172	6,061	2,099	12	3,962 R	74.2%	25.7%	74.3%	25.7%
93,019	MARSHALL	19,905	16,523	3,345	37	13,178 R	83.0%	16.8%	83.2%	16.8%
412,992	MOBILE	83,568	48,651	34,835	82	13,816 R	58.2%	41.7%	58.3%	41.7%
23,068	MONROE	6,083	3,500	2,580	3	920 R	57.5%	42.4%	57.6%	42.4%
229,363	MONTGOMERY	57,302	23,811	33,366	125	9,555 D	41.6%	58.2%	41.6%	58.4%
119,490	MORGAN	29,212	22,428	6,708	76	15,720 R	76.8%	23.0%	77.0%	23.0%
10,591	PERRY	3,596	962	2,633	1	1,671 D	26.8%	73.2%	26.8%	73.2%
19,746	PICKENS	6,055	3,528	2,525	2	1,003 R	58.3%	41.7%	58.3%	41.7%
32,899	PIKE	9,164	5,330	3,821	13	1,509 R	58.2%	41.7%	58.2%	41.8%
22,913	RANDOLPH	6,004	4,076	1,917	11	2,159 R	67.9%	31.9%	68.0%	32.0%
52,947	RUSSELL	9,202	4,440	4,758	4	318 D	48.3%	51.7%	48.3%	51.7%
195,085	SHELBY	50,716	40,297	10,324	95	29,973 R	79.5%	20.4%	79.6%	20.4%
83,593	ST. CLAIR	19,469	15,921	3,522	26	12,399 R	81.8%	18.1%	81.9%	18.1%
13,763	SUMTER	4,156	1,051	3,101	4	2,050 D	25.3%	74.6%	25.3%	74.7%

ALABAMA

GOVERNOR 2014

2010 Census Population	County	Total Vote	Republican (Bentley)	Democratic (Griffith)	Other	Rep.-Dem. Plurality		Percentage			
---	---	---	---	---	---	---	---	Total Vote		Major Vote	
								Rep.	Dem.	Rep.	Dem.
82,291	TALLADEGA	19,231	11,335	7,877	19	3,458 R		58.9%	41.0%	59.0%	41.0%
41,616	TALLAPOOSA	12,053	8,002	4,041	10	3,961 R		66.4%	33.5%	66.4%	33.6%
194,656	TUSCALOOSA	42,653	25,369	17,196	88	8,173 R		59.5%	40.3%	59.6%	40.4%
67,023	WALKER	17,097	12,317	4,750	30	7,567 R		72.0%	27.8%	72.2%	27.8%
17,581	WASHINGTON	5,006	3,263	1,742	1	1,521 R		65.2%	34.8%	65.2%	34.8%
11,670	WILCOX	4,264	1,347	2,913	4	1,566 D		31.6%	68.3%	31.6%	68.4%
24,484	WINSTON	6,753	5,353	1,391	9	3,962 R		79.3%	20.6%	79.4%	20.6%
4,779,736	*TOTAL*	*1,180,413*	*750,231*	*427,787*	*2,395*	*322,444 R*		*63.6%*	*36.2%*	*63.7%*	*36.3%*

ALABAMA

SENATOR 2014

2010 Census Population	County	Total Vote	Republican (Sessions)	Democratic	Other	Rep.-Dem. Plurality		Rep.	Percentage of Total Vote			
---	---	---	---	---	---	---	---	---	Dem.	Rep.	Dem.
54,571	AUTAUGA	10,514	10,345		169	10,345 R		98.4%		100.0%	
182,265	BALDWIN	39,845	39,135		710	39,135 R		98.2%		100.0%	
27,457	BARBOUR	3,555	3,475		80	3,475 R		97.7%		100.0%	
22,915	BIBB	3,965	3,901		64	3,901 R		98.4%		100.0%	
57,322	BLOUNT	12,803	12,674		129	12,674 R		99.0%		100.0%	
10,914	BULLOCK	899	852		47	852 R		94.8%		100.0%	
20,947	BUTLER	3,450	3,391		59	3,391 R		98.3%		100.0%	
118,572	CALHOUN	19,800	19,264		536	19,264 R		97.3%		100.0%	
34,215	CHAMBERS	4,798	4,670		128	4,670 R		97.3%		100.0%	
25,989	CHEROKEE	5,249	5,193		56	5,193 R		98.9%		100.0%	
43,643	CHILTON	9,634	9,546		88	9,546 R		99.1%		100.0%	
13,859	CHOCTAW	2,472	2,428		44	2,428 R		98.2%		100.0%	
25,833	CLARKE	5,163	5,083		80	5,083 R		98.5%		100.0%	
13,932	CLAY	3,453	3,394		59	3,394 R		98.3%		100.0%	
14,972	CLEBURNE	3,258	3,222		36	3,222 R		98.9%		100.0%	
49,948	COFFEE	9,005	8,888		117	8,888 R		98.7%		100.0%	
54,428	COLBERT	10,328	10,065		263	10,065 R		97.5%		100.0%	
13,228	CONECUH	2,420	2,372		48	2,372 R		98.0%		100.0%	
11,539	COOSA	2,493	2,434		59	2,434 R		97.6%		100.0%	
37,765	COVINGTON	6,543	6,496		47	6,496 R		99.3%		100.0%	
13,906	CRENSHAW	3,203	3,159		44	3,159 R		98.6%		100.0%	
80,406	CULLMAN	17,457	17,298		159	17,298 R		99.1%		100.0%	
50,251	DALE	8,903	8,735		168	8,735 R		98.1%		100.0%	
43,820	DALLAS	5,150	4,825		325	4,825 R		93.7%		100.0%	
71,109	DEKALB	12,562	12,445		117	12,445 R		99.1%		100.0%	
79,303	ELMORE	16,912	16,660		252	16,660 R		98.5%		100.0%	
38,319	ESCAMBIA	6,410	6,323		87	6,323 R		98.6%		100.0%	
104,430	ETOWAH	19,673	19,224		449	19,224 R		97.7%		100.0%	
17,241	FAYETTE	5,213	5,166		47	5,166 R		99.1%		100.0%	
31,704	FRANKLIN	5,274	5,185		89	5,185 R		98.3%		100.0%	
26,790	GENEVA	6,216	6,143		73	6,143 R		98.8%		100.0%	
9,045	GREENE	663	629		34	629 R		94.9%		100.0%	
15,760	HALE	2,208	2,142		66	2,142 R		97.0%		100.0%	
17,302	HENRY	3,507	3,437		70	3,437 R		98.0%		100.0%	
101,547	HOUSTON	18,539	18,212		327	18,212 R		98.2%		100.0%	
53,227	JACKSON	8,592	8,413		179	8,413 R		97.9%		100.0%	
658,466	JEFFERSON	96,181	91,243		4,938	91,243 R		94.9%		100.0%	
14,564	LAMAR	3,430	3,387		43	3,387 R		98.7%		100.0%	
92,709	LAUDERDALE	17,028	16,508		520	16,508 R		96.9%		100.0%	
34,339	LAWRENCE	6,190	6,091		99	6,091 R		98.4%		100.0%	

ALABAMA

SENATOR 2014

2010 Census Population	County	Total Vote	Republican (Sessions)	Democratic	Other	Rep.-Dem. Plurality	Rep.	Percentage of Total Vote Dem.	Percentage of Total Vote Rep.	Percentage of Total Vote Dem.
140,247	LEE	18,128	17,514		614	17,514 R	96.6%		100.0%	
82,782	LIMESTONE	18,159	17,740		419	17,740 R	97.7%		100.0%	
11,299	LOWNDES	1,401	1,344		57	1,344 R	95.9%		100.0%	
21,452	MACON	1,260	1,133		127	1,133 R	89.9%		100.0%	
334,811	MADISON	65,032	62,126		2,906	62,126 R	95.5%		100.0%	
21,027	MARENGO	3,465	3,408		57	3,408 R	98.4%		100.0%	
30,776	MARION	6,543	6,467		76	6,467 R	98.8%		100.0%	
93,019	MARSHALL	16,789	16,589		200	16,589 R	98.8%		100.0%	
412,992	MOBILE	52,745	51,264		1,481	51,264 R	97.2%		100.0%	
23,068	MONROE	3,742	3,688		54	3,688 R	98.6%		100.0%	
229,363	MONTGOMERY	28,819	27,252		1,567	27,252 R	94.6%		100.0%	
119,490	MORGAN	23,428	23,008		420	23,008 R	98.2%		100.0%	
10,591	PERRY	1,114	1,079		35	1,079 R	96.9%		100.0%	
19,746	PICKENS	3,736	3,652		84	3,652 R	97.8%		100.0%	
32,899	PIKE	6,113	5,949		164	5,949 R	97.3%		100.0%	
22,913	RANDOLPH	4,176	4,119		57	4,119 R	98.6%		100.0%	
52,947	RUSSELL	4,961	4,756		205	4,756 R	95.9%		100.0%	
195,085	SHELBY	43,181	42,275		906	42,275 R	97.9%		100.0%	
83,593	ST. CLAIR	16,858	16,648		210	16,648 R	98.8%		100.0%	
13,763	SUMTER	1,257	1,206		51	1,206 R	95.9%		100.0%	
82,291	TALLADEGA	12,783	12,465		318	12,465 R	97.5%		100.0%	
41,616	TALLAPOOSA	8,666	8,552		114	8,552 R	98.7%		100.0%	
194,656	TUSCALOOSA	28,334	27,260		1,074	27,260 R	96.2%		100.0%	
67,023	WALKER	13,864	13,600		264	13,600 R	98.1%		100.0%	
17,581	WASHINGTON	3,426	3,393		33	3,393 R	99.0%		100.0%	
11,670	WILCOX	1,528	1,494		34	1,494 R	97.8%		100.0%	
24,484	WINSTON	5,624	5,572		52	5,572 R	99.1%		100.0%	
4,779,736	TOTAL	818,090	795,606		22,484	795,606 R	97.3%		100.0%	

ALABAMA

HOUSE OF REPRESENTATIVES

CD	Year	Total Vote	Republican Vote	Republican Candidate	Democratic Vote	Democratic Candidate	Other Vote	Rep.-Dem. Plurality	Total Vote Rep.	Total Vote Dem.	Major Vote Rep.	Major Vote Dem.
1	2014	152,234	103,758	BYRNE, BRADLEY*	48,278	LEFLORE, BURTON R.	198	55,480 R	68.2%	31.7%	68.2%	31.8%
1	2012	200,676	196,374	BONNER, JOSIAH ROBBINS "JO" JR.*			4,302	196,374 R	97.9%		100.0%	
2	2014	167,952	113,103	ROBY, MARTHA*	54,692	WRIGHT, ERICK	157	58,411 R	67.3%	32.6%	67.4%	32.6%
2	2012	283,953	180,591	ROBY, MARTHA*	103,092	FORD, THERESE	270	77,499 R	63.6%	36.3%	63.7%	36.3%
3	2014	156,620	103,558	ROGERS, MIKE*	52,816	SMITH, JESSE TREMAIN	246	50,742 R	66.1%	33.7%	66.2%	33.8%
3	2012	273,930	175,306	ROGERS, MIKE*	98,141	HARRIS, JOHN ANDREW	483	77,165 R	64.0%	35.8%	64.1%	35.9%
4	2014	134,752	132,831	ADERHOLT, ROBERT B.*			1,921	132,831 R	98.6%		100.0%	
4	2012	269,118	199,071	ADERHOLT, ROBERT B.*	69,706	BOMAN, DANIEL H.	341	129,365 R	74.0%	25.9%	74.1%	25.9%
5	2014	154,974	115,338	BROOKS, MO*			39,636	115,338 R	74.4%		100.0%	
5	2012	291,293	189,185	BROOKS, MO*	101,772	HOLLEY, CHARLIE L.	336	87,413 R	64.9%	34.9%	65.0%	35.0%
6	2014	178,449	135,945	PALMER, GARY J.	42,291	LESTER, MARK	213	93,654 R	76.2%	23.7%	76.3%	23.7%
6	2012	308,102	219,262	BACHUS, SPENCER*	88,267	BAILEY, PENNY "COLONEL"	573	130,995 R	71.2%	28.6%	71.3%	28.7%
7	2014	135,899			133,687	SEWELL, TERRI A.*	2,212	133,687 D		98.4%		100.0%
7	2012	306,558	73,835	CHAMBERLAIN, DON	232,520	SEWELL, TERRI A.*	203	158,685 D	24.1%	75.8%	24.1%	75.9%
TOTAL	2014	1,080,880	704,533		331,764		44,583	372,769 R	65.2%	30.7%	68.0%	32.0%
TOTAL	2012	1,933,630	1,233,624		693,498		6,508	540,126 R	63.8%	35.9%	64.0%	36.0%

Note: An asterisk (*) denotes incumbent.

ALABAMA

GENERAL AND PRIMARY ELECTIONS

2014 GENERAL ELECTIONS: OTHER VOTES

Governor Other vote was 2,395 scattered write-in

Senate Other vote was 22,484 scattered write-in

House Other vote was:

CD 1	198 scattered write-in
CD 2	157 scattered write-in
CD 3	246 scattered write-in
CD 4	1,921 scattered write-in
CD 5	39,005 Unaffiliated (Mark Bray), 631 scattered write-in
CD 6	213 scattered write-in
CD 7	2,212 scattered write-in

2014 PRIMARY ELECTIONS: SUPPLEMENTARY INFORMATION

Primary	June 3, 2014	**Registration**	2,961,790	No Party Registration
Primary Runoff	July 15, 2014	(as of May 31, 2014 – includes 115,741 inactive registrants)		

Primary Type Open—Any registered voter could vote in either the Democratic or Republican primary, although any voter who participated in the Republican primary could not vote in the Democratic runoff. There was no such restriction on participation in the Republican runoff.

	REPUBLICAN PRIMARIES			DEMOCRATIC PRIMARIES		
Senator	Sessions, Jeff*	Unopposed				
Governor	Bentley, Robert*	388,247	89.3%	Griffith, Parker	115,433	63.9%
	George, Stacy Lee	25,134	5.8%	Bass, Kevin	65,225	36.1%
	Starkey, Bob	21,144	4.9%			
	TOTAL	434,525		TOTAL	180,658	
Congressional District 1	Byrne, Bradley*	Unopposed		LeFlore, Burton R.	Unopposed	
Congressional District 2	Roby, Martha*	Unopposed		Wright, Erick	Unopposed	
Congressional District 3	Rogers, Mike*	50,372	75.9%	Smith, Jesse Tremain	Unopposed	
	Casson, Thomas	15,999	24.1%			
	TOTAL	66,371				
Congressional District 4	Aderholt, Robert B.*	Unopposed				
Congressional District 5	Brooks, Mo*	49,117	80.3%			
	Hill Sr., Jerry Wayne	12,038	19.7%			
	TOTAL	61,155				

ALABAMA

GENERAL AND PRIMARY ELECTIONS

	REPUBLICAN PRIMARIES			DEMOCRATIC PRIMARIES		
Congressional District 6	DeMarco, Paul	30,894	32.7%	Vise, Avery	Unopposed	
	Palmer, Gary J.	18,655	19.7%			
	Beason, Scott	14,451	15.3%			
	Mathis, Chad	14,420	15.3%			
	Brooke, Will W.	13,130	13.9%			
	Vigneulle, Tom R.	2,397	2.5%			
	Shattuck, Robert	587	0.6%			
	TOTAL	94,534				
	PRIMARY RUNOFF					
	Palmer, Gary J.	47,524	63.5%			
	DeMarco, Paul	27,329	36.5%			
	TOTAL	74,853				
Congressional District 7				Sewell, Terri A.*	74,953	83.9%
				Johnson, Tamara Harris	14,374	16.1%
				TOTAL	89,327	

Note: Democratic primary winner Avery Vise withdrew from the race after the primary election, and was replaced on the general election ballot by Mark Lester. An asterisk (*) denotes incumbent.

ALASKA

One member At Large

Alaska reports election results by legislative district. The districts indicated were first effective for the 2014 elections.

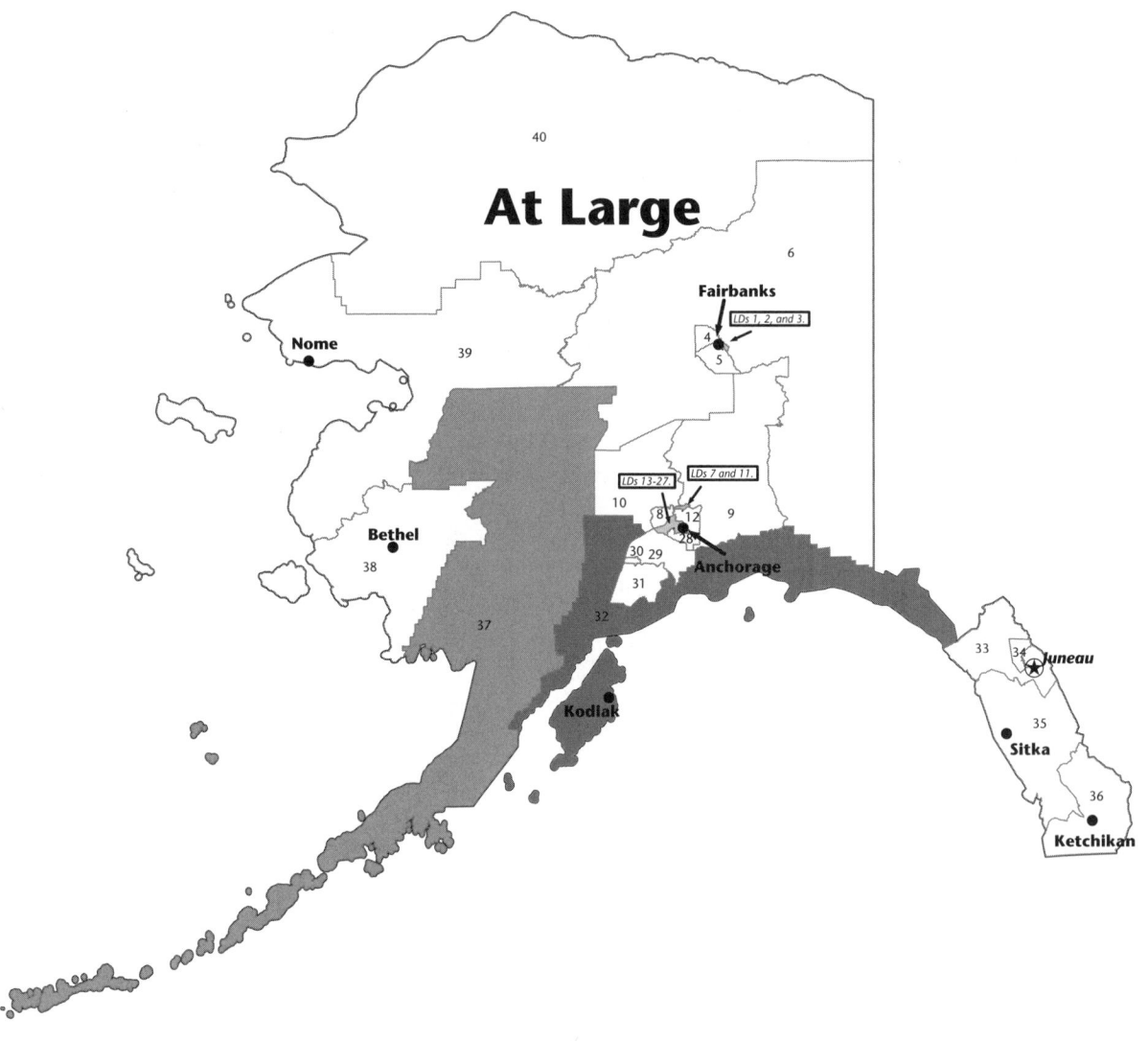

40

At Large

6

Fairbanks

LDs 1, 2, and 3.

4
5

Nome

39

LDs 13-27.

LDs 7 and 11.

10

8 12
28
9

Bethel

30 29

38

31

Anchorage

37

32

33 34 *Juneau*

Kodiak

35

Sitka

36

Ketchikan

Alaska includes more islands to the west of those that are illustrated on this map.

ALASKA

GOVERNOR

Bill Walker (I) Elected 2014 to a four-year term.

SENATORS (2 Republicans)

Lisa Murkowski (R). Reelected 2010 to a six-year term as a write-in candidate. Previously elected 2004. Had been appointed December 20, 2002, to fill the vacancy created by the resignation of her father, Frank H. Murkowski (R), to become governor of Alaska.

Daniel Sullivan (R). Elected 2014 to a six-year term.

REPRESENTATIVE (1 Republican)

At Large. Don Young (R)

POSTWAR VOTE FOR PRESIDENT

Year	Total Vote	Republican		Democratic		Other Vote	Rep.-Dem. Plurality	Percentage			
								Total Vote		Major Vote	
		Vote	Candidate	Vote	Candidate			Rep.	Dem.	Rep.	Dem.
2012	300,495	164,676	Romney, W. Mitt	122,640	Obama, Barack H.*	13,179	42,036 R	54.8%	40.8%	57.3%	42.7%
2008	326,197	193,841	McCain, John S. III	123,594	Obama, Barack H.	8,762	70,247 R	59.4%	37.9%	61.1%	38.9%
2004	312,598	190,889	Bush, George W.*	111,025	Kerry, John F.	10,684	79,864 R	61.1%	35.5%	63.2%	36.8%
2000**	285,560	167,398	Bush, George W.	79,004	Gore, Albert Jr.	39,158	88,394 R	58.6%	27.7%	67.9%	32.1%
1996**	241,620	122,746	Dole, Robert "Bob"	80,380	Clinton, Bill*	38,494	42,366 R	50.8%	33.3%	60.4%	39.6%
1992**	258,506	102,000	Bush, George H.*	78,294	Clinton, Bill	78,212	23,706 R	39.5%	30.3%	56.6%	43.4%
1988	200,116	119,251	Bush, George H.	72,584	Dukakis, Michael S.	8,281	46,667 R	59.6%	36.3%	62.2%	37.8%
1984	207,605	138,377	Reagan, Ronald*	62,007	Mondale, Walter F.	7,221	76,370 R	66.7%	29.9%	69.1%	30.9%
1980**	158,445	86,112	Reagan, Ronald	41,842	Carter, Jimmy*	30,491	44,270 R	54.3%	26.4%	67.3%	32.7%
1976	123,574	71,555	Ford, Gerald R.*	44,058	Carter, Jimmy	7,961	27,497 R	57.9%	35.7%	61.9%	38.1%
1972	95,219	55,349	Nixon, Richard M.*	32,967	McGovern, George S.	6,903	22,382 R	58.1%	34.6%	62.7%	37.3%
1968**	83,035	37,600	Nixon, Richard M.	35,411	Humphrey, Hubert Horatio Jr.	10,024	2,189 R	45.3%	42.6%	51.5%	48.5%
1964	67,259	22,930	Goldwater, Barry M. Sr.	44,329	Johnson, Lyndon B.*		21,399 D	34.1%	65.9%	34.1%	65.9%
1960	60,762	30,953	Nixon, Richard M.	29,809	Kennedy, John F.		1,144 R	50.9%	49.1%	50.9%	49.1%

Note: An asterisk (*) denotes incumbent. **In past elections, the other vote included: 2000 - 28,747 Green (Ralph Nader); 1996 - 26,333 Reform (Ross Perot); 1992 - 73,481 Independent (Perot); 1980 - 18,479 Libertarian (Ed Clark) and 11,155 Independent (John Anderson); 1968 - 10,024 American Independent (George Wallace). Alaska was formally admitted as a state in January 1959.

ALASKA

POSTWAR VOTE FOR GOVERNOR

Year	Total Vote	Republican Vote	Republican Candidate	Democratic Vote	Democratic Candidate	Other Vote	Rep.-Dem. Plurality	Total Vote Rep.	Total Vote Dem.	Major Vote Rep.	Major Vote Dem.
2014**	279,958	128,435	Parnell, Sean R.*			151,523	128,435 R#	45.9%		100.0%	
2010	256,192	151,318	Parnell, Sean R.*	96,519	Berkowitz, Ethan A.	8,355	54,799 R	59.1%	37.7%	61.1%	38.9%
2006	237,322	114,697	Palin, Sarah H.	97,238	Knowles, Tony	25,387	17,459 R	48.3%	41.0%	54.1%	45.9%
2002	231,484	129,279	Murkowski, Frank H.	94,216	Ulmer, Fran	7,989	35,063 R	55.8%	40.7%	57.8%	42.2%
1998**	220,177	39,331	Lindauer, John	112,879	Knowles, Tony*	67,967	73,548 D	17.9%	51.3%	25.8%	74.2%
1994**	213,435	87,157	Campbell, James O.	87,693	Knowles, Tony*	38,585	536 D	40.8%	41.1%	49.8%	50.2%
1990**	194,750	50,991	Sturgulewski, Arliss	60,201	Knowles, Tony	83,558	9,210 D#	26.2%	30.9%	45.9%	54.1%
1986	179,555	76,515	Sturgulewski, Arliss	84,943	Cowper, Steve	18,097	8,428 D	42.6%	47.3%	47.4%	52.6%
1982**	194,885	72,291	Fink, Tom	89,918	Sheffield, Bill	32,676	17,627 D	37.1%	46.1%	44.6%	55.4%
1978**	126,910	49,580	Hammond, Jay S.*	25,656	Croft, Chancy	51,674	23,924 R	39.1%	20.2%	65.9%	34.1%
1974	96,163	45,840	Hammond, Jay S.	45,553	Egan, William A.*	4,770	287 R	47.7%	47.4%	50.2%	49.8%
1970	80,779	37,264	Miller, Keith	42,309	Egan, William A.	1,206	5,045 D	46.1%	52.4%	46.8%	53.2%
1966	66,294	33,145	Hickel, Walter J.	32,065	Egan, William A.*	1,084	1,080 R	50.0%	48.4%	50.8%	49.2%
1962	56,681	27,054	Stepovich, Mike	29,627	Egan, William A.*		2,573 D	47.7%	52.3%	47.7%	52.3%
1958	48,968	19,299	Butrovich, John Jr.	29,189	Egan, William A.	480	9,890 D	39.4%	59.6%	39.8%	60.2%

Note: An asterisk (*) denotes incumbent. A pound sign (#) indicates (1990) Alaska Independent candidate Walter Hickel's victory over the Democratic candidate Tony Knowles, and (2014) Independent candidate Bill Walker's victory over the Republican candidate Sean Parnell. **In past elections, the other vote included: 2014 - 134,658 Independent (Bill Walker) was elected with 48.1 percent of the vote; 1998 - 40,209 write-in (Robin Taylor), who finished second; 1994 - 27,838 Alaskan Independence (John B. "Jack" Coghill); 1990 - 75,721 Alaskan Independence (Walter J. Hickel); 1982 - 29,067 Libertarian (Richard L. Randolph); 1978 - 33,555 write-in (Hickel) and 15,656 Alaskans for Kelly (Tom Kelly). Hickel won the 1990 election with 38.9 percent of the total vote and finished second in 1978.

POSTWAR VOTE FOR SENATOR

Year	Total Vote	Republican Vote	Republican Candidate	Democratic Vote	Democratic Candidate	Other Vote	Rep.-Dem. Plurality	Total Vote Rep.	Total Vote Dem.	Major Vote Rep.	Major Vote Dem.
2014	282,400	135,445	Sullivan, Daniel	129,431	Begich, Mark*	17,524	6,014 R	48.0%	45.8%	51.1%	48.9%
2010**	255,474	90,839	Miller, Joe	60,045	McAdams, Scott T.	104,590	30,794 R	35.6%	23.5%	60.2%	39.8%
2008	317,723	147,814	Stevens, Ted*	151,767	Begich, Mark	18,142	3,953 D	46.5%	47.8%	49.3%	50.7%
2004	308,315	149,773	Murkowski, Lisa A.*	140,424	Knowles, Tony	18,118	9,349 R	48.6%	45.5%	51.6%	48.4%
2002	229,548	179,438	Stevens, Ted*	24,133	Vondersaar, Frank	25,977	155,305 R	78.2%	10.5%	88.1%	11.9%
1998	221,807	165,227	Murkowski, Frank H.*	43,743	Sonneman, Joseph	12,837	121,484 R	74.5%	19.7%	79.1%	20.9%
1996**	231,916	177,893	Stevens, Ted*	23,977	Obermeyer, Theresa N.	30,046	153,916 R	76.7%	10.3%	88.1%	11.9%
1992	239,714	127,163	Murkowski, Frank H.	92,065	Smith, Tony	20,486	35,098 R	53.0%	38.4%	58.0%	42.0%
1990	189,957	125,806	Stevens, Ted	61,152	Beasley, Michael	2,999	64,654 R	66.2%	32.2%	67.3%	32.7%
1986	180,801	97,674	Murkowski, Frank H.*	79,727	Olds, Glenn	3,400	17,947 R	54.0%	44.1%	55.1%	44.9%
1984	206,438	146,919	Stevens, Ted*	58,804	Havelock, John E.	715	88,115 R	71.2%	28.5%	71.4%	28.6%
1980	156,762	84,159	Murkowski, Frank H.	72,007	Gruening, Clark S.	596	12,152 R	53.7%	45.9%	53.9%	46.1%
1978	122,741	92,783	Stevens, Ted*	29,574	Hobbs, Donald W.	384	63,209 R	75.6%	24.1%	75.8%	24.2%
1974	93,275	38,914	Lewis, C. R.	54,361	Gravel, Mike		15,447 D	41.7%	58.3%	41.7%	58.3%
1972	96,007	74,216	Stevens, Ted*	21,791	Guess, Gene		52,425 R	77.3%	22.7%	77.3%	22.7%
1970S	80,364	47,908	Stevens, Ted*	32,456	Kay, Wendell P.		15,452 R	59.6%	40.4%	59.6%	40.4%
1968	80,931	30,286	Rasmuson, Elmer	36,527	Gravel, Mike	14,118	6,241 D	37.4%	45.1%	45.3%	54.7%
1966	65,250	15,961	McKinley, Lee L.	49,289	Bartlett, E. L.*		33,328 D	24.5%	75.5%	24.5%	75.5%
1962	58,181	24,354	Stevens, Ted	33,827	Gruening, Ernest		9,473 D	41.9%	58.1%	41.9%	58.1%
1960	59,978	21,937	McKinley, Lee L.	38,041	Bartlett, E. L.*		16,104 D	36.6%	63.4%	36.6%	63.4%
1958	48,837	7,299	Robertson, R. E.	40,939	Bartlett, E. L.	599	33,640 D	14.9%	83.8%	15.1%	84.9%
1958	49,525	23,462	Stepovich, Mike	26,063	Gruening, Ernest		2,601 D	47.4%	52.6%	47.4%	52.6%

Note: An asterisk (*) denotes incumbent. **In past elections, the other vote included: 2010 - 101,091 Republican write-in (Lisa Murkowski), who won reelection with 39.6 percent of the vote; 1996 - 29,037 Green (Jed Whittaker), who finished second. The 1970 election was for a short term to fill a vacancy. The two 1958 elections were held to indeterminate terms and the Senate later determined by lot that Senator Gruening would serve four years, Senator Bartlett two. The plurality for 2010 shows the difference between the official Republican and Democratic candidates.

ALASKA

GOVERNOR 2014

2010 Census Population	Election District	Total Vote	Republican (Parnell)	Democratic	Independent (Walker)	Other	Rep.-Ind. Plurality	Total Vote Rep.	Dem.	Ind.
17,726	Election District 1	5,849	2,478		2,978	393	500 I	42.4%		50.9%
17,738	Election District 2	3,796	1,912		1,646	238	266 R	50.4%		43.4%
17,673	Election District 3	6,053	3,416		2,287	350	1129 R	56.4%		37.8%
17,786	Election District 4	8,603	3,068		5,122	413	2054 I	35.7%		59.5%
17,837	Election District 5	6,933	2,721		3,801	411	1080 I	39.2%		54.8%
17,807	Election District 6	7,036	3,222		3,347	467	125 I	45.8%		47.6%
17,703	Election District 7	6,964	3,924		2,675	365	1249 R	56.3%		38.4%
17,830	Election District 8	6,450	3,649		2,426	375	1223 R	56.6%		37.6%
17,739	Election District 9	7,543	3,675		3,463	405	212 R	48.7%		45.9%
17,827	Election District 10	7,605	4,133		2,983	489	1150 R	54.3%		39.2%
17,716	Election District 11	8,206	4,600		3,222	384	1378 R	56.1%		39.3%
17,671	Election District 12	8,243	4,661		3,216	366	1445 R	56.5%		39.0%
17,678	Election District 13	4,724	2,644		1,777	303	867 R	56.0%		37.6%
17,818	Election District 14	8,848	4,959		3,537	352	1422 R	56.0%		40.0%
17,672	Election District 15	4,071	1,895		1,846	330	49 R	46.5%		45.3%
17,806	Election District 16	6,544	2,670		3,409	465	739 I	40.8%		52.1%
17,797	Election District 17	5,976	2,284		3,281	411	997 I	38.2%		54.9%
17,925	Election District 18	7,036	2,449		4,120	467	1671 I	34.8%		58.6%
17,692	Election District 19	4,439	1,543		2,493	403	950 I	34.8%		56.2%
17,718	Election District 20	6,540	2,018		4,097	425	2079 I	30.9%		62.6%
17,642	Election District 21	8,068	3,165		4,480	423	1315 I	39.2%		55.5%
17,755	Election District 22	7,777	3,709		3,713	355	4 I	47.7%		47.7%
17,809	Election District 23	6,220	2,710		3,146	364	436 I	43.6%		50.6%
17,702	Election District 24	8,622	4,292		3,976	354	316 R	49.8%		46.1%
17,924	Election District 25	7,220	3,226		3,573	421	347 I	44.7%		49.5%
17,693	Election District 26	8,111	4,240		3,486	385	754 R	52.3%		43.0%
17,678	Election District 27	8,054	3,573		4,051	430	478 I	44.4%		50.3%
17,778	Election District 28	10,455	5,147		4,984	324	163 R	49.2%		47.7%
18,026	Election District 29	8,016	4,659		2,890	467	1769 R	58.1%		36.1%
18,021	Election District 30	7,721	4,755		2,587	379	2168 R	61.6%		33.5%
17,971	Election District 31	8,555	3,844		4,263	448	419 I	44.9%		49.8%
18,077	Election District 32	6,137	2,472		3,243	422	771 I	40.3%		52.8%
17,635	Election District 33	9,187	2,857		5,837	493	2980 I	31.1%		63.5%
17,668	Election District 34	8,619	3,966		4,257	396	291 I	46.0%		49.4%
17,825	Election District 35	7,943	3,229		4,047	667	818 I	40.7%		51.0%
17,874	Election District 36	7,080	3,358		3,257	465	101 R	47.4%		46.0%
17,448	Election District 37	5,077	1,931		2,618	528	687 I	38.0%		51.6%
17,546	Election District 38	5,260	1,617		3,004	639	1387 I	30.7%		57.1%
17,677	Election District 39	5,872	2,132		3,147	593	1015 I	36.3%		53.6%
17,323	Election District 40	4,505	1,632		2,373	500	741 I	36.2%		52.7%
710,231	Total	279,958	128,435		134,658	16,865	6223 I	45.9%		48.1%

Note: *Population totals represent Census 2010 data applied to district boundaries that were re-drawn in 2013 and in place for the 2014 elections.

ALASKA

SENATOR 2014

2010 Census Population	Election District	Total Vote	Republican (Sullivan)	Democratic (Begich)	Other	Rep.-Dem. Plurality	Percentage Total Vote Rep.	Dem.	Major Vote Rep.	Dem.
17,726	Election District 1	5,908	2,611	2,923	374	312 D	44.2%	49.5%	47.2%	52.8%
17,738	Election District 2	3,826	2,160	1,420	246	740 R	56.5%	37.1%	60.3%	39.7%
17,673	Election District 3	6,096	4,081	1,604	411	2,477 R	66.9%	26.3%	71.8%	28.2%
17,786	Election District 4	8,670	3,620	4,593	457	973 D	41.8%	53.0%	44.1%	55.9%
17,837	Election District 5	7,011	3,099	3,518	394	419 D	44.2%	50.2%	46.8%	53.2%

24

ALASKA

SENATOR 2014

2010 Census Population	Election District	Total Vote	Republican (Sullivan)	Democratic (Begich)	Other	Rep.-Dem. Plurality	Total Vote		Major Vote	
							Rep.	Dem.	Rep.	Dem.
17,807	Election District 6	7,092	3,667	2,949	476	718 R	51.7%	41.6%	55.4%	44.6%
17,703	Election District 7	6,978	4,518	1,860	600	2,658 R	64.7%	26.7%	70.8%	29.2%
17,830	Election District 8	6,483	4,322	1,588	573	2,734 R	66.7%	24.5%	73.1%	26.9%
17,739	Election District 9	7,531	4,558	2,396	577	2,162 R	60.5%	31.8%	65.5%	34.5%
17,827	Election District 10	7,632	4,669	2,319	644	2,350 R	61.2%	30.4%	66.8%	33.2%
17,716	Election District 11	8,242	5,168	2,514	560	2,654 R	62.7%	30.5%	67.3%	32.7%
17,671	Election District 12	8,265	5,323	2,404	538	2,919 R	64.4%	29.1%	68.9%	31.1%
17,678	Election District 13	4,824	2,979	1,530	315	1,449 R	61.8%	31.7%	66.1%	33.9%
17,818	Election District 14	8,907	5,488	3,035	384	2,453 R	61.6%	34.1%	64.4%	35.6%
17,672	Election District 15	4,115	1,864	2,006	245	142 D	45.3%	48.7%	48.2%	51.8%
17,806	Election District 16	6,638	2,707	3,562	369	855 D	40.8%	53.7%	43.2%	56.8%
17,797	Election District 17	6,092	2,353	3,322	417	969 D	38.6%	54.5%	41.5%	58.5%
17,925	Election District 18	7,137	2,442	4,270	425	1,828 D	34.2%	59.8%	36.4%	63.6%
17,692	Election District 19	4,532	1,293	2,945	294	1,652 D	28.5%	65.0%	30.5%	69.5%
17,718	Election District 20	6,656	2,005	4,322	329	2,317 D	30.1%	64.9%	31.7%	68.3%
17,642	Election District 21	8,155	3,341	4,442	372	1,101 D	41.0%	54.5%	42.9%	57.1%
17,755	Election District 22	7,835	3,919	3,480	436	439 R	50.0%	44.4%	53.0%	47.0%
17,809	Election District 23	6,302	2,746	3,162	394	416 D	43.6%	50.2%	46.5%	53.5%
17,702	Election District 24	8,673	4,597	3,738	338	859 R	53.0%	43.1%	55.2%	44.8%
17,924	Election District 25	7,305	3,338	3,544	423	206 D	45.7%	48.5%	48.5%	51.5%
17,693	Election District 26	8,182	4,399	3,435	348	964 R	53.8%	42.0%	56.2%	43.8%
17,678	Election District 27	8,136	3,639	4,081	416	442 D	44.7%	50.2%	47.1%	52.9%
17,778	Election District 28	10,519	5,465	4,737	317	728 R	52.0%	45.0%	53.6%	46.4%
18,026	Election District 29	8,075	5,075	2,403	597	2,672 R	62.8%	29.8%	67.9%	32.1%
18,021	Election District 30	7,772	5,024	2,232	516	2,792 R	64.6%	28.7%	69.2%	30.8%
17,971	Election District 31	8,631	4,296	3,772	563	524 R	49.8%	43.7%	53.2%	46.8%
18,077	Election District 32	6,204	2,722	3,045	437	323 D	43.9%	49.1%	47.2%	52.8%
17,635	Election District 33	9,265	2,615	6,204	446	3,589 D	28.2%	67.0%	29.7%	70.3%
17,668	Election District 34	8,650	3,647	4,481	522	834 D	42.2%	51.8%	44.9%	55.1%
17,825	Election District 35	8,068	3,164	4,291	613	1,127 D	39.2%	53.2%	42.4%	57.6%
17,874	Election District 36	7,143	3,672	2,948	523	724 R	51.4%	41.3%	55.5%	44.5%
17,448	Election District 37	5,133	1,458	3,319	356	1,861 D	28.4%	64.7%	30.5%	69.5%
17,546	Election District 38	5,287	862	4,084	341	3,222 D	16.3%	77.2%	17.4%	82.6%
17,677	Election District 39	5,911	1,265	4,144	502	2,879 D	21.4%	70.1%	23.4%	76.6%
17,323	Election District 40	4,519	1,274	2,809	436	1,535 D	28.2%	62.2%	31.2%	68.8%
710,231	TOTAL	282,400	135,445	129,431	17,524	6,014 R	48.0%	45.8%	51.1%	48.9%

Note: *Population totals represent Census 2010 data applied to district boundaries that were re-drawn in 2013 and in place for the 2014 elections.

ALASKA

HOUSE OF REPRESENTATIVES

CD	Year	Total Vote	Republican Vote	Republican Candidate	Democratic Vote	Democratic Candidate	Other Vote	Rep.-Dem. Plurality	Total Vote Rep.	Total Vote Dem.	Major Vote Rep.	Major Vote Dem.
At Large	2014	279,741	142,572	YOUNG, DON*	114,602	DUNBAR, FORREST	22,567	27,970 R	51.0%	41.0%	55.4%	44.6%
At Large	2012	289,804	185,296	YOUNG, DON*	82,927	CISSNA, SHARON M.	21,581	102,369 R	63.9%	28.6%	69.1%	30.9%
At Large	2010	254,335	175,384	YOUNG, DON*	77,606	CRAWFORD, HARRY T.	1,345	97,778 R	69.0%	30.5%	69.3%	30.7%
At Large	2008	316,978	158,939	YOUNG, DON*	142,560	BERKOWITZ, ETHAN A.	15,479	16,379 R	50.1%	45.0%	52.7%	47.3%
At Large	2006	234,645	132,743	YOUNG, DON*	93,879	BENSON, DIANE E.	8,023	38,864 R	56.6%	40.0%	58.6%	41.4%
At Large	2004	299,996	213,216	YOUNG, DON*	67,074	HIGGINS, THOMAS M.	19,706	146,142 R	71.1%	22.4%	76.1%	23.9%
At Large	2002	227,725	169,685	YOUNG, DON*	39,357	GREENE, CLIFFORD	18,683	130,328 R	74.5%	17.3%	81.2%	18.8%
At Large	2000	274,393	190,862	YOUNG, DON*	45,372	GREENE, CLIFFORD	38,159	145,490 R	69.6%	16.5%	80.8%	19.2%
At Large	1998	223,300	139,676	YOUNG, DON*	77,232	DUNCAN, JIM	6,392	62,444 R	62.6%	34.6%	64.4%	35.6%
At Large	1996	233,700	138,834	YOUNG, DON*	85,114	LINCOLN, GEORGIANNA	9,752	53,720 R	59.4%	36.4%	62.0%	38.0%

ALASKA
HOUSE OF REPRESENTATIVES

			Republican		Democratic		Other	Rep.-Dem.	Percentage			
									Total Vote		Major Vote	
CD	Year	Total Vote	Vote	Candidate	Vote	Candidate	Vote	Plurality	Rep.	Dem.	Rep.	Dem.
At Large	1994	208,240	118,537	YOUNG, DON*	68,172	SMITH, TONY	21,531	50,365 R	56.9%	32.7%	63.5%	36.5%
At Large	1992	239,116	111,849	YOUNG, DON*	102,378	DEVENS, JOHN S.	24,889	9,471 R	46.8%	42.8%	52.2%	47.8%
At Large	1990	191,647	99,003	YOUNG, DON*	91,677	DEVENS, JOHN S.	967	7,326 R	51.7%	47.8%	51.9%	48.1%
At Large	1988	192,955	120,595	YOUNG, DON*	71,881	GRUENSTEIN, PETER	479	48,714 R	62.5%	37.3%	62.7%	37.3%
At Large	1986	180,277	101,799	YOUNG, DON*	74,053	BEGICH, PEGGE	4,425	27,746 R	56.5%	41.1%	57.9%	42.1%
At Large	1984	206,437	113,582	YOUNG, DON*	86,052	BEGICH, PEGGE	6,803	27,530 R	55.0%	41.7%	56.9%	43.1%
At Large	1982	181,084	128,274	YOUNG, DON*	52,011	CARLSON, DAVE	799	76,263 R	70.8%	28.7%	71.2%	28.8%
At Large	1980	154,618	114,089	YOUNG, DON*	39,922	PARNELL, KEVIN	607	74,167 R	73.8%	25.8%	74.1%	25.9%
At Large	1978	124,187	68,811	YOUNG, DON*	55,176	RODEY, PATRICK	200	13,635 R	55.4%	44.4%	55.5%	44.5%
At Large	1976	118,208	83,722	YOUNG, DON*	34,194	HOPSON, EBEN	292	49,528 R	70.8%	28.9%	71.0%	29.0%
At Large	1974	95,921	51,641	YOUNG, DON*	44,280	HENSLEY, WILLIAM L.		7,361 R	53.8%	46.2%	53.8%	46.2%
At Large	1972	95,401	41,750	YOUNG, DON	53,651	BEGICH, NICHOLAS J.*		11,901 D	43.8%	56.2%	43.8%	56.2%
At Large	1970	80,084	35,947	MURKOWSKI, FRANK H.	44,137	BEGICH, NICHOLAS J.		8,190 D	44.9%	55.1%	44.9%	55.1%
At Large	1968	80,362	43,577	POLLOCK, HOWARD W.*	36,785	BEGICH, NICHOLAS J.		6,792 R	54.2%	45.8%	54.2%	45.8%
At Large	1966	65,907	34,040	POLLOCK, HOWARD W.	31,867	RIVERS, RALPH J.*		2,173 R	51.6%	48.4%	51.6%	48.4%
At Large	1964	67,156	32,566	THOMAS, LOWELL	34,590	RIVERS, RALPH J.*		2,024 D	48.5%	51.5%	48.5%	51.5%
At Large	1962	58,591	26,638	THOMAS, LOWELL	31,953	RIVERS, RALPH J.*		5,315 D	45.5%	54.5%	45.5%	54.5%
At Large	1960	59,063	25,517	RETTIG, R. L.	33,546	RIVERS, RALPH J.*		8,029 D	43.2%	56.8%	43.2%	56.8%
At Large	1958	48,644	20,699	BENSON, HENRY A.	27,945	RIVERS, RALPH J.		7,246 D	42.6%	57.4%	42.6%	57.4%

Note: An asterisk (*) denotes incumbent.

ALASKA
GENERAL AND PRIMARY ELECTIONS

2014 GENERAL ELECTIONS: OTHER VOTES

Governor Other vote was 134,658 Non Affiliated (Bill Walker), 8,985 Libertarian (Carolyn F. "Care" Clift), 6,987 Constitution (J. R. Myers), 893 scattered write-in

Senate Other vote was 10,512 Libertarian (Mark Fish), 5,636 Non Affiliated (Ted Gianoutsos), 1,376 scattered write-in

House Other vote was:

At Large 21,290 Libertarian (Jim C. McDermott), 1,277 scattered write-in

2014 PRIMARY ELECTIONS: SUPPLEMENTARY INFORMATION

Primary	August 19, 2014	**Registration** (as of August 3, 2014)	495,012	Republican	133,155
				Democratic	69,131
				Alaskan Independence	16,247
				Libertarian	7,219
				Green	1,781
				Veterans	1,144
				Constitution	203
				Nonpartisan	84,152
				Undeclared	181,980

Primary Type Any registered voter could participate in the Democratic primary. The Republican primary was restricted to registered Republican, Undeclared, and Nonpartisan voters. (Undeclared voters may be associated with a party but do not wish to declare which one. Nonpartisan voters are not associated with any party.) Democratic candidates were listed on the primary ballot together with candidates of the Alaskan Independence and Libertarian parties. The high vote-getter of each party went onto the general election ballot. Republican candidates were listed on a primary ballot of their own.

ALASKA

GENERAL AND PRIMARY ELECTIONS

		REPUBLICAN PRIMARIES			DEMOCRATIC PRIMARIES	
Senator	Sullivan, Daniel	44,740	40.1%	Begich, Mark*	58,092	96.6%
	Miller, Joe	35,904	32.1%	Bryk, William	2,024	3.4%
	Treadwell, Mead	27,807	24.9%			
	Jaramillo, John M.	3,246	2.9%			
	TOTAL	111,697		TOTAL	60,116	
Governor	Parnell, Sean R.*	80,903	75.9%	Mallott, Byron	42,327	80.1%
	Millette, Russ	11,296	10.6%	Stoddard, Phil	10,514	19.9%
	Snowden, Brad	10,594	9.9%			
	Heikes, Gerald L. "Tap"	3,855	3.6%			
	TOTAL	106,648		TOTAL	52,841	
Congressional At Large	Young, Don*	79,393	74.3%	Dunbar, Forrest	38,735	80.9%
	Cox, John R.	14,497	13.6%	Vondersaar, Frank	9,132	19.1%
	Seaward, David	7,604	7.1%			
	Dohner, David	5,373	5.0%			
	TOTAL	106,867		TOTAL	47,867	

Note: After the primary election, Democrat Byron Mallott withdrew from the race in order to run for lieutenant governor on the Independent ticket headed by Bill Walker. Consequently, the Democrats did not run a candidate in the general election. An asterisk (*) denotes incumbent.

ARIZONA

Congressional districts first established for elections held in 2012

9 members

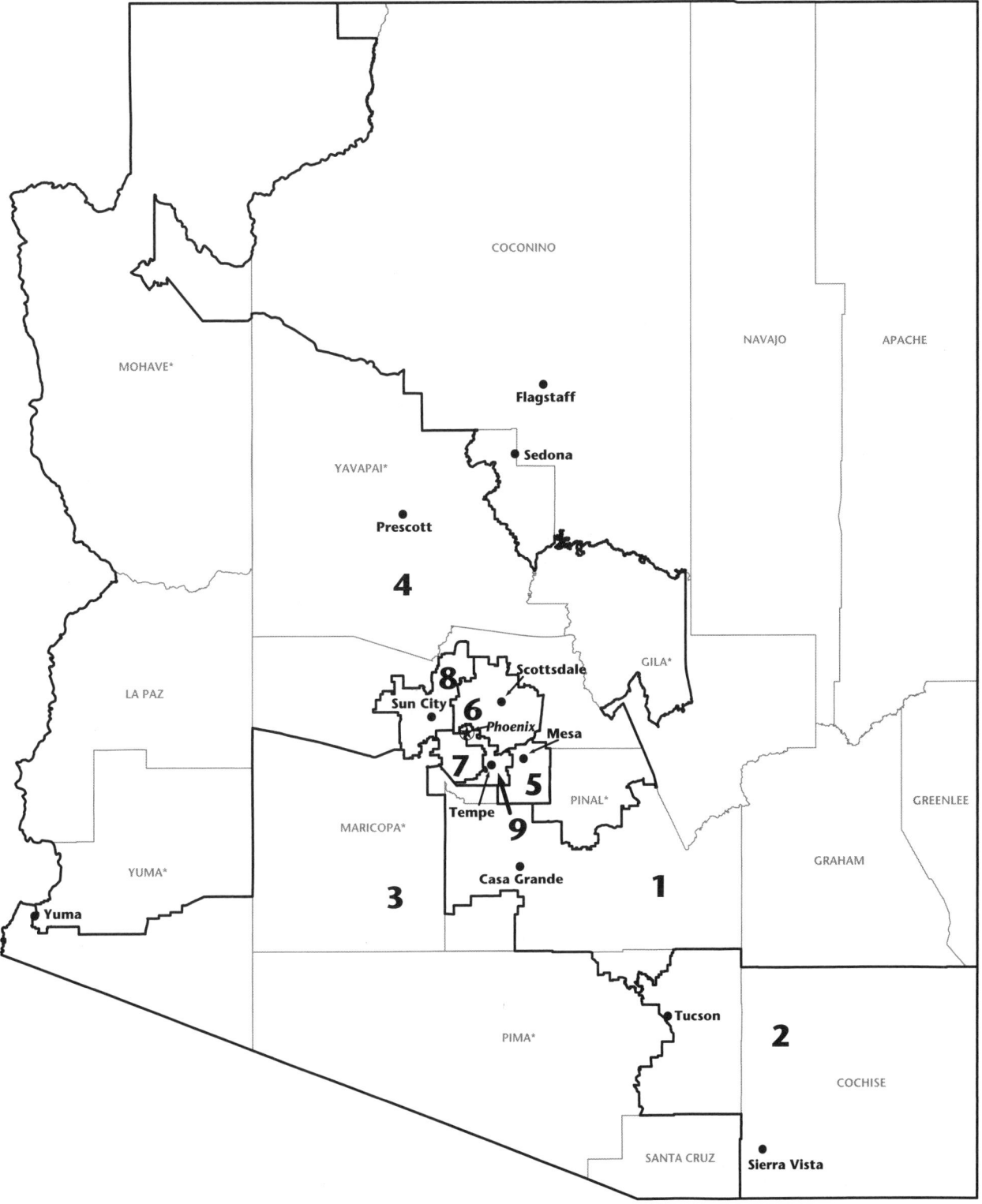

* Asterisk indicates a county whose boundaries include parts of two or more congressional districts.

ARIZONA
Greater Phoenix Area

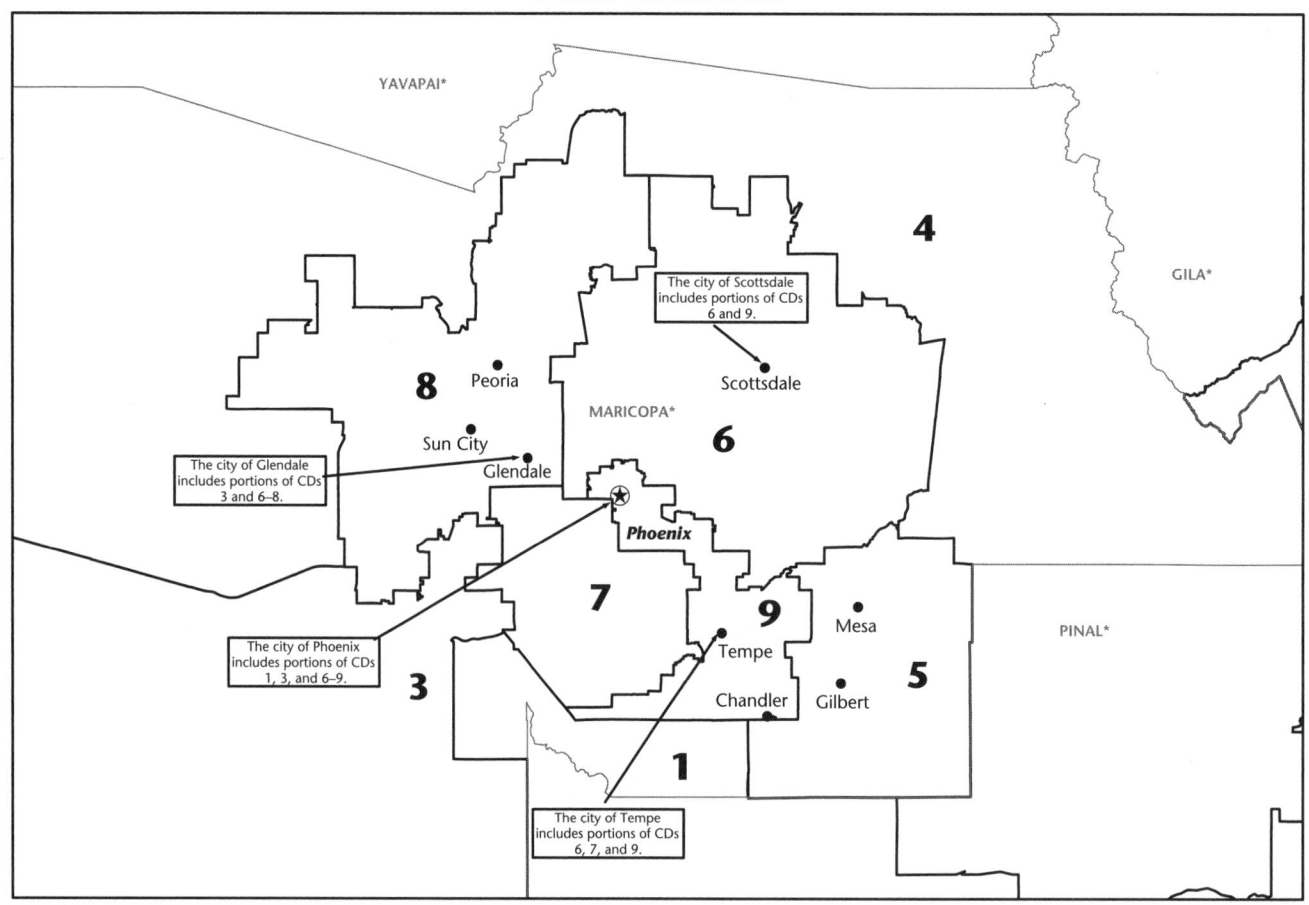

YAVAPAI*

4

GILA*

The city of Scottsdale includes portions of CDs 6 and 9.

Peoria

8

Scottsdale

MARICOPA*

Sun City

6

The city of Glendale includes portions of CDs 3 and 6–8.

Glendale

Phoenix

The city of Phoenix includes portions of CDs 1, 3, and 6–9.

7

9

Mesa

PINAL*

3

Tempe

5

1

Chandler

Gilbert

The city of Tempe includes portions of CDs 6, 7, and 9.

ARIZONA

GOVERNOR
Doug Ducey (R). Elected 2014 to a four-year term.

SENATORS (2 Republicans)
Jeff Flake (R). Elected 2012 to a six-year term.

John McCain (R). Reelected 2010 to a six-year term. Previously elected 2004, 1998, 1992, 1986.

REPRESENTATIVES (5 Republicans, 4 Democrats)
1. Ann Kirkpatrick (D)
2. Martha McSally (R)
3. Raúl M. Grijalva (D)
4. Paul A. Gosar (R)
5. Matt Salmon (R)
6. David Schweikert (R)
7. Ruben Gallego (D)
8. Trent Franks (R)
9. Kyrsten Sinema (D)

POSTWAR VOTE FOR PRESIDENT

		Republican		Democratic		Other	Rep.-Dem.	Total Vote		Major Vote	
Year	Total Vote	Vote	Candidate	Vote	Candidate	Vote	Plurality	Rep.	Dem.	Rep.	Dem.
2012	2,299,254	1,233,654	Romney, W. Mitt	1,025,232	Obama, Barack H.*	40,368	208,422 R	53.7%	44.6%	54.6%	45.4%
2008	2,293,475	1,230,111	McCain, John S. III	1,034,707	Obama, Barack H.	28,657	195,404 R	53.6%	45.1%	54.3%	45.7%
2004	2,012,585	1,104,294	Bush, George W.*	893,524	Kerry, John F.	14,767	210,770 R	54.9%	44.4%	55.3%	44.7%
2000**	1,532,016	781,652	Bush, George W.	685,341	Gore, Albert Jr.	65,023	96,311 R	51.0%	44.7%	53.3%	46.7%
1996**	1,404,405	622,073	Dole, Robert "Bob"	653,288	Clinton, Bill*	129,044	31,215 D	44.3%	46.5%	48.8%	51.2%
1992**	1,486,975	572,086	Bush, George H.*	543,050	Clinton, Bill	371,839	29,036 R	38.5%	36.5%	51.3%	48.7%
1988	1,171,873	702,541	Bush, George H.	454,029	Dukakis, Michael S.	15,303	248,512 R	60.0%	38.7%	60.7%	39.3%
1984	1,025,897	681,416	Reagan, Ronald*	333,854	Mondale, Walter F.	10,627	347,562 R	66.4%	32.5%	67.1%	32.9%
1980**	873,945	529,688	Reagan, Ronald	246,843	Carter, Jimmy*	97,414	282,845 R	60.6%	28.2%	68.2%	31.8%
1976	742,719	418,642	Ford, Gerald R.*	295,602	Carter, Jimmy	28,475	123,040 R	56.4%	39.8%	58.6%	41.4%
1972	622,926	402,812	Nixon, Richard M.*	198,540	McGovern, George S.	21,574	204,272 R	64.7%	31.9%	67.0%	33.0%
1968**	486,936	266,721	Nixon, Richard M.	170,514	Humphrey, Hubert Horatio Jr.	49,701	96,207 R	54.8%	35.0%	61.0%	39.0%
1964	480,770	242,535	Goldwater, Barry M. Sr.	237,753	Johnson, Lyndon B.*	482	4,782 R	50.4%	49.5%	50.5%	49.5%
1960	398,491	221,241	Nixon, Richard M.	176,781	Kennedy, John F.	469	44,460 R	55.5%	44.4%	55.6%	44.4%
1956	290,173	176,990	Eisenhower, Dwight D.*	112,880	Stevenson, Adlai E. II	303	64,110 R	61.0%	38.9%	61.1%	38.9%
1952	260,570	152,042	Eisenhower, Dwight D.	108,528	Stevenson, Adlai E. II		43,514 R	58.3%	41.7%	58.3%	41.7%
1948	177,065	77,597	Dewey, Thomas E.	95,251	Truman, Harry S.*	4,217	17,654 D	43.8%	53.8%	44.9%	55.1%

Note: An asterisk (*) denotes incumbent. **In past elections, the other vote included: 2000 - 45,645 Green (Ralph Nader); 1996 - 112,072 Reform (Ross Perot); 1992 - 353,741 Independent (Perot); 1980 - 76,952 Independent (John Anderson); 1968 - 46,573 American Independent (George Wallace).

ARIZONA

POSTWAR VOTE FOR GOVERNOR

Year	Total Vote	Republican Vote	Republican Candidate	Democratic Vote	Democratic Candidate	Other Vote	Rep.-Dem. Plurality	Total Vote Rep.	Total Vote Dem.	Major Vote Rep.	Major Vote Dem.
2014	1,506,416	805,062	Ducey, Doug	626,921	Duval, Fred	74,433	178,141 R	53.4%	41.6%	56.2%	43.8%
2010	1,728,081	938,934	Brewer, Jan*	733,935	Goddard, Terry	55,212	204,999 R	54.3%	42.5%	56.1%	43.9%
2006	1,533,645	543,528	Munsil, Len	959,830	Napolitano, Janet*	30,287	416,302 D	35.4%	62.6%	36.2%	63.8%
2002	1,226,111	554,465	Salmon, Matt	566,284	Napolitano, Janet	105,362	11,819 D	45.2%	46.2%	49.5%	50.5%
1998	1,017,616	620,188	Hull, Jane Dee*	361,552	Johnson, Paul	35,876	258,636 R	60.9%	35.5%	63.2%	36.8%
1994	1,129,607	593,492	Symington, Fife*	500,702	Basha, Eddie	35,413	92,790 R	52.5%	44.3%	54.2%	45.8%
1991S	940,737	492,569	Symington, Fife	448,168	Goddard, Terry		44,401 R	52.4%	47.6%	52.4%	47.6%
1986**	866,984	343,913	Mecham, Evan	298,986	Warner, Carolyn	224,085	44,927 R	39.7%	34.5%	53.5%	46.5%
1982	726,364	235,877	Corbet, Leo	453,795	Babbitt, Bruce*	36,692	217,918 D	32.5%	62.5%	34.2%	65.8%
1978	538,556	241,093	Mecham, Evan	282,605	Babbitt, Bruce*	14,858	41,512 D	44.8%	52.5%	46.0%	54.0%
1974	552,202	273,674	Williams, Jack R.*	278,375	Castro, Raul H.	153	4,701 D	49.6%	50.4%	49.6%	50.4%
1970**	411,409	209,522	Williams, Jack R.*	201,887	Castro, Raul H.		7,635 R	50.9%	49.1%	50.9%	49.1%
1968	483,998	279,923	Williams, Jack R.*	204,075	Goddard, Sam		75,848 R	57.8%	42.2%	57.8%	42.2%
1966	378,342	203,438	Williams, Jack R.	174,904	Goddard, Sam*		28,534 R	53.8%	46.2%	53.8%	46.2%
1964	473,502	221,404	Kleindienst, Richard	252,098	Goddard, Sam		30,694 D	46.8%	53.2%	46.8%	53.2%
1962	365,841	200,578	Fannin, Paul*	165,263	Goddard, Sam		35,315 R	54.8%	45.2%	54.8%	45.2%
1960	397,107	235,502	Fannin, Paul*	161,605	Ackerman, Lee		73,897 R	59.3%	40.7%	59.3%	40.7%
1958	290,465	160,136	Fannin, Paul	130,329	Morrison, Robert		29,807 R	55.1%	44.9%	55.1%	44.9%
1956	288,592	116,744	Griffen, Horace B.	171,848	McFarland, Ernest W.*		55,104 D	40.5%	59.5%	40.5%	59.5%
1954	243,970	115,866	Pyle, Howard*	128,104	McFarland, Ernest W.		12,238 D	47.5%	52.5%	47.5%	52.5%
1952	260,285	156,592	Pyle, Howard*	103,693	Haldiman, Joe C.		52,899 R	60.2%	39.8%	60.2%	39.8%
1950	195,227	99,109	Pyle, Howard	96,118	Frohmiller, Ana		2,991 R	50.8%	49.2%	50.8%	49.2%
1948	175,767	70,419	Brockett, Bruce D.	104,008	Garvey, Dan E.	1,340	33,589 D	40.1%	59.2%	40.4%	59.6%
1946	122,462	48,867	Brockett, Bruce D.	73,595	Osborn, Sidney P.*		24,728 D	39.9%	60.1%	39.9%	60.1%

Note: An asterisk (*) denotes incumbent. **In 1990 neither major party candidate won an absolute majority, therefore a runoff election was held February 26, 1991; the vote above is for the February runoff. In the November 1990 election, a total of 1,055,406 votes were cast as follows: 523,984 (49.6%) Republican (Fife Symington); 519,691 (49.2%) Democratic (Terry Goddard); 11,731 (1.1%) Other. In past elections, the other vote included: 1986 - 224,085 Independent (Bill Schulz). The term of office for Arizona's governor was increased from two to four years effective with the 1970 election.

POSTWAR VOTE FOR SENATOR

Year	Total Vote	Republican Vote	Republican Candidate	Democratic Vote	Democratic Candidate	Other Vote	Rep.-Dem. Plurality	Total Vote Rep.	Total Vote Dem.	Major Vote Rep.	Major Vote Dem.
2012	2,243,422	1,104,457	Flake, Jeff	1,036,542	Carmona, Richard	102,423	67,915 R	49.2%	46.2%	51.6%	48.4%
2010	1,708,484	1,005,615	McCain, John S. III*	592,011	Glassman, Rodney	110,858	413,604 R	58.9%	34.7%	62.9%	37.1%
2006	1,526,782	814,398	Kyl, Jon*	664,141	Pederson, Jim	48,243	150,257 R	53.3%	43.5%	55.1%	44.9%
2004	1,961,677	1,505,372	McCain, John S. III*	404,507	Starky, Stuart Marc	51,798	1,100,865 R	76.7%	20.6%	78.8%	21.2%
2000	1,397,076	1,108,196	Kyl, Jon*			288,880	1,108,196 R	79.3%		100.0%	
1998	1,013,280	696,577	McCain, John S. III*	275,224	Ranger, Ed	41,479	421,353 R	68.7%	27.2%	71.7%	28.3%
1994	1,119,060	600,999	Kyl, Jon	442,510	Coopersmith, Sam	75,551	158,489 R	53.7%	39.5%	57.6%	42.4%
1992**	1,382,051	771,395	McCain, John S. III*	436,321	Sargent, Claire	174,335	335,074 R	55.8%	31.6%	63.9%	36.1%
1988	1,164,539	478,060	DeGreen, Keith	660,403	DeConcini, Dennis*	26,076	182,343 D	41.1%	56.7%	42.0%	58.0%
1986	862,921	521,850	McCain, John S. III	340,965	Kimball, Richard	106	180,885 R	60.5%	39.5%	60.5%	39.5%
1982	723,885	291,749	Dunn, Pete	411,970	DeConcini, Dennis*	20,166	120,221 D	40.3%	56.9%	41.5%	58.5%
1980	874,178	432,371	Goldwater, Barry M. Sr.*	422,972	Schulz, Bill	18,835	9,399 R	49.5%	48.4%	50.5%	49.5%
1976	741,210	321,236	Steiger, Sam	400,334	DeConcini, Dennis	19,640	79,098 D	43.3%	54.0%	44.5%	55.5%
1974	549,919	320,396	Goldwater, Barry M. Sr.*	229,523	Marshall, Jonathan		90,873 R	58.3%	41.7%	58.3%	41.7%
1970	407,796	228,284	Fannin, Paul*	179,512	Grossman, Sam		48,772 R	56.0%	44.0%	56.0%	44.0%
1968	479,945	274,607	Goldwater, Barry M. Sr.	205,338	Elson, Roy L.		69,269 R	57.2%	42.8%	57.2%	42.8%
1964	468,788	241,084	Fannin, Paul	227,704	Elson, Roy L.		13,380 R	51.4%	48.6%	51.4%	48.6%
1962	362,605	163,388	Mecham, Evan	199,217	Hayden, Carl*		35,829 D	45.1%	54.9%	45.1%	54.9%
1958	293,623	164,593	Goldwater, Barry M. Sr.*	129,030	McFarland, Ernest W.		35,563 R	56.1%	43.9%	56.1%	43.9%
1956	278,263	107,447	Jones, Ross F.	170,816	Hayden, Carl*		63,369 D	38.6%	61.4%	38.6%	61.4%
1952	257,401	132,063	Goldwater, Barry M. Sr.	125,338	McFarland, Ernest W.*		6,725 R	51.3%	48.7%	51.3%	48.7%
1950	185,092	68,846	Brockett, Bruce	116,246	Hayden, Carl*		47,400 D	37.2%	62.8%	37.2%	62.8%
1946	116,239	35,022	Powers, Ward S.	80,415	McFarland, Ernest W.*	802	45,393 D	30.1%	69.2%	30.3%	69.7%

Note: An asterisk (*) denotes incumbent. **In past elections, the other vote included: 1992 - 145,361 Independent (Evan Mecham). The Democratic Party did not run a candidate in the 2000 Senate election.

ARIZONA

GOVERNOR 2014

2010 Census Population	County	Total Vote	Republican (Ducey)	Democratic (Duval)	Other	Rep.-Dem. Plurality	Percentage Total Vote Rep.	Dem.	Major Vote Rep.	Dem.
71,518	APACHE	20,584	5,871	13,562	1,151	7,691 D	28.5%	65.9%	30.2%	69.8%
131,346	COCHISE	36,461	21,662	12,709	2,090	8,953 R	59.4%	34.9%	63.0%	37.0%
134,421	COCONINO	36,939	14,528	20,212	2,199	5,684 D	39.3%	54.7%	41.8%	58.2%
53,597	GILA	15,839	9,610	5,253	976	4,357 R	60.7%	33.2%	64.7%	35.3%
37,220	GRAHAM	7,266	4,985	1,919	362	3,066 R	68.6%	26.4%	72.2%	27.8%
8,437	GREENLEE	1,921	995	792	134	203 R	51.8%	41.2%	55.7%	44.3%
20,489	LA PAZ	3,484	2,388	846	250	1,542 R	68.5%	24.3%	73.8%	26.2%
3,817,117	MARICOPA	857,778	469,200	346,879	41,699	122,321 R	54.7%	40.4%	57.5%	42.5%
200,186	MOHAVE	46,675	33,150	10,662	2,863	22,488 R	71.0%	22.8%	75.7%	24.3%
107,449	NAVAJO	27,349	13,569	12,128	1,652	1,441 R	49.6%	44.3%	52.8%	47.2%
980,263	PIMA	270,670	122,966	136,302	11,402	13,336 D	45.4%	50.4%	47.4%	52.6%
375,770	PINAL	71,473	41,313	26,131	4,029	15,182 R	57.8%	36.6%	61.3%	38.7%
47,420	SANTA CRUZ	9,324	3,175	5,819	330	2,644 D	34.1%	62.4%	35.3%	64.7%
211,033	YAVAPAI	74,154	46,806	23,210	4,138	23,596 R	63.1%	31.3%	66.9%	33.1%
195,751	YUMA	26,499	14,844	10,497	1,158	4,347 R	56.0%	39.6%	58.6%	41.4%
6,392,017	TOTAL	1,506,416	805,062	626,921	74,433	178,141 R	53.4%	41.6%	56.2%	43.8%

ARIZONA

HOUSE OF REPRESENTATIVES

CD	Year	Total Vote	Republican Vote	Candidate	Democratic Vote	Candidate	Other Vote	Rep.-Dem. Plurality	Percentage Total Vote Rep.	Dem.	Major Vote Rep.	Dem.
1	2014	185,114	87,723	TOBIN, ANDY	97,391	KIRKPATRICK, ANN*		9,668 D	47.4%	52.6%	47.4%	52.6%
1	2012	251,595	113,594	PATON, JONATHAN	122,774	KIRKPATRICK, ANN	15,227	9,180 D	45.1%	48.8%	48.1%	51.9%
2	2014	219,351	109,704	MCSALLY, MARTHA	109,543	BARBER, RON*	104	161 R	50.0%	49.9%	50.0%	50.0%
2	2012	292,279	144,884	MCSALLY, MARTHA	147,338	BARBER, RON*	57	2,454 D	49.6%	50.4%	49.6%	50.4%
3	2014	104,428	46,185	SAUCEDO MERCER, GABRIELLA	58,192	GRIJALVA, RAÚL M.*	51	12,007 D	44.2%	55.7%	44.2%	55.8%
3	2012	168,698	62,663	SAUCEDO MERCER, GABRIELLA	98,468	GRIJALVA, RAÚL M.*	7,567	35,805 D	37.1%	58.4%	38.9%	61.1%
4	2014	175,179	122,560	GOSAR, PAUL A.*	45,179	WEISSER, MIKEL	7,440	77,381 R	70.0%	25.8%	73.1%	26.9%
4	2012	243,760	162,907	GOSAR, PAUL A.*	69,154	ROBINSON, JOHNNIE	11,699	93,753 R	66.8%	28.4%	70.2%	29.8%
5	2014	179,463	124,867	SALMON, MATT*	54,596	WOODS, JAMES ISSAC		70,271 R	69.6%	30.4%	69.6%	30.4%
5	2012	273,059	183,470	SALMON, MATT	89,589	MORGAN, SPENCER		93,881 R	67.2%	32.8%	67.2%	32.8%
6	2014	199,776	129,578	SCHWEIKERT, DAVID*	70,198	WILLIAMSON, W. JOHN		59,380 R	64.9%	35.1%	64.9%	35.1%
6	2012	293,177	179,706	SCHWEIKERT, DAVID*	97,666	JETTE, MATTHEW	15,805	82,040 R	61.3%	33.3%	64.8%	35.2%
7	2014	72,452			54,235	GALLEGO, RUBEN	18,217	54,235 D		74.9%		100.0%
7	2012	127,827			104,489	PASTOR, ED*	23,338	104,489 D		81.7%		100.0%
8	2014	169,776	128,710	FRANKS, TRENT*			41,066	128,710 R	75.8%		100.0%	
8	2012	272,791	172,809	FRANKS, TRENT*	95,635	SCHARER, GENE	4,347	77,174 R	63.3%	35.1%	64.4%	35.6%
9	2014	162,062	67,841	ROGERS, WENDY	88,609	SINEMA, KYRSTEN*	5,612	20,768 D	41.9%	54.7%	43.4%	56.6%
9	2012	250,131	111,630	PARKER, VERNON B.	121,881	SINEMA, KYRSTEN	16,620	10,251 D	44.6%	48.7%	47.8%	52.2%
TOTAL	2014	1,467,601	817,168		577,943		72,490	239,225 R	55.7%	39.4%	58.6%	41.4%
TOTAL	2012	2,173,317	1,131,663		946,994		94,660	184,669 R	52.1%	43.6%	54.4%	45.6%

Note: An asterisk (*) denotes incumbent.

ARIZONA

GENERAL AND PRIMARY ELECTIONS

2014 GENERAL ELECTIONS: OTHER VOTES

Governor	Other vote was 57,337 Libertarian (Barry J. Hess), 15,432 Americans Elect (J.L. Mealer), 1,520 Write-in (J. Johnson), 50 Write-in (Brian Bailey), 43 Write-in (Alice Novoa), 29 Write-in (Cary Dolego), 15 Write-in (Curtis Woolsey), 7 Write-in (Diana-Elizabeth R.R. Kennedy)
House	Other vote was:
CD 2	56 Write-in (Sampson U. Ramirez), 48 Write-in (Sydney Dudikoff)
CD 3	43 Write-in (F. Sanchez), 8 Write-in (Lee Thomspon)
CD 4	7,440 Libertarian (Chris Rike)
CD 7	10,715 Libertarian (Joe Cobb), 3,856 Americans Elect (Rebecca DeWitt), 3,496 Independent (Jose Penalosa), 129 Write-in (Gary Dunn), 17 Write-in (Gustavo Ortega), 4 Write-in (Samuel Esquivel)
CD 8	41,066 Americans Elect (Stephen Dolgos)
CD 9	5,612 Libertarian (Powell E. Gammill)

2014 PRIMARY ELECTIONS: SUPPLEMENTARY INFORMATION

Primary	August 26, 2014	**Registration** (as of August 26, 2014)	3,247,146	Republican Democratic Libertarian Americans Elect Other	1,122,723 944,665 26,915 399 1,152,444

Primary Type Semi-open—Registered Democrats and Republicans could vote only in their party's primary. But voters not registered with any political party could participate in either the Democratic or Republican primary.

	REPUBLICAN PRIMARIES			DEMOCRATIC PRIMARIES		
Governor	Ducey, Doug	200,607	37.2%	Duval, Fred	271,276	100.0%
	Smith, Scott	119,107	22.1%			
	Jones, Christine	89,922	16.7%			
	Bennett, Ken	62,010	11.5%			
	Thomas, Andrew P.	43,822	8.1%			
	Riggs, Frank	24,168	4.5%			
	Aloisi, Mike	27				
	Lukasik, Alice	27				
	TOTAL	*539,690*		*TOTAL*	*271,276*	
Congressional District 1	Tobin, Andy	18,814	35.8%	Kirkpatrick, Ann*	51,393	100.0%
	Kiehne, Gary	18,407	35.1%			
	Kwasman, Adam Charles	15,266	29.1%			
	TOTAL	*52,487*		*TOTAL*	*51,393*	
Congressional District 2	McSally, Martha	45,492	69.4%	Barber, Ron*	49,039	100.0%
	Wooten, Charles A. "Chuck"	14,995	22.9%			
	Kais, Shelley	5,103	7.8%			
	TOTAL	*65,590*		*TOTAL*	*49,039*	
Congressional District 3	Saucedo Mercer, Gabriella	18,823	100.0%	Grijalva, Raúl M.*	28,758	100.0%
	TOTAL	*18,823*		*TOTAL*	*28,758*	
Congressional District 4	Gosar, Paul A.*	65,354	100.0%	Weisser, Mikel	19,643	100.0%
	TOTAL	*65,354*		*TOTAL*	*19,643*	

ARIZONA

GENERAL AND PRIMARY ELECTIONS

	REPUBLICAN PRIMARIES			DEMOCRATIC PRIMARIES		
Congressional District 5	Salmon, Matt*	71,690	100.0%	Woods, James Issac	20,249	100.0%
	TOTAL	*71,690*		*TOTAL*	*20,249*	
Congressional District 6	Schweikert, David*	69,902	100.0%	Williamson, W. John	25,306	100.0%
	TOTAL	*69,902*		*TOTAL*	*25,306*	
Congressional District 7				Gallego, Ruben	14,936	48.9%
				Wilcox, Mary Rose	11,077	36.3%
				Camacho, Randy Robert	2,330	7.6%
				Maupin, Jarrett Martin Jr.	2,199	7.2%
				TOTAL	*30,542*	
Congressional District 8	Franks, Trent*	53,771	73.3%			
	Van Steenwyk, Clair	19,629	26.7%			
	TOTAL	*73,400*				
Congressional District 9	Rogers, Wendy	30,484	60.6%	Sinema, Kyrsten*	31,900	100.0%
	Walter, Andrew	19,808	39.4%			
	TOTAL	*50,292*		*TOTAL*	*31,900*	

Note: An asterisk (*) denotes incumbent.

ARKANSAS

Congressional districts first established for elections held in 2012

4 members

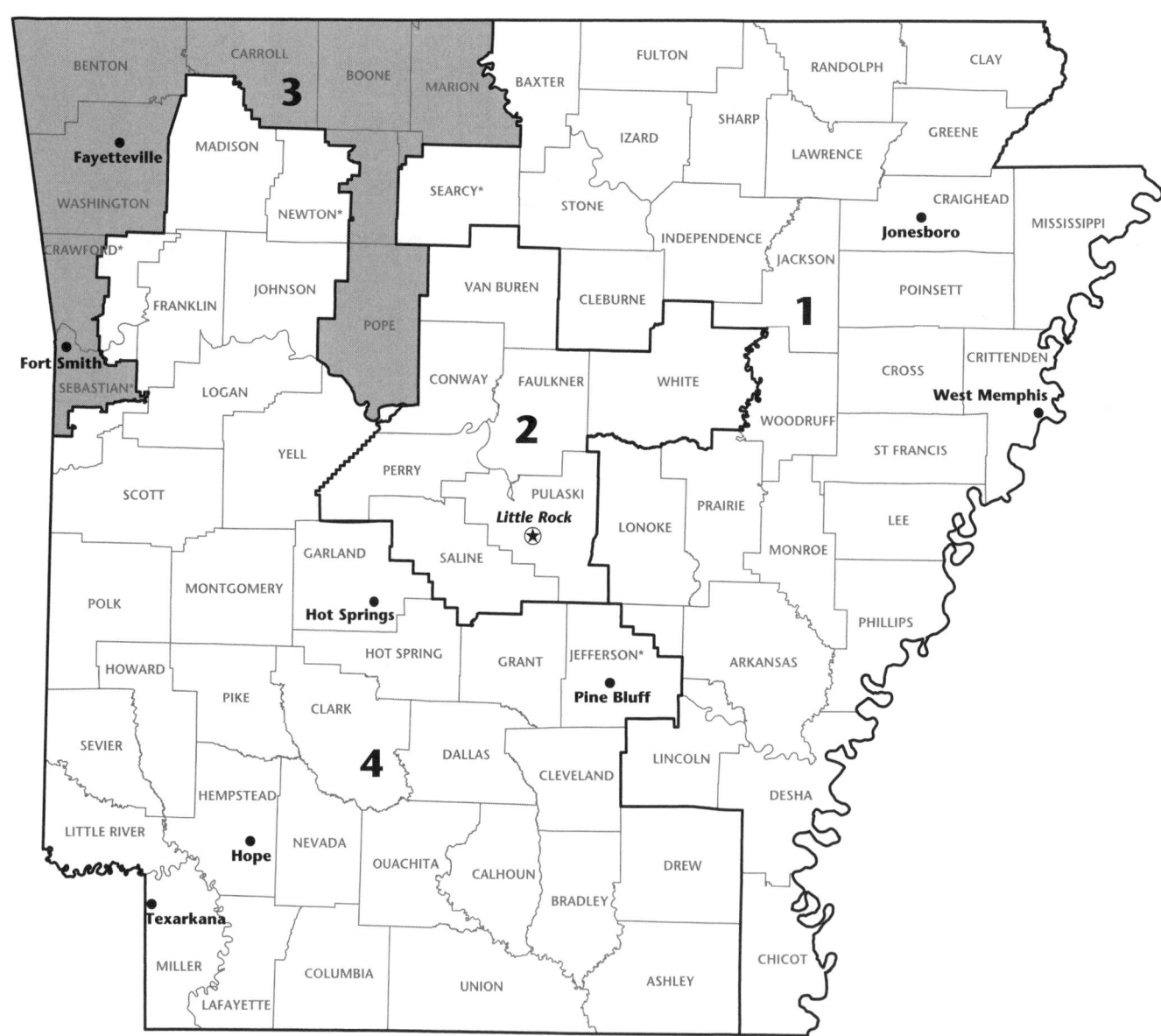

* Asterisk indicates a county whose boundaries include parts of two or more congressional districts.

ARKANSAS

GOVERNOR
Asa Hutchinson (R). Elected 2014 to a four-year term.

SENATORS (2 Republicans)
John Boozman (R). Elected 2010 to a six-year term.

Tom Cotton (R). Elected 2014 to a six-year term.

REPRESENTATIVES (4 Republicans)
1. Eric A. "Rick" Crawford (R)
2. J. French Hill (R)
3. Steve Womack (R)
4. Bruce Westerman (R)

POSTWAR VOTE FOR PRESIDENT

| | | Republican | | Democratic | | Other | Rep.-Dem. | Percentage | | | |
| | | | | | | | | Total Vote | | Major Vote | |
Year	Total Vote	Vote	Candidate	Vote	Candidate	Vote	Plurality	Rep.	Dem.	Rep.	Dem.
2012	1,069,468	647,744	Romney, W. Mitt	394,409	Obama, Barack H.*	27,315	253,335 R	60.6%	36.9%	62.2%	37.8%
2008	1,086,617	638,017	McCain, John S. III	422,310	Obama, Barack H.	26,290	215,707 R	58.7%	38.9%	60.2%	39.8%
2004	1,054,945	572,898	Bush, George W.*	469,953	Kerry, John F.	12,094	102,945 R	54.3%	44.5%	54.9%	45.1%
2000**	921,781	472,940	Bush, George W.	422,768	Gore, Albert Jr.	26,073	50,172 R	51.3%	45.9%	52.8%	47.2%
1996**	884,262	325,416	Dole, Robert "Bob"	475,171	Clinton, Bill*	83,675	149,755 D	36.8%	53.7%	40.6%	59.4%
1992**	950,653	337,324	Bush, George H.*	505,823	Clinton, Bill	107,506	168,499 D	35.5%	53.2%	40.0%	60.0%
1988	827,738	466,578	Bush, George H.	349,237	Dukakis, Michael S.	11,923	117,341 R	56.4%	42.2%	57.2%	42.8%
1984	884,406	534,774	Reagan, Ronald*	338,646	Mondale, Walter F.	10,986	196,128 R	60.5%	38.3%	61.2%	38.8%
1980**	837,582	403,164	Reagan, Ronald	398,041	Carter, Jimmy*	36,377	5,123 R	48.1%	47.5%	50.3%	49.7%
1976	767,535	267,903	Ford, Gerald R.*	498,604	Carter, Jimmy	1,028	230,701 D	34.9%	65.0%	35.0%	65.0%
1972	651,320	448,541	Nixon, Richard M.*	199,892	McGovern, George S.	2,887	248,649 R	68.9%	30.7%	69.2%	30.8%
1968**	619,969	190,759	Nixon, Richard M.	188,228	Humphrey, Hubert Horatio Jr.	240,982	2,531 R#	30.8%	30.4%	50.3%	49.7%
1964	560,426	243,264	Goldwater, Barry M. Sr.	314,197	Johnson, Lyndon B.*	2,965	70,933 D	43.4%	56.1%	43.6%	56.4%
1960	428,509	184,508	Nixon, Richard M.	215,049	Kennedy, John F.	28,952	30,541 D	43.1%	50.2%	46.2%	53.8%
1956	406,572	186,287	Eisenhower, Dwight D.*	213,277	Stevenson, Adlai E. II	7,008	26,990 D	45.8%	52.5%	46.6%	53.4%
1952	404,800	177,155	Eisenhower, Dwight D.	226,300	Stevenson, Adlai E. II	1,345	49,145 D	43.8%	55.9%	43.9%	56.1%
1948**	242,475	50,959	Dewey, Thomas E.	149,659	Truman, Harry S.*	41,857	98,700 D	21.0%	61.7%	25.4%	74.6%

Note: An asterisk (*) denotes incumbent. A pound sign (#) indicates that the state was carried by a third party candidate or independent electoral slate. **In past elections, the other vote included: 2000 - 13,421 Green (Ralph Nader); 1996 - 69,884 Reform (Ross Perot); 1992 - 99,132 Independent (Perot); 1980 - 22,468 Independent (John Anderson); 1968 - 240,982 American Independent (Wallace); 1948 - 40,068 States' Rights (Strom Thurmond). Wallace carried Arkansas in 1968 with 38.9 percent of the vote.

ARKANSAS

POSTWAR VOTE FOR GOVERNOR

Year	Total Vote	Republican Vote	Republican Candidate	Democratic Vote	Democratic Candidate	Other Vote	Rep.-Dem. Plurality	Percentage Total Vote Rep.	Percentage Total Vote Dem.	Percentage Major Vote Rep.	Percentage Major Vote Dem.
2014	848,592	470,429	Hutchinson, Asa	352,115	Ross, Mike	26,048	118,314 R	55.4%	41.5%	57.2%	42.8%
2010	781,333	262,784	Keet, Jim	503,336	Beebe, Mike D.*	15,213	240,552 D	33.6%	64.4%	34.3%	65.7%
2006	774,680	315,040	Hutchinson, Asa	430,765	Beebe, Mike D.	28,875	115,725 D	40.7%	55.6%	42.2%	57.8%
2002	805,696	427,082	Huckabee, Mike*	378,250	Fisher, Jimmie Lou	364	48,832 R	53.0%	46.9%	53.0%	47.0%
1998	728,619	430,919	Huckabee, Mike*	278,155	King, James	19,545	152,764 R	59.1%	38.2%	60.8%	39.2%
1994	716,840	287,904	Nelson, Sheffield	428,936	Tucker, Jim Guy*		141,032 D	40.2%	59.8%	40.2%	59.8%
1990	696,412	295,925	Nelson, Sheffield	400,386	Clinton, Bill*	101	104,461 D	42.5%	57.5%	42.5%	57.5%
1986**	688,851	248,727	White, Frank D.	439,882	Clinton, Bill*	242	191,155 D	36.1%	63.9%	36.1%	63.9%
1984	886,548	331,987	Freeman, Woody	554,561	Clinton, Bill*		222,574 D	37.4%	62.6%	37.4%	62.6%
1982	789,351	357,496	White, Frank D.*	431,855	Clinton, Bill		74,359 D	45.3%	54.7%	45.3%	54.7%
1980	838,925	435,684	White, Frank D.	403,241	Clinton, Bill*		32,443 R	51.9%	48.1%	51.9%	48.1%
1978	528,912	193,746	Lowe, A. Lynn	335,101	Clinton, Bill	65	141,355 D	36.6%	63.4%	36.6%	63.4%
1976	726,949	121,716	Griffith, Leon	605,083	Pryor, David H.*	150	483,367 D	16.7%	83.2%	16.7%	83.3%
1974	545,974	187,872	Coon, Ken	358,018	Pryor, David H.	84	170,146 D	34.4%	65.6%	34.4%	65.6%
1972	648,069	159,177	Blaylock, Len E.	488,892	Bumpers, Dale*		329,715 D	24.6%	75.4%	24.6%	75.4%
1970	608,198	196,418	Rockefeller, Winthrop*	375,648	Bumpers, Dale	36,132	179,230 D	32.3%	61.8%	34.3%	65.7%
1968	615,590	322,777	Rockefeller, Winthrop*	292,813	Crank, Marion		29,964 R	52.4%	47.6%	52.4%	47.6%
1966	563,527	306,324	Rockefeller, Winthrop	257,203	Johnson, James Douglas		49,121 R	54.4%	45.6%	54.4%	45.6%
1964	592,113	254,561	Rockefeller, Winthrop	337,489	Faubus, Orval E.*	63	82,928 D	43.0%	57.0%	43.0%	57.0%
1962	308,092	82,349	Ricketts, Willis	225,743	Faubus, Orval E.*		143,394 D	26.7%	73.3%	26.7%	73.3%
1960	421,985	129,921	Britt, Henry M.	292,064	Faubus, Orval E.*		162,143 D	30.8%	69.2%	30.8%	69.2%
1958	286,886	50,288	Johnson, George W.	236,598	Faubus, Orval E.*		186,310 D	17.5%	82.5%	17.5%	82.5%
1956	399,012	77,215	Mitchell, Roy	321,797	Faubus, Orval E.*		244,582 D	19.4%	80.6%	19.4%	80.6%
1954	335,176	127,004	Remmel, Pratt C.	208,121	Faubus, Orval E.	51	81,117 D	37.9%	62.1%	37.9%	62.1%
1952	391,592	49,292	Speck, Jefferson W.	342,292	Cherry, Francis	8	293,000 D	12.6%	87.4%	12.6%	87.4%
1950	317,081	50,303	Speck, Jefferson W.	266,778	McMath, Sidney S.*		216,475 D	15.9%	84.1%	15.9%	84.1%
1948	244,271	26,500	Black, Charles R.	217,771	McMath, Sidney S.		191,271 D	10.8%	89.2%	10.8%	89.2%
1946	152,162	24,133	Mills, W. T.	128,029	Laney, Ben*		103,896 D	15.9%	84.1%	15.9%	84.1%

Note: An asterisk (*) denotes incumbent. **The term of office for Arkansas governor was increased from two to four years effective with the 1986 election.

POSTWAR VOTE FOR SENATOR

Year	Total Vote	Republican Vote	Republican Candidate	Democratic Vote	Democratic Candidate	Other Vote	Rep.-Dem. Plurality	Percentage Total Vote Rep.	Percentage Total Vote Dem.	Percentage Major Vote Rep.	Percentage Major Vote Dem.
2014	847,505	478,819	Cotton, Tom	334,174	Pryor, Mark*	34,512	144,645 R	56.5%	39.4%	58.9%	41.1%
2010	779,957	451,618	Boozman, John	288,156	Lincoln, Blanche L.*	40,183	163,462 R	57.9%	36.9%	61.0%	39.0%
2008**	1,011,754			804,678	Pryor, Mark*	207,076	804,678 D		79.5%		100.0%
2004	1,039,349	458,036	Holt, Jim L.	580,973	Lincoln, Blanche L.*	340	122,937 D	44.1%	55.9%	44.1%	55.9%
2002	803,959	370,653	Hutchinson, Tim*	433,306	Pryor, Mark		62,653 D	46.1%	53.9%	46.1%	53.9%
1998	700,644	295,870	Boozman, Fay	385,878	Lincoln, Blanche L.	18,896	90,008 D	42.2%	55.1%	43.4%	56.6%
1996	846,183	445,942	Hutchinson, Tim	400,241	Bryant, Winston		45,701 R	52.7%	47.3%	52.7%	47.3%
1992	920,008	366,373	Huckabee, Mike	553,635	Bumpers, Dale*		187,262 D	39.8%	60.2%	39.8%	60.2%
1990**	494,735			493,910	Pryor, David H.*	825	493,910 D		99.8%		100.0%
1986	695,487	262,313	Hutchinson, Asa	433,122	Bumpers, Dale*	52	170,809 D	37.7%	62.3%	37.7%	62.3%
1984	875,956	373,615	Bethune, Ed	502,341	Pryor, David H.*		128,726 D	42.7%	57.3%	42.7%	57.3%
1980	808,812	330,576	Clark, Bill	477,905	Bumpers, Dale*	331	147,329 D	40.9%	59.1%	40.9%	59.1%
1978	522,239	84,722	Kelly, Tom	399,916	Pryor, David H.	37,601	315,194 D	16.2%	76.6%	17.5%	82.5%
1974	543,082	82,026	Jones, John Harris	461,056	Bumpers, Dale		379,030 D	15.1%	84.9%	15.1%	84.9%
1972	634,636	248,238	Babbitt, Wayne H.	386,398	McClellan, John L.*		138,160 D	39.1%	60.9%	39.1%	60.9%
1968	591,704	241,739	Bernard, Charles T.	349,965	Fulbright, J. William*		108,226 D	40.9%	59.1%	40.9%	59.1%
1966**					McClellan, John L.*		D				
1962	312,880	98,013	Jones, Kenneth	214,867	Fulbright, J. William*		116,854 D	31.3%	68.7%	31.3%	68.7%
1960**					McClellan, John L.*		D				
1956	399,695	68,016	Henley, Ben C.	331,679	Fulbright, J. William*		263,663 D	17.0%	83.0%	17.0%	83.0%
1954	291,058			291,058	McClellan, John L.*		291,058 D		100.0%		100.0%
1950	302,582			302,582	Fulbright, J. William*		302,582 D		100.0%		100.0%
1948	231,922			216,401	McClellan, John L.*	15,521	216,401 D		93.3%		100.0%

Note: An asterisk (*) denotes incumbent. **In past elections, the other vote included: 2008 - 207,076 Green (Rebekah Kennedy), who finished second. In 1990 the vote for Senator David H. Pryor was not canvassed in seven counties because he was unopposed. Senator John L. McClellan was reelected in 1960 and in 1966, but his vote was not canvassed in many counties. The Republican Party did not run a candidate in the 1948, 1950, 1954, 1960, 1966, 1990, and 2008 Senate elections.

ARKANSAS
GOVERNOR 2014

2010 Census Population	County	Total Vote	Republican (Hutchinson)	Democratic (Ross)	Other	Rep.-Dem. Plurality	Percentage Total Vote Rep.	Dem.	Major Vote Rep.	Dem.
19,019	ARKANSAS	5,096	2,676	2,317	103	359 R	52.5%	45.5%	53.6%	46.4%
21,853	ASHLEY	6,246	3,037	3,077	132	40 D	48.6%	49.3%	49.7%	50.3%
41,513	BAXTER	14,951	9,693	4,681	577	5,012 R	64.8%	31.3%	67.4%	32.6%
221,339	BENTON	62,941	43,535	17,122	2,284	26,413 R	69.2%	27.2%	71.8%	28.2%
36,903	BOONE	10,982	7,363	3,107	512	4,256 R	67.0%	28.3%	70.3%	29.7%
11,508	BRADLEY	2,906	1,360	1,498	48	138 D	46.8%	51.5%	47.6%	52.4%
5,368	CALHOUN	1,645	862	740	43	122 R	52.4%	45.0%	53.8%	46.2%
27,446	CARROLL	8,087	4,635	3,095	357	1,540 R	57.3%	38.3%	60.0%	40.0%
11,800	CHICOT	3,503	1,024	2,437	42	1,413 D	29.2%	69.6%	29.6%	70.4%
22,995	CLARK	6,971	2,834	4,014	123	1,180 D	40.7%	57.6%	41.4%	58.6%
16,083	CLAY	4,017	1,943	1,912	162	31 R	48.4%	47.6%	50.4%	49.6%
25,970	CLEBURNE	9,877	6,670	2,797	410	3,873 R	67.5%	28.3%	70.5%	29.5%
8,689	CLEVELAND	2,735	1,558	1,103	74	455 R	57.0%	40.3%	58.5%	41.5%
24,552	COLUMBIA	8,012	4,306	3,541	165	765 R	53.7%	44.2%	54.9%	45.1%
21,273	CONWAY	6,355	3,366	2,822	167	544 R	53.0%	44.4%	54.4%	45.6%
96,443	CRAIGHEAD	25,357	14,218	10,342	797	3,876 R	56.1%	40.8%	57.9%	42.1%
61,948	CRAWFORD	16,227	11,180	4,426	621	6,754 R	68.9%	27.3%	71.6%	28.4%
50,902	CRITTENDEN	10,621	4,497	5,845	279	1,348 D	42.3%	55.0%	43.5%	56.5%
17,870	CROSS	5,266	2,899	2,240	127	659 R	55.1%	42.5%	56.4%	43.6%
8,116	DALLAS	2,387	1,076	1,274	37	198 D	45.1%	53.4%	45.8%	54.2%
13,008	DESHA	3,409	1,057	2,297	55	1,240 D	31.0%	67.4%	31.5%	68.5%
18,509	DREW	5,244	2,535	2,620	89	85 D	48.3%	50.0%	49.2%	50.8%
113,237	FAULKNER	33,941	20,540	12,227	1,174	8,313 R	60.5%	36.0%	62.7%	37.3%
18,125	FRANKLIN	5,512	3,488	1,859	165	1,629 R	63.3%	33.7%	65.2%	34.8%
12,245	FULTON	3,383	1,867	1,394	122	473 R	55.2%	41.2%	57.3%	42.7%
96,024	GARLAND	30,916	17,729	12,118	1,069	5,611 R	57.3%	39.2%	59.4%	40.6%
17,853	GRANT	5,352	3,327	1,853	172	1,474 R	62.2%	34.6%	64.2%	35.8%
42,090	GREENE	11,085	6,355	4,321	409	2,034 R	57.3%	39.0%	59.5%	40.5%
22,609	HEMPSTEAD	5,396	2,662	2,637	97	25 R	49.3%	48.9%	50.2%	49.8%
32,923	HOT SPRING	9,433	4,963	4,154	316	809 R	52.6%	44.0%	54.4%	45.6%
13,789	HOWARD	3,679	1,768	1,851	60	83 D	48.1%	50.3%	48.9%	51.1%
36,647	INDEPENDENCE	10,649	6,634	3,623	392	3,011 R	62.3%	34.0%	64.7%	35.3%
13,696	IZARD	4,355	2,470	1,702	183	768 R	56.7%	39.1%	59.2%	40.8%
17,997	JACKSON	4,151	1,981	2,045	125	64 D	47.7%	49.3%	49.2%	50.8%
77,435	JEFFERSON	20,178	6,473	13,447	258	6,974 D	32.1%	66.6%	32.5%	67.5%
25,540	JOHNSON	6,567	3,742	2,572	253	1,170 R	57.0%	39.2%	59.3%	40.7%
7,645	LAFAYETTE	2,418	1,177	1,200	41	23 D	48.7%	49.6%	49.5%	50.5%
17,415	LAWRENCE	4,605	2,340	2,079	186	261 R	50.8%	45.1%	53.0%	47.0%
10,424	LEE	2,647	898	1,713	36	815 D	33.9%	64.7%	34.4%	65.6%
14,134	LINCOLN	3,087	1,476	1,531	80	55 D	47.8%	49.6%	49.1%	50.9%
13,171	LITTLE RIVER	4,100	2,001	2,005	94	4 D	48.8%	48.9%	50.0%	50.0%
22,353	LOGAN	6,504	3,918	2,378	208	1,540 R	60.2%	36.6%	62.2%	37.8%
68,356	LONOKE	19,548	13,385	5,568	595	7,817 R	68.5%	28.5%	70.6%	29.4%
15,717	MADISON	5,177	3,171	1,820	186	1,351 R	61.3%	35.2%	63.5%	36.5%
16,653	MARION	5,008	3,185	1,571	252	1,614 R	63.6%	31.4%	67.0%	33.0%
43,462	MILLER	11,485	7,031	4,241	213	2,790 R	61.2%	36.9%	62.4%	37.6%
46,480	MISSISSIPPI	10,230	4,321	5,526	383	1,205 D	42.2%	54.0%	43.9%	56.1%
8,149	MONROE	2,387	1,026	1,309	52	283 D	43.0%	54.8%	43.9%	56.1%
9,487	MONTGOMERY	2,925	1,711	1,113	101	598 R	58.5%	38.1%	60.6%	39.4%
8,997	NEVADA	2,776	1,085	1,657	34	572 D	39.1%	59.7%	39.6%	60.4%
8,330	NEWTON	3,032	1,903	970	159	933 R	62.8%	32.0%	66.2%	33.8%
26,120	OUACHITA	7,920	3,456	4,340	124	884 D	43.6%	54.8%	44.3%	55.7%
10,445	PERRY	3,597	2,074	1,386	137	688 R	57.7%	38.5%	59.9%	40.1%
21,757	PHILLIPS	5,756	1,888	3,713	155	1,825 D	32.8%	64.5%	33.7%	66.3%
11,291	PIKE	3,116	1,746	1,302	68	444 R	56.0%	41.8%	57.3%	42.7%
24,583	POINSETT	6,368	3,423	2,730	215	693 R	53.8%	42.9%	55.6%	44.4%
20,662	POLK	6,369	4,110	1,965	294	2,145 R	64.5%	30.9%	67.7%	32.3%
61,754	POPE	17,087	11,412	5,085	590	6,327 R	66.8%	29.8%	69.2%	30.8%
8,715	PRAIRIE	2,659	1,563	1,019	77	544 R	58.8%	38.3%	60.5%	39.5%
382,748	PULASKI	127,689	53,050	71,804	2,835	18,754 D	41.5%	56.2%	42.5%	57.5%

ARKANSAS

GOVERNOR 2014

2010 Census Population	County	Total Vote	Republican (Hutchinson)	Democratic (Ross)	Other	Rep.-Dem. Plurality	Percentage			
							Total Vote		Major Vote	
							Rep.	Dem.	Rep.	Dem.
17,969	RANDOLPH	5,060	2,600	2,220	240	380 R	51.4%	43.9%	53.9%	46.1%
107,118	SALINE	39,729	25,823	12,555	1,351	13,268 R	65.0%	31.6%	67.3%	32.7%
11,233	SCOTT	3,099	1,919	1,073	107	846 R	61.9%	34.6%	64.1%	35.9%
8,195	SEARCY	3,064	2,174	765	125	1,409 R	71.0%	25.0%	74.0%	26.0%
125,744	SEBASTIAN	31,864	20,875	9,971	1,018	10,904 R	65.5%	31.3%	67.7%	32.3%
17,058	SEVIER	3,554	1,908	1,549	97	359 R	53.7%	43.6%	55.2%	44.8%
17,264	SHARP	5,681	3,396	2,031	254	1,365 R	59.8%	35.8%	62.6%	37.4%
28,258	ST. FRANCIS	5,963	2,161	3,681	121	1,520 D	36.2%	61.7%	37.0%	63.0%
12,394	STONE	4,518	2,809	1,516	193	1,293 R	62.2%	33.6%	64.9%	35.1%
41,639	UNION	12,424	6,626	5,555	243	1,071 R	53.3%	44.7%	54.4%	45.6%
17,295	VAN BUREN	5,932	3,582	2,112	238	1,470 R	60.4%	35.6%	62.9%	37.1%
203,065	WASHINGTON	54,540	30,134	22,420	1,986	7,714 R	55.3%	41.1%	57.3%	42.7%
77,076	WHITE	21,871	15,007	6,120	744	8,887 R	68.6%	28.0%	71.0%	29.0%
7,260	WOODRUFF	2,146	757	1,342	47	585 D	35.3%	62.5%	36.1%	63.9%
22,185	YELL	5,225	2,985	2,070	170	915 R	57.1%	39.6%	59.1%	40.9%
2,915,918	TOTAL	848,592	470,429	352,115	26,048	118,314 R	55.4%	41.5%	57.2%	42.8%

ARKANSAS

SENATOR 2014

2010 Census Population	County	Total Vote	Republican (Cotton)	Democratic (Pryor)	Other	Rep.-Dem. Plurality	Percentage			
							Total Vote		Major Vote	
							Rep.	Dem.	Rep.	Dem.
19,019	ARKANSAS	5,087	2,590	2,358	139	232 R	50.9%	46.4%	52.3%	47.7%
21,853	ASHLEY	6,221	3,267	2,775	179	492 R	52.5%	44.6%	54.1%	45.9%
41,513	BAXTER	14,968	9,950	4,364	654	5,586 R	66.5%	29.2%	69.5%	30.5%
221,339	BENTON	62,925	42,358	17,511	3,056	24,847 R	67.3%	27.8%	70.8%	29.2%
36,903	BOONE	11,002	7,578	2,884	540	4,694 R	68.9%	26.2%	72.4%	27.6%
11,508	BRADLEY	2,889	1,469	1,323	97	146 R	50.8%	45.8%	52.6%	47.4%
5,368	CALHOUN	1,634	898	664	72	234 R	55.0%	40.6%	57.5%	42.5%
27,446	CARROLL	8,078	4,698	2,985	395	1,713 R	58.2%	37.0%	61.1%	38.9%
11,800	CHICOT	3,500	1,149	2,284	67	1,135 D	32.8%	65.3%	33.5%	66.5%
22,995	CLARK	6,959	3,122	3,625	212	503 D	44.9%	52.1%	46.3%	53.7%
16,083	CLAY	3,998	2,253	1,573	172	680 R	56.4%	39.3%	58.9%	41.1%
25,970	CLEBURNE	9,874	6,636	2,686	552	3,950 R	67.2%	27.2%	71.2%	28.8%
8,689	CLEVELAND	2,724	1,668	939	117	729 R	61.2%	34.5%	64.0%	36.0%
24,552	COLUMBIA	7,928	4,610	3,094	224	1,516 R	58.1%	39.0%	59.8%	40.2%
21,273	CONWAY	6,345	3,393	2,703	249	690 R	53.5%	42.6%	55.7%	44.3%
96,443	CRAIGHEAD	25,311	15,247	9,055	1,009	6,192 R	60.2%	35.8%	62.7%	37.3%
61,948	CRAWFORD	16,207	11,134	4,242	831	6,892 R	68.7%	26.2%	72.4%	27.6%
50,902	CRITTENDEN	10,681	4,527	5,901	253	1,374 D	42.4%	55.2%	43.4%	56.6%
17,870	CROSS	5,272	2,982	2,143	147	839 R	56.6%	40.6%	58.2%	41.8%
8,116	DALLAS	2,368	1,166	1,134	68	32 R	49.2%	47.9%	50.7%	49.3%
13,008	DESHA	3,398	1,211	2,082	105	871 D	35.6%	61.3%	36.8%	63.2%
18,509	DREW	5,222	2,675	2,378	169	297 R	51.2%	45.5%	52.9%	47.1%
113,237	FAULKNER	33,893	20,588	11,885	1,420	8,703 R	60.7%	35.1%	63.4%	36.6%
18,125	FRANKLIN	5,477	3,357	1,854	266	1,503 R	61.3%	33.9%	64.4%	35.6%
12,245	FULTON	3,383	2,005	1,234	144	771 R	59.3%	36.5%	61.9%	38.1%
96,024	GARLAND	30,866	18,567	11,126	1,173	7,441 R	60.2%	36.0%	62.5%	37.5%
17,853	GRANT	5,343	3,490	1,615	238	1,875 R	65.3%	30.2%	68.4%	31.6%
42,090	GREENE	11,099	6,865	3,675	559	3,190 R	61.9%	33.1%	65.1%	34.9%
22,609	HEMPSTEAD	5,375	3,080	2,140	155	940 R	57.3%	39.8%	59.0%	41.0%
32,923	HOT SPRING	9,394	5,260	3,661	473	1,599 R	56.0%	39.0%	59.0%	41.0%

ARKANSAS

SENATOR 2014

2010 Census Population	County	Total Vote	Republican (Cotton)	Democratic (Pryor)	Other	Rep.-Dem. Plurality	Percentage Total Vote Rep.	Dem.	Major Vote Rep.	Dem.
13,789	HOWARD	3,660	2,082	1,485	93	597 R	56.9%	40.6%	58.4%	41.6%
36,647	INDEPENDENCE	10,618	6,615	3,407	596	3,208 R	62.3%	32.1%	66.0%	34.0%
13,696	IZARD	4,351	2,595	1,550	206	1,045 R	59.6%	35.6%	62.6%	37.4%
17,997	JACKSON	4,144	2,103	1,808	233	295 R	50.7%	43.6%	53.8%	46.2%
77,435	JEFFERSON	20,144	6,568	13,145	431	6,577 D	32.6%	65.3%	33.3%	66.7%
25,540	JOHNSON	6,539	3,638	2,488	413	1,150 R	55.6%	38.0%	59.4%	40.6%
7,645	LAFAYETTE	2,405	1,367	973	65	394 R	56.8%	40.5%	58.4%	41.6%
17,415	LAWRENCE	4,578	2,593	1,731	254	862 R	56.6%	37.8%	60.0%	40.0%
10,424	LEE	2,665	871	1,737	57	866 D	32.7%	65.2%	33.4%	66.6%
14,134	LINCOLN	3,079	1,538	1,427	114	111 R	50.0%	46.3%	51.9%	48.1%
13,171	LITTLE RIVER	4,070	2,295	1,620	155	675 R	56.4%	39.8%	58.6%	41.4%
22,353	LOGAN	6,468	3,932	2,132	404	1,800 R	60.8%	33.0%	64.8%	35.2%
68,356	LONOKE	19,507	13,330	5,368	809	7,962 R	68.3%	27.5%	71.3%	28.7%
15,717	MADISON	5,159	3,102	1,755	302	1,347 R	60.1%	34.0%	63.9%	36.1%
16,653	MARION	5,027	3,328	1,428	271	1,900 R	66.2%	28.4%	70.0%	30.0%
43,462	MILLER	11,454	7,581	3,636	237	3,945 R	66.2%	31.7%	67.6%	32.4%
46,480	MISSISSIPPI	10,318	4,523	5,349	446	826 D	43.8%	51.8%	45.8%	54.2%
8,149	MONROE	2,401	1,025	1,292	84	267 D	42.7%	53.8%	44.2%	55.8%
9,487	MONTGOMERY	2,900	1,834	940	126	894 R	63.2%	32.4%	66.1%	33.9%
8,997	NEVADA	2,754	1,405	1,280	69	125 R	51.0%	46.5%	52.3%	47.7%
8,330	NEWTON	2,974	1,923	908	143	1,015 R	64.7%	30.5%	67.9%	32.1%
26,120	OUACHITA	7,951	3,748	3,999	204	251 D	47.1%	50.3%	48.4%	51.6%
10,445	PERRY	3,587	2,108	1,258	221	850 R	58.8%	35.1%	62.6%	37.4%
21,757	PHILLIPS	5,771	1,774	3,792	205	2,018 D	30.7%	65.7%	31.9%	68.1%
11,291	PIKE	3,102	2,015	971	116	1,044 R	65.0%	31.3%	67.5%	32.5%
24,583	POINSETT	6,352	3,689	2,336	327	1,353 R	58.1%	36.8%	61.2%	38.8%
20,662	POLK	6,344	4,446	1,511	387	2,935 R	70.1%	23.8%	74.6%	25.4%
61,754	POPE	17,092	11,611	4,687	794	6,924 R	67.9%	27.4%	71.2%	28.8%
8,715	PRAIRIE	2,658	1,539	998	121	541 R	57.9%	37.5%	60.7%	39.3%
382,748	PULASKI	127,607	52,142	71,905	3,560	19,763 D	40.9%	56.3%	42.0%	58.0%
17,969	RANDOLPH	5,059	2,951	1,842	266	1,109 R	58.3%	36.4%	61.6%	38.4%
107,118	SALINE	39,647	25,756	12,153	1,738	13,603 R	65.0%	30.7%	67.9%	32.1%
11,233	SCOTT	3,083	1,964	925	194	1,039 R	63.7%	30.0%	68.0%	32.0%
8,195	SEARCY	3,055	2,144	755	156	1,389 R	70.2%	24.7%	74.0%	26.0%
125,744	SEBASTIAN	31,856	20,573	9,870	1,413	10,703 R	64.6%	31.0%	67.6%	32.4%
17,058	SEVIER	3,546	2,243	1,176	127	1,067 R	63.3%	33.2%	65.6%	34.4%
17,264	SHARP	5,643	3,534	1,788	321	1,746 R	62.6%	31.7%	66.4%	33.6%
28,258	ST. FRANCIS	6,047	2,198	3,752	97	1,554 D	36.3%	62.0%	36.9%	63.1%
12,394	STONE	4,513	2,805	1,478	230	1,327 R	62.2%	32.7%	65.5%	34.5%
41,639	UNION	12,381	7,253	4,818	310	2,435 R	58.6%	38.9%	60.1%	39.9%
17,295	VAN BUREN	5,905	3,648	1,957	300	1,691 R	61.8%	33.1%	65.1%	34.9%
203,065	WASHINGTON	54,463	29,454	22,285	2,724	7,169 R	54.1%	40.9%	56.9%	43.1%
77,076	WHITE	21,846	15,296	5,507	1,043	9,789 R	70.0%	25.2%	73.5%	26.5%
7,260	WOODRUFF	2,151	749	1,299	103	550 D	34.8%	60.4%	36.6%	63.4%
22,185	YELL	5,210	3,138	1,760	312	1,378 R	60.2%	33.8%	64.1%	35.9%
2,915,918	TOTAL	847,505	478,819	334,174	34,512	144,645 R	56.5%	39.4%	58.9%	41.1%

ARKANSAS

HOUSE OF REPRESENTATIVES

CD	Year	Total Vote	Republican		Democratic		Other Vote	Rep.-Dem. Plurality	Percentage			
									Total Vote		Major Vote	
			Vote	Candidate	Vote	Candidate			Rep.	Dem.	Rep.	Dem.
1	2014	196,256	124,139	CRAWFORD, Eric A. "RICK"*	63,555	MCPHERSON, JACKIE	8,562	60,584 R	63.3%	32.4%	66.1%	33.9%
1	2012	246,843	138,800	CRAWFORD, Eric A. "RICK"*	96,601	ELLINGTON, SCOTT	11,442	42,199 R	56.2%	39.1%	59.0%	41.0%
2	2014	237,330	123,073	HILL, J. FRENCH	103,477	HAYS, PATRICK	10,780	19,596 R	51.9%	43.6%	54.3%	45.7%
2	2012	286,598	158,175	GRIFFIN, TIM*	113,156	RULE, HERB	15,267	45,019 R	55.2%	39.5%	58.3%	41.7%
3	2014	190,935	151,630	WOMACK, STEVE*			39,305	151,630 R	79.4%		100.0%	
3	2012	245,660	186,467	WOMACK, STEVE*			59,193	186,467 R	75.9%		100.0%	
4	2014	206,131	110,789	WESTERMAN, BRUCE	87,742	WITT, JAMES LEE	7,600	23,047 R	53.7%	42.6%	55.8%	44.2%
4	2012	258,953	154,149	COTTON, TOM	95,013	JEFFRESS, GENE	9,791	59,136 R	59.5%	36.7%	61.9%	38.1%
TOTAL	2014	830,652	509,631		254,774		66,247	254,857 R	61.4%	30.7%	66.7%	33.3%
TOTAL	2012	1,038,054	637,591		304,770		95,693	332,821 R	61.4%	29.4%	67.7%	32.3%

Note: An asterisk (*) denotes incumbent.

ARKANSAS

GENERAL AND PRIMARY ELECTIONS

2014 GENERAL ELECTIONS: OTHER VOTES

Governor   Other vote was 16,319 Libertarian (Frank Gilbert), 9,729 Green (Josh Drake)

Senate   Other vote was 17,210 Libertarian (Nathan LaFrance), 16,797 Green (Mark H. Swaney), 505 scattered write-in

House   Other vote was:

CD 1   8,562 Libertarian (Brian Scott Willhite)
CD 2   10,780 Libertarian (Debbie Standiford)
CD 3   39,305 Libertarian (Grant Brand)
CD 4   7,598 Libertarian (Ken Hamilton), 2 scattered write-in

2014 PRIMARY ELECTIONS: SUPPLEMENTARY INFORMATION

Primary   May 20, 2014   **Registration**   1,624,187   No Party Registration
(as of May 20 , 2014)

Primary Runoff June 10, 2014

Primary Type   Any registered voter could participate in either the Democratic or Republican primary. However, if they participated in one party's primary they could not vote in the runoff of the other party.

	REPUBLICAN PRIMARIES			DEMOCRATIC PRIMARIES		
Senator	Cotton, Tom	Unopposed		Pryor, Mark*	Unopposed	
Governor	Hutchinson, Asa	130,752	73.0%	Ross, Mike	129,437	84.4%
	Coleman, Curtis	48,473	27.0%	Bryant, Lynette "Doc"	23,906	15.6%
	TOTAL	179,225		TOTAL	153,343	
Congressional District 1	Crawford, Eric A. "Rick"*	Unopposed		McPherson, Jackie	Unopposed	

ARKANSAS

GENERAL AND PRIMARY ELECTIONS

	REPUBLICAN PRIMARIES			DEMOCRATIC PRIMARIES	
Congressional District 2	Hill, J. French	29,916	55.1%	Hays, Patrick	Unopposed
	Clemmer, Ann	12,400	22.8%		
	Reynolds, Conrad	11,994	22.1%		
	TOTAL	*54,310*			
Congressional District 3	Womack, Steve*	Unopposed			
Congressional District 4	Westerman, Bruce	18,719	54.5%	Witt, James Lee	Unopposed
	Moll, Tommy	15,659	45.5%		
	TOTAL	*34,378*			

Note: An asterisk (*) denotes incumbent.

42

CALIFORNIA

Congressional districts first established for elections held in 2012

53 members

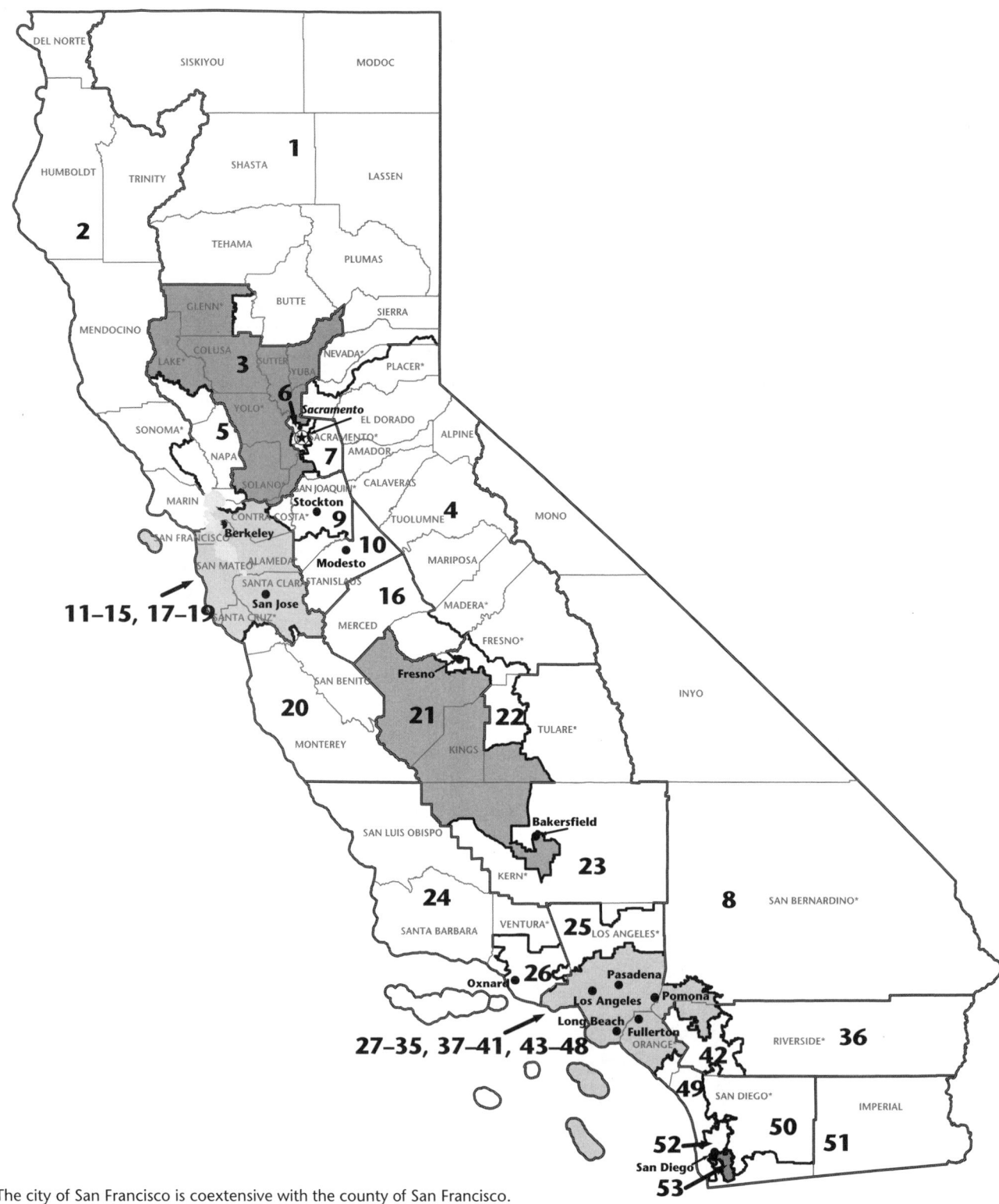

The city of San Francisco is coextensive with the county of San Francisco.

* Asterisk indicates a county whose boundaries include parts of two or more congressional districts.

CALIFORNIA

Greater San Francisco Bay Area

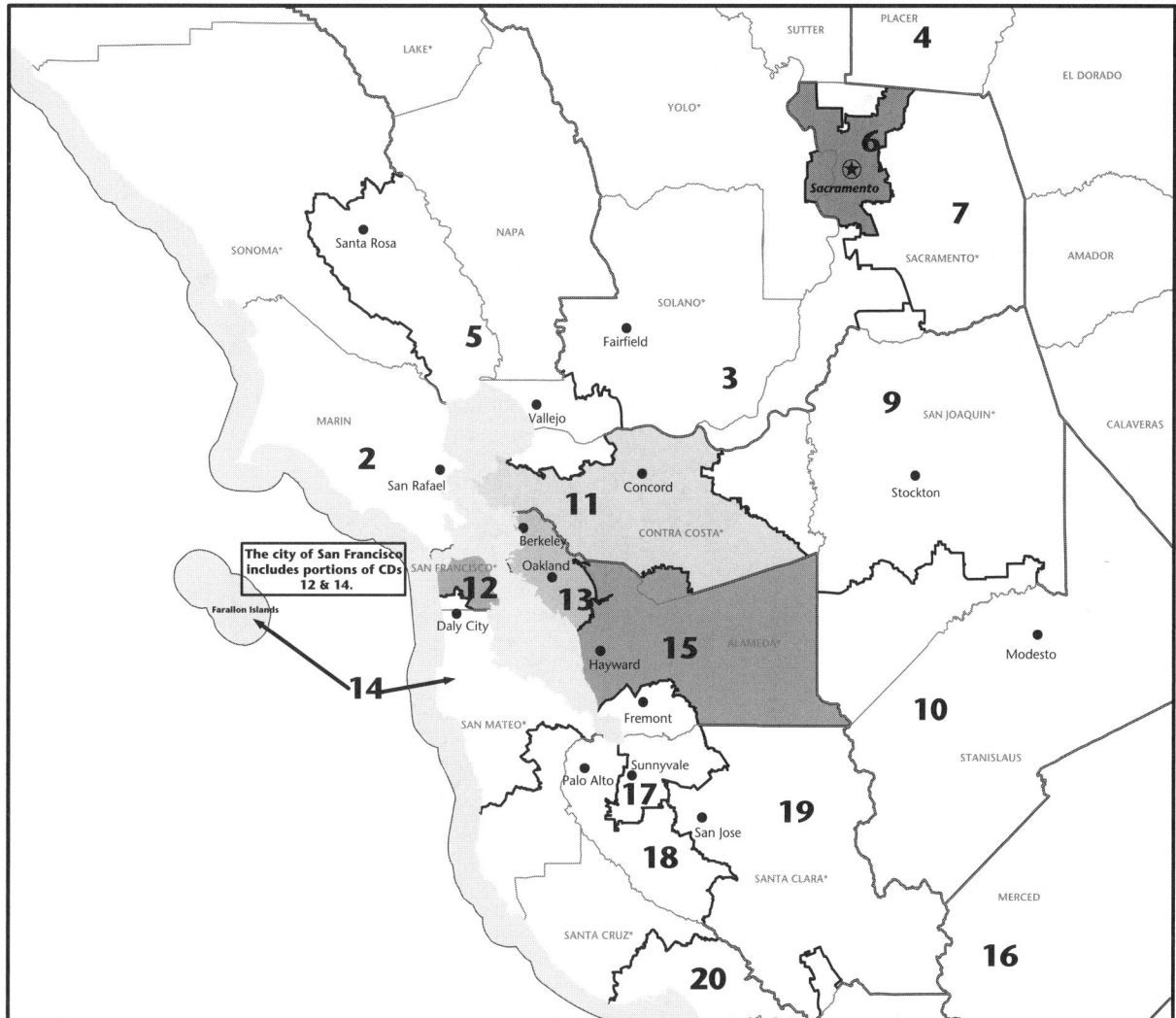

The city of San Francisco includes portions of CDs 12 & 14.

* Asterisk indicates a county whose boundaries include parts of two or more congressional districts.

CALIFORNIA

Greater Los Angeles, San Diego Areas

25
LOS ANGELES*
8
Santa Clarita
VENTURA*
SAN BERNARDINO*
26 Simi Valley
28
27
Rancho Cucamonga
San Bernardino
Thousand Oaks
29 30
Glendale Pasadena El Monte Pomona
Ontario 35 31
33
32
24
37 40 38 39
Riverside Moreno Valley
Inglewood

The city of Los Angeles includes portions of CDs 25, 28–30, 33, 34, 37, 40, 43–44.

34
43 44
Corona 41
36
Fullerton
Torrance
Anaheim 46 Orange
RIVERSIDE*
Long Beach
45
47
Garden Grove Irvine ORANGE*
42
Huntington Beach 48
Santa Ana

CD 24 includes Santa Barbara Island

CD 47 includes Catalina Island & San Clemente Island.

49
Oceanside
Escondido
50
52 SAN DIEGO* IMPERIAL

The city of San Diego includes portions of CDs 49–53.

53
51
Chula Vista

* Asterisk indicates a county whose boundaries include parts of two or more congressional districts.

CALIFORNIA

GOVERNOR
Edmund G. "Jerry" Brown Jr. (D). Re-elected 2014 to a four-year term. Previously elected 2010, 1978, 1974.

SENATORS (2 Democrats)
Barbara Boxer (D). Reelected 2010 to a six-year term. Previously elected 2004, 1998, 1992.

Dianne Feinstein (D). Reelected 2012 to a six-year term. Previously elected 2006, 2000, 1994, and 1992 to fill the remaining two years of the term vacated when Senator Pete Wilson (R) was elected governor in November 1990.

REPRESENTATIVES (14 Republicans, 39 Democrats)

1. Doug LaMalfa (R)
2. Jared Huffman (D)
3. John Garamendi (D)
4. Tom McClintock (R)
5. Mike Thompson (D)
6. Doris O. Matsui (D)
7. Ami Bera (D)
8. Paul Cook (R)
9. Jerry McNerney (D)
10. Jeff Denham (R)
11. Mark DeSaulnier (D)
12. Nancy Pelosi (D)
13. Barbara Lee (D)
14. Jackie Speier (D)
15. Eric Swalwell (D)
16. Jim Costa (D)
17. Michael M. Honda (D)
18. Anna G. Eshoo (D)
19. Zoe Lofgren (D)
20. Sam Farr (D)
21. David G. Valadao (R)
22. Devin Nunes (R)
23. Kevin McCarthy (R)
24. Lois Capps (D)
25. Stephen Knight (R)
26. Julia Brownley (D)
27. Judy Chu (D)
28. Adam B. Schiff (D)
29. Tony Cárdenas (D)
30. Brad Sherman (D)
31. Pete Aguilar (D)
32. Grace F. Napolitano (D)
33. Ted Lieu (D)
34. Xavier Becerra (D)
35. Norma J. Torres (D)
36. Raul Ruiz (D)
37. Karen Bass (D)
38. Linda J. Sánchez (D)
39. Edward R. Royce (R)
40. Lucille Roybal-Allard (D)
41. Mark Takano (D)
42. Ken Calvert (R)
43. Maxine Waters (D)
44. Janice Hahn (D)
45. Mimi Walters (R)
46. Loretta Sanchez (D)
47. Alan S. Lowenthal (D)
48. Dana Rohrabacher (R)
49. Darrell E. Issa (R)
50. Duncan D. Hunter (R)
51. Juan Vargas (D)
52. Scott H. Peters (D)
53. Susan A. Davis (D)

POSTWAR VOTE FOR PRESIDENT

Year	Total Vote	Republican		Democratic		Other Vote	Rep.-Dem. Plurality	Percentage			
		Vote	Candidate	Vote	Candidate			Total Vote		Major Vote	
								Rep.	Dem.	Rep.	Dem.
2012	13,038,547	4,839,958	Romney, W. Mitt	7,854,285	Obama, Barack H.*	344,304	3,014,327 D	37.1%	60.2%	38.1%	61.9%
2008	13,561,900	5,011,781	McCain, John S. III	8,274,473	Obama, Barack H.	275,646	3,262,692 D	37.0%	61.0%	37.7%	62.3%
2004	12,421,852	5,509,826	Bush, George W.*	6,745,485	Kerry, John F.	166,541	1,235,659 D	44.4%	54.3%	45.0%	55.0%
2000**	10,965,856	4,567,429	Bush, George W.	5,861,203	Gore, Albert Jr.	537,224	1,293,774 D	41.7%	53.4%	43.8%	56.2%
1996**	10,019,484	3,828,380	Dole, Robert "Bob"	5,119,835	Clinton, Bill*	1,071,269	1,291,455 D	38.2%	51.1%	42.8%	57.2%
1992**	11,131,721	3,630,574	Bush, George H.*	5,121,325	Clinton, Bill	2,379,822	1,490,751 D	32.6%	46.0%	41.5%	58.5%
1988	9,887,065	5,054,917	Bush, George H.	4,702,233	Dukakis, Michael S.	129,915	352,684 R	51.1%	47.6%	51.8%	48.2%
1984	9,505,423	5,467,009	Reagan, Ronald*	3,922,519	Mondale, Walter F.	115,895	1,544,490 R	57.5%	41.3%	58.2%	41.8%
1980**	8,587,063	4,524,858	Reagan, Ronald	3,083,661	Carter, Jimmy*	978,544	1,441,197 R	52.7%	35.9%	59.5%	40.5%
1976	7,867,117	3,882,244	Ford, Gerald R.*	3,742,284	Carter, Jimmy	242,589	139,960 R	49.3%	47.6%	50.9%	49.1%
1972	8,367,862	4,602,096	Nixon, Richard M.*	3,475,847	McGovern, George S.	289,919	1,126,249 R	55.0%	41.5%	57.0%	43.0%
1968**	7,251,587	3,467,664	Nixon, Richard M.	3,244,318	Humphrey, Hubert Horatio Jr.	539,605	223,346 R	47.8%	44.7%	51.7%	48.3%
1964	7,057,586	2,879,108	Goldwater, Barry M. Sr.	4,171,877	Johnson, Lyndon B.*	6,601	1,292,769 D	40.8%	59.1%	40.8%	59.2%
1960	6,506,578	3,259,722	Nixon, Richard M.	3,224,099	Kennedy, John F.	22,757	35,623 R	50.1%	49.6%	50.3%	49.7%
1956	5,466,355	3,027,668	Eisenhower, Dwight D.*	2,420,135	Stevenson, Adlai E. II	18,552	607,533 R	55.4%	44.3%	55.6%	44.4%
1952	5,141,849	2,897,310	Eisenhower, Dwight D.	2,197,548	Stevenson, Adlai E. II	46,991	699,762 R	56.3%	42.7%	56.9%	43.1%
1948	4,021,538	1,895,269	Dewey, Thomas E.	1,913,134	Truman, Harry S.*	213,135	17,865 D	47.1%	47.6%	49.8%	50.2%

Note: An asterisk (*) denotes incumbent. **In past elections, the other vote included: 2000 - 418,707 Green (Ralph Nader); 1996 - 697,847 Reform (Ross Perot); 1992 - 2,296,006 Independent (Perot); 1980 - 739,833 Independent (John Anderson); 1968 - 487,270 American Independent (George Wallace).

CALIFORNIA

POSTWAR VOTE FOR GOVERNOR

		Republican		Democratic		Other Vote	Rep.-Dem. Plurality	Percentage			
								Total Vote		Major Vote	
Year	Total Vote	Vote	Candidate	Vote	Candidate			Rep.	Dem.	Rep.	Dem.
2014	7,317,581	2,929,213	Kashkari, Neel	4,388,368	Brown, Edmund G.*		1,459,155 D	40.0%	60.0%	40.0%	60.0%
2010	10,095,185	4,127,391	Whitman, Meg	5,428,149	Brown, Edmund G.	539,645	1,300,758 D	40.9%	53.8%	43.2%	56.8%
2006	8,679,416	4,850,157	Schwarzenegger, Arnold*	3,376,732	Angelides, Phil	452,527	1,473,425 R	55.9%	38.9%	59.0%	41.0%
2003S	8,657,915	4,206,284	Schwarzenegger, Arnold	2,724,874	Bustamante, Cruz	1,726,757	1,481,410 R	48.6%	31.5%	60.7%	39.3%
2002	7,476,311	3,169,801	Simon, Bill	3,533,490	Davis, Gray*	773,020	363,689 D	42.4%	47.3%	47.3%	52.7%
1998	8,385,196	3,218,030	Lungren, Dan	4,860,702	Davis, Gray	306,464	1,642,672 D	38.4%	58.0%	39.8%	60.2%
1994	8,665,375	4,781,766	Wilson, Pete*	3,519,799	Brown, Kathleen	363,810	1,261,967 R	55.2%	40.6%	57.6%	42.4%
1990	7,699,467	3,791,904	Wilson, Pete	3,525,197	Feinstein, Dianne	382,366	266,707 R	49.2%	45.8%	51.8%	48.2%
1986	7,443,551	4,506,601	Deukmejian, George*	2,781,714	Bradley, Tom	155,236	1,724,887 R	60.5%	37.4%	61.8%	38.2%
1982	7,876,698	3,881,014	Deukmejian, George	3,787,669	Bradley, Tom	208,015	93,345 R	49.3%	48.1%	50.6%	49.4%
1978	6,922,378	2,526,534	Younger, Evelle J.	3,878,812	Brown, Edmund G.*	517,032	1,352,278 D	36.5%	56.0%	39.4%	60.6%
1974	6,248,070	2,952,954	Flournoy, Houston I.	3,131,648	Brown, Edmund G.	163,468	178,694 D	47.3%	50.1%	48.5%	51.5%
1970	6,510,272	3,439,664	Reagan, Ronald*	2,938,807	Unruh, Jess	131,801	500,857 R	52.8%	45.1%	53.9%	46.1%
1966	6,503,445	3,742,913	Reagan, Ronald	2,749,174	Brown, Edmund G.	11,358	993,739 R	57.6%	42.3%	57.7%	42.3%
1962	5,853,270	2,740,351	Nixon, Richard M.	3,037,109	Brown, Edmund G.*	75,810	296,758 D	46.8%	51.9%	47.4%	52.6%
1958	5,255,777	2,110,911	Knowland, William F.	3,140,076	Brown, Edmund G.	4,790	1,029,165 D	40.2%	59.7%	40.2%	59.8%
1954	4,030,368	2,290,519	Knight, Goodwin J.*	1,739,368	Graves, Richard Perrin	481	551,151 R	56.8%	43.2%	56.8%	43.2%
1950	3,796,090	2,461,754	Warren, Earl*	1,333,856	Roosevelt, James	480	1,127,898 R	64.8%	35.1%	64.9%	35.1%
1946**	2,738,978	2,344,542	Warren, Earl*			213,857	2,344,542 R	91.6%		100.0%	

Note: An asterisk (*) denotes incumbent. **The 2003 election was for a short term to fill a vacancy created by voter approval of a measure to remove Governor Gray Davis (D) from office. The measure passed by a vote of 4,976,274 votes (55.4 percent) for recall to 4,007,783 (44.6 percent) against recall. In the same election, more than 100 candidates ran for the right to succeed Davis. No primary election was held to cull the field. All candidates, regardless of party, ran together on the same ballot. The winner, Arnold Schwarzenegger, is listed as the Republican candidate. The leading Democratic vote-getter, Cruz Bustamante, is listed as the Democratic candidate. The percentages given are for Schwarzenegger and Bustamante. The leading "Other" candidate was Republican Tom McClintock, who received 1,161,287 votes (13.4 percent of the total). The percentage columns are for Schwarzenegger and Bustamante and do not include additional candidates. In 1946 the Republican candidate won both major party nominations.

POSTWAR VOTE FOR SENATOR

		Republican		Democratic		Other Vote	Rep.-Dem. Plurality	Percentage			
								Total Vote		Major Vote	
Year	Total Vote	Vote	Candidate	Vote	Candidate			Rep.	Dem.	Rep.	Dem.
2012	12,578,511	4,713,887	Emken, Elizabeth	7,864,624	Feinstein, Dianne*		3,150,737 D	37.5%	62.5%	37.5%	62.5%
2010	9,999,860	4,217,386	Fiorina, Carly	5,218,137	Boxer, Barbara*	564,337	1,000,751 D	42.2%	52.2%	44.7%	55.3%
2006	8,541,476	2,990,822	Mountjoy, Dick	5,076,289	Feinstein, Dianne*	474,365	2,085,467 D	35.0%	59.4%	37.1%	62.9%
2004	12,053,295	4,555,922	Jones, Bill	6,955,728	Boxer, Barbara*	541,645	2,399,806 D	37.8%	57.7%	39.6%	60.4%
2000	10,623,614	3,886,853	Campbell, Tom	5,932,522	Feinstein, Dianne*	804,239	2,045,669 D	36.6%	55.8%	39.6%	60.4%
1998	8,314,953	3,576,351	Fong, Matt	4,411,705	Boxer, Barbara*	326,897	835,354 D	43.0%	53.1%	44.8%	55.2%
1994	8,514,089	3,817,025	Huffington, Michael	3,979,152	Feinstein, Dianne*	717,912	162,127 D	44.8%	46.7%	49.0%	51.0%
1992	10,799,703	4,644,182	Sargent, Claire	5,173,467	Boxer, Barbara	982,054	529,285 D	43.0%	47.9%	47.3%	52.7%
1992S	10,782,743	4,093,501	Seymour, John*	5,853,651	Feinstein, Dianne	835,591	1,760,150 D	38.0%	54.3%	41.2%	58.8%
1988	9,743,598	5,143,409	Wilson, Pete*	4,287,253	McCarthy, Leo T.	312,936	856,156 R	52.8%	44.0%	54.5%	45.5%
1986	7,398,522	3,541,804	Zschau, Ed	3,646,672	Cranston, Alan*	210,046	104,868 D	47.9%	49.3%	49.3%	50.7%
1982	7,805,538	4,022,565	Wilson, Pete	3,494,968	Brown, Edmund G.	288,005	527,597 R	51.5%	44.8%	53.5%	46.5%
1980	8,327,481	3,093,426	Gann, Paul	4,705,399	Cranston, Alan*	528,656	1,611,973 D	37.1%	56.5%	39.7%	60.3%
1976	7,472,268	3,748,973	Hayakawa, S. I.	3,502,862	Tunney, John V.*	220,433	246,111 R	50.2%	46.9%	51.7%	48.3%
1974	6,102,432	2,210,267	Richardson, H. L.	3,693,160	Cranston, Alan*	199,005	1,482,893 D	36.2%	60.5%	37.4%	62.6%
1970	6,492,157	2,877,617	Murphy, George*	3,496,558	Tunney, John V.	117,982	618,941 D	44.3%	53.9%	45.1%	54.9%
1968	7,102,465	3,329,148	Rafferty, Max	3,680,352	Cranston, Alan	92,965	351,204 D	46.9%	51.8%	47.5%	52.5%
1964	7,041,821	3,628,555	Murphy, George	3,411,912	Salinger, Pierre*	1,354	216,643 R	51.5%	48.5%	51.5%	48.5%
1962	5,647,952	3,180,483	Kuchel, Thomas H.*	2,452,839	Richards, Richard	14,630	727,644 R	56.3%	43.4%	56.5%	43.5%
1958	5,135,221	2,204,337	Knight, Goodwin J.	2,927,693	Engle, Clair	3,191	723,356 D	42.9%	57.0%	43.0%	57.0%
1956	5,361,467	2,892,918	Kuchel, Thomas H.*	2,445,816	Richards, Richard	22,733	447,102 R	54.0%	45.6%	54.2%	45.8%
1954S	3,929,668	2,090,836	Kuchel, Thomas H.*	1,788,071	Yorty, Samuel W.	50,761	302,765 R	53.2%	45.5%	53.9%	46.1%
1952**	4,542,548	3,982,448	Knowland, William F.*			560,100	3,982,448 R	87.7%		100.0%	
1950	3,686,315	2,183,454	Nixon, Richard M.	1,502,507	Douglas, Helen Gahagan	354	680,947 R	59.2%	40.8%	59.2%	40.8%
1946	2,639,465	1,428,067	Knowland, William F.*	1,167,161	Rogers, Will Jr.	44,237	260,906 R	54.1%	44.2%	55.0%	45.0%

Note: An asterisk (*) denotes incumbent. **In past elections, the other vote included: 1952 - 542,270 Progressive (Reuben W. Borough), who finished second. The Republican candidate that year (William F. Knowland) won both major party nominations. The 1954 election was for a short term to fill a vacancy, as was one of the 1992 elections.

CALIFORNIA

GOVERNOR 2014

2010 Census Population	County	Total Vote	Republican (Kashkari)	Democratic (Brown)	Other	Rep.-Dem. Plurality	Percentage Total Vote Rep.	Dem.	Major Vote Rep.	Dem.
1,510,271	ALAMEDA	356,674	63,593	293,081		229,488 D	17.8%	82.2%	17.8%	82.2%
1,175	ALPINE	459	175	284		109 D	38.1%	61.9%	38.1%	61.9%
38,091	AMADOR	12,753	7,071	5,682		1,389 R	55.4%	44.6%	55.4%	44.6%
220,000	BUTTE	61,769	32,249	29,520		2,729 R	52.2%	47.8%	52.2%	47.8%
45,578	CALAVERAS	15,711	8,841	6,870		1,971 R	56.3%	43.7%	56.3%	43.7%
21,419	COLUSA	4,187	2,398	1,789		609 R	57.3%	42.7%	57.3%	42.7%
1,049,025	CONTRA COSTA	254,063	79,660	174,403		94,743 D	31.4%	68.6%	31.4%	68.6%
28,610	DEL NORTE	7,027	3,539	3,488		51 R	50.4%	49.6%	50.4%	49.6%
181,058	EL DORADO	61,359	33,443	27,916		5,527 R	54.5%	45.5%	54.5%	45.5%
930,450	FRESNO	159,887	83,744	76,143		7,601 R	52.4%	47.6%	52.4%	47.6%
28,122	GLENN	5,957	3,908	2,049		1,859 R	65.6%	34.4%	65.6%	34.4%
134,623	HUMBOLDT	37,149	13,146	24,003		10,857 D	35.4%	64.6%	35.4%	64.6%
174,528	IMPERIAL	20,941	7,484	13,457		5,973 D	35.7%	64.3%	35.7%	64.3%
18,546	INYO	5,429	3,112	2,317		795 R	57.3%	42.7%	57.3%	42.7%
839,631	KERN	132,686	78,417	54,269		24,148 R	59.1%	40.9%	59.1%	40.9%
152,982	KINGS	22,327	13,575	8,752		4,823 R	60.8%	39.2%	60.8%	39.2%
64,665	LAKE	17,497	6,775	10,722		3,947 D	38.7%	61.3%	38.7%	61.3%
34,895	LASSEN	6,822	4,609	2,213		2,396 R	67.6%	32.4%	67.6%	32.4%
9,818,605	LOS ANGELES	1,463,328	485,186	978,142		492,956 D	33.2%	66.8%	33.2%	66.8%
150,865	MADERA	26,799	16,825	9,974		6,851 R	62.8%	37.2%	62.8%	37.2%
252,409	MARIN	87,898	18,147	69,751		51,604 D	20.6%	79.4%	20.6%	79.4%
18,251	MARIPOSA	6,537	4,038	2,499		1,539 R	61.8%	38.2%	61.8%	38.2%
87,841	MENDOCINO	24,165	6,825	17,340		10,515 D	28.2%	71.8%	28.2%	71.8%
255,793	MERCED	37,793	18,848	18,945		97 D	49.9%	50.1%	49.9%	50.1%
9,686	MODOC	2,831	2,061	770		1,291 R	72.8%	27.2%	72.8%	27.2%
14,202	MONO	3,074	1,442	1,632		190 D	46.9%	53.1%	46.9%	53.1%
415,057	MONTEREY	73,906	22,591	51,315		28,724 D	30.6%	69.4%	30.6%	69.4%
136,484	NAPA	37,905	12,059	25,846		13,787 D	31.8%	68.2%	31.8%	68.2%
98,764	NEVADA	38,395	17,419	20,976		3,557 D	45.4%	54.6%	45.4%	54.6%
3,010,232	ORANGE	620,524	344,817	275,707		69,110 R	55.6%	44.4%	55.6%	44.4%
348,432	PLACER	112,845	61,604	51,241		10,363 R	54.6%	45.4%	54.6%	45.4%
20,007	PLUMAS	7,105	4,139	2,966		1,173 R	58.3%	41.7%	58.3%	41.7%
2,189,641	RIVERSIDE	351,145	185,805	165,340		20,465 R	52.9%	47.1%	52.9%	47.1%
1,418,788	SACRAMENTO	324,758	122,342	202,416		80,074 D	37.7%	62.3%	37.7%	62.3%
55,269	SAN BENITO	13,623	4,969	8,654		3,685 D	36.5%	63.5%	36.5%	63.5%
2,035,210	SAN BERNARDINO	286,875	152,458	134,417		18,041 R	53.1%	46.9%	53.1%	46.9%
3,095,313	SAN DIEGO	678,361	331,942	346,419		14,477 D	48.9%	51.1%	48.9%	51.1%
805,235	SAN FRANCISCO	223,187	26,442	196,745		170,303 D	11.8%	88.2%	11.8%	88.2%
685,306	SAN JOAQUIN	116,945	54,331	62,614		8,283 D	46.5%	53.5%	46.5%	53.5%
269,637	SAN LUIS OBISPO	85,792	39,186	46,606		7,420 D	45.7%	54.3%	45.7%	54.3%
718,451	SAN MATEO	159,895	39,615	120,280		80,665 D	24.8%	75.2%	24.8%	75.2%
423,895	SANTA BARBARA	111,415	46,503	64,912		18,409 D	41.7%	58.3%	41.7%	58.3%
1,781,642	SANTA CLARA	395,845	107,113	288,732		181,619 D	27.1%	72.9%	27.1%	72.9%
262,382	SANTA CRUZ	72,476	15,499	56,977		41,478 D	21.4%	78.6%	21.4%	78.6%
177,223	SHASTA	56,516	35,007	21,509		13,498 R	61.9%	38.1%	61.9%	38.1%
3,240	SIERRA	1,536	857	679		178 R	55.8%	44.2%	55.8%	44.2%
44,900	SISKIYOU	13,820	7,717	6,103		1,614 R	55.8%	44.2%	55.8%	44.2%
413,344	SOLANO	89,628	31,754	57,874		26,120 D	35.4%	64.6%	35.4%	64.6%
483,878	SONOMA	143,577	36,249	107,328		71,079 D	25.2%	74.8%	25.2%	74.8%
514,453	STANISLAUS	90,352	43,786	46,566		2,780 D	48.5%	51.5%	48.5%	51.5%
94,737	SUTTER	20,332	11,644	8,688		2,956 R	57.3%	42.7%	57.3%	42.7%
63,463	TEHAMA	15,360	9,952	5,408		4,544 R	64.8%	35.2%	64.8%	35.2%
13,786	TRINITY	3,874	2,163	1,711		452 R	55.8%	44.2%	55.8%	44.2%
442,179	TULARE	61,704	37,996	23,708		14,288 R	61.6%	38.4%	61.6%	38.4%
55,365	TUOLUMNE	17,009	9,058	7,951		1,107 R	53.3%	46.7%	53.3%	46.7%
823,318	VENTURA	199,869	93,797	106,072		12,275 D	46.9%	53.1%	46.9%	53.1%
200,849	YOLO	45,474	14,043	31,431		17,388 D	30.9%	69.1%	30.9%	69.1%
72,155	YUBA	12,411	7,245	5,166		2,079 R	58.4%	41.6%	58.4%	41.6%
37,253,956	TOTAL	7,317,581	2,929,213	4,388,368		1,459,155 D	40.0%	60.0%	40.0%	60.0%

CALIFORNIA

HOUSE OF REPRESENTATIVES

CD	Year	Total Vote	Republican Vote	Republican Candidate	Democratic Vote	Democratic Candidate	Other Vote	Rep.-Dem. Plurality	Total Vote Rep.	Total Vote Dem.	Major Vote Rep.	Major Vote Dem.
1	2014	216,372	132,052	LAMALFA, DOUG*	84,320	HALL, HEIDI		47,732 R	61.0%	39.0%	61.0%	39.0%
1	2012	294,213	168,827	LAMALFA, DOUG	125,386	REED, JIM		43,441 R	57.4%	42.6%	57.4%	42.6%
2	2014	217,524	54,400	MENSING, DALE	163,124	HUFFMAN, JARED*		108,724 D	25.0%	75.0%	25.0%	75.0%
2	2012	317,526	91,310	ROBERTS, DANIEL W.	226,216	HUFFMAN, JARED		134,906 D	28.8%	71.2%	28.8%	71.2%
3	2014	150,260	71,036	LOGUE, DAN	79,224	GARAMENDI, JOHN*		8,188 D	47.3%	52.7%	47.3%	52.7%
3	2012	233,968	107,086	VANN, KIM	126,882	GARAMENDI, JOHN*		19,796 D	45.8%	54.2%	45.8%	54.2%
4	2014	211,134	126,784	MCCLINTOCK, TOM*			84,350	126,784 R	60.0%		100.0%	
4	2012	323,688	197,803	MCCLINTOCK, TOM*	125,885	UPPAL, JACK		71,918 R	61.1%	38.9%	61.1%	38.9%
5	2014	171,148			129,613	THOMPSON, MIKE*	41,535	129,613 D		75.7%		100.0%
5	2012	272,417	69,545	LOFTIN, RANDY	202,872	THOMPSON, MIKE*		133,327 D	25.5%	74.5%	25.5%	74.5%
6	2014	133,456	36,448	MCCRAY, JOSEPH SR.	97,008	MATSUI, DORIS O.*		60,560 D	27.3%	72.7%	27.3%	72.7%
6	2012	214,073	53,406	MCCRAY, JOSEPH SR.	160,667	MATSUI, DORIS O.*		107,261 D	24.9%	75.1%	24.9%	75.1%
7	2014	183,587	91,066	OSE, DOUG	92,521	BERA, AMI*		1,455 D	49.6%	50.4%	49.6%	50.4%
7	2012	273,291	132,050	LUNGREN, DAN*	141,241	BERA, AMI		9,191 D	48.3%	51.7%	48.3%	51.7%
8	2014	114,536	77,480	COOK, PAUL*	37,056	CONAWAY, ROBERT DEAN "BOB"		40,424 R	67.6%	32.4%	67.6%	32.4%
8	2012	179,644	103,093	COOK, PAUL			76,551	103,093 R	57.4%		100.0%	
9	2014	121,204	57,729	AMADOR, ANTONIO C. "TONY"	63,475	MCNERNEY, JERRY*		5,746 D	47.6%	52.4%	47.6%	52.4%
9	2012	213,077	94,704	GILL, RICKY	118,373	MCNERNEY, JERRY*		23,669 D	44.4%	55.6%	44.4%	55.6%
10	2014	125,705	70,582	DENHAM, JEFF*	55,123	EGGMAN, MICHAEL		15,459 R	56.1%	43.9%	56.1%	43.9%
10	2012	209,199	110,265	DENHAM, JEFF*	98,934	HERNANDEZ, JOSE		11,331 R	52.7%	47.3%	52.7%	47.3%
11	2014	174,662	57,160	PHAN-QUANG, TUE	117,502	DESAULNIER, MARK		60,342 D	32.7%	67.3%	32.7%	67.3%
11	2012	287,879	87,136	FULLER, VIRGINIA	200,743	MILLER, GEORGE*		113,607 D	30.3%	69.7%	30.3%	69.7%
12	2014	192,264	32,197	DENNIS, JOHN	160,067	PELOSI, NANCY*		127,870 D	16.7%	83.3%	16.7%	83.3%
12	2012	298,187	44,478	DENNIS, JOHN	253,709	PELOSI, NANCY*		209,231 D	14.9%	85.1%	14.9%	85.1%
13	2014	190,431	21,940	SUNDEEN, DAKIN	168,491	LEE, BARBARA*		146,551 D	11.5%	88.5%	11.5%	88.5%
13	2012	288,582			250,436	LEE, BARBARA*	38,146	250,436 D		86.8%		100.0%
14	2014	149,146	34,757	CHEW, ROBIN	114,389	SPEIER, JACKIE*		79,632 D	23.3%	76.7%	23.3%	76.7%
14	2012	258,283	54,455	BACIGALUPI, DEBORAH "DEBBIE"	203,828	SPEIER, JACKIE*		149,373 D	21.1%	78.9%	21.1%	78.9%
15	2014	142,906	43,150	BUSSELL, HUGH	99,756	SWALWELL, ERIC*		56,606 D	30.2%	69.8%	30.2%	69.8%
15	2012	231,034			120,388	SWALWELL, ERIC	110,646	120,388 D		52.1%		100.0%
16	2014	91,220	44,943	TACHERRA, JOHNNY M.	46,277	COSTA, JIM*		1,334 D	49.3%	50.7%	49.3%	50.7%
16	2012	147,450	62,801	WHELAN, BRIAN DANIEL	84,649	COSTA, JIM*		21,848 D	42.6%	57.4%	42.6%	57.4%
17	2014	134,408			69,561	HONDA, MICHAEL M.*	64,847	69,561 D		51.8%		100.0%
17	2012	216,728	57,336	LI, EVELYN	159,392	HONDA, MICHAEL M.*		102,056 D	26.5%	73.5%	26.5%	73.5%
18	2014	196,386	63,326	FOX, RICHARD B.	133,060	ESHOO, ANNA G.*		69,734 D	32.2%	67.8%	32.2%	67.8%
18	2012	301,934	89,103	CHAPMAN, DAVE	212,831	ESHOO, ANNA G.*		123,728 D	29.5%	70.5%	29.5%	70.5%
19	2014	127,788			85,888	LOFGREN, ZOE*	41,900	85,888 D		67.2%		100.0%
19	2012	221,613	59,313	MURRAY, ROBERT	162,300	LOFGREN, ZOE*		102,987 D	26.8%	73.2%	26.8%	73.2%
20	2014	141,044			106,034	FARR, SAM*	35,010	106,034 D		75.2%		100.0%
20	2012	233,562	60,566	TAYLOR, JEFF	172,996	FARR, SAM*		112,430 D	25.9%	74.1%	25.9%	74.1%
21	2014	79,377	45,907	VALADAO, DAVID G.*	33,470	RENTERIA, AMANDA		12,437 R	57.8%	42.2%	57.8%	42.2%
21	2012	116,283	67,164	VALADAO, DAVID G.	49,119	HERNANDEZ, JOHN		18,045 R	57.8%	42.2%	57.8%	42.2%
22	2014	133,342	96,053	NUNES, DEVIN*	37,289	AGUILERA-MARRERO, SUZANNA "SAM"		58,764 R	72.0%	28.0%	72.0%	28.0%
22	2012	213,941	132,386	NUNES, DEVIN*	81,555	LEE, OTTO		50,831 R	61.9%	38.1%	61.9%	38.1%
23	2014	134,043	100,317	MCCARTHY, KEVIN*	33,726	GARCIA, RAUL		66,591 R	74.8%	25.2%	74.8%	25.2%
23	2012	216,003	158,161	MCCARTHY, KEVIN*			57,842	158,161 R	73.2%		100.0%	
24	2014	198,794	95,566	MITCHUM, CHRIS	103,228	CAPPS, LOIS*		7,662 D	48.1%	51.9%	48.1%	51.9%
24	2012	284,495	127,746	MALDONADO, ABEL	156,749	CAPPS, LOIS*		29,003 D	44.9%	55.1%	44.9%	55.1%
25	2014	114,072	60,847	KNIGHT, STEPHEN			53,225	60,847 R	53.3%		100.0%	
25	2012	236,575	129,593	MCKEON, HOWARD P. "BUCK"*	106,982	ROGERS, LEE C.		22,611 R	54.8%	45.2%	54.8%	45.2%
26	2014	169,829	82,653	GORELL, JEFF	87,176	BROWNLEY, JULIA*		4,523 D	48.7%	51.3%	48.7%	51.3%
26	2012	263,935	124,863	STRICKLAND, TONY	139,072	BROWNLEY, JULIA		14,209 D	47.3%	52.7%	47.3%	52.7%
27	2014	127,580	51,852	ORSWELL, JACK	75,728	CHU, JUDY*		23,876 D	40.6%	59.4%	40.6%	59.4%
27	2012	241,008	86,817	ORSWELL, JACK	154,191	CHU, JUDY*		67,374 D	36.0%	64.0%	36.0%	64.0%
28	2014	120,264			91,996	SCHIFF, ADAM B.*	28,268	91,996 D		76.5%		100.0%
28	2012	246,711	58,008	JENNERJAHN, PHIL	188,703	SCHIFF, ADAM B.*		130,695 D	23.5%	76.5%	23.5%	76.5%

CALIFORNIA

HOUSE OF REPRESENTATIVES

			Republican		Democratic				Percentage			
									Total Vote		Major Vote	
CD	Year	Total Vote	Vote	Candidate	Vote	Candidate	Other Vote	Rep.-Dem. Plurality	Rep.	Dem.	Rep.	Dem.
29	2014	67,141	17,045	LEADER, WILLIAM O'CALLAGHAN	50,096	CÁRDENAS, TONY*		33,051 D	25.4%	74.6%	25.4%	74.6%
29	2012	150,281			111,287	CÁRDENAS, TONY	38,994	111,287 D		74.1%		100.0%
30	2014	131,883	45,315	REED, MARK	86,568	SHERMAN, BRAD*		41,253 D	34.4%	65.6%	34.4%	65.6%
30	2012	247,851			149,456	SHERMAN, BRAD*	98,395	149,456 D		60.3%		100.0%
31	2014	99,784	48,162	CHABOT, PAUL	51,622	AGUILAR, PETE		3,460 D	48.3%	51.7%	48.3%	51.7%
31	2012	161,219	88,964	MILLER, GARY G.*			72,255	88,964 R	55.2%		100.0%	
32	2014	84,406	34,053	ALAS, ARTURO ENRIQUE	50,353	NAPOLITANO, GRACE F.*		16,300 D	40.3%	59.7%	40.3%	59.7%
32	2012	190,111	65,208	MILLER, DAVID L.	124,903	NAPOLITANO, GRACE F.*		59,695 D	34.3%	65.7%	34.3%	65.7%
33	2014	183,031	74,700	CARR, ELAN S.	108,331	LIEU, TED		33,631 D	40.8%	59.2%	40.8%	59.2%
33	2012	318,520			171,860	WAXMAN, HENRY A.*	146,660	171,860 D		54.0%		100.0%
34	2014	61,621			44,697	BECERRA, XAVIER*	16,924	44,697 D		72.5%		100.0%
34	2012	140,590	20,223	SMITH, STEPHEN	120,367	BECERRA, XAVIER*		100,144 D	14.4%	85.6%	14.4%	85.6%
35	2014	62,475			39,502	TORRES, NORMA J.	22,973	39,502 D		63.2%		100.0%
35	2012	142,680			79,698	MCLEOD, GLORIA NEGRETE	62,982	79,698 D		55.9%		100.0%
36	2014	134,139	61,457	NESTANDE, BRIAN	72,682	RUIZ, RAUL*		11,225 D	45.8%	54.2%	45.8%	54.2%
36	2012	208,142	97,953	BONO MACK, MARY*	110,189	RUIZ, RAUL		12,236 D	47.1%	52.9%	47.1%	52.9%
37	2014	114,838	18,051	KING, R. ADAM	96,787	BASS, KAREN*		78,736 D	15.7%	84.3%	15.7%	84.3%
37	2012	239,580	32,541	OSBORNE, MORGAN	207,039	BASS, KAREN*		174,498 D	13.6%	86.4%	13.6%	86.4%
38	2014	98,480	40,288	CAMPOS, BENJAMIN	58,192	SÁNCHEZ, LINDA T.*		17,904 D	40.9%	59.1%	40.9%	59.1%
38	2012	215,087	69,807	CAMPOS, BENJAMIN	145,280	SÁNCHEZ, LINDA T.*		75,473 D	32.5%	67.5%	32.5%	67.5%
39	2014	133,225	91,319	ROYCE, EDWARD R.*	41,906	ANDERSON, PETER		49,413 R	68.5%	31.5%	68.5%	31.5%
39	2012	251,967	145,607	ROYCE, EDWARD R.*	106,360	CHEN, JAY		39,247 R	57.8%	42.2%	57.8%	42.2%
40	2014	49,379			30,208	ROYBAL-ALLARD, LUCILLE*	19,171	30,208 D		61.2%		100.0%
40	2012	125,553			73,940	ROYBAL-ALLARD, LUCILLE*	51,613	73,940 D		58.9%		100.0%
41	2014	82,884	35,936	ADAMS, STEVE	46,948	TAKANO, MARK*		11,012 D	43.4%	56.6%	43.4%	56.6%
41	2012	175,652	72,074	TAVAGLIONE, JOHN	103,578	TAKANO, MARK		31,504 D	41.0%	59.0%	41.0%	59.0%
42	2014	113,390	74,540	CALVERT, KEN*	38,850	SHERIDAN, TIM		35,690 R	65.7%	34.3%	65.7%	34.3%
42	2012	214,947	130,245	CALVERT, KEN*	84,702	WILLIAMSON, MICHAEL		45,543 R	60.6%	39.4%	60.6%	39.4%
43	2014	98,202	28,521	WOOD JR., JOHN	69,681	WATERS, MAXINE*		41,160 D	29.0%	71.0%	29.0%	71.0%
43	2012	200,894			143,123	WATERS, MAXINE*	57,771	143,123 D		71.2%		100.0%
44	2014	68,862			59,670	HAHN, JANICE*	9,192	59,670 D		86.7%		100.0%
44	2012	165,898			99,909	HAHN, JANICE	65,989	99,909 D		60.2%		100.0%
45	2014	162,902	106,083	WALTERS, MIMI	56,819	LEAVENS, DREW		49,264 R	65.1%	34.9%	65.1%	34.9%
45	2012	293,231	171,417	CAMPBELL, JOHN*	121,814	KANG, SUKHEE		49,603 R	58.5%	41.5%	58.5%	41.5%
46	2014	83,315	33,577	NICK, ADAM	49,738	SANCHEZ, LORETTA*		16,161 D	40.3%	59.7%	40.3%	59.7%
46	2012	149,815	54,121	HAYDEN, JERRY	95,694	SANCHEZ, LORETTA*		41,573 D	36.1%	63.9%	36.1%	63.9%
47	2014	123,400	54,309	WHALLON, ANDY	69,091	LOWENTHAL, ALAN S.*		14,782 D	44.0%	56.0%	44.0%	56.0%
47	2012	230,012	99,919	DELONG, GARY	130,093	LOWENTHAL, ALAN S.		30,174 D	43.4%	56.6%	43.4%	56.6%
48	2014	174,795	112,082	ROHRABACHER, DANA*	62,713	SAVARY, SUE		49,369 R	64.1%	35.9%	64.1%	35.9%
48	2012	290,502	177,144	ROHRABACHER, DANA*	113,358	VARASTEH, RON		63,786 R	61.0%	39.0%	61.0%	39.0%
49	2014	163,142	98,161	ISSA, DARRELL E.*	64,981	PEISER, DAVE		33,180 R	60.2%	39.8%	60.2%	39.8%
49	2012	274,618	159,725	ISSA, DARRELL E.*	114,893	TETALMAN, JERRY		44,832 R	58.2%	41.8%	58.2%	41.8%
50	2014	157,299	111,997	HUNTER, DUNCAN D.*	45,302	KIMBER, JAMES H.		66,695 R	71.2%	28.8%	71.2%	28.8%
50	2012	258,293	174,838	HUNTER, DUNCAN D.*	83,455	SECOR, DAVID B.		91,383 R	67.7%	32.3%	67.7%	32.3%
51	2014	81,950	25,577	MEADE, STEPHEN	56,373	VARGAS, JUAN*		30,796 D	31.2%	68.8%	31.2%	68.8%
51	2012	159,398	45,464	CRIMMINS, MICHAEL	113,934	VARGAS, JUAN		68,470 D	28.5%	71.5%	28.5%	71.5%
52	2014	191,572	92,746	DEMAIO, CARL	98,826	PETERS, SCOTT H.*		6,080 D	48.4%	51.6%	48.4%	51.6%
52	2012	295,910	144,459	BILBRAY, BRIAN P.*	151,451	PETERS, SCOTT H.		6,992 D	48.8%	51.2%	48.8%	51.2%
53	2014	148,044	60,940	WILSKE, LARRY	87,104	DAVIS, SUSAN A.*		26,164 D	41.2%	58.8%	41.2%	58.8%
53	2012	268,307	103,482	POPADITCH, NICK	164,825	DAVIS, SUSAN A.*		61,343 D	38.6%	61.4%	38.6%	61.4%
TOTAL	2014	7,132,641	2,813,104		3,902,142		417,395	1,089,038 D	39.4%	54.7%	41.9%	58.1%
TOTAL	2012	12,204,357	4,381,206		6,945,307		877,844	2,564,101 D	35.9%	56.9%	38.7%	61.3%

Note: An asterisk (*) denotes incumbent.

For notes on 2012 elections with two candidates of the same party running on the general election ballot please consult *America Votes 30*.

CALIFORNIA

GENERAL AND PRIMARY ELECTIONS

2014 GENERAL ELECTIONS: OTHER VOTES

House	Other vote was:
CD 5	41,535 Independent (James Hinton)
CD 20	35,010 Independent (Ronald Paul Kabat)
CD 28	28,268 Independent (Steve Stokes)
CD 44	9,192 Peace and Freedom (Adam Shbeita)

2014 PRIMARY ELECTIONS: SUPPLEMENTARY INFORMATION

Primary	June 3, 2014	Registration (as of May 19, 2014)	17,722,006	Democratic	7,692,670
				Republican	5,036,610
				American Independent	475,914
				Libertarian	116,733
				Green	109,674
				Peace and Freedom	78,345
				Americans Elect	3,674
				Other	459,171
				No Party Preference	3,749,215

Primary Type Open—Any registered voter could participate in the "top two" primary, in which candidates of all parties (and independents) run together on the same ballot and the top two finishers in each primary race advanced to the general election.

ALL-PARTY PRIMARIES

Governor	Brown, Edmund G. "Jerry" Jr.* (Democrat)	2,354,769	54.3%
	Kashkari, Neel (Republican)	839,767	19.4%
	Donnelly, Tim (Republican)	643,236	14.8%
	Blount, Andrew (Republican)	89,749	2.1%
	Champ, Glenn (Republican)	76,066	1.8%
	Rodriquez, Luis J. (Green)	66,872	1.5%
	Sheehan, Cindy L. (Peace and Freedom)	52,707	1.2%
	Winston, Alma Marie (Republican)	46,042	1.1%
	Newman, Robert (No Party)	44,120	1.0%
	Agbede, Akinyemi (Democrat)	37,024	0.9%
	Aguirre, Richard (Republican)	35,125	0.8%
	Ambrozewicz, Bogdan "Bo" (No Party)	14,929	0.3%
	Buycks, Janel Hyeshia (No Party)	12,136	0.3%
	Christian, Rakesh Kumar (No Party)	11,142	0.3%
	Leicht, Joe (No Party)	9,307	0.2%
	Bernal, Karen Jill (Write-in)	17	
	Wildstar, Nickolas (Write-in)	17	
	Walls, Jimelle L. (Write-in)	3	
	TOTAL	*4,333,028*	
Congressional District 1	LaMalfa, Doug* (Republican)	75,317	53.4%
	Hall, Heidi (Democrat)	42,481	30.1%
	Cheadle, Gregory (Republican)	13,909	9.9%
	Levine, Dan (Democrat)	9,213	6.5%
	TOTAL	*140,920*	
Congressional District 2	Huffman, Jared* (Democrat)	99,186	67.9%
	Mensing, Dale (Republican)	32,614	22.3%
	Caffrey, Andy (Democrat)	14,245	9.8%
	TOTAL	*146,045*	

CALIFORNIA

GENERAL AND PRIMARY ELECTIONS

ALL-PARTY PRIMARIES

Congressional District 3	Garamendi, John* (Democrat)	54,672	53.5%
	Logue, Dan (Republican)	47,560	46.5%
	TOTAL	102,232	
Congressional District 4	McClintock, Tom* (Republican)	80,999	56.2%
	Moore, Arthur "Art" (Republican)	32,855	22.8%
	Gerlach, Jeffrey D. (No Party)	30,300	21.0%
	TOTAL	144,154	
Congressional District 5	Thompson, Mike* (Democrat)	88,709	80.4%
	Hinton, James (No Party)	12,292	11.1%
	Van Raam, Douglas S. (No Party)	9,279	8.4%
	TOTAL	110,280	
Congressional District 6	Matsui, Doris O.* (Democrat)	62,640	73.6%
	McCray, Joseph Sr. (Republican)	22,465	26.4%
	TOTAL	85,105	
Congressional District 7	Bera, Ami* (Democrat)	51,878	46.7%
	Ose, Doug (Republican)	29,307	26.4%
	Birman, Igor (Republican)	19,431	17.5%
	Emken, Elizabeth (Republican)	7,924	7.1%
	Tuma, Douglas Arthur (Libertarian)	1,629	1.5%
	Tufi, Phill A. (No Party)	869	0.8%
	TOTAL	111,038	
Congressional District 8	Cook, Paul* (Republican)	40,007	58.1%
	Conaway, Robert Dean "Bob" (Democrat)	12,885	18.7%
	Hannosh, Paul (Republican)	9,037	13.1%
	Lee, Odessia (Democrat)	6,930	10.1%
	TOTAL	68,859	
Congressional District 9	McNerney, Jerry* (Democrat)	38,295	49.4%
	Amador, Antonio C. "Tony" (Republican)	20,424	26.3%
	Colangelo, Steve Anthony (Republican)	14,195	18.3%
	Davis, Karen "Mathews" (Republican)	4,637	6.0%
	TOTAL	77,551	
Congressional District 10	Denham, Jeff* (Republican)	44,237	58.9%
	Eggman, Michael (Democrat)	19,804	26.4%
	Barkley, Michael "Mike" (Democrat)	11,005	14.7%
	Christensen, David Paul (Write-in)	2	
	TOTAL	75,048	
Congressional District 11	DeSaulnier, Mark (Democrat)	59,605	58.8%
	Phan-Quang, Tue (Republican)	28,242	27.9%
	Sudduth, Cheryl (Democrat)	4,913	4.8%
	Daysog, Tony (Democrat)	3,482	3.4%
	Ramey, Jason (No Party)	2,673	2.6%
	Ingersol, Ki (Democrat)	2,313	2.3%
	Fuller, Virginia (Write-in)	140	0.1%
	TOTAL	101,368	
Congressional District 12	Pelosi, Nancy* (Democrat)	79,816	73.6%
	Dennis, John (Republican)	12,922	11.9%
	Hermanson, Barry (Green)	6,156	5.7%
	Peterson, David (Democrat)	3,774	3.5%
	Lara, Frank (Peace and Freedom)	2,107	1.9%
	Steger, Michael (Democrat)	1,514	1.4%
	Thorsson, A.J. "Desmond" (No Party)	1,270	1.2%
	Welles, Jim (No Party)	879	0.8%
	TOTAL	108,438	

CALIFORNIA

GENERAL AND PRIMARY ELECTIONS

ALL-PARTY PRIMARIES

Congressional District 13	Lee, Barbara* (Democrat)	77,461	82.6%
	Sundeen, Dakin (Republican)	9,533	10.2%
	Jelincic, Justin (Democrat)	4,602	4.9%
	Allen, Lawrence N. (Peace and Freedom)	2,190	2.3%
	TOTAL	*93,786*	
Congressional District 14	Speier, Jackie* (Democrat)	66,800	77.4%
	Chew, Robin (Republican)	19,482	22.6%
	TOTAL	*86,282*	
Congressional District 15	Swalwell, Eric* (Democrat)	42,419	49.1%
	Bussell, Hugh (Republican)	22,228	25.7%
	Corbett, Ellen (Democrat)	21,798	25.2%
	TOTAL	*86,445*	
Congressional District 16	Costa, Jim* (Democrat)	25,586	44.3%
	Tacherra, Johnny M. (Republican)	12,542	21.7%
	Crass, Steve M. (Republican)	8,877	15.4%
	Levey, Mel (Republican)	4,565	7.9%
	Garcia-Botelho, Joanna Lynn (Republican)	3,827	6.6%
	Melton, Job Emanuel (Democrat)	2,370	4.1%
	TOTAL	*57,767*	
Congressional District 17	Honda, Michael M.* (Democrat)	43,607	48.2%
	Khanna, Ro (Democrat)	25,384	28.0%
	Singh, Vanila (Republican)	15,359	17.0%
	VanLandingham, Joel (Republican)	6,154	6.8%
	TOTAL	*90,504*	
Congressional District 18	Eshoo, Anna G.* (Democrat)	81,295	67.6%
	Fox, Richard B. (Republican)	27,111	22.5%
	Anderson, Bruce Gordon (Republican)	9,644	8.0%
	Braun, Oscar Alejandro (Republican)	2,190	1.8%
	TOTAL	*120,240*	
Congressional District 19	Lofgren, Zoe* (Democrat)	63,845	76.0%
	Murray, Robert (Democrat)	20,132	24.0%
	TOTAL	*83,977*	
Congressional District 20	Farr, Sam* (Democrat)	67,528	73.8%
	Kabat, Ronald Paul (No Party)	23,950	26.2%
	TOTAL	*91,478*	
Congressional District 21	Valadao, David G.* (Republican)	28,773	63.0%
	Renteria, Amanda (Democrat)	11,682	25.6%
	Hernandez, John (Democrat)	5,232	11.5%
	TOTAL	*45,687*	
Congressional District 22	Nunes, Devin* (Republican)	60,499	67.9%
	Aguilera-Marrero, Suzanna "Sam" (Democrat)	22,198	24.9%
	Catano, John P. (Republican)	6,403	7.2%
	TOTAL	*89,100*	
Congressional District 23	McCarthy, Kevin* (Republican)	58,334	99.1%
	Garcia, Raul (Write-in)	313	0.5%
	Biglay, Mike (Write-in)	157	0.3%
	Porter, Ronald L. (Write-in)	36	0.1%
	Lightfoot, Gail K. (Write-in)	31	0.1%
	TOTAL	*58,871*	

CALIFORNIA

GENERAL AND PRIMARY ELECTIONS

ALL-PARTY PRIMARIES

Congressional District 24	Capps, Lois* (Democrat)	58,198	43.7%
	Mitchum, Chris (Republican)	21,059	15.8%
	Fareed, Justin (Republican)	20,445	15.3%
	Francisco, Dale (Republican)	15,575	11.7%
	Allen, Bradley "Brad" (Republican)	9,269	7.0%
	Marshall, Sandra (Democrat)	4,646	3.5%
	Coyne Jr., Paul H. (Democrat)	2,144	1.6%
	Isakson, Steve (No Party)	1,249	0.9%
	Stuart, Cynthia A. "Alexis" (Republican)	678	0.5%
	TOTAL	*133,263*	
Congressional District 25	Strickland, Tony (Republican)	19,090	29.6%
	Knight, Stephen (Republican)	18,327	28.4%
	Rogers, Lee (Democrat)	14,315	22.2%
	Thomas, Evan (Democrat)	6,149	9.5%
	Castagna, Troy (Republican)	3,805	5.9%
	Bruce, David Koster (Libertarian)	1,214	1.9%
	Mussack, Michael (No Party)	933	1.4%
	Singh, Navraj (Republican)	699	1.1%
	TOTAL	*64,532*	
Congressional District 26	Brownley, Julia* (Democrat)	38,854	45.5%
	Gorell, Jeff (Republican)	38,021	44.5%
	Dagnesses, Rafael (Republican)	6,536	7.7%
	Kmiec, Douglas William (No Party)	1,980	2.3%
	TOTAL	*85,391*	
Congressional District 27	Chu, Judy* (Democrat)	39,915	60.4%
	Orswell, Jack (Republican)	26,205	39.6%
	TOTAL	*66,120*	
Congressional District 28	Schiff, Adam B.* (Democrat)	46,004	74.5%
	Stokes, Steve (No Party)	11,078	17.9%
	Genovese, Sal (Democrat)	4,643	7.5%
	Yousuf, Sam (Write-in)	38	0.1%
	TOTAL	*61,763*	
Congressional District 29	Cardenas, Tony* (Democrat)	19,566	62.8%
	Leader, William O'Callaghan (Republican)	8,025	25.8%
	Gamble, Venice (Democrat)	3,542	11.4%
	TOTAL	*31,133*	
Congressional District 30	Sherman, Brad* (Democrat)	40,787	57.9%
	Reed, Mark (Republican)	14,129	20.1%
	Kleinman, Pablo (Republican)	8,808	12.5%
	Litchman, Marc (Democrat)	4,251	6.0%
	Powelson, Michael W. (Green)	2,352	3.3%
	Rab, A. (Write-in)	76	0.1%
	TOTAL	*70,403*	
Congressional District 31	Chabot, Paul (Republican)	14,163	26.6%
	Aguilar, Pete (Democrat)	9,242	17.4%
	Gooch, Lesli (Republican)	9,033	17.0%
	Reyes, Eloise Gomez (Democrat)	8,461	15.9%
	Baca, Joe (Democrat)	5,954	11.2%
	Tillman, Danny (Democrat)	4,659	8.7%
	Downing, Ryan (Republican)	1,737	3.3%
	TOTAL	*53,249*	
Congressional District 32	Napolitano, Grace F.* (Democrat)	24,639	60.0%
	Alas, Arturo Enrique (Republican)	16,459	40.0%
	TOTAL	*41,098*	

CALIFORNIA

GENERAL AND PRIMARY ELECTIONS

ALL-PARTY PRIMARIES

Congressional District 33	Carr, Elan S. (Republican)	23,476	21.6%
	Lieu, Ted (Democrat)	20,432	18.8%
	Greuel, Wendy (Democrat)	17,988	16.6%
	Williamson, Marianne (No Party)	14,335	13.2%
	Miller, Matt L. (Democrat)	13,005	12.0%
	Gilani, Lily (Republican)	7,673	7.1%
	Mottus, Kevin N. (Republican)	2,561	2.4%
	Mulvaney, Barbara (Democrat)	2,516	2.3%
	Kanuth, David (Democrat)	1,554	1.4%
	Holmes, Kristie (Democrat)	994	0.9%
	Herd, Mark Matthew (Libertarian)	883	0.8%
	Sachs, Michael Ian (Green)	732	0.7%
	Shapiro, Michael (Democrat)	650	0.6%
	Fox, Tom (No Party)	509	0.5%
	Obagi, Zein E. (Democrat)	477	0.4%
	Flaherty, Vincent (Democrat)	345	0.3%
	Graf, James (Democrat)	327	0.3%
	Roske, Brent C. (No Party)	188	0.2%
	Milonopoulos, Theo (Write-in)	1	
	TOTAL	*108,646*	
Congressional District 34	Becerra, Xavier* (Democrat)	22,878	73.8%
	Edwards, Adrienne Nicole (Democrat)	4,474	14.4%
	Johnson, Howard (Peace and Freedom)	3,587	11.6%
	Smith, Jonathan Turner (Write-in)	48	0.2%
	TOTAL	*30,987*	
Congressional District 35	Torres, Norma J. (Democrat)	17,996	65.7%
	Gagnier, Christina (Democrat)	4,081	14.9%
	Heydenfeldt, Scott (Democrat)	2,574	9.4%
	Vieyra, Anthony W. (Democrat)	2,183	8.0%
	Lopez, Benjamin "Ben" (Write-in)	567	2.1%
	TOTAL	*27,401*	
Congressional District 36	Ruiz, Raul* (Democrat)	41,443	50.3%
	Nestande, Brian (Republican)	28,662	34.8%
	Haynes, Ray (Republican)	12,232	14.9%
	TOTAL	*82,337*	
Congressional District 37	Bass, Karen* (Democrat)	47,639	79.6%
	King, R. Adam (Republican)	8,530	14.3%
	Evans, Mervin L. (Democrat)	3,677	6.1%
	TOTAL	*59,846*	
Congressional District 38	Sanchez, Linda T.* (Democrat)	27,149	57.5%
	Campos, Benjamin (Republican)	20,046	42.5%
	TOTAL	*47,195*	
Congressional District 39	Royce, Edward R.* (Republican)	49,071	70.6%
	Anderson, Peter (Democrat)	20,480	29.4%
	TOTAL	*69,551*	
Congressional District 40	Roybal-Allard, Lucille* (Democrat)	13,745	66.4%
	Sanchez, David (Democrat)	6,968	33.6%
	TOTAL	*20,713*	
Congressional District 41	Takano, Mark* (Democrat)	19,648	44.7%
	Adams, Steve (Republican)	16,264	37.0%
	Franco, Veronica (Democrat)	4,509	10.2%
	Girard, Yvonne Terrell (Republican)	3,581	8.1%
	TOTAL	*44,002*	

CALIFORNIA

GENERAL AND PRIMARY ELECTIONS

ALL-PARTY PRIMARIES

Congressional District 42	Calvert, Ken* (Republican)	37,506	67.5%
	Sheridan, Tim (Democrat)	8,788	15.8%
	Marquez, Chris (Democrat)	6,118	11.0%
	Condley, Kerri (Democrat)	3,150	5.7%
	Harvey, Floyd (Write-in)	8	
	TOTAL	55,570	
Congressional District 43	Waters, Maxine* (Democrat)	33,746	67.2%
	Wood Jr., John (Republican)	16,440	32.8%
	Cook, Brandon M. (Write-in)	12	
	TOTAL	50,198	
Congressional District 44	Hahn, Janice* (Democrat)	25,641	100.0%
	Shbeita, Adam (Write-in)	5	
	TOTAL	25,646	
Congressional District 45	Walters, Mimi (Republican)	39,631	45.1%
	Leavens, Drew (Democrat)	24,721	28.1%
	Raths, Greg G. (Republican)	21,284	24.2%
	Salehi, Al (No Party)	2,317	2.6%
	TOTAL	87,953	
Congressional District 46	Sanchez, Loretta* (Democrat)	20,172	50.6%
	Nick, Adam (Republican)	7,234	18.1%
	Cullum, John J. (Republican)	5,666	14.2%
	Vazquez, Carlos (Republican)	4,969	12.5%
	Atalla, Ehab (Democrat)	1,835	4.6%
	TOTAL	39,876	
Congressional District 47	Lowenthal, Alan S.* (Democrat)	44,019	57.1%
	Whallon, Andy (Republican)	33,093	42.9%
	Brogan, George (Write-in)	3	
	TOTAL	77,115	
Congressional District 48	Rohrabacher, Dana* (Republican)	52,431	56.1%
	Savary, Sue (Democrat)	18,242	19.5%
	Leece, Wendy (Republican)	11,082	11.9%
	Burns, David (Democrat)	6,142	6.6%
	Banuelos, Robert J. (Democrat)	5,591	6.0%
	TOTAL	93,488	
Congressional District 49	Issa, Darrell E.* (Republican)	56,558	61.9%
	Peiser, Dave (Democrat)	25,946	28.4%
	Isagawa, Noboru (Write-in)	8,887	9.7%
	Moore, Johnny (Write-in)	16	
	TOTAL	91,407	
Congressional District 50	Hunter, Duncan D.* (Republican)	62,371	70.4%
	Kimber, James H. (Democrat)	21,552	24.3%
	Benoit, Michael (Libertarian)	4,634	5.2%
	TOTAL	88,557	
Congressional District 51	Vargas, Juan* (Democrat)	35,812	68.3%
	Meade, Stephen (Republican)	16,403	31.3%
	Griffes, Ernest (Write-in)	184	0.4%
	TOTAL	52,399	

CALIFORNIA

GENERAL AND PRIMARY ELECTIONS

ALL-PARTY PRIMARIES

Congressional District 52	Peters, Scott H.* (Democrat)	53,926	42.3%
	DeMaio, Carl (Republican)	44,954	35.3%
	Jorgensen, Kirk (Republican)	23,588	18.5%
	Simon, Fred J. (Republican)	5,040	4.0%
	TOTAL	127,508	
Congressional District 53	Davis, Susan A.* (Democrat)	50,041	56.3%
	Wilske, Larry (Republican)	18,384	20.7%
	True, Wayne (Republican)	9,182	10.3%
	Edwards, John R. (Republican)	3,986	4.5%
	Marchese, Joel A. (Republican)	2,729	3.1%
	Stieringer, Jim G. (Republican)	2,106	2.4%
	Campbell, John W. (No Party)	1,596	1.8%
	Bobb, Christina (No Party)	929	1.0%
	TOTAL	88,953	

Note: An asterisk (*) denotes incumbent.

COLORADO

Congressional districts first established for elections held in 2012

7 members

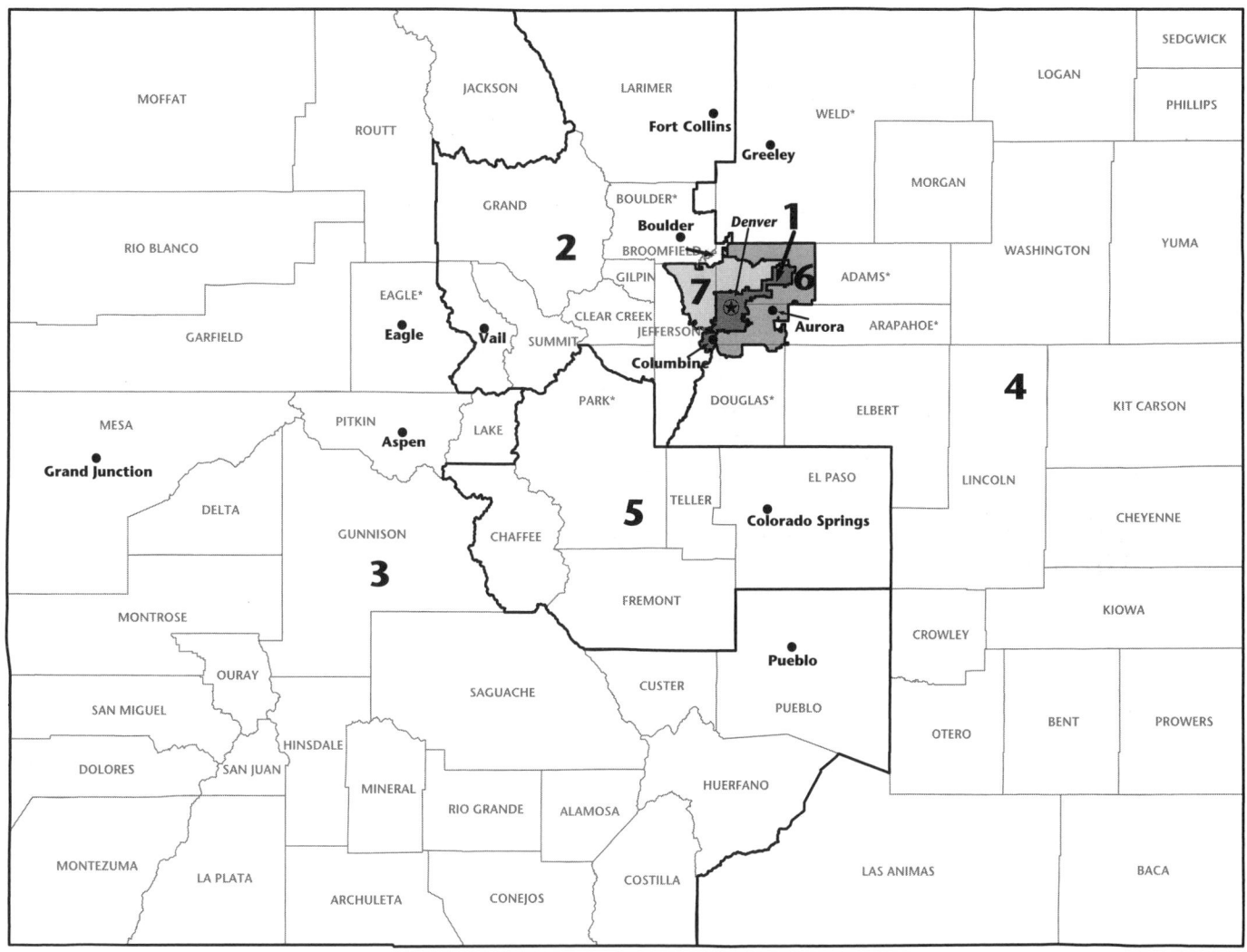

* Asterisk indicates a county whose boundaries include parts of two or more congressional districts.

COLORADO
Denver Area

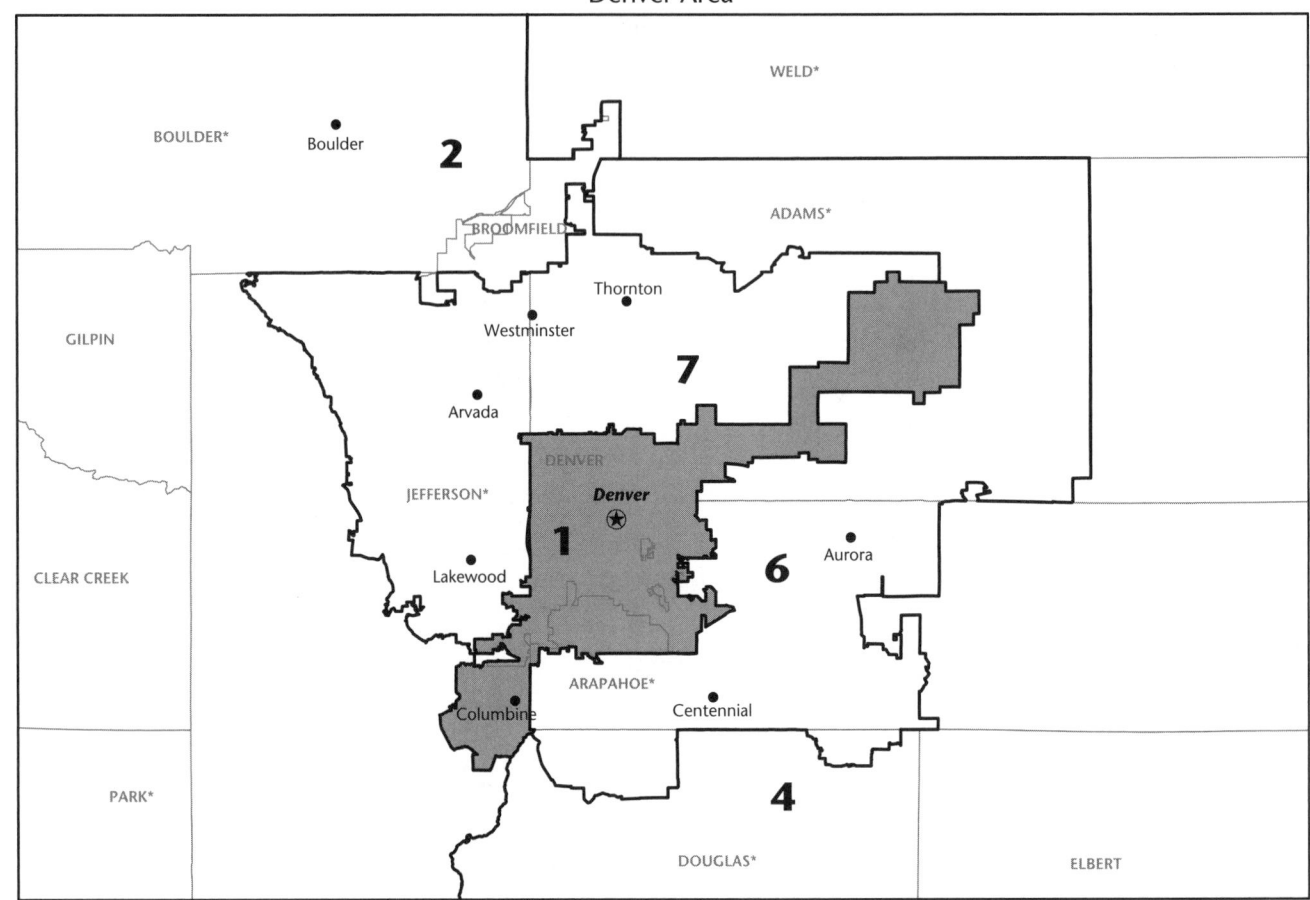

* Asterisk indicates a county whose boundaries include parts of two or more congressional districts.

COLORADO

GOVERNOR
John Hickenlooper (D). Re-elected 2014 to a four-year term. Previously elected 2010.

SENATORS (1 Democrat, 1 Republican)
Michael F. Bennet (D). Elected 2010 to a six-year term. Sworn in as senator January 22, 2009, to fill the vacancy created by the resignation of Ken Salazar (D) to become U.S. secretary of interior.

Cory Gardner (R). Elected 2014 to a six-year term.

REPRESENTATIVES (4 Republicans, 3 Democrats)
1. Diana DeGette (D)
2. Jared Polis (D)
3. Scott R. Tipton (R)
4. Ken Buck (R)
5. Doug Lamborn (R)
6. Mike Coffman (R)
7. Ed Perlmutter (D)

POSTWAR VOTE FOR PRESIDENT

		Republican		Democratic		Other Vote	Rep.-Dem. Plurality	Percentage			
								Total Vote		Major Vote	
Year	Total Vote	Vote	Candidate	Vote	Candidate			Rep.	Dem.	Rep.	Dem.
2012	2,569,522	1,185,243	Romney, W. Mitt	1,323,102	Obama, Barack H.*	61,177	137,859 D	46.1%	51.5%	47.3%	52.7%
2008	2,401,462	1,073,629	McCain, John S. III	1,288,633	Obama, Barack H.	39,200	215,004 D	44.7%	53.7%	45.4%	54.6%
2004	2,130,330	1,101,255	Bush, George W.*	1,001,732	Kerry, John F.	27,343	99,523 R	51.7%	47.0%	52.4%	47.6%
2000**	1,741,368	883,748	Bush, George W.	738,227	Gore, Albert Jr.	119,393	145,521 R	50.8%	42.4%	54.5%	45.5%
1996**	1,510,704	691,848	Dole, Robert "Bob"	671,152	Clinton, Bill*	147,704	20,696 R	45.8%	44.4%	50.8%	49.2%
1992**	1,569,180	562,850	Bush, George H.*	629,681	Clinton, Bill	376,649	66,831 D	35.9%	40.1%	47.2%	52.8%
1988	1,372,394	728,177	Bush, George H.	621,453	Dukakis, Michael S.	22,764	106,724 R	53.1%	45.3%	54.0%	46.0%
1984	1,295,380	821,817	Reagan, Ronald*	454,975	Mondale, Walter F.	18,588	366,842 R	63.4%	35.1%	64.4%	35.6%
1980**	1,184,415	652,264	Reagan, Ronald	367,973	Carter, Jimmy*	164,178	284,291 R	55.1%	31.1%	63.9%	36.1%
1976	1,081,554	584,367	Ford, Gerald R.*	460,353	Carter, Jimmy	36,834	124,014 R	54.0%	42.6%	55.9%	44.1%
1972	953,884	597,189	Nixon, Richard M.*	329,980	McGovern, George S.	26,715	267,209 R	62.6%	34.6%	64.4%	35.6%
1968**	811,199	409,345	Nixon, Richard M.	335,174	Humphrey, Hubert Horatio Jr.	66,680	74,171 R	50.5%	41.3%	55.0%	45.0%
1964	776,986	296,767	Goldwater, Barry M. Sr.	476,024	Johnson, Lyndon B.*	4,195	179,257 D	38.2%	61.3%	38.4%	61.6%
1960	736,236	402,242	Nixon, Richard M.	330,629	Kennedy, John F.	3,365	71,613 R	54.6%	44.9%	54.9%	45.1%
1956	657,074	394,479	Eisenhower, Dwight D.*	257,997	Stevenson, Adlai E. II	4,598	136,482 R	60.0%	39.3%	60.5%	39.5%
1952	630,103	379,782	Eisenhower, Dwight D.	245,504	Stevenson, Adlai E. II	4,817	134,278 R	60.3%	39.0%	60.7%	39.3%
1948	515,237	239,714	Dewey, Thomas E.	267,288	Truman, Harry S.*	8,235	27,574 D	46.5%	51.9%	47.3%	52.7%

Note: An asterisk (*) denotes incumbent. **In past elections, the other vote included: 2000 - 91,434 Green (Ralph Nader); 1996 - 99,629 Reform (Ross Perot); 1992 - 366,010 Independent (Perot); 1980 - 130,633 Independent (John Anderson); 1968 - 60,813 American Independent (George Wallace).

COLORADO

POSTWAR VOTE FOR GOVERNOR

Year	Total Vote	Republican Vote	Republican Candidate	Democratic Vote	Democratic Candidate	Other Vote	Rep.-Dem. Plurality	Total Vote Rep.	Total Vote Dem.	Major Vote Rep.	Major Vote Dem.
2014	2,041,607	938,195	Beauprez, Bob	1,006,433	Hickenlooper, John*	96,979	68,238 D	46.0%	49.3%	48.2%	51.8%
2010**	1,788,001	199,062	Maes, Dan	912,189	Hickenlooper, John	676,750	713,127 D	11.1%	51.0%	17.9%	82.1%
2006	1,558,387	625,886	Beauprez, Bob	888,096	Ritter, Bill Jr.	44,405	262,210 D	40.2%	57.0%	41.3%	58.7%
2002	1,412,602	884,583	Owens, Bill*	475,373	Heath, Rollie	52,646	409,210 R	62.6%	33.7%	65.0%	35.0%
1998	1,323,530	649,688	Owens, Bill	639,358	Schoettler, Gail	34,484	10,330 R	49.1%	48.3%	50.4%	49.6%
1994	1,116,307	432,042	Benson, Bruce	619,205	Romer, Roy*	65,060	187,163 D	38.7%	55.5%	41.1%	58.9%
1990	1,011,272	358,403	Andrews, John	626,032	Romer, Roy*	26,837	267,629 D	35.4%	61.9%	36.4%	63.6%
1986	1,058,928	434,420	Strickland, Ted	616,325	Romer, Roy	8,183	181,905 D	41.0%	58.2%	41.3%	58.7%
1982	956,021	302,740	Fuhr, John D.	627,960	Lamm, Richard D.*	25,321	325,220 D	31.7%	65.7%	32.5%	67.5%
1978	823,807	317,292	Strickland, Ted	483,985	Lamm, Richard D.*	22,530	166,693 D	38.5%	58.7%	39.6%	60.4%
1974	828,968	378,907	Vanderhoof, John D.*	441,199	Lamm, Richard D.	8,862	62,292 D	45.7%	53.2%	46.2%	53.8%
1970	668,496	350,690	Love, John A.*	302,432	Hogan, Mark	15,374	48,258 R	52.5%	45.2%	53.7%	46.3%
1966	660,063	356,730	Love, John A.*	287,132	Knous, Robert L.	16,201	69,598 R	54.0%	43.5%	55.4%	44.6%
1962	616,481	349,342	Love, John A.	262,890	McNichols, Stephen L.R.*	4,249	86,452 R	56.7%	42.6%	57.1%	42.9%
1958**	549,808	228,643	Burch, Palmer L.	321,165	McNichols, Stephen L.R.*		92,522 D	41.6%	58.4%	41.6%	58.4%
1956	645,233	313,950	Brotzman, Donald G.	331,283	McNichols, Stephen L.R.		17,333 D	48.7%	51.3%	48.7%	51.3%
1954	489,540	227,335	Brotzman, Donald G.	262,205	Johnson, Edwin C.		34,870 D	46.4%	53.6%	46.4%	53.6%
1952	613,034	349,924	Thornton, Dan*	260,044	Metzger, John W.	3,066	89,880 R	57.1%	42.4%	57.4%	42.6%
1950	450,994	236,472	Thornton, Dan	212,976	Johnson, Walter W.	1,546	23,496 R	52.4%	47.2%	52.6%	47.4%
1948	501,680	168,928	Hamil, David A.	332,752	Knous, William Lee*		163,824 D	33.7%	66.3%	33.7%	66.3%
1946	335,087	160,483	Lavington, Leon E.	174,604	Knous, William Lee		14,121 D	47.9%	52.1%	47.9%	52.1%

Note: An asterisk (*) denotes incumbent. **In past elections, the other vote included: 2010 - 651,232 American Constitution (Tom Tancredo), who finished second. The term of office of Colorado's governor was increased from two to four years effective with the 1958 election.

POSTWAR VOTE FOR SENATOR

Year	Total Vote	Republican Vote	Republican Candidate	Democratic Vote	Democratic Candidate	Other Vote	Rep.-Dem. Plurality	Total Vote Rep.	Total Vote Dem.	Major Vote Rep.	Major Vote Dem.
2014	2,041,058	983,891	Gardner, Cory	944,203	Udall, Mark*	112,964	39,688 R	48.2%	46.3%	51.0%	49.0%
2010	1,772,570	822,802	Buck, Ken	851,778	Bennet, Michael F.*	97,990	28,976 D	46.4%	48.1%	49.1%	50.9%
2008	2,331,712	990,784	Schaffer, Bob	1,231,049	Udall, Mark	109,879	240,265 D	42.5%	52.8%	44.6%	55.4%
2004	2,107,554	980,668	Coors, Pete	1,081,188	Salazar, Ken	45,698	100,520 D	46.5%	51.3%	47.6%	52.4%
2002	1,416,082	717,893	Allard, Wayne*	648,130	Strickland, Tom	50,059	69,763 R	50.7%	45.8%	52.6%	47.4%
1998	1,327,235	829,370	Campbell, Ben Nighthorse*	464,754	Lamm, Dottie	33,111	364,616 R	62.5%	35.0%	64.1%	35.9%
1996	1,469,611	750,325	Allard, Wayne	677,600	Strickland, Tom	41,686	72,725 R	51.1%	46.1%	52.5%	47.5%
1992	1,552,289	662,893	Considine, Terry	803,725	Campbell, Ben Nighthorse	85,671	140,832 D	42.7%	51.8%	45.2%	54.8%
1990	1,022,027	569,048	Brown, Hank	425,746	Heath, Josie	27,233	143,302 R	55.7%	41.7%	57.2%	42.8%
1986	1,060,765	512,994	Kramer, Ken	529,449	Wirth, Timothy E.	18,322	16,455 D	48.4%	49.9%	49.2%	50.8%
1984	1,297,809	833,821	Armstrong, William L.*	449,327	Dick, Nancy	14,661	384,494 R	64.2%	34.6%	65.0%	35.0%
1980	1,173,646	571,295	Buchanan, Mary E.	590,501	Hart, Gary W.*	11,850	19,206 D	48.7%	50.3%	49.2%	50.8%
1978	819,150	480,596	Armstrong, William L.	330,247	Haskell, Floyd K.*	8,307	150,349 R	58.7%	40.3%	59.3%	40.7%
1974	824,166	325,508	Dominick, Peter H.*	471,691	Hart, Gary W.	26,967	146,183 D	39.5%	57.2%	40.8%	59.2%
1972	926,093	447,957	Alott, Gordon Llewellyn*	457,545	Haskell, Floyd K.	20,591	9,588 D	48.4%	49.4%	49.5%	50.5%
1968	785,536	459,952	Dominick, Peter H.*	325,584	McNichols, Stephen L.R.		134,368 R	58.6%	41.4%	58.6%	41.4%
1966	634,837	368,307	Alott, Gordon Llewellyn*	266,198	Romer, Roy	332	102,109 R	58.0%	41.9%	58.0%	42.0%
1962	613,444	328,655	Dominick, Peter H.	279,586	Carroll, John Albert*	5,203	49,069 R	53.6%	45.6%	54.0%	46.0%
1960	727,633	389,428	Alott, Gordon Llewellyn*	334,854	Knous, Robert L.	3,351	54,574 R	53.5%	46.0%	53.8%	46.2%
1956	636,974	317,102	Thornton, Dan	319,872	Carroll, John Albert		2,770 D	49.8%	50.2%	49.8%	50.2%
1954	484,188	248,502	Alott, Gordon Llewellyn	235,686	Carroll, John Albert		12,816 R	51.3%	48.7%	51.3%	48.7%
1950	450,176	239,734	Millikin, Eugene D.*	210,442	Carroll, John Albert		29,292 R	53.3%	46.7%	53.3%	46.7%
1948	510,121	165,069	Nicholson, Will F.	340,719	Johnson, Edwin C.*	4,333	175,650 D	32.4%	66.8%	32.6%	67.4%

Note: An asterisk (*) denotes incumbent.

COLORADO
GOVERNOR 2014

2010 Census Population	County	Total Vote	Republican (Beauprez)	Democratic (Hickenlooper)	Other	Rep.-Dem. Plurality		Percentage			
								Total Vote		Major Vote	
								Rep.	Dem.	Rep.	Dem.
441,603	ADAMS	130,606	58,011	65,450	7,145	7,439	D	44.4%	50.1%	47.0%	53.0%
15,445	ALAMOSA	5,167	2,238	2,632	297	394	D	43.3%	50.9%	46.0%	54.0%
572,003	ARAPAHOE	223,899	98,374	116,445	9,080	18,071	D	43.9%	52.0%	45.8%	54.2%
12,084	ARCHULETA	5,463	3,032	2,153	278	879	R	55.5%	39.4%	58.5%	41.5%
3,788	BACA	1,866	1,354	406	106	948	R	72.6%	21.8%	76.9%	23.1%
6,499	BENT	1,580	937	548	95	389	R	59.3%	34.7%	63.1%	36.9%
294,567	BOULDER	141,760	36,868	96,565	8,327	59,697	D	26.0%	68.1%	27.6%	72.4%
55,889	BROOMFIELD	27,610	12,240	14,100	1,270	1,860	D	44.3%	51.1%	46.5%	53.5%
17,809	CHAFFEE	8,933	4,306	4,211	416	95	R	48.2%	47.1%	50.6%	49.4%
1,836	CHEYENNE	1,037	814	165	58	649	R	78.5%	15.9%	83.1%	16.9%
9,088	CLEAR CREEK	4,682	1,967	2,455	260	488	D	42.0%	52.4%	44.5%	55.5%
8,256	CONEJOS	3,495	1,642	1,727	126	85	D	47.0%	49.4%	48.7%	51.3%
3,524	COSTILLA	1,419	401	941	77	540	D	28.3%	66.3%	29.9%	70.1%
5,823	CROWLEY	1,337	884	336	117	548	R	66.1%	25.1%	72.5%	27.5%
4,255	CUSTER	2,522	1,656	765	101	891	R	65.7%	30.3%	68.4%	31.6%
30,952	DELTA	13,461	8,801	3,944	716	4,857	R	65.4%	29.3%	69.1%	30.9%
600,158	DENVER	231,985	50,257	172,290	9,438	122,033	D	21.7%	74.3%	22.6%	77.4%
2,064	DOLORES	971	635	280	56	355	R	65.4%	28.8%	69.4%	30.6%
285,465	DOUGLAS	138,186	81,706	52,187	4,293	29,519	R	59.1%	37.8%	61.0%	39.0%
52,197	EAGLE	17,404	6,449	10,253	702	3,804	D	37.1%	58.9%	38.6%	61.4%
622,263	EL PASO	227,878	139,140	76,678	12,060	62,462	R	61.1%	33.6%	64.5%	35.5%
23,086	ELBERT	12,495	9,099	2,797	599	6,302	R	72.8%	22.4%	76.5%	23.5%
46,824	FREMONT	17,214	11,121	4,927	1,166	6,194	R	64.6%	28.6%	69.3%	30.7%
56,389	GARFIELD	19,372	9,583	8,840	949	743	R	49.5%	45.6%	52.0%	48.0%
5,441	GILPIN	2,897	1,198	1,441	258	243	D	41.4%	49.7%	45.4%	54.6%
14,843	GRAND	6,840	3,525	3,020	295	505	R	51.5%	44.2%	53.9%	46.1%
15,324	GUNNISON	6,936	2,562	3,960	414	1,398	D	36.9%	57.1%	39.3%	60.7%
843	HINSDALE	518	295	203	20	92	R	56.9%	39.2%	59.2%	40.8%
6,711	HUERFANO	3,193	1,445	1,548	200	103	D	45.3%	48.5%	48.3%	51.7%
1,394	JACKSON	762	575	164	23	411	R	75.5%	21.5%	77.8%	22.2%
534,543	JEFFERSON	256,437	114,398	130,196	11,843	15,798	D	44.6%	50.8%	46.8%	53.2%
1,398	KIOWA	757	604	113	40	491	R	79.8%	14.9%	84.2%	15.8%
8,270	KIT CARSON	3,097	2,327	647	123	1,680	R	75.1%	20.9%	78.2%	21.8%
51,334	LA PLATA	22,784	9,658	12,017	1,109	2,359	D	42.4%	52.7%	44.6%	55.4%
7,310	LAKE	2,473	903	1,385	185	482	D	36.5%	56.0%	39.5%	60.5%
299,630	LARIMER	144,851	65,054	72,550	7,247	7,496	D	44.9%	50.1%	47.3%	52.7%
15,507	LAS ANIMAS	5,586	2,721	2,562	303	159	R	48.7%	45.9%	51.5%	48.5%
5,467	LINCOLN	2,021	1,525	406	90	1,119	R	75.5%	20.1%	79.0%	21.0%
22,709	LOGAN	7,773	5,438	2,027	308	3,411	R	70.0%	26.1%	72.8%	27.2%
146,723	MESA	57,898	35,236	19,859	2,803	15,377	R	60.9%	34.3%	64.0%	36.0%
712	MINERAL	604	294	277	33	17	R	48.7%	45.9%	51.5%	48.5%
13,795	MOFFAT	4,882	3,794	853	235	2,941	R	77.7%	17.5%	81.6%	18.4%
25,535	MONTEZUMA	9,660	5,672	3,383	605	2,289	R	58.7%	35.0%	62.6%	37.4%
41,276	MONTROSE	16,610	10,907	4,971	732	5,936	R	65.7%	29.9%	68.7%	31.3%
28,159	MORGAN	8,860	5,861	2,646	353	3,215	R	66.2%	29.9%	68.9%	31.1%
18,831	OTERO	6,696	3,714	2,599	383	1,115	R	55.5%	38.8%	58.8%	41.2%
4,436	OURAY	2,678	1,151	1,434	93	283	D	43.0%	53.5%	44.5%	55.5%
16,206	PARK	8,054	4,624	2,958	472	1,666	R	57.4%	36.7%	61.0%	39.0%
4,442	PHILLIPS	1,994	1,442	477	75	965	R	72.3%	23.9%	75.1%	24.9%
17,148	PITKIN	7,689	1,877	5,505	307	3,628	D	24.4%	71.6%	25.4%	74.6%
12,551	PROWERS	3,981	2,728	1,052	201	1,676	R	68.5%	26.4%	72.2%	27.8%
159,063	PUEBLO	59,568	26,696	29,591	3,281	2,895	D	44.8%	49.7%	47.4%	52.6%
6,666	RIO BLANCO	2,715	2,166	434	115	1,732	R	79.8%	16.0%	83.3%	16.7%
11,982	RIO GRANDE	4,480	2,437	1,800	243	637	R	54.4%	40.2%	57.5%	42.5%
23,509	ROUTT	10,480	4,005	6,092	383	2,087	D	38.2%	58.1%	39.7%	60.3%
6,108	SAGUACHE	2,386	860	1,312	214	452	D	36.0%	55.0%	39.6%	60.4%
699	SAN JUAN	449	177	243	29	66	D	39.4%	54.1%	42.1%	57.9%
7,359	SAN MIGUEL	3,243	821	2,190	232	1,369	D	25.3%	67.5%	27.3%	72.7%
2,379	SEDGWICK	1,209	806	342	61	464	R	66.7%	28.3%	70.2%	29.8%
27,994	SUMMIT	11,514	3,705	7,306	503	3,601	D	32.2%	63.5%	33.6%	66.4%

COLORADO

GOVERNOR 2014

2010 Census Population	County	Total Vote	Republican (Beauprez)	Democratic (Hickenlooper)	Other	Rep.-Dem. Plurality	Percentage			
							Total Vote		Major Vote	
							Rep.	Dem.	Rep.	Dem.
23,350	TELLER	11,303	7,364	3,241	698	4,123 R	65.2%	28.7%	69.4%	30.6%
4,814	WASHINGTON	2,355	1,915	365	75	1,550 R	81.3%	15.5%	84.0%	16.0%
252,825	WELD	90,774	52,844	33,375	4,555	19,469 R	58.2%	36.8%	61.3%	38.7%
10,043	YUMA	4,258	3,356	794	108	2,562 R	78.8%	18.6%	80.9%	19.1%
5,029,196	TOTAL	2,041,607	938,195	1,006,433	96,979	68,238 D	46.0%	49.3%	48.2%	51.8%

COLORADO

SENATOR 2014

2010 Census Population	County	Total Vote	Republican (Gardner)	Democratic (Udall)	Other	Rep.-Dem. Plurality	Percentage			
							Total Vote		Major Vote	
							Rep.	Dem.	Rep.	Dem.
441,603	ADAMS	130,613	58,614	62,296	9,703	3,682 D	44.9%	47.7%	48.5%	51.5%
15,445	ALAMOSA	5,146	2,350	2,440	356	90 D	45.7%	47.4%	49.1%	50.9%
572,003	ARAPAHOE	223,546	103,915	107,347	12,284	3,432 D	46.5%	48.0%	49.2%	50.8%
12,084	ARCHULETA	5,453	3,103	2,030	320	1,073 R	56.9%	37.2%	60.5%	39.5%
3,788	BACA	1,859	1,374	353	132	1,021 R	73.9%	19.0%	79.6%	20.4%
6,499	BENT	1,565	949	503	113	446 R	60.6%	32.1%	65.4%	34.6%
294,567	BOULDER	142,321	38,931	97,612	5,778	58,681 D	27.4%	68.6%	28.5%	71.5%
55,889	BROOMFIELD	27,611	12,833	13,309	1,469	476 D	46.5%	48.2%	49.1%	50.9%
17,809	CHAFFEE	8,902	4,393	4,025	484	368 R	49.3%	45.2%	52.2%	47.8%
1,836	CHEYENNE	1,038	848	122	68	726 R	81.7%	11.8%	87.4%	12.6%
9,088	CLEAR CREEK	4,650	1,987	2,344	319	357 D	42.7%	50.4%	45.9%	54.1%
8,256	CONEJOS	3,465	1,659	1,621	185	38 R	47.9%	46.8%	50.6%	49.4%
3,524	COSTILLA	1,401	396	912	93	516 D	28.3%	65.1%	30.3%	69.7%
5,823	CROWLEY	1,340	878	344	118	534 R	65.5%	25.7%	71.8%	28.2%
4,255	CUSTER	2,516	1,659	740	117	919 R	65.9%	29.4%	69.2%	30.8%
30,952	DELTA	13,440	9,199	3,504	737	5,695 R	68.4%	26.1%	72.4%	27.6%
600,158	DENVER	231,553	56,789	163,783	10,981	106,994 D	24.5%	70.7%	25.7%	74.3%
2,064	DOLORES	966	653	246	67	407 R	67.6%	25.5%	72.6%	27.4%
285,465	DOUGLAS	137,809	86,626	45,163	6,020	41,463 R	62.9%	32.8%	65.7%	34.3%
52,197	EAGLE	17,347	7,102	9,438	807	2,336 D	40.9%	54.4%	42.9%	57.1%
622,263	EL PASO	228,154	141,475	73,208	13,471	68,267 R	62.0%	32.1%	65.9%	34.1%
23,086	ELBERT	12,459	9,137	2,556	766	6,581 R	73.3%	20.5%	78.1%	21.9%
46,824	FREMONT	17,221	11,085	4,773	1,363	6,312 R	64.4%	27.7%	69.9%	30.1%
56,389	GARFIELD	19,309	9,894	8,387	1,028	1,507 R	51.2%	43.4%	54.1%	45.9%
5,441	GILPIN	2,875	1,169	1,450	256	281 D	40.7%	50.4%	44.6%	55.4%
14,843	GRAND	6,799	3,638	2,795	366	843 R	53.5%	41.1%	56.6%	43.4%
15,324	GUNNISON	6,933	2,671	3,840	422	1,169 D	38.5%	55.4%	41.0%	59.0%
843	HINSDALE	523	307	191	25	116 R	58.7%	36.5%	61.6%	38.4%
6,711	HUERFANO	3,197	1,449	1,504	244	55 D	45.3%	47.0%	49.1%	50.9%
1,394	JACKSON	735	531	163	41	368 R	72.2%	22.2%	76.5%	23.5%
534,543	JEFFERSON	256,144	120,240	121,109	14,795	869 D	46.9%	47.3%	49.8%	50.2%
1,398	KIOWA	761	616	107	38	509 R	80.9%	14.1%	85.2%	14.8%
8,270	KIT CARSON	3,100	2,448	487	165	1,961 R	79.0%	15.7%	83.4%	16.6%
51,334	LA PLATA	22,879	10,174	11,852	853	1,678 D	44.5%	51.8%	46.2%	53.8%
7,310	LAKE	2,442	906	1,311	225	405 D	37.1%	53.7%	40.9%	59.1%
299,630	LARIMER	145,672	69,198	68,659	7,815	539 R	47.5%	47.1%	50.2%	49.8%
15,507	LAS ANIMAS	5,564	2,803	2,380	381	423 R	50.4%	42.8%	54.1%	45.9%
5,467	LINCOLN	1,998	1,557	321	120	1,236 R	77.9%	16.1%	82.9%	17.1%
22,709	LOGAN	7,720	5,662	1,591	467	4,071 R	73.3%	20.6%	78.1%	21.9%
146,723	MESA	57,491	39,313	15,410	2,768	23,903 R	68.4%	26.8%	71.8%	28.2%

COLORADO

SENATOR 2014

2010 Census Population	County	Total Vote	Republican (Gardner)	Democratic (Udall)	Other	Rep.-Dem. Plurality	Percentage Total Vote Rep.	Dem.	Major Vote Rep.	Dem.
712	MINERAL	601	304	254	43	50 R	50.6%	42.3%	54.5%	45.5%
13,795	MOFFAT	4,874	3,727	826	321	2,901 R	76.5%	16.9%	81.9%	18.1%
25,535	MONTEZUMA	9,697	5,784	3,353	560	2,431 R	59.6%	34.6%	63.3%	36.7%
41,276	MONTROSE	16,649	11,907	4,071	671	7,836 R	71.5%	24.5%	74.5%	25.5%
28,159	MORGAN	8,812	6,119	2,164	529	3,955 R	69.4%	24.6%	73.9%	26.1%
18,831	OTERO	6,641	3,814	2,332	495	1,482 R	57.4%	35.1%	62.1%	37.9%
4,436	OURAY	2,689	1,234	1,355	100	121 D	45.9%	50.4%	47.7%	52.3%
16,206	PARK	8,035	4,673	2,827	535	1,846 R	58.2%	35.2%	62.3%	37.7%
4,442	PHILLIPS	1,977	1,516	357	104	1,159 R	76.7%	18.1%	80.9%	19.1%
17,148	PITKIN	7,749	2,106	5,409	234	3,303 D	27.2%	69.8%	28.0%	72.0%
12,551	PROWERS	3,981	2,874	887	220	1,987 R	72.2%	22.3%	76.4%	23.6%
159,063	PUEBLO	59,657	27,571	27,877	4,209	306 D	46.2%	46.7%	49.7%	50.3%
6,666	RIO BLANCO	2,721	2,214	361	146	1,853 R	81.4%	13.3%	86.0%	14.0%
11,982	RIO GRANDE	4,442	2,534	1,566	342	968 R	57.0%	35.3%	61.8%	38.2%
23,509	ROUTT	10,452	4,278	5,639	535	1,361 D	40.9%	54.0%	43.1%	56.9%
6,108	SAGUACHE	2,377	861	1,307	209	446 D	36.2%	55.0%	39.7%	60.3%
699	SAN JUAN	462	182	255	25	73 D	39.4%	55.2%	41.6%	58.4%
7,359	SAN MIGUEL	3,257	870	2,226	161	1,356 D	26.7%	68.3%	28.1%	71.9%
2,379	SEDGWICK	1,206	853	262	91	591 R	70.7%	21.7%	76.5%	23.5%
27,994	SUMMIT	11,532	4,046	6,957	529	2,911 D	35.1%	60.3%	36.8%	63.2%
23,350	TELLER	11,267	7,337	3,158	772	4,179 R	65.1%	28.0%	69.9%	30.1%
4,814	WASHINGTON	2,358	2,055	237	66	1,818 R	87.2%	10.1%	89.7%	10.3%
252,825	WELD	90,811	54,823	29,785	6,203	25,038 R	60.4%	32.8%	64.8%	35.2%
10,043	YUMA	4,294	3,678	512	104	3,166 R	85.7%	11.9%	87.8%	12.2%
5,029,196	TOTAL	2,041,058	983,891	944,203	112,964	39,688 R	48.2%	46.3%	51.0%	49.0%

COLORADO

HOUSE OF REPRESENTATIVES

CD	Year	Total Vote	Republican Vote	Candidate	Democratic Vote	Candidate	Other Vote	Rep.-Dem. Plurality	Percentage Total Vote Rep.	Dem.	Major Vote Rep.	Dem.
1	2014	278,494	80,682	WALSH, MARTIN H.	183,281	DEGETTE, DIANA*	14,531	102,599 D	29.0%	65.8%	30.6%	69.4%
1	2012	348,228	93,217	STROUD, DANNY	237,579	DEGETTE, DIANA*	17,432	144,362 D	26.8%	68.2%	28.2%	71.8%
2	2014	345,945	149,645	LEING, GEORGE	196,300	POLIS, JARED*		46,655 D	43.3%	56.7%	43.3%	56.7%
2	2012	421,580	162,639	LUNDBERG, KEVIN	234,758	POLIS, JARED*	24,183	72,119 D	38.6%	55.7%	40.9%	59.1%
3	2014	281,141	163,011	TIPTON, SCOTT R.*	100,364	TAPIA, ABEL	17,766	62,647 R	58.0%	35.7%	61.9%	38.1%
3	2012	347,574	185,291	TIPTON, SCOTT R.*	142,920	PACE, SAL	19,363	42,371 R	53.3%	41.1%	56.5%	43.5%
4	2014	286,507	185,292	BUCK, KEN	83,727	MEYERS, VIC	17,488	101,565 R	64.7%	29.2%	68.9%	31.1%
4	2012	342,336	200,006	GARDNER, CORY*	125,800	SHAFFER, BRANDON	16,530	74,206 R	58.4%	36.7%	61.4%	38.6%
5	2014	262,855	157,182	LAMBORN, DOUG*	105,673	HALTER JR., IRVING LESLIE "IRV"		51,509 R	59.8%	40.2%	59.8%	40.2%
5	2012	307,237	199,639	LAMBORN, DOUG*			107,598	199,639 R	65.0%		100.0%	
6	2014	276,440	143,467	COFFMAN, MIKE*	118,847	ROMANOFF, ANDREW	14,126	24,620 R	51.9%	43.0%	54.7%	45.3%
6	2012	342,914	163,938	COFFMAN, MIKE*	156,937	MIKLOSI, JOE	22,039	7,001 R	47.8%	45.8%	51.1%	48.9%
7	2014	269,143	120,918	YTTERBERG, DON	148,225	PERLMUTTER, ED*		27,307 D	44.9%	55.1%	44.9%	55.1%
7	2012	340,970	139,066	COORS, JOE	182,460	PERLMUTTER, ED*	19,444	43,394 D	40.8%	53.5%	43.3%	56.7%
TOTAL	2014	2,000,525	1,000,197		936,417		63,911	63,780 R	50.0%	46.8%	51.6%	48.4%
TOTAL	2012	2,450,839	1,143,796		1,080,454		226,589	63,342 R	46.7%	44.1%	51.4%	48.6%

Note: An asterisk (*) denotes incumbent.

COLORADO

GENERAL AND PRIMARY ELECTIONS

2014 GENERAL ELECTIONS: OTHER VOTES

Governor Other vote was 39,590 Libertarian (Matthew Hess), 27,391 Green (Harry Hempy), 24,042 Independent (Mike Dunafon), 5,923 Independent (Paul Noel Fiorino), 33 Write-in (Marcus Giavanni)

Senate Other vote was 52,876 Libertarian (Gaylon Kent), 29,472 Independent (Steve Shogan), 24,151 Independent (Raul Acosta), 6,427 Unity Party of Colorado (Bill Hammons), 21 Write-in (Donald Willoughby), 17 Write-in (Kathleen Rosewater Cunningham)

House Other vote was:

CD 1 9,292 Libertarian (Frank Atwood), 5,236 Independent (Danny Stroud), 2 Write-in (Daniel Kirschler), 1 Write-in (Logan Blackburn)
CD 3 11,294 Independent (Tisha Casida), 6,472 Libertarian (Travis Mero)
CD 4 9,472 Libertarian (Jess Loban), 8,016 Independent (Grant Doherty)
CD 6 8,623 Libertarian (Norm Olsen), 5,503 Green (Gary Swing)

2014 PRIMARY ELECTIONS: SUPPLEMENTARY INFORMATION

Primary	June 24, 2014	**Registration** (as of June 2, 2014 – includes 652,337 inactive registrants)	3,553,148	Republican	1,119,500
				Democratic	1,099,207
				Libertarian	28,097
				Green	10,351
				American Constitution	8,076
				Unaffiliated	1,287,917

Primary Type Semi-open—Registered Democrats and Republicans could vote only in their party's primary. Any other registered voter could participate in either the Democratic or Republican primary but in the process had to declare his or her affiliation with that party.

	REPUBLICAN PRIMARIES			**DEMOCRATIC PRIMARIES**		
Senator	Gardner, Cory	338,324	100.0%	Udall, Mark*	213,746	100.0%
	TOTAL	338,324		TOTAL	213,746	
Governor	Beauprez, Bob	116,333	30.2%	Hickenlooper, John*	214,403	100.0%
	Tancredo, Tom	102,830	26.7%			
	Gessler, Scott	89,213	23.2%			
	Kopp, Mike	76,373	19.9%			
	TOTAL	384,749		TOTAL	214,403	
Congressional District 1	Walsh, Martin H.	21,519	100.0%	DeGette, Diana*	43,514	100.0%
	Cunningham, Kathleen	1				
	TOTAL	21,520		TOTAL	43,514	
Congressional District 2	Leing, George	43,481	100.0%	Polis, Jared*	37,759	100.0%
	TOTAL	43,481		TOTAL	37,759	
Congressional District 3	Tipton, Scott R.*	46,177	74.5%	Tapia, Abel	29,931	100.0%
	Cox, David L.	15,773	25.5%			
	TOTAL	61,950		TOTAL	29,931	
Congressional District 4	Buck, Ken	32,714	44.2%	Meyers, Vic	20,883	99.9%
	Renfroe, Scott	17,722	23.9%	Chapin, Dan	29	0.1%
	Kirkmeyer, Barbara	12,155	16.4%			
	Laffey, Stephen P.	11,433	15.4%			
	TOTAL	74,024		TOTAL	20,912	

COLORADO

GENERAL AND PRIMARY ELECTIONS

	REPUBLICAN PRIMARIES			DEMOCRATIC PRIMARIES		
Congressional District 5	Lamborn, Doug*	38,741	52.6%	Halter Jr., Irving Leslie "Irv"	16,412	100.0%
	Rayburn, Bentley B.	34,967	47.4%			
	TOTAL	73,708		TOTAL	16,412	
Congressional District 6	Coffman, Mike*	43,737	100.0%	Romanoff, Andrew	24,267	100.0%
	TOTAL	43,737		TOTAL	24,267	
Congressional District 7	Ytterberg, Don	34,817	100.0%	Perlmutter, Ed*	30,659	100.0%
	TOTAL	34,817		TOTAL	30,659	

Note: An asterisk (*) denotes incumbent.

CONNECTICUT

Congressional districts first established for elections held in 2012
5 members

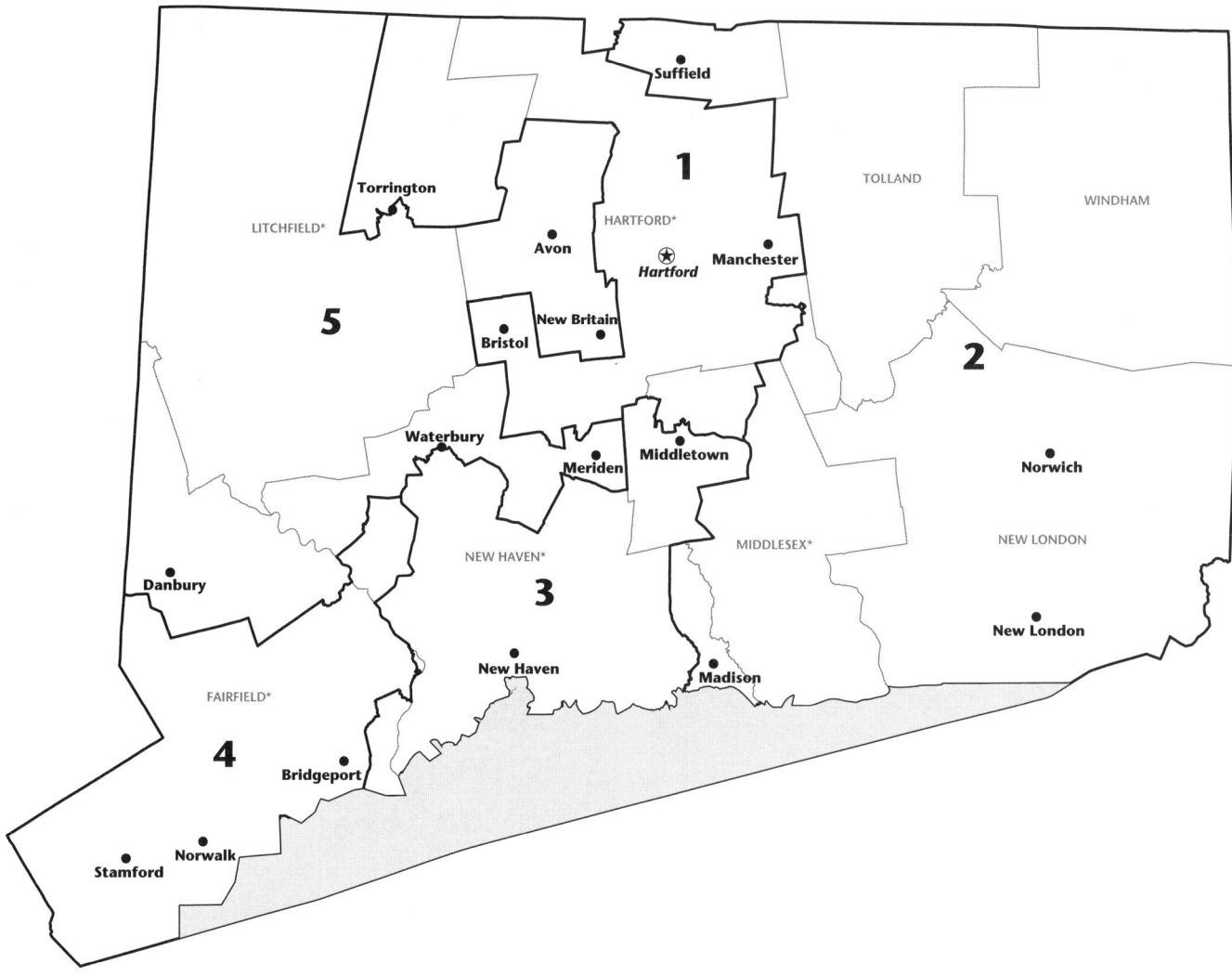

* Asterisk indicates a county whose boundaries include parts of two or more congressional districts.

CONNECTICUT

GOVERNOR
Dan Malloy (D). Reelected 2014 to a four-year term. Previously elected 2010.

SENATORS (2 Democrats)
Richard Blumenthal (D). Elected 2010 to a six-year term.

Christopher Murphy (D). Elected 2012 to a six-year term.

REPRESENTATIVES (5 Democrats)
1. John B. Larson (D)
2. Joe Courtney (D)
3. Rosa L. DeLauro (D)
4. James A. Himes (D)
5. Elizabeth H. Esty (D)

POSTWAR VOTE FOR PRESIDENT

Year	Total Vote	Republican		Democratic		Other Vote	Rep.-Dem. Plurality	Percentage			
								Total Vote		Major Vote	
		Vote	Candidate	Vote	Candidate			Rep.	Dem.	Rep.	Dem.
2012	1,558,960	634,892	Romney, W. Mitt	905,083	Obama, Barack H.*	18,985	270,191 D	40.7%	58.1%	41.2%	58.8%
2008	1,646,792	629,428	McCain, John S. III	997,772	Obama, Barack H.	19,592	368,344 D	38.2%	60.6%	38.7%	61.3%
2004	1,578,769	693,826	Bush, George W.*	857,488	Kerry, John F.	27,455	163,662 D	43.9%	54.3%	44.7%	55.3%
2000**	1,459,525	561,094	Bush, George W.	816,015	Gore, Albert Jr.	82,416	254,921 D	38.4%	55.9%	40.7%	59.3%
1996**	1,392,614	483,109	Dole, Robert "Bob"	735,740	Clinton, Bill*	173,765	252,631 D	34.7%	52.8%	39.6%	60.4%
1992**	1,616,332	578,313	Bush, George H.*	682,318	Clinton, Bill	355,701	104,005 D	35.8%	42.2%	45.9%	54.1%
1988	1,443,394	750,241	Bush, George H.	676,584	Dukakis, Michael S.	16,569	73,657 R	52.0%	46.9%	52.6%	47.4%
1984	1,466,900	890,877	Reagan, Ronald*	569,597	Mondale, Walter F.	6,426	321,280 R	60.7%	38.8%	61.0%	39.0%
1980**	1,406,285	677,210	Reagan, Ronald	541,732	Carter, Jimmy*	187,343	135,478 R	48.2%	38.5%	55.6%	44.4%
1976	1,381,526	719,261	Ford, Gerald R.*	647,895	Carter, Jimmy	14,370	71,366 R	52.1%	46.9%	52.6%	47.4%
1972	1,384,277	810,763	Nixon, Richard M.*	555,498	McGovern, George S.	18,016	255,265 R	58.6%	40.1%	59.3%	40.7%
1968**	1,256,232	556,721	Nixon, Richard M.	621,561	Humphrey, Hubert Horatio Jr.	77,950	64,840 D	44.3%	49.5%	47.2%	52.8%
1964	1,218,578	390,996	Goldwater, Barry M. Sr.	826,269	Johnson, Lyndon B.*	1,313	435,273 D	32.1%	67.8%	32.1%	67.9%
1960	1,222,883	565,813	Nixon, Richard M.	657,055	Kennedy, John F.	15	91,242 D	46.3%	53.7%	46.3%	53.7%
1956	1,117,121	711,837	Eisenhower, Dwight D.*	405,079	Stevenson, Adlai E. II	205	306,758 R	63.7%	36.3%	63.7%	36.3%
1952	1,096,911	611,012	Eisenhower, Dwight D.	481,649	Stevenson, Adlai E. II	4,250	129,363 R	55.7%	43.9%	55.9%	44.1%
1948	883,518	437,754	Dewey, Thomas E.	423,297	Truman, Harry S.*	22,467	14,457 R	49.5%	47.9%	50.8%	49.2%

Note: An asterisk (*) denotes incumbent. **In past elections, the other vote included: 2000 - 64,452 Green (Ralph Nader); 1996 - 139,523 Reform (Ross Perot); 1992 - 348,771 Independent (Perot); 1980 - 171,807 Independent (John Anderson); 1968 - 76,650 American Independent (George Wallace).

CONNECTICUT

POSTWAR VOTE FOR GOVERNOR

Year	Total Vote	Republican Vote	Republican Candidate	Democratic Vote	Democratic Candidate	Other Vote	Rep.-Dem. Plurality	Percentage Total Vote Rep.	Dem.	Major Vote Rep.	Dem.
2014	1,092,773	526,295	Foley, Tom C.	554,314	Malloy, Dan*	12,164	28,019 D	48.2%	50.7%	48.7%	51.3%
2010	1,145,799	560,874	Foley, Tom C.	567,278	Malloy, Dan	17,647	6,404 D	49.0%	49.5%	49.7%	50.3%
2006	1,123,466	710,048	Rell, M. Jodi*	398,220	DeStefano, John Jr.	15,198	311,828 R	63.2%	35.4%	64.1%	35.9%
2002	1,022,998	573,958	Rowland, John G.*	448,984	Curry, Bill	56	124,974 R	56.1%	43.9%	56.1%	43.9%
1998	999,537	628,707	Rowland, John G.*	354,187	Kennelly, Barbara B.	16,643	274,520 R	62.9%	35.4%	64.0%	36.0%
1994**	1,147,084	415,201	Rowland, John G.	375,133	Curry, Bill	356,750	40,068 R	36.2%	32.7%	52.5%	47.5%
1990**	1,142,101	427,840	Rowland, John G.	237,641	Morrison, Bruce A.	476,620	190,199 R#	37.5%	20.8%	64.3%	35.7%
1986	993,692	408,489	Belaga, Julie D.	575,638	O'Neill, William A.*	9,565	167,149 D	41.1%	57.9%	41.5%	58.5%
1982	1,083,876	497,773	Rome, Lewis B.	578,264	O'Neill, William A.*	7,839	80,491 D	45.9%	53.4%	46.3%	53.7%
1978	1,036,608	422,316	Sarasin, Ronald A.	613,109	Grasso, Ella T.*	1,183	190,793 D	40.7%	59.1%	40.8%	59.2%
1974	1,102,773	440,169	Steele, Robert H.	643,490	Grasso, Ella T.	19,114	203,321 D	39.9%	58.4%	40.6%	59.4%
1970	1,082,797	582,160	Meskill, Thomas J.	500,561	Daddario, Emilio Q.	76	81,599 R	53.8%	46.2%	53.8%	46.2%
1966	1,008,557	446,536	Gengras, E. Clayton	561,599	Dempsey, John N.*	422	115,063 D	44.3%	55.7%	44.3%	55.7%
1962	1,031,902	482,852	Alsop, John	549,027	Dempsey, John N.*	23	66,175 D	46.8%	53.2%	46.8%	53.2%
1958	974,509	360,644	Zeller, Fred R.	607,012	Ribicoff, Abraham A.*	6,853	246,368 D	37.0%	62.3%	37.3%	62.7%
1954	936,753	460,528	Lodge, Henry Cabot Jr.*	463,643	Ribicoff, Abraham A.	12,582	3,115 D	49.2%	49.5%	49.8%	50.2%
1950**	878,735	436,418	Lodge, Henry Cabot Jr.	419,404	Bowles, Chester*	22,913	17,014 R	49.7%	47.7%	51.0%	49.0%
1948	875,620	429,071	Shannon, James C.*	431,746	Bowles, Chester	14,803	2,675 D	49.0%	49.3%	49.8%	50.2%
1946	683,831	371,852	McConaughy, James L.	276,335	Snow, Wilbert*	35,644	95,517 R	54.4%	40.4%	57.4%	42.6%

Note: An asterisk (*) denotes incumbent. A pound sign (#) indicates that the state was carried by a third party candidate or independent electoral slate. **In past elections, the other vote included: 1994 - 216,585 A Connecticut Party (Elaine Strong Groark); 130,128 Independent (Tom Scott); 1990 - 460,576 A Connecticut Party (Lowell P. Weicker Jr.). Weicker won the 1990 election with 40.4 percent of the total vote. The term of office for Connecticut's governor was increased from two to four years effective with the 1950 election.

POSTWAR VOTE FOR SENATOR

Year	Total Vote	Republican Vote	Republican Candidate	Democratic Vote	Democratic Candidate	Other Vote	Rep.-Dem. Plurality	Percentage Total Vote Rep.	Dem.	Major Vote Rep.	Dem.
2012	1,511,764	651,089	McMahon, Linda E.	828,761	Murphy, Christopher	31,914	177,672 D	43.1%	54.8%	44.0%	56.0%
2010	1,153,115	498,341	McMahon, Linda E.	636,040	Blumenthal, Richard	18,734	137,699 D	43.2%	55.2%	43.9%	56.1%
2006**	1,134,780	109,198	Schlesinger, Alan	450,844	Lamont, Ned	574,738	341,646 D#	9.6%	39.7%	19.5%	80.5%
2004	1,424,726	457,749	Orchulli, Jack	945,347	Dodd, Christopher J.*	21,630	487,598 D	32.1%	66.4%	32.6%	67.4%
2000	1,311,261	448,077	Giordano, Phil	828,902	Lieberman, Joseph I.*	34,282	380,825 D	34.2%	63.2%	35.1%	64.9%
1998	964,457	312,177	Franks, Gary A.	628,306	Dodd, Christopher J.*	23,974	316,129 D	32.4%	65.1%	33.2%	66.8%
1994	1,079,767	334,833	Labriola, Jerry Jr.	723,842	Lieberman, Joseph I.*	21,092	389,009 D	31.0%	67.0%	31.6%	68.4%
1992	1,500,709	572,036	Johnson, Brook	882,569	Dodd, Christopher J.*	46,104	310,533 D	38.1%	58.8%	39.3%	60.7%
1988	1,383,526	678,454	Weicker, Lowell P. Jr.*	688,499	Lieberman, Joseph I.	16,573	10,045 D	49.0%	49.8%	49.6%	50.4%
1986	976,933	340,438	Eddy, Roger W.	632,695	Dodd, Christopher J.*	3,800	292,257 D	34.8%	64.8%	35.0%	65.0%
1982	1,083,613	545,987	Weicker, Lowell P. Jr.*	499,146	Moffett, Anthony T.	38,480	46,841 R	50.4%	46.1%	52.2%	47.8%
1980	1,356,075	581,884	Buckley, James L.	763,969	Dodd, Christopher J.	10,222	182,085 D	42.9%	56.3%	43.2%	56.8%
1976	1,361,666	785,683	Weicker, Lowell P. Jr.*	561,018	Schaffer, Gloria	14,965	224,665 R	57.7%	41.2%	58.3%	41.7%
1974	1,084,918	372,055	Brannen, James H.	690,820	Ribicoff, Abraham A.*	22,043	318,765 D	34.3%	63.7%	35.0%	65.0%
1970**	1,089,353	454,721	Weicker, Lowell P. Jr.	368,111	Duffey, Joseph D.	266,521	86,610 R	41.7%	33.8%	55.3%	44.7%
1968	1,206,537	551,455	May, Edwin H. Jr.	655,043	Ribicoff, Abraham A.*	39	103,588 D	45.7%	54.3%	45.7%	54.3%
1964	1,208,163	426,939	Lodge, Henry Cabot Jr.	781,008	Dodd, Thomas J.*	216	354,069 D	35.3%	64.6%	35.3%	64.7%
1962	1,029,301	501,694	Seely-Brown, Horace Jr.	527,522	Ribicoff, Abraham J.	85	25,828 D	48.7%	51.3%	48.7%	51.3%
1958	965,463	410,622	Purtell, William A.*	554,841	Dodd, Thomas J.		144,219 D	42.5%	57.5%	42.5%	57.5%
1956	1,113,819	610,829	Bush, Prescott S.*	479,460	Dodd, Thomas J.	23,530	131,369 R	54.8%	43.0%	56.0%	44.0%
1952	1,093,467	573,854	Purtell, William A.	485,066	Benton, William*	34,547	88,788 R	52.5%	44.4%	54.2%	45.8%
1952S	1,093,268	559,465	Bush, Prescott S.	530,505	Ribicoff, Abraham A.	3,298	28,960 R	51.2%	48.5%	51.3%	48.7%
1950	877,827	409,053	Talbot, Joseph E.	453,646	McMahon, Brien*	15,128	44,593 D	46.6%	51.7%	47.4%	52.6%
1950S	877,135	430,311	Bush, Prescott S.	431,413	Benton, William	15,411	1,102 D	49.1%	49.2%	49.9%	50.1%
1946	682,921	381,328	Baldwin, Raymond E.*	276,424	Tone, Joseph M.	25,169	104,904 R	55.8%	40.5%	58.0%	42.0%

Note: An asterisk (*) denotes incumbent. A pound sign (#) indicates that the state was carried by a third party candidate or independent electoral slate. **In past elections, the other vote included: 2006 - 564,095 Connecticut For Lieberman (Joseph I. Lieberman); 1970 - 266,497 Independent (Thomas J. Dodd). Lieberman won the 2006 election with 49.7 percent of the vote. One each of the 1950 and 1952 elections were for short terms to fill a vacancy.

CONNECTICUT

GOVERNOR 2014

2010 Census Population	County	Total Vote	Republican (Foley)	Democratic (Malloy)	Other	Rep.-Dem. Plurality		Percentage			
								Total Vote		Major Vote	
								Rep.	Dem.	Rep.	Dem.
916,829	FAIRFIELD	258,873	128,629	128,714	1,530	85	D	49.7%	49.7%	50.0%	50.0%
894,014	HARTFORD	276,765	125,722	148,096	2,947	22,374	D	45.4%	53.5%	45.9%	54.1%
189,927	LITCHFIELD	69,248	40,992	27,282	974	13,710	R	59.2%	39.4%	60.0%	40.0%
165,676	MIDDLESEX	63,653	31,342	31,478	833	136	D	49.2%	49.5%	49.9%	50.1%
862,477	NEW HAVEN	254,754	116,068	135,973	2,713	19,905	D	45.6%	53.4%	46.1%	53.9%
274,055	NEW LONDON	83,781	39,666	42,983	1,132	3,317	D	47.3%	51.3%	48.0%	52.0%
152,691	TOLLAND	51,940	27,315	23,887	738	3,428	R	52.6%	46.0%	53.3%	46.7%
118,428	WINDHAM	33,051	16,561	15,901	589	660	R	50.1%	48.1%	51.0%	49.0%
	Votes Not Reported by County	708			708						
3,574,097	TOTAL	1,092,773	526,295	554,314	12,164	28,019	D	48.2%	50.7%	48.7%	51.3%

Note: Write-in vote was aggregated on a statewide basis.

2010 Census Population	City/Town	Total Vote	Republican (Foley)	Democratic (Malloy)	Other	Rep.-Dem. Plurality		Percentage			
								Total Vote		Major Vote	
								Rep.	Dem.	Rep.	Dem.
19,249	ANSONIA	4,807	2,291	2,454	62	163	D	47.7%	51.1%	48.3%	51.7%
20,486	BLOOMFIELD	8,362	1,744	6,580	38	4,836	D	20.9%	78.7%	21.0%	79.0%
28,026	BRANFORD	10,771	4,730	5,935	106	1,205	D	43.9%	55.1%	44.4%	55.6%
144,229	BRIDGEPORT	21,578	4,623	16,863	92	12,240	D	21.4%	78.1%	21.5%	78.5%
60,477	BRISTOL	17,672	9,124	8,282	266	842	R	51.6%	46.9%	52.4%	47.6%
29,261	CHESHIRE	11,541	6,339	5,058	144	1,281	R	54.9%	43.8%	55.6%	44.4%
80,893	DANBURY	16,087	7,668	8,267	152	599	D	47.7%	51.4%	48.1%	51.9%
20,732	DARIEN	7,113	4,872	2,226	15	2,646	R	68.5%	31.3%	68.6%	31.4%
51,252	EAST HARTFORD	12,069	4,044	7,887	138	3,843	D	33.5%	65.3%	33.9%	66.1%
29,257	EAST HAVEN	8,092	3,685	4,323	84	638	D	45.5%	53.4%	46.0%	54.0%
44,654	ENFIELD	12,372	6,649	5,553	170	1,096	R	53.7%	44.9%	54.5%	45.5%
59,404	FAIRFIELD	20,864	10,875	9,882	107	993	R	52.1%	47.4%	52.4%	47.6%
25,340	FARMINGTON	10,488	5,648	4,753	87	895	R	53.9%	45.3%	54.3%	45.7%
34,427	GLASTONBURY	14,426	7,804	6,506	116	1,298	R	54.1%	45.1%	54.5%	45.5%
61,171	GREENWICH	19,090	11,544	7,474	72	4,070	R	60.5%	39.2%	60.7%	39.3%
40,115	GROTON	9,818	4,448	5,258	112	810	D	45.3%	53.6%	45.8%	54.2%
22,375	GUILFORD	9,928	4,285	5,540	103	1,255	D	43.2%	55.8%	43.6%	56.4%
60,960	HAMDEN	19,210	5,933	13,121	156	7,188	D	30.9%	68.3%	31.1%	68.9%
124,775	HARTFORD	17,207	1,865	15,257	85	13,392	D	10.8%	88.7%	10.9%	89.1%
58,241	MANCHESTER	16,311	7,138	8,971	202	1,833	D	43.8%	55.0%	44.3%	55.7%
26,543	MANSFIELD	5,609	1,688	3,857	64	2,169	D	30.1%	68.8%	30.4%	69.6%
60,868	MERIDEN	14,512	6,260	8,023	229	1,763	D	43.1%	55.3%	43.8%	56.2%
47,648	MIDDLETOWN	14,143	5,310	8,675	158	3,365	D	37.5%	61.3%	38.0%	62.0%
52,759	MILFORD	18,388	9,358	8,830	200	528	R	50.9%	48.0%	51.5%	48.5%
31,862	NAUGATUCK	8,342	5,101	3,096	145	2,005	R	61.1%	37.1%	62.2%	37.8%
73,206	NEW BRITAIN	13,142	4,356	8,631	155	4,275	D	33.1%	65.7%	33.5%	66.5%
129,779	NEW HAVEN	26,792	3,491	23,183	118	19,692	D	13.0%	86.5%	13.1%	86.9%
27,620	NEW LONDON	5,067	1,406	3,614	47	2,208	D	27.7%	71.3%	28.0%	72.0%
28,142	NEW MILFORD	8,634	4,790	3,736	108	1,054	R	55.5%	43.3%	56.2%	43.8%
30,562	NEWINGTON	11,021	5,234	5,634	153	400	D	47.5%	51.1%	48.2%	51.8%
27,560	NEWTOWN	10,255	5,250	4,931	74	319	R	51.2%	48.1%	51.6%	48.4%
24,093	NORTH HAVEN	9,375	4,923	4,363	89	560	R	52.5%	46.5%	53.0%	47.0%
85,603	NORWALK	22,230	9,413	12,705	112	3,292	D	42.3%	57.2%	42.6%	57.4%
40,493	NORWICH	8,332	3,323	4,874	135	1,551	D	39.9%	58.5%	40.5%	59.5%
24,638	RIDGEFIELD	9,344	5,271	4,031	42	1,240	R	56.4%	43.1%	56.7%	43.3%
39,559	SHELTON	13,466	8,201	5,126	139	3,075	R	60.9%	38.1%	61.5%	38.5%
23,511	SIMSBURY	10,447	5,752	4,613	82	1,139	R	55.1%	44.2%	55.5%	44.5%
25,709	SOUTH WINDSOR	10,071	5,012	4,925	134	87	R	49.8%	48.9%	50.4%	49.6%
43,069	SOUTHINGTON	16,077	9,122	6,728	227	2,394	R	56.7%	41.8%	57.6%	42.4%
122,643	STAMFORD	29,439	11,890	17,388	161	5,498	D	40.4%	59.1%	40.6%	59.4%

CONNECTICUT

GOVERNOR 2014

2010 Census Population	City/Town	Total Vote	Republican (Foley)	Democratic (Malloy)	Other	Rep.-Dem. Plurality	Percentage			
							Total Vote		Major Vote	
							Rep.	Dem.	Rep.	Dem.
51,384	STRATFORD	15,778	7,345	8,285	148	940 D	46.6%	52.5%	47.0%	53.0%
36,383	TORRINGTON	10,531	6,272	4,073	186	2,199 R	59.6%	38.7%	60.6%	39.4%
36,018	TRUMBULL	13,386	7,598	5,685	103	1,913 R	56.8%	42.5%	57.2%	42.8%
29,179	VERNON	9,030	4,490	4,428	112	62 R	49.7%	49.0%	50.3%	49.7%
45,135	WALLINGFORD	15,763	8,353	7,222	188	1,131 R	53.0%	45.8%	53.6%	46.4%
110,366	WATERBURY	20,416	9,336	10,831	249	1,495 D	45.7%	53.1%	46.3%	53.7%
22,514	WATERTOWN	8,535	5,661	2,747	127	2,914 R	66.3%	32.2%	67.3%	32.7%
63,268	WEST HARTFORD	23,786	8,793	14,817	176	6,024 D	37.0%	62.3%	37.2%	62.8%
55,564	WEST HAVEN	13,806	4,750	8,896	160	4,146 D	34.4%	64.4%	34.8%	65.2%
26,391	WESTPORT	9,974	4,534	5,416	24	882 D	45.5%	54.3%	45.6%	54.4%
26,668	WETHERSFIELD	10,619	5,260	5,255	104	5 R	49.5%	49.5%	50.0%	50.0%
25,268	WINDHAM	5,160	1,752	3,297	111	1,545 D	34.0%	63.9%	34.7%	65.3%
29,044	WINDSOR	11,187	3,781	7,308	98	3,527 D	33.8%	65.3%	34.1%	65.9%

CONNECTICUT

HOUSE OF REPRESENTATIVES

CD	Year	Total Vote	Republican		Democratic		Other Vote	Rep.-Dem. Plurality	Percentage			
			Vote	Candidate	Vote	Candidate			Total Vote		Major Vote	
									Rep.	Dem.	Rep.	Dem.
1	2014	217,881	78,609	COREY, MATTHEW M.	135,825	LARSON, JOHN B.*	3,447	57,216 D	36.1%	62.3%	36.7%	63.3%
1	2012	297,061	82,321	DECKER, JOHN HENRY	206,973	LARSON, JOHN B.*	7,767	124,652 D	27.7%	69.7%	28.5%	71.5%
2	2014	227,936	80,837	HOPKINS-CAVANAGH, LORI	141,948	COURTNEY, JOE*	5,151	61,111 D	35.5%	62.3%	36.3%	63.7%
2	2012	299,960	88,103	FORMICA, PAUL	204,708	COURTNEY, JOE*	7,149	116,605 D	29.4%	68.2%	30.1%	69.9%
3	2014	209,939	69,454	BROWN, JAMES E.	140,485	DELAURO, ROSA L.*		71,031 D	33.1%	66.9%	33.1%	66.9%
3	2012	291,301	73,726	WINSLEY, WAYNE	217,573	DELAURO, ROSA L.*	2	143,847 D	25.3%	74.7%	25.3%	74.7%
4	2014	198,800	91,922	DEBICELLA, DAN	106,873	HIMES, JAMES A.*	5	14,951 D	46.2%	53.8%	46.2%	53.8%
4	2012	293,432	117,503	OBSITNIK, STEVE	175,929	HIMES, JAMES A.*		58,426 D	40.0%	60.0%	40.0%	60.0%
5	2014	213,301	97,767	GREENBERG, MARK	113,564	ESTY, ELIZABETH H.*	1,970	15,797 D	45.8%	53.2%	46.3%	53.7%
5	2012	284,757	138,637	RORABACK, ANDREW	146,098	ESTY, ELIZABETH H.	22	7,461 D	48.7%	51.3%	48.7%	51.3%
TOTAL	2014	1,067,857	418,589		638,695		10,573	220,106 D	39.2%	59.8%	39.6%	60.4%
TOTAL	2012	1,466,511	500,290		951,281		14,940	450,991 D	34.1%	64.9%	34.5%	65.5%

Note: An asterisk (*) denotes incumbent.

CONNECTICUT

GENERAL AND PRIMARY ELECTIONS

2014 GENERAL ELECTIONS: OTHER VOTES

Governor   Other vote was 11,456 Independent (Joe Visconti), 708 scattered write-in

House   Other vote was:

CD 1   3,447 Green (Jeffery Russell)

CD 2   2,602 Libertarian (Daniel J. Reale), 2,549 Green (William Clyde)

CD 4   3 Write-in (Stephen A. Miller), 2 Write-in (Sophie E. Pastore)

CD 5   1,970 Independent (John Pistone)

CONNECTICUT

GENERAL AND PRIMARY ELECTIONS

2014 PRIMARY ELECTIONS: SUPPLEMENTARY INFORMATION

Primary	August 12, 2014	**Registration** (as of October 29, 2013 – includes 154,830 inactive registrants)	2,172,403	Democratic Republican Other Unaffiliated	798,478 436,550 19,840 917,535

Primary Type Closed—Only registered Democrats and Republicans could vote in their party's primary. (The statewide party registration figures in October 2013 add to 2,172,403, but the total is listed on the Connecticut election web site as 2,172,400.)

	REPUBLICAN PRIMARIES			DEMOCRATIC PRIMARIES	
Governor	Foley, Tom C. Mckinney, John P. *TOTAL*	44,144 35,282 *79,426*	55.6% 44.4%	Malloy, Dan*	Unopposed
Congressional District 1	Corey, Matthew M.	Unopposed		Larson, John B.*	Unopposed
Congressional District 2	Hopkins-Cavanagh, Lori	Unopposed		Courtney, Joe*	Unopposed
Congressional District 3	Brown, James E.	Unopposed		DeLauro, Rosa L.*	Unopposed
Congressional District 4	Debicella, Dan	Unopposed		Himes, James A.*	Unopposed
Congressional District 5	Greenberg, Mark	Unopposed		Esty, Elizabeth H.*	Unopposed

Note: An asterisk (*) denotes incumbent.

DELAWARE

One member At Large

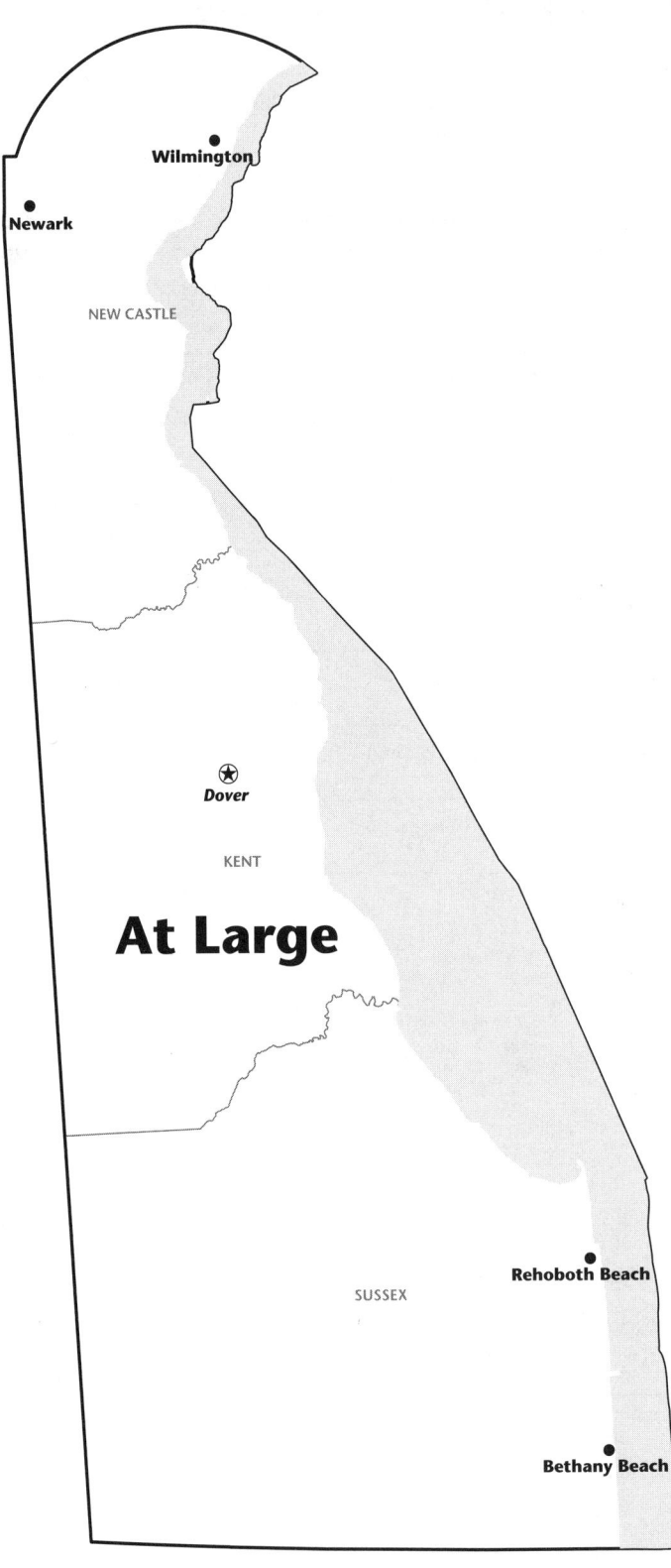

DELAWARE

GOVERNOR
Jack Markell (D). Reelected 2012 to a four-year term. Previously elected 2008.

SENATORS (2 Democrats)
Thomas R. Carper (D). Reelected 2012 to a six-year term. Previously elected 2006, 2000.

Christopher A. Coons (D). Elected 2010 to a six-year term.

REPRESENTATIVE (1 Democrat)
At Large. John C. Carney, Jr. (D)

POSTWAR VOTE FOR PRESIDENT

Year	Total Vote	Republican Vote	Republican Candidate	Democratic Vote	Democratic Candidate	Other Vote	Rep.-Dem. Plurality	Total Vote Rep.	Total Vote Dem.	Major Vote Rep.	Major Vote Dem.
2012	413,921	165,484	Romney, W. Mitt	242,584	Obama, Barack H.*	5,853	77,100 D	40.0%	58.6%	40.6%	59.4%
2008	412,412	152,374	McCain, John S. III	255,459	Obama, Barack H.	4,579	103,085 D	36.9%	61.9%	37.4%	62.6%
2004	375,190	171,660	Bush, George W.*	200,152	Kerry, John F.	3,378	28,492 D	45.8%	53.3%	46.2%	53.8%
2000**	327,622	137,288	Bush, George W.	180,068	Gore, Albert Jr.	10,266	42,780 D	41.9%	55.0%	43.3%	56.7%
1996**	271,084	99,062	Dole, Robert "Bob"	140,355	Clinton, Bill*	31,667	41,293 D	36.5%	51.8%	41.4%	58.6%
1992**	289,735	102,313	Bush, George H.*	126,054	Clinton, Bill	61,368	23,741 D	35.3%	43.5%	44.8%	55.2%
1988	249,891	139,639	Bush, George H.	108,647	Dukakis, Michael S.	1,605	30,992 R	55.9%	43.5%	56.2%	43.8%
1984	254,572	152,190	Reagan, Ronald*	101,656	Mondale, Walter F.	726	50,534 R	59.8%	39.9%	60.0%	40.0%
1980**	235,900	111,252	Reagan, Ronald	105,754	Carter, Jimmy*	18,894	5,498 R	47.2%	44.8%	51.3%	48.7%
1976	235,834	109,831	Ford, Gerald R.*	122,596	Carter, Jimmy	3,407	12,765 D	46.6%	52.0%	47.3%	52.7%
1972	235,516	140,357	Nixon, Richard M.*	92,283	McGovern, George S.	2,876	48,074 R	59.6%	39.2%	60.3%	39.7%
1968**	214,367	96,714	Nixon, Richard M.	89,194	Humphrey, Hubert Horatio Jr.	28,459	7,520 R	45.1%	41.6%	52.0%	48.0%
1964	201,320	78,078	Goldwater, Barry M. Sr.	122,704	Johnson, Lyndon B.*	538	44,626 D	38.8%	60.9%	38.9%	61.1%
1960	196,683	96,373	Nixon, Richard M.	99,590	Kennedy, John F.	720	3,217 D	49.0%	50.6%	49.2%	50.8%
1956	177,988	98,057	Eisenhower, Dwight D.*	79,421	Stevenson, Adlai E. II	510	18,636 R	55.1%	44.6%	55.3%	44.7%
1952	174,025	90,059	Eisenhower, Dwight D.	83,315	Stevenson, Adlai E. II	651	6,744 R	51.8%	47.9%	51.9%	48.1%
1948	139,073	69,588	Dewey, Thomas E.	67,813	Truman, Harry S.*	1,672	1,775 R	50.0%	48.8%	50.6%	49.4%

Note: An asterisk (*) denotes incumbent. **In past elections, the other vote included: 2000 - 8,307 Green (Ralph Nader); 1996 - 28,719 Reform (Ross Perot); 1992 - 59,213 Independent (Perot); 1980 - 16,288 Independent (John Anderson); 1968 - 28,459 American Independent (George Wallace).

DELAWARE

POSTWAR VOTE FOR GOVERNOR

Year	Total Vote	Republican		Democratic		Other Vote	Rep.-Dem. Plurality	Percentage			
								Total Vote		Major Vote	
		Vote	Candidate	Vote	Candidate			Rep.	Dem.	Rep.	Dem.
2012	398,033	113,793	Cragg, Jeffrey	275,993	Markell, Jack*	8,247	162,200 D	28.6%	69.3%	29.2%	70.8%
2008	395,204	126,662	Lee, William Swain	266,861	Markell, Jack	1,681	140,199 D	32.0%	67.5%	32.2%	67.8%
2004	365,008	167,115	Lee, William Swain	185,687	Minner, Ruth Ann*	12,206	18,572 D	45.8%	50.9%	47.4%	52.6%
2000	323,688	128,603	Burris, John M.	191,695	Minner, Ruth Ann	3,390	63,092 D	39.7%	59.2%	40.2%	59.8%
1996	271,122	82,654	Rzewnicki, Janet C.	188,300	Carper, Thomas R.*	168	105,646 D	30.5%	69.5%	30.5%	69.5%
1992	277,058	90,725	Scott, B. Gary	179,365	Carper, Thomas R.	6,968	88,640 D	32.7%	64.7%	33.6%	66.4%
1988	239,969	169,733	Castle, Michael N.*	70,236	Kreshtoll, Jacob		99,497 R	70.7%	29.3%	70.7%	29.3%
1984	243,565	135,250	Castle, Michael N.	108,315	Quillen, William T.		26,935 R	55.5%	44.5%	55.5%	44.5%
1980	225,081	159,004	du Pont, Pierre S. IV*	64,217	Gordy, William J.	1,860	94,787 R	70.6%	28.5%	71.2%	28.8%
1976	229,563	130,531	du Pont, Pierre S. IV	97,480	Tribbitt, Sherman W.*	1,552	33,051 R	56.9%	42.5%	57.2%	42.8%
1972	228,722	109,583	Peterson, Russell W.*	117,274	Tribbitt, Sherman W.	1,865	7,691 D	47.9%	51.3%	48.3%	51.7%
1968	206,834	104,474	Peterson, Russell W.	102,360	Terry, Charles L. Jr.*		2,114 R	50.5%	49.5%	50.5%	49.5%
1964	200,171	97,374	Buckson, David P.	102,797	Terry, Charles L. Jr.		5,423 D	48.6%	51.4%	48.6%	51.4%
1960	194,835	94,043	Rollins, John W.	100,792	Carvel, Elbert N.		6,749 D	48.3%	51.7%	48.3%	51.7%
1956	177,012	91,965	Boggs, James Caleb*	85,047	McConnell, J. H. Tyler		6,918 R	52.0%	48.0%	52.0%	48.0%
1952	170,749	88,977	Boggs, James Caleb	81,772	Carvel, Elbert N.*		7,205 R	52.1%	47.9%	52.1%	47.9%
1948	140,335	64,996	George, Hyland P.	75,339	Carvel, Elbert N.		10,343 D	46.3%	53.7%	46.3%	53.7%

Note: An asterisk (*) denotes incumbent.

POSTWAR VOTE FOR SENATOR

Year	Total Vote	Republican		Democratic		Other Vote	Rep.-Dem. Plurality	Percentage			
								Total Vote		Major Vote	
		Vote	Candidate	Vote	Candidate			Rep.	Dem.	Rep.	Dem.
2014	234,038	98,823	Wade, Kevin	130,655	Coons, Christopher A.*	4,560	31,832 D	42.2%	55.8%	43.1%	56.9%
2012	399,607	115,700	Wade, Kevin	265,415	Carper, Thomas R.*	18,492	149,715 D	29.0%	66.4%	30.4%	69.6%
2010S	307,402	123,053	O'Donnell, Christine	174,012	Coons, Christopher A.	10,337	50,959 D	40.0%	56.6%	41.4%	58.6%
2008	398,134	140,595	O'Donnell, Christine	257,539	Biden, Joseph R. Jr.*		116,944 D	35.3%	64.7%	35.3%	64.7%
2006	254,099	69,734	Ting, Jan	170,567	Carper, Thomas R.*	13,798	100,833 D	27.4%	67.1%	29.0%	71.0%
2002	232,314	94,793	Clatworthy, Raymond J.	135,253	Biden, Joseph R. Jr.*	2,268	40,460 D	40.8%	58.2%	41.2%	58.8%
2000	327,017	142,891	Roth, William V.*	181,566	Carper, Thomas R.	2,560	38,675 D	43.7%	55.5%	44.0%	56.0%
1996	275,591	105,088	Clatworthy, Raymond J.	165,465	Biden, Joseph R. Jr.*	5,038	60,377 D	38.1%	60.0%	38.8%	61.2%
1994	199,029	111,088	Roth, William V.*	84,554	Oberly, Charles M.	3,387	26,534 R	55.8%	42.5%	56.8%	43.2%
1990	180,152	64,554	Brady, M. Jane	112,918	Biden, Joseph R. Jr.*	2,680	48,364 D	35.8%	62.7%	36.4%	63.6%
1988	243,493	151,115	Roth, William V.*	92,378	Woo, S. B.		58,737 R	62.1%	37.9%	62.1%	37.9%
1984	245,932	98,101	Burris, John M.	147,831	Biden, Joseph R. Jr.*		49,730 D	39.9%	60.1%	39.9%	60.1%
1982	190,960	105,357	Roth, William V.*	84,413	Levinson, David N.	1,190	20,944 R	55.2%	44.2%	55.5%	44.5%
1978	162,072	66,479	Baxter, James H.	93,930	Biden, Joseph R. Jr.*	1,663	27,451 D	41.0%	58.0%	41.4%	58.6%
1976	224,859	125,502	Roth, William V.*	98,055	Maloney, Thomas C.	1,302	27,447 R	55.8%	43.6%	56.1%	43.9%
1972	229,828	112,844	Boggs, James Caleb*	116,006	Biden, Joseph R. Jr.	978	3,162 D	49.1%	50.5%	49.3%	50.7%
1970	161,439	94,979	Roth, William V.	64,740	Zimmerman, Jacob	1,720	30,239 R	58.8%	40.1%	59.5%	40.5%
1966	164,531	97,268	Boggs, James Caleb*	67,263	Tunnell, James M. Jr.		30,005 R	59.1%	40.9%	59.1%	40.9%
1964	200,703	103,782	Williams, John J.*	96,850	Carvel, Elbert N.	71	6,932 R	51.7%	48.3%	51.7%	48.3%
1960	194,964	98,874	Boggs, James Caleb	96,090	Frear, J. Allen Jr.*		2,784 R	50.7%	49.3%	50.7%	49.3%
1958	154,432	82,280	Williams, John J.*	72,152	Carvel, Elbert N.		10,128 R	53.3%	46.7%	53.3%	46.7%
1954	144,900	62,389	Warburton, Herbert B.	82,511	Frear, J. Allen Jr.*		20,122 D	43.1%	56.9%	43.1%	56.9%
1952	170,705	93,020	Williams, John J.*	77,685	du Pont Bayard, Alexis I.		15,335 R	54.5%	45.5%	54.5%	45.5%
1948	141,362	68,246	Buck, Clayton Douglass*	71,888	Frear, J. Allen Jr.	1,228	3,642 D	48.3%	50.9%	48.7%	51.3%
1946	113,513	62,603	Williams, John J.	50,910	Tunnell, James M.*		11,693 R	55.2%	44.8%	55.2%	44.8%

Note: An asterisk (*) denotes incumbent.

DELAWARE

SENATOR 2014

2010 Census Population	County	Total Vote	Republican (Wade)	Democratic (Coons)	Other	Rep.-Dem. Plurality	Percentage			
							Total Vote		Major Vote	
							Rep.	Dem.	Rep.	Dem.
162,310	KENT	39,426	19,527	19,218	681	309 R	49.5%	48.7%	50.4%	49.6%
538,479	NEW CASTLE	133,162	45,229	84,985	2,948	39,756 D	34.0%	63.8%	34.7%	65.3%
197,145	SUSSEX	61,450	34,067	26,452	931	7,615 R	55.4%	43.0%	56.3%	43.7%
897,934	TOTAL	234,038	98,823	130,655	4,560	31,832 D	42.2%	55.8%	43.1%	56.9%

DELAWARE

HOUSE OF REPRESENTATIVES

CD	Year	Total Vote	Republican		Democratic		Other Vote	Rep.-Dem. Plurality	Percentage			
			Vote	Candidate	Vote	Candidate			Total Vote		Major Vote	
									Rep.	Dem.	Rep.	Dem.
At Large	2014	231,617	85,146	IZZO, ROSE	137,251	CARNEY, JOHN C. JR.*	9,220	52,105 D	36.8%	59.3%	38.3%	61.7%
At Large	2012	388,059	129,757	KOVACH, THOMAS H.	249,933	CARNEY, JOHN C. JR.*	8,369	120,176 D	33.4%	64.4%	34.2%	65.8%
At Large	2010	305,636	125,442	URQUHART, GLEN	173,543	CARNEY, JOHN C. JR.	6,651	48,101 D	41.0%	56.8%	42.0%	58.0%
At Large	2008	385,457	235,437	CASTLE, MICHAEL N.*	146,434	HARTLEY-NAGLE, KAREN	3,586	89,003 R	61.1%	38.0%	61.7%	38.3%
At Large	2006	251,694	143,897	CASTLE, MICHAEL N.*	97,565	SPIVACK, DENNIS	10,232	46,332 R	57.2%	38.8%	59.6%	40.4%
At Large	2004	356,045	245,978	CASTLE, MICHAEL N.*	105,716	DONNELLY, PAUL	4,351	140,262 R	69.1%	29.7%	69.9%	30.1%
At Large	2002	228,405	164,605	CASTLE, MICHAEL N.*	61,011	MILLER, MICHEAL C.	2,789	103,594 R	72.1%	26.7%	73.0%	27.0%
At Large	2000	313,171	211,797	CASTLE, MICHAEL N.*	96,488	MILLER, MICHEAL C.	4,886	115,309 R	67.6%	30.8%	68.7%	31.3%
At Large	1998	180,527	119,811	CASTLE, MICHAEL N.*	57,446	WILLIAMS, DENNIS E.	3,270	62,365 R	66.4%	31.8%	67.6%	32.4%
At Large	1996	266,836	185,576	CASTLE, MICHAEL N.*	73,253	WILLIAMS, DENNIS E.	8,007	112,323 R	69.5%	27.5%	71.7%	28.3%
At Large	1994	195,037	137,960	CASTLE, MICHAEL N.*	51,803	DESANTIS, CAROL ANN	5,274	86,157 R	70.7%	26.6%	72.7%	27.3%
At Large	1992	276,157	153,037	CASTLE, MICHAEL N.	117,426	WOO, S. B.	5,694	35,611 R	55.4%	42.5%	56.6%	43.4%
At Large	1990	177,432	58,037	WILLIAMS, RALPH O.	116,274	CARPER, THOMAS R.*	3,121	58,237 D	32.7%	65.5%	33.3%	66.7%
At Large	1988	234,517	76,179	KRAPF, JAMES P.	158,338	CARPER, THOMAS R.*		82,159 D	32.5%	67.5%	32.5%	67.5%
At Large	1986	160,757	53,767	NEUBERGER, THOMAS S.	106,351	CARPER, THOMAS R.*	639	52,584 D	33.4%	66.2%	33.6%	66.4%
At Large	1984	243,014	100,650	DUPONT, ELISE	142,070	CARPER, THOMAS R.*	294	41,420 D	41.4%	58.5%	41.5%	58.5%
At Large	1982	188,064	87,153	EVANS, THOMAS B.*	98,533	CARPER, THOMAS R.	2,378	11,380 D	46.3%	52.4%	46.9%	53.1%
At Large	1980	216,629	133,842	EVANS, THOMAS B.*	81,227	MAXWELL, ROBERT L.	1,560	52,615 R	61.8%	37.5%	62.2%	37.8%
At Large	1978	157,566	91,689	EVANS, THOMAS B.*	64,863	HINDES, GARY E.	1,014	26,826 R	58.2%	41.2%	58.6%	41.4%
At Large	1976	214,799	110,677	EVANS, THOMAS B.	102,431	SHIPLEY, SAMUEL L.	1,691	8,246 R	51.5%	47.7%	51.9%	48.1%
At Large	1974	160,328	93,826	DU PONT, PIERRE S. IV*	63,490	SOLES, JAMES	3,012	30,336 R	58.5%	39.6%	59.6%	40.4%
At Large	1972	225,851	141,237	DU PONT, PIERRE S. IV*	83,230	HANDLOFF, NORMA	1,384	58,007 R	62.5%	36.9%	62.9%	37.1%
At Large	1970	160,313	86,125	DU PONT, PIERRE S. IV	71,429	DANIELLO, JOHN D.	2,759	14,696 R	53.7%	44.6%	54.7%	45.3%
At Large	1968	200,820	117,827	ROTH, WILLIAM V.*	82,993	MCDOWELL, HARRIS B. JR.		34,834 R	58.7%	41.3%	58.7%	41.3%
At Large	1966	163,093	90,961	ROTH, WILLIAM V.	72,132	MCDOWELL, HARRIS B. JR.*		18,829 R	55.8%	44.2%	55.8%	44.2%
At Large	1964	198,691	86,254	SNOWDEN, JAMES H.	112,361	MCDOWELL, HARRIS B. JR.*	76	26,107 R	43.4%	56.6%	43.4%	56.6%
At Large	1962	153,356	71,934	WILLIAMS, WILMER F.	81,166	MCDOWELL, HARRIS B. JR.*	256	9,232 D	46.9%	52.9%	47.0%	53.0%
At Large	1960	194,564	96,337	MCKINSTRY, JAMES T.	98,227	MCDOWELL, HARRIS B. JR.*		1,890 D	49.5%	50.5%	49.5%	50.5%
At Large	1958	152,896	76,099	HASKELL, HARRY G. JR.*	76,797	MCDOWELL, HARRIS B. JR.*		698 D	49.8%	50.2%	49.8%	50.2%
At Large	1956	176,182	91,538	HASKELL, HARRY G. JR.	84,644	MCDOWELL, HARRIS B. JR.*		6,894 R	52.0%	48.0%	52.0%	48.0%
At Large	1954	144,236	65,035	MARTIN, LILLIAN I.	79,201	MCDOWELL, HARRIS B. JR.		14,166 D	45.1%	54.9%	45.1%	54.9%
At Large	1952	170,015	88,285	WARBURTON, H. B.	81,730	SCANNELL, JOSEPH S.		6,555 R	51.9%	48.1%	51.9%	48.1%
At Large	1950	129,404	73,313	BOGGS, JAMES CALEB*	56,091	WINCHESTER, H. M.		17,222 R	56.7%	43.3%	56.7%	43.3%
At Large	1948	140,535	71,127	BOGGS, JAMES CALEB*	68,909	MCGUIGAN, J. CARL	499	2,218 R	50.6%	49.0%	50.8%	49.2%
At Large	1946	112,621	63,516	BOGGS, JAMES CALEB	49,105	TRAYNOR, PHILIP A.*		14,411 R	56.4%	43.6%	56.4%	43.6%

Note: An asterisk (*) denotes incumbent.

DELAWARE

GENERAL AND PRIMARY ELECTIONS

2014 GENERAL ELECTIONS: OTHER VOTES

Senate   Other vote was 4,560 Green (Andrew Richard Groff)

House   Other vote was:

At Large   4,801 Green (Bernard August), 4,419 Libertarian (Scott Gesty)

2014 PRIMARY ELECTIONS: SUPPLEMENTARY INFORMATION

Primary	September 9, 2014	**Registration** (as of September 1, 2014)	641,032	Democratic	305,191
				Republican	179,988
				Other	155,853

Primary Type   Closed—Only registered Democrats and Republicans could vote in their party's primary.

	REPUBLICAN PRIMARIES			DEMOCRATIC PRIMARIES	
Senator	Wade, Kevin	18,181	75.7%	Coons, Christopher A.*	Unopposed
	Smink, Carl	5,848	24.3%		
	TOTAL	24,029			
Congressional At Large	Izzo, Rose	Unopposed		Carney, John C. Jr.*	Unopposed

Note: An asterisk (*) denotes incumbent.

FLORIDA

Congressional districts first established for elections held in 2012

27 members

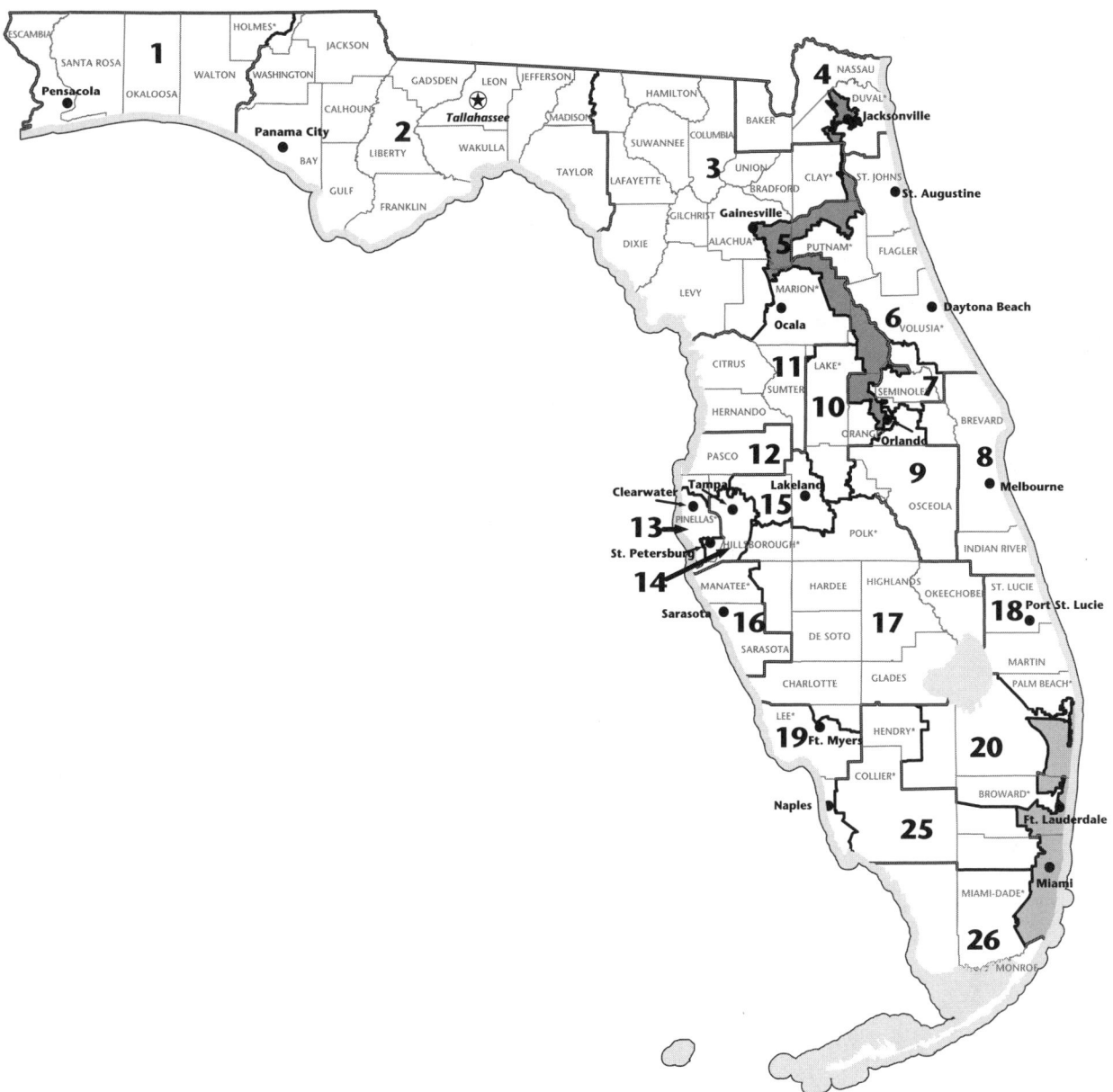

* Asterisk indicates a county whose boundaries include parts of two or more congressional districts.

FLORIDA

St.Petersburg, Tampa, Fort Myers Areas

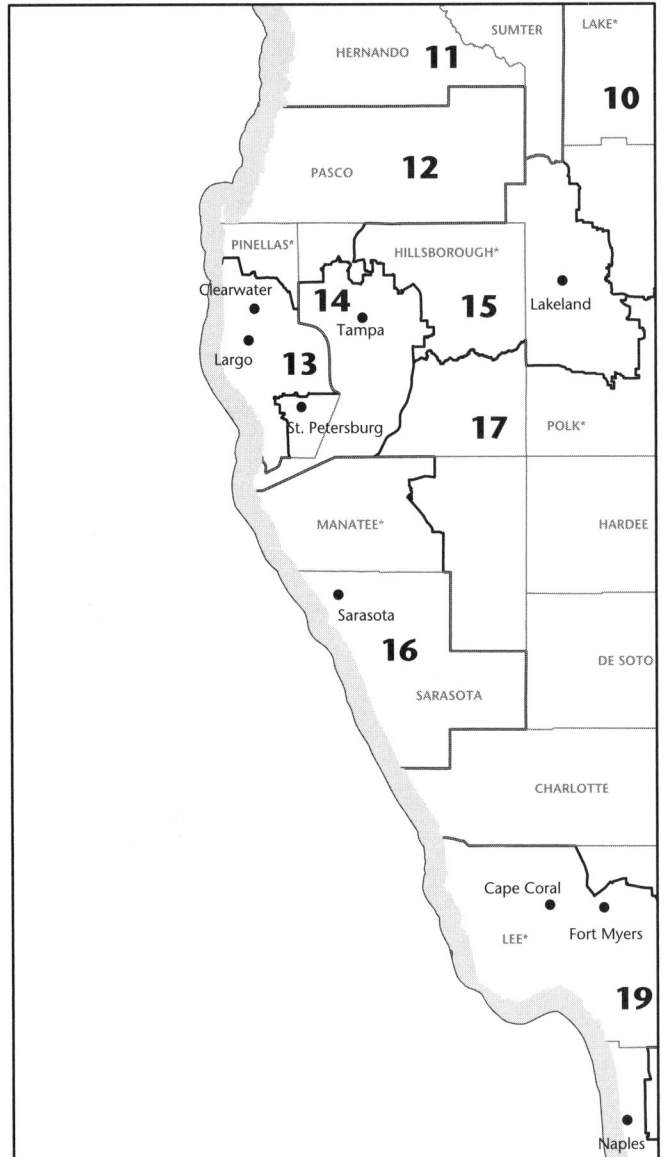

* Asterisk indicates a county whose boundaries include parts of two or more congressional districts.

FLORIDA

Greater Miami, Fort Lauderdale Areas

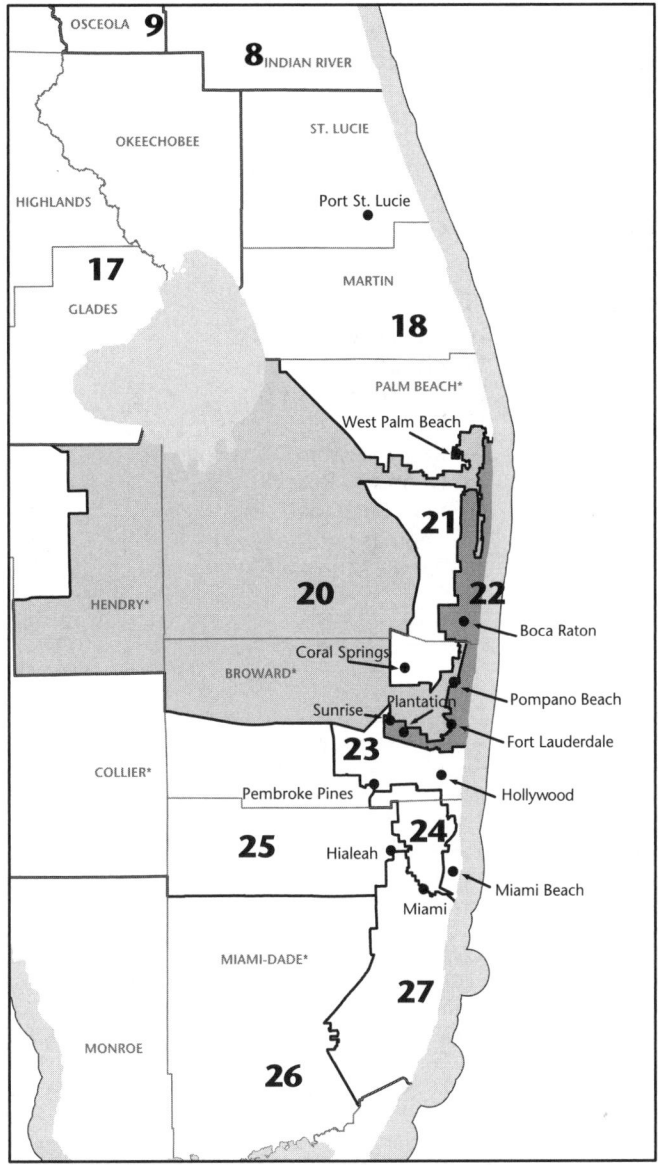

* Asterisk indicates a county whose boundaries include parts of two or more congressional districts.

FLORIDA

GOVERNOR

Rick Scott (R). Elected 2014 to a four-year term. Previously elected 2010.

SENATORS (1 Republican, 1 Democrat)

Bill Nelson (D). Reelected 2012 to a six-year term. Previously elected 2006, 2000.

Marco Rubio (R). Elected 2010 to a six-year term.

REPRESENTATIVES (17 Republicans, 10 Democrats)

1. Jeff Miller (R)
2. Gwen Graham (D)
3. Ted S. Yoho (R)
4. Ander Crenshaw (R)
5. Corrine Brown (D)
6. Ron DeSantis (R)
7. John L. Mica (R)
8. Bill Posey (R)
9. Alan Grayson (D)
10. Daniel Webster (R)
11. Richard B. Nugent (R)
12. Gus M. Bilirakis (R)
13. David W. Jolly (R)
14. Kathy Castor (D)
15. Dennis A. Ross (R)
16. Vern Buchanan (R)
17. Thomas J. Rooney (R)
18. Patrick Murphy (D)
19. Curt Clawson (R)
20. Alcee L. Hastings (D)
21. Theodore E. Deutch (D)
22. Lois Frankel (D)
23. Debbie Wasserman Schultz (D)
24. Frederica S. Wilson (D)
25. Mario Diaz-Balart (R)
26. Carlos Curbelo (R)
27. Ileana Ros-Lehtinen (R)

POSTWAR VOTE FOR PRESIDENT

| Year | Total Vote | Republican | | Democratic | | Other Vote | Rep.-Dem. Plurality | Total Vote | | Major Vote | |
		Vote	Candidate	Vote	Candidate			Rep.	Dem.	Rep.	Dem.
2012	8,474,179	4,163,447	Romney, W. Mitt	4,237,756	Obama, Barack H.*	72,976	74,309 D	49.1%	50.0%	49.6%	50.4%
2008	8,390,744	4,045,624	McCain, John S. III	4,282,074	Obama, Barack H.	63,046	236,450 D	48.2%	51.0%	48.6%	51.4%
2004	7,609,810	3,964,522	Bush, George W.*	3,583,544	Kerry, John F.	61,744	380,978 R	52.1%	47.1%	52.5%	47.5%
2000**	5,963,110	2,912,790	Bush, George W.	2,912,253	Gore, Albert Jr.	138,067	537 R	48.8%	48.8%	50.0%	50.0%
1996**	5,303,794	2,244,536	Dole, Robert "Bob"	2,546,870	Clinton, Bill*	512,388	302,334 D	42.3%	48.0%	46.8%	53.2%
1992**	5,314,392	2,173,310	Bush, George H.*	2,072,698	Clinton, Bill	1,068,384	100,612 R	40.9%	39.0%	51.2%	48.8%
1988	4,302,313	2,618,885	Bush, George H.	1,656,701	Dukakis, Michael S.	26,727	962,184 R	60.9%	38.5%	61.3%	38.7%
1984	4,180,051	2,730,350	Reagan, Ronald*	1,448,816	Mondale, Walter F.	885	1,281,534 R	65.3%	34.7%	65.3%	34.7%
1980**	3,686,930	2,046,951	Reagan, Ronald	1,419,475	Carter, Jimmy*	220,504	627,476 R	55.5%	38.5%	59.1%	40.9%
1976	3,150,631	1,469,531	Ford, Gerald R.*	1,636,000	Carter, Jimmy	45,100	166,469 D	46.6%	51.9%	47.3%	52.7%
1972	2,583,283	1,857,759	Nixon, Richard M.*	718,117	McGovern, George S.	7,407	1,139,642 R	71.9%	27.8%	72.1%	27.9%
1968**	2,187,805	886,804	Nixon, Richard M.	676,794	Humphrey, Hubert Horatio Jr.	624,207	210,010 R	40.5%	30.9%	56.7%	43.3%
1964	1,854,481	905,941	Goldwater, Barry M. Sr.	948,540	Johnson, Lyndon B.*		42,599 D	48.9%	51.1%	48.9%	51.1%
1960	1,544,176	795,476	Nixon, Richard M.	748,700	Kennedy, John F.		46,776 R	51.5%	48.5%	51.5%	48.5%
1956	1,125,762	643,849	Eisenhower, Dwight D.*	480,371	Stevenson, Adlai E. II	1,542	163,478 R	57.2%	42.7%	57.3%	42.7%
1952	989,337	544,036	Eisenhower, Dwight D.	444,950	Stevenson, Adlai E. II	351	99,086 R	55.0%	45.0%	55.0%	45.0%
1948**	577,643	194,280	Dewey, Thomas E.	281,988	Truman, Harry S.*	101,375	87,708 D	33.6%	48.8%	40.8%	59.2%

Note: An asterisk (*) denotes incumbent. **In past elections, the other vote included: 2000 - 97,488 Green (Ralph Nader); 1996 - 483,870 Reform (Ross Perot); 1992 - 1,053,067 Independent (Perot); 1980 - 189,692 Independent (John Anderson); 1968 - 624,207 American Independent (George Wallace); 1948 - 89,755 States' Rights (Strom Thurmond).

FLORIDA

POSTWAR VOTE FOR GOVERNOR

Year	Total Vote	Republican Vote	Republican Candidate	Democratic Vote	Democratic Candidate	Other Vote	Rep.-Dem. Plurality	Total Vote Rep.	Total Vote Dem.	Major Vote Rep.	Major Vote Dem.
2014	5,951,561	2,865,343	Scott, Rick*	2,801,198	Crist, Charlie	285,020	64,145 R	48.1%	47.1%	50.6%	49.4%
2010	5,359,735	2,619,335	Scott, Rick	2,557,785	Sink, Alex	182,615	61,550 R	48.9%	47.7%	50.6%	49.4%
2006	4,829,270	2,519,845	Crist, Charlie	2,178,289	Davis, Jim	131,136	341,556 R	52.2%	45.1%	53.6%	46.4%
2002	5,100,581	2,856,845	Bush, Jeb*	2,201,427	McBride, Bill	42,309	655,418 R	56.0%	43.2%	56.5%	43.5%
1998	3,964,441	2,191,105	Bush, Jeb	1,773,054	MacKay, Kenneth H. "Buddy"*	282	418,051 R	55.3%	44.7%	55.3%	44.7%
1994	4,206,659	2,071,068	Bush, Jeb	2,135,008	Chiles, Lawton*	583	63,940 D	49.2%	50.8%	49.2%	50.8%
1990	3,530,871	1,535,068	Martinez, Bob*	1,995,206	Chiles, Lawton	597	460,138 D	43.5%	56.5%	43.5%	56.5%
1986	3,386,171	1,847,525	Martinez, Bob	1,538,620	Pajcic, Steve	26	308,905 R	54.6%	45.4%	54.6%	45.4%
1982	2,688,566	949,013	Bafalis, L. A.	1,739,553	Graham, Bob*		790,540 D	35.3%	64.7%	35.3%	64.7%
1978	2,530,468	1,123,888	Eckerd, Jack M.	1,406,580	Graham, Bob		282,692 D	44.4%	55.6%	44.4%	55.6%
1974	1,828,392	709,438	Thomas, Jerry	1,118,954	Askew, Reubin*		409,516 D	38.8%	61.2%	38.8%	61.2%
1970	1,730,813	746,243	Kirk, Claude R. Jr.*	984,305	Askew, Reubin	265	238,062 D	43.1%	56.9%	43.1%	56.9%
1966	1,489,661	821,190	Kirk, Claude R. Jr.	668,233	High, Robert King	238	152,957 R	55.1%	44.9%	55.1%	44.9%
1964**	1,663,481	686,297	Holley, Charles R.	933,554	Burns, Haydon	43,630	247,257 D	41.3%	56.1%	42.4%	57.6%
1960	1,419,343	569,936	Petersen, George C.	849,407	Bryant, Farris		279,471 D	40.2%	59.8%	40.2%	59.8%
1956	1,014,733	266,980	Washburn, William A. Jr.	747,753	Collins, Leroy*		480,773 D	26.3%	73.7%	26.3%	73.7%
1954S	357,783	69,852	Watson, J. Tom	287,769	Collins, Leroy	162	217,917 D	19.5%	80.4%	19.5%	80.5%
1952	834,518	210,009	Swan, Harry S.	624,463	McCarty, Daniel T.	46	414,454 D	25.2%	74.8%	25.2%	74.8%
1948	457,638	76,153	Acker, Bert L.	381,459	Warren, Fuller	26	305,306 D	16.6%	83.4%	16.6%	83.4%

Note: An asterisk (*) denotes incumbent. **The 1964 election was for a two-year term to permit shifting the vote for governor to non-presidential years. The 1954 election was for a short term to fill a vacancy.

POSTWAR VOTE FOR SENATOR

Year	Total Vote	Republican Vote	Republican Candidate	Democratic Vote	Democratic Candidate	Other Vote	Rep.-Dem. Plurality	Total Vote Rep.	Total Vote Dem.	Major Vote Rep.	Major Vote Dem.
2012	8,189,946	3,458,267	Mack, Connie IV	4,523,451	Nelson, Bill*	208,228	1,065,184 D	42.2%	55.2%	43.3%	56.7%
2010**	5,411,106	2,645,743	Rubio, Marco	1,092,936	Meek, Kendrick B.	1,672,427	1,552,807 R	48.9%	20.2%	70.8%	29.2%
2006	4,793,534	1,826,127	Harris, Katherine	2,890,548	Nelson, C. W. "Bill"*	76,859	1,064,421 D	38.1%	60.3%	38.7%	61.3%
2004	7,429,894	3,672,864	Martinez, Mel	3,590,201	Castor, Betty	166,829	82,663 R	49.4%	48.3%	50.6%	49.4%
2000	5,856,731	2,705,348	McCollum, Bill	2,989,487	Nelson, C. W. "Bill"	161,896	284,139 D	46.2%	51.0%	47.5%	52.5%
1998	3,900,162	1,463,755	Crist, Charlie	2,436,407	Graham, Bob*		972,652 D	37.5%	62.5%	37.5%	62.5%
1994	4,106,176	2,894,726	Mack, Connie III*	1,210,412	Rodham, Hugh E.	1,038	1,684,314 R	70.5%	29.5%	70.5%	29.5%
1992	4,962,290	1,716,505	Grant, Bill	3,245,565	Graham, Bob*	220	1,529,060 D	34.6%	65.4%	34.6%	65.4%
1988	4,068,209	2,051,071	Mack, Connie III	2,016,553	MacKay, Buddy	585	34,518 R	50.4%	49.6%	50.4%	49.6%
1986	3,429,996	1,552,376	Hawkins, Paula*	1,877,543	Graham, Bob	77	325,167 D	45.3%	54.7%	45.3%	54.7%
1982	2,653,419	1,015,330	Poole, Van B.	1,637,667	Chiles, Lawton*	422	622,337 D	38.3%	61.7%	38.3%	61.7%
1980	3,528,028	1,822,460	Hawkins, Paula	1,705,409	Gunter, Bill	159	117,051 R	51.7%	48.3%	51.7%	48.3%
1976	2,857,534	1,057,886	Grady, John	1,799,518	Chiles, Lawton*	130	741,632 D	37.0%	63.0%	37.0%	63.0%
1974**	1,800,539	736,674	Eckerd, Jack M.	781,031	Stone, Richard	282,834	44,357 D	40.9%	43.4%	48.5%	51.5%
1970	1,675,378	772,817	Cramer, William C.	902,438	Chiles, Lawton	123	129,621 D	46.1%	53.9%	46.1%	53.9%
1968	2,024,136	1,131,499	Gurney, Edward J.	892,637	Collins, Leroy		238,862 R	55.9%	44.1%	55.9%	44.1%
1964	1,560,337	562,212	Kirk, Claude R. Jr.	997,585	Holland, Spessard L.*	540	435,373 D	36.0%	63.9%	36.0%	64.0%
1962	939,207	281,381	Rupert, Emerson H.	657,633	Smathers, George A.*	193	376,252 D	30.0%	70.0%	30.0%	70.0%
1958	542,069	155,956	Hyzer, Leland	386,113	Holland, Spessard L.*		230,157 D	28.8%	71.2%	28.8%	71.2%
1956	655,418			655,418	Smathers, George A.*		655,418 D		100.0%		100.0%
1952	617,800			616,665	Holland, Spessard L.*	1,135	616,665 D		99.8%		100.0%
1950	313,487	74,228	Booth, John P.	238,987	Smathers, George A.	272	164,759 D	23.7%	76.2%	23.7%	76.3%
1946	198,645	42,413	Schad, J. Harry	156,232	Holland, Spessard L.		113,819 D	21.4%	78.6%	21.4%	78.6%

Note: An asterisk (*) denotes incumbent. **In past elections, the other vote included: 2010 - 1,607,549 Independent (Charlie Crist), who placed second; 1974 - 282,659 American (John Grady). The Republican Party did not run a candidate in the 1952 and 1956 Senate elections.

FLORIDA
GOVERNOR 2014

2010 Census Population	Absentee County	Total Vote	Republican (Scott)	Democratic (Crist)	Other	Rep.-Dem. Plurality	Percentage Total Vote Rep.	Dem.	Major Vote Rep.	Dem.
247,336	ALACHUA	78,153	31,097	44,052	3,004	12,955 D	39.8%	56.4%	41.4%	58.6%
27,115	BAKER	8,444	5,956	2,100	388	3,856 R	70.5%	24.9%	73.9%	26.1%
168,852	BAY	57,050	40,956	12,990	3,104	27,966 R	71.8%	22.8%	75.9%	24.1%
28,520	BRADFORD	8,543	5,525	2,594	424	2,931 R	64.7%	30.4%	68.1%	31.9%
543,376	BREVARD	221,772	116,620	91,018	14,134	25,602 R	52.6%	41.0%	56.2%	43.8%
1,748,066	BROWARD	468,893	138,394	318,950	11,549	180,556 D	29.5%	68.0%	30.3%	69.7%
14,625	CALHOUN	4,187	2,676	1,202	309	1,474 R	63.9%	28.7%	69.0%	31.0%
159,978	CHARLOTTE	67,118	35,236	26,963	4,919	8,273 R	52.5%	40.2%	56.7%	43.3%
141,236	CITRUS	58,320	31,305	22,424	4,591	8,881 R	53.7%	38.4%	58.3%	41.7%
190,865	CLAY	68,139	49,330	15,948	2,861	33,382 R	72.4%	23.4%	75.6%	24.4%
321,520	COLLIER	113,620	75,337	35,281	3,002	40,056 R	66.3%	31.1%	68.1%	31.9%
67,531	COLUMBIA	18,374	11,604	5,812	958	5,792 R	63.2%	31.6%	66.6%	33.4%
34,862	DESOTO	7,512	3,681	3,294	537	387 R	49.0%	43.8%	52.8%	47.2%
16,422	DIXIE	5,360	3,345	1,657	358	1,688 R	62.4%	30.9%	66.9%	33.1%
864,263	DUVAL	270,033	146,407	112,026	11,600	34,381 R	54.2%	41.5%	56.7%	43.3%
297,619	ESCAMBIA	97,951	60,719	33,434	3,798	27,285 R	62.0%	34.1%	64.5%	35.5%
95,696	FLAGLER	37,858	19,996	15,994	1,868	4,002 R	52.8%	42.2%	55.6%	44.4%
11,549	FRANKLIN	4,306	2,505	1,633	168	872 R	58.2%	37.9%	60.5%	39.5%
46,389	GADSDEN	17,594	4,798	12,425	371	7,627 D	27.3%	70.6%	27.9%	72.1%
16,939	GILCHRIST	5,963	4,129	1,485	349	2,644 R	69.2%	24.9%	73.5%	26.5%
12,884	GLADES	3,020	1,815	1,042	163	773 R	60.1%	34.5%	63.5%	36.5%
15,863	GULF	5,169	3,476	1,432	261	2,044 R	67.2%	27.7%	70.8%	29.2%
14,799	HAMILTON	3,718	1,958	1,622	138	336 R	52.7%	43.6%	54.7%	45.3%
27,731	HARDEE	5,391	3,207	1,751	433	1,456 R	59.5%	32.5%	64.7%	35.3%
39,140	HENDRY	6,696	3,749	2,626	321	1,123 R	56.0%	39.2%	58.8%	41.2%
172,778	HERNANDO	63,976	30,635	28,622	4,719	2,013 R	47.9%	44.7%	51.7%	48.3%
98,786	HIGHLANDS	31,978	18,888	11,070	2,020	7,818 R	59.1%	34.6%	63.0%	37.0%
1,229,226	HILLSBOROUGH	371,968	170,127	180,168	21,673	10,041 D	45.7%	48.4%	48.6%	51.4%
19,927	HOLMES	5,713	4,301	1,052	360	3,249 R	75.3%	18.4%	80.3%	19.7%
138,028	INDIAN RIVER	52,502	30,719	19,248	2,535	11,471 R	58.5%	36.7%	61.5%	38.5%
49,746	JACKSON	15,106	8,745	5,711	650	3,034 R	57.9%	37.8%	60.5%	39.5%
14,761	JEFFERSON	6,305	2,840	3,291	174	451 D	45.0%	52.2%	46.3%	53.7%
8,870	LAFAYETTE	2,599	1,710	752	137	958 R	65.8%	28.9%	69.5%	30.5%
297,052	LAKE	112,515	63,009	42,811	6,695	20,198 R	56.0%	38.0%	59.5%	40.5%
618,754	LEE	210,301	121,962	79,454	8,885	42,508 R	58.0%	37.8%	60.6%	39.4%
275,487	LEON	108,134	38,289	66,739	3,106	28,450 D	35.4%	61.7%	36.5%	63.5%
40,801	LEVY	13,295	8,408	4,172	715	4,236 R	63.2%	31.4%	66.8%	33.2%
8,365	LIBERTY	2,672	1,562	901	209	661 R	58.5%	33.7%	63.4%	36.6%
19,224	MADISON	6,359	3,131	3,024	204	107 R	49.2%	47.6%	50.9%	49.1%
322,833	MANATEE	119,558	61,871	49,515	8,172	12,356 R	51.7%	41.4%	55.5%	44.5%
331,298	MARION	119,854	66,220	46,351	7,283	19,869 R	55.3%	38.7%	58.8%	41.2%
146,318	MARTIN	61,222	33,836	24,616	2,770	9,220 R	55.3%	40.2%	57.9%	42.1%
2,496,435	MIAMI-DADE	521,452	205,017	304,721	11,714	99,704 D	39.3%	58.4%	40.2%	59.8%
73,090	MONROE	28,505	13,096	14,305	1,104	1,209 D	45.9%	50.2%	47.8%	52.2%
73,314	NASSAU	30,693	22,105	7,229	1,359	14,876 R	72.0%	23.6%	75.4%	24.6%
180,822	OKALOOSA	61,163	46,162	12,129	2,872	34,033 R	75.5%	19.8%	79.2%	20.8%
39,996	OKEECHOBEE	8,894	5,016	3,311	567	1,705 R	56.4%	37.2%	60.2%	39.8%
1,145,956	ORANGE	307,664	128,014	164,570	15,080	36,556 D	41.6%	53.5%	43.8%	56.2%
268,685	OSCEOLA	68,469	29,431	35,457	3,581	6,026 D	43.0%	51.8%	45.4%	54.6%
1,320,134	PALM BEACH	419,468	160,413	246,730	12,325	86,317 D	38.2%	58.8%	39.4%	60.6%
464,697	PASCO	160,716	75,222	72,363	13,131	2,859 R	46.8%	45.0%	51.0%	49.0%
916,542	PINELLAS	351,854	144,271	183,930	23,653	39,659 D	41.0%	52.3%	44.0%	56.0%
602,095	POLK	191,957	98,224	79,481	14,252	18,743 R	51.2%	41.4%	55.3%	44.7%
74,364	PUTNAM	22,710	13,903	7,335	1,472	6,568 R	61.2%	32.3%	65.5%	34.5%
151,372	SANTA ROSA	53,316	39,933	10,815	2,568	29,118 R	74.9%	20.3%	78.7%	21.3%
379,448	SARASOTA	161,457	78,678	73,706	9,073	4,972 R	48.7%	45.7%	51.6%	48.4%
422,718	SEMINOLE	144,780	73,355	62,786	8,639	10,569 R	50.7%	43.4%	53.9%	46.1%
190,039	ST. JOHNS	86,499	58,150	24,921	3,428	33,229 R	67.2%	28.8%	70.0%	30.0%
277,789	ST. LUCIE	88,997	38,006	46,422	4,569	8,416 D	42.7%	52.2%	45.0%	55.0%

FLORIDA

GOVERNOR 2014

2010 Census Population	Absentee County	Total Vote	Republican (Scott)	Democratic (Crist)	Other	Rep.-Dem. Plurality	Total Vote Rep.	Total Vote Dem.	Major Vote Rep.	Major Vote Dem.
93,420	SUMTER	55,160	37,633	15,867	1,660	21,766 R	68.2%	28.8%	70.3%	29.7%
41,551	SUWANNEE	12,777	8,445	3,597	735	4,848 R	66.1%	28.2%	70.1%	29.9%
22,570	TAYLOR	6,676	4,266	2,115	295	2,151 R	63.9%	31.7%	66.9%	33.1%
15,535	UNION	5,010	2,780	1,905	325	875 R	55.5%	38.0%	59.3%	40.7%
494,593	VOLUSIA	175,873	85,749	79,315	10,809	6,434 R	48.8%	45.1%	51.9%	48.1%
30,776	WAKULLA	11,560	6,444	4,560	556	1,884 R	55.7%	39.4%	58.6%	41.4%
55,043	WALTON	20,414	15,168	4,347	899	10,821 R	74.3%	21.3%	77.7%	22.3%
24,896	WASHINGTON	8,256	5,788	2,029	439	3,759 R	70.1%	24.6%	74.0%	26.0%
18,801,310	TOTAL	5,951,561	2,865,343	2,801,198	285,020	64,145 R	48.1%	47.1%	50.6%	49.4%

FLORIDA

HOUSE OF REPRESENTATIVES

CD	Year	Total Vote	Rep. Vote	Republican Candidate	Dem. Vote	Democratic Candidate	Other Vote	Rep.-Dem. Plurality	Total Rep.	Total Dem.	Major Rep.	Major Dem.
1	2014	235,343	165,086	MILLER, JEFF*	54,976	BRYAN, JAMES "JIM"	15,281	110,110 R	70.1%	23.4%	75.0%	25.0%
1	2012	342,594	238,440	MILLER, JEFF*	92,961	BRYAN, JAMES "JIM"	11,193	145,479 R	69.6%	27.1%	71.9%	28.1%
2	2014	249,780	123,262	SOUTHERLAND, STEVE*	126,096	GRAHAM, GWEN	422	2,834 D	49.3%	50.5%	49.4%	50.6%
2	2012	333,718	175,856	SOUTHERLAND, STEVE*	157,634	LAWSON, AL	228	18,222 R	52.7%	47.2%	52.7%	47.3%
3	2014	228,809	148,691	YOHO, TED S.*	73,910	WHEELER, MARIHELEN HADDOCK	6,208	74,781 R	65.0%	32.3%	66.8%	33.2%
3	2012	315,669	204,331	YOHO, TED S.	102,468	GAILLOT, J.R.	8,870	101,863 R	64.7%	32.5%	66.6%	33.4%
4	2014	227,253	177,887	CRENSHAW, ANDER*			49,366	177,887 R	78.3%		100.0%	
4	2012	315,470	239,988	CRENSHAW, ANDER*			75,482	239,988 R	76.1%		100.0%	
5	2014	171,577	59,237	SCURRY-SMITH, GLOREATHA "GLO"	112,340	BROWN, CORRINE*		53,103 D	34.5%	65.5%	34.5%	65.5%
5	2012	269,153	70,700	KOLB, LEANNE	190,472	BROWN, CORRINE*	7,981	119,772 D	26.3%	70.8%	27.1%	72.9%
6	2014	265,817	166,254	DESANTIS, RON*	99,563	COX, DAVID		66,691 R	62.5%	37.5%	62.5%	37.5%
6	2012	342,451	195,962	DESANTIS, RON	146,489	BEAVEN, HEATHER		49,473 R	57.2%	42.8%	57.2%	42.8%
7	2014	227,164	144,474	MICA, JOHN L.*	73,011	NEUMAN, WESLEY RYAN "WES"	9,679	71,463 R	63.6%	32.1%	66.4%	33.6%
7	2012	316,010	185,518	MICA, JOHN L.*	130,479	KENDALL, JASON H.	13	55,039 R	58.7%	41.3%	58.7%	41.3%
8	2014	274,513	180,728	POSEY, BILL*	93,724	ROTHBLATT, GABRIEL	61	87,004 R	65.8%	34.1%	65.9%	34.1%
8	2012	348,909	205,432	POSEY, BILL*	130,870	ROBERTS, SHANNON	12,607	74,562 R	58.9%	37.5%	61.1%	38.9%
9	2014	173,878	74,963	PLATT, CAROL	93,850	GRAYSON, ALAN*	5,065	18,887 D	43.1%	54.0%	44.4%	55.6%
9	2012	263,747	98,856	LONG, TODD	164,891	GRAYSON, ALAN		66,035 D	37.5%	62.5%	37.5%	62.5%
10	2014	232,574	143,128	WEBSTER, DANIEL*	89,426	MCKENNA, MICHAEL PATRICK	20	53,702 R	61.5%	38.5%	61.5%	38.5%
10	2012	318,269	164,649	WEBSTER, DANIEL*	153,574	DEMINGS, VAL B.	46	11,075 R	51.7%	48.3%	51.7%	48.3%
11	2014	272,294	181,508	NUGENT, RICHARD B.*	90,786	KOLLER, DAVID C.		90,722 R	66.7%	33.3%	66.7%	33.3%
11	2012	338,663	218,360	NUGENT, RICHARD B.*	120,303	WERDER, H. DAVID		98,057 R	64.5%	35.5%	64.5%	35.5%
12	2014			BILIRAKIS, GUS M.*				R				
12	2012	330,167	209,604	BILIRAKIS, GUS M.*	108,770	SNOW, JONATHAN MICHAEL	11,793	100,834 R	63.5%	32.9%	65.8%	34.2%
13	2014	223,576	168,172	JOLLY, DAVID W.*			55,404	168,172 R	75.2%		100.0%	
13	2012	329,347	189,605	YOUNG, C.W. BILL*	139,742	EHRLICH, JESSICA		49,863 R	57.6%	42.4%	57.6%	42.4%
14	2014					CASTOR, KATHY*		D				
14	2012	280,601	83,480	OTERO, EVELIO "EJ"	197,121	CASTOR, KATHY*		113,641 D	29.8%	70.2%	29.8%	70.2%
15	2014	213,582	128,750	ROSS, DENNIS A.*	84,832	COHN, ALAN MICHAEL		43,918 R	60.3%	39.7%	60.3%	39.7%
15	2012			ROSS, DENNIS A.				R				
16	2014	274,829	169,126	BUCHANAN, VERN*	105,483	LAWRENCE, HENRY	220	63,643 R	61.5%	38.4%	61.6%	38.4%
16	2012	349,076	187,147	BUCHANAN, VERN*	161,929	FITZGERALD, KEITH		25,218 R	53.6%	46.4%	53.6%	46.4%
17	2014	223,756	141,493	ROONEY, THOMAS J.*	82,263	BRONSON, WILLIAM		59,230 R	63.2%	36.8%	63.2%	36.8%
17	2012	282,271	165,488	ROONEY, THOMAS J.*	116,766	BRONSON, WILLIAM	17	48,722 R	58.6%	41.4%	58.6%	41.4%
18	2014	253,374	101,896	DOMINO, CARL J.	151,478	MURPHY, PATRICK*		49,582 D	40.2%	59.8%	40.2%	59.8%
18	2012	330,665	164,353	WEST, ALLEN*	166,257	MURPHY, PATRICK	55	1,904 D	49.7%	50.3%	49.7%	50.3%

FLORIDA

HOUSE OF REPRESENTATIVES

| | | | Republican | | Democratic | | | | Percentage | | | |
| | | | | | | | Other Vote | Rep.-Dem. Plurality | Total Vote | | Major Vote | |
CD	Year	Total Vote	Vote	Candidate	Vote	Candidate			Rep.	Dem.	Rep.	Dem.
19	2014	246,861	159,354	CLAWSON, CURT*	80,824	FREEMAN, APRIL	6,683	78,530 R	64.6%	32.7%	66.3%	33.7%
19	2012	306,216	189,833	RADEL, TREY	109,746	ROACH, JIM	6,637	80,087 R	62.0%	35.8%	63.4%	36.6%
20	2014	157,466	28,968	BONNER, JAY	128,498	HASTINGS, ALCEE L.*		99,530 D	18.4%	81.6%	18.4%	81.6%
20	2012	244,285			214,727	HASTINGS, ALCEE L.*	29,558	214,727 D		87.9%		100.0%
21	2014	153,970			153,395	DEUTCH, Theodore E.*	575	153,395 D		99.6%		100.0%
21	2012	284,400			221,263	DEUTCH, Theodore E.*	63,137	221,263 D		77.8%		100.0%
22	2014	216,096	90,685	SPAIN, PAUL DOUGLAS	125,404	FRANKEL, LOIS*	7	34,719 D	42.0%	58.0%	42.0%	58.0%
22	2012	313,071	142,050	HASNER, ADAM	171,021	FRANKEL, LOIS		28,971 D	45.4%	54.6%	45.4%	54.6%
23	2014	164,788	61,519	KAUFMAN, JOSEPH "JOE"	103,269	WASSERMAN SCHULTZ, DEBBIE*		41,750 D	37.3%	62.7%	37.3%	62.7%
23	2012	275,430	98,096	HARRINGTON, KAREN	174,205	WASSERMAN SCHULTZ, DEBBIE*	3,129	76,109 D	35.6%	63.2%	36.0%	64.0%
24	2014	149,918	15,239	NEREE, DUFIRSTSON	129,192	WILSON, FREDERICA S.*	5,487	113,953 D	10.2%	86.2%	10.6%	89.4%
24	2012					WILSON, FREDERICA S.		D				
25	2014			DIAZ-BALART, MARIO*				R				
25	2012	200,229	151,466	DIAZ-BALART, MARIO*			48,763	151,466 R	75.6%		100.0%	
26	2014	161,337	83,031	CURBELO, CARLOS	78,306	GARCIA, JOE*		4,725 R	51.5%	48.5%	51.5%	48.5%
26	2012	252,957	108,820	RIVERA, DAVID*	135,694	GARCIA, JOE	8,443	26,874 D	43.0%	53.6%	44.5%	55.5%
27	2014			ROS-LEHTINEN, ILEANA*				R				
27	2012	230,171	138,488	ROS-LEHTINEN, ILEANA*	85,020	YEVANCEY, MANNY	6,663	53,468 R	60.2%	36.9%	62.0%	38.0%
TOTAL	2014	4,998,555	2,713,451		2,130,626		154,478	582,825 R	54.3%	42.6%	56.0%	44.0%
TOTAL	2012	7,513,539	3,826,522		3,392,402		294,615	434,120 R	50.9%	45.2%	53.0%	47.0%

Note: An asterisk (*) denotes incumbent. No vote in a district indicates that the winning candidate for completely unopposed and no vote was totalized.

FLORIDA

GENERAL AND PRIMARY ELECTIONS

2014 GENERAL ELECTIONS: OTHER VOTES

Governor　　Other vote was 223,356 Libertarian (Adrian Wyllie), 41,341 Unaffiliated (Glenn Burkett), 20,186 Unaffiliated (Farid Khavari), 137 scattered write-in

House　　Other vote was:

CD 1　　15,281 No Party Affiliation (Mark Wichern)

CD 2　　422 Write-in (Luther Lee)

CD 3　　6,208 No Party Affiliation (Howard "Term Limits" Lawson)

CD 4　　35,663 No Party Affiliation (Paula Moser-Bartlett), 13,690 No Party Affiliation (Gary L. Koniz), 13 Write-in (Deborah Katz Pueschel)

CD 7　　9,679 No Party Affiliation (Al Krulick)

CD 8　　61 Write-in (Christopher L. Duncan)

CD 9　　5,060 No Party Affiliation (Marko Milakovich), 5 Write-in (Leon Leo Ray)

CD 10　　20 Write-in (David B. Falstad)

CD 13　　55,318 Libertarian (Lucas Overby), 86 Write-in (Michael Stephen Levinson)

CD 16　　220 Write-in (Joe Newman)

CD 19　　6,671 Libertarian (Ray Netherwood), 12 Write-in (Timothy J. Rossano)

CD 21　　575 Write-in (W. Michael Trout)

CD 22　　7 Write-in (Raymond Schamis)

CD 24　　5,487 No Party Affiliation (Luis E. Fernandez)

FLORIDA

GENERAL AND PRIMARY ELECTIONS

2014 PRIMARY ELECTIONS: SUPPLEMENTARY INFORMATION

Primary	August 26, 2014	**Registration** (as of July 28, 2014)	11,807,507	Democratic	4,599,326
				Republican	4,144,186
				Independent Party of Florida	265,012
				Independence Party of Florida	49,511
				Libertarian	22,716
				Green	5,750
				Other Parties	5,270
				No Party Affiliation	2,715,736

Primary Type Closed—Only registered Democrats and Republicans could vote in their party's primary, with the exception of races where there were to be no other candidates (including write-ins) on the general election ballot. Then, the contested primary would be open to all voters.

	REPUBLICAN PRIMARIES			DEMOCRATIC PRIMARIES		
Governor	Scott, Rick*	831,887	87.6%	Crist, Charlie	623,001	74.4%
	Cuevas-Neunder, Elizabeth	100,496	10.6%	Rich, Nan	214,795	25.6%
	Adeshina, Yinka	16,761	1.8%			
	TOTAL	949,144		TOTAL	837,796	
Congressional District 1	Miller, Jeff*	44,784	75.3%	Bryan, James "Jim"	Unopposed	
	Krause, John E.	14,660	24.7%			
	TOTAL	59,444				
Congressional District 2	Southerland, Steve*	Unopposed		Graham, Gwen	Unopposed	
Congressional District 3	Yoho, Ted S.*	37,486	79.4%	Wheeler, Marihelen Haddock	Unopposed	
	Rush, Jacob Anthony "Jake"	9,739	20.6%			
	TOTAL	47,225				
Congressional District 4	Crenshaw, Ander*	38,613	70.9%			
	Shoaf, J. Ryman	15,817	29.1%			
	TOTAL	54,430				
Congressional District 5	Scurry-Smith, Gloreatha "Glo"	10,968	63.0%	Brown, Corrine*	Unopposed	
	Lowe, Thuy "Twee"	6,451	37.0%			
	TOTAL	17,419				
Congressional District 6	DeSantis, Ron*	Unopposed		Cox, David	Unopposed	
Congressional District 7	Mica, John L.*	32,084	72.1%	Neuman, Wesley Ryan "Wes"	Unopposed	
	Smith, David A.	8,316	18.7%			
	Oehlrich, Donald Paul "Don"	2,285	5.1%			
	Shirley, Kelly	1,786	4.0%			
	TOTAL	44,471				
Congressional District 8	Posey, Bill*	Unopposed		Rothblatt, Gabriel	Unopposed	

FLORIDA

GENERAL AND PRIMARY ELECTIONS

	REPUBLICAN PRIMARIES			DEMOCRATIC PRIMARIES		
Congressional District 9	Platt, Carol	11,542	54.6%	Grayson, Alan*	18,641	74.3%
	Bonilla, Jorge L. Jr.	6,293	29.8%	Ruiz, Nicholas	6,441	25.7%
	Vivaldi, Peter	3,301	15.6%			
	TOTAL	*21,136*		*TOTAL*	*25,082*	
Congressional District 10	Webster, Daniel*	Unopposed		McKenna, Michael Patrick	11,912	49.7%
				Modarres, Shayan	7,324	30.6%
				Ferree, William M. "Bill"	4,718	19.7%
				TOTAL	*23,954*	
Congressional District 11	Nugent, Richard B.*	Unopposed		Koller, David C.	Unopposed	
Congressional District 12	Bilirakis, Gus M.*	Unopposed				
Congressional District 13	Jolly, David W.*	Unopposed				
Congressional District 14				Castor, Kathy*	Unopposed	
Congressional District 15	Ross, Dennis A.*	Unopposed		Cohn, Alan Michael	Unopposed	
Congressional District 16	Buchanan, Vern*	Unopposed		Lawrence, Henry	Unopposed	
Congressional District 17	Rooney, Thomas J.*	Unopposed		Bronson, William	Unopposed	
Congressional District 18	Domino, Carl J.	15,805	38.4%	Murphy, Patrick*	Unopposed	
	Schlesinger, Alan	9,920	24.1%			
	Hires, Beverly Joy	5,760	14.0%			
	Lara, Brian	5,361	13.0%			
	Turnquest, Calvin Deon	2,757	6.7%			
	Wukoson, Nick Robert	1,594	3.9%			
	TOTAL	*41,197*				
Congressional District 19	Clawson, Curt*	Unopposed		Freeman, April	Unopposed	
Congressional District 20	Bonner, Jay	Unopposed		Hastings, Alcee L.*	29,236	79.2%
				Enright, Jean L.	5,256	14.2%
				McCline, Jameel	2,424	6.6%
				TOTAL	*36,916*	
Congressional District 21				Deutch, Theodore E.*	31,080	91.6%
				Morel, Emmanuel G.	2,845	8.4%
				TOTAL	*33,925*	
Congressional District 22	Spain, Paul Douglas	7,492	42.6%	Frankel, Lois*	Unopposed	
	McGee, Andrea Leigh	6,073	34.5%			
	Wagie, David William	4,017	22.8%			
	TOTAL	*17,582*				
Congressional District 23	Kaufman, Joseph "Joe"	6,299	62.6%	Wasserman Schultz, Debbie*	Unopposed	
	Garcia, Juan	3,764	37.4%			
	TOTAL	*10,063*				

FLORIDA

GENERAL AND PRIMARY ELECTIONS

	REPUBLICAN PRIMARIES			DEMOCRATIC PRIMARIES		
Congressional District 24	Neree, Dufirstson	Unopposed		Wilson, Frederica S.*	35,456	80.4%
				Etienne, Michael A.	8,628	19.6%
				TOTAL	*44,084*	
Congressional District 25	Diaz-Balart, Mario*	Unopposed				
Congressional District 26	Curbelo, Carlos	13,861	47.0%	Garcia, Joe*	Unopposed	
	MacDougall, Ed	7,455	25.3%			
	Martinez, Joe	5,136	17.4%			
	Rivera, David	2,209	7.5%			
	Palomares-Starbuck, Lorenzo "Larry"	824	2.8%			
	TOTAL	*29,485*				
Congressional District 27	Ros-Lehtinen, Ileana*	Unopposed				

Note: An asterisk (*) denotes incumbent.

GEORGIA

Congressional districts first established for elections held in 2012

14 members

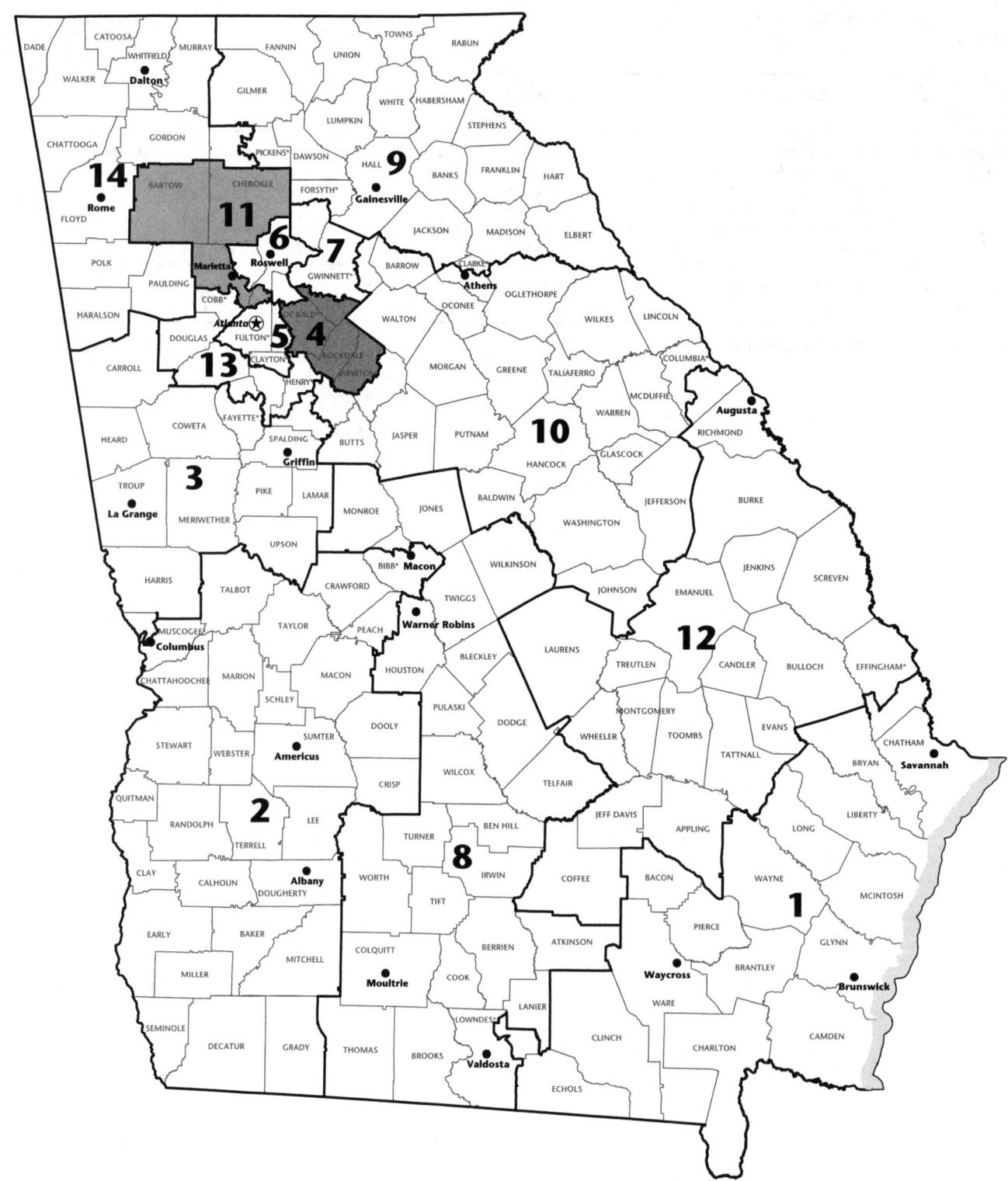

* Asterisk indicates a county whose boundaries include parts of two or more congressional districts.

GEORGIA
Atlanta Area

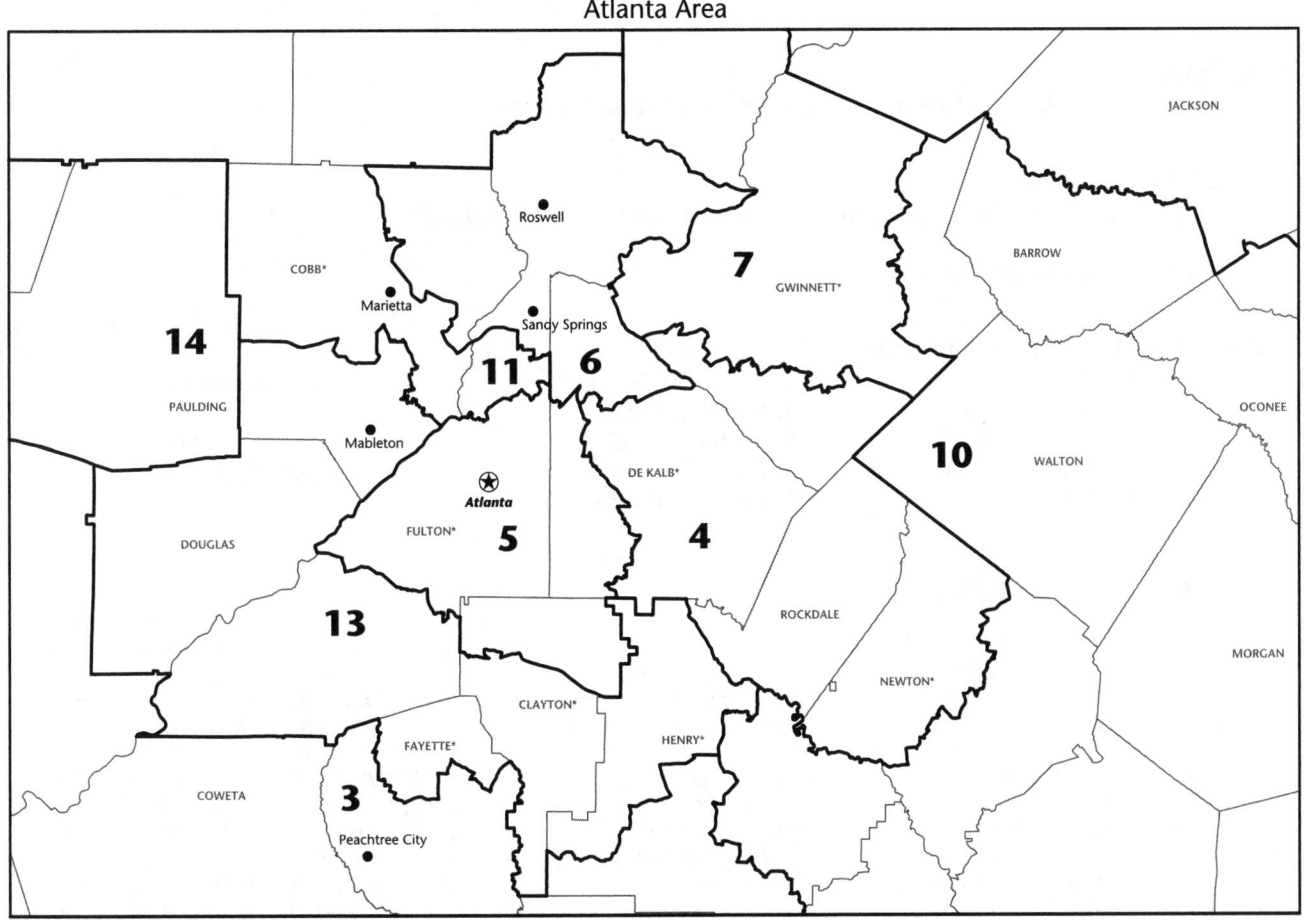

* Asterisk indicates a county whose boundaries include parts of two or more congressional districts.

GEORGIA

GOVERNOR

Nathan Deal (R). Reelected 2014 to a four-year term. Previously elected 2010.

SENATORS (2 Republicans)

Johnny Isakson (R). Reelected 2010 to a six-year term. Previously elected 2004.

David A. Perdue (R). Elected 2014 to a six-year term.

REPRESENTATIVES (10 Republicans, 4 Democrats)

1. Earl L. "Buddy" Carter (R)
2. Sanford D. Bishop Jr. (D)
3. Lynn A. Westmoreland (R)
4. Henry C. "Hank" Johnson Jr. (D)
5. John Lewis (D)
6. Tom Price (R)
7. Rob Woodall (R)
8. Austin Scott (R)
9. Doug Collins (R)
10. Jody B. Hice (R)
11. Barry Loudermilk (R)
12. Rick W. Allen (R)
13. David Scott (D)
14. Tom Graves (R)

POSTWAR VOTE FOR PRESIDENT

| Year | Total Vote | Republican | | Democratic | | Other Vote | Rep.-Dem. Plurality | Percentage | | | |
| | | Vote | Candidate | Vote | Candidate | | | Total Vote | | Major Vote | |
								Rep.	Dem.	Rep.	Dem.
2012	3,900,050	2,078,688	Romney, W. Mitt	1,773,827	Obama, Barack H.*	47,535	304,861 R	53.3%	45.5%	54.0%	46.0%
2008	3,924,486	2,048,759	McCain, John S. III	1,844,123	Obama, Barack H.	31,604	204,636 R	52.2%	47.0%	52.6%	47.4%
2004	3,301,875	1,914,254	Bush, George W.*	1,366,149	Kerry, John F.	21,472	548,105 R	58.0%	41.4%	58.4%	41.6%
2000**	2,596,645	1,419,720	Bush, George W.	1,116,230	Gore, Albert Jr.	60,695	303,490 R	54.7%	43.0%	56.0%	44.0%
1996**	2,299,071	1,080,843	Dole, Robert "Bob"	1,053,849	Clinton, Bill*	164,379	26,994 R	47.0%	45.8%	50.6%	49.4%
1992**	2,321,125	995,252	Bush, George H.*	1,008,966	Clinton, Bill	316,907	13,714 D	42.9%	43.5%	49.7%	50.3%
1988	1,812,672	1,081,331	Bush, George H.	717,792	Dukakis, Michael S.	13,549	363,539 R	59.7%	39.6%	60.1%	39.9%
1984	1,776,120	1,068,722	Reagan, Ronald*	706,628	Mondale, Walter F.	770	362,094 R	60.2%	39.8%	60.2%	39.8%
1980**	1,596,695	654,168	Reagan, Ronald	890,733	Carter, Jimmy*	51,794	236,565 D	41.0%	55.8%	42.3%	57.7%
1976	1,467,458	483,743	Ford, Gerald R.*	979,409	Carter, Jimmy	4,306	495,666 D	33.0%	66.7%	33.1%	66.9%
1972	1,174,772	881,496	Nixon, Richard M.*	289,529	McGovern, George S.	3,747	591,967 R	75.0%	24.6%	75.3%	24.7%
1968**	1,250,266	380,111	Nixon, Richard M.	334,440	Humphrey, Hubert Horatio Jr.	535,715	45,671 R#	30.4%	26.7%	53.2%	46.8%
1964	1,139,335	616,584	Goldwater, Barry M. Sr.	522,556	Johnson, Lyndon B.*	195	94,028 R	54.1%	45.9%	54.1%	45.9%
1960	733,349	274,472	Nixon, Richard M.	458,638	Kennedy, John F.	239	184,166 D	37.4%	62.5%	37.4%	62.6%
1956	669,655	222,778	Eisenhower, Dwight D.*	444,688	Stevenson, Adlai E. II	2,189	221,910 D	33.3%	66.4%	33.4%	66.6%
1952	655,785	198,961	Eisenhower, Dwight D.	456,823	Stevenson, Adlai E. II	1	257,862 D	30.3%	69.7%	30.3%	69.7%
1948**	418,844	76,691	Dewey, Thomas E.	254,646	Truman, Harry S.*	87,507	177,955 D	18.3%	60.8%	23.1%	76.9%

Note: An asterisk (*) denotes incumbent. A pound sign (#) indicates that the state was carried by a third part candidate or independent electoral slate. **In past elections, the other vote included: 2000 - 13,273 Green (Ralph Nader); 1996 - 146,337 Reform (Ross Perot); 1992 - 309,657 Independent (Perot); 1980 - 36,055 Independent (John Anderson); 1968 - 535,550 American Independent (George Wallace); 1948 - 85,135 States' Rights (Strom Thurmond, who placed second statewide). Wallace carried Georgia in 1968 with 42.8 percent of the vote.

GEORGIA

POSTWAR VOTE FOR GOVERNOR

Year	Total Vote	Republican Vote	Republican Candidate	Democratic Vote	Democratic Candidate	Other Vote	Rep.-Dem. Plurality	Total Vote Rep.	Total Vote Dem.	Major Vote Rep.	Major Vote Dem.
2014	2,550,648	1,345,237	Deal, Nathan*	1,144,794	Carter, Jason J.	60,617	200,443 R	52.7%	44.9%	54.0%	46.0%
2010	2,576,161	1,365,832	Deal, Nathan	1,107,011	Barnes, Roy E.	103,318	258,821 R	53.0%	43.0%	55.2%	44.8%
2006	2,122,258	1,229,724	Perdue, Sonny*	811,049	Taylor, Mark	81,485	418,675 R	57.9%	38.2%	60.3%	39.7%
2002	2,027,177	1,041,700	Perdue, Sonny	937,070	Barnes, Roy E.*	48,407	104,630 R	51.4%	46.2%	52.6%	47.4%
1998	1,792,808	790,201	Millner, Guy	941,076	Barnes, Roy E.	61,531	150,875 D	44.1%	52.5%	45.6%	54.4%
1994	1,545,328	756,371	Millner, Guy	788,926	Miller, Zell*	31	32,555 D	48.9%	51.1%	48.9%	51.1%
1990	1,449,682	645,625	Isakson, Johnny	766,662	Miller, Zell	37,395	121,037 D	44.5%	52.9%	45.7%	54.3%
1986	1,175,114	346,512	Davis, Guy	828,465	Harris, Joe Frank*	137	481,953 D	29.5%	70.5%	29.5%	70.5%
1982	1,169,043	434,496	Bell, Robert H.	734,092	Harris, Joe Frank	455	299,596 D	37.2%	62.8%	37.2%	62.8%
1978	662,862	128,139	Cook, Rodney M.	534,572	Busbee, George*	151	406,433 D	19.3%	80.6%	19.3%	80.7%
1974	936,438	289,113	Thompson, Ronnie	646,777	Busbee, George	548	357,664 D	30.9%	69.1%	30.9%	69.1%
1970	1,046,663	424,983	Suit, Hal	620,419	Carter, Jimmy	1,261	195,436 D	40.6%	59.3%	40.7%	59.3%
1966**	975,019	453,665	Callaway, Howard H.	450,626	Maddox, Lester	70,728	3,039 R	46.5%	46.2%	50.2%	49.8%
1962	311,691			311,524	Sanders, Carl E.	167	311,524 D		99.9%		100.0%
1958	168,497			168,414	Vandiver, S. Ernest	83	168,414 D		100.0%		100.0%
1954	331,966			331,899	Griffin, S. Marvin	67	331,899 D		100.0%		100.0%
1950	234,430			230,771	Talmadge, Herman E.*	3,659	230,771 D		98.4%		100.0%
1948S	363,764			354,712	Talmadge, Herman E.	9,052	354,712 D		97.5%		100.0%
1946	146,191			144,067	Talmadge, Eugene	2,124	144,067 D		98.5%		100.0%

Note: An asterisk (*) denotes incumbent. **In 1966 in the absence of a majority for any candidate, the State Legislature elected Democrat Lester Maddox to a four-year term. The 1948 election was for a short term to fill a vacancy. The Republican Party did not run a candidate in the 1946, 1948, 1950, 1954, 1958, and 1962 gubernatorial elections.

POSTWAR VOTE FOR SENATOR

Year	Total Vote	Republican Vote	Republican Candidate	Democratic Vote	Democratic Candidate	Other Vote	Rep.-Dem. Plurality	Total Vote Rep.	Total Vote Dem.	Major Vote Rep.	Major Vote Dem.
2014	2,567,805	1,358,088	Perdue, David	1,160,811	Nunn, Michelle	48,906	197,277 R	52.9%	45.2%	53.9%	46.1%
2010	2,555,258	1,489,904	Isakson, Johnny*	996,516	Thurmond, Michael	68,838	493,388 R	58.3%	39.0%	59.9%	40.1%
2008**	3,752,485	1,867,097	Chambliss, Saxby*	1,757,393	Martin, Jim	127,995	109,704 R	49.8%	46.8%	51.5%	48.5%
2008S	2,137,956	1,228,033	Chambliss, Saxby*	909,923	Martin, Jim		318,110 R	57.4%	42.6%	57.4%	42.6%
2004	3,220,981	1,864,202	Isakson, Johnny	1,287,690	Majette, Denise L.	69,089	576,512 R	57.9%	40.0%	59.1%	40.9%
2002	2,030,608	1,071,464	Chambliss, Saxby	932,156	Cleland, Max*	26,988	139,308 R	52.8%	45.9%	53.5%	46.5%
2000S	2,428,510	920,478	Mattingly, Mack F.	1,413,224	Miller, Zell*	94,808	492,746 D	37.9%	58.2%	39.4%	60.6%
1998	1,753,911	918,540	Coverdell, Paul*	791,904	Coles, Michael	43,467	126,636 R	52.4%	45.2%	53.7%	46.3%
1996	2,259,232	1,073,969	Millner, Guy	1,103,993	Cleland, Max	81,270	30,024 D	47.5%	48.9%	49.3%	50.7%
1992**	2,251,587	1,073,282	Coverdell, Paul	1,108,416	Fowler, Wyche Jr.*	69,889	35,134 D	47.7%	49.2%	49.2%	50.8%
1992S	1,253,991	635,114	Coverdell, Paul	618,877	Fowler, Wyche Jr.*		16,237 R	50.6%	49.4%	50.6%	49.4%
1990	1,033,517			1,033,439	Nunn, Sam*	78	1,033,439 D		100.0%		100.0%
1986	1,225,008	601,241	Mattingly, Mack F.*	623,707	Fowler, Wyche Jr.	60	22,466 D	49.1%	50.9%	49.1%	50.9%
1984	1,681,344	337,196	Hicks, John Michael	1,344,104	Nunn, Sam*	44	1,006,908 D	20.1%	79.9%	20.1%	79.9%
1980	1,580,340	803,686	Mattingly, Mack F.	776,143	Talmadge, Herman E.*	511	27,543 R	50.9%	49.1%	50.9%	49.1%
1978	645,164	108,808	Stokes, John W.	536,320	Nunn, Sam*	36	427,512 D	16.9%	83.1%	16.9%	83.1%
1974	874,555	246,866	Johnson, Jerry R.	627,376	Talmadge, Herman E.*	313	380,510 D	28.2%	71.7%	28.2%	71.8%
1972	1,178,708	542,331	Thompson, S. Fletcher	635,970	Nunn, Sam	407	93,639 D	46.0%	54.0%	46.0%	54.0%
1968	1,141,889	256,796	Patton, E. Earl	885,093	Talmadge, Herman E.*		628,297 D	22.5%	77.5%	22.5%	77.5%
1966	631,330			631,002	Russell, Richard Brevard Jr.*	328	631,002 D		99.9%		100.0%
1962	306,250			306,250	Talmadge, Herman E.*		306,250 D		100.0%		100.0%
1960	576,495			576,140	Russell, Richard Brevard Jr.*	355	576,140 D		99.9%		100.0%
1956	541,267			541,094	Talmadge, Herman E.	173	541,094 D		100.0%		100.0%
1954	333,936			333,917	Russell, Richard Brevard Jr.*	19	333,917 D		100.0%		100.0%
1950	261,293			261,290	George, Walter F.*	3	261,290 D		100.0%		100.0%
1948	362,504			362,104	Russell, Richard Brevard Jr.*	400	362,104 D		99.9%		100.0%

Note: An asterisk (*) denotes incumbent. **The 2000 election was for a short term to fill a vacancy. In 1992 and 2008, no candidate drew a majority of the general election vote required by state law, forcing runoff elections whose results are listed above for each year. In 2008 the November general election vote was 1,867,097 (49.8%) Republican (Saxby Chambliss); 1,757,393 (46.8%) Democratic (Jim Martin); and 127,995 (3.4%) Other. In 1992 the November general election vote was 1,073,282 (47.7%) Republican (Paul Coverdell); 1,108,416 (49.2%) Democratic (Wyche Fowler); and 69,889 (3.1%) Other. The 2008 runoff was held December 2; the 1992 runoff took place on November 24. The Republican Party did not run a candidate in the 1948, 1950, 1954, 1956, 1960, 1962, 1966, and 1990 Senate elections.

GEORGIA
GOVERNOR 2014

2010 Census Population	County	Total Vote	Republican (Deal)	Democratic (Carter)	Other	Rep.-Dem. Plurality	Percentage Total Vote Rep.	Dem.	Major Vote Rep.	Dem.
18,236	APPLING	4,408	3,192	1,124	92	2,068 R	72.4%	25.5%	74.0%	26.0%
8,375	ATKINSON	1,628	1,008	565	55	443 R	61.9%	34.7%	64.1%	35.9%
11,096	BACON	2,194	1,678	440	76	1,238 R	76.5%	20.1%	79.2%	20.8%
3,451	BAKER	989	491	481	17	10 R	49.6%	48.6%	50.5%	49.5%
45,720	BALDWIN	10,503	4,975	5,318	210	343 D	47.4%	50.6%	48.3%	51.7%
18,395	BANKS	4,334	3,583	625	126	2,958 R	82.7%	14.4%	85.1%	14.9%
69,367	BARROW	16,109	11,794	3,746	569	8,048 R	73.2%	23.3%	75.9%	24.1%
100,157	BARTOW	22,770	16,425	5,618	727	10,807 R	72.1%	24.7%	74.5%	25.5%
17,634	BEN HILL	3,453	1,901	1,465	87	436 R	55.1%	42.4%	56.5%	43.5%
19,286	BERRIEN	3,922	2,851	939	132	1,912 R	72.7%	23.9%	75.2%	24.8%
155,547	BIBB	42,571	17,447	24,552	572	7,105 D	41.0%	57.7%	41.5%	58.5%
13,063	BLECKLEY	3,245	2,256	909	80	1,347 R	69.5%	28.0%	71.3%	28.7%
18,411	BRANTLEY	2,977	2,306	567	104	1,739 R	77.5%	19.0%	80.3%	19.7%
16,243	BROOKS	4,642	2,448	2,114	80	334 R	52.7%	45.5%	53.7%	46.3%
30,233	BRYAN	7,950	5,515	2,218	217	3,297 R	69.4%	27.9%	71.3%	28.7%
70,217	BULLOCH	13,854	8,689	4,897	268	3,792 R	62.7%	35.3%	64.0%	36.0%
23,316	BURKE	5,869	2,832	2,943	94	111 D	48.3%	50.1%	49.0%	51.0%
23,655	BUTTS	6,106	3,993	1,970	143	2,023 R	65.4%	32.3%	67.0%	33.0%
6,694	CALHOUN	1,451	612	819	20	207 D	42.2%	56.4%	42.8%	57.2%
50,513	CAMDEN	9,741	6,400	3,063	278	3,337 R	65.7%	31.4%	67.6%	32.4%
10,998	CANDLER	2,200	1,449	714	37	735 R	65.9%	32.5%	67.0%	33.0%
110,527	CARROLL	26,066	17,420	7,897	749	9,523 R	66.8%	30.3%	68.8%	31.2%
63,942	CATOOSA	13,920	10,122	3,349	449	6,773 R	72.7%	24.1%	75.1%	24.9%
12,171	CHARLTON	2,011	1,287	658	66	629 R	64.0%	32.7%	66.2%	33.8%
265,128	CHATHAM	68,715	30,996	36,302	1,417	5,306 D	45.1%	52.8%	46.1%	53.9%
11,267	CHATTAHOOCHEE	693	310	365	18	55 D	44.7%	52.7%	45.9%	54.1%
26,015	CHATTOOGA	4,824	2,858	1,774	192	1,084 R	59.2%	36.8%	61.7%	38.3%
214,346	CHEROKEE	66,718	50,073	14,322	2,323	35,751 R	75.1%	21.5%	77.8%	22.2%
116,714	CLARKE	25,536	8,370	16,560	606	8,190 D	32.8%	64.8%	33.6%	66.4%
3,183	CLAY	930	387	538	5	151 D	41.6%	57.8%	41.8%	58.2%
259,424	CLAYTON	62,288	9,897	51,510	881	41,613 D	15.9%	82.7%	16.1%	83.9%
6,798	CLINCH	1,168	728	407	33	321 R	62.3%	34.8%	64.1%	35.9%
688,078	COBB	213,077	118,613	88,349	6,115	30,264 R	55.7%	41.5%	57.3%	42.7%
42,356	COFFEE	8,183	5,240	2,754	189	2,486 R	64.0%	33.7%	65.5%	34.5%
45,498	COLQUITT	7,904	5,577	2,117	210	3,460 R	70.6%	26.8%	72.5%	27.5%
124,053	COLUMBIA	40,180	28,388	10,405	1,387	17,983 R	70.7%	25.9%	73.2%	26.8%
17,212	COOK	3,539	2,221	1,234	84	987 R	62.8%	34.9%	64.3%	35.7%
127,317	COWETA	37,171	25,924	10,145	1,102	15,779 R	69.7%	27.3%	71.9%	28.1%
12,630	CRAWFORD	3,248	2,056	1,127	65	929 R	63.3%	34.7%	64.6%	35.4%
23,439	CRISP	4,983	3,057	1,831	95	1,226 R	61.3%	36.7%	62.5%	37.5%
16,633	DADE	3,436	2,450	859	127	1,591 R	71.3%	25.0%	74.0%	26.0%
22,330	DAWSON	7,284	6,020	1,064	200	4,956 R	82.6%	14.6%	85.0%	15.0%
27,842	DECATUR	6,054	3,289	2,668	97	621 R	54.3%	44.1%	55.2%	44.8%
691,893	DEKALB	210,639	44,676	162,274	3,689	117,598 D	21.2%	77.0%	21.6%	78.4%
21,796	DODGE	5,082	3,135	1,812	135	1,323 R	61.7%	35.7%	63.4%	36.6%
14,918	DOOLY	2,685	1,306	1,342	37	36 D	48.6%	50.0%	49.3%	50.7%
94,565	DOUGHERTY	23,474	7,502	15,635	337	8,133 D	32.0%	66.6%	32.4%	67.6%
132,403	DOUGLAS	37,501	17,397	19,248	856	1,851 D	46.4%	51.3%	47.5%	52.5%
11,008	EARLY	3,166	1,606	1,514	46	92 R	50.7%	47.8%	51.5%	48.5%
4,034	ECHOLS	623	478	134	11	344 R	76.7%	21.5%	78.1%	21.9%
52,250	EFFINGHAM	12,580	9,339	2,929	312	6,410 R	74.2%	23.3%	76.1%	23.9%
20,166	ELBERT	4,683	2,821	1,757	105	1,064 R	60.2%	37.5%	61.6%	38.4%
22,598	EMANUEL	4,967	3,160	1,706	101	1,454 R	63.6%	34.3%	64.9%	35.1%
11,000	EVANS	2,149	1,373	739	37	634 R	63.9%	34.4%	65.0%	35.0%
23,682	FANNIN	6,904	5,220	1,544	140	3,676 R	75.6%	22.4%	77.2%	22.8%
106,567	FAYETTE	42,080	25,989	15,047	1,044	10,942 R	61.8%	35.8%	63.3%	36.7%
96,317	FLOYD	20,822	13,335	6,742	745	6,593 R	64.0%	32.4%	66.4%	33.6%
175,511	FORSYTH	56,571	44,895	10,030	1,646	34,865 R	79.4%	17.7%	81.7%	18.3%
22,084	FRANKLIN	4,702	3,750	838	114	2,912 R	79.8%	17.8%	81.7%	18.3%
920,581	FULTON	265,671	92,489	168,010	5,172	75,521 D	34.8%	63.2%	35.5%	64.5%

GEORGIA
GOVERNOR 2014

2010 Census Population	County	Total Vote	Republican (Deal)	Democratic (Carter)	Other	Rep.-Dem. Plurality		Percentage Total Vote		Major Vote	
								Rep.	Dem.	Rep.	Dem.
28,292	GILMER	7,826	5,956	1,609	261	4,347	R	76.1%	20.6%	78.7%	21.3%
3,082	GLASCOCK	789	631	134	24	497	R	80.0%	17.0%	82.5%	17.5%
79,626	GLYNN	20,023	13,118	6,493	412	6,625	R	65.5%	32.4%	66.9%	33.1%
55,186	GORDON	10,325	7,456	2,500	369	4,956	R	72.2%	24.2%	74.9%	25.1%
25,011	GRADY	5,532	3,374	2,028	130	1,346	R	61.0%	36.7%	62.5%	37.5%
15,994	GREENE	6,523	4,184	2,241	98	1,943	R	64.1%	34.4%	65.1%	34.9%
805,321	GWINNETT	198,207	107,746	85,137	5,324	22,609	R	54.4%	43.0%	55.9%	44.1%
43,041	HABERSHAM	9,648	7,688	1,701	259	5,987	R	79.7%	17.6%	81.9%	18.1%
179,684	HALL	43,841	34,320	8,399	1,122	25,921	R	78.3%	19.2%	80.3%	19.7%
9,429	HANCOCK	2,398	498	1,869	31	1,371	D	20.8%	77.9%	21.0%	79.0%
28,780	HARALSON	6,813	5,127	1,434	252	3,693	R	75.3%	21.0%	78.1%	21.9%
32,024	HARRIS	10,242	6,986	3,009	247	3,977	R	68.2%	29.4%	69.9%	30.1%
25,213	HART	6,782	4,637	1,967	178	2,670	R	68.4%	29.0%	70.2%	29.8%
11,834	HEARD	2,481	1,773	640	68	1,133	R	71.5%	25.8%	73.5%	26.5%
203,922	HENRY	63,014	30,636	31,053	1,325	417	D	48.6%	49.3%	49.7%	50.3%
139,900	HOUSTON	37,347	22,168	14,335	844	7,833	R	59.4%	38.4%	60.7%	39.3%
9,538	IRWIN	2,321	1,548	713	60	835	R	66.7%	30.7%	68.5%	31.5%
60,485	JACKSON	15,991	12,560	2,935	496	9,625	R	78.5%	18.4%	81.1%	18.9%
13,900	JASPER	3,842	2,556	1,195	91	1,361	R	66.5%	31.1%	68.1%	31.9%
15,068	JEFF DAVIS	2,988	2,114	808	66	1,306	R	70.7%	27.0%	72.3%	27.7%
16,930	JEFFERSON	4,507	2,027	2,427	53	400	D	45.0%	53.8%	45.5%	54.5%
8,340	JENKINS	1,910	1,117	763	30	354	R	58.5%	39.9%	59.4%	40.6%
9,980	JOHNSON	2,292	1,487	761	44	726	R	64.9%	33.2%	66.1%	33.9%
28,669	JONES	8,067	4,829	3,101	137	1,728	R	59.9%	38.4%	60.9%	39.1%
18,317	LAMAR	4,966	3,144	1,715	107	1,429	R	63.3%	34.5%	64.7%	35.3%
10,078	LANIER	1,432	846	543	43	303	R	59.1%	37.9%	60.9%	39.1%
48,434	LAURENS	12,876	7,733	4,897	246	2,836	R	60.1%	38.0%	61.2%	38.8%
28,298	LEE	8,850	6,414	2,217	219	4,197	R	72.5%	25.1%	74.3%	25.7%
63,453	LIBERTY	8,894	3,331	5,395	168	2,064	D	37.5%	60.7%	38.2%	61.8%
7,996	LINCOLN	2,670	1,704	901	65	803	R	63.8%	33.7%	65.4%	34.6%
14,464	LONG	2,128	1,233	833	62	400	R	57.9%	39.1%	59.7%	40.3%
109,233	LOWNDES	21,268	11,801	9,080	387	2,721	R	55.5%	42.7%	56.5%	43.5%
29,966	LUMPKIN	7,657	5,755	1,642	260	4,113	R	75.2%	21.4%	77.8%	22.2%
14,740	MACON	3,008	997	1,970	41	973	D	33.1%	65.5%	33.6%	66.4%
28,120	MADISON	7,545	5,433	1,869	243	3,564	R	72.0%	24.8%	74.4%	25.6%
8,742	MARION	2,145	1,068	1,025	52	43	R	49.8%	47.8%	51.0%	49.0%
21,875	MCDUFFIE	5,976	3,557	2,269	150	1,288	R	59.5%	38.0%	61.1%	38.9%
14,333	MCINTOSH	3,837	2,085	1,661	91	424	R	54.3%	43.3%	55.7%	44.3%
21,992	MERIWETHER	6,063	3,141	2,802	120	339	R	51.8%	46.2%	52.9%	47.1%
6,125	MILLER	1,426	1,028	373	25	655	R	72.1%	26.2%	73.4%	26.6%
23,498	MITCHELL	4,937	2,474	2,366	97	108	R	50.1%	47.9%	51.1%	48.9%
26,424	MONROE	8,575	5,813	2,595	167	3,218	R	67.8%	30.3%	69.1%	30.9%
9,123	MONTGOMERY	2,285	1,594	627	64	967	R	69.8%	27.4%	71.8%	28.2%
17,868	MORGAN	6,310	4,302	1,877	131	2,425	R	68.2%	29.7%	69.6%	30.4%
39,628	MURRAY	6,051	4,168	1,639	244	2,529	R	68.9%	27.1%	71.8%	28.2%
189,885	MUSCOGEE	41,008	16,042	24,192	774	8,150	D	39.1%	59.0%	39.9%	60.1%
99,958	NEWTON	28,202	13,605	14,067	530	462	D	48.2%	49.9%	49.2%	50.8%
32,808	OCONEE	13,539	9,399	3,740	400	5,659	R	69.4%	27.6%	71.5%	28.5%
14,899	OGLETHORPE	4,088	2,669	1,301	118	1,368	R	65.3%	31.8%	67.2%	32.8%
142,324	PAULDING	36,258	24,514	10,635	1,109	13,879	R	67.6%	29.3%	69.7%	30.3%
27,695	PEACH	7,237	3,614	3,514	109	100	R	49.9%	48.6%	50.7%	49.3%
29,431	PICKENS	8,823	6,918	1,641	264	5,277	R	78.4%	18.6%	80.8%	19.2%
18,758	PIERCE	3,896	3,134	674	88	2,460	R	80.4%	17.3%	82.3%	17.7%
17,869	PIKE	5,598	4,347	1,073	178	3,274	R	77.7%	19.2%	80.2%	19.8%
41,475	POLK	7,990	5,322	2,387	281	2,935	R	66.6%	29.9%	69.0%	31.0%
12,010	PULASKI	2,350	1,492	812	46	680	R	63.5%	34.6%	64.8%	35.2%
21,218	PUTNAM	6,268	4,359	1,809	100	2,550	R	69.5%	28.9%	70.7%	29.3%
2,513	QUITMAN	593	269	309	15	40	D	45.4%	52.1%	46.5%	53.5%
16,276	RABUN	5,453	4,007	1,279	167	2,728	R	73.5%	23.5%	75.8%	24.2%

GEORGIA

GOVERNOR 2014

2010 Census Population	County	Total Vote	Republican (Deal)	Democratic (Carter)	Other	Rep.-Dem. Plurality		Percentage			
								Total Vote		Major Vote	
								Rep.	Dem.	Rep.	Dem.
7,719	RANDOLPH	2,118	993	1,110	15	117	D	46.9%	52.4%	47.2%	52.8%
200,549	RICHMOND	47,743	17,232	29,722	789	12,490	D	36.1%	62.3%	36.7%	63.3%
85,215	ROCKDALE	26,572	10,684	15,424	464	4,740	D	40.2%	58.0%	40.9%	59.1%
5,010	SCHLEY	1,260	894	343	23	551	R	71.0%	27.2%	72.3%	27.7%
14,593	SCREVEN	3,754	2,034	1,653	67	381	R	54.2%	44.0%	55.2%	44.8%
8,729	SEMINOLE	2,209	1,357	805	47	552	R	61.4%	36.4%	62.8%	37.2%
64,073	SPALDING	16,692	10,122	6,118	452	4,004	R	60.6%	36.7%	62.3%	37.7%
26,175	STEPHENS	5,136	3,832	1,151	153	2,681	R	74.6%	22.4%	76.9%	23.1%
6,058	STEWART	1,212	431	766	15	335	D	35.6%	63.2%	36.0%	64.0%
32,819	SUMTER	7,998	3,572	4,344	82	772	D	44.7%	54.3%	45.1%	54.9%
6,865	TALBOT	2,147	778	1,335	34	557	D	36.2%	62.2%	36.8%	63.2%
1,717	TALIAFERRO	557	217	332	8	115	D	39.0%	59.6%	39.5%	60.5%
25,520	TATTNALL	4,220	2,934	1,205	81	1,729	R	69.5%	28.6%	70.9%	29.1%
8,906	TAYLOR	2,188	1,184	961	43	223	R	54.1%	43.9%	55.2%	44.8%
16,500	TELFAIR	2,701	1,453	1,191	57	262	R	53.8%	44.1%	55.0%	45.0%
9,315	TERRELL	3,248	1,428	1,773	47	345	D	44.0%	54.6%	44.6%	55.4%
44,720	THOMAS	10,927	6,389	4,342	196	2,047	R	58.5%	39.7%	59.5%	40.5%
40,118	TIFT	8,484	5,593	2,691	200	2,902	R	65.9%	31.7%	67.5%	32.5%
27,223	TOOMBS	5,535	3,840	1,584	111	2,256	R	69.4%	28.6%	70.8%	29.2%
10,471	TOWNS	4,264	3,152	1,031	81	2,121	R	73.9%	24.2%	75.4%	24.6%
6,885	TREUTLEN	1,506	907	572	27	335	R	60.2%	38.0%	61.3%	38.7%
67,044	TROUP	15,657	9,261	6,062	334	3,199	R	59.1%	38.7%	60.4%	39.6%
8,930	TURNER	2,261	1,271	924	66	347	R	56.2%	40.9%	57.9%	42.1%
9,023	TWIGGS	2,883	1,250	1,580	53	330	D	43.4%	54.8%	44.2%	55.8%
21,356	UNION	7,743	5,915	1,622	206	4,293	R	76.4%	20.9%	78.5%	21.5%
27,153	UPSON	7,071	4,431	2,453	187	1,978	R	62.7%	34.7%	64.4%	35.6%
68,756	WALKER	12,339	8,664	3,257	418	5,407	R	70.2%	26.4%	72.7%	27.3%
83,768	WALTON	25,840	19,845	5,364	631	14,481	R	76.8%	20.8%	78.7%	21.3%
36,312	WARE	6,655	4,427	2,079	149	2,348	R	66.5%	31.2%	68.0%	32.0%
5,834	WARREN	1,485	670	791	24	121	D	45.1%	53.3%	45.9%	54.1%
21,187	WASHINGTON	6,049	2,881	3,102	66	221	D	47.6%	51.3%	48.2%	51.8%
30,099	WAYNE	6,133	4,232	1,727	174	2,505	R	69.0%	28.2%	71.0%	29.0%
2,799	WEBSTER	777	410	357	10	53	R	52.8%	45.9%	53.5%	46.5%
7,421	WHEELER	1,501	876	594	31	282	R	58.4%	39.6%	59.6%	40.4%
27,144	WHITE	7,665	5,985	1,417	263	4,568	R	78.1%	18.5%	80.9%	19.1%
102,599	WHITFIELD	15,794	10,564	4,511	719	6,053	R	66.9%	28.6%	70.1%	29.9%
9,255	WILCOX	1,870	1,218	610	42	608	R	65.1%	32.6%	66.6%	33.4%
10,593	WILKES	3,086	1,691	1,337	58	354	R	54.8%	43.3%	55.8%	44.2%
9,563	WILKINSON	3,141	1,544	1,552	45	8	D	49.2%	49.4%	49.9%	50.1%
21,679	WORTH	5,173	3,629	1,398	146	2,231	R	70.2%	27.0%	72.2%	27.8%
9,687,653	TOTAL	2,550,648	1,345,237	1,144,794	60,617	200,443	R	52.7%	44.9%	54.0%	46.0%

GEORGIA

SENATOR 2014

2010 Census Population	County	Total Vote	Republican (Perdue)	Democratic (Nunn)	Other	Rep.-Dem. Plurality		Percentage			
								Total Vote		Major Vote	
								Rep.	Dem.	Rep.	Dem.
18,236	APPLING	4,442	3,298	1,059	85	2,239	R	74.2%	23.8%	75.7%	24.3%
8,375	ATKINSON	1,633	1,073	503	57	570	R	65.7%	30.8%	68.1%	31.9%
11,096	BACON	2,224	1,769	395	60	1,374	R	79.5%	17.8%	81.7%	18.3%
3,451	BAKER	994	484	487	23	3	D	48.7%	49.0%	49.8%	50.2%
45,720	BALDWIN	10,635	4,998	5,453	184	455	D	47.0%	51.3%	47.8%	52.2%

GEORGIA
SENATOR 2014

2010 Census Population	County	Total Vote	Republican (Perdue)	Democratic (Nunn)	Other	Rep.-Dem. Plurality	Total Vote Rep.	Total Vote Dem.	Major Vote Rep.	Major Vote Dem.
18,395	BANKS	4,324	3,591	623	110	2,968 R	83.0%	14.4%	85.2%	14.8%
69,367	BARROW	16,213	11,988	3,746	479	8,242 R	73.9%	23.1%	76.2%	23.8%
100,157	BARTOW	22,884	16,842	5,437	605	11,405 R	73.6%	23.8%	75.6%	24.4%
17,634	BEN HILL	3,512	2,043	1,403	66	640 R	58.2%	39.9%	59.3%	40.7%
19,286	BERRIEN	3,954	2,967	874	113	2,093 R	75.0%	22.1%	77.2%	22.8%
155,547	BIBB	42,961	17,572	24,901	488	7,329 D	40.9%	58.0%	41.4%	58.6%
13,063	BLECKLEY	3,278	2,337	873	68	1,464 R	71.3%	26.6%	72.8%	27.2%
18,411	BRANTLEY	2,994	2,459	465	70	1,994 R	82.1%	15.5%	84.1%	15.9%
16,243	BROOKS	4,649	2,564	2,013	72	551 R	55.2%	43.3%	56.0%	44.0%
30,233	BRYAN	8,010	5,628	2,217	165	3,411 R	70.3%	27.7%	71.7%	28.3%
70,217	BULLOCH	13,930	8,623	5,066	241	3,557 R	61.9%	36.4%	63.0%	37.0%
23,316	BURKE	5,947	2,798	3,054	95	256 D	47.0%	51.4%	47.8%	52.2%
23,655	BUTTS	6,155	4,138	1,880	137	2,258 R	67.2%	30.5%	68.8%	31.2%
6,694	CALHOUN	1,462	617	827	18	210 D	42.2%	56.6%	42.7%	57.3%
50,513	CAMDEN	9,876	6,637	3,069	170	3,568 R	67.2%	31.1%	68.4%	31.6%
10,998	CANDLER	2,211	1,458	717	36	741 R	65.9%	32.4%	67.0%	33.0%
110,527	CARROLL	26,221	17,652	7,857	712	9,795 R	67.3%	30.0%	69.2%	30.8%
63,942	CATOOSA	13,949	10,695	2,856	398	7,839 R	76.7%	20.5%	78.9%	21.1%
12,171	CHARLTON	2,023	1,396	585	42	811 R	69.0%	28.9%	70.5%	29.5%
265,128	CHATHAM	69,609	30,565	37,935	1,109	7,370 D	43.9%	54.5%	44.6%	55.4%
11,267	CHATTAHOOCHEE	707	336	351	20	15 D	47.5%	49.6%	48.9%	51.1%
26,015	CHATTOOGA	4,800	3,138	1,466	196	1,672 R	65.4%	30.5%	68.2%	31.8%
214,346	CHEROKEE	67,015	51,111	14,116	1,788	36,995 R	76.3%	21.1%	78.4%	21.6%
116,714	CLARKE	25,702	8,380	16,787	535	8,407 D	32.6%	65.3%	33.3%	66.7%
3,183	CLAY	947	399	535	13	136 D	42.1%	56.5%	42.7%	57.3%
259,424	CLAYTON	62,943	9,352	52,876	715	43,524 D	14.9%	84.0%	15.0%	85.0%
6,798	CLINCH	1,176	814	340	22	474 R	69.2%	28.9%	70.5%	29.5%
688,078	COBB	213,523	118,147	90,659	4,717	27,488 R	55.3%	42.5%	56.6%	43.4%
42,356	COFFEE	8,268	5,417	2,658	193	2,759 R	65.5%	32.1%	67.1%	32.9%
45,498	COLQUITT	8,043	5,800	2,082	161	3,718 R	72.1%	25.9%	73.6%	26.4%
124,053	COLUMBIA	40,163	28,657	10,765	741	17,892 R	71.4%	26.8%	72.7%	27.3%
17,212	COOK	3,568	2,320	1,171	77	1,149 R	65.0%	32.8%	66.5%	33.5%
127,317	COWETA	37,396	26,182	10,268	946	15,914 R	70.0%	27.5%	71.8%	28.2%
12,630	CRAWFORD	3,287	2,112	1,119	56	993 R	64.3%	34.0%	65.4%	34.6%
23,439	CRISP	5,068	3,129	1,865	74	1,264 R	61.7%	36.8%	62.7%	37.3%
16,633	DADE	3,421	2,577	725	119	1,852 R	75.3%	21.2%	78.0%	22.0%
22,330	DAWSON	7,313	6,097	1,082	134	5,015 R	83.4%	14.8%	84.9%	15.1%
27,842	DECATUR	6,072	3,457	2,519	96	938 R	56.9%	41.5%	57.8%	42.2%
691,893	DEKALB	211,844	42,892	166,142	2,810	123,250 D	20.2%	78.4%	20.5%	79.5%
21,796	DODGE	5,197	3,400	1,657	140	1,743 R	65.4%	31.9%	67.2%	32.8%
14,918	DOOLY	2,717	1,323	1,368	26	45 D	48.7%	50.3%	49.2%	50.8%
94,565	DOUGHERTY	23,735	7,547	15,937	251	8,390 D	31.8%	67.1%	32.1%	67.9%
132,403	DOUGLAS	37,771	17,401	19,560	810	2,159 D	46.1%	51.8%	47.1%	52.9%
11,008	EARLY	3,188	1,648	1,510	30	138 R	51.7%	47.4%	52.2%	47.8%
4,034	ECHOLS	623	513	96	14	417 R	82.3%	15.4%	84.2%	15.8%
52,250	EFFINGHAM	12,646	9,340	3,032	274	6,308 R	73.9%	24.0%	75.5%	24.5%
20,166	ELBERT	4,737	2,975	1,698	64	1,277 R	62.8%	35.8%	63.7%	36.3%
22,598	EMANUEL	5,000	3,216	1,694	90	1,522 R	64.3%	33.9%	65.5%	34.5%
11,000	EVANS	2,165	1,369	758	38	611 R	63.2%	35.0%	64.4%	35.6%
23,682	FANNIN	6,933	5,240	1,542	151	3,698 R	75.6%	22.2%	77.3%	22.7%
106,567	FAYETTE	42,303	26,174	15,360	769	10,814 R	61.9%	36.3%	63.0%	37.0%
96,317	FLOYD	20,957	13,902	6,448	607	7,454 R	66.3%	30.8%	68.3%	31.7%
175,511	FORSYTH	56,815	45,163	10,353	1,299	34,810 R	79.5%	18.2%	81.4%	18.6%
22,084	FRANKLIN	4,733	3,785	839	109	2,946 R	80.0%	17.7%	81.9%	18.1%
920,581	FULTON	267,550	90,427	173,523	3,600	83,096 D	33.8%	64.9%	34.3%	65.7%
28,292	GILMER	7,889	6,104	1,592	193	4,512 R	77.4%	20.2%	79.3%	20.7%
3,082	GLASCOCK	801	645	135	21	510 R	80.5%	16.9%	82.7%	17.3%
79,626	GLYNN	20,273	13,511	6,519	243	6,992 R	66.6%	32.2%	67.5%	32.5%
55,186	GORDON	10,313	7,719	2,224	370	5,495 R	74.8%	21.6%	77.6%	22.4%
25,011	GRADY	5,559	3,567	1,876	116	1,691 R	64.2%	33.7%	65.5%	34.5%

GEORGIA

SENATOR 2014

2010 Census Population	County	Total Vote	Republican (Perdue)	Democratic (Nunn)	Other	Rep.-Dem. Plurality		Percentage			
								Total Vote		Major Vote	
								Rep.	Dem.	Rep.	Dem.
15,994	GREENE	6,541	4,110	2,350	81	1,760	R	62.8%	35.9%	63.6%	36.4%
805,321	GWINNETT	199,325	107,895	87,129	4,301	20,766	R	54.1%	43.7%	55.3%	44.7%
43,041	HABERSHAM	9,690	7,656	1,766	268	5,890	R	79.0%	18.2%	81.3%	18.7%
179,684	HALL	43,914	33,573	9,204	1,137	24,369	R	76.5%	21.0%	78.5%	21.5%
9,429	HANCOCK	2,435	489	1,928	18	1,439	D	20.1%	79.2%	20.2%	79.8%
28,780	HARALSON	6,826	5,256	1,318	252	3,938	R	77.0%	19.3%	80.0%	20.0%
32,024	HARRIS	10,357	7,306	2,878	173	4,428	R	70.5%	27.8%	71.7%	28.3%
25,213	HART	6,765	4,668	1,946	151	2,722	R	69.0%	28.8%	70.6%	29.4%
11,834	HEARD	2,489	1,802	617	70	1,185	R	72.4%	24.8%	74.5%	25.5%
203,922	HENRY	63,520	30,983	31,414	1,123	431	D	48.8%	49.5%	49.7%	50.3%
139,900	HOUSTON	37,829	22,875	14,340	614	8,535	R	60.5%	37.9%	61.5%	38.5%
9,538	IRWIN	2,336	1,604	689	43	915	R	68.7%	29.5%	70.0%	30.0%
60,485	JACKSON	16,028	12,730	2,902	396	9,828	R	79.4%	18.1%	81.4%	18.6%
13,900	JASPER	3,858	2,563	1,213	82	1,350	R	66.4%	31.4%	67.9%	32.1%
15,068	JEFF DAVIS	2,996	2,189	733	74	1,456	R	73.1%	24.5%	74.9%	25.1%
16,930	JEFFERSON	4,567	2,024	2,496	47	472	D	44.3%	54.7%	44.8%	55.2%
8,340	JENKINS	1,938	1,120	786	32	334	R	57.8%	40.6%	58.8%	41.2%
9,980	JOHNSON	2,313	1,539	742	32	797	R	66.5%	32.1%	67.5%	32.5%
28,669	JONES	8,148	4,982	3,018	148	1,964	R	61.1%	37.0%	62.3%	37.7%
18,317	LAMAR	5,010	3,197	1,700	113	1,497	R	63.8%	33.9%	65.3%	34.7%
10,078	LANIER	1,422	878	506	38	372	R	61.7%	35.6%	63.4%	36.6%
48,434	LAURENS	12,982	7,913	4,877	192	3,036	R	61.0%	37.6%	61.9%	38.1%
28,298	LEE	8,918	6,636	2,134	148	4,502	R	74.4%	23.9%	75.7%	24.3%
63,453	LIBERTY	9,021	3,259	5,621	141	2,362	D	36.1%	62.3%	36.7%	63.3%
7,996	LINCOLN	2,681	1,721	894	66	827	R	64.2%	33.3%	65.8%	34.2%
14,464	LONG	2,146	1,258	824	64	434	R	58.6%	38.4%	60.4%	39.6%
109,233	LOWNDES	21,456	12,513	8,673	270	3,840	R	58.3%	40.4%	59.1%	40.9%
29,966	LUMPKIN	7,699	5,824	1,642	233	4,182	R	75.6%	21.3%	78.0%	22.0%
14,740	MACON	3,044	1,017	1,983	44	966	D	33.4%	65.1%	33.9%	66.1%
28,120	MADISON	7,584	5,554	1,810	220	3,744	R	73.2%	23.9%	75.4%	24.6%
8,742	MARION	2,173	1,145	995	33	150	R	52.7%	45.8%	53.5%	46.5%
21,875	MCDUFFIE	6,066	3,612	2,349	105	1,263	R	59.5%	38.7%	60.6%	39.4%
14,333	MCINTOSH	3,863	2,092	1,685	86	407	R	54.2%	43.6%	55.4%	44.6%
21,992	MERIWETHER	6,100	3,189	2,802	109	387	R	52.3%	45.9%	53.2%	46.8%
6,125	MILLER	1,427	1,064	341	22	723	R	74.6%	23.9%	75.7%	24.3%
23,498	MITCHELL	4,999	2,555	2,369	75	186	R	51.1%	47.4%	51.9%	48.1%
26,424	MONROE	8,655	5,919	2,599	137	3,320	R	68.4%	30.0%	69.5%	30.5%
9,123	MONTGOMERY	2,295	1,612	636	47	976	R	70.2%	27.7%	71.7%	28.3%
17,868	MORGAN	6,348	4,346	1,888	114	2,458	R	68.5%	29.7%	69.7%	30.3%
39,628	MURRAY	6,051	4,621	1,231	199	3,390	R	76.4%	20.3%	79.0%	21.0%
189,885	MUSCOGEE	41,494	16,600	24,249	645	7,649	D	40.0%	58.4%	40.6%	59.4%
99,958	NEWTON	28,388	13,650	14,230	508	580	D	48.1%	50.1%	49.0%	51.0%
32,808	OCONEE	13,569	9,487	3,747	335	5,740	R	69.9%	27.6%	71.7%	28.3%
14,899	OGLETHORPE	4,125	2,725	1,299	101	1,426	R	66.1%	31.5%	67.7%	32.3%
142,324	PAULDING	36,494	25,068	10,494	932	14,574	R	68.7%	28.8%	70.5%	29.5%
27,695	PEACH	7,334	3,729	3,510	95	219	R	50.8%	47.9%	51.5%	48.5%
29,431	PICKENS	8,890	7,087	1,586	217	5,501	R	79.7%	17.8%	81.7%	18.3%
18,758	PIERCE	3,960	3,345	568	47	2,777	R	84.5%	14.3%	85.5%	14.5%
17,869	PIKE	5,635	4,458	1,036	141	3,422	R	79.1%	18.4%	81.1%	18.9%
41,475	POLK	8,065	5,540	2,197	328	3,343	R	68.7%	27.2%	71.6%	28.4%
12,010	PULASKI	2,386	1,548	800	38	748	R	64.9%	33.5%	65.9%	34.1%
21,218	PUTNAM	6,313	4,343	1,868	102	2,475	R	68.8%	29.6%	69.9%	30.1%
2,513	QUITMAN	618	302	299	17	3	R	48.9%	48.4%	50.2%	49.8%
16,276	RABUN	5,462	3,940	1,381	141	2,559	R	72.1%	25.3%	74.0%	26.0%
7,719	RANDOLPH	2,143	1,015	1,112	16	97	D	47.4%	51.9%	47.7%	52.3%
200,549	RICHMOND	48,294	16,934	30,709	651	13,775	D	35.1%	63.6%	35.5%	64.5%
85,215	ROCKDALE	26,734	10,633	15,723	378	5,090	D	39.8%	58.8%	40.3%	59.7%
5,010	SCHLEY	1,275	930	320	25	610	R	72.9%	25.1%	74.4%	25.6%
14,593	SCREVEN	3,787	2,024	1,700	63	324	R	53.4%	44.9%	54.4%	45.6%
8,729	SEMINOLE	2,237	1,388	804	45	584	R	62.0%	35.9%	63.3%	36.7%

GEORGIA

SENATOR 2014

2010 Census Population	County	Total Vote	Republican (Perdue)	Democratic (Nunn)	Other	Rep.-Dem. Plurality	Percentage			
							Total Vote		Major Vote	
							Rep.	Dem.	Rep.	Dem.
64,073	SPALDING	16,821	10,237	6,189	395	4,048 R	60.9%	36.8%	62.3%	37.7%
26,175	STEPHENS	5,194	3,915	1,140	139	2,775 R	75.4%	21.9%	77.4%	22.6%
6,058	STEWART	1,232	475	736	21	261 D	38.6%	59.7%	39.2%	60.8%
32,819	SUMTER	8,014	3,674	4,253	87	579 D	45.8%	53.1%	46.3%	53.7%
6,865	TALBOT	2,165	804	1,312	49	508 D	37.1%	60.6%	38.0%	62.0%
1,717	TALIAFERRO	574	213	348	13	135 D	37.1%	60.6%	38.0%	62.0%
25,520	TATTNALL	4,237	2,932	1,229	76	1,703 R	69.2%	29.0%	70.5%	29.5%
8,906	TAYLOR	2,208	1,260	917	31	343 R	57.1%	41.5%	57.9%	42.1%
16,500	TELFAIR	2,744	1,524	1,168	52	356 R	55.5%	42.6%	56.6%	43.4%
9,315	TERRELL	3,293	1,442	1,802	49	360 D	43.8%	54.7%	44.5%	55.5%
44,720	THOMAS	11,005	6,725	4,151	129	2,574 R	61.1%	37.7%	61.8%	38.2%
40,118	TIFT	8,574	5,856	2,587	131	3,269 R	68.3%	30.2%	69.4%	30.6%
27,223	TOOMBS	5,560	3,927	1,539	94	2,388 R	70.6%	27.7%	71.8%	28.2%
10,471	TOWNS	4,297	3,116	1,113	68	2,003 R	72.5%	25.9%	73.7%	26.3%
6,885	TREUTLEN	1,534	942	562	30	380 R	61.4%	36.6%	62.6%	37.4%
67,044	TROUP	15,769	9,366	6,093	310	3,273 R	59.4%	38.6%	60.6%	39.4%
8,930	TURNER	2,287	1,341	910	36	431 R	58.6%	39.8%	59.6%	40.4%
9,023	TWIGGS	2,923	1,251	1,614	58	363 D	42.8%	55.2%	43.7%	56.3%
21,356	UNION	7,777	5,875	1,722	180	4,153 R	75.5%	22.1%	77.3%	22.7%
27,153	UPSON	7,116	4,581	2,380	155	2,201 R	64.4%	33.4%	65.8%	34.2%
68,756	WALKER	12,378	9,331	2,662	385	6,669 R	75.4%	21.5%	77.8%	22.2%
83,768	WALTON	26,028	20,073	5,427	528	14,646 R	77.1%	20.9%	78.7%	21.3%
36,312	WARE	6,697	4,697	1,911	89	2,786 R	70.1%	28.5%	71.1%	28.9%
5,834	WARREN	1,502	655	824	23	169 D	43.6%	54.9%	44.3%	55.7%
21,187	WASHINGTON	6,109	2,843	3,183	83	340 D	46.5%	52.1%	47.2%	52.8%
30,099	WAYNE	6,206	4,375	1,676	155	2,699 R	70.5%	27.0%	72.3%	27.7%
2,799	WEBSTER	775	429	332	14	97 R	55.4%	42.8%	56.4%	43.6%
7,421	WHEELER	1,529	924	572	33	352 R	60.4%	37.4%	61.8%	38.2%
27,144	WHITE	7,682	5,948	1,512	222	4,436 R	77.4%	19.7%	79.7%	20.3%
102,599	WHITFIELD	15,866	11,556	3,817	493	7,739 R	72.8%	24.1%	75.2%	24.8%
9,255	WILCOX	1,909	1,291	595	23	696 R	67.6%	31.2%	68.5%	31.5%
10,593	WILKES	3,116	1,692	1,385	39	307 R	54.3%	44.4%	55.0%	45.0%
9,563	WILKINSON	3,195	1,580	1,570	45	10 R	49.5%	49.1%	50.2%	49.8%
21,679	WORTH	5,220	3,725	1,378	117	2,347 R	71.4%	26.4%	73.0%	27.0%
9,687,653	TOTAL	2,567,805	1,358,088	1,160,811	48,906	197,277 R	52.9%	45.2%	53.9%	46.1%

GEORGIA

HOUSE OF REPRESENTATIVES

CD	Year	Total Vote	Republican		Democratic		Other Vote	Rep.-Dem. Plurality	Percentage			
			Vote	Candidate	Vote	Candidate			Total Vote		Major Vote	
									Rep.	Dem.	Rep.	Dem.
1	2014	156,512	95,337	CARTER, EARL L. "BUDDY"	61,175	REESE, BRIAN CORWIN		34,162 R	60.9%	39.1%	60.9%	39.1%
1	2012	249,580	157,181	KINGSTON, JACK*	92,399	MESSINGER, LESLI		64,782 R	63.0%	37.0%	63.0%	37.0%
2	2014	162,900	66,537	DUKE, GREG	96,363	BISHOP, SANFORD D. Jr.*		29,826 D	40.8%	59.2%	40.8%	59.2%
2	2012	255,161	92,410	HOUSE, JOHN	162,751	BISHOP, SANFORD D. Jr.*		70,341 D	36.2%	63.8%	36.2%	63.8%
3	2014	156,277	156,277	WESTMORELAND, LYNN A.*				156,277 R	100.0%		100.0%	
3	2012	232,485	232,380	WESTMORELAND, LYNN A.*			105	232,380 R	100.0%		100.0%	
4	2014	161,320			161,211	JOHNSON, HENRY C. "HANK" Jr.*	109	161,211 D		99.9%		100.0%
4	2012	283,962	75,041	VAUGHN, J. CHRIS	208,861	JOHNSON, HENRY C. "HANK" Jr.*	60	133,820 D	26.4%	73.6%	26.4%	73.6%
5	2014	170,326			170,326	LEWIS, JOHN*		170,326 D		100.0%		100.0%
5	2012	277,689	43,335	STOPECK, HOWARD	234,330	LEWIS, JOHN*	24	190,995 D	15.6%	84.4%	15.6%	84.4%

GEORGIA

HOUSE OF REPRESENTATIVES

CD	Year	Total Vote	Republican		Democratic		Other Vote	Rep.-Dem. Plurality	Percentage			
									Total Vote		Major Vote	
			Vote	Candidate	Vote	Candidate			Rep.	Dem.	Rep.	Dem.
6	2014	210,504	139,018	PRICE, TOM*	71,486	MONTIGEL, ROBERT		67,532 R	66.0%	34.0%	66.0%	34.0%
6	2012	294,034	189,669	PRICE, TOM*	104,365	KAZANOW, JEFF		85,304 R	64.5%	35.5%	64.5%	35.5%
7	2014	173,669	113,557	WOODALL, ROB*	60,112	WIGHT, THOMAS D.		53,445 R	65.4%	34.6%	65.4%	34.6%
7	2012	252,066	156,689	WOODALL, ROB*	95,377	REILLY, STEVE		61,312 R	62.2%	37.8%	62.2%	37.8%
8	2014	130,057	129,938	SCOTT, AUSTIN*			119	129,938 R	99.9%		100.0%	
8	2012	197,789	197,789	SCOTT, AUSTIN*				197,789 R	100.0%		100.0%	
9	2014	181,047	146,059	COLLINS, DOUG*	34,988	VOGEL, DAVID D.		111,071 R	80.7%	19.3%	80.7%	19.3%
9	2012	252,153	192,101	COLLINS, DOUG	60,052	COOLEY, JODY		132,049 R	76.2%	23.8%	76.2%	23.8%
10	2014	196,480	130,703	HICE, JODY B.	65,777	DIOUS, IVORY KENNETH "KEN"		64,926 R	66.5%	33.5%	66.5%	33.5%
10	2012	211,466	211,065	BROUN, PAUL*			401	211,065 R	99.8%		100.0%	
11	2014	161,532	161,532	LOUDERMILK, BARRY				161,532 R	100.0%		100.0%	
11	2012	287,351	196,968	GINGREY, PHIL*	90,353	THOMPSON, PATRICK	30	106,615 R	68.5%	31.4%	68.6%	31.4%
12	2014	166,814	91,336	ALLEN, RICK W.	75,478	BARROW, JOHN*		15,858 R	54.8%	45.2%	54.8%	45.2%
12	2012	259,121	119,973	ANDERSON, LEE	139,148	BARROW, JOHN*		19,175 D	46.3%	53.7%	46.3%	53.7%
13	2014	159,445			159,445	SCOTT, DAVID*		159,445 D		100.0%		100.0%
13	2012	281,538	79,550	MALIK, S.	201,988	SCOTT, DAVID*		122,438 D	28.3%	71.7%	28.3%	71.7%
14	2014	118,782	118,782	GRAVES, TOM*				118,782 R	100.0%		100.0%	
14	2012	219,192	159,947	GRAVES, TOM*	59,245	GRANT, DANIEL "DANNY"		100,702 R	73.0%	27.0%	73.0%	27.0%
TOTAL	2014	2,305,665	1,349,076		956,361		228	392,715 R	58.5%	41.5%	58.5%	41.5%
TOTAL	2012	3,553,587	2,104,098		1,448,869		620	655,229 R	59.2%	40.8%	59.2%	40.8%

Note: An asterisk (*) denotes incumbent.

GEORGIA

GENERAL AND PRIMARY ELECTIONS

2014 GENERAL ELECTIONS: OTHER VOTES

Governor	Other vote was 60,185 Libertarian (Andrew T. Hunt), 420 Write-in (David C. Byrne), 10 Write-in (Matthew Jamison), 2 Write-in (Chancey Andrell Porter)
Senate	Other vote was 48,862 Libertarian (Amanda Swafford), 21 Write-in (Anantha Reddy Muscu), 14 Write-in (Mary H. Schroder), 9 Write-in (Brian Russell Brown)
House	Other vote was:
CD 4	109 Write-in (Raymond L. Davis)
CD 8	119 Write-in (Ronald L. Cain)

2014 PRIMARY ELECTIONS: SUPPLEMENTARY INFORMATION

Primary	May 20, 2014	Registration	5,048,825	No Party Registration
Primary Runoff	July 22, 2014	(as of May 20, 2014)		

Primary Type	Open—Any registered voter could participate in either the Democratic or Republican primary, although if voters voted in one party's primary they could not participate in a primary runoff of the other party. Voters who did not participate in the primary could vote in either party's runoff.

GEORGIA

GENERAL AND PRIMARY ELECTIONS

	REPUBLICAN PRIMARIES			DEMOCRATIC PRIMARIES		
Senator	Perdue, David	185,466	30.6%	Nunn, Michelle	246,369	75.0%
	Kingston, Jack	156,157	25.8%	Miles, Ollisteen "Steen"	39,418	12.0%
	Handel, Karen	132,944	22.0%	Robinson, Todd Anthony	31,822	9.7%
	Gingrey, Phil	60,735	10.0%	Radulovacki, Branko "Rad"	11,101	3.4%
	Broun, Paul	58,297	9.6%			
	Grayson, Derrick E.	6,045	1.0%			
	Gardner, Arthur A. "Art"	5,711	0.9%			
	TOTAL	*605,355*		*TOTAL*	*328,710*	
	PRIMARY RUNOFF					
	Perdue, David	245,951	50.9%			
	Kingston, Jack	237,448	49.1%			
	TOTAL	*483,399*				
Governor	Deal, Nathan*	430,170	72.1%	Carter, Jason J.	304,243	100.0%
	Pennington, David E.	99,548	16.7%			
	Barge, John D.	66,500	11.2%			
	TOTAL	*596,218*		*TOTAL*	*304,243*	
Congressional District 1	Carter, Earl L. "Buddy"	18,971	36.2%	Tavio, Amy L.	6,148	34.0%
	Johnson, Robert Eugene "Bob"	11,890	22.7%	Reese, Brian Corwin	6,122	33.8%
	McCallum, John A.	10,715	20.5%	Smith, Marc Anthony	5,836	32.2%
	Chapman, Jeff	6,918	13.2%			
	Carter, Darwin	2,819	5.4%			
	Martin, Earl Thomas	1,063	2.0%			
	TOTAL	*52,376*		*TOTAL*	*18,106*	
	PRIMARY RUNOFF			**PRIMARY RUNOFF**		
	Carter, Earl L. "Buddy"	22,871	53.8%	Reese, Brian Corwin	6,531	63.1%
	Johnson, Robert Eugene "Bob"	19,632	46.2%	Tavio, Amy L.	3,821	36.9%
	TOTAL	*42,503*		*TOTAL*	*10,352*	
Congressional District 2	Duke, Greg	16,468	69.4%	Bishop, Sanford D. Jr.*	39,941	100.0%
	Childs, Vivian L.	7,252	30.6%			
	TOTAL	*23,720*		*TOTAL*	*39,941*	
Congressional District 3	Westmoreland, Lynn A.*	37,106	69.5%			
	Flanegan, "Chip"	16,294	30.5%			
	TOTAL	*53,400*				
Congressional District 4				Johnson, Henry C. "Hank" Jr.*	26,514	54.8%
				Brown, Tom	21,909	45.2%
				TOTAL	*48,423*	
Congressional District 5				Lewis, John*	48,001	100.0%
				TOTAL	*48,001*	
Congressional District 6	Price, Tom*	44,074	100.0%	Montigel, Robert	11,493	100.0%
	TOTAL	*44,074*		*TOTAL*	*11,493*	
Congressional District 7	Woodall, Rob*	33,804	100.0%	Wight, Thomas D.	7,141	100.0%
	TOTAL	*33,804*		*TOTAL*	*7,141*	
Congressional District 8	Scott, Austin*	36,073	100.0%			
	TOTAL	*36,073*				
Congressional District 9	Collins, Doug*	49,951	80.2%	Vogel, David D.	6,415	100.0%
	Fontaine, Bernard "Bernie"	12,315	19.8%			
	TOTAL	*62,266*		*TOTAL*	*6,415*	

GEORGIA

GENERAL AND PRIMARY ELECTIONS

REPUBLICAN PRIMARIES			DEMOCRATIC PRIMARIES		
Congressional District 10	Hice, Jody B.	17,408	33.5%	Dious, Ivory Kenneth "Ken"	15,965	100.0%
	Collins, Mike A.	17,143	33.0%			
	Sheldon, Donna H.	7,972	15.3%			
	Gerrard, Gary	3,830	7.4%			
	Simpson, Stephen K.	2,423	4.7%			
	Swan, S. Mitchell	2,167	4.2%			
	Slowinski, Brian	1,027	2.0%			
	TOTAL	51,970		TOTAL	15,965	
	PRIMARY RUNOFF					
	Hice, Jody B.	26,975	54.3%			
	Collins, Mike A.	22,684	45.7%			
	TOTAL	49,659				
Congressional District 11	Loudermilk, Barry	20,862	36.6%			
	Barr, Bob	14,704	25.8%			
	Pridemore, Tricia	9,745	17.1%			
	Lindsey, Edward "Ed"	8,448	14.8%			
	Mrozinski, Larry	2,288	4.0%			
	Levene, Allan	962	1.7%			
	TOTAL	57,009				
	PRIMARY RUNOFF					
	Loudermilk, Barry	34,667	66.1%			
	Barr, Bob	17,807	33.9%			
	TOTAL	52,474				
Congressional District 12	Allen, Rick W.	25,093	54.0%	Barrow, John*	26,324	100.0%
	Yu, Eugene	7,677	16.5%			
	Dutton, Delvis William	6,644	14.3%			
	Stone, John	5,826	12.5%			
	Vann, Diane	1,237	2.7%	TOTAL	26,324	
	TOTAL	46,477				
Congressional District 13				Scott, David*	29,486	82.2%
				Owens, Michael C.	6,367	17.8%
				TOTAL	35,853	
Congressional District 14	Graves, Tom*	32,343	74.1%			
	Herron, Ken	11,324	25.9%			
	TOTAL	43,667				

Note: An asterisk (*) denotes incumbent.

HAWAII

Congressional districts first established for elections held in 2012

2 members

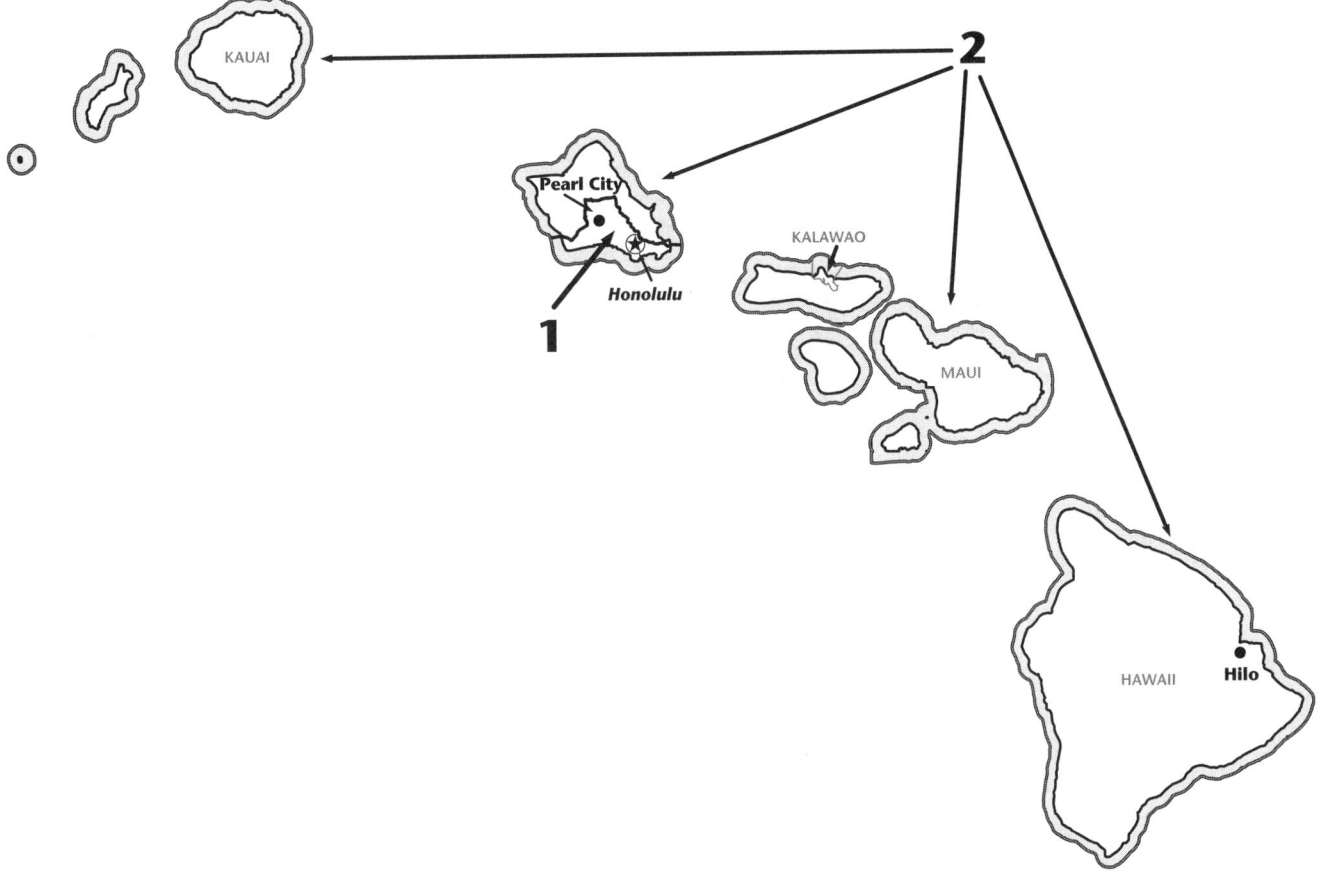

Hawaii includes more islands to the west of those that are illustrated on this map.

HAWAII

GOVERNOR
David Ige (D). Elected 2014 to a four-year term.

SENATORS (2 Democrats)
Mazie K. Hirono (D). Elected 2012 to a six-year term.

Brian Schatz (D). Elected November 4, 2014, in a special election following the death of Senator Daniel K. Inouye. Schatz was initially appointed December 27, 2012, to fill the vacancy.

REPRESENTATIVES (2 Democrats)
1. Mark Takai (D) 2. Tulsi Gabbard (D)

POSTWAR VOTE FOR PRESIDENT

| | | Republican | | Democratic | | | | Percentage | | | |
| | | | | | | | | Total Vote | | Major Vote | |
Year	Total Vote	Vote	Candidate	Vote	Candidate	Other Vote	Rep.-Dem. Plurality	Rep.	Dem.	Rep.	Dem.
2012	434,697	121,015	Romney, W. Mitt	306,658	Obama, Barack H.*	7,024	185,643 D	27.8%	70.5%	28.3%	71.7%
2008	453,568	120,566	McCain, John S. III	325,871	Obama, Barack H.	7,131	205,305 D	26.6%	71.8%	27.0%	73.0%
2004	429,013	194,191	Bush, George W.*	231,708	Kerry, John F.	3,114	37,517 D	45.3%	54.0%	45.6%	54.4%
2000**	367,951	137,845	Bush, George W.	205,286	Gore, Albert Jr.	24,820	67,441 D	37.5%	55.8%	40.2%	59.8%
1996**	360,120	113,943	Dole, Robert "Bob"	205,012	Clinton, Bill*	41,165	91,069 D	31.6%	56.9%	35.7%	64.3%
1992**	372,842	136,822	Bush, George H.*	179,310	Clinton, Bill	56,710	42,488 D	36.7%	48.1%	43.3%	56.7%
1988	354,461	158,625	Bush, George H.	192,364	Dukakis, Michael S.	3,472	33,739 D	44.8%	54.3%	45.2%	54.8%
1984	335,846	185,050	Reagan, Ronald*	147,154	Mondale, Walter F.	3,642	37,896 R	55.1%	43.8%	55.7%	44.3%
1980**	303,287	130,112	Reagan, Ronald	135,879	Carter, Jimmy*	37,296	5,767 D	42.9%	44.8%	48.9%	51.1%
1976	291,301	140,003	Ford, Gerald R.*	147,375	Carter, Jimmy	3,923	7,372 D	48.1%	50.6%	48.7%	51.3%
1972	270,274	168,865	Nixon, Richard M.*	101,409	McGovern, George S.		67,456 R	62.5%	37.5%	62.5%	37.5%
1968**	236,218	91,425	Nixon, Richard M.	141,324	Humphrey, Hubert Horatio Jr.	3,469	49,899 D	38.7%	59.8%	39.3%	60.7%
1964	207,271	44,022	Goldwater, Barry M. Sr.	163,249	Johnson, Lyndon B.*		119,227 D	21.2%	78.8%	21.2%	78.8%
1960	184,705	92,295	Nixon, Richard M.	92,410	Kennedy, John F.		115 D	50.0%	50.0%	50.0%	50.0%

Note: An asterisk (*) denotes incumbent. **In past elections, the other vote included: 2000 - 21,623 Green (Ralph Nader); 1996 - 27,358 Reform (Ross Perot); 1992 - 53,003 Independent (Perot); 1980 - 32,021 Independent (John Anderson); 1968 - 3,469 American Independent (George Wallace). Hawaii was formally admitted as a state in August 1959.

HAWAII

POSTWAR VOTE FOR GOVERNOR

Year	Total Vote	Republican Vote	Republican Candidate	Democratic Vote	Democratic Candidate	Other Vote	Rep.-Dem. Plurality	Total Vote Rep.	Total Vote Dem.	Major Vote Rep.	Major Vote Dem.
2014**	366,210	135,775	Aiona, Duke	181,106	Ige, David Yutaka	49,329	45,331 D	37.1%	49.5%	42.8%	57.2%
2010	382,563	157,311	Aiona, Duke	222,724	Abercrombie, Neil	2,528	65,413 D	41.1%	58.2%	41.4%	58.6%
2006	344,315	215,313	Lingle, Linda*	121,717	Iwase, Randy	7,285	93,596 R	62.5%	35.4%	63.9%	36.1%
2002	382,110	197,009	Lingle, Linda	179,647	Hirono, Mazie K.	5,454	17,362 R	51.6%	47.0%	52.3%	47.7%
1998	407,556	198,952	Lingle, Linda	204,206	Cayetano, Benjamin J.*	4,398	5,254 D	48.8%	50.1%	49.3%	50.7%
1994**	369,013	107,908	Saiki, Patricia	134,978	Cayetano, Benjamin J.	126,127	27,070 D	29.2%	36.6%	44.4%	55.6%
1990	340,132	131,310	Hemmings, Fred	203,491	Waihee, John*	5,331	72,181 D	38.6%	59.8%	39.2%	60.8%
1986	334,115	160,460	Anderson, D. G.	173,655	Waihee, John		13,195 D	48.0%	52.0%	48.0%	52.0%
1982**	311,853	81,507	Anderson, D. G.	141,043	Ariyoshi, George R.*	89,303	59,536 D	26.1%	45.2%	36.6%	63.4%
1978	281,587	124,610	Leopold, John	153,394	Ariyoshi, George R.*	3,583	28,784 D	44.3%	54.5%	44.8%	55.2%
1974	249,650	113,388	Crossley, Randolph	136,262	Ariyoshi, George R.		22,874 D	45.4%	54.6%	45.4%	54.6%
1970	239,061	101,249	King, Samuel P.	137,812	Burns, John A.*		36,563 D	42.4%	57.6%	42.4%	57.6%
1966	213,164	104,324	Crossley, Randolph	108,840	Burns, John A.*		4,516 D	48.9%	51.1%	48.9%	51.1%
1962	196,015	81,707	Quinn, Willam F.*	114,308	Burns, John A.		32,601 D	41.7%	58.3%	41.7%	58.3%
1959**	168,662	86,213	Quinn, Willam F.	82,074	Burns, John A.	375	4,139 R	51.1%	48.7%	51.2%	48.8%

Note: An asterisk (*) denotes incumbent. **In past elections, the other vote included: 2014 - 42,934 Mufi Hannemann (Independent); 1994 - 113,158 Best Party (Frank F. Fasi); 1982 - 89,303 Independent Democrat (Fasi). In both 1982 and 1994, Fasi finished second. The 1959 election was for a short term pending the regular vote in 1962.

POSTWAR VOTE FOR SENATOR

Year	Total Vote	Republican Vote	Republican Candidate	Democratic Vote	Democratic Candidate	Other Vote	Rep.-Dem. Plurality	Total Vote Rep.	Total Vote Dem.	Major Vote Rep.	Major Vote Dem.
2014	353,774	98,006	Cavasso, Cam	246,827	Schatz, Brian*	8,941	148,821 D	27.7%	69.8%	28.4%	71.6%
2012	430,483	160,994	Lingle, Linda	269,489	Hirono, Mazie K.		108,495 D	37.4%	62.6%	37.4%	62.6%
2010	370,583	79,939	Cavasso, Cam	277,228	Inouye, Daniel K.*	13,416	197,289 D	21.6%	74.8%	22.4%	77.6%
2006	342,842	126,097	Thielen, Cynthia	210,330	Akaka, Daniel K.*	6,415	84,233 D	36.8%	61.3%	37.5%	62.5%
2004	415,347	87,172	Cavasso, Cam	313,629	Inouye, Daniel K.*	14,546	226,457 D	21.0%	75.5%	21.7%	78.3%
2000	345,623	84,701	Carroll, John	251,215	Akaka, Daniel K.*	9,707	166,514 D	24.5%	72.7%	25.2%	74.8%
1998	398,124	70,964	Young, Crystal	315,252	Inouye, Daniel K.*	11,908	244,288 D	17.8%	79.2%	18.4%	81.6%
1994	356,902	86,320	Hustace, Maria M.	256,189	Akaka, Daniel K.*	14,393	169,869 D	24.2%	71.8%	25.2%	74.8%
1992**	363,662	97,928	Reed, Rick	208,266	Inouye, Daniel K.*	57,468	110,338 D	26.9%	57.3%	32.0%	68.0%
1990S	349,666	155,978	Saiki, Patricia	188,901	Akaka, Daniel K.	4,787	32,923 D	44.6%	54.0%	45.2%	54.8%
1988	323,876	66,987	Hustace, Maria M.	247,941	Matsunaga, Spark M.*	8,948	180,954 D	20.7%	76.6%	21.3%	78.7%
1986	328,797	86,910	Hutchinson, Frank	241,887	Inouye, Daniel K.*		154,977 D	26.4%	73.6%	26.4%	73.6%
1982	306,410	52,071	Brown, Clarence J.	245,386	Matsunaga, Spark M.*	8,953	193,315 D	17.0%	80.1%	17.5%	82.5%
1980	288,006	53,068	Brown, Cooper	224,485	Inouye, Daniel K.*	10,453	171,417 D	18.4%	77.9%	19.1%	80.9%
1976	302,092	122,724	Quinn, Willam F.	162,305	Matsunaga, Spark M.	17,063	39,581 D	40.6%	53.7%	43.1%	56.9%
1974**	250,221			207,454	Inouye, Daniel K.*	42,767	207,454 D		82.9%		100.0%
1970	240,760	124,163	Fong, Hiram L.*	116,597	Heftel, Cecil		7,566 R	51.6%	48.4%	51.6%	48.4%
1968	226,927	34,008	Thiessen, Wayne C.	189,248	Inouye, Daniel K.*	3,671	155,240 D	15.0%	83.4%	15.2%	84.8%
1964	208,814	110,747	Fong, Hiram L.*	96,789	Gill, Thomas P.	1,278	13,958 R	53.0%	46.4%	53.4%	46.6%
1962	196,361	60,067	Dillingham, Ben	136,294	Inouye, Daniel K.		76,227 D	30.6%	69.4%	30.6%	69.4%
1959S**	163,875	79,123	Tsukiyama, Wilfred C.	83,700	Long, Oren E.	1,052	4,577 D	48.3%	51.1%	48.6%	51.4%
1959S	164,808	87,161	Fong, Hiram L.	77,647	Fasi, Frank F.		9,514 R	52.9%	47.1%	52.9%	47.1%

Note: An asterisk (*) denotes incumbent. **In past elections, the other vote was: 1992 - 49,921 Green (Linda B. Martin); 1974 - 42,767 Peoples (James D. Kimmel), who finished second. The 1990 election was for a short term to fill a vacancy. The two 1959 elections were held to indeterminate terms and the Senate later determined by lot that Senator Long would serve a short term, Senator Fong a long term. The Republican Party did not run a Senate candidate in the 1974 election.

HAWAII

GOVERNOR 2014

2010 Census Population	County	Total Vote	Republican (Aiona)	Democratic (Ige)	Independent (Hannemann)	Other	Rep.-Dem. Plurality	Percentage Total Vote Rep.	Total Vote Dem.	Major Vote Rep.	Major Vote Dem.
185,079	HAWAII	49,812	15,387	25,674	7,308	1,443	10,287 D	30.9%	51.5%	37.5%	62.5%
953,207	HONOLULU	247,972	100,279	119,312	25,085	3,296	19,033 D	40.4%	48.1%	45.7%	54.3%
67,091	KAUAI	23,429	7,495	12,451	2,900	583	4,956 D	32.0%	53.1%	37.6%	62.4%
154,834	MAUI	44,997	12,614	23,669	7,641	1,073	11,055 D	28.0%	52.6%	34.8%	65.2%
1,360,211	TOTAL	366,210	135,775	181,106	42,934	6,395	45,331 D	37.1%	49.5%	42.8%	57.2%

HAWAII

SENATOR 2014

2010 Census Population	County	Total Vote	Republican (Cavasso)	Democratic (Schatz)	Other	Rep.-Dem. Plurality	Percentage Total Vote Rep.	Total Vote Dem.	Major Vote Rep.	Major Vote Dem.
185,079	HAWAII	48,483	11,093	35,509	1,881	24,416 D	22.9%	73.2%	23.8%	76.2%
953,207	HONOLULU	239,787	71,487	163,411	4,889	91,924 D	29.8%	68.1%	30.4%	69.6%
67,091	KAUAI	21,976	5,250	16,189	537	10,939 D	23.9%	73.7%	24.5%	75.5%
154,834	MAUI	43,467	10,165	31,668	1,634	21,503 D	23.4%	72.9%	24.3%	75.7%
	Overseas Vote	61	11	50		39 D	18.0%	82.0%	18.0%	82.0%
1,360,211	TOTAL	353,774	98,006	246,827	8,941	148,821 D	27.7%	69.8%	28.4%	71.6%

HAWAII

HOUSE OF REPRESENTATIVES

CD	Year	Total Vote	Republican Vote	Republican Candidate	Democratic Vote	Democratic Candidate	Other Vote	Rep.-Dem. Plurality	Percentage Total Vote Rep.	Total Vote Dem.	Major Vote Rep.	Major Vote Dem.
1	2014	179,844	86,454	DJOU, CHARLES	93,390	TAKAI, MARK		6,936 D	48.1%	51.9%	48.1%	51.9%
1	2012	213,329	96,824	DJOU, CHARLES	116,505	HANABUSA, COLLEEN*		19,681 D	45.4%	54.6%	45.4%	54.6%
2	2014	180,333	33,630	CROWLEY, KAWIKA	142,010	GABBARD, TULSI*	4,693	108,380 D	18.6%	78.7%	19.1%	80.9%
2	2012	209,210	40,707	CROWLEY, KAWIKA	168,503	GABBARD, TULSI		127,796 D	19.5%	80.5%	19.5%	80.5%
TOTAL	2014	360,177	120,084		235,400		4,693	115,316 D	33.3%	65.4%	33.8%	66.2%
TOTAL	2012	422,539	137,531		285,008			147,477 D	32.5%	67.5%	32.5%	67.5%

Note: An asterisk (*) denotes incumbent.

HAWAII

GENERAL AND PRIMARY ELECTIONS

2014 GENERAL ELECTIONS: OTHER VOTES

Governor   Other vote was 42,934 Independent (Mufi Hannemann), 6,395 Libertarian (Jeff Davis)

Senate   Other vote was 8,941 Libertarian (Michael Kokoski)

House   Other vote was:

CD 2   4,693 Libertarian (Joe Kent)

2014 PRIMARY ELECTIONS: SUPPLEMENTARY INFORMATION

Primary   August 9, 2014   **Registration**   697,033   No Party Registration
(as of August 9, 2014)

Primary Type   Open—Any registered voter could participate in the party primary of his or her choice.

	REPUBLICAN PRIMARIES			DEMOCRATIC PRIMARIES		
Governor	Aiona, Duke	41,832	97.2%	Ige, David Y.	157,050	67.4%
	Gregory, Stuart	640	1.5%	Abercrombie, Neil*	73,507	31.5%
	Collins, Charles "Trump"	580	1.3%	Tanabe, Van K.	2,622	1.1%
	TOTAL	*43,052*		*TOTAL*	*233,179*	
	Cavasso, Cam	25,874	72.3%	Schatz, Brian	115,445	49.4%
	Roco, John	4,425	12.4%	Hanabusa, Colleen	113,663	48.6%
	Friel, Harry J.	3,477	9.7%	Evans, Brian	4,842	2.1%
	Pirkowski, Eddie	2,033	5.7%			
	TOTAL	*35,809*		*TOTAL*	*233,950*	
Congressional District 1	Djou, Charles	20,802	96.4%	Takai, Mark	52,736	44.5%
	Levene, Allan	777	3.6%	Kim, Donna Mercado	33,678	28.4%
				Chang, Stanley	12,135	10.2%
				Anderson, Ikaika	7,937	6.7%
				Espero, Will	4,555	3.8%
				Manahan, Joey	4,495	3.8%
				Xian, Kathryn	3,039	2.6%
	TOTAL	*21,579*		*TOTAL*	*118,575*	
Congressional District 2	Crowley, Kawika	9,094	56.8%	Gabbard, Tulsi*	92,032	100.0%
	Capelouto, Marissa	6,926	43.2%			
	TOTAL	*16,020*		*TOTAL*	*92,032*	

Note: An asterisk (*) denotes incumbent.

IDAHO

Congressional districts first established for elections held in 2012

2 members

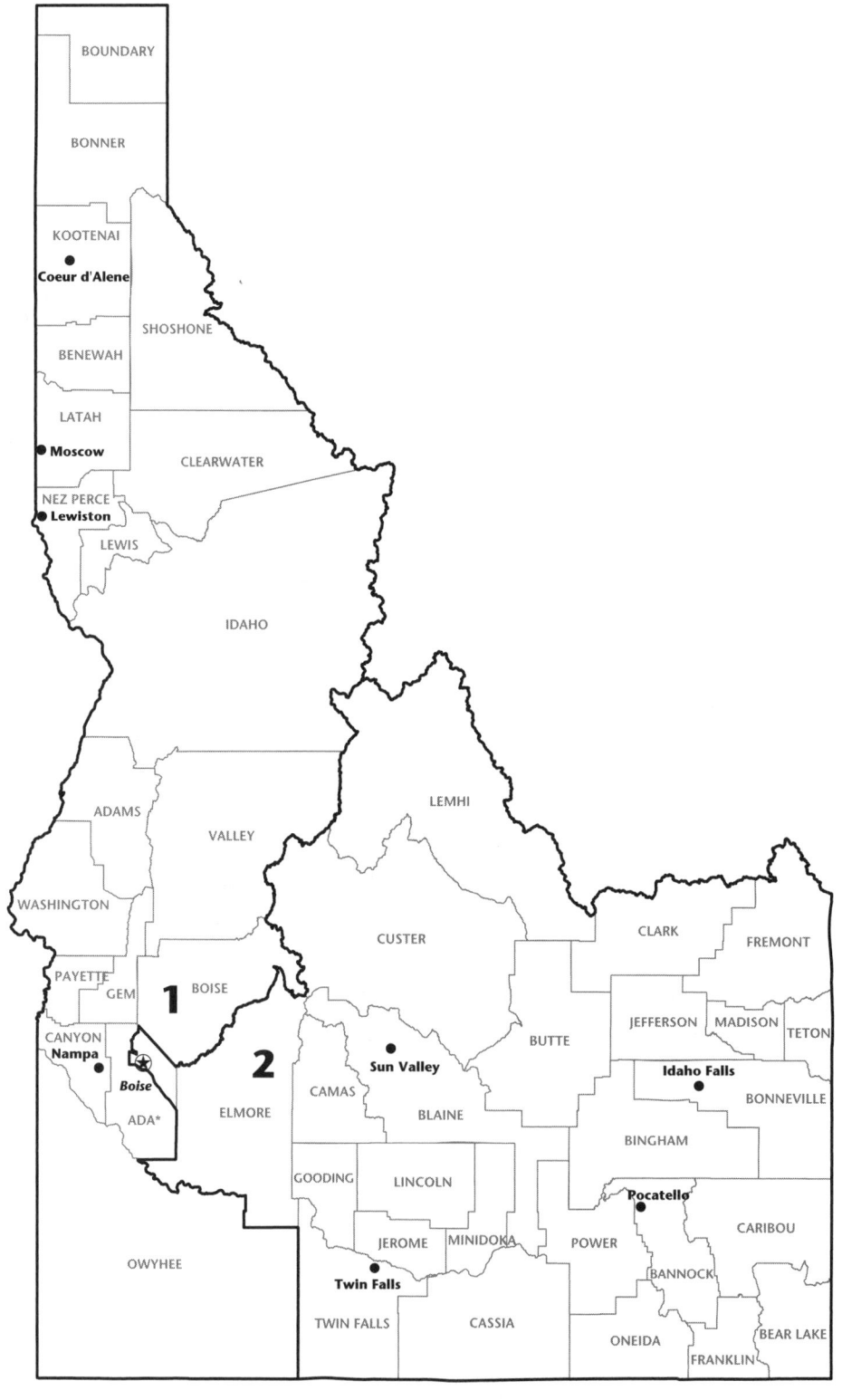

* Asterisk indicates a county whose boundaries include parts of two or more congressional districts.

IDAHO

GOVERNOR

C. L. "Butch" Otter (R). Reelected 2014 to a four-year term. Previously elected 2010, 2006.

SENATORS (2 Republicans)

Mike Crapo (R). Reelected 2010 to a six-year term. Previously elected 2004, 1998.

James E. Risch (R). Re-elected 2014 to a six-year term. Previously elected 2008.

REPRESENTATIVES (2 Republicans)

1. Raúl R. Labrador (R)   2. Michael K. Simpson (R)

POSTWAR VOTE FOR PRESIDENT

| | | Republican | | Democratic | | Other Vote | Rep.-Dem. Plurality | Percentage | | | |
| | | | | | | | | Total Vote | | Major Vote | |
Year	Total Vote	Vote	Candidate	Vote	Candidate			Rep.	Dem.	Rep.	Dem.
2012	652,346	420,911	Romney, W. Mitt	212,787	Obama, Barack H.*	18,648	208,124 R	64.5%	32.6%	66.4%	33.6%
2008	655,122	403,012	McCain, John S. III	236,440	Obama, Barack H.	15,670	166,572 R	61.5%	36.1%	63.0%	37.0%
2004	598,447	409,235	Bush, George W.*	181,098	Kerry, John F.	8,114	228,137 R	68.4%	30.3%	69.3%	30.7%
2000**	501,621	336,937	Bush, George W.	138,637	Gore, Albert Jr.	26,047	198,300 R	67.2%	27.6%	70.8%	29.2%
1996**	491,719	256,595	Dole, Robert "Bob"	165,443	Clinton, Bill*	69,681	91,152 R	52.2%	33.6%	60.8%	39.2%
1992**	482,142	202,645	Bush, George H.*	137,013	Clinton, Bill	142,484	65,632 R	42.0%	28.4%	59.7%	40.3%
1988	408,968	253,881	Bush, George H.	147,272	Dukakis, Michael S.	7,815	106,609 R	62.1%	36.0%	63.3%	36.7%
1984	411,144	297,523	Reagan, Ronald*	108,510	Mondale, Walter F.	5,111	189,013 R	72.4%	26.4%	73.3%	26.7%
1980**	437,431	290,699	Reagan, Ronald	110,192	Carter, Jimmy*	36,540	180,507 R	66.5%	25.2%	72.5%	27.5%
1976	344,071	204,151	Ford, Gerald R.*	126,549	Carter, Jimmy	13,371	77,602 R	59.3%	36.8%	61.7%	38.3%
1972	310,379	199,384	Nixon, Richard M.*	80,826	McGovern, George S.	30,169	118,558 R	64.2%	26.0%	71.2%	28.8%
1968**	291,183	165,369	Nixon, Richard M.	89,273	Humphrey, Hubert Horatio Jr.	36,541	76,096 R	56.8%	30.7%	64.9%	35.1%
1964	292,477	143,557	Goldwater, Barry M. Sr.	148,920	Johnson, Lyndon B.*		5,363 D	49.1%	50.9%	49.1%	50.9%
1960	300,450	161,597	Nixon, Richard M.	138,853	Kennedy, John F.		22,744 R	53.8%	46.2%	53.8%	46.2%
1956	272,989	166,979	Eisenhower, Dwight D.*	105,868	Stevenson, Adlai E. II	142	61,111 R	61.2%	38.8%	61.2%	38.8%
1952	276,254	180,707	Eisenhower, Dwight D.	95,081	Stevenson, Adlai E. II	466	85,626 R	65.4%	34.4%	65.5%	34.5%
1948	214,816	101,514	Dewey, Thomas E.	107,370	Truman, Harry S.*	5,932	5,856 D	47.3%	50.0%	48.6%	51.4%

Note: An asterisk (*) denotes incumbent. **In past elections, the other vote included: 2000 - 12,292 Green (Ralph Nader); 1996 - 62,518 Reform (Ross Perot); 1992 - 130,395 Independent (Perot); 1980 - 27,058 Independent (John Anderson); 1968 - 36,541 American Independent (George Wallace).

IDAHO

POSTWAR VOTE FOR GOVERNOR

Year	Total Vote	Republican		Democratic		Other Vote	Rep.-Dem. Plurality	Percentage			
								Total Vote		Major Vote	
		Vote	Candidate	Vote	Candidate			Rep.	Dem.	Rep.	Dem.
2014	439,830	235,405	Otter, C. L. "Butch"*	169,556	Balukoff, A. J.	34,869	65,849 R	53.5%	38.6%	58.1%	41.9%
2010	452,535	267,483	Otter, C. L. "Butch"*	148,680	Allred, Keith	36,372	118,803 R	59.1%	32.9%	64.3%	35.7%
2006	450,850	237,437	Otter, C. L. "Butch"	198,845	Brady, Jerry M.	14,568	38,592 R	52.7%	44.1%	54.4%	45.6%
2002	411,477	231,566	Kempthorne, Dirk*	171,711	Brady, Jerry M.	8,200	59,855 R	56.3%	41.7%	57.4%	42.6%
1998	381,248	258,095	Kempthorne, Dirk	110,815	Huntley, Robert C.	12,338	147,280 R	67.7%	29.1%	70.0%	30.0%
1994	413,346	216,123	Batt, Phil	181,363	Echohawk, Larry	15,860	34,760 R	52.3%	43.9%	54.4%	45.6%
1990	320,610	101,937	Fairchild, Roger	218,673	Andrus, Cecil D.*		116,736 D	31.8%	68.2%	31.8%	68.2%
1986	387,426	189,794	Leroy, David H.	193,429	Andrus, Cecil D.	4,203	3,635 D	49.0%	49.9%	49.5%	50.5%
1982	326,522	161,157	Batt, Phil	165,365	Evans, John V.*		4,208 D	49.4%	50.6%	49.4%	50.6%
1978	288,566	114,149	Larsen, Allan	169,540	Evans, John V.*	4,877	55,391 D	39.6%	58.8%	40.2%	59.8%
1974	259,632	68,731	Murphy, Jack M.	184,142	Andrus, Cecil D.*	6,759	115,411 D	26.5%	70.9%	27.2%	72.8%
1970	245,112	117,108	Samuelson, Don*	128,004	Andrus, Cecil D.		10,896 D	47.8%	52.2%	47.8%	52.2%
1966**	252,593	104,586	Samuelson, Don	93,744	Andrus, Cecil D.	54,263	10,842 R	41.4%	37.1%	52.7%	47.3%
1962	255,454	139,578	Smylie, Robert E.*	115,876	Smith, Vernon K.		23,702 R	54.6%	45.4%	54.6%	45.4%
1958	239,046	121,810	Smylie, Robert E.*	117,236	Derr, A. M.		4,574 R	51.0%	49.0%	51.0%	49.0%
1954	228,685	124,038	Smylie, Robert E.	104,647	Hamilton, Clark		19,391 R	54.2%	45.8%	54.2%	45.8%
1950	204,792	107,642	Jordan, Len B.	97,150	Wright, Calvin E.		10,492 R	52.6%	47.4%	52.6%	47.4%
1946	181,364	102,233	Robins, Charles A.	79,131	Williams, Arnold*		23,102 R	56.4%	43.6%	56.4%	43.6%

Note: An asterisk (*) denotes incumbent. **In past elections, the other vote included: 1966 - 30,913 Independent (Perry Swisher).

POSTWAR VOTE FOR SENATOR

Year	Total Vote	Republican		Democratic		Other Vote	Rep.-Dem. Plurality	Percentage			
								Total Vote		Major Vote	
		Vote	Candidate	Vote	Candidate			Rep.	Dem.	Rep.	Dem.
2014	437,170	285,596	Risch, James E.*	151,574	Mitchell, Nels		134,022 R	65.3%	34.7%	65.3%	34.7%
2010	449,530	319,953	Crapo, Mike*	112,057	Sullivan, P. Tom	17,520	207,896 R	71.2%	24.9%	74.1%	25.9%
2008	644,780	371,744	Risch, James E.	219,903	Larocco, Larry	53,133	151,841 R	57.7%	34.1%	62.8%	37.2%
2004**	503,932	499,796	Crapo, Mike*			4,136	499,796 R	99.2%		100.0%	
2002	408,544	266,215	Craig, Larry E.*	132,975	Blinken, Alan	9,354	133,240 R	65.2%	32.5%	66.7%	33.3%
1998	378,174	262,966	Crapo, Michael D.	107,375	Mauk, Bill	7,833	155,591 R	69.5%	28.4%	71.0%	29.0%
1996	497,233	283,532	Craig, Larry E.*	198,422	Minnick, Walt	15,279	85,110 R	57.0%	39.9%	58.8%	41.2%
1992	478,504	270,468	Kempthorne, Dirk	208,036	Stallings, Richard		62,432 R	56.5%	43.5%	56.5%	43.5%
1990	315,936	193,641	Craig, Larry E.	122,295	Twilegar, Ron J.		71,346 R	61.3%	38.7%	61.3%	38.7%
1986	382,024	196,958	Symms, Steven D.*	185,066	Evans, John V.		11,892 R	51.6%	48.4%	51.6%	48.4%
1984	406,168	293,193	McClure, James A.*	105,591	Busch, Peter M.	7,384	187,602 R	72.2%	26.0%	73.5%	26.5%
1980	439,647	218,701	Symms, Steven D.	214,439	Church, Frank*	6,507	4,262 R	49.7%	48.8%	50.5%	49.5%
1978	284,047	194,412	McClure, James A.*	89,635	Jensen, Dwight		104,777 R	68.4%	31.6%	68.4%	31.6%
1974	258,847	109,072	Smith, Robert L.	145,140	Church, Frank*	4,635	36,068 D	42.1%	56.1%	42.9%	57.1%
1972	309,602	161,804	McClure, James A.	140,913	Davis, William E. Bud	6,885	20,891 R	52.3%	45.5%	53.5%	46.5%
1968	287,876	114,394	Hansen, George V.	173,482	Church, Frank*		59,088 D	39.7%	60.3%	39.7%	60.3%
1966	252,456	139,819	Jordan, Len B.*	112,637	Harding, Ralph R.		27,182 R	55.4%	44.6%	55.4%	44.6%
1962	258,786	117,129	Hawley, Jack	141,657	Church, Frank*		24,528 D	45.3%	54.7%	45.3%	54.7%
1962S	257,677	131,279	Jordan, Len B.*	126,398	Pfost, Gracie B.		4,881 R	50.9%	49.1%	50.9%	49.1%
1960	292,096	152,648	Dworshak, Henry C.*	139,448	McLaughlin, R. F.		13,200 R	52.3%	47.7%	52.3%	47.7%
1956	265,292	102,781	Welker, Herman*	149,096	Church, Frank	13,415	46,315 D	38.7%	56.2%	40.8%	59.2%
1954	226,408	142,269	Dworshak, Henry C.*	84,139	Taylor, Glen H.		58,130 R	62.8%	37.2%	62.8%	37.2%
1950	201,417	124,237	Welker, Herman	77,180	Clark, D. Worth		47,057 R	61.7%	38.3%	61.7%	38.3%
1950S	201,700	104,608	Dworshak, Henry C.	97,092	Burtenshaw, Claude		7,516 R	51.9%	48.1%	51.9%	48.1%
1948	214,188	103,868	Dworshak, Henry C.*	107,000	Miller, Bert H.	3,320	3,132 D	48.5%	50.0%	49.3%	50.7%
1946S	180,152	105,523	Dworshak, Henry C.	74,629	Donart, George E.		30,894 R	58.6%	41.4%	58.6%	41.4%

Note: An asterisk (*) denotes incumbent. **In 2004 there was no candidate on the Democratic line. A write-in candidate, who was a Democrat, received 4,136 votes, which are listed in the Other Vote column. The 1946 election and one each of the 1950 and 1962 elections were for short terms to fill vacancies.

IDAHO

GOVERNOR 2014

2010 Census Population	County	Total Vote	Republican (Otter)	Democratic (Balukoff)	Other	Rep.-Dem. Plurality	Total Vote Rep.	Total Vote Dem.	Major Vote Rep.	Major Vote Dem.
392,365	ADA	129,678	55,407	66,347	7,924	10,940 D	42.7%	51.2%	45.5%	54.5%
3,976	ADAMS	1,408	907	373	128	534 R	64.4%	26.5%	70.9%	29.1%
82,839	BANNOCK	22,454	10,282	10,355	1,817	73 D	45.8%	46.1%	49.8%	50.2%
5,986	BEAR LAKE	1,892	1,378	317	197	1,061 R	72.8%	16.8%	81.3%	18.7%
9,285	BENEWAH	2,671	1,421	781	469	640 R	53.2%	29.2%	64.5%	35.5%
45,607	BINGHAM	10,644	6,725	2,942	977	3,783 R	63.2%	27.6%	69.6%	30.4%
21,376	BLAINE	7,096	2,401	4,363	332	1,962 D	33.8%	61.5%	35.5%	64.5%
7,028	BOISE	2,703	1,607	846	250	761 R	59.5%	31.3%	65.5%	34.5%
40,877	BONNER	12,799	6,907	4,410	1,482	2,497 R	54.0%	34.5%	61.0%	39.0%
104,234	BONNEVILLE	27,000	15,295	9,377	2,328	5,918 R	56.6%	34.7%	62.0%	38.0%
10,972	BOUNDARY	3,359	1,997	850	512	1,147 R	59.5%	25.3%	70.1%	29.9%
2,891	BUTTE	1,126	759	260	107	499 R	67.4%	23.1%	74.5%	25.5%
1,117	CAMAS	437	273	125	39	148 R	62.5%	28.6%	68.6%	31.4%
188,923	CANYON	44,421	27,124	13,536	3,761	13,588 R	61.1%	30.5%	66.7%	33.3%
6,963	CARIBOU	1,955	1,331	450	174	881 R	68.1%	23.0%	74.7%	25.3%
22,952	CASSIA	5,450	3,832	1,162	456	2,670 R	70.3%	21.3%	76.7%	23.3%
982	CLARK	238	167	48	23	119 R	70.2%	20.2%	77.7%	22.3%
8,761	CLEARWATER	2,653	1,455	943	255	512 R	54.8%	35.5%	60.7%	39.3%
4,368	CUSTER	1,794	1,109	441	244	668 R	61.8%	24.6%	71.5%	28.5%
27,038	ELMORE	5,259	3,170	1,664	425	1,506 R	60.3%	31.6%	65.6%	34.4%
12,786	FRANKLIN	2,890	2,163	393	334	1,770 R	74.8%	13.6%	84.6%	15.4%
13,242	FREMONT	4,106	2,932	821	353	2,111 R	71.4%	20.0%	78.1%	21.9%
16,719	GEM	5,231	3,543	1,230	458	2,313 R	67.7%	23.5%	74.2%	25.8%
15,464	GOODING	3,955	2,474	1,163	318	1,311 R	62.6%	29.4%	68.0%	32.0%
16,267	IDAHO	5,657	3,495	1,509	653	1,986 R	61.8%	26.7%	69.8%	30.2%
26,140	JEFFERSON	7,046	5,006	1,336	704	3,670 R	71.0%	19.0%	78.9%	21.1%
22,374	JEROME	4,408	2,797	1,247	364	1,550 R	63.5%	28.3%	69.2%	30.8%
138,494	KOOTENAI	37,083	22,194	11,750	3,139	10,444 R	59.8%	31.7%	65.4%	34.6%
37,244	LATAH	11,737	4,542	6,321	874	1,779 D	38.7%	53.9%	41.8%	58.2%
7,936	LEMHI	2,937	1,970	667	300	1,303 R	67.1%	22.7%	74.7%	25.3%
3,821	LEWIS	1,214	662	428	124	234 R	54.5%	35.3%	60.7%	39.3%
5,208	LINCOLN	1,336	826	421	89	405 R	61.8%	31.5%	66.2%	33.8%
37,536	MADISON	6,822	4,671	1,482	669	3,189 R	68.5%	21.7%	75.9%	24.1%
20,069	MINIDOKA	4,630	3,087	1,182	361	1,905 R	66.7%	25.5%	72.3%	27.7%
39,265	NEZ PERCE	11,261	5,369	5,142	750	227 R	47.7%	45.7%	51.1%	48.9%
4,286	ONEIDA	1,098	807	179	112	628 R	73.5%	16.3%	81.8%	18.2%
11,526	OWYHEE	2,578	1,887	479	212	1,408 R	73.2%	18.6%	79.8%	20.2%
22,623	PAYETTE	5,705	3,862	1,378	465	2,484 R	67.7%	24.2%	73.7%	26.3%
7,817	POWER	2,104	1,208	707	189	501 R	57.4%	33.6%	63.1%	36.9%
12,765	SHOSHONE	3,384	1,658	1,383	343	275 R	49.0%	40.9%	54.5%	45.5%
10,170	TETON	3,935	1,678	1,977	280	299 D	42.6%	50.2%	45.9%	54.1%
77,230	TWIN FALLS	18,924	11,023	6,477	1,424	4,546 R	58.2%	34.2%	63.0%	37.0%
9,862	VALLEY	3,547	1,851	1,484	212	367 R	52.2%	41.8%	55.5%	44.5%
10,198	WASHINGTON	3,205	2,153	810	242	1,343 R	67.2%	25.3%	72.7%	27.3%
1,567,582	TOTAL	439,830	235,405	169,556	34,869	65,849 R	53.5%	38.6%	58.1%	41.9%

IDAHO

SENATOR 2014

2010 Census Population	County	Total Vote	Republican (Risch)	Democratic (Mitchell)	Other	Rep.-Dem. Plurality	Percentage Total Vote Rep.	Dem.	Major Vote Rep.	Dem.
392,365	ADA	128,827	69,404	59,423		9,981 R	53.9%	46.1%	53.9%	46.1%
3,976	ADAMS	1,397	1,022	375		647 R	73.2%	26.8%	73.2%	26.8%
82,839	BANNOCK	22,331	12,980	9,351		3,629 R	58.1%	41.9%	58.1%	41.9%
5,986	BEAR LAKE	1,888	1,599	289		1,310 R	84.7%	15.3%	84.7%	15.3%
9,285	BENEWAH	2,643	1,924	719		1,205 R	72.8%	27.2%	72.8%	27.2%
45,607	BINGHAM	10,591	8,013	2,578		5,435 R	75.7%	24.3%	75.7%	24.3%
21,376	BLAINE	7,040	2,854	4,186		1,332 D	40.5%	59.5%	40.5%	59.5%
7,028	BOISE	2,682	1,902	780		1,122 R	70.9%	29.1%	70.9%	29.1%
40,877	BONNER	12,681	8,462	4,219		4,243 R	66.7%	33.3%	66.7%	33.3%
104,234	BONNEVILLE	26,804	19,240	7,564		11,676 R	71.8%	28.2%	71.8%	28.2%
10,972	BOUNDARY	3,302	2,517	785		1,732 R	76.2%	23.8%	76.2%	23.8%
2,891	BUTTE	1,135	895	240		655 R	78.9%	21.1%	78.9%	21.1%
1,117	CAMAS	429	329	100		229 R	76.7%	23.3%	76.7%	23.3%
188,923	CANYON	44,307	32,063	12,244		19,819 R	72.4%	27.6%	72.4%	27.6%
6,963	CARIBOU	1,945	1,618	327		1,291 R	83.2%	16.8%	83.2%	16.8%
22,952	CASSIA	5,440	4,616	824		3,792 R	84.9%	15.1%	84.9%	15.1%
982	CLARK	232	195	37		158 R	84.1%	15.9%	84.1%	15.9%
8,761	CLEARWATER	2,637	1,876	761		1,115 R	71.1%	28.9%	71.1%	28.9%
4,368	CUSTER	1,781	1,361	420		941 R	76.4%	23.6%	76.4%	23.6%
27,038	ELMORE	5,233	3,690	1,543		2,147 R	70.5%	29.5%	70.5%	29.5%
12,786	FRANKLIN	2,839	2,527	312		2,215 R	89.0%	11.0%	89.0%	11.0%
13,242	FREMONT	4,076	3,356	720		2,636 R	82.3%	17.7%	82.3%	17.7%
16,719	GEM	5,197	3,961	1,236		2,725 R	76.2%	23.8%	76.2%	23.8%
15,464	GOODING	3,933	2,912	1,021		1,891 R	74.0%	26.0%	74.0%	26.0%
16,267	IDAHO	5,617	4,371	1,246		3,125 R	77.8%	22.2%	77.8%	22.2%
26,140	JEFFERSON	7,058	5,968	1,090		4,878 R	84.6%	15.4%	84.6%	15.4%
22,374	JEROME	4,374	3,294	1,080		2,214 R	75.3%	24.7%	75.3%	24.7%
138,494	KOOTENAI	36,944	25,681	11,263		14,418 R	69.5%	30.5%	69.5%	30.5%
37,244	LATAH	11,639	5,826	5,813		13 R	50.1%	49.9%	50.1%	49.9%
7,936	LEMHI	2,927	2,273	654		1,619 R	77.7%	22.3%	77.7%	22.3%
3,821	LEWIS	1,200	893	307		586 R	74.4%	25.6%	74.4%	25.6%
5,208	LINCOLN	1,335	972	363		609 R	72.8%	27.2%	72.8%	27.2%
37,536	MADISON	6,788	5,902	886		5,016 R	86.9%	13.1%	86.9%	13.1%
20,069	MINIDOKA	4,603	3,622	981		2,641 R	78.7%	21.3%	78.7%	21.3%
39,265	NEZ PERCE	11,160	6,974	4,186		2,788 R	62.5%	37.5%	62.5%	37.5%
4,286	ONEIDA	1,092	918	174		744 R	84.1%	15.9%	84.1%	15.9%
11,526	OWYHEE	2,577	2,117	460		1,657 R	82.1%	17.9%	82.1%	17.9%
22,623	PAYETTE	5,687	4,366	1,321		3,045 R	76.8%	23.2%	76.8%	23.2%
7,817	POWER	2,076	1,441	635		806 R	69.4%	30.6%	69.4%	30.6%
12,765	SHOSHONE	3,281	1,874	1,407		467 R	57.1%	42.9%	57.1%	42.9%
10,170	TETON	3,900	1,991	1,909		82 R	51.1%	48.9%	51.1%	48.9%
77,230	TWIN FALLS	18,798	13,309	5,489		7,820 R	70.8%	29.2%	70.8%	29.2%
9,862	VALLEY	3,542	2,067	1,475		592 R	58.4%	41.6%	58.4%	41.6%
10,198	WASHINGTON	3,202	2,421	781		1,640 R	75.6%	24.4%	75.6%	24.4%
1,567,582	TOTAL	437,170	285,596	151,574		134,022 R	65.3%	34.7%	65.3%	34.7%

IDAHO

HOUSE OF REPRESENTATIVES

| CD | Year | Total Vote | Republican | | Democratic | | Other Vote | Rep.-Dem. Plurality | Percentage | | | |
| | | | Vote | Candidate | Vote | Candidate | | | Total Vote | | Major Vote | |
									Rep.	Dem.	Rep.	Dem.
1	2014	220,864	143,580	LABRADOR, RAUL R.*	77,277	RINGO, SHIRLEY G.	7	66,303 R	65.0%	35.0%	65.0%	35.0%
1	2012	316,724	199,402	LABRADOR, RAUL R.*	97,450	FARRIS, JIMMY	19,872	101,952 R	63.0%	30.8%	67.2%	32.8%
2	2014	214,293	131,492	SIMPSON, MICHAEL K.*	82,801	STALLINGS, RICHARD		48,691 R	61.4%	38.6%	61.4%	38.6%
2	2012	318,494	207,412	SIMPSON, MICHAEL K.*	110,847	LEFAVOUR, NICOLE	235	96,565 R	65.1%	34.8%	65.2%	34.8%
TOTAL	2014	435,157	275,072		160,078		7	114,994 R	63.2%	36.8%	63.2%	36.8%
TOTAL	2012	635,218	406,814		208,297		20,107	198,517 R	64.0%	32.8%	66.1%	33.9%

Note: An asterisk (*) denotes incumbent.

IDAHO

GENERAL AND PRIMARY ELECTIONS

2014 GENERAL ELECTIONS: OTHER VOTES

Governor   Other vote was 17,884 Libertarian (John T. Bujak), 8,801 Independent (Jill Humble), 5,219 Constitution (Steven D. Pankey), 2,870 Independent (Pro-Life), 95 scattered write-ins

Senotor

House
  CD 1   Other vote was:
      7 Write-in (Reed C. McCandless)

2014 PRIMARY ELECTIONS: SUPPLEMENTARY INFORMATION

Primary	May 20, 2014	**Registration** (as of May 1, 2014)	742,937	Republican	244,488
				Democratic	57,330
				Libertarian	3,514
				Constitution	1,751
				Unaffiliated	435,854

Primary Type   Open—Any registered voter could participate in the Democratic primary. Only registered Republicans could vote in the Republican primary.

	REPUBLICAN PRIMARIES			DEMOCRATIC PRIMARIES		
Senator	Risch, James E.*	119,209	79.9%	Mitchell, Nels	16,908	69.6%
	Anderson, Jeremy "T"	29,939	20.1%	Bryk, William	7,378	30.4%
	TOTAL	149,148		TOTAL	24,286	
Governor	Otter, C. L. "Butch"*	79,779	51.4%	Balukoff, A.J.	16,751	65.3%
	Fulcher, Russell M.	67,694	43.6%	Kerr, Terry	8,887	34.7%
	Brown, Harley D.	5,084	3.3%			
	Bayes, Walt	2,753	1.8%			
	TOTAL	155,310		TOTAL	25,638	
Congressional District 1	Labrador, Raul R.*	56,206	78.6%	Ringo, Shirley G.	9,047	82.0%
	Marie, Lisa	5,164	7.2%	Barone, Ryan Andrew	1,981	18.0%
	Greenway, Michael	3,494	4.9%			
	McCandless, Reed C.	3,373	4.7%			
	Blackwell, Sean	3,304	4.6%			
	TOTAL	71,541		TOTAL	11,028	
Congressional District 2	Simpson, Michael K.*	48,632	61.6%	Stallings, Richard	14,547	100.0%
	Smith, Bryan D.	30,263	38.4%			
	TOTAL	78,895		TOTAL	14,547	

Note: An asterisk (*) denotes incumbent.

ILLINOIS

Congressional districts first established for elections held in 2012

18 members

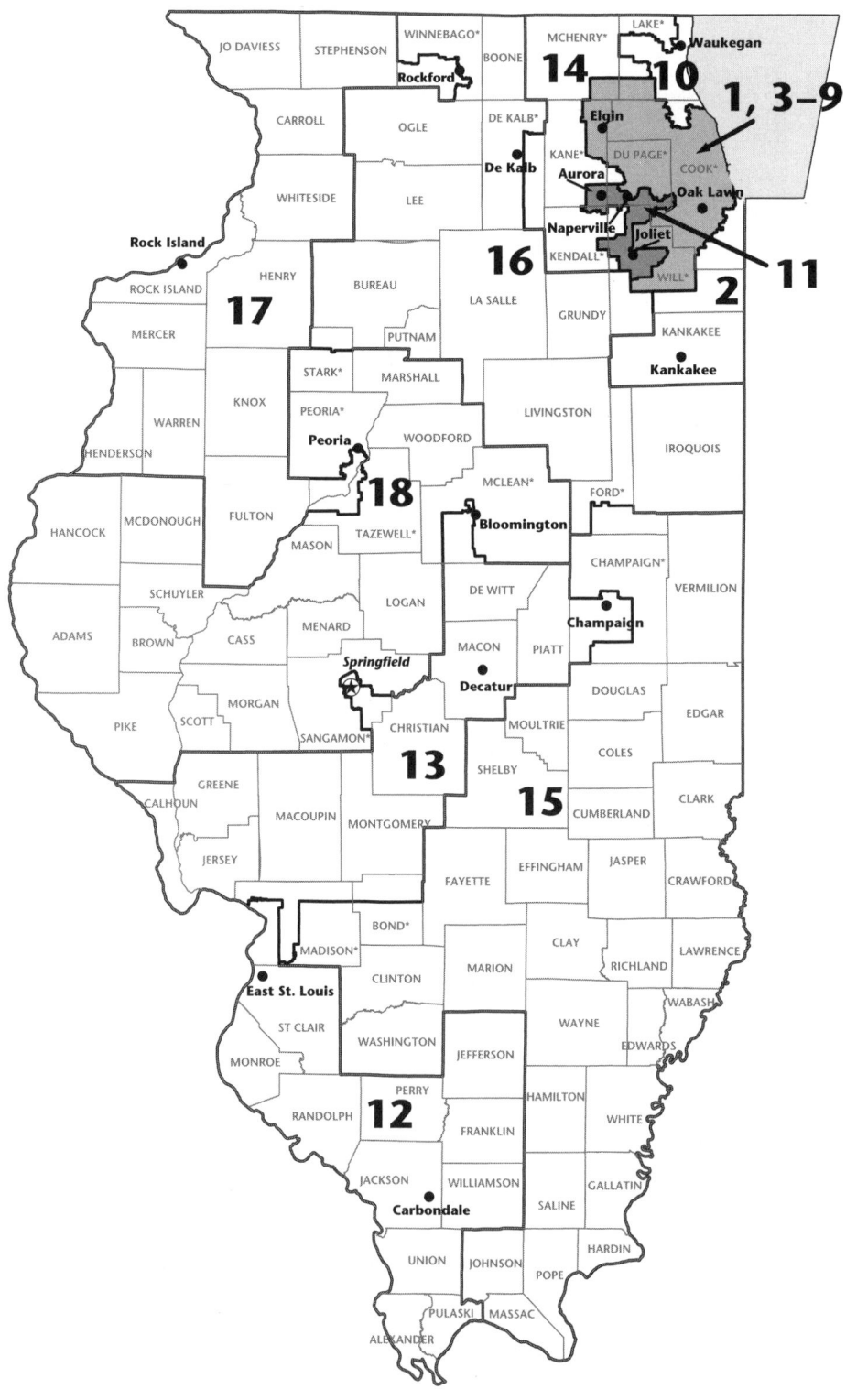

* Asterisk indicates a county whose boundaries include parts of two or more congressional districts.

ILLINOIS
Chicago Area

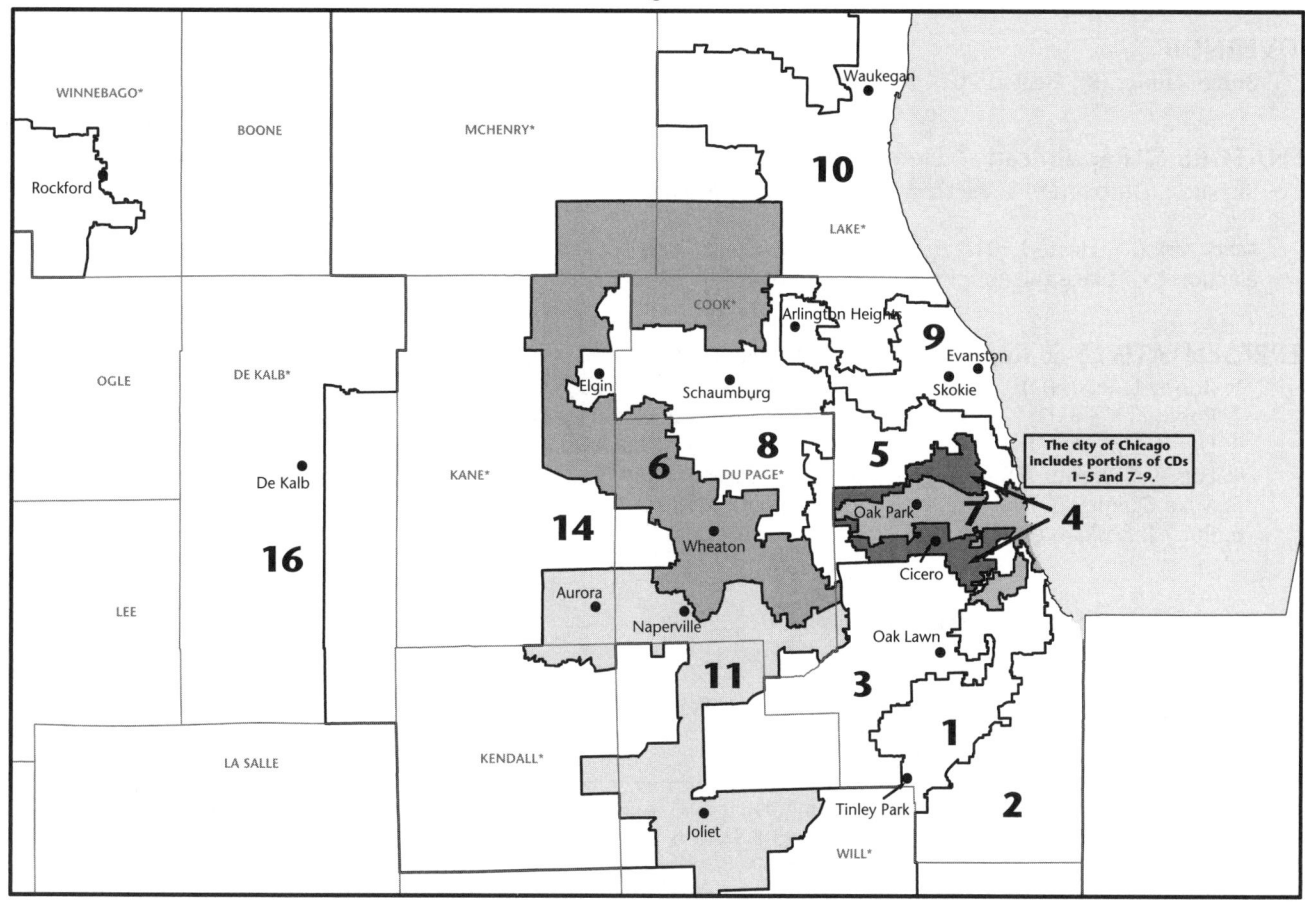

* Asterisk indicates a county whose boundaries include parts of two or more congressional districts.

ILLINOIS

GOVERNOR
Bruce Rauner (R). Elected 2014 to a four-year term.

SENATORS (1 Republican, 1 Democrat)
Richard J. Durbin (D). Re-elected 2014 to a six-year term. Previously elected 2008, 2002, 1996.

Mark Kirk (R). Elected 2010 to a six-year term. Also won special election held in conjunction with the 2010 general election to replace the appointed senator, Roland Burris (D).

REPRESENTATIVES (8 Republicans, 10 Democrats)
1. Bobby L. Rush (D)
2. Robin L. Kelly (D)
3. Daniel Lipinski (D)
4. Luis V. Gutiérrez (D)
5. Mike Quigley (D)
6. Peter J. Roskam (R)
7. Danny K. Davis (D)
8. Tammy Duckworth (D)
9. Janice D. Schakowsky (D)
10. Robert J. Dold (R)
11. Bill Foster (D)
12. Mike Bost (R)
13. Rodney Davis (R)
14. Randy Hultgren (R)
15. John Shimkus (R)
16. Adam Kinzinger (R)
17. Cheri Bustos (D)
18. Darin LaHood (R)

POSTWAR VOTE FOR PRESIDENT

		Republican		Democratic		Other	Rep.-Dem.	Total Vote		Major Vote	
Year	Total Vote	Vote	Candidate	Vote	Candidate	Vote	Plurality	Rep.	Dem.	Rep.	Dem.
2012	5,242,014	2,135,216	Romney, W. Mitt	3,019,512	Obama, Barack H.*	87,286	884,296 D	40.7%	57.6%	41.4%	58.6%
2008	5,522,371	2,031,179	McCain, John S. III	3,419,348	Obama, Barack H.	71,844	1,388,169 D	36.8%	61.9%	37.3%	62.7%
2004	5,274,322	2,345,946	Bush, George W.*	2,891,550	Kerry, John F.	36,826	545,604 D	44.5%	54.8%	44.8%	55.2%
2000**	4,742,123	2,019,421	Bush, George W.	2,589,026	Gore, Albert Jr.	133,676	569,605 D	42.6%	54.6%	43.8%	56.2%
1996**	4,311,391	1,587,021	Dole, Robert "Bob"	2,341,744	Clinton, Bill*	382,626	754,723 D	36.8%	54.3%	40.4%	59.6%
1992**	5,050,157	1,734,096	Bush, George H.*	2,453,350	Clinton, Bill	862,711	719,254 D	34.3%	48.6%	41.4%	58.6%
1988	4,559,120	2,310,939	Bush, George H.	2,215,940	Dukakis, Michael S.	32,241	94,999 R	50.7%	48.6%	51.0%	49.0%
1984	4,819,088	2,707,103	Reagan, Ronald*	2,086,499	Mondale, Walter F.	25,486	620,604 R	56.2%	43.3%	56.5%	43.5%
1980**	4,749,721	2,358,049	Reagan, Ronald	1,981,413	Carter, Jimmy*	410,259	376,636 R	49.6%	41.7%	54.3%	45.7%
1976	4,718,914	2,364,269	Ford, Gerald R.*	2,271,295	Carter, Jimmy	83,350	92,974 R	50.1%	48.1%	51.0%	49.0%
1972	4,723,236	2,788,179	Nixon, Richard M.*	1,913,472	McGovern, George S.	21,585	874,707 R	59.0%	40.5%	59.3%	40.7%
1968**	4,619,749	2,174,774	Nixon, Richard M.	2,039,814	Humphrey, Hubert Horatio Jr.	405,161	134,960 R	47.1%	44.2%	51.6%	48.4%
1964	4,702,841	1,905,946	Goldwater, Barry M. Sr.	2,796,833	Johnson, Lyndon B.*	62	890,887 D	40.5%	59.5%	40.5%	59.5%
1960	4,757,409	2,368,988	Nixon, Richard M.	2,377,846	Kennedy, John F.	10,575	8,858 D	49.8%	50.0%	49.9%	50.1%
1956	4,407,407	2,623,327	Eisenhower, Dwight D.*	1,775,682	Stevenson, Adlai E. II	8,398	847,645 R	59.5%	40.3%	59.6%	40.4%
1952	4,481,058	2,457,327	Eisenhower, Dwight D.	2,013,920	Stevenson, Adlai E. II	9,811	443,407 R	54.8%	44.9%	55.0%	45.0%
1948	3,984,046	1,961,103	Dewey, Thomas E.	1,994,715	Truman, Harry S.*	28,228	33,612 D	49.2%	50.1%	49.6%	50.4%

Note: An asterisk (*) denotes incumbent. **In past elections, the other vote included: 2000 - 103,759 Green (Ralph Nader); 1996 - 346,408 Reform (Ross Perot); 1992 - 840,515 Independent (Perot); 1980 - 346,754 Independent (John Anderson); 1968 - 390,958 American Independent (George Wallace).

ILLINOIS

POSTWAR VOTE FOR GOVERNOR

Year	Total Vote	Republican		Democratic		Other Vote	Rep.-Dem. Plurality	Percentage			
								Total Vote		Major Vote	
		Vote	Candidate	Vote	Candidate			Rep.	Dem.	Rep.	Dem.
2014	3,627,690	1,823,627	Rauner, Bruce	1,681,343	Quinn, Pat*	122,720	142,284 R	50.3%	46.3%	52.0%	48.0%
2010	3,729,989	1,713,385	Brady, Bill	1,745,219	Quinn, Pat*	271,385	31,834 D	45.9%	46.8%	49.5%	50.5%
2006**	3,487,989	1,369,315	Topinka, Judy Baar	1,736,731	Blagojevich, Rod R.*	381,943	367,416 D	39.3%	49.8%	44.1%	55.9%
2002	3,538,891	1,594,960	Ryan, Jim	1,847,040	Blagojevich, Rod R.	96,891	252,080 D	45.1%	52.2%	46.3%	53.7%
1998	3,358,705	1,714,094	Ryan, George H.	1,594,191	Poshard, Glenn	50,420	119,903 R	51.0%	47.5%	51.8%	48.2%
1994	3,106,566	1,984,318	Edgar, Jim*	1,069,850	Netsch, Dawn C.	52,398	914,468 R	63.9%	34.4%	65.0%	35.0%
1990	3,257,410	1,653,126	Edgar, Jim	1,569,217	Hartigan, Neil F.	35,067	83,909 R	50.7%	48.2%	51.3%	48.7%
1986**	3,143,978	1,655,849	Thompson, James R.*	208,830	Fairchild, Mark	1,279,299	1,447,019 R	52.7%	6.6%	88.8%	11.2%
1982	3,673,681	1,816,101	Thompson, James R.*	1,811,027	Stevenson, Adlai E. II	46,553	5,074 R	49.4%	49.3%	50.1%	49.9%
1978	3,150,095	1,859,684	Thompson, James R.*	1,263,134	Bakalis, Michael	27,277	596,550 R	59.0%	40.1%	59.6%	40.4%
1976**	4,635,728	3,000,395	Thompson, James R.	1,606,989	Howlett, Michael J.	28,344	1,393,406 R	64.7%	34.7%	65.1%	34.9%
1972	4,678,802	2,293,809	Ogilvie, Richard B.*	2,371,301	Walker, Daniel	13,692	77,492 D	49.0%	50.7%	49.2%	50.8%
1968	4,506,000	2,307,295	Ogilvie, Richard B.	2,179,501	Shapiro, Samuel H.	19,204	127,794 R	51.2%	48.4%	51.4%	48.6%
1964	4,657,500	2,239,095	Percy, Charles H.	2,418,394	Kerner, Otto*	11	179,299 D	48.1%	51.9%	48.1%	51.9%
1960	4,674,187	2,070,479	Stratton, William G.*	2,594,731	Kerner, Otto	8,977	524,252 D	44.3%	55.5%	44.4%	55.6%
1956	4,314,611	2,171,786	Stratton, William G.*	2,134,909	Austin, Richard B.	7,916	36,877 R	50.3%	49.5%	50.4%	49.6%
1952	4,415,864	2,317,363	Stratton, William G.	2,089,721	Dixon, Sherwood	8,780	227,642 R	52.5%	47.3%	52.6%	47.4%
1948	3,940,257	1,678,007	Green, Dwight H.*	2,250,074	Stevenson, Adlai E. II	12,176	572,067 D	42.6%	57.1%	42.7%	57.3%

Note: An asterisk (*) denotes incumbent. **In past elections, the other vote included: 2006 - 361,336 Green (Rich Whitney); 1986 - 1,256,626 Illinois Solidarity (Adlai E. Stevenson III). In 1986 there was no Democratic candidate for governor on the ballot. Mark Fairchild, a supporter of Lyndon H. LaRouche Jr., was the "paired" Democratic candidate for lt. governor and the Democratic vote was cast for this ticket of "no name" and Fairchild. Running on the Illinois Solidarity line, Stevenson finished second with 40.0 percent of the vote. The 1976 vote was for a two-year term to permit shifting the election for governor to non-presidential years.

POSTWAR VOTE FOR SENATOR

Year	Total Vote	Republican		Democratic		Other Vote	Rep.-Dem. Plurality	Percentage			
								Total Vote		Major Vote	
		Vote	Candidate	Vote	Candidate			Rep.	Dem.	Rep.	Dem.
2014	3,603,519	1,538,522	Oberweis, James D.	1,929,637	Durbin, Richard J.*	135,360	391,115 D	42.7%	53.5%	44.4%	55.6%
2010	3,704,473	1,778,698	Kirk, Mark Steven	1,719,478	Giannoulias, Alexander	206,297	59,220 R	48.0%	46.4%	50.8%	49.2%
2008	5,329,884	1,520,621	Sauerberg, Steve	3,615,844	Durbin, Richard J.*	193,419	2,095,223 D	28.5%	67.8%	29.6%	70.4%
2004	5,141,520	1,390,690	Keyes, Alan	3,597,456	Obama, Barack H.	153,374	2,206,766 D	27.0%	70.0%	27.9%	72.1%
2002	3,486,851	1,325,703	Durkin, Jim	2,103,766	Durbin, Richard J.*	57,382	778,063 D	38.0%	60.3%	38.7%	61.3%
1998	3,392,845	1,709,041	Fitzgerald, Peter G.	1,610,496	Moseley-Braun, Carol*	73,308	98,545 R	50.4%	47.5%	51.5%	48.5%
1996	4,250,722	1,728,824	Salvi, Al	2,384,028	Durbin, Richard J.	137,870	655,204 D	40.7%	56.1%	42.0%	58.0%
1992	4,939,558	2,126,833	Williamson, Richard S.	2,631,229	Moseley-Braun, Carol	181,496	504,396 D	43.1%	53.3%	44.7%	55.3%
1990	3,251,005	1,135,628	Martin, Lynn	2,115,377	Simon, Paul*		979,749 D	34.9%	65.1%	34.9%	65.1%
1986	3,122,883	1,053,734	Koehler, Judy	2,033,783	Dixon, Alan J.*	35,366	980,049 D	33.7%	65.1%	34.1%	65.9%
1984	4,787,473	2,308,039	Percy, Charles H.*	2,397,303	Simon, Paul	82,131	89,264 D	48.2%	50.1%	49.1%	50.9%
1980	4,580,029	1,946,296	O'Neal, David C.	2,565,302	Dixon, Alan J.	68,431	619,006 D	42.5%	56.0%	43.1%	56.9%
1978	3,184,764	1,698,711	Percy, Charles H.*	1,448,187	Seith, Alex	37,866	250,524 R	53.3%	45.5%	54.0%	46.0%
1974	2,914,666	1,084,884	Burditt, George M.	1,811,496	Stevenson, Adlai E. II*	18,286	726,612 D	37.2%	62.2%	37.5%	62.5%
1972	4,608,380	2,867,078	Percy, Charles H.*	1,721,031	Pucinski, Roman C.	20,271	1,146,047 R	62.2%	37.3%	62.5%	37.5%
1970S	3,599,272	1,519,718	Smith, Ralph T.*	2,065,054	Stevenson, Adlai E. II	14,500	545,336 D	42.2%	57.4%	42.4%	57.6%
1968	4,449,757	2,358,947	Dirksen, Everett Mckinley*	2,073,242	Clark, William G.	17,568	285,705 R	53.0%	46.6%	53.2%	46.8%
1966	3,822,725	2,100,449	Percy, Charles H.	1,678,147	Douglas, Paul H.*	44,129	422,302 R	54.9%	43.9%	55.6%	44.4%
1962	3,709,216	1,961,202	Dirksen, Everett Mckinley*	1,748,007	Yates, Sidney R.	7	213,195 R	52.9%	47.1%	52.9%	47.1%
1960	4,632,796	2,093,846	Witwer, Samuel W.	2,530,943	Douglas, Paul H.*	8,007	437,097 D	45.2%	54.6%	45.3%	54.7%
1956	4,264,830	2,307,352	Dirksen, Everett Mckinley*	1,949,883	Stengel, Richard	7,595	357,469 R	54.1%	45.7%	54.2%	45.8%
1954	3,368,025	1,563,683	Meek, Joseph T.	1,804,338	Douglas, Paul H.*	4	240,655 D	46.4%	53.6%	46.4%	53.6%
1950	3,622,673	1,951,984	Dirksen, Everett Mckinley	1,657,630	Lucas, Scott W.*	13,059	294,354 R	53.9%	45.8%	54.1%	45.9%
1948	3,900,285	1,740,026	Brooks, C. Wayland*	2,147,754	Douglas, Paul H.	12,505	407,728 D	44.6%	55.1%	44.8%	55.2%

Note: An asterisk (*) denotes incumbent. **The 1970 election was for a short term to fill a vacancy.

ILLINOIS

GOVERNOR 2014

2010 Census Population	County	Total Vote	Republican (Rauner)	Democratic (Quinn)	Other	Rep.-Dem. Plurality	Total Vote		Major Vote	
							Rep.	Dem.	Rep.	Dem.
67,103	ADAMS	22,456	17,146	4,342	968	12,804 R	76.4%	19.3%	79.8%	20.2%
8,238	ALEXANDER	2,329	1,137	1,015	177	122 R	48.8%	43.6%	52.8%	47.2%
17,768	BOND	4,899	3,082	1,442	375	1,640 R	62.9%	29.4%	68.1%	31.9%
54,165	BOONE	15,247	9,529	5,029	689	4,500 R	62.5%	33.0%	65.5%	34.5%
6,937	BROWN	1,584	1,120	364	100	756 R	70.7%	23.0%	75.5%	24.5%
34,978	BUREAU	12,716	7,258	4,731	727	2,527 R	57.1%	37.2%	60.5%	39.5%
5,089	CALHOUN	1,963	1,157	683	123	474 R	58.9%	34.8%	62.9%	37.1%
15,387	CARROLL	5,527	3,621	1,582	324	2,039 R	65.5%	28.6%	69.6%	30.4%
13,642	CASS	3,769	2,242	1,249	278	993 R	59.5%	33.1%	64.2%	35.8%
201,081	CHAMPAIGN	54,479	29,918	22,314	2,247	7,604 R	54.9%	41.0%	57.3%	42.7%
34,800	CHRISTIAN	11,545	7,462	3,265	818	4,197 R	64.6%	28.3%	69.6%	30.4%
16,335	CLARK	5,197	3,805	1,083	309	2,722 R	73.2%	20.8%	77.8%	22.2%
13,815	CLAY	3,927	2,948	721	258	2,227 R	75.1%	18.4%	80.3%	19.7%
37,762	CLINTON	12,746	9,699	2,270	777	7,429 R	76.1%	17.8%	81.0%	19.0%
53,873	COLES	14,731	9,507	4,376	848	5,131 R	64.5%	29.7%	68.5%	31.5%
5,194,675	COOK	1,345,139	447,388	870,866	26,885	423,478 D	33.3%	64.7%	33.9%	66.1%
19,817	CRAWFORD	6,310	4,375	1,505	430	2,870 R	69.3%	23.9%	74.4%	25.6%
11,048	CUMBERLAND	3,932	2,739	926	267	1,813 R	69.7%	23.6%	74.7%	25.3%
16,561	DE WITT	5,486	3,859	1,299	328	2,560 R	70.3%	23.7%	74.8%	25.2%
105,160	DEKALB	28,176	16,246	10,944	986	5,302 R	57.7%	38.8%	59.7%	40.3%
19,980	DOUGLAS	5,988	4,522	1,156	310	3,366 R	75.5%	19.3%	79.6%	20.4%
916,924	DU PAGE	286,215	174,041	105,374	6,800	68,667 R	60.8%	36.8%	62.3%	37.7%
18,576	EDGAR	6,295	4,491	1,435	369	3,056 R	71.3%	22.8%	75.8%	24.2%
6,721	EDWARDS	2,299	1,862	314	123	1,548 R	81.0%	13.7%	85.6%	14.4%
34,242	EFFINGHAM	12,187	9,352	2,272	563	7,080 R	76.7%	18.6%	80.5%	19.5%
22,140	FAYETTE	6,549	4,638	1,481	430	3,157 R	70.8%	22.6%	75.8%	24.2%
14,081	FORD	4,484	3,401	854	229	2,547 R	75.8%	19.0%	79.9%	20.1%
39,561	FRANKLIN	12,648	7,677	4,104	867	3,573 R	60.7%	32.4%	65.2%	34.8%
37,069	FULTON	11,048	5,173	4,976	899	197 R	46.8%	45.0%	51.0%	49.0%
5,589	GALLATIN	1,840	1,145	564	131	581 R	62.2%	30.7%	67.0%	33.0%
13,886	GREENE	4,297	2,820	1,159	318	1,661 R	65.6%	27.0%	70.9%	29.1%
50,063	GRUNDY	16,529	9,760	6,073	696	3,687 R	59.0%	36.7%	61.6%	38.4%
8,457	HAMILTON	3,143	2,136	780	227	1,356 R	68.0%	24.8%	73.3%	26.7%
19,104	HANCOCK	5,979	4,271	1,343	365	2,928 R	71.4%	22.5%	76.1%	23.9%
4,320	HARDIN	1,434	922	419	93	503 R	64.3%	29.2%	68.8%	31.2%
7,331	HENDERSON	2,623	1,559	912	152	647 R	59.4%	34.8%	63.1%	36.9%
50,486	HENRY	17,686	10,829	5,958	899	4,871 R	61.2%	33.7%	64.5%	35.5%
29,718	IROQUOIS	9,452	7,329	1,723	400	5,606 R	77.5%	18.2%	81.0%	19.0%
60,218	JACKSON	15,945	8,114	6,876	955	1,238 R	50.9%	43.1%	54.1%	45.9%
9,698	JASPER	4,086	2,897	936	253	1,961 R	70.9%	22.9%	75.6%	24.4%
38,827	JEFFERSON	12,366	8,281	3,310	775	4,971 R	67.0%	26.8%	71.4%	28.6%
22,985	JERSEY	8,024	5,215	2,292	517	2,923 R	65.0%	28.6%	69.5%	30.5%
22,678	JO DAVIESS	7,781	4,726	2,700	355	2,026 R	60.7%	34.7%	63.6%	36.4%
12,582	JOHNSON	4,564	3,170	1,099	295	2,071 R	69.5%	24.1%	74.3%	25.7%
515,269	KANE	125,444	75,835	46,363	3,246	29,472 R	60.5%	37.0%	62.1%	37.9%
113,449	KANKAKEE	34,091	20,449	12,431	1,211	8,018 R	60.0%	36.5%	62.2%	37.8%
114,736	KENDALL	32,359	19,946	11,361	1,052	8,585 R	61.6%	35.1%	63.7%	36.3%
52,919	KNOX	16,098	8,311	6,925	862	1,386 R	51.6%	43.0%	54.5%	45.5%
113,924	LA SALLE	35,388	19,843	13,871	1,674	5,972 R	56.1%	39.2%	58.9%	41.1%
703,462	LAKE	200,827	116,277	79,939	4,611	36,338 R	57.9%	39.8%	59.3%	40.7%
16,833	LAWRENCE	4,132	2,670	1,216	246	1,454 R	64.6%	29.4%	68.7%	31.3%
36,031	LEE	11,241	6,527	4,061	653	2,466 R	58.1%	36.1%	61.6%	38.4%
38,950	LIVINGSTON	11,103	7,335	3,073	695	4,262 R	66.1%	27.7%	70.5%	29.5%
30,305	LOGAN	8,659	5,864	2,201	594	3,663 R	67.7%	25.4%	72.7%	27.3%
110,768	MACON	33,365	20,467	11,345	1,553	9,122 R	61.3%	34.0%	64.3%	35.7%
47,765	MACOUPIN	15,655	9,278	5,169	1,208	4,109 R	59.3%	33.0%	64.2%	35.8%
269,282	MADISON	79,157	46,075	28,444	4,638	17,631 R	58.2%	35.9%	61.8%	38.2%
39,437	MARION	11,778	8,683	2,291	804	6,392 R	73.7%	19.5%	79.1%	20.9%
12,640	MARSHALL	4,236	2,666	1,285	285	1,381 R	62.9%	30.3%	67.5%	32.5%
14,666	MASON	5,266	2,952	1,891	423	1,061 R	56.1%	35.9%	61.0%	39.0%

ILLINOIS

GOVERNOR 2014

2010 Census Population	County	Total Vote	Republican (Rauner)	Democratic (Quinn)	Other	Rep.-Dem. Plurality	Percentage Total Vote Rep.	Dem.	Major Vote Rep.	Dem.
15,429	MASSAC	4,278	2,828	1,268	182	1,560 R	66.1%	29.6%	69.0%	31.0%
32,612	MCDONOUGH	8,564	5,242	2,842	480	2,400 R	61.2%	33.2%	64.8%	35.2%
308,760	MCHENRY	93,996	61,827	29,116	3,053	32,711 R	65.8%	31.0%	68.0%	32.0%
169,572	MCLEAN	50,468	31,646	16,600	2,222	15,046 R	62.7%	32.9%	65.6%	34.4%
12,705	MENARD	4,866	3,239	1,371	256	1,868 R	66.6%	28.2%	70.3%	29.7%
16,434	MERCER	6,554	3,823	2,377	354	1,446 R	58.3%	36.3%	61.7%	38.3%
32,957	MONROE	12,559	8,843	3,138	578	5,705 R	70.4%	25.0%	73.8%	26.2%
30,104	MONTGOMERY	8,693	5,260	2,752	681	2,508 R	60.5%	31.7%	65.7%	34.3%
35,547	MORGAN	11,105	7,192	3,182	731	4,010 R	64.8%	28.7%	69.3%	30.7%
14,846	MOULTRIE	4,546	3,261	1,021	264	2,240 R	71.7%	22.5%	76.2%	23.8%
53,497	OGLE	17,064	11,236	5,015	813	6,221 R	65.8%	29.4%	69.1%	30.9%
186,494	PEORIA	52,074	28,127	21,232	2,715	6,895 R	54.0%	40.8%	57.0%	43.0%
22,350	PERRY	7,200	4,481	2,294	425	2,187 R	62.2%	31.9%	66.1%	33.9%
16,729	PIATT	7,053	4,975	1,702	376	3,273 R	70.5%	24.1%	74.5%	25.5%
16,430	PIKE	5,747	4,110	1,268	369	2,842 R	71.5%	22.1%	76.4%	23.6%
4,470	POPE	1,567	1,057	409	101	648 R	67.5%	26.1%	72.1%	27.9%
6,161	PULASKI	2,569	1,487	917	165	570 R	57.9%	35.7%	61.9%	38.1%
6,006	PUTNAM	2,555	1,264	1,096	195	168 R	49.5%	42.9%	53.6%	46.4%
33,476	RANDOLPH	11,129	6,607	3,838	684	2,769 R	59.4%	34.5%	63.3%	36.7%
16,233	RICHLAND	4,967	3,525	1,171	271	2,354 R	71.0%	23.6%	75.1%	24.9%
147,546	ROCK ISLAND	44,940	22,680	20,495	1,765	2,185 R	50.5%	45.6%	52.5%	47.5%
24,913	SALINE	7,771	4,839	2,375	557	2,464 R	62.3%	30.6%	67.1%	32.9%
197,465	SANGAMON	71,504	39,692	27,822	3,990	11,870 R	55.5%	38.9%	58.8%	41.2%
7,544	SCHUYLER	3,297	2,051	990	256	1,061 R	62.2%	30.0%	67.4%	32.6%
5,355	SCOTT	2,178	1,538	480	160	1,058 R	70.6%	22.0%	76.2%	23.8%
22,363	SHELBY	8,087	5,726	1,780	581	3,946 R	70.8%	22.0%	76.3%	23.7%
270,056	ST. CLAIR	76,317	39,438	33,474	3,405	5,964 R	51.7%	43.9%	54.1%	45.9%
5,994	STARK	1,913	1,246	537	130	709 R	65.1%	28.1%	69.9%	30.1%
47,711	STEPHENSON	14,646	9,338	4,558	750	4,780 R	63.8%	31.1%	67.2%	32.8%
135,394	TAZEWELL	43,408	26,991	13,538	2,879	13,453 R	62.2%	31.2%	66.6%	33.4%
17,808	UNION	6,137	3,900	1,887	350	2,013 R	63.5%	30.7%	67.4%	32.6%
81,625	VERMILION	21,632	14,028	6,290	1,314	7,738 R	64.8%	29.1%	69.0%	31.0%
11,947	WABASH	3,849	2,809	885	155	1,924 R	73.0%	23.0%	76.0%	24.0%
17,707	WARREN	5,461	3,281	1,923	257	1,358 R	60.1%	35.2%	63.0%	37.0%
14,716	WASHINGTON	5,721	4,354	1,004	363	3,350 R	76.1%	17.5%	81.3%	18.7%
16,760	WAYNE	5,764	4,899	625	240	4,274 R	85.0%	10.8%	88.7%	11.3%
14,665	WHITE	5,994	4,358	1,339	297	3,019 R	72.7%	22.3%	76.5%	23.5%
58,498	WHITESIDE	17,422	9,436	7,125	861	2,311 R	54.2%	40.9%	57.0%	43.0%
677,560	WILL	196,444	109,319	81,548	5,577	27,771 R	55.6%	41.5%	57.3%	42.7%
66,357	WILLIAMSON	20,387	13,081	6,177	1,129	6,904 R	64.2%	30.3%	67.9%	32.1%
295,266	WINNEBAGO	78,879	44,785	30,691	3,403	14,094 R	56.8%	38.9%	59.3%	40.7%
38,664	WOODFORD	13,966	10,061	3,209	696	6,852 R	72.0%	23.0%	75.8%	24.2%
12,830,632	TOTAL	3,627,690	1,823,627	1,681,343	122,720	142,284 R	50.3%	46.3%	52.0%	48.0%

ILLINOIS

SENATOR 2014

2010 Census Population	County	Total Vote	Republican (Oberweis)	Democratic (Durbin)	Other	Rep.-Dem. Plurality		Total Vote Rep.	Total Vote Dem.	Major Vote Rep.	Major Vote Dem.
67,103	ADAMS	22,406	15,277	6,307	822	8,970	R	68.2%	28.1%	70.8%	29.2%
8,238	ALEXANDER	2,318	846	1,361	111	515	D	36.5%	58.7%	38.3%	61.7%
17,768	BOND	4,923	2,689	2,001	233	688	R	54.6%	40.6%	57.3%	42.7%
54,165	BOONE	15,211	8,704	5,735	772	2,969	R	57.2%	37.7%	60.3%	39.7%
6,937	BROWN	1,577	1,030	476	71	554	R	65.3%	30.2%	68.4%	31.6%
34,978	BUREAU	12,661	6,798	5,329	534	1,469	R	53.7%	42.1%	56.1%	43.9%
5,089	CALHOUN	1,973	904	1,003	66	99	D	45.8%	50.8%	47.4%	52.6%
15,387	CARROLL	5,552	3,131	2,161	260	970	R	56.4%	38.9%	59.2%	40.8%
13,642	CASS	3,775	2,002	1,586	187	416	R	53.0%	42.0%	55.8%	44.2%
201,081	CHAMPAIGN	54,501	25,958	26,489	2,054	531	D	47.6%	48.6%	49.5%	50.5%
34,800	CHRISTIAN	11,610	6,896	4,189	525	2,707	R	59.4%	36.1%	62.2%	37.8%
16,335	CLARK	5,206	3,437	1,507	262	1,930	R	66.0%	28.9%	69.5%	30.5%
13,815	CLAY	3,917	2,587	1,132	198	1,455	R	66.0%	28.9%	69.6%	30.4%
37,762	CLINTON	12,660	7,428	4,657	575	2,771	R	58.7%	36.8%	61.5%	38.5%
53,873	COLES	14,770	8,483	5,625	662	2,858	R	57.4%	38.1%	60.1%	39.9%
5,194,675	COOK	1,333,018	345,255	945,635	42,128	600,380	D	25.9%	70.9%	26.7%	73.3%
19,817	CRAWFORD	6,302	3,922	2,032	348	1,890	R	62.2%	32.2%	65.9%	34.1%
11,048	CUMBERLAND	3,927	2,376	1,334	217	1,042	R	60.5%	34.0%	64.0%	36.0%
16,561	DE WITT	5,475	3,437	1,766	272	1,671	R	62.8%	32.3%	66.1%	33.9%
105,160	DEKALB	28,114	14,096	12,551	1,467	1,545	R	50.1%	44.6%	52.9%	47.1%
19,980	DOUGLAS	5,993	3,859	1,897	237	1,962	R	64.4%	31.7%	67.0%	33.0%
916,924	DU PAGE	285,610	144,505	129,941	11,164	14,564	R	50.6%	45.5%	52.7%	47.3%
18,576	EDGAR	6,241	3,555	2,395	291	1,160	R	57.0%	38.4%	59.7%	40.3%
6,721	EDWARDS	2,258	1,608	558	92	1,050	R	71.2%	24.7%	74.2%	25.8%
34,242	EFFINGHAM	12,197	8,303	3,493	401	4,810	R	68.1%	28.6%	70.4%	29.6%
22,140	FAYETTE	6,553	4,104	2,183	266	1,921	R	62.6%	33.3%	65.3%	34.7%
14,081	FORD	4,477	3,034	1,256	187	1,778	R	67.8%	28.1%	70.7%	29.3%
39,561	FRANKLIN	12,680	6,375	5,723	582	652	R	50.3%	45.1%	52.7%	47.3%
37,069	FULTON	11,076	4,655	5,885	536	1,230	D	42.0%	53.1%	44.2%	55.8%
5,589	GALLATIN	1,826	830	905	91	75	D	45.5%	49.6%	47.8%	52.2%
13,886	GREENE	4,348	2,319	1,822	207	497	R	53.3%	41.9%	56.0%	44.0%
50,063	GRUNDY	16,493	8,655	6,982	856	1,673	R	52.5%	42.3%	55.3%	44.7%
8,457	HAMILTON	3,109	1,671	1,288	150	383	R	53.7%	41.4%	56.5%	43.5%
19,104	HANCOCK	5,989	3,851	1,898	240	1,953	R	64.3%	31.7%	67.0%	33.0%
4,320	HARDIN	1,447	811	581	55	230	R	56.0%	40.2%	58.3%	41.7%
7,331	HENDERSON	2,597	1,217	1,259	121	42	D	46.9%	48.5%	49.2%	50.8%
50,486	HENRY	17,674	9,464	7,556	654	1,908	R	53.5%	42.8%	55.6%	44.4%
29,718	IROQUOIS	9,435	6,548	2,481	406	4,067	R	69.4%	26.3%	72.5%	27.5%
60,218	JACKSON	16,210	6,962	8,534	714	1,572	D	42.9%	52.6%	44.9%	55.1%
9,698	JASPER	4,060	2,377	1,476	207	901	R	58.5%	36.4%	61.7%	38.3%
38,827	JEFFERSON	12,321	6,738	5,018	565	1,720	R	54.7%	40.7%	57.3%	42.7%
22,985	JERSEY	7,969	4,434	3,176	359	1,258	R	55.6%	39.9%	58.3%	41.7%
22,678	JO DAVIESS	7,719	4,138	3,220	361	918	R	53.6%	41.7%	56.2%	43.8%
12,582	JOHNSON	4,547	2,924	1,418	205	1,506	R	64.3%	31.2%	67.3%	32.7%
515,269	KANE	124,831	64,014	55,253	5,564	8,761	R	51.3%	44.3%	53.7%	46.3%
113,449	KANKAKEE	33,888	17,434	14,830	1,624	2,604	R	51.4%	43.8%	54.0%	46.0%
114,736	KENDALL	32,230	17,263	13,244	1,723	4,019	R	53.6%	41.1%	56.6%	43.4%
52,919	KNOX	16,097	7,213	8,240	644	1,027	D	44.8%	51.2%	46.7%	53.3%
113,924	LA SALLE	35,352	18,482	14,950	1,920	3,532	R	52.3%	42.3%	55.3%	44.7%
703,462	LAKE	193,450	90,958	95,886	6,606	4,928	D	47.0%	49.6%	48.7%	51.3%
16,833	LAWRENCE	4,095	2,400	1,456	239	944	R	58.6%	35.6%	62.2%	37.8%
36,031	LEE	11,254	6,346	4,345	563	2,001	R	56.4%	38.6%	59.4%	40.6%
38,950	LIVINGSTON	11,170	7,236	3,447	487	3,789	R	64.8%	30.9%	67.7%	32.3%
30,305	LOGAN	8,625	5,588	2,679	358	2,909	R	64.8%	31.1%	67.6%	32.4%
110,768	MACON	33,467	19,063	13,098	1,306	5,965	R	57.0%	39.1%	59.3%	40.7%
47,765	MACOUPIN	15,768	7,811	7,163	794	648	R	49.5%	45.4%	52.2%	47.8%
269,282	MADISON	79,210	40,116	35,566	3,528	4,550	R	50.6%	44.9%	53.0%	47.0%
39,437	MARION	11,818	6,476	4,782	560	1,694	R	54.8%	40.5%	57.5%	42.5%
12,640	MARSHALL	4,252	2,554	1,525	173	1,029	R	60.1%	35.9%	62.6%	37.4%
14,666	MASON	5,285	2,532	2,474	279	58	R	47.9%	46.8%	50.6%	49.4%

ILLINOIS

SENATOR 2014

2010 Census Population	County	Total Vote	Republican (Oberweis)	Democratic (Durbin)	Other	Rep.-Dem. Plurality	Percentage Total Vote Rep.	Dem.	Major Vote Rep.	Dem.
15,429	MASSAC	4,253	2,543	1,570	140	973 R	59.8%	36.9%	61.8%	38.2%
32,612	MCDONOUGH	8,578	4,818	3,422	338	1,396 R	56.2%	39.9%	58.5%	41.5%
308,760	MCHENRY	93,578	53,601	35,445	4,532	18,156 R	57.3%	37.9%	60.2%	39.8%
169,572	MCLEAN	50,486	29,885	18,967	1,634	10,918 R	59.2%	37.6%	61.2%	38.8%
12,705	MENARD	4,886	3,140	1,595	151	1,545 R	64.3%	32.6%	66.3%	33.7%
16,434	MERCER	6,512	3,165	3,036	311	129 R	48.6%	46.6%	51.0%	49.0%
32,957	MONROE	12,539	7,663	4,441	435	3,222 R	61.1%	35.4%	63.3%	36.7%
30,104	MONTGOMERY	8,764	4,914	3,422	428	1,492 R	56.1%	39.0%	58.9%	41.1%
35,547	MORGAN	11,171	6,212	4,534	425	1,678 R	55.6%	40.6%	57.8%	42.2%
14,846	MOULTRIE	4,559	2,884	1,480	195	1,404 R	63.3%	32.5%	66.1%	33.9%
53,497	OGLE	17,002	10,602	5,611	789	4,991 R	62.4%	33.0%	65.4%	34.6%
186,494	PEORIA	52,131	26,824	23,832	1,475	2,992 R	51.5%	45.7%	53.0%	47.0%
22,350	PERRY	7,241	3,592	3,400	249	192 R	49.6%	47.0%	51.4%	48.6%
16,729	PIATT	7,084	4,271	2,499	314	1,772 R	60.3%	35.3%	63.1%	36.9%
16,430	PIKE	5,755	3,509	2,019	227	1,490 R	61.0%	35.1%	63.5%	36.5%
4,470	POPE	1,561	951	537	73	414 R	60.9%	34.4%	63.9%	36.1%
6,161	PULASKI	2,559	1,132	1,329	98	197 D	44.2%	51.9%	46.0%	54.0%
6,006	PUTNAM	2,526	1,232	1,163	131	69 R	48.8%	46.0%	51.4%	48.6%
33,476	RANDOLPH	11,205	5,544	5,235	426	309 R	49.5%	46.7%	51.4%	48.6%
16,233	RICHLAND	4,935	3,244	1,466	225	1,778 R	65.7%	29.7%	68.9%	31.1%
147,546	ROCK ISLAND	45,010	19,406	24,143	1,461	4,737 D	43.1%	53.6%	44.6%	55.4%
24,913	SALINE	7,728	4,043	3,337	348	706 R	52.3%	43.2%	54.8%	45.2%
197,465	SANGAMON	72,041	38,189	31,214	2,638	6,975 R	53.0%	43.3%	55.0%	45.0%
7,544	SCHUYLER	3,262	1,726	1,378	158	348 R	52.9%	42.2%	55.6%	44.4%
5,355	SCOTT	2,174	1,243	827	104	416 R	57.2%	38.0%	60.0%	40.0%
22,363	SHELBY	8,102	5,147	2,537	418	2,610 R	63.5%	31.3%	67.0%	33.0%
270,056	ST. CLAIR	76,605	34,877	38,813	2,915	3,936 D	45.5%	50.7%	47.3%	52.7%
5,994	STARK	1,909	1,135	682	92	453 R	59.5%	35.7%	62.5%	37.5%
47,711	STEPHENSON	14,488	8,080	5,728	680	2,352 R	55.8%	39.5%	58.5%	41.5%
135,394	TAZEWELL	43,590	26,574	15,511	1,505	11,063 R	61.0%	35.6%	63.1%	36.9%
17,808	UNION	6,148	3,161	2,761	226	400 R	51.4%	44.9%	53.4%	46.6%
81,625	VERMILION	21,632	11,610	9,112	910	2,498 R	53.7%	42.1%	56.0%	44.0%
11,947	WABASH	3,812	2,403	1,232	177	1,171 R	63.0%	32.3%	66.1%	33.9%
17,707	WARREN	5,466	2,857	2,420	189	437 R	52.3%	44.3%	54.1%	45.9%
14,716	WASHINGTON	5,666	3,532	1,885	249	1,647 R	62.3%	33.3%	65.2%	34.8%
16,760	WAYNE	5,741	4,189	1,289	263	2,900 R	73.0%	22.5%	76.5%	23.5%
14,665	WHITE	5,925	3,519	2,138	268	1,381 R	59.4%	36.1%	62.2%	37.8%
58,498	WHITESIDE	17,571	8,331	8,517	723	186 D	47.4%	48.5%	49.4%	50.6%
677,560	WILL	192,637	93,138	91,471	8,028	1,667 R	48.3%	47.5%	50.5%	49.5%
66,357	WILLIAMSON	20,320	11,880	7,686	754	4,194 R	58.5%	37.8%	60.7%	39.3%
295,266	WINNEBAGO	78,859	40,239	35,436	3,184	4,803 R	51.0%	44.9%	53.2%	46.8%
38,664	WOODFORD	13,991	9,838	3,758	395	6,080 R	70.3%	26.9%	72.4%	27.6%
12,830,632	TOTAL	3,603,519	1,538,522	1,929,637	135,360	391,115 D	42.7%	53.5%	44.4%	55.6%

ILLINOIS

HOUSE OF REPRESENTATIVES

CD	Year	Total Vote	Republican			Democratic			Other Vote	Rep.-Dem. Plurality	Percentage			
			Vote		Candidate	Vote		Candidate			Total Vote		Major Vote	
											Rep.	Dem.	Rep.	Dem.
1	2014	222,017	59,749		TILLMAN, JIMMY LEE	162,268		RUSH, BOBBY L.*		102,519 D	26.9%	73.1%	26.9%	73.1%
1	2012	320,844	83,989		PELOQUIN, DONALD E.	236,854		RUSH, BOBBY L.*	1	152,865 D	26.2%	73.8%	26.2%	73.8%
2	2014	204,266	43,799		WALLACE, ERIC M.	160,337		KELLY, ROBIN L.*	130	116,538 D	21.4%	78.5%	21.5%	78.5%
2	2012	297,712	69,115		WOODWORTH, BRIAN	188,303		JACKSON, JESSE L. JR.*	40,294	119,188 D	23.2%	63.3%	26.8%	73.2%
3	2014	180,855	64,091		BRANNIGAN, SHARON M.	116,764		LIPINSKI, DANIEL*		52,673 D	35.4%	64.6%	35.4%	64.6%
3	2012	246,398	77,653		GRABOWSKI, RICHARD	168,738		LIPINSKI, DANIEL*	7	91,085 D	31.5%	68.5%	31.5%	68.5%
4	2014	101,944	22,278		CONCEPCION, HECTOR	79,666		GUTIERREZ, LUIS V.*		57,388 D	21.9%	78.1%	21.9%	78.1%
4	2012	160,509	27,279		CONCEPCION, HECTOR	133,226		GUTIERREZ, LUIS V.*	4	105,947 D	17.0%	83.0%	17.0%	83.0%
5	2014	184,019	56,350		KOLBER, VINCENT A. "VINCE"	116,364		QUIGLEY, MIKE*	11,305	60,014 D	30.6%	63.2%	32.6%	67.4%
5	2012	270,377	77,289		SCHMITT, DAN	177,729		QUIGLEY, MIKE*	15,359	100,440 D	28.6%	65.7%	30.3%	69.7%
6	2014	238,752	160,287		ROSKAM, PETER J.*	78,465		MASON, MICHAEL		81,822 R	67.1%	32.9%	67.1%	32.9%
6	2012	326,129	193,138		ROSKAM, PETER J.*	132,991		COOLIDGE, LESLIE		60,147 R	59.2%	40.8%	59.2%	40.8%
7	2014	182,278	27,168		BUMPERS, ROBERT L.	155,110		DAVIS, DANNY K.*		127,942 D	14.9%	85.1%	14.9%	85.1%
7	2012	286,435	31,466		ZAK, RITA	242,439		DAVIS, DANNY K.*	12,530	210,973 D	11.0%	84.6%	11.5%	88.5%
8	2014	151,056	66,878		KAIFESH, LAWRENCE JOSEPH "LARRY"	84,178		DUCKWORTH, TAMMY*		17,300 D	44.3%	55.7%	44.3%	55.7%
8	2012	225,066	101,860		WALSH, JOE*	123,206		DUCKWORTH, TAMMY		21,346 D	45.3%	54.7%	45.3%	54.7%
9	2014	213,450	72,384		ATANUS, SUSANNE	141,000		SCHAKOWSKY, JANICE D.*	66	68,616 D	33.9%	66.1%	33.9%	66.1%
9	2012	293,807	98,924		WOLFE, TIMOTHY	194,869		SCHAKOWSKY, JANICE D.*	14	95,945 D	33.7%	66.3%	33.7%	66.3%
10	2014	187,128	95,992		DOLD, ROBERT J.	91,136		SCHNEIDER, BRAD*		4,856 R	51.3%	48.7%	51.3%	48.7%
10	2012	264,454	130,564		DOLD, ROBERT J.*	133,890		SCHNEIDER, BRAD		3,326 D	49.4%	50.6%	49.4%	50.6%
11	2014	174,772	81,335		SENGER, DARLENE	93,436		FOSTER, BILL*	1	12,101 D	46.5%	53.5%	46.5%	53.5%
11	2012	254,295	105,348		BIGGERT, JUDY*	148,928		FOSTER, BILL	19	43,580 D	41.4%	58.6%	41.4%	58.6%
12	2014	209,738	110,038		BOST, MIKE	87,860		ENYART, WILLIAM*	11,840	22,178 R	52.5%	41.9%	55.6%	44.4%
12	2012	303,949	129,902		PLUMMER, JASON	157,000		ENYART, WILLIAM	17,047	27,098 D	42.7%	51.7%	45.3%	54.7%
13	2014	210,272	123,337		DAVIS, RODNEY*	86,935		CALLIS, ANN E.		36,402 R	58.7%	41.3%	58.7%	41.3%
13	2012	294,385	137,034		DAVIS, RODNEY	136,032		GILL, DAVID M.	21,319	1,002 R	46.5%	46.2%	50.2%	49.8%
14	2014	222,230	145,369		HULTGREN, RANDY*	76,861		ANDERSON, DENNIS		68,508 R	65.4%	34.6%	65.4%	34.6%
14	2012	301,954	177,603		HULTGREN, RANDY*	124,351		ANDERSON, DENNIS		53,252 R	58.8%	41.2%	58.8%	41.2%
15	2014	221,926	166,274		SHIMKUS, JOHN*	55,652		THORSLAND, ERIC		110,622 R	74.9%	25.1%	74.9%	25.1%
15	2012	299,937	205,775		SHIMKUS, JOHN*	94,162		MICHAEL, ANGELA		111,613 R	68.6%	31.4%	68.6%	31.4%
16	2014	217,198	153,388		KINZINGER, ADAM*	63,810		OLSEN, RANDALL WAYNE		89,578 R	70.6%	29.4%	70.6%	29.4%
16	2012	294,090	181,789		KINZINGER, ADAM*	112,301		ROHL, WANDA		69,488 R	61.8%	38.2%	61.8%	38.2%
17	2014	199,361	88,785		SCHILLING, BOBBY	110,560		BUSTOS, CHERI*	16	21,775 D	44.5%	55.5%	44.5%	55.5%
17	2012	288,161	134,623		SCHILLING, BOBBY*	153,519		BUSTOS, CHERI	19	18,896 D	46.7%	53.3%	46.7%	53.3%
18	2014	246,740	184,363		SCHOCK, AARON*	62,377		MILLER, DARREL ERVIN		121,986 R	74.7%	25.3%	74.7%	25.3%
18	2012	329,631	244,467		SCHOCK, AARON*	85,164		WATERWORTH, STEVE		159,303 R	74.2%	25.8%	74.2%	25.8%
TOTAL	2014	3,568,002	1,721,865			1,822,779			23,358	100,914 D	48.3%	51.1%	48.6%	51.4%
TOTAL	2012	5,058,133	2,207,818			2,743,702			106,613	535,884 D	43.6%	54.2%	44.6%	55.4%

Note: An asterisk (*) denotes incumbent.

ILLINOIS

GENERAL AND PRIMARY ELECTIONS

2014 GENERAL ELECTIONS: OTHER VOTES

Governor   Other vote was 121,534 Libertarian (Chad Grimm), 684 Write-in (Scott Summers), 256 Write-in (Robert "Chico" Perez), 134 Write-in (Mark Smith), 112 scattered write-in

Senate   Other vote was 135,316 Libertarian (Sharon Hansen), 44 scattered write-in

ILLINOIS

GENERAL AND PRIMARY ELECTIONS

House   Other vote was:

CD 2   130 Write-in (Marcus Lewis)
CD 5   11,305 Green (Nancy Wade)
CD 9   66 Write-in (Phil Collins)
CD 11   1 Write-in (Constant "Connor" Vlakancic)
CD 12   11,840 Green (Paula Bradshaw)
CD 17   16 Write-in (Bill Fawell)

2014 PRIMARY ELECTIONS: SUPPLEMENTARY INFORMATION

Primary March 18, 2014   **Registration** 7,505,002   No Party Registration
(as of March 18, 2014)

Primary Type Open—Any registered voter could participate in the primary of either party.

	REPUBLICAN PRIMARIES			DEMOCRATIC PRIMARIES		
Senator	Oberweis, James D.	423,097	56.1%	Durbin, Richard J.*	429,041	100.0%
	Truax, Douglas Lee	331,237	43.9%			
	Procarione, Sherry	54				
	TOTAL	754,388		TOTAL	429,041	
Governor	Rauner, Bruce	328,934	40.1%	Quinn, Pat*	321,818	71.9%
	Dillard, Kirk W.	305,120	37.2%	Hardiman, Tio	125,500	28.1%
	Brady, Bill	123,708	15.1%			
	Rutherford, Dan	61,948	7.6%			
	TOTAL	819,710		TOTAL	447,318	
Congressional District 1	Tillman, Jimmy Lee	17,188	100.0%	Rush, Bobby L.*	47,627	100.0%
	TOTAL	17,188		TOTAL	47,627	
Congressional District 2	Wallace, Eric M.	16,096	100.0%	Kelly, Robin L.*	40,286	100.0%
	TOTAL	16,096		TOTAL	40,286	
Congressional District 3	Brannigan, Sharon M.	18,358	62.7%	Lipinski, Daniel*	28,883	100.0%
	Harris, Diane M.	10,937	37.3%			
	TOTAL	29,295		TOTAL	28,883	
Congressional District 4	Concepcion, Hector	6,637	100.0%	Gutierrez, Luis V.*	21,625	74.3%
				Eidenberg, Alexandra	4,796	16.5%
				Zavala, Jorge	2,670	9.2%
	TOTAL	6,637		TOTAL	29,091	
Congressional District 5	White, Fredrick K.	21	100.0%	Quigley, Mike*	26,364	100.0%
	TOTAL	21		TOTAL	26,364	
Congressional District 6	Roskam, Peter J.*	65,332	100.0%	Mason, Michael	8,615	100.0%
	TOTAL	65,332		TOTAL	8,615	
Congressional District 7	Bumpers, Robert L.	7,289	100.0%	Davis, Danny K.*	43,061	100.0%
	TOTAL	7,289		TOTAL	43,061	

ILLINOIS

GENERAL AND PRIMARY ELECTIONS

	REPUBLICAN PRIMARIES			DEMOCRATIC PRIMARIES		
Congressional District 8	Kaifesh, Lawrence Joseph "Larry"	24,657	71.5%	Duckworth, Tammy*	10,661	100.0%
	Goel, Manju	9,827	28.5%			
	TOTAL	34,484		TOTAL	10,661	
Congressional District 9	Atanus, Susanne	15,575	52.4%	Schakowsky, Janice D.*	31,576	100.0%
	Williams III, David Earl	14,148	47.6%			
	TOTAL	29,723		TOTAL	31,576	
Congressional District 10	Dold, Robert J.	32,124	100.0%	Schneider, Brad*	11,945	100.0%
	TOTAL	32,124		TOTAL	11,945	
Congressional District 11	Senger, Darlene	13,290	36.9%	Foster, Bill*	12,461	100.0%
	Balkema, Chris	12,024	33.4%			
	Miller, Albert "Bert"	9,460	26.3%			
	Bayne, Ian L.	1,253	3.5%			
	TOTAL	36,027		TOTAL	12,461	
Congressional District 12	Bost, Mike	33,066	100.0%	Enyart, William*	31,015	100.0%
	TOTAL	33,066		TOTAL	31,015	
Congressional District 13	Davis, Rodney*	27,816	54.6%	Callis, Ann E.	17,322	54.7%
	Harold, Erika	20,951	41.1%	Gollin, George	9,935	31.3%
	Firsching, Michael	2,147	4.2%	Green, David L.	4,438	14.0%
	TOTAL	50,914		TOTAL	31,695	
Congressional District 14	Hultgren, Randy*	57,665	100.0%	Anderson, Dennis	5,184	65.8%
				Hosta, John J.	2,691	34.2%
	TOTAL	57,665		TOTAL	7,875	
Congressional District 15	Shimkus, John M.*	66,453	100.0%	Thorsland, Eric	17,108	100.0%
	TOTAL	66,453		TOTAL	17,108	
Congressional District 16	Kinzinger, Adam*	56,593	78.4%	Olsen, Randall Wayne	12,077	100.0%
	Hale, David J.	15,558	21.6%			
	TOTAL	72,151		TOTAL	12,077	
Congressional District 17	Schilling, Bobby	41,063	100.0%	Bustos, Cheri*	21,923	100.0%
	TOTAL	41,063		TOTAL	21,923	
Congressional District 18	Schock, Aaron*	82,412	100.0%	Miller, Darrel Ervin	6,763	54.3%
				Mellon, Rob	5,692	45.7%
	TOTAL	82,412		TOTAL	12,455	

Note: An asterisk (*) denotes incumbent.

INDIANA

Congressional districts first established for elections held in 2012

9 members

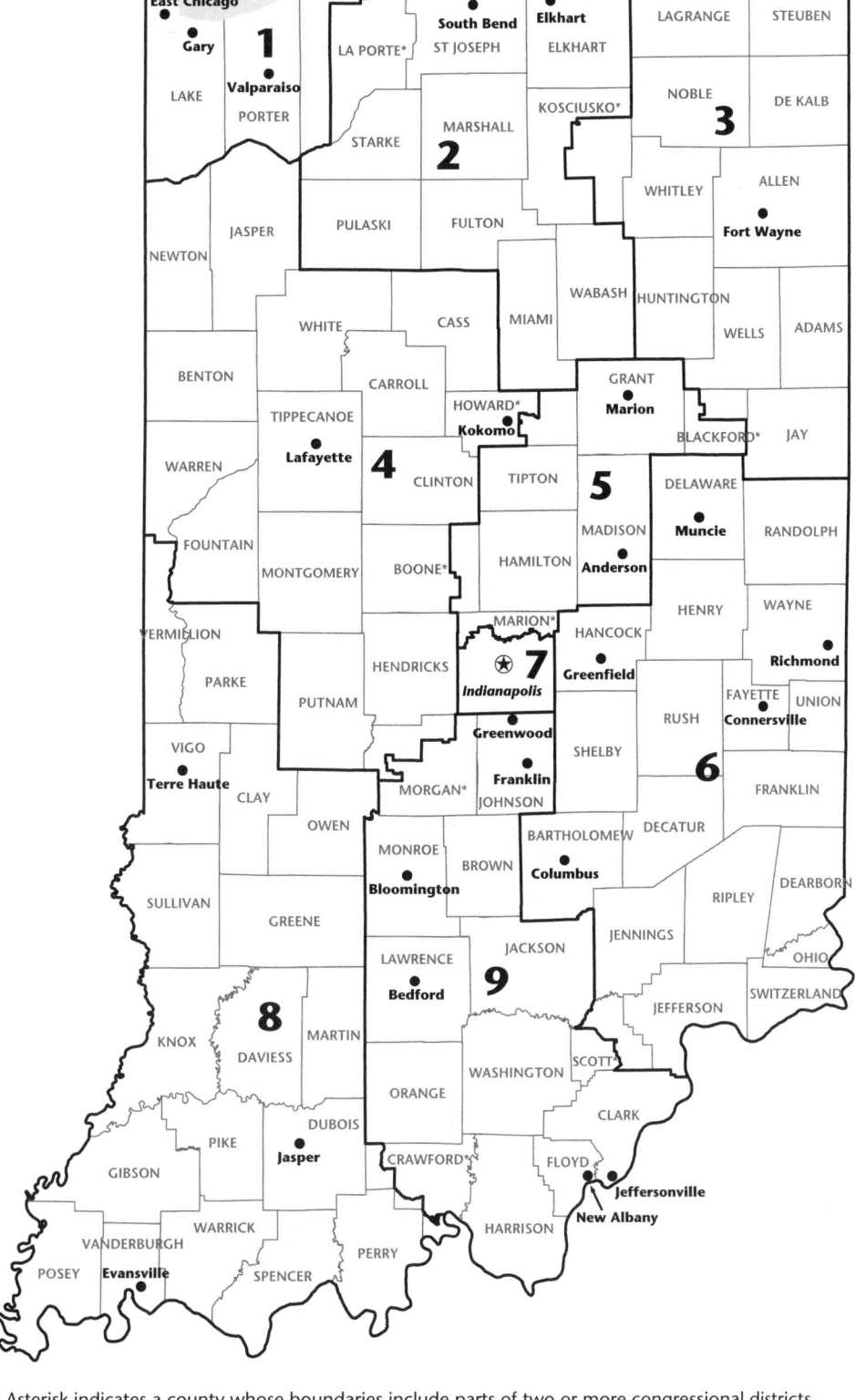

* Asterisk indicates a county whose boundaries include parts of two or more congressional districts.

INDIANA

GOVERNOR
Mike Pence (R). Elected 2012 to a four-year term.

SENATORS (1 Republican, 1 Democrat)
Daniel Coats (R). Elected 2010 to a six-year term. Previously elected 1992, 1990.

Joe Donnelly (D). Elected 2012 to a six-year term.

REPRESENTATIVES (7 Republicans, 2 Democrats)
1. Peter J. Visclosky (D)
2. Jackie Walorski (R)
3. Marlin A. Stutzman (R)
4. Todd Rokita (R)
5. Susan W. Brooks (R)
6. Luke Messer (R)
7. André Carson (D)
8. Larry Bucshon (R)
9. Todd C. Young (R)

POSTWAR VOTE FOR PRESIDENT

| | | Republican | | Democratic | | Other | Rep.-Dem. | Percentage | | | |
| | | | | | | | | Total Vote | | Major Vote | |
Year	Total Vote	Vote	Candidate	Vote	Candidate	Vote	Plurality	Rep.	Dem.	Rep.	Dem.
2012	2,624,534	1,420,543	Romney, W. Mitt	1,152,887	Obama, Barack H.*	51,104	267,656 R	54.1%	43.9%	55.2%	44.8%
2008	2,751,054	1,345,648	McCain, John S. III	1,374,039	Obama, Barack H.	31,367	28,391 D	48.9%	49.9%	49.5%	50.5%
2004	2,468,002	1,479,438	Bush, George W.*	969,011	Kerry, John F.	19,553	510,427 R	59.9%	39.3%	60.4%	39.6%
2000**	2,199,305	1,245,836	Bush, George W.	901,980	Gore, Albert Jr.	51,489	343,856 R	56.6%	41.0%	58.0%	42.0%
1996**	2,135,842	1,006,693	Dole, Robert "Bob"	887,424	Clinton, Bill*	241,725	119,269 R	47.1%	41.5%	53.1%	46.9%
1992**	2,305,871	989,375	Bush, George H.*	848,420	Clinton, Bill	468,076	140,955 R	42.9%	36.8%	53.8%	46.2%
1988	2,168,621	1,297,763	Bush, George H.	860,643	Dukakis, Michael S.	10,215	437,120 R	59.8%	39.7%	60.1%	39.9%
1984	2,233,069	1,377,230	Reagan, Ronald*	841,481	Mondale, Walter F.	14,358	535,749 R	61.7%	37.7%	62.1%	37.9%
1980**	2,242,033	1,255,656	Reagan, Ronald	844,197	Carter, Jimmy*	142,180	411,459 R	56.0%	37.7%	59.8%	40.2%
1976	2,220,362	1,183,958	Ford, Gerald R.*	1,014,714	Carter, Jimmy	21,690	169,244 R	53.3%	45.7%	53.8%	46.2%
1972	2,125,529	1,405,154	Nixon, Richard M.*	708,568	McGovern, George S.	11,807	696,586 R	66.1%	33.3%	66.5%	33.5%
1968**	2,123,597	1,067,885	Nixon, Richard M.	806,659	Humphrey, Hubert Horatio Jr.	249,053	261,226 R	50.3%	38.0%	57.0%	43.0%
1964	2,091,606	911,118	Goldwater, Barry M. Sr.	1,170,848	Johnson, Lyndon B.*	9,640	259,730 D	43.6%	56.0%	43.8%	56.2%
1960	2,135,360	1,175,120	Nixon, Richard M.	952,358	Kennedy, John F.	7,882	222,762 R	55.0%	44.6%	55.2%	44.8%
1956	1,974,607	1,182,811	Eisenhower, Dwight D.*	783,908	Stevenson, Adlai E. II	7,888	398,903 R	59.9%	39.7%	60.1%	39.9%
1952	1,955,049	1,136,259	Eisenhower, Dwight D.	801,530	Stevenson, Adlai E. II	17,260	334,729 R	58.1%	41.0%	58.6%	41.4%
1948	1,656,212	821,079	Dewey, Thomas E.	807,831	Truman, Harry S.*	27,302	13,248 R	49.6%	48.8%	50.4%	49.6%

Note: An asterisk (*) denotes incumbent. **In past elections, the other vote included: 2000 - 18,531 Green (Ralph Nader); 1996 - 224,299 Reform (Ross Perot); 1992 - 455,934 Independent (Perot); 1980 - 111,639 Independent (John Anderson); 1968 - 243,108 American Independent (George Wallace).

INDIANA

POSTWAR VOTE FOR GOVERNOR

Year	Total Vote	Republican Vote	Republican Candidate	Democratic Vote	Democratic Candidate	Other Vote	Rep.-Dem. Plurality	Total Vote Rep.	Total Vote Dem.	Major Vote Rep.	Major Vote Dem.
2012	2,577,329	1,275,424	Pence, Mike	1,200,016	Gregg, John R.	101,889	75,408 R	49.5%	46.6%	51.5%	48.5%
2008	2,703,752	1,563,885	Daniels, Mitch*	1,082,463	Thompson, Jill Long	57,404	481,422 R	57.8%	40.0%	59.1%	40.9%
2004	2,448,498	1,302,912	Daniels, Mitch	1,113,900	Kernan, Joseph E.	31,686	189,012 R	53.2%	45.5%	53.9%	46.1%
2000	2,179,413	908,285	McIntosh, David M.	1,232,525	O'Bannon, Frank*	38,603	324,240 D	41.7%	56.6%	42.4%	57.6%
1996	2,110,047	986,982	Goldsmith, Stephen	1,087,128	O'Bannon, Frank	35,937	100,146 D	46.8%	51.5%	47.6%	52.4%
1992	2,229,116	822,533	Pearson, Linley E.	1,382,151	Bayh, Evan*	24,432	559,618 D	36.9%	62.0%	37.3%	62.7%
1988	2,140,781	1,002,207	Mutz, John M.	1,138,574	Bayh, Evan		136,367 D	46.8%	53.2%	46.8%	53.2%
1984	2,197,988	1,146,497	Orr, Robert D.*	1,036,922	Townsend, W. Wayne	14,569	109,575 R	52.2%	47.2%	52.5%	47.5%
1980	2,178,403	1,257,383	Orr, Robert D.	913,116	Hillenbrand, John A.	7,904	344,267 R	57.7%	41.9%	57.9%	42.1%
1976	2,175,324	1,236,555	Bowen, Otis R.*	927,243	Conrad, Larry A.	11,526	309,312 R	56.8%	42.6%	57.1%	42.9%
1972	2,120,847	1,203,903	Bowen, Otis R.	900,489	Welsh, Matthew E.	16,455	303,414 R	56.8%	42.5%	57.2%	42.8%
1968	2,049,063	1,080,262	Whitcomb, Edgar D.	965,816	Rock, Robert L.	2,985	114,446 R	52.7%	47.1%	52.8%	47.2%
1964	2,073,058	901,342	Ristine, Richard O.	1,164,763	Branigin, Roger D.	6,953	263,421 D	43.5%	56.2%	43.6%	56.4%
1960	2,128,965	1,049,540	Parker, Crawford F.	1,072,717	Welsh, Matthew E.	6,708	23,177 D	49.3%	50.4%	49.5%	50.5%
1956	1,954,290	1,086,868	Handley, Harold W.	859,393	Tucker, Ralph	8,029	227,475 R	55.6%	44.0%	55.8%	44.2%
1952	1,931,869	1,075,685	Craig, George N.	841,984	Watkins, John A.	14,200	233,701 R	55.7%	43.6%	56.1%	43.9%
1948	1,652,321	745,892	Creighton, Hobart	884,995	Schricker, Henry F.	21,434	139,103 D	45.1%	53.6%	45.7%	54.3%

Note: An asterisk (*) denotes incumbent.

POSTWAR VOTE FOR SENATOR

Year	Total Vote	Republican Vote	Republican Candidate	Democratic Vote	Democratic Candidate	Other Vote	Rep.-Dem. Plurality	Total Vote Rep.	Total Vote Dem.	Major Vote Rep.	Major Vote Dem.
2012	2,560,102	1,133,621	Mourdock, Richard E.	1,281,181	Donnelly, Joe S.	145,300	147,560 D	44.3%	50.0%	46.9%	53.1%
2010	1,744,481	952,116	Coats, Daniel	697,775	Ellsworth, Brad	94,590	254,341 R	54.6%	40.0%	57.7%	42.3%
2006**	1,341,111	1,171,553	Lugar, Richard G.*			169,558	1,171,553 R	87.4%		100.0%	
2004	2,428,233	903,913	Scott, Marvin B.	1,496,976	Bayh, Evan*	27,344	593,063 D	37.2%	61.6%	37.6%	62.4%
2000	2,145,209	1,427,944	Lugar, Richard G.*	683,273	Johnson, David L.	33,992	744,671 R	66.6%	31.9%	67.6%	32.4%
1998	1,588,617	552,732	Helmke, Paul	1,012,244	Bayh, Evan	23,641	459,512 D	34.8%	63.7%	35.3%	64.7%
1994	1,543,568	1,039,625	Lugar, Richard G.*	470,799	Jontz, Jim	33,144	568,826 R	67.4%	30.5%	68.8%	31.2%
1992	2,211,426	1,267,972	Coats, Daniel*	900,148	Hogsett, Joseph H.	43,306	367,824 R	57.3%	40.7%	58.5%	41.5%
1990S	1,504,302	806,048	Coats, Daniel	696,639	Hill, Baron P.	1,615	109,409 R	53.6%	46.3%	53.6%	46.4%
1988	2,099,303	1,430,525	Lugar, Richard G.*	668,778	Wickes, Jack		761,747 R	68.1%	31.9%	68.1%	31.9%
1986	1,545,563	936,143	Quayle, John Danforth*	595,192	Long, Jill Lynette	14,228	340,951 R	60.6%	38.5%	61.1%	38.9%
1982	1,817,287	978,301	Lugar, Richard G.*	828,400	Fithian, Floyd	10,586	149,901 R	53.8%	45.6%	54.1%	45.9%
1980	2,198,376	1,182,414	Quayle, John Danforth	1,015,962	Bayh, Birch Evan*		166,452 R	53.8%	46.2%	53.8%	46.2%
1976	2,171,187	1,275,833	Lugar, Richard G.	878,522	Hartke, R. Vance*	16,832	397,311 R	58.8%	40.5%	59.2%	40.8%
1974	1,752,978	814,117	Lugar, Richard G.	889,269	Bayh, Birch Evan*	49,592	75,152 D	46.4%	50.7%	47.8%	52.2%
1970	1,737,697	866,707	Roudebush, Richard	870,990	Hartke, R. Vance*		4,283 D	49.9%	50.1%	49.9%	50.1%
1968	2,053,118	988,571	Ruckelshaus, William	1,060,456	Bayh, Birch Evan*	4,091	71,885 D	48.1%	51.7%	48.2%	51.8%
1964	2,076,963	941,519	Bontrager, D. Russell	1,128,505	Hartke, R. Vance*	6,939	186,986 D	45.3%	54.3%	45.5%	54.5%
1962	1,800,038	894,547	Capehart, Homer E.*	905,491	Bayh, Birch Evan		10,944 D	49.7%	50.3%	49.7%	50.3%
1958	1,724,598	731,635	Handley, Harold W.	973,636	Hartke, R. Vance	19,327	242,001 D	42.4%	56.5%	42.9%	57.1%
1956	1,963,986	1,084,262	Capehart, Homer E.*	871,781	Wickard, Claude R.	7,943	212,481 R	55.2%	44.4%	55.4%	44.6%
1952	1,946,118	1,020,605	Jenner, William E.*	911,169	Schricker, Henry F.	14,344	109,436 R	52.4%	46.8%	52.8%	47.2%
1950	1,598,724	844,303	Capehart, Homer E.*	741,025	Campbell, Alex M.	13,396	103,278 R	52.8%	46.4%	53.3%	46.7%
1946	1,347,434	739,809	Jenner, William E.	584,288	Townsend, M. Clifford	23,337	155,521 R	54.9%	43.4%	55.9%	44.1%

Note: An asterisk (*) denotes incumbent. **In past elections, the other vote included: 2006 - 168,820 Libertarian (Steve Osborn), who finished second. The 1990 election was for a short term to fill a vacancy. The Democratic Party did not run a candidate in the 2006 senate election.

INDIANA

HOUSE OF REPRESENTATIVES

CD	Year	Total Vote	Republican		Democratic		Other Vote	Rep.-Dem. Plurality	Percentage			
									Total Vote		Major Vote	
			Vote	Candidate	Vote	Candidate			Rep.	Dem.	Rep.	Dem.
1	2014	142,293	51,000	LEYVA, MARK J.	86,579	VISCLOSKY, PETER J.*	4,714	35,579 D	35.8%	60.8%	37.1%	62.9%
1	2012	279,034	91,291	PHELPS, JOEL	187,743	VISCLOSKY, PETER J.*		96,452 D	32.7%	67.3%	32.7%	67.3%
2	2014	145,200	85,583	WALORSKI, JACKIE*	55,590	BOCK, JOE	4,027	29,993 R	58.9%	38.3%	60.6%	39.4%
2	2012	273,475	134,033	WALORSKI, JACKIE	130,113	MULLEN, BRENDAN	9,329	3,920 R	49.0%	47.6%	50.7%	49.3%
3	2014	148,793	102,889	STUTZMAN, MARLIN A.*	39,771	KUHNLE, JUSTIN	6,133	63,118 R	69.1%	26.7%	72.1%	27.9%
3	2012	280,235	187,872	STUTZMAN, MARLIN A.*	92,363	BOYD, KEVIN		95,509 R	67.0%	33.0%	67.0%	33.0%
4	2014	142,054	94,998	ROKITA, TODD*	47,056	DALE, JOHN		47,942 R	66.9%	33.1%	66.9%	33.1%
4	2012	272,268	168,688	ROKITA, TODD*	93,015	NELSON, TARA E.	10,565	75,673 R	62.0%	34.2%	64.5%	35.5%
5	2014	161,440	105,277	BROOKS, SUSAN W.*	49,756	DENNEY, SHAWN A.	6,407	55,521 R	65.2%	30.8%	67.9%	32.1%
5	2012	333,359	194,570	BROOKS, SUSAN W.	125,347	RESKE, SCOTT	13,442	69,223 R	58.4%	37.6%	60.8%	39.2%
6	2014	155,071	102,187	MESSER, LUKE*	45,509	HEITZMAN, SUSAN HALL	7,375	56,678 R	65.9%	29.3%	69.2%	30.8%
6	2012	275,253	162,613	MESSER, LUKE	96,678	BOOKOUT, BRAD	15,962	65,935 R	59.1%	35.1%	62.7%	37.3%
7	2014	112,261	46,887	PING, CATHERINE "CAT"	61,443	CARSON, ANDRE*	3,931	14,556 D	41.8%	54.7%	43.3%	56.7%
7	2012	257,950	95,828	MAY, CARLOS	162,122	CARSON, ANDRE*		66,294 D	37.1%	62.9%	37.1%	62.9%
8	2014	171,315	103,344	BUCSHON, LARRY	61,384	SPANGLER, TOM	6,587	41,960 R	60.3%	35.8%	62.7%	37.3%
8	2012	283,992	151,533	BUCSHON, LARRY*	122,325	CROOKS, DAVE	10,134	29,208 R	53.4%	43.1%	55.3%	44.7%
9	2014	162,387	101,594	YOUNG, TODD C.*	55,016	BAILEY, BILL	5,777	46,578 R	62.6%	33.9%	64.9%	35.1%
9	2012	298,180	165,332	YOUNG, TODD C.*	132,848	YODER, SHELLI		32,484 R	55.4%	44.6%	55.4%	44.6%
TOTAL	2014	1,340,814	793,759		502,104		44,951	291,655 R	59.2%	37.4%	61.3%	38.7%
TOTAL	2012	2,553,746	1,351,760		1,142,554		59,432	209,206 R	52.9%	44.7%	54.2%	45.8%

Note: An asterisk (*) denotes incumbent.

INDIANA

GENERAL AND PRIMARY ELECTIONS

2014 GENERAL ELECTIONS: OTHER VOTES

House   Other vote was:

CD 1   4,714 Libertarian (Donna Dunn)
CD 2   4,027 Libertarian (Jeff Petermann)
CD 3   6,133 Libertarian (Scott Wise)
CD 5   6,407 Libertarian (John Krom)
CD 6   7,375 Libertarian (Eric Miller)
CD 7   3,931 Libertarian (Chris Mayo)
CD 8   6,587 Libertarian (Andrew M. "Andy" Horning)
CD 9   5,777 Libertarian (R. Mike Frey)

2014 PRIMARY ELECTIONS: SUPPLEMENTARY INFORMATION

Primary   May 6, 2014   **Registration**   4,571,744   No Party Registration
                                  (as of May 6, 2014)

Primary Type   Open—Any registered voter could participate in the primary of either party, although he or she could be challenged based on party affiliation. When voters challenged, they must execute a statement saying that they voted for a majority of the party's candidates in the previous general election. If they did not vote in the previous general election, they must indicate that they will vote for a majority of the party's candidates in the next general election.

INDIANA

GENERAL AND PRIMARY ELECTIONS

	REPUBLICAN PRIMARIES			DEMOCRATIC PRIMARIES		
Congressional District 1	Leyva, Mark J.	12,738	100.0%	Visclosky, Peter J.*	34,446	100.0%
	TOTAL	*12,738*		*TOTAL*	*34,446*	
Congressional District 2	Walorski, Jackie*	28,641	100.0%	Bock, Joe	11,103	58.1%
				Morrison, Dan	3,540	18.5%
				Kern, Bob	2,634	13.8%
				Carpenter, Douglas M.	1,837	9.6%
	TOTAL	*28,641*		*TOTAL*	*19,114*	
Congressional District 3	Stutzman, Marlin A.*	48,837	81.7%	Kuhnle, Justin	2,893	34.9%
	Baringer, Mark William	5,868	9.8%	Schrader, Thomas Allen	2,805	33.8%
	Mahoney III, James E. "Jim"	5,094	8.5%	Redmond, Jim	2,597	31.3%
	TOTAL	*59,799*		*TOTAL*	*8,295*	
Congressional District 4	Rokita, Todd*	43,179	71.2%	Dale, John	3,742	42.2%
	Grant, Kevin Jay	17,472	28.8%	Day, Roger D.	2,266	25.5%
				Blaydes, Jeffrey Oliver	1,332	15.0%
				Pollchik, Howard Joseph	778	8.8%
				Futrell, John L.	754	8.5%
	TOTAL	*60,651*		*TOTAL*	*8,872*	
Congressional District 5	Brooks, Susan W.*	34,996	72.7%	Denney, Shawn A.	6,141	41.9%
	Stockdale, David S.	7,327	15.2%	Ford, David William	4,856	33.1%
	Campbell, David M. "Mike"	5,790	12.0%	Davidson, Allen Ray	3,660	25.0%
	TOTAL	*48,113*		*TOTAL*	*14,657*	
Congressional District 6	Messer, Luke*	49,094	100.0%	Heitzman, Susan Hall	9,078	48.3%
				Siekman, Lane	5,574	29.6%
				Westerfield, Corrine Nicole	4,151	22.1%
	TOTAL	*49,094*		*TOTAL*	*18,803*	
Congressional District 7	Ping, Catherine "Cat"	4,882	35.1%	Carson, Andre*	19,446	89.1%
	Harmon, Wayne E.	3,258	23.4%	Godfrey, Curtis	1,209	5.5%
	Miniear, JD	2,840	20.4%	Ajabu, Mmoja	782	3.6%
	Smith, Gordon E.	1,872	13.5%	Pullins, Pierre Quincy	390	1.8%
	Magee, Erin Kent	1,057	7.6%			
	TOTAL	*13,909*		*TOTAL*	*21,827*	
Congressional District 8	Bucshon, Larry*	30,967	74.9%	Spangler, Tom	23,055	100.0%
	McNeil, Andrew T.	10,405	25.1%			
	TOTAL	*41,372*		*TOTAL*	*23,055*	
Congressional District 9	Young, Todd C.*	30,402	79.4%	Bailey, Bill	10,394	45.4%
	Heil, Kathy Lowe	4,607	12.0%	McClure, James R. Jr.	5,737	25.1%
	Jones, Mark G.	3,293	8.6%	Miller, J. S.	3,561	15.6%
				Thomas, William Joseph	3,206	14.0%
	TOTAL	*38,302*		*TOTAL*	*22,898*	

Note: An asterisk (*) denotes incumbent.

IOWA

Congressional districts first established for elections held in 2012

4 members

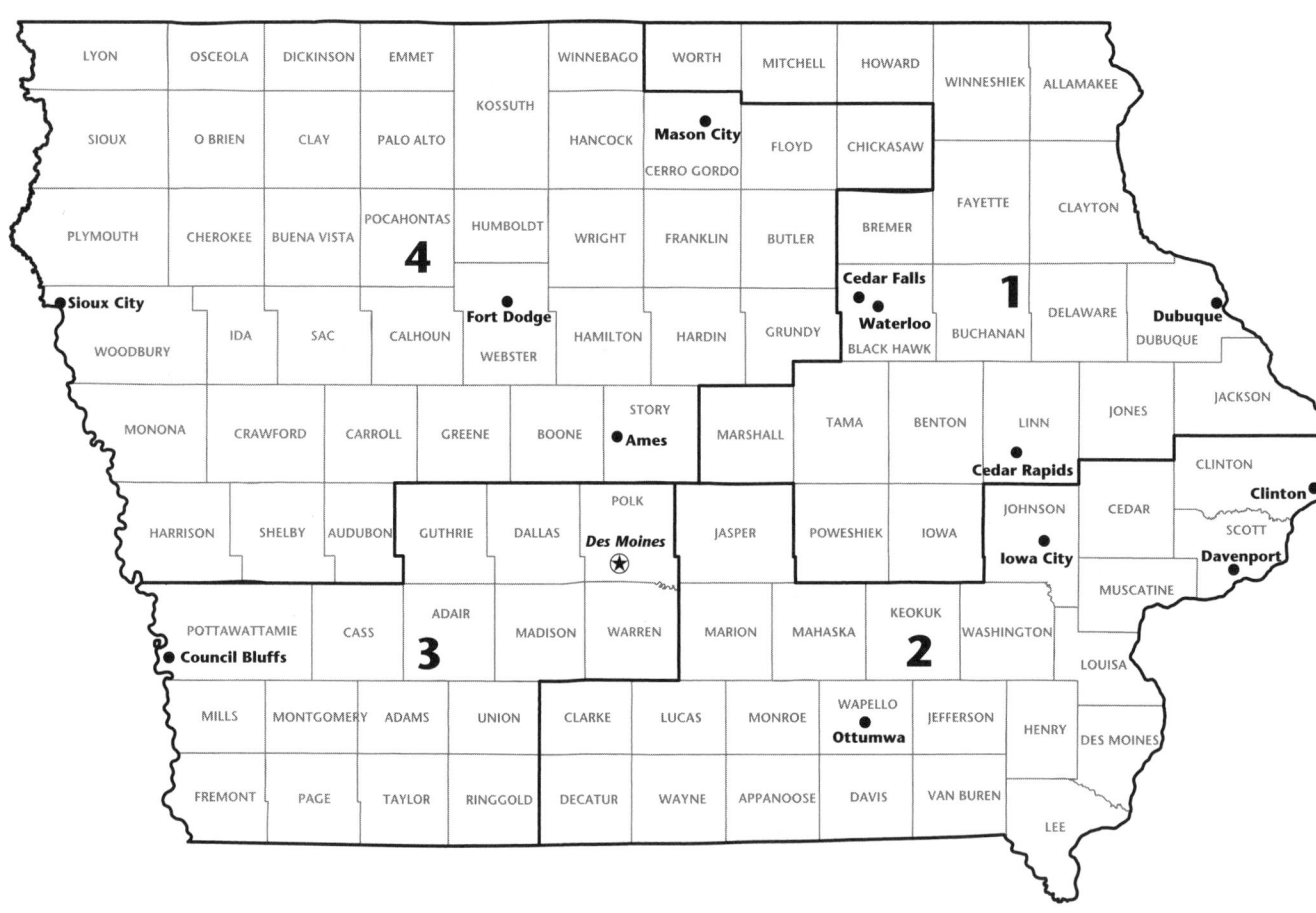

IOWA

GOVERNOR
Terry E. Branstad (R). Reelected 2014 to a four-year term. Previously elected 2010, 1994, 1990, 1986, 1982.

SENATORS (2 Republicans)
Joni Ernst (R). Elected 2014 to a six-year term.

Chuck Grassley (R). Reelected 2010 to a six-year term. Previously elected 2004, 1998, 1992, 1986, 1980.

REPRESENTATIVES (3 Republicans, 1 Democrat)
1. Rod Blum (R)
2. David Loebsack (D)
3. David Young (R)
4. Steve King (R)

POSTWAR VOTE FOR PRESIDENT

| | | Republican | | Democratic | | | | Percentage | | | |
| | | | | | | Other | Rep.-Dem. | Total Vote | | Major Vote | |
Year	Total Vote	Vote	Candidate	Vote	Candidate	Vote	Plurality	Rep.	Dem.	Rep.	Dem.
2012	1,582,180	730,617	Romney, W. Mitt	822,544	Obama, Barack H.*	29,019	91,927 D	46.2%	52.0%	47.0%	53.0%
2008	1,537,123	682,379	McCain, John S. III	828,940	Obama, Barack H.	25,804	146,561 D	44.4%	53.9%	45.2%	54.8%
2004	1,506,908	751,957	Bush, George W.*	741,898	Kerry, John F.	13,053	10,059 R	49.9%	49.2%	50.3%	49.7%
2000**	1,315,563	634,373	Bush, George W.	638,517	Gore, Albert Jr.	42,673	4,144 D	48.2%	48.5%	49.8%	50.2%
1996**	1,234,075	492,644	Dole, Robert "Bob"	620,258	Clinton, Bill*	121,173	127,614 D	39.9%	50.3%	44.3%	55.7%
1992**	1,354,607	504,891	Bush, George H.*	586,353	Clinton, Bill	263,363	81,462 D	37.3%	43.3%	46.3%	53.7%
1988	1,225,614	545,355	Bush, George H.	670,557	Dukakis, Michael S.	9,702	125,202 D	44.5%	54.7%	44.9%	55.1%
1984	1,319,805	703,088	Reagan, Ronald*	605,620	Mondale, Walter F.	11,097	97,468 R	53.3%	45.9%	53.7%	46.3%
1980**	1,317,661	676,026	Reagan, Ronald	508,672	Carter, Jimmy*	132,963	167,354 R	51.3%	38.6%	57.1%	42.9%
1976	1,279,306	632,863	Ford, Gerald R.*	619,931	Carter, Jimmy	26,512	12,932 R	49.5%	48.5%	50.5%	49.5%
1972	1,225,944	706,207	Nixon, Richard M.*	496,206	McGovern, George S.	23,531	210,001 R	57.6%	40.5%	58.7%	41.3%
1968**	1,167,931	619,106	Nixon, Richard M.	476,699	Humphrey, Hubert Horatio Jr.	72,126	142,407 R	53.0%	40.8%	56.5%	43.5%
1964	1,184,539	449,148	Goldwater, Barry M. Sr.	733,030	Johnson, Lyndon B.*	2,361	283,882 D	37.9%	61.9%	38.0%	62.0%
1960	1,273,810	722,381	Nixon, Richard M.	550,565	Kennedy, John F.	864	171,816 R	56.7%	43.2%	56.7%	43.3%
1956	1,234,564	729,187	Eisenhower, Dwight D.*	501,858	Stevenson, Adlai E. II	3,519	227,329 R	59.1%	40.7%	59.2%	40.8%
1952	1,268,773	808,906	Eisenhower, Dwight D.	451,513	Stevenson, Adlai E. II	8,354	357,393 R	63.8%	35.6%	64.2%	35.8%
1948	1,038,264	494,018	Dewey, Thomas E.	522,380	Truman, Harry S.*	21,866	28,362 D	47.6%	50.3%	48.6%	51.4%

Note: An asterisk (*) denotes incumbent. **In past elections, the other vote included: 2000 - 29,374 Green (Ralph Nader); 1996 - 105,159 Reform (Ross Perot); 1992 - 253,468 Independent (Perot); 1980 - 115,633 Independent (John Anderson); 1968 - 66,422 American Independent (George Wallace).

IOWA

POSTWAR VOTE FOR GOVERNOR

| Year | Total Vote | Republican | | Democratic | | Other Vote | Rep.-Dem. Plurality | Percentage | | | |
| | | Vote | Candidate | Vote | Candidate | | | Total Vote | | Major Vote | |
								Rep.	Dem.	Rep.	Dem.
2014	1,129,057	666,032	Branstad, Terry E.*	420,787	Hatch, Jack	42,238	245,245 R	59.0%	37.3%	61.3%	38.7%
2010	1,122,013	592,494	Branstad, Terry E.	484,798	Culver, Chet*	44,721	107,696 R	52.8%	43.2%	55.0%	45.0%
2006	1,053,255	467,425	Nussle, Jim	569,021	Culver, Chet	16,809	101,596 D	44.4%	54.0%	45.1%	54.9%
2002	1,025,802	456,612	Gross, Doug	540,449	Vilsack, Tom*	28,741	83,837 D	44.5%	52.7%	45.8%	54.2%
1998	956,418	444,787	Lightfoot, Jim Ross	500,231	Vilsack, Tom	11,400	55,444 D	46.5%	52.3%	47.1%	52.9%
1994	997,248	566,395	Branstad, Terry E.*	414,453	Campbell, Bonnie J.	16,400	151,942 R	56.8%	41.6%	57.7%	42.3%
1990	976,483	591,852	Branstad, Terry E.*	379,372	Avenson, Donald D.	5,259	212,480 R	60.6%	38.9%	60.9%	39.1%
1986	910,623	472,712	Branstad, Terry E.*	436,987	Junkins, Lowell L.	924	35,725 R	51.9%	48.0%	52.0%	48.0%
1982	1,038,229	548,313	Branstad, Terry E.	483,291	Conlin, Roxanne	6,625	65,022 R	52.8%	46.5%	53.2%	46.8%
1978	843,190	491,713	Ray, Robert E.*	345,519	Fitzgerald, Jerome D.	5,958	146,194 R	58.3%	41.0%	58.7%	41.3%
1974**	920,458	534,518	Ray, Robert E.*	377,553	Schaben, James F.	8,387	156,965 R	58.1%	41.0%	58.6%	41.4%
1972	1,210,222	707,177	Ray, Robert E.*	487,282	Franzenburg, Paul	15,763	219,895 R	58.4%	40.3%	59.2%	40.8%
1970	791,241	403,394	Ray, Robert E.*	368,911	Fulton, Robert	18,936	34,483 R	51.0%	46.6%	52.2%	47.8%
1968	1,135,988	613,827	Ray, Robert E.	521,216	Franzenburg, Paul	945	92,611 R	54.0%	45.9%	54.1%	45.9%
1966	893,175	394,518	Murray, William G.	494,259	Hughes, Harold E.*	4,398	99,741 D	44.2%	55.3%	44.4%	55.6%
1964	1,167,734	365,131	Hultman, Evan	794,610	Hughes, Harold E.*	7,993	429,479 D	31.3%	68.0%	31.5%	68.5%
1962	819,854	388,955	Erbe, Norman A.*	430,899	Hughes, Harold E.		41,944 D	47.4%	52.6%	47.4%	52.6%
1960	1,237,089	645,026	Erbe, Norman A.	592,063	McManus, E. J.		52,963 R	52.1%	47.9%	52.1%	47.9%
1958	859,095	394,071	Murray, William G.	465,024	Loveless, Herschel C.*		70,953 D	45.9%	54.1%	45.9%	54.1%
1956	1,204,235	587,383	Hoegh, Leo A.*	616,852	Loveless, Herschel C.		29,469 D	48.8%	51.2%	48.8%	51.2%
1954	848,592	435,944	Hoegh, Leo A.	410,255	Herring, Clyde E.	2,393	25,689 R	51.4%	48.3%	51.5%	48.5%
1952	1,230,045	638,388	Beardsley, William*	587,671	Loveless, Herschel C.	3,986	50,717 R	51.9%	47.8%	52.1%	47.9%
1950	857,213	506,642	Beardsley, William*	347,176	Gillette, Lester S.	3,395	159,466 R	59.1%	40.5%	59.3%	40.7%
1948	994,833	553,900	Beardsley, William	434,432	Switzer, Carroll O.	6,501	119,468 R	55.7%	43.7%	56.0%	44.0%
1946	631,681	362,592	Blue, Robert D.	266,190	Miles, Frank	2,899	96,402 R	57.4%	42.1%	57.7%	42.3%

Note: An asterisk (*) denotes incumbent. **The term of office of Iowa's governor was increased from two to four years effective with the 1974 election.

POSTWAR VOTE FOR SENATOR

| Year | Total Vote | Republican | | Democratic | | Other Vote | Rep.-Dem. Plurality | Percentage | | | |
| | | Vote | Candidate | Vote | Candidate | | | Total Vote | | Major Vote | |
								Rep.	Dem.	Rep.	Dem.
2014	1,129,700	588,575	Ernst, Joni	494,370	Braley, Bruce	46,755	94,205 R	52.1%	43.8%	54.3%	45.7%
2010	1,116,063	718,215	Grassley, Chuck*	371,686	Conlin, Roxanne	26,162	346,529 R	64.4%	33.3%	65.9%	34.1%
2008	1,502,918	560,006	Reed, Christopher	941,665	Harkin, Tom*	1,247	381,659 D	37.3%	62.7%	37.3%	62.7%
2004	1,479,228	1,038,175	Grassley, Chuck*	412,365	Small, Arthur A.	28,688	625,810 R	70.2%	27.9%	71.6%	28.4%
2002	1,023,075	447,892	Ganske, Greg	554,278	Harkin, Tom*	20,905	106,386 D	43.8%	54.2%	44.7%	55.3%
1998	947,907	648,480	Grassley, Chuck*	289,049	Osterberg, David	10,378	359,431 R	68.4%	30.5%	69.2%	30.8%
1996	1,224,054	571,807	Lightfoot, Jim Ross	634,166	Harkin, Tom*	18,081	62,359 D	46.7%	51.8%	47.4%	52.6%
1992	1,292,494	899,761	Grassley, Chuck*	351,561	Lloyd-Jones, Jean	41,172	548,200 R	69.6%	27.2%	71.9%	28.1%
1990	983,933	446,869	Tauke, Tom	535,975	Harkin, Tom*	1,089	89,106 D	45.4%	54.5%	45.5%	54.5%
1986	891,762	588,880	Grassley, Chuck*	299,406	Roehrick, John P.	3,476	289,474 R	66.0%	33.6%	66.3%	33.7%
1984	1,292,700	564,381	Jepsen, Roger W.*	716,883	Harkin, Tom	11,436	152,502 D	43.7%	55.5%	44.0%	56.0%
1980	1,277,034	683,014	Grassley, Chuck	581,545	Culver, John C.*	12,475	101,469 R	53.5%	45.5%	54.0%	46.0%
1978	824,654	421,598	Jepsen, Roger W.	395,066	Clark, Richard*	7,990	26,532 R	51.1%	47.9%	51.6%	48.4%
1974	889,561	420,546	Stanley, David M.	462,947	Culver, John C.	6,068	42,401 D	47.3%	52.0%	47.6%	52.4%
1972	1,203,333	530,525	Miller, Jack*	662,637	Clark, Richard	10,171	132,112 D	44.1%	55.1%	44.5%	55.5%
1968	1,144,086	568,469	Stanley, David M.	574,884	Hughes, Harold E.	733	6,415 D	49.7%	50.2%	49.7%	50.3%
1966	857,496	522,339	Miller, Jack*	324,114	Smith, E. B.	11,043	198,225 R	60.9%	37.8%	61.7%	38.3%
1962	807,972	431,364	Hickenlooper, Bourke B.*	376,602	Smith, E. B.	6	54,762 R	53.4%	46.6%	53.4%	46.6%
1960	1,237,582	642,463	Miller, Jack	595,119	Loveless, Herschel C.		47,344 R	51.9%	48.1%	51.9%	48.1%
1956	1,178,655	635,499	Hickenlooper, Bourke B.*	543,156	Evans, R. M.		92,343 R	53.9%	46.1%	53.9%	46.1%
1954	847,355	442,409	Martin, Thomas E.	402,712	Gillette, Guy M.*	2,234	39,697 R	52.2%	47.5%	52.3%	47.7%
1950	858,523	470,613	Hickenlooper, Bourke B.*	383,766	Loveland, Albert J.	4,144	86,847 R	54.8%	44.7%	55.1%	44.9%
1948	1,000,412	415,778	Wilson, George*	578,226	Gillette, Guy M.	6,408	162,448 D	41.6%	57.8%	41.8%	58.2%

Note: An asterisk (*) denotes incumbent.

IOWA
GOVERNOR 2014

2010 Census Population	County	Total Vote	Republican (Branstad)	Democratic (Hatch)	Other	Rep.-Dem. Plurality	Percentage Total Vote Rep.	Percentage Total Vote Dem.	Percentage Major Vote Rep.	Percentage Major Vote Dem.
7,682	ADAIR	3,162	2,153	872	137	1,281 R	68.1%	27.6%	71.2%	28.8%
4,029	ADAMS	1,712	1,230	419	63	811 R	71.8%	24.5%	74.6%	25.4%
14,330	ALLAMAKEE	5,268	3,393	1,725	150	1,668 R	64.4%	32.7%	66.3%	33.7%
12,887	APPANOOSE	4,430	2,882	1,350	198	1,532 R	65.1%	30.5%	68.1%	31.9%
6,119	AUDUBON	2,442	1,654	706	82	948 R	67.7%	28.9%	70.1%	29.9%
26,076	BENTON	10,285	6,382	3,514	389	2,868 R	62.1%	34.2%	64.5%	35.5%
131,090	BLACK HAWK	46,546	23,633	21,506	1,407	2,127 R	50.8%	46.2%	52.4%	47.6%
26,306	BOONE	10,569	5,922	4,171	476	1,751 R	56.0%	39.5%	58.7%	41.3%
24,276	BREMER	10,045	6,083	3,661	301	2,422 R	60.6%	36.4%	62.4%	37.6%
20,958	BUCHANAN	7,893	4,498	3,118	277	1,380 R	57.0%	39.5%	59.1%	40.9%
20,260	BUENA VISTA	5,883	4,096	1,568	219	2,528 R	69.6%	26.7%	72.3%	27.7%
14,867	BUTLER	5,777	3,888	1,673	216	2,215 R	67.3%	29.0%	69.9%	30.1%
9,670	CALHOUN	4,033	2,660	1,025	348	1,635 R	66.0%	25.4%	72.2%	27.8%
20,816	CARROLL	8,114	5,370	2,452	292	2,918 R	66.2%	30.2%	68.7%	31.3%
13,956	CASS	5,039	3,542	1,331	166	2,211 R	70.3%	26.4%	72.7%	27.3%
18,499	CEDAR	7,327	4,632	2,484	211	2,148 R	63.2%	33.9%	65.1%	34.9%
44,151	CERRO GORDO	17,065	10,308	6,351	406	3,957 R	60.4%	37.2%	61.9%	38.1%
12,072	CHEROKEE	4,857	3,544	1,199	114	2,345 R	73.0%	24.7%	74.7%	25.3%
12,439	CHICKASAW	4,944	3,046	1,756	142	1,290 R	61.6%	35.5%	63.4%	36.6%
9,286	CLARKE	3,273	2,092	1,051	130	1,041 R	63.9%	32.1%	66.6%	33.4%
16,667	CLAY	6,043	4,355	1,521	167	2,834 R	72.1%	25.2%	74.1%	25.9%
18,129	CLAYTON	7,032	4,449	2,368	215	2,081 R	63.3%	33.7%	65.3%	34.7%
49,116	CLINTON	17,237	10,473	6,247	517	4,226 R	60.8%	36.2%	62.6%	37.4%
17,096	CRAWFORD	4,808	3,431	1,161	216	2,270 R	71.4%	24.1%	74.7%	25.3%
66,135	DALLAS	28,983	18,815	9,072	1,096	9,743 R	64.9%	31.3%	67.5%	32.5%
8,753	DAVIS	2,962	1,971	876	115	1,095 R	66.5%	29.6%	69.2%	30.8%
8,457	DECATUR	2,622	1,717	768	137	949 R	65.5%	29.3%	69.1%	30.9%
17,764	DELAWARE	6,911	4,604	2,131	176	2,473 R	66.6%	30.8%	68.4%	31.6%
40,325	DES MOINES	13,644	7,328	5,958	358	1,370 R	53.7%	43.7%	55.2%	44.8%
16,667	DICKINSON	7,299	5,294	1,889	116	3,405 R	72.5%	25.9%	73.7%	26.3%
93,653	DUBUQUE	36,295	21,049	14,295	951	6,754 R	58.0%	39.4%	59.6%	40.4%
10,302	EMMET	3,553	2,458	968	127	1,490 R	69.2%	27.2%	71.7%	28.3%
20,880	FAYETTE	7,831	4,745	2,815	271	1,930 R	60.6%	35.9%	62.8%	37.2%
16,303	FLOYD	6,035	3,788	2,083	164	1,705 R	62.8%	34.5%	64.5%	35.5%
10,680	FRANKLIN	3,934	2,796	980	158	1,816 R	71.1%	24.9%	74.0%	26.0%
7,441	FREMONT	2,434	1,671	626	137	1,045 R	68.7%	25.7%	72.7%	27.3%
9,336	GREENE	3,633	2,297	1,169	167	1,128 R	63.2%	32.2%	66.3%	33.7%
12,453	GRUNDY	5,328	3,761	1,340	227	2,421 R	70.6%	25.2%	73.7%	26.3%
10,954	GUTHRIE	4,370	2,896	1,251	223	1,645 R	66.3%	28.6%	69.8%	30.2%
15,673	HAMILTON	5,714	3,630	1,870	214	1,760 R	63.5%	32.7%	66.0%	34.0%
11,341	HANCOCK	4,383	3,218	996	169	2,222 R	73.4%	22.7%	76.4%	23.6%
17,534	HARDIN	6,809	4,328	2,122	359	2,206 R	63.6%	31.2%	67.1%	32.9%
14,928	HARRISON	5,003	3,442	1,191	370	2,251 R	68.8%	23.8%	74.3%	25.7%
20,145	HENRY	6,712	4,466	2,062	184	2,404 R	66.5%	30.7%	68.4%	31.6%
9,566	HOWARD	3,417	2,186	1,116	115	1,070 R	64.0%	32.7%	66.2%	33.8%
9,815	HUMBOLDT	3,892	2,765	995	132	1,770 R	71.0%	25.6%	73.5%	26.5%
7,089	IDA	2,726	2,161	517	48	1,644 R	79.3%	19.0%	80.7%	19.3%
16,355	IOWA	6,764	4,420	2,086	258	2,334 R	65.3%	30.8%	67.9%	32.1%
19,848	JACKSON	7,640	4,986	2,471	183	2,515 R	65.3%	32.3%	66.9%	33.1%
36,842	JASPER	14,984	8,245	5,918	821	2,327 R	55.0%	39.5%	58.2%	41.8%
16,843	JEFFERSON	6,321	3,169	2,856	296	313 R	50.1%	45.2%	52.6%	47.4%
130,882	JOHNSON	52,238	19,775	30,684	1,779	10,909 D	37.9%	58.7%	39.2%	60.8%
20,638	JONES	7,749	4,581	2,899	269	1,682 R	59.1%	37.4%	61.2%	38.8%
10,511	KEOKUK	3,736	2,641	981	114	1,660 R	70.7%	26.3%	72.9%	27.1%
15,543	KOSSUTH	6,636	4,509	1,911	216	2,598 R	67.9%	28.8%	70.2%	29.8%
35,862	LEE	10,716	5,647	4,638	431	1,009 R	52.7%	43.3%	54.9%	45.1%
211,226	LINN	86,321	44,586	39,036	2,699	5,550 R	51.7%	45.2%	53.3%	46.7%
11,387	LOUISA	3,400	2,297	993	110	1,304 R	67.6%	29.2%	69.8%	30.2%
8,898	LUCAS	3,212	2,102	945	165	1,157 R	65.4%	29.4%	69.0%	31.0%
11,581	LYON	4,362	3,787	491	84	3,296 R	86.8%	11.3%	88.5%	11.5%

IOWA

GOVERNOR 2014

2010 Census Population	County	Total Vote	Republican (Branstad)	Democratic (Hatch)	Other	Rep.-Dem. Plurality	Percentage			
							Total Vote		Major Vote	
							Rep.	Dem.	Rep.	Dem.
15,679	MADISON	6,526	4,210	1,980	336	2,230 R	64.5%	30.3%	68.0%	32.0%
22,381	MAHASKA	7,805	5,648	1,809	348	3,839 R	72.4%	23.2%	75.7%	24.3%
33,309	MARION	13,362	8,794	4,000	568	4,794 R	65.8%	29.9%	68.7%	31.3%
40,648	MARSHALL	13,718	7,202	5,958	558	1,244 R	52.5%	43.4%	54.7%	45.3%
15,059	MILLS	4,915	3,362	1,193	360	2,169 R	68.4%	24.3%	73.8%	26.2%
10,776	MITCHELL	4,169	2,993	1,089	87	1,904 R	71.8%	26.1%	73.3%	26.7%
9,243	MONONA	3,794	2,798	910	86	1,888 R	73.7%	24.0%	75.5%	24.5%
7,970	MONROE	2,934	1,974	827	133	1,147 R	67.3%	28.2%	70.5%	29.5%
10,740	MONTGOMERY	3,805	2,791	772	242	2,019 R	73.4%	20.3%	78.3%	21.7%
42,745	MUSCATINE	13,144	8,051	4,563	530	3,488 R	61.3%	34.7%	63.8%	36.2%
14,398	O'BRIEN	5,441	4,562	794	85	3,768 R	83.8%	14.6%	85.2%	14.8%
6,462	OSCEOLA	2,215	1,847	310	58	1,537 R	83.4%	14.0%	85.6%	14.4%
15,932	PAGE	4,833	3,545	1,097	191	2,448 R	73.3%	22.7%	76.4%	23.6%
9,421	PALO ALTO	3,678	2,492	1,087	99	1,405 R	67.8%	29.6%	69.6%	30.4%
24,986	PLYMOUTH	9,225	7,366	1,695	164	5,671 R	79.8%	18.4%	81.3%	18.7%
7,310	POCAHONTAS	2,872	1,991	736	145	1,255 R	69.3%	25.6%	73.0%	27.0%
430,640	POLK	164,258	82,490	73,904	7,864	8,586 R	50.2%	45.0%	52.7%	47.3%
93,158	POTTAWATTAMIE	26,208	16,646	8,023	1,539	8,623 R	63.5%	30.6%	67.5%	32.5%
18,914	POWESHIEK	7,450	4,134	3,017	299	1,117 R	55.5%	40.5%	57.8%	42.2%
5,131	RINGGOLD	2,081	1,447	552	82	895 R	69.5%	26.5%	72.4%	27.6%
10,350	SAC	3,856	2,815	899	142	1,916 R	73.0%	23.3%	75.8%	24.2%
165,224	SCOTT	61,559	37,488	22,415	1,656	15,073 R	60.9%	36.4%	62.6%	37.4%
12,167	SHELBY	4,288	3,217	943	128	2,274 R	75.0%	22.0%	77.3%	22.7%
33,704	SIOUX	13,426	12,236	1,013	177	11,223 R	91.1%	7.5%	92.4%	7.6%
89,542	STORY	32,845	16,725	14,566	1,554	2,159 R	50.9%	44.3%	53.4%	46.6%
17,767	TAMA	6,625	3,249	3,031	345	218 R	49.0%	45.8%	51.7%	48.3%
6,317	TAYLOR	2,198	1,598	527	73	1,071 R	72.7%	24.0%	75.2%	24.8%
12,534	UNION	2,083	1,397	569	117	828 R	67.1%	27.3%	71.1%	28.9%
7,570	VAN BUREN	2,864	2,013	718	133	1,295 R	70.3%	25.1%	73.7%	26.3%
35,625	WAPELLO	10,937	5,986	4,461	490	1,525 R	54.7%	40.8%	57.3%	42.7%
46,225	WARREN	19,565	11,509	7,123	933	4,386 R	58.8%	36.4%	61.8%	38.2%
21,704	WASHINGTON	8,260	5,268	2,654	338	2,614 R	63.8%	32.1%	66.5%	33.5%
6,403	WAYNE	2,177	1,512	576	89	936 R	69.5%	26.5%	72.4%	27.6%
38,013	WEBSTER	13,059	7,862	4,627	570	3,235 R	60.2%	35.4%	63.0%	37.0%
10,866	WINNEBAGO	4,258	3,130	1,039	89	2,091 R	73.5%	24.4%	75.1%	24.9%
21,056	WINNESHIEK	8,264	4,795	3,272	197	1,523 R	58.0%	39.6%	59.4%	40.6%
102,172	WOODBURY	30,286	19,840	9,542	904	10,298 R	65.5%	31.5%	67.5%	32.5%
7,598	WORTH	3,100	2,004	1,002	94	1,002 R	64.6%	32.3%	66.7%	33.3%
13,229	WRIGHT	4,621	3,198	1,266	157	1,932 R	69.2%	27.4%	71.6%	28.4%
3,046,355	TOTAL	1,129,057	666,032	420,787	42,238	245,245 R	59.0%	37.3%	61.3%	38.7%

IOWA

SENATOR 2014

2010 Census Population	County	Total Vote	Republican (Ernst)	Democratic (Braley)	Other	Rep.-Dem. Plurality	Percentage			
							Total Vote		Major Vote	
							Rep.	Dem.	Rep.	Dem.
7,682	ADAIR	3,142	1,967	989	186	978 R	62.6%	31.5%	66.5%	33.5%
4,029	ADAMS	1,687	1,111	494	82	617 R	65.9%	29.3%	69.2%	30.8%
14,330	ALLAMAKEE	5,235	2,762	2,177	296	585 R	52.8%	41.6%	55.9%	44.1%
12,887	APPANOOSE	4,388	2,531	1,595	262	936 R	57.7%	36.3%	61.3%	38.7%
6,119	AUDUBON	2,423	1,461	851	111	610 R	60.3%	35.1%	63.2%	36.8%

IOWA
SENATOR 2014

2010 Census Population	County	Total Vote	Republican (Ernst)	Democratic (Braley)	Other	Rep.-Dem. Plurality	Percentage Total Vote Rep.	Dem.	Major Vote Rep.	Dem.
26,076	BENTON	10,237	5,883	3,933	421	1,950 R	57.5%	38.4%	59.9%	40.1%
131,090	BLACK HAWK	46,746	21,007	24,311	1,428	3,304 D	44.9%	52.0%	46.4%	53.6%
26,306	BOONE	10,542	5,639	4,430	473	1,209 R	53.5%	42.0%	56.0%	44.0%
24,276	BREMER	10,049	5,487	4,207	355	1,280 R	54.6%	41.9%	56.6%	43.4%
20,958	BUCHANAN	7,881	3,945	3,538	398	407 R	50.1%	44.9%	52.7%	47.3%
20,260	BUENA VISTA	5,846	3,522	2,037	287	1,485 R	60.2%	34.8%	63.4%	36.6%
14,867	BUTLER	5,788	3,630	1,944	214	1,686 R	62.7%	33.6%	65.1%	34.9%
9,670	CALHOUN	3,996	2,543	1,257	196	1,286 R	63.6%	31.5%	66.9%	33.1%
20,816	CARROLL	8,035	4,728	2,907	400	1,821 R	58.8%	36.2%	61.9%	38.1%
13,956	CASS	5,011	3,292	1,528	191	1,764 R	65.7%	30.5%	68.3%	31.7%
18,499	CEDAR	7,333	4,017	2,986	330	1,031 R	54.8%	40.7%	57.4%	42.6%
44,151	CERRO GORDO	17,056	7,600	8,894	562	1,294 D	44.6%	52.1%	46.1%	53.9%
12,072	CHEROKEE	4,828	3,036	1,512	280	1,524 R	62.9%	31.3%	66.8%	33.2%
12,439	CHICKASAW	4,931	2,623	2,036	272	587 R	53.2%	41.3%	56.3%	43.7%
9,286	CLARKE	3,269	1,865	1,198	206	667 R	57.1%	36.6%	60.9%	39.1%
16,667	CLAY	6,000	3,793	1,906	301	1,887 R	63.2%	31.8%	66.6%	33.4%
18,129	CLAYTON	7,008	3,810	2,893	305	917 R	54.4%	41.3%	56.8%	43.2%
49,116	CLINTON	17,192	8,054	8,339	799	285 D	46.8%	48.5%	49.1%	50.9%
17,096	CRAWFORD	4,710	2,889	1,548	273	1,341 R	61.3%	32.9%	65.1%	34.9%
66,135	DALLAS	28,920	17,205	10,763	952	6,442 R	59.5%	37.2%	61.5%	38.5%
8,753	DAVIS	2,919	1,727	1,031	161	696 R	59.2%	35.3%	62.6%	37.4%
8,457	DECATUR	2,591	1,496	857	238	639 R	57.7%	33.1%	63.6%	36.4%
17,764	DELAWARE	6,916	4,052	2,620	244	1,432 R	58.6%	37.9%	60.7%	39.3%
40,325	DES MOINES	13,612	6,317	6,795	500	478 D	46.4%	49.9%	48.2%	51.8%
16,667	DICKINSON	7,250	4,558	2,431	261	2,127 R	62.9%	33.5%	65.2%	34.8%
93,653	DUBUQUE	36,405	16,517	18,439	1,449	1,922 D	45.4%	50.6%	47.3%	52.7%
10,302	EMMET	3,508	1,988	1,234	286	754 R	56.7%	35.2%	61.7%	38.3%
20,880	FAYETTE	7,828	4,054	3,455	319	599 R	51.8%	44.1%	54.0%	46.0%
16,303	FLOYD	6,009	2,727	3,013	269	286 D	45.4%	50.1%	47.5%	52.5%
10,680	FRANKLIN	3,907	2,470	1,221	216	1,249 R	63.2%	31.3%	66.9%	33.1%
7,441	FREMONT	2,427	1,513	799	115	714 R	62.3%	32.9%	65.4%	34.6%
9,336	GREENE	3,633	2,068	1,370	195	698 R	56.9%	37.7%	60.2%	39.8%
12,453	GRUNDY	5,313	3,626	1,516	171	2,110 R	68.2%	28.5%	70.5%	29.5%
10,954	GUTHRIE	4,351	2,739	1,367	245	1,372 R	63.0%	31.4%	66.7%	33.3%
15,673	HAMILTON	5,689	3,379	2,035	275	1,344 R	59.4%	35.8%	62.4%	37.6%
11,341	HANCOCK	4,380	2,652	1,530	198	1,122 R	60.5%	34.9%	63.4%	36.6%
17,534	HARDIN	6,774	4,082	2,364	328	1,718 R	60.3%	34.9%	63.3%	36.7%
14,928	HARRISON	4,968	3,074	1,650	244	1,424 R	61.9%	33.2%	65.1%	34.9%
20,145	HENRY	6,640	4,012	2,320	308	1,692 R	60.4%	34.9%	63.4%	36.6%
9,566	HOWARD	3,373	1,503	1,709	161	206 D	44.6%	50.7%	46.8%	53.2%
9,815	HUMBOLDT	3,882	2,575	1,137	170	1,438 R	66.3%	29.3%	69.4%	30.6%
7,089	IDA	2,718	1,881	714	123	1,167 R	69.2%	26.3%	72.5%	27.5%
16,355	IOWA	6,750	3,933	2,530	287	1,403 R	58.3%	37.5%	60.9%	39.1%
19,848	JACKSON	7,624	3,771	3,382	471	389 R	49.5%	44.4%	52.7%	47.3%
36,842	JASPER	14,956	7,779	6,350	827	1,429 R	52.0%	42.5%	55.1%	44.9%
16,843	JEFFERSON	6,302	2,761	3,237	304	476 D	43.8%	51.4%	46.0%	54.0%
130,882	JOHNSON	52,447	16,749	34,103	1,595	17,354 D	31.9%	65.0%	32.9%	67.1%
20,638	JONES	7,746	4,092	3,323	331	769 R	52.8%	42.9%	55.2%	44.8%
10,511	KEOKUK	3,708	2,388	1,161	159	1,227 R	64.4%	31.3%	67.3%	32.7%
15,543	KOSSUTH	6,603	4,013	2,279	311	1,734 R	60.8%	34.5%	63.8%	36.2%
35,862	LEE	10,655	4,924	5,274	457	350 D	46.2%	49.5%	48.3%	51.7%
211,226	LINN	86,482	39,116	44,186	3,180	5,070 D	45.2%	51.1%	47.0%	53.0%
11,387	LOUISA	3,381	2,019	1,207	155	812 R	59.7%	35.7%	62.6%	37.4%
8,898	LUCAS	3,183	1,944	1,029	210	915 R	61.1%	32.3%	65.4%	34.6%
11,581	LYON	4,335	3,647	588	100	3,059 R	84.1%	13.6%	86.1%	13.9%
15,679	MADISON	6,531	3,967	2,226	338	1,741 R	60.7%	34.1%	64.1%	35.9%
22,381	MAHASKA	7,787	5,334	2,091	362	3,243 R	68.5%	26.9%	71.8%	28.2%
33,309	MARION	13,339	8,387	4,401	551	3,986 R	62.9%	33.0%	65.6%	34.4%
40,648	MARSHALL	13,659	7,049	6,041	569	1,008 R	51.6%	44.2%	53.9%	46.1%
15,059	MILLS	4,906	3,281	1,376	249	1,905 R	66.9%	28.0%	70.5%	29.5%

IOWA

SENATOR 2014

2010 Census Population	County	Total Vote	Republican (Ernst)	Democratic (Braley)	Other	Rep.-Dem. Plurality	Percentage			
							Total Vote		Major Vote	
							Rep.	Dem.	Rep.	Dem.
10,776	MITCHELL	4,127	2,117	1,865	145	252 R	51.3%	45.2%	53.2%	46.8%
9,243	MONONA	3,733	2,172	1,272	289	900 R	58.2%	34.1%	63.1%	36.9%
7,970	MONROE	2,896	1,749	970	177	779 R	60.4%	33.5%	64.3%	35.7%
10,740	MONTGOMERY	3,802	2,803	892	107	1,911 R	73.7%	23.5%	75.9%	24.1%
42,745	MUSCATINE	13,075	6,767	5,685	623	1,082 R	51.8%	43.5%	54.3%	45.7%
14,398	O'BRIEN	5,429	4,151	1,093	185	3,058 R	76.5%	20.1%	79.2%	20.8%
6,462	OSCEOLA	2,165	1,682	399	84	1,283 R	77.7%	18.4%	80.8%	19.2%
15,932	PAGE	4,823	3,416	1,270	137	2,146 R	70.8%	26.3%	72.9%	27.1%
9,421	PALO ALTO	3,625	2,050	1,362	213	688 R	56.6%	37.6%	60.1%	39.9%
24,986	PLYMOUTH	9,202	6,678	2,182	342	4,496 R	72.6%	23.7%	75.4%	24.6%
7,310	POCAHONTAS	2,850	1,877	828	145	1,049 R	65.9%	29.1%	69.4%	30.6%
430,640	POLK	164,432	75,545	82,720	6,167	7,175 D	45.9%	50.3%	47.7%	52.3%
93,158	POTTAWATTAMIE	26,216	15,118	9,692	1,406	5,426 R	57.7%	37.0%	60.9%	39.1%
18,914	POWESHIEK	7,475	3,696	3,455	324	241 R	49.4%	46.2%	51.7%	48.3%
5,131	RINGGOLD	2,071	1,294	613	164	681 R	62.5%	29.6%	67.9%	32.1%
10,350	SAC	3,810	2,508	1,103	199	1,405 R	65.8%	29.0%	69.5%	30.5%
165,224	SCOTT	61,548	30,518	29,091	1,939	1,427 R	49.6%	47.3%	51.2%	48.8%
12,167	SHELBY	4,255	2,922	1,173	160	1,749 R	68.7%	27.6%	71.4%	28.6%
33,704	SIOUX	13,363	11,611	1,475	277	10,136 R	86.9%	11.0%	88.7%	11.3%
89,542	STORY	32,959	15,272	16,376	1,311	1,104 D	46.3%	49.7%	48.3%	51.7%
17,767	TAMA	6,613	3,495	2,819	299	676 R	52.9%	42.6%	55.4%	44.6%
6,317	TAYLOR	2,181	1,508	584	89	924 R	69.1%	26.8%	72.1%	27.9%
12,534	UNION	4,279	2,554	1,504	221	1,050 R	59.7%	35.1%	62.9%	37.1%
7,570	VAN BUREN	2,841	1,758	944	139	814 R	61.9%	33.2%	65.1%	34.9%
35,625	WAPELLO	10,918	5,326	4,993	599	333 R	48.8%	45.7%	51.6%	48.4%
46,225	WARREN	19,497	10,861	7,784	852	3,077 R	55.7%	39.9%	58.3%	41.7%
21,704	WASHINGTON	8,233	4,781	3,098	354	1,683 R	58.1%	37.6%	60.7%	39.3%
6,403	WAYNE	2,162	1,343	704	115	639 R	62.1%	32.6%	65.6%	34.4%
38,013	WEBSTER	13,018	6,991	5,374	653	1,617 R	53.7%	41.3%	56.5%	43.5%
10,866	WINNEBAGO	4,198	2,231	1,766	201	465 R	53.1%	42.1%	55.8%	44.2%
21,056	WINNESHIEK	8,243	3,958	3,933	352	25 R	48.0%	47.7%	50.2%	49.8%
102,172	WOODBURY	30,273	17,022	11,625	1,626	5,397 R	56.2%	38.4%	59.4%	40.6%
7,598	WORTH	3,081	1,382	1,555	144	173 D	44.9%	50.5%	47.1%	52.9%
13,229	WRIGHT	4,567	2,855	1,507	205	1,348 R	62.5%	33.0%	65.5%	34.5%
3,046,355	TOTAL	1,129,700	588,575	494,370	46,755	94,205 R	52.1%	43.8%	54.3%	45.7%

IOWA

HOUSE OF REPRESENTATIVES

CD	Year	Total Vote	Republican Vote	Republican Candidate	Democratic Vote	Democratic Candidate	Other Vote	Rep.-Dem. Plurality	Percentage			
									Total Vote		Major Vote	
									Rep.	Dem.	Rep.	Dem.
1	2014	289,306	147,762	BLUM, ROD	141,145	MURPHY, PAT	399	6,617 R	51.1%	48.8%	51.1%	48.9%
1	2012	390,849	162,465	LANGE, BENJAMIN M.	222,422	BRALEY, BRUCE*	5,962	59,957 D	41.6%	56.9%	42.2%	57.8%
2	2014	273,329	129,455	MILLER-MEEKS, MARIANNETTE	143,431	LOEBSACK, DAVID*	443	13,976 D	47.4%	52.5%	47.4%	52.6%
2	2012	381,275	161,977	ARCHER, JOHN	211,863	LOEBSACK, DAVID*	7,435	49,886 D	42.5%	55.6%	43.3%	56.7%
3	2014	282,066	148,814	YOUNG, DAVID	119,109	APPEL, STACI	14,143	29,705 R	52.8%	42.2%	55.5%	44.5%
3	2012	386,842	202,000	LATHAM, TOM*	168,632	BOSWELL, LEONARD L.	16,210	33,368 R	52.2%	43.6%	54.5%	45.5%
4	2014	275,633	169,834	KING, STEVE*	105,504	MOWRER, JIM	295	64,330 R	61.6%	38.3%	61.7%	38.3%
4	2012	377,883	200,063	KING, STEVE*	169,470	VILSACK, CHRISTIE	8,350	30,593 R	52.9%	44.8%	54.1%	45.9%
TOTAL	2014	1,120,334	595,865		509,189		15,280	86,676 R	53.2%	45.4%	53.9%	46.1%
TOTAL	2012	1,536,849	726,505		772,387		37,957	45,882 D	47.3%	50.3%	48.5%	51.5%

Note: An asterisk (*) denotes incumbent.

IOWA

GENERAL AND PRIMARY ELECTIONS

2014 GENERAL ELECTIONS: OTHER VOTES

Governor   Other vote was 20,321 Libertarian (Lee Hieb), 10,582 New Independent (Jim Hennager), 10,240 Iowa (Jonathan Narcisse), 1,095 scattered write-in

Senate   Other vote was 26,815 Independent (Rick Stewart), 8,232 Libertarian (Douglas Butzier), 5,873 Other (Bob Quast), 4,724 No Party (Ruth Smith), 1,111 scattered write-in

House   Other vote was:

CD 1	399 scattered write-in
CD 2	443 scattered write-in
CD 3	9,054 Libertarian (Edward Benedict Wright), 4,360 No Party (Bryan Jack Holder), 729 scattered write-in
CD 4	295 scattered write-in

2014 PRIMARY ELECTIONS: SUPPLEMENTARY INFORMATION

Primary   June 3, 2014

Registration (as of June 2, 2014 – includes 204,033 inactive registrants)   2,120,816

Democratic	665,225
Republican	650,459
No Party	800,343
Other	4,789

Primary Type   Semi-open—Registered Democrats and Republicans could vote only in their party's primary, although any registered voter (including those not affiliated with either party) could participate in either party's primary by changing his or her registration to that party on primary day.

	REPUBLICAN PRIMARIES			DEMOCRATIC PRIMARIES		
Senator	Ernst, Joni	88,535	56.1%	Braley, Bruce	62,600	99.1%
	Clovis, Sam	28,418	18.0%	Write-In	545	0.9%
	Jacobs, Mark	26,523	16.8%			
	Whitaker, Matt	11,884	7.5%			
	Schaben, Scott	2,233	1.4%			
	Write-In	155	0.1%			
	TOTAL	*157,748*		*TOTAL*	*63,145*	
Governor	Branstad, Terry E.*	129,752	83.0%	Hatch, Jack	60,385	99.2%
	Hoefling, Thomas	26,299	16.8%	Write-In	466	0.8%
	Write-In	294	0.2%			
	TOTAL	*156,345*		*TOTAL*	*60,851*	
Congressional District 1	Blum, Rod	16,886	54.9%	Murphy, Pat	10,189	36.7%
	Rathje, Steve	11,420	37.1%	Vernon, Monica	6,559	23.6%
	Boliver, Gail E.	2,413	7.8%	Dandekar, Swati	5,076	18.3%
	Write-In	42	0.1%	Kajtazovic, Anesa	4,067	14.7%
				O'Brien, Dave	1,846	6.7%
				Write-In	18	0.1%
	TOTAL	*30,761*		*TOTAL*	*27,755*	
Congressional District 2	Miller-Meeks, Mariannette	15,043	49.4%	Loebsack, David*	17,154	99.3%
	Lofgren, Mark S.	11,634	38.2%	Write-In	117	0.7%
	Waldren, Matthew C.	3,746	12.3%			
	Write-In	52	0.2%			
	TOTAL	*30,475*		*TOTAL*	*17,271*	

IOWA

GENERAL AND PRIMARY ELECTIONS

	REPUBLICAN PRIMARIES			DEMOCRATIC PRIMARIES		
Congressional	Zaun, Brad	10,522	24.7%	Appel, Staci	9,233	99.2%
District 3	Cramer, Robert	9,032	21.2%	Write-In	75	0.8%
	Schultz, Matt	8,464	19.9%			
	Shaw, Monte	7,220	17.0%			
	Young, David	6,604	15.5%			
	Grandanette, Joe	661	1.6%			
	Write-In	42	0.1%			
	TOTAL	*42,545*		*TOTAL*	*9,308*	
Congressional	King, Steve*	43,098	99.1%	Mowrer, Jim	9,900	99.6%
District 4	Write-In	382	0.9%	Write-In	42	0.4%
	TOTAL	*43,480*		*TOTAL*	*9,942*	

Note: An asterisk (*) denotes incumbent.

KANSAS

Congressional districts first established for elections held in 2012
4 members

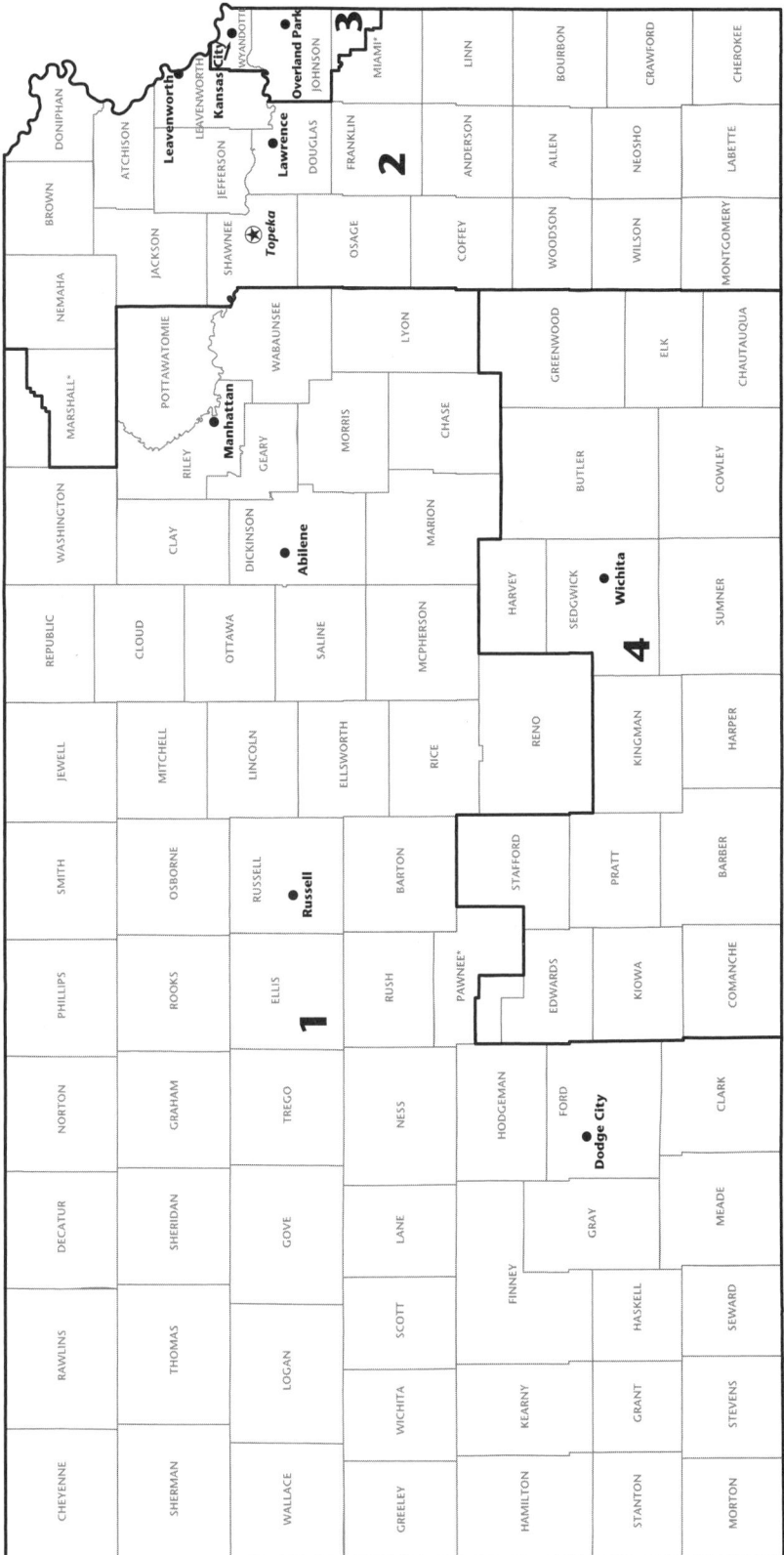

KANSAS

GOVERNOR
Sam Brownback (R). Re-elected 2014 to a four-year term. Previously elected 2010.

SENATORS (2 Republicans)
Jerry Moran (R). Elected 2010 to a six-year term.

Pat Roberts (R). Re-elected 2014 to a six-year term. Previously elected 2008, 2002, 1996.

REPRESENTATIVES (4 Republicans)
1. Tim Huelskamp (R)
2. Lynn Jenkins (R)
3. Kevin Yoder (R)
4. Mike Pompeo (R)

POSTWAR VOTE FOR PRESIDENT

| | | Republican | | Democratic | | Other | Rep.-Dem. | Percentage | | | |
| | | | | | | | | Total Vote | | Major Vote | |
Year	Total Vote	Vote	Candidate	Vote	Candidate	Vote	Plurality	Rep.	Dem.	Rep.	Dem.
2012	1,159,971	692,634	Romney, W. Mitt	440,726	Obama, Barack H.*	26,611	251,908 R	59.7%	38.0%	61.1%	38.9%
2008	1,235,872	699,655	McCain, John S. III	514,765	Obama, Barack H.	21,452	184,890 R	56.6%	41.7%	57.6%	42.4%
2004	1,187,756	736,456	Bush, George W.*	434,993	Kerry, John F.	16,307	301,463 R	62.0%	36.6%	62.9%	37.1%
2000**	1,072,218	622,332	Bush, George W.	399,276	Gore, Albert Jr.	50,610	223,056 R	58.0%	37.2%	60.9%	39.1%
1996**	1,074,300	583,245	Dole, Robert "Bob"	387,659	Clinton, Bill*	103,396	195,586 R	54.3%	36.1%	60.1%	39.9%
1992**	1,157,335	449,951	Bush, George H.*	390,434	Clinton, Bill	316,950	59,517 R	38.9%	33.7%	53.5%	46.5%
1988	993,044	554,049	Bush, George H.	422,636	Dukakis, Michael S.	16,359	131,413 R	55.8%	42.6%	56.7%	43.3%
1984	1,021,991	677,296	Reagan, Ronald*	333,149	Mondale, Walter F.	11,546	344,147 R	66.3%	32.6%	67.0%	33.0%
1980**	979,795	566,812	Reagan, Ronald	326,150	Carter, Jimmy*	86,833	240,662 R	57.9%	33.3%	63.5%	36.5%
1976	957,845	502,752	Ford, Gerald R.*	430,421	Carter, Jimmy	24,672	72,331 R	52.5%	44.9%	53.9%	46.1%
1972	916,095	619,812	Nixon, Richard M.*	270,287	McGovern, George S.	25,996	349,525 R	67.7%	29.5%	69.6%	30.4%
1968**	872,783	478,674	Nixon, Richard M.	302,996	Humphrey, Hubert Horatio Jr.	91,113	175,678 R	54.8%	34.7%	61.2%	38.8%
1964	857,901	386,579	Goldwater, Barry M. Sr.	464,028	Johnson, Lyndon B.*	7,294	77,449 D	45.1%	54.1%	45.4%	54.6%
1960	928,825	561,474	Nixon, Richard M.	363,213	Kennedy, John F.	4,138	198,261 R	60.4%	39.1%	60.7%	39.3%
1956	866,243	566,878	Eisenhower, Dwight D.*	296,317	Stevenson, Adlai E. II	3,048	270,561 R	65.4%	34.2%	65.7%	34.3%
1952	896,166	616,302	Eisenhower, Dwight D.	273,296	Stevenson, Adlai E. II	6,568	343,006 R	68.8%	30.5%	69.3%	30.7%
1948	788,819	423,039	Dewey, Thomas E.	351,902	Truman, Harry S.*	13,878	71,137 R	53.6%	44.6%	54.6%	45.4%

Note: An asterisk (*) denotes incumbent. **In past elections, the other vote included: 2000 - 36,086 Green (Ralph Nader); 1996 - 92,639 Reform (Ross Perot); 1992 - 312,358 Independent (Perot); 1980 - 68,231 Independent (John Anderson); 1968 - 88,921 American Independent (George Wallace).

KANSAS

POSTWAR VOTE FOR GOVERNOR

Year	Total Vote	Republican Vote	Republican Candidate	Democratic Vote	Democratic Candidate	Other Vote	Rep.-Dem. Plurality	Total Vote Rep.	Total Vote Dem.	Major Vote Rep.	Major Vote Dem.
2014	869,502	433,196	Brownback, Sam*	401,100	Davis, Paul	35,206	32,096 R	49.8%	46.1%	51.9%	48.1%
2010	838,790	530,760	Brownback, Sam	270,166	Holland, Tom	37,864	260,594 R	63.3%	32.2%	66.3%	33.7%
2006	849,700	343,586	Barnett, Jim	491,993	Sebelius, Kathleen*	14,121	148,407 D	40.4%	57.9%	41.1%	58.9%
2002	835,692	376,830	Shallenburger, Tim	441,858	Sebelius, Kathleen	17,004	65,028 D	45.1%	52.9%	46.0%	54.0%
1998	742,665	544,882	Graves, Bill*	168,243	Sawyer, Tom	29,540	376,639 R	73.4%	22.7%	76.4%	23.6%
1994	821,030	526,113	Graves, Bill	294,733	Slattery, Jim	184	231,380 R	64.1%	35.9%	64.1%	35.9%
1990	783,325	333,589	Hayden, Mike*	380,609	Finney, Joan	69,127	47,020 D	42.6%	48.6%	46.7%	53.3%
1986	840,605	436,267	Hayden, Mike	404,338	Docking, Thomas R.		31,929 R	51.9%	48.1%	51.9%	48.1%
1982	763,263	339,356	Hardage, Sam	405,772	Carlin, John*	18,135	66,416 D	44.5%	53.2%	45.5%	54.5%
1978	736,246	348,015	Bennett, Robert F.*	363,835	Carlin, John	24,396	15,820 D	47.3%	49.4%	48.9%	51.1%
1974**	783,875	387,792	Bennett, Robert F.	384,115	Miller, Vern	11,968	3,677 R	49.5%	49.0%	50.2%	49.8%
1972	921,550	341,438	Kay, Morris	571,256	Docking, Robert*	8,856	229,818 D	37.1%	62.0%	37.4%	62.6%
1970	745,196	333,227	Frizzell, Kent	404,611	Docking, Robert*	7,358	71,384 D	44.7%	54.3%	45.2%	54.8%
1968	862,473	410,673	Harman, Rick	447,269	Docking, Robert*	4,531	36,596 D	47.6%	51.9%	47.9%	52.1%
1966	692,955	304,325	Avery, William H.*	380,030	Docking, Robert	8,600	75,705 D	43.9%	54.8%	44.5%	55.5%
1964	850,414	432,667	Avery, William H.	400,264	Wiles, Harry G.	17,483	32,403 R	50.9%	47.1%	51.9%	48.1%
1962	638,798	341,257	Anderson, John Jr.*	291,285	Saffels, Dale E.	6,256	49,972 R	53.4%	45.6%	54.0%	46.0%
1960	922,522	511,534	Anderson, John Jr.	402,261	Docking, George*	8,727	109,273 R	55.4%	43.6%	56.0%	44.0%
1958	735,939	313,036	Reed, Clyde M.	415,506	Docking, George*	7,397	102,470 D	42.5%	56.5%	43.0%	57.0%
1956	864,935	364,340	Shaw, Warren W.	479,701	Docking, George	20,894	115,361 D	42.1%	55.5%	43.2%	56.8%
1954	622,633	329,868	Hall, Fred	286,218	Docking, George	6,547	43,650 R	53.0%	46.0%	53.5%	46.5%
1952	872,139	491,338	Arn, Edward F.*	363,482	Rooney, Charles	17,319	127,856 R	56.3%	41.7%	57.5%	42.5%
1950	619,310	333,001	Arn, Edward F.	275,494	Anderson, Kenneth T.	10,815	57,507 R	53.8%	44.5%	54.7%	45.3%
1948	760,407	433,396	Carlson, Frank*	307,485	Carpenter, Randolph	19,526	125,911 R	57.0%	40.4%	58.5%	41.5%
1946	577,694	309,064	Carlson, Frank	254,283	Woodring, Harry H.	14,347	54,781 R	53.5%	44.0%	54.9%	45.1%

Note: An asterisk (*) denotes incumbent. **The term of office of Kansas's governor was increased from two to four years effective with the 1974 election.

POSTWAR VOTE FOR SENATOR

Year	Total Vote	Republican Vote	Republican Candidate	Democratic Vote	Democratic Candidate	Other Vote	Rep.-Dem. Plurality	Total Vote Rep.	Total Vote Dem.	Major Vote Rep.	Major Vote Dem.
2014	866,191	460,350	Roberts, Pat*			405,841	460,350 R	53.1%		100.0%	
2010	837,692	587,175	Moran, Jerry	220,971	Johnston, Lisa	29,546	366,204 R	70.1%	26.4%	72.7%	27.3%
2008	1,210,690	727,121	Roberts, Pat*	441,399	Slattery, Jim	42,170	285,722 R	60.1%	36.5%	62.2%	37.8%
2004	1,129,022	780,863	Brownback, Sam*	310,337	Jones, Lee	37,822	470,526 R	69.2%	27.5%	71.6%	28.4%
2002	776,850	641,075	Roberts, Pat*			135,775	641,075 R	82.5%		100.0%	
1998	727,236	474,639	Brownback, Sam*	229,718	Feleciano, Paul Jr.	22,879	244,921 R	65.3%	31.6%	67.4%	32.6%
1996	1,052,300	652,677	Roberts, Pat	362,380	Thompson, Sally	37,243	290,297 R	62.0%	34.4%	64.3%	35.7%
1996S	1,064,716	574,021	Brownback, Sam	461,344	Docking, Jill	29,351	112,677 R	53.9%	43.3%	55.4%	44.6%
1992	1,126,447	706,246	Dole, Robert "Bob"*	349,525	O'Dell, Gloria	70,676	356,721 R	62.7%	31.0%	66.9%	33.1%
1990	786,235	578,605	Kassebaum, Nancy Landon*	207,491	Williams, Dick	139	371,114 R	73.6%	26.4%	73.6%	26.4%
1986	823,566	576,902	Dole, Robert "Bob"*	246,664	MacDonald, Guy		330,238 R	70.0%	30.0%	70.0%	30.0%
1984	996,729	757,402	Kassebaum, Nancy Landon*	211,664	Maher, James R.	27,663	545,738 R	76.0%	21.2%	78.2%	21.8%
1980	938,957	598,686	Dole, Robert "Bob"*	340,271	Simpson, John		258,415 R	63.8%	36.2%	63.8%	36.2%
1978	748,839	403,354	Kassebaum, Nancy Landon	317,602	Roy, William R.	27,883	85,752 R	53.9%	42.4%	55.9%	44.1%
1974	794,437	403,983	Dole, Robert "Bob"*	390,451	Roy, William R.	3	13,532 R	50.9%	49.1%	50.9%	49.1%
1972	871,702	622,591	Pearson, James B.*	200,764	Tetzlaff, Arch O.	48,347	421,827 R	71.4%	23.0%	75.6%	24.4%
1968	817,096	490,911	Dole, Robert "Bob"	315,911	Robinson, William I.	10,274	175,000 R	60.1%	38.7%	60.8%	39.2%
1966	671,345	350,077	Pearson, James B.*	303,223	Breeding, J. Floyd	18,045	46,854 R	52.1%	45.2%	53.6%	46.4%
1962	622,232	388,500	Carlson, Frank*	223,630	Smith, K. L.	10,102	164,870 R	62.4%	35.9%	63.5%	36.5%
1962S	613,250	344,689	Pearson, James B.*	260,756	Aylward, Paul L.	7,805	83,933 R	56.2%	42.5%	56.9%	43.1%
1960	888,592	485,499	Schoeppel, Andrew F.*	388,895	Theis, Frank	14,198	96,604 R	54.6%	43.8%	55.5%	44.5%
1956	825,280	477,822	Carlson, Frank*	333,939	Hart, George	13,519	143,883 R	57.9%	40.5%	58.9%	41.1%
1954	618,063	348,144	Schoeppel, Andrew F.*	258,575	McGill, George	11,344	89,569 R	56.3%	41.8%	57.4%	42.6%
1950	619,104	335,880	Carlson, Frank*	271,365	Aiken, Paul	11,859	64,515 R	54.3%	43.8%	55.3%	44.7%
1948	716,342	393,412	Schoeppel, Andrew F.	305,987	McGill, George	16,943	87,425 R	54.9%	42.7%	56.3%	43.7%

Note: An asterisk (*) denotes incumbent. **In past elections, the other vote included: 2014 - 368,372 Independent (Greg Orman). One of the 1996 and 1962 elections was for a short term to fill a vacancy. The Democratic Party did not run a candidate in the 2014 and 2002 senate elections.

KANSAS

GOVERNOR 2014

2010 Census Population	County	Total Vote	Republican (Brownback)	Democratic (Davis)	Other	Rep.-Dem. Plurality		Percentage Total Vote Rep.	Total Vote Dem.	Major Vote Rep.	Major Vote Dem.
13,371	ALLEN	4,460	2,268	1,981	211	287	R	50.9%	44.4%	53.4%	46.6%
8,102	ANDERSON	2,571	1,484	940	147	544	R	57.7%	36.6%	61.2%	38.8%
16,924	ATCHISON	4,768	2,461	2,129	178	332	R	51.6%	44.7%	53.6%	46.4%
4,861	BARBER	1,749	1,157	520	72	637	R	66.2%	29.7%	69.0%	31.0%
27,674	BARTON	8,076	4,973	2,769	334	2,204	R	61.6%	34.3%	64.2%	35.8%
15,173	BOURBON	5,050	3,010	1,844	196	1,166	R	59.6%	36.5%	62.0%	38.0%
9,984	BROWN	3,200	1,825	1,236	139	589	R	57.0%	38.6%	59.6%	40.4%
65,880	BUTLER	20,770	11,803	8,006	961	3,797	R	56.8%	38.5%	59.6%	40.4%
2,790	CHASE	1,081	586	440	55	146	R	54.2%	40.7%	57.1%	42.9%
3,669	CHAUTAUQUA	1,112	758	280	74	478	R	68.2%	25.2%	73.0%	27.0%
21,603	CHEROKEE	6,039	3,552	2,262	225	1,290	R	58.8%	37.5%	61.1%	38.9%
2,726	CHEYENNE	1,063	804	219	40	585	R	75.6%	20.6%	78.6%	21.4%
2,215	CLARK	830	556	240	34	316	R	67.0%	28.9%	69.8%	30.2%
8,535	CLAY	3,143	1,872	1,125	146	747	R	59.6%	35.8%	62.5%	37.5%
9,533	CLOUD	3,203	1,889	1,176	138	713	R	59.0%	36.7%	61.6%	38.4%
8,601	COFFEY	3,159	1,818	1,167	174	651	R	57.5%	36.9%	60.9%	39.1%
1,891	COMANCHE	680	462	187	31	275	R	67.9%	27.5%	71.2%	28.8%
36,311	COWLEY	9,853	4,769	4,618	466	151	R	48.4%	46.9%	50.8%	49.2%
39,134	CRAWFORD	10,740	4,652	5,732	356	1,080	D	43.3%	53.4%	44.8%	55.2%
2,961	DECATUR	1,233	904	292	37	612	R	73.3%	23.7%	75.6%	24.4%
19,754	DICKINSON	6,448	3,824	2,204	420	1,620	R	59.3%	34.2%	63.4%	36.6%
7,945	DONIPHAN	2,266	1,491	668	107	823	R	65.8%	29.5%	69.1%	30.9%
110,826	DOUGLAS	37,943	9,545	27,424	974	17,879	D	25.2%	72.3%	25.8%	74.2%
3,037	EDWARDS	1,151	766	347	38	419	R	66.6%	30.1%	68.8%	31.2%
2,882	ELK	1,095	622	401	72	221	R	56.8%	36.6%	60.8%	39.2%
28,452	ELLIS	9,525	5,072	4,085	368	987	R	53.2%	42.9%	55.4%	44.6%
6,497	ELLSWORTH	2,293	1,258	925	110	333	R	54.9%	40.3%	57.6%	42.4%
36,776	FINNEY	6,788	4,144	2,406	238	1,738	R	61.0%	35.4%	63.3%	36.7%
33,848	FORD	6,186	3,824	2,088	274	1,736	R	61.8%	33.8%	64.7%	35.3%
25,992	FRANKLIN	7,871	4,166	3,285	420	881	R	52.9%	41.7%	55.9%	44.1%
34,362	GEARY	5,028	2,574	2,200	254	374	R	51.2%	43.8%	53.9%	46.1%
2,695	GOVE	1,133	810	286	37	524	R	71.5%	25.2%	73.9%	26.1%
2,597	GRAHAM	1,165	743	365	57	378	R	63.8%	31.3%	67.1%	32.9%
7,829	GRANT	1,777	1,157	507	113	650	R	65.1%	28.5%	69.5%	30.5%
6,006	GRAY	1,639	1,113	452	74	661	R	67.9%	27.6%	71.1%	28.9%
1,247	GREELEY	560	383	154	23	229	R	68.4%	27.5%	71.3%	28.7%
6,689	GREENWOOD	2,237	1,365	745	127	620	R	61.0%	33.3%	64.7%	35.3%
2,690	HAMILTON	711	462	226	23	236	R	65.0%	31.8%	67.2%	32.8%
6,034	HARPER	2,003	1,234	671	98	563	R	61.6%	33.5%	64.8%	35.2%
34,684	HARVEY	11,672	5,840	5,454	378	386	R	50.0%	46.7%	51.7%	48.3%
4,256	HASKELL	1,052	774	242	36	532	R	73.6%	23.0%	76.2%	23.8%
1,916	HODGEMAN	853	636	195	22	441	R	74.6%	22.9%	76.5%	23.5%
13,462	JACKSON	4,831	2,315	2,296	220	19	R	47.9%	47.5%	50.2%	49.8%
19,126	JEFFERSON	6,567	3,073	3,246	248	173	D	46.8%	49.4%	48.6%	51.4%
3,077	JEWELL	1,120	747	296	77	451	R	66.7%	26.4%	71.6%	28.4%
544,179	JOHNSON	192,752	94,787	92,416	5,549	2,371	R	49.2%	47.9%	50.6%	49.4%
3,977	KEARNY	1,004	716	262	26	454	R	71.3%	26.1%	73.2%	26.8%
7,858	KINGMAN	2,870	1,724	1,002	144	722	R	60.1%	34.9%	63.2%	36.8%
2,553	KIOWA	902	608	259	35	349	R	67.4%	28.7%	70.1%	29.9%
21,607	LABETTE	5,739	3,017	2,492	230	525	R	52.6%	43.4%	54.8%	45.2%
1,750	LANE	762	509	220	33	289	R	66.8%	28.9%	69.8%	30.2%
76,227	LEAVENWORTH	19,971	10,217	8,872	882	1,345	R	51.2%	44.4%	53.5%	46.5%
3,241	LINCOLN	1,179	737	400	42	337	R	62.5%	33.9%	64.8%	35.2%
9,656	LINN	3,086	1,978	977	131	1,001	R	64.1%	31.7%	66.9%	33.1%
2,756	LOGAN	1,053	766	236	51	530	R	72.7%	22.4%	76.4%	23.6%
33,690	LYON	8,991	3,520	5,053	418	1,533	D	39.2%	56.2%	41.1%	58.9%
12,660	MARION	4,418	2,553	1,634	231	919	R	57.8%	37.0%	61.0%	39.0%
10,117	MARSHALL	3,721	1,990	1,563	168	427	R	53.5%	42.0%	56.0%	44.0%
29,180	MCPHERSON	10,158	5,561	4,183	414	1,378	R	54.7%	41.2%	57.1%	42.9%
4,575	MEADE	1,430	994	381	55	613	R	69.5%	26.6%	72.3%	27.7%

KANSAS

GOVERNOR 2014

2010 Census Population	County	Total Vote	Republican (Brownback)	Democratic (Davis)	Other	Rep.-Dem. Plurality	Total Vote Rep.	Total Vote Dem.	Major Vote Rep.	Major Vote Dem.
32,787	MIAMI	10,527	6,107	4,021	399	2,086 R	58.0%	38.2%	60.3%	39.7%
6,373	MITCHELL	2,328	1,464	765	99	699 R	62.9%	32.9%	65.7%	34.3%
35,471	MONTGOMERY	8,713	5,495	2,853	365	2,642 R	63.1%	32.7%	65.8%	34.2%
5,923	MORRIS	2,112	1,000	912	200	88 R	47.3%	43.2%	52.3%	47.7%
3,233	MORTON	906	597	268	41	329 R	65.9%	29.6%	69.0%	31.0%
10,178	NEMAHA	4,203	2,616	1,444	143	1,172 R	62.2%	34.4%	64.4%	35.6%
16,512	NEOSHO	4,865	2,644	2,007	214	637 R	54.3%	41.3%	56.8%	43.2%
3,107	NESS	1,180	880	260	40	620 R	74.6%	22.0%	77.2%	22.8%
5,671	NORTON	1,824	1,216	518	90	698 R	66.7%	28.4%	70.1%	29.9%
16,295	OSAGE	5,804	2,871	2,573	360	298 R	49.5%	44.3%	52.7%	47.3%
3,858	OSBORNE	1,445	919	440	86	479 R	63.6%	30.4%	67.6%	32.4%
6,091	OTTAWA	2,348	1,500	677	171	823 R	63.9%	28.8%	68.9%	31.1%
6,973	PAWNEE	2,145	1,126	938	81	188 R	52.5%	43.7%	54.6%	45.4%
5,642	PHILLIPS	2,524	1,753	633	138	1,120 R	69.5%	25.1%	73.5%	26.5%
21,604	POTTAWATOMIE	8,092	4,989	2,633	470	2,356 R	61.7%	32.5%	65.5%	34.5%
9,656	PRATT	3,150	1,719	1,298	133	421 R	54.6%	41.2%	57.0%	43.0%
2,519	RAWLINS	1,158	872	242	44	630 R	75.3%	20.9%	78.3%	21.7%
64,511	RENO	19,069	9,772	8,478	819	1,294 R	51.2%	44.5%	53.5%	46.5%
4,980	REPUBLIC	2,016	1,290	615	111	675 R	64.0%	30.5%	67.7%	32.3%
10,083	RICE	2,977	1,769	1,064	144	705 R	59.4%	35.7%	62.4%	37.6%
71,115	RILEY	15,492	6,784	8,035	673	1,251 D	43.8%	51.9%	45.8%	54.2%
5,181	ROOKS	2,028	1,416	506	106	910 R	69.8%	25.0%	73.7%	26.3%
3,307	RUSH	1,332	814	452	66	362 R	61.1%	33.9%	64.3%	35.7%
6,970	RUSSELL	2,582	1,581	867	134	714 R	61.2%	33.6%	64.6%	35.4%
55,606	SALINE	17,501	8,479	7,830	1,192	649 R	48.4%	44.7%	52.0%	48.0%
4,936	SCOTT	1,728	1,271	385	72	886 R	73.6%	22.3%	76.8%	23.2%
498,365	SEDGWICK	142,774	69,868	66,719	6,187	3,149 R	48.9%	46.7%	51.2%	48.8%
22,952	SEWARD	3,295	2,225	925	145	1,300 R	67.5%	28.1%	70.6%	29.4%
177,934	SHAWNEE	61,929	23,621	35,826	2,482	12,205 D	38.1%	57.9%	39.7%	60.3%
2,556	SHERIDAN	1,062	776	254	32	522 R	73.1%	23.9%	75.3%	24.7%
6,010	SHERMAN	2,012	1,453	479	80	974 R	72.2%	23.8%	75.2%	24.8%
3,853	SMITH	1,728	1,135	509	84	626 R	65.7%	29.5%	69.0%	31.0%
4,437	STAFFORD	1,524	950	513	61	437 R	62.3%	33.7%	64.9%	35.1%
2,235	STANTON	709	521	161	27	360 R	73.5%	22.7%	76.4%	23.6%
5,724	STEVENS	1,419	946	419	54	527 R	66.7%	29.5%	69.3%	30.7%
24,132	SUMNER	7,350	3,814	3,146	390	668 R	51.9%	42.8%	54.8%	45.2%
7,900	THOMAS	2,710	1,747	844	119	903 R	64.5%	31.1%	67.4%	32.6%
3,001	TREGO	1,191	764	376	51	388 R	64.1%	31.6%	67.0%	33.0%
7,053	WABAUNSEE	2,870	1,443	912	515	531 R	50.3%	31.8%	61.3%	38.7%
1,485	WALLACE	630	510	93	27	417 R	81.0%	14.8%	84.6%	15.4%
5,799	WASHINGTON	2,291	1,547	641	103	906 R	67.5%	28.0%	70.7%	29.3%
2,234	WICHITA	763	596	136	31	460 R	78.1%	17.8%	81.4%	18.6%
9,409	WILSON	2,615	1,703	806	106	897 R	65.1%	30.8%	67.9%	32.1%
3,309	WOODSON	1,078	613	418	47	195 R	56.9%	38.8%	59.5%	40.5%
157,505	WYANDOTTE	28,773	8,802	18,928	1,043	10,126 D	30.6%	65.8%	31.7%	68.3%
2,853,118	TOTAL	869,502	433,196	401,100	35,206	32,096 R	49.8%	46.1%	51.9%	48.1%

KANSAS

SENATOR 2014

2010 Census Population	County	Total Vote	Republican (Roberts)	Democratic	Independent (Orman)	Other	Rep.-Ind. Plurality	Percentage Total Vote Rep.	Dem.	Ind.
13,371	ALLEN	4,428	2,531		1,564	333	967 R	57.2%		35.3%
8,102	ANDERSON	2,537	1,554		826	157	728 R	61.3%		32.6%
16,924	ATCHISON	4,729	2,490		1,953	286	537 R	52.7%		41.3%
4,861	BARBER	1,706	1,196		447	63	749 R	70.1%		26.2%
27,674	BARTON	8,070	5,403		2,313	354	3,090 R	67.0%		28.7%
15,173	BOURBON	4,958	3,190		1,456	312	1,734 R	64.3%		29.4%
9,984	BROWN	3,188	2,074		964	150	1,110 R	65.1%		30.2%
65,880	BUTLER	20,737	12,387		7,413	937	4,974 R	59.7%		35.7%
2,790	CHASE	1,083	649		377	57	272 R	59.9%		34.8%
3,669	CHAUTAUQUA	1,107	837		221	49	616 R	75.6%		20.0%
21,603	CHEROKEE	5,934	3,675		1,800	459	1,875 R	61.9%		30.3%
2,726	CHEYENNE	1,049	823		196	30	627 R	78.5%		18.7%
2,215	CLARK	818	607		177	34	430 R	74.2%		21.6%
8,535	CLAY	3,156	2,156		869	131	1,287 R	68.3%		27.5%
9,533	CLOUD	3,197	2,123		906	168	1,217 R	66.4%		28.3%
8,601	COFFEY	3,144	2,025		951	168	1,074 R	64.4%		30.2%
1,891	COMANCHE	696	496		163	37	333 R	71.3%		23.4%
36,311	COWLEY	9,814	5,292		3,947	575	1,345 R	53.9%		40.2%
39,134	CRAWFORD	10,465	5,136		4,539	790	597 R	49.1%		43.4%
2,961	DECATUR	1,222	943		231	48	712 R	77.2%		18.9%
19,754	DICKINSON	6,451	4,160		1,951	340	2,209 R	64.5%		30.2%
7,945	DONIPHAN	2,243	1,555		552	136	1,003 R	69.3%		24.6%
110,826	DOUGLAS	37,758	11,116		25,315	1,327	14,199 I	29.4%		67.0%
3,037	EDWARDS	1,147	806		294	47	512 R	70.3%		25.6%
2,882	ELK	1,084	680		318	86	362 R	62.7%		29.3%
28,452	ELLIS	9,513	5,730		3,368	415	2,362 R	60.2%		35.4%
6,497	ELLSWORTH	2,273	1,410		750	113	660 R	62.0%		33.0%
36,776	FINNEY	6,776	4,446		2,028	302	2,418 R	65.6%		29.9%
33,848	FORD	6,179	4,126		1,814	239	2,312 R	66.8%		29.4%
25,992	FRANKLIN	7,860	4,374		3,024	462	1,350 R	55.6%		38.5%
34,362	GEARY	4,983	2,779		1,974	230	805 R	55.8%		39.6%
2,695	GOVE	1,130	857		228	45	629 R	75.8%		20.2%
2,597	GRAHAM	1,143	799		298	46	501 R	69.9%		26.1%
7,829	GRANT	1,772	1,275		413	84	862 R	72.0%		23.3%
6,006	GRAY	1,639	1,210		360	69	850 R	73.8%		22.0%
1,247	GREELEY	566	426		113	27	313 R	75.3%		20.0%
6,689	GREENWOOD	2,233	1,432		644	157	788 R	64.1%		28.8%
2,690	HAMILTON	717	546		150	21	396 R	76.2%		20.9%
6,034	HARPER	2,011	1,352		538	121	814 R	67.2%		26.8%
34,684	HARVEY	11,644	6,169		5,051	424	1,118 R	53.0%		43.4%
4,256	HASKELL	1,051	829		187	35	642 R	78.9%		17.8%
1,916	HODGEMAN	770	581		169	20	412 R	75.5%		21.9%
13,462	JACKSON	4,801	2,553		2,014	234	539 R	53.2%		41.9%
19,126	JEFFERSON	6,566	3,421		2,878	267	543 R	52.1%		43.8%
3,077	JEWELL	1,120	850		216	54	634 R	75.9%		19.3%
544,179	JOHNSON	192,677	94,843		92,849	4,985	1,994 R	49.2%		48.2%
3,977	KEARNY	1,007	763		214	30	549 R	75.8%		21.3%
7,858	KINGMAN	2,862	1,858		875	129	983 R	64.9%		30.6%
2,553	KIOWA	898	687		185	26	502 R	76.5%		20.6%
21,607	LABETTE	5,672	3,214		2,086	372	1,128 R	56.7%		36.8%
1,750	LANE	764	580		159	25	421 R	75.9%		20.8%
76,227	LEAVENWORTH	19,872	10,411		8,561	900	1,850 R	52.4%		43.1%
3,241	LINCOLN	1,276	925		299	52	626 R	72.5%		23.4%
9,656	LINN	3,193	2,032		973	188	1,059 R	63.6%		30.5%
2,756	LOGAN	1,049	798		202	49	596 R	76.1%		19.3%
33,690	LYON	8,917	4,261		4,254	402	7 R	47.8%		47.7%
12,660	MARION	4,429	2,847		1,363	219	1,484 R	64.3%		30.8%
10,117	MARSHALL	3,703	2,250		1,295	158	955 R	60.8%		35.0%
29,180	MCPHERSON	10,138	6,043		3,588	507	2,455 R	59.6%		35.4%
4,575	MEADE	1,401	1,035		314	52	721 R	73.9%		22.4%

KANSAS
SENATOR 2014

2010 Census Population	County	Total Vote	Republican (Roberts)	Democratic	Independent (Orman)	Other	Rep.-Ind. Plurality	Percentage Total Vote Rep.	Dem.	Ind.
32,787	MIAMI	10,510	6,090		4,012	408	2,078 R	57.9%		38.2%
6,373	MITCHELL	2,256	1,635		527	94	1,108 R	72.5%		23.4%
35,471	MONTGOMERY	8,613	5,997		2,213	403	3,784 R	69.6%		25.7%
5,923	MORRIS	2,035	1,196		723	116	473 R	58.8%		35.5%
3,233	MORTON	910	699		176	35	523 R	76.8%		19.3%
10,178	NEMAHA	4,212	2,890		1,134	188	1,756 R	68.6%		26.9%
16,512	NEOSHO	4,808	2,905		1,565	338	1,340 R	60.4%		32.5%
3,107	NESS	1,178	917		220	41	697 R	77.8%		18.7%
5,671	NORTON	1,816	1,339		390	87	949 R	73.7%		21.5%
16,295	OSAGE	5,791	3,198		2,278	315	920 R	55.2%		39.3%
3,858	OSBORNE	1,447	1,046		329	72	717 R	72.3%		22.7%
6,091	OTTAWA	2,322	1,683		503	136	1,180 R	72.5%		21.7%
6,973	PAWNEE	2,162	1,373		697	92	676 R	63.5%		32.2%
5,642	PHILLIPS	2,547	1,926		504	117	1,422 R	75.6%		19.8%
21,604	POTTAWATOMIE	8,093	5,408		2,338	347	3,070 R	66.8%		28.9%
9,656	PRATT	3,126	1,968		1,006	152	962 R	63.0%		32.2%
2,519	RAWLINS	1,166	944		176	46	768 R	81.0%		15.1%
64,511	RENO	18,870	10,489		7,425	956	3,064 R	55.6%		39.3%
4,980	REPUBLIC	2,000	1,421		483	96	938 R	71.1%		24.2%
10,083	RICE	2,989	1,899		936	154	963 R	63.5%		31.3%
71,115	RILEY	15,449	7,779		7,182	488	597 R	50.4%		46.5%
5,181	ROOKS	2,027	1,510		396	121	1,114 R	74.5%		19.5%
3,307	RUSH	1,325	888		370	67	518 R	67.0%		27.9%
6,970	RUSSELL	2,574	1,739		704	131	1,035 R	67.6%		27.4%
55,606	SALINE	17,429	9,694		6,720	1,015	2,974 R	55.6%		38.6%
4,936	SCOTT	1,739	1,363		296	80	1,067 R	78.4%		17.0%
498,365	SEDGWICK	142,351	72,506		62,527	7,318	9,979 R	50.9%		43.9%
22,952	SEWARD	3,279	2,399		729	151	1,670 R	73.2%		22.2%
177,934	SHAWNEE	61,728	26,566		32,770	2,392	6,204 I	43.0%		53.1%
2,556	SHERIDAN	1,051	815		200	36	615 R	77.5%		19.0%
6,010	SHERMAN	2,008	1,511		426	71	1,085 R	75.2%		21.2%
3,853	SMITH	1,727	1,272		365	90	907 R	73.7%		21.1%
4,437	STAFFORD	1,520	1,027		421	72	606 R	67.6%		27.7%
2,235	STANTON	707	560		119	28	441 R	79.2%		16.8%
5,724	STEVENS	1,425	1,119		240	66	879 R	78.5%		16.8%
24,132	SUMNER	7,372	4,268		2,650	454	1,618 R	57.9%		35.9%
7,900	THOMAS	2,704	1,956		636	112	1,320 R	72.3%		23.5%
3,001	TREGO	1,189	813		309	67	504 R	68.4%		26.0%
7,053	WABAUNSEE	2,864	1,769		922	173	847 R	61.8%		32.2%
1,485	WALLACE	630	545		68	17	477 R	86.5%		10.8%
5,799	WASHINGTON	2,293	1,684		496	113	1,188 R	73.4%		21.6%
2,234	WICHITA	763	617		115	31	502 R	80.9%		15.1%
9,409	WILSON	2,602	1,799		656	147	1,143 R	69.1%		25.2%
3,309	WOODSON	1,066	676		305	85	371 R	63.4%		28.6%
157,505	WYANDOTTE	28,192	8,836		17,938	1,418	9,102 I	31.3%		63.6%
2,853,118	TOTAL	866,191	460,350		368,372	37,469	91,978 R	53.1%		55.5%

KANSAS

HOUSE OF REPRESENTATIVES

CD	Year	Total Vote	Republican		Democratic		Other Vote	Rep.-Dem. Plurality	Percentage			
									Total Vote		Major Vote	
			Vote	Candidate	Vote	Candidate			Rep.	Dem.	Rep.	Dem.
1	2014	204,161	138,764	HUELSKAMP, TIM*	65,397	SHEROW, JAMES E.		73,367 R	68.0%	32.0%	68.0%	32.0%
1	2012	211,337	211,337	HUELSKAMP, TIM*				211,337 R	100.0%		100.0%	
2	2014	225,686	128,742	JENKINS, LYNN*	87,153	WAKEFIELD, MARGIE	9,791	41,589 R	57.0%	38.6%	59.6%	40.4%
2	2012	293,718	167,463	JENKINS, LYNN*	113,735	SCHLINGENSIEPEN, TOBIAS	12,520	53,728 R	57.0%	38.7%	59.6%	40.4%
3	2014	224,077	134,493	YODER, KEVIN*	89,584	KULTALA, KELLY		44,909 R	60.0%	40.0%	60.0%	40.0%
3	2012	293,762	201,087	YODER, KEVIN*			92,675	201,087 R	68.5%		100.0%	
4	2014	208,153	138,757	POMPEO, MIKE*	69,396	SCHUCKMAN, PERRY		69,361 R	66.7%	33.3%	66.7%	33.3%
4	2012	258,922	161,094	POMPEO, MIKE*	81,770	TILLMAN, ROBERT	16,058	79,324 R	62.2%	31.6%	66.3%	33.7%
TOTAL	2014	862,077	540,756		311,530		9,791	229,226 R	62.7%	36.1%	63.4%	36.6%
TOTAL	2012	1,057,739	740,981		195,505		121,253	545,476 R	70.1%	18.5%	79.1%	20.9%

Note: An asterisk (*) denotes incumbent.

KANSAS

GENERAL AND PRIMARY ELECTIONS

2014 GENERAL ELECTIONS: OTHER VOTES

Governor Other vote was 35,206 Libertarian (Keen A. Umbehr)

Senate Other vote was 368,372 Independent (Greg Orman), 37,469 Libertarian (Randall Batson)

House Other vote was:

CD 2 9,791 Libertarian (Christopher Clemmons)

2014 PRIMARY ELECTIONS: SUPPLEMENTARY INFORMATION

Primary	August 5, 2014	**Registration** (as of July 15, 2014)	1,735,395	Republican	765,398
				Democratic	422,181
				Libertarian	12,656
				Unaffiliated	535,160

Primary Type Semi-open—Registered Democrats and Republicans could vote only in their party's primary. "Unaffiliated" voters could participate in either primary, although they had to change their registration to that party on primary day.

	REPUBLICAN PRIMARIES			DEMOCRATIC PRIMARIES		
Senator	Roberts, Pat*	127,089	48.1%	Taylor, Chadwick "Chad"	35,067	53.3%
	Wolf, Milton	107,799	40.8%	Wiesner, Patrick	30,752	46.7%
	Smith, Della Jean "D.J."	15,288	5.8%			
	Zahnter, Alvin E.	14,164	5.4%			
	TOTAL	264,340		TOTAL	65,819	

Notes: An asterisk (*) denotes incumbent. Taylor withdrew from teh race after the primary. There was no Democratic candidate in the general election.

KANSAS

GENERAL AND PRIMARY ELECTIONS

	REPUBLICAN PRIMARIES			DEMOCRATIC PRIMARIES		
Governor	Brownback, Sam*	166,687	63.2%	Davis, Paul	66,357	100.0%
	Winn, Jennifer	96,907	36.8%			
	TOTAL	263,594		TOTAL	66,357	
Congressional District 1	Huelskamp, Tim*	42,847	55.0%	Sherow, James E.	8,209	65.7%
	LaPolice, Alan	35,108	45.0%	Whitney, Bryan	4,293	34.3%
	TOTAL	77,955		TOTAL	12,502	
Congressional District 2	Jenkins, Lynn*	41,850	69.1%	Wakefield, Margie	18,337	100.0%
	Tucker, Joshua Joel	18,680	30.9%			
	TOTAL	60,530		TOTAL	18,337	
Congressional District 3	Yoder, Kevin*	47,319	100.0%	Kultala, Kelly	14,189	68.5%
				Marselus, Reginald "Reggie"	6,524	31.5%
	TOTAL	47,319		TOTAL	20,713	
Congressional District 4	Pompeo, Mike*	43,564	62.6%	Schuckman, Perry	11,408	100.0%
	Tiahrt, Todd	25,977	37.4%			
	TOTAL	69,541		TOTAL	11,408	

Note: An asterisk (*) denotes incumbent.

KENTUCKY

Congressional districts first established for elections held in 2012

6 members

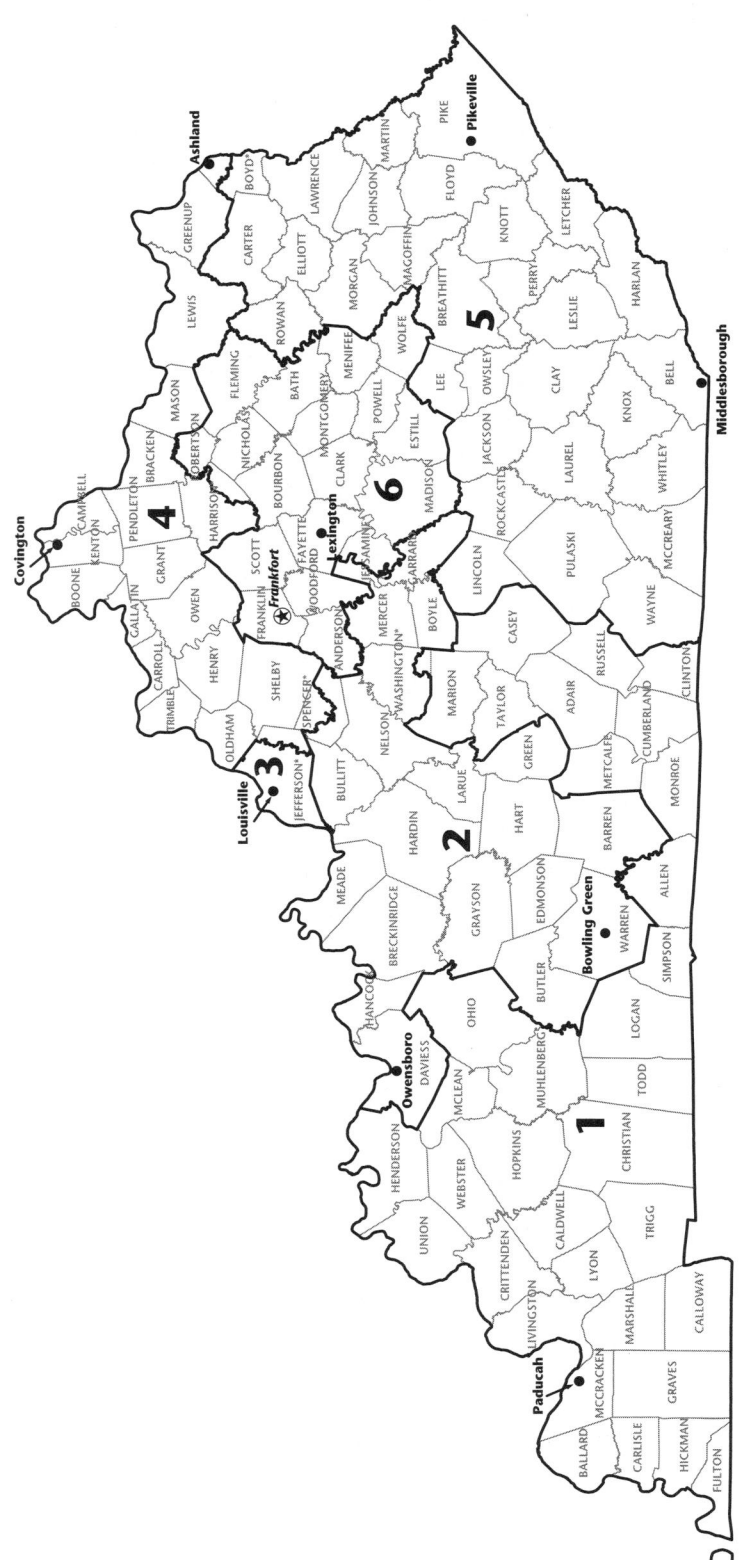

* Asterisk indicates a county whose boundaries include parts of two or more congressional districts.

KENTUCKY

GOVERNOR
Steven L. Beshear (D). Reelected 2011 to a four-year term. Previously elected 2007.

SENATORS (2 Republicans)
Mitch McConnell (R). Reelected 2014 to a six-year term. Previously elected 2008, 2002, 1996, 1990, 1984.

Rand Paul (R). Elected 2010 to a six-year term.

REPRESENTATIVES (5 Republicans, 1 Democrat)
1. Ed Whitfield (R)
2. Brett Guthrie (R)
3. John A. Yarmuth (D)
4. Thomas Massie (R)
5. Harold Rogers (R)
6. Andy Barr (R)

POSTWAR VOTE FOR PRESIDENT

| | | Republican | | Democratic | | | | Percentage | | | |
| | | | | | | Other | Rep.-Dem. | Total Vote | | Major Vote | |
Year	Total Vote	Vote	Candidate	Vote	Candidate	Vote	Plurality	Rep.	Dem.	Rep.	Dem.
2012	1,797,212	1,087,190	Romney, W. Mitt	679,370	Obama, Barack H.*	30,652	407,820 R	60.5%	37.8%	61.5%	38.5%
2008	1,826,620	1,048,462	McCain, John S. III	751,985	Obama, Barack H.	26,173	296,477 R	57.4%	41.2%	58.2%	41.8%
2004	1,795,882	1,069,439	Bush, George W.*	712,733	Kerry, John F.	13,710	356,706 R	59.5%	39.7%	60.0%	40.0%
2000**	1,544,187	872,492	Bush, George W.	638,898	Gore, Albert Jr.	32,797	233,594 R	56.5%	41.4%	57.7%	42.3%
1996**	1,388,708	623,283	Dole, Robert "Bob"	636,614	Clinton, Bill*	128,811	13,331 D	44.9%	45.8%	49.5%	50.5%
1992**	1,492,900	617,178	Bush, George H.*	665,104	Clinton, Bill	210,618	47,926 D	41.3%	44.6%	48.1%	51.9%
1988	1,322,517	734,281	Bush, George H.	580,368	Dukakis, Michael S.	7,868	153,913 R	55.5%	43.9%	55.9%	44.1%
1984	1,369,345	821,702	Reagan, Ronald*	539,539	Mondale, Walter F.	8,104	282,163 R	60.0%	39.4%	60.4%	39.6%
1980**	1,294,627	635,274	Reagan, Ronald	616,417	Carter, Jimmy*	42,936	18,857 R	49.1%	47.6%	50.8%	49.2%
1976	1,167,142	531,852	Ford, Gerald R.*	615,717	Carter, Jimmy	19,573	83,865 D	45.6%	52.8%	46.3%	53.7%
1972	1,067,499	676,446	Nixon, Richard M.*	371,159	McGovern, George S.	19,894	305,287 R	63.4%	34.8%	64.6%	35.4%
1968**	1,055,893	462,411	Nixon, Richard M.	397,541	Humphrey, Hubert Horatio Jr.	195,941	64,870 R	43.8%	37.6%	53.8%	46.2%
1964	1,046,105	372,977	Goldwater, Barry M. Sr.	669,659	Johnson, Lyndon B.*	3,469	296,682 D	35.7%	64.0%	35.8%	64.2%
1960	1,124,462	602,607	Nixon, Richard M.	521,855	Kennedy, John F.		80,752 R	53.6%	46.4%	53.6%	46.4%
1956	1,053,805	572,192	Eisenhower, Dwight D.*	476,453	Stevenson, Adlai E. II	5,160	95,739 R	54.3%	45.2%	54.6%	45.4%
1952	993,148	495,029	Eisenhower, Dwight D.	495,729	Stevenson, Adlai E. II	2,390	700 D	49.8%	49.9%	50.0%	50.0%
1948	822,658	341,210	Dewey, Thomas E.	466,756	Truman, Harry S.*	14,692	125,546 D	41.5%	56.7%	42.2%	57.8%

Note: An asterisk (*) denotes incumbent. **In past elections, the other vote included: 2000 - 23,192 Green (Ralph Nader); 1996 - 120,396 Reform (Ross Perot); 1992 - 203,944 Independent (Perot); 1980 - 31,127 Independent (John Anderson); 1968 - 193,098 American Independent (George Wallace).

KENTUCKY

POSTWAR VOTE FOR GOVERNOR

Year	Total Vote	Republican Vote	Republican Candidate	Democratic Vote	Democratic Candidate	Other Vote	Rep.-Dem. Plurality	Total Vote Rep.	Total Vote Dem.	Major Vote Rep.	Major Vote Dem.
2011	833,139	294,034	Williams, David Lynn	464,245	Beshear, Steven L.*	74,860	170,211 D	35.3%	55.7%	38.8%	61.2%
2007	1,055,325	435,773	Fletcher, Ernest*	619,552	Beshear, Steven L.		183,779 D	41.3%	58.7%	41.3%	58.7%
2003	1,083,443	596,284	Fletcher, Ernest	487,159	Chandler, Ben		109,125 R	55.0%	45.0%	55.0%	45.0%
1999**	580,074	128,788	Martin, Peppy	352,099	Patton, Paul E.*	99,187	223,311 D	22.2%	60.7%	26.8%	73.2%
1995	983,979	479,227	Forgy, Larry	500,787	Patton, Paul E.	3,965	21,560 D	48.7%	50.9%	48.9%	51.1%
1991	834,920	294,452	Harper, John	540,468	Jones, Brereton C.		246,016 D	35.3%	64.7%	35.3%	64.7%
1987	777,815	273,141	Harper, John	504,674	Wilkinson, Wallace G.		231,533 D	35.1%	64.9%	35.1%	64.9%
1983	1,030,628	454,650	Bunning, Jim	561,674	Collins, Martha Layne	14,304	107,024 D	44.1%	54.5%	44.7%	55.3%
1979	939,366	381,278	Nunn, Louie B.	558,088	Brown, J. Y. Jr.		176,810 D	40.6%	59.4%	40.6%	59.4%
1975	748,157	277,998	Gable, Robert E.	470,159	Carroll, Julian*		192,161 D	37.2%	62.8%	37.2%	62.8%
1971	930,792	412,653	Emberton, Thomas	470,722	Ford, Wendell H.	47,417	58,069 D	44.3%	50.6%	46.7%	53.3%
1967	886,146	453,323	Nunn, Louie B.	425,674	Ward, Henry	7,149	27,649 R	51.2%	48.0%	51.6%	48.4%
1963	886,047	436,496	Nunn, Louie B.	449,551	Breathitt, Edward T.		13,055 D	49.3%	50.7%	49.3%	50.7%
1959	853,005	336,456	Robsion, John M. Jr.	516,549	Combs, Bert T.		180,093 D	39.4%	60.6%	39.4%	60.6%
1955	778,488	322,671	Denney, Edwin R.	451,647	Chandler, Happy	4,170	128,976 D	41.4%	58.0%	41.7%	58.3%
1951	634,359	288,014	Siler, Eugene	346,345	Wetherby, Lawrence W.		58,331 D	45.4%	54.6%	45.4%	54.6%
1947	675,551	287,756	Dummit, Eldon S.	387,795	Clements, Earle C.		100,039 D	42.6%	57.4%	42.6%	57.4%

Note: An asterisk (*) denotes incumbent. **In past elections, the other vote included: 1999 - 88,930 Reform (Gatewood Galbraith).

POSTWAR VOTE FOR SENATOR

Year	Total Vote	Republican Vote	Republican Candidate	Democratic Vote	Democratic Candidate	Other Vote	Rep.-Dem. Plurality	Total Vote Rep.	Total Vote Dem.	Major Vote Rep.	Major Vote Dem.
2014	1,435,868	806,787	McConnell, Mitch*	584,698	Grimes, Alison Lundergan	44,383	222,089 R	56.2%	40.7%	58.0%	42.0%
2010	1,356,468	755,411	Paul, Rand	599,843	Conway, Jack	1,214	155,568 R	55.7%	44.2%	55.7%	44.3%
2008	1,800,821	953,816	McConnell, A. Mitch*	847,005	Lunsford, Bruce		106,811 R	53.0%	47.0%	53.0%	47.0%
2004	1,724,362	873,507	Bunning, Jim*	850,855	Mongiardo, Frank Daniel		22,652 R	50.7%	49.3%	50.7%	49.3%
2002	1,131,475	731,679	McConnell, A. Mitch*	399,634	Weinberg, Lois Combs	162	332,045 R	64.7%	35.3%	64.7%	35.3%
1998	1,145,414	569,817	Bunning, Jim	563,051	Baesler, Scott	12,546	6,766 R	49.7%	49.2%	50.3%	49.7%
1996	1,307,046	724,794	McConnell, A. Mitch*	560,012	Beshear, Steven L.	22,240	164,782 R	55.5%	42.8%	56.4%	43.6%
1992	1,330,858	476,604	Williams, David Lynn	836,888	Ford, Wendell H.*	17,366	360,284 D	35.8%	62.9%	36.3%	63.7%
1990	916,010	478,034	McConnell, A. Mitch*	437,976	Sloane, Harvey		40,058 R	52.2%	47.8%	52.2%	47.8%
1986	677,280	173,330	Andrews, Jackson M.	503,775	Ford, Wendell H.*	175	330,445 D	25.6%	74.4%	25.6%	74.4%
1984	1,292,407	644,990	McConnell, A. Mitch	639,721	Huddleston, Walter*	7,696	5,269 R	49.9%	49.5%	50.2%	49.8%
1980	1,106,890	386,029	Foust, Mary Louise	720,861	Ford, Wendell H.*		334,832 D	34.9%	65.1%	34.9%	65.1%
1978	476,783	175,766	Guenthner, Louie	290,730	Huddleston, Walter*	10,287	114,964 D	36.9%	61.0%	37.7%	62.3%
1974	745,994	328,982	Cook, Marlow W.*	399,406	Ford, Wendell H.	17,606	70,424 D	44.1%	53.5%	45.2%	54.8%
1972	1,037,861	494,337	Nunn, Louie B.	528,550	Huddleston, Walter	14,974	34,213 D	47.6%	50.9%	48.3%	51.7%
1968	942,865	484,260	Cook, Marlow W.	448,960	Peden, Katherine	9,645	35,300 R	51.4%	47.6%	51.9%	48.1%
1966	749,884	483,805	Cooper, John Sherman*	266,079	Brown, John Young		217,726 R	64.5%	35.5%	64.5%	35.5%
1962	820,088	432,648	Morton, Thruston B.*	387,440	Wyatt, Wilson W.		45,208 R	52.8%	47.2%	52.8%	47.2%
1960	1,088,377	644,087	Cooper, John Sherman*	444,290	Johnson, Keen		199,797 R	59.2%	40.8%	59.2%	40.8%
1956	1,006,825	506,903	Morton, Thruston B.	499,922	Clements, Earle C.*		6,981 R	50.3%	49.7%	50.3%	49.7%
1956S	1,011,645	538,505	Cooper, John Sherman	473,140	Wetherby, Lawrence W.		65,365 R	53.2%	46.8%	53.2%	46.8%
1954	797,057	362,948	Cooper, John Sherman*	434,109	Barkley, Alben W.		71,161 D	45.5%	54.5%	45.5%	54.5%
1952S	960,228	494,576	Cooper, John Sherman	465,652	Underwood, Thomas R.		28,924 R	51.5%	48.5%	51.5%	48.5%
1950	612,617	278,368	Dawson, Charles I.	334,249	Clements, Earle C.*		55,881 D	45.4%	54.6%	45.4%	54.6%
1948	794,469	383,776	Cooper, John Sherman	408,256	Chapman, Virgil	2,437	24,480 D	48.3%	51.4%	48.5%	51.5%
1946S	615,119	327,652	Cooper, John Sherman	285,829	Brown, John Young	1,638	41,823 R	53.3%	46.5%	53.4%	46.6%

Note: An asterisk (*) denotes incumbent. **The elections in 1946 and 1952 as well as one in 1956 were for short terms to fill vacancies.

KENTUCKY
SENATOR 2014

2010 Census Population	County	Total Vote	Republican (McConnell)	Democratic (Grimes)	Other	Rep.-Dem. Plurality	Percentage Total Vote Rep.	Dem.	Major Vote Rep.	Dem.
18,656	ADAIR	7,162	4,900	2,023	239	2,877 R	68.4%	28.2%	70.8%	29.2%
19,956	ALLEN	6,564	4,410	1,875	279	2,535 R	67.2%	28.6%	70.2%	29.8%
21,421	ANDERSON	8,804	5,164	3,158	482	2,006 R	58.7%	35.9%	62.1%	37.9%
8,249	BALLARD	3,591	2,249	1,223	119	1,026 R	62.6%	34.1%	64.8%	35.2%
42,173	BARREN	13,962	8,268	5,091	603	3,177 R	59.2%	36.5%	61.9%	38.1%
11,591	BATH	3,835	1,777	1,890	168	113 D	46.3%	49.3%	48.5%	51.5%
28,691	BELL	8,251	5,757	2,206	288	3,551 R	69.8%	26.7%	72.3%	27.7%
118,811	BOONE	34,202	23,191	9,779	1,232	13,412 R	67.8%	28.6%	70.3%	29.7%
19,985	BOURBON	6,644	3,494	2,907	243	587 R	52.6%	43.8%	54.6%	45.4%
49,542	BOYD	14,638	7,264	6,841	533	423 R	49.6%	46.7%	51.5%	48.5%
28,432	BOYLE	9,617	5,437	3,892	288	1,545 R	56.5%	40.5%	58.3%	41.7%
8,488	BRACKEN	2,572	1,575	898	99	677 R	61.2%	34.9%	63.7%	36.3%
13,878	BREATHITT	4,655	2,430	2,062	163	368 R	52.2%	44.3%	54.1%	45.9%
20,059	BRECKINRIDGE	7,211	4,120	2,830	261	1,290 R	57.1%	39.2%	59.3%	40.7%
74,319	BULLITT	24,326	14,717	8,847	762	5,870 R	60.5%	36.4%	62.5%	37.5%
12,690	BUTLER	4,077	2,873	1,085	119	1,788 R	70.5%	26.6%	72.6%	27.4%
12,984	CALDWELL	5,031	3,089	1,743	199	1,346 R	61.4%	34.6%	63.9%	36.1%
37,191	CALLOWAY	12,390	7,263	4,676	451	2,587 R	58.6%	37.7%	60.8%	39.2%
90,336	CAMPBELL	29,697	17,607	10,971	1,119	6,636 R	59.3%	36.9%	61.6%	38.4%
5,104	CARLISLE	2,212	1,386	777	49	609 R	62.7%	35.1%	64.1%	35.9%
10,811	CARROLL	3,452	1,683	1,649	120	34 R	48.8%	47.8%	50.5%	49.5%
27,720	CARTER	8,591	4,479	3,748	364	731 R	52.1%	43.6%	54.4%	45.6%
15,955	CASEY	5,041	3,699	1,174	168	2,525 R	73.4%	23.3%	75.9%	24.1%
73,955	CHRISTIAN	15,289	9,317	5,516	456	3,801 R	60.9%	36.1%	62.8%	37.2%
35,613	CLARK	12,447	7,131	4,882	434	2,249 R	57.3%	39.2%	59.4%	40.6%
21,730	CLAY	6,127	4,597	1,325	205	3,272 R	75.0%	21.6%	77.6%	22.4%
10,272	CLINTON	4,128	3,156	838	134	2,318 R	76.5%	20.3%	79.0%	21.0%
9,315	CRITTENDEN	3,363	2,283	953	127	1,330 R	67.9%	28.3%	70.6%	29.4%
6,856	CUMBERLAND	2,981	2,079	778	124	1,301 R	69.7%	26.1%	72.8%	27.2%
96,656	DAVIESS	32,698	18,228	13,433	1,037	4,795 R	55.7%	41.1%	57.6%	42.4%
12,161	EDMONSON	4,231	2,731	1,370	130	1,361 R	64.5%	32.4%	66.6%	33.4%
7,852	ELLIOTT	2,134	898	1,153	83	255 D	42.1%	54.0%	43.8%	56.2%
14,672	ESTILL	4,661	2,881	1,588	192	1,293 R	61.8%	34.1%	64.5%	35.5%
295,803	FAYETTE	96,900	44,073	50,332	2,495	6,259 D	45.5%	51.9%	46.7%	53.3%
14,348	FLEMING	4,931	2,863	1,920	148	943 R	58.1%	38.9%	59.9%	40.1%
39,451	FLOYD	13,079	6,914	5,734	431	1,180 R	52.9%	43.8%	54.7%	45.3%
49,285	FRANKLIN	19,706	8,329	10,534	843	2,205 D	42.3%	53.5%	44.2%	55.8%
6,813	FULTON	1,953	1,087	804	62	283 R	55.7%	41.2%	57.5%	42.5%
8,589	GALLATIN	2,650	1,530	1,028	92	502 R	57.7%	38.8%	59.8%	40.2%
16,912	GARRARD	5,504	3,764	1,562	178	2,202 R	68.4%	28.4%	70.7%	29.3%
24,662	GRANT	6,338	4,126	1,938	274	2,188 R	65.1%	30.6%	68.0%	32.0%
37,121	GRAVES	13,116	8,365	4,359	392	4,006 R	63.8%	33.2%	65.7%	34.3%
25,746	GRAYSON	7,888	5,048	2,553	287	2,495 R	64.0%	32.4%	66.4%	33.6%
11,258	GREEN	4,807	3,198	1,454	155	1,744 R	66.5%	30.2%	68.7%	31.3%
36,910	GREENUP	11,820	6,077	5,378	365	699 R	51.4%	45.5%	53.1%	46.9%
8,565	HANCOCK	3,723	1,882	1,707	134	175 R	50.6%	45.9%	52.4%	47.6%
105,543	HARDIN	30,539	17,551	11,975	1,013	5,576 R	57.5%	39.2%	59.4%	40.6%
29,278	HARLAN	8,966	6,451	2,199	316	4,252 R	71.9%	24.5%	74.6%	25.4%
18,846	HARRISON	5,799	3,228	2,243	328	985 R	55.7%	38.7%	59.0%	41.0%
18,199	HART	5,771	3,296	2,248	227	1,048 R	57.1%	39.0%	59.5%	40.5%
46,250	HENDERSON	13,953	7,119	6,479	355	640 R	51.0%	46.4%	52.4%	47.6%
15,416	HENRY	5,875	3,281	2,382	212	899 R	55.8%	40.5%	57.9%	42.1%
4,902	HICKMAN	1,926	1,156	707	63	449 R	60.0%	36.7%	62.1%	37.9%
46,920	HOPKINS	15,965	10,405	5,087	473	5,318 R	65.2%	31.9%	67.2%	32.8%
13,494	JACKSON	4,565	3,555	856	154	2,699 R	77.9%	18.8%	80.6%	19.4%
741,096	JEFFERSON	258,547	108,786	144,761	5,000	35,975 D	42.1%	56.0%	42.9%	57.1%
48,586	JESSAMINE	17,103	10,822	5,567	714	5,255 R	63.3%	32.5%	66.0%	34.0%
23,356	JOHNSON	8,086	5,608	2,152	326	3,456 R	69.4%	26.6%	72.3%	27.7%
159,720	KENTON	46,542	28,297	16,661	1,584	11,636 R	60.8%	35.8%	62.9%	37.1%
16,346	KNOTT	4,342	2,578	1,661	103	917 R	59.4%	38.3%	60.8%	39.2%

KENTUCKY

SENATOR 2014

2010 Census Population	County	Total Vote	Republican (McConnell)	Democratic (Grimes)	Other	Rep.-Dem. Plurality	Percentage Total Vote Rep.	Dem.	Major Vote Rep.	Dem.
31,883	KNOX	10,211	6,977	2,951	283	4,026 R	68.3%	28.9%	70.3%	29.7%
14,193	LARUE	4,741	2,966	1,608	167	1,358 R	62.6%	33.9%	64.8%	35.2%
58,849	LAUREL	17,082	12,613	3,997	472	8,616 R	73.8%	23.4%	75.9%	24.1%
15,860	LAWRENCE	5,168	3,128	1,842	198	1,286 R	60.5%	35.6%	62.9%	37.1%
7,887	LEE	2,625	1,729	799	97	930 R	65.9%	30.4%	68.4%	31.6%
11,310	LESLIE	4,293	3,513	684	96	2,829 R	81.8%	15.9%	83.7%	16.3%
24,519	LETCHER	7,543	4,787	2,495	261	2,292 R	63.5%	33.1%	65.7%	34.3%
13,870	LEWIS	3,429	2,383	951	95	1,432 R	69.5%	27.7%	71.5%	28.5%
24,742	LINCOLN	7,431	4,565	2,590	276	1,975 R	61.4%	34.9%	63.8%	36.2%
9,519	LIVINGSTON	3,895	2,374	1,389	132	985 R	60.9%	35.7%	63.1%	36.9%
26,835	LOGAN	7,665	4,719	2,706	240	2,013 R	61.6%	35.3%	63.6%	36.4%
8,314	LYON	3,638	2,096	1,425	117	671 R	57.6%	39.2%	59.5%	40.5%
82,916	MADISON	26,842	15,472	10,407	963	5,065 R	57.6%	38.8%	59.8%	40.2%
13,333	MAGOFFIN	6,340	3,662	2,523	155	1,139 R	57.8%	39.8%	59.2%	40.8%
19,820	MARION	5,905	2,498	3,267	140	769 D	42.3%	55.3%	43.3%	56.7%
31,448	MARSHALL	13,306	7,886	4,977	443	2,909 R	59.3%	37.4%	61.3%	38.7%
12,929	MARTIN	4,140	3,077	925	138	2,152 R	74.3%	22.3%	76.9%	23.1%
17,490	MASON	5,620	3,279	2,192	149	1,087 R	58.3%	39.0%	59.9%	40.1%
65,565	MCCRACKEN	23,864	15,043	8,262	559	6,781 R	63.0%	34.6%	64.5%	35.5%
18,306	MCCREARY	5,001	3,508	1,275	218	2,233 R	70.1%	25.5%	73.3%	26.7%
9,531	MCLEAN	3,789	2,217	1,457	115	760 R	58.5%	38.5%	60.3%	39.7%
28,602	MEADE	9,230	5,123	3,793	314	1,330 R	55.5%	41.1%	57.5%	42.5%
6,306	MENIFEE	2,577	1,183	1,291	103	108 D	45.9%	50.1%	47.8%	52.2%
21,331	MERCER	7,917	4,901	2,602	414	2,299 R	61.9%	32.9%	65.3%	34.7%
10,099	METCALFE	4,032	2,294	1,550	188	744 R	56.9%	38.4%	59.7%	40.3%
10,963	MONROE	4,682	3,472	1,021	189	2,451 R	74.2%	21.8%	77.3%	22.7%
26,499	MONTGOMERY	8,884	4,711	3,837	336	874 R	53.0%	43.2%	55.1%	44.9%
13,923	MORGAN	4,224	2,230	1,817	177	413 R	52.8%	43.0%	55.1%	44.9%
31,499	MUHLENBERG	9,694	5,192	4,249	253	943 R	53.6%	43.8%	55.0%	45.0%
43,437	NELSON	14,964	7,663	6,883	418	780 R	51.2%	46.0%	52.7%	47.3%
7,135	NICHOLAS	2,245	1,005	1,147	93	142 D	44.8%	51.1%	46.7%	53.3%
23,842	OHIO	8,985	5,460	3,236	289	2,224 R	60.8%	36.0%	62.8%	37.2%
60,316	OLDHAM	23,374	15,049	7,746	579	7,303 R	64.4%	33.1%	66.0%	34.0%
10,841	OWEN	4,058	2,495	1,383	180	1,112 R	61.5%	34.1%	64.3%	35.7%
4,755	OWSLEY	2,115	1,458	574	83	884 R	68.9%	27.1%	71.8%	28.2%
14,877	PENDLETON	4,250	2,715	1,304	231	1,411 R	63.9%	30.7%	67.6%	32.4%
28,712	PERRY	9,614	6,179	3,098	337	3,081 R	64.3%	32.2%	66.6%	33.4%
65,024	PIKE	18,880	11,840	6,531	509	5,309 R	62.7%	34.6%	64.4%	35.6%
12,613	POWELL	4,396	2,156	2,022	218	134 R	49.0%	46.0%	51.6%	48.4%
63,063	PULASKI	21,594	15,610	5,263	721	10,347 R	72.3%	24.4%	74.8%	25.2%
2,282	ROBERTSON	794	459	314	21	145 R	57.8%	39.5%	59.4%	40.6%
17,056	ROCKCASTLE	5,097	3,803	1,122	172	2,681 R	74.6%	22.0%	77.2%	22.8%
23,333	ROWAN	7,391	3,453	3,667	271	214 D	46.7%	49.6%	48.5%	51.5%
17,565	RUSSELL	6,743	4,779	1,685	279	3,094 R	70.9%	25.0%	73.9%	26.1%
47,173	SCOTT	16,844	9,371	6,767	706	2,604 R	55.6%	40.2%	58.1%	41.9%
42,074	SHELBY	15,150	9,220	5,525	405	3,695 R	60.9%	36.5%	62.5%	37.5%
17,327	SIMPSON	4,776	2,738	1,887	151	851 R	57.3%	39.5%	59.2%	40.8%
17,061	SPENCER	7,464	4,766	2,445	253	2,321 R	63.9%	32.8%	66.1%	33.9%
24,512	TAYLOR	9,672	6,119	3,271	282	2,848 R	63.3%	33.8%	65.2%	34.8%
12,460	TODD	3,696	2,368	1,180	148	1,188 R	64.1%	31.9%	66.7%	33.3%
14,339	TRIGG	5,266	3,328	1,765	173	1,563 R	63.2%	33.5%	65.3%	34.7%
8,809	TRIMBLE	3,045	1,678	1,282	85	396 R	55.1%	42.1%	56.7%	43.3%
15,007	UNION	5,130	3,171	1,824	135	1,347 R	61.8%	35.6%	63.5%	36.5%
113,792	WARREN	33,170	19,460	12,671	1,039	6,789 R	58.7%	38.2%	60.6%	39.4%
11,717	WASHINGTON	4,575	2,655	1,775	145	880 R	58.0%	38.8%	59.9%	40.1%
20,813	WAYNE	6,877	4,229	2,340	308	1,889 R	61.5%	34.0%	64.4%	35.6%
13,621	WEBSTER	4,500	2,854	1,512	134	1,342 R	63.4%	33.6%	65.4%	34.6%
35,637	WHITLEY	9,662	6,879	2,485	298	4,394 R	71.2%	25.7%	73.5%	26.5%
7,355	WOLFE	2,388	1,134	1,180	74	46 D	47.5%	49.4%	49.0%	51.0%
24,939	WOODFORD	10,407	5,573	4,470	364	1,103 R	53.6%	43.0%	55.5%	44.5%
4,339,367	TOTAL	1,435,868	806,787	584,698	44,383	222,089 R	56.2%	40.7%	58.0%	42.0%

KENTUCKY
HOUSE OF REPRESENTATIVES

CD	Year	Total Vote	Republican Vote	Candidate	Democratic Vote	Candidate	Other Vote	Rep.-Dem. Plurality	Total Vote Rep.	Total Vote Dem.	Major Vote Rep.	Major Vote Dem.
1	2014	236,618	173,022	WHITFIELD, ED*	63,596	HATCHETT, CHARLES KENDALL		109,426 R	73.1%	26.9%	73.1%	26.9%
1	2012	287,155	199,956	WHITFIELD, ED*	87,199	HATCHETT, CHARLES KENDALL		112,757 R	69.6%	30.4%	69.6%	30.4%
2	2014	226,834	156,936	GUTHRIE, BRETT*	69,898	LEACH, RON		87,038 R	69.2%	30.8%	69.2%	30.8%
2	2012	282,267	181,508	GUTHRIE, BRETT*	89,541	WILLIAMS, DAVID LYNN	11,218	91,967 R	64.3%	31.7%	67.0%	33.0%
3	2014	247,355	87,981	MACFARLANE, MICHAEL	157,056	YARMUTH, JOHN A.*	2,318	69,075 D	35.6%	63.5%	35.9%	64.1%
3	2012	322,656	111,452	WICKER, BROOKS	206,385	YARMUTH, JOHN A.*	4,819	94,933 D	34.5%	64.0%	35.1%	64.9%
4	2014	222,158	150,464	MASSIE, THOMAS*	71,694	NEWBERRY, PETER		78,770 R	67.7%	32.3%	67.7%	32.3%
4	2012	299,444	186,036	MASSIE, THOMAS*	104,734	ADKINS, WILLIAM R. "BILL"	8,674	81,302 R	62.1%	35.0%	64.0%	36.0%
5	2014	218,967	171,350	ROGERS, HAROLD*	47,617	STEPP, KENNETH		123,733 R	78.3%	21.7%	78.3%	21.7%
5	2012	250,855	195,408	ROGERS, HAROLD*	55,447	STEPP, KENNETH		139,961 R	77.9%	22.1%	77.9%	22.1%
6	2014	245,694	147,404	BARR, ANDY*	98,290	JENSEN, ELISABETH		49,114 R	60.0%	40.0%	60.0%	40.0%
6	2012	303,000	153,222	BARR, ANDY*	141,438	CHANDLER, BEN*	8,340	11,784 R	50.6%	46.7%	52.0%	48.0%
TOTAL	2014	1,397,626	887,157		508,151		2,318	379,006 R	63.5%	36.4%	63.6%	36.4%
TOTAL	2012	1,745,377	1,027,582		684,744		33,051	342,838 R	58.9%	39.2%	60.0%	40.0%

Note: An asterisk (*) denotes incumbent.

KENTUCKY
GENERAL AND PRIMARY ELECTIONS

2014 GENERAL ELECTIONS: OTHER VOTES

Senate Other vote was 44,240 Libertarian (David M. Patterson), 143 scattered write-in

House Other vote was:

CD 3 2,318 Independent (Gregory Peter Puccetti)

2014 PRIMARY ELECTIONS: SUPPLEMENTARY INFORMATION

Primary	May 20, 2014	**Registration** (as of May 20, 2014)	3,105,349	Democratic	1,672,664
				Republican	1,196,183
				Other	236,502

Primary Type Closed—Only registered Democrats and Republicans could vote in their party's primary.

	REPUBLICAN PRIMARIES			DEMOCRATIC PRIMARIES		
Senator	McConnell, Mitch*	213,753	60.2%	Grimes, Alison Lundergan	307,821	76.5%
	Bevin, Matt G.	125,787	35.4%	Leichty, Gregory Brent	32,602	8.1%
	Sterling, Shawna	7,214	2.0%	Farnsley, Burrel Charles	32,310	8.0%
	Payne, Chris	5,338	1.5%	Recktenwald, Tom	29,791	7.4%
	Copas, James Bradley "Brad"	3,024	0.9%			
	TOTAL	355,116		TOTAL	402,524	
Congressional District 1	Whitfield, Ed*	Unopposed		Hatchett, Charles Kendall	38,055	55.5%
				Bolin, Wesley Seaton	30,528	44.5%
				TOTAL	68,583	

KENTUCKY

GENERAL AND PRIMARY ELECTIONS

	REPUBLICAN PRIMARIES		DEMOCRATIC PRIMARIES		
Congressional District 2	Guthrie, Brett*	Unopposed	Leach, Ron	Unopposed	
Congressional District 3	Macfarlane, Michael	Unopposed	Yarmuth, John A.*	52,026	87.0%
			Pierce, E. Ray	7,747	13.0%
			TOTAL	59,773	
Congressional District 4	Massie, Thomas*	Unopposed	Newberry, Peter	Unopposed	
Congressional District 5	Rogers, Harold*	Unopposed	Stepp, Kenneth	38,949	58.8%
			Wilson, Billy Ray	27,246	41.2%
			TOTAL	66,195	
Congressional District 6	Barr, Andy*	Unopposed	Jensen, Elisabeth	46,727	60.9%
			Young, Geoff M.	30,035	39.1%
			TOTAL	76,762	

Note: An asterisk (*) denotes incumbent.

LOUISIANA

Congressional districts first established for elections held in 2012

6 members

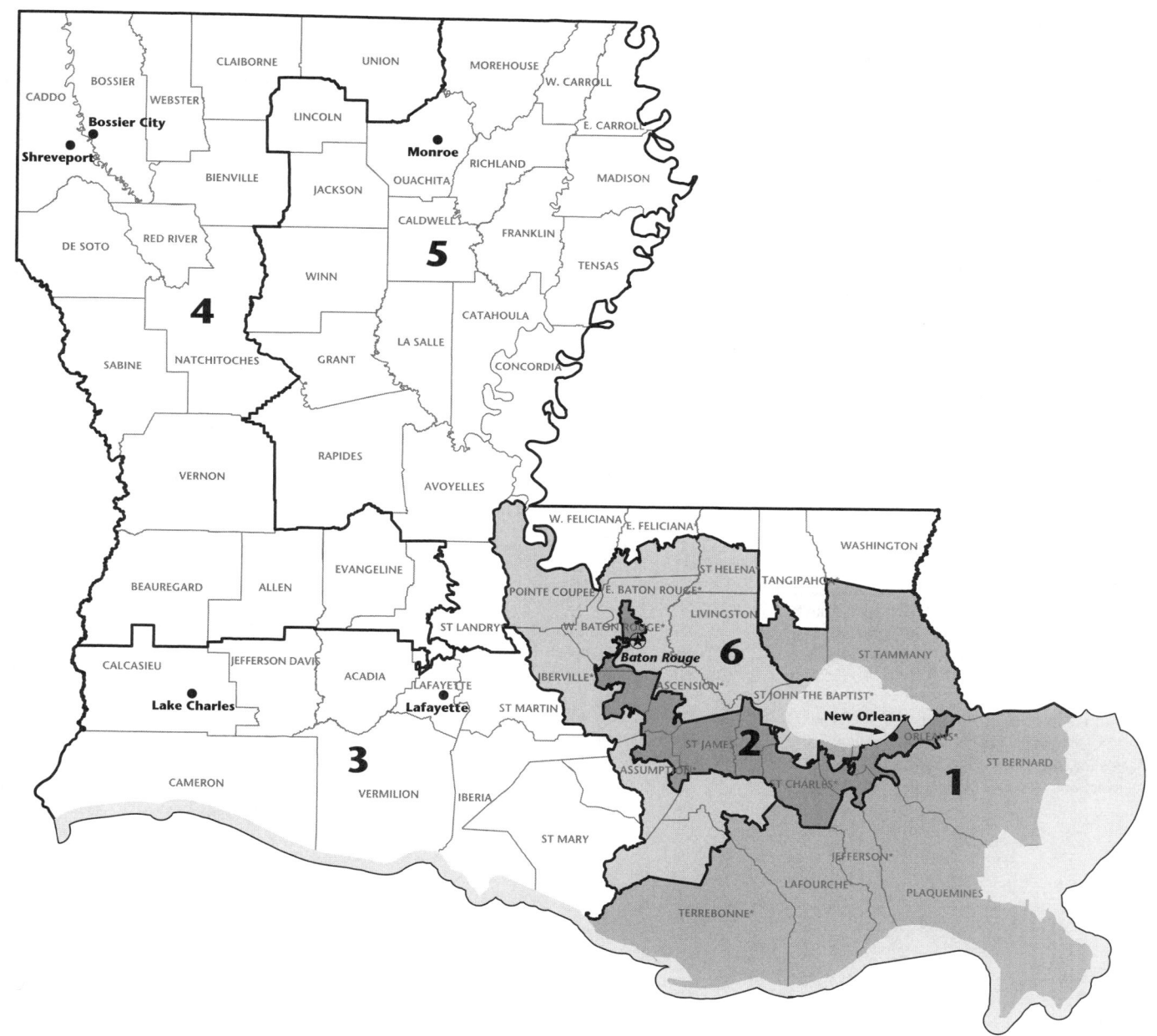

* Asterisk indicates a county whose boundaries include parts of two or more congressional districts.

LOUISIANA

GOVERNOR
Bobby Jindal (R). Reelected 2011 to a four-year term. Previously elected 2007.

SENATORS (2 Republicans)
Bill Cassidy (R). Elected 2014 to a six-year term.

David Vitter (R). Reelected 2010 to a six-year term. Previously elected 2004.

REPRESENTATIVES (5 Republicans, 1 Democrat)
1. Steve Scalise (R)
2. Cedric L. Richmond (D)
3. Charles W. Boustany Jr. (R)
4. John Fleming (R)
5. Ralph Lee Abraham (R)
6. Garret Graves (R)

POSTWAR VOTE FOR PRESIDENT

		Republican		Democratic		Other Vote	Rep.-Dem. Plurality	Total Vote		Major Vote	
Year	Total Vote	Vote	Candidate	Vote	Candidate			Rep.	Dem.	Rep.	Dem.
2012	1,994,065	1,152,262	Romney, W. Mitt	809,141	Obama, Barack H.*	32,662	343,121 R	57.8%	40.6%	58.7%	41.3%
2008	1,960,761	1,148,275	McCain, John S. III	782,989	Obama, Barack H.	29,497	365,286 R	58.6%	39.9%	59.5%	40.5%
2004	1,943,106	1,102,169	Bush, George W.*	820,299	Kerry, John F.	20,638	281,870 R	56.7%	42.2%	57.3%	42.7%
2000**	1,765,656	927,871	Bush, George W.	792,344	Gore, Albert Jr.	45,441	135,527 R	52.6%	44.9%	53.9%	46.1%
1996**	1,783,959	712,586	Dole, Robert "Bob"	927,837	Clinton, Bill*	143,536	215,251 D	39.9%	52.0%	43.4%	56.6%
1992**	1,790,017	733,386	Bush, George H.*	815,971	Clinton, Bill	240,660	82,585 D	41.0%	45.6%	47.3%	52.7%
1988	1,628,202	883,702	Bush, George H.	717,460	Dukakis, Michael S.	27,040	166,242 R	54.3%	44.1%	55.2%	44.8%
1984	1,706,822	1,037,299	Reagan, Ronald*	651,586	Mondale, Walter F.	17,937	385,713 R	60.8%	38.2%	61.4%	38.6%
1980**	1,548,591	792,853	Reagan, Ronald	708,453	Carter, Jimmy*	47,285	84,400 R	51.2%	45.7%	52.8%	47.2%
1976	1,278,539	587,446	Ford, Gerald R.*	661,365	Carter, Jimmy	29,728	73,919 D	45.9%	51.7%	47.0%	53.0%
1972	1,051,491	686,852	Nixon, Richard M.*	298,142	McGovern, George S.	66,497	388,710 R	65.3%	28.4%	69.7%	30.3%
1968**	1,097,450	257,535	Nixon, Richard M.	309,615	Humphrey, Hubert Horatio Jr.	530,300	52,080 D#	23.5%	28.2%	45.4%	54.6%
1964	896,293	509,225	Goldwater, Barry M. Sr.	387,068	Johnson, Lyndon B.*		122,157 R	56.8%	43.2%	56.8%	43.2%
1960**	807,891	230,980	Nixon, Richard M.	407,339	Kennedy, John F.	169,572	176,359 D	28.6%	50.4%	36.2%	63.8%
1956	617,544	329,047	Eisenhower, Dwight D.*	243,977	Stevenson, Adlai E. II	44,520	85,070 R	53.3%	39.5%	57.4%	42.6%
1952	651,952	306,925	Eisenhower, Dwight D.	345,027	Stevenson, Adlai E. II		38,102 D	47.1%	52.9%	47.1%	52.9%
1948**	416,336	72,657	Dewey, Thomas E.	136,344	Truman, Harry S.*	207,335	63,687 D#	17.5%	32.7%	34.8%	65.2%

Note: An asterisk (*) denotes incumbent. A pound sign (#) indicates that the state was carried by a third party candidate. **In past elections, the other vote included: 2000 - 20,473 Green (Ralph Nader); 1996 - 123,293 Reform (Ross Perot); 1992 - 211,478 Independent (Perot); 1980 - 26,345 Independent (John Anderson); 1968 - 530,300 American Independent (George Wallace); 1960 - 169,572 Unpledged Independent Electors; 1948 - 204,290 States' Rights (Strom Thurmond). Wallace carried Louisiana in 1968 with 48.3 percent of the vote. Thurmond won the state in 1948 with 49.1 percent.

LOUISIANA

POSTWAR VOTE FOR GOVERNOR

Year	Total Vote	Republican Vote	Republican Candidate	Democratic Vote	Democratic Candidate	Other Vote	Rep.-Dem. Plurality	Total Vote Rep.	Total Vote Dem.	Major Vote Rep.	Major Vote Dem.
2011	1,023,163	673,239	Jindal, Bobby*	182,925	Hollis, Tara	166,999	490,314 R	65.8%	17.9%	78.6%	21.4%
2007**	1,297,840	699,275	Jindal, Bobby	226,476	Boasso, Walter J.	372,089	472,799 R	53.9%	17.5%	75.5%	24.5%
2003**	1,407,842	676,484	Jindal, Bobby	731,358	Kathleen, Babineaux		54,874 D	48.1%	51.9%	48.1%	51.9%
1999	1,295,205	805,203	Foster, Mike*	382,445	Jefferson, William J.	107,557	422,758 R	62.2%	29.5%	67.8%	32.2%
1995**	1,550,360	984,499	Foster, Mike	565,861	Fields, Cleo		418,638 R	63.5%	36.5%	63.5%	36.5%
1991**	1,728,040	671,009	Duke, David E.	1,057,031	Edwards, Edwin W.		386,022 D	38.8%	61.2%	38.8%	61.2%
1987**	1,558,730	287,780	Livingston, Bob	516,078	Roemer, Charles	754,872	228,298 D	18.5%	33.1%	35.8%	64.2%
1983	1,615,905	588,508	Treen, David Conner*	1,006,561	Edwards, Edwin W.	20,836	418,053 D	36.4%	62.3%	36.9%	63.1%
1979**	1,371,825	690,691	Treen, David Conner	681,134	Lambert, Louis		9,557 R	50.3%	49.7%	50.3%	49.7%
1975	430,095			430,095	Edwards, Edwin W.*		430,095 D		100.0%		100.0%
1972	1,121,570	480,424	Treen, David Conner	641,146	Edwards, Edwin W.		160,722 D	42.8%	57.2%	42.8%	57.2%
1968	372,762			372,762	McKeithen, John J.*		372,762 D		100.0%		100.0%
1964	773,390	297,753	Lyons, Charlton H. Sr.	469,589	McKeithen, John J.	6,048	171,836 D	38.5%	60.7%	38.8%	61.2%
1960	506,562	86,135	Grevemberg, F. C.	407,907	Davis, Jimmie H.	12,520	321,772 D	17.0%	80.5%	17.4%	82.6%
1956	172,291			172,291	Long, Earl K.		172,291 D		100.0%		100.0%
1952	118,723			118,723	Kennon, Robert F.		118,723 D		100.0%		100.0%
1948	76,566			76,566	Long, Earl K.		76,566 D		100.0%		100.0%

Note: An asterisk (*) denotes incumbent. **Since the 1970s, Louisiana has had a two-tier election system for governor in which all candidates, regardless of party, run together in an open election. A candidate who wins a majority of the vote is elected. If no candidate receives 50 percent, a runoff is held between the top two finishers. The results of the runoff are listed in this chart for 1979, 1991, 1995, and 2003. In elections that did not require a runoff, the leading Democratic and Republican candidates are listed with their votes from the first-round, open election. The votes for other candidates are listed in the "Other Vote" column, regardless of whether they were Democratic, Republican, or independent. In past elections, the other vote included: 2007 - 186,682 No Party (John Georges), 161,665 Democrat (Foster Campbell); 1987 - 437,801 Democrat (Edwin W. Edwards). In 1987, Edwards withdrew after finishing second in the initial round of voting. Democrat Charles Roemer finished first with 33.1 percent and with Edwards's withdrawal, no runoff was held. The major party vote percentages are calculated for the top vote-getter for each party only; it does not include additional members of the same party. The Republican Party did not run a candidate in the 1948, 1952, 1956, 1968, and 1975 gubernatorial elections.

POSTWAR VOTE FOR SENATOR

Year	Total Vote	Republican Vote	Republican Candidate	Democratic Vote	Democratic Candidate	Other Vote	Rep.-Dem. Plurality	Total Vote Rep.	Total Vote Dem.	Major Vote Rep.	Major Vote Dem.
2014	1,472,044	603,048	Cassidy, Bill	619,402	Landrieu, Mary L.*	249,594	16,354 D	41.0%	42.1%	49.3%	50.7%
2014S	1,273,589	712,379	Cassidy, Bill	561,210	Landrieu, Mary L.*		151,169 R	55.9%	44.1%	55.9%	44.1%
2010**	1,264,994	715,415	Vitter, David B.*	476,572	Melancon, Charlie R.	73,007	238,843 R	56.6%	37.7%	60.0%	40.0%
2008	1,896,554	867,177	Kennedy, John	988,298	Landrieu, Mary L.*	41,099	121,121 D	45.7%	52.1%	46.7%	53.3%
2004**	1,848,056	943,014	Vitter, David B.	542,150	John, Chris	362,892	400,864 R	51.0%	29.3%	63.5%	36.5%
2002**	1,235,296	596,642	Terrell, Suzanne Haik	638,654	Landrieu, Mary L.*		42,012 D	48.3%	51.7%	48.3%	51.7%
1998	969,165	306,516	Donelon, Jim	620,502	Breaux, John B.*	42,047	313,886 D	31.6%	64.0%	33.1%	66.9%
1996**	1,700,102	847,157	Jenkins, Louis E. "Woody" Jr.	852,945	Landrieu, Mary L.		5,788 D	49.8%	50.2%	49.8%	50.2%
1992	843,037	69,986	Stockstill, Lyle	616,021	Breaux, John B.*	157,030	546,035 D	8.3%	73.1%	10.2%	89.8%
1990	1,396,113	607,391	Duke, David E.	752,902	Johnston, J. Bennett*	35,820	145,511 D	43.5%	53.9%	44.7%	55.3%
1986**	1,369,897	646,311	Moore, W. Henson	723,586	Breaux, John B.		77,275 D	47.2%	52.8%	47.2%	52.8%
1984	977,473	86,546	Ross, Robert M.	838,181	Johnston, J. Bennett*	52,746	751,635 D	8.9%	85.7%	9.4%	90.6%
1980**	841,013	13,739	Bardwell, Jerry C.	484,770	Long, Russell B.*	342,504	471,031 D		57.5%		100.0%
1978**	839,669			498,773	Johnston, J. Bennett*	340,896	498,773 D		59.4%		100.0%
1974	434,643			434,643	Long, Russell B.*		434,643 D		100.0%		100.0%
1972**	1,084,904	206,846	Toledano, Ben C.	598,987	Johnston, J. Bennett	279,071	392,141 D	19.1%	55.2%	25.7%	74.3%
1968	518,586			518,586	Long, Russell B.*		518,586 D		100.0%		100.0%
1966	437,695			437,695	Ellender, Allen J.*		437,695 D		100.0%		100.0%
1962	421,904	103,066	O'Hearn, Taylor Walters	318,838	Long, Russell B.*		215,772 D	24.4%	75.6%	24.4%	75.6%
1960	541,928	109,698	Reese, George W. Jr.	432,228	Ellender, Allen J.*	2	322,530 D	20.2%	79.8%	20.2%	79.8%
1956	335,564			335,564	Long, Russell B.*		335,564 D		100.0%		100.0%
1954	207,115			207,115	Ellender, Allen J.*		207,115 D		100.0%		100.0%
1950	251,838	30,931	Gerth, Charles S.	220,907	Long, Russell B.*		189,976 D	12.3%	87.7%	12.3%	87.7%
1948	330,324			330,315	Ellender, Allen J.	9	330,315 D		100.0%		100.0%
1948S	407,685	102,339	Clarke, Clem S.	305,346	Long, Russell B.		203,007 D	25.1%	74.9%	25.1%	74.9%

Note: An asterisk (*) denotes incumbent. **In 2008 and 2010, Louisiana used the more typical system of party primaries followed by a general election to fill seats in Congress. From 1978 through 2004, and again in 2014 Senate seats were decided in open elections in which candidates of all parties ran together on the same ballot. If no candidate won a majority of the vote in the first round, a runoff was held between the top two vote-getters, regardless of party. The Senate elections in 1986, 1996, 2002, and 2014 were decided by a runoff, with the results of the runoff listed in this chart. In elections that did not require a runoff, the leading Democratic and Republican candidates are listed with their votes in the first-round, open election. The votes for other candidates are listed in the "Other Vote" column, regardless of whether they were Democratic, Republican, or independent. In past elections, the other vote included: 2004 - 275,821 Democrat (John Kennedy); 1980 - 325,922 Democrat (Louis Jenkins), who finished second; 1978 - 340,896 Democrat (Louis Jenkins), who finished second; 1972 - 250,161 Independent (John J. McKeithen), who finished second. One of the 1948 elections was for a short term to fill a vacancy. The major party vote percentages are calculated for the top vote-getter for each party only; it does not include additional members of the same party. The Republican Party did not run a candidate in Senate elections in 1948, 1954, 1956, 1966, 1968, 1974, and 1978.

LOUISIANA

SENATOR 2014 RUN-OFF

2010 Census Population	Parish	Total Vote	Republican (Cassidy)	Democratic (Landrieu)	Other	Rep.-Dem. Plurality	Percentage			
							Total Vote		Major Vote	
							Rep.	Dem.	Rep.	Dem.
61,773	ACADIA	18,041	13,290	4,751		8,539 R	73.7%	26.3%	73.7%	26.3%
25,764	ALLEN	5,286	3,646	1,640		2,006 R	69.0%	31.0%	69.0%	31.0%
107,215	ASCENSION	32,109	20,534	11,575		8,959 R	64.0%	36.0%	64.0%	36.0%
23,421	ASSUMPTION	6,672	3,292	3,380		88 D	49.3%	50.7%	49.3%	50.7%
42,073	AVOYELLES	11,817	7,406	4,411		2,995 R	62.7%	37.3%	62.7%	37.3%
35,654	BEAUREGARD	8,695	6,878	1,817		5,061 R	79.1%	20.9%	79.1%	20.9%
14,353	BIENVILLE	4,844	2,357	2,487		130 D	48.7%	51.3%	48.7%	51.3%
116,979	BOSSIER	28,328	20,691	7,637		13,054 R	73.0%	27.0%	73.0%	27.0%
254,969	CADDO	69,765	31,952	37,813		5,861 D	45.8%	54.2%	45.8%	54.2%
192,768	CALCASIEU	48,381	30,511	17,870		12,641 R	63.1%	36.9%	63.1%	36.9%
10,132	CALDWELL	3,063	2,291	772		1,519 R	74.8%	25.2%	74.8%	25.2%
6,839	CAMERON	1,947	1,545	402		1,143 R	79.4%	20.6%	79.4%	20.6%
10,407	CATAHOULA	3,277	2,158	1,119		1,039 R	65.9%	34.1%	65.9%	34.1%
17,195	CLAIBORNE	4,660	2,503	2,157		346 R	53.7%	46.3%	53.7%	46.3%
20,822	CONCORDIA	5,361	3,083	2,278		805 R	57.5%	42.5%	57.5%	42.5%
26,656	DE SOTO	8,508	4,591	3,917		674 R	54.0%	46.0%	54.0%	46.0%
440,171	EAST BATON ROUGE	131,389	62,118	69,271		7,153 D	47.3%	52.7%	47.3%	52.7%
7,759	EAST CARROLL	2,789	913	1,876		963 D	32.7%	67.3%	32.7%	67.3%
20,267	EAST FELICIANA	7,283	3,653	3,630		23 R	50.2%	49.8%	50.2%	49.8%
33,984	EVANGELINE	10,437	6,336	4,101		2,235 R	60.7%	39.3%	60.7%	39.3%
20,767	FRANKLIN	6,523	4,509	2,014		2,495 R	69.1%	30.9%	69.1%	30.9%
22,309	GRANT	5,325	4,398	927		3,471 R	82.6%	17.4%	82.6%	17.4%
73,240	IBERIA	20,390	12,738	7,652		5,086 R	62.5%	37.5%	62.5%	37.5%
33,387	IBERVILLE	12,915	5,378	7,537		2,159 D	41.6%	58.4%	41.6%	58.4%
16,274	JACKSON	5,241	3,264	1,977		1,287 R	62.3%	37.7%	62.3%	37.7%
432,552	JEFFERSON	109,715	58,179	51,536		6,643 R	53.0%	47.0%	53.0%	47.0%
31,594	JEFFERSON DAVIS	8,140	5,781	2,359		3,422 R	71.0%	29.0%	71.0%	29.0%
14,890	LA SALLE	4,283	3,763	520		3,243 R	87.9%	12.1%	87.9%	12.1%
221,578	LAFAYETTE	62,834	42,537	20,297		22,240 R	67.7%	32.3%	67.7%	32.3%
96,318	LAFOURCHE	23,236	14,876	8,360		6,516 R	64.0%	36.0%	64.0%	36.0%
46,735	LINCOLN	12,061	7,187	4,874		2,313 R	59.6%	40.4%	59.6%	40.4%
128,026	LIVINGSTON	32,799	27,212	5,587		21,625 R	83.0%	17.0%	83.0%	17.0%
12,093	MADISON	3,116	1,244	1,872		628 D	39.9%	60.1%	39.9%	60.1%
27,979	MOREHOUSE	8,252	4,338	3,914		424 R	52.6%	47.4%	52.6%	47.4%
39,566	NATCHITOCHES	10,291	5,674	4,617		1,057 R	55.1%	44.9%	55.1%	44.9%
343,829	ORLEANS	103,031	15,590	87,441		71,851 D	15.1%	84.9%	15.1%	84.9%
153,720	OUACHITA	43,219	26,799	16,420		10,379 R	62.0%	38.0%	62.0%	38.0%
23,042	PLAQUEMINES	7,673	4,342	3,331		1,011 R	56.6%	43.4%	56.6%	43.4%
22,802	POINTE COUPEE	7,967	3,824	4,143		319 D	48.0%	52.0%	48.0%	52.0%
131,613	RAPIDES	38,389	25,123	13,266		11,857 R	65.4%	34.6%	65.4%	34.6%
9,091	RED RIVER	2,804	1,423	1,381		42 R	50.7%	49.3%	50.7%	49.3%
20,725	RICHLAND	7,109	4,442	2,667		1,775 R	62.5%	37.5%	62.5%	37.5%
24,233	SABINE	6,165	4,838	1,327		3,511 R	78.5%	21.5%	78.5%	21.5%
35,897	ST. BERNARD	9,394	4,636	4,758		122 D	49.4%	50.6%	49.4%	50.6%
52,780	ST. CHARLES	15,846	9,059	6,787		2,272 R	57.2%	42.8%	57.2%	42.8%
11,203	ST. HELENA	4,286	1,610	2,676		1,066 D	37.6%	62.4%	37.6%	62.4%
22,102	ST. JAMES	8,200	2,919	5,281		2,362 D	35.6%	64.4%	35.6%	64.4%
45,924	ST. JOHN THE BAPTIST	12,986	4,031	8,955		4,924 D	31.0%	69.0%	31.0%	69.0%
83,384	ST. LANDRY	27,606	13,616	13,990		374 D	49.3%	50.7%	49.3%	50.7%
52,160	ST. MARTIN	16,248	9,817	6,431		3,386 R	60.4%	39.6%	60.4%	39.6%
54,650	ST. MARY	13,585	7,773	5,812		1,961 R	57.2%	42.8%	57.2%	42.8%
233,740	ST. TAMMANY	76,510	54,915	21,595		33,320 R	71.8%	28.2%	71.8%	28.2%
121,097	TANGIPAHOA	31,472	19,149	12,323		6,826 R	60.8%	39.2%	60.8%	39.2%
5,252	TENSAS	1,767	796	971		175 D	45.0%	55.0%	45.0%	55.0%
111,860	TERREBONNE	26,223	16,732	9,491		7,241 R	63.8%	36.2%	63.8%	36.2%
22,721	UNION	6,953	4,965	1,988		2,977 R	71.4%	28.6%	71.4%	28.6%
57,999	VERMILION	14,760	11,201	3,559		7,642 R	75.9%	24.1%	75.9%	24.1%
52,334	VERNON	9,777	7,854	1,923		5,931 R	80.3%	19.7%	80.3%	19.7%
47,168	WASHINGTON	12,047	7,144	4,903		2,241 R	59.3%	40.7%	59.3%	40.7%
41,207	WEBSTER	12,011	7,126	4,885		2,241 R	59.3%	40.7%	59.3%	40.7%

LOUISIANA

SENATOR 2014 RUN-OFF

2010 Census Population	Parish	Total Vote	Republican (Cassidy)	Democratic (Landrieu)	Other	Rep.-Dem. Plurality	Total Vote Rep.	Total Vote Dem.	Major Vote Rep.	Major Vote Dem.
23,788	WEST BATON ROUGE	8,462	4,314	4,148		166 R	51.0%	49.0%	51.0%	49.0%
11,604	WEST CARROLL	3,004	2,422	582		1,840 R	80.6%	19.4%	80.6%	19.4%
15,625	WEST FELICIANA	4,158	2,231	1,927		304 R	53.7%	46.3%	53.7%	46.3%
15,313	WINN	4,164	2,862	1,302		1,560 R	68.7%	31.3%	68.7%	31.3%
4,533,372	TOTAL	1,273,589	712,379	561,210		151,169 R	55.9%	44.1%	55.9%	44.1%

LOUISIANA

HOUSE OF REPRESENTATIVES

CD	Year	Total Vote	Republican Vote	Republican Candidate	Democratic Vote	Democratic Candidate	Other Vote	Rep.-Dem. Plurality	Total Vote Rep.	Total Vote Dem.	Major Vote Rep.	Major Vote Dem.
1	2014	244,004	189,250	SCALISE, STEVE*	24,761	MENDOZA, M. V. VINNY	29,993	164,489 R	77.6%	10.1%	88.4%	11.6%
1	2012	290,410	193,496	SCALISE, STEVE*	61,703	MENDOZA, M. V. VINNY	35,211	131,793 R	66.6%	21.2%	75.8%	24.2%
2	2014	221,570			152,201	RICHMOND, CEDRIC L.*	69,369	152,201 D		68.7%		100.0%
2	2012	287,354	38,801	BAILEY, DWAYNE	158,501	RICHMOND, CEDRIC L.*	90,052	119,700 D	13.5%	55.2%	19.7%	80.3%
3	2014	236,268	185,867	BOUSTANY, CHARLES W. JR.*			50,401		78.7%		100.0%	
3	2012	311,393	139,123	BOUSTANY, CHARLES W. JR.	67,070	RICHARD, RON	105,200	72,053 R	44.7%	21.5%	67.5%	32.5%
4	2014	207,919	152,683	FLEMING, JOHN*			55,236		73.4%		100.0%	
4	2012	249,531	187,894	FLEMING, JOHN*			61,637		75.3%		100.0%	
5**	2014	209,622	134,616	ABRAHAM, RALPH LEE	75,006	MAYO, JAMIE		59,610 R	64.2%	35.8%	64.2%	35.8%
5	2012	260,216	202,536	ALEXANDER, RODNEY*			57,680		77.8%		100.0%	
6**	2014	222,990	139,209	GRAVES, GARRET	83,781	EDWARDS, EDWIN W.		55,428 R	62.4%	37.6%	62.4%	37.6%
6	2012	306,713	243,553	CASSIDY, BILL*			63,160		79.4%		100.0%	
TOTAL	2014	1,342,373	823,684		394,840		123,849	428,844 R	61.4%	29.4%	67.6%	32.4%
TOTAL	2012	1,705,617	1,005,403		287,274		412,940	718,129 R	58.9%	16.8%	77.8%	22.2%

Note: An asterisk (*) denotes incumbent. ** Indicates results of a runoff.

LOUISIANA

GENERAL AND PRIMARY ELECTIONS

2014 GENERAL ELECTIONS: OTHER VOTES

Senate See "First-Round Vote" table.

House Other vote was:

CD 1 21,286 Democrat (Lee A. Dugas), 8,707 Libertarian (Jeff Sanford)

CD 2 37,805 Democrat (Gary Landrieu), 16,327 No Party (David Graham Brooks), 15,237 Libertarian (Samuel Davenport)

CD 3 28,342 No Party (Russell Richard), 22,059 Republican (Bryan Barrilleaux)

CD 4 55,236 Libertarian (Randall Lord)

CD 5 See "First-Round Vote" table.

CD 6 See "First-Round Vote" table.

LOUISIANA

GENERAL AND PRIMARY ELECTIONS

2014 PRIMARY ELECTIONS: SUPPLEMENTARY INFORMATION

Primary	November 4, 2014	**Registration** (as of November 1, 2014)	2,935,143	Democratic	1,373,264
				Republican	812,696
				Other Parties	749,183

Primary Type For governor and other federal offices, Louisiana has a two-tier electoral system open to all voters, with a first round of voting (sometimes called an open or "jungle" primary) that features candidates from all parties running together on the same ballot. A candidate who wins a majority of the vote in the first round is elected. Otherwise, there is a runoff held several weeks later between the top two finishers.

Primary Data See "First-Round Vote" table

FIRST-ROUND VOTE (NOV. 4, 2014)

Senate	Mary L. Landrieu (D)*#	619,402	42.1%
	Bill Cassidy (R)#	603,048	41.0%
	Rob Maness (R)	202,556	13.8%
	Thomas Clements (R)	14,173	1.0%
	Brannon Lee McMorris (Libertarian)	13,034	0.9%
	Wayne Ables (D)	11,323	0.8%
	William P. Waymire Jr. (D)	4,673	0.3%
	Vallian Senegal (D)	3,835	0.3%
	TOTAL	*1,472,044*	
Congressional District 5	Jamie Mayo (D)#	67,611	28.2%
	Ralph Lee Abraham (R)#	55,489	23.2%
	Zach Dasher (R)	53,628	22.4%
	Vance M. McAllister (R)*	26,606	11.1%
	Clyde C. Hiolloway (R)	17,877	7.5%
	Harris Brown (R)	9,890	4.1%
	Ed Tarpley (R)	4,594	1.9%
	Charles Saucier (Libertarian)	2,201	0.9%
	Eliot S. Barron (Green)	1,655	0.7%
	TOTAL	*239,551*	
Congressional District 6	Edwin W. Edwards (D)#	77,866	30.1%
	Garret Graves (R)#	70,715	27.4%
	Paul Dietzel II (R)	35,024	13.6%
	Dan Claitor (R)	26,524	10.3%
	Lenar Whitney (R)	19,151	7.4%
	Richard Lieberman (D)	7,309	2.8%
	Craig McCulloch (R)	5,815	2.2%
	Robert Lamar "Bob" Bell (R)	5,182	2.0%
	Peter Williams (D)	4,037	1.6%
	Rufus Holt Craig Jr. (Libertarian)	3,561	1.4%
	Norman "Norm" Clark (R)	1,848	0.7%
	Trey Thomas (R)	1,447	0.6%
	TOTAL	*258,479*	

Note: The table above lists the first-round results for contests that were eventually decided in a December 6, 2014 runoff. A pound sign (#) indicates the candidates in each race who qualified for the runoff.

MAINE

Congressional districts first established for elections held in 2012

2 members

AROOSTOOK

Presque Isle

PISCATAQUIS

SOMERSET

2

PENOBSCOT

FRANKLIN

Orono

Bangor

WASHINGTON

OXFORD

Farmington

Waterville

KENNEBEC

WALDO

HANCOCK

Augusta

ANDROSCOGGIN

LINCOLN

KNOX

Lewiston

Rockland

SAGADAHOC

1

Brunswick

CUMBERLAND

Portland

Saco

Kennebunkport

YORK

* Asterisk indicates a county whose boundaries include parts of two or more congressional districts.

MAINE

GOVERNOR
Paul LePage (R). Re-elected 2014 to a four-year term. Previously elected 2010.

SENATORS (1 Republican, 1 Independent)
Susan M. Collins (R). Reelected 2014 to a six-year term. Previously elected 2008, 2002, 1996.

Angus S. King Jr. (Ind.). Elected 2012 to a six-year term.

REPRESENTATIVES (1 Democrat, 1 Republican)
1. Chellie Pingree (D)   2. Bruce Poliquin (R)

POSTWAR VOTE FOR PRESIDENT

		Republican		Democratic		Other Vote	Rep.-Dem. Plurality	Total Vote		Major Vote	
Year	Total Vote	Vote	Candidate	Vote	Candidate			Rep.	Dem.	Rep.	Dem.
2012	713,180	292,276	Romney, W. Mitt	401,306	Obama, Barack H.*	19,598	109,030 D	41.0%	56.3%	42.1%	57.9%
2008	731,163	295,273	McCain, John S. III	421,923	Obama, Barack H.	13,967	126,650 D	40.4%	57.7%	41.2%	58.8%
2004	740,752	330,201	Bush, George W.*	396,842	Kerry, John F.	13,709	66,641 D	44.6%	53.6%	45.4%	54.6%
2000**	651,817	286,616	Bush, George W.	319,951	Gore, Albert Jr.	45,250	33,335 D	44.0%	49.1%	47.3%	52.7%
1996**	605,897	186,378	Dole, Robert "Bob"	312,788	Clinton, Bill*	106,731	126,410 D	30.8%	51.6%	37.3%	62.7%
1992**	679,499	206,504	Bush, George H.*	263,420	Clinton, Bill	209,575	56,916 D	30.4%	38.8%	43.9%	56.1%
1988	555,035	307,131	Bush, George H.	243,569	Dukakis, Michael S.	4,335	63,562 R	55.3%	43.9%	55.8%	44.2%
1984	553,144	336,500	Reagan, Ronald*	214,515	Mondale, Walter F.	2,129	121,985 R	60.8%	38.8%	61.1%	38.9%
1980**	523,011	238,522	Reagan, Ronald	220,974	Carter, Jimmy*	63,515	17,548 R	45.6%	42.3%	51.9%	48.1%
1976	483,216	236,320	Ford, Gerald R.*	232,279	Carter, Jimmy	14,617	4,041 R	48.9%	48.1%	50.4%	49.6%
1972	417,042	256,458	Nixon, Richard M.*	160,584	McGovern, George S.		95,874 R	61.5%	38.5%	61.5%	38.5%
1968**	392,936	169,254	Nixon, Richard M.	217,312	Humphrey, Hubert Horatio Jr.	6,370	48,058 D	43.1%	55.3%	43.8%	56.2%
1964	380,965	118,701	Goldwater, Barry M. Sr.	262,264	Johnson, Lyndon B.*		143,563 D	31.2%	68.8%	31.2%	68.8%
1960	421,767	240,608	Nixon, Richard M.	181,159	Kennedy, John F.		59,449 R	57.0%	43.0%	57.0%	43.0%
1956	351,706	249,238	Eisenhower, Dwight D.*	102,468	Stevenson, Adlai E. II		146,770 R	70.9%	29.1%	70.9%	29.1%
1952	351,786	232,353	Eisenhower, Dwight D.	118,806	Stevenson, Adlai E. II	627	113,547 R	66.0%	33.8%	66.2%	33.8%
1948	264,787	150,234	Dewey, Thomas E.	111,916	Truman, Harry S.*	2,637	38,318 R	56.7%	42.3%	57.3%	42.7%

Note: An asterisk (*) denotes incumbent. **In past elections, the other vote included: 2000 - 37,127 Green (Ralph Nader); 1996 - 85,970 Reform (Ross Perot); 1992 - 206,820 Independent (Perot), who placed second; 1980 - 53,327 Independent (John Anderson); 1968 - 6,370 American Independent (George Wallace).

MAINE

POSTWAR VOTE FOR GOVERNOR

Year	Total Vote	Republican Vote	Candidate	Democratic Vote	Candidate	Other Vote	Rep.-Dem. Plurality	Percentage Total Vote Rep.	Dem.	Major Vote Rep.	Dem.
2014	611,227	294,519	LePage, Paul*	265,114	Michaud, Michael H.	51,594	29,405 R	48.2%	43.4%	52.6%	47.4%
2010**	572,766	218,065	LePage, Paul	109,387	Mitchell, Elizabeth H. "Libby"	245,314	108,678 R	38.1%	19.1%	66.6%	33.4%
2006**	550,865	166,425	Woodcock, Chandler E.	209,927	Baldacci, John*	174,513	43,502 D	30.2%	38.1%	44.2%	55.8%
2002	505,190	209,496	Cianchette, Peter E.	238,179	Baldacci, John	57,515	28,683 D	41.5%	47.1%	46.8%	53.2%
1998**	421,009	79,716	Longley, James B. Jr.	50,506	Connolly, Thomas J.	290,787	29,210 R#	18.9%	12.0%	61.2%	38.8%
1994**	511,308	117,990	Collins, Susan M.	172,951	Brennan, Joseph E.	220,367	54,961 D#	23.1%	33.8%	40.6%	59.4%
1990	522,492	243,766	McKernan, John R.*	230,038	Brennan, Joseph E.	48,688	13,728 R	46.7%	44.0%	51.4%	48.6%
1986**	426,861	170,312	McKernan, John R.	128,744	Tierney, James	127,805	41,568 R	39.9%	30.2%	56.9%	43.1%
1982	460,295	172,949	Cragin, Charles L.	281,066	Brennan, Joseph E.*	6,280	108,117 D	37.6%	61.1%	38.1%	61.9%
1978**	370,258	126,862	Palmer, Linwood E.	176,493	Brennan, Joseph E.	66,903	49,631 D	34.3%	47.7%	41.8%	58.2%
1974**	363,945	84,176	Erwin, James S.*	132,219	Mitchell, George J.	147,550	48,043 D#	23.1%	36.3%	38.9%	61.1%
1970	325,386	162,248	Erwin, James S.	163,138	Curtis, Kenneth M.*		890 D	49.9%	50.1%	49.9%	50.1%
1966	323,838	151,802	Reed, John H.*	172,036	Curtis, Kenneth M.		20,234 D	46.9%	53.1%	46.9%	53.1%
1962	292,725	146,604	Reed, John H.*	146,121	Dolloff, Maynard C.		483 R	50.1%	49.9%	50.1%	49.9%
1960S	417,215	219,768	Reed, John H.	197,447	Coffin, Frank M.		22,321 R	52.7%	47.3%	52.7%	47.3%
1958**	280,245	134,572	Hildreth, Horace A.	145,673	Clauson, Clinton A.		11,101 D	48.0%	52.0%	48.0%	52.0%
1956	304,649	124,395	Trafton, Willis A. Jr.	180,254	Muskie, Edmund S.*		55,859 D	40.8%	59.2%	40.8%	59.2%
1954	248,971	113,298	Cross, Burton M.*	135,673	Muskie, Edmund S.		22,375 D	45.5%	54.5%	45.5%	54.5%
1952	248,441	128,532	Cross, Burton M.	82,538	Oliver, James C.	37,371	45,994 R	51.7%	33.2%	60.9%	39.1%
1950	241,177	145,823	Payne, Frederick G.*	94,304	Grant, Earle S.	1,050	51,519 R	60.5%	39.1%	60.7%	39.3%
1948	222,500	145,956	Payne, Frederick G.	76,544	Lausier, Louis B.		69,412 R	65.6%	34.4%	65.6%	34.4%
1946	179,951	110,327	Hildreth, Horace A.	69,624	Clark, F. Davis		40,703 R	61.3%	38.7%	61.3%	38.7%

Note: An asterisk (*) denotes incumbent. A pound sign (#) indicates that an independant candidate was elected. **In past elections, the other vote included: 2010 - 208,270 Independent (Eliot R. Cutler), who placed second; 2006 - 118,715 Independent Maine Course (Barbara Merrill); 1998 - 246,772 Independent (Angus King), who was reelected with 58.6 percent of the total vote; 1994 - 180,829 Independent (King), who was elected with 35.4 percent of the total vote; 1986 - 64,317 Independent (Sherry F. Huber), 63,474 Independent (John E. Menario); 1978 - 65,889 Independent (Herman C. Frankland); 1974 - 142,464 Independent (James B. Longley), who was elected with 39.1 percent of the total vote. The 1960 election was for a short term to fill a vacancy. The term of office of Maine's governor was increased from two to four years effective with the 1958 election.

POSTWAR VOTE FOR SENATOR

Year	Total Vote	Republican Vote	Candidate	Democratic Vote	Candidate	Other Vote	Rep.-Dem. Plurality	Percentage Total Vote Rep.	Dem.	Major Vote Rep.	Dem.
2014	604,008	413,495	Collins, Susan M.*	190,244	Bellows, Shenna	269	223,251 R	68.5%	31.5%	68.5%	31.5%
2012**	700,599	215,399	Summers, Charles E.	92,900	Dill, Cynthia Ann	392,300	122,499 R#	30.7%	13.3%	69.9%	30.1%
2008	724,430	444,300	Collins, Susan M.*	279,510	Allen, Tom	620	164,790 R	61.3%	38.6%	61.4%	38.6%
2006	543,981	402,598	Snowe, Olympia J.*	111,984	Bright, Jean Hay	29,399	290,614 R	74.0%	20.6%	78.2%	21.8%
2002	504,899	295,041	Collins, Susan M.*	209,858	Pingree, Chellie		85,183 R	58.4%	41.6%	58.4%	41.6%
2000	634,872	437,689	Snowe, Olympia J.*	197,183	Lawrence, Mark W.		240,506 R	68.9%	31.1%	68.9%	31.1%
1996	606,777	298,422	Collins, Susan M.	266,226	Brennan, Joseph E.	42,129	32,196 R	49.2%	43.9%	52.9%	47.1%
1994	511,733	308,244	Snowe, Olympia J.	186,042	Andrews, Thomas H.	17,447	122,202 R	60.2%	36.4%	62.4%	37.6%
1990	520,320	319,167	Cohen, William S.*	201,053	Rolde, Neil	100	118,114 R	61.3%	38.6%	61.4%	38.6%
1988	557,375	104,758	Wyman, Jasper S.	452,590	Mitchell, George J.*	27	347,832 D	18.8%	81.2%	18.8%	81.2%
1984	551,406	404,414	Cohen, William S.*	142,626	Mitchell, Elizabeth H. "Libby"	4,366	261,788 R	73.3%	25.9%	73.9%	26.1%
1982	459,715	179,882	Emery, David F.	279,819	Mitchell, George J.	14	99,937 D	39.1%	60.9%	39.1%	60.9%
1978	375,172	212,294	Cohen, William S.	127,327	Hathaway, William D.*	35,551	84,967 R	56.6%	33.9%	62.5%	37.5%
1976	486,254	193,489	Monks, Robert A. G.	292,704	Muskie, Edmund S.*	61	99,215 D	39.8%	60.2%	39.8%	60.2%
1972	421,310	197,040	Smith, Margaret Chase*	224,270	Hathaway, William D.		27,230 D	46.8%	53.2%	46.8%	53.2%
1970	323,860	123,906	Bishop, Neil S.	199,954	Muskie, Edmund S.*		76,048 D	38.3%	61.7%	38.3%	61.7%
1966	319,535	188,291	Smith, Margaret Chase*	131,136	Violette, Elmer H.	108	57,155 R	58.9%	41.0%	58.9%	41.1%
1964	380,551	127,040	McIntire, Clifford G.	253,511	Muskie, Edmund S.*		126,471 D	33.4%	66.6%	33.4%	66.6%
1960	416,699	256,890	Smith, Margaret Chase*	159,809	Cormier, Lucia M.		97,081 R	61.6%	38.4%	61.6%	38.4%
1958	284,364	111,522	Payne, Frederick G.*	172,842	Muskie, Edmund S.		61,320 D	39.2%	60.8%	39.2%	60.8%
1954	246,605	144,530	Smith, Margaret Chase*	102,075	Fullam, Paul A.		42,455 R	58.6%	41.4%	58.6%	41.4%
1952	237,164	139,205	Payne, Frederick G.	82,665	Dube, Roger P.	15,294	56,540 R	58.7%	34.9%	62.7%	37.3%
1948	223,256	159,182	Smith, Margaret Chase	64,074	Scolten, Adrian H.		95,108 R	71.3%	28.7%	71.3%	28.7%
1946	175,014	111,215	Brewster, Ralph O.*	63,799	MacDonald, Peter M.		47,416 R	63.5%	36.5%	63.5%	36.5%

Note: An asterisk (*) denotes incumbent. A pound sign (#) indicates that an independant candidate was elected. **In past elections, the other vote included: 2012 - 370,580 Independent (Angus King), who received 52.9 percent of the total vote and was elected.

MAINE

GOVERNOR 2014

2010 Census Population	County	Total Vote	Republican (LePage)	Democratic (Michaud)	Other	Rep.-Dem. Plurality	Percentage			
							Total Vote		Major Vote	
							Rep.	Dem.	Rep.	Dem.
107,702	ANDROSCOGGIN	45,920	25,987	16,376	3,557	9,611 R	56.6%	35.7%	61.3%	38.7%
71,870	AROOSTOOK	28,856	13,725	12,398	2,733	1,327 R	47.6%	43.0%	52.5%	47.5%
281,674	CUMBERLAND	141,007	55,932	72,217	12,858	16,285 D	39.7%	51.2%	43.6%	56.4%
30,768	FRANKLIN	14,265	7,591	5,426	1,248	2,165 R	53.2%	38.0%	58.3%	41.7%
54,418	HANCOCK	26,294	12,016	12,007	2,271	9 R	45.7%	45.7%	50.0%	50.0%
122,151	KENNEBEC	56,714	28,336	24,129	4,249	4,207 R	50.0%	42.5%	54.0%	46.0%
39,736	KNOX	18,891	8,425	8,911	1,555	486 D	44.6%	47.2%	48.6%	51.4%
34,457	LINCOLN	18,141	9,157	7,633	1,351	1,524 R	50.5%	42.1%	54.5%	45.5%
57,833	OXFORD	26,400	14,902	9,269	2,229	5,633 R	56.4%	35.1%	61.7%	38.3%
153,923	PENOBSCOT	64,112	33,190	26,210	4,712	6,980 R	51.8%	40.9%	55.9%	44.1%
17,535	PISCATAQUIS	8,179	4,736	2,810	633	1,926 R	57.9%	34.4%	62.8%	37.2%
35,293	SAGADAHOC	18,577	8,760	8,264	1,553	496 R	47.2%	44.5%	51.5%	48.5%
52,228	SOMERSET	22,203	12,194	8,422	1,587	3,772 R	54.9%	37.9%	59.1%	40.9%
38,786	WALDO	18,475	8,862	8,167	1,446	695 R	48.0%	44.2%	52.0%	48.0%
32,856	WASHINGTON	14,002	7,390	5,452	1,160	1,938 R	52.8%	38.9%	57.5%	42.5%
197,131	YORK	88,335	43,055	36,905	8,375	6,150 R	48.7%	41.8%	53.8%	46.2%
	Votes Not Reported by County	856	261	518	77	257 D	30.5%	60.5%	33.5%	66.5%
1,328,361	TOTAL	611,227	294,519	265,114	51,594	29,405 R	48.2%	43.4%	52.6%	47.4%

2010 Census Population	City/Town	Total Vote	Republican (LePage)	Democratic (Michaud)	Other	Rep.-Dem. Plurality	Percentage			
							Total Vote		Major Vote	
							Rep.	Dem.	Rep.	Dem.
23,055	AUBURN	9,583	4,944	3,823	816	1,121 R	51.6%	39.9%	56.4%	43.6%
19,136	AUGUSTA	7,745	3,364	3,738	643	374 D	43.4%	48.3%	47.4%	52.6%
33,039	BANGOR	11,871	4,813	6,022	1,036	1,209 D	40.5%	50.7%	44.4%	55.6%
8,514	BATH	3,812	1,396	2,083	333	687 D	36.6%	54.6%	40.1%	59.9%
6,668	BELFAST	3,149	1,086	1,808	255	722 D	34.5%	57.4%	37.5%	62.5%
7,246	BERWICK	2,551	1,446	887	218	559 R	56.7%	34.8%	62.0%	38.0%
21,277	BIDDEFORD	7,728	3,375	3,598	755	223 D	43.7%	46.6%	48.4%	51.6%
9,482	BREWER	4,148	2,177	1,672	299	505 R	52.5%	40.3%	56.6%	43.4%
20,278	BRUNSWICK	10,090	3,439	5,896	755	2,457 D	34.1%	58.4%	36.8%	63.2%
8,034	BUXTON	3,960	2,277	1,382	301	895 R	57.5%	34.9%	62.2%	37.8%
4,850	CAMDEN	2,843	831	1,758	254	927 D	29.2%	61.8%	32.1%	67.9%
9,015	CAPE ELIZABETH	5,559	1,793	2,986	780	1,193 D	32.3%	53.7%	37.5%	62.5%
8,189	CARIBOU	3,190	1,532	1,326	332	206 R	48.0%	41.6%	53.6%	46.4%
7,211	CUMBERLAND TOWN	4,561	1,980	2,051	530	71 D	43.4%	45.0%	49.1%	50.9%
6,204	ELIOT	3,022	1,340	1,322	360	18 R	44.3%	43.7%	50.3%	49.7%
7,741	ELLSWORTH	3,472	1,764	1,401	307	363 R	50.8%	40.4%	55.7%	44.3%
6,735	FAIRFIELD	2,779	1,432	1,147	200	285 R	51.5%	41.3%	55.5%	44.5%
11,185	FALMOUTH	6,650	2,880	3,022	748	142 D	43.3%	45.4%	48.8%	51.2%
7,760	FARMINGTON	3,148	1,421	1,449	278	28 D	45.1%	46.0%	49.5%	50.5%
7,879	FREEPORT	4,681	1,720	2,482	479	762 D	36.7%	53.0%	40.9%	59.1%
5,800	GARDINER	2,699	1,201	1,228	270	27 D	44.5%	45.5%	49.4%	50.6%
16,381	GORHAM	7,550	3,716	3,212	622	504 R	49.2%	42.5%	53.6%	46.4%
7,761	GRAY	3,986	2,211	1,415	360	796 R	55.5%	35.5%	61.0%	39.0%
7,257	HAMPDEN	3,359	1,772	1,335	252	437 R	52.8%	39.7%	57.0%	43.0%
4,740	HARPSWELL	3,048	1,338	1,473	237	135 D	43.9%	48.3%	47.6%	52.4%
6,123	HOULTON	2,063	1,011	861	191	150 R	49.0%	41.7%	54.0%	46.0%
4,851	JAY	2,243	1,110	944	189	166 R	49.5%	42.1%	54.0%	46.0%
10,798	KENNEBUNK	5,975	2,540	2,790	645	250 D	42.5%	46.7%	47.7%	52.3%
9,490	KITTERY	3,945	1,353	2,090	502	737 D	34.3%	53.0%	39.3%	60.7%
36,592	LEWISTON	13,504	6,846	5,541	1,117	1,305 R	50.7%	41.0%	55.3%	44.7%

MAINE

GOVERNOR 2014

2010 Census Population	City/Town	Total Vote	Republican (LePage)	Democratic (Michaud)	Other	Rep.-Dem. Plurality	Percentage			
							Total Vote		Major Vote	
							Rep.	Dem.	Rep.	Dem.
2,314	LIMESTONE	654	287	309	58	22 D	43.9%	47.2%	48.2%	51.8%
5,085	LINCOLN TOWN	2,047	1,211	677	159	534 R	59.2%	33.1%	64.1%	35.9%
9,009	LISBON	4,111	2,480	1,322	309	1,158 R	60.3%	32.2%	65.2%	34.8%
4,506	MILLINOCKET	2,061	852	1,052	157	200 D	41.3%	51.0%	44.7%	55.3%
6,240	OAKLAND	2,836	1,458	1,143	235	315 R	51.4%	40.3%	56.1%	43.9%
8,624	OLD ORCHARD BEACH	4,296	1,773	2,114	409	341 D	41.3%	49.2%	45.6%	54.4%
7,840	OLD TOWN	3,142	1,274	1,616	252	342 D	40.5%	51.4%	44.1%	55.9%
10,362	ORONO	3,496	1,008	2,165	323	1,157 D	28.8%	61.9%	31.8%	68.2%
66,194	PORTLAND	29,960	6,724	20,833	2,403	14,109 D	22.4%	69.5%	24.4%	75.6%
9,692	PRESQUE ISLE	3,429	1,579	1,464	386	115 R	46.0%	42.7%	51.9%	48.1%
7,297	ROCKLAND	2,676	1,019	1,427	230	408 D	38.1%	53.3%	41.7%	58.3%
5,841	RUMFORD	2,337	1,226	928	183	298 R	52.5%	39.7%	56.9%	43.1%
18,482	SACO	8,289	3,716	3,822	751	106 D	44.8%	46.1%	49.3%	50.7%
20,798	SANFORD	7,409	3,660	3,020	729	640 R	49.4%	40.8%	54.8%	45.2%
18,919	SCARBOROUGH	10,408	4,977	4,398	1,033	579 R	47.8%	42.3%	53.1%	46.9%
8,589	SKOWHEGAN	3,463	1,649	1,596	218	53 R	47.6%	46.1%	50.8%	49.2%
7,220	SOUTH BERWICK	2,963	1,280	1,408	275	128 D	43.2%	47.5%	47.6%	52.4%
25,002	SOUTH PORTLAND	12,375	3,916	7,239	1,220	3,323 D	31.6%	58.5%	35.1%	64.9%
9,874	STANDISH	4,389	2,567	1,505	317	1,062 R	58.5%	34.3%	63.0%	37.0%
8,784	TOPSHAM	5,007	2,275	2,281	451	6 D	45.4%	45.6%	49.9%	50.1%
15,722	WATERVILLE	5,644	2,179	3,068	397	889 D	38.6%	54.4%	41.5%	58.5%
9,589	WELLS	4,970	2,481	2,050	439	431 R	49.9%	41.2%	54.8%	45.2%
17,494	WESTBROOK	7,656	3,174	3,823	659	649 D	41.5%	49.9%	45.4%	54.6%
17,001	WINDHAM	7,753	4,178	2,898	677	1,280 R	53.9%	37.4%	59.0%	41.0%
7,794	WINSLOW	3,729	1,970	1,479	280	491 R	52.8%	39.7%	57.1%	42.9%
6,092	WINTHROP	3,120	1,483	1,376	261	107 R	47.5%	44.1%	51.9%	48.1%
8,349	YARMOUTH	4,695	1,672	2,478	545	806 D	35.6%	52.8%	40.3%	59.7%
12,529	YORK TOWN	6,879	2,939	3,166	774	227 D	42.7%	46.0%	48.1%	51.9%

MAINE

SENATOR 2014

2010 Census Population	County	Total Vote	Republican (Collins)	Democratic (Bellows)	Other	Rep.-Dem. Plurality	Percentage			
							Total Vote		Major Vote	
							Rep.	Dem.	Rep.	Dem.
107,702	ANDROSCOGGIN	45,344	32,649	12,680	15	19,969 R	72.0%	28.0%	72.0%	28.0%
71,870	AROOSTOOK	28,419	22,182	6,217	20	15,965 R	78.1%	21.9%	78.1%	21.9%
281,674	CUMBERLAND	139,566	86,495	53,036	35	33,459 R	62.0%	38.0%	62.0%	38.0%
30,768	FRANKLIN	14,077	9,847	4,215	15	5,632 R	70.0%	29.9%	70.0%	30.0%
54,418	HANCOCK	26,037	16,411	9,618	8	6,793 R	63.0%	36.9%	63.0%	37.0%
122,151	KENNEBEC	56,040	38,748	17,279	13	21,469 R	69.1%	30.8%	69.2%	30.8%
39,736	KNOX	18,665	11,622	7,006	37	4,616 R	62.3%	37.5%	62.4%	37.6%
34,457	LINCOLN	17,983	12,321	5,646	16	6,675 R	68.5%	31.4%	68.6%	31.4%
57,833	OXFORD	26,068	18,545	7,511	12	11,034 R	71.1%	28.8%	71.2%	28.8%
153,923	PENOBSCOT	63,253	46,611	16,614	28	29,997 R	73.7%	26.3%	73.7%	26.3%
17,535	PISCATAQUIS	8,042	6,174	1,862	6	4,312 R	76.8%	23.2%	76.8%	23.2%
35,293	SAGADAHOC	18,394	12,715	5,666	13	7,049 R	69.1%	30.8%	69.2%	30.8%
52,228	SOMERSET	21,899	15,820	6,068	11	9,752 R	72.2%	27.7%	72.3%	27.7%
38,786	WALDO	18,202	11,816	6,379	7	5,437 R	64.9%	35.0%	64.9%	35.1%
32,856	WASHINGTON	13,786	9,801	3,978	7	5,823 R	71.1%	28.9%	71.1%	28.9%
197,131	YORK	87,382	61,313	26,045	24	35,268 R	70.2%	29.8%	70.2%	29.8%
	Votes Not Reported by County	851	425	424	2	1 R	49.9%	49.8%	50.1%	49.9%
1,328,361	TOTAL	604,008	413,495	190,244	269	223,251 R	68.5%	31.5%	68.5%	31.5%

MAINE

SENATOR 2014

2010 Census Population	City/Town	Total Vote	Republican (Collins)	Democratic (Bellows)	Other	Rep.-Dem. Plurality	Percentage			
							Total Vote		Major Vote	
							Rep.	Dem.	Rep.	Dem.
23,055	AUBURN	9,494	6,596	2,895	3	3,701 R	69.5%	30.5%	69.5%	30.5%
19,136	AUGUSTA	7,656	5,062	2,594		2,468 R	66.1%	33.9%	66.1%	33.9%
33,039	BANGOR	11,716	7,758	3,951	7	3,807 R	66.2%	33.7%	66.3%	33.7%
8,514	BATH	3,784	2,374	1,410		964 R	62.7%	37.3%	62.7%	37.3%
6,668	BELFAST	3,107	1,671	1,436		235 R	53.8%	46.2%	53.8%	46.2%
7,246	BERWICK	2,520	1,944	576		1,368 R	77.1%	22.9%	77.1%	22.9%
21,277	BIDDEFORD	7,672	5,144	2,526	2	2,618 R	67.0%	32.9%	67.1%	32.9%
9,482	BREWER	4,130	3,116	1,014		2,102 R	75.4%	24.6%	75.4%	24.6%
20,278	BRUNSWICK	10,017	5,710	4,303	4	1,407 R	57.0%	43.0%	57.0%	43.0%
8,034	BUXTON	3,914	2,927	985	2	1,942 R	74.8%	25.2%	74.8%	25.2%
4,850	CAMDEN	2,806	1,425	1,381		44 R	50.8%	49.2%	50.8%	49.2%
9,015	CAPE ELIZABETH	5,501	3,307	2,194		1,113 R	60.1%	39.9%	60.1%	39.9%
8,189	CARIBOU	3,145	2,515	630		1,885 R	80.0%	20.0%	80.0%	20.0%
7,211	CUMBERLAND TOWN	4,526	3,201	1,325		1,876 R	70.7%	29.3%	70.7%	29.3%
6,204	ELIOT	2,986	2,044	941	1	1,103 R	68.5%	31.5%	68.5%	31.5%
7,741	ELLSWORTH	3,437	2,344	1,093		1,251 R	68.2%	31.8%	68.2%	31.8%
6,735	FAIRFIELD	2,752	1,894	858		1,036 R	68.8%	31.2%	68.8%	31.2%
11,185	FALMOUTH	6,608	4,462	2,146		2,316 R	67.5%	32.5%	67.5%	32.5%
7,760	FARMINGTON	3,112	2,091	1,009	12	1,082 R	67.2%	32.4%	67.5%	32.5%
7,879	FREEPORT	4,629	2,797	1,831	1	966 R	60.4%	39.6%	60.4%	39.6%
5,800	GARDINER	2,680	1,809	870	1	939 R	67.5%	32.5%	67.5%	32.5%
16,381	GORHAM	7,482	5,367	2,114	1	3,253 R	71.7%	28.3%	71.7%	28.3%
7,761	GRAY	3,925	2,960	961	4	1,999 R	75.4%	24.5%	75.5%	24.5%
7,257	HAMPDEN	3,326	2,483	843		1,640 R	74.7%	25.3%	74.7%	25.3%
4,740	HARPSWELL	3,019	1,957	1,062		895 R	64.8%	35.2%	64.8%	35.2%
6,123	HOULTON	2,040	1,656	377	7	1,279 R	81.2%	18.5%	81.5%	18.5%
4,851	JAY	2,224	1,438	786		652 R	64.7%	35.3%	64.7%	35.3%
10,798	KENNEBUNK	5,919	3,979	1,940		2,039 R	67.2%	32.8%	67.2%	32.8%
9,490	KITTERY	3,907	2,335	1,572		763 R	59.8%	40.2%	59.8%	40.2%
36,592	LEWISTON	13,301	9,000	4,301		4,699 R	67.7%	32.3%	67.7%	32.3%
2,314	LIMESTONE	648	478	170		308 R	73.8%	26.2%	73.8%	26.2%
5,085	LINCOLN TOWN	2,014	1,626	387	1	1,239 R	80.7%	19.2%	80.8%	19.2%
9,009	LISBON	4,051	3,094	954	3	2,140 R	76.4%	23.5%	76.4%	23.6%
4,506	MILLINOCKET	2,028	1,448	577	3	871 R	71.4%	28.5%	71.5%	28.5%
6,240	OAKLAND	2,807	2,010	797		1,213 R	71.6%	28.4%	71.6%	28.4%
8,624	OLD ORCHARD BEACH	4,255	2,743	1,502	10	1,241 R	64.5%	35.3%	64.6%	35.4%
7,840	OLD TOWN	3,099	2,127	970	2	1,157 R	68.6%	31.3%	68.7%	31.3%
10,362	ORONO	3,446	2,077	1,368	1	709 R	60.3%	39.7%	60.3%	39.7%
66,194	PORTLAND	29,584	13,273	16,305	6	3,032 D	44.9%	55.1%	44.9%	55.1%
9,692	PRESQUE ISLE	3,389	2,604	784	1	1,820 R	76.8%	23.1%	76.9%	23.1%
7,297	ROCKLAND	2,638	1,486	1,152		334 R	56.3%	43.7%	56.3%	43.7%
5,841	RUMFORD	2,324	1,562	762		800 R	67.2%	32.8%	67.2%	32.8%
18,482	SACO	8,181	5,574	2,606	1	2,968 R	68.1%	31.9%	68.1%	31.9%
20,798	SANFORD	7,313	5,147	2,165	1	2,982 R	70.4%	29.6%	70.4%	29.6%
18,919	SCARBOROUGH	10,319	7,365	2,950	4	4,415 R	71.4%	28.6%	71.4%	28.6%
8,589	SKOWHEGAN	3,409	2,365	1,044		1,321 R	69.4%	30.6%	69.4%	30.6%
7,220	SOUTH BERWICK	2,933	1,955	978		977 R	66.7%	33.3%	66.7%	33.3%
25,002	SOUTH PORTLAND	12,241	6,835	5,404	2	1,431 R	55.8%	44.1%	55.8%	44.2%
9,874	STANDISH	4,338	3,242	1,094	2	2,148 R	74.7%	25.2%	74.8%	25.2%
8,784	TOPSHAM	4,954	3,454	1,499	1	1,955 R	69.7%	30.3%	69.7%	30.3%
15,722	WATERVILLE	5,564	3,283	2,281		1,002 R	59.0%	41.0%	59.0%	41.0%
9,589	WELLS	4,927	3,528	1,399		2,129 R	71.6%	28.4%	71.6%	28.4%
17,494	WESTBROOK	7,584	4,922	2,657	5	2,265 R	64.9%	35.0%	64.9%	35.1%
17,001	WINDHAM	7,679	5,598	2,080	1	3,518 R	72.9%	27.1%	72.9%	27.1%
7,794	WINSLOW	3,679	2,636	1,043		1,593 R	71.6%	28.4%	71.6%	28.4%
6,092	WINTHROP	3,097	2,121	976		1,145 R	68.5%	31.5%	68.5%	31.5%
8,349	YARMOUTH	4,661	2,993	1,668		1,325 R	64.2%	35.8%	64.2%	35.8%
12,529	YORK TOWN	6,823	4,627	2,195	1	2,432 R	67.8%	32.2%	67.8%	32.2%

MAINE

HOUSE OF REPRESENTATIVES

CD	Year	Total Vote	Republican Vote	Candidate	Democratic Vote	Candidate	Other Vote	Rep.-Dem. Plurality	Total Vote Rep.	Total Vote Dem.	Major Vote Rep.	Major Vote Dem.
1	2014	308,898	94,751	MISIUK, ISAAC J.	186,674	PINGREE, CHELLIE*	27,473	91,923 D	30.7%	60.4%	33.7%	66.3%
1	2012	364,803	128,440	COURTNEY, JONATHAN T. E.	236,363	PINGREE, CHELLIE*		107,923 D	35.2%	64.8%	35.2%	64.8%
2	2014	283,448	133,308	POLIQUIN, BRUCE	118,556	CAIN, EMILY ANN	31,584	14,752 R	47.0%	41.8%	52.9%	47.1%
2	2012	328,998	137,542	RAYE, KEVIN L.	191,456	MICHAUD, MICHAEL H.*		53,914 D	41.8%	58.2%	41.8%	58.2%
TOTAL	2014	592,346	228,059		305,230		59,057	77,171 D	38.5%	51.5%	42.8%	57.2%
TOTAL	2012	693,801	265,982		427,819			161,837 D	38.3%	61.7%	38.3%	61.7%

Note: An asterisk (*) denotes incumbent.

MAINE

GENERAL AND PRIMARY ELECTIONS

2014 GENERAL ELECTIONS: OTHER VOTES

Governor Other vote was 51,515 Independent (Eliot R. Cutler), 79 scattered write-in

Senate Other vote was 269 scattered write-in

House Other vote was:

CD 1 27,410 Independent (Richard Paul Murphy), 63 scattered write-in
CD 2 31,336 Independent (Blaine Richardson), 248 scattered write-in

2014 PRIMARY ELECTIONS: SUPPLEMENTARY INFORMATION

Primary June 10, 2014 **Registration** (as of June 10, 2014 – includes 26,726 inactive registrants) 985,166

Democratic 314,617
Republican 266,865
Green Independent 39,004
Unenrolled 364,680

Primary Type Semi-open—Registered voters in a political party could participate only in their party's primary. "Unenrolled" and new voters could vote in either party's primary by enrolling in that party on primary day.

	REPUBLICAN PRIMARIES			DEMOCRATIC PRIMARIES		
Senator	Collins, Susan M.*	53,416	98.9%	Bellows, Shenna	47,909	100.0%
	Write-In	615	1.1%			
	TOTAL	54,031		TOTAL	47,909	
Governor	LePage, Paul R.*	50,856	100.0%	Michaud, Michael H.	56,286	100.0%
	TOTAL	50,856		TOTAL	56,286	
Congressional District 1	Misiuk, Isaac J.	17,061	100.0%	Pingree, Chellie*	30,950	100.0%
	TOTAL	17,061		TOTAL	30,950	
Congressional District 2	Poliquin, Bruce	19,736	56.8%	Cain, Emily Ann	19,906	71.0%
	Raye, Kevin L.	14,987	43.2%	Jackson, Troy	8,116	29.0%
	TOTAL	34,723		TOTAL	28,022	

Note: An asterisk (*) denotes incumbent.

MARYLAND

Congressional districts first established for elections held in 2012
8 members

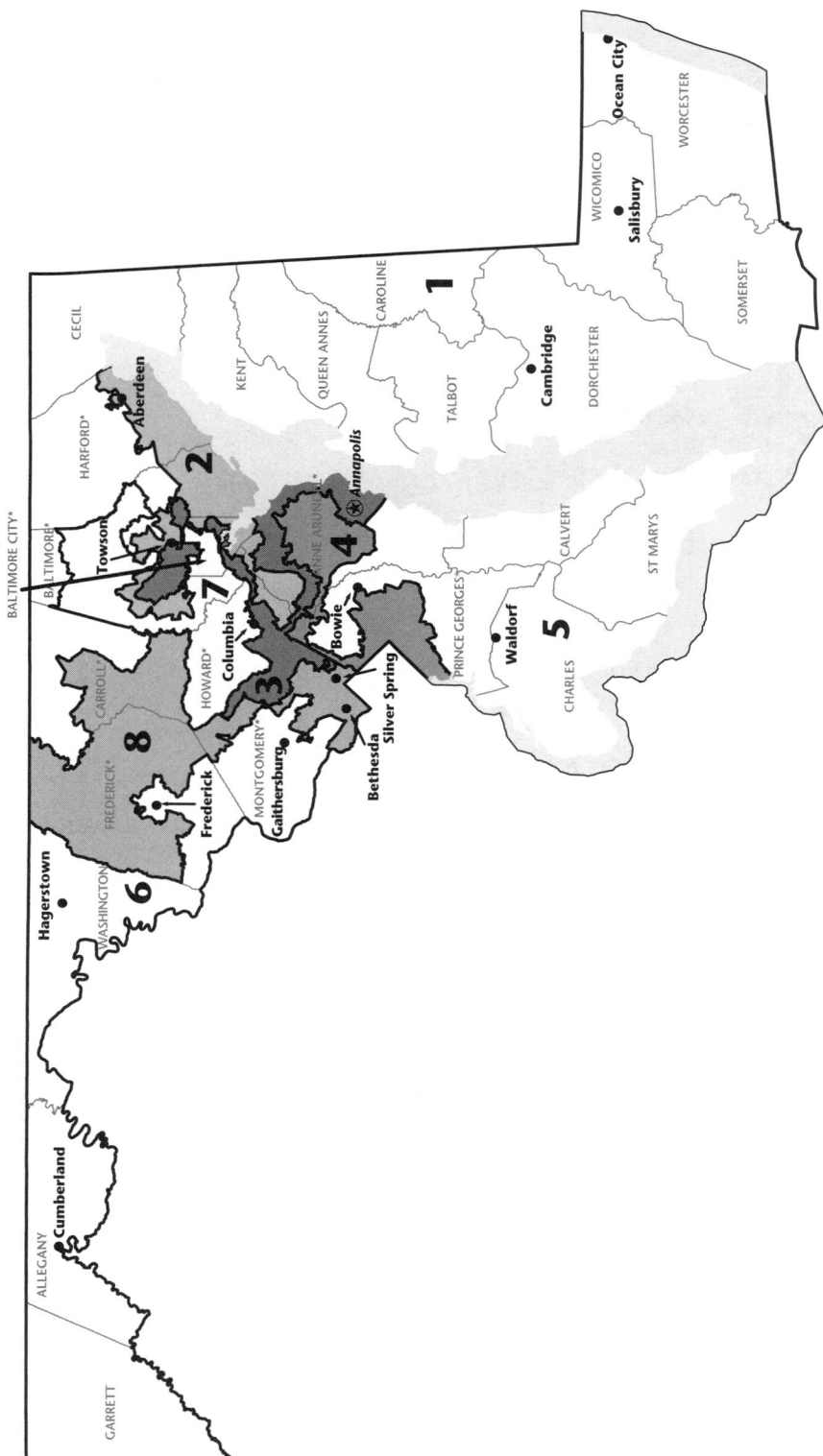

The city of Baltimore City is an independent city that is treated as a county equivalent.

* Asterisk indicates a county whose boundaries include parts of two or more congressional districts.

MARYLAND
Baltimore, Washington, D.C., Areas

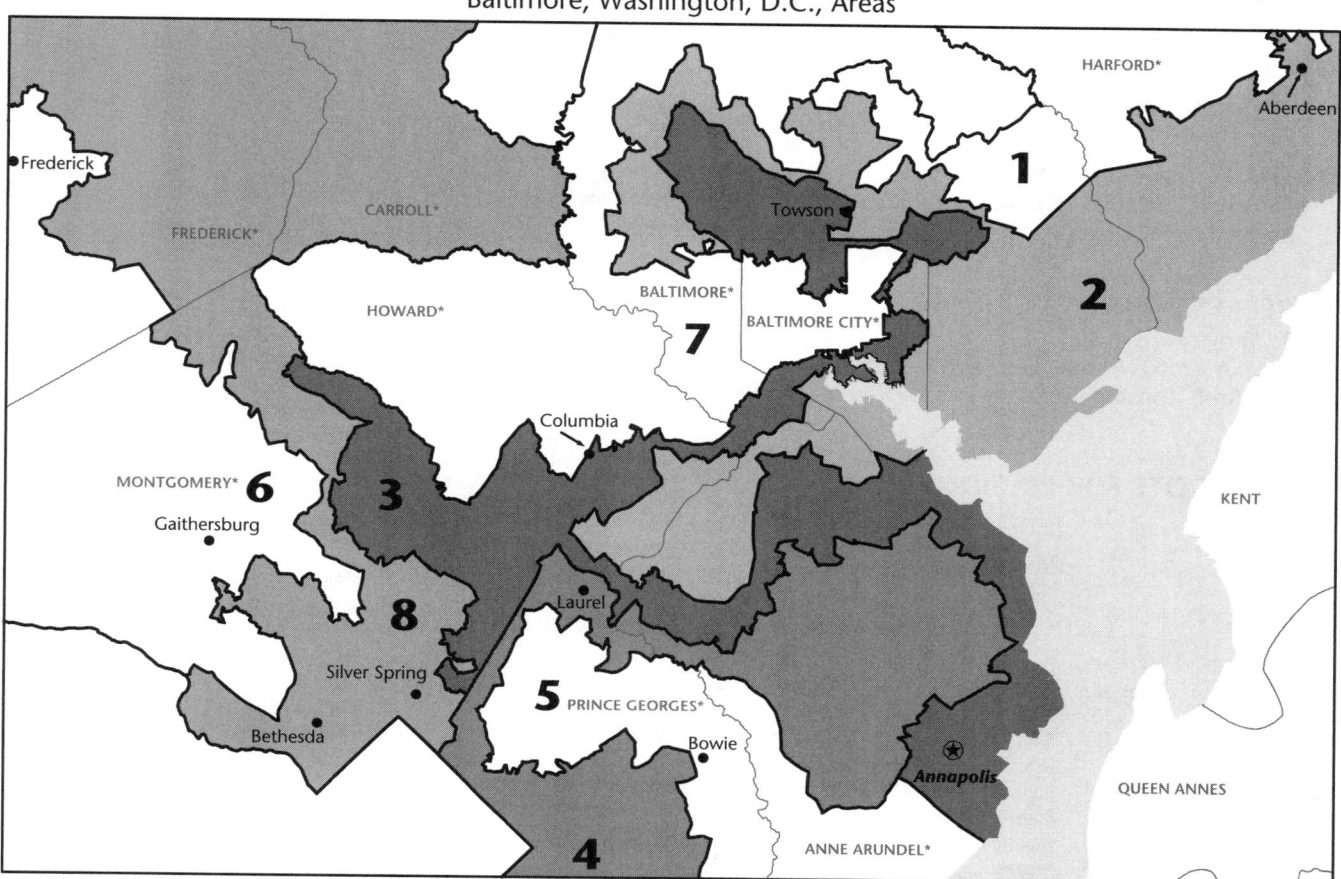

* Asterisk indicates a county whose boundaries include parts of two or more congressional districts.

MARYLAND

GOVERNOR
Larry Hogan (R). Elected 2014 to a four-year term.

SENATORS (2 Democrats)
Benjamin L. Cardin (D). Re-elected 2012 to a six-year term. Previously elected 2006.
Barbara A. Mikulski (D). Re-elected 2010 to a six-year term. Previously elected 2004, 1998, 1992, 1986.

REPRESENTATIVES (1 Republican, 7 Democrats)
1. Andy Harris (R)
2. C. A. Dutch Ruppersberger (D)
3. John P. Sarbanes (D)
4. Donna F. Edwards (D)
5. Steny H. Hoyer (D)
6. John K. Delaney (D)
7. Elijah E. Cummings (D)
8. Chris Van Hollen (D)

POSTWAR VOTE FOR PRESIDENT

| Year | Total Vote | Republican | | Democratic | | Other Vote | Rep.-Dem. Plurality | Total Vote | | Major Vote | |
		Vote	Candidate	Vote	Candidate			Rep.	Dem.	Rep.	Dem.
2012	2,707,327	971,869	Romney, W. Mitt	1,677,844	Obama, Barack H.*	57,614	705,975 D	35.9%	62.0%	36.7%	63.3%
2008	2,631,596	959,862	McCain, John S. III	1,629,467	Obama, Barack H.	42,267	669,605 D	36.5%	61.9%	37.1%	62.9%
2004	2,386,678	1,024,703	Bush, George W.*	1,334,493	Kerry, John F.	27,482	309,790 D	42.9%	55.9%	43.4%	56.6%
2000**	2,020,480	813,797	Bush, George W.	1,140,782	Gore, Albert Jr.	65,901	326,985 D	40.3%	56.5%	41.6%	58.4%
1996**	1,780,870	681,530	Dole, Robert "Bob"	966,207	Clinton, Bill*	133,133	284,677 D	38.3%	54.3%	41.4%	58.6%
1992**	1,985,046	707,094	Bush, George H.*	988,571	Clinton, Bill	289,381	281,477 D	35.6%	49.8%	41.7%	58.3%
1988	1,714,358	876,167	Bush, George H.	826,304	Dukakis, Michael S.	11,887	49,863 R	51.1%	48.2%	51.5%	48.5%
1984	1,675,873	879,918	Reagan, Ronald*	787,935	Mondale, Walter F.	8,020	91,983 R	52.5%	47.0%	52.8%	47.2%
1980**	1,540,496	680,606	Reagan, Ronald	726,161	Carter, Jimmy*	133,729	45,555 D	44.2%	47.1%	48.4%	51.6%
1976	1,439,897	672,661	Ford, Gerald R.*	759,612	Carter, Jimmy	7,624	86,951 D	46.7%	52.8%	47.0%	53.0%
1972	1,353,812	829,305	Nixon, Richard M.*	505,781	McGovern, George S.	18,726	323,524 R	61.3%	37.4%	62.1%	37.9%
1968**	1,235,039	517,995	Nixon, Richard M.	538,310	Humphrey, Hubert Horatio Jr.	178,734	20,315 D	41.9%	43.6%	49.0%	51.0%
1964	1,116,457	385,495	Goldwater, Barry M. Sr.	730,912	Johnson, Lyndon B.*	50	345,417 D	34.5%	65.5%	34.5%	65.5%
1960	1,055,349	489,538	Nixon, Richard M.	565,808	Kennedy, John F.	3	76,270 D	46.4%	53.6%	46.4%	53.6%
1956	932,827	559,738	Eisenhower, Dwight D.*	372,613	Stevenson, Adlai E. II	476	187,125 R	60.0%	39.9%	60.0%	40.0%
1952	902,074	499,424	Eisenhower, Dwight D.	395,337	Stevenson, Adlai E. II	7,313	104,087 R	55.4%	43.8%	55.8%	44.2%
1948	596,748	294,814	Dewey, Thomas E.	286,521	Truman, Harry S.*	15,413	8,293 R	49.4%	48.0%	50.7%	49.3%

Note: An asterisk (*) denotes incumbent. **In past elections, the other vote included: 2000 - 53,768 Green (Ralph Nader); 1996 - 115,812 Reform (Ross Perot); 1992 - 281,414 Independent (Perot); 1980 - 119,537 Independent (John Anderson); 1968 - 178,734 American Independent (George Wallace).

MARYLAND

POSTWAR VOTE FOR GOVERNOR

Year	Total Vote	Republican		Democratic		Other Vote	Rep.-Dem. Plurality	Percentage			
								Total Vote		Major Vote	
		Vote	Candidate	Vote	Candidate			Rep.	Dem.	Rep.	Dem.
2014	1,733,177	884,400	Hogan, Larry	818,890	Brown, Anthony G.	29,887	65,510 R	51.0%	47.2%	51.9%	48.1%
2010	1,857,880	776,319	Ehrlich, Robert L. "Bob" Jr.	1,044,961	O'Malley, Martin*	36,600	268,642 D	41.8%	56.2%	42.6%	57.4%
2006	1,788,316	825,464	Ehrlich, Robert L. "Bob" Jr.*	942,279	O'Malley, Martin	20,573	116,815 D	46.2%	52.7%	46.7%	53.3%
2002	1,706,179	879,592	Ehrlich, Robert L. "Bob" Jr.	813,422	Townsend, Kathleen Kennedy	13,165	66,170 R	51.6%	47.7%	52.0%	48.0%
1998	1,535,978	688,357	Sauerbrey, Ellen R.	846,972	Glendening, Parris N.*	649	158,615 D	44.8%	55.1%	44.8%	55.2%
1994	1,410,300	702,101	Sauerbrey, Ellen R.	708,094	Glendening, Parris N.	105	5,993 D	49.8%	50.2%	49.8%	50.2%
1990	1,111,088	446,980	Shepard, William S.	664,015	Schaefer, William D.*	93	217,035 D	40.2%	59.8%	40.2%	59.8%
1986	1,101,476	194,185	Mooney, Thomas J.	907,291	Schaefer, William D.		713,106 D	17.6%	82.4%	17.6%	82.4%
1982	1,139,149	432,826	Pascal, Robert A.	705,910	Hughes, Harry R.*	413	273,084 D	38.0%	62.0%	38.0%	62.0%
1978	1,011,963	293,635	Beall, John Glenn Jr.	718,328	Hughes, Harry R.		424,693 D	29.0%	71.0%	29.0%	71.0%
1974	949,097	346,449	Gore, Louise	602,648	Mandel, Marvin*		256,199 D	36.5%	63.5%	36.5%	63.5%
1970	973,099	314,336	Blair, C. Stanley	639,579	Mandel, Marvin*	19,184	325,243 D	32.3%	65.7%	33.0%	67.0%
1966	919,760	455,318	Agnew, Spiro T.	373,543	Mahoney, George P.	90,899	81,775 R	49.5%	40.6%	54.9%	45.1%
1962	769,347	341,271	Small, Frank Jr.	428,071	Tawes, J. Millard*	5	86,800 D	44.4%	55.6%	44.4%	55.6%
1958	763,234	278,173	Devereux, James Patrick	485,061	Tawes, J. Millard		206,888 D	36.4%	63.6%	36.4%	63.6%
1954	700,484	381,451	McKeldin, Theodore R.*	319,033	Byrd, Harry Clifton		62,418 R	54.5%	45.5%	54.5%	45.5%
1950	645,631	369,807	McKeldin, Theodore R.	275,824	Lane, William Preston		93,983 R	57.3%	42.7%	57.3%	42.7%
1946	489,836	221,752	McKeldin, Theodore R.	268,084	Lane, William Preston		46,332 D	45.3%	54.7%	45.3%	54.7%

Note: An asterisk (*) denotes incumbent.

POSTWAR VOTE FOR SENATOR

Year	Total Vote	Republican		Democratic		Other Vote	Rep.-Dem. Plurality	Percentage			
								Total Vote		Major Vote	
		Vote	Candidate	Vote	Candidate			Rep.	Dem.	Rep.	Dem.
2012**	2,633,234	693,291	Bongino, Daniel John	1,474,028	Cardin, Benjamin L.*	465,915	780,737 D	26.3%	56.0%	32.0%	68.0%
2010	1,833,858	655,666	Wartotz, Eric	1,140,531	Mikulski, Barbara A.*	37,661	484,865 D	35.8%	62.2%	36.5%	63.5%
2006	1,781,139	787,182	Steele, Michael	965,477	Cardin, Benjamin L.	28,480	178,295 D	44.2%	54.2%	44.9%	55.1%
2004	2,323,183	783,055	Pipkin, Edward J.	1,504,691	Mikulski, Barbara A.*	35,437	721,636 D	33.7%	64.8%	34.2%	65.8%
2000	1,946,898	715,178	Rappaport, Paul H.	1,230,013	Sarbanes, Paul S.*	1,707	514,835 D	36.7%	63.2%	36.8%	63.2%
1998	1,507,447	444,637	Pierpont, Ross Z.	1,062,810	Mikulski, Barbara A.*		618,173 D	29.5%	70.5%	29.5%	70.5%
1994	1,369,104	559,908	Brock, William E.	809,125	Sarbanes, Paul S.*	71	249,217 D	40.9%	59.1%	40.9%	59.1%
1992	1,841,735	533,688	Keyes, Alan	1,307,610	Mikulski, Barbara A.*	437	773,922 D	29.0%	71.0%	29.0%	71.0%
1988	1,617,065	617,537	Keyes, Alan	999,166	Sarbanes, Paul S.*	362	381,629 D	38.2%	61.8%	38.2%	61.8%
1986	1,112,637	437,411	Chavez, Linda	675,225	Mikulski, Barbara A.	1	237,814 D	39.3%	60.7%	39.3%	60.7%
1982	1,114,690	407,334	Hogan, Lawrence J.	707,356	Sarbanes, Paul S.*		300,022 D	36.5%	63.5%	36.5%	63.5%
1980	1,286,088	850,970	Mathias, Charles McCurdy Jr.*	435,118	Conroy, Edward T.		415,852 R	66.2%	33.8%	66.2%	33.8%
1976	1,365,568	530,439	Beall, John Glenn Jr.*	772,101	Sarbanes, Paul S.	63,028	241,662 D	38.8%	56.5%	40.7%	59.3%
1974	877,786	503,223	Mathias, Charles McCurdy Jr.*	374,563	Mikulski, Barbara A.		128,660 R	57.3%	42.7%	57.3%	42.7%
1970	956,370	484,960	Beall, John Glenn Jr.	460,422	Tydings, Joseph D.*	10,988	24,538 R	50.7%	48.1%	51.3%	48.7%
1968**	1,133,727	541,893	Mathias, Charles McCurdy Jr.	443,367	Brewster, Daniel B.*	148,467	98,526 R	47.8%	39.1%	55.0%	45.0%
1964	1,081,049	402,393	Beall, James Glenn*	678,649	Tydings, Joseph D.	7	276,256 D	37.2%	62.8%	37.2%	62.8%
1962	708,855	269,131	Miller, Edward T.	439,723	Brewster, Daniel B.	1	170,592 D	38.0%	62.0%	38.0%	62.0%
1958	749,291	382,021	Beall, James Glenn*	367,270	D'Alesandro, Thomas Jr.		14,751 R	51.0%	49.0%	51.0%	49.0%
1956	892,167	473,059	Butler, John Marshall*	419,108	Mahoney, George P.		53,951 R	53.0%	47.0%	53.0%	47.0%
1952	856,193	449,823	Beall, James Glenn	406,370	Mahoney, George P.		43,453 R	52.5%	47.5%	52.5%	47.5%
1950	615,614	326,291	Butler, John Marshall	283,180	Tydings, Millard E.*	6,143	43,111 R	53.0%	46.0%	53.5%	46.5%
1946	472,232	235,000	Markey, David John	237,232	O'Conor, Herbert R.		2,232 D	49.8%	50.2%	49.8%	50.2%

Note: An asterisk (*) denotes incumbent. **In past elections, the other vote included: 2012 - 430,934 Independent (S. Rob Sobhani); 1968 - 148,467 Independent (George P. Mahoney).

MARYLAND

GOVERNOR 2014

2010 Census Population	County	Total Vote	Republican (Hogan)	Democratic (Brown)	Other	Rep.-Dem. Plurality	Total Vote Rep.	Total Vote Dem.	Major Vote Rep.	Major Vote Dem.
75,087	ALLEGANY	20,478	15,410	4,629	439	10,781 R	75.3%	22.6%	76.9%	23.1%
537,656	ANNE ARUNDEL	180,338	119,195	58,001	3,142	61,194 R	66.1%	32.2%	67.3%	32.7%
805,029	BALTIMORE	264,143	155,936	102,734	5,473	53,202 R	59.0%	38.9%	60.3%	39.7%
620,961	BALTIMORE CITY	140,686	30,845	106,213	3,628	75,368 D	21.9%	75.5%	22.5%	77.5%
88,737	CALVERT	32,904	22,739	9,579	586	13,160 R	69.1%	29.1%	70.4%	29.6%
33,066	CAROLINE	9,208	7,144	1,931	133	5,213 R	77.6%	21.0%	78.7%	21.3%
167,134	CARROLL	64,419	52,951	10,349	1,119	42,602 R	82.2%	16.1%	83.7%	16.3%
101,108	CECIL	26,766	20,699	5,467	600	15,232 R	77.3%	20.4%	79.1%	20.9%
146,551	CHARLES	47,469	22,268	24,601	600	2,333 D	46.9%	51.8%	47.5%	52.5%
32,618	DORCHESTER	10,660	7,276	3,252	132	4,024 R	68.3%	30.5%	69.1%	30.9%
233,385	FREDERICK	80,072	50,715	27,682	1,675	23,033 R	63.3%	34.6%	64.7%	35.3%
30,097	GARRETT	9,182	7,319	1,634	229	5,685 R	79.7%	17.8%	81.7%	18.3%
244,826	HARFORD	91,460	69,986	19,814	1,660	50,172 R	76.5%	21.7%	77.9%	22.1%
287,085	HOWARD	105,453	54,353	49,227	1,873	5,126 R	51.5%	46.7%	52.5%	47.5%
20,197	KENT	7,756	5,009	2,603	144	2,406 R	64.6%	33.6%	65.8%	34.2%
971,777	MONTGOMERY	264,819	97,312	163,694	3,813	66,382 D	36.7%	61.8%	37.3%	62.7%
863,420	PRINCE GEORGES	219,572	32,619	184,950	2,003	152,331 D	14.9%	84.2%	15.0%	85.0%
47,798	QUEEN ANNES	19,426	15,436	3,757	233	11,679 R	79.5%	19.3%	80.4%	19.6%
26,470	SOMERSET	6,701	4,488	2,135	78	2,353 R	67.0%	31.9%	67.8%	32.2%
105,151	ST. MARYS	32,557	23,675	8,203	679	15,472 R	72.7%	25.2%	74.3%	25.7%
37,782	TALBOT	15,226	10,616	4,420	190	6,196 R	69.7%	29.0%	70.6%	29.4%
147,430	WASHINGTON	38,821	28,469	9,661	691	18,808 R	73.3%	24.9%	74.7%	25.3%
98,733	WICOMICO	25,924	16,669	8,833	422	7,836 R	64.3%	34.1%	65.4%	34.6%
51,454	WORCESTER	19,137	13,271	5,521	345	7,750 R	69.3%	28.8%	70.6%	29.4%
5,773,552	TOTAL	1,733,177	884,400	818,890	29,887	65,510 R	51.0%	47.2%	51.9%	48.1%

MARYLAND

HOUSE OF REPRESENTATIVES

CD	Year	Total Vote	Republican Vote	Republican Candidate	Democratic Vote	Democratic Candidate	Other Vote	Rep.-Dem. Plurality	Total Vote Rep.	Total Vote Dem.	Major Vote Rep.	Major Vote Dem.
1	2014	250,418	176,342	HARRIS, ANDY*	73,843	TILGHMAN, BILL	233	102,499 R	70.4%	29.5%	70.5%	29.5%
1	2012	337,760	214,204	HARRIS, ANDY*	92,812	ROSEN, WENDY	30,744	121,392 R	63.4%	27.5%	69.8%	30.2%
2	2014	196,354	70,411	BANACH, DAVID	120,412	RUPPERSBERGER, C. A. DUTCH*	5,531	50,001 D	35.9%	61.3%	36.9%	63.1%
2	2012	295,940	92,071	JACOBS, NANCY C.	194,088	RUPPERSBERGER, C. A. DUTCH*	9,781	102,017 D	31.1%	65.6%	32.2%	67.8%
3	2014	215,946	87,029	LONG, CHARLES A.	128,594	SARBANES, JOHN P.*	323	41,565 D	40.3%	59.5%	40.4%	59.6%
3	2012	319,859	94,549	KNOWLES, ERIC DELANO	213,747	SARBANES, JOHN P.*	11,563	119,198 D	29.6%	66.8%	30.7%	69.3%
4	2014	191,837	54,217	HOYT, NANCY	134,628	EDWARDS, DONNA F.*	2,992	80,411 D	28.3%	70.2%	28.7%	71.3%
4	2012	311,512	64,560	LOUDON, FAITH M.	240,385	EDWARDS, DONNA F.*	6,567	175,825 D	20.7%	77.2%	21.2%	78.8%
5	2014	226,040	80,752	CHAFFEE, CHRIS	144,725	HOYER, STENY H.*	563	63,973 D	35.7%	64.0%	35.8%	64.2%
5	2012	343,820	95,271	O'DONNELL, TONY	238,618	HOYER, STENY H.*	9,931	143,347 D	27.7%	69.4%	28.5%	71.5%
6	2014	190,536	91,930	BONGINO, DANIEL JOHN	94,704	DELANEY, JOHN K.*	3,902	2,774 D	48.2%	49.7%	49.3%	50.7%
6	2012	309,549	117,313	BARTLETT, ROSCOE G.*	181,921	DELANEY, JOHN K.	10,315	64,608 D	37.9%	58.8%	39.2%	60.8%
7	2014	206,809	55,860	VAUGHN, CORROGAN R.	144,639	CUMMINGS, ELIJAH E.*	6,310	88,779 D	27.0%	69.9%	27.9%	72.1%
7	2012	323,818	67,405	MIRABILE, FRANK C.	247,770	CUMMINGS, ELIJAH E.*	8,643	180,365 D	20.8%	76.5%	21.4%	78.6%
8	2014	225,097	87,859	WALLACE, DAVE	136,722	VAN HOLLEN, CHRIS*	516	48,863 D	39.0%	60.7%	39.1%	60.9%
8	2012	343,256	113,033	TIMMERMAN, KENNETH R.	217,531	VAN HOLLEN, CHRIS*	12,692	104,498 D	32.9%	63.4%	34.2%	65.8%
TOTAL	2014	1,703,037	704,400		978,267		20,370	273,867 D	41.4%	57.4%	41.9%	58.1%
TOTAL	2012	2,585,514	858,406		1,626,872		100,236	768,466 D	33.2%	62.9%	34.5%	65.5%

Note: An asterisk (*) denotes incumbent.

MARYLAND

GENERAL AND PRIMARY ELECTIONS

2014 GENERAL ELECTIONS: OTHER VOTES

Governor   Other vote was 25,382 Libertarian (Shawn Quinn), 4,505 scattered write-in

House   Other vote was:

CD 1	233 scattered write-in
CD 2	5,326 Green (Ian Andrew Schlakman), 205 scattered write-in
CD 3	323 scattered write-in
CD 4	2,795 Libertarian (Arvin Vohra), 197 scattered write-in
CD 5	336 scattered write-in, 227 Write-in (Dennis L. Fritz)
CD 6	3,762 Green (George Gluck), 140 scattered write-in
CD 7	6,103 Libertarian (Scott Soffen), 207 scattered write-in
CD 8	398 scattered write-in, 102 Write-in (Andrew Wildman), 16 Write-in (Lih Young)

2014 PRIMARY ELECTIONS: SUPPLEMENTARY INFORMATION

Primary   June 24, 2014   **Registration** (as of June 7, 2014)   3,392,600

Democratic	2,051,319
Republican	950,195
Libertarian	7,113
Green	4,052
Other	16,062
Unaffiliated	363,859

Primary Type   Closed—Only registered Democrats and Republicans could vote in their party's primary.

	REPUBLICAN PRIMARIES			DEMOCRATIC PRIMARIES		
Governor	Hogan, Larry	92,376	43.0%	Brown, Anthony G.	249,398	51.4%
	Craig, David R.	62,639	29.1%	Gansler, Doug	117,383	24.2%
	Lollar, Charles	33,292	15.5%	Mizeur, Heather	104,721	21.6%
	George, Ron	26,628	12.4%	Walsh, Cindy A.	6,863	1.4%
				Smith, Charles U.	3,507	0.7%
				Jaffe, Ralph	3,221	0.7%
	TOTAL	*214,935*		*TOTAL*	*485,093*	
Congressional District 1	Harris, Andy*	45,477	77.9%	Tilghman, Bill	19,937	57.1%
	Goff, Jonathan	12,913	22.1%	LaFerla, John	14,965	42.9%
	TOTAL	*58,390*		*TOTAL*	*34,902*	
Congressional District 2	Banach, David	14,990	100.0%	Ruppersberger, C. A. Dutch*	43,614	77.6%
				Rundquist, Paul	6,450	11.5%
				Taylor, Blaine	6,164	11.0%
	TOTAL	*14,990*		*TOTAL*	*56,228*	
Congressional District 3	Long, Charles A.	7,597	43.6%	Sarbanes, John P.*	54,926	85.2%
	Harris, Thomas E. "Pinkston"	7,303	41.9%	Molyett, Matthew	9,564	14.8%
	Jackson, Michael P.	2,524	14.5%			
	TOTAL	*17,424*		*TOTAL*	*64,490*	
Congressional District 4	Hoyt, Nancy	5,368	37.6%	Edwards, Donna F.*	53,648	87.0%
	Holmes, Greg	3,469	24.3%	Christopher, Warren	8,021	13.0%
	McDermott, George E.	2,740	19.2%			
	Graziani, John R.	2,695	18.9%			
	TOTAL	*14,272*		*TOTAL*	*61,669*	

MARYLAND

GENERAL AND PRIMARY ELECTIONS

	REPUBLICAN PRIMARIES			DEMOCRATIC PRIMARIES		
Congressional District 5	Chaffee, Chris	8,137	41.6%	Hoyer, Steny H.*	57,240	100.0%
	Arness, Mark Kenneth	6,050	30.9%			
	Potter, Tom	5,374	27.5%			
	TOTAL	19,561		TOTAL	57,240	
Congressional District 6	Bongino, Daniel John	23,933	83.5%	Delaney, John K.*	33,289	100.0%
	Painter, Harold W.	4,718	16.5%			
	TOTAL	28,651		TOTAL	33,289	
Congressional District 7	Vaughn, Corrogan R.	6,293	54.8%	Cummings, Elijah E.*	69,790	90.6%
	Bly, Raymond J.	5,195	45.2%	Alexander, Bryant	4,786	6.2%
				Dickson Jr., Fred Donald	2,460	3.2%
	TOTAL	11,488		TOTAL	77,036	
Congressional District 8	Wallace, Dave	22,648	100.0%	Van Hollen, Chris*	60,556	91.3%
				English, George	3,834	5.8%
				Young, Lih	1,950	2.9%
	TOTAL	22,648		TOTAL	66,340	

Note: An asterisk (*) denotes incumbent.

MASSACHUSETTS

Congressional districts first established for elections held in 2012
9 members

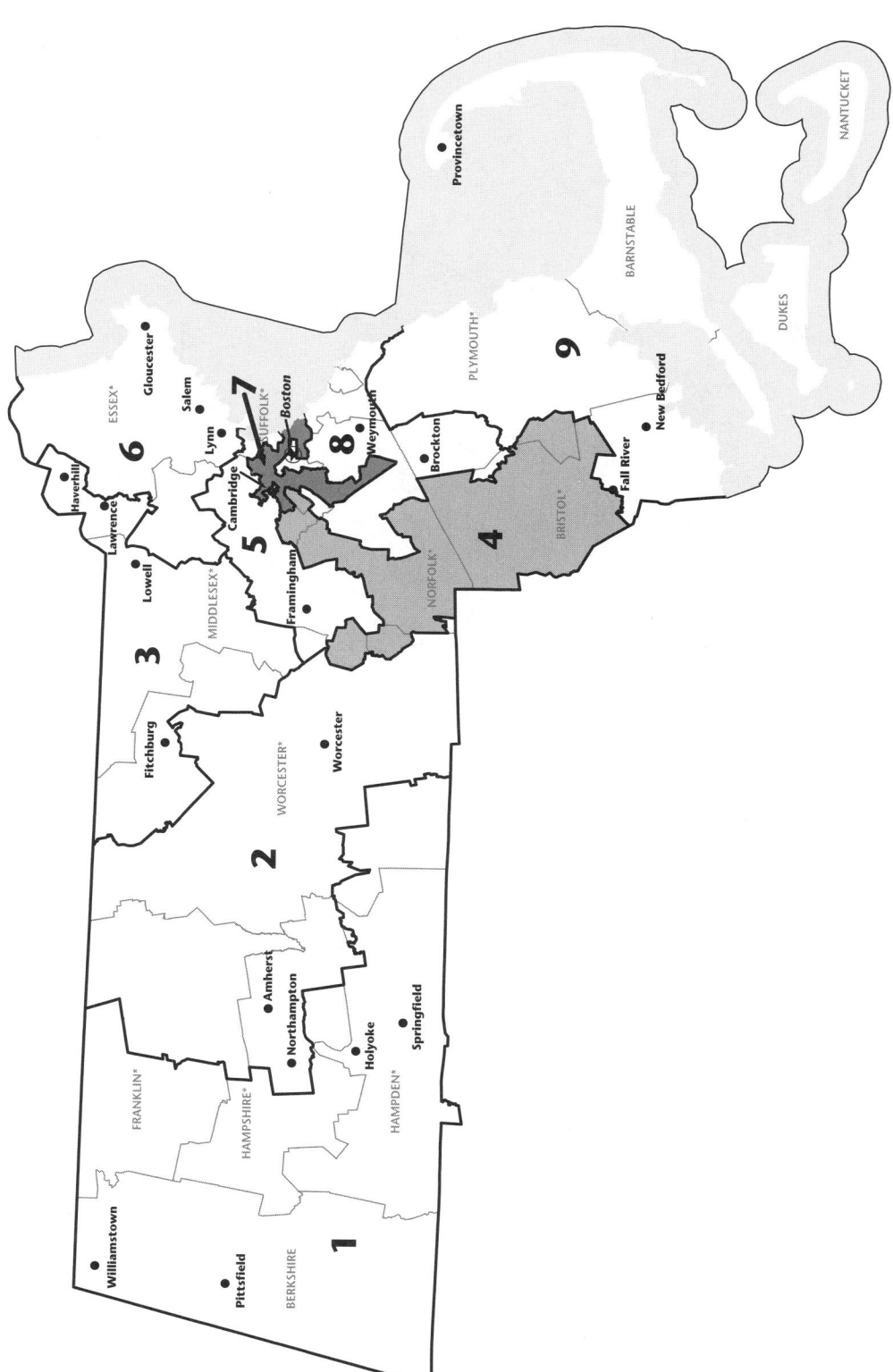

* Asterisk indicates a county whose boundaries include parts of two or more congressional districts.

MASSACHUSETTS
Boston Area

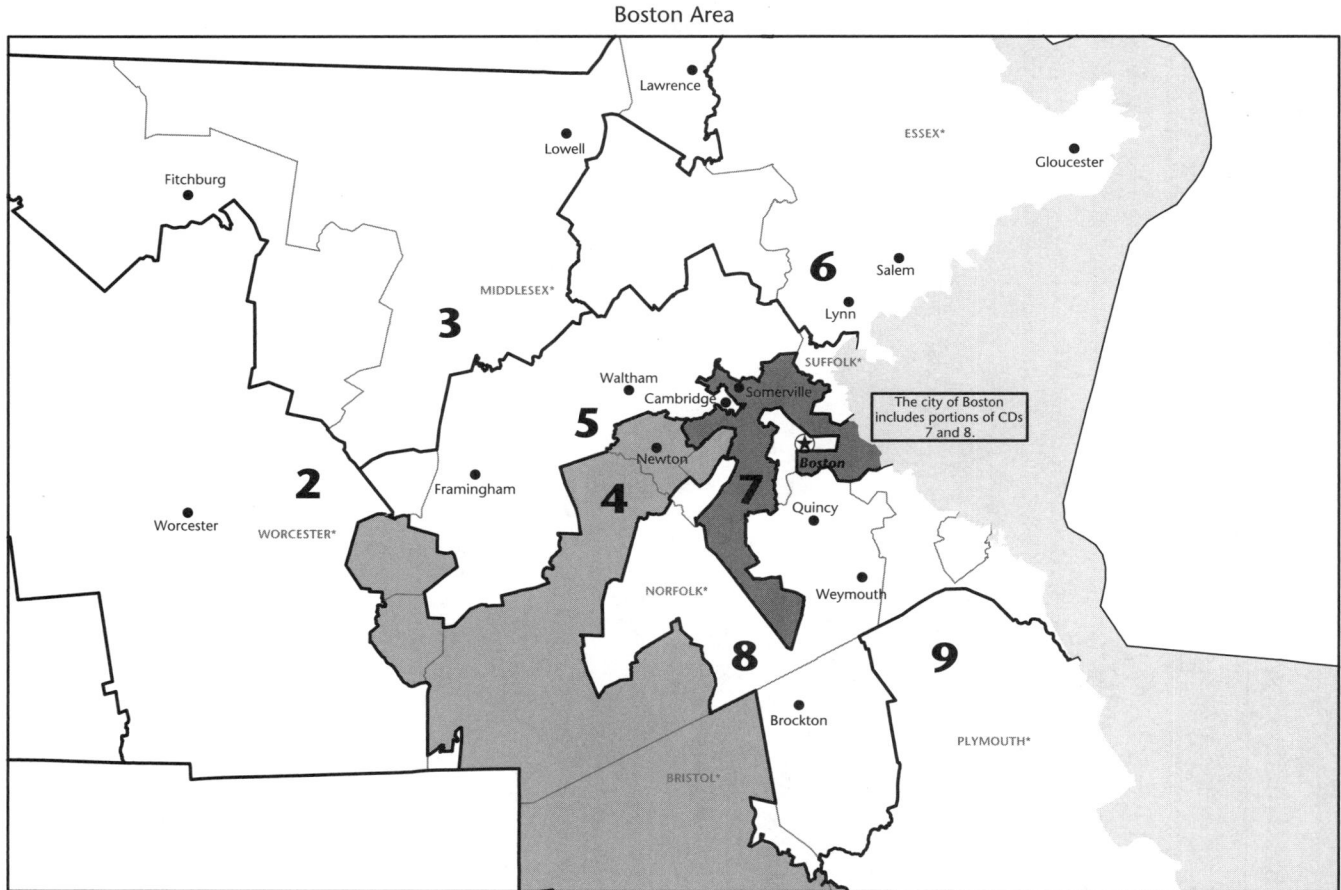

* Asterisk indicates a county whose boundaries include parts of two or more congressional districts.

MASSACHUSETTS

GOVERNOR
Charlie Baker (R). Elected 2014 to a four-year term.

SENATORS (2 Democrats)
Edward J. Markey (D). Reelected 2014 to a full six-year term. Previously elected June 25, 2013, to serve the remainder of the term vacated by the January 2013 resignation of John Kerry to become secretary of state. William "Mo" Cowan (D) had been appointed on January 30, 2013, to fill the vacant seat until the June 2013 special election.

Elizabeth Warren (D). Elected 2012 to a six-year term.

REPRESENTATIVES (9 Democrats)
1. Richard E. Neal (D)
2. James P. McGovern (D)
3. Niki Tsongas (D)
4. Joseph P. Kennedy III (D)
5. Katherine M. Clark (D)
6. Seth Moulton (D)
7. Michael E. Capuano (D)
8. Stephen F. Lynch (D)
9. William R. Keating (D)

POSTWAR VOTE FOR PRESIDENT

Year	Total Vote	Republican		Democratic		Other Vote	Rep.-Dem. Plurality	Percentage			
								Total Vote		Major Vote	
		Vote	Candidate	Vote	Candidate			Rep.	Dem.	Rep.	Dem.
2012	3,167,767	1,188,314	Romney, W. Mitt	1,921,290	Obama, Barack H.*	58,163	732,976 D	37.5%	60.7%	38.2%	61.8%
2008	3,080,985	1,108,854	McCain, John S. III	1,904,097	Obama, Barack H.	68,034	795,243 D	36.0%	61.8%	36.8%	63.2%
2004	2,912,388	1,071,109	Bush, George W.*	1,803,800	Kerry, John F.	37,479	732,691 D	36.8%	61.9%	37.3%	62.7%
2000**	2,702,984	878,502	Bush, George W.	1,616,487	Gore, Albert Jr.	207,995	737,985 D	32.5%	59.8%	35.2%	64.8%
1996**	2,556,785	718,107	Dole, Robert "Bob"	1,571,763	Clinton, Bill*	266,915	853,656 D	28.1%	61.5%	31.4%	68.6%
1992**	2,773,700	805,049	Bush, George H.*	1,318,662	Clinton, Bill	649,989	513,613 D	29.0%	47.5%	37.9%	62.1%
1988	2,632,805	1,194,635	Bush, George H.	1,401,415	Dukakis, Michael S.	36,755	206,780 D	45.4%	53.2%	46.0%	54.0%
1984	2,559,453	1,310,936	Reagan, Ronald*	1,239,606	Mondale, Walter F.	8,911	71,330 R	51.2%	48.4%	51.4%	48.6%
1980**	2,524,298	1,057,631	Reagan, Ronald	1,053,802	Carter, Jimmy*	412,865	3,829 R	41.9%	41.7%	50.1%	49.9%
1976	2,547,558	1,030,276	Ford, Gerald R.*	1,429,475	Carter, Jimmy	87,807	399,199 D	40.4%	56.1%	41.9%	58.1%
1972	2,458,756	1,112,078	Nixon, Richard M.*	1,332,540	McGovern, George S.	14,138	220,462 D	45.2%	54.2%	45.5%	54.5%
1968**	2,331,752	766,844	Nixon, Richard M.	1,469,218	Humphrey, Hubert Horatio Jr.	95,690	702,374 D	32.9%	63.0%	34.3%	65.7%
1964	2,344,798	549,727	Goldwater, Barry M. Sr.	1,786,422	Johnson, Lyndon B.*	8,649	1,236,695 D	23.4%	76.2%	23.5%	76.5%
1960	2,469,480	976,750	Nixon, Richard M.	1,487,174	Kennedy, John F.	5,556	510,424 D	39.6%	60.2%	39.6%	60.4%
1956	2,348,506	1,393,197	Eisenhower, Dwight D.*	948,190	Stevenson, Adlai E. II	7,119	445,007 R	59.3%	40.4%	59.5%	40.5%
1952	2,383,398	1,292,325	Eisenhower, Dwight D.	1,083,525	Stevenson, Adlai E. II	7,548	208,800 R	54.2%	45.5%	54.4%	45.6%
1948	2,107,146	909,370	Dewey, Thomas E.	1,151,788	Truman, Harry S.*	45,988	242,418 D	43.2%	54.7%	44.1%	55.9%

Note: An asterisk (*) denotes incumbent. **In past elections, the other vote included: 2000 - 173,564 Green (Ralph Nader); 1996 - 227,217 Reform (Ross Perot); 1992 - 630,731 Independent (Perot); 1980 - 382,539 Independent (John Anderson); 1968 - 87,088 American Independent (George Wallace).

MASSACHUSETTS

POSTWAR VOTE FOR GOVERNOR

Year	Total Vote	Republican		Democratic		Other Vote	Rep.-Dem. Plurality	Percentage			
		Vote	Candidate	Vote	Candidate			Total Vote		Major Vote	
								Rep.	Dem.	Rep.	Dem.
2014	2,158,326	1,044,573	Baker, Charlie	1,004,408	Coakley, Martha	109,345	40,165 R	48.4%	46.5%	51.0%	49.0%
2010	2,297,039	964,866	Baker, Charlie	1,112,283	Patrick, Deval*	219,890	147,417 D	42.0%	48.4%	46.5%	53.5%
2006	2,219,779	784,342	Healey, Kerry	1,234,984	Patrick, Deval	200,453	450,642 D	35.3%	55.6%	38.8%	61.2%
2002	2,194,179	1,091,988	Romney, W. Mitt	985,981	O'Brien, Shannon P.	116,210	106,007 R	49.8%	44.9%	52.6%	47.4%
1998	1,903,336	967,160	Cellucci, Argeo Paul*	901,843	Harshbarger, Scott	34,333	65,317 R	50.8%	47.4%	51.7%	48.3%
1994	2,255,150	1,599,141	Weld, William F.*	636,138	Roosevelt, Mark	19,871	963,003 R	70.9%	28.2%	71.5%	28.5%
1990	2,342,927	1,175,817	Weld, William F.	1,099,878	Silber, John	67,232	75,939 R	50.2%	46.9%	51.7%	48.3%
1986	1,684,079	525,364	Kariotis, George	1,157,786	Dukakis, Michael S.*	929	632,422 D	31.2%	68.7%	31.2%	68.8%
1982	2,050,254	749,679	Sears, John W.	1,219,109	Dukakis, Michael S.	81,466	469,430 D	36.6%	59.5%	38.1%	61.9%
1978	1,962,251	926,072	Hatch, Francis W.	1,030,294	King, Edward J.	5,885	104,222 D	47.2%	52.5%	47.3%	52.7%
1974	1,854,798	784,353	Sargent, Francis W.*	992,284	Dukakis, Michael S.	78,161	207,931 D	42.3%	53.5%	44.1%	55.9%
1970	1,867,906	1,058,623	Sargent, Francis W.*	799,269	White, Kevin H.	10,014	259,354 R	56.7%	42.8%	57.0%	43.0%
1966**	2,041,177	1,277,358	Volpe, John A.*	752,720	McCormack, Edward J.	11,099	524,638 R	62.6%	36.9%	62.9%	37.1%
1964	2,340,130	1,176,462	Volpe, John A.	1,153,416	Bellotti, Francis X.	10,252	23,046 R	50.3%	49.3%	50.5%	49.5%
1962	2,109,089	1,047,891	Volpe, John A.*	1,053,322	Peabody, Endicott	7,876	5,431 D	49.7%	49.9%	49.9%	50.1%
1960	2,417,133	1,269,295	Volpe, John A.	1,130,810	Ward, Joseph D.	17,028	138,485 R	52.5%	46.8%	52.9%	47.1%
1958	1,899,117	818,463	Gibbons, Charles	1,067,020	Furcolo, Foster*	13,634	248,557 D	43.1%	56.2%	43.4%	56.6%
1956	2,339,884	1,096,759	Whittier, Sumner G.	1,234,618	Furcolo, Foster	8,507	137,859 D	46.9%	52.8%	47.0%	53.0%
1954	1,903,774	985,339	Herter, Christian A.*	910,087	Murphy, Robert F.	8,348	75,252 R	51.8%	47.8%	52.0%	48.0%
1952	2,356,298	1,175,955	Herter, Christian A.	1,161,499	Dever, Paul A.*	18,844	14,456 R	49.9%	49.3%	50.3%	49.7%
1950	1,910,180	824,069	Coolidge, Arthur W.	1,074,570	Dever, Paul A.	11,541	250,501 D	43.1%	56.3%	43.4%	56.6%
1948	2,099,250	849,895	Bradford, Robert F.*	1,239,247	Dever, Paul A.	10,108	389,352 D	40.5%	59.0%	40.7%	59.3%
1946	1,683,452	911,152	Bradford, Robert F.	762,743	Tobin, Maurice J.*	9,557	148,409 R	54.1%	45.3%	54.4%	45.6%

Note: An asterisk (*) denotes incumbent. **The term of office of Massachusetts's governor was increased from two to four years effective with the 1966 election.

POSTWAR VOTE FOR SENATOR

Year	Total Vote	Republican		Democratic		Other Vote	Rep.-Dem. Plurality	Percentage			
		Vote	Candidate	Vote	Candidate			Total Vote		Major Vote	
								Rep.	Dem.	Rep.	Dem.
2014	2,084,972	791,950	Herr, Brian J.	1,289,944	Markey, Edward J.*	3,078	497,994 D	38.0%	61.9%	38.0%	62.0%
2013S	1,177,790	525,307	Gomez, Gabriel E.	645,429	Markey, Edward J.	7,054	120,122 D	44.6%	54.8%	44.9%	55.1%
2012	3,156,553	1,458,048	Brown, Scott P.*	1,696,346	Warren, Elizabeth	2,159	238,298 D	46.2%	53.7%	46.2%	53.8%
2010S	2,252,582	1,168,178	Brown, Scott P.	1,060,861	Coakley, Martha	23,543	107,317 R	51.9%	47.1%	52.4%	47.6%
2008	2,994,247	926,044	Beatty, Jeffrey K.	1,971,974	Kerry, John F.*	96,229	1,045,930 D	30.9%	65.9%	32.0%	68.0%
2006	2,165,490	661,532	Chase, Kenneth G.	1,500,738	Kennedy, Edward M.*	3,220	839,206 D	30.5%	69.3%	30.6%	69.4%
2002**	2,006,758			1,605,976	Kerry, John F.*	400,782	1,605,976 D		80.0%		100.0%
2000**	2,599,420	334,341	Robinson, Jack E. III	1,889,494	Kennedy, Edward M.*	375,585	1,555,153 D	12.9%	72.7%	15.0%	85.0%
1996	2,555,886	1,142,837	Weld, William F.	1,334,345	Kerry, John F.*	78,704	191,508 D	44.7%	52.2%	46.1%	53.9%
1994	2,179,964	894,005	Romney, W. Mitt	1,266,011	Kennedy, Edward M.*	19,948	372,006 D	41.0%	58.1%	41.4%	58.6%
1990	2,316,212	992,917	Rappaport, Jim	1,321,712	Kerry, John F.*	1,583	328,795 D	42.9%	57.1%	42.9%	57.1%
1988	2,606,225	884,267	Malone, Joseph D.	1,693,344	Kennedy, Edward M.*	28,614	809,077 D	33.9%	65.0%	34.3%	65.7%
1984	2,530,195	1,136,806	Shamie, Raymond	1,392,981	Kerry, John F.	408	256,175 D	44.9%	55.1%	44.9%	55.1%
1982	2,050,769	784,602	Shamie, Raymond	1,247,084	Kennedy, Edward M.*	19,083	462,482 D	38.3%	60.8%	38.6%	61.4%
1978	1,985,700	890,584	Brooke, Edward W. III*	1,093,283	Tsongas, Paul E.	1,833	202,699 D	44.8%	55.1%	44.9%	55.1%
1976	2,491,255	722,641	Robertson, Michael	1,726,657	Kennedy, Edward M.*	41,957	1,004,016 D	29.0%	69.3%	29.5%	70.5%
1972	2,370,676	1,505,932	Brooke, Edward W. III*	823,278	Droney, John J.	41,466	682,654 R	63.5%	34.7%	64.7%	35.3%
1970	1,935,607	715,978	Spaulding, Josiah A.	1,202,856	Kennedy, Edward M.*	16,773	486,878 D	37.0%	62.1%	37.3%	62.7%
1966	1,999,949	1,213,473	Brooke, Edward W. III	774,761	Peabody, Endicott	11,715	438,712 R	60.7%	38.7%	61.0%	39.0%
1964	2,312,028	587,663	Whitmore, Howard Jr.	1,716,907	Kennedy, Edward M.*	7,458	1,129,244 D	25.4%	74.3%	25.5%	74.5%
1962S	2,097,085	877,669	Lodge, George C.	1,162,611	Kennedy, Edward M.	56,805	284,942 D	41.9%	55.4%	43.0%	57.0%
1960	2,417,813	1,358,556	Saltonstall, Leverett*	1,050,725	O'Connor, Thomas J. Jr.	8,532	307,831 R	56.2%	43.5%	56.4%	43.6%
1958	1,862,041	488,318	Celeste, Vincent J.	1,362,926	Kennedy, John F.*	10,797	874,608 D	26.2%	73.2%	26.4%	73.6%
1954	1,892,710	956,605	Saltonstall, Leverett*	927,899	Furcolo, Foster	8,206	28,706 R	50.5%	49.0%	50.8%	49.2%
1952	2,360,425	1,141,247	Lodge, Henry Cabot Jr.*	1,211,984	Kennedy, John F.	7,194	70,737 D	48.3%	51.3%	48.5%	51.5%
1948	2,055,798	1,088,475	Saltonstall, Leverett*	954,398	Fitzgerald, John I.	12,925	134,077 R	52.9%	46.4%	53.3%	46.7%
1946	1,662,063	989,736	Lodge, Henry Cabot Jr.	660,200	Walsh, David I.*	12,127	329,536 R	59.5%	39.7%	60.0%	40.0%

Note: An asterisk (*) denotes incumbent. **In past elections, the other vote included: 2002 - 369,807 Libertarian (Michael E. Cloud); 2000 - 308,748 Libertarian (Carla Howell). The Republican Party did not run a candidate in the 2002 Senate election. The 1962, 2010 and 2013 elections were for short terms to fill a vacancy.

MASSACHUSETTS

GOVERNOR 2014

2010 Census Population	County	Total Vote	Republican (Baker)	Democratic (Coakley)	Other	Rep.-Dem. Plurality	Total Vote Rep.	Total Vote Dem.	Major Vote Rep.	Major Vote Dem.
215,888	BARNSTABLE	97,779	52,251	41,525	4,003	10,726 R	53.4%	42.5%	55.7%	44.3%
131,219	BERKSHIRE	39,569	11,201	26,207	2,161	15,006 D	28.3%	66.2%	29.9%	70.1%
548,285	BRISTOL	146,157	72,641	66,045	7,471	6,596 R	49.7%	45.2%	52.4%	47.6%
16,535	DUKES	7,303	2,493	4,477	333	1,984 D	34.1%	61.3%	35.8%	64.2%
743,159	ESSEX	255,570	135,365	109,776	10,429	25,589 R	53.0%	43.0%	55.2%	44.8%
71,372	FRANKLIN	26,310	8,826	15,077	2,407	6,251 D	33.5%	57.3%	36.9%	63.1%
463,490	HAMPDEN	134,729	64,850	54,751	15,128	10,099 R	48.1%	40.6%	54.2%	45.8%
158,080	HAMPSHIRE	54,948	19,103	30,982	4,863	11,879 D	34.8%	56.4%	38.1%	61.9%
1,503,085	MIDDLESEX	525,671	238,750	264,319	22,602	25,569 D	45.4%	50.3%	47.5%	52.5%
10,172	NANTUCKET	3,680	1,717	1,817	146	100 D	46.7%	49.4%	48.6%	51.4%
670,850	NORFOLK	251,722	133,328	107,891	10,503	25,437 R	53.0%	42.9%	55.3%	44.7%
494,919	PLYMOUTH	179,254	102,551	68,141	8,562	34,410 R	57.2%	38.0%	60.1%	39.9%
722,023	SUFFOLK	181,583	57,754	116,610	7,219	58,856 D	31.8%	64.2%	33.1%	66.9%
798,552	WORCESTER	254,051	143,743	96,790	13,518	46,953 R	56.6%	38.1%	59.8%	40.2%
6,547,629	TOTAL	2,158,326	1,044,573	1,004,408	109,345	40,165 R	48.4%	46.5%	51.0%	49.0%

2010 Census Population	City/Town	Total Vote	Republican (Baker)	Democratic (Coakley)	Other	Rep.-Dem. Plurality	Total Vote Rep.	Total Vote Dem.	Major Vote Rep.	Major Vote Dem.
21,924	ACTON	8,665	3,776	4,534	355	758 D	43.6%	52.3%	45.4%	54.6%
28,438	AGAWAM	10,102	5,778	3,148	1,176	2,630 R	57.2%	31.2%	64.7%	35.3%
37,819	AMHERST	7,787	1,269	6,092	426	4,823 D	16.3%	78.2%	17.2%	82.8%
33,201	ANDOVER	13,121	7,862	4,869	390	2,993 R	59.9%	37.1%	61.8%	38.2%
42,844	ARLINGTON	19,520	6,243	12,435	842	6,192 D	32.0%	63.7%	33.4%	66.6%
43,593	ATTLEBORO	12,174	6,652	4,953	569	1,699 R	54.6%	40.7%	57.3%	42.7%
45,193	BARNSTABLE	18,649	10,670	7,222	757	3,448 R	57.2%	38.7%	59.6%	40.4%
24,729	BELMONT	10,247	4,303	5,623	321	1,320 D	42.0%	54.9%	43.4%	56.6%
39,502	BEVERLY	14,589	7,538	6,394	657	1,144 R	51.7%	43.8%	54.1%	45.9%
40,243	BILLERICA	14,100	8,248	5,121	731	3,127 R	58.5%	36.3%	61.7%	38.3%
617,594	BOSTON	158,840	47,653	104,995	6,192	57,342 D	30.0%	66.1%	31.2%	68.8%
35,744	BRAINTREE	14,268	8,223	5,462	583	2,761 R	57.6%	38.3%	60.1%	39.9%
93,810	BROCKTON	21,184	7,433	12,792	959	5,359 D	35.1%	60.4%	36.8%	63.2%
58,732	BROOKLINE	18,671	5,567	12,488	616	6,921 D	29.8%	66.9%	30.8%	69.2%
24,498	BURLINGTON	9,241	5,205	3,659	377	1,546 R	56.3%	39.6%	58.7%	41.3%
105,162	CAMBRIDGE	32,360	5,589	25,525	1,246	19,936 D	17.3%	78.9%	18.0%	82.0%
21,561	CANTON	8,701	5,026	3,337	338	1,689 R	57.8%	38.4%	60.1%	39.9%
33,802	CHELMSFORD	14,041	8,198	5,140	703	3,058 R	58.4%	36.6%	61.5%	38.5%
55,298	CHICOPEE	15,803	7,604	5,951	2,248	1,653 R	48.1%	37.7%	56.1%	43.9%
17,668	CONCORD	8,205	3,440	4,518	247	1,078 D	41.9%	55.1%	43.2%	56.8%
26,493	DANVERS	10,076	5,975	3,668	433	2,307 R	59.3%	36.4%	62.0%	38.0%
34,032	DARTMOUTH	9,275	4,514	4,299	462	215 R	48.7%	46.4%	51.2%	48.8%
24,729	DEDHAM	9,805	5,107	4,299	399	808 R	52.1%	43.8%	54.3%	45.7%
29,457	DRACUT	10,495	6,614	3,416	465	3,198 R	63.0%	32.5%	65.9%	34.1%
23,112	EASTON	8,206	4,992	2,890	324	2,102 R	60.8%	35.2%	63.3%	36.7%
41,667	EVERETT	9,153	3,500	5,279	374	1,779 D	38.2%	57.7%	39.9%	60.1%
88,857	FALL RIVER	16,584	6,036	9,616	932	3,580 D	36.4%	58.0%	38.6%	61.4%
31,531	FALMOUTH	14,303	7,137	6,584	582	553 R	49.9%	46.0%	52.0%	48.0%
40,318	FITCHBURG	8,965	4,601	3,720	644	881 R	51.3%	41.5%	55.3%	44.7%
68,318	FRAMINGHAM	18,844	8,156	9,825	863	1,669 D	43.3%	52.1%	45.4%	54.6%
31,635	FRANKLIN	12,162	7,325	4,254	583	3,071 R	60.2%	35.0%	63.3%	36.7%
28,789	GLOUCESTER	10,987	5,139	5,325	523	186 D	46.8%	48.5%	49.1%	50.9%
60,879	HAVERHILL	18,569	9,994	7,647	928	2,347 R	53.8%	41.2%	56.7%	43.3%
22,157	HINGHAM	10,370	6,295	3,712	363	2,583 R	60.7%	35.8%	62.9%	37.1%
39,880	HOLYOKE	10,233	3,641	5,508	1,084	1,867 D	35.6%	53.8%	39.8%	60.2%

MASSACHUSETTS

GOVERNOR 2014

2010 Census Population	City/Town	Total Vote	Republican (Baker)	Democratic (Coakley)	Other	Rep.-Dem. Plurality	Percentage			
							Total Vote		Major Vote	
							Rep.	Dem.	Rep.	Dem.
76,377	LAWRENCE	13,636	3,700	9,414	522	5,714 D	27.1%	69.0%	28.2%	71.8%
40,759	LEOMINSTER	12,507	7,029	4,724	754	2,305 R	56.2%	37.8%	59.8%	40.2%
31,394	LEXINGTON	13,166	5,054	7,748	364	2,694 D	38.4%	58.8%	39.5%	60.5%
106,519	LOWELL	20,644	9,038	10,478	1,128	1,440 D	43.8%	50.8%	46.3%	53.7%
90,329	LYNN	20,494	8,020	11,636	838	3,616 D	39.1%	56.8%	40.8%	59.2%
59,450	MALDEN	13,975	5,222	8,092	661	2,870 D	37.4%	57.9%	39.2%	60.8%
19,808	MARBLEHEAD	9,729	5,530	3,957	242	1,573 R	56.8%	40.7%	58.3%	41.7%
38,499	MARLBOROUGH	11,543	6,038	4,939	566	1,099 R	52.3%	42.8%	55.0%	45.0%
25,132	MARSHFIELD	11,069	6,854	3,777	438	3,077 R	61.9%	34.1%	64.5%	35.5%
56,173	MEDFORD	19,327	7,002	11,453	872	4,451 D	36.2%	59.3%	37.9%	62.1%
26,983	MELROSE	11,724	5,520	5,709	495	189 D	47.1%	48.7%	49.2%	50.8%
47,255	METHUEN	14,207	8,272	5,397	538	2,875 R	58.2%	38.0%	60.5%	39.5%
27,999	MILFORD	9,098	5,080	3,601	417	1,479 R	55.8%	39.6%	58.5%	41.5%
27,003	MILTON	11,736	5,750	5,648	338	102 R	49.0%	48.1%	50.4%	49.6%
33,006	NATICK	13,557	6,458	6,523	576	65 D	47.6%	48.1%	49.7%	50.3%
28,886	NEEDHAM	13,287	6,628	6,247	412	381 R	49.9%	47.0%	51.5%	48.5%
95,072	NEW BEDFORD	17,492	5,547	10,882	1,063	5,335 D	31.7%	62.2%	33.8%	66.2%
85,146	NEWTON	32,772	12,089	19,068	1,615	6,979 D	36.9%	58.2%	38.8%	61.2%
28,352	NORTH ANDOVER	10,558	6,655	3,553	350	3,102 R	63.0%	33.7%	65.2%	34.8%
28,712	NORTH ATTLEBOROUGH	9,221	5,814	3,004	403	2,810 R	63.1%	32.6%	65.9%	34.1%
28,549	NORTHAMPTON	11,530	2,228	8,526	776	6,298 D	19.3%	73.9%	20.7%	79.3%
28,602	NORWOOD	10,541	5,677	4,405	459	1,272 R	53.9%	41.8%	56.3%	43.7%
51,251	PEABODY	19,306	10,524	7,883	899	2,641 R	54.5%	40.8%	57.2%	42.8%
44,737	PITTSFIELD	11,409	3,155	7,559	695	4,404 D	27.7%	66.3%	29.4%	70.6%
56,468	PLYMOUTH	21,420	12,301	8,079	1,040	4,222 R	57.4%	37.7%	60.4%	39.6%
92,271	QUINCY	27,002	13,404	12,255	1,343	1,149 R	49.6%	45.4%	52.2%	47.8%
32,112	RANDOLPH	9,325	3,090	5,834	401	2,744 D	33.1%	62.6%	34.6%	65.4%
24,747	READING	10,703	6,064	4,284	355	1,780 R	56.7%	40.0%	58.6%	41.4%
51,755	REVERE	11,395	5,312	5,547	536	235 D	46.6%	48.7%	48.9%	51.1%
41,340	SALEM	13,250	5,528	7,052	670	1,524 D	41.7%	53.2%	43.9%	56.1%
26,628	SAUGUS	9,927	5,667	3,827	433	1,840 R	57.1%	38.6%	59.7%	40.3%
18,133	SCITUATE	8,632	5,044	3,136	452	1,908 R	58.4%	36.3%	61.7%	38.3%
35,608	SHREWSBURY	13,422	8,247	4,711	464	3,536 R	61.4%	35.1%	63.6%	36.4%
75,754	SOMERVILLE	22,474	4,918	16,351	1,205	11,433 D	21.9%	72.8%	23.1%	76.9%
153,060	SPRINGFIELD	33,119	10,256	19,312	3,551	9,056 D	31.0%	58.3%	34.7%	65.3%
21,437	STONEHAM	9,126	5,002	3,834	290	1,168 R	54.8%	42.0%	56.6%	43.4%
26,962	STOUGHTON	9,329	4,752	4,140	437	612 R	50.9%	44.4%	53.4%	46.6%
55,874	TAUNTON	14,584	7,039	6,682	863	357 R	48.3%	45.8%	51.3%	48.7%
28,961	TEWKSBURY	11,313	6,989	3,875	449	3,114 R	61.8%	34.3%	64.3%	35.7%
24,932	WAKEFIELD	10,682	6,094	4,189	399	1,905 R	57.0%	39.2%	59.3%	40.7%
24,070	WALPOLE	10,665	6,765	3,474	426	3,291 R	63.4%	32.6%	66.1%	33.9%
60,632	WALTHAM	16,582	7,431	8,396	755	965 D	44.8%	50.6%	47.0%	53.0%
31,915	WATERTOWN	11,597	4,152	6,934	511	2,782 D	35.8%	59.8%	37.5%	62.5%
27,982	WELLESLEY	11,069	6,139	4,660	270	1,479 R	55.5%	42.1%	56.8%	43.2%
28,391	WEST SPRINGFIELD	8,305	4,582	2,759	964	1,823 R	55.2%	33.2%	62.4%	37.6%
41,094	WESTFIELD	12,559	6,992	4,075	1,492	2,917 R	55.7%	32.4%	63.2%	36.8%
53,743	WEYMOUTH	20,132	10,954	8,041	1,137	2,913 R	54.4%	39.9%	57.7%	42.3%
21,374	WINCHESTER	9,699	5,346	4,077	276	1,269 R	55.1%	42.0%	56.7%	43.3%
38,120	WOBURN	13,753	7,381	5,772	600	1,609 R	53.7%	42.0%	56.1%	43.9%
181,045	WORCESTER	38,452	16,091	20,297	2,064	4,206 D	41.8%	52.8%	44.2%	55.8%
23,793	YARMOUTH	10,099	5,426	4,164	509	1,262 R	53.7%	41.2%	56.6%	43.4%

MASSACHUSETTS

SENATOR SPECIAL 2013

2010 Census Population	County	Total Vote	Republican (Gomez)	Democratic (Markey)	Other	Rep.-Dem. Plurality	Percentage Total Vote Rep.	Dem.	Major Vote Rep.	Dem.
215,888	BARNSTABLE	60,231	32,020	27,982	229	4,038 R	53.2%	46.5%	53.4%	46.6%
131,219	BERKSHIRE	21,737	5,817	15,809	111	9,992 D	26.8%	72.7%	26.9%	73.1%
548,285	BRISTOL	68,980	34,722	33,791	467	931 R	50.3%	49.0%	50.7%	49.3%
16,535	DUKES	4,316	1,338	2,965	13	1,627 D	31.0%	68.7%	31.1%	68.9%
743,159	ESSEX	129,307	63,248	65,339	720	2,091 D	48.9%	50.5%	49.2%	50.8%
71,372	FRANKLIN	16,223	5,276	10,830	117	5,554 D	32.5%	66.8%	32.8%	67.2%
463,490	HAMPDEN	65,787	34,504	30,894	389	3,610 R	52.4%	47.0%	52.8%	47.2%
158,080	HAMPSHIRE	35,022	10,952	23,818	252	12,866 D	31.3%	68.0%	31.5%	68.5%
1,503,085	MIDDLESEX	305,137	116,716	186,651	1,770	69,935 D	38.3%	61.2%	38.5%	61.5%
10,172	NANTUCKET	1,996	877	1,114	5	237 D	43.9%	55.8%	44.0%	56.0%
670,850	NORFOLK	139,788	66,339	72,565	884	6,226 D	47.5%	51.9%	47.8%	52.2%
494,919	PLYMOUTH	90,783	51,649	38,588	546	13,061 R	56.9%	42.5%	57.2%	42.8%
722,023	SUFFOLK	104,300	25,924	77,683	693	51,759 D	24.9%	74.5%	25.0%	75.0%
798,552	WORCESTER	134,183	75,925	57,400	858	18,525 R	56.6%	42.8%	56.9%	43.1%
6,547,629	TOTAL	1,177,790	525,307	645,429	7,054	120,122 D	44.6%	54.8%	44.9%	55.1%

2010 Census Population	City/Town	Total Vote	Republican (Gomez)	Democratic (Markey)	Other	Rep.-Dem. Plurality	Percentage Total Vote Rep.	Dem.	Major Vote Rep.	Dem.
21,924	ACTON	5,131	1,692	3,420	19	1,728 D	33.0%	66.7%	33.1%	66.9%
28,438	AGAWAM	4,774	3,009	1,743	22	1,266 R	63.0%	36.5%	63.3%	36.7%
37,819	AMHERST	5,151	567	4,561	23	3,994 D	11.0%	88.5%	11.1%	88.9%
33,201	ANDOVER	6,879	3,721	3,130	28	591 R	54.1%	45.5%	54.3%	45.7%
42,844	ARLINGTON	12,987	3,254	9,655	78	6,401 D	25.1%	74.3%	25.2%	74.8%
43,593	ATTLEBORO	5,361	2,873	2,461	27	412 R	53.6%	45.9%	53.9%	46.1%
45,193	BARNSTABLE	11,326	6,580	4,712	34	1,868 R	58.1%	41.6%	58.3%	41.7%
24,729	BELMONT	6,798	2,191	4,576	31	2,385 D	32.2%	67.3%	32.4%	67.6%
39,502	BEVERLY	7,143	3,321	3,787	35	466 D	46.5%	53.0%	46.7%	53.3%
40,243	BILLERICA	6,890	4,098	2,753	39	1,345 R	59.5%	40.0%	59.8%	40.2%
617,594	BOSTON	92,294	21,457	70,223	614	48,766 D	23.2%	76.1%	23.4%	76.6%
35,744	BRAINTREE	7,628	4,373	3,191	64	1,182 R	57.3%	41.8%	57.8%	42.2%
93,810	BROCKTON	10,651	3,751	6,817	83	3,066 D	35.2%	64.0%	35.5%	64.5%
58,732	BROOKLINE	12,770	2,260	10,480	30	8,220 D	17.7%	82.1%	17.7%	82.3%
24,498	BURLINGTON	4,621	2,455	2,135	31	320 R	53.1%	46.2%	53.5%	46.5%
105,162	CAMBRIDGE	21,108	2,248	18,759	101	16,511 D	10.6%	88.9%	10.7%	89.3%
21,561	CANTON	4,750	2,500	2,226	24	274 R	52.6%	46.9%	52.9%	47.1%
33,802	CHELMSFORD	7,767	4,383	3,347	37	1,036 R	56.4%	43.1%	56.7%	43.3%
55,298	CHICOPEE	7,363	3,945	3,352	66	593 R	53.6%	45.5%	54.1%	45.9%
17,668	CONCORD	5,323	1,674	3,635	14	1,961 D	31.4%	68.3%	31.5%	68.5%
26,493	DANVERS	4,791	2,621	2,137	33	484 R	54.7%	44.6%	55.1%	44.9%
34,032	DARTMOUTH	4,518	2,271	2,226	21	45 R	50.3%	49.3%	50.5%	49.5%
24,729	DEDHAM	5,778	2,846	2,885	47	39 D	49.3%	49.9%	49.7%	50.3%
29,457	DRACUT	5,190	3,349	1,807	34	1,542 R	64.5%	34.8%	65.0%	35.0%
23,112	EASTON	3,796	2,198	1,581	17	617 R	57.9%	41.6%	58.2%	41.8%
41,667	EVERETT	4,709	1,440	3,222	47	1,782 D	30.6%	68.4%	30.9%	69.1%
88,857	FALL RIVER	7,011	2,421	4,519	71	2,098 D	34.5%	64.5%	34.9%	65.1%
31,531	FALMOUTH	9,133	4,411	4,676	46	265 D	48.3%	51.2%	48.5%	51.5%
40,318	FITCHBURG	4,325	2,395	1,900	30	495 R	55.4%	43.9%	55.8%	44.2%
68,318	FRAMINGHAM	11,198	4,043	7,090	65	3,047 D	36.1%	63.3%	36.3%	63.7%
31,635	FRANKLIN	5,437	3,065	2,334	38	731 R	56.4%	42.9%	56.8%	43.2%
28,789	GLOUCESTER	5,652	2,394	3,230	28	836 D	42.4%	57.1%	42.6%	57.4%
60,879	HAVERHILL	9,055	4,997	4,002	56	995 R	55.2%	44.2%	55.5%	44.5%
22,157	HINGHAM	6,050	3,318	2,695	37	623 R	54.8%	44.5%	55.2%	44.8%
39,880	HOLYOKE	4,815	1,849	2,944	22	1,095 D	38.4%	61.1%	38.6%	61.4%

MASSACHUSETTS
SENATOR SPECIAL 2013

2010 Census Population	City/Town	Total Vote	Republican (Gomez)	Democratic (Markey)	Other	Rep.-Dem. Plurality	Percentage Total Vote Rep.	Dem.	Major Vote Rep.	Dem.
76,377	LAWRENCE	6,206	1,653	4,500	53	2,847 D	26.6%	72.5%	26.9%	73.1%
40,759	LEOMINSTER	6,139	3,692	2,410	37	1,282 R	60.1%	39.3%	60.5%	39.5%
31,394	LEXINGTON	9,231	2,309	6,887	35	4,578 D	25.0%	74.6%	25.1%	74.9%
106,519	LOWELL	9,900	4,152	5,662	86	1,510 D	41.9%	57.2%	42.3%	57.7%
90,329	LYNN	10,067	3,369	6,632	66	3,263 D	33.5%	65.9%	33.7%	66.3%
59,450	MALDEN	8,155	2,198	5,892	65	3,694 D	27.0%	72.3%	27.2%	72.8%
19,808	MARBLEHEAD	5,703	2,647	3,029	27	382 D	46.4%	53.1%	46.6%	53.4%
38,499	MARLBOROUGH	6,185	2,997	3,145	43	148 D	48.5%	50.8%	48.8%	51.2%
25,132	MARSHFIELD	5,426	3,266	2,144	16	1,122 R	60.2%	39.5%	60.4%	39.6%
56,173	MEDFORD	11,339	3,557	7,694	88	4,137 D	31.4%	67.9%	31.6%	68.4%
26,983	MELROSE	6,644	2,676	3,933	35	1,257 D	40.3%	59.2%	40.5%	59.5%
47,255	METHUEN	6,428	3,861	2,530	37	1,331 R	60.1%	39.4%	60.4%	39.6%
27,999	MILFORD	4,075	2,101	1,949	25	152 R	51.6%	47.8%	51.9%	48.1%
27,003	MILTON	7,064	3,111	3,907	46	796 D	44.0%	55.3%	44.3%	55.7%
33,006	NATICK	7,751	3,051	4,666	34	1,615 D	39.4%	60.2%	39.5%	60.5%
28,886	NEEDHAM	8,252	3,051	5,174	27	2,123 D	37.0%	62.7%	37.1%	62.9%
95,072	NEW BEDFORD	7,661	2,591	5,007	63	2,416 D	33.8%	65.4%	34.1%	65.9%
85,146	NEWTON	21,888	5,398	16,389	101	10,991 D	24.7%	74.9%	24.8%	75.2%
28,352	NORTH ANDOVER	5,266	3,140	2,105	21	1,035 R	59.6%	40.0%	59.9%	40.1%
28,712	NORTH ATTLEBOROUGH	7,225	4,273	2,868	84	1,405 R	59.1%	39.7%	59.8%	40.2%
28,549	NORTHAMPTON	10,772	2,086	8,552	134	6,466 D	19.4%	79.4%	19.6%	80.4%
28,602	NORWOOD	5,779	2,987	2,748	44	239 R	51.7%	47.6%	52.1%	47.9%
51,251	PEABODY	9,632	4,849	4,703	80	146 R	50.3%	48.8%	50.8%	49.2%
44,737	PITTSFIELD	6,046	1,601	4,414	31	2,813 D	26.5%	73.0%	26.6%	73.4%
56,468	PLYMOUTH	10,790	6,232	4,491	67	1,741 R	57.8%	41.6%	58.1%	41.9%
92,271	QUINCY	15,264	7,197	7,897	170	700 D	47.2%	51.7%	47.7%	52.3%
32,112	RANDOLPH	5,111	1,523	3,548	40	2,025 D	29.8%	69.4%	30.0%	70.0%
24,747	READING	5,320	2,689	2,606	25	83 R	50.5%	49.0%	50.8%	49.2%
51,755	REVERE	5,940	2,322	3,568	50	1,246 D	39.1%	60.1%	39.4%	60.6%
41,340	SALEM	6,530	2,400	4,090	40	1,690 D	36.8%	62.6%	37.0%	63.0%
26,628	SAUGUS	4,822	2,630	2,163	29	467 R	54.5%	44.9%	54.9%	45.1%
18,133	SCITUATE	5,011	2,898	2,082	31	816 R	57.8%	41.5%	58.2%	41.8%
35,608	SHREWSBURY	7,186	4,052	3,107	27	945 R	56.4%	43.2%	56.6%	43.4%
75,754	SOMERVILLE	14,028	2,281	11,614	133	9,333 D	16.3%	82.8%	16.4%	83.6%
153,060	SPRINGFIELD	15,690	5,194	10,400	96	5,206 D	33.1%	66.3%	33.3%	66.7%
21,437	STONEHAM	5,240	2,557	2,665	18	108 D	48.8%	50.9%	49.0%	51.0%
26,962	STOUGHTON	4,933	2,393	2,515	25	122 D	48.5%	51.0%	48.8%	51.2%
55,874	TAUNTON	6,721	3,355	3,335	31	20 R	49.9%	49.6%	50.1%	49.9%
28,961	TEWKSBURY	5,455	3,289	2,121	45	1,168 R	60.3%	38.9%	60.8%	39.2%
24,932	WAKEFIELD	5,574	2,893	2,648	33	245 R	51.9%	47.5%	52.2%	47.8%
24,070	WALPOLE	5,217	3,140	2,038	39	1,102 R	60.2%	39.1%	60.6%	39.4%
60,632	WALTHAM	9,350	3,730	5,567	53	1,837 D	39.9%	59.5%	40.1%	59.9%
31,915	WATERTOWN	6,915	1,907	4,972	36	3,065 D	27.6%	71.9%	27.7%	72.3%
27,982	WELLESLEY	7,335	3,151	4,164	20	1,013 D	43.0%	56.8%	43.1%	56.9%
28,391	WEST SPRINGFIELD	4,040	2,450	1,567	23	883 R	60.6%	38.8%	61.0%	39.0%
41,094	WESTFIELD	5,932	3,691	2,213	28	1,478 R	62.2%	37.3%	62.5%	37.5%
53,743	WEYMOUTH	10,123	5,504	4,523	96	981 R	54.4%	44.7%	54.9%	45.1%
21,374	WINCHESTER	6,392	2,932	3,438	22	506 D	45.9%	53.8%	46.0%	54.0%
38,120	WOBURN	7,486	3,921	3,494	71	427 R	52.4%	46.7%	52.9%	47.1%
181,045	WORCESTER	21,160	8,601	12,408	151	3,807 D	40.6%	58.6%	40.9%	59.1%
23,793	YARMOUTH	6,269	3,469	2,782	18	687 R	55.3%	44.4%	55.5%	44.5%
4,437,403	TOTAL	744,841	294,987	445,167	4,687	150,180 D	39.6%	59.8%	39.9%	60.1%

MASSACHUSETTS

SENATOR 2014

2010 Census Population	County	Total Vote	Republican (Herr)	Democratic (Markey)	Other	Rep.-Dem. Plurality	Total Vote Rep.	Total Vote Dem.	Major Vote Rep.	Major Vote Dem.
215,888	BARNSTABLE	95,911	44,534	51,317	60	6,783 D	46.4%	53.5%	46.5%	53.5%
131,219	BERKSHIRE	38,523	9,626	28,871	26	19,245 D	25.0%	74.9%	25.0%	75.0%
548,285	BRISTOL	141,889	57,513	84,226	150	26,713 D	40.5%	59.4%	40.6%	59.4%
16,535	DUKES	7,175	2,010	5,161	4	3,151 D	28.0%	71.9%	28.0%	72.0%
743,159	ESSEX	247,116	99,944	146,869	303	46,925 D	40.4%	59.4%	40.5%	59.5%
71,372	FRANKLIN	25,712	6,899	18,785	28	11,886 D	26.8%	73.1%	26.9%	73.1%
463,490	HAMPDEN	128,776	51,664	76,816	296	25,152 D	40.1%	59.7%	40.2%	59.8%
158,080	HAMPSHIRE	53,552	15,036	38,451	65	23,415 D	28.1%	71.8%	28.1%	71.9%
1,503,085	MIDDLESEX	511,884	173,537	337,553	794	164,016 D	33.9%	65.9%	34.0%	66.0%
10,172	NANTUCKET	3,622	1,386	2,233	3	847 D	38.3%	61.7%	38.3%	61.7%
670,850	NORFOLK	242,444	98,027	144,086	331	46,059 D	40.4%	59.4%	40.5%	59.5%
494,919	PLYMOUTH	173,571	81,740	91,682	149	9,942 D	47.1%	52.8%	47.1%	52.9%
722,023	SUFFOLK	169,435	34,189	134,704	542	100,515 D	20.2%	79.5%	20.2%	79.8%
798,552	WORCESTER	245,362	115,845	129,190	327	13,345 D	47.2%	52.7%	47.3%	52.7%
6,547,629	TOTAL	2,084,972	791,950	1,289,944	3,078	497,994 D	38.0%	61.9%	38.0%	62.0%

2010 Census Population	City/Town	Total Vote	Republican (Herr)	Democratic (Markey)	Other	Rep.-Dem. Plurality	Total Vote Rep.	Total Vote Dem.	Major Vote Rep.	Major Vote Dem.
21,924	ACTON	8,490	2,774	5,701	15	2,927 D	32.7%	67.1%	32.7%	67.3%
28,438	AGAWAM	9,672	4,722	4,933	17	211 D	48.8%	51.0%	48.9%	51.1%
37,819	AMHERST	7,679	852	6,809	18	5,957 D	11.1%	88.7%	11.1%	88.9%
33,201	ANDOVER	12,794	6,176	6,615	3	439 D	48.3%	51.7%	48.3%	51.7%
42,844	ARLINGTON	19,115	4,216	14,884	15	10,668 D	22.1%	77.9%	22.1%	77.9%
43,593	ATTLEBORO	11,796	5,388	6,397	11	1,009 D	45.7%	54.2%	45.7%	54.3%
45,193	BARNSTABLE	18,306	9,134	9,156	16	22 D	49.9%	50.0%	49.9%	50.1%
24,729	BELMONT	9,962	2,866	7,082	14	4,216 D	28.8%	71.1%	28.8%	71.2%
39,502	BEVERLY	14,092	5,392	8,699	1	3,307 D	38.3%	61.7%	38.3%	61.7%
40,243	BILLERICA	13,721	6,513	7,190	18	677 D	47.5%	52.4%	47.5%	52.5%
617,594	BOSTON	147,791	28,138	119,145	508	91,007 D	19.0%	80.6%	19.1%	80.9%
35,744	BRAINTREE	13,608	5,910	7,674	24	1,764 D	43.4%	56.4%	43.5%	56.5%
93,810	BROCKTON	20,316	5,364	14,939	13	9,575 D	26.4%	73.5%	26.4%	73.6%
58,732	BROOKLINE	18,298	3,438	14,848	12	11,410 D	18.8%	81.1%	18.8%	81.2%
24,498	BURLINGTON	8,966	3,976	4,979	11	1,003 D	44.3%	55.5%	44.4%	55.6%
105,162	CAMBRIDGE	31,802	3,208	28,524	70	25,316 D	10.1%	89.7%	10.1%	89.9%
21,561	CANTON	8,353	3,676	4,671	6	995 D	44.0%	55.9%	44.0%	56.0%
33,802	CHELMSFORD	13,567	6,414	7,134	19	720 D	47.3%	52.6%	47.3%	52.7%
55,298	CHICOPEE	15,315	5,828	9,435	52	3,607 D	38.1%	61.6%	38.2%	61.8%
17,668	CONCORD	8,035	2,524	5,508	3	2,984 D	31.4%	68.6%	31.4%	68.6%
26,493	DANVERS	9,754	4,395	5,346	13	951 D	45.1%	54.8%	45.1%	54.9%
34,032	DARTMOUTH	9,097	3,280	5,811	6	2,531 D	36.1%	63.9%	36.1%	63.9%
24,729	DEDHAM	9,340	3,624	5,706	10	2,082 D	38.8%	61.1%	38.8%	61.2%
29,457	DRACUT	10,217	5,138	5,022	57	116 R	50.3%	49.2%	50.6%	49.4%
23,112	EASTON	7,931	3,921	3,996	14	75 D	49.4%	50.4%	49.5%	50.5%
41,667	EVERETT	8,731	1,970	6,747	14	4,777 D	22.6%	77.3%	22.6%	77.4%
88,857	FALL RIVER	16,062	4,670	11,383	9	6,713 D	29.1%	70.9%	29.1%	70.9%
31,531	FALMOUTH	14,043	5,973	8,061	9	2,088 D	42.5%	57.4%	42.6%	57.4%
40,318	FITCHBURG	8,558	3,569	4,983	6	1,414 D	41.7%	58.2%	41.7%	58.3%
68,318	FRAMINGHAM	18,431	5,996	12,409	26	6,413 D	32.5%	67.3%	32.6%	67.4%
31,635	FRANKLIN	11,706	5,804	5,886	16	82 D	49.6%	50.3%	49.6%	50.4%
28,789	GLOUCESTER	10,611	3,844	6,752	15	2,908 D	36.2%	63.6%	36.3%	63.7%
60,879	HAVERHILL	17,974	7,803	10,132	39	2,329 D	43.4%	56.4%	43.5%	56.5%
22,157	HINGHAM	10,013	4,785	5,228		443 D	47.8%	52.2%	47.8%	52.2%
39,880	HOLYOKE	9,763	2,681	7,065	17	4,384 D	27.5%	72.4%	27.5%	72.5%

MASSACHUSETTS
SENATOR 2014

2010 Census Population	City/Town	Total Vote	Republican (Herr)	Democratic (Markey)	Other	Rep.-Dem. Plurality	Percentage			
							Total Vote		Major Vote	
							Rep.	Dem.	Rep.	Dem.
76,377	LAWRENCE	12,931	2,483	10,396	52	7,913 D	19.2%	80.4%	19.3%	80.7%
40,759	LEOMINSTER	12,031	5,559	6,453	19	894 D	46.2%	53.6%	46.3%	53.7%
31,394	LEXINGTON	12,868	3,336	9,526	6	6,190 D	25.9%	74.0%	25.9%	74.1%
106,519	LOWELL	19,744	6,232	13,446	66	7,214 D	31.6%	68.1%	31.7%	68.3%
90,329	LYNN	19,671	5,162	14,450	59	9,288 D	26.2%	73.5%	26.3%	73.7%
59,450	MALDEN	13,635	3,132	10,476	27	7,344 D	23.0%	76.8%	23.0%	77.0%
19,808	MARBLEHEAD	9,400	3,800	5,595	5	1,795 D	40.4%	59.5%	40.4%	59.6%
38,499	MARLBOROUGH	11,272	4,752	6,512	8	1,760 D	42.2%	57.8%	42.2%	57.8%
25,132	MARSHFIELD	10,728	5,437	5,278	13	159 R	50.7%	49.2%	50.7%	49.3%
56,173	MEDFORD	18,826	4,818	13,973	35	9,155 D	25.6%	74.2%	25.6%	74.4%
26,983	MELROSE	11,403	3,767	7,619	17	3,852 D	33.0%	66.8%	33.1%	66.9%
47,255	METHUEN	13,820	6,384	7,424	12	1,040 D	46.2%	53.7%	46.2%	53.8%
27,999	MILFORD	8,705	3,906	4,781	18	875 D	44.9%	54.9%	45.0%	55.0%
27,003	MILTON	11,147	3,921	7,201	25	3,280 D	35.2%	64.6%	35.3%	64.7%
33,006	NATICK	13,280	4,823	8,449	8	3,626 D	36.3%	63.6%	36.3%	63.7%
28,886	NEEDHAM	12,829	4,531	8,279	19	3,748 D	35.3%	64.5%	35.4%	64.6%
95,072	NEW BEDFORD	17,121	4,070	13,017	34	8,947 D	23.8%	76.0%	23.8%	76.2%
85,146	NEWTON	31,781	7,745	23,983	53	16,238 D	24.4%	75.5%	24.4%	75.6%
28,352	NORTH ANDOVER	10,283	5,226	5,044	13	182 R	50.8%	49.1%	50.9%	49.1%
28,712	NORTH ATTLEBOROUGH	8,962	4,718	4,240	4	478 R	52.6%	47.3%	52.7%	47.3%
28,549	NORTHAMPTON	11,295	1,514	9,769	12	8,255 D	13.4%	86.5%	13.4%	86.6%
28,602	NORWOOD	10,173	4,216	5,940	17	1,724 D	41.4%	58.4%	41.5%	58.5%
51,251	PEABODY	18,650	7,344	11,279	27	3,935 D	39.4%	60.5%	39.4%	60.6%
44,737	PITTSFIELD	11,061	2,622	8,433	6	5,811 D	23.7%	76.2%	23.7%	76.3%
56,468	PLYMOUTH	20,784	10,229	10,535	20	306 D	49.2%	50.7%	49.3%	50.7%
92,271	QUINCY	25,852	9,110	16,669	73	7,559 D	35.2%	64.5%	35.3%	64.7%
32,112	RANDOLPH	8,943	2,102	6,824	17	4,722 D	23.5%	76.3%	23.5%	76.5%
24,747	READING	10,354	4,480	5,871	3	1,391 D	43.3%	56.7%	43.3%	56.7%
51,755	REVERE	10,852	3,095	7,731	26	4,636 D	28.5%	71.2%	28.6%	71.4%
41,340	SALEM	12,776	3,587	9,180	9	5,593 D	28.1%	71.9%	28.1%	71.9%
26,628	SAUGUS	9,565	3,983	5,579	3	1,596 D	41.6%	58.3%	41.7%	58.3%
18,133	SCITUATE	8,335	4,001	4,331	3	330 D	48.0%	52.0%	48.0%	52.0%
35,608	SHREWSBURY	12,857	6,084	6,766	7	682 D	47.3%	52.6%	47.3%	52.7%
75,754	SOMERVILLE	22,011	2,920	19,000	91	16,080 D	13.3%	86.3%	13.3%	86.7%
153,060	SPRINGFIELD	31,304	7,444	23,734	126	16,290 D	23.8%	75.8%	23.9%	76.1%
21,437	STONEHAM	8,836	3,446	5,387	3	1,941 D	39.0%	61.0%	39.0%	61.0%
26,962	STOUGHTON	9,002	3,500	5,497	5	1,997 D	38.9%	61.1%	38.9%	61.1%
55,874	TAUNTON	13,818	5,363	8,423	32	3,060 D	38.8%	61.0%	38.9%	61.1%
28,961	TEWKSBURY	11,017	5,220	5,780	17	560 D	47.4%	52.5%	47.5%	52.5%
24,932	WAKEFIELD	10,338	4,382	5,931	25	1,549 D	42.4%	57.4%	42.5%	57.5%
24,070	WALPOLE	10,234	5,172	5,048	14	124 R	50.5%	49.3%	50.6%	49.4%
60,632	WALTHAM	16,031	5,154	10,860	17	5,706 D	32.2%	67.7%	32.2%	67.8%
31,915	WATERTOWN	11,339	2,810	8,503	26	5,693 D	24.8%	75.0%	24.8%	75.2%
27,982	WELLESLEY	10,736	4,496	6,240		1,744 D	41.9%	58.1%	41.9%	58.1%
28,391	WEST SPRINGFIELD	7,882	3,698	4,173	11	475 D	46.9%	52.9%	47.0%	53.0%
41,094	WESTFIELD	12,029	5,825	6,194	10	369 D	48.4%	51.5%	48.5%	51.5%
53,743	WEYMOUTH	19,422	8,205	11,176	41	2,971 D	42.2%	57.5%	42.3%	57.7%
21,374	WINCHESTER	9,463	3,762	5,701		1,939 D	39.8%	60.2%	39.8%	60.2%
38,120	WOBURN	13,341	5,314	8,003	24	2,689 D	39.8%	60.0%	39.9%	60.1%
181,045	WORCESTER	36,927	11,923	24,897	107	12,974 D	32.3%	67.4%	32.4%	67.6%
23,793	YARMOUTH	9,906	4,675	5,225	6	550 D	47.2%	52.7%	47.2%	52.8%

MASSACHUSETTS

HOUSE OF REPRESENTATIVES

CD	Year	Total Vote	Republican		Democratic		Other Vote	Rep.-Dem. Plurality	Percentage			
									Total Vote		Major Vote	
			Vote	Candidate	Vote	Candidate			Rep.	Dem.	Rep.	Dem.
1	2014	171,110			167,612	NEAL, RICHARD E.*	3,498	167,612 D		98.0%		100.0%
1	2012	266,133			261,936	NEAL, RICHARD E.*	4,197	261,936 D		98.4%		100.0%
2	2014	172,745			169,640	MCGOVERN, JAMES P.*	3,105	169,640 D		98.2%		100.0%
2	2012	263,335			259,257	MCGOVERN, JAMES P.*	4,078	259,257 D		98.5%		100.0%
3	2014	220,946	81,638	WOFFORD, ROSEANN EHRHARD	139,104	TSONGAS, NIKI*	204	57,466 D	36.9%	63.0%	37.0%	63.0%
3	2012	321,753	109,372	GOLNIK, JONATHAN A.	212,119	TSONGAS, NIKI*	262	102,747 D	34.0%	65.9%	34.0%	66.0%
4	2014	188,098			184,158	KENNEDY, JOSEPH P. III*	3,940	184,158 D		97.9%		100.0%
4	2012	362,245	129,936	BIELAT, SEAN	221,303	KENNEDY, JOSEPH P. III	11,006	91,367 D	35.9%	61.1%	37.0%	63.0%
5	2014	185,260			182,100	CLARK, KATHERINE M.*	3,160	182,100 D		98.3%		100.0%
5	2012	341,109	82,944	TIERNEY, TOM	257,490	MARKEY, EDWARD J.*	675	174,546 D	24.3%	75.5%	24.4%	75.6%
6	2014	272,219	111,989	TISEI, RICHARD	149,638	MOULTON, SETH	10,592	37,649 D	41.1%	55.0%	42.8%	57.2%
6	2012	374,807	176,612	TISEI, RICHARD	180,942	TIERNEY, JOHN F.*	17,253	4,330 D	47.1%	48.3%	49.4%	50.6%
7	2014	144,546			142,133	CAPUANO, MICHAEL E.*	2,413	142,133 D		98.3%		100.0%
7	2012	252,836			210,794	CAPUANO, MICHAEL E.*	42,042	210,794 D		83.4%		100.0%
8	2014	203,351			200,644	LYNCH, STEPHEN F.*	2,707	200,644 D		98.7%		100.0%
8	2012	346,811	82,242	SELVAGGI, JOE	263,999	LYNCH, STEPHEN F.*	570	181,757 D	23.7%	76.1%	23.8%	76.2%
9	2014	255,541	114,971	CHAPMAN, JOHN C.	140,413	KEATING, WILLIAM R.*	157	25,442 D	45.0%	54.9%	45.0%	55.0%
9	2012	362,405	116,531	SHELDON, CHRISTOPHER	212,754	KEATING, WILLIAM R.*	33,120	96,223 D	32.2%	58.7%	35.4%	64.6%
TOTAL	2014	1,813,816	308,598		1,475,442		29,776	1,166,844 D	17.0%	81.3%	17.3%	82.7%
TOTAL	2012	2,891,434	697,637		2,080,594		113,203	1,382,957 D	24.1%	72.0%	25.1%	74.9%

Note: An asterisk (*) denotes incumbent.

MASSACHUSETTS

GENERAL AND PRIMARY ELECTIONS

2014 GENERAL ELECTIONS: OTHER VOTES

Governor   Other vote was 71,814 United Independent (Evan Falchuk), 19,378 Independent (Scott Lively), 16,295 Independent (Jeffrey McCormick), 1,858 scattered write-in

Senate (2014)   Other vote was 3,078 scattered write-in

Senate (2013)   Other vote was 4,550 Twelve Visions (Richard A. Heos), 2,504 scattered write-in

House   Other vote was:

CD 1   3,498 scattered write-in
CD 2   3,105 scattered write-in
CD 3   204 scattered write-in
CD 4   3,940 scattered write-in
CD 5   1 Write-in (William F. Wilt), 3,159 scattered write-in
CD 6   10,373 Independent (Christopher John Stockwell), 219 scattered write-in
CD 7   2,413 scattered write-in
CD 8   2,707 scattered write-in
CD 9   157 scattered write-in

MASSACHUSETTS

GENERAL AND PRIMARY ELECTIONS

2014 PRIMARY ELECTIONS: SUPPLEMENTARY INFORMATION

Primary	September 9, 2014	**Registration** (as of August 20, 2014)	4,260,569	Democratic Republican Other Unenrolled	1,509,269 466,487 22,242 2,262,571	

Primary Type   Semi-open—Registered Democrats and Republicans could vote only in their party's primary. "Unenrolled" voters could participate in either party's primary.

	REPUBLICAN PRIMARIES			**DEMOCRATIC PRIMARIES**		
Senator	Herr, Brian J.	117,216	99.3%	Markey, Edward J.*	402,433	98.3%
	Write-In	872	0.7%	Write-In	6,986	1.7%
	TOTAL	118,088		TOTAL	409,419	
Governor	Baker, Charlie	116,004	74.1%	Coakley, Martha	229,156	42.4%
	Fisher, Mark R.	40,240	25.7%	Grossman, Steven	196,594	36.4%
	Write-In	336	0.2%	Berwick, Donald M.	113,988	21.1%
				Write-In	995	0.2%
	TOTAL	156,580		TOTAL	540,733	
Congressional District 1	Write-In	1,059	100.0%	Neal, Richard E.*	43,225	99.1%
				Write-In	406	0.9%
	TOTAL	1,059		TOTAL	43,631	
Congressional District 2	Write-In	1,351	100.0%	McGovern, James P.*	39,852	99.3%
				Write-In	288	0.7%
	TOTAL	1,351		TOTAL	40,140	
Congressional District 3	Wofford, Roseann Ehrhard	12,731	99.3%	Tsongas, Niki*	39,152	99.0%
	Write-In	85	0.7%	Write-In	402	1.0%
	TOTAL	12,816		TOTAL	39,554	
Congressional District 4	Write-In	1,072	100.0%	Kennedy, Joseph P. III*	44,606	99.2%
				Write-In	357	0.8%
	TOTAL	1,072		TOTAL	44,963	
Congressional District 5	Write-In	1,266	100.0%	Clark, Katherine M.*	57,014	81.2%
				Schwartz, Sheldon	13,070	18.6%
				Write-In	140	0.2%
	TOTAL	1,266		TOTAL	70,224	
Congressional District 6	Tisei, Richard	18,227	99.2%	Moulton, Seth	36,575	50.8%
	Write-In	143	0.8%	Tierney, John F.*	28,915	40.1%
				Defranco, Marisa A.	4,293	6.0%
				Devine, John Patrick	1,527	2.1%
				Gutta, John	691	1.0%
				Write-In	36	
	TOTAL	18,370		TOTAL	72,037	
Congressional District 7	Write-In	734	100.0%	Capuano, Michael E.*	45,292	98.7%
				Write-In	578	1.3%
	TOTAL	734		TOTAL	45,870	
Congressional District 8	Write-In	1,488	100.0%	Lynch, Stephen F.*	51,077	99.0%
				Write-In	499	1.0%
	TOTAL	1,488		TOTAL	51,576	
Congressional District 9	Chapman, John C.	9,567	32.3%	Keating, William R.*	42,716	99.2%
	Alliegro, Mark C.	9,049	30.6%	Write-In	345	0.8%
	Shores, Daniel L.	6,973	23.6%			
	Cogliano, Vincent Anthony Jr.	3,917	13.2%			
	Write-In	69	0.2%			
	TOTAL	29,575		TOTAL	43,061	

Note: An asterisk (*) denotes incumbent.

MICHIGAN

Congressional districts first established for elections held in 2012

14 members

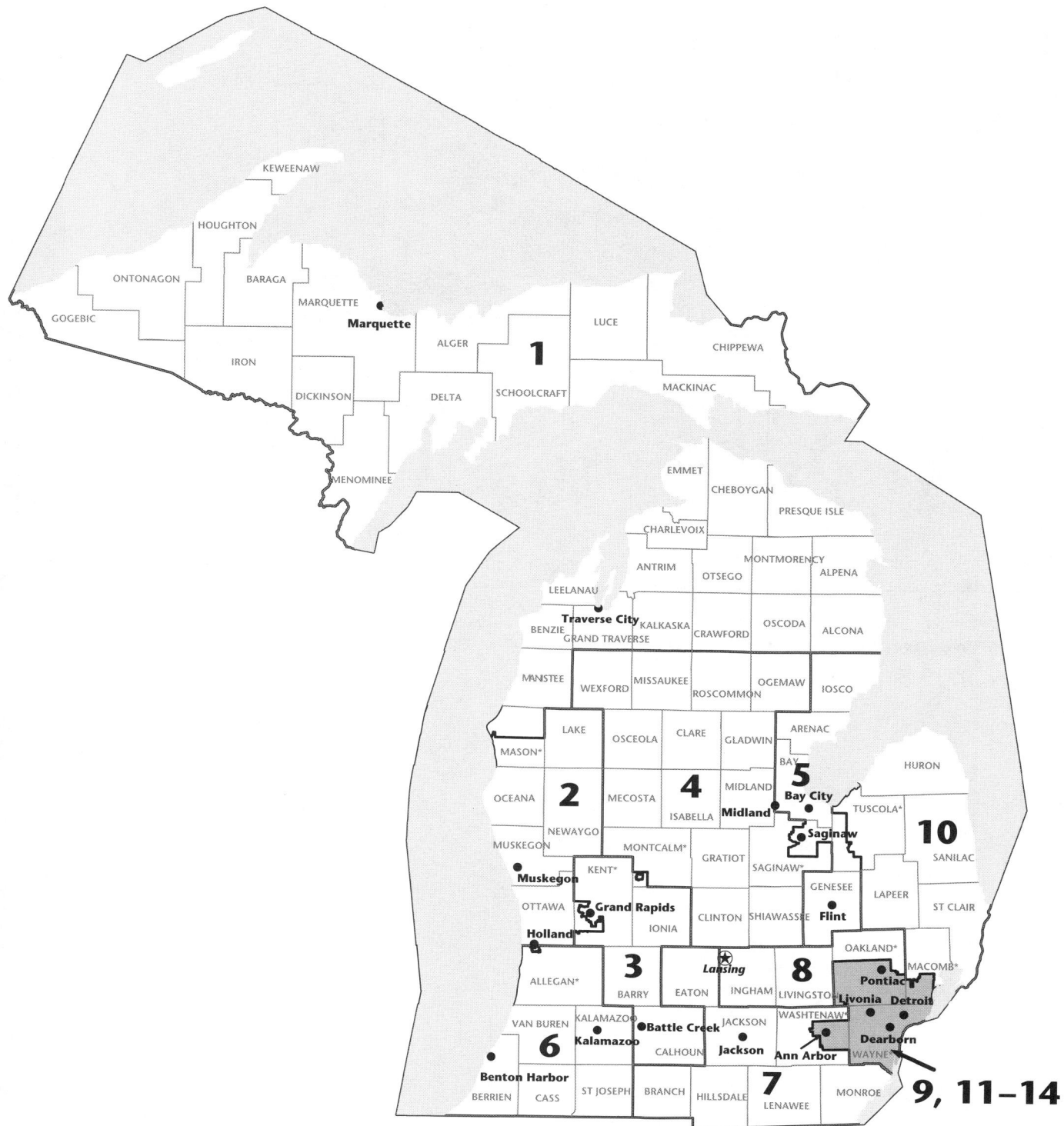

KEWEENAW

HOUGHTON

ONTONAGON

BARAGA

GOGEBIC

MARQUETTE

Marquette

IRON

DICKINSON

DELTA

ALGER

SCHOOLCRAFT

LUCE

1

CHIPPEWA

MACKINAC

MENOMINEE

EMMET

CHEBOYGAN

PRESQUE ISLE

CHARLEVOIX

LEELANAU

ANTRIM

OTSEGO

MONTMORENCY

ALPENA

Traverse City KALKASKA

BENZIE

GRAND TRAVERSE

CRAWFORD

OSCODA

ALCONA

MANISTEE

WEXFORD

MISSAUKEE

ROSCOMMON

OGEMAW

IOSCO

MASON*

LAKE

OSCEOLA

CLARE

GLADWIN

ARENAC

BAY

HURON

OCEANA

2

MECOSTA

4

MIDLAND

5 Bay City

TUSCOLA*

10

NEWAYGO

ISABELLA

Midland

Saginaw

SANILAC

MUSKEGON

MONTCALM*

GRATIOT

SAGINAW*

Muskegon

KENT*

GENESEE

LAPEER

ST CLAIR

OTTAWA

Grand Rapids

IONIA

CLINTON

SHIAWASSEE

Flint

Holland

OAKLAND*

MACOMB*

ALLEGAN*

3

Lansing

8

Pontiac

LIVINGSTON

Livonia Detroit

BARRY

EATON

INGHAM

WASHTENAW*

VAN BUREN

KALAMAZOO

JACKSON

Dearborn

Battle Creek

Kalamazoo

CALHOUN

Jackson

Ann Arbor

WAYNE

6

9, 11–14

Benton Harbor

BERRIEN

CASS

ST JOSEPH

BRANCH

HILLSDALE

7

LENAWEE

MONROE

* Asterisk indicates a county whose boundaries include parts of two or more congressional districts.

MICHIGAN
Detroit Area

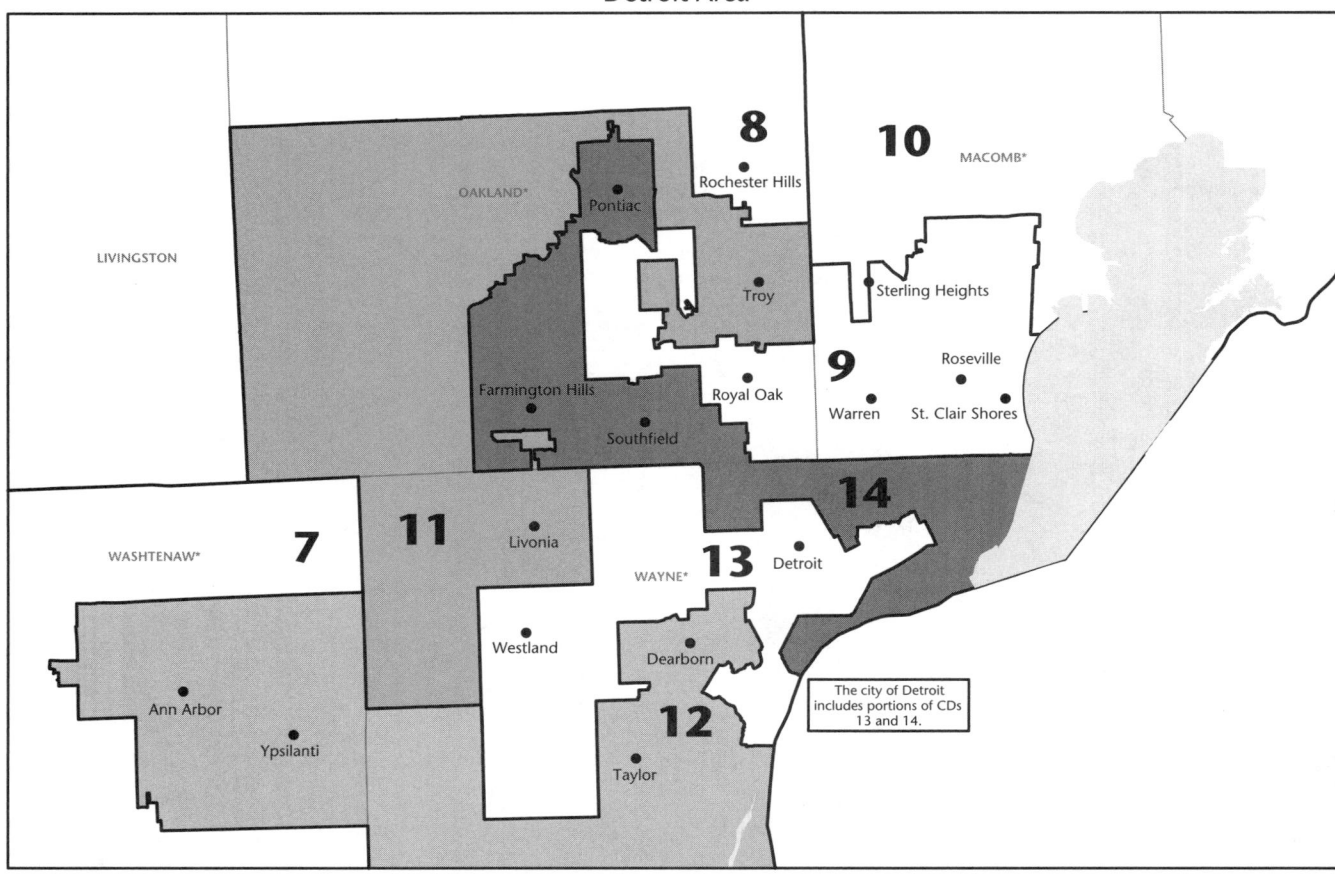

* Asterisk indicates a county whose boundaries include parts of two or more congressional districts.

MICHIGAN

GOVERNOR

Rick Snyder (R). Reelected 2014 to a four-year term. Previously elected 2010.

SENATORS (2 Democrats)

Gary Peters (D). Elected 2014 to a six-year term.

Debbie Stabenow (D). Reelected 2012 to a six-year term. Previously elected 2006, 2000.

REPRESENTATIVES (9 Republicans, 5 Democrats)

1. Dan Benishek (R)
2. Bill Huizenga (R)
3. Justin Amash (R)
4. John R. Moolenaar (R)
5. Daniel T. Kildee (D)
6. Fred Upton (R)
7. Tim Walberg (R)
8. Mike Bishop (R)
9. Sander M. Levin (D)
10. Candice S. Miller (R)
11. David A. Trott (R)
12. Debbie Dingell (D)
13. John Conyers Jr. (D)
14. Brenda L. Lawrence (D)

POSTWAR VOTE FOR PRESIDENT

Year	Total Vote	Republican Vote	Candidate	Democratic Vote	Candidate	Other Vote	Rep.-Dem. Plurality	Total Vote Rep.	Total Vote Dem.	Major Vote Rep.	Major Vote Dem.
2012	4,730,961	2,115,256	Romney, W. Mitt	2,564,569	Obama, Barack H.*	51,136	449,313 D	44.7%	54.2%	45.2%	54.8%
2008	5,001,766	2,048,639	McCain, John S. III	2,872,579	Obama, Barack H.	80,548	823,940 D	41.0%	57.4%	41.6%	58.4%
2004	4,839,252	2,313,746	Bush, George W.*	2,479,183	Kerry, John F.	46,323	165,437 D	47.8%	51.2%	48.3%	51.7%
2000**	4,232,711	1,953,139	Bush, George W.	2,170,418	Gore, Albert Jr.	109,154	217,279 D	46.1%	51.3%	47.4%	52.6%
1996**	3,848,844	1,481,212	Dole, Robert "Bob"	1,989,653	Clinton, Bill*	377,979	508,441 D	38.5%	51.7%	42.7%	57.3%
1992**	4,274,673	1,554,940	Bush, George H.*	1,871,182	Clinton, Bill	848,551	316,242 D	36.4%	43.8%	45.4%	54.6%
1988	3,669,163	1,965,486	Bush, George H.	1,675,783	Dukakis, Michael S.	27,894	289,703 R	53.6%	45.7%	54.0%	46.0%
1984	3,801,658	2,251,571	Reagan, Ronald*	1,529,638	Mondale, Walter F.	20,449	721,933 R	59.2%	40.2%	59.5%	40.5%
1980**	3,909,725	1,915,225	Reagan, Ronald	1,661,532	Carter, Jimmy*	332,968	253,693 R	49.0%	42.5%	53.5%	46.5%
1976	3,653,749	1,893,742	Ford, Gerald R.*	1,696,714	Carter, Jimmy	63,293	197,028 R	51.8%	46.4%	52.7%	47.3%
1972	3,489,727	1,961,721	Nixon, Richard M.*	1,459,435	McGovern, George S.	68,571	502,286 R	56.2%	41.8%	57.3%	42.7%
1968**	3,306,250	1,370,665	Nixon, Richard M.	1,593,082	Humphrey, Hubert Horatio Jr.	342,503	222,417 D	41.5%	48.2%	46.2%	53.8%
1964	3,203,102	1,060,152	Goldwater, Barry M. Sr.	2,136,615	Johnson, Lyndon B.*	6,335	1,076,463 D	33.1%	66.7%	33.2%	66.8%
1960	3,318,097	1,620,428	Nixon, Richard M.	1,687,269	Kennedy, John F.	10,400	66,841 D	48.8%	50.9%	49.0%	51.0%
1956	3,080,468	1,713,647	Eisenhower, Dwight D.*	1,359,898	Stevenson, Adlai E. II	6,923	353,749 R	55.6%	44.1%	55.8%	44.2%
1952	2,798,592	1,551,529	Eisenhower, Dwight D.	1,230,657	Stevenson, Adlai E. II	16,406	320,872 R	55.4%	44.0%	55.8%	44.2%
1948	2,109,609	1,038,595	Dewey, Thomas E.	1,003,448	Truman, Harry S.*	67,566	35,147 R	49.2%	47.6%	50.9%	49.1%

Note: An asterisk (*) denotes incumbent. **In past elections, the other vote included: 2000 - 84,165 Green (Ralph Nader); 1996 - 336,670 Reform (Ross Perot); 1992 - 824,813 Independent (Perot); 1980 - 275,223 Independent (John Anderson); 1968 - 331,968 American Independent (George Wallace).

MICHIGAN

POSTWAR VOTE FOR GOVERNOR

Year	Total Vote	Republican Vote	Republican Candidate	Democratic Vote	Democratic Candidate	Other Vote	Rep.-Dem. Plurality	Total Vote Rep.	Total Vote Dem.	Major Vote Rep.	Major Vote Dem.
2014	3,156,531	1,607,399	Snyder, Rick*	1,479,057	Schauer, Mark H.	70,075	128,342 R	50.9%	46.9%	52.1%	47.9%
2010	3,226,088	1,874,834	Snyder, Rick	1,287,320	Bernero, Virg	63,934	587,514 R	58.1%	39.9%	59.3%	40.7%
2006	3,801,256	1,608,086	DeVos, Dick	2,142,513	Granholm, Jennifer M.*	50,657	534,427 D	42.3%	56.4%	42.9%	57.1%
2002	3,177,565	1,506,104	Posthumus, Dick	1,633,796	Granholm, Jennifer M.	37,665	127,692 D	47.4%	51.4%	48.0%	52.0%
1998	3,027,104	1,883,005	Engler, John*	1,143,574	Fieger, Geoffrey	525	739,431 R	62.2%	37.8%	62.2%	37.8%
1994	3,089,077	1,899,101	Engler, John*	1,188,438	Wolpe, Howard	1,538	710,663 R	61.5%	38.5%	61.5%	38.5%
1990	2,564,563	1,276,134	Engler, John	1,258,539	Blanchard, James J.*	29,890	17,595 R	49.8%	49.1%	50.3%	49.7%
1986	2,396,564	753,647	Lucas, William	1,632,138	Blanchard, James J.*	10,779	878,491 D	31.4%	68.1%	31.6%	68.4%
1982	3,040,008	1,369,582	Headlee, Richard H.	1,561,291	Blanchard, James J.	109,135	191,709 D	45.1%	51.4%	46.7%	53.3%
1978	2,867,212	1,628,485	Milliken, William G.*	1,237,256	Fitzgerald, William	1,471	391,229 R	56.8%	43.2%	56.8%	43.2%
1974	2,657,020	1,356,865	Milliken, William G.*	1,242,250	Levin, Sander M.	57,905	114,615 R	51.1%	46.8%	52.2%	47.8%
1970	2,656,093	1,338,711	Milliken, William G.*	1,294,600	Levin, Sander M.	22,782	44,111 R	50.4%	48.7%	50.8%	49.2%
1966**	2,461,909	1,490,430	Romney, George W.*	963,383	Ferency, Zolton A.	8,096	527,047 R	60.5%	39.1%	60.7%	39.3%
1964	3,158,102	1,764,355	Romney, George W.*	1,381,442	Staebler, Neil	12,305	382,913 R	55.9%	43.7%	56.1%	43.9%
1962	2,764,839	1,420,086	Romney, George W.	1,339,513	Swainson, John B.*	5,240	80,573 R	51.4%	48.4%	51.5%	48.5%
1960	3,255,991	1,602,022	Bagwell, Paul D.	1,643,634	Swainson, John B.	10,335	41,612 D	49.2%	50.5%	49.4%	50.6%
1958	2,312,184	1,078,089	Bagwell, Paul D.	1,225,533	Williams, G. Mennen*	8,562	147,444 D	46.6%	53.0%	46.8%	53.2%
1956	3,049,651	1,376,376	Cobo, Albert E.	1,666,689	Williams, G. Mennen*	6,586	290,313 D	45.1%	54.7%	45.2%	54.8%
1954	2,187,027	963,300	Leonard, Donald S.	1,216,308	Williams, G. Mennen*	7,419	253,008 D	44.0%	55.6%	44.2%	55.8%
1952	2,865,980	1,423,275	Alger, Fred M. Jr.	1,431,893	Williams, G. Mennen*	10,812	8,618 D	49.7%	50.0%	49.8%	50.2%
1950	1,879,382	933,998	Kelly, Harry F.	935,152	Williams, G. Mennen	10,232	1,154 D	49.7%	49.8%	50.0%	50.0%
1948	2,113,122	964,810	Sigler, Kim*	1,128,664	Williams, G. Mennen	19,648	163,854 D	45.7%	53.4%	46.1%	53.9%
1946	1,665,475	1,003,878	Sigler, Kim	644,540	Van Wagoner, Murray D.	17,057	359,338 R	60.3%	38.7%	60.9%	39.1%

Note: An asterisk (*) denotes incumbent. **The term of office of Michigan's governor was increased from two to four years effective with the 1966 election.

POSTWAR VOTE FOR SENATOR

Year	Total Vote	Republican Vote	Republican Candidate	Democratic Vote	Democratic Candidate	Other Vote	Rep.-Dem. Plurality	Total Vote Rep.	Total Vote Dem.	Major Vote Rep.	Major Vote Dem.
2014	3,121,775	1,290,199	Land, Terri Lynn	1,704,936	Peters, Gary	126,640	414,737 D	41.3%	54.6%	43.1%	56.9%
2012	4,652,918	1,767,386	Hoekstra, Peter	2,735,826	Stabenow, Debbie*	149,706	968,440 D	38.0%	58.8%	39.2%	60.8%
2008	4,848,620	1,641,070	Hoogendyk, Jack Jr.	3,038,386	Levin, Carl*	169,164	1,397,316 D	33.8%	62.7%	35.1%	64.9%
2006	3,780,142	1,559,597	Bouchard, Michael	2,151,278	Stabenow, Debbie*	69,267	591,681 D	41.3%	56.9%	42.0%	58.0%
2002	3,129,281	1,185,545	Raczkowski, Andrew	1,896,614	Levin, Carl*	47,128	711,069 D	37.9%	60.6%	38.5%	61.5%
2000	4,167,685	1,994,693	Abraham, Spencer*	2,061,952	Stabenow, Debbie	111,040	67,259 D	47.9%	49.5%	49.2%	50.8%
1996	3,762,575	1,500,106	Romney, Ronna	2,195,738	Levin, Carl*	66,731	695,632 D	39.9%	58.4%	40.6%	59.4%
1994	3,043,385	1,578,770	Abraham, Spencer	1,300,960	Carr, M. Robert	163,655	277,810 R	51.9%	42.7%	54.8%	45.2%
1990	2,560,494	1,055,695	Schuette, Bill	1,471,753	Levin, Carl*	33,046	416,058 D	41.2%	57.5%	41.8%	58.2%
1988	3,505,985	1,348,219	Dunn, Jim	2,116,865	Riegle, Donald Wayne Jr.*	40,901	768,646 D	38.5%	60.4%	38.9%	61.1%
1984	3,700,938	1,745,302	Lousma, Jack	1,915,831	Levin, Carl*	39,805	170,529 D	47.2%	51.8%	47.7%	52.3%
1982	2,994,334	1,223,288	Ruppe, Philip E.	1,728,793	Riegle, Donald Wayne Jr.*	42,253	505,505 D	40.9%	57.7%	41.4%	58.6%
1978	2,846,630	1,362,165	Griffin, Robert P.*	1,484,193	Levin, Carl	272	122,028 D	47.9%	52.1%	47.9%	52.1%
1976	3,484,664	1,635,087	Esch, Marvin L.	1,831,031	Riegle, Donald Wayne Jr.	18,546	195,944 D	46.9%	52.5%	47.2%	52.8%
1972	3,406,906	1,781,065	Griffin, Robert P.*	1,577,178	Kelley, Frank J.	48,663	203,887 R	52.3%	46.3%	53.0%	47.0%
1970	2,610,763	858,438	Romney, Lenore	1,744,672	Hart, Philip A.*	7,653	886,234 D	32.9%	66.8%	33.0%	67.0%
1966	2,439,365	1,363,530	Griffin, Robert P.*	1,069,484	Williams, G. Mennen	6,351	294,046 R	55.9%	43.8%	56.0%	44.0%
1964	3,101,667	1,096,272	Peterson, Elly M.	1,996,912	Hart, Philip A.*	8,483	900,640 D	35.3%	64.4%	35.4%	64.6%
1960	3,226,647	1,548,873	Bentley, Alvin M.	1,669,179	McNamara, Patrick V.*	8,595	120,306 D	48.0%	51.7%	48.1%	51.9%
1958	2,271,644	1,046,963	Potter, Charles E.*	1,216,966	Hart, Philip A.	7,715	170,003 D	46.1%	53.6%	46.2%	53.8%
1954	2,144,840	1,049,420	Ferguson, Homer*	1,088,550	McNamara, Patrick V.	6,870	39,130 D	48.9%	50.8%	49.1%	50.9%
1952	2,821,133	1,428,352	Potter, Charles E.	1,383,416	Moody, Blair	9,365	44,936 R	50.6%	49.0%	50.8%	49.2%
1948	2,062,097	1,045,156	Ferguson, Homer*	1,000,329	Hook, Frank E.	16,612	44,827 R	50.7%	48.5%	51.1%	48.9%
1946	1,618,720	1,085,570	Vandenberg, Arthur H.*	517,923	Lee, James H.	15,227	567,647 R	67.1%	32.0%	67.7%	32.3%

Note: An asterisk (*) denotes incumbent.

MICHIGAN
GOVERNOR 2014

2010 Census Population	County	Total Vote	Republican (Snyder)	Democratic (Schauer)	Other	Rep.-Dem. Plurality		Percentage			
								Total Vote		Major Vote	
								Rep.	Dem.	Rep.	Dem.
10,942	ALCONA	4,466	2,529	1,806	131	723 R		56.6%	40.4%	58.3%	41.7%
9,601	ALGER	3,283	1,520	1,646	117	126 D		46.3%	50.1%	48.0%	52.0%
111,408	ALLEGAN	35,453	23,301	11,187	965	12,114 R		65.7%	31.6%	67.6%	32.4%
29,598	ALPENA	9,620	4,810	4,546	264	264 R		50.0%	47.3%	51.4%	48.6%
23,580	ANTRIM	9,519	5,881	3,407	231	2,474 R		61.8%	35.8%	63.3%	36.7%
15,899	ARENAC	5,378	2,708	2,459	211	249 R		50.4%	45.7%	52.4%	47.6%
8,860	BARAGA	2,487	1,180	1,249	58	69 D		47.4%	50.2%	48.6%	51.4%
59,173	BARRY	20,064	12,824	6,760	480	6,064 R		63.9%	33.7%	65.5%	34.5%
107,771	BAY	38,202	17,899	19,307	996	1,408 D		46.9%	50.5%	48.1%	51.9%
17,525	BENZIE	7,227	3,823	3,183	221	640 R		52.9%	44.0%	54.6%	45.4%
156,813	BERRIEN	43,479	24,173	18,042	1,264	6,131 R		55.6%	41.5%	57.3%	42.7%
45,248	BRANCH	11,291	7,050	3,907	334	3,143 R		62.4%	34.6%	64.3%	35.7%
136,146	CALHOUN	37,966	20,425	16,709	832	3,716 R		53.8%	44.0%	55.0%	45.0%
52,293	CASS	13,422	7,521	5,425	476	2,096 R		56.0%	40.4%	58.1%	41.9%
25,949	CHARLEVOIX	10,549	6,255	3,998	296	2,257 R		59.3%	37.9%	61.0%	39.0%
26,152	CHEBOYGAN	9,579	5,287	4,005	287	1,282 R		55.2%	41.8%	56.9%	43.1%
38,520	CHIPPEWA	11,078	5,590	5,166	322	424 R		50.5%	46.6%	52.0%	48.0%
30,926	CLARE	9,261	4,660	4,210	391	450 R		50.3%	45.5%	52.5%	47.5%
75,382	CLINTON	29,118	15,946	12,723	449	3,223 R		54.8%	43.7%	55.6%	44.4%
14,074	CRAWFORD	4,758	2,656	1,962	140	694 R		55.8%	41.2%	57.5%	42.5%
37,069	DELTA	13,418	7,072	6,054	292	1,018 R		52.7%	45.1%	53.9%	46.1%
26,168	DICKINSON	8,573	5,025	3,374	174	1,651 R		58.6%	39.4%	59.8%	40.2%
107,759	EATON	41,041	20,026	20,263	752	237 D		48.8%	49.4%	49.7%	50.3%
32,694	EMMET	13,020	8,063	4,580	377	3,483 R		61.9%	35.2%	63.8%	36.2%
425,790	GENESEE	131,596	48,896	79,566	3,134	30,670 D		37.2%	60.5%	38.1%	61.9%
25,692	GLADWIN	8,606	4,579	3,735	292	844 R		53.2%	43.4%	55.1%	44.9%
16,427	GOGEBIC	5,048	2,306	2,628	114	322 D		45.7%	52.1%	46.7%	53.3%
86,986	GRAND TRAVERSE	33,366	19,461	12,992	913	6,469 R		58.3%	38.9%	60.0%	40.0%
42,476	GRATIOT	10,939	5,670	4,986	283	684 R		51.8%	45.6%	53.2%	46.8%
46,688	HILLSDALE	13,313	8,309	4,598	406	3,711 R		62.4%	34.5%	64.4%	35.6%
36,628	HOUGHTON	10,360	5,581	4,449	330	1,132 R		53.9%	42.9%	55.6%	44.4%
33,118	HURON	11,831	7,143	4,377	311	2,766 R		60.4%	37.0%	62.0%	38.0%
280,895	INGHAM	87,019	35,392	50,002	1,625	14,610 D		40.7%	57.5%	41.4%	58.6%
63,905	IONIA	18,010	10,424	7,093	493	3,331 R		57.9%	39.4%	59.5%	40.5%
25,887	IOSCO	9,457	5,095	4,063	299	1,032 R		53.9%	43.0%	55.6%	44.4%
11,817	IRON	4,223	2,262	1,839	122	423 R		53.6%	43.5%	55.2%	44.8%
70,311	ISABELLA	16,438	8,031	7,871	536	160 R		48.9%	47.9%	50.5%	49.5%
160,248	JACKSON	46,233	25,672	19,563	998	6,109 R		55.5%	42.3%	56.8%	43.2%
250,331	KALAMAZOO	81,160	41,409	37,524	2,227	3,885 R		51.0%	46.2%	52.5%	47.5%
17,153	KALKASKA	5,781	3,330	2,202	249	1,128 R		57.6%	38.1%	60.2%	39.8%
602,622	KENT	188,372	116,967	67,289	4,116	49,678 R		62.1%	35.7%	63.5%	36.5%
2,156	KEWEENAW	1,114	639	444	31	195 R		57.4%	39.9%	59.0%	41.0%
11,539	LAKE	3,520	1,745	1,656	119	89 R		49.6%	47.0%	51.3%	48.7%
88,319	LAPEER	29,629	17,024	11,614	991	5,410 R		57.5%	39.2%	59.4%	40.6%
21,708	LEELANAU	11,006	6,172	4,600	234	1,572 R		56.1%	41.8%	57.3%	42.7%
99,892	LENAWEE	29,074	15,576	12,664	834	2,912 R		53.6%	43.6%	55.2%	44.8%
180,967	LIVINGSTON	70,022	47,113	21,484	1,425	25,629 R		67.3%	30.7%	68.7%	31.3%
6,631	LUCE	1,913	1,046	810	57	236 R		54.7%	42.3%	56.4%	43.6%
11,113	MACKINAC	4,509	2,414	1,996	99	418 R		53.5%	44.3%	54.7%	45.3%
840,978	MACOMB	265,103	142,836	116,651	5,616	26,185 R		53.9%	44.0%	55.0%	45.0%
24,733	MANISTEE	9,256	4,362	4,652	242	290 D		47.1%	50.3%	48.4%	51.6%
67,077	MARQUETTE	22,254	9,264	12,458	532	3,194 D		41.6%	56.0%	42.6%	57.4%
28,705	MASON	10,063	5,455	4,330	278	1,125 R		54.2%	43.0%	55.7%	44.3%
42,798	MECOSTA	11,697	6,491	4,854	352	1,637 R		55.5%	41.5%	57.2%	42.8%
24,029	MENOMINEE	6,500	3,635	2,729	136	906 R		55.9%	42.0%	57.1%	42.9%
83,629	MIDLAND	29,026	17,669	10,607	750	7,062 R		60.9%	36.5%	62.5%	37.5%
14,849	MISSAUKEE	4,884	3,209	1,541	134	1,668 R		65.7%	31.6%	67.6%	32.4%
152,021	MONROE	46,999	24,271	21,447	1,281	2,824 R		51.6%	45.6%	53.1%	46.9%
63,342	MONTCALM	17,173	9,866	6,686	621	3,180 R		57.5%	38.9%	59.6%	40.4%
9,765	MONTMORENCY	3,540	1,912	1,497	131	415 R		54.0%	42.3%	56.1%	43.9%

MICHIGAN

GOVERNOR 2014

2010 Census Population	County	Total Vote	Republican (Snyder)	Democratic (Schauer)	Other	Rep.-Dem. Plurality	Percentage			
							Total Vote		Major Vote	
							Rep.	Dem.	Rep.	Dem.
172,188	MUSKEGON	49,071	22,879	24,752	1,440	1,873 D	46.6%	50.4%	48.0%	52.0%
48,460	NEWAYGO	14,528	8,980	5,031	517	3,949 R	61.8%	34.6%	64.1%	35.9%
1,202,362	OAKLAND	446,666	247,876	191,375	7,415	56,501 R	55.5%	42.8%	56.4%	43.6%
26,570	OCEANA	8,284	4,999	3,045	240	1,954 R	60.3%	36.8%	62.1%	37.9%
21,699	OGEMAW	6,983	3,622	3,095	266	527 R	51.9%	44.3%	53.9%	46.1%
6,780	ONTONAGON	2,535	1,295	1,156	84	139 R	51.1%	45.6%	52.8%	47.2%
23,528	OSCEOLA	7,238	4,337	2,642	259	1,695 R	59.9%	36.5%	62.1%	37.9%
8,640	OSCODA	2,778	1,498	1,158	122	340 R	53.9%	41.7%	56.4%	43.6%
24,164	OTSEGO	8,545	5,085	3,211	249	1,874 R	59.5%	37.6%	61.3%	38.7%
263,801	OTTAWA	89,549	65,892	21,956	1,701	43,936 R	73.6%	24.5%	75.0%	25.0%
13,376	PRESQUE ISLE	5,264	2,743	2,365	156	378 R	52.1%	44.9%	53.7%	46.3%
24,449	ROSCOMMON	9,204	4,861	4,070	273	791 R	52.8%	44.2%	54.4%	45.6%
200,169	SAGINAW	67,145	30,266	35,370	1,509	5,104 D	45.1%	52.7%	46.1%	53.9%
43,114	SANILAC	12,642	7,986	4,288	368	3,698 R	63.2%	33.9%	65.1%	34.9%
8,485	SCHOOLCRAFT	2,889	1,507	1,321	61	186 R	52.2%	45.7%	53.3%	46.7%
70,648	SHIAWASSEE	24,286	12,266	11,251	769	1,015 R	50.5%	46.3%	52.2%	47.8%
163,040	ST. CLAIR	51,762	28,666	21,546	1,550	7,120 R	55.4%	41.6%	57.1%	42.9%
61,295	ST. JOSEPH	14,907	9,124	5,308	475	3,816 R	61.2%	35.6%	63.2%	36.8%
55,729	TUSCOLA	17,904	9,804	7,530	570	2,274 R	54.8%	42.1%	56.6%	43.4%
76,258	VAN BUREN	22,228	12,310	9,250	668	3,060 R	55.4%	41.6%	57.1%	42.9%
344,791	WASHTENAW	120,912	50,394	68,275	2,243	17,881 D	41.7%	56.5%	42.5%	57.5%
1,820,584	WAYNE	509,884	177,691	323,762	8,431	146,071 D	34.8%	63.5%	35.4%	64.6%
32,735	WEXFORD	10,041	5,868	3,835	338	2,033 R	58.4%	38.2%	60.5%	39.5%
9,883,640	TOTAL	3,156,531	1,607,399	1,479,057	70,075	128,342 R	50.9%	46.9%	52.1%	47.9%

MICHIGAN

SENATOR 2014

2010 Census Population	County	Total Vote	Republican (Land)	Democratic (Peters)	Other	Rep.-Dem. Plurality	Percentage			
							Total Vote		Major Vote	
							Rep.	Dem.	Rep.	Dem.
10,942	ALCONA	4,441	2,330	1,983	128	347 R	52.5%	44.7%	54.0%	46.0%
9,601	ALGER	3,251	1,520	1,621	110	101 D	46.8%	49.9%	48.4%	51.6%
111,408	ALLEGAN	35,210	19,739	13,667	1,804	6,072 R	56.1%	38.8%	59.1%	40.9%
29,598	ALPENA	9,550	4,497	4,782	271	285 D	47.1%	50.1%	48.5%	51.5%
23,580	ANTRIM	9,455	5,134	3,937	384	1,197 R	54.3%	41.6%	56.6%	43.4%
15,899	ARENAC	5,282	2,153	2,827	302	674 D	40.8%	53.5%	43.2%	56.8%
8,860	BARAGA	2,470	1,227	1,176	67	51 R	49.7%	47.6%	51.1%	48.9%
59,173	BARRY	19,897	10,501	8,262	1,134	2,239 R	52.8%	41.5%	56.0%	44.0%
107,771	BAY	37,766	14,083	21,934	1,749	7,851 D	37.3%	58.1%	39.1%	60.9%
17,525	BENZIE	7,185	3,342	3,557	286	215 D	46.5%	49.5%	48.4%	51.6%
156,813	BERRIEN	43,088	24,746	16,968	1,374	7,778 R	57.4%	39.4%	59.3%	40.7%
45,248	BRANCH	11,173	6,099	4,475	599	1,624 R	54.6%	40.1%	57.7%	42.3%
136,146	CALHOUN	37,543	16,582	19,038	1,923	2,456 D	44.2%	50.7%	46.6%	53.4%
52,293	CASS	13,340	8,025	4,828	487	3,197 R	60.2%	36.2%	62.4%	37.6%
25,949	CHARLEVOIX	10,443	5,470	4,568	405	902 R	52.4%	43.7%	54.5%	45.5%
26,152	CHEBOYGAN	9,481	4,680	4,400	401	280 R	49.4%	46.4%	51.5%	48.5%
38,520	CHIPPEWA	10,974	5,191	5,340	443	149 D	47.3%	48.7%	49.3%	50.7%
30,926	CLARE	9,170	4,090	4,475	605	385 D	44.6%	48.8%	47.8%	52.2%
75,382	CLINTON	28,743	13,397	14,411	935	1,014 D	46.6%	50.1%	48.2%	51.8%
14,074	CRAWFORD	4,691	2,323	2,132	236	191 R	49.5%	45.4%	52.1%	47.9%

MICHIGAN
SENATOR 2014

2010 Census Population	County	Total Vote	Republican (Land)	Democratic (Peters)	Other	Rep.-Dem. Plurality	Percentage Total Vote Rep.	Dem.	Major Vote Rep.	Dem.
37,069	DELTA	13,296	6,863	6,114	319	749 R	51.6%	46.0%	52.9%	47.1%
26,168	DICKINSON	8,478	4,915	3,366	197	1,549 R	58.0%	39.7%	59.4%	40.6%
107,759	EATON	40,630	17,068	22,070	1,492	5,002 D	42.0%	54.3%	43.6%	56.4%
32,694	EMMET	12,906	6,932	5,497	477	1,435 R	53.7%	42.6%	55.8%	44.2%
425,790	GENESEE	130,773	39,895	86,097	4,781	46,202 D	30.5%	65.8%	31.7%	68.3%
25,692	GLADWIN	8,556	3,813	4,272	471	459 D	44.6%	49.9%	47.2%	52.8%
16,427	GOGEBIC	4,971	2,269	2,566	136	297 D	45.6%	51.6%	46.9%	53.1%
86,986	GRAND TRAVERSE	32,947	16,575	15,029	1,343	1,546 R	50.3%	45.6%	52.4%	47.6%
42,476	GRATIOT	10,798	4,815	5,523	460	708 D	44.6%	51.1%	46.6%	53.4%
46,688	HILLSDALE	13,152	7,623	4,891	638	2,732 R	58.0%	37.2%	60.9%	39.1%
36,628	HOUGHTON	10,314	5,390	4,620	304	770 R	52.3%	44.8%	53.8%	46.2%
33,118	HURON	11,603	5,962	5,190	451	772 R	51.4%	44.7%	53.5%	46.5%
280,895	INGHAM	86,281	27,541	55,895	2,845	28,354 D	31.9%	64.8%	33.0%	67.0%
63,905	IONIA	17,742	8,581	8,189	972	392 R	48.4%	46.2%	51.2%	48.8%
25,887	IOSCO	9,368	3,974	4,918	476	944 D	42.4%	52.5%	44.7%	55.3%
11,817	IRON	4,188	2,166	1,877	145	289 R	51.7%	44.8%	53.6%	46.4%
70,311	ISABELLA	16,267	6,582	8,869	816	2,287 D	40.5%	54.5%	42.6%	57.4%
160,248	JACKSON	45,669	21,616	22,094	1,959	478 D	47.3%	48.4%	49.5%	50.5%
250,331	KALAMAZOO	80,282	32,663	43,453	4,166	10,790 D	40.7%	54.1%	42.9%	57.1%
17,153	KALKASKA	5,721	2,905	2,448	368	457 R	50.8%	42.8%	54.3%	45.7%
602,622	KENT	186,882	97,314	81,904	7,664	15,410 R	52.1%	43.8%	54.3%	45.7%
2,156	KEWEENAW	1,097	620	447	30	173 R	56.5%	40.7%	58.1%	41.9%
11,539	LAKE	3,488	1,492	1,780	216	288 D	42.8%	51.0%	45.6%	54.4%
88,319	LAPEER	29,271	14,411	13,184	1,676	1,227 R	49.2%	45.0%	52.2%	47.8%
21,708	LEELANAU	10,930	5,243	5,340	347	97 D	48.0%	48.9%	49.5%	50.5%
99,892	LENAWEE	28,614	14,913	12,584	1,117	2,329 R	52.1%	44.0%	54.2%	45.8%
180,967	LIVINGSTON	68,877	37,633	27,872	3,372	9,761 R	54.6%	40.5%	57.5%	42.5%
6,631	LUCE	1,904	992	835	77	157 R	52.1%	43.9%	54.3%	45.7%
11,113	MACKINAC	4,468	2,221	2,082	165	139 R	49.7%	46.6%	51.6%	48.4%
840,978	MACOMB	261,008	108,147	140,600	12,261	32,453 D	41.4%	53.9%	43.5%	56.5%
24,733	MANISTEE	9,164	3,921	4,867	376	946 D	42.8%	53.1%	44.6%	55.4%
67,077	MARQUETTE	22,100	8,867	12,616	617	3,749 D	40.1%	57.1%	41.3%	58.7%
28,705	MASON	9,967	4,849	4,720	398	129 R	48.7%	47.4%	50.7%	49.3%
42,798	MECOSTA	11,598	5,763	5,224	611	539 R	49.7%	45.0%	52.5%	47.5%
24,029	MENOMINEE	6,423	3,662	2,607	154	1,055 R	57.0%	40.6%	58.4%	41.6%
83,629	MIDLAND	28,693	14,891	12,690	1,112	2,201 R	51.9%	44.2%	54.0%	46.0%
14,849	MISSAUKEE	4,875	3,044	1,605	226	1,439 R	62.4%	32.9%	65.5%	34.5%
152,021	MONROE	46,045	20,838	22,957	2,250	2,119 D	45.3%	49.9%	47.6%	52.4%
63,342	MONTCALM	17,030	8,198	7,744	1,088	454 R	48.1%	45.5%	51.4%	48.6%
9,765	MONTMORENCY	3,514	1,771	1,557	186	214 R	50.4%	44.3%	53.2%	46.8%
172,188	MUSKEGON	48,619	18,307	27,784	2,528	9,477 D	37.7%	57.1%	39.7%	60.3%
48,460	NEWAYGO	14,450	7,769	5,815	866	1,954 R	53.8%	40.2%	57.2%	42.8%
1,202,362	OAKLAND	441,330	179,474	246,241	15,615	66,767 D	40.7%	55.8%	42.2%	57.8%
26,570	OCEANA	8,164	4,190	3,514	460	676 R	51.3%	43.0%	54.4%	45.6%
21,699	OGEMAW	6,897	2,980	3,511	406	531 D	43.2%	50.9%	45.9%	54.1%
6,780	ONTONAGON	2,514	1,263	1,174	77	89 R	50.2%	46.7%	51.8%	48.2%
23,528	OSCEOLA	7,172	3,930	2,823	419	1,107 R	54.8%	39.4%	58.2%	41.8%
8,640	OSCODA	2,745	1,367	1,194	184	173 R	49.8%	43.5%	53.4%	46.6%
24,164	OTSEGO	8,465	4,564	3,523	378	1,041 R	53.9%	41.6%	56.4%	43.6%
263,801	OTTAWA	88,860	57,927	27,700	3,233	30,227 R	65.2%	31.2%	67.7%	32.3%
13,376	PRESQUE ISLE	5,226	2,427	2,596	203	169 D	46.4%	49.7%	48.3%	51.7%
24,449	ROSCOMMON	9,053	4,152	4,371	530	219 D	45.9%	48.3%	48.7%	51.3%
200,169	SAGINAW	66,459	24,747	39,436	2,276	14,689 D	37.2%	59.3%	38.6%	61.4%
43,114	SANILAC	12,547	6,771	5,143	633	1,628 R	54.0%	41.0%	56.8%	43.2%
8,485	SCHOOLCRAFT	2,865	1,478	1,313	74	165 R	51.6%	45.8%	53.0%	47.0%
70,648	SHIAWASSEE	23,956	10,132	12,682	1,142	2,550 D	42.3%	52.9%	44.4%	55.6%
163,040	ST. CLAIR	51,187	23,467	24,828	2,892	1,361 D	45.8%	48.5%	48.6%	51.4%
61,295	ST. JOSEPH	14,820	7,891	6,102	827	1,789 R	53.2%	41.2%	56.4%	43.6%
55,729	TUSCOLA	17,743	8,481	8,471	791	10 R	47.8%	47.7%	50.0%	50.0%
76,258	VAN BUREN	21,992	10,046	10,663	1,283	617 D	45.7%	48.5%	48.5%	51.5%

MICHIGAN

SENATOR 2014

2010 Census Population	County	Total Vote	Republican (Land)	Democratic (Peters)	Other	Rep.-Dem. Plurality	Total Vote Rep.	Total Vote Dem.	Major Vote Rep.	Major Vote Dem.
344,791	WASHTENAW	119,822	35,155	80,617	4,050	45,462 D	29.3%	67.3%	30.4%	69.6%
1,820,584	WAYNE	503,913	126,423	360,641	16,849	234,218 D	25.1%	71.6%	26.0%	74.0%
32,735	WEXFORD	9,933	5,191	4,220	522	971 R	52.3%	42.5%	55.2%	44.8%
9,883,640	TOTAL	3,121,775	1,290,199	1,704,936	126,640	414,737 D	41.3%	54.6%	43.1%	56.9%

MICHIGAN

HOUSE OF REPRESENTATIVES

CD	Year	Total Vote	Republican Vote	Republican Candidate	Democratic Vote	Democratic Candidate	Other Vote	Rep.-Dem. Plurality	Total Vote Rep.	Total Vote Dem.	Major Vote Rep.	Major Vote Dem.
1	2014	250,131	130,414	BENISHEK, DAN*	113,263	CANNON, JERRY	6,454	17,151 R	52.1%	45.3%	53.5%	46.5%
1	2012	347,037	167,060	BENISHEK, DAN*	165,179	MCDOWELL, GARY	14,798	1,881 R	48.1%	47.6%	50.3%	49.7%
2	2014	213,072	135,568	HUIZENGA, BILL*	70,851	VANDERSTELT, DEAN	6,653	64,717 R	63.6%	33.3%	65.7%	34.3%
2	2012	318,267	194,653	HUIZENGA, BILL*	108,973	GERMAN, WILLIE JR.	14,641	85,680 R	61.2%	34.2%	64.1%	35.9%
3	2014	217,165	125,754	AMASH, JUSTIN*	84,720	GOODRICH, BOB	6,691	41,034 R	57.9%	39.0%	59.7%	40.3%
3	2012	326,283	171,675	AMASH, JUSTIN*	144,108	PESTKA, STEVE	10,500	27,567 R	52.6%	44.2%	54.4%	45.6%
4	2014	219,423	123,962	MOOLENAAR, JOHN R.	85,777	HOLMES, JEFF	9,684	38,185 R	56.5%	39.1%	59.1%	40.9%
4	2012	312,949	197,386	CAMP, DAVE*	104,996	WIRTH, DEBRA FREIDELL	10,567	92,390 R	63.1%	33.6%	65.3%	34.7%
5	2014	222,138	69,222	HARDWICK, ALLEN	148,182	KILDEE, DANIEL T.*	4,734	78,960 D	31.2%	66.7%	31.8%	68.2%
5	2012	330,146	103,931	SLEZAK, JIM	214,531	KILDEE, DANIEL T.	11,684	110,600 D	31.5%	65.0%	32.6%	67.4%
6	2014	208,976	116,801	UPTON, FRED*	84,391	CLEMENTS, PAUL C.	7,784	32,410 R	55.9%	40.4%	58.1%	41.9%
6	2012	320,475	174,955	UPTON, FRED*	136,563	O'BRIEN, MIKE	8,957	38,392 R	54.6%	42.6%	56.2%	43.8%
7	2014	223,685	119,564	WALBERG, TIM*	92,083	BYRNES, PAM	12,038	27,481 R	53.5%	41.2%	56.5%	43.5%
7	2012	318,069	169,668	WALBERG, TIM*	136,849	HASKELL, KURT R.	11,552	32,819 R	53.3%	43.0%	55.4%	44.6%
8	2014	243,125	132,739	BISHOP, MIKE	102,269	SCHERTZING, ERIC	8,117	30,470 R	54.6%	42.1%	56.5%	43.5%
8	2012	345,054	202,217	ROGERS, MIKE*	128,657	ENDERLE, LANCE	14,180	73,560 R	58.6%	37.3%	61.1%	38.9%
9	2014	225,757	81,470	BRIKHO, GEORGE	136,342	LEVIN, SANDER M.*	7,945	54,872 D	36.1%	60.4%	37.4%	62.6%
9	2012	337,316	114,760	VOLARIC, DON	208,846	LEVIN, SANDER M.*	13,710	94,086 D	34.0%	61.9%	35.5%	64.5%
10	2014	228,692	157,069	MILLER, CANDICE S.*	67,143	STADLER, CHUCK	4,480	89,926 R	68.7%	29.4%	70.1%	29.9%
10	2012	328,612	226,075	MILLER, CANDICE S.*	97,734	STADLER, CHUCK	4,803	128,341 R	68.8%	29.7%	69.8%	30.2%
11	2014	251,238	140,435	TROTT, DAVID A.	101,681	MCKENZIE, BOBBY	9,122	38,754 R	55.9%	40.5%	58.0%	42.0%
11	2012	358,139	181,788	BENTIVOLIO, KERRY	158,879	TAJ, SYED	17,472	22,909 R	50.8%	44.4%	53.4%	46.6%
12	2014	206,660	64,716	BOWMAN, TERRENCE "TERRY"	134,346	DINGELL, DEBBIE	7,598	69,630 D	31.3%	65.0%	32.5%	67.5%
12	2012	319,223	92,472	KALLGREN, CYNTHIA	216,884	DINGELL, JOHN D. JR.*	9,867	124,412 D	29.0%	67.9%	29.9%	70.1%
13	2014	166,947	27,234	GORMAN, JEFF	132,710	CONYERS, JOHN JR.*	7,003	105,476 D	16.3%	79.5%	17.0%	83.0%
13	2012	284,270	38,769	SAWICKI, HARRY	235,336	CONYERS, JOHN JR.*	10,165	196,567 D	13.6%	82.8%	14.1%	85.9%
14	2014	212,468	41,801	BARR, CHRISTINA	165,272	LAWRENCE, BRENDA L.	5,395	123,471 D	19.7%	77.8%	20.2%	79.8%
14	2012	328,792	51,395	HAULER, JOHN	270,450	PETERS, GARY*	6,947	219,055 D	15.6%	82.3%	16.0%	84.0%
TOTAL	2014	3,089,477	1,466,749		1,519,030		103,698	52,281 D	47.5%	49.2%	49.1%	50.9%
TOTAL	2012	4,574,632	2,086,804		2,327,985		159,843	241,181 D	45.6%	50.9%	47.3%	52.7%

Note: An asterisk (*) denotes incumbent.

MICHIGAN

GENERAL AND PRIMARY ELECTIONS

2014 GENERAL ELECTIONS: OTHER VOTES

Governor	Other vote was 35,723 Libertarian (Mary Buzuma), 19,368 U.S. Taxpayers (Mark McFarlin), 14,934 Green (Paul Homeniuk), 50 scattered write-in
Senate	Other vote was 62,897 Libertarian (Jim Fulner), 37,529 U.S. Taxpayers (Richard Matkin), 26,137 Green (Chris Wahmhoff), 77 scattered write-in
House	Other vote was:
CD 1	3,823 Libertarian (Loel Gnadt), 2,631 Green (Ellis Boal)
CD 2	3,877 Libertarian (Ronald Welch), 2,776 U.S. Taxpayers (Ronald E. Graeser)
CD 3	6,691 Green (Tonya Duncan)
CD 4	4,990 U.S. Taxpayers (George Zimmer), 4,694 Libertarian (William Tyler White)
CD 5	4,734 Libertarian (Harold H. Jones)
CD 6	5,530 Libertarian (Erwin J. Haas), 2,254 Green (John Lawrence)
CD 7	4,531 Libertarian (Kenneth L. Proctor), 4,369 No Party Affiliation (David Bernard Swartout), 3,138 U.S. Taxpayers (Rick Strawcutter)
CD 8	4,557 Libertarian (James Weeks), 1,880 Greenback (Jim Casha), 1,680 Natural Law (Jeremy Burgess)
CD 9	4,792 Libertarian (Gregory Creswell), 3,153 Green (John McDermott)
CD 10	4,480 Green (Harley G. Mikkelson)
CD 11	7,711 Libertarian (John Tatar), 1,411 Write-in (Kerry Bentivolio)
CD 12	5,039 No Party Affiliation (Gary Walkowicz), 2,559 Libertarian (Bhagwan Dashairya)
CD 13	3,537 Libertarian (Chris Sharer), 3,466 No Party Affiliation (Sam Johnson)
CD 14	3,366 Libertarian (Leonard Schwartz), 1,999 Green (Stephen Boyle), 30 Write-in (Calvin Pruden)

2014 PRIMARY ELECTIONS: SUPPLEMENTARY INFORMATION

Primary	August 5, 2014	**Registration** (as of July 7, 2014 – includes 877,345 inactive registrants)	7,413,142	No Party Registration
Primary Type	Open—Any registered voter could participate in the primary of either party.			

	REPUBLICAN PRIMARIES			DEMOCRATIC PRIMARIES		
Senator	Land, Terri Lynn	588,084	100.0%	Peters, Gary	504,102	100.0%
	TOTAL	*588,084*		*TOTAL*	*504,102*	
Governor	Snyder, Rick*	617,720	100.0%	Schauer, Mark H.	513,263	100.0%
	TOTAL	*617,720*		*TOTAL*	*513,263*	
Congressional District 1	Benishek, Dan*	49,540	69.7%	Cannon, Jerry	31,104	100.0%
	Arcand, Alan	21,497	30.3%			
	TOTAL	*71,037*		*TOTAL*	*31,104*	
Congressional District 2	Huizenga, Bill*	54,416	100.0%	Vanderstelt, Dean	19,957	100.0%
	TOTAL	*54,416*		*TOTAL*	*19,957*	
Congressional District 3	Amash, Justin*	39,706	57.4%	Goodrich, Bob	20,378	100.0%
	Ellis, Brian	29,422	42.6%			
	TOTAL	*69,128*		*TOTAL*	*20,378*	

MICHIGAN

GENERAL AND PRIMARY ELECTIONS

	REPUBLICAN PRIMARIES			DEMOCRATIC PRIMARIES		
Congressional District 4	Moolenaar, John R.	34,399	52.4%	Holmes, Jeff	23,496	100.0%
	Mitchell, Paul	23,844	36.3%			
	Konetchy, Peter D.	7,408	11.3%			
	TOTAL	65,651		TOTAL	23,496	
Congressional District 5	Hardwick, Allen	13,557	51.3%	Kildee, Daniel T.*	46,065	100.0%
	Whitmire, Tom	12,859	48.7%			
	TOTAL	26,416		TOTAL	46,065	
Congressional District 6	Upton, Fred*	37,731	71.2%	Clements, Paul C.	19,894	100.0%
	Bussler, Jim	15,283	28.8%			
	TOTAL	53,014		TOTAL	19,894	
Congressional District 7	Walberg, Tim*	38,046	79.3%	Byrnes, Pam	25,048	100.0%
	North, Douglas Radcliffe	9,934	20.7%			
	TOTAL	47,980		TOTAL	25,048	
Congressional District 8	Bishop, Mike	35,422	60.3%	Schertzing, Eric	13,535	42.8%
	McMillin, Tom	23,358	39.7%	Grettenberger, Susan	11,921	37.7%
				Darga, Ken	3,103	9.8%
				Hank, Jeffrey	3,054	9.7%
	TOTAL	58,780		TOTAL	31,613	
Congressional District 9	Brikho, George	30,678	100.0%	Levin, Sander M.*	40,877	100.0%
	TOTAL	30,678		TOTAL	40,877	
Congressional District 10	Miller, Candice S.*	55,272	100.0%	Stadler, Chuck	25,820	100.0%
	TOTAL	55,272		TOTAL	25,820	
Congressional District 11	Trott, David A.	42,008	66.4%	McKenzie, Bobby	13,441	34.3%
	Bentivolio, Kerry*	21,254	33.6%	Kumar, Anil	12,479	31.8%
				Skinner, Nancy	10,371	26.5%
				Roberts, Bill	2,906	7.4%
	TOTAL	63,262		TOTAL	39,197	
Congressional District 12	Bowman, Terrence "Terry"	18,793	100.0%	Dingell, Debbie	45,162	77.7%
				Mullins, Raymond	12,994	22.3%
	TOTAL	18,793		TOTAL	58,156	
Congressional District 13	Gorman, Jeff	6,696	100.0%	Conyers, John Jr.*	42,005	73.9%
				Sheffield, Horace	14,850	26.1%
	TOTAL	6,696		TOTAL	56,855	
Congressional District 14	Barr, Christina	12,611	100.0%	Lawrence, Brenda L.	26,387	35.6%
				Hobbs, Rudy	23,996	32.4%
				Clarke, Hansen	22,866	30.9%
				Foster, Burgess	831	1.1%
	TOTAL	12,611		TOTAL	74,080	

Note: An asterisk (*) denotes incumbent.

MINNESOTA

Congressional districts first established for elections held in 2012

8 members

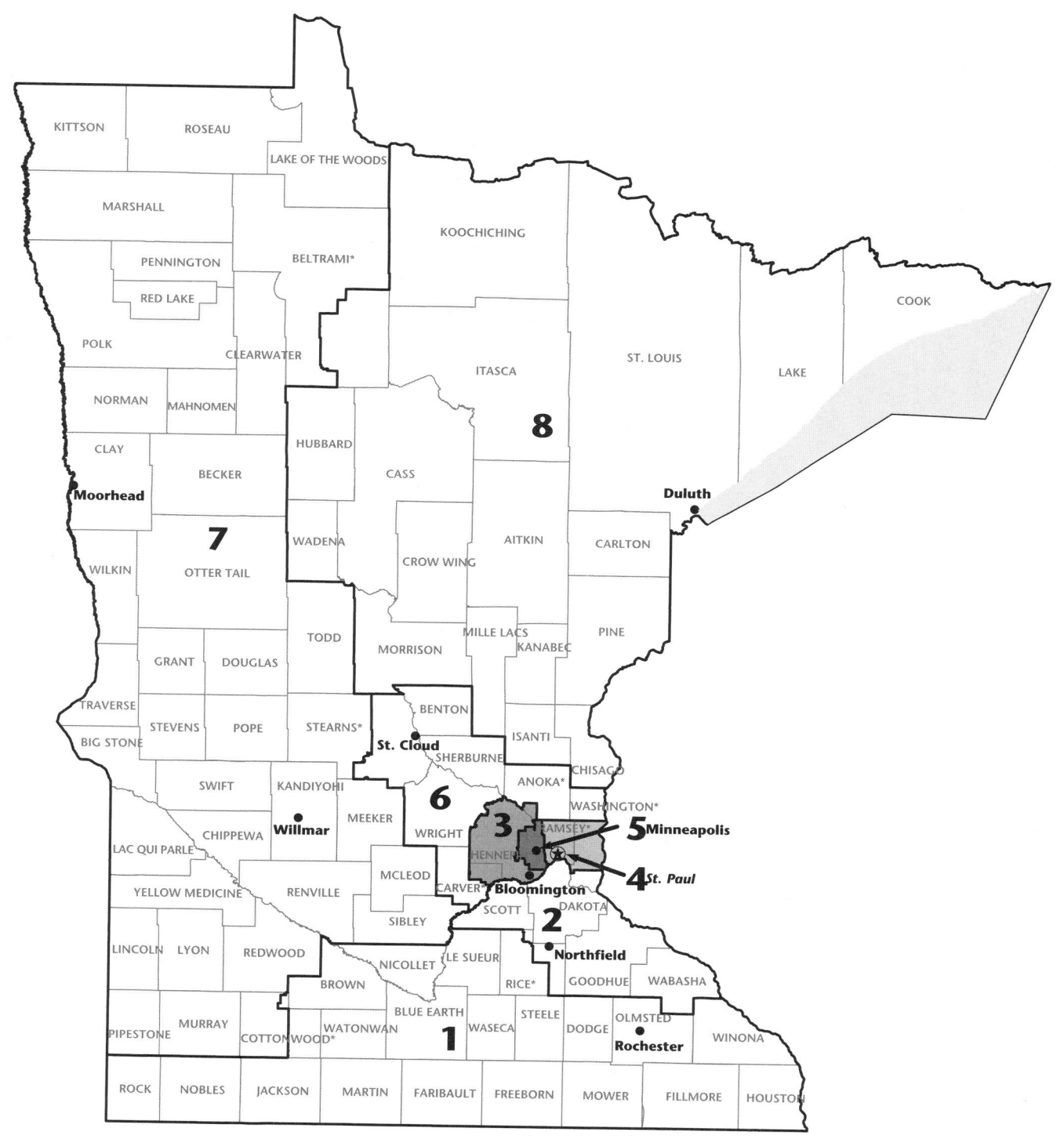

* Asterisk indicates a county whose boundaries include parts of two or more congressional districts.

MINNESOTA
Minneapolis–St. Paul Area

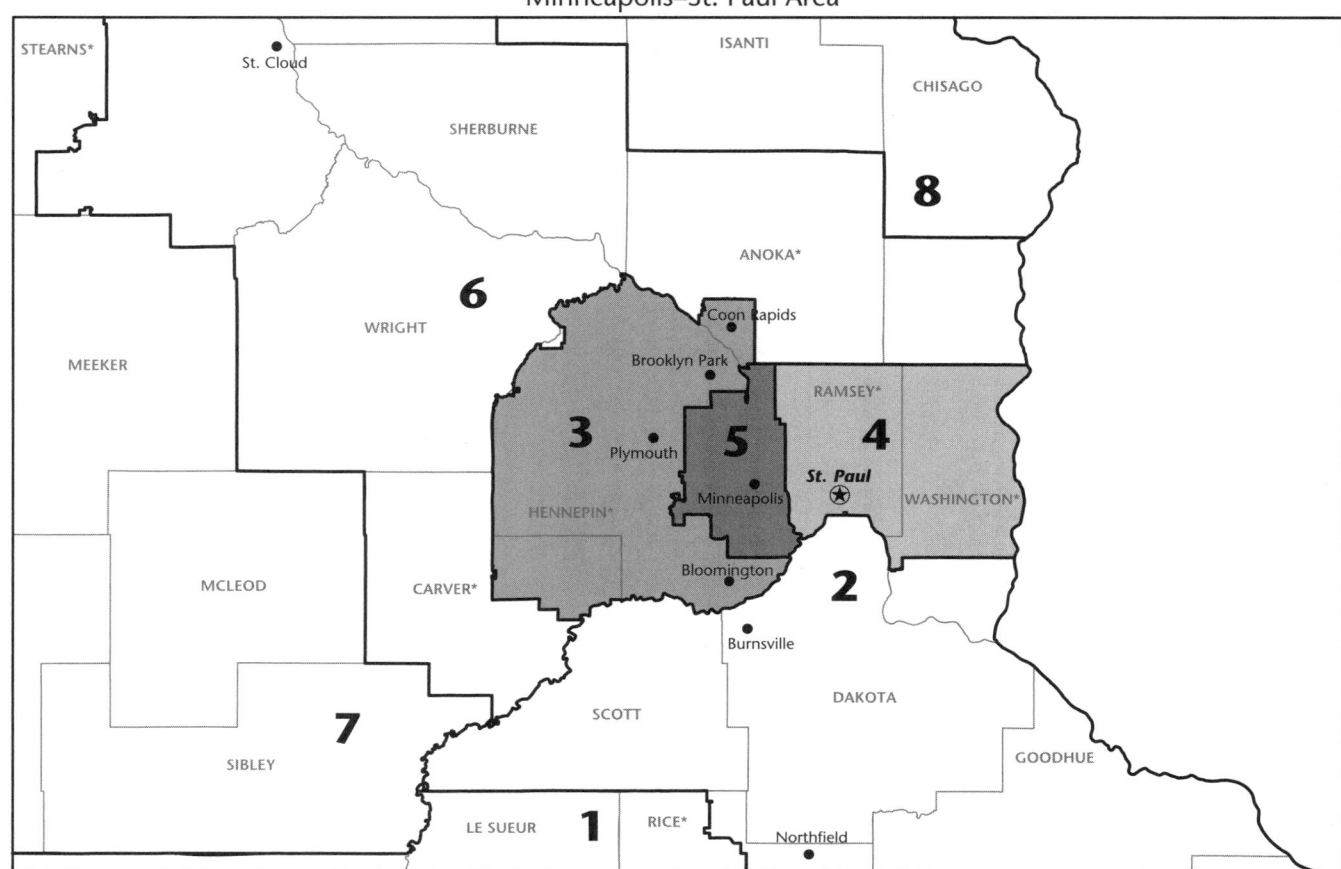

* Asterisk indicates a county whose boundaries include parts of two or more congressional districts.

MINNESOTA

GOVERNOR
Mark Dayton (D). Reelected 2014 to a four-year term. Previously elected 2010.

SENATORS (2 Democrats)
Al Franken (D). Reelected 2014 to a six-year term. Previously elected 2008.

Amy Klobuchar (D). Reelected 2012 to a six-year term. Previously elected 2006.

REPRESENTATIVES (3 Republicans, 5 Democrats)
1. Timothy J. Walz (D)
2. John Kline (R)
3. Erik Paulsen (R)
4. Betty McCollum (D)
5. Keith Ellison (D)
6. Tom Emmer (R)
7. Collin C. Peterson (D)
8. Richard M. Nolan (D)

POSTWAR VOTE FOR PRESIDENT

| | | Republican | | Democratic | | | | Percentage | | | |
| | | | | | | | | Total Vote | | Major Vote | |
Year	Total Vote	Vote	Candidate	Vote	Candidate	Other Vote	Rep.-Dem. Plurality	Rep.	Dem.	Rep.	Dem.
2012	2,936,561	1,320,225	Romney, W. Mitt	1,546,167	Obama, Barack H.*	70,169	225,942 D	45.0%	52.7%	46.1%	53.9%
2008	2,910,369	1,275,409	McCain, John S. III	1,573,354	Obama, Barack H.	61,606	297,945 D	43.8%	54.1%	44.8%	55.2%
2004	2,828,387	1,346,695	Bush, George W.*	1,445,014	Kerry, John F.	36,678	98,319 D	47.6%	51.1%	48.2%	51.8%
2000**	2,438,685	1,109,659	Bush, George W.	1,168,266	Gore, Albert Jr.	160,760	58,607 D	45.5%	47.9%	48.7%	51.3%
1996**	2,192,640	766,476	Dole, Robert "Bob"	1,120,438	Clinton, Bill*	305,726	353,962 D	35.0%	51.1%	40.6%	59.4%
1992**	2,347,948	747,841	Bush, George H.*	1,020,997	Clinton, Bill	579,110	273,156 D	31.9%	43.5%	42.3%	57.7%
1988	2,096,790	962,337	Bush, George H.	1,109,471	Dukakis, Michael S.	24,982	147,134 D	45.9%	52.9%	46.4%	53.6%
1984	2,084,449	1,032,603	Reagan, Ronald*	1,036,364	Mondale, Walter F.	15,482	3,761 D	49.5%	49.7%	49.9%	50.1%
1980**	2,051,980	873,268	Reagan, Ronald	954,174	Carter, Jimmy*	224,538	80,906 D	42.6%	46.5%	47.8%	52.2%
1976	1,949,931	819,395	Ford, Gerald R.*	1,070,440	Carter, Jimmy	60,096	251,045 D	42.0%	54.9%	43.4%	56.6%
1972	1,741,652	898,269	Nixon, Richard M.*	802,346	McGovern, George S.	41,037	95,923 R	51.6%	46.1%	52.8%	47.2%
1968**	1,588,506	658,643	Nixon, Richard M.	857,738	Humphrey, Hubert Horatio Jr.	72,125	199,095 D	41.5%	54.0%	43.4%	56.6%
1964	1,554,462	559,624	Goldwater, Barry M. Sr.	991,117	Johnson, Lyndon B.*	3,721	431,493 D	36.0%	63.8%	36.1%	63.9%
1960	1,541,887	757,915	Nixon, Richard M.	779,933	Kennedy, John F.	4,039	22,018 D	49.2%	50.6%	49.3%	50.7%
1956	1,340,005	719,302	Eisenhower, Dwight D.*	617,525	Stevenson, Adlai E. II	3,178	101,777 R	53.7%	46.1%	53.8%	46.2%
1952	1,379,483	763,211	Eisenhower, Dwight D.	608,458	Stevenson, Adlai E. II	7,814	154,753 R	55.3%	44.1%	55.6%	44.4%
1948	1,212,226	483,617	Dewey, Thomas E.	692,966	Truman, Harry S.*	35,643	209,349 D	39.9%	57.2%	41.1%	58.9%

Note: An asterisk (*) denotes incumbent. **In past elections, the other vote included: 2000 - 126,696 Green (Nader); 1996 - 257,704 Reform (Ross Perot); 1992 - 562,506 Independent (Perot); 1980 - 174,990 Independent (John Anderson); 1968 - 68,931 American Independent (George Wallace).

MINNESOTA

POSTWAR VOTE FOR GOVERNOR

Year	Total Vote	Republican		Democratic		Other Vote	Rep.-Dem. Plurality	Percentage			
		Vote	Candidate	Vote	Candidate			Total Vote		Major Vote	
								Rep.	Dem.	Rep.	Dem.
2014	1,975,406	879,257	Johnson, Jeff	989,113	Dayton, Mark*	107,036	109,856 D	44.5%	50.1%	47.1%	52.9%
2010**	2,107,021	910,462	Emmer, Tom	919,232	Dayton, Mark	277,327	8,770 D	43.2%	43.6%	49.8%	50.2%
2006	2,202,937	1,028,568	Pawlenty, Tim*	1,007,460	Hatch, Mike	166,909	21,108 R	46.7%	45.7%	50.5%	49.5%
2002**	2,252,473	999,473	Pawlenty, Tim	821,268	Moe, Roger D.	431,732	178,205 R	44.4%	36.5%	54.9%	45.1%
1998**	2,090,518	716,880	Coleman, Norm	587,060	Humphrey, Hubert Horatio "Skip" III	786,578	129,820 R#	34.3%	28.1%	55.0%	45.0%
1994	1,765,590	1,094,165	Carlson, Arne*	589,344	Marty, John	82,081	504,821 R	62.0%	33.4%	65.0%	35.0%
1990	1,806,777	895,988	Carlson, Arne	836,218	Perpich, Rudy*	74,571	59,770 R	49.6%	46.3%	51.7%	48.3%
1986	1,415,989	606,755	Ludeman, Cal R.	790,138	Perpich, Rudy*	19,096	183,383 D	42.9%	55.8%	43.4%	56.6%
1982	1,789,539	715,796	Whitney, Wheelock	1,049,104	Perpich, Rudy*	24,639	333,308 D	40.0%	58.6%	40.6%	59.4%
1978	1,585,702	830,019	Quie, Albert H.	718,244	Perpich, Rudy*	37,439	111,775 R	52.3%	45.3%	53.6%	46.4%
1974	1,252,898	367,722	Johnson, John W.	786,787	Anderson, Wendell R.*	98,389	419,065 D	29.3%	62.8%	31.9%	68.1%
1970	1,365,443	621,780	Head, Douglas M.	737,921	Anderson, Wendell R.	5,742	116,141 D	45.5%	54.0%	45.7%	54.3%
1966	1,295,058	680,593	Levander, Harold	607,943	Rolvaag, Karl F.*	6,522	72,650 R	52.6%	46.9%	52.8%	47.2%
1962**	1,246,904	619,751	Andersen, Elmer L.*	619,842	Rolvaag, Karl F.	7,311	91 D	49.7%	49.7%	50.0%	50.0%
1960	1,550,265	783,813	Andersen, Elmer L.	760,934	Freeman, Orville L.	5,518	22,879 R	50.6%	49.1%	50.7%	49.3%
1958	1,159,915	490,731	MacKinnon, George	658,326	Freeman, Orville L.*	10,858	167,595 D	42.3%	56.8%	42.7%	57.3%
1956	1,422,161	685,196	Nelsen, Ancher	731,180	Freeman, Orville L.*	5,785	45,984 D	48.2%	51.4%	48.4%	51.6%
1954	1,151,417	538,865	Anderson, C. Elmer*	607,099	Freeman, Orville L.	5,453	68,234 D	46.8%	52.7%	47.0%	53.0%
1952	1,418,869	785,125	Anderson, C. Elmer	624,480	Freeman, Orville L.	9,264	160,645 R	55.3%	44.0%	55.7%	44.3%
1950	1,046,632	635,800	Youngdahl, Luther W.*	400,637	Peterson, Harry H.	10,195	235,163 R	60.7%	38.3%	61.3%	38.7%
1948	1,210,874	643,572	Youngdahl, Luther W.*	545,746	Halsted, Charles L.	21,556	97,826 R	53.1%	45.1%	54.1%	45.9%
1946	880,348	519,067	Youngdahl, Luther W.	349,565	Barker, Harold H.	11,716	169,502 R	59.0%	39.7%	59.8%	40.2%

Note: An asterisk (*) denotes incumbent. A pound sign (#) indicates that the state was carried by a third party candidate. **In past elections, the other vote included: 2010 - 251,487 Independence (Tom Horner); 2002 - 364,534 Independence (Timothy J. Penny); 1998 - 773,403 Reform (Jesse Ventura), who was elected with 37.0 percent of the total vote. The term of office of Minnesota's governor was increased from two to four years effective with the 1962 election.

POSTWAR VOTE FOR SENATOR

Year	Total Vote	Republican		Democratic		Other Vote	Rep.-Dem. Plurality	Percentage			
		Vote	Candidate	Vote	Candidate			Total Vote		Major Vote	
								Rep.	Dem.	Rep.	Dem.
2014	1,981,528	850,227	McFadden, Mike	1,053,205	Franken, Al*	78,096	202,978 D	42.9%	53.2%	44.7%	55.3%
2012	2,843,207	867,974	Bills, Kurt	1,854,595	Klobuchar, Amy*	120,638	986,621 D	30.5%	65.2%	31.9%	68.1%
2008**	2,862,142	1,212,206	Coleman, Norm*	1,212,431	Franken, Al	437,505	225 D	42.4%	42.4%	50.0%	50.0%
2006	2,202,772	835,653	Kennedy, Mark	1,278,849	Klobuchar, Amy	88,270	443,196 D	37.9%	58.1%	39.5%	60.5%
2002**	2,254,639	1,116,697	Coleman, Norm	1,067,246	Mondale, Walter F.	70,696	49,451 R	49.5%	47.3%	51.1%	48.9%
2000	2,419,520	1,047,474	Grams, Rod*	1,181,553	Dayton, Mark	190,493	134,079 D	43.3%	48.8%	47.0%	53.0%
1996	2,183,062	901,282	Boschwitz, Rudy	1,098,493	Wellstone, Paul D.*	183,287	197,211 D	41.3%	50.3%	45.1%	54.9%
1994	1,772,929	869,653	Grams, Rod	781,860	Wynia, Ann	121,416	87,793 R	49.1%	44.1%	52.7%	47.3%
1990	1,808,045	864,375	Boschwitz, Rudy*	911,999	Wellstone, Paul D.	31,671	47,624 D	47.8%	50.4%	48.7%	51.3%
1988	2,093,953	1,176,210	Durenberger, David*	856,694	Humphrey, Hubert Horatio "Skip" III	61,049	319,516 R	56.2%	40.9%	57.9%	42.1%
1984	2,066,143	1,199,926	Boschwitz, Rudy*	852,844	Growe, Joan Anderson	13,373	347,082 R	58.1%	41.3%	58.5%	41.5%
1982	1,804,676	949,207	Durenberger, David*	840,401	Dayton, Mark	15,068	108,806 R	52.6%	46.6%	53.0%	47.0%
1978	1,580,778	894,092	Boschwitz, Rudy	638,375	Anderson, Wendell R.*	48,311	255,717 R	56.6%	40.4%	58.3%	41.7%
1978S	1,560,724	957,908	Durenberger, David	538,675	Short, Robert E.	64,141	419,233 R	61.4%	34.5%	64.0%	36.0%
1976	1,912,068	478,611	Brekke, Gerald W.	1,290,736	Humphrey, Hubert Horatio Jr.*	142,721	812,125 D	25.0%	67.5%	27.1%	72.9%
1972	1,731,653	742,121	Hansen, Philip	981,340	Mondale, Walter F.*	8,192	239,219 D	42.9%	56.7%	43.1%	56.9%
1970	1,364,887	568,025	MacGregor, Clark	788,256	Humphrey, Hubert Horatio Jr.*	8,606	220,231 D	41.6%	57.8%	41.9%	58.1%
1966	1,271,426	574,868	Forsythe, Robert A.	685,840	Mondale, Walter F.	10,718	110,972 D	45.2%	53.9%	45.6%	54.4%
1964	1,543,600	605,933	Whitney, Wheelock	931,363	McCarthy, Eugene J.*	6,304	325,430 D	39.3%	60.3%	39.4%	60.6%
1960	1,536,839	648,586	Peterson, P. Kenneth	884,168	Humphrey, Hubert Horatio Jr.*	4,085	235,582 D	42.2%	57.5%	42.3%	57.7%
1958	1,150,883	536,629	Thye, Edward J.	608,847	McCarthy, Eugene J.	5,407	72,218 D	46.6%	52.9%	46.8%	53.2%
1954	1,138,952	479,619	Bjornson, Val	642,193	Humphrey, Hubert Horatio Jr.*	17,140	162,574 D	42.1%	56.4%	42.8%	57.2%
1952	1,387,419	785,649	Thye, Edward J.*	590,011	Carlson, William E.	11,759	195,638 R	56.6%	42.5%	57.1%	42.9%
1948	1,217,250	482,801	Ball, Joseph H.*	729,494	Humphrey, Hubert Horatio Jr.	4,955	246,693 D	39.7%	59.9%	39.8%	60.2%
1946	878,731	517,775	Thye, Edward J.	349,520	Jorgenson, Theodore	11,436	168,255 R	58.9%	39.8%	59.7%	40.3%

Note: An asterisk (*) denotes incumbent. **In past elections, the other vote included: 2008 - 437,505 Independence (Dean Barkley). In October 2002 the Democratic incumbent, Paul Wellstone, was killed in an airplane crash. Walter F. Mondale was named to replace him on the general election ballot. One of the 1978 elections was for a short term to fill a vacancy.

MINNESOTA
GOVERNOR 2014

2010 Census Population	County	Total Vote	Republican (Johnson)	Democratic (Dayton)	Other	Rep.-Dem. Plurality		Rep.	Dem.	Rep.	Dem.
16,202	AITKIN	7,232	3,319	3,533	380	214	D	45.9%	48.9%	48.4%	51.6%
330,844	ANOKA	117,688	59,250	52,062	6,376	7,188	R	50.3%	44.2%	53.2%	46.8%
32,504	BECKER	11,976	6,539	4,738	699	1,801	R	54.6%	39.6%	58.0%	42.0%
44,442	BELTRAMI	15,367	6,520	7,819	1,028	1,299	D	42.4%	50.9%	45.5%	54.5%
38,451	BENTON	13,076	6,976	5,246	854	1,730	R	53.3%	40.1%	57.1%	42.9%
5,269	BIG STONE	2,112	930	1,065	117	135	D	44.0%	50.4%	46.6%	53.4%
64,013	BLUE EARTH	20,054	8,500	10,107	1,447	1,607	D	42.4%	50.4%	45.7%	54.3%
25,893	BROWN	9,321	4,998	3,739	584	1,259	R	53.6%	40.1%	57.2%	42.8%
35,386	CARLTON	13,827	4,776	8,176	875	3,400	D	34.5%	59.1%	36.9%	63.1%
91,042	CARVER	36,815	21,842	13,328	1,645	8,514	R	59.3%	36.2%	62.1%	37.9%
28,567	CASS	12,234	6,432	5,104	698	1,328	R	52.6%	41.7%	55.8%	44.2%
12,441	CHIPPEWA	4,654	2,116	2,284	254	168	D	45.5%	41.7%	48.1%	51.9%
53,887	CHISAGO	20,180	10,645	8,380	1,155	2,265	R	52.8%	41.5%	56.0%	44.0%
58,999	CLAY	17,816	7,139	9,573	1,104	2,434	D	40.1%	53.7%	42.7%	57.3%
8,695	CLEARWATER	2,882	1,547	1,163	172	384	R	53.7%	40.4%	57.1%	42.9%
5,176	COOK	2,896	919	1,769	208	850	D	31.7%	61.1%	34.2%	65.8%
11,687	COTTONWOOD	4,288	2,225	1,823	240	402	R	51.9%	42.5%	55.0%	45.0%
62,500	CROW WING	26,810	14,005	11,290	1,515	2,715	R	52.2%	42.1%	55.4%	44.6%
398,552	DAKOTA	152,137	72,714	72,052	7,371	662	R	47.8%	47.4%	50.2%	49.8%
20,087	DODGE	7,631	4,190	2,900	541	1,290	R	54.9%	38.0%	59.1%	40.9%
36,009	DOUGLAS	15,288	8,471	6,028	789	2,443	R	55.4%	39.4%	58.4%	41.6%
14,553	FARIBAULT	5,415	2,795	2,297	323	498	R	51.6%	42.4%	54.9%	45.1%
20,866	FILLMORE	8,296	4,058	3,710	528	348	R	48.9%	44.7%	52.2%	47.8%
31,255	FREEBORN	12,385	5,414	6,205	766	791	D	43.7%	50.1%	46.6%	53.4%
46,183	GOODHUE	17,252	8,833	7,516	903	1,317	R	51.2%	43.6%	54.0%	46.0%
6,018	GRANT	2,848	1,245	1,436	167	191	D	43.7%	50.4%	46.4%	53.6%
1,152,425	HENNEPIN	448,812	160,966	265,820	22,026	104,854	D	35.9%	59.2%	37.7%	62.3%
19,027	HOUSTON	7,802	3,607	3,672	523	65	D	46.2%	47.1%	49.6%	50.4%
20,428	HUBBARD	8,691	4,584	3,660	447	924	R	52.7%	42.1%	55.6%	44.4%
37,816	ISANTI	13,894	7,539	5,498	857	2,041	R	54.3%	39.6%	57.8%	42.2%
45,058	ITASCA	18,896	7,460	10,395	1,041	2,935	D	39.5%	55.0%	41.8%	58.2%
10,266	JACKSON	3,864	2,045	1,575	244	470	R	52.9%	40.8%	56.5%	43.5%
16,239	KANABEC	6,202	3,060	2,707	435	353	R	49.3%	43.6%	53.1%	46.9%
42,239	KANDIYOHI	16,640	8,322	7,528	790	794	R	50.0%	45.2%	52.5%	47.5%
4,552	KITTSON	1,940	770	1,060	110	290	D	39.7%	54.6%	42.1%	57.9%
13,311	KOOCHICHING	5,298	1,903	3,056	339	1,153	D	35.9%	57.7%	38.4%	61.6%
7,259	LAC QUI PARLE	2,979	1,319	1,513	147	194	D	44.3%	50.8%	46.6%	53.4%
10,866	LAKE	5,122	1,792	3,030	300	1,238	D	35.0%	59.2%	37.2%	62.8%
4,045	LAKE OF THE WOODS	1,885	984	755	146	229	R	52.2%	40.1%	56.6%	43.4%
27,703	LE SUEUR	9,699	4,826	4,283	590	543	R	49.8%	44.2%	53.0%	47.0%
5,896	LINCOLN	2,320	1,087	1,047	186	40	R	46.9%	45.1%	50.9%	49.1%
25,857	LYON	8,359	4,407	3,460	492	947	R	52.7%	41.4%	56.0%	44.0%
5,413	MAHNOMEN	1,690	624	941	125	317	D	36.9%	55.7%	39.9%	60.1%
9,439	MARSHALL	4,041	1,884	1,916	241	32	D	46.6%	47.4%	49.6%	50.4%
20,840	MARTIN	7,813	4,449	2,850	514	1,599	R	56.9%	36.5%	61.0%	39.0%
36,651	MCLEOD	12,385	7,009	4,547	829	2,462	R	56.6%	36.7%	60.7%	39.3%
23,300	MEEKER	9,135	4,811	3,697	627	1,114	R	52.7%	40.5%	56.5%	43.5%
26,097	MILLE LACS	8,936	4,498	3,867	571	631	R	50.3%	43.3%	53.8%	46.2%
33,198	MORRISON	12,854	7,081	4,993	780	2,088	R	55.1%	38.8%	58.6%	41.4%
39,163	MOWER	11,791	5,064	6,005	722	941	D	42.9%	50.9%	45.7%	54.3%
8,725	MURRAY	3,537	1,763	1,510	264	253	R	49.8%	42.7%	53.9%	46.1%
32,727	NICOLLET	11,770	4,927	6,044	799	1,117	D	41.9%	51.4%	44.9%	55.1%
21,378	NOBLES	6,007	3,026	2,619	362	407	R	50.4%	43.6%	53.6%	46.4%
6,852	NORMAN	2,402	813	1,429	160	616	D	33.8%	59.5%	36.3%	63.7%
144,248	OLMSTED	50,291	24,928	22,718	2,645	2,210	R	49.6%	45.2%	52.3%	47.7%
57,303	OTTER TAIL	22,102	12,533	8,494	1,075	4,039	R	56.7%	38.4%	59.6%	40.4%
13,930	PENNINGTON	5,087	2,325	2,356	406	31	D	45.7%	46.3%	49.7%	50.3%
29,750	PINE	10,384	4,762	4,960	662	198	D	45.9%	47.8%	49.0%	51.0%
9,596	PIPESTONE	3,784	2,211	1,296	277	915	R	58.4%	34.2%	63.0%	37.0%
31,600	POLK	9,749	4,742	4,476	531	266	R	48.6%	45.9%	51.4%	48.6%

MINNESOTA

GOVERNOR 2014

2010 Census Population	County	Total Vote	Republican (Johnson)	Democratic (Dayton)	Other	Rep.-Dem. Plurality		Percentage			
								Total Vote		Major Vote	
								Rep.	Dem.	Rep.	Dem.
10,995	POPE	4,927	2,297	2,351	279	54	D	46.6%	47.7%	49.4%	50.6%
508,640	RAMSEY	180,225	57,295	113,223	9,707	55,928	D	31.8%	62.8%	33.6%	66.4%
4,089	RED LAKE	1,456	624	724	108	100	D	42.9%	49.7%	46.3%	53.7%
16,059	REDWOOD	5,489	3,123	2,025	341	1,098	R	56.9%	36.9%	60.7%	39.3%
15,730	RENVILLE	5,717	2,808	2,563	346	245	R	49.1%	44.8%	52.3%	47.7%
64,142	RICE	21,390	9,048	11,121	1,221	2,073	D	42.3%	52.0%	44.9%	55.1%
9,687	ROCK	3,133	1,804	1,137	192	667	R	57.6%	36.3%	61.3%	38.7%
15,629	ROSEAU	5,374	3,136	1,925	313	1,211	R	58.4%	35.8%	62.0%	38.0%
129,928	SCOTT	45,084	25,586	17,142	2,356	8,444	R	56.8%	38.0%	59.9%	40.1%
88,499	SHERBURNE	30,373	17,795	10,784	1,794	7,011	R	58.6%	35.5%	62.3%	37.7%
15,226	SIBLEY	5,991	3,268	2,244	479	1,024	R	54.5%	37.5%	59.3%	40.7%
200,226	ST. LOUIS	81,311	26,423	50,484	4,404	24,061	D	32.5%	62.1%	34.4%	65.6%
150,642	STEARNS	51,017	26,753	21,242	3,022	5,511	R	52.4%	41.6%	55.7%	44.3%
36,576	STEELE	12,541	6,576	5,245	720	1,331	R	52.4%	41.8%	55.6%	44.4%
9,726	STEVENS	4,234	1,966	2,027	241	61	D	46.4%	47.9%	49.2%	50.8%
9,783	SWIFT	4,106	1,665	2,189	252	524	D	40.6%	53.3%	43.2%	56.8%
24,895	TODD	8,802	4,708	3,558	536	1,150	R	53.5%	40.4%	57.0%	43.0%
3,558	TRAVERSE	1,521	617	811	93	194	D	40.6%	53.3%	43.2%	56.8%
21,676	WABASHA	8,360	4,228	3,635	497	593	R	50.6%	43.5%	53.8%	46.2%
13,843	WADENA	5,099	2,932	1,877	290	1,055	R	57.5%	36.8%	61.0%	39.0%
19,136	WASECA	6,555	3,224	2,890	441	334	R	49.2%	44.1%	52.7%	47.3%
238,136	WASHINGTON	95,650	46,922	44,451	4,277	2,471	R	49.1%	46.5%	51.4%	48.6%
11,211	WATONWAN	3,691	1,687	1,764	240	77	D	45.7%	47.8%	48.9%	51.1%
6,576	WILKIN	2,312	1,198	988	126	210	R	51.8%	42.7%	54.8%	45.2%
51,461	WINONA	15,832	6,977	7,829	1,026	852	D	44.1%	49.5%	47.1%	52.9%
124,700	WRIGHT	44,600	26,172	15,901	2,527	10,271	R	58.7%	35.7%	62.2%	37.8%
10,438	YELLOW MEDICINE	3,975	1,906	1,863	206	43	R	47.9%	46.9%	50.6%	49.4%
5,303,925	TOTAL	1,975,406	879,257	989,113	107,036	109,856	D	44.5%	50.1%	47.1%	52.9%

MINNESOTA

SENATOR 2014

2010 Census Population	County	Total Vote	Republican (McFadden)	Democratic (Franken)	Other	Rep.-Dem. Plurality		Percentage			
								Total Vote		Major Vote	
								Rep.	Dem.	Rep.	Dem.
16,202	AITKIN	7,264	3,200	3,788	276	588	D	44.1%	52.1%	45.8%	54.2%
330,844	ANOKA	117,866	57,906	55,410	4,550	2,496	R	49.1%	47.0%	51.1%	48.9%
32,504	BECKER	12,023	5,941	5,396	686	545	R	49.4%	44.9%	52.4%	47.6%
44,442	BELTRAMI	15,433	6,456	8,252	725	1,796	D	41.8%	53.5%	43.9%	56.1%
38,451	BENTON	13,169	6,565	5,877	727	688	R	49.9%	44.6%	52.8%	47.2%
5,269	BIG STONE	2,122	851	1,166	105	315	D	40.1%	54.9%	42.2%	57.8%
64,013	BLUE EARTH	20,116	8,194	10,866	1,056	2,672	D	40.7%	54.0%	43.0%	57.0%
25,893	BROWN	9,344	4,657	4,270	417	387	R	49.8%	45.7%	52.2%	47.8%
35,386	CARLTON	13,880	4,666	8,633	581	3,967	D	33.6%	62.2%	35.1%	64.9%
91,042	CARVER	36,938	21,323	14,424	1,191	6,899	R	57.7%	39.0%	59.6%	40.4%
28,567	CASS	12,276	6,246	5,445	585	801	R	50.9%	44.4%	53.4%	46.6%
12,441	CHIPPEWA	4,666	2,001	2,460	205	459	D	42.9%	52.7%	44.9%	55.1%
53,887	CHISAGO	20,277	10,456	8,979	842	1,477	R	51.6%	44.3%	53.8%	46.2%
58,999	CLAY	17,898	6,908	10,229	761	3,321	D	38.6%	57.2%	40.3%	59.7%
8,695	CLEARWATER	2,898	1,536	1,196	166	340	R	53.0%	41.3%	56.2%	43.8%

MINNESOTA
SENATOR 2014

2010 Census Population	County	Total Vote	Republican (McFadden)	Democratic (Franken)	Other	Rep.-Dem. Plurality		Percentage			
								Total Vote		Major Vote	
								Rep.	Dem.	Rep.	Dem.
5,176	COOK	2,919	945	1,852	122	907	D	32.4%	63.4%	33.8%	66.2%
11,687	COTTONWOOD	4,304	2,077	1,982	245	95	R	48.3%	46.1%	51.2%	48.8%
62,500	CROW WING	26,908	13,715	12,049	1,144	1,666	R	51.0%	44.8%	53.2%	46.8%
398,552	DAKOTA	152,469	71,509	75,860	5,100	4,351	D	46.9%	49.8%	48.5%	51.5%
20,087	DODGE	7,677	3,816	3,354	507	462	R	49.7%	43.7%	53.2%	46.8%
36,009	DOUGLAS	15,369	7,853	6,879	637	974	R	51.1%	44.8%	53.3%	46.7%
14,553	FARIBAULT	5,431	2,615	2,502	314	113	R	48.1%	46.1%	51.1%	48.9%
20,866	FILLMORE	8,361	3,429	4,366	566	937	D	41.0%	52.2%	44.0%	56.0%
31,255	FREEBORN	12,416	5,125	6,719	572	1,594	D	41.3%	54.1%	43.3%	56.7%
46,183	GOODHUE	17,283	8,315	8,176	792	139	R	48.1%	47.3%	50.4%	49.6%
6,018	GRANT	2,865	1,165	1,554	146	389	D	40.7%	54.2%	42.8%	57.2%
1,152,425	HENNEPIN	449,612	158,269	278,240	13,103	119,971	D	35.2%	61.9%	36.3%	63.7%
19,027	HOUSTON	7,841	3,523	3,697	621	174	D	44.9%	47.1%	48.8%	51.2%
20,428	HUBBARD	8,719	4,462	3,880	377	582	R	51.2%	44.5%	53.5%	46.5%
37,816	ISANTI	13,937	7,269	6,022	646	1,247	R	52.2%	43.2%	54.7%	45.3%
45,058	ITASCA	18,976	7,447	10,781	748	3,334	D	39.2%	56.8%	40.9%	59.1%
10,266	JACKSON	3,872	1,892	1,741	239	151	R	48.9%	45.0%	52.1%	47.9%
16,239	KANABEC	6,220	2,912	2,983	325	71	D	46.8%	48.0%	49.4%	50.6%
42,239	KANDIYOHI	16,695	7,877	8,190	628	313	D	47.2%	49.1%	49.0%	51.0%
4,552	KITTSON	1,951	725	1,136	90	411	D	37.2%	58.2%	39.0%	61.0%
13,311	KOOCHICHING	5,351	1,936	3,108	307	1,172	D	36.2%	58.1%	38.4%	61.6%
7,259	LAC QUI PARLE	2,986	1,236	1,620	130	384	D	41.4%	54.3%	43.3%	56.7%
10,866	LAKE	5,139	1,752	3,170	217	1,418	D	34.1%	61.7%	35.6%	64.4%
4,045	LAKE OF THE WOODS	1,891	969	806	116	163	R	51.2%	42.6%	54.6%	45.4%
27,703	LE SUEUR	9,743	4,568	4,754	421	186	D	46.9%	48.8%	49.0%	51.0%
5,896	LINCOLN	2,333	1,041	1,100	192	59	D	44.6%	47.1%	48.6%	51.4%
25,857	LYON	8,371	4,178	3,799	394	379	R	49.9%	45.4%	52.4%	47.6%
5,413	MAHNOMEN	1,717	598	999	120	401	D	34.8%	58.2%	37.4%	62.6%
9,439	MARSHALL	4,087	1,796	2,054	237	258	D	43.9%	50.3%	46.6%	53.4%
20,840	MARTIN	7,855	4,188	3,200	467	988	R	53.3%	40.7%	56.7%	43.3%
36,651	MCLEOD	12,416	6,549	5,186	681	1,363	R	52.7%	41.8%	55.8%	44.2%
23,300	MEEKER	9,150	4,480	4,128	542	352	R	49.0%	45.1%	52.0%	48.0%
26,097	MILLE LACS	8,964	4,211	4,303	450	92	D	47.0%	48.0%	49.5%	50.5%
33,198	MORRISON	12,954	6,594	5,676	684	918	R	50.9%	43.8%	53.7%	46.3%
39,163	MOWER	11,848	4,571	6,672	605	2,101	D	38.6%	56.3%	40.7%	59.3%
8,725	MURRAY	3,535	1,626	1,606	303	20	R	46.0%	45.4%	50.3%	49.7%
32,727	NICOLLET	11,788	4,698	6,514	576	1,816	D	39.9%	55.3%	41.9%	58.1%
21,378	NOBLES	6,025	2,973	2,596	456	377	R	49.3%	43.1%	53.4%	46.6%
6,852	NORMAN	2,461	855	1,471	135	616	D	34.7%	59.8%	36.8%	63.2%
144,248	OLMSTED	50,460	23,375	24,757	2,328	1,382	D	46.3%	49.1%	48.6%	51.4%
57,303	OTTER TAIL	22,174	11,910	9,243	1,021	2,667	R	53.7%	41.7%	56.3%	43.7%
13,930	PENNINGTON	5,132	2,290	2,515	327	225	D	44.6%	49.0%	47.7%	52.3%
29,750	PINE	10,425	4,531	5,360	534	829	D	43.5%	51.4%	45.8%	54.2%
9,596	PIPESTONE	3,813	2,119	1,384	310	735	R	55.6%	36.3%	60.5%	39.5%
31,600	POLK	9,805	4,522	4,778	505	256	D	46.1%	48.7%	48.6%	51.4%
10,995	POPE	4,944	2,143	2,595	206	452	D	43.3%	52.5%	45.2%	54.8%
508,640	RAMSEY	180,893	56,010	118,768	6,115	62,758	D	31.0%	65.7%	32.0%	68.0%
4,089	RED LAKE	1,469	605	779	85	174	D	41.2%	53.0%	43.7%	56.3%
16,059	REDWOOD	5,516	2,848	2,342	326	506	R	51.6%	42.5%	54.9%	45.1%
15,730	RENVILLE	5,742	2,556	2,911	275	355	D	44.5%	50.7%	46.8%	53.2%
64,142	RICE	21,493	8,603	12,045	845	3,442	D	40.0%	56.0%	41.7%	58.3%
9,687	ROCK	3,156	1,793	1,141	222	652	R	56.8%	36.2%	61.1%	38.9%
15,629	ROSEAU	5,405	3,043	2,083	279	960	R	56.3%	38.5%	59.4%	40.6%
129,928	SCOTT	45,202	24,963	18,597	1,642	6,366	R	55.2%	41.1%	57.3%	42.7%
88,499	SHERBURNE	30,449	17,390	11,745	1,314	5,645	R	57.1%	38.6%	59.7%	40.3%
15,226	SIBLEY	6,013	2,995	2,632	386	363	R	49.8%	43.8%	53.2%	46.8%
200,226	ST. LOUIS	81,598	26,114	52,347	3,137	26,233	D	32.0%	64.2%	33.3%	66.7%
150,642	STEARNS	51,246	25,329	23,607	2,310	1,722	R	49.4%	46.1%	51.8%	48.2%
36,576	STEELE	12,576	6,147	5,797	632	350	R	48.9%	46.1%	51.5%	48.5%
9,726	STEVENS	4,250	1,878	2,216	156	338	D	44.2%	52.1%	45.9%	54.1%

MINNESOTA

SENATOR 2014

2010 Census Population	County	Total Vote	Republican (McFadden)	Democratic (Franken)	Other	Rep.-Dem. Plurality	Percentage			
							Total Vote		Major Vote	
							Rep.	Dem.	Rep.	Dem.
9,783	SWIFT	4,124	1,591	2,345	188	754 D	38.6%	56.9%	40.4%	59.6%
24,895	TODD	8,847	4,398	3,958	491	440 R	49.7%	44.7%	52.6%	47.4%
3,558	TRAVERSE	1,533	572	882	79	310 D	37.3%	57.5%	39.3%	60.7%
21,676	WABASHA	8,384	3,836	4,043	505	207 D	45.8%	48.2%	48.7%	51.3%
13,843	WADENA	5,124	2,841	2,041	242	800 R	55.4%	39.8%	58.2%	41.8%
19,136	WASECA	6,580	3,017	3,205	358	188 D	45.9%	48.7%	48.5%	51.5%
238,136	WASHINGTON	95,921	45,475	47,350	3,096	1,875 D	47.4%	49.4%	49.0%	51.0%
11,211	WATONWAN	3,705	1,563	1,943	199	380 D	42.2%	52.4%	44.6%	55.4%
6,576	WILKIN	2,333	1,147	1,045	141	102 R	49.2%	44.8%	52.3%	47.7%
51,461	WINONA	15,872	6,690	8,252	930	1,562 D	42.1%	52.0%	44.8%	55.2%
124,700	WRIGHT	44,742	25,496	17,326	1,920	8,170 R	57.0%	38.7%	59.5%	40.5%
10,438	YELLOW MEDICINE	3,993	1,772	2,057	164	285 D	44.4%	51.5%	46.3%	53.7%
5,303,925	TOTAL	1,981,528	850,227	1,053,205	78,096	202,978 D	42.9%	53.2%	44.7%	55.3%

MINNESOTA

HOUSE OF REPRESENTATIVES

CD	Year	Total Vote	Republican		Democratic		Other Vote	Rep.-Dem. Plurality	Percentage			
			Vote	Candidate	Vote	Candidate			Total Vote		Major Vote	
									Rep.	Dem.	Rep.	Dem.
1	2014	226,695	103,536	HAGEDORN, JAMES "JIM"	122,851	WALZ, TIMOTHY J.*	308	19,315 D	45.7%	54.2%	45.7%	54.3%
1	2012	335,880	142,164	QUIST, ALLEN	193,211	WALZ, TIMOTHY J.*	505	51,047 D	42.3%	57.5%	42.4%	57.6%
2	2014	245,848	137,778	KLINE, JOHN*	95,565	OBERMUELLER, MIKE	12,505	42,213 R	56.0%	38.9%	59.0%	41.0%
2	2012	358,446	193,587	KLINE, JOHN*	164,338	OBERMUELLER, MIKE	521	29,249 R	54.0%	45.8%	54.1%	45.9%
3	2014	269,585	167,515	PAULSEN, ERIK*	101,846	SUND, SHARON	224	65,669 R	62.1%	37.8%	62.2%	37.8%
3	2012	382,705	222,335	PAULSEN, ERIK*	159,937	BARNES, BRIAN	433	62,398 R	58.1%	41.8%	58.2%	41.8%
4	2014	241,637	79,492	WAHLGREN, SHARNA	147,857	MCCOLLUM, BETTY*	14,288	68,365 D	32.9%	61.2%	35.0%	65.0%
4	2012	347,991	109,659	HERNANDEZ, TONY	216,685	MCCOLLUM, BETTY*	21,647	107,026 D	31.5%	62.3%	33.6%	66.4%
5	2014	236,010	56,577	DAGGETT, DOUG J.	167,079	ELLISON, KEITH*	12,354	110,502 D	24.0%	70.8%	25.3%	74.7%
5	2012	351,969	88,753	FIELDS, CHRIS	262,102	ELLISON, KEITH*	1,114	173,349 D	25.2%	74.5%	25.3%	74.7%
6	2014	236,846	133,328	EMMER, TOM	90,926	PERSKE, JOE	12,592	42,402 R	56.3%	38.4%	59.5%	40.5%
6	2012	355,153	179,240	BACHMANN, MICHELE*	174,944	GRAVES, JIM	969	4,296 R	50.5%	49.3%	50.6%	49.4%
7	2014	240,835	109,955	WESTROM, TORREY NORMAN	130,546	PETERSON, COLLIN C.*	334	20,591 D	45.7%	54.2%	45.7%	54.3%
7	2012	327,576	114,151	BYBERG, LEE	197,791	PETERSON, COLLIN C.*	15,634	83,640 D	34.8%	60.4%	36.6%	63.4%
8	2014	266,083	125,358	MILLS, STEWART	129,090	NOLAN, RICHARD M.*	11,635	3,732 D	47.1%	48.5%	49.3%	50.7%
8	2012	353,663	160,520	CRAVAACK, CHIP*	191,976	NOLAN, RICHARD M.	1,167	31,456 D	45.4%	54.3%	45.5%	54.5%
TOTAL	2014	1,963,539	913,539		985,760		64,240	72,221 D	46.5%	50.2%	48.1%	51.9%
TOTAL	2012	2,813,383	1,210,409		1,560,984		41,990	350,575 D	43.0%	55.5%	43.7%	56.3%

Note: An asterisk (*) denotes incumbent.

MINNESOTA

GENERAL AND PRIMARY ELECTIONS

2014 GENERAL ELECTIONS: OTHER VOTES

Governor   Other vote was 56,900 Independence (Hannah Nicollet), 31,259 Grassroots - Legalize Cannabis (Chris Wright), 18,082 Libertarian (Chris Holbrook), 795 scattered write-in

Senate   Other vote was 47,530 Independence (Steve Carlson), 29,685 Libertarian (Heather Johnson), 881 scattered write-in

MINNESOTA

GENERAL AND PRIMARY ELECTIONS

House　　Other vote was:

CD 1　　308 scattered write-in
CD 2　　12,319 Independence (Paula Overby), 186 scattered write-in
CD 3　　224 scattered write-in
CD 4　　14,059 Independence (David "Dave" Thomas), 229 scattered write-in
CD 5　　12,001 Independence (Lee Bauer), 353 scattered write-in
CD 6　　12,457 Independence (John Denney), 135 scattered write-in
CD 7　　334 scattered write-in
CD 8　　11,450 Green (Ray "Skip" Sandman), 185 scattered write-in

2014 PRIMARY ELECTIONS: SUPPLEMENTARY INFORMATION

Primary　August 12, 2014　　**Registration** (as of August 12, 2014)　　3,130,855　　No Party Registration

Primary Type　Open—Any registered voter could participate in the party primary of their choice.

	REPUBLICAN PRIMARIES			DEMOCRATIC PRIMARIES		
Senator	McFadden, Mike	129,601	71.7%	Franken, Al*	182,720	94.5%
	Abeler, James J. "Jim"	26,714	14.8%	Henningsgard, Sandra	10,627	5.5%
	Carlson, David	16,449	9.1%			
	Munro, Patrick D.	5,058	2.8%			
	Savior, Ole	2,840	1.6%			
	TOTAL	*180,662*		*TOTAL*	*193,347*	
Governor	Johnson, Jeff	55,836	30.3%	Dayton, Mark*	177,849	93.0%
	Zellers, Kurt	44,046	23.9%	Davis, Leslie	8,530	4.5%
	Seifert, Marty	38,851	21.1%	Dahn, Bill	4,880	2.6%
	Honour, Scott	38,377	20.8%			
	Anderson, Merrill	7,000	3.8%			
	TOTAL	*184,110*		*TOTAL*	*191,259*	
Congressional District 1	Hagedorn, James "Jim"	12,748	54.0%	Walz, Timothy J.*	19,983	100.0%
	Miller, Aaron	10,870	46.0%			
	TOTAL	*23,618*		*TOTAL*	*19,983*	
Congressional District 2	Kline, John*	18,236	100.0%	Obermueller, Mike	12,361	82.5%
				Roberts, Michael J.	2,622	17.5%
	TOTAL	*18,236*		*TOTAL*	*14,983*	
Congressional District 3	Paulsen, Erik*	Unopposed		Sund, Sharon	Unopposed	
Congressional District 4	Wahlgren, Sharna	Unopposed		McCollum, Betty*	Unopposed	
Congressional District 5	Daggett, Doug J.	Unopposed		Ellison, Keith*	Unopposed	
Congressional District 6	Emmer, Tom	19,557	73.3%	Perske, Joe	10,070	100.0%
	Sivarajah, Rhonda	7,125	26.7%			
	TOTAL	*26,682*		*TOTAL*	*10,070*	
Congressional District 7	Westrom, Torrey Norman	Unopposed		Peterson, Collin C.*	Unopposed	
Congressional District 8	Mills, Stewart	Unopposed		Nolan, Richard M.*	Unopposed	

Note: An asterisk (*) denotes incumbent.

MISSISSIPPI

Congressional districts first established for elections held in 2012

4 members

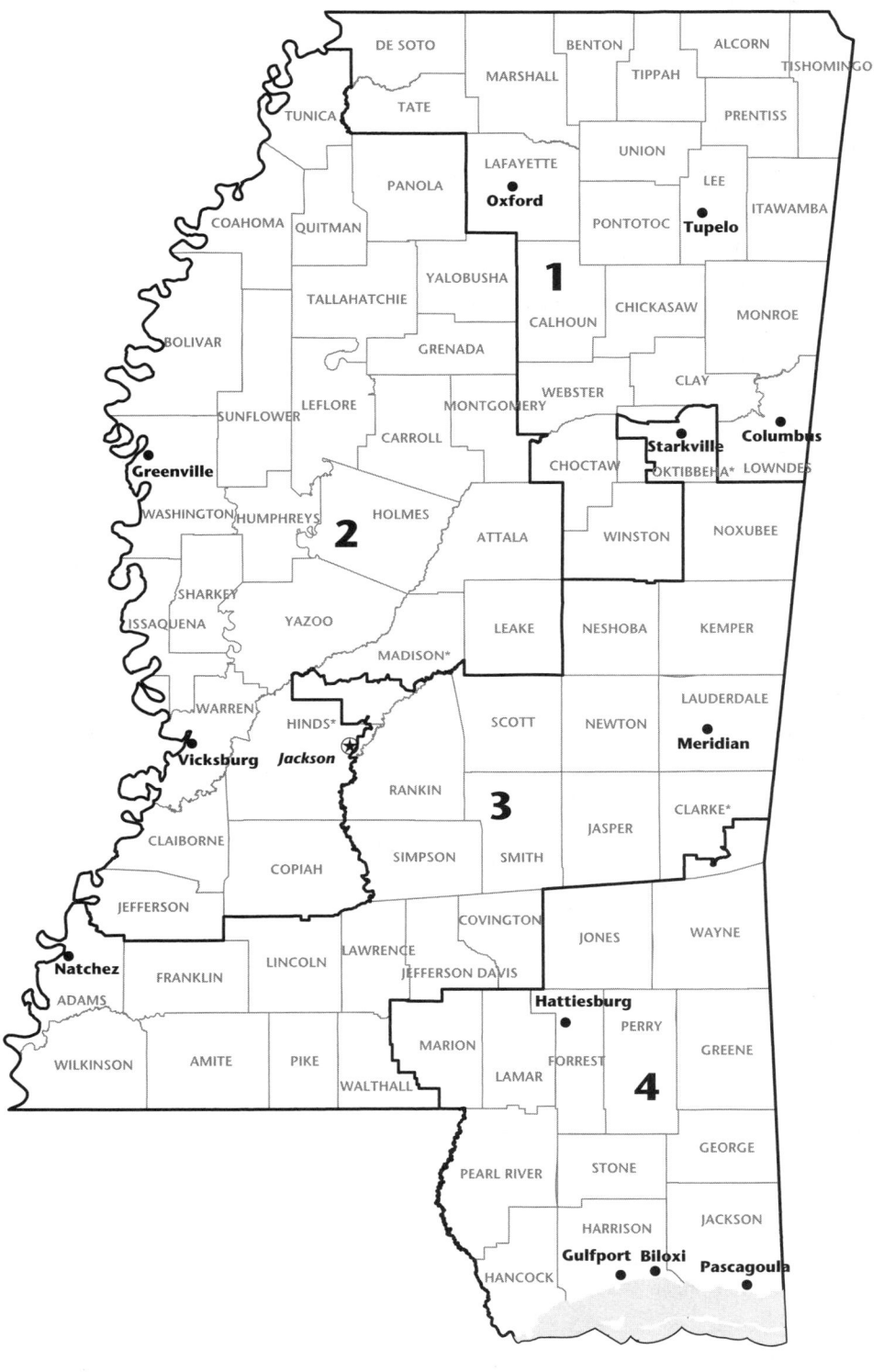

* Asterisk indicates a county whose boundaries include parts of two or more congressional districts.

MISSISSIPPI

GOVERNOR
Phil Bryant (R). Elected 2011 to a four-year term.

SENATORS (2 Republicans)
Thad Cochran (R). Reelected 2014 to a six-year term. Previously elected 2008, 2002, 1996, 1990, 1984, 1978.

Roger F. Wicker (R). Reelected 2012 to a six-year term. Previously elected 2008 to fill the final four years of the term vacated by the December 2007 resignation of Senator C. Trent Lott. Wicker had been appointed to fill the vacancy and was sworn in as senator on December 31, 2007.

REPRESENTATIVES (3 Republicans, 1 Democrat)
1. Trent Kelly (R)
2. Bennie G. Thompson (D)
3. Gregg Harper (R)
4. Steven M. Palazzo (R)

POSTWAR VOTE FOR PRESIDENT

| | | Republican | | Democratic | | | | Percentage | | | |
| | | | | | | | | Total Vote | | Major Vote | |
Year	Total Vote	Vote	Candidate	Vote	Candidate	Other Vote	Rep.-Dem. Plurality	Rep.	Dem.	Rep.	Dem.
2012	1,285,584	710,746	Romney, W. Mitt	562,949	Obama, Barack H.*	11,889	147,797 R	55.3%	43.8%	55.8%	44.2%
2008	1,289,865	724,597	McCain, John S. III	554,662	Obama, Barack H.	10,606	169,935 R	56.2%	43.0%	56.6%	43.4%
2004	1,152,145	684,981	Bush, George W.*	458,094	Kerry, John F.	9,070	226,887 R	59.5%	39.8%	59.9%	40.1%
2000**	994,184	572,844	Bush, George W.	404,614	Gore, Albert Jr.	16,726	168,230 R	57.6%	40.7%	58.6%	41.4%
1996**	893,857	439,838	Dole, Robert "Bob"	394,022	Clinton, Bill*	59,997	45,816 R	49.2%	44.1%	52.7%	47.3%
1992**	981,793	487,793	Bush, George H.*	400,258	Clinton, Bill	93,742	87,535 R	49.7%	40.8%	54.9%	45.1%
1988	931,527	557,890	Bush, George H.	363,921	Dukakis, Michael S.	9,716	193,969 R	59.9%	39.1%	60.5%	39.5%
1984	941,104	582,377	Reagan, Ronald*	352,192	Mondale, Walter F.	6,535	230,185 R	61.9%	37.4%	62.3%	37.7%
1980**	892,620	441,089	Reagan, Ronald	429,281	Carter, Jimmy*	22,250	11,808 R	49.4%	48.1%	50.7%	49.3%
1976	769,361	366,846	Ford, Gerald R.*	381,309	Carter, Jimmy	21,206	14,463 D	47.7%	49.6%	49.0%	51.0%
1972	645,963	505,125	Nixon, Richard M.*	126,782	McGovern, George S.	14,056	378,343 R	78.2%	19.6%	79.9%	20.1%
1968**	654,509	88,516	Nixon, Richard M.	150,644	Humphrey, Hubert Horatio Jr.	415,349	62,128 D#	13.5%	23.0%	37.0%	63.0%
1964	409,146	356,528	Goldwater, Barry M. Sr.	52,618	Johnson, Lyndon B.*		303,910 R	87.1%	12.9%	87.1%	12.9%
1960**	298,171	73,561	Nixon, Richard M.	108,362	Kennedy, John F.	116,248	34,801 D#	24.7%	36.3%	40.4%	59.6%
1956	248,104	60,685	Eisenhower, Dwight D.*	144,453	Stevenson, Adlai E. II	42,966	83,768 D	24.5%	58.2%	29.6%	70.4%
1952	285,532	112,966	Eisenhower, Dwight D.	172,566	Stevenson, Adlai E. II		59,600 D	39.6%	60.4%	39.6%	60.4%
1948**	192,190	5,043	Dewey, Thomas E.	19,384	Truman, Harry S.*	167,763	14,341 D#	2.6%	10.1%	20.6%	79.4%

Note: An asterisk (*) denotes incumbent. A pound sign (#) indicates that the state was carried by a third party candidate or independent electoral state. **In past elections, the other vote included: 2000 - 8,122 Green (Ralph Nader); 1996 - 52,222 Reform (Ross Perot); 1992 - 85,626 Independent (Perot); 1980 - 12,036 Independent (John Anderson); 1968 - 415,349 American Independent (George Wallace); 1960 - 116,248 Unpledged Independent Democratic electors; 1948 - 167,538 States' Rights (Strom Thurmond). Thurmond won Mississippi in 1948 with 87.2 percent of the vote. The slate of Unpledged Independent Democratic electors carried the state in 1960 with 39.0 percent. Wallace won Mississippi in 1968 with 63.5 percent of the vote.

MISSISSIPPI

POSTWAR VOTE FOR GOVERNOR

Year	Total Vote	Republican Vote	Republican Candidate	Democratic Vote	Democratic Candidate	Other Vote	Rep.-Dem. Plurality	Total Vote Rep.	Total Vote Dem.	Major Vote Rep.	Major Vote Dem.
2011	893,468	544,851	Bryant, Phil	348,617	DuPree, Johnny L.		196,234 R	61.0%	39.0%	61.0%	39.0%
2007	744,039	430,807	Barbour, Haley*	313,232	Eaves, John Arthur Jr.		117,575 R	57.9%	42.1%	57.9%	42.1%
2003	894,487	470,404	Barbour, Haley	409,787	Musgrove, Ronnie*	14,296	60,617 R	52.6%	45.8%	53.4%	46.6%
1999**	763,938	370,691	Parker, Mike	379,034	Musgrove, Ronnie	14,213	8,343 D	48.5%	49.6%	49.4%	50.6%
1995	819,471	455,261	Fordice, Kirk*	364,210	Molpus, Dick		91,051 R	55.6%	44.4%	55.6%	44.4%
1991	711,188	361,500	Fordice, Kirk	338,435	Mabus, Ray*	11,253	23,065 R	50.8%	47.6%	51.6%	48.4%
1987	721,695	336,006	Reed, Jack R.	385,689	Mabus, Ray		49,683 D	46.6%	53.4%	46.6%	53.4%
1983	742,737	288,764	Bramlett, Leon	409,209	Allain, William A.	44,764	120,445 D	38.9%	55.1%	41.4%	58.6%
1979	677,322	263,702	Carmichael, Gil	413,620	Winter, William		149,918 D	38.9%	61.1%	38.9%	61.1%
1975	708,033	319,632	Carmichael, Gil	369,568	Finch, Cliff	18,833	49,936 D	45.1%	52.2%	46.4%	53.6%
1971**	780,537			601,122	Waller, William L.	179,415			77.0%		100.0%
1967	448,696	133,378	Phillips, Rubel L.	315,318	Williams, John Bell		181,940 D	29.7%	70.3%	29.7%	70.3%
1963	363,971	138,515	Phillips, Rubel L.	225,456	Johnson, Paul B. Jr.		86,941 D	38.1%	61.9%	38.1%	61.9%
1959	57,671			57,671	Barnett, Ross R.		57,671 D		100.0%		100.0%
1955	40,707			40,707	Coleman, James P.		40,707 D		100.0%		100.0%
1951	43,422			43,422	White, Hugh L.		43,422 D		100.0%		100.0%
1947	166,095			161,993	Wright, Fielding L.	4,102	161,993 D		97.5%		100.0%

Note: An asterisk (*) denotes incumbent. **In past elections, the other vote included: 1971 - 172,762 Independent (Charles Evers), who finished second. In 1999 no candidate received a majority of the vote. Democrat Ronnie Musgrove was elected in January 2000 by the Mississippi House of Representatives. The Republican Party did not run a gubernatorial candidate in 1947, 1951, 1955, 1959, and 1971.

POSTWAR VOTE FOR SENATOR

Year	Total Vote	Republican Vote	Republican Candidate	Democratic Vote	Democratic Candidate	Other Vote	Rep.-Dem. Plurality	Total Vote Rep.	Total Vote Dem.	Major Vote Rep.	Major Vote Dem.
2014	631,858	378,481	Cochran, Thad*	239,439	Childers, Travis	13,938	139,042 R	59.9%	37.9%	61.3%	38.7%
2012	1,241,568	709,626	Wicker, Roger F.*	503,467	Gore, Albert N. Jr.	28,475	206,159 R	57.2%	40.6%	58.5%	41.5%
2008S	1,243,473	683,409	Wicker, Roger F.*	560,064	Musgrove, Ronnie		123,345 R	55.0%	45.0%	55.0%	45.0%
2008	1,247,026	766,111	Cochran, Thad*	480,915	Fleming, Erik R.		285,196 R	61.4%	38.6%	61.4%	38.6%
2006	610,921	388,399	Lott, C. Trent*	213,000	Fleming, Erik R.	9,522	175,399 R	63.6%	34.9%	64.6%	35.4%
2002**	630,495	533,269	Cochran, Thad*			97,226	533,269 R	84.6%		100.0%	
2000	994,144	654,941	Lott, C. Trent*	314,090	Brown, Troy	25,113	340,851 R	65.9%	31.6%	67.6%	32.4%
1996	878,662	624,154	Cochran, Thad*	240,647	Hunt, James W. "Bootie"	13,861	383,507 R	71.0%	27.4%	72.2%	27.8%
1994	608,085	418,333	Lott, C. Trent*	189,752	Harper, Ken		228,581 R	68.8%	31.2%	68.8%	31.2%
1990	274,244	274,244	Cochran, Thad*				274,244 R	100.0%		100.0%	
1988	946,719	510,380	Lott, C. Trent	436,339	Dowdy, Wayne		74,041 R	53.9%	46.1%	53.9%	46.1%
1984	952,240	580,314	Cochran, Thad*	371,926	Winter, William		208,388 R	60.9%	39.1%	60.9%	39.1%
1982	645,026	230,927	Barbour, Haley	414,099	Stennis, John*		183,172 D	35.8%	64.2%	35.8%	64.2%
1978**	583,936	263,089	Cochran, Thad	185,454	Dantin, Maurice	135,393	77,635 R	45.1%	31.8%	58.7%	41.3%
1976	554,433			554,433	Stennis, John*		554,433 D		100.0%		100.0%
1972	645,746	249,779	Carmichael, Gil	375,102	Eastland, James O.*	20,865	125,323 D	38.7%	58.1%	40.0%	60.0%
1970**	324,215			286,622	Stennis, John*	37,593	286,622 D		88.4%		100.0%
1966	394,541	105,652	Walker, Prentiss	258,248	Eastland, James O.*	30,641	152,596 D	26.8%	65.5%	29.0%	71.0%
1964	343,364			343,364	Stennis, John*		343,364 D		100.0%		100.0%
1960	266,148	21,807	Moore, Joe A.	244,341	Eastland, James O.*		222,534 D	8.2%	91.8%	8.2%	91.8%
1958	61,039			61,039	Stennis, John*		61,039 D		100.0%		100.0%
1954	105,526	4,678	White, James A.	100,848	Eastland, James O.*		96,170 D	4.4%	95.6%	4.4%	95.6%
1952	233,919			233,919	Stennis, John*		233,919 D		100.0%		100.0%
1948	151,478			151,478	Eastland, James O.*		151,478 D		100.0%		100.0%
1947S**	193,086			32,068	Stennis, John	141,018	D				
1946	46,747			46,747	Bilbo, Theodore G.*		46,747 D		100.0%		100.0%

Note: An asterisk (*) denotes incumbent. **In past elections, the other vote included: 2002 - 97,226 Reform (Shawn O'Hara), who finished second; 1978 - 133,646 Independent (Charles Evers). The 1947 election and one of the 2008 elections were for short terms to fill a vacancy. Both special elections were held without party designation or nomination. In 1947 John Stennis received 52,068 votes (26.9 percent of the total vote) and won the election with a plurality of 6,343 votes. Other candidates that year included: 45,725 W. M. Colmer; 43,642 Forrest B. Jackson; 27,159 Paul B. Johnson; 24,492 John E. Rankin. The Republican Party did not run a candidate in Senate elections in 1946, 1948, 1952, 1958, 1964, 1970, and 1976. The Democratic Party did not run a candidate in Senate elections in 1990 and 2002.

MISSISSIPPI
SENATOR 2014

2010 Census Population	County	Total Vote	Republican (Cochran)	Democratic (Childers)	Other	Rep.-Dem. Plurality		Percentage			
								Total Vote		Major Vote	
								Rep.	Dem.	Rep.	Dem.
32,297	ADAMS	8,615	4,360	4,142	113	218	R	50.6%	48.1%	51.3%	48.7%
37,057	ALCORN	6,077	4,300	1,686	91	2,614	R	70.8%	27.7%	71.8%	28.2%
13,131	AMITE	3,940	2,306	1,529	105	777	R	58.5%	38.8%	60.1%	39.9%
19,564	ATTALA	4,159	2,508	1,575	76	933	R	60.3%	37.9%	61.4%	38.6%
8,729	BENTON	1,919	920	970	29	50	D	47.9%	50.5%	48.7%	51.3%
34,145	BOLIVAR	8,514	3,996	4,410	108	414	D	46.9%	51.8%	47.5%	52.5%
14,962	CALHOUN	3,406	2,136	1,224	46	912	R	62.7%	35.9%	63.6%	36.4%
10,597	CARROLL	3,088	2,127	902	59	1,225	R	68.9%	29.2%	70.2%	29.8%
17,392	CHICKASAW	4,300	2,002	2,269	29	267	D	46.6%	52.8%	46.9%	53.1%
8,547	CHOCTAW	2,277	1,521	713	43	808	R	66.8%	31.3%	68.1%	31.9%
9,604	CLAIBORNE	2,179	551	1,610	18	1,059	D	25.3%	73.9%	25.5%	74.5%
16,732	CLARKE	4,133	2,760	1,275	98	1,485	R	66.8%	30.8%	68.4%	31.6%
20,634	CLAY	6,371	2,797	3,522	52	725	D	43.9%	55.3%	44.3%	55.7%
26,151	COAHOMA	4,961	2,218	2,670	73	452	D	44.7%	53.8%	45.4%	54.6%
29,449	COPIAH	6,415	3,330	2,950	135	380	R	51.9%	46.0%	53.0%	47.0%
19,568	COVINGTON	5,117	2,940	2,000	177	940	R	57.5%	39.1%	59.5%	40.5%
161,252	DE SOTO	25,312	16,920	7,535	857	9,385	R	66.8%	29.8%	69.2%	30.8%
74,934	FORREST	14,346	9,196	4,766	384	4,430	R	64.1%	33.2%	65.9%	34.1%
8,118	FRANKLIN	2,278	1,445	794	39	651	R	63.4%	34.9%	64.5%	35.5%
22,578	GEORGE	4,353	3,331	728	294	2,603	R	76.5%	16.7%	82.1%	17.9%
14,400	GREENE	2,375	1,708	517	150	1,191	R	71.9%	21.8%	76.8%	23.2%
21,906	GRENADA	5,572	3,111	2,377	84	734	R	55.8%	42.7%	56.7%	43.3%
43,929	HANCOCK	9,177	6,699	2,004	474	4,695	R	73.0%	21.8%	77.0%	23.0%
187,105	HARRISON	33,604	22,113	10,269	1,222	11,844	R	65.8%	30.6%	68.3%	31.7%
245,285	HINDS	51,184	20,975	29,609	600	8,634	D	41.0%	57.8%	41.5%	58.5%
19,198	HOLMES	4,422	1,313	3,069	40	1,756	D	29.7%	69.4%	30.0%	70.0%
9,375	HUMPHREYS	2,268	990	1,262	16	272	D	43.7%	55.6%	44.0%	56.0%
1,406	ISSAQUENA	379	196	181	2	15	R	51.7%	47.8%	52.0%	48.0%
23,401	ITAWAMBA	4,798	3,259	1,452	87	1,807	R	67.9%	30.3%	69.2%	30.8%
139,668	JACKSON	30,455	21,393	8,065	997	13,328	R	70.2%	26.5%	72.6%	27.4%
17,062	JASPER	4,680	2,073	2,493	114	420	D	44.3%	53.3%	45.4%	54.6%
7,726	JEFFERSON	1,915	444	1,455	16	1,011	D	23.2%	76.0%	23.4%	76.6%
12,487	JEFFERSON DAVIS	3,985	1,644	2,264	77	620	D	41.3%	56.8%	42.1%	57.9%
67,761	JONES	16,726	9,444	6,540	742	2,904	R	56.5%	39.1%	59.1%	40.9%
10,456	KEMPER	2,315	1,043	1,244	28	201	D	45.1%	53.7%	45.6%	54.4%
47,351	LAFAYETTE	9,728	6,311	3,278	139	3,033	R	64.9%	33.7%	65.8%	34.2%
55,658	LAMAR	13,598	10,399	2,786	413	7,613	R	76.5%	20.5%	78.9%	21.1%
80,261	LAUDERDALE	14,702	10,359	4,109	234	6,250	R	70.5%	27.9%	71.6%	28.4%
12,929	LAWRENCE	3,391	2,142	1,183	66	959	R	63.2%	34.9%	64.4%	35.6%
23,805	LEAKE	4,686	2,667	1,923	96	744	R	56.9%	41.0%	58.1%	41.9%
82,910	LEE	18,865	11,792	6,790	283	5,002	R	62.5%	36.0%	63.5%	36.5%
32,317	LEFLORE	5,839	2,472	3,332	35	860	D	42.3%	57.1%	42.6%	57.4%
34,869	LINCOLN	7,415	5,278	1,987	150	3,291	R	71.2%	26.8%	72.6%	27.4%
59,779	LOWNDES	14,626	8,245	6,229	152	2,016	R	56.4%	42.6%	57.0%	43.0%
95,203	MADISON	24,386	16,359	7,737	290	8,622	R	67.1%	31.7%	67.9%	32.1%
27,088	MARION	6,195	4,067	1,997	131	2,070	R	65.6%	32.2%	67.1%	32.9%
37,144	MARSHALL	7,283	3,130	4,007	146	877	D	43.0%	55.0%	43.9%	56.1%
36,989	MONROE	7,776	4,552	3,150	74	1,402	R	58.5%	40.5%	59.1%	40.9%
10,925	MONTGOMERY	2,746	1,539	1,154	53	385	R	56.0%	42.0%	57.1%	42.9%
29,676	NESHOBA	6,140	4,526	1,495	119	3,031	R	73.7%	24.3%	75.2%	24.8%
21,720	NEWTON	5,015	3,602	1,308	105	2,294	R	71.8%	26.1%	73.4%	26.6%
11,545	NOXUBEE	2,842	863	1,958	21	1,095	D	30.4%	68.9%	30.6%	69.4%
47,671	OKTIBBEHA	9,087	5,340	3,683	64	1,657	R	58.8%	40.5%	59.2%	40.8%
34,707	PANOLA	6,813	3,535	3,165	113	370	R	51.9%	46.5%	52.8%	47.2%
55,834	PEARL RIVER	10,755	7,943	2,096	716	5,847	R	73.9%	19.5%	79.1%	20.9%
12,250	PERRY	2,738	1,814	798	126	1,016	R	66.3%	29.1%	69.4%	30.6%
40,404	PIKE	7,821	4,203	3,481	137	722	R	53.7%	44.5%	54.7%	45.3%
29,957	PONTOTOC	6,511	4,539	1,830	142	2,709	R	69.7%	28.1%	71.3%	28.7%
25,276	PRENTISS	5,282	2,588	2,635	59	47	D	49.0%	49.9%	49.6%	50.4%
8,223	QUITMAN	2,512	998	1,464	50	466	D	39.7%	58.3%	40.5%	59.5%

MISSISSIPPI

SENATOR 2014

2010 Census Population	County	Total Vote	Republican (Cochran)	Democratic (Childers)	Other	Rep.-Dem. Plurality	Total Vote Rep.	Total Vote Dem.	Major Vote Rep.	Major Vote Dem.
141,617	RANKIN	32,120	24,552	6,840	728	17,712 R	76.4%	21.3%	78.2%	21.8%
28,264	SCOTT	5,012	3,117	1,803	92	1,314 R	62.2%	36.0%	63.4%	36.6%
4,916	SHARKEY	1,111	539	560	12	21 D	48.5%	50.4%	49.0%	51.0%
27,503	SIMPSON	6,965	4,347	2,502	116	1,845 R	62.4%	35.9%	63.5%	36.5%
16,491	SMITH	4,292	2,890	1,276	126	1,614 R	67.3%	29.7%	69.4%	30.6%
17,786	STONE	4,026	2,886	980	160	1,906 R	71.7%	24.3%	74.7%	25.3%
29,450	SUNFLOWER	5,088	2,002	3,032	54	1,030 D	39.3%	59.6%	39.8%	60.2%
15,378	TALLAHATCHIE	2,892	1,340	1,509	43	169 D	46.3%	52.2%	47.0%	53.0%
28,886	TATE	4,970	3,159	1,676	135	1,483 R	63.6%	33.7%	65.3%	34.7%
22,232	TIPPAH	4,841	3,243	1,513	85	1,730 R	67.0%	31.3%	68.2%	31.8%
19,593	TISHOMINGO	4,623	3,088	1,425	110	1,663 R	66.8%	30.8%	68.4%	31.6%
10,778	TUNICA	1,663	642	995	26	353 D	38.6%	59.8%	39.2%	60.8%
27,134	UNION	5,720	3,996	1,655	69	2,341 R	69.9%	28.9%	70.7%	29.3%
15,443	WALTHALL	3,981	2,289	1,598	94	691 R	57.5%	40.1%	58.9%	41.1%
48,773	WARREN	11,130	6,480	4,448	202	2,032 R	58.2%	40.0%	59.3%	40.7%
51,137	WASHINGTON	8,680	3,987	4,586	107	599 D	45.9%	52.8%	46.5%	53.5%
20,747	WAYNE	4,322	2,384	1,773	165	611 R	55.2%	41.0%	57.3%	42.7%
10,253	WEBSTER	2,815	2,116	661	38	1,455 R	75.2%	23.5%	76.2%	23.8%
9,878	WILKINSON	2,133	841	1,267	25	426 D	39.4%	59.4%	39.9%	60.1%
19,198	WINSTON	4,995	2,783	2,155	57	628 R	55.7%	43.1%	56.4%	43.6%
12,678	YALOBUSHA	3,223	1,710	1,465	48	245 R	53.1%	45.5%	53.9%	46.1%
28,065	YAZOO	4,889	2,758	2,074	57	684 R	56.4%	42.4%	57.1%	42.9%
2,967,297	TOTAL	631,858	378,481	239,439	13,938	139,042 R	59.9%	37.9%	61.3%	38.7%

MISSISSIPPI

HOUSE OF REPRESENTATIVES

CD	Year	Total Vote	Republican Vote	Republican Candidate	Democratic Vote	Democratic Candidate	Other Vote	Rep.-Dem. Plurality	Total Vote Rep.	Total Vote Dem.	Major Vote Rep.	Major Vote Dem.
1	2014	151,111	102,622	NUNNELEE, ALAN*	43,713	DICKEY, RON E.	4,776	58,909 R	67.9%	28.9%	70.1%	29.9%
1	2012	309,177	186,760	NUNNELEE, ALAN*	114,076	MORRIS, BRAD	8,341	72,684 R	60.4%	36.9%	62.1%	37.9%
2	2014	148,646			100,688	THOMPSON, BENNIE G.*	47,958	100,688 D		67.7%		100.0%
2	2012	320,244	99,160	MARCY, BILL	214,978	THOMPSON, BENNIE G.*	6,106	115,818 D	31.0%	67.1%	31.6%	68.4%
3	2014	170,946	117,771	HARPER, GREGG*	47,744	MAGEE, DOUGLAS MACARTHUR "DOUG"	5,431	70,027 R	68.9%	27.9%	71.2%	28.8%
3	2012	293,322	234,717	HARPER, GREGG*			58,605	234,717 R	80.0%		100.0%	
4	2014	155,576	108,776	PALAZZO, STEVEN M.*	37,869	MOORE, MATT	8,931	70,907 R	69.9%	24.3%	74.2%	25.8%
4	2012	285,432	182,998	PALAZZO, STEVEN M.*	82,344	MOORE, MATT	20,090	100,654 R	64.1%	28.8%	69.0%	31.0%
TOTAL	2014	626,279	329,169		230,014		67,096	99,155 R	52.6%	36.7%	58.9%	41.1%
TOTAL	2012	1,208,175	703,635		411,398		93,142	292,237 R	58.2%	34.1%	63.1%	36.9%

Note: An asterisk (*) denotes incumbent.

MISSISSIPPI

GENERAL AND PRIMARY ELECTIONS

2014 GENERAL ELECTIONS: OTHER VOTES

Senate   Other vote was 13,938 Reform (Shawn O'Hara)

House   Other vote was:

CD 1   3,830 Libertarian (Danny Bedwell), 946 Reform (Lajena Walley)
CD 2   36,465 Independent (Troy Ray), 11,493 Reform (Shelley Shoemake)
CD 3   3,890 Independent (Roger Gerrard), 1,541 Reform (Barbara Dale Washer)
CD 4   3,684 Independent (Cindy Burleson), 3,473 Libertarian (Joey Robinson), 917 Reform (Eli "Sarge" Jackson), 857 Independent (Ed Reich)

2014 PRIMARY ELECTIONS: SUPPLEMENTARY INFORMATION

Primary   June 3, 2014   **Registration**   1,864,751   No Party Registration
(as of June 3, 2014)

Primary Type   Open—Any registered voter could participate in the party primary of his or her choice. But any voter who cast a ballot in the primary of one party could not vote in the runoff of the other party.

	REPUBLICAN PRIMARIES			DEMOCRATIC PRIMARIES		
Senator	McDaniel, Chris	157,728	49.5%	Childers, Travis	63,548	74.0%
	Cochran, Thad*	156,313	49.0%	Marcy, Bill	10,361	12.1%
	Carey, Thomas	4,854	1.5%	Compton, William Bond Jr.	8,465	9.9%
				Rawl, Jonathan	3,492	4.1%
	TOTAL	*318,895*		*TOTAL*	*85,866*	
	PRIMARY RUNOFF					
	Cochran, Thad*	194,972	51.0%			
	McDaniel, Chris	187,249	49.0%			
	TOTAL	*382,221*				
Congressional District 1	Nunnelee, Alan*	56,556	100.0%	Dickey, Ron E.	9,741	66.0%
				Weathers, Rex N.	5,022	34.0%
	TOTAL	*56,556*		*TOTAL*	*14,763*	
Congressional District 2				Thompson, Bennie G.*	41,618	95.7%
				Fairconetue, Damien	1,860	4.3%
				TOTAL	*43,478*	
Congressional District 3	Harper, Gregg*	85,674	92.2%	Magee, Douglas MacArthur "Doug"	7,738	48.2%
	Caraway, Hardy	7,258	7.8%	Quinn, Dennis C.	5,820	36.3%
				Liljeberg, Jim	2,490	15.5%
	TOTAL	*92,932*		*TOTAL*	*16,048*	
				PRIMARY RUNOFF		
				Magee, Douglas MacArthur "Doug"	4,925	52.5%
				Quinn, Dennis C.	4,462	47.5%
				TOTAL	*9,387*	
Congressional District 4	Palazzo, Steven M.*	54,268	50.5%	Moore, Matt	6,355	55.7%
	Taylor, Gene	46,133	43.0%	Causey, Trish	5,063	44.3%
	Carter, Tom G.	4,955	4.6%			
	Kelly, Tavish	1,129	1.1%			
	Vincent, Ron	904	0.8%			
	TOTAL	*107,389*		*TOTAL*	*11,418*	

Note: An asterisk (*) denotes incumbent.

MISSOURI

Congressional districts first established for elections held in 2012

8 members

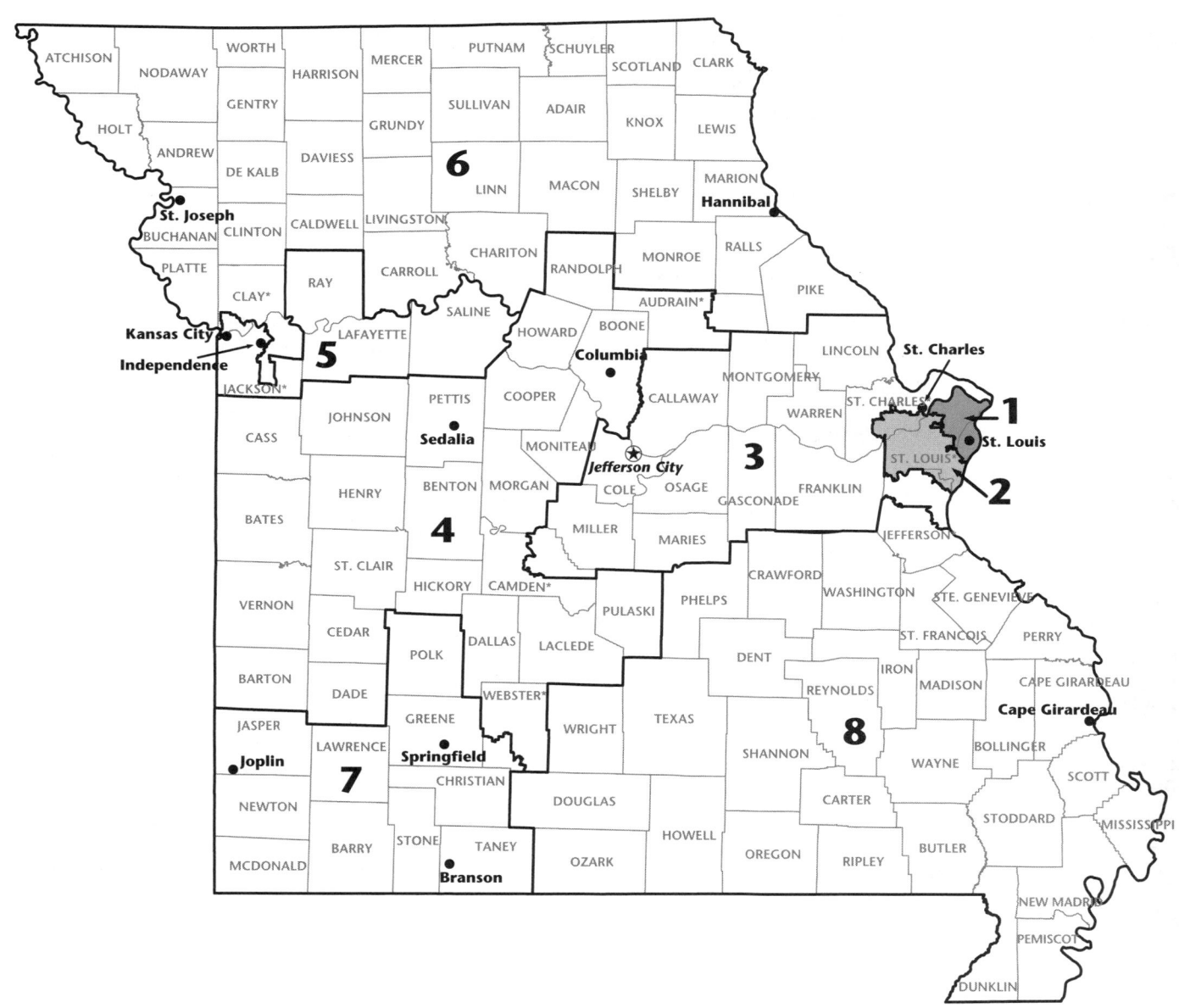

The city of St. Louis is an independent city that is treated as a county equivalent; so is Kansas City for voting purposes.

* Asterisk indicates a county whose boundaries include parts of two or more congressional districts.

MISSOURI

GOVERNOR
Jeremiah W. "Jay" Nixon (D). Reelected 2012 to a four-year term. Previously elected 2008.

SENATORS (1 Republican, 1 Democrat)
Roy Blunt (R). Elected 2010 to a six-year term.

Claire McCaskill (D). Reelected 2012 to a six-year term. Previously elected 2006.

REPRESENTATIVES (6 Republicans, 2 Democrats)
1. William Lacy Clay (D)
2. Ann Wagner (R)
3. Blaine Luetkemeyer (R)
4. Vicky Hartzler (R)
5. Emanuel Cleaver (D)
6. Sam Graves (R)
7. Billy Long (R)
8. Jason Smith (R)

POSTWAR VOTE FOR PRESIDENT

| | | Republican | | Democratic | | Other | Rep.-Dem. | Percentage | | | |
| | | | | | | | | Total Vote | | Major Vote | |
Year	Total Vote	Vote	Candidate	Vote	Candidate	Vote	Plurality	Rep.	Dem.	Rep.	Dem.
2012	2,757,323	1,482,440	Romney, W. Mitt	1,223,796	Obama, Barack H.*	51,087	258,644 R	53.8%	44.4%	54.8%	45.2%
2008	2,925,205	1,445,814	McCain, John S. III	1,441,911	Obama, Barack H.	37,480	3,903 R	49.4%	49.3%	50.1%	49.9%
2004	2,731,364	1,455,713	Bush, George W.*	1,259,171	Kerry, John F.	16,480	196,542 R	53.3%	46.1%	53.6%	46.4%
2000**	2,359,892	1,189,924	Bush, George W.	1,111,138	Gore, Albert Jr.	58,830	78,786 R	50.4%	47.1%	51.7%	48.3%
1996**	2,158,065	890,016	Dole, Robert "Bob"	1,025,935	Clinton, Bill*	242,114	135,919 D	41.2%	47.5%	46.5%	53.5%
1992**	2,391,565	811,159	Bush, George H.*	1,053,873	Clinton, Bill	526,533	242,714 D	33.9%	44.1%	43.5%	56.5%
1988	2,093,713	1,084,953	Bush, George H.	1,001,619	Dukakis, Michael S.	7,141	83,334 R	51.8%	47.8%	52.0%	48.0%
1984	2,122,783	1,274,188	Reagan, Ronald*	848,583	Mondale, Walter F.	12	425,605 R	60.0%	40.0%	60.0%	40.0%
1980**	2,099,824	1,074,181	Reagan, Ronald	931,182	Carter, Jimmy*	94,461	142,999 R	51.2%	44.3%	53.6%	46.4%
1976	1,953,600	927,443	Ford, Gerald R.*	998,387	Carter, Jimmy	27,770	70,944 D	47.5%	51.1%	48.2%	51.8%
1972	1,855,803	1,153,852	Nixon, Richard M.*	697,147	McGovern, George S.	4,804	456,705 R	62.2%	37.6%	62.3%	37.7%
1968**	1,809,502	811,932	Nixon, Richard M.	791,444	Humphrey, Hubert Horatio Jr.	206,126	20,488 R	44.9%	43.7%	50.6%	49.4%
1964	1,817,879	653,535	Goldwater, Barry M. Sr.	1,164,344	Johnson, Lyndon B.*		510,809 D	36.0%	64.0%	36.0%	64.0%
1960	1,934,422	962,221	Nixon, Richard M.	972,201	Kennedy, John F.		9,980 D	49.7%	50.3%	49.7%	50.3%
1956	1,832,562	914,289	Eisenhower, Dwight D.*	918,273	Stevenson, Adlai E. II		3,984 D	49.9%	50.1%	49.9%	50.1%
1952	1,892,062	959,429	Eisenhower, Dwight D.	929,830	Stevenson, Adlai E. II	2,803	29,599 R	50.7%	49.1%	50.8%	49.2%
1948	1,578,628	655,039	Dewey, Thomas E.	917,315	Truman, Harry S.*	6,274	262,276 D	41.5%	58.1%	41.7%	58.3%

Note: An asterisk (*) denotes incumbent. **In past elections, the other vote included: 2000 - 38,515 Green (Ralph Nader); 1996 - 217,188 Reform (Ross Perot); 1992 - 518,741 Independent (Perot); 1980 - 77,920 Independent (John Anderson); 1968 - 206,126 American Independent (George Wallace).

MISSOURI

POSTWAR VOTE FOR GOVERNOR

Year	Total Vote	Republican Vote	Republican Candidate	Democratic Vote	Democratic Candidate	Other Vote	Rep.-Dem. Plurality	Total Vote Rep.	Total Vote Dem.	Major Vote Rep.	Major Vote Dem.
2012	2,727,883	1,160,265	Spence, David "Dave"	1,494,056	Nixon, Jay W.*	73,562	333,791 D	42.5%	54.8%	43.7%	56.3%
2008	2,877,778	1,136,364	Hulshof, Kenny	1,680,611	Nixon, Jay W.	60,803	544,247 D	39.5%	58.4%	40.3%	59.7%
2004	2,719,599	1,382,419	Blunt, Matt	1,301,442	McCaskill, Claire	35,738	80,977 R	50.8%	47.9%	51.5%	48.5%
2000	2,346,830	1,131,307	Talent, James M.	1,152,752	Holden, Bob	62,771	21,445 D	48.2%	49.1%	49.5%	50.5%
1996	2,142,518	866,268	Kelly, Margaret	1,224,801	Carnahan, Mel*	51,449	358,533 D	40.4%	57.2%	41.4%	58.6%
1992	2,343,999	968,574	Webster, William L.	1,375,425	Carnahan, Mel		406,851 D	41.3%	58.7%	41.3%	58.7%
1988	2,085,928	1,339,531	Ashcroft, John*	724,919	Hearnes, Betty C.	21,478	614,612 R	64.2%	34.8%	64.9%	35.1%
1984	2,108,210	1,194,506	Ashcroft, John	913,700	Rothman, Kenneth J.	4	280,806 R	56.7%	43.3%	56.7%	43.3%
1980	2,088,028	1,098,950	Bond, Kit	981,884	Teasdale, Joseph P.*	7,194	117,066 R	52.6%	47.0%	52.8%	47.2%
1976	1,933,575	958,110	Bond, Kit*	971,184	Teasdale, Joseph P.	4,281	13,074 D	49.6%	50.2%	49.7%	50.3%
1972	1,865,683	1,029,451	Bond, Kit	832,751	Dowd, Edward L.	3,481	196,700 R	55.2%	44.6%	55.3%	44.7%
1968	1,764,602	691,797	Roos, Lawrence K.	1,072,805	Hearnes, Warren E.*		381,008 D	39.2%	60.8%	39.2%	60.8%
1964	1,789,600	678,949	Shepley, Ethan A. H.	1,110,651	Hearnes, Warren E.		431,702 D	37.9%	62.1%	37.9%	62.1%
1960	1,887,326	792,131	Farmer, Edward G.	1,095,195	Dalton, John M.		303,064 D	42.0%	58.0%	42.0%	58.0%
1956	1,808,338	866,810	Hocker, Lon	941,528	Blair, James T. Jr.		74,718 D	47.9%	52.1%	47.9%	52.1%
1952	1,870,998	886,270	Elliott, Howard	983,169	Donnelly, Phil M.	1,559	96,899 D	47.4%	52.5%	47.4%	52.6%
1948	1,567,338	670,064	Thompson, Murray E.	893,092	Smith, Forrest	4,182	223,028 D	42.8%	57.0%	42.9%	57.1%

Note: An asterisk (*) denotes incumbent.

POSTWAR VOTE FOR SENATOR

Year	Total Vote	Republican Vote	Republican Candidate	Democratic Vote	Democratic Candidate	Other Vote	Rep.-Dem. Plurality	Total Vote Rep.	Total Vote Dem.	Major Vote Rep.	Major Vote Dem.
2012	2,725,793	1,066,159	Akin, Todd	1,494,125	McCaskill, Claire*	165,509	427,966 D	39.1%	54.8%	41.6%	58.4%
2010	1,943,899	1,054,160	Blunt, Roy	789,736	Carnahan, Robin	100,003	264,424 R	54.2%	40.6%	57.2%	42.8%
2006	2,128,459	1,006,941	Talent, James M.*	1,055,255	McCaskill, Claire	66,263	48,314 D	47.3%	49.6%	48.8%	51.2%
2004	2,706,402	1,518,089	Bond, Kit*	1,158,261	Farmer, Nancy	30,052	359,828 R	56.1%	42.8%	56.7%	43.3%
2002S	1,877,620	935,032	Talent, James M.	913,778	Carnahan, Jean*	28,810	21,254 R	49.8%	48.7%	50.6%	49.4%
2000**	2,361,586	1,142,852	Ashcroft, John*	1,191,812	Carnahan, Mel	26,922	48,960 D	48.4%	50.5%	49.0%	51.0%
1998	1,576,857	830,625	Bond, Kit*	690,208	Nixon, Jay W.	56,024	140,417 R	52.7%	43.8%	54.6%	45.4%
1994	1,775,116	1,060,149	Ashcroft, John	633,697	Wheat, Alan	81,270	426,452 R	59.7%	35.7%	62.6%	37.4%
1992	2,354,925	1,221,901	Bond, Kit*	1,057,967	Rothman-Serot, Geri	75,057	163,934 R	51.9%	44.9%	53.6%	46.4%
1988	2,078,875	1,407,416	Danforth, John C.*	660,045	Nixon, Jay W.	11,414	747,371 R	67.7%	31.8%	68.1%	31.9%
1986	1,477,327	777,612	Bond, Kit	699,624	Woods, Harriett	91	77,988 R	52.6%	47.4%	52.6%	47.4%
1982	1,543,521	784,876	Danforth, John C.*	758,629	Woods, Harriett	16	26,247 R	50.8%	49.1%	50.9%	49.1%
1980	2,066,965	985,399	McNary, Gene	1,074,859	Eagleton, Thomas F.*	6,707	89,460 D	47.7%	52.0%	47.8%	52.2%
1976	1,914,777	1,090,067	Danforth, John C.*	813,571	Hearnes, Warren E.	11,139	276,496 R	56.9%	42.5%	57.3%	42.7%
1974	1,224,303	480,900	Curtis, Thomas B.	735,433	Eagleton, Thomas F.*	7,970	254,533 D	39.3%	60.1%	39.5%	60.5%
1970	1,283,912	617,903	Danforth, John C.	655,431	Symington, Stuart*	10,578	37,528 D	48.1%	51.0%	48.5%	51.5%
1968	1,737,958	850,544	Curtis, Thomas B.	887,414	Eagleton, Thomas F.		36,870 D	48.9%	51.1%	48.9%	51.1%
1964	1,783,043	596,377	Bradshaw, Jean Paul	1,186,666	Symington, Stuart*		590,289 D	33.4%	66.6%	33.4%	66.6%
1962	1,222,259	555,330	Kemper, Crosby	666,929	Long, Edward V.*		111,599 D	45.4%	54.6%	45.4%	54.6%
1960S	1,880,232	880,576	Hocker, Lon	999,656	Long, Edward V.		119,080 D	46.8%	53.2%	46.8%	53.2%
1958	1,173,930	393,847	Palmer, Hazel	780,083	Symington, Stuart*		386,236 D	33.5%	66.5%	33.5%	66.5%
1956	1,800,984	785,048	Douglas, Herbert	1,015,936	Hennings, Thomas Carey Jr.*		230,888 D	43.6%	56.4%	43.6%	56.4%
1952	1,868,083	858,170	Kem, James P.*	1,008,523	Symington, Stuart	1,390	150,353 D	45.9%	54.0%	46.0%	54.0%
1950	1,279,631	593,139	Donnell, Forrest C.*	685,732	Hennings, Thomas Carey Jr.	760	92,593 D	46.4%	53.6%	46.4%	53.6%
1946	1,084,100	572,556	Kem, James P.	511,544	Briggs, Frank		61,012 R	52.8%	47.2%	52.8%	47.2%

Note: An asterisk (*) denotes incumbent. **In 2000 the Democratic candidate, Mel Carnahan, was killed in an airplane crash in October but his name remained on the ballot and he won the election in November. Subsequently, his widow, Jean Carnahan, was appointed to fill the seat until an election could be held in 2002 for the remaining four years of the term. The 1960 and 2002 elections were for short terms to fill a vacancy.

MISSOURI

HOUSE OF REPRESENTATIVES

CD	Year	Total Vote	Republican		Democratic		Other Vote	Rep.-Dem. Plurality	Percentage			
			Vote	Candidate	Vote	Candidate			Total Vote		Major Vote	
									Rep.	Dem.	Rep.	Dem.
1	2014	163,494	35,273	ELDER, DANIEL J.	119,315	CLAY, WILLIAM LACY*	8,906	84,042 D	21.6%	73.0%	22.8%	77.2%
1	2012	340,583	60,832	HAMLIN, ROBYN	267,927	CLAY, WILLIAM LACY*	11,824	207,095 D	17.9%	78.7%	18.5%	81.5%
2	2014	231,117	148,191	WAGNER, ANN*	75,384	LIEBER, ARTHUR	7,542	72,807 R	64.1%	32.6%	66.3%	33.7%
2	2012	394,448	236,971	WAGNER, ANN	146,272	KOENEN, GLENN	11,205	90,699 R	60.1%	37.1%	61.8%	38.2%
3	2014	191,620	130,940	LUETKEMEYER, BLAINE*	52,021	DENTON, COURTNEY	8,659	78,919 R	68.3%	27.1%	71.6%	28.4%
3	2012	338,385	214,843	LUETKEMEYER, BLAINE*	111,189	MAYER, ERIC C.	12,353	103,654 R	63.5%	32.9%	65.9%	34.1%
4	2014	176,286	120,014	HARTZLER, VICKY*	46,464	IRVIN, NATE A.	9,808	73,550 R	68.1%	26.4%	72.1%	27.9%
4	2012	318,723	192,237	HARTZLER, VICKY*	113,120	HENSLEY, TERESA	13,366	79,117 R	60.3%	35.5%	63.0%	37.0%
5	2014	153,635	69,071	TURK, JACOB	79,256	CLEAVER, EMANUEL*	5,308	10,185 D	45.0%	51.6%	46.6%	53.4%
5	2012	330,942	122,149	TURK, JACOB	200,290	CLEAVER, EMANUEL*	8,503	78,141 D	36.9%	60.5%	37.9%	62.1%
6	2014	186,970	124,616	GRAVES, SAM*	55,157	HEDGE, W. A. "BILL"	7,197	69,459 R	66.7%	29.5%	69.3%	30.7%
6	2012	333,688	216,906	GRAVES, SAM*	108,503	YARBER, KYLE	8,279	108,403 R	65.0%	32.5%	66.7%	33.3%
7	2014	163,957	104,054	LONG, BILLY*	47,282	EVANS, JIM	12,621	56,772 R	63.5%	28.8%	68.8%	31.2%
7	2012	318,740	203,565	LONG, BILLY*	98,498	EVANS, JIM	16,677	105,067 R	63.9%	30.9%	67.4%	32.6%
8	2014	159,224	106,124	SMITH, JASON*	38,721	STOCKER, BARBARA HAMILL	14,379	67,403 R	66.7%	24.3%	73.3%	26.7%
8	2012	300,391	216,083	EMERSON, JO ANN*	73,755	RUSHIN, JACK	10,553	142,328 R	71.9%	24.6%	74.6%	25.4%
TOTAL	2014	1,426,303	838,283		513,600		74,420	324,683 R	58.8%	36.0%	62.0%	38.0%
TOTAL	2012	2,675,900	1,463,586		1,119,554		92,760	344,032 R	54.7%	41.8%	56.7%	43.3%

Note: An asterisk (*) denotes incumbent.

MISSOURI

GENERAL AND PRIMARY ELECTIONS

2014 GENERAL ELECTIONS: OTHER VOTES

House	Other vote was:
CD 1	8,906 Libertarian (Robb E. Cunningham)
CD 2	7,542 Libertarian (Bill Slantz)
CD 3	8,593 Libertarian (Steven Hedrick), 66 Write-in (Harold Davis)
CD 4	9,793 Libertarian (Herschel Young), 15 Write-in (Gregory A. Cowan)
CD 5	5,308 Libertarian (Roy Welborn)
CD 6	7,197 Libertarian (Russ Lee Monchil)
CD 7	12,584 Libertarian (Kevin Craig), 32 Write-in (Nikolas Bruce), 3 Write-in (John C. Hagerty), 2 Write-in (Martin Lindstedt)
CD 8	6,821 Independent (Terry Lynn Hampton), 3,799 Constitution (Doug Enyart), 3,759 Libertarian (Rick Vandeven)

2014 PRIMARY ELECTIONS: SUPPLEMENTARY INFORMATION

Primary August 5, 2014 **Registration** (as of August 1, 2014) 4,065,162 No Party Registration

Primary Type Open—Any registered voter could participate in the party primary of his or her choice.

MISSOURI

GENERAL AND PRIMARY ELECTIONS

	REPUBLICAN PRIMARIES			DEMOCRATIC PRIMARIES		
Congressional District 1	Elder, Daniel J.	4,196	39.3%	Clay, William Lacy*	69,650	100.0%
	Baker, Martin D.	3,659	34.2%			
	Koehr, David	2,833	26.5%			
	TOTAL	10,688		TOTAL	69,650	
Congressional District 2	Wagner, Ann*	55,322	100.0%	Lieber, Arthur	54,557	100.0%
	TOTAL	55,322		TOTAL	54,557	
Congressional District 3	Luetkemeyer, Blaine*	71,030	79.5%	Denton, Courtney	15,987	57.1%
	Morris, John	9,786	10.9%	Steinman, Velma	11,988	42.9%
	Steinman, Leonard	8,580	9.6%			
	TOTAL	89,396		TOTAL	27,975	
Congressional District 4	Hartzler, Vicky*	65,404	74.7%	Irvin, Nate A.	26,831	100.0%
	Webb, John	22,131	25.3%			
	TOTAL	87,535		TOTAL	26,831	
Congressional District 5	Turk, Jacob	24,615	68.6%	Cleaver, Emanuel*	44,296	82.0%
	Lindsey, Bill	5,020	14.0%	Memoly, Mark	2,988	5.5%
	Burris, Michael Craig	4,797	13.4%	Lindsey, Charles	2,687	5.0%
	Knox, Berton A.	1,453	4.0%	Holmes, Eric	2,584	4.8%
				Gough, Bob	1,438	2.7%
	TOTAL	35,885		TOTAL	53,993	
Congressional District 6	Graves, Sam*	56,789	76.6%	Hedge, W. A. "Bill"	18,109	51.7%
	Ryan, Christopher	8,745	11.8%	Fields, Edward Dwayne	9,706	27.7%
	Reid, Kyle	4,364	5.9%	Crose, Gary Lynn	7,241	20.7%
	Tharp, Brian L.	4,244	5.7%			
	TOTAL	74,142		TOTAL	35,056	
Congressional District 7	Long, Billy*	55,505	62.4%	Evans, Jim	8,671	53.8%
	Works, Marshall	33,498	37.6%	Williams, Genevieve	7,457	46.2%
	TOTAL	89,003		TOTAL	16,128	
Congressional District 8	Smith, Jason*	66,511	100.0%	Stocker, Barbara Hamill	28,303	100.0%
	TOTAL	66,511		TOTAL	28,303	

Note: An asterisk (*) denotes incumbent.

MONTANA

One member At Large

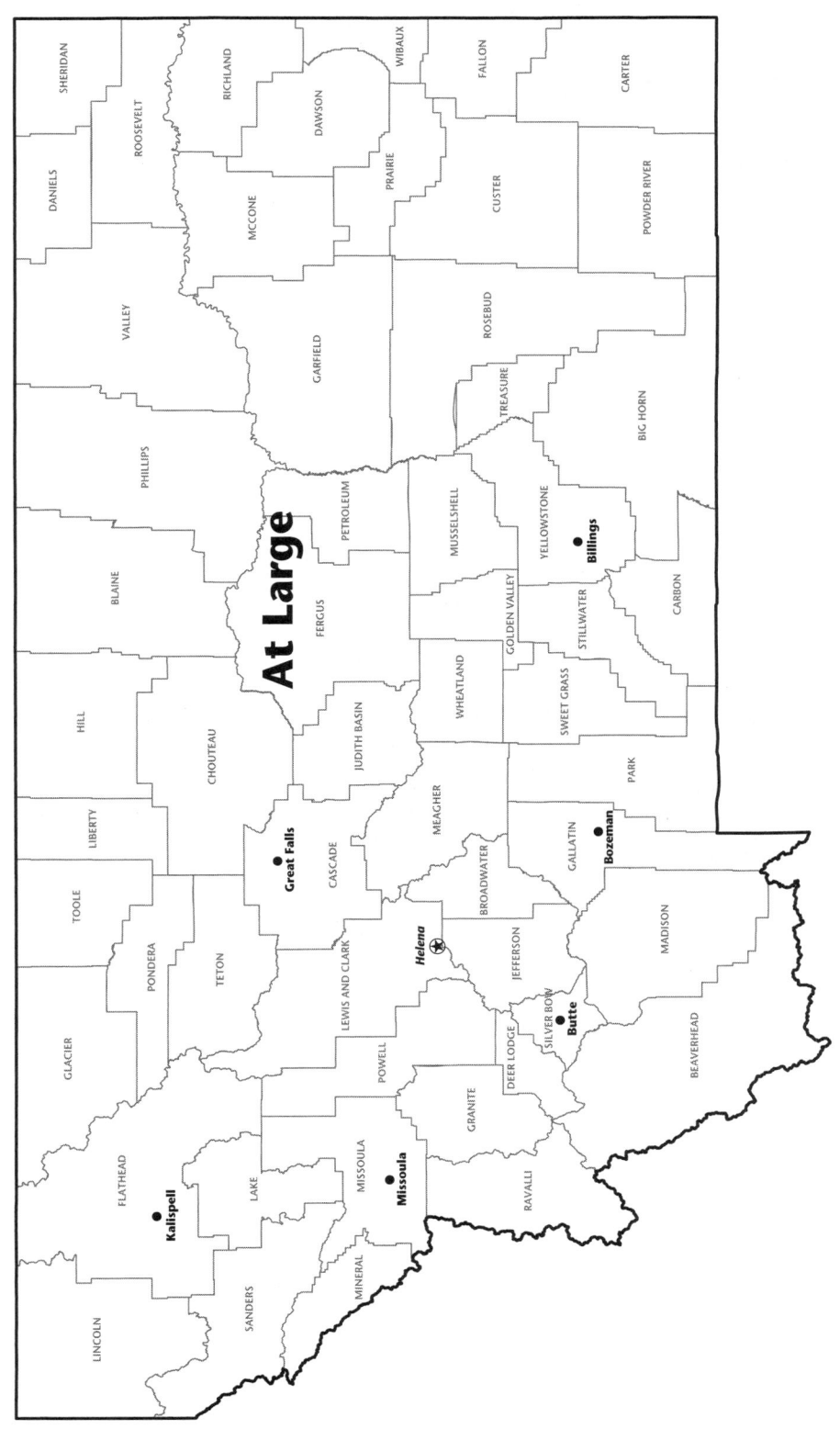

MONTANA

GOVERNOR
Steve Bullock (D). Elected 2012 to a four-year term.

SENATORS (1 Democrat, 1 Republican)
Steve Daines (R). Elected 2014 to a six-year term.

Jon Tester (D). Reelected 2012 to a six-year term. Previously elected 2006.

REPRESENTATIVE (1 Republican)
At Large. Ryan K. Zinke (R)

POSTWAR VOTE FOR PRESIDENT

| | | Republican | | Democratic | | Other Vote | Rep.-Dem. Plurality | Percentage | | | |
| | | | | | | | | Total Vote | | Major Vote | |
Year	Total Vote	Vote	Candidate	Vote	Candidate			Rep.	Dem.	Rep.	Dem.
2012	484,048	267,928	Romney, W. Mitt	201,839	Obama, Barack H.*	14,281	66,089 R	55.4%	41.7%	57.0%	43.0%
2008	490,302	242,763	McCain, John S. III	231,667	Obama, Barack H.	15,872	11,096 R	49.5%	47.2%	51.2%	48.8%
2004	450,445	266,063	Bush, George W.*	173,710	Kerry, John F.	10,672	92,353 R	59.1%	38.6%	60.5%	39.5%
2000**	410,997	240,178	Bush, George W.	137,126	Gore, Albert Jr.	33,693	103,052 R	58.4%	33.4%	63.7%	36.3%
1996**	407,261	179,652	Dole, Robert "Bob"	167,922	Clinton, Bill*	59,687	11,730 R	44.1%	41.2%	51.7%	48.3%
1992**	410,611	144,207	Bush, George H.*	154,507	Clinton, Bill	111,897	10,300 D	35.1%	37.6%	48.3%	51.7%
1988	365,674	190,412	Bush, George H.	168,936	Dukakis, Michael S.	6,326	21,476 R	52.1%	46.2%	53.0%	47.0%
1984	384,377	232,450	Reagan, Ronald*	146,742	Mondale, Walter F.	5,185	85,708 R	60.5%	38.2%	61.3%	38.7%
1980**	363,952	206,814	Reagan, Ronald	118,032	Carter, Jimmy*	39,106	88,782 R	56.8%	32.4%	63.7%	36.3%
1976	328,734	173,703	Ford, Gerald R.*	149,259	Carter, Jimmy	5,772	24,444 R	52.8%	45.4%	53.8%	46.2%
1972	317,603	183,976	Nixon, Richard M.*	120,197	McGovern, George S.	13,430	63,779 R	57.9%	37.8%	60.5%	39.5%
1968**	274,404	138,835	Nixon, Richard M.	114,117	Humphrey, Hubert Horatio Jr.	21,452	24,718 R	50.6%	41.6%	54.9%	45.1%
1964	278,628	113,032	Goldwater, Barry M. Sr.	164,246	Johnson, Lyndon B.*	1,350	51,214 D	40.6%	58.9%	40.8%	59.2%
1960	277,579	141,841	Nixon, Richard M.	134,891	Kennedy, John F.	847	6,950 R	51.1%	48.6%	51.3%	48.7%
1956	271,171	154,933	Eisenhower, Dwight D.*	116,238	Stevenson, Adlai E. II		38,695 R	57.1%	42.9%	57.1%	42.9%
1952	265,037	157,394	Eisenhower, Dwight D.	106,213	Stevenson, Adlai E. II	1,430	51,181 R	59.4%	40.1%	59.7%	40.3%
1948	224,278	96,770	Dewey, Thomas E.	119,071	Truman, Harry S.*	8,437	22,301 D	43.1%	53.1%	44.8%	55.2%

Note: An asterisk (*) denotes incumbent. **In past elections, the other vote included: 2000 - 24,437 Green (Ralph Nader); 1996 - 55,229 Reform (Ross Perot); 1992 - 107,225 Independent (Perot); 1980 - 29,281 Independent (John Anderson); 1968 - 20,015 American Independent (George Wallace).

MONTANA

POSTWAR VOTE FOR GOVERNOR

Year	Total Vote	Republican Vote	Republican Candidate	Democratic Vote	Democratic Candidate	Other Vote	Rep.-Dem. Plurality	Total Vote Rep.	Total Vote Dem.	Major Vote Rep.	Major Vote Dem.
2012	483,489	228,879	Hill, Rick	236,450	Bullock, Steve	18,160	7,571 D	47.3%	48.9%	49.2%	50.8%
2008	486,734	158,268	Brown, Roy	318,670	Schweitzer, Brian*	9,796	160,402 D	32.5%	65.5%	33.2%	66.8%
2004	446,146	205,313	Brown, Bob	225,016	Schweitzer, Brian	15,817	19,703 D	46.0%	50.4%	47.7%	52.3%
2000	410,192	209,135	Martz, Judy	193,131	O'Keefe, Mark	7,926	16,004 R	51.0%	47.1%	52.0%	48.0%
1996**	405,175	320,768	Racicot, Marc*	84,407	Jacobson, Judy		236,361 R	79.2%	20.8%	79.2%	20.8%
1992	407,842	209,401	Racicot, Marc	198,421	Bradley, Dorothy	20	10,980 R	51.3%	48.7%	51.3%	48.7%
1988	367,021	190,604	Stephens, Stan	169,313	Judge, Thomas L.	7,104	21,291 R	51.9%	46.1%	53.0%	47.0%
1984	378,970	100,070	Goodover, Pat M.	266,578	Schwinden, Ted*	12,322	166,508 D	26.4%	70.3%	27.3%	72.7%
1980	360,470	160,896	Ramirez, Jack	199,574	Schwinden, Ted		38,678 D	44.6%	55.4%	44.6%	55.4%
1976	316,720	115,848	Woodahi, Robert	195,420	Judge, Thomas L.*	5,452	79,572 D	36.6%	61.7%	37.2%	62.8%
1972	318,754	146,231	Smith, Ed	172,523	Judge, Thomas L.		26,292 D	45.9%	54.1%	45.9%	54.1%
1968	278,112	116,432	Babcock, Tim M.*	150,481	Anderson, Forrest H.	11,199	34,049 D	41.9%	54.1%	43.6%	56.4%
1964	280,975	144,113	Babcock, Tim M.	136,862	Renne, Roland		7,251 R	51.3%	48.7%	51.3%	48.7%
1960	279,881	154,230	Nutter, Donald G.	125,651	Cannon, Paul		28,579 R	55.1%	44.9%	55.1%	44.9%
1956	270,366	138,878	Aronson, John Hugo*	131,488	Olsen, Arnold		7,390 R	51.4%	48.6%	51.4%	48.6%
1952	263,792	134,423	Aronson, John Hugo	129,369	Bonner, John W.*		5,054 R	51.0%	49.0%	51.0%	49.0%
1948	222,964	97,792	Ford, Samuel C.*	124,267	Bonner, John W.	905	26,475 D	43.9%	55.7%	44.0%	56.0%

Note: An asterisk (*) denotes incumbent. **In 1996 the Democratic vote total included 7,936 absentee ballots cast for the party's initial gubernatorial candidate, Chet Blaylock, who died that October.

POSTWAR VOTE FOR SENATOR

Year	Total Vote	Republican Vote	Republican Candidate	Democratic Vote	Democratic Candidate	Other Vote	Rep.-Dem. Plurality	Total Vote Rep.	Total Vote Dem.	Major Vote Rep.	Major Vote Dem.
2014	369,826	213,709	Daines, Steve	148,184	Curtis, Amanda	7,933	65,525 R	57.8%	40.1%	59.1%	40.9%
2012	486,066	218,051	Rehberg, Dennis "Denny"	236,123	Tester, Jon*	31,892	18,072 D	44.9%	48.6%	48.0%	52.0%
2008	477,658	129,369	Kelleher, Bob	348,289	Baucus, Max S.*		218,920 D	27.1%	72.9%	27.1%	72.9%
2006	406,505	196,283	Burns, Conrad*	199,845	Tester, Jon	10,377	3,562 D	48.3%	49.2%	49.6%	50.4%
2002	326,537	103,611	Taylor, Mike	204,853	Baucus, Max S.*	18,073	101,242 D	31.7%	62.7%	33.6%	66.4%
2000	411,601	208,082	Burns, Conrad*	194,430	Schweitzer, Brian	9,089	13,652 R	50.6%	47.2%	51.7%	48.3%
1996	407,490	182,111	Rehberg, Dennis "Denny"	201,935	Baucus, Max S.*	23,444	19,824 D	44.7%	49.6%	47.4%	52.6%
1994	350,409	218,542	Burns, Conrad*	131,845	Mudd, Jack	22	86,697 R	62.4%	37.6%	62.4%	37.6%
1990	319,336	93,836	Kolstad, Allen C.	217,563	Baucus, Max S.*	7,937	123,727 D	29.4%	68.1%	30.1%	69.9%
1988	365,254	189,445	Burns, Conrad	175,809	Melcher, John*		13,636 R	51.9%	48.1%	51.9%	48.1%
1984	379,155	154,308	Cozzens, Chuck	215,704	Baucus, Max S.*	9,143	61,396 D	40.7%	56.9%	41.7%	58.3%
1982	321,062	133,789	Williams, Larry	174,861	Melcher, John*	12,412	41,072 D	41.7%	54.5%	43.3%	56.7%
1978	287,942	127,589	Williams, Larry	160,353	Baucus, Max S.		32,764 D	44.3%	55.7%	44.3%	55.7%
1976	321,445	115,213	Burger, Stanley C.	206,232	Melcher, John		91,019 D	35.8%	64.2%	35.8%	64.2%
1972	314,925	151,316	Hibbard, Henry S.	163,609	Metcalf, Lee*		12,293 D	48.0%	52.0%	48.0%	52.0%
1970	247,869	97,809	Wallace, Harold E.	150,060	Mansfield, Mike*		52,251 D	39.5%	60.5%	39.5%	60.5%
1966	259,863	121,697	Babcock, Tim M.	138,166	Metcalf, Lee*		16,469 D	46.8%	53.2%	46.8%	53.2%
1964	280,010	99,367	Blewett, Alex	180,643	Mansfield, Mike*		81,276 D	35.5%	64.5%	35.5%	64.5%
1960	276,612	136,281	Fjare, Orvin B.	140,331	Metcalf, Lee		4,050 D	49.3%	50.7%	49.3%	50.7%
1958	229,483	54,573	Welch, Lou W.	174,910	Mansfield, Mike*		120,337 D	23.8%	76.2%	23.8%	76.2%
1954	227,454	112,863	D'Ewart, Wesley A.	114,591	Murray, James E.*		1,728 D	49.6%	50.4%	49.6%	50.4%
1952	262,297	127,360	Ecton, Zales N.*	133,109	Mansfield, Mike	1,828	5,749 D	48.6%	50.7%	48.9%	51.1%
1948	221,003	94,458	Davis, Tom J.	125,193	Murray, James E.*	1,352	30,735 D	42.7%	56.6%	43.0%	57.0%
1946	190,566	101,901	Ecton, Zales N.	86,476	Erickson, Leif	2,189	15,425 R	53.5%	45.4%	54.1%	45.9%

Note: An asterisk (*) denotes incumbent.

MONTANA

SENATOR 2014

2010 Census Population	County	Total Vote	Republican (Daines)	Democratic (Curtis)	Other	Rep.-Dem. Plurality	Percentage Total Vote Rep.	Dem.	Major Vote Rep.	Dem.
9,246	BEAVERHEAD	4,025	2,790	1,141	94	1,649 R	69.3%	28.3%	71.0%	29.0%
12,865	BIG HORN	3,754	1,806	1,888	60	82 D	48.1%	50.3%	48.9%	51.1%
6,491	BLAINE	1,870	920	935	15	15 D	49.2%	50.0%	49.6%	50.4%
5,612	BROADWATER	2,561	1,902	603	56	1,299 R	74.3%	23.5%	75.9%	24.1%
10,078	CARBON	4,696	2,926	1,680	90	1,246 R	62.3%	35.8%	63.5%	36.5%
1,160	CARTER	622	551	59	12	492 R	88.6%	9.5%	90.3%	9.7%
81,327	CASCADE	26,231	14,704	11,045	482	3,659 R	56.1%	42.1%	57.1%	42.9%
5,813	CHOUTEAU	2,147	1,445	669	33	776 R	67.3%	31.2%	68.4%	31.6%
11,699	CUSTER	4,080	2,585	1,406	89	1,179 R	63.4%	34.5%	64.8%	35.2%
1,751	DANIELS	817	602	179	36	423 R	73.7%	21.9%	77.1%	22.9%
8,966	DAWSON	3,254	2,297	877	80	1,420 R	70.6%	27.0%	72.4%	27.6%
9,298	DEER LODGE	3,345	1,133	2,134	78	1,001 D	33.9%	63.8%	34.7%	65.3%
2,890	FALLON	1,139	913	162	64	751 R	80.2%	14.2%	84.9%	15.1%
11,586	FERGUS	4,961	3,449	1,417	95	2,032 R	69.5%	28.6%	70.9%	29.1%
90,928	FLATHEAD	32,039	21,437	10,013	589	11,424 R	66.9%	31.3%	68.2%	31.8%
89,513	GALLATIN	35,570	18,756	15,984	830	2,772 R	52.7%	44.9%	54.0%	46.0%
1,206	GARFIELD	588	513	64	11	449 R	87.2%	10.9%	88.9%	11.1%
13,399	GLACIER	3,211	1,319	1,825	67	506 D	41.1%	56.8%	42.0%	58.0%
884	GOLDEN VALLEY	444	334	90	20	244 R	75.2%	20.3%	78.8%	21.2%
3,079	GRANITE	1,516	997	470	49	527 R	65.8%	31.0%	68.0%	32.0%
16,096	HILL	5,035	2,683	2,255	97	428 R	53.3%	44.8%	54.3%	45.7%
11,406	JEFFERSON	5,247	3,330	1,798	119	1,532 R	63.5%	34.3%	64.9%	35.1%
2,072	JUDITH BASIN	1,010	720	275	15	445 R	71.3%	27.2%	72.4%	27.6%
28,746	LAKE	9,992	5,740	4,038	214	1,702 R	57.4%	40.4%	58.7%	41.3%
63,395	LEWIS AND CLARK	26,087	13,455	12,102	530	1,353 R	51.6%	46.4%	52.6%	47.4%
2,339	LIBERTY	872	618	236	18	382 R	70.9%	27.1%	72.4%	27.6%
19,687	LINCOLN	7,342	5,204	1,904	234	3,300 R	70.9%	25.9%	73.2%	26.8%
7,691	MADISON	3,635	2,549	1,014	72	1,535 R	70.1%	27.9%	71.5%	28.5%
1,734	MCCONE	862	653	189	20	464 R	75.8%	21.9%	77.6%	22.4%
1,891	MEAGHER	785	590	182	13	408 R	75.2%	23.2%	76.4%	23.6%
4,223	MINERAL	1,537	981	504	52	477 R	63.8%	32.8%	66.1%	33.9%
109,299	MISSOULA	42,250	17,459	23,852	939	6,393 D	41.3%	56.5%	42.3%	57.7%
4,538	MUSSELSHELL	2,059	1,572	442	45	1,130 R	76.3%	21.5%	78.1%	21.9%
15,636	PARK	6,991	3,943	2,846	202	1,097 R	56.4%	40.7%	58.1%	41.9%
494	PETROLEUM	239	200	36	3	164 R	83.7%	15.1%	84.7%	15.3%
4,253	PHILLIPS	1,750	1,379	337	34	1,042 R	78.8%	19.3%	80.4%	19.6%
6,153	PONDERA	2,174	1,474	666	34	808 R	67.8%	30.6%	68.9%	31.1%
1,743	POWDER RIVER	873	705	157	11	548 R	80.8%	18.0%	81.8%	18.2%
7,027	POWELL	2,327	1,550	705	72	845 R	66.6%	30.3%	68.7%	31.3%
1,179	PRAIRIE	604	458	134	12	324 R	75.8%	22.2%	77.4%	22.6%
40,212	RAVALLI	16,900	11,040	5,512	348	5,528 R	65.3%	32.6%	66.7%	33.3%
9,746	RICHLAND	3,337	2,557	693	87	1,864 R	76.6%	20.8%	78.7%	21.3%
10,425	ROOSEVELT	2,666	1,339	1,268	59	71 R	50.2%	47.6%	51.4%	48.6%
9,233	ROSEBUD	2,624	1,669	900	55	769 R	63.6%	34.3%	65.0%	35.0%
11,413	SANDERS	4,586	3,197	1,247	142	1,950 R	69.7%	27.2%	71.9%	28.1%
3,384	SHERIDAN	1,390	909	447	34	462 R	65.4%	32.2%	67.0%	33.0%
34,200	SILVER BOW	12,781	4,095	8,451	235	4,356 D	32.0%	66.1%	32.6%	67.4%
9,117	STILLWATER	3,750	2,692	991	67	1,701 R	71.8%	26.4%	73.1%	26.9%
3,651	SWEET GRASS	1,642	1,257	353	32	904 R	76.6%	21.5%	78.1%	21.9%
6,073	TETON	2,729	1,819	857	53	962 R	66.7%	31.4%	68.0%	32.0%
5,324	TOOLE	1,663	1,193	433	37	760 R	71.7%	26.0%	73.4%	26.6%
718	TREASURE	385	271	104	10	167 R	70.4%	27.0%	72.3%	27.7%
7,369	VALLEY	3,333	2,193	1,055	85	1,138 R	65.8%	31.7%	67.5%	32.5%
2,168	WHEATLAND	741	538	187	16	351 R	72.6%	25.2%	74.2%	25.8%
1,017	WIBAUX	467	365	94	8	271 R	78.2%	20.1%	79.5%	20.5%
147,972	YELLOWSTONE	52,291	31,933	19,279	1,079	12,654 R	61.1%	36.9%	62.4%	37.6%
989,415	TOTAL	369,826	213,709	148,184	7,933	65,525 R	57.8%	40.1%	59.1%	40.9%

MONTANA
HOUSE OF REPRESENTATIVES

			Republican		Democratic		Other Vote	Rep.-Dem. Plurality	Total Vote		Major Vote	
CD	Year	Total Vote	Vote	Candidate	Vote	Candidate			Rep.	Dem.	Rep.	Dem.
At Large	2014	367,963	203,871	ZINKE, RYAN K.	148,690	LEWIS, JOHN	15,402	55,181 R	55.4%	40.4%	57.8%	42.2%
At Large	2012	479,740	255,468	DAINES, STEVE	204,939	GILLAN, KIM	19,333	50,529 R	53.3%	42.7%	55.5%	44.5%
At Large	2010	360,341	217,696	REHBERG, DENNIS "DENNY"*	121,954	MCDONALD, DENNIS	20,691	95,742 R	60.4%	33.8%	64.1%	35.9%
At Large	2008	480,900	308,470	REHBERG, DENNIS "DENNY"*	155,930	DRISCOLL, JOHN	16,500	152,540 R	64.1%	32.4%	66.4%	33.6%
At Large	2006	406,134	239,124	REHBERG, DENNIS "DENNY"*	158,916	LINDEEN, MONICA	8,094	80,208 R	58.9%	39.1%	60.1%	39.9%
At Large	2004	444,230	286,076	REHBERG, DENNIS "DENNY"*	145,606	VELAZQUEZ, TRACY E.	12,548	140,470 R	64.4%	32.8%	66.3%	33.7%
At Large	2002	331,321	214,100	REHBERG, DENNIS "DENNY"*	108,233	KELLY, STEVE	8,988	105,867 R	64.6%	32.7%	66.4%	33.6%
At Large	2000	410,523	211,418	REHBERG, DENNIS "DENNY"	189,971	KEENAN, NANCY	9,134	21,447 R	51.5%	46.3%	52.7%	47.3%
At Large	1998	331,551	175,748	HILL, RICK*	147,073	DESCHAMPS, DUSTY	8,730	28,675 R	53.0%	44.4%	54.4%	45.6%
At Large	1996	404,426	211,975	HILL, RICK	174,516	YELLOWTAIL, BILL	17,935	37,459 R	52.4%	43.2%	54.8%	45.2%
At Large	1994	352,133	148,715	JAMISON, CY	171,372	WILLIAMS, JOHN PATRICK "PAT"*	32,046	22,657 D	42.2%	48.7%	46.5%	53.5%
At Large	1992	403,735	189,570	MARLENEE, RON*	203,711	WILLIAMS, JOHN PATRICK "PAT"*	10,454	14,141 D	47.0%	50.5%	48.2%	51.8%

Note: An asterisk (*) denotes incumbent.

MONTANA
GENERAL AND PRIMARY ELECTIONS

2014 GENERAL ELECTIONS: OTHER VOTES

Senate Other vote was 7,933 Libertarian (Roger Roots)

House Other vote was:

At Large 15,402 Libertarian (Mike Fellows)

2014 PRIMARY ELECTIONS: SUPPLEMENTARY INFORMATION

Primary June 3, 2014 **Registration** (as of June 3, 2014) 659,921 No Party Registration

Primary Type Open—Any registered voter could participate in the party primary of his or her choice.

	REPUBLICAN PRIMARIES			DEMOCRATIC PRIMARIES		
Senator	Daines, Steve	110,565	83.4%	Walsh, John*	48,665	64.0%
	Cundiff, Susan	11,909	9.0%	Bohlinger, John	17,187	22.6%
	Edmunds, Champ	10,151	7.7%	Adams, Dirk S.	10,139	13.3%
				Write-In	11	
	TOTAL	132,625		TOTAL	76,002	
Congressional At Large	Zinke, Ryan K.	43,766	33.3%	Lewis, John	42,588	59.8%
	Stapleton, Corey	38,591	29.3%	Driscoll, John	28,580	40.2%
	Rosendale, Matt	37,965	28.8%			
	Arntzen, Elsie	9,011	6.8%			
	Turiano, Drew	2,290	1.7%			
	TOTAL	131,623		TOTAL	71,168	

Notes: An asterisk (*) denotes incumbent. Democratic primary candidate John Walsh withdrew from the race after the primary. He was replaced as the Democratic candidate by Amanda Curtis.

NEBRASKA

Congressional districts first established for elections held in 2012

3 members

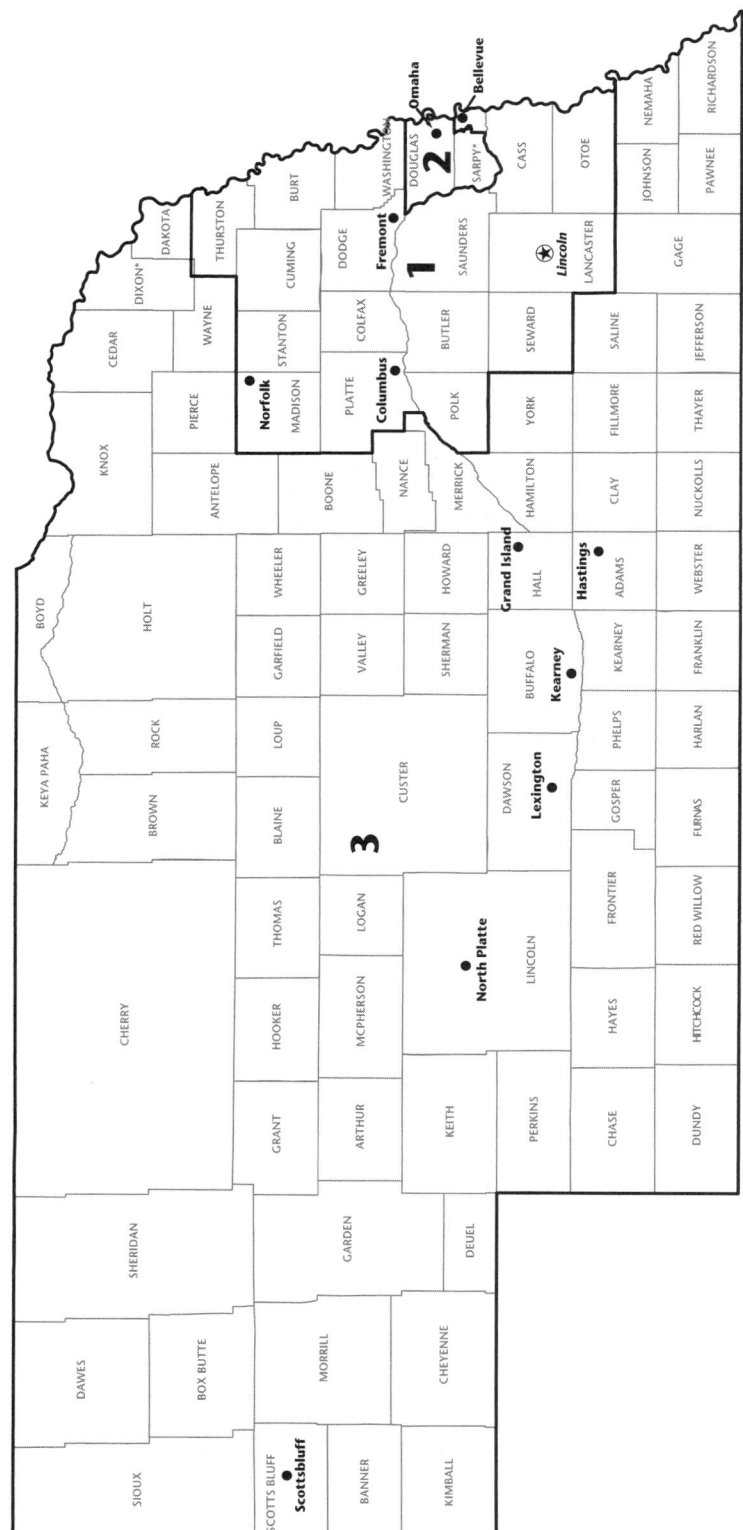

NEBRASKA

GOVERNOR
Pete Ricketts (R). Elected 2014 to a four-year term.

SENATORS (2 Republicans)
Deb Fischer (R). Elected 2012 to a six-year term.

Ben Sasse (R). Elected 2014 to a six-year term.

REPRESENTATIVES (2 Republicans, 1 Democrat)
1. Jeff Fortenberry (R)   2. Brad Ashford (D)   3. Adrian Smith (R)

POSTWAR VOTE FOR PRESIDENT

| | | Republican | | Democratic | | | | Percentage | | | |
| | | | | | | | | Total Vote | | Major Vote | |
Year	Total Vote	Vote	Candidate	Vote	Candidate	Other Vote	Rep.-Dem. Plurality	Rep.	Dem.	Rep.	Dem.
2012	794,379	475,064	Romney, W. Mitt	302,081	Obama, Barack H.*	17,234	172,983 R	59.8%	38.0%	61.1%	38.9%
2008	801,281	452,979	McCain, John S. III	333,319	Obama, Barack H.	14,983	119,660 R	56.5%	41.6%	57.6%	42.4%
2004	778,186	512,814	Bush, George W.*	254,328	Kerry, John F.	11,044	258,486 R	65.9%	32.7%	66.8%	33.2%
2000**	697,019	433,862	Bush, George W.	231,780	Gore, Albert Jr.	31,377	202,082 R	62.2%	33.3%	65.2%	34.8%
1996**	677,415	363,467	Dole, Robert "Bob"	236,761	Clinton, Bill*	77,187	126,706 R	53.7%	35.0%	60.6%	39.4%
1992**	737,546	343,678	Bush, George H.*	216,864	Clinton, Bill	177,004	126,814 R	46.6%	29.4%	61.3%	38.7%
1988	661,465	397,956	Bush, George H.	259,235	Dukakis, Michael S.	4,274	138,721 R	60.2%	39.2%	60.6%	39.4%
1984	652,090	460,054	Reagan, Ronald*	187,866	Mondale, Walter F.	4,170	272,188 R	70.6%	28.8%	71.0%	29.0%
1980**	640,854	419,937	Reagan, Ronald	166,851	Carter, Jimmy*	54,066	253,086 R	65.5%	26.0%	71.6%	28.4%
1976	607,668	359,705	Ford, Gerald R.*	233,692	Carter, Jimmy	14,271	126,013 R	59.2%	38.5%	60.6%	39.4%
1972	576,289	406,298	Nixon, Richard M.*	169,991	McGovern, George S.		236,307 R	70.5%	29.5%	70.5%	29.5%
1968**	536,851	321,163	Nixon, Richard M.	170,784	Humphrey, Hubert Horatio Jr.	44,904	150,379 R	59.8%	31.8%	65.3%	34.7%
1964	584,154	276,847	Goldwater, Barry M. Sr.	307,307	Johnson, Lyndon B.*		30,460 D	47.4%	52.6%	47.4%	52.6%
1960	613,095	380,553	Nixon, Richard M.	232,542	Kennedy, John F.		148,011 R	62.1%	37.9%	62.1%	37.9%
1956	577,137	378,108	Eisenhower, Dwight D.*	199,029	Stevenson, Adlai E. II		179,079 R	65.5%	34.5%	65.5%	34.5%
1952	609,660	421,603	Eisenhower, Dwight D.	188,057	Stevenson, Adlai E. II		233,546 R	69.2%	30.8%	69.2%	30.8%
1948	488,940	264,774	Dewey, Thomas E.	224,165	Truman, Harry S.*	1	40,609 R	54.2%	45.8%	54.2%	45.8%

Note: An asterisk (*) denotes incumbent. **In past elections, the other vote included: 2000 - 24,540 Green (Ralph Nader); 1996 - 71,278 Reform (Ross Perot); 1992 - 174,104 Independent (Perot); 1980 - 44,993 Independent (John Anderson); 1968 - 44,904 American Independent (George Wallace).

NEBRASKA

POSTWAR VOTE FOR GOVERNOR

Year	Total Vote	Republican		Democratic		Other Vote	Rep.-Dem. Plurality	Percentage			
								Total Vote		Major Vote	
		Vote	Candidate	Vote	Candidate			Rep.	Dem.	Rep.	Dem.
2014	540,202	308,751	Ricketts, Pete	211,905	Hassebrook, Chuck	19,546	96,846 R	57.2%	39.2%	59.3%	40.7%
2010	487,988	360,645	Heineman, Dave*	127,343	Meister, Mike		233,302 R	73.9%	26.1%	73.9%	26.1%
2006	593,357	435,507	Heineman, Dave*	145,115	Hahn, David	12,735	290,392 R	73.4%	24.5%	75.0%	25.0%
2002	480,991	330,349	Johanns, Mike*	132,348	Dean, Stormy	18,294	198,001 R	68.7%	27.5%	71.4%	28.6%
1998	545,238	293,910	Johanns, Mike	250,678	Hoppner, Bill	650	43,232 R	53.9%	46.0%	54.0%	46.0%
1994	579,561	148,230	Spence, Gene	423,270	Nelson, Earl "Ben"*	8,061	275,040 D	25.6%	73.0%	25.9%	74.1%
1990	586,542	288,741	Orr, Kay*	292,771	Nelson, Earl "Ben"	5,030	4,030 D	49.2%	49.9%	49.7%	50.3%
1986	564,422	298,325	Orr, Kay	265,156	Boosalis, Helen	941	33,169 R	52.9%	47.0%	52.9%	47.1%
1982	547,902	270,203	Thone, Charles*	277,436	Kerrey, Bob	263	7,233 D	49.3%	50.6%	49.3%	50.7%
1978	492,423	275,473	Thone, Charles	216,754	Whelan, Gerald T.	196	58,719 R	55.9%	44.0%	56.0%	44.0%
1974	451,306	159,780	Marvel, Richard D.	267,012	Exon, J. James*	24,514	107,232 D	35.4%	59.2%	37.4%	62.6%
1970	461,619	201,994	Tiemann, Norbert T.*	248,552	Exon, J. James	11,073	46,558 D	43.8%	53.8%	44.8%	55.2%
1966**	486,396	299,245	Tiemann, Norbert T.	186,985	Sorensen, Philip C.	166	112,260 R	61.5%	38.4%	61.5%	38.5%
1964	578,090	231,029	Burney, Dwight W.	347,026	Morrison, Frank B.*	35	115,997 D	40.0%	60.0%	40.0%	60.0%
1962	464,585	221,885	Seaton, Fred A.	242,669	Morrison, Frank B.*	31	20,784 D	47.8%	52.2%	47.8%	52.2%
1960	598,971	287,302	Cooper, John R.	311,344	Morrison, Frank B.	325	24,042 D	48.0%	52.0%	48.0%	52.0%
1958	421,067	209,705	Anderson, Victor E.*	211,345	Brooks, Ralph G.	17	1,640 D	49.8%	50.2%	49.8%	50.2%
1956	567,916	308,285	Anderson, Victor E.*	228,048	Sorrell, Frank	31,583	80,237 R	54.3%	40.2%	57.5%	42.5%
1954	414,841	250,080	Anderson, Victor E.	164,753	Ritchie, William	8	85,327 R	60.3%	39.7%	60.3%	39.7%
1952	594,814	365,409	Crosby, Robert B.	229,400	Raecke, Walter R.	5	136,009 R	61.4%	38.6%	61.4%	38.6%
1950	449,728	247,089	Peterson, Val*	202,638	Raecke, Walter R.	1	44,451 R	54.9%	45.1%	54.9%	45.1%
1948	476,352	286,119	Peterson, Val*	190,214	Sorrell, Frank	19	95,905 R	60.1%	39.9%	60.1%	39.9%
1946	380,835	249,468	Peterson, Val	131,367	Sorrell, Frank		118,101 R	65.5%	34.5%	65.5%	34.5%

Note: An asterisk (*) denotes incumbent. **The term of office of Nebraska's governor was increased from two to four years effective with the 1966 election.

POSTWAR VOTE FOR SENATOR

Year	Total Vote	Republican		Democratic		Other Vote	Rep.-Dem. Plurality	Percentage			
								Total Vote		Major Vote	
		Vote	Candidate	Vote	Candidate			Rep.	Dem.	Rep.	Dem.
2014	540,337	347,636	Sasse, Ben	170,127	Domina, David A.	22,574	177,509 R	64.3%	31.5%	67.1%	32.9%
2012	788,572	455,593	Fischer, Deb	332,979	Kerrey, Bob		122,614 R	57.8%	42.2%	57.8%	42.2%
2008	792,511	455,854	Johanns, Mike	317,456	Kleeb, Scott	19,201	138,398 R	57.5%	40.1%	58.9%	41.1%
2006	592,316	213,928	Ricketts, Pete	378,388	Nelson, Earl "Ben"*		164,460 D	36.1%	63.9%	36.1%	63.9%
2002	480,217	397,438	Hagel, Chuck*	70,290	Matulka, Charlie A.	12,489	327,148 R	82.8%	14.6%	85.0%	15.0%
2000	692,344	337,967	Stenberg, Don	353,097	Nelson, Earl "Ben"	1,280	15,130 D	48.8%	51.0%	48.9%	51.1%
1996	676,789	379,933	Hagel, Chuck	281,904	Nelson, Earl "Ben"	14,952	98,029 R	56.1%	41.7%	57.4%	42.6%
1994	579,205	260,668	Stoney, Jan	317,297	Kerrey, Bob*	1,240	56,629 D	45.0%	54.8%	45.1%	54.9%
1990	593,828	243,013	Daub, Harold J.	349,779	Exon, J. James*	1,036	106,766 D	40.9%	58.9%	41.0%	59.0%
1988	667,860	278,250	Karnes, David	378,717	Kerrey, Bob	10,893	100,467 D	41.7%	56.7%	42.4%	57.6%
1984	639,668	307,147	Hoch, Nancy	332,217	Exon, J. James*	304	25,070 D	48.0%	51.9%	48.0%	52.0%
1982	545,647	155,760	Keck, Jim	363,350	Zorinsky, Edward*	26,537	207,590 D	28.5%	66.6%	30.0%	70.0%
1978	494,368	159,806	Shasteen, Donald	334,276	Exon, J. James	286	174,470 D	32.3%	67.6%	32.3%	67.7%
1976	598,314	284,284	McCollister, John Y.	313,809	Zorinsky, Edward	221	29,525 D	47.5%	52.4%	47.5%	52.5%
1972	568,580	301,841	Curtis, Carl T.*	265,922	Carpenter, Terry	817	35,919 R	53.1%	46.8%	53.2%	46.8%
1970	458,966	240,894	Hruska, Roman L.*	217,681	Morrison, Frank B.	391	23,213 R	52.5%	47.4%	52.5%	47.5%
1966	485,101	296,116	Curtis, Carl T.*	187,950	Morrison, Frank B.	1,035	108,166 R	61.0%	38.7%	61.2%	38.8%
1964	563,401	345,772	Hruska, Roman L.*	217,605	Arndt, Raymond W.	24	128,167 R	61.4%	38.6%	61.4%	38.6%
1960	598,743	352,748	Curtis, Carl T.*	245,837	Conrad, Robert B.	158	106,911 R	58.9%	41.1%	58.9%	41.1%
1958	417,385	232,227	Hruska, Roman L.	185,152	Morrison, Frank B.	6	47,075 R	55.6%	44.4%	55.6%	44.4%
1954	418,691	255,695	Curtis, Carl T.	162,990	Neville, Keith	6	92,705 R	61.1%	38.9%	61.1%	38.9%
1954S	411,225	250,341	Hruska, Roman L.	160,881	Green, James F.	3	89,460 R	60.9%	39.1%	60.9%	39.1%
1952	591,749	408,971	Butler, Hugh*	164,660	Long, Stanley D.	18,118	244,311 R	69.1%	27.8%	71.3%	28.7%
1952S	581,750	369,841	Griswold, Dwight	211,898	Ritchie, William	11	157,943 R	63.6%	36.4%	63.6%	36.4%
1948	471,895	267,575	Wherry, Kenneth S.*	204,320	Carpenter, Terry		63,255 R	56.7%	43.3%	56.7%	43.3%
1946	382,959	271,208	Butler, Hugh*	111,751	Mekota, John E.		159,457 R	70.8%	29.2%	70.8%	29.2%

Note: An asterisk (*) denotes incumbent. **One each of the 1952 and 1954 elections was for a short term to fill a vacancy.

NEBRASKA

GOVERNOR 2014

2010 Census Population	County	Total Vote	Republican (Ricketts)	Democratic (Hassebrook)	Other	Rep.-Dem. Plurality	Percentage			
							Total Vote		Major Vote	
							Rep.	Dem.	Rep.	Dem.
31,364	ADAMS	8,577	5,065	3,173	339	1,892 R	59.1%	37.0%	61.5%	38.5%
6,685	ANTELOPE	2,487	1,602	797	88	805 R	64.4%	32.0%	66.8%	33.2%
460	ARTHUR	181	143	31	7	112 R	79.0%	17.1%	82.2%	17.8%
690	BANNER	292	242	37	13	205 R	82.9%	12.7%	86.7%	13.3%
478	BLAINE	201	157	38	6	119 R	78.1%	18.9%	80.5%	19.5%
5,505	BOONE	2,171	1,342	764	65	578 R	61.8%	35.2%	63.7%	36.3%
11,308	BOX BUTTE	3,030	2,033	852	145	1,181 R	67.1%	28.1%	70.5%	29.5%
2,099	BOYD	938	602	299	37	303 R	64.2%	31.9%	66.8%	33.2%
3,145	BROWN	1,112	761	293	58	468 R	68.4%	26.3%	72.2%	27.8%
46,102	BUFFALO	13,311	8,616	4,131	564	4,485 R	64.7%	31.0%	67.6%	32.4%
6,858	BURT	2,859	1,305	1,449	105	144 D	45.6%	50.7%	47.4%	52.6%
8,395	BUTLER	3,125	1,826	1,171	128	655 R	58.4%	37.5%	60.9%	39.1%
25,241	CASS	8,599	5,107	3,057	435	2,050 R	59.4%	35.6%	62.6%	37.4%
8,852	CEDAR	3,024	2,050	876	98	1,174 R	67.8%	29.0%	70.1%	29.9%
3,966	CHASE	1,392	1,030	321	41	709 R	74.0%	23.1%	76.2%	23.8%
5,713	CHERRY	2,227	1,749	382	96	1,367 R	78.5%	17.2%	82.1%	17.9%
9,998	CHEYENNE	2,852	2,137	612	103	1,525 R	74.9%	21.5%	77.7%	22.3%
6,542	CLAY	2,148	1,348	698	102	650 R	62.8%	32.5%	65.9%	34.1%
10,515	COLFAX	1,972	1,121	772	79	349 R	56.8%	39.1%	59.2%	40.8%
9,139	CUMING	2,903	1,780	1,038	85	742 R	61.3%	35.8%	63.2%	36.8%
10,939	CUSTER	4,191	2,741	1,249	201	1,492 R	65.4%	29.8%	68.7%	31.3%
21,006	DAKOTA	3,754	2,141	1,487	126	654 R	57.0%	39.6%	59.0%	41.0%
9,182	DAWES	2,723	1,904	681	138	1,223 R	69.9%	25.0%	73.7%	26.3%
24,326	DAWSON	5,536	3,653	1,664	219	1,989 R	66.0%	30.1%	68.7%	31.3%
1,941	DEUEL	696	555	104	37	451 R	79.7%	14.9%	84.2%	15.8%
6,000	DIXON	1,944	1,237	649	58	588 R	63.6%	33.4%	65.6%	34.4%
36,691	DODGE	10,422	5,756	4,166	500	1,590 R	55.2%	40.0%	58.0%	42.0%
517,110	DOUGLAS	144,520	74,049	65,979	4,492	8,070 R	51.2%	45.7%	52.9%	47.1%
2,008	DUNDY	695	531	136	28	395 R	76.4%	19.6%	79.6%	20.4%
5,890	FILLMORE	2,298	1,330	872	96	458 R	57.9%	37.9%	60.4%	39.6%
3,225	FRANKLIN	1,343	838	440	65	398 R	62.4%	32.8%	65.6%	34.4%
2,756	FRONTIER	951	656	255	40	401 R	69.0%	26.8%	72.0%	28.0%
4,959	FURNAS	1,668	1,100	477	91	623 R	65.9%	28.6%	69.8%	30.2%
22,311	GAGE	7,329	3,802	3,195	332	607 R	51.9%	43.6%	54.3%	45.7%
2,057	GARDEN	634	498	112	24	386 R	78.5%	17.7%	81.6%	18.4%
2,049	GARFIELD	722	498	203	21	295 R	69.0%	28.1%	71.0%	29.0%
2,044	GOSPER	743	513	206	24	307 R	69.0%	27.7%	71.3%	28.7%
614	GRANT	268	216	37	15	179 R	80.6%	13.8%	85.4%	14.6%
2,538	GREELEY	812	437	335	40	102 R	53.8%	41.3%	56.6%	43.4%
58,607	HALL	13,920	7,741	5,558	621	2,183 R	55.6%	39.9%	58.2%	41.8%
9,124	HAMILTON	3,638	2,393	1,077	168	1,316 R	65.8%	29.6%	69.0%	31.0%
3,423	HARLAN	1,329	881	385	63	496 R	66.3%	29.0%	69.6%	30.4%
967	HAYES	455	348	88	19	260 R	76.5%	19.3%	79.8%	20.2%
2,908	HITCHCOCK	1,153	780	325	48	455 R	67.6%	28.2%	70.6%	29.4%
10,435	HOLT	3,673	2,424	1,108	141	1,316 R	66.0%	30.2%	68.6%	31.4%
736	HOOKER	285	218	57	10	161 R	76.5%	20.0%	79.3%	20.7%
6,274	HOWARD	2,082	1,133	832	117	301 R	54.4%	40.0%	57.7%	42.3%
7,547	JEFFERSON	2,568	1,434	1,018	116	416 R	55.8%	39.6%	58.5%	41.5%
5,217	JOHNSON	1,689	887	728	74	159 R	52.5%	43.1%	54.9%	45.1%
6,489	KEARNEY	2,578	1,704	777	97	927 R	66.1%	30.1%	68.7%	31.3%
8,368	KEITH	2,606	1,996	517	93	1,479 R	76.6%	19.8%	79.4%	20.6%
824	KEYA PAHA	381	275	92	14	183 R	72.2%	24.1%	74.9%	25.1%
3,821	KIMBALL	1,221	916	240	65	676 R	75.0%	19.7%	79.2%	20.8%
8,701	KNOX	3,196	2,063	1,019	114	1,044 R	64.5%	31.9%	66.9%	33.1%
285,407	LANCASTER	86,081	41,216	42,323	2,542	1,107 D	47.9%	49.2%	49.3%	50.7%
36,288	LINCOLN	10,656	6,872	3,372	412	3,500 R	64.5%	31.6%	67.1%	32.9%
763	LOGAN	350	272	66	12	206 R	77.7%	18.9%	80.5%	19.5%
632	LOUP	321	202	103	16	99 R	62.9%	32.1%	66.2%	33.8%
34,876	MADISON	9,302	6,293	2,628	381	3,665 R	67.7%	28.3%	70.5%	29.5%
539	MCPHERSON	241	178	49	14	129 R	73.9%	20.3%	78.4%	21.6%

NEBRASKA

GOVERNOR 2014

2010 Census Population	County	Total Vote	Republican (Ricketts)	Democratic (Hassebrook)	Other	Rep.-Dem. Plurality	Percentage			
							Total Vote		Major Vote	
							Rep.	Dem.	Rep.	Dem.
7,845	MERRICK	2,899	1,813	948	138	865 R	62.5%	32.7%	65.7%	34.3%
5,042	MORRILL	1,545	1,184	301	60	883 R	76.6%	19.5%	79.7%	20.3%
3,735	NANCE	1,170	615	501	54	114 R	52.6%	42.8%	55.1%	44.9%
7,248	NEMAHA	2,402	1,409	877	116	532 R	58.7%	36.5%	61.6%	38.4%
4,500	NUCKOLLS	1,520	865	587	68	278 R	56.9%	38.6%	59.6%	40.4%
15,740	OTOE	5,421	3,251	1,938	232	1,313 R	60.0%	35.7%	62.7%	37.3%
2,773	PAWNEE	1,085	672	376	37	296 R	61.9%	34.7%	64.1%	35.9%
2,970	PERKINS	1,041	764	252	25	512 R	73.4%	24.2%	75.2%	24.8%
9,188	PHELPS	3,340	2,310	904	126	1,406 R	69.2%	27.1%	71.9%	28.1%
7,266	PIERCE	2,348	1,702	570	76	1,132 R	72.5%	24.3%	74.9%	25.1%
32,237	PLATTE	9,268	6,133	2,823	312	3,310 R	66.2%	30.5%	68.5%	31.5%
5,406	POLK	1,762	1,197	509	56	688 R	67.9%	28.9%	70.2%	29.8%
11,055	RED WILLOW	3,516	2,489	878	149	1,611 R	70.8%	25.0%	73.9%	26.1%
8,363	RICHARDSON	2,588	1,512	964	112	548 R	58.4%	37.2%	61.1%	38.9%
1,526	ROCK	620	416	176	28	240 R	67.1%	28.4%	70.3%	29.7%
14,200	SALINE	3,690	1,638	1,913	139	275 D	44.4%	51.8%	46.1%	53.9%
158,840	SARPY	44,747	26,932	16,078	1,737	10,854 R	60.2%	35.9%	62.6%	37.4%
20,780	SAUNDERS	7,287	4,378	2,609	300	1,769 R	60.1%	35.8%	62.7%	37.3%
36,970	SCOTTS BLUFF	9,688	6,671	2,676	341	3,995 R	68.9%	27.6%	71.4%	28.6%
16,750	SEWARD	5,468	3,224	2,066	178	1,158 R	59.0%	37.8%	60.9%	39.1%
5,469	SHERIDAN	1,723	1,388	261	74	1,127 R	80.6%	15.1%	84.2%	15.8%
3,152	SHERMAN	1,326	637	625	64	12 R	48.0%	47.1%	50.5%	49.5%
1,311	SIOUX	535	449	69	17	380 R	83.9%	12.9%	86.7%	13.3%
6,129	STANTON	1,730	1,183	493	54	690 R	68.4%	28.5%	70.6%	29.4%
5,228	THAYER	1,960	1,158	707	95	451 R	59.1%	36.1%	62.1%	37.9%
647	THOMAS	310	242	59	9	183 R	78.1%	19.0%	80.4%	19.6%
6,940	THURSTON	1,448	626	796	26	170 D	43.2%	55.0%	44.0%	56.0%
4,260	VALLEY	1,630	1,011	559	60	452 R	62.0%	34.3%	64.4%	35.6%
20,234	WASHINGTON	6,873	4,354	2,256	263	2,098 R	63.3%	32.8%	65.9%	34.1%
9,595	WAYNE	2,686	1,744	865	77	879 R	64.9%	32.2%	66.8%	33.2%
3,812	WEBSTER	1,276	756	479	41	277 R	59.2%	37.5%	61.2%	38.8%
818	WHEELER	413	255	141	17	114 R	61.7%	34.1%	64.4%	35.6%
13,665	YORK	4,512	3,076	1,249	187	1,827 R	68.2%	27.7%	71.1%	28.9%
1,826,341	TOTAL	540,202	308,751	211,905	19,546	96,846 R	57.2%	39.2%	59.3%	40.7%

NEBRASKA

SENATOR 2014

2010 Census Population	County	Total Vote	Republican (Sasse)	Democratic (Domina)	Other	Rep.-Dem. Plurality	Percentage			
							Total Vote		Major Vote	
							Rep.	Dem.	Rep.	Dem.
31,364	ADAMS	8,602	5,906	2,322	374	3,584 R	68.7%	27.0%	71.8%	28.2%
6,685	ANTELOPE	2,542	1,845	632	65	1,213 R	72.6%	24.9%	74.5%	25.5%
460	ARTHUR	180	144	29	7	115 R	80.0%	16.1%	83.2%	16.8%
690	BANNER	288	249	31	8	218 R	86.5%	10.8%	88.9%	11.1%
478	BLAINE	203	147	24	32	123 R	72.4%	11.8%	86.0%	14.0%
5,505	BOONE	2,205	1,643	466	96	1,177 R	74.5%	21.1%	77.9%	22.1%
11,308	BOX BUTTE	3,028	2,060	836	132	1,224 R	68.0%	27.6%	71.1%	28.9%
2,099	BOYD	948	712	206	30	506 R	75.1%	21.7%	77.6%	22.4%
3,145	BROWN	1,126	883	176	67	707 R	78.4%	15.6%	83.4%	16.6%
46,102	BUFFALO	13,350	9,953	2,168	1,229	7,785 R	74.6%	16.2%	82.1%	17.9%

NEBRASKA

SENATOR 2014

2010 Census Population	County	Total Vote	Republican (Sasse)	Democratic (Domina)	Other	Rep.-Dem. Plurality	Percentage			
							Total Vote		Major Vote	
							Rep.	Dem.	Rep.	Dem.
6,858	BURT	2,836	1,816	934	86	882 R	64.0%	32.9%	66.0%	34.0%
8,395	BUTLER	3,107	2,377	601	129	1,776 R	76.5%	19.3%	79.8%	20.2%
25,241	CASS	8,590	6,062	2,209	319	3,853 R	70.6%	25.7%	73.3%	26.7%
8,852	CEDAR	3,053	1,916	1,060	77	856 R	62.8%	34.7%	64.4%	35.6%
3,966	CHASE	1,402	1,205	127	70	1,078 R	85.9%	9.1%	90.5%	9.5%
5,713	CHERRY	2,229	1,769	326	134	1,443 R	79.4%	14.6%	84.4%	15.6%
9,998	CHEYENNE	2,847	2,241	496	110	1,745 R	78.7%	17.4%	81.9%	18.1%
6,542	CLAY	2,166	1,687	380	99	1,307 R	77.9%	17.5%	81.6%	18.4%
10,515	COLFAX	1,972	1,405	506	61	899 R	71.2%	25.7%	73.5%	26.5%
9,139	CUMING	2,885	2,144	667	74	1,477 R	74.3%	23.1%	76.3%	23.7%
10,939	CUSTER	4,272	2,536	420	1,316	2,116 R	59.4%	9.8%	85.8%	14.2%
21,006	DAKOTA	3,730	2,208	1,357	165	851 R	59.2%	36.4%	61.9%	38.1%
9,182	DAWES	2,706	1,912	662	132	1,250 R	70.7%	24.5%	74.3%	25.7%
24,326	DAWSON	5,554	4,220	942	392	3,278 R	76.0%	17.0%	81.8%	18.2%
1,941	DEUEL	690	555	90	45	465 R	80.4%	13.0%	86.0%	14.0%
6,000	DIXON	1,931	1,280	597	54	683 R	66.3%	30.9%	68.2%	31.8%
36,691	DODGE	10,492	7,324	2,840	328	4,484 R	69.8%	27.1%	72.1%	27.9%
517,110	DOUGLAS	143,974	81,226	58,917	3,831	22,309 R	56.4%	40.9%	58.0%	42.0%
2,008	DUNDY	692	591	69	32	522 R	85.4%	10.0%	89.5%	10.5%
5,890	FILLMORE	2,308	1,635	588	85	1,047 R	70.8%	25.5%	73.5%	26.5%
3,225	FRANKLIN	1,358	1,084	187	87	897 R	79.8%	13.8%	85.3%	14.7%
2,756	FRONTIER	967	805	116	46	689 R	83.2%	12.0%	87.4%	12.6%
4,959	FURNAS	1,665	1,344	214	107	1,130 R	80.7%	12.9%	86.3%	13.7%
22,311	GAGE	7,340	4,705	2,330	305	2,375 R	64.1%	31.7%	66.9%	33.1%
2,057	GARDEN	633	508	84	41	424 R	80.3%	13.3%	85.8%	14.2%
2,049	GARFIELD	730	558	125	47	433 R	76.4%	17.1%	81.7%	18.3%
2,044	GOSPER	744	543	111	90	432 R	73.0%	14.9%	83.0%	17.0%
614	GRANT	274	199	53	22	146 R	72.6%	19.3%	79.0%	21.0%
2,538	GREELEY	820	556	230	34	326 R	67.8%	28.0%	70.7%	29.3%
58,607	HALL	13,922	9,214	4,057	651	5,157 R	66.2%	29.1%	69.4%	30.6%
9,124	HAMILTON	3,640	2,847	622	171	2,225 R	78.2%	17.1%	82.1%	17.9%
3,423	HARLAN	1,344	1,074	199	71	875 R	79.9%	14.8%	84.4%	15.6%
967	HAYES	458	399	33	26	366 R	87.1%	7.2%	92.4%	7.6%
2,908	HITCHCOCK	1,171	977	142	52	835 R	83.4%	12.1%	87.3%	12.7%
10,435	HOLT	3,719	2,675	922	122	1,753 R	71.9%	24.8%	74.4%	25.6%
736	HOOKER	294	212	44	38	168 R	72.1%	15.0%	82.8%	17.2%
6,274	HOWARD	2,089	1,452	546	91	906 R	69.5%	26.1%	72.7%	27.3%
7,547	JEFFERSON	2,586	1,827	669	90	1,158 R	70.6%	25.9%	73.2%	26.8%
5,217	JOHNSON	1,672	1,082	531	59	551 R	64.7%	31.8%	67.1%	32.9%
6,489	KEARNEY	2,597	2,044	361	192	1,683 R	78.7%	13.9%	85.0%	15.0%
8,368	KEITH	2,616	2,083	361	172	1,722 R	79.6%	13.8%	85.2%	14.8%
824	KEYA PAHA	380	315	53	12	262 R	82.9%	13.9%	85.6%	14.4%
3,821	KIMBALL	1,207	972	170	65	802 R	80.5%	14.1%	85.1%	14.9%
8,701	KNOX	3,175	2,100	923	152	1,177 R	66.1%	29.1%	69.5%	30.5%
285,407	LANCASTER	86,033	44,462	37,265	4,306	7,197 R	51.7%	43.3%	54.4%	45.6%
36,288	LINCOLN	10,695	7,750	2,456	489	5,294 R	72.5%	23.0%	75.9%	24.1%
763	LOGAN	354	290	40	24	250 R	81.9%	11.3%	87.9%	12.1%
632	LOUP	317	230	52	35	178 R	72.6%	16.4%	81.6%	18.4%
34,876	MADISON	9,384	6,476	2,636	272	3,840 R	69.0%	28.1%	71.1%	28.9%
539	MCPHERSON	248	190	40	18	150 R	76.6%	16.1%	82.6%	17.4%
7,845	MERRICK	2,899	2,211	553	135	1,658 R	76.3%	19.1%	80.0%	20.0%
5,042	MORRILL	1,546	1,255	236	55	1,019 R	81.2%	15.3%	84.2%	15.8%
3,735	NANCE	1,178	818	318	42	500 R	69.4%	27.0%	72.0%	28.0%
7,248	NEMAHA	2,399	1,730	554	115	1,176 R	72.1%	23.1%	75.7%	24.3%
4,500	NUCKOLLS	1,527	1,175	278	74	897 R	76.9%	18.2%	80.9%	19.1%
15,740	OTOE	5,408	3,828	1,372	208	2,456 R	70.8%	25.4%	73.6%	26.4%
2,773	PAWNEE	1,093	788	276	29	512 R	72.1%	25.3%	74.1%	25.9%
2,970	PERKINS	1,042	862	128	52	734 R	82.7%	12.3%	87.1%	12.9%
9,188	PHELPS	3,388	2,725	473	190	2,252 R	80.4%	14.0%	85.2%	14.8%
7,266	PIERCE	2,357	1,843	445	69	1,398 R	78.2%	18.9%	80.6%	19.4%

NEBRASKA

SENATOR 2014

2010 Census Population	County	Total Vote	Republican (Sasse)	Democratic (Domina)	Other	Rep.-Dem. Plurality	Percentage			
							Total Vote		Major Vote	
							Rep.	Dem.	Rep.	Dem.
32,237	PLATTE	9,291	7,282	1,725	284	5,557 R	78.4%	18.6%	80.8%	19.2%
5,406	POLK	1,769	1,384	318	67	1,066 R	78.2%	18.0%	81.3%	18.7%
11,055	RED WILLOW	3,528	2,941	442	145	2,499 R	83.4%	12.5%	86.9%	13.1%
8,363	RICHARDSON	2,579	1,901	591	87	1,310 R	73.7%	22.9%	76.3%	23.7%
1,526	ROCK	632	496	104	32	392 R	78.5%	16.5%	82.7%	17.3%
14,200	SALINE	3,680	2,184	1,357	139	827 R	59.3%	36.9%	61.7%	38.3%
158,840	SARPY	44,708	30,281	13,163	1,264	17,118 R	67.7%	29.4%	69.7%	30.3%
20,780	SAUNDERS	7,303	5,174	1,871	258	3,303 R	70.8%	25.6%	73.4%	26.6%
36,970	SCOTTS BLUFF	9,709	7,106	2,205	398	4,901 R	73.2%	22.7%	76.3%	23.7%
16,750	SEWARD	5,489	3,860	1,365	264	2,495 R	70.3%	24.9%	73.9%	26.1%
5,469	SHERIDAN	1,730	1,453	207	70	1,246 R	84.0%	12.0%	87.5%	12.5%
3,152	SHERMAN	1,305	896	295	114	601 R	68.7%	22.6%	75.2%	24.8%
1,311	SIOUX	532	444	73	15	371 R	83.5%	13.7%	85.9%	14.1%
6,129	STANTON	1,739	1,256	427	56	829 R	72.2%	24.6%	74.6%	25.4%
5,228	THAYER	1,974	1,476	421	77	1,055 R	74.8%	21.3%	77.8%	22.2%
647	THOMAS	313	246	46	21	200 R	78.6%	14.7%	84.2%	15.8%
6,940	THURSTON	1,420	713	663	44	50 R	50.2%	46.7%	51.8%	48.2%
4,260	VALLEY	1,638	1,216	346	76	870 R	74.2%	21.1%	77.8%	22.2%
20,234	WASHINGTON	6,907	5,105	1,613	189	3,492 R	73.9%	23.4%	76.0%	24.0%
9,595	WAYNE	2,682	1,729	863	90	866 R	64.5%	32.2%	66.7%	33.3%
3,812	WEBSTER	1,287	948	299	40	649 R	73.7%	23.2%	76.0%	24.0%
818	WHEELER	408	309	76	23	233 R	75.7%	18.6%	80.3%	19.7%
13,665	YORK	4,537	3,377	774	386	2,603 R	74.4%	17.1%	81.4%	18.6%
1,826,341	TOTAL	540,337	347,636	170,127	22,574	177,509 R	64.3%	31.5%	67.1%	32.9%

NEBRASKA

HOUSE OF REPRESENTATIVES

CD	Year	Total Vote	Republican		Democratic		Other Vote	Rep.-Dem. Plurality	Percentage			
			Vote	Candidate	Vote	Candidate			Total Vote		Major Vote	
									Rep.	Dem.	Rep.	Dem.
1	2014	179,057	123,219	FORTENBERRY, JEFF*	55,838	CRAWFORD, DENNIS P.		67,381 R	68.8%	31.2%	68.8%	31.2%
1	2012	256,095	174,889	FORTENBERRY, JEFF*	81,206	REIMAN, KOREY L.		93,683 R	68.3%	31.7%	68.3%	31.7%
2	2014	171,509	78,157	TERRY, LEE*	83,872	ASHFORD, BRAD	9,480	5,715 D	45.6%	48.9%	48.2%	51.8%
2	2012	263,731	133,964	TERRY, LEE*	129,767	EWING, JOHN W. JR.		4,197 R	50.8%	49.2%	50.8%	49.2%
3	2014	184,964	139,440	SMITH, ADRIAN*	45,524	SULLIVAN, MARK		93,916 R	75.4%	24.6%	75.4%	24.6%
3	2012	252,689	187,423	SMITH, ADRIAN*	65,266	SULLIVAN, MARK		122,157 R	74.2%	25.8%	74.2%	25.8%
TOTAL	2014	535,530	340,816		185,234		9,480	155,582 R	63.6%	34.6%	64.8%	35.2%
TOTAL	2012	772,515	496,276		276,239			220,037 R	64.2%	35.8%	64.2%	35.8%

Note: An asterisk (*) denotes incumbent.

NEBRASKA

GENERAL AND PRIMARY ELECTIONS

2014 GENERAL ELECTIONS: OTHER VOTES

Governor	Other vote was 19,001 Libertarian (Mark G. Elworth), 545 scattered write-in
Senate	Other vote was 15,868 By Petition (Jim Jenkins), 6,260 By Petition (Todd F. Watson), 446 scattered write-in
House	Other vote was:
CD 2	9,021 Libertarian (Steven C. Laird), 459 scattered write-in

2014 PRIMARY ELECTIONS: SUPPLEMENTARY INFORMATION

Primary	May 13, 2014	**Registration** (as of May 13, 2014)	1,152,144	Republican	556,523
				Democratic	358,965
				Libertarian	5,034
				Nonpartisan	231,622

Primary Type   Semi-open—Registered Democrats and Republicans could vote only in their party's primary. Voters registered as Nonpartisan could participate in either party's primary for the Senate and House (but not for governor).

	REPUBLICAN PRIMARIES			**DEMOCRATIC PRIMARIES**		
Senator	Sasse, Ben	110,802	49.3%	Domina, David A.	45,648	67.6%
	Dinsdale, Sid	50,494	22.5%	Marvin, Larry	21,904	32.4%
	Osborn, Shane	47,338	21.1%			
	McLeay, Bart	12,840	5.7%			
	Johnson, Clifton R.	3,310	1.5%			
	TOTAL	*224,784*		*TOTAL*	*67,552*	
Governor	Ricketts, Pete	58,671	26.6%	Hassebrook, Chuck	65,620	100.0%
	Bruning, Jon	56,324	25.5%			
	McCoy, Beau	46,196	20.9%			
	Foley, Mike	42,394	19.2%			
	Carlson, Tom	9,080	4.1%			
	Slone, Bryan	8,265	3.7%			
	TOTAL	*220,930*		*TOTAL*	*65,620*	
Congressional District 1	Fortenberry, Jeff*	63,673	86.1%	Crawford, Dennis P.	24,140	100.0%
	Turek, Jessica Lynn	5,902	8.0%			
	Parker, Dennis L.	4,407	6.0%			
	TOTAL	*73,982*		*TOTAL*	*24,140*	
Congressional District 2	Terry, Lee*	25,812	52.9%	Ashford, Brad	16,989	81.4%
	Frei, Dan	22,970	47.1%	Aupperle, Mark	3,872	18.6%
	TOTAL	*48,782*		*TOTAL*	*20,861*	
Congressional District 3	Smith, Adrian*	67,113	68.1%	Sullivan, Mark	20,069	100.0%
	Brewer, Tom	31,436	31.9%			
	TOTAL	*98,549*		*TOTAL*	*20,069*	

Note: An asterisk (*) denotes incumbent.

NEVADA

Congressional districts first established for elections held in 2012

4 members

The city of Carson City is an independent city that is treated as a county equivalent; the label is included only for the city.

* Asterisk indicates a county whose boundaries include parts of two or more congressional districts.

NEVADA
Greater Las Vegas Area

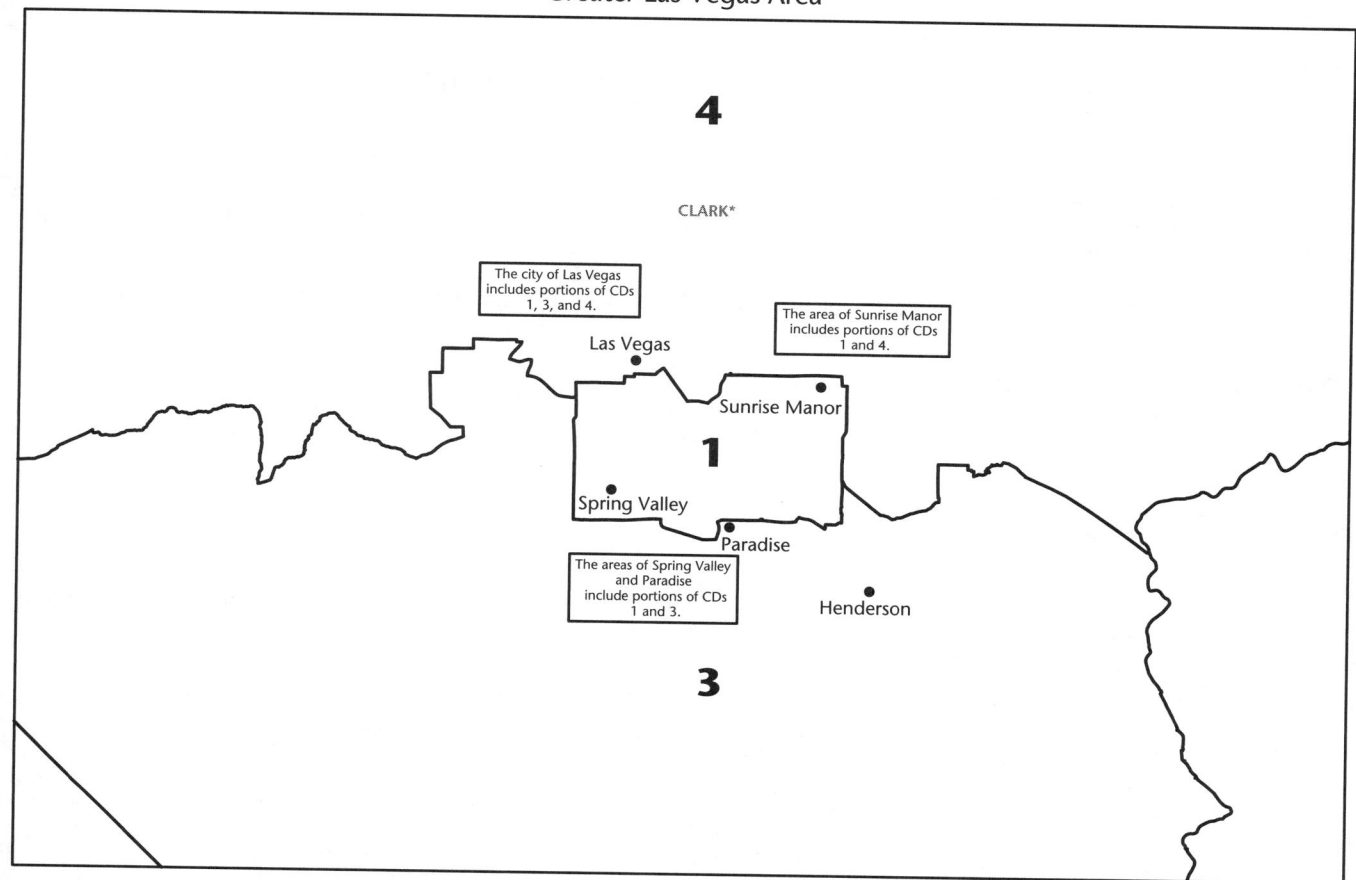

4

CLARK*

The city of Las Vegas includes portions of CDs 1, 3, and 4.

The area of Sunrise Manor includes portions of CDs 1 and 4.

Las Vegas

Sunrise Manor

1

Spring Valley

Paradise

The areas of Spring Valley and Paradise include portions of CDs 1 and 3.

Henderson

3

* Asterisk indicates a county whose boundaries include parts of two or more congressional districts.

NEVADA

GOVERNOR
Brian Sandoval (R). Reelected 2014 to a four-year term. Previously elected 2010.

SENATORS (1 Republican, 1 Democrat)
Dean Heller (R). Elected 2012 to a six-year term. Sworn into office May 9, 2011, following the resignation of John Ensign (R), who was under investigation by the Senate Ethics Committee as to whether he tried to illegally cover up an extramarital affair with a former staff member.

Harry Reid (D). Reelected 2010 to a six-year term. Previously elected 2004, 1998, 1992, 1986

REPRESENTATIVES (3 Republicans, 1 Democrat)
1. Dina Titus (D)
2. Mark E. Amodei (R)
3. Joseph J. Heck (R)
4. Cresent Hardy (R)

POSTWAR VOTE FOR PRESIDENT

| | | Republican | | Democratic | | | | Total Vote | | Major Vote | |
| | | | | | | Other | Rep.-Dem. | | | | |
Year	Total Vote	Vote	Candidate	Vote	Candidate	Vote	Plurality	Rep.	Dem.	Rep.	Dem.
2012	1,014,918	463,567	Romney, W. Mitt	531,373	Obama, Barack H.*	19,978	67,806 D	45.7%	52.4%	46.6%	53.4%
2008	967,848	412,827	McCain, John S. III	533,736	Obama, Barack H.	21,285	120,909 D	42.7%	55.1%	43.6%	56.4%
2004	829,587	418,690	Bush, George W.*	397,190	Kerry, John F.	13,707	21,500 R	50.5%	47.9%	51.3%	48.7%
2000**	608,970	301,575	Bush, George W.	279,978	Gore, Albert Jr.	27,417	21,597 R	49.5%	46.0%	51.9%	48.1%
1996**	464,279	199,244	Dole, Robert "Bob"	203,974	Clinton, Bill*	61,061	4,730 D	42.9%	43.9%	49.4%	50.6%
1992**	506,318	175,828	Bush, George H.*	189,148	Clinton, Bill	141,342	13,320 D	34.7%	37.4%	48.2%	51.8%
1988	350,067	206,040	Bush, George H.	132,738	Dukakis, Michael S.	11,289	73,302 R	58.9%	37.9%	60.8%	39.2%
1984	286,667	188,770	Reagan, Ronald*	91,655	Mondale, Walter F.	6,242	97,115 R	65.8%	32.0%	67.3%	32.7%
1980**	247,885	155,017	Reagan, Ronald	66,666	Carter, Jimmy*	26,202	88,351 R	62.5%	26.9%	69.9%	30.1%
1976	201,876	101,273	Ford, Gerald R.*	92,479	Carter, Jimmy	8,124	8,794 R	50.2%	45.8%	52.3%	47.7%
1972	181,766	115,750	Nixon, Richard M.*	66,016	McGovern, George S.		49,734 R	63.7%	36.3%	63.7%	36.3%
1968**	154,218	73,188	Nixon, Richard M.	60,598	Humphrey, Hubert Horatio Jr.	20,432	12,590 R	47.5%	39.3%	54.7%	45.3%
1964	135,433	56,094	Goldwater, Barry M. Sr.	79,339	Johnson, Lyndon B.*		23,245 D	41.4%	58.6%	41.4%	58.6%
1960	107,267	52,387	Nixon, Richard M.	54,880	Kennedy, John F.		2,493 D	48.8%	51.2%	48.8%	51.2%
1956	96,689	56,049	Eisenhower, Dwight D.*	40,640	Stevenson, Adlai E. II		15,409 R	58.0%	42.0%	58.0%	42.0%
1952	82,190	50,502	Eisenhower, Dwight D.	31,688	Stevenson, Adlai E. II		18,814 R	61.4%	38.6%	61.4%	38.6%
1948	62,117	29,357	Dewey, Thomas E.	31,291	Truman, Harry S.*	1,469	1,934 D	47.3%	50.4%	48.4%	51.6%

Note: An asterisk (*) denotes incumbent. **In past elections, the other vote included: 2000 - 15,008 Green (Ralph Nader); 1996 - 43,986 Reform (Ross Perot); 1992 - 132,580 Independent (Perot); 1980 - 17,651 Independent (John Anderson); 1968 - 20,432 American Independent (George Wallace).

NEVADA

POSTWAR VOTE FOR GOVERNOR

Year	Total Vote	Republican Vote	Republican Candidate	Democratic Vote	Democratic Candidate	Other Vote	Rep.-Dem. Plurality	Percentage Total Vote Rep.	Percentage Total Vote Dem.	Percentage Major Vote Rep.	Percentage Major Vote Dem.
2014	547,349	386,340	Sandoval, Brian*	130,722	Goodman, Robert "Bob"	30,287	255,618 R	70.6%	23.9%	74.7%	25.3%
2010	716,529	382,350	Sandoval, Brian	298,171	Reid, Rory	36,008	84,179 R	53.4%	41.6%	56.2%	43.8%
2006	582,158	279,003	Gibbons, James A. "Jim"	255,684	Titus, Dina	47,471	23,319 R	47.9%	43.9%	52.2%	47.8%
2002	504,079	344,001	Guinn, Kenny*	110,935	Neal, Joe	49,143	233,066 R	68.2%	22.0%	75.6%	24.4%
1998	433,630	223,892	Guinn, Kenny	182,281	Jones, Jan Laverty	27,457	41,611 R	51.6%	42.0%	55.1%	44.9%
1994	379,676	156,875	Gibbons, James A. "Jim"	200,026	Miller, Robert J.*	22,775	43,151 D	41.3%	52.7%	44.0%	56.0%
1990	320,743	95,789	Gallaway, Jim	207,878	Miller, Robert J.*	17,076	112,089 D	29.9%	64.8%	31.5%	68.5%
1986	260,375	65,081	Cafferata, Patty	187,268	Bryan, Richard H.*	8,026	122,187 D	25.0%	71.9%	25.8%	74.2%
1982	239,751	100,104	List, Robert F.*	128,132	Bryan, Richard H.	11,515	28,028 D	41.8%	53.4%	43.9%	56.1%
1978	192,445	108,097	List, Robert F.	76,361	Rose, Robert E.	7,987	31,736 R	56.2%	39.7%	58.6%	41.4%
1974**	169,358	28,959	Crumpler, Shirley	114,114	O'Callaghan, Mike*	26,285	85,155 D	17.1%	67.4%	20.2%	79.8%
1970	146,991	64,400	Fike, Ed	70,697	O'Callaghan, Mike	11,894	6,297 D	43.8%	48.1%	47.7%	52.3%
1966	137,677	71,807	Laxalt, Paul	65,870	Sawyer, Grant*		5,937 R	52.2%	47.8%	52.2%	47.8%
1962	96,929	32,145	Gragson, Oran K.	64,784	Sawyer, Grant*		32,639 D	33.2%	66.8%	33.2%	66.8%
1958	84,889	34,025	Russell, Charles H.*	50,864	Sawyer, Grant		16,839 D	40.1%	59.9%	40.1%	59.9%
1954	78,462	41,665	Russell, Charles H.*	36,797	Pittman, Vail		4,868 R	53.1%	46.9%	53.1%	46.9%
1950	61,773	35,609	Russell, Charles H.	26,164	Pittman, Vail*		9,445 R	57.6%	42.4%	57.6%	42.4%
1946	49,902	21,247	Jepson, Melvin E.	28,655	Pittman, Vail		7,408 D	42.6%	57.4%	42.6%	57.4%

Note: An asterisk (*) denotes incumbent. **In past elections, the other vote included: 1974 - 26,285 Independent American (James Ray Houston).

POSTWAR VOTE FOR SENATOR

Year	Total Vote	Republican Vote	Republican Candidate	Democratic Vote	Democratic Candidate	Other Vote	Rep.-Dem. Plurality	Percentage Total Vote Rep.	Percentage Total Vote Dem.	Percentage Major Vote Rep.	Percentage Major Vote Dem.
2012	997,805	457,656	Heller, Dean*	446,080	Berkley, Shelley	94,069	11,576 R	45.9%	44.7%	50.6%	49.4%
2010	721,404	321,361	Angle, Sharron E.	362,785	Reid, Harry*	37,258	41,424 D	44.5%	50.3%	47.0%	53.0%
2006	582,572	322,501	Ensign, John*	238,796	Carter, Jack	21,275	83,705 R	55.4%	41.0%	57.5%	42.5%
2004	810,068	284,640	Ziser, Richard	494,805	Reid, Harry*	30,623	210,165 D	35.1%	61.1%	36.5%	63.5%
2000	600,250	330,687	Ensign, John	238,260	Bernstein, Ed	31,303	92,427 R	55.1%	39.7%	58.1%	41.9%
1998	435,790	208,222	Ensign, John	208,650	Reid, Harry*	18,918	428 D	47.8%	47.9%	49.9%	50.1%
1994	380,530	156,020	Furman, Hal	193,804	Bryan, Richard H.*	30,706	37,784 D	41.0%	50.9%	44.6%	55.4%
1992	495,887	199,413	Dahl, Demar	253,150	Reid, Harry*	43,324	53,737 D	40.2%	51.0%	44.1%	55.9%
1988	349,649	161,336	Hecht, Chic*	175,548	Bryan, Richard H.	12,765	14,212 D	46.1%	50.2%	47.9%	52.1%
1986	261,932	116,606	Santini, James	130,955	Reid, Harry	14,371	14,349 D	44.5%	50.0%	47.1%	52.9%
1982	240,394	120,377	Hecht, Chic	114,720	Cannon, Howard W.*	5,297	5,657 R	50.1%	47.7%	51.2%	48.8%
1980	246,436	144,224	Laxalt, Paul*	92,129	Gojack, Mary	10,083	52,095 R	58.5%	37.4%	61.0%	39.0%
1976	201,980	63,471	Towell, David	127,295	Cannon, Howard W.*	11,214	63,824 D	31.4%	63.0%	33.3%	66.7%
1974	169,473	79,605	Laxalt, Paul	78,981	Reid, Harry	10,887	624 R	47.0%	46.6%	50.2%	49.8%
1970	147,768	60,838	Raggio, William J.	85,187	Cannon, Howard W.*	1,743	24,349 D	41.2%	57.6%	41.7%	58.3%
1968	152,690	69,068	Fike, Ed	83,622	Bible, Alan Harvey*		14,554 D	45.2%	54.8%	45.2%	54.8%
1964	134,624	67,288	Laxalt, Paul	67,336	Cannon, Howard W.*		48 D	50.0%	50.0%	50.0%	50.0%
1962	97,192	33,749	Wright, William B.	63,443	Bible, Alan Harvey*		29,694 D	34.7%	65.3%	34.7%	65.3%
1958	84,492	35,760	Malone, George W.*	48,732	Cannon, Howard W.		12,972 D	42.3%	57.7%	42.3%	57.7%
1956	96,389	45,712	Young, Cliff	50,677	Bible, Alan Harvey*		4,965 D	47.4%	52.6%	47.4%	52.6%
1954S	77,513	32,470	Brown, Ernest S.	45,043	Bible, Alan Harvey		12,573 D	41.9%	58.1%	41.9%	58.1%
1952	81,090	41,906	Malone, George W.*	39,184	Mechling, Thomas B.		2,722 R	51.7%	48.3%	51.7%	48.3%
1950	61,762	25,933	Marshall, George E.	35,829	McCarran, Patrick A.*		9,896 D	42.0%	58.0%	42.0%	58.0%
1946	50,354	27,801	Malone, George W.	22,553	Bunker, Berkeley L.		5,248 R	55.2%	44.8%	55.2%	44.8%

Note: An asterisk (*) denotes incumbent. **The 1954 election was for a short term to fill a vacancy.

NEVADA

GOVERNOR 2014

2010 Census Population	County	Total Vote	Republican (Sandoval)	Democratic (Goodman)	Other	Rep.-Dem. Plurality	Percentage			
							Total Vote		Major Vote	
							Rep.	Dem.	Rep.	Dem.
55,274	CARSON CITY	15,647	12,108	2,410	1,129	9,698 R	77.4%	15.4%	83.4%	16.6%
24,877	CHURCHILL	7,455	6,356	666	433	5,690 R	85.3%	8.9%	90.5%	9.5%
1,951,269	CLARK	337,687	223,433	97,097	17,157	126,336 R	66.2%	28.8%	69.7%	30.3%
46,997	DOUGLAS	18,026	14,910	2,174	942	12,736 R	82.7%	12.1%	87.3%	12.7%
48,818	ELKO	10,200	8,038	1,119	1,043	6,919 R	78.8%	11.0%	87.8%	12.2%
783	ESMERALDA	355	273	42	40	231 R	76.9%	11.8%	86.7%	13.3%
1,987	EUREKA	700	533	53	114	480 R	76.1%	7.6%	91.0%	9.0%
16,528	HUMBOLDT	4,349	3,633	459	257	3,174 R	83.5%	10.6%	88.8%	11.2%
5,775	LANDER	1,763	1,475	163	125	1,312 R	83.7%	9.2%	90.0%	10.0%
5,345	LINCOLN	1,609	1,323	146	140	1,177 R	82.2%	9.1%	90.1%	9.9%
51,980	LYON	14,181	11,659	1,643	879	10,016 R	82.2%	11.6%	87.6%	12.4%
4,772	MINERAL	1,406	1,102	210	94	892 R	78.4%	14.9%	84.0%	16.0%
43,946	NYE	12,167	9,095	2,005	1,067	7,090 R	74.8%	16.5%	81.9%	18.1%
6,753	PERSHING	1,556	1,228	174	154	1,054 R	78.9%	11.2%	87.6%	12.4%
4,010	STOREY	1,896	1,462	265	169	1,197 R	77.1%	14.0%	84.7%	15.3%
421,407	WASHOE	115,565	87,739	21,598	6,228	66,141 R	75.9%	18.7%	80.2%	19.8%
10,030	WHITE PINE	2,787	1,973	498	316	1,475 R	70.8%	17.9%	79.8%	20.2%
2,700,551	TOTAL	547,349	386,340	130,722	30,287	255,618 R	70.6%	23.9%	74.7%	25.3%

NEVADA

HOUSE OF REPRESENTATIVES

CD	Year	Total Vote	Republican		Democratic		Other Vote	Rep.-Dem. Plurality	Percentage			
			Vote	Candidate	Vote	Candidate			Total Vote		Major Vote	
									Rep.	Dem.	Rep.	Dem.
1	2014	80,299	30,413	TEIJEIRO, ANNETTE	45,643	TITUS, DINA*	4,243	15,230 D	37.9%	56.8%	40.0%	60.0%
1	2012	179,278	56,521	EDWARDS, CHRIS	113,967	TITUS, DINA	8,790	57,446 D	31.5%	63.6%	33.2%	66.8%
2	2014	186,210	122,402	AMODEI, MARK E.*	52,016	SPEES, KRISTEN	11,792	70,386 R	65.7%	27.9%	70.2%	29.8%
2	2012	281,449	162,213	AMODEI, MARK E.*	102,019	KOEPNICK, SAMUEL	17,217	60,194 R	57.6%	36.2%	61.4%	38.6%
3	2014	145,719	88,528	HECK, JOSEPH J.*	52,644	BILBRAY, ERIN	4,547	35,884 R	60.8%	36.1%	62.7%	37.3%
3	2012	272,523	137,244	HECK, JOSEPH J.*	116,823	OCEGUERA, JOHN	18,456	20,421 R	50.4%	42.9%	54.0%	46.0%
4	2014	130,781	63,466	HARDY, CRESENT	59,844	HORSFORD, STEVEN A.*	7,471	3,622 R	48.5%	45.8%	51.5%	48.5%
4	2012	240,492	101,261	TARKANIAN, DANNY	120,501	HORSFORD, STEVEN A.	18,730	19,240 D	42.1%	50.1%	45.7%	54.3%
TOTAL	2014	543,009	304,809		210,147		28,053	94,662 R	56.1%	38.7%	59.2%	40.8%
TOTAL	2012	973,742	457,239		453,310		63,193	3,929 R	47.0%	46.6%	50.2%	49.8%

Note: An asterisk (*) denotes incumbent.

NEVADA

GENERAL AND PRIMARY ELECTIONS

2014 GENERAL ELECTIONS: OTHER VOTES

Governor   Other vote was 15,751 No Party ("None Of These Candidates"), 14,536 Independent American (David Lory VanDerBeek)

House   Other vote was:

CD 1   2,617 Libertarian (Richard Charles), 1,626 Independent American (Kamau Bakari)

CD 2   11,792 Independent American (Janine Hansen)

CD 3   1,637 Independent (David Goossen), 1,566 Libertarian (Randy Kimmick), 1,344 Independent (Steven St. John)

CD 4   4,119 Libertarian (Steve Brown), 3,352 Independent American (Russell Best)

2014 PRIMARY ELECTIONS: SUPPLEMENTARY INFORMATION

Primary	June 10, 2014	**Registration** (as of May 20, 2014 – includes 270,482 inactive registrants)	1,424,417	Democratic	591,818
				Republican	479,825
				Independent American	70,258
				Libertarian	11,296
				Other	9,789
				Nonpartisan	261,431

Primary Type   Closed—Only registered Democrats and Republicans could vote in their party's primary.

	REPUBLICAN PRIMARIES			DEMOCRATIC PRIMARIES		
Governor	Sandoval, Brian*	105,857	89.9%	"None Of These Candidates"	21,725	30.0%
	Hamilton, Eddie ("In Liberty")	3,758	3.2%	Goodman, Robert "Bob"	17,961	24.8%
	"None Of These Candidates"	3,509	3.0%	Frye, Stephen H.	8,231	11.3%
	Tarbell, William	1,966	1.7%	Rutledge, John	6,039	8.3%
	Tighe, Thomas J.	1,495	1.3%	Chang, Charles "Charlie"	5,619	7.7%
	Marinch, Gary A.	1,195	1.0%	Hyepock, Chris	4,743	6.5%
				Rheinhart, Allen	3,605	5.0%
				Shabazz, Abdul H.	2,731	3.8%
				Conquest, Frederick L.	1,867	2.6%
	TOTAL	*117,780*		*TOTAL*	*72,521*	
Congressional District 1	Teijeiro, Annette	6,083	54.7%	Titus, Dina*	12,966	86.0%
	Padilla, Jose	5,045	45.3%	Peters, Herb	2,106	14.0%
	TOTAL	*11,128*		*TOTAL*	*15,072*	
Congressional District 2	Amodei, Mark E.*	Unopposed		Spees, Kristen	8,206	38.3%
				Dempsey, Brian	6,804	31.8%
				Alm, Vance	3,225	15.1%
				Lee, Ed	3,164	14.8%
				TOTAL	*21,399*	
Congressional District 3	Heck, Joseph J.*	Unopposed		Bilbray, Erin	13,204	84.0%
				Campbell, Zachary "Mr. Z"	2,511	16.0%
				TOTAL	*15,715*	
Congressional District 4	Hardy, Cresent	10,398	42.6%	Horsford, Steven A.*	16,269	84.3%
	Innis, Niger	8,077	33.1%	Budetich, Mark J. Jr.	1,532	7.9%
	Monroe, Mike	5,393	22.1%	Zeller, Sid	1,498	7.8%
	Poliak, Carlo	523	2.1%			
	TOTAL	*24,391*		*TOTAL*	*19,299*	

Note: An asterisk (*) denotes incumbent.

NEW HAMPSHIRE

Congressional districts first established for elections held in 2012

2 members

* Asterisk indicates a county whose boundaries include parts of two or more congressional districts.

NEW HAMPSHIRE

GOVERNOR

Maggie Hassan (D). Re-elected 2014 to a two-year term. Previously elected 2012.

SENATORS (1 Republican, 1 Democrat)

Kelly Ayotte (R). Elected 2010 to a six-year term.
Leanne Shaheen (D). Reelected 2014 to a six-year term. Previously elected 2008.

REPRESENTATIVES (1 Republican, 1 Democrat)

1. Frank C. Guinta (R) 2. Ann M. Kuster (D)

POSTWAR VOTE FOR PRESIDENT

		Republican		Democratic				Total Vote		Major Vote	
Year	Total Vote	Vote	Candidate	Vote	Candidate	Other Vote	Rep.-Dem. Plurality	Rep.	Dem.	Rep.	Dem.
2012	710,972	329,918	Romney, W. Mitt	369,561	Obama, Barack H.*	11,493	39,643 D	46.4%	52.0%	47.2%	52.8%
2008	710,970	316,534	McCain, John S. III	384,826	Obama, Barack H.	9,610	68,292 D	44.5%	54.1%	45.1%	54.9%
2004	677,738	331,237	Bush, George W.*	340,511	Kerry, John F.	5,990	9,274 D	48.9%	50.2%	49.3%	50.7%
2000**	569,081	273,559	Bush, George W.	266,348	Gore, Albert Jr.	29,174	7,211 R	48.1%	46.8%	50.7%	49.3%
1996**	499,175	196,532	Dole, Robert "Bob"	246,214	Clinton, Bill*	56,429	49,682 D	39.4%	49.3%	44.4%	55.6%
1992**	537,943	202,484	Bush, George H.*	209,040	Clinton, Bill	126,419	6,556 D	37.6%	38.9%	49.2%	50.8%
1988	451,074	281,537	Bush, George H.	163,696	Dukakis, Michael S.	5,841	117,841 R	62.4%	36.3%	63.2%	36.8%
1984	389,066	267,051	Reagan, Ronald*	120,395	Mondale, Walter F.	1,620	146,656 R	68.6%	30.9%	68.9%	31.1%
1980**	383,990	221,705	Reagan, Ronald	108,864	Carter, Jimmy*	53,421	112,841 R	57.7%	28.4%	67.1%	32.9%
1976	339,618	185,935	Ford, Gerald R.*	147,635	Carter, Jimmy	6,048	38,300 R	54.7%	43.5%	55.7%	44.3%
1972	334,055	213,724	Nixon, Richard M.*	116,435	McGovern, George S.	3,896	97,289 R	64.0%	34.9%	64.7%	35.3%
1968**	297,298	154,903	Nixon, Richard M.	130,589	Humphrey, Hubert Horatio Jr.	11,806	24,314 R	52.1%	43.9%	54.3%	45.7%
1964	288,093	104,029	Goldwater, Barry M. Sr.	184,064	Johnson, Lyndon B.*		80,035 D	36.1%	63.9%	36.1%	63.9%
1960	295,761	157,989	Nixon, Richard M.	137,772	Kennedy, John F.		20,217 R	53.4%	46.6%	53.4%	46.6%
1956	266,994	176,519	Eisenhower, Dwight D.*	90,364	Stevenson, Adlai E. II	111	86,155 R	66.1%	33.8%	66.1%	33.9%
1952	272,950	166,287	Eisenhower, Dwight D.	106,663	Stevenson, Adlai E. II		59,624 R	60.9%	39.1%	60.9%	39.1%
1948	231,440	121,299	Dewey, Thomas E.	107,995	Truman, Harry S.*	2,146	13,304 R	52.4%	46.7%	52.9%	47.1%

Note: An asterisk (*) denotes incumbent. **In past elections, the other vote included: 2000 - 22,198 Green (Ralph Nader); 1996 - 48,390 Reform (Ross Perot); 1992 - 121,337 Independent (Perot); 1980 - 49,693 Independent (John Anderson); 1968 - 11,173 American Independent (George Wallace).

NEW HAMPSHIRE

POSTWAR VOTE FOR GOVERNOR

Year	Total Vote	Republican Vote	Republican Candidate	Democratic Vote	Democratic Candidate	Other Vote	Rep.-Dem. Plurality	Total Vote Rep.	Total Vote Dem.	Major Vote Rep.	Major Vote Dem.
2014	486,183	230,610	Havenstein, Walt	254,666	Hassan, Maggie*	907	24,056 D	47.4%	52.4%	47.5%	52.5%
2012	693,877	295,026	Lamontagne, Ovide M.	378,934	Hassan, Maggie	19,917	83,908 D	42.5%	54.6%	43.8%	56.2%
2010	456,588	205,616	Stephen, John A.	240,346	Lynch, John*	10,626	34,730 D	45.0%	52.6%	46.1%	53.9%
2008	682,910	188,555	Kenney, Joseph D.	479,042	Lynch, John*	15,313	290,487 D	27.6%	70.1%	28.2%	71.8%
2006	403,679	104,288	Coburn, Jim	298,760	Lynch, John*	631	194,472 D	25.8%	74.0%	25.9%	74.1%
2004	667,020	325,981	Benson, Craig*	340,299	Lynch, John	740	14,318 D	48.9%	51.0%	48.9%	51.1%
2002	442,976	259,663	Benson, Craig	169,277	Fernald, Mark D.	14,036	90,386 R	58.6%	38.2%	60.5%	39.5%
2000	564,953	246,952	Humphrey, Gordon John	275,038	Shaheen, Jeanne*	42,963	28,086 D	43.7%	48.7%	47.3%	52.7%
1998	318,940	98,473	Lucas, Jay	210,769	Shaheen, Jeanne*	9,698	112,296 D	30.9%	66.1%	31.8%	68.2%
1996	497,040	196,321	Lamontagne, Ovide M.	284,175	Shaheen, Jeanne	16,544	87,854 D	39.5%	57.2%	40.9%	59.1%
1994	311,882	218,134	Merrill, Steve*	79,686	King, Wayne D.	14,062	138,448 R	69.9%	25.6%	73.2%	26.8%
1992	516,170	289,170	Merrill, Steve	206,232	Arnesen, Deborah A.	20,768	82,938 R	56.0%	40.0%	58.4%	41.6%
1990	295,018	177,773	Gregg, Judd*	101,923	Grandmaison, J. Joseph	15,322	75,850 R	60.3%	34.5%	63.6%	36.4%
1988	441,923	267,064	Gregg, Judd	172,543	McEachern, Paul*	2,316	94,521 R	60.4%	39.0%	60.8%	39.2%
1986	251,107	134,824	Sununu, John H.*	116,142	McEachern, Paul	141	18,682 R	53.7%	46.3%	53.7%	46.3%
1984	383,910	256,574	Sununu, John H.*	127,156	Spirou, Chris	180	129,418 R	66.8%	33.1%	66.9%	33.1%
1982	282,588	145,389	Sununu, John H.	132,317	Gallen, Hugh J.*	4,882	13,072 R	51.4%	46.8%	52.4%	47.6%
1980	384,031	156,178	Thomson, Meldrim Jr.	226,436	Gallen, Hugh J.*	1,417	70,258 D	40.7%	59.0%	40.8%	59.2%
1978	269,587	122,464	Thomson, Meldrim Jr.*	133,133	Gallen, Hugh J.	13,990	10,669 D	45.4%	49.4%	47.9%	52.1%
1976	342,669	197,589	Thomson, Meldrim Jr.*	145,015	Spanos, Harry V.	65	52,574 R	57.7%	42.3%	57.7%	42.3%
1974	226,665	115,933	Thomson, Meldrim Jr.*	110,591	Leonard, Richard W.	141	5,342 R	51.1%	48.8%	51.2%	48.8%
1972**	323,102	133,702	Thomson, Meldrim Jr.	126,107	Crowley, Roger J.	63,293	7,595 R	41.4%	39.0%	51.5%	48.5%
1970	222,441	102,298	Peterson, Walter R.*	98,098	Crowley, Roger J.	22,045	4,200 R	46.0%	44.1%	51.0%	49.0%
1968	285,342	149,902	Peterson, Walter R.	135,378	Bussiere, Emile R.	62	14,524 R	52.5%	47.4%	52.5%	47.5%
1966	233,642	107,259	Gregg, Hugh	125,882	King, John W.*	501	18,623 D	45.9%	53.9%	46.0%	54.0%
1964	285,863	94,824	Pillsbury, John	190,863	King, John W.*	176	96,039 D	33.2%	66.8%	33.2%	66.8%
1962	230,048	94,567	Pillsbury, John	135,481	King, John W.		40,914 D	41.1%	58.9%	41.1%	58.9%
1960	290,527	161,123	Powell, Wesley*	129,404	Boutin, Bernard L.		31,719 R	55.5%	44.5%	55.5%	44.5%
1958	206,745	106,790	Powell, Wesley	99,955	Boutin, Bernard L.		6,835 R	51.7%	48.3%	51.7%	48.3%
1956	258,695	141,578	Dwinell, Lane*	117,117	Shaw, John		24,461 R	54.7%	45.3%	54.7%	45.3%
1954	194,631	107,287	Dwinell, Lane	87,344	Shaw, John		19,943 R	55.1%	44.9%	55.1%	44.9%
1952	265,715	167,791	Gregg, Hugh	97,924	Craig, William H.		69,867 R	63.1%	36.9%	63.1%	36.9%
1950	191,239	108,907	Adams, Sherman*	82,258	Bingham, Robert P.	74	26,649 R	56.9%	43.0%	57.0%	43.0%
1948	222,571	116,212	Adams, Sherman	105,207	Hill, Herbert W.	1,152	11,005 R	52.2%	47.3%	52.5%	47.5%
1946	163,451	103,204	Dale, Charles M.	60,247	Keefe, F. Clyde		42,957 R	63.1%	36.9%	63.1%	36.9%

Note: An asterisk (*) denotes incumbent. **In past elections, the other vote included: 1972 - 63,199 Independent (Malcolm McLane).

NEW HAMPSHIRE

POSTWAR VOTE FOR SENATOR

Year	Total Vote	Republican Vote	Republican Candidate	Democratic Vote	Democratic Candidate	Other Vote	Rep.-Dem. Plurality	Total Vote Rep.	Total Vote Dem.	Major Vote Rep.	Major Vote Dem.
2014	488,159	235,347	Brown, Scott P.	251,184	Shaheen, Jeanne*	1,628	15,837 D	48.2%	51.5%	48.4%	51.6%
2010	455,149	273,218	Ayotte, Kelly	167,545	Hodes, Paul W.	14,386	105,673 R	60.0%	36.8%	62.0%	38.0%
2008	694,787	314,403	Sununu, John E.*	358,438	Shaheen, Jeanne	21,946	44,035 D	45.3%	51.6%	46.7%	53.3%
2004	657,086	434,847	Gregg, Judd*	221,549	Haddock, Dorris R. "Granny D"	690	213,298 R	66.2%	33.7%	66.2%	33.8%
2002	447,135	227,229	Sununu, John E.	207,478	Shaheen, Jeanne	12,428	19,751 R	50.8%	46.4%	52.3%	47.7%
1998	314,956	213,477	Gregg, Judd*	88,883	Condodemetraky, George	12,596	124,594 R	67.8%	28.2%	70.6%	29.4%
1996	491,966	242,304	Smith, Robert C.*	227,397	Swett, Dick	22,265	14,907 R	49.3%	46.2%	51.6%	48.4%
1992	518,416	249,591	Gregg, Judd	234,982	Rauh, John	33,843	14,609 R	48.1%	45.3%	51.5%	48.5%
1990	291,393	189,792	Smith, Robert C.	91,299	Durkin, John A.	10,302	98,493 R	65.1%	31.3%	67.5%	32.5%
1986	244,797	154,090	Rudman, Warren B.*	79,225	Peabody, Endicott	11,482	74,865 R	62.9%	32.4%	66.0%	34.0%
1984	384,406	225,828	Humphrey, Gordon John*	157,447	D'Amours, Norman E.	1,131	68,381 R	58.7%	41.0%	58.9%	41.1%
1980	375,060	195,559	Rudman, Warren B.	179,455	Durkin, John A.*	46	16,104 R	52.1%	47.8%	52.1%	47.9%
1978	263,779	133,745	Humphrey, Gordon John	127,945	McIntyre, Thomas J.*	2,089	5,800 R	50.7%	48.5%	51.1%	48.9%
1975S	262,682	113,007	Wyman, Louis C.	140,778	Durkin, John A.	8,897	27,771 D	43.0%	53.6%	44.5%	55.5%
1974**	223,363	110,926	Wyman, Louis C.	110,924	Durkin, John A.	1,513	2 R	49.7%	49.7%	50.0%	50.0%
1972	324,354	139,852	Powell, Wesley	184,495	McIntyre, Thomas J.*	7	44,643 D	43.1%	56.9%	43.1%	56.9%
1968	286,989	170,163	Cotton, Norris R.*	116,816	King, John W.	10	53,347 R	59.3%	40.7%	59.3%	40.7%
1966	229,305	105,241	Thyng, Harrison R.	123,888	McIntyre, Thomas J.*	176	18,647 D	45.9%	54.0%	45.9%	54.1%
1962	224,479	134,035	Cotton, Norris R.*	90,444	Catalfo, Alfred Jr.		43,591 R	59.7%	40.3%	59.7%	40.3%
1962S	224,811	107,199	Bass, Perkins	117,612	McIntyre, Thomas J.		10,413 D	47.7%	52.3%	47.7%	52.3%
1960	287,545	173,521	Bridges, Styles*	114,024	Hill, Herbert W.		59,497 R	60.3%	39.7%	60.3%	39.7%
1956	251,943	161,424	Cotton, Norris R.*	90,519	Pickett, Laurence M.		70,905 R	64.1%	35.9%	64.1%	35.9%
1954	194,536	117,150	Bridges, Styles*	77,386	Morin, Gerard L.		39,764 R	60.2%	39.8%	60.2%	39.8%
1954S	189,558	114,068	Cotton, Norris R.	75,490	Betley, Stanley J.		38,578 R	60.2%	39.8%	60.2%	39.8%
1950	190,573	106,142	Tobey, Charles W.*	72,473	Kelley, Emmet J.	11,958	33,669 R	55.7%	38.0%	59.4%	40.6%
1948	222,898	129,600	Bridges, Styles*	91,760	Fortin, Alfred E.	1,538	37,840 R	58.1%	41.2%	58.5%	41.5%

Note: An asterisk (*) denotes incumbent. **Following the closely contested 1974 election, neither candidate was seated and the 1975 special election was held for the remaining years of that term. One each of the 1954 and 1962 elections was for a short term to fill a vacancy.

NEW HAMPSHIRE

GOVERNOR 2014

2010 Census Population	County	Total Vote	Republican (Havenstein)	Democratic (Hassan)	Other	Rep.-Dem. Plurality	Total Vote Rep.	Total Vote Dem.	Major Vote Rep.	Major Vote Dem.
60,088	BELKNAP	23,713	12,603	11,069	41	1,534 R	53.1%	46.7%	53.2%	46.8%
47,818	CARROLL	20,680	10,316	10,332	32	16 D	49.9%	50.0%	50.0%	50.0%
77,117	CHESHIRE	27,124	10,611	16,440	73	5,829 D	39.1%	60.6%	39.2%	60.8%
33,055	COOS	10,595	4,151	6,429	15	2,278 D	39.2%	60.7%	39.2%	60.8%
89,118	GRAFTON	33,039	12,884	20,155		7,271 D	39.0%	61.0%	39.0%	61.0%
400,721	HILLSBOROUGH	137,893	70,041	67,525	327	2,516 R	50.8%	49.0%	50.9%	49.1%
146,445	MERRIMACK	57,100	24,608	32,365	127	7,757 D	43.1%	56.7%	43.2%	56.8%
295,223	ROCKINGHAM	118,451	60,538	57,743	170	2,795 R	51.1%	48.7%	51.2%	48.8%
123,143	STRAFFORD	42,156	18,026	24,032	98	6,006 D	42.8%	57.0%	42.9%	57.1%
43,742	SULLIVAN	15,432	6,832	8,576	24	1,744 D	44.3%	55.6%	44.3%	55.7%
1,316,470	TOTAL	486,183	230,610	254,666	907	24,056 D	47.4%	52.4%	47.5%	52.5%

NEW HAMPSHIRE

GOVERNOR 2014

2010 Census Population	City/Town	Total Vote	Republican (Havenstein)	Democratic (Hassan)	Other	Rep.-Dem. Plurality	Percentage			
							Total Vote		Major Vote	
							Rep.	Dem.	Rep.	Dem.
11,201	AMHERST	5,591	3,008	2,575	8	433 R	53.8%	46.1%	53.9%	46.1%
6,751	ATKINSON	3,163	1,835	1,323	5	512 R	58.0%	41.8%	58.1%	41.9%
8,576	BARRINGTON	3,439	1,607	1,822	10	215 D	46.7%	53.0%	46.9%	53.1%
21,203	BEDFORD	9,562	5,809	3,736	17	2,073 R	60.8%	39.1%	60.9%	39.1%
7,356	BELMONT	2,321	1,252	1,065	4	187 R	53.9%	45.9%	54.0%	46.0%
10,051	BERLIN	2,714	751	1,955	8	1,204 D	27.7%	72.0%	27.8%	72.2%
7,519	BOW	3,814	1,752	2,062		310 D	45.9%	54.1%	45.9%	54.1%
13,355	CLAREMONT	3,720	1,513	2,198	9	685 D	40.7%	59.1%	40.8%	59.2%
42,695	CONCORD	15,443	4,973	10,430	40	5,457 D	32.2%	67.5%	32.3%	67.7%
10,115	CONWAY	3,286	1,337	1,948	1	611 D	40.7%	59.3%	40.7%	59.3%
33,109	DERRY	10,144	5,563	4,581		982 R	54.8%	45.2%	54.8%	45.2%
29,987	DOVER	10,936	4,132	6,787	17	2,655 D	37.8%	62.1%	37.8%	62.2%
14,638	DURHAM	4,184	1,233	2,946	5	1,713 D	29.5%	70.4%	29.5%	70.5%
6,411	EPPING	2,408	1,185	1,218	5	33 D	49.2%	50.6%	49.3%	50.7%
14,306	EXETER	6,500	2,378	4,122		1,744 D	36.6%	63.4%	36.6%	63.4%
6,786	FARMINGTON	1,884	958	917	9	41 R	50.8%	48.7%	51.1%	48.9%
8,477	FRANKLIN	2,432	1,158	1,260	14	102 D	47.6%	51.8%	47.9%	52.1%
7,126	GILFORD	3,351	1,718	1,625	8	93 R	51.3%	48.5%	51.4%	48.6%
17,651	GOFFSTOWN	6,171	3,255	2,905	11	350 R	52.7%	47.1%	52.8%	47.2%
8,523	HAMPSTEAD	3,801	2,238	1,559	4	679 R	58.9%	41.0%	58.9%	41.1%
15,430	HAMPTON	6,977	3,378	3,592	7	214 D	48.4%	51.5%	48.5%	51.5%
11,260	HANOVER	4,616	1,000	3,611	5	2,611 D	21.7%	78.2%	21.7%	78.3%
7,684	HOLLIS	3,858	2,150	1,703	5	447 R	55.7%	44.1%	55.8%	44.2%
13,451	HOOKSETT	5,100	2,702	2,398		304 R	53.0%	47.0%	53.0%	47.0%
24,467	HUDSON	8,198	4,659	3,521	18	1,138 R	56.8%	42.9%	57.0%	43.0%
5,457	JAFFREY	1,919	873	1,040	6	167 D	45.5%	54.2%	45.6%	54.4%
23,409	KEENE	7,575	2,280	5,274	21	2,994 D	30.1%	69.6%	30.2%	69.8%
6,025	KINGSTON	2,350	1,317	1,032	1	285 R	56.0%	43.9%	56.1%	43.9%
15,951	LACONIA	5,389	2,727	2,655	7	72 R	50.6%	49.3%	50.7%	49.3%
13,151	LEBANON	4,680	1,397	3,280	3	1,883 D	29.9%	70.1%	29.9%	70.1%
8,271	LITCHFIELD	3,188	1,848	1,332	8	516 R	58.0%	41.8%	58.1%	41.9%
5,928	LITTLETON	1,987	893	1,089	5	196 D	44.9%	54.8%	45.1%	54.9%
24,129	LONDONDERRY	8,848	4,990	3,828	30	1,162 R	56.4%	43.3%	56.6%	43.4%
109,565	MANCHESTER	30,404	13,511	16,782	111	3,271 D	44.4%	55.2%	44.6%	55.4%
25,494	MERRIMACK TOWN	9,888	5,562	4,326		1,236 R	56.2%	43.8%	56.2%	43.8%
15,115	MILFORD	5,375	2,684	2,669	22	15 R	49.9%	49.7%	50.1%	49.9%
86,494	NASHUA	26,546	12,347	14,139	60	1,792 D	46.5%	53.3%	46.6%	53.4%
8,936	NEWMARKET	3,417	1,239	2,169	9	930 D	36.3%	63.5%	36.4%	63.6%
6,507	NEWPORT	1,957	1,019	932	6	87 R	52.1%	47.6%	52.2%	47.8%
12,897	PELHAM	4,535	2,782	1,747	6	1,035 R	61.3%	38.5%	61.4%	38.6%
7,115	PEMBROKE	2,681	1,233	1,441	7	208 D	46.0%	53.7%	46.1%	53.9%
6,284	PETERBOROUGH	2,891	997	1,893	1	896 D	34.5%	65.5%	34.5%	65.5%
7,609	PLAISTOW	2,714	1,568	1,145	1	423 R	57.8%	42.2%	57.8%	42.2%
6,990	PLYMOUTH	1,846	644	1,198	4	554 D	34.9%	64.9%	35.0%	65.0%
20,779	PORTSMOUTH	9,190	2,747	6,424	19	3,677 D	29.9%	69.9%	30.0%	70.0%
10,138	RAYMOND	3,278	1,845	1,422	11	423 R	56.3%	43.4%	56.5%	43.5%
29,752	ROCHESTER	9,478	4,593	4,854	31	261 D	48.5%	51.2%	48.6%	51.4%
28,776	SALEM	9,916	5,432	4,465	19	967 R	54.8%	45.0%	54.9%	45.1%
8,693	SEABROOK	2,607	1,434	1,169	4	265 R	55.0%	44.8%	55.1%	44.9%
11,766	SOMERSWORTH	3,332	1,357	1,966	9	609 D	40.7%	59.0%	40.8%	59.2%
7,230	SWANZEY	2,370	1,022	1,348		326 D	43.1%	56.9%	43.1%	56.9%
8,785	WEARE	3,189	1,776	1,405	8	371 R	55.7%	44.1%	55.8%	44.2%
13,592	WINDHAM	5,743	3,507	2,229	7	1,278 R	61.1%	38.8%	61.1%	38.9%
6,269	WOLFEBORO	3,209	1,774	1,435		339 R	55.3%	44.7%	55.3%	44.7%

NEW HAMPSHIRE

SENATOR 2014

2010 Census Population	County	Total Vote	Republican (Brown)	Democratic (Shaheen)	Other	Rep.-Dem. Plurality	Percentage Total Vote Rep.	Dem.	Major Vote Rep.	Dem.
60,088	BELKNAP	23,738	12,566	11,097	75	1,469 R	52.9%	46.7%	53.1%	46.9%
47,818	CARROLL	20,696	10,150	10,502	44	352 D	49.0%	50.7%	49.1%	50.9%
77,117	CHESHIRE	27,212	10,598	16,468	146	5,870 D	38.9%	60.5%	39.2%	60.8%
33,055	COOS	10,640	3,998	6,611	31	2,613 D	37.6%	62.1%	37.7%	62.3%
89,118	GRAFTON	33,257	12,654	20,496	107	7,842 D	38.0%	61.6%	38.2%	61.8%
400,721	HILLSBOROUGH	138,300	70,529	67,191	580	3,338 R	51.0%	48.6%	51.2%	48.8%
146,445	MERRIMACK	57,181	24,597	32,413	171	7,816 D	43.0%	56.7%	43.1%	56.9%
295,223	ROCKINGHAM	119,290	65,056	53,934	300	11,122 R	54.5%	45.2%	54.7%	45.3%
123,143	STRAFFORD	42,385	18,541	23,710	134	5,169 D	43.7%	55.9%	43.9%	56.1%
43,742	SULLIVAN	15,460	6,658	8,762	40	2,104 D	43.1%	56.7%	43.2%	56.8%
1,316,470	TOTAL	488,159	235,347	251,184	1,628	15,837 D	48.2%	51.5%	48.4%	51.6%

2010 Census Population	City/Town	Total Vote	Republican (Brown)	Democratic (Shaheen)	Other	Rep.-Dem. Plurality	Percentage Total Vote Rep.	Dem.	Major Vote Rep.	Dem.
11,201	AMHERST	5,602	3,019	2,559	24	460 R	53.9%	45.7%	54.1%	45.9%
6,751	ATKINSON	3,208	2,023	1,180	5	843 R	63.1%	36.8%	63.2%	36.8%
8,576	BARRINGTON	3,442	1,623	1,801	18	178 D	47.2%	52.3%	47.4%	52.6%
21,203	BEDFORD	9,570	5,935	3,599	36	2,336 R	62.0%	37.6%	62.3%	37.7%
7,356	BELMONT	2,331	1,259	1,069	3	190 R	54.0%	45.9%	54.1%	45.9%
10,051	BERLIN	2,742	701	2,029	12	1,328 D	25.6%	74.0%	25.7%	74.3%
7,519	BOW	3,802	1,769	2,033		264 D	46.5%	53.5%	46.5%	53.5%
13,355	CLAREMONT	3,748	1,473	2,263	12	790 D	39.3%	60.4%	39.4%	60.6%
42,695	CONCORD	15,519	5,143	10,334	42	5,191 D	33.1%	66.6%	33.2%	66.8%
10,115	CONWAY	3,293	1,284	2,005	4	721 D	39.0%	60.9%	39.0%	61.0%
33,109	DERRY	10,186	5,867	4,319		1,548 R	57.6%	42.4%	57.6%	42.4%
29,987	DOVER	10,991	4,332	6,635	24	2,303 D	39.4%	60.4%	39.5%	60.5%
14,638	DURHAM	4,231	1,305	2,913	13	1,608 D	30.8%	68.8%	30.9%	69.1%
6,411	EPPING	2,399	1,204	1,188	7	16 R	50.2%	49.5%	50.3%	49.7%
14,306	EXETER	6,526	2,641	3,885		1,244 D	40.5%	59.5%	40.5%	59.5%
6,786	FARMINGTON	1,871	959	912		47 R	51.3%	48.7%	51.3%	48.7%
8,477	FRANKLIN	2,446	1,121	1,298	27	177 D	45.8%	53.1%	46.3%	53.7%
7,126	GILFORD	3,352	1,793	1,549	10	244 R	53.5%	46.2%	53.7%	46.3%
17,651	GOFFSTOWN	6,198	3,275	2,899	24	376 R	52.8%	46.8%	53.0%	47.0%
8,523	HAMPSTEAD	3,836	2,444	1,380	12	1,064 R	63.7%	36.0%	63.9%	36.1%
15,430	HAMPTON	7,062	3,776	3,272	14	504 R	53.5%	46.3%	53.6%	46.4%
11,260	HANOVER	4,705	1,042	3,652	11	2,610 D	22.1%	77.6%	22.2%	77.8%
7,684	HOLLIS	3,861	2,122	1,731	8	391 R	55.0%	44.8%	55.1%	44.9%
13,451	HOOKSETT	5,078	2,763	2,315		448 R	54.4%	45.6%	54.4%	45.6%
24,467	HUDSON	8,268	4,717	3,504	47	1,213 R	57.1%	42.4%	57.4%	42.6%
5,457	JAFFREY	1,926	865	1,054	7	189 D	44.9%	54.7%	45.1%	54.9%
23,409	KEENE	7,645	2,359	5,242	44	2,883 D	30.9%	68.6%	31.0%	69.0%
6,025	KINGSTON	2,367	1,397	962	8	435 R	59.0%	40.6%	59.2%	40.8%
15,951	LACONIA	5,402	2,779	2,609	14	170 R	51.4%	48.3%	51.6%	48.4%
13,151	LEBANON	4,726	1,381	3,330	15	1,949 D	29.2%	70.5%	29.3%	70.7%
8,271	LITCHFIELD	3,200	1,863	1,326	11	537 R	58.2%	41.4%	58.4%	41.6%
5,928	LITTLETON	1,986	907	1,074	5	167 D	45.7%	54.1%	45.8%	54.2%
24,129	LONDONDERRY	8,870	5,185	3,646	39	1,539 R	58.5%	41.1%	58.7%	41.3%
109,565	MANCHESTER	30,484	13,799	16,518	167	2,719 D	45.3%	54.2%	45.5%	54.5%
25,494	MERRIMACK TOWN	9,883	5,480	4,403		1,077 R	55.4%	44.6%	55.4%	44.6%
15,115	MILFORD	5,371	2,618	2,716	37	98 D	48.7%	50.6%	49.1%	50.9%
86,494	NASHUA	26,708	12,461	14,148	99	1,687 D	46.7%	53.0%	46.8%	53.2%
8,936	NEWMARKET	3,435	1,330	2,095	10	765 D	38.7%	61.0%	38.8%	61.2%
6,507	NEWPORT	1,959	945	1,002	12	57 D	48.2%	51.1%	48.5%	51.5%
12,897	PELHAM	4,602	2,949	1,640	13	1,309 R	64.1%	35.6%	64.3%	35.7%

NEW HAMPSHIRE

SENATOR 2014

2010 Census Population	City/Town	Total Vote	Republican (Brown)	Democratic (Shaheen)	Other	Rep.-Dem. Plurality	Percentage			
							Total Vote		Major Vote	
							Rep.	Dem.	Rep.	Dem.
7,115	PEMBROKE	2,681	1,241	1,430	10	189 D	46.3%	53.3%	46.5%	53.5%
6,284	PETERBOROUGH	2,879	995	1,878	6	883 D	34.6%	65.2%	34.6%	65.4%
7,609	PLAISTOW	2,736	1,702	1,029	5	673 R	62.2%	37.6%	62.3%	37.7%
6,990	PLYMOUTH	1,857	624	1,221	12	597 D	33.6%	65.8%	33.8%	66.2%
20,779	PORTSMOUTH	9,271	3,020	6,228	23	3,208 D	32.6%	67.2%	32.7%	67.3%
10,138	RAYMOND	3,310	1,887	1,373	50	514 R	57.0%	41.5%	57.9%	42.1%
29,752	ROCHESTER	9,511	4,668	4,809	34	141 D	49.1%	50.6%	49.3%	50.7%
28,776	SALEM	10,074	6,174	3,874	26	2,300 R	61.3%	38.5%	61.4%	38.6%
8,693	SEABROOK	2,661	1,635	1,021	5	614 R	61.4%	38.4%	61.6%	38.4%
11,766	SOMERSWORTH	3,356	1,441	1,900	15	459 D	42.9%	56.6%	43.1%	56.9%
7,230	SWANZEY	2,355	1,024	1,331		307 D	43.5%	56.5%	43.5%	56.5%
8,785	WEARE	3,189	1,762	1,402	25	360 R	55.3%	44.0%	55.7%	44.3%
13,592	WINDHAM	5,813	3,741	2,061	11	1,680 R	64.4%	35.5%	64.5%	35.5%
6,269	WOLFEBORO	3,221	1,775	1,446		329 R	55.1%	44.9%	55.1%	44.9%

NEW HAMPSHIRE

HOUSE OF REPRESENTATIVES

CD	Year	Total Vote	Republican		Democratic		Other Vote	Rep.-Dem. Plurality	Percentage			
			Vote	Candidate	Vote	Candidate			Total Vote		Major Vote	
									Rep.	Dem.	Rep.	Dem.
1	2014	242,736	125,508	GUINTA, FRANK C.	116,769	SHEA-PORTER, CAROL*	459	8,739 R	51.7%	48.1%	51.8%	48.2%
1	2012	345,022	158,659	GUINTA, FRANK C.*	171,650	SHEA-PORTER, CAROL	14,713	12,991 D	46.0%	49.8%	48.0%	52.0%
2	2014	238,184	106,871	GARCIA, MARILINDA	130,700	KUSTER, ANN M.*	613	23,829 D	44.9%	54.9%	45.0%	55.0%
2	2012	337,394	152,977	BASS, CHARLES*	169,275	KUSTER, ANN M.	15,142	16,298 D	45.3%	50.2%	47.5%	52.5%
TOTAL	2014	480,920	232,379		247,469		1,072	15,090 D	48.3%	51.5%	48.4%	51.6%
TOTAL	2012	682,416	311,636		340,925		29,855	29,289 D	45.7%	50.0%	47.8%	52.2%

Note: An asterisk (*) denotes incumbent.

NEW HAMPSHIRE

GENERAL AND PRIMARY ELECTIONS

2014 GENERAL ELECTIONS: OTHER VOTES

Governor   Other vote was 907 scattered write-in

Senate   Other vote was 1,628 scattered write-in

House   Other vote was:

CD 1   459 scattered write-in
CD 2   613 scattered write-in

NEW HAMPSHIRE

GENERAL AND PRIMARY ELECTIONS

2014 PRIMARY ELECTIONS: SUPPLEMENTARY INFORMATION

Primary September 9, 2014   **Registration** (as of September 9, 2014)   868,182   Republican 264,502 / Democratic 235,948 / Undeclared 367,732

Primary Type Semi-open—Registered Democrats and Republicans could vote only in their party's primary. "Undeclared" voters could participate in either party's primary.

REPUBLICAN PRIMARIES			DEMOCRATIC PRIMARIES		
Senator					
Brown, Scott P.	59,147	49.9%	Shaheen, Jeanne*	39,282	97.8%
Rubens, Jim	27,252	23.0%	Write-In	875	2.2%
Smith, Robert "Bob"	26,762	22.6%			
Kelly, Walter	1,392	1.2%			
Heghmann, Bob	789	0.7%			
Martin, Andy	738	0.6%			
Farnham, Mark	737	0.6%			
Dziedzic, Miro	515	0.4%			
Beloin, Gerard	503	0.4%			
Write-In	403	0.3%			
D'Arcy, Robert	399	0.3%			
TOTAL	118,637		TOTAL	40,157	
Governor					
Havenstein, Walt	62,766	55.3%	Hassan, Maggie*	39,185	93.1%
Hemingway, Andrew	42,005	37.0%	Freeman, Ian	1,719	4.1%
Greene, Daniel	5,362	4.7%	Terrio, Clecia	704	1.7%
Smolin, Jonathan	2,620	2.3%	Write-In	488	1.2%
Write-In	731	0.6%			
TOTAL	113,484		TOTAL	42,096	
Congressional District 1					
Guinta, Frank C.	29,246	49.0%	Shea-Porter, Carol*	16,956	98.1%
Innis, Daniel E.	24,342	40.8%	Write-In	327	1.9%
Kelly, Brendan	4,999	8.4%			
Jabour, Everett	996	1.7%			
Write-In	123	0.2%			
TOTAL	59,706		TOTAL	17,283	
Congressional District 2					
Garcia, Marilinda	27,285	49.2%	Kuster, Ann M.*	21,269	98.6%
Lambert, Gary	15,196	27.4%	Write-In	300	1.4%
Lawrence, James "Jim"	10,327	18.6%			
Little, Mike	2,489	4.5%			
Write-In	165	0.3%			
TOTAL	55,462		TOTAL	21,569	

Note: An asterisk (*) denotes incumbent.

NEW JERSEY

Congressional districts first established for elections held in 2012

12 members

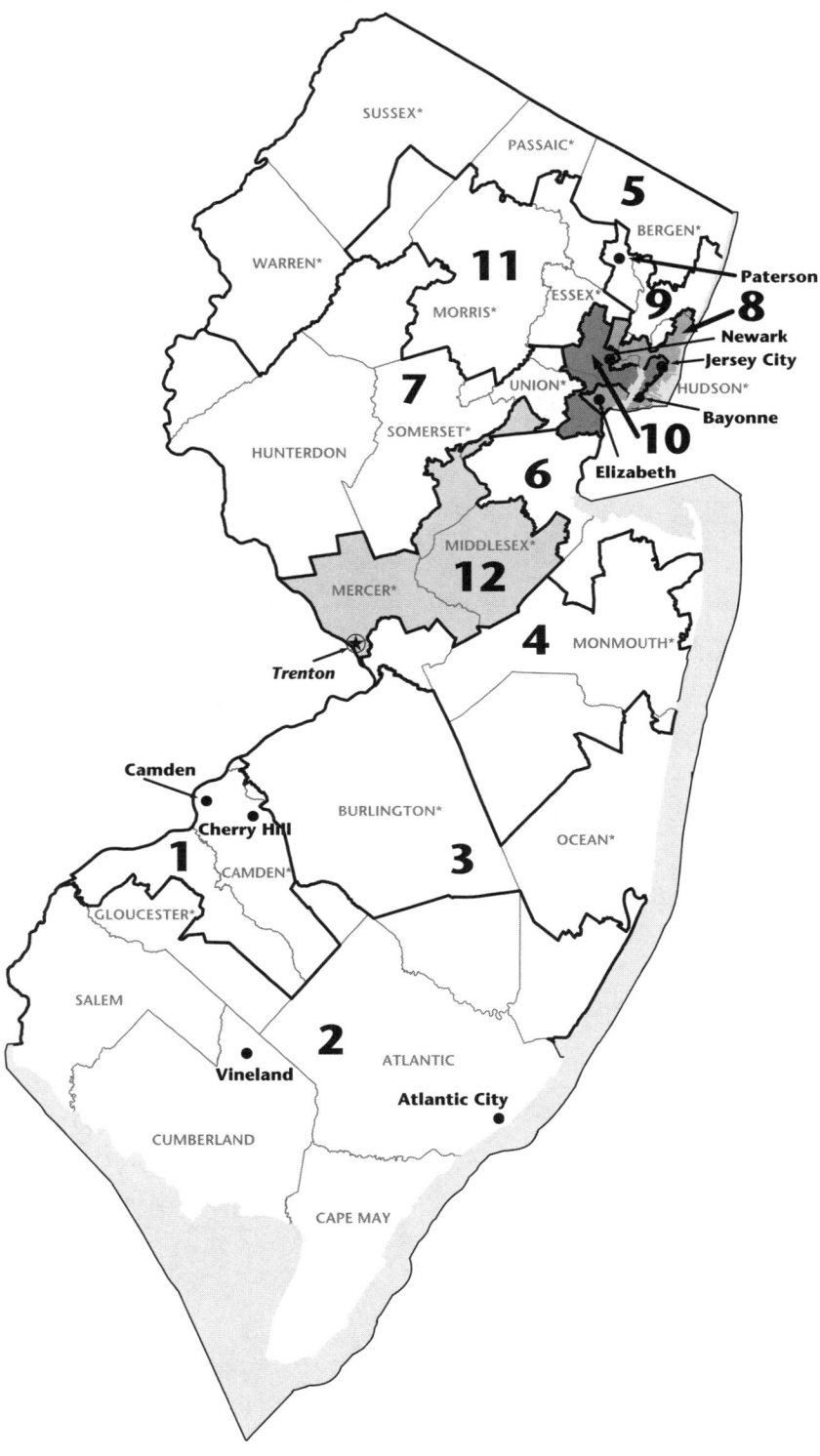

* Asterisk indicates a county whose boundaries include parts of two or more congressional districts.

NEW JERSEY
Northern New Jersey Gateway Area

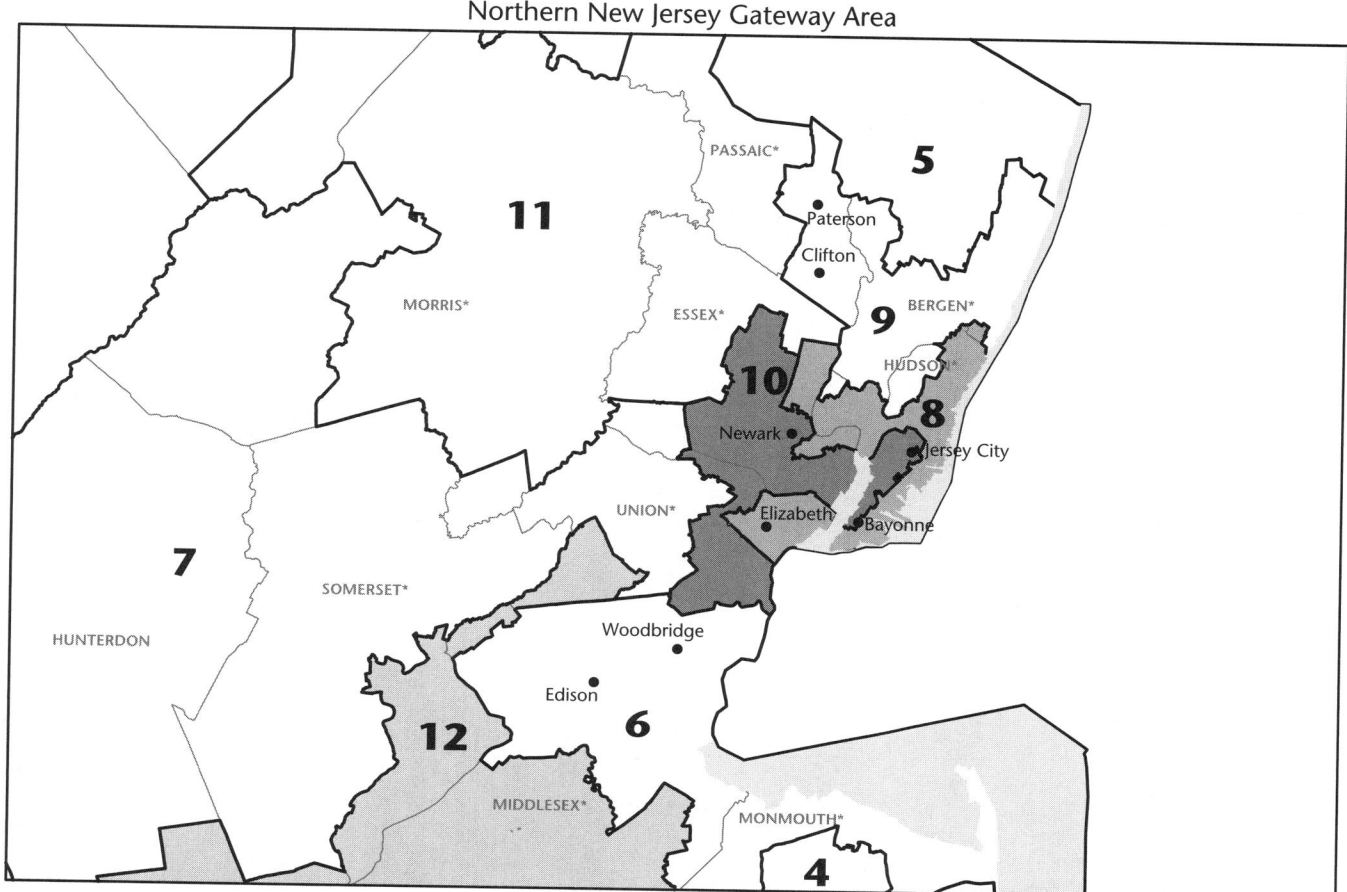

* Asterisk indicates a county whose boundaries include parts of two or more congressional districts.

NEW JERSEY

GOVERNOR
Chris Christie (R). Reelected 2013 to a four-year term. Previously elected 2009.

SENATORS (2 Democrats)
Cory A. Booker (D). Reelected 2014 to a six-year term. Previously elected October 16, 2013, to serve the remainder of the term vacated by the June 2013 death of Frank Lautenberg (D). Jeff Chiesa (R) had been appointed June 6, 2013, to fill the vacant seat until the October 2013 special election.

Robert Menendez (D). Reelected 2012 to a six-year term. Previously elected 2006.

REPRESENTATIVES (6 Republicans, 6 Democrats)
1. Donald Norcross (D)
2. Frank A. LoBiondo (R)
3. Thomas McArthur (R)
4. Christopher H. Smith (R)
5. Scott Garrett (R)
6. Frank Pallone Jr. (D)
7. Leonard Lance (R)
8. Albio Sires (D)
9. Bill Pascrell Jr. (D)
10. Donald M. Payne Jr. (D)
11. Rodney P. Frelinghuysen (R)
12. Bonnie Watson Coleman (D)

POSTWAR VOTE FOR PRESIDENT

		Republican		Democratic		Other Vote	Rep.-Dem. Plurality	Percentage			
								Total Vote		Major Vote	
Year	Total Vote	Vote	Candidate	Vote	Candidate			Rep.	Dem.	Rep.	Dem.
2012	3,640,292	1,477,568	Romney, W. Mitt	2,125,101	Obama, Barack H.*	37,623	647,533 D	40.6%	58.4%	41.0%	59.0%
2008	3,868,237	1,613,207	McCain, John S. III	2,215,422	Obama, Barack H.	39,608	602,215 D	41.7%	57.3%	42.1%	57.9%
2004	3,611,691	1,670,003	Bush, George W.*	1,911,430	Kerry, John F.	30,258	241,427 D	46.2%	52.9%	46.6%	53.4%
2000**	3,187,226	1,284,173	Bush, George W.	1,788,850	Gore, Albert Jr.	114,203	504,677 D	40.3%	56.1%	41.8%	58.2%
1996**	3,075,807	1,103,078	Dole, Robert "Bob"	1,652,329	Clinton, Bill*	320,400	549,251 D	35.9%	53.7%	40.0%	60.0%
1992**	3,343,594	1,356,865	Bush, George H.*	1,436,206	Clinton, Bill	550,523	79,341 D	40.6%	43.0%	48.6%	51.4%
1988	3,099,553	1,743,192	Bush, George H.	1,320,352	Dukakis, Michael S.	36,009	422,840 R	56.2%	42.6%	56.9%	43.1%
1984	3,217,862	1,933,630	Reagan, Ronald*	1,261,323	Mondale, Walter F.	22,909	672,307 R	60.1%	39.2%	60.5%	39.5%
1980**	2,975,684	1,546,557	Reagan, Ronald	1,147,364	Carter, Jimmy*	281,763	399,193 R	52.0%	38.6%	57.4%	42.6%
1976	3,014,472	1,509,688	Ford, Gerald R.*	1,444,653	Carter, Jimmy	60,131	65,035 R	50.1%	47.9%	51.1%	48.9%
1972	2,997,229	1,845,502	Nixon, Richard M.*	1,102,211	McGovern, George S.	49,516	743,291 R	61.6%	36.8%	62.6%	37.4%
1968**	2,875,395	1,325,467	Nixon, Richard M.	1,264,206	Humphrey, Hubert Horatio Jr.	285,722	61,261 R	46.1%	44.0%	51.2%	48.8%
1964	2,847,663	964,174	Goldwater, Barry M. Sr.	1,868,231	Johnson, Lyndon B.*	15,258	904,057 D	33.9%	65.6%	34.0%	66.0%
1960	2,773,111	1,363,324	Nixon, Richard M.	1,385,415	Kennedy, John F.	24,372	22,091 D	49.2%	50.0%	49.6%	50.4%
1956	2,484,312	1,606,942	Eisenhower, Dwight D.*	850,337	Stevenson, Adlai E. II	27,033	756,605 R	64.7%	34.2%	65.4%	34.6%
1952	2,418,554	1,373,613	Eisenhower, Dwight D.	1,015,902	Stevenson, Adlai E. II	29,039	357,711 R	56.8%	42.0%	57.5%	42.5%
1948	1,949,555	981,124	Dewey, Thomas E.	895,455	Truman, Harry S.*	72,976	85,669 R	50.3%	45.9%	52.3%	47.7%

Note: An asterisk (*) denotes incumbent. **In past elections, the other vote included: 2000 - 94,554 Green (Ralph Nader); 1996 - 262,134 Reform (Ross Perot); 1992 - 521,829 Independent (Perot); 1980 - 234,632 Independent (John Anderson); 1968 - 262,187 American Independent (George Wallace).

NEW JERSEY

POSTWAR VOTE FOR GOVERNOR

| Year | Total Vote | Republican | | Democratic | | Other Vote | Rep.-Dem. Plurality | Percentage | | | |
| | | Vote | Candidate | Vote | Candidate | | | Total Vote | | Major Vote | |
								Rep.	Dem.	Rep.	Dem.
2013	2,120,866	1,278,932	Christie, Chris*	809,978	Buono, Barbara	31,956	468,954 R	60.3%	38.2%	61.2%	38.8%
2009	2,423,792	1,174,445	Christie, Chris	1,087,731	Corzine, Jon S.*	161,616	86,714 R	48.5%	44.9%	51.9%	48.1%
2005	2,290,099	985,271	Forrester, Doug	1,224,551	Corzine, Jon S.	80,277	239,280 D	43.0%	53.5%	44.6%	55.4%
2001	2,227,165	928,174	Schundler, Bret	1,256,853	McGreevey, James	42,138	328,679 D	41.7%	56.4%	42.5%	57.5%
1997	2,418,344	1,133,394	Whitman, Christine T.*	1,107,968	McGreevey, James	176,982	25,426 R	46.9%	45.8%	50.6%	49.4%
1993	2,505,964	1,236,124	Whitman, Christine T.	1,210,031	Florio, James J.*	59,809	26,093 R	49.3%	48.3%	50.5%	49.5%
1989	2,253,800	838,553	Courter, James A.	1,379,973	Florio, James J.	35,274	541,420 D	37.2%	61.2%	37.8%	62.2%
1985	1,972,624	1,372,631	Kean, Thomas H.*	578,402	Shapiro, Peter	21,591	794,229 R	69.6%	29.3%	70.4%	29.6%
1981	2,317,239	1,145,999	Kean, Thomas H.	1,144,202	Florio, James J.	27,038	1,797 R	49.5%	49.4%	50.0%	50.0%
1977	2,126,264	888,880	Bateman, Raymond H.	1,184,564	Byrne, Brendan T.*	52,820	295,684 D	41.8%	55.7%	42.9%	57.1%
1973	2,122,010	676,235	Sandman, Charles W.	1,414,613	Byrne, Brendan T.	31,162	738,378 D	31.9%	66.7%	32.3%	67.7%
1969	2,366,606	1,411,905	Cahill, William T.	911,003	Meyner, Robert B.	43,698	500,902 R	59.7%	38.5%	60.8%	39.2%
1965	2,229,583	915,996	Dumont, Wayne Jr.	1,279,568	Hughes, Richard J.*	34,019	363,572 D	41.1%	57.4%	41.7%	58.3%
1961	2,152,662	1,049,274	Mitchell, James P.	1,084,194	Hughes, Richard J.	19,194	34,920 D	48.7%	50.4%	49.2%	50.8%
1957	2,018,488	897,321	Forbes, Malcolm Stevenson Sr.	1,101,130	Meyner, Robert B.*	20,037	203,809 D	44.5%	54.6%	44.9%	55.1%
1953	1,810,812	809,068	Troast, Paul L.	962,710	Meyner, Robert B.	39,034	153,642 D	44.7%	53.2%	45.7%	54.3%
1949**	1,718,788	885,882	Driscoll, Alfred Eastlack*	810,022	Wene, Elmer H.	22,884	75,860 R	51.5%	47.1%	52.2%	47.8%
1946	1,414,527	807,378	Driscoll, Alfred Eastlack	585,960	Hansen, Lewis G.	21,189	221,418 R	57.1%	41.4%	57.9%	42.1%

Note: An asterisk (*) denotes incumbent. **The term of office of New Jersey's governor was increased from three to four years effective with the 1949 election.

POSTWAR VOTE FOR SENATOR

| Year | Total Vote | Republican | | Democratic | | Other Vote | Rep.-Dem. Plurality | Percentage | | | |
| | | Vote | Candidate | Vote | Candidate | | | Total Vote | | Major Vote | |
								Rep.	Dem.	Rep.	Dem.
2014	1,869,535	791,297	Bell, Jeffrey	1,043,866	Booker, Cory A.*	34,372	252,569 D	42.3%	55.8%	43.1%	56.9%
2013S	1,348,659	593,684	Lonegan, Steven M.	740,742	Booker, Cory A.	14,233	147,058 D	44.0%	54.9%	44.5%	55.5%
2012	3,374,668	1,329,405	Kyrillos, Joe	1,985,783	Menendez, Robert*	59,480	656,378 D	39.4%	58.8%	40.1%	59.9%
2008	3,482,445	1,461,025	Zimmer, Dick	1,951,218	Lautenberg, Frank R.*	70,202	490,193 D	42.0%	56.0%	42.8%	57.2%
2006	2,250,070	997,775	Kean, Tom Jr.	1,200,843	Menendez, Robert*	51,452	203,068 D	44.3%	53.4%	45.4%	54.6%
2002	2,112,604	928,439	Forrester, Douglas R.	1,138,193	Lautenberg, Frank R.	45,972	209,754 D	43.9%	53.9%	44.9%	55.1%
2000	3,015,662	1,420,267	Franks, Bob	1,511,237	Corzine, Jon S.	84,158	90,970 D	47.1%	50.1%	48.4%	51.6%
1996	2,884,106	1,227,817	Zimmer, Dick	1,519,328	Torricelli, Robert G.	136,961	291,511 D	42.6%	52.7%	44.7%	55.3%
1994	2,054,887	966,244	Haytaian, Garabed	1,033,487	Lautenberg, Frank R.*	55,156	67,243 D	47.0%	50.3%	48.3%	51.7%
1990	1,938,454	918,874	Whitman, Christine T.	977,810	Bradley, Bill Warren*	41,770	58,936 D	47.4%	50.4%	48.4%	51.6%
1988	2,987,634	1,349,937	Dawkins, Peter M.	1,599,905	Lautenberg, Frank R.*	37,792	249,968 D	45.2%	53.6%	45.8%	54.2%
1984	3,096,456	1,080,100	Mochary, Mary V.	1,986,644	Bradley, Bill Warren*	29,712	906,544 D	34.9%	64.2%	35.2%	64.8%
1982	2,193,945	1,047,626	Fenwick, Millicent	1,117,549	Lautenberg, Frank R.	28,770	69,923 D	47.8%	50.9%	48.4%	51.6%
1978	1,957,515	844,200	Bell, Jeffrey	1,082,960	Bradley, Bill Warren	30,355	238,760 D	43.1%	55.3%	43.8%	56.2%
1976	2,771,387	1,054,505	Norcross, David F.	1,681,140	Williams, Harrison A. Jr.*	35,742	626,635 D	38.0%	60.7%	38.5%	61.5%
1972	2,791,907	1,743,854	Case, Clifford P.*	963,573	Kerbs, Paul J.	84,480	780,281 R	62.5%	34.5%	64.4%	35.6%
1970	2,142,105	903,026	Gross, Nelson G.	1,157,074	Williams, Harrison A. Jr.*	82,005	254,048 D	42.2%	54.0%	43.8%	56.2%
1966	2,130,688	1,278,843	Case, Clifford P.*	788,021	Wilentz, Warren W.	63,824	490,822 R	60.0%	37.0%	61.9%	38.1%
1964	2,709,575	1,011,280	Shanley, Bernard M.	1,677,515	Williams, Harrison A. Jr.*	20,780	666,235 D	37.3%	61.9%	37.6%	62.4%
1960	7,934,990	4,451,496	Case, Clifford P.*	3,454,155	Lord, Thorn	29,339	997,341 R	56.1%	43.5%	56.3%	43.7%
1958	1,881,329	882,287	Kean, Robert Winthrop	966,832	Williams, Harrison A. Jr.	32,210	84,545 D	46.9%	51.4%	47.7%	52.3%
1954	1,770,557	861,528	Case, Clifford P.*	858,158	Howell, Charles R.	50,871	3,370 R	48.7%	48.5%	50.1%	49.9%
1952	2,318,232	1,286,782	Smith, H. Alexander*	1,011,187	Alexander, Archibald S.	20,263	275,595 R	55.5%	43.6%	56.0%	44.0%
1948	1,869,882	934,720	Hendrickson, Robert C.	884,414	Alexander, Archibald S.	50,748	50,306 R	50.0%	47.3%	51.4%	48.6%
1946	1,367,155	799,808	Smith, H. Alexander*	548,458	Brunner, George E.	18,889	251,350 R	58.5%	40.1%	59.3%	40.7%

Note: An asterisk (*) denotes incumbent. The 2013 election was for a short term to fill a vacancy.

NEW JERSEY

GOVERNOR 2013

2010 Census Population	County	Total Vote	Republican (Christie)	Democratic (Buono)	Other	Rep.-Dem. Plurality	Percentage			
							Total Vote		Major Vote	
							Rep.	Dem.	Rep.	Dem.
274,549	ATLANTIC	70,698	43,975	25,557	1,166	18,418 R	62.2%	36.1%	63.2%	36.8%
905,116	BERGEN	226,069	136,178	87,376	2,515	48,802 R	60.2%	38.7%	60.9%	39.1%
448,734	BURLINGTON	127,079	79,220	46,161	1,698	33,059 R	62.3%	36.3%	63.2%	36.8%
513,657	CAMDEN	117,877	64,545	51,546	1,786	12,999 R	54.8%	43.7%	55.6%	44.4%
97,265	CAPE MAY	32,848	23,531	8,798	519	14,733 R	71.6%	26.8%	72.8%	27.2%
156,898	CUMBERLAND	31,667	17,943	13,129	595	4,814 R	56.7%	41.5%	57.7%	42.3%
783,969	ESSEX	154,805	57,353	95,747	1,705	38,394 D	37.0%	61.9%	37.5%	62.5%
288,288	GLOUCESTER	78,985	50,640	27,060	1,285	23,580 R	64.1%	34.3%	65.2%	34.8%
634,266	HUDSON	97,585	42,567	53,386	1,632	10,819 D	43.6%	54.7%	44.4%	55.6%
128,349	HUNTERDON	42,559	31,292	10,425	842	20,867 R	73.5%	24.5%	75.0%	25.0%
366,513	MERCER	93,433	48,530	43,282	1,621	5,248 R	51.9%	46.3%	52.9%	47.1%
809,858	MIDDLESEX	174,312	101,619	70,225	2,468	31,394 R	58.3%	40.3%	59.1%	40.9%
630,380	MONMOUTH	174,647	123,417	48,477	2,753	74,940 R	70.7%	27.8%	71.8%	28.2%
492,276	MORRIS	141,094	98,888	39,824	2,382	59,064 R	70.1%	28.2%	71.3%	28.7%
576,567	OCEAN	166,022	125,781	37,930	2,311	87,851 R	75.8%	22.8%	76.8%	23.2%
501,226	PASSAIC	101,823	53,858	46,825	1,140	7,033 R	52.9%	46.0%	53.5%	46.5%
66,083	SALEM	19,132	12,748	5,889	495	6,859 R	66.6%	30.8%	68.4%	31.6%
323,444	SOMERSET	87,313	58,981	26,913	1,419	32,068 R	67.6%	30.8%	68.7%	31.3%
149,265	SUSSEX	41,996	29,873	10,704	1,419	19,169 R	71.1%	25.5%	73.6%	26.4%
536,499	UNION	113,564	58,135	53,869	1,560	4,266 R	51.2%	47.4%	51.9%	48.1%
108,692	WARREN	27,358	19,858	6,855	645	13,003 R	72.6%	25.1%	74.3%	25.7%
8,791,894	TOTAL	2,120,866	1,278,932	809,978	31,956	468,954 R	60.3%	38.2%	61.2%	38.8%

NEW JERSEY

SENATOR SPECIAL 2013

2010 Census Population	County	Total Vote	Republican (Lonegan)	Democratic (Booker)	Other	Rep.-Dem. Plurality	Percentage			
							Total Vote		Major Vote	
							Rep.	Dem.	Rep.	Dem.
274,549	ATLANTIC	38,572	18,637	19,469	466	832 D	48.3%	50.5%	48.9%	51.1%
905,116	BERGEN	145,302	61,622	82,526	1,154	20,904 D	42.4%	56.8%	42.7%	57.3%
448,734	BURLINGTON	77,648	34,224	42,543	881	8,319 D	44.1%	54.8%	44.6%	55.4%
513,657	CAMDEN	72,984	24,758	47,474	752	22,716 D	33.9%	65.0%	34.3%	65.7%
97,265	CAPE MAY	17,736	10,432	7,080	224	3,352 R	58.8%	39.9%	59.6%	40.4%
156,898	CUMBERLAND	15,782	7,496	8,069	217	573 D	47.5%	51.1%	48.2%	51.8%
783,969	ESSEX	118,569	24,929	92,384	1,256	67,455 D	21.0%	77.9%	21.2%	78.8%
288,288	GLOUCESTER	42,661	20,871	21,240	550	369 D	48.9%	49.8%	49.6%	50.4%
634,266	HUDSON	61,320	12,830	47,683	807	34,853 D	20.9%	77.8%	21.2%	78.8%
128,349	HUNTERDON	28,647	17,593	10,781	273	6,812 R	61.4%	37.6%	62.0%	38.0%
366,513	MERCER	58,810	18,576	38,934	1,300	20,358 D	31.6%	66.2%	32.3%	67.7%
809,858	MIDDLESEX	106,106	43,644	61,362	1,100	17,718 D	41.1%	57.8%	41.6%	58.4%
630,380	MONMOUTH	109,463	59,059	49,340	1,064	9,719 R	54.0%	45.1%	54.5%	45.5%
492,276	MORRIS	96,752	54,665	41,317	770	13,348 R	56.5%	42.7%	57.0%	43.0%
576,567	OCEAN	105,739	68,166	36,665	908	31,501 R	64.5%	34.7%	65.0%	35.0%
501,226	PASSAIC	63,334	25,263	37,378	693	12,115 D	39.9%	59.0%	40.3%	59.7%
66,083	SALEM	9,623	5,598	3,903	122	1,695 R	58.2%	40.6%	58.9%	41.1%
323,444	SOMERSET	58,346	29,304	28,539	503	765 R	50.2%	48.9%	50.7%	49.3%
149,265	SUSSEX	27,355	17,796	9,252	307	8,544 R	65.1%	33.8%	65.8%	34.2%
536,499	UNION	76,838	27,152	48,991	695	21,839 D	35.3%	63.8%	35.7%	64.3%
108,692	WARREN	17,072	11,069	5,812	191	5,257 R	64.8%	34.0%	65.6%	34.4%
8,791,894	TOTAL	1,348,659	593,684	740,742	14,233	147,058 D	44.0%	54.9%	44.5%	55.5%

NEW JERSEY

SENATOR 2014

2010 Census Population	County	Total Vote	Republican (Bell)	Democratic (Booker)	Other	Rep.-Dem. Plurality	Percentage			
							Total Vote		Major Vote	
							Rep.	Dem.	Rep.	Dem.
274,549	ATLANTIC	63,307	29,422	32,566	1,319	3,144 D	46.5%	51.4%	47.5%	52.5%
905,116	BERGEN	217,210	89,597	124,409	3,204	34,812 D	41.2%	57.3%	41.9%	58.1%
448,734	BURLINGTON	119,206	52,721	64,730	1,755	12,009 D	44.2%	54.3%	44.9%	55.1%
513,657	CAMDEN	113,154	37,543	73,881	1,730	36,338 D	33.2%	65.3%	33.7%	66.3%
97,265	CAPE MAY	28,179	16,178	11,572	429	4,606 R	57.4%	41.1%	58.3%	41.7%
156,898	CUMBERLAND	27,822	12,455	14,830	537	2,375 D	44.8%	53.3%	45.6%	54.4%
783,969	ESSEX	137,974	29,527	106,472	1,975	76,945 D	21.4%	77.2%	21.7%	78.3%
288,288	GLOUCESTER	70,304	31,717	37,131	1,456	5,414 D	45.1%	52.8%	46.1%	53.9%
634,266	HUDSON	86,981	16,707	68,165	2,109	51,458 D	19.2%	78.4%	19.7%	80.3%
128,349	HUNTERDON	36,814	21,709	14,241	864	7,468 R	59.0%	38.7%	60.4%	39.6%
366,513	MERCER	79,749	25,749	52,476	1,524	26,727 D	32.3%	65.8%	32.9%	67.1%
809,858	MIDDLESEX	139,655	53,679	83,732	2,244	30,053 D	38.4%	60.0%	39.1%	60.9%
630,380	MONMOUTH	149,291	79,417	67,011	2,863	12,406 R	53.2%	44.9%	54.2%	45.8%
492,276	MORRIS	116,415	64,688	49,920	1,807	14,768 R	55.6%	42.9%	56.4%	43.6%
576,567	OCEAN	137,967	79,254	55,631	3,082	23,623 R	57.4%	40.3%	58.8%	41.2%
501,226	PASSAIC	86,653	32,612	52,533	1,508	19,921 D	37.6%	60.6%	38.3%	61.7%
66,083	SALEM	18,097	9,304	8,060	733	1,244 R	51.4%	44.5%	53.6%	46.4%
323,444	SOMERSET	76,407	37,835	37,124	1,448	711 R	49.5%	48.6%	50.5%	49.5%
149,265	SUSSEX	36,060	22,292	12,722	1,046	9,570 R	61.8%	35.3%	63.7%	36.3%
536,499	UNION	104,647	34,741	68,051	1,855	33,310 D	33.2%	65.0%	33.8%	66.2%
108,692	WARREN	23,643	14,150	8,609	884	5,541 R	59.8%	36.4%	62.2%	37.8%
8,791,894	TOTAL	1,869,535	791,297	1,043,866	34,372	252,569 D	42.3%	55.8%	43.1%	56.9%

NEW JERSEY

HOUSE OF REPRESENTATIVES

CD	Year	Total Vote	Republican		Democratic		Other Vote	Rep.-Dem. Plurality	Percentage			
			Vote	Candidate	Vote	Candidate			Total Vote		Major Vote	
									Rep.	Dem.	Rep.	Dem.
1	2014	162,492	64,073	COBB, GARRY W.	93,315	NORCROSS, DONALD	5,104	29,242 D	39.4%	57.4%	40.7%	59.3%
1	2012	308,519	92,459	HORTON, GREGORY W.	210,470	ANDREWS, ROBERT E.*	5,590	118,011 D	30.0%	68.2%	30.5%	69.5%
2	2014	177,148	108,875	LOBIONDO, FRANK A.*	66,026	HUGHES, WILLIAM J. JR.	2,247	42,849 R	61.5%	37.3%	62.2%	37.8%
2	2012	289,072	166,679	LOBIONDO, FRANK A.*	116,463	SHOBER, CASSANDRA	5,930	50,216 R	57.7%	40.3%	58.9%	41.1%
3	2014	186,103	100,471	MACARTHUR, THOMAS	82,537	BELGARD, AIMEE	3,095	17,934 R	54.0%	44.4%	54.9%	45.1%
3	2012	324,406	174,257	RUNYAN, JON*	145,509	ADLER, SHELLEY	4,640	28,748 R	53.7%	44.9%	54.5%	45.5%
4	2014	174,849	118,826	SMITH, CHRISTOPHER H.*	54,415	SCOLAVINO, RUBEN	1,608	64,411 R	68.0%	31.1%	68.6%	31.4%
4	2012	306,249	195,146	SMITH, CHRISTOPHER H.*	107,992	FROELICH, BRIAN P.	3,111	87,154 R	63.7%	35.3%	64.4%	35.6%
5	2014	188,921	104,678	GARRETT, SCOTT*	81,808	CHO, ROY	2,435	22,870 R	55.4%	43.3%	56.1%	43.9%
5	2012	304,377	167,503	GARRETT, SCOTT*	130,102	GUSSEN, ADAM	6,772	37,401 R	55.0%	42.7%	56.3%	43.7%
6	2014	120,457	46,891	WILKINSON, ANTHONY E.	72,190	PALLONE, FRANK JR.*	1,376	25,299 D	38.9%	59.9%	39.4%	60.6%
6	2012	239,638	84,360	LITTLE, ANNA C.	151,782	PALLONE, FRANK JR.*	3,496	67,422 D	35.2%	63.3%	35.7%	64.3%
7	2014	175,997	104,287	LANCE, LEONARD*	68,232	KOVACH, JANICE	3,478	36,055 R	59.3%	38.8%	60.4%	39.6%
7	2012	307,395	175,704	LANCE, LEONARD*	123,090	CHIVUKULA, UPENDRA J.	8,601	52,614 R	57.2%	40.0%	58.8%	41.2%
8	2014	79,518	15,141	TISCORNIA, JUDE ANTHONY	61,510	SIRES, ALBIO*	2,867	46,369 D	19.0%	77.4%	19.8%	80.2%
8	2012	167,800	31,767	KARCZEWSKI, MARIA	130,857	SIRES, ALBIO*	5,176	99,090 D	18.9%	78.0%	19.5%	80.5%
9	2014	120,459	36,246	PAUL, DIERDRE	82,498	PASCRELL, BILL JR.*	1,715	46,252 D	30.1%	68.5%	30.5%	69.5%
9	2012	220,148	55,094	BOTEACH, SHMULEY	162,834	PASCRELL, BILL JR.*	2,220	107,740 D	25.0%	74.0%	25.3%	74.7%
10	2014	112,123	14,154	DENTLEY, YOLANDA	95,734	PAYNE, DONALD M. JR.*	2,235	81,580 D	12.6%	85.4%	12.9%	87.1%
10	2012	230,060	24,271	KELEMEN, BRIAN C.	201,435	PAYNE, DONALD M. JR.	4,354	177,164 D	10.5%	87.6%	10.8%	89.2%
11	2014	174,932	109,455	FRELINGHUYSEN, RODNEY P.*	65,477	DUNEC, MARK S.		43,978 R	62.6%	37.4%	62.6%	37.4%
11	2012	309,899	182,239	FRELINGHUYSEN, RODNEY P.*	123,935	ARVANITES, JOHN	3,725	58,304 R	58.8%	40.0%	59.5%	40.5%

NEW JERSEY

HOUSE OF REPRESENTATIVES

CD	Year	Total Vote	Republican Vote	Republican Candidate	Democratic Vote	Democratic Candidate	Other Vote	Rep.-Dem. Plurality	Total Vote Rep.	Total Vote Dem.	Major Vote Rep.	Major Vote Dem.
										Percentage		
12	2014	148,366	54,168	ECK, ALIETA	90,430	COLEMAN, BONNIE WATSON	3,768	36,262 D	36.5%	61.0%	37.5%	62.5%
12	2012	274,391	80,907	BECK, ERIC A.	189,938	HOLT, RUSH D.*	3,546	109,031 D	29.5%	69.2%	29.9%	70.1%
TOTAL	2014	1,821,365	877,265		914,172		29,928	36,907 D	48.2%	50.2%	49.0%	51.0%
TOTAL	2012	3,281,954	1,430,386		1,794,407		57,161	364,021 D	43.6%	54.7%	44.4%	55.6%

Note: An asterisk (*) denotes incumbent.

NEW JERSEY

GENERAL AND PRIMARY ELECTIONS

2014 GENERAL ELECTIONS: OTHER VOTES

Senate
Other vote was 16,721 Libertarian (Joseph "Joe" Baratelli), 5,704 Economic Growth (Hank Schroeder), 4,513 Independent (Jeff Boss), 3,890 Democrat-Republican (Eugene Martin Lavergne), 3,544 Independent (Antonio Nico Sabas)

House
Other vote was:

CD 1
1,784 We Deserve Better (Scot John Tomaszewski), 1,134 Stop Boss Politics (Robert Shapiro), 1,103 Change Is Needed (Margaret Chapman), 634 Of the People (Mike Berman), 449 Democrat-Republican (Donald E. Letton)

CD 2
663 D-R Party (Alexander Spano), 612 Independent (Gary Stein), 501 American Labor (Costantino Rozzo), 471 Independent (Bayode Olabisi)

CD 3
3,095 D-R Party (Frederick John Lavergne)

CD 4
1,608 D-R Party (Scott Neuman)

CD 5
2,435 For Americans (Mark Quick)

CD 6
1,376 Libertarian (Dorit Goikhman)

CD 7
3,478 Libertarian (Jim Gawron)

CD 8
1,192 Politicans Are Crooks (Herbert H. Shaw), 1,022 Wake Up USA (Pablo Olivera), 653 9/11 Truth Needed (Robert Thorne)

CD 9
1,715 Seeking Inclusion (Nestor Montilla)

CD 10
1,237 Bullying Breaks Hearts (Gwendolyn Franklin), 998 Future. Vision (Dark Angel)

CD 12
1,330 Legalize Marijuana (Don Dezarn), 890 Green (Steven Welzer), 567 Truth Vision Hope (Kenneth J. Cody), 531 Start the Conversation (Jack Freudenheim), 450 D-R Party (Allen J. Cannon)

2014 PRIMARY ELECTIONS: SUPPLEMENTARY INFORMATION

Primary	June 3, 2014	**Registration** (as of May 31, 2014)	5,462,041	Democratic	1,789,833
				Republican	1,076,988
				Libertarian	2,388
				Green	1,248
				Conservative	653
				U.S. Constitution	172
				Reform	64
				Natural Law	37
				Unaffiliated	2,590,658

Primary Type
Semi-open—Registered Democrats and Republicans could vote only in their party's primary. "Unaffiliated" voters could participate in either party's primary if they were willing to become a member of that party.

NEW JERSEY

GENERAL AND PRIMARY ELECTIONS

	REPUBLICAN PRIMARIES			DEMOCRATIC PRIMARIES		
Senator	Bell, Jeffrey	42,728	29.4%	Booker, Cory A.*	202,129	100.0%
	Pezzullo, Richard J.	38,130	26.2%			
	Goldberg, Brian D.	36,266	25.0%			
	Sabrin, Murray	28,183	19.4%			
	TOTAL	145,307		TOTAL	202,129	
Governor (2013)	Christie, Chris*	205,666	91.9%	Buono, Barbara	173,714	88.1%
	Grossman, Seth	18,095	8.1%	Webster, Troy	23,457	11.9%
	TOTAL	223,761		TOTAL	197,171	
Congressional District 1	Cobb, Garry W.	6,405	68.3%	Norcross, Donald	18,504	72.1%
	Gustafson, Claire	1,337	14.3%	Broomell Jr., Frank	3,871	15.1%
	McManus, Gerard	863	9.2%	Minor, Frank W.	3,303	12.9%
	Lucas, Lee	767	8.2%			
	TOTAL	9,372		TOTAL	25,678	
Congressional District 2	LoBiondo, Frank A.*	14,294	82.5%	Hughes, William J. Jr.	11,455	81.8%
	Assad, Mike	3,037	17.5%	Cole, David H.	2,554	18.2%
	TOTAL	17,331		TOTAL	14,009	
Congressional District 3	MacArthur, Thomas	15,908	59.9%	Belgard, Aimee	12,425	83.8%
	Lonegan, Steven M.	10,643	40.1%	Kleinhendler, Howard	1,705	11.5%
				Todd, Bruce	700	4.7%
	TOTAL	26,551		TOTAL	14,830	
Congressional District 4	Smith, Christopher H.*	14,810	100.0%	Scolavino, Ruben	8,122	100.0%
	TOTAL	14,810		TOTAL	8,122	
Congressional District 5	Garrett, Scott*	15,972	100.0%	Cho, Roy	9,529	90.2%
				Sare, Diane	1,031	9.8%
	TOTAL	15,972		TOTAL	10,560	
Congressional District 6	Wilkinson, Anthony E.	4,816	100.0%	Pallone, Frank Jr.*	11,358	100.0%
	TOTAL	4,816		TOTAL	11,358	
Congressional District 7	Lance, Leonard*	15,900	54.4%	Kovach, Janice	8,768	100.0%
	Larsen, David	13,308	45.6%			
	TOTAL	29,208		TOTAL	8,768	
Congressional District 8	Tiscornia, Jude Anthony	1,973	100.0%	Sires, Albio*	25,641	100.0%
	TOTAL	1,973		TOTAL	25,641	
Congressional District 9	Paul, Dierdre	4,474	100.0%	Pascrell, Bill Jr.*	12,907	100.0%
	TOTAL	4,474		TOTAL	12,907	
Congressional District 10	Dentley, Yolanda	1,490	100.0%	Payne, Donald M. Jr.*	24,490	91.3%
				Toussaint, Robert Louis	1,291	4.8%
				Fraser, Aaron	697	2.6%
				Vaughn III, Curtis Alphonzo	360	1.3%
	TOTAL	1,490		TOTAL	26,838	
Congressional District 11	Frelinghuysen, Rodney P.*	15,697	66.7%	Dunec, Mark S.	6,949	76.0%
	Van Glahn, Rick	7,828	33.3%	Murphy, Brian	1,122	12.3%
				Brogowski, Lee Anne	1,078	11.8%
	TOTAL	23,525		TOTAL	9,149	
Congressional District 12	Eck, Alieta	6,617	100.0%	Coleman, Bonnie Watson	15,603	43.0%
				Greenstein, Linda	10,089	27.8%
				Chivukula, Upendra J.	7,890	21.8%
				Zwicker, Andrew	2,668	7.4%
	TOTAL	6,617		TOTAL	36,250	

Note: An asterisk (*) denotes incumbent.

NEW MEXICO

Congressional districts first established for elections held in 2012

3 members

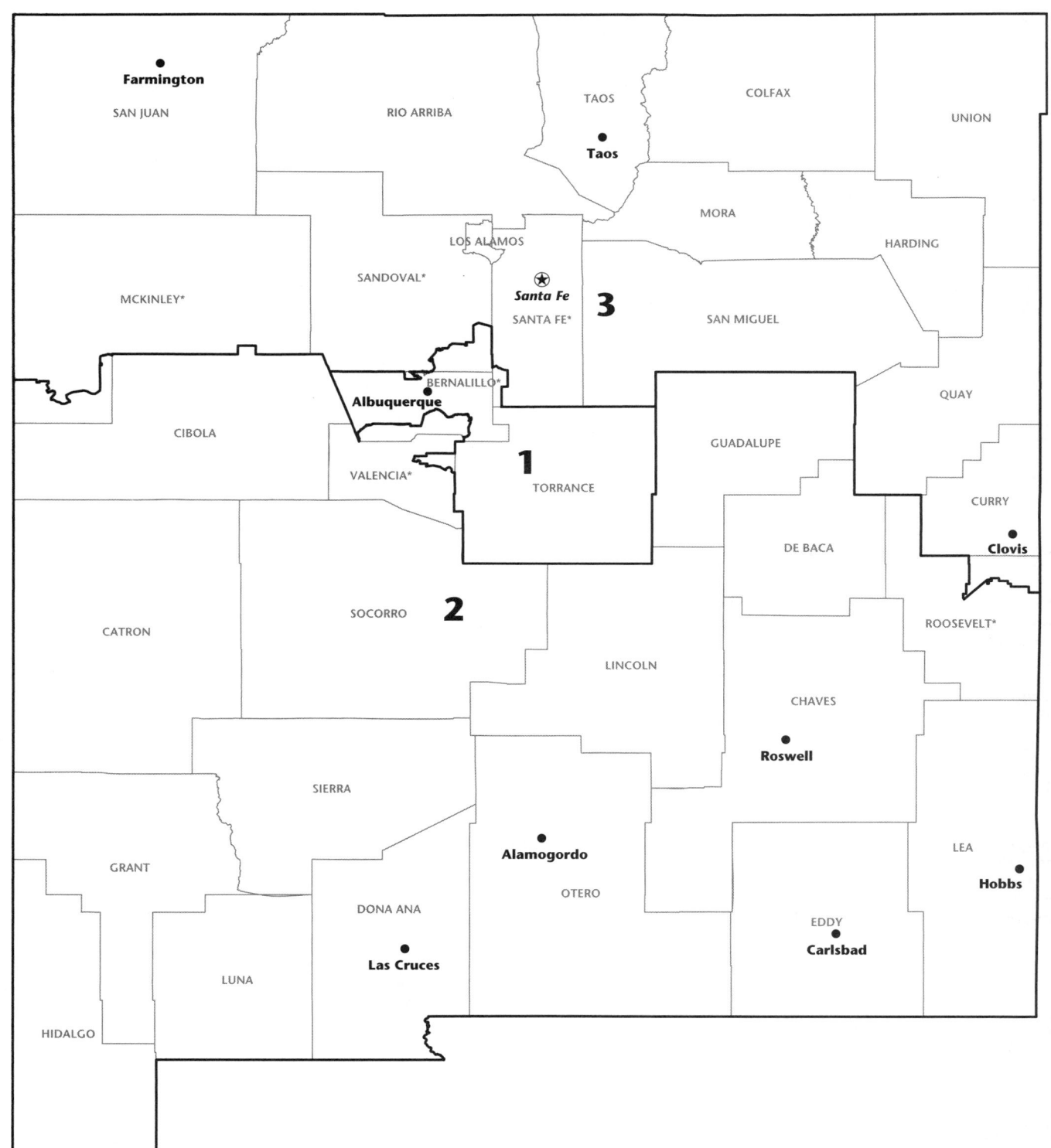

* Asterisk indicates a county whose boundaries include parts of two or more congressional districts.

NEW MEXICO

GOVERNOR
Susana Martinez (R). Re-elected 2014 to a four-year term. Previously elected 2010.

SENATORS (2 Democrats)
Martin Heinrich (D). Elected 2012 to a six-year term.

Tom Udall (D). Re-elected 2014 to a six-year term. Previously elected 2008.

REPRESENTATIVES (1 Republican, 2 Democrats)
1. Michelle Lujan Grisham (D)   2. Steve Pearce (R)   3. Ben Ray Luján (D)

POSTWAR VOTE FOR PRESIDENT

Year	Total Vote	Republican		Democratic		Other Vote	Rep.-Dem. Plurality	Percentage			
								Total Vote		Major Vote	
		Vote	Candidate	Vote	Candidate			Rep.	Dem.	Rep.	Dem.
2012	783,757	335,788	Romney, W. Mitt	415,335	Obama, Barack H.*	32,634	79,547 D	42.8%	53.0%	44.7%	55.3%
2008	830,158	346,832	McCain, John S. III	472,422	Obama, Barack H.	10,904	125,590 D	41.8%	56.9%	42.3%	57.7%
2004	756,304	376,930	Bush, George W.*	370,942	Kerry, John F.	8,432	5,988 R	49.8%	49.0%	50.4%	49.6%
2000**	598,605	286,417	Bush, George W.	286,783	Gore, Albert Jr.	25,405	366 D	47.8%	47.9%	50.0%	50.0%
1996**	556,074	232,751	Dole, Robert "Bob"	273,495	Clinton, Bill*	49,828	40,744 D	41.9%	49.2%	46.0%	54.0%
1992**	569,986	212,824	Bush, George H.*	261,617	Clinton, Bill	95,545	48,793 D	37.3%	45.9%	44.9%	55.1%
1988	521,287	270,341	Bush, George H.	244,497	Dukakis, Michael S.	6,449	25,844 R	51.9%	46.9%	52.5%	47.5%
1984	514,370	307,101	Reagan, Ronald*	201,769	Mondale, Walter F.	5,500	105,332 R	59.7%	39.2%	60.3%	39.7%
1980**	456,971	250,779	Reagan, Ronald	167,826	Carter, Jimmy*	38,366	82,953 R	54.9%	36.7%	59.9%	40.1%
1976	418,409	211,419	Ford, Gerald R.*	201,148	Carter, Jimmy	5,842	10,271 R	50.5%	48.1%	51.2%	48.8%
1972	386,241	235,606	Nixon, Richard M.*	141,084	McGovern, George S.	9,551	94,522 R	61.0%	36.5%	62.5%	37.5%
1968**	327,350	169,692	Nixon, Richard M.	130,081	Humphrey, Hubert Horatio Jr.	27,577	39,611 R	51.8%	39.7%	56.6%	43.4%
1964	328,645	132,838	Goldwater, Barry M. Sr.	194,015	Johnson, Lyndon B.*	1,792	61,177 D	40.4%	59.0%	40.6%	59.4%
1960	311,107	153,733	Nixon, Richard M.	156,027	Kennedy, John F.	1,347	2,294 D	49.4%	50.2%	49.6%	50.4%
1956	253,926	146,788	Eisenhower, Dwight D.*	106,098	Stevenson, Adlai E. II	1,040	40,690 R	57.8%	41.8%	58.0%	42.0%
1952	238,608	132,170	Eisenhower, Dwight D.	105,661	Stevenson, Adlai E. II	777	26,509 R	55.4%	44.3%	55.6%	44.4%
1948	187,063	80,303	Dewey, Thomas E.	105,464	Truman, Harry S.*	1,296	25,161 D	42.9%	56.4%	43.2%	56.8%

Note: An asterisk (*) denotes incumbent. **In past elections, the other vote included: 2000 - 21,251 Green (Ralph Nader); 1996 - 32,257 Reform (Ross Perot); 1992 - 91,895 Independent (Perot); 1980 - 29,459 Independent (John Anderson); 1968 - 25,737 American Independent (George Wallace).

NEW MEXICO

POSTWAR VOTE FOR GOVERNOR

		Republican		Democratic		Other Vote	Rep.-Dem. Plurality	Percentage			
								Total Vote		Major Vote	
Year	Total Vote	Vote	Candidate	Vote	Candidate			Rep.	Dem.	Rep.	Dem.
2014	512,805	293,443	Martinez, Susana*	219,362	King, Gary K.		74,081 R	57.2%	42.8%	57.2%	42.8%
2010	602,827	321,219	Martinez, Susana	280,614	Denish, Diane D.	994	40,605 R	53.3%	46.5%	53.4%	46.6%
2006	559,170	174,364	Dendahl, John	384,806	Richardson, Bill*		210,442 D	31.2%	68.8%	31.2%	68.8%
2002	484,233	189,074	Sanchez, John A.	268,693	Richardson, Bill	26,466	79,619 D	39.0%	55.5%	41.3%	58.7%
1998	498,703	271,948	Johnson, Gary E.*	226,755	Chavez, Martin J.		45,193 R	54.5%	45.5%	54.5%	45.5%
1994**	467,621	232,945	Johnson, Gary E.	186,686	King, Bruce*	47,990	46,259 R	49.8%	39.9%	55.5%	44.5%
1990	411,232	185,692	Bond, Frank	224,564	King, Bruce	976	38,872 D	45.2%	54.6%	45.3%	54.7%
1986	394,833	209,455	Carruthers, Garrey E.	185,378	Powell, Ray B.		24,077 R	53.0%	47.0%	53.0%	47.0%
1982	407,466	191,626	Irick, John B.	215,840	Anaya, Toney		24,214 D	47.0%	53.0%	47.0%	53.0%
1978	345,577	170,848	Skeen, Joseph R.	174,631	King, Bruce	98	3,783 D	49.4%	50.5%	49.5%	50.5%
1974	328,742	160,430	Skeen, Joseph R.	164,172	Apodaca, Jerry	4,140	3,742 D	48.8%	49.9%	49.4%	50.6%
1970**	290,375	134,640	Domenici, Peter V.	148,835	King, Bruce	6,900	14,195 D	46.4%	51.3%	47.5%	52.5%
1968	318,975	160,140	Cargo, David F.*	157,230	Chavez, Fabian	1,605	2,910 R	50.2%	49.3%	50.5%	49.5%
1966	260,232	134,625	Cargo, David F.	125,587	Lusk, T. E.	20	9,038 R	51.7%	48.3%	51.7%	48.3%
1964	318,042	126,540	Tucker, Merle H.	191,497	Campbell, Jack M.*	5	64,957 D	39.8%	60.2%	39.8%	60.2%
1962	247,135	116,184	Mechem, Edwin L.*	130,933	Campbell, Jack M.	18	14,749 D	47.0%	53.0%	47.0%	53.0%
1960	305,542	153,765	Mechem, Edwin L.	151,777	Burroughs, John*		1,988 R	50.3%	49.7%	50.3%	49.7%
1958	205,048	101,567	Mechem, Edwin L.*	103,481	Burroughs, John		1,914 D	49.5%	50.5%	49.5%	50.5%
1956	251,751	131,488	Mechem, Edwin L.	120,263	Simms, John F. Jr.*		11,225 R	52.2%	47.8%	52.2%	47.8%
1954	193,956	83,373	Stockton, Alvin	110,583	Simms, John F. Jr.		27,210 D	43.0%	57.0%	43.0%	57.0%
1952	240,150	129,116	Mechem, Edwin L.*	111,034	Grantham, Everett		18,082 R	53.8%	46.2%	53.8%	46.2%
1950	180,205	96,846	Mechem, Edwin L.	83,359	Miles, John E.		13,487 R	53.7%	46.3%	53.7%	46.3%
1948	189,992	86,023	Lujan, Manuel	103,969	Mabry, Thomas J.*		17,946 D	45.3%	54.7%	45.3%	54.7%
1946	132,630	62,575	Safford, Edward L.	70,055	Mabry, Thomas J.		7,480 D	47.2%	52.8%	47.2%	52.8%

Note: An asterisk (*) denotes incumbent. **In past elections, the other vote included: 1994 - 47,990 Green (Roberto Mondragon). The term of New Mexico's governor was increased from two to four years effective with the 1970 election.

POSTWAR VOTE FOR SENATOR

		Republican		Democratic		Other Vote	Rep.-Dem. Plurality	Percentage			
								Total Vote		Major Vote	
Year	Total Vote	Vote	Candidate	Vote	Candidate			Rep.	Dem.	Rep.	Dem.
2014	515,506	229,097	Weh, Allen	286,409	Udall, Tom*		57,312 D	44.4%	55.6%	44.4%	55.6%
2012	775,792	351,259	Wilson, Heather A.	395,717	Heinrich, Martin	28,816	44,458 D	45.3%	51.0%	47.0%	53.0%
2008	823,650	318,522	Pearce, Steve	505,128	Udall, Tom		186,606 D	38.7%	61.3%	38.7%	61.3%
2006	558,550	163,826	McCulloch, Allen	394,365	Bingaman, Jeff*	359	230,539 D	29.3%	70.6%	29.3%	70.7%
2002	483,340	314,301	Domenici, Peter V.*	169,039	Tristani, Gloria		145,262 R	65.0%	35.0%	65.0%	35.0%
2000	589,526	225,517	Redmond, Bill	363,744	Bingaman, Jeff*	265	138,227 D	38.3%	61.7%	38.3%	61.7%
1996	551,821	357,171	Domenici, Peter V.*	164,356	Trujillo, Art	30,294	192,815 R	64.7%	29.8%	68.5%	31.5%
1994	463,196	213,025	McMillan, Colin R.	249,989	Bingaman, Jeff*	182	36,964 D	46.0%	54.0%	46.0%	54.0%
1990	406,938	296,712	Domenici, Peter V.*	110,033	Benavides, Tom R.	193	186,679 R	72.9%	27.0%	72.9%	27.1%
1988	508,598	186,579	Valentine, William	321,983	Bingaman, Jeff*	36	135,404 D	36.7%	63.3%	36.7%	63.3%
1984	502,634	361,371	Domenici, Peter V.*	141,253	Pratt, Judith A.	10	220,118 R	71.9%	28.1%	71.9%	28.1%
1982	404,810	187,128	Schmitt, Harrison*	217,682	Bingaman, Jeff		30,554 D	46.2%	53.8%	46.2%	53.8%
1978	343,554	183,442	Domenici, Peter V.*	160,045	Anaya, Toney	67	23,397 R	53.4%	46.6%	53.4%	46.6%
1976	413,141	234,681	Schmitt, Harrison	176,382	Montoya, Joseph M.*	2,078	58,299 R	56.8%	42.7%	57.1%	42.9%
1972	378,330	204,253	Domenici, Peter V.	173,815	Daniels, Jack	262	30,438 R	54.0%	45.9%	54.0%	46.0%
1970	289,906	135,004	Carter, Anderson	151,486	Montoya, Joseph M.*	3,416	16,482 D	46.6%	52.3%	47.1%	52.9%
1966	258,203	120,988	Carter, Anderson	137,205	Anderson, Clinton P.*	10	16,217 D	46.9%	53.1%	46.9%	53.1%
1964	325,774	147,562	Mechem, Edwin L.	178,209	Montoya, Joseph M.	3	30,647 D	45.3%	54.7%	45.3%	54.7%
1960	300,551	109,897	Colwes, William	190,654	Anderson, Clinton P.*		80,757 D	36.6%	63.4%	36.6%	63.4%
1958	203,323	75,827	Atchley, Forrest S.	127,496	Chavez, Dennis*		51,669 D	37.3%	62.7%	37.3%	62.7%
1954	194,422	83,071	Mechem, Edwin L.	111,351	Anderson, Clinton P.*		28,280 D	42.7%	57.3%	42.7%	57.3%
1952	239,711	117,168	Hurley, Patrick J.	122,543	Chavez, Dennis*		5,375 D	48.9%	51.1%	48.9%	51.1%
1948	188,495	80,226	Hurley, Patrick J.	108,269	Anderson, Clinton P.		28,043 D	42.6%	57.4%	42.6%	57.4%
1946	133,282	64,632	Hurley, Patrick J.	68,650	Chavez, Dennis*		4,018 D	48.5%	51.5%	48.5%	51.5%

Note: An asterisk (*) denotes incumbent.

NEW MEXICO

GOVERNOR 2014

2010 Census Population	County	Total Vote	Republican (Martinez)	Democratic (King)	Other	Rep.-Dem. Plurality	Percentage			
							Total Vote		Major Vote	
							Rep.	Dem.	Rep.	Dem.
662,564	BERNALILLO	169,942	93,442	76,500		16,942 R	55.0%	45.0%	55.0%	45.0%
3,725	CATRON	1,715	1,413	302		1,111 R	82.4%	17.6%	82.4%	17.6%
65,645	CHAVES	13,005	10,094	2,911		7,183 R	77.6%	22.4%	77.6%	22.4%
27,213	CIBOLA	5,683	3,296	2,387		909 R	58.0%	42.0%	58.0%	42.0%
13,750	COLFAX	4,257	2,806	1,451		1,355 R	65.9%	34.1%	65.9%	34.1%
48,376	CURRY	7,964	5,628	2,336		3,292 R	70.7%	29.3%	70.7%	29.3%
2,022	DE BACA	798	615	183		432 R	77.1%	22.9%	77.1%	22.9%
209,233	DONA ANA	41,339	22,161	19,178		2,983 R	53.6%	46.4%	53.6%	46.4%
53,829	EDDY	11,627	9,046	2,581		6,465 R	77.8%	22.2%	77.8%	22.2%
29,514	GRANT	9,122	4,965	4,157		808 R	54.4%	45.6%	54.4%	45.6%
4,687	GUADALUPE	1,874	1,105	769		336 R	59.0%	41.0%	59.0%	41.0%
695	HARDING	519	349	170		179 R	67.2%	32.8%	67.2%	32.8%
4,894	HIDALGO	1,478	1,001	477		524 R	67.7%	32.3%	67.7%	32.3%
64,727	LEA	9,087	7,070	2,017		5,053 R	77.8%	22.2%	77.8%	22.2%
20,497	LINCOLN	6,187	4,904	1,283		3,621 R	79.3%	20.7%	79.3%	20.7%
17,950	LOS ALAMOS	7,901	4,773	3,128		1,645 R	60.4%	39.6%	60.4%	39.6%
25,095	LUNA	4,849	3,169	1,680		1,489 R	65.4%	34.6%	65.4%	34.6%
71,492	MCKINLEY	14,858	7,465	7,393		72 R	50.2%	49.8%	50.2%	49.8%
4,881	MORA	2,115	962	1,153		191 D	45.5%	54.5%	45.5%	54.5%
63,797	OTERO	12,808	9,825	2,983		6,842 R	76.7%	23.3%	76.7%	23.3%
9,041	QUAY	2,678	1,820	858		962 R	68.0%	32.0%	68.0%	32.0%
40,246	RIO ARRIBA	10,141	4,490	5,651		1,161 D	44.3%	55.7%	44.3%	55.7%
19,846	ROOSEVELT	3,784	2,534	1,250		1,284 R	67.0%	33.0%	67.0%	33.0%
130,044	SAN JUAN	29,958	22,461	7,497		14,964 R	75.0%	25.0%	75.0%	25.0%
29,393	SAN MIGUEL	8,002	3,247	4,755		1,508 D	40.6%	59.4%	40.6%	59.4%
131,561	SANDOVAL	38,466	23,805	14,661		9,144 R	61.9%	38.1%	61.9%	38.1%
144,170	SANTA FE	48,360	15,702	32,658		16,956 D	32.5%	67.5%	32.5%	67.5%
11,988	SIERRA	3,691	2,684	1,007		1,677 R	72.7%	27.3%	72.7%	27.3%
17,866	SOCORRO	5,313	3,050	2,263		787 R	57.4%	42.6%	57.4%	42.6%
32,937	TAOS	10,638	3,695	6,943		3,248 D	34.7%	65.3%	34.7%	65.3%
16,383	TORRANCE	4,633	3,038	1,595		1,443 R	65.6%	34.4%	65.6%	34.4%
4,549	UNION	1,390	984	406		578 R	70.8%	29.2%	70.8%	29.2%
76,569	VALENCIA	18,623	11,844	6,779		5,065 R	63.6%	36.4%	63.6%	36.4%
2,059,179	TOTAL	512,805	293,443	219,362		74,081 R	57.2%	42.8%	57.2%	42.8%

NEW MEXICO

SENATOR 2014

2010 Census Population	County	Total Vote	Republican (Weh)	Democratic (Udall)	Other	Rep.-Dem. Plurality	Percentage			
							Total Vote		Major Vote	
							Rep.	Dem.	Rep.	Dem.
662,564	BERNALILLO	171,511	73,751	97,760		24,009 D	43.0%	57.0%	43.0%	57.0%
3,725	CATRON	1,699	1,156	543		613 R	68.0%	32.0%	68.0%	32.0%
65,645	CHAVES	12,984	8,801	4,183		4,618 R	67.8%	32.2%	67.8%	32.2%
27,213	CIBOLA	5,683	2,045	3,638		1,593 D	36.0%	64.0%	36.0%	64.0%
13,750	COLFAX	4,272	1,878	2,394		516 D	44.0%	56.0%	44.0%	56.0%
48,376	CURRY	8,024	5,612	2,412		3,200 R	69.9%	30.1%	69.9%	30.1%
2,022	DE BACA	783	462	321		141 R	59.0%	41.0%	59.0%	41.0%
209,233	DONA ANA	41,261	18,150	23,111		4,961 D	44.0%	56.0%	44.0%	56.0%
53,829	EDDY	11,589	7,545	4,044		3,501 R	65.1%	34.9%	65.1%	34.9%
29,514	GRANT	9,186	3,863	5,323		1,460 D	42.1%	57.9%	42.1%	57.9%

NEW MEXICO

SENATOR 2014

2010 Census Population	County	Total Vote	Republican (Weh)	Democratic (Udall)	Other	Rep.-Dem. Plurality	Percentage			
							Total Vote		Major Vote	
							Rep.	Dem.	Rep.	Dem.
4,687	GUADALUPE	1,833	455	1,378		923 D	24.8%	75.2%	24.8%	75.2%
695	HARDING	516	256	260		4 D	49.6%	50.4%	49.6%	50.4%
4,894	HIDALGO	1,451	667	784		117 D	46.0%	54.0%	46.0%	54.0%
64,727	LEA	9,099	6,739	2,360		4,379 R	74.1%	25.9%	74.1%	25.9%
20,497	LINCOLN	6,166	4,035	2,131		1,904 R	65.4%	34.6%	65.4%	34.6%
17,950	LOS ALAMOS	7,968	3,534	4,434		900 D	44.4%	55.6%	44.4%	55.6%
25,095	LUNA	4,855	2,388	2,467		79 D	49.2%	50.8%	49.2%	50.8%
71,492	MCKINLEY	14,815	3,481	11,334		7,853 D	23.5%	76.5%	23.5%	76.5%
4,881	MORA	2,113	585	1,528		943 D	27.7%	72.3%	27.7%	72.3%
63,797	OTERO	12,767	8,158	4,609		3,549 R	63.9%	36.1%	63.9%	36.1%
9,041	QUAY	2,682	1,557	1,125		432 R	58.1%	41.9%	58.1%	41.9%
40,246	RIO ARRIBA	10,168	2,503	7,665		5,162 D	24.6%	75.4%	24.6%	75.4%
19,846	ROOSEVELT	3,785	2,531	1,254		1,277 R	66.9%	33.1%	66.9%	33.1%
130,044	SAN JUAN	30,041	18,137	11,904		6,233 R	60.4%	39.6%	60.4%	39.6%
29,393	SAN MIGUEL	8,041	1,842	6,199		4,357 D	22.9%	77.1%	22.9%	77.1%
131,561	SANDOVAL	38,698	18,558	20,140		1,582 D	48.0%	52.0%	48.0%	52.0%
144,170	SANTA FE	49,075	11,418	37,657		26,239 D	23.3%	76.7%	23.3%	76.7%
11,988	SIERRA	3,695	2,120	1,575		545 R	57.4%	42.6%	57.4%	42.6%
17,866	SOCORRO	5,289	2,152	3,137		985 D	40.7%	59.3%	40.7%	59.3%
32,937	TAOS	10,724	2,026	8,698		6,672 D	18.9%	81.1%	18.9%	81.1%
16,383	TORRANCE	4,623	2,624	1,999		625 R	56.8%	43.2%	56.8%	43.2%
4,549	UNION	1,379	874	505		369 R	63.4%	36.6%	63.4%	36.6%
76,569	VALENCIA	18,731	9,194	9,537		343 D	49.1%	50.9%	49.1%	50.9%
2,059,179	TOTAL	515,506	229,097	286,409		57,312 D	44.4%	55.6%	44.4%	55.6%

NEW MEXICO

HOUSE OF REPRESENTATIVES

CD	Year	Total Vote	Republican		Democratic		Other Vote	Rep.-Dem. Plurality	Percentage			
			Vote	Candidate	Vote	Candidate			Total Vote		Major Vote	
									Rep.	Dem.	Rep.	Dem.
1	2014	180,032	74,558	FRESE, MICHAEL H.	105,474	GRISHAM, MICHELLE LUJAN*		30,916 D	41.4%	58.6%	41.4%	58.6%
1	2012	275,856	112,473	ARNOLD-JONES, JANICE E.	162,924	GRISHAM, MICHELLE LUJAN	459	50,451 D	40.8%	59.1%	40.8%	59.2%
2	2014	147,777	95,209	PEARCE, STEVE*	52,499	LARA, ROXANNE "ROCKY"	69	42,710 R	64.4%	35.5%	64.5%	35.5%
2	2012	225,515	133,180	PEARCE, STEVE*	92,162	ERHARD, EVELYN MADRID	173	41,018 R	59.1%	40.9%	59.1%	40.9%
3	2014	184,076	70,775	BYRD, JEFFERSON L.	113,249	LUJAN, BEN RAY*	52	42,474 D	38.4%	61.5%	38.5%	61.5%
·3	2012	264,719	97,616	BYRD, JEFFERSON L.	167,103	LUJAN, BEN RAY*		69,487 D	36.9%	63.1%	36.9%	63.1%
TOTAL	2014	511,885	240,542		271,222		121	30,680 D	47.0%	53.0%	47.0%	53.0%
TOTAL	2012	766,090	343,269		422,189		632	78,920 D	44.8%	55.1%	44.8%	55.2%

Note: An asterisk (*) denotes incumbent.

NEW MEXICO

GENERAL AND PRIMARY ELECTIONS

2014 GENERAL ELECTIONS: OTHER VOTES

House   Other vote was:

CD 1   69 Write-in (Jack McGrann)
CD 2   52 Write-in (Thomas F. Hook)

2014 PRIMARY ELECTIONS: SUPPLEMENTARY INFORMATION

Primary	June 3, 2014	**Registration** (as of June 2, 2014)	1,275,665	Democratic Republican Other Declined to State	597,518 398,735 38,727 240,685

Primary Type   Closed—Only registered Democrats and Republicans could vote in their party's primary.

	REPUBLICAN PRIMARIES			DEMOCRATIC PRIMARIES		
Senator	Weh, Allen Clements, David Kale *TOTAL*	41,566 24,413 *65,979*	63.0% 37.0%	Udall, Tom* *TOTAL*	113,502 *113,502*	100.0%
Governor	Martinez, Susana* *TOTAL*	64,413 *64,413*	100.0%	King, Gary K. Webber, Alan M. Rael, Lawrence D. Morales, Howie C. Lopez, Linda M. Martinez, Mario J. Chavez, Phillip George *TOTAL*	43,918 28,406 24,878 17,863 10,288 16 2 *125,371*	35.0% 22.7% 19.8% 14.2% 8.2%
Congressional District 1	Frese, Michael H. Priem, Richard G. *TOTAL*	13,300 7,054 *20,354*	65.3% 34.7%	Grisham, Michelle Lujan* *TOTAL*	29,133 *29,133*	100.0%
Congressional District 2	Pearce, Steve* *TOTAL*	24,598 *24,598*	100.0%	Lara, Roxanne "Rocky" *TOTAL*	21,751 *21,751*	100.0%
Congressional District 3	Byrd, Jefferson L. *TOTAL*	15,690 *15,690*	100.0%	Lujan, Ben Ray* Blanch Jr., Robert J. *TOTAL*	50,709 7,207 *57,916*	87.6% 12.4%

Note: An asterisk (*) denotes incumbent.

NEW YORK

Congressional districts first established for elections held in 2012
27 members

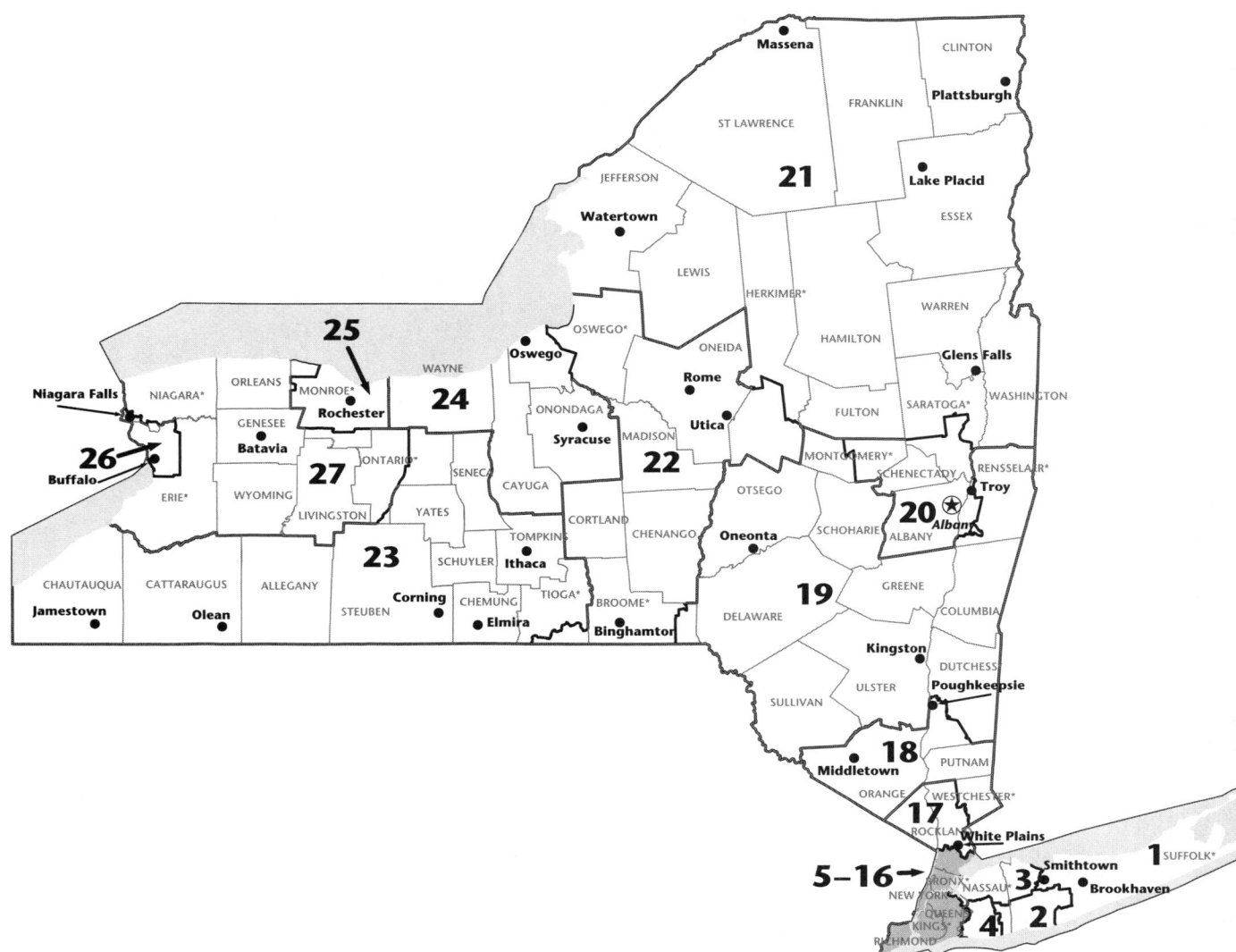

* Asterisk indicates a county whose boundaries include parts of two or more congressional districts.

NEW YORK
New York City Area

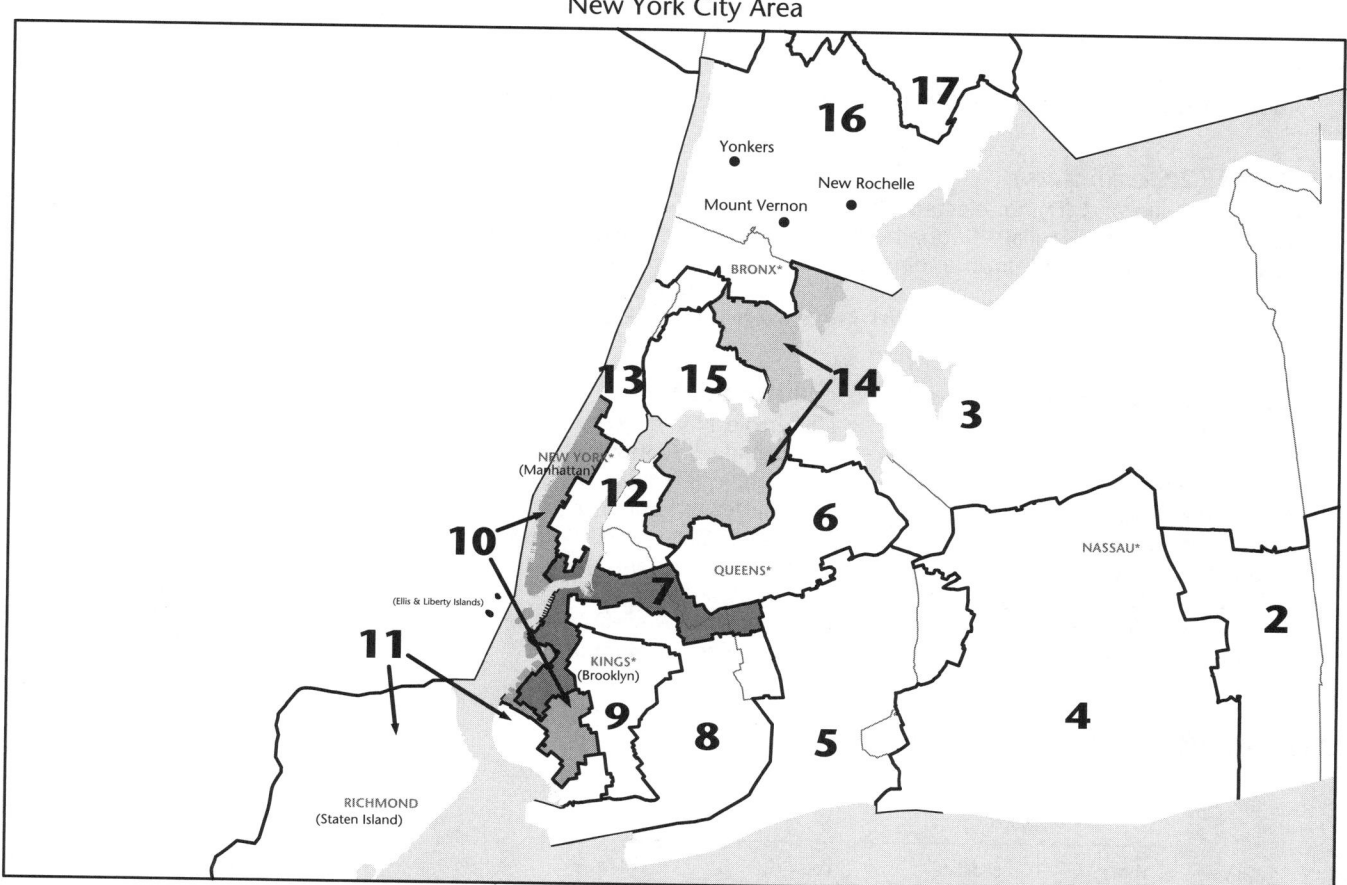

* Asterisk indicates a county whose boundaries include parts of two or more congressional districts.

NEW YORK

GOVERNOR

Andrew Cuomo (D). Re-elected 2014 to a four-year term. Previously elected 2010.

SENATORS (2 Democrats)

Kirsten E. Gillibrand (D). Re-elected 2012 to a six-year term. Previously elected 2010 to fill the remaining two years of the term vacated by Hillary Rodham Clinton (D), who resigned in January 2009 to become U.S. secretary of state. Gillibrand sworn in as senator January 27, 2009, shortly after the vacancy occurred.

Charles E. Schumer (D). Reelected 2010 to a six-year term. Previously elected 2004, 1998.

REPRESENTATIVES (9 Republicans, 18 Democrats)

1. Lee M. Zeldin (R)
2. Pete T. King (R)
3. Steve Israel (D)
4. Kathleen M. Rice (D)
5. Gregory W. Meeks (D)
6. Grace Meng (D)
7. Nydia M. Velázquez (D)
8. Hakeem S. Jeffries (D)
9. Yvette D. Clarke (D)
10. Jerrold Nadler (D)
11. Daniel M. Donovan Jr. (R)
12. Carolyn B. Maloney (D)
13. Charles B. Rangel (D)
14. Joseph Crowley (D)
15. José E. Serrano (D)
16. Eliot L. Engel (D)
17. Nita M. Lowey (D)
18. Sean Patrick Maloney (D)
19. Christopher P. Gibson (R)
20. Paul Tonko (D)
21. Elise M. Stefanik (R)
22. Richard L. Hanna (R)
23. Tom Reed (R)
24. John Katko (R)
25. Louise M. Slaughter (D)
26. Brian Higgins (D)
27. Chris Collins (R)

POSTWAR VOTE FOR PRESIDENT

Year	Total Vote	Republican		Democratic		Other Vote	Rep.-Dem. Plurality	Percentage			
								Total Vote		Major Vote	
		Vote	Candidate	Vote	Candidate			Rep.	Dem.	Rep.	Dem.
2012	7,081,159	2,490,431	Romney, W. Mitt	4,485,741	Obama, Barack H.*	104,987	1,995,310 D	35.2%	63.3%	35.7%	64.3%
2008	7,640,931	2,752,771	McCain, John S. III	4,804,945	Obama, Barack H.	83,215	2,052,174 D	36.0%	62.9%	36.4%	63.6%
2004	7,391,036	2,962,567	Bush, George W.*	4,314,280	Kerry, John F.	114,189	1,351,713 D	40.1%	58.4%	40.7%	59.3%
2000**	6,821,999	2,403,374	Bush, George W.	4,107,697	Gore, Albert Jr.	310,928	1,704,323 D	35.2%	60.2%	36.9%	63.1%
1996**	6,316,129	1,933,492	Dole, Robert "Bob"	3,756,177	Clinton, Bill*	626,460	1,822,685 D	30.6%	59.5%	34.0%	66.0%
1992**	6,926,925	2,346,649	Bush, George H.*	3,444,450	Clinton, Bill	1,135,826	1,097,801 D	33.9%	49.7%	40.5%	59.5%
1988	6,485,683	3,081,871	Bush, George H.	3,347,882	Dukakis, Michael S.	55,930	266,011 D	47.5%	51.6%	47.9%	52.1%
1984	6,806,810	3,664,763	Reagan, Ronald*	3,119,609	Mondale, Walter F.	22,438	545,154 R	53.8%	45.8%	54.0%	46.0%
1980**	6,201,959	2,893,831	Reagan, Ronald	2,728,372	Carter, Jimmy*	579,756	165,459 R	46.7%	44.0%	51.5%	48.5%
1976	6,534,170	3,100,791	Ford, Gerald R.*	3,389,558	Carter, Jimmy	43,821	288,767 D	47.5%	51.9%	47.8%	52.2%
1972	7,165,919	4,192,778	Nixon, Richard M.*	2,951,084	McGovern, George S.	22,057	1,241,694 R	58.5%	41.2%	58.7%	41.3%
1968**	6,791,688	3,007,932	Nixon, Richard M.	3,378,470	Humphrey, Hubert Horatio Jr.	405,286	370,538 D	44.3%	49.7%	47.1%	52.9%
1964	7,166,275	2,243,559	Goldwater, Barry M. Sr.	4,913,102	Johnson, Lyndon B.*	9,614	2,669,543 D	31.3%	68.6%	31.3%	68.7%
1960	7,291,079	3,446,419	Nixon, Richard M.	3,830,085	Kennedy, John F.	14,575	383,666 D	47.3%	52.5%	47.4%	52.6%
1956	7,095,971	4,345,506	Eisenhower, Dwight D.*	2,747,944	Stevenson, Adlai E. II	2,521	1,597,562 R	61.2%	38.7%	61.3%	38.7%
1952	7,128,239	3,952,813	Eisenhower, Dwight D.	3,104,601	Stevenson, Adlai E. II	70,825	848,212 R	55.5%	43.6%	56.0%	44.0%
1948**	6,177,337	2,841,163	Dewey, Thomas E.	2,780,204	Truman, Harry S.*	555,970	60,959 R	46.0%	45.0%	50.5%	49.5%

Note: An asterisk (*) denotes incumbent. **In past elections, the other vote included: 2000 - 244,030 Green (Ralph Nader); 1996 - 503,458 Reform (Ross Perot); 1992 - 1,090,721 Independent (Perot); 1980 - 467,801 Independent (John Anderson); 1968 - 358,864 American Independent (George Wallace); 1948 - 509,559 Progressive (Henry Wallace).

NEW YORK

POSTWAR VOTE FOR GOVERNOR

Year	Total Vote	Republican Vote	Candidate	Democratic Vote	Candidate	Other Vote	Rep.-Dem. Plurality	Rep. Total	Dem. Total	Rep. Major	Dem. Major
2014	3,819,086	1,537,077	Astorino, Rob	2,069,480	Cuomo, Andrew*	212,529	532,403 D	40.2%	54.2%	42.6%	57.4%
2010	4,658,825	1,548,184	Paladino, Carl	2,911,721	Cuomo, Andrew	198,920	1,363,537 D	33.2%	62.5%	34.7%	65.3%
2006	4,437,220	1,274,335	Faso, John	3,086,709	Spitzer, Eliot	76,176	1,812,374 D	28.7%	69.6%	29.2%	70.8%
2002**	4,579,078	2,262,255	Pataki, George E.*	1,534,064	McCall, H. Carl	782,759	728,191 R	49.4%	33.5%	59.6%	40.4%
1998	4,735,236	2,571,991	Pataki, George E.*	1,570,317	Vallone, Peter F.	592,928	1,001,674 R	54.3%	33.2%	62.1%	37.9%
1994	5,208,762	2,538,702	Pataki, George E.	2,364,904	Cuomo, Mario M.*	305,156	173,798 R	48.7%	45.4%	51.8%	48.2%
1990**	4,056,896	865,948	Rinfret, Pierre A.	2,157,087	Cuomo, Mario M.*	1,033,861	1,291,139 D	21.3%	53.2%	28.6%	71.4%
1986	4,294,124	1,363,810	O'Rourke, Andrew P.	2,775,229	Cuomo, Mario M.*	155,085	1,411,419 D	31.8%	64.6%	32.9%	67.1%
1982	5,254,891	2,494,827	Lehrman, Lew	2,675,213	Cuomo, Mario M.	84,851	180,386 D	47.5%	50.9%	48.3%	51.7%
1978	4,768,820	2,156,404	Duryea, Perry B.	2,429,272	Carey, Hugh L.*	183,144	272,868 D	45.2%	50.9%	47.0%	53.0%
1974	5,293,176	2,219,667	Wilson, Malcolm*	3,028,503	Carey, Hugh L.	45,006	808,836 D	41.9%	57.2%	42.3%	57.7%
1970	6,013,064	3,151,432	Rockefeller, Nelson A.*	2,421,426	Goldberg, Arthur J.	440,206	730,006 R	52.4%	40.3%	56.5%	43.5%
1966**	6,006,246	2,690,626	Rockefeller, Nelson A.*	2,298,363	O'Connor, Frank	1,017,257	392,263 R	44.8%	38.3%	53.9%	46.1%
1962	5,805,631	3,081,587	Rockefeller, Nelson A.*	2,552,418	Morgenthau, Robert M.	171,626	529,169 R	53.1%	44.0%	54.7%	45.3%
1958	5,712,665	3,126,929	Rockefeller, Nelson A.	2,553,895	Harriman, Averell*	31,841	573,034 R	54.7%	44.7%	55.0%	45.0%
1954	5,161,942	2,549,613	Ives, Irving M.	2,560,738	Harriman, Averell	51,591	11,125 D	49.4%	49.6%	49.9%	50.1%
1950	5,308,889	2,819,523	Dewey, Thomas E.*	2,246,855	Lynch, Walter A.	242,511	572,668 R	53.1%	42.3%	55.7%	44.3%
1946	4,964,552	2,825,633	Dewey, Thomas E.*	2,138,482	Mead, James M.	437	687,151 R	56.9%	43.1%	56.9%	43.1%

Note: An asterisk (*) denotes incumbent. **In past elections, the other vote included: 2002 - 654,016 Independence (B. Thomas Golisano); 1990 - 827,614 Conservative (Herbert I. London); 1966 - 510,023 Conservative (Paul L. Adams), 507,234 Liberal (Franklin Roosevelt Jr.).

POSTWAR VOTE FOR SENATOR

Year	Total Vote	Republican Vote	Candidate	Democratic Vote	Candidate	Other Vote	Rep.-Dem. Plurality	Rep. Total	Dem. Total	Rep. Major	Dem. Major
2012	6,679,678	1,758,702	Long, Wendy	4,822,330	Gillibrand, Kirsten E.*	98,646	3,063,628 D	26.3%	72.2%	26.7%	73.3%
2010	4,596,796	1,480,423	Townsend, Jay	3,047,880	Schumer, Charles E.*	68,493	1,567,457 D	32.2%	66.3%	32.7%	67.3%
2010S	4,508,771	1,582,693	DioGuardi, Joseph J.	2,837,684	Gillibrand, Kirsten E.*	88,394	1,254,991 D	35.1%	62.9%	35.8%	64.2%
2006	4,490,053	1,392,189	Spencer, John	3,008,428	Clinton, Hillary Rodham*	89,436	1,616,239 D	31.0%	67.0%	31.6%	68.4%
2004	6,702,875	1,625,069	Mills, Howard D.	4,769,824	Schumer, Charles E.*	307,982	3,144,755 D	24.2%	71.2%	25.4%	74.6%
2000	6,779,839	2,915,730	Lazio, Rick A.	3,747,310	Clinton, Hillary Rodham	116,799	831,580 D	43.0%	55.3%	43.8%	56.2%
1998	4,670,805	2,058,988	D'Amato, Alfonse M.*	2,551,065	Schumer, Charles E.	60,752	492,077 D	44.1%	54.6%	44.7%	55.3%
1994	4,794,601	1,988,308	Castro, Bernadette	2,646,541	Moynihan, Daniel Patrick*	159,752	658,233 D	41.5%	55.2%	42.9%	57.1%
1992	6,458,826	3,166,994	D'Amato, Alfonse M.*	3,086,200	Abrams, Robert	205,632	80,794 R	49.0%	47.8%	50.6%	49.4%
1988	6,040,980	1,875,784	McMillan, Robert	4,048,649	Moynihan, Daniel Patrick*	116,547	2,172,865 D	31.1%	67.0%	31.7%	68.3%
1986	4,179,447	2,378,197	D'Amato, Alfonse M.*	1,723,216	Green, Mark J.	78,034	654,981 R	56.9%	41.2%	58.0%	42.0%
1982	4,967,729	1,696,766	Sullivan, Florence M.	3,232,146	Moynihan, Daniel Patrick*	38,817	1,535,380 D	34.2%	65.1%	34.4%	65.6%
1980**	6,014,914	2,699,652	D'Amato, Alfonse M.	2,618,661	Holtzman, Elizabeth	696,601	80,991 R	44.9%	43.5%	50.8%	49.2%
1976	6,319,755	2,836,633	Buckley, James L.*	3,422,594	Moynihan, Daniel Patrick	60,528	585,961 D	44.9%	54.2%	45.3%	54.7%
1974	5,163,600	2,340,188	Javits, Jacob K.*	1,973,781	Clark, Ramsey	849,631	366,407 R	45.3%	38.2%	54.2%	45.8%
1970**	5,904,782	1,434,472	Goodell, Charles E.*	2,171,232	Ottinger, Richard L.	2,299,078	736,760 D**	24.3%	36.8%	39.8%	60.2%
1968**	6,574,415	3,269,772	Javits, Jacob K.*	2,150,695	O'Dwyer, Paul	1,153,948	1,119,077 R	49.7%	32.7%	60.3%	39.7%
1964	7,151,686	3,104,056	Keating, Kenneth B.*	3,823,749	Kennedy, Robert F.	223,881	719,693 D	43.4%	53.5%	44.8%	55.2%
1962	5,703,168	3,272,417	Javits, Jacob K.*	2,289,323	Donovan, James B.	141,428	983,094 R	57.4%	40.1%	58.8%	41.2%
1958	5,602,088	2,842,942	Keating, Kenneth B.	2,709,950	Hogan, Frank S.	49,196	132,992 R	50.7%	48.4%	51.2%	48.8%
1956	6,991,136	3,723,933	Javits, Jacob K.	3,265,159	Wagner, Robert Ferdinand	2,044	458,774 R	53.3%	46.7%	53.3%	46.7%
1952	6,980,259	3,853,934	Ives, Irving M.*	2,521,736	Cashmore, John	604,589	1,332,198 R	55.2%	36.1%	60.4%	39.6%
1950	5,228,403	2,367,353	Hanley, Joe R.	2,632,313	Lehman, Herbert H.*	228,737	264,960 D	45.3%	50.3%	47.4%	52.6%
1949S	4,966,878	2,384,381	Dulles, John Foster	2,582,438	Lehman, Herbert H.	59	198,057 D	48.0%	52.0%	48.0%	52.0%
1946	4,867,564	2,559,365	Ives, Irving M.	2,308,112	Lehman, Herbert H.	87	251,253 R	52.6%	47.4%	52.6%	47.4%

Note: An asterisk (*) denotes incumbent. **In past elections, the other vote included: 1980 - 664,544 Liberal (Jacob K. Javits); 1970 - 2,288,190 Conservative (James L. Buckley); 1968 - 1,139,402 Conservative (Buckley). Buckley won the 1970 election with 38.8 percent of the total vote. The 1949 election and one of the 2010 elections were for short terms to fill a vacancy.

NEW YORK
GOVERNOR 2014

2010 Census Population	County	Total Vote	Republican (Astorino)	Democratic (Cuomo)	Other	Rep.-Dem. Plurality		Percentage			
								Total Vote		Major Vote	
								Rep.	Dem.	Rep.	Dem.
304,204	ALBANY	86,321	35,061	38,498	12,762	3,437	D	40.6%	44.6%	47.7%	52.3%
48,946	ALLEGANY	11,891	8,393	3,036	462	5,357	R	70.6%	25.5%	73.4%	26.6%
1,385,108	BRONX	138,767	15,288	120,007	3,472	104,719	D	11.0%	86.5%	11.3%	88.7%
200,600	BROOME	52,150	22,353	26,371	3,426	4,018	D	42.9%	50.6%	45.9%	54.1%
80,317	CATTARAUGUS	19,026	11,885	6,425	716	5,460	R	62.5%	33.8%	64.9%	35.1%
80,026	CAYUGA	21,161	10,570	9,177	1,414	1,393	R	50.0%	43.4%	53.5%	46.5%
134,905	CHAUTAUQUA	34,274	19,771	13,163	1,340	6,608	R	57.7%	38.4%	60.0%	40.0%
88,830	CHEMUNG	22,765	13,540	8,535	690	5,005	R	59.5%	37.5%	61.3%	38.7%
50,477	CHENANGO	11,993	6,784	4,356	853	2,428	R	56.6%	36.3%	60.9%	39.1%
82,128	CLINTON	19,442	7,697	10,809	936	3,112	D	39.6%	55.6%	41.6%	58.4%
63,096	COLUMBIA	20,562	9,772	8,403	2,387	1,369	R	47.5%	40.9%	53.8%	46.2%
49,336	CORTLAND	11,778	6,422	4,396	960	2,026	R	54.5%	37.3%	59.4%	40.6%
47,980	DELAWARE	12,761	7,446	4,341	974	3,105	R	58.3%	34.0%	63.2%	36.8%
297,488	DUTCHESS	75,535	37,832	33,306	4,397	4,526	R	50.1%	44.1%	53.2%	46.8%
919,040	ERIE	239,720	103,801	125,617	10,302	21,816	D	43.3%	52.4%	45.2%	54.8%
39,370	ESSEX	10,812	4,422	5,722	668	1,300	D	40.9%	52.9%	43.6%	56.4%
51,599	FRANKLIN	10,370	4,698	5,057	615	359	D	45.3%	48.8%	48.2%	51.8%
55,531	FULTON	13,597	8,907	3,964	726	4,943	R	65.5%	29.2%	69.2%	30.8%
60,079	GENESEE	16,163	11,320	4,285	558	7,035	R	70.0%	26.5%	72.5%	27.5%
49,221	GREENE	15,210	9,175	4,920	1,115	4,255	R	60.3%	32.3%	65.1%	34.9%
4,836	HAMILTON	2,397	1,611	647	139	964	R	67.2%	27.0%	71.3%	28.7%
64,519	HERKIMER	15,157	8,755	5,325	1,077	3,430	R	57.8%	35.1%	62.2%	37.8%
116,229	JEFFERSON	23,725	11,853	10,700	1,172	1,153	R	50.0%	45.1%	52.6%	47.4%
2,504,700	KINGS	301,010	44,726	236,357	19,927	191,631	D	14.9%	78.5%	15.9%	84.1%
27,087	LEWIS	6,797	4,073	2,343	381	1,730	R	59.9%	34.5%	63.5%	36.5%
65,393	LIVINGSTON	18,456	12,663	4,985	808	7,678	R	68.6%	27.0%	71.8%	28.2%
73,442	MADISON	18,336	9,656	7,135	1,545	2,521	R	52.7%	38.9%	57.5%	42.5%
744,344	MONROE	201,757	96,933	94,595	10,229	2,338	R	48.0%	46.9%	50.6%	49.4%
50,219	MONTGOMERY	12,759	7,534	4,464	761	3,070	R	59.0%	35.0%	62.8%	37.2%
1,339,532	NASSAU	319,100	140,842	168,570	9,688	27,728	D	44.1%	52.8%	45.5%	54.5%
1,585,873	NEW YORK	255,549	32,656	203,080	19,813	170,424	D	12.8%	79.5%	13.9%	86.1%
216,469	NIAGARA	53,238	28,877	22,622	1,739	6,255	R	54.2%	42.5%	56.1%	43.9%
234,878	ONEIDA	51,008	25,045	22,621	3,342	2,424	R	49.1%	44.3%	52.5%	47.5%
467,026	ONONDAGA	134,653	53,487	69,579	11,587	16,092	D	39.7%	51.7%	43.5%	56.5%
107,931	ONTARIO	32,123	19,336	11,247	1,540	8,089	R	60.2%	35.0%	63.2%	36.8%
372,813	ORANGE	86,466	45,137	37,617	3,712	7,520	R	52.2%	43.5%	54.5%	45.5%
42,883	ORLEANS	9,415	6,778	2,318	319	4,460	R	72.0%	24.6%	74.5%	25.5%
122,109	OSWEGO	28,900	16,033	11,017	1,850	5,016	R	55.5%	38.1%	59.3%	40.7%
62,259	OTSEGO	15,941	8,032	6,097	1,812	1,935	R	50.4%	38.2%	56.8%	43.2%
99,710	PUTNAM	27,456	15,042	11,325	1,089	3,717	R	54.8%	41.2%	57.0%	43.0%
2,230,722	QUEENS	240,457	50,600	179,742	10,115	129,142	D	21.0%	74.8%	22.0%	78.0%
159,429	RENSSELAER	46,454	24,848	16,481	5,125	8,367	R	53.5%	35.5%	60.1%	39.9%
468,730	RICHMOND	79,985	34,180	43,725	2,080	9,545	D	42.7%	54.7%	43.9%	56.1%
311,687	ROCKLAND	72,789	32,914	37,453	2,422	4,539	D	45.2%	51.5%	46.8%	53.2%
219,607	SARATOGA	67,987	37,105	24,866	6,016	12,239	R	54.6%	36.6%	59.9%	40.1%
154,727	SCHENECTADY	43,667	21,445	17,713	4,509	3,732	R	49.1%	40.6%	54.8%	45.2%
32,749	SCHOHARIE	9,828	6,240	2,741	847	3,499	R	63.5%	27.9%	69.5%	30.5%
18,343	SCHUYLER	5,981	3,660	1,890	431	1,770	R	61.2%	31.6%	65.9%	34.1%
35,251	SENECA	9,188	5,263	3,330	595	1,933	R	57.3%	36.2%	61.2%	38.8%
111,944	ST. LAWRENCE	24,778	11,766	11,407	1,605	359	R	47.5%	46.0%	50.8%	49.2%
98,990	STEUBEN	27,606	18,250	8,458	898	9,792	R	66.1%	30.6%	68.3%	31.7%
1,493,350	SUFFOLK	323,640	156,351	155,031	12,258	1,320	R	48.3%	47.9%	50.2%	49.8%
77,547	SULLIVAN	17,379	10,005	6,278	1,096	3,727	R	57.6%	36.1%	61.4%	38.6%
51,125	TIOGA	13,516	7,636	5,082	798	2,554	R	56.5%	37.6%	60.0%	40.0%
101,564	TOMPKINS	25,974	7,552	13,850	4,572	6,298	D	29.1%	53.3%	35.3%	64.7%
182,493	ULSTER	52,188	23,934	22,080	6,174	1,854	R	45.9%	42.3%	52.0%	48.0%
65,707	WARREN	19,093	10,605	6,767	1,721	3,838	R	55.5%	35.4%	61.0%	39.0%
63,216	WASHINGTON	14,932	8,699	4,866	1,367	3,833	R	58.3%	32.6%	64.1%	35.9%
93,772	WAYNE	24,915	16,690	7,130	1,095	9,560	R	67.0%	28.6%	70.1%	29.9%
949,113	WESTCHESTER	222,278	92,441	123,017	6,820	30,576	D	41.6%	55.3%	42.9%	57.1%
42,155	WYOMING	11,374	8,596	2,455	323	6,141	R	75.6%	21.6%	77.8%	22.2%
25,348	YATES	6,536	4,091	2,086	359	2,005	R	62.6%	31.9%	66.2%	33.8%
19,378,102	TOTAL	3,819,086	1,537,077	2,069,480	212,529	532,403	D	40.2%	54.2%	42.6%	57.4%

NEW YORK

HOUSE OF REPRESENTATIVES

CD	Year	Total Vote	Republican		Democratic		Other Vote	Rep.-Dem. Plurality	Percentage			
			Vote	Candidate	Vote	Candidate			Total Vote		Major Vote	
									Rep.	Dem.	Rep.	Dem.
1	2014	172,865	94,035	ZELDIN, LEE M.	78,722	BISHOP, TIMOTHY H.*	108	15,313 R	54.4%	45.5%	54.4%	45.6%
1	2012	278,659	132,304	ALTSCHULER, RANDY	146,179	BISHOP, TIMOTHY H.*	176	13,875 D	47.5%	52.5%	47.5%	52.5%
2	2014	139,330	95,177	KING, PETER T.*	41,814	MAHER, PATRICIA M.	2,339	53,363 R	68.3%	30.0%	69.5%	30.5%
2	2012	242,943	142,309	KING, PETER T.*	100,545	FALCONE, VIVIANNE	89	41,764 R	58.6%	41.4%	58.6%	41.4%
3	2014	164,375	74,269	LALLY, GRANT M.	90,032	ISRAEL, STEVE*	74	15,763 D	45.2%	54.8%	45.2%	54.8%
3	2012	273,171	113,203	LABATE, STEPHEN	157,880	ISRAEL, STEVE*	2,088	44,677 D	41.4%	57.8%	41.8%	58.2%
4	2014	170,099	80,127	BLAKEMAN, BRUCE	89,793	RICE, KATHLEEN M.	179	9,666 D	47.1%	52.8%	47.2%	52.8%
4	2012	265,300	85,693	BECKER, FRANCIS X. JR.	163,955	MCCARTHY, CAROLYN*	15,652	78,262 D	32.3%	61.8%	34.3%	65.7%
5	2014	79,821			75,712	MEEKS, GREGORY W.*	4,109	75,712 D		94.9%		100.0%
5	2012	187,141	17,875	JENNINGS, ALLAN JR.	167,836	MEEKS, GREGORY W.*	1,430	149,961 D	9.6%	89.7%	9.6%	90.4%
6	2014	55,963			55,368	MENG, GRACE*	595	55,368 D		98.9%		100.0%
6	2012	164,374	50,846	HALLORAN, DANIEL	111,501	MENG, GRACE	2,027	60,655 D	30.9%	67.8%	31.3%	68.7%
7	2014	63,812	5,713	FERNANDEZ, JOSE LUIS	56,593	VELAZQUEZ, NYDIA M.*	1,506	50,880 D	9.0%	88.7%	9.2%	90.8%
7	2012	152,111			143,930	VELAZQUEZ, NYDIA M.*	8,181	143,930 D		94.6%		100.0%
8	2014	83,999			77,255	JEFFRIES, HAKEEM S.*	6,744	77,255 D		92.0%		100.0%
8	2012	204,207	17,650	BELLONE, ALAN	184,039	JEFFRIES, HAKEEM S.	2,518	166,389 D	8.6%	90.1%	8.8%	91.2%
9	2014	92,569			82,659	CLARKE, YVETTE D.*	9,910	82,659 D		89.3%		100.0%
9	2012	213,431	24,164	CAVANAGH, DANIEL	186,141	CLARKE, YVETTE D.*	3,126	161,977 D	11.3%	87.2%	11.5%	88.5%
10	2014	101,881			89,080	NADLER, JERROLD*	12,801	89,080 D		87.4%		100.0%
10	2012	205,349	39,413	CHAN, MICHAEL	165,743	NADLER, JERROLD*	193	126,330 D	19.2%	80.7%	19.2%	80.8%
11	2014	107,363	58,886	GRIMM, MICHAEL G.*	45,244	RECCHIA JR., DOMENIC M.	3,233	13,642 R	54.8%	42.1%	56.6%	43.4%
11	2012	197,635	103,118	GRIMM, MICHAEL G.*	92,430	MURPHY, MARK	2,087	10,688 R	52.2%	46.8%	52.7%	47.3%
12	2014	113,429	22,731	DI IORIO, NICHOLAS S.	90,603	MALONEY, CAROLYN B.*	95	67,872 D	20.0%	79.9%	20.1%	79.9%
12	2012	241,426	46,841	WIGHT, CHRISTOPHER	194,370	MALONEY, CAROLYN B.*	215	147,529 D	19.4%	80.5%	19.4%	80.6%
13	2014	78,353			68,396	RANGEL, CHARLES B.*	9,957	68,396 D		87.3%		100.0%
13	2012	192,913	12,147	SCHLEY, CRAIG	175,016	RANGEL, CHARLES B.*	5,750	162,869 D	6.3%	90.7%	6.5%	93.5%
14	2014	57,204			50,352	CROWLEY, JOSEPH*	6,852	50,352 D		88.0%		100.0%
14	2012	145,190	21,755	GIBBONS, WILLIAM JR.	120,761	CROWLEY, JOSEPH*	2,674	99,006 D	15.0%	83.2%	15.3%	84.7%
15	2014	56,563			54,906	SERRANO, JOSE E.*	1,657	54,906 D		97.1%		100.0%
15	2012	157,115	4,427	DELLA VALLE, FRANK	152,661	SERRANO, JOSE E.*	27	148,234 D	2.8%	97.2%	2.8%	97.2%
16	2014	100,391			99,658	ENGEL, ELIOT L.*	733	99,658 D		99.3%		100.0%
16	2012	236,553	53,935	MCLAUGHLIN, JOSEPH	179,562	ENGEL, ELIOT L.*	3,056	125,627 D	22.8%	75.9%	23.1%	76.9%
17	2014	174,054	75,781	DAY, CHRIS	98,150	LOWEY, NITA M.*	123	22,369 D	43.5%	56.4%	43.6%	56.4%
17	2012	266,205	91,899	CARVIN, JOE	171,417	LOWEY, NITA M.*	2,889	79,518 D	34.5%	64.4%	34.9%	65.1%
18	2014	179,091	85,660	HAYWORTH, NAN	88,993	MALONEY, SEAN PATRICK*	4,438	3,333 D	47.8%	49.7%	49.0%	51.0%
18	2012	277,063	133,049	HAYWORTH, NAN*	143,845	MALONEY, SEAN PATRICK	169	10,796 D	48.0%	51.9%	48.1%	51.9%
19	2014	204,173	131,594	GIBSON, CHRISTOPHER P.*	72,470	ELDRIDGE, SEAN	109	59,124 R	64.5%	35.5%	64.5%	35.5%
19	2012	284,679	150,245	GIBSON, CHRISTOPHER P.*	134,295	SCHREIBMAN, JULIAN	139	15,950 R	52.8%	47.2%	52.8%	47.2%
20	2014	204,329	79,104	FISCHER, JIM	125,111	TONKO, PAUL*	114	46,007 D	38.7%	61.2%	38.7%	61.3%
20	2012	297,314	93,778	DIETERICH, ROBERT	203,401	TONKO, PAUL*	135	109,623 D	31.5%	68.4%	31.6%	68.4%
21	2014	174,668	96,226	STEFANIK, ELISE M.	59,063	WOOLF, AARON	19,379	37,163 R	55.1%	33.8%	62.0%	38.0%
21	2012	252,556	121,646	DOHENY, MATTHEW A.	126,631	OWENS, WILLIAM L. "BILL"*	4,279	4,985 D	48.2%	50.1%	49.0%	51.0%
22	2014	131,932	129,851	HANNA, RICHARD L.*			2,081	129,851 R	98.4%		100.0%	
22	2012	260,863	157,941	HANNA, RICHARD L.*	102,080	LAMB, DAN	842	55,861 R	60.5%	39.1%	60.7%	39.3%
23	2014	183,481	113,130	REED, TOM*	70,242	ROBERTSON, MARTHA	109	42,888 R	61.7%	38.3%	61.7%	38.3%
23	2012	265,282	137,669	REED, TOM*	127,535	SHINAGAWA, NATE	78	10,134 R	51.9%	48.1%	51.9%	48.1%
24	2014	199,222	118,474	KATKO, JOHN	80,304	MAFFEI, DANIEL B.*	444	38,170 R	59.5%	40.3%	59.6%	40.4%
24	2012	292,988	127,054	BUERKLE, ANN MARIE*	143,044	MAFFEI, DANIEL B.	22,890	15,990 D	43.4%	48.8%	47.0%	53.0%
25	2014	192,971	95,932	ASSINI, MARK W.	96,803	SLAUGHTER, LOUISE M.*	236	871 D	49.7%	50.2%	49.8%	50.2%
25	2012	313,452	133,389	BROOKS, MAGGIE	179,810	SLAUGHTER, LOUISE M.*	253	46,421 D	42.6%	57.4%	42.6%	57.4%
26	2014	166,124	52,909	WEPPNER, KATHLEEN "KATHY"	113,210	HIGGINS, BRIAN*	5	60,301 D	31.8%	68.1%	31.9%	68.1%
26	2012	284,271	71,666	MADIGAN, MICHAEL H.	212,588	HIGGINS, BRIAN*	17	140,922 D	25.2%	74.8%	25.2%	74.8%
27	2014	203,645	144,675	COLLINS, CHRIS*	58,911	O'DONNELL, JIM	59	85,764 R	71.0%	28.9%	71.1%	28.9%
27	2012	317,534	161,220	COLLINS, CHRIS	156,219	HOCHUL, KATHY COURTNEY*	95	5,001 R	50.8%	49.2%	50.8%	49.2%
TOTAL	2014	3,651,707	1,554,274		2,009,444		87,989	455,170 D	42.6%	55.0%	43.6%	56.4%
TOTAL	2012	6,469,725	2,245,236		4,143,414		81,075	1,898,178 D	34.7%	64.0%	35.1%	64.9%

Note: An asterisk (*) denotes incumbent.

NEW YORK

GENERAL AND PRIMARY ELECTIONS

2014 GENERAL ELECTIONS: OTHER VOTES

Governor   Other vote was 184,419 Green (Howie Hawkins), 16,769 Libertarian (Michael McDermott), 6,378 Write-in, 4,963 Sapient Party (Steven Cohn)

House   Other vote was:

CD 1	108 scattered write-in
CD 2	2,281 Green (William D. Stevenson), 58 scattered write-in
CD 3	74 scattered write-in
CD 4	179 scattered write-in
CD 5	3,870 Allen 4 Congress (Allen F. Steinhardt), 239 scattered write-in
CD 6	595 scattered write-in
CD 7	1,398 Conservative (Allan E. Romaguera), 108 scattered write-in
CD 8	6,673 Conservative (Alan Bellone), 71 scattered write-in
CD 9	9,727 Conservative (Daniel Cavanagh), 183 scattered write-in
CD 10	12,042 Conservative (Ross Brady), 554 Flourish Every Person (Michael J. Dilger), 205 scattered write-in
CD 11	2,687 Green (Henry Bardel), 546 scattered write-in
CD 12	95 scattered write-in
CD 13	9,806 Green (Daniel Vila Rivera), 151 scattered write-in
CD 14	6,735 Conservative (Elizabeth Perri), 117 scattered write-in
CD 15	1,047 Conservative (Eduardo Ramirez), 568 Green (William Edstrom), 42 scattered write-in
CD 16	733 scattered write-in
CD 17	123 scattered write-in
CD 18	4,294 Mr. Smith for Congress (Scott A. Smith), 144 scattered write-in
CD 19	109 scattered write-in
CD 20	114 scattered write-in
CD 21	19,238 Green (Matthew J. Funiciello), 141 scattered write-in
CD 22	2,081 scattered write-in
CD 23	109 scattered write-in
CD 24	444 scattered write-in
CD 25	236 scattered write-in
CD 26	5 scattered write-in
CD 27	59 scattered write-in

NEW YORK

GENERAL AND PRIMARY ELECTIONS

2014 PRIMARY ELECTIONS: SUPPLEMENTARY INFORMATION

Primary	June 24, 2014 (Congress) September 9, 2014 (Governor)	**Registration** (as of April 1, 2014 – includes 873,222 inactive registrants)	11,810,858	Democratic Republican Independence Conservative Working Families Green Other Parties Unaffiliated	5,873,844 2,785,773 482,356 156,317 48,110 24,237 5,173 2,435,048

NEW YORK

GENERAL AND PRIMARY ELECTIONS

Primary Type   Closed—Only registered Democrats and Republicans could vote in their party's primary.

	REPUBLICAN PRIMARIES			DEMOCRATIC PRIMARIES		
Governor	Astorino, Rob	Unopposed		Cuomo, Andrew*	361,380	62.9%
				Teachout, Zephyr	192,210	33.5%
				Credico, Randy	20,760	3.6%
				TOTAL	*574,350*	
Congressional District 1	Zeldin, Lee M.	10,283	61.3%	Bishop, Timothy H.*	Unopposed	
	Demos, George C.	6,482	38.7%			
	TOTAL	*16,765*				
Congressional District 2	King, Peter T.*	Unopposed		Maher, Patricia M.	Unopposed	
Congressional District 3	Lally, Grant M.	3,439	50.1%	Israel, Steve*	Unopposed	
	Labate, Stephen	3,428	49.9%			
	TOTAL	*6,867*				
Congressional District 4	Blakeman, Bruce	9,083	66.0%	Rice, Kathleen M.	7,770	57.3%
	Scaturro, Frank	4,687	34.0%	Abrahams, Kevan	5,791	42.7%
	TOTAL	*13,770*		*TOTAL*	*13,561*	
Congressional District 5				Meeks, Gregory W.*	8,119	80.1%
				Marthone, Joseph R.	2,023	19.9%
				TOTAL	*10,142*	
Congressional District 6				Meng, Grace*	Unopposed	
Congressional District 7	Fernandez, Jose Luis	Unopposed		Velazquez, Nydia*	7,627	80.2%
				Kurzon, Jeff	1,796	18.9%
				Write-In,	84	0.9%
				TOTAL	*9,507*	
Congressional District 8				Jeffries, Hakeem S.*	Unopposed	
Congressional District 9				Clarke, Yvette D.*	Unopposed	
Congressional District 10				Nadler, Jerrold*	Unopposed	
Congressional District 11	Grimm, Michael G.*	Unopposed		Recchia Jr., Domenic M.	Unopposed	
Congressional District 12	Di Iorio, Nicholas S.	Unopposed		Maloney, Carolyn B.*		
Congressional District 13				Rangel, Charles B.*	23,865	47.5%
				Espaillat, Adriano	21,607	43.0%
				Walrond Jr., Michael A.	3,971	7.9%
				Garcia, Yolanda	599	1.2%
				Write-In	192	0.4%
				TOTAL	*50,234*	
Congressional District 14				Crowley, Joseph*	Unopposed	
Congressional District 15				Serrano, Jose E.*	10,346	84.4%
				Sloan, Sam	1,004	8.2%
				Write-In	914	7.5%
				TOTAL	*12,264*	

NEW YORK

GENERAL AND PRIMARY ELECTIONS

	REPUBLICAN PRIMARIES			DEMOCRATIC PRIMARIES	
Congressional District 16				Engel, Eliot L.*	Unopposed
Congressional District 17	Day, Chris	Unopposed		Lowey, Nita M.*	Unopposed
Congressional District 18	Hayworth, Nan	Unopposed		Maloney, Sean Patrick*	Unopposed
Congressional District 19	Gibson, Christopher P.*	Unopposed		Eldridge, Sean	Unopposed
Congressional District 20	Fischer, Jim	Unopposed		Tonko, Paul*	Unopposed
Congressional District 21	Stefanik, Elise M. Doheny, Matthew A. TOTAL	16,489 10,620 27,109	60.8% 39.2%	Woolf, Aaron	Unopposed
Congressional District 22	Hanna, Richard L.* Tenney, Claudia TOTAL	16,119 14,000 30,119	53.5% 46.5%		
Congressional District 23	Reed, Tom*	Unopposed		Robertson, Martha	Unopposed
Congressional District 24	Katko, John	Unopposed		Maffei, Daniel B.*	Unopposed
Congressional District 25	Assini, Mark W.	Unopposed		Slaughter, Louise M.*	Unopposed
Congressional District 26	Weppner, Kathleen "Kathy"	Unopposed		Higgins, Brian*	Unopposed
Congressional District 27	Collins, Chris*	Unopposed		O'Donnell, Jim	Unopposed

Note: An asterisk (*) denotes incumbent.

NORTH CAROLINA

Congressional districts first established for elections held in 2012

13 members

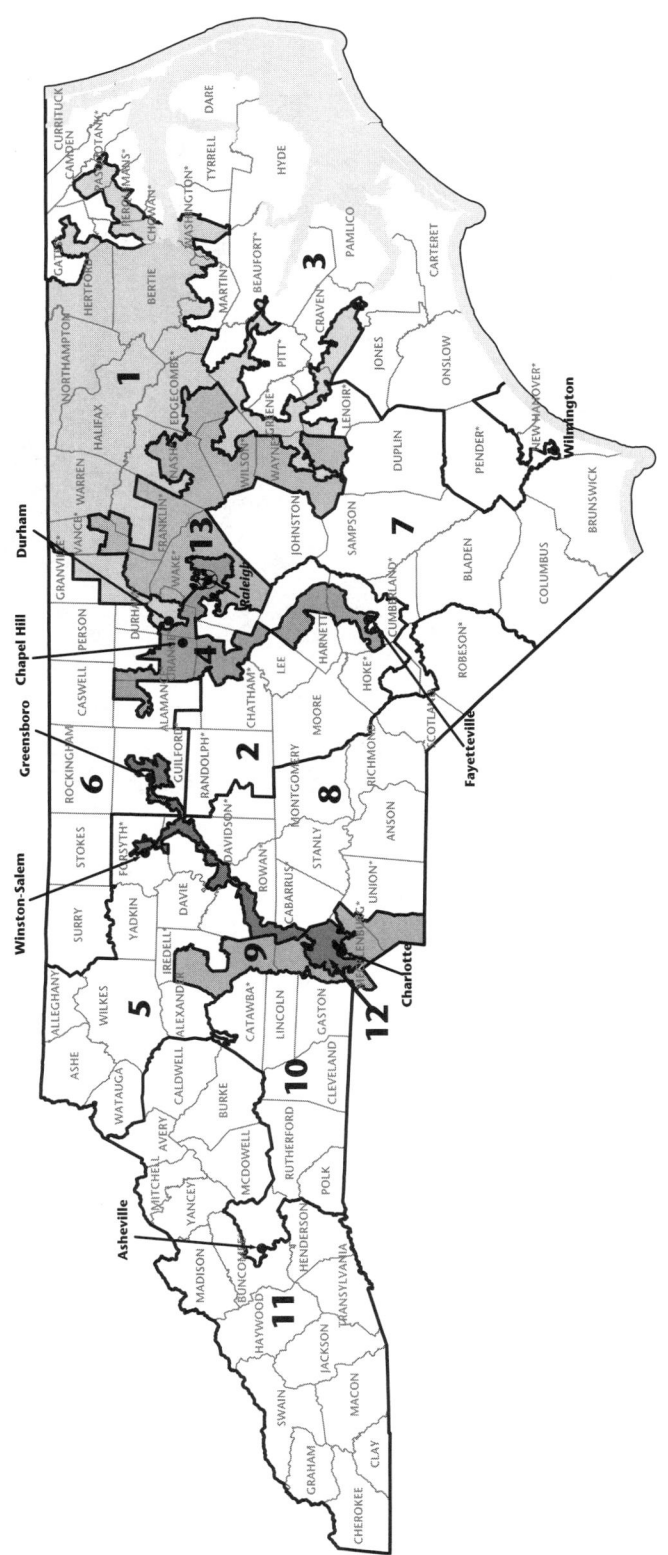

* Asterisk indicates a county whose boundaries include parts of two or more congressional districts.

NORTH CAROLINA

Central North Carolina Area

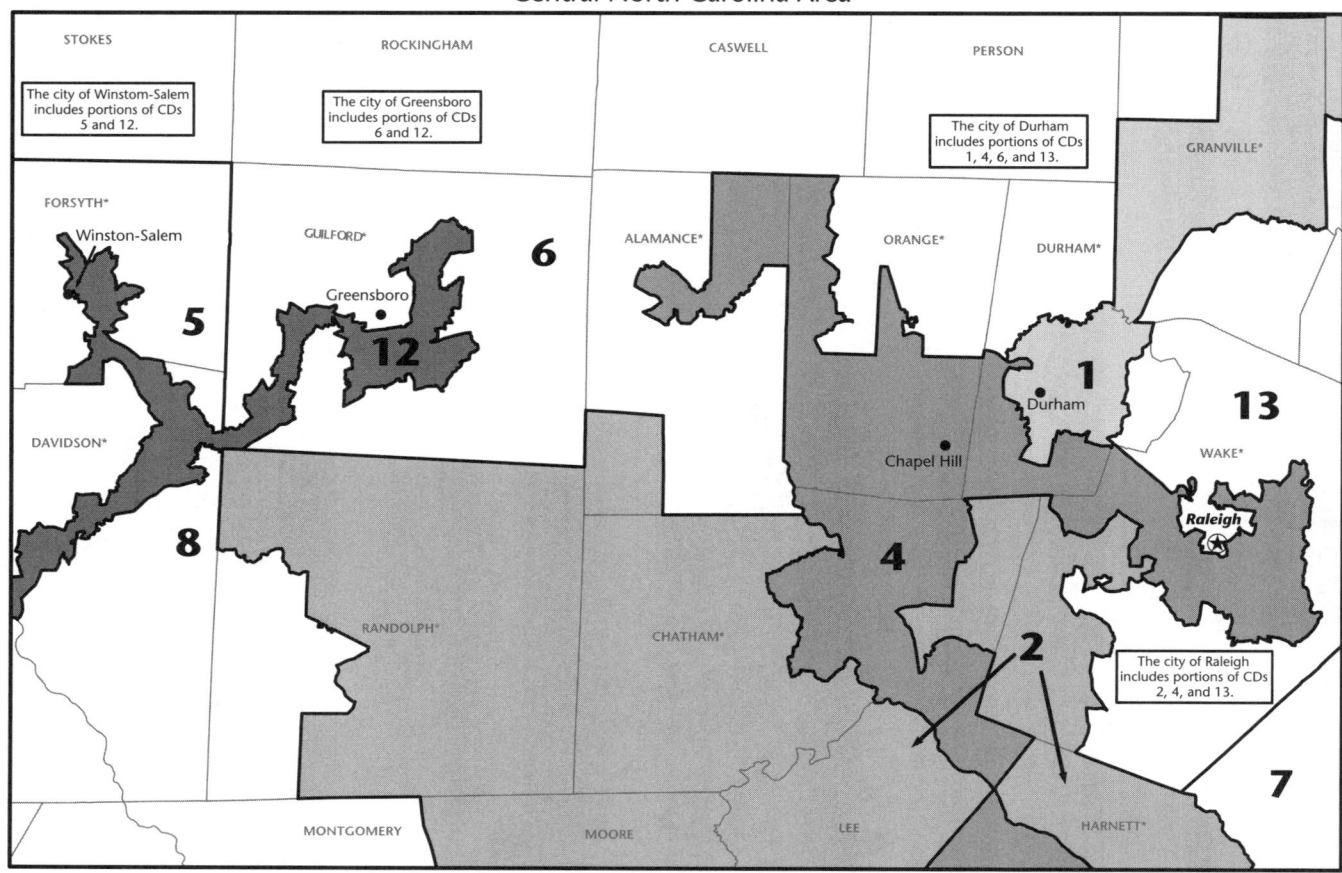

STOKES

The city of Winstom-Salem includes portions of CDs 5 and 12.

ROCKINGHAM

The city of Greensboro includes portions of CDs 6 and 12.

CASWELL

PERSON

The city of Durham includes portions of CDs 1, 4, 6, and 13.

GRANVILLE*

FORSYTH*

Winston-Salem

5

GUILFORD*

Greensboro

12

6

ALAMANCE*

ORANGE*

DURHAM*

1

Durham

13

WAKE*

DAVIDSON*

8

Chapel Hill

4

Raleigh

RANDOLPH*

CHATHAM*

2

The city of Raleigh includes portions of CDs 2, 4, and 13.

MONTGOMERY

MOORE

LEE

HARNETT*

7

* Asterisk indicates a county whose boundaries include parts of two or more congressional districts.

NORTH CAROLINA

GOVERNOR
Pat McCrory (R). Elected 2012 to a four-year term.

SENATORS (2 Republicans)
Richard Burr (R). Re-elected 2010 to a six-year term. Previously elected 2004.

Thom Tills (R). Elected 2014 to a six-year term.

REPRESENTATIVES (10 Republicans, 3 Democrats)
1. G. K. Butterfield (D)
2. Renee L. Ellmers (R)
3. Walter B. Jones Jr. (R)
4. David E. Price (D)
5. Virginia Foxx (R)
6. Mark Walker (R)
7. David Rouzer (R)
8. Richard Hudson (R)
9. Robert Pittenger (R)
10. Patrick T. McHenry (R)
11. Mark Meadows (R)
12. Alma S. Adams (D)
13. George Holding (R)

POSTWAR VOTE FOR PRESIDENT

| Year | Total Vote | Republican | | Democratic | | Other Vote | Rep.-Dem. Plurality | Percentage | | | |
| | | | | | | | | Total Vote | | Major Vote | |
		Vote	Candidate	Vote	Candidate			Rep.	Dem.	Rep.	Dem.
2012	4,505,372	2,270,395	Romney, W. Mitt	2,178,391	Obama, Barack H.*	56,586	92,004 R	50.4%	48.4%	51.0%	49.0%
2008	4,310,789	2,128,474	McCain, John S. III	2,142,651	Obama, Barack H.	39,664	14,177 D	49.4%	49.7%	49.8%	50.2%
2004	3,501,007	1,961,166	Bush, George W.*	1,525,849	Kerry, John F.	13,992	435,317 R	56.0%	43.6%	56.2%	43.8%
2000	2,911,262	1,631,163	Bush, George W.	1,257,692	Gore, Albert Jr.	22,407	373,471 R	56.0%	43.2%	56.5%	43.5%
1996**	2,515,807	1,225,938	Dole, Robert "Bob"	1,107,849	Clinton, Bill*	182,020	118,089 R	48.7%	44.0%	52.5%	47.5%
1992**	2,611,850	1,134,661	Bush, George H.*	1,114,042	Clinton, Bill	363,147	20,619 R	43.4%	42.7%	50.5%	49.5%
1988	2,134,370	1,237,258	Bush, George H.	890,167	Dukakis, Michael S.	6,945	347,091 R	58.0%	41.7%	58.2%	41.8%
1984	2,175,361	1,346,481	Reagan, Ronald*	824,287	Mondale, Walter F.	4,593	522,194 R	61.9%	37.9%	62.0%	38.0%
1980**	1,855,833	915,018	Reagan, Ronald	875,635	Carter, Jimmy*	65,180	39,383 R	49.3%	47.2%	51.1%	48.9%
1976	1,677,914	741,960	Ford, Gerald R.*	926,365	Carter, Jimmy	9,589	184,405 D	44.2%	55.2%	44.5%	55.5%
1972	1,518,612	1,054,889	Nixon, Richard M.*	438,705	McGovern, George S.	25,018	616,184 R	69.5%	28.9%	70.6%	29.4%
1968**	1,587,493	627,192	Nixon, Richard M.	464,113	Humphrey, Hubert Horatio Jr.	496,188	163,079 R	39.5%	29.2%	57.5%	42.5%
1964	1,424,983	624,844	Goldwater, Barry M. Sr.	800,139	Johnson, Lyndon B.*		175,295 D	43.8%	56.2%	43.8%	56.2%
1960	1,368,556	655,420	Nixon, Richard M.	713,136	Kennedy, John F.		57,716 D	47.9%	52.1%	47.9%	52.1%
1956	1,165,592	575,062	Eisenhower, Dwight D.*	590,530	Stevenson, Adlai E. II		15,468 D	49.3%	50.7%	49.3%	50.7%
1952	1,210,910	558,107	Eisenhower, Dwight D.	652,803	Stevenson, Adlai E. II		94,696 D	46.1%	53.9%	46.1%	53.9%
1948**	791,209	258,572	Dewey, Thomas E.	459,070	Truman, Harry S.*	73,567	200,498 D	32.7%	58.0%	36.0%	64.0%

Note: An asterisk (*) denotes incumbent. **In past elections, the other vote included: 1996 - 168,059 Reform (Ross Perot); 1992 - 357,864 Independent (Perot); 1980 - 52,800 Independent (John Anderson); 1968 - 496,188 American Independent (George Wallace), who finished second; 1948 - 69,652 States' Rights (Strom Thurmond).

NORTH CAROLINA

POSTWAR VOTE FOR GOVERNOR

Year	Total Vote	Republican Vote	Republican Candidate	Democratic Vote	Democratic Candidate	Other Vote	Rep.-Dem. Plurality	Total Vote Rep.	Total Vote Dem.	Major Vote Rep.	Major Vote Dem.
2012	4,468,295	2,440,707	McCrory, Pat	1,931,580	Dalton, Walter H.	96,008	509,127 R	54.6%	43.2%	55.8%	44.2%
2008	4,268,941	2,001,168	McCrory, Pat	2,146,189	Perdue, Bev	121,584	145,021 D	46.9%	50.3%	48.3%	51.7%
2004	3,486,688	1,495,021	Ballantine, Patrick J.	1,939,154	Easley, Mike*	52,513	444,133 D	42.9%	55.6%	43.5%	56.5%
2000	2,942,062	1,360,960	Vinroot, Richard	1,530,324	Easley, Mike	50,778	169,364 D	46.3%	52.0%	47.1%	52.9%
1996	2,566,185	1,097,053	Hayes, Robert "Robin"	1,436,638	Hunt, James B. Jr.*	32,494	339,585 D	42.8%	56.0%	43.3%	56.7%
1992	2,595,184	1,121,955	Gardner, James C.	1,368,246	Hunt, James B. Jr.	104,983	246,291 D	43.2%	52.7%	45.1%	54.9%
1988	2,180,205	1,222,338	Martin, James G.*	957,867	Jordan, Robert B.		264,471 R	56.1%	43.9%	56.1%	43.9%
1984	2,226,727	1,208,167	Martin, James G.	1,011,209	Edmisten, Rufus	7,351	196,958 R	54.3%	45.4%	54.4%	45.6%
1980	1,847,432	691,449	Lake, Beverly	1,143,145	Hunt, James B. Jr.*	12,838	451,696 D	37.4%	61.9%	37.7%	62.3%
1976	1,663,814	564,092	Flaherty, David T.	1,081,293	Hunt, James B. Jr.	18,429	517,201 D	33.9%	65.0%	34.3%	65.7%
1972	1,504,785	767,470	Holshouser, James E. Jr.	729,104	Bowles, Hargrove Skipper Jr.	8,211	38,366 R	51.0%	48.5%	51.3%	48.7%
1968	1,558,308	737,075	Gardner, James C.	821,233	Scott, Robert W.		84,158 D	47.3%	52.7%	47.3%	52.7%
1964	1,396,508	606,165	Gavin, Robert L.	790,343	Moore, Dan K.		184,178 D	43.4%	56.6%	43.4%	56.6%
1960	1,350,360	613,975	Gavin, Robert L.	735,248	Sanford, Terry	1,137	121,273 D	45.5%	54.4%	45.5%	54.5%
1956	1,135,859	375,379	Hayes, Kyle	760,480	Hodges, Luther H.		385,101 D	33.0%	67.0%	33.0%	67.0%
1952	1,179,635	383,329	Seawell, Herbert F. Jr.	796,306	Umstead, William B.		412,977 D	32.5%	67.5%	32.5%	67.5%
1948	780,525	206,166	Pritchard, George M.	570,995	Scott, W. Kerr	3,364	364,829 D	26.4%	73.2%	26.5%	73.5%

Note: An asterisk (*) denotes incumbent.

POSTWAR VOTE FOR SENATOR

Year	Total Vote	Republican Vote	Republican Candidate	Democratic Vote	Democratic Candidate	Other Vote	Rep.-Dem. Plurality	Total Vote Rep.	Total Vote Dem.	Major Vote Rep.	Major Vote Dem.
2014	2,915,281	1,423,259	Tillis, Thom	1,377,651	Hagan, Kay*	114,371	45,608 R	48.8%	47.3%	50.8%	49.2%
2010	2,660,079	1,458,046	Burr, Richard*	1,145,074	Marshall, Elaine	56,959	312,972 R	54.8%	43.0%	56.0%	44.0%
2008	4,271,970	1,887,510	Dole, Elizabeth*	2,249,311	Hagan, Kay	135,149	361,801 D	44.2%	52.7%	45.6%	54.4%
2004	3,472,082	1,791,450	Burr, Richard	1,632,527	Bowles, Erskine B.	48,105	158,923 R	51.6%	47.0%	52.3%	47.7%
2002	2,331,181	1,248,664	Dole, Elizabeth	1,047,983	Bowles, Erskine B.	34,534	200,681 R	53.6%	45.0%	54.4%	45.6%
1998	2,012,143	945,943	Faircloth, Lauch*	1,029,237	Edwards, John	36,963	83,294 D	47.0%	51.2%	47.9%	52.1%
1996	2,556,456	1,345,833	Helms, Jesse*	1,173,875	Gantt, Harvey B.	36,748	171,958 R	52.6%	45.9%	53.4%	46.6%
1992	2,577,891	1,297,892	Faircloth, Lauch	1,194,015	Sanford, Terry*	85,984	103,877 R	50.3%	46.3%	52.1%	47.9%
1990	2,069,585	1,087,331	Helms, Jesse*	981,573	Gantt, Harvey B.	681	105,758 R	52.5%	47.4%	52.6%	47.4%
1986	1,591,330	767,668	Broyhill, James Thomas*	823,662	Sanford, Terry		55,994 D	48.2%	51.8%	48.2%	51.8%
1984	2,239,051	1,156,768	Helms, Jesse*	1,070,488	Hunt, James B. Jr.	11,795	86,280 R	51.7%	47.8%	51.9%	48.1%
1980	1,797,665	898,064	East, John P.	887,653	Morgan, Robert*	11,948	10,411 R	50.0%	49.4%	50.3%	49.7%
1978	1,135,814	619,151	Helms, Jesse*	516,663	Ingram, John		102,488 R	54.5%	45.5%	54.5%	45.5%
1974	1,020,367	377,618	Stevens, William E.	633,775	Morgan, Robert	8,974	256,157 D	37.0%	62.1%	37.3%	62.7%
1972	1,472,541	795,248	Helms, Jesse	677,293	Galifianakis, Nick		117,955 R	54.0%	46.0%	54.0%	46.0%
1968	1,437,340	566,934	Somers, Robert V.	870,406	Ervin, Sam James Jr.*		303,472 D	39.4%	60.6%	39.4%	60.6%
1966	901,978	400,502	Shallcross, John S.	501,440	Jordan, B. Everett*	36	100,938 D	44.4%	55.6%	44.4%	55.6%
1962	813,155	321,635	Greene, Claude L. Jr.	491,520	Ervin, Sam James Jr.*		169,885 D	39.6%	60.4%	39.6%	60.4%
1960	1,291,485	497,964	Hayes, Kyle	793,521	Jordan, B. Everett*		295,557 D	38.6%	61.4%	38.6%	61.4%
1958S	616,469	184,977	Clarke, Richard C. Jr.	431,492	Jordan, B. Everett*		246,515 D	30.0%	70.0%	30.0%	70.0%
1956	1,098,828	367,475	Johnson, Joel A.	731,353	Ervin, Sam James Jr.*		363,878 D	33.4%	66.6%	33.4%	66.6%
1954	619,634	211,322	West, Paul C.	408,312	Scott, W. Kerr		196,990 D	34.1%	65.9%	34.1%	65.9%
1954S	410,574			410,574	Ervin, Sam James Jr.*				100.0%		100.0%
1950	548,277	171,804	Leavitt, Halsey B.	376,473	Hoey, Clyde R.*		204,669 D	31.3%	68.7%	31.3%	68.7%
1950S	544,924	177,753	Gavin, E. L.	364,912	Smith, Willis	2,259	187,159 D	32.6%	67.0%	32.8%	67.2%
1948	764,559	220,307	Wilkinson, John A.	540,762	Broughton, J. Melville*	3,490	320,455 D	28.8%	70.7%	28.9%	71.1%

Note: An asterisk (*) denotes incumbent. **One each of the 1950 and 1954 elections as well as the 1958 election were for short terms to fill vacancies. The Republican Party did not run a Senate candidate in the 1954 election for the short term.

NORTH CAROLINA

SENATOR 2014

2010 Census Population	County	Total Vote	Republican (Tillis)	Democratic (Hagan)	Other	Rep.-Dem. Plurality	Percentage			
							Total Vote		Major Vote	
							Rep.	Dem.	Rep.	Dem.
151,131	ALAMANCE	44,328	24,380	18,145	1,803	6,235 R	55.0%	40.9%	57.3%	42.7%
37,198	ALEXANDER	11,899	7,925	3,088	886	4,837 R	66.6%	26.0%	72.0%	28.0%
11,155	ALLEGHANY	4,191	2,496	1,356	339	1,140 R	59.6%	32.4%	64.8%	35.2%
26,948	ANSON	6,761	2,374	4,149	238	1,775 D	35.1%	61.4%	36.4%	63.6%
27,281	ASHE	9,506	5,658	3,225	623	2,433 R	59.5%	33.9%	63.7%	36.3%
17,797	AVERY	5,088	3,718	1,133	237	2,585 R	73.1%	22.3%	76.6%	23.4%
47,759	BEAUFORT	17,774	9,737	7,071	966	2,666 R	54.8%	39.8%	57.9%	42.1%
21,282	BERTIE	6,433	2,218	4,050	165	1,832 D	34.5%	63.0%	35.4%	64.6%
35,190	BLADEN	11,347	5,041	5,639	667	598 D	44.4%	49.7%	47.2%	52.8%
107,431	BRUNSWICK	40,843	22,882	15,739	2,222	7,143 R	56.0%	38.5%	59.2%	40.8%
238,318	BUNCOMBE	86,879	33,872	49,455	3,552	15,583 D	39.0%	56.9%	40.6%	59.4%
90,912	BURKE	24,631	14,203	8,837	1,591	5,366 R	57.7%	35.9%	61.6%	38.4%
178,011	CABARRUS	51,804	29,366	20,070	2,368	9,296 R	56.7%	38.7%	59.4%	40.6%
83,029	CALDWELL	21,026	13,309	6,258	1,459	7,051 R	63.3%	29.8%	68.0%	32.0%
9,980	CAMDEN	3,214	1,960	1,144	110	816 R	61.0%	35.6%	63.1%	36.9%
66,469	CARTERET	25,152	16,507	7,500	1,145	9,007 R	65.6%	29.8%	68.8%	31.2%
23,719	CASWELL	7,147	3,485	3,441	221	44 R	48.8%	48.1%	50.3%	49.7%
154,358	CATAWBA	44,076	27,445	14,295	2,336	13,150 R	62.3%	32.4%	65.8%	34.2%
63,505	CHATHAM	27,765	11,921	14,994	850	3,073 D	42.9%	54.0%	44.3%	55.7%
27,444	CHEROKEE	9,475	6,374	2,713	388	3,661 R	67.3%	28.6%	70.1%	29.9%
14,793	CHOWAN	5,220	2,821	2,264	135	557 R	54.0%	43.4%	55.5%	44.5%
10,587	CLAY	4,501	3,011	1,320	170	1,691 R	66.9%	29.3%	69.5%	30.5%
98,078	CLEVELAND	27,896	15,534	10,977	1,385	4,557 R	55.7%	39.3%	58.6%	41.4%
58,098	COLUMBUS	14,941	7,050	6,899	992	151 R	47.2%	46.2%	50.5%	49.5%
103,505	CRAVEN	30,736	17,583	11,967	1,186	5,616 R	57.2%	38.9%	59.5%	40.5%
319,431	CUMBERLAND	76,075	30,902	42,620	2,553	11,718 D	40.6%	56.0%	42.0%	58.0%
23,547	CURRITUCK	7,581	5,066	2,250	265	2,816 R	66.8%	29.7%	69.2%	30.8%
33,920	DARE	12,878	7,262	5,208	408	2,054 R	56.4%	40.4%	58.2%	41.8%
162,878	DAVIDSON	43,012	29,274	11,862	1,876	17,412 R	68.1%	27.6%	71.2%	28.8%
41,240	DAVIE	13,883	9,521	3,745	617	5,776 R	68.6%	27.0%	71.8%	28.2%
58,505	DUPLIN	12,786	6,844	5,464	478	1,380 R	53.5%	42.7%	55.6%	44.4%
267,587	DURHAM	93,333	19,828	71,508	1,997	51,680 D	21.2%	76.6%	21.7%	78.3%
56,552	EDGECOMBE	17,012	5,157	11,436	419	6,279 D	30.3%	67.2%	31.1%	68.9%
350,670	FORSYTH	108,807	49,559	56,008	3,240	6,449 D	45.5%	51.5%	46.9%	53.1%
60,619	FRANKLIN	19,862	9,765	9,131	966	634 R	49.2%	46.0%	51.7%	48.3%
206,086	GASTON	54,782	33,167	19,060	2,555	14,107 R	60.5%	34.8%	63.5%	36.5%
12,197	GATES	3,355	1,628	1,644	83	16 D	48.5%	49.0%	49.8%	50.2%
8,861	GRAHAM	3,328	2,046	997	285	1,049 R	61.5%	30.0%	67.2%	32.8%
59,916	GRANVILLE	16,454	7,366	8,504	584	1,138 D	44.8%	51.7%	46.4%	53.6%
21,362	GREENE	5,817	2,911	2,680	226	231 R	50.0%	46.1%	52.1%	47.9%
488,406	GUILFORD	164,172	68,805	91,228	4,139	22,423 D	41.9%	55.6%	43.0%	57.0%
54,691	HALIFAX	17,482	6,107	10,865	510	4,758 D	34.9%	62.1%	36.0%	64.0%
114,678	HARNETT	27,133	15,419	10,565	1,149	4,854 R	56.8%	38.9%	59.3%	40.7%
59,036	HAYWOOD	18,896	9,791	8,088	1,017	1,703 R	51.8%	42.8%	54.8%	45.2%
106,740	HENDERSON	36,345	21,749	13,180	1,416	8,569 R	59.8%	36.3%	62.3%	37.7%
24,669	HERTFORD	6,372	1,864	4,393	115	2,529 D	29.3%	68.9%	29.8%	70.2%
46,952	HOKE	10,382	4,015	5,970	397	1,955 D	38.7%	57.5%	40.2%	59.8%
5,810	HYDE	1,784	795	890	99	95 D	44.6%	49.9%	47.2%	52.8%
159,437	IREDELL	50,510	31,252	16,300	2,958	14,952 R	61.9%	32.3%	65.7%	34.3%
40,271	JACKSON	10,874	5,072	5,225	577	153 D	46.6%	48.1%	49.3%	50.7%
168,878	JOHNSTON	49,908	30,520	17,235	2,153	13,285 R	61.2%	34.5%	63.9%	36.1%
10,153	JONES	3,964	2,028	1,733	203	295 R	51.2%	43.7%	53.9%	46.1%
57,866	LEE	15,694	7,959	6,966	769	993 R	50.7%	44.4%	53.3%	46.7%
59,495	LENOIR	18,522	8,802	9,086	634	284 D	47.5%	49.1%	49.2%	50.8%
78,265	LINCOLN	23,848	15,860	6,690	1,298	9,170 R	66.5%	28.1%	70.3%	29.7%
33,922	MACON	11,793	6,781	4,341	671	2,440 R	57.5%	36.8%	61.0%	39.0%
20,764	MADISON	7,654	3,668	3,504	482	164 R	47.9%	45.8%	51.1%	48.9%
24,505	MARTIN	8,298	3,676	4,302	320	626 D	44.3%	51.8%	46.1%	53.9%
44,996	MCDOWELL	11,048	6,920	3,402	726	3,518 R	62.6%	30.8%	67.0%	33.0%
919,628	MECKLENBURG	265,275	100,975	156,946	7,354	55,971 D	38.1%	59.2%	39.1%	60.9%

NORTH CAROLINA

SENATOR 2014

2010 Census Population	County	Total Vote	Republican (Tillis)	Democratic (Hagan)	Other	Rep.-Dem. Plurality	Percentage Total Vote Rep.	Dem.	Major Vote Rep.	Dem.
15,579	MITCHELL	5,212	3,715	1,268	229	2,447 R	71.3%	24.3%	74.6%	25.4%
27,798	MONTGOMERY	8,080	4,304	3,320	456	984 R	53.3%	41.1%	56.5%	43.5%
88,247	MOORE	32,898	20,473	11,333	1,092	9,140 R	62.2%	34.4%	64.4%	35.6%
95,840	NASH	34,210	16,869	16,325	1,016	544 R	49.3%	47.7%	50.8%	49.2%
202,667	NEW HANOVER	66,385	31,519	31,441	3,425	78 R	47.5%	47.4%	50.1%	49.9%
22,099	NORTHAMPTON	6,626	2,108	4,365	153	2,257 D	31.8%	65.9%	32.6%	67.4%
177,772	ONSLOW	31,493	19,830	10,126	1,537	9,704 R	63.0%	32.2%	66.2%	33.8%
133,801	ORANGE	52,826	12,779	38,705	1,342	25,926 D	24.2%	73.3%	24.8%	75.2%
13,144	PAMLICO	5,419	3,012	2,195	212	817 R	55.6%	40.5%	57.8%	42.2%
40,661	PASQUOTANK	10,184	4,498	5,487	199	989 D	44.2%	53.9%	45.0%	55.0%
52,217	PENDER	16,380	9,093	6,303	984	2,790 R	55.5%	38.5%	59.1%	40.9%
13,453	PERQUIMANS	4,109	2,500	1,532	77	968 R	60.8%	37.3%	62.0%	38.0%
39,464	PERSON	12,678	6,666	5,452	560	1,214 R	52.6%	43.0%	55.0%	45.0%
168,148	PITT	45,405	21,202	22,734	1,469	1,532 D	46.7%	50.1%	48.3%	51.7%
20,510	POLK	7,522	4,155	3,079	288	1,076 R	55.2%	40.9%	57.4%	42.6%
141,752	RANDOLPH	36,765	26,899	8,198	1,668	18,701 R	73.2%	22.3%	76.6%	23.4%
46,639	RICHMOND	12,929	5,668	6,515	746	847 D	43.8%	50.4%	46.5%	53.5%
134,168	ROBESON	24,731	10,751	13,086	894	2,335 D	43.5%	52.9%	45.1%	54.9%
93,643	ROCKINGHAM	28,113	15,990	10,555	1,568	5,435 R	56.9%	37.5%	60.2%	39.8%
138,428	ROWAN	39,047	23,230	13,532	2,285	9,698 R	59.5%	34.7%	63.2%	36.8%
67,810	RUTHERFORD	19,453	11,719	6,624	1,110	5,095 R	60.2%	34.1%	63.9%	36.1%
63,431	SAMPSON	17,376	9,278	7,409	689	1,869 R	53.4%	42.6%	55.6%	44.4%
36,157	SCOTLAND	10,112	4,153	5,629	330	1,476 D	41.1%	55.7%	42.5%	57.5%
60,585	STANLY	19,235	12,497	5,431	1,307	7,066 R	65.0%	28.2%	69.7%	30.3%
47,401	STOKES	14,200	9,503	3,752	945	5,751 R	66.9%	26.4%	71.7%	28.3%
73,673	SURRY	19,276	12,291	5,905	1,080	6,386 R	63.8%	30.6%	67.5%	32.5%
13,981	SWAIN	4,370	2,045	1,964	361	81 R	46.8%	44.9%	51.0%	49.0%
33,090	TRANSYLVANIA	13,108	6,945	5,479	684	1,466 R	53.0%	41.8%	55.9%	44.1%
4,407	TYRRELL	1,231	591	569	71	22 R	48.0%	46.2%	50.9%	49.1%
201,292	UNION	58,897	37,601	19,057	2,239	18,544 R	63.8%	32.4%	66.4%	33.6%
45,422	VANCE	13,996	5,031	8,525	440	3,494 D	35.9%	60.9%	37.1%	62.9%
900,993	WAKE	326,426	136,236	180,033	10,157	43,797 D	41.7%	55.2%	43.1%	56.9%
20,972	WARREN	6,642	2,033	4,441	168	2,408 D	30.6%	66.9%	31.4%	68.6%
13,228	WASHINGTON	4,605	1,768	2,649	188	881 D	38.4%	57.5%	40.0%	60.0%
51,079	WATAUGA	16,968	8,232	7,831	905	401 R	48.5%	46.2%	51.2%	48.8%
122,623	WAYNE	32,958	17,865	14,009	1,084	3,856 R	54.2%	42.5%	56.0%	44.0%
69,340	WILKES	18,576	12,564	4,897	1,115	7,667 R	67.6%	26.4%	72.0%	28.0%
81,234	WILSON	25,756	11,750	13,325	681	1,575 D	45.6%	51.7%	46.9%	53.1%
38,406	YADKIN	11,301	8,329	2,357	615	5,972 R	73.7%	20.9%	77.9%	22.1%
17,818	YANCEY	8,231	4,343	3,459	429	884 R	52.8%	42.0%	55.7%	44.3%
9,535,483	TOTAL	2,915,281	1,423,259	1,377,651	114,371	45,608 R	48.8%	47.3%	50.8%	49.2%

NORTH CAROLINA

HOUSE OF REPRESENTATIVES

CD	Year	Total Vote	Republican Vote	Candidate	Democratic Vote	Candidate	Other Vote	Rep.-Dem. Plurality	Percentage Total Vote Rep.	Dem.	Major Vote Rep.	Dem.
1	2014	210,323	55,990	RICH, ARTHUR	154,333	BUTTERFIELD, G. K.*		98,343 D	26.6%	73.4%	26.6%	73.4%
1	2012	338,066	77,288	DILAURO, PETE	254,644	BUTTERFIELD, G. K.*	6,134	177,356 D	22.9%	75.3%	23.3%	76.7%
2	2014	207,607	122,128	ELLMERS, RENEE L.*	85,479	AIKEN, CLAY		36,649 R	58.8%	41.2%	58.8%	41.2%
2	2012	311,397	174,066	ELLMERS, RENEE L.*	128,973	WILKINS, STEVE	8,358	45,093 R	55.9%	41.4%	57.4%	42.6%

NORTH CAROLINA
HOUSE OF REPRESENTATIVES

CD	Year	Total Vote	Republican Vote	Republican Candidate	Democratic Vote	Democratic Candidate	Other Vote	Rep.-Dem. Plurality	Total Vote Rep.	Total Vote Dem.	Major Vote Rep.	Major Vote Dem.
3	2014	205,597	139,415	JONES, WALTER B. JR.*	66,182	ADAME, MARSHALL		73,233 R	67.8%	32.2%	67.8%	32.2%
3	2012	309,885	195,571	JONES, WALTER B. JR.*	114,314	ANDERSON, ERIK		81,257 R	63.1%	36.9%	63.1%	36.9%
4	2014	227,362	57,416	WRIGHT, PAUL	169,946	PRICE, DAVID E.*		112,530 D	25.3%	74.7%	25.3%	74.7%
4	2012	348,485	88,951	D'ANNUNZIO, TIM	259,534	PRICE, DAVID E.*		170,583 D	25.5%	74.5%	25.5%	74.5%
5	2014	228,252	139,279	FOXX, VIRGINIA*	88,973	BRANNON, JOSHUA "JOSH"		50,306 R	61.0%	39.0%	61.0%	39.0%
5	2012	349,197	200,945	FOXX, VIRGINIA*	148,252	MOTSINGER, ELISABETH		52,693 R	57.5%	42.5%	57.5%	42.5%
6	2014	251,070	147,312	WALKER, MARK	103,758	FJELD, LAURA		43,554 R	58.7%	41.3%	58.7%	41.3%
6	2012	364,583	222,116	COBLE, HOWARD*	142,467	FORIEST, TONY		79,649 R	60.9%	39.1%	60.9%	39.1%
7	2014	226,504	134,431	ROUZER, DAVID	84,054	BARFIELD JR., JONATHAN	8,019	50,377 R	59.4%	37.1%	61.5%	38.5%
7	2012	336,736	168,041	ROUZER, DAVID	168,695	MCINTYRE, MIKE*		654 D	49.9%	50.1%	49.9%	50.1%
8	2014	187,422	121,568	HUDSON, RICHARD*	65,854	BLUE, ANTONIO		55,714 R	64.9%	35.1%	64.9%	35.1%
8	2012	302,280	160,695	HUDSON, RICHARD	137,139	KISSELL, LARRY*	4,446	23,556 R	53.2%	45.4%	54.0%	46.0%
9	2014	173,668	163,080	PITTENGER, ROBERT*			10,588	163,080 R	93.9%		100.0%	
9	2012	375,690	194,537	PITTENGER, ROBERT	171,503	ROBERTS, JENNIFER	9,650	23,034 R	51.8%	45.7%	53.1%	46.9%
10	2014	218,796	133,504	MCHENRY, PATRICK T.*	85,292	MACQUEEN IV, TATE		48,212 R	61.0%	39.0%	61.0%	39.0%
10	2012	334,849	190,826	MCHENRY, PATRICK T.*	144,023	KEEVER, PATRICIA R. "PATSY"		46,803 R	57.0%	43.0%	57.0%	43.0%
11	2014	230,024	144,682	MEADOWS, MARK*	85,342	HILL, THOMAS		59,340 R	62.9%	37.1%	62.9%	37.1%
11	2012	331,426	190,319	MEADOWS, MARK	141,107	ROGERS, HAYDEN		49,212 R	57.4%	42.6%	57.4%	42.6%
12	2014	172,664	42,568	COAKLEY, VINCE	130,096	ADAMS, ALMA S.		87,528 D	24.7%	75.3%	24.7%	75.3%
12	2012	310,908	63,317	BROSCH, JACK	247,591	WATT, MELVIN*		184,274 D	20.4%	79.6%	20.4%	79.6%
13	2014	268,709	153,991	HOLDING, GEORGE*	114,718	CLEARY, BRENDA		39,273 R	57.3%	42.7%	57.3%	42.7%
13	2012	370,610	210,495	HOLDING, GEORGE	160,115	MALONE, CHARLES		50,380 R	56.8%	43.2%	56.8%	43.2%
TOTAL	2014	2,807,998	1,555,364		1,234,027		18,607	321,337 R	55.4%	43.9%	55.8%	44.2%
TOTAL	2012	4,384,112	2,137,167		2,218,357		28,588	81,190 D	48.7%	50.6%	49.1%	50.9%

Note: An asterisk (*) denotes incumbent.

NORTH CAROLINA
GENERAL AND PRIMARY ELECTIONS

2014 GENERAL ELECTIONS: OTHER VOTES

Senate Other vote was 109,100 Libertarian (Sean Haugh), 4,307 Scattered Write-in, 621 Write-in (John Rhodes), 201 Write-in (David Waddell), 142 Write-in (Barry Gurney)

House Other vote was:

CD 7 7,850 Libertarian (J. Wesley Casteen), 169 Write-in (Miscellaneous)
CD 9 8,219 Scattered Write-in, 2,369 Write-in (Shawn Eckles)

2014 PRIMARY ELECTIONS: SUPPLEMENTARY INFORMATION

Primary	May 6, 2014	**Registration**	6,516,126	Democratic	2,754,823
Primary Runoff	July 15, 2014	(as of May 6, 2014)		Republican	1,995,779
				Libertarian	23,541
				Unaffiliated	1,741,983

Primary Type Semi-open—Registered Democrats and Republicans could vote only in their party's primary. Unaffiliated voters could participate in the primary of any recognized party. However, if a voter cast a ballot in one party's primary, he or she could not participate in the runoff of another party.

NORTH CAROLINA

GENERAL AND PRIMARY ELECTIONS

	REPUBLICAN PRIMARIES			DEMOCRATIC PRIMARIES		
Senator	Tillis, Thom	223,174	45.7%	Hagan, Kay*	372,209	77.2%
	Brannon, Greg	132,630	27.1%	Stewart, Will	66,903	13.9%
	Harris, Mark	85,727	17.5%	Reeves, Ernest Tyrone	43,257	9.0%
	Grant, Heather	22,971	4.7%			
	Snyder, Jim	9,414	1.9%			
	Alexander, Ted	9,258	1.9%			
	Bradshaw, Alex Lee	3,528	0.7%			
	Kryn, Edward	1,853	0.4%			
	TOTAL	488,555		TOTAL	482,369	
Congressional District 1	Rich, Arthur	5,519	51.3%	Butterfield, G. K.*	60,847	81.1%
	Shypulefski, John Brent "Brent"	5,232	48.7%	Whittacre, Dan	14,147	18.9%
	TOTAL	10,751		TOTAL	74,994	
Congressional District 2	Ellmers, Renee L.*	21,412	58.7%	Aiken, Clay	11,678	40.9%
	Roche, Frank	15,045	41.3%	Crisco Sr., Keith	11,288	39.5%
				Morris, Toni	5,616	19.6%
	TOTAL	36,457		TOTAL	28,582	
Congressional District 3	Jones, Walter B. Jr.*	22,616	50.9%	Adame, Marshall	Unopposed	
	Griffin, Taylor	20,024	45.1%			
	Novinec, Al "Big Al"	1,798	4.0%			
	TOTAL	44,438				
Congressional District 4	Wright, Paul	Unopposed		Price, David E.*	Unopposed	
Congressional District 5	Foxx, Virginia*	49,572	75.4%	Brannon, Joshua "Josh"	8,010	33.1%
	Doyle, Philip	16,175	24.6%	Henley, Gardenia M.	6,417	26.5%
				Holleman, Michael W.	5,618	23.2%
				Stinson, William Clinton "Will"	4,189	17.3%
	TOTAL	65,747		TOTAL	24,234	
				PRIMARY RUNOFF		
				Brannon, Joshua "Josh"	2,748	65.6%
				Henley, Gardenia M.	1,443	34.4%
				TOTAL	4,191	
Congressional District 6	Berger Jr., Phil	15,127	34.3%	Fjeld, Laura	19,066	56.2%
	Walker, Mark	11,123	25.2%	Davis, Bruce	14,882	43.8%
	VonCannon, Bruce	5,055	11.5%			
	Matheny, Bryan Zachary "Zack"	5,043	11.4%			
	Phillips, Jeff	3,494	7.9%			
	Webb, Don	1,899	4.3%			
	Causey, John Michael "Mike"	1,427	3.2%			
	Kopf, Kenneth Albert "Kenn"	510	1.2%			
	Sutherland, Charlie	458	1.0%			
	TOTAL	44,136		TOTAL	33,948	
	PRIMARY RUNOFF					
	Walker, Mark	18,965	59.9%			
	Berger Jr., Phil	12,722	40.1%			
	TOTAL	31,687				
Congressional District 7	Rouzer, David	23,010	53.0%	Barfield Jr., Jonathan	21,966	58.3%
	White, Haywood "Woody"	17,389	40.1%	Martin Jr., Walter	15,741	41.7%
	Andrade, Chris	3,000	6.9%			
	TOTAL	43,399		TOTAL	37,707	
Congressional District 8	Hudson, Richard*	Unopposed		Blue, Antonio	Unopposed	
Congressional District 9	Pittenger, Robert*	29,505	67.6%			
	Steinberg, Mike	14,146	32.4%			
	TOTAL	43,651				

NORTH CAROLINA

GENERAL AND PRIMARY ELECTIONS

	REPUBLICAN PRIMARIES			DEMOCRATIC PRIMARIES		
Congressional District 10	McHenry, Patrick T.*	29,400	78.0%	MacQueen IV, Tate	Unopposed	
	Lynch, Richard	8,273	22.0%			
	TOTAL	37,673				
Congressional District 11	Meadows, Mark*	Unopposed		Hill, Thomas	16,819	54.1%
				Ruehl, Keith	14,272	45.9%
				TOTAL	31,091	
Congressional District 12	Coakley, Vince	8,652	78.0%	Adams, Alma S.	15,235	44.0%
	Threatt, Leon	2,439	22.0%	Graham, Malcolm	8,180	23.6%
				Battle, George	4,342	12.5%
				Brandon, Marcus	2,856	8.2%
				Mitchell, James "Smuggie"	1,775	5.1%
				Osborne, Curtis C.	1,733	5.0%
	TOTAL	11,091		Patel, Rajive	502	1.4%
				TOTAL	34,623	
Congressional District 13	Holding, George*	Unopposed		Cleary, Brenda	24,631	70.4%
				Conlon, Virginia	6,308	18.0%
				Sanyal, Arunava "Ron"	4,052	11.6%
				TOTAL	34,991	

Note: An asterisk (*) denotes incumbent.

NORTH DAKOTA

One member At Large

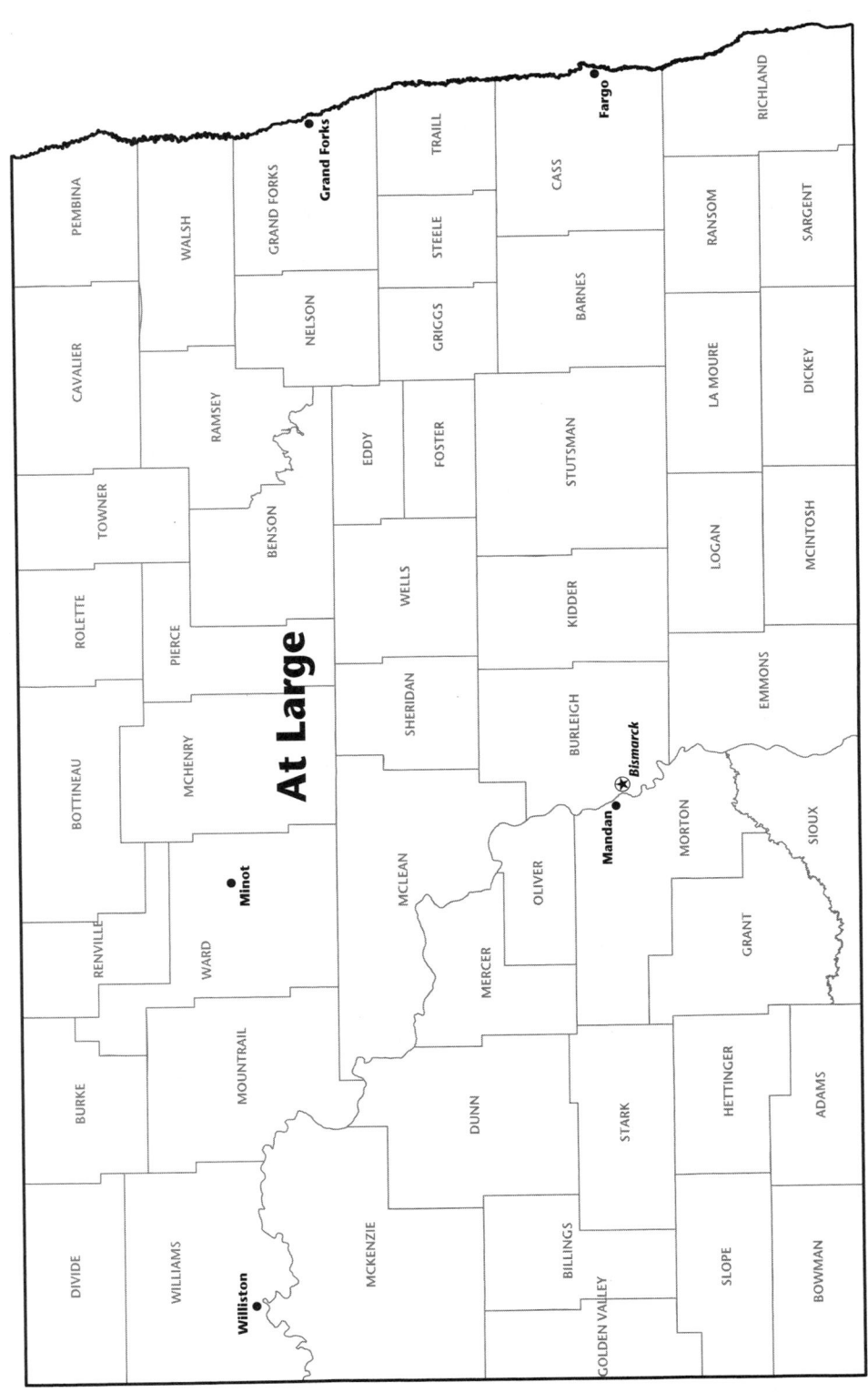

NORTH DAKOTA

GOVERNOR
Jack Dalrymple (R). Elected 2012 to a four-year term. Initially sworn in as governor December 7, 2010, to fill the vacancy created by the resignation of John Hoeven (R) following Hoeven's election to the Senate.

SENATORS (1 Republican, 1 Democrat)
Heidi Heitkamp (D). Elected 2012 to a six-year term.

John Hoeven (R). Elected 2010 to a six-year term.

REPRESENTATIVES (1 Republican)
At Large. Kevin Cramer (R)

POSTWAR VOTE FOR PRESIDENT

| | | Republican | | Democratic | | | | Percentage | | | |
| | | | | | | | | Total Vote | | Major Vote | |
Year	Total Vote	Vote	Candidate	Vote	Candidate	Other Vote	Rep.-Dem. Plurality	Rep.	Dem.	Rep.	Dem.
2012	322,627	188,163	Romney, W. Mitt	124,827	Obama, Barack H.*	9,637	63,336 R	58.3%	38.7%	60.1%	39.9%
2008	316,621	168,601	McCain, John S. III	141,278	Obama, Barack H.	6,742	27,323 R	53.3%	44.6%	54.4%	45.6%
2004	312,833	196,651	Bush, George W.*	111,052	Kerry, John F.	5,130	85,599 R	62.9%	35.5%	63.9%	36.1%
2000**	288,256	174,852	Bush, George W.	95,284	Gore, Albert Jr.	18,120	79,568 R	60.7%	33.1%	64.7%	35.3%
1996**	266,411	125,050	Dole, Robert "Bob"	106,905	Clinton, Bill*	34,456	18,145 R	46.9%	40.1%	53.9%	46.1%
1992**	308,133	136,244	Bush, George H.*	99,168	Clinton, Bill	72,721	37,076 R	44.2%	32.2%	57.9%	42.1%
1988	297,261	166,559	Bush, George H.	127,739	Dukakis, Michael S.	2,963	38,820 R	56.0%	43.0%	56.6%	43.4%
1984	308,971	200,336	Reagan, Ronald*	104,429	Mondale, Walter F.	4,206	95,907 R	64.8%	33.8%	65.7%	34.3%
1980**	301,545	193,695	Reagan, Ronald	79,189	Carter, Jimmy*	28,661	114,506 R	64.2%	26.3%	71.0%	29.0%
1976	297,188	153,470	Ford, Gerald R.*	136,078	Carter, Jimmy	7,640	17,392 R	51.6%	45.8%	53.0%	47.0%
1972	280,514	174,109	Nixon, Richard M.*	100,384	McGovern, George S.	6,021	73,725 R	62.1%	35.8%	63.4%	36.6%
1968**	247,882	138,669	Nixon, Richard M.	94,769	Humphrey, Hubert Horatio Jr.	14,444	43,900 R	55.9%	38.2%	59.4%	40.6%
1964	258,389	108,207	Goldwater, Barry M. Sr.	149,784	Johnson, Lyndon B.*	398	41,577 D	41.9%	58.0%	41.9%	58.1%
1960	278,431	154,310	Nixon, Richard M.	123,963	Kennedy, John F.	158	30,347 R	55.4%	44.5%	55.5%	44.5%
1956	253,991	156,766	Eisenhower, Dwight D.*	96,742	Stevenson, Adlai E. II	483	60,024 R	61.7%	38.1%	61.8%	38.2%
1952	270,127	191,712	Eisenhower, Dwight D.	76,694	Stevenson, Adlai E. II	1,721	115,018 R	71.0%	28.4%	71.4%	28.6%
1948	220,716	115,139	Dewey, Thomas E.	95,812	Truman, Harry S.*	9,765	19,327 R	52.2%	43.4%	54.6%	45.4%

Note: An asterisk (*) denotes incumbent. **In past elections, the other vote included: 2000 - 9,486 Green (Ralph Nader); 1996 - 32,515 Reform (Ross Perot); 1992 - 71,084 Independent (Perot); 1980 - 23,640 Independent (John Anderson); 1968 - 14,244 American Independent (George Wallace).

NORTH DAKOTA

POSTWAR VOTE FOR GOVERNOR

Year	Total Vote	Republican Vote	Republican Candidate	Democratic Vote	Democratic Candidate	Other Vote	Rep.-Dem. Plurality	Total Vote Rep.	Total Vote Dem.	Major Vote Rep.	Major Vote Dem.
2012	317,812	200,526	Dalrymple, Jack*	109,047	Taylor, Ryan M.	8,239	91,479 R	63.1%	34.3%	64.8%	35.2%
2008	315,692	235,009	Hoeven, John*	74,279	Mathern, Tim	6,404	160,730 R	74.4%	23.5%	76.0%	24.0%
2004	309,873	220,803	Hoeven, John*	84,877	Satrom, Joe	4,193	135,926 R	71.3%	27.4%	72.2%	27.8%
2000	289,412	159,255	Hoeven, John	130,144	Heitkamp, Heidi	13	29,111 R	55.0%	45.0%	55.0%	45.0%
1996	264,298	174,937	Schafer, Edward T.*	89,349	Kaldor, Lee	12	85,588 R	66.2%	33.8%	66.2%	33.8%
1992	304,861	176,398	Schafer, Edward T.	123,845	Spaeth, Nicholas	4,618	52,553 R	57.9%	40.6%	58.8%	41.2%
1988	299,080	119,986	Mallberg, Leon L.	179,094	Sinner, George A.*		59,108 D	40.1%	59.9%	40.1%	59.9%
1984	314,382	140,460	Olson, Allen I.	173,922	Sinner, George A.		33,462 D	44.7%	55.3%	44.7%	55.3%
1980	302,621	162,230	Olson, Allen I.	140,391	Link, Arthur A.*		21,839 R	53.6%	46.4%	53.6%	46.4%
1976	297,249	138,321	Elkin, Richard	153,309	Link, Arthur A.*	5,619	14,988 D	46.5%	51.6%	47.4%	52.6%
1972	281,931	138,032	Davis, John E.	143,899	Link, Arthur A.	5,867	5,867 D	49.0%	51.0%	49.0%	51.0%
1968	247,998	108,380	McCarney, Robert P.	135,955	Guy, William L.*	3,663	27,575 D	43.7%	54.8%	44.4%	55.6%
1964**	262,661	116,247	Halcrow, Don	146,414	Guy, William L.*		30,167 D	44.3%	55.7%	44.3%	55.7%
1962	228,509	113,251	Andrews, Mark	115,258	Guy, William L.*		2,007 D	49.6%	50.4%	49.6%	50.4%
1960	275,375	122,486	Dahl, C. P.	136,148	Guy, William L.	16,741	13,662 D	44.5%	49.4%	47.4%	52.6%
1958	210,599	111,836	Davis, John E.*	98,763	Lord, John F.		13,073 R	53.1%	46.9%	53.1%	46.9%
1956	252,435	147,566	Davis, John E.	104,869	Warner, Wallace E.		42,697 R	58.5%	41.5%	58.5%	41.5%
1954	193,501	124,253	Brunsdale, Norman*	69,248	Bymers, Cornelius		55,005 R	64.2%	35.8%	64.2%	35.8%
1952	253,934	199,944	Brunsdale, Norman*	53,990	Johnson, Ole S.		145,954 R	78.7%	21.3%	78.7%	21.3%
1950	183,772	121,822	Brunsdale, Norman	61,950	Byerly, Clyde G.		59,872 R	66.3%	33.7%	66.3%	33.7%
1948	214,958	131,764	Aandahl, Fred G.*	80,655	Henry, Howard	2,539	51,109 R	61.3%	37.5%	62.0%	38.0%
1946	169,391	116,672	Aandahl, Fred G.*	52,719	Burdick, Quentin N.		63,953 R	68.9%	31.1%	68.9%	31.1%

Note: An asterisk (*) denotes incumbent. **The term of office of North Dakota's governor was increased from two to four years effective with the 1964 election.

POSTWAR VOTE FOR SENATOR

Year	Total Vote	Republican Vote	Republican Candidate	Democratic Vote	Democratic Candidate	Other Vote	Rep.-Dem. Plurality	Total Vote Rep.	Total Vote Dem.	Major Vote Rep.	Major Vote Dem.
2012	320,851	158,282	Berg, Rick	161,163	Heitkamp, Heidi	1,406	2,881 D	49.3%	50.2%	49.5%	50.5%
2010	238,812	181,689	Hoeven, John	52,955	Potter, Tracy	4,168	128,734 R	76.1%	22.2%	77.4%	22.6%
2006	218,152	64,417	Grotberg, Dwight	150,146	Conrad, Kent*	3,589	85,729 D	29.5%	68.8%	30.0%	70.0%
2004	310,696	98,553	Liffrig, Mike G.	212,143	Dorgan, Byron L.*		113,590 D	31.7%	68.3%	31.7%	68.3%
2000	287,539	111,069	Sand, Duane	176,470	Conrad, Kent*		65,401 D	38.6%	61.4%	38.6%	61.4%
1998	213,358	75,013	Nalewaja, Donna	134,747	Dorgan, Byron L.*	3,598	59,734 D	35.2%	63.2%	35.8%	64.2%
1994	236,547	99,390	Clayburg, Ben	137,157	Conrad, Kent*		37,767 D	42.0%	58.0%	42.0%	58.0%
1992	303,957	118,162	Sydness, Steve	179,347	Dorgan, Byron L.	6,448	61,185 D	38.9%	59.0%	39.7%	60.3%
1992S	163,311	55,194	Dalrymple, Jack	103,246	Conrad, Kent*	4,871	48,052 D	33.8%	63.2%	34.8%	65.2%
1988	289,170	112,937	Striden, Earl	171,899	Burdick, Quentin N.*	4,334	58,962 D	39.1%	59.4%	39.6%	60.4%
1986	288,998	141,797	Andrews, Mark*	143,932	Conrad, Kent	3,269	2,135 D	49.1%	49.8%	49.6%	50.4%
1982	262,465	89,304	Knorr, Gene	164,873	Burdick, Quentin N.*	8,288	75,569 D	34.0%	62.8%	35.1%	64.9%
1980	299,272	210,347	Andrews, Mark	86,650	Johanneson, Kent	2,267	123,689 R	70.3%	29.0%	70.8%	29.2%
1976	283,062	103,466	Stroup, Richard	175,772	Burdick, Quentin N.*	3,824	72,306 D	36.6%	62.1%	37.1%	62.9%
1974	235,661	114,117	Young, Milton R.*	113,931	Guy, William L.	7,613	186 R	48.4%	48.3%	50.0%	50.0%
1970	219,560	82,996	Kleppe, Tom	134,519	Burdick, Quentin N.*	2,045	51,523 D	37.8%	61.3%	38.2%	61.8%
1968	239,776	154,968	Young, Milton R.*	80,815	Lashkowitz, Herschel	3,993	74,153 R	64.6%	33.7%	65.7%	34.3%
1964	258,945	109,681	Kleppe, Tom	149,264	Burdick, Quentin N.*		39,583 D	42.4%	57.6%	42.4%	57.6%
1962	223,737	135,705	Young, Milton R.*	88,032	Lanier, William		47,673 R	60.7%	39.3%	60.7%	39.3%
1960S	210,349	103,475	Davis, John E.	104,593	Burdick, Quentin N.	2,281	1,118 D	49.2%	49.7%	49.7%	50.3%
1958	204,635	117,070	Langer, William*	84,892	Vendsel, Raymond	2,673	32,178 R	57.2%	41.5%	58.0%	42.0%
1956	244,161	155,305	Young, Milton R.*	87,919	Burdick, Quentin N.	937	67,386 R	63.6%	36.0%	63.9%	36.1%
1952**	237,995	157,907	Langer, William*	55,347	Morrison, Harold A.	24,741	102,560 R	66.3%	23.3%	74.0%	26.0%
1950	186,716	126,209	Young, Milton R.*	60,507	O'Brien, Harry		65,702 R	67.6%	32.4%	67.6%	32.4%
1946**	165,382	88,210	Langer, William*	38,368	Larson, Abner B.	38,804	49,842 R	53.3%	23.2%	69.7%	30.3%
1946S**	136,852	75,998	Young, Milton R.*	37,507	Lanier, William	23,347	38,491 R	55.5%	27.4%	67.0%	33.0%

Note: An asterisk (*) denotes incumbent. **In past elections, the other vote included: 1952 - 24,741 Independent (Fred G. Aandahl); 1946 - 38,804 Independent (Arthur E. Thompson), who finished second; 1946 Special - 20,848 Independent (Gerald P. Nye). One of the 1992 elections was for a short term to fill a vacancy and the special election was held in December. The 1946 and 1960 special elections were held in June for short terms to fill vacancies.

NORTH DAKOTA

HOUSE OF REPRESENTATIVES

| | | | Republican | | Democratic | | | | Percentage | | | |
| | | | | | | | Other | Rep.-Dem. | Total Vote | | Major Vote | |
CD	Year	Total Vote	Vote	Candidate	Vote	Candidate	Vote	Plurality	Rep.	Dem.	Rep.	Dem.
At Large	2014	248,670	138,100	CRAMER, KEVIN*	95,678	SINNER, GEORGE	14,892	42,422 R	55.5%	38.5%	59.1%	40.9%
At Large	2012	316,071	173,433	CRAMER, KEVIN	131,869	GULLESON, PAM	10,769	41,564 R	54.9%	41.7%	56.8%	43.2%
At Large	2010	237,137	129,802	BERG, RICK	106,542	POMEROY, EARL*	793	23,260 R	54.7%	44.9%	54.9%	45.1%
At Large	2008	313,965	119,388	SAND, DUANE	194,577	POMEROY, EARL*		75,189 D	38.0%	62.0%	38.0%	62.0%
At Large	2006	217,621	74,687	MECHTEL, MATT	142,934	POMEROY, EARL*		68,247 D	34.3%	65.7%	34.3%	65.7%
At Large	2004	310,814	125,684	SAND, DUANE	185,130	POMEROY, EARL*		59,446 D	40.4%	59.6%	40.4%	59.6%
At Large	2002	231,030	109,957	CLAYBURGH, RICK	121,073	POMEROY, EARL*		11,116 D	47.6%	52.4%	47.6%	52.4%
At Large	2000	285,658	127,251	DORSO, JOHN	151,173	POMEROY, EARL*	7,234	23,922 D	44.5%	52.9%	45.7%	54.3%
At Large	1998	212,888	87,511	CRAMER, KEVIN	119,668	POMEROY, EARL*	5,709	32,157 D	41.1%	56.2%	42.2%	57.8%
At Large	1996	263,010	113,684	CRAMER, KEVIN	144,833	POMEROY, EARL*	4,493	31,149 D	43.2%	55.1%	44.0%	56.0%
At Large	1994	235,389	105,988	PORTER, GARY	123,134	POMEROY, EARL*	6,267	17,146 D	45.0%	52.3%	46.3%	53.7%
At Large	1992	297,898	117,442	KORSMO, JOHN T.	169,273	POMEROY, EARL	11,183	51,831 D	39.4%	56.8%	41.0%	59.0%
At Large	1990	233,979	81,443	SCHAFER, EDWARD T.	152,530	DORGAN, BYRON L.*	6	71,087 D	34.8%	65.2%	34.8%	65.2%
At Large	1988	299,982	84,475	SYDNESS, STEVE	212,583	DORGAN, BYRON L.*	2,924	128,108 D	28.2%	70.9%	28.4%	71.6%
At Large	1986	286,361	66,989	VINJE, SYVER	216,258	DORGAN, BYRON L.*	3,114	149,269 D	23.4%	75.5%	23.7%	76.3%
At Large	1984	308,729	65,761	ALTENBURG, LOIS I.	242,968	DORGAN, BYRON L.*		177,207 D	21.3%	78.7%	21.3%	78.7%
At Large	1982	260,499	72,241	JONES, KENT	186,534	DORGAN, BYRON L.*	1,724	114,293 D	27.7%	71.6%	27.9%	72.1%
At Large	1980	293,076	124,707	SMYKOWSKI, JIM	166,437	DORGAN, BYRON L.	1,932	41,730 D	42.6%	56.8%	42.8%	57.2%
At Large	1978	220,348	147,746	ANDREWS, MARK*	68,016	HAGEN, BRUCE	4,586	79,730 R	67.1%	30.9%	68.5%	31.5%
At Large	1976	289,881	181,018	ANDREWS, MARK*	104,263	OMDAHL, LLOYD B.	4,600	76,755 R	62.4%	36.0%	63.5%	36.5%
At Large	1974	233,688	130,184	ANDREWS, MARK*	103,504	DORGAN, BYRON L.		26,680 R	55.7%	44.3%	55.7%	44.3%
At Large	1972	268,721	195,360	ANDREWS, MARK*	72,850	ISTA, RICHARD	511	122,510 R	72.7%	27.1%	72.8%	27.2%

Note: An asterisk (*) denotes incumbent.

NORTH DAKOTA

GENERAL AND PRIMARY ELECTIONS

2014 GENERAL ELECTIONS: OTHER VOTES

House

Other vote was:

At Large   14,531 Libertarian (Robert J. "Jack" Seaman), 361 scattered write-in

2014 PRIMARY ELECTIONS: SUPPLEMENTARY INFORMATION

Primary   June 10, 2014   **Registration**   No Party Registration
(No Formal Registration)

Primary Type   Open—Any person of voting age (18 years old at the time of the primary election) could participate in the primary of either party. As of June 10, 2014, North Dakota's estimated voting-age population was 545,020.

	REPUBLICAN PRIMARIES			DEMOCRATIC PRIMARIES		
Congressional At Large	Cramer, Kevin*	50,188	99.7%	Sinner, George	30,102	99.8%
	Write-In	151	0.3%	Write-In	52	0.2%
	TOTAL	*50,339*		*TOTAL*	*30,154*	

Note: An asterisk (*) denotes incumbent.

OHIO

Congressional districts first established for elections held in 2012

16 members

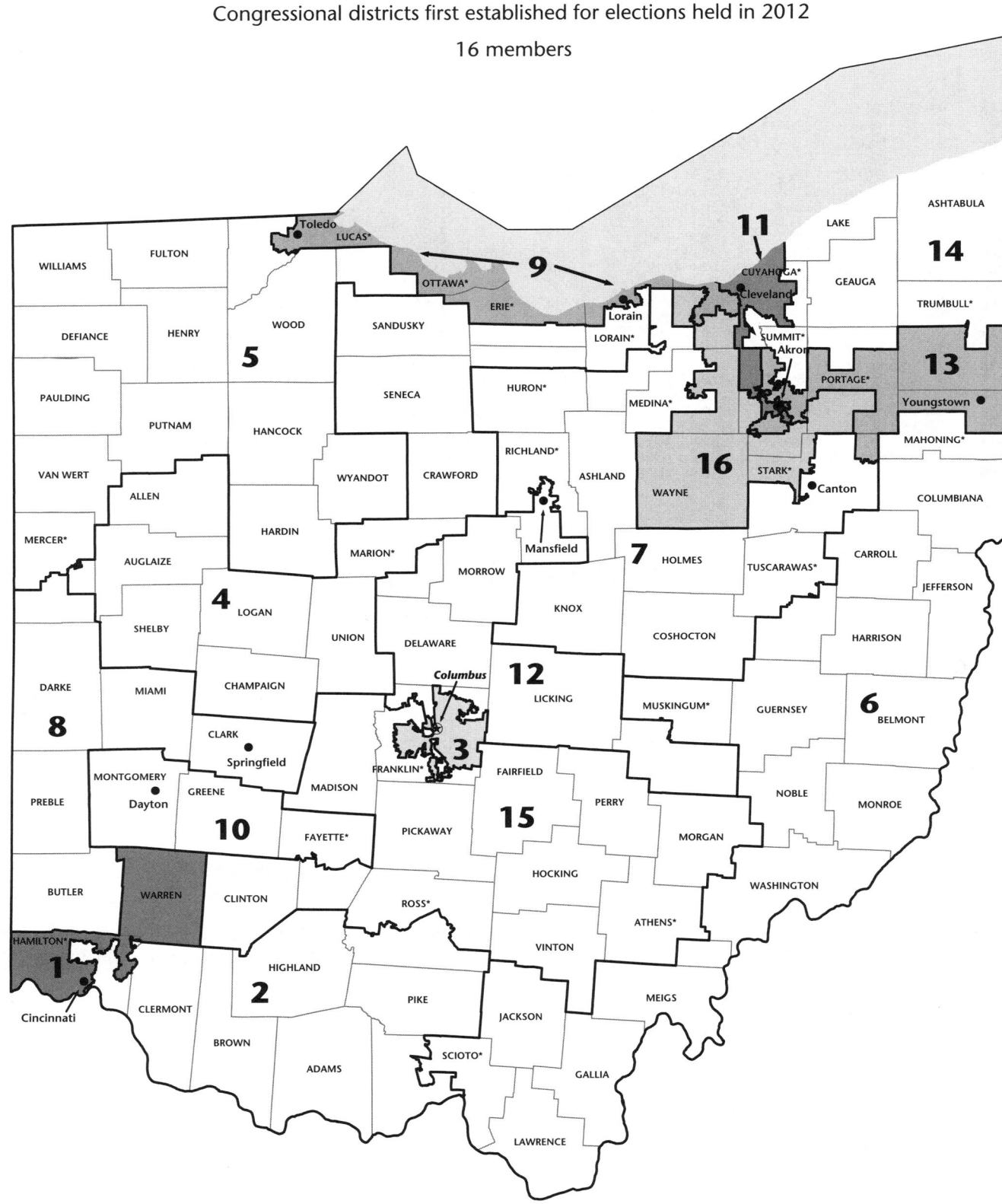

* Asterisk indicates a county whose boundaries include parts of two or more congressional districts.

OHIO
Cleveland Area

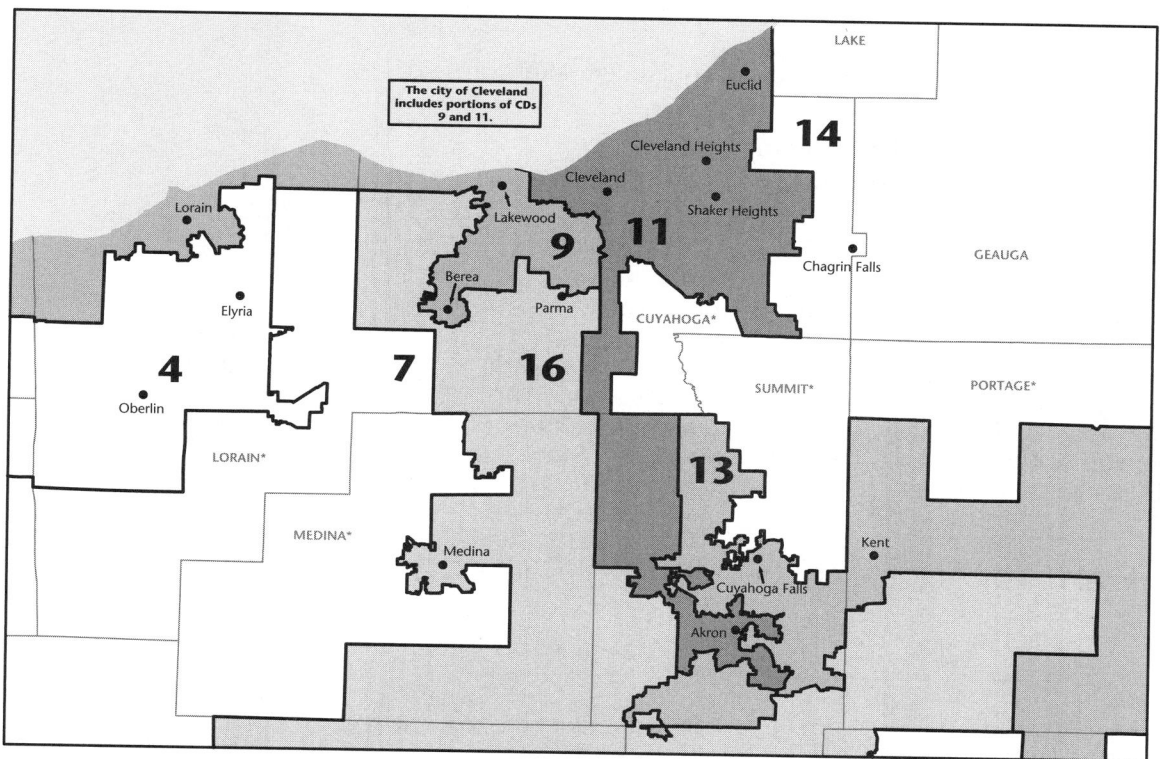

Columbus Area

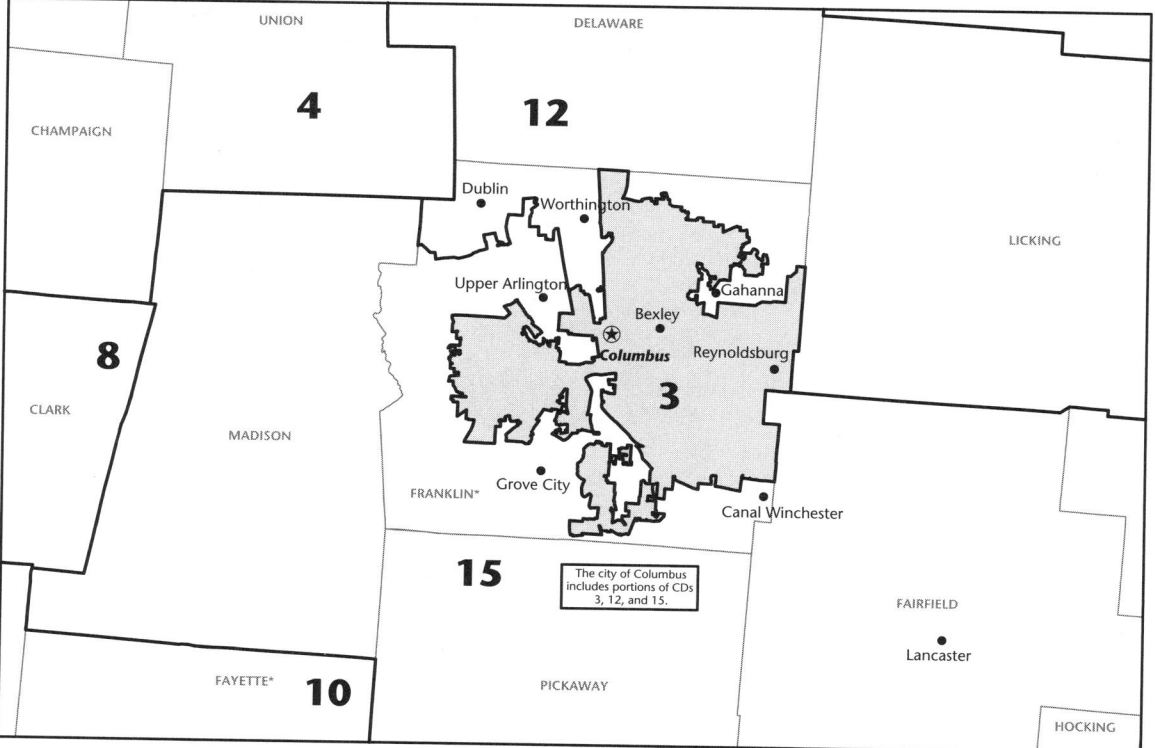

* Asterisk indicates a county whose boundaries include parts of two or more congressional districts.

OHIO

GOVERNOR

John Kasich (R). Reelected 2014 to a four-year term. Previously elected 2010.

SENATORS (1 Republican, 1 Democrat)

Sherrod Brown (D). Reelected 2012 to a six-year term. Previously elected 2006.

Rob Portman (R). Elected 2010 to a six-year term.

REPRESENTATIVES (12 Republicans, 4 Democrats)

1. Steve Chabot (R)
2. Brad R. Wenstrup (R)
3. Joyce Beatty (D)
4. Jim Jordan (R)
5. Robert E. Latta (R)
6. Bill Johnson (R)
7. Bob Gibbs (R)
8. John A. Boehner (R)
9. Marcy Kaptur (D)
10. Michael R. Turner (R)
11. Marcia L. Fudge (D)
12. Patrick J. Tiberi (R)
13. Tim Ryan (D)
14. David P. Joyce (R)
15. Steve Stivers (R)
16. James B. Renacci (R)

POSTWAR VOTE FOR PRESIDENT

Year	Total Vote	Republican		Democratic		Other Vote	Rep.-Dem. Plurality	Percentage			
		Vote	Candidate	Vote	Candidate			Total Vote		Major Vote	
								Rep.	Dem.	Rep.	Dem.
2012	5,580,840	2,661,433	Romney, W. Mitt	2,827,710	Obama, Barack H.*	91,697	166,277 D	47.7%	50.7%	48.5%	51.5%
2008	5,708,350	2,677,820	McCain, John S. III	2,940,044	Obama, Barack H.	90,486	262,224 D	46.9%	51.5%	47.7%	52.3%
2004	5,627,908	2,859,768	Bush, George W.*	2,741,167	Kerry, John F.	26,973	118,601 R	50.8%	48.7%	51.1%	48.9%
2000**	4,701,998	2,350,363	Bush, George W.	2,183,628	Gore, Albert Jr.	168,007	166,735 R	50.0%	46.4%	51.8%	48.2%
1996**	4,534,434	1,859,883	Dole, Robert "Bob"	2,148,222	Clinton, Bill*	526,329	288,339 D	41.0%	47.4%	46.4%	53.6%
1992**	4,939,967	1,894,310	Bush, George H.*	1,984,942	Clinton, Bill	1,060,715	90,632 D	38.3%	40.2%	48.8%	51.2%
1988	4,393,699	2,416,549	Bush, George H.	1,939,629	Dukakis, Michael S.	37,521	476,920 R	55.0%	44.1%	55.5%	44.5%
1984	4,547,619	2,678,560	Reagan, Ronald*	1,825,440	Mondale, Walter F.	43,619	853,120 R	58.9%	40.1%	59.5%	40.5%
1980**	4,283,603	2,206,545	Reagan, Ronald	1,752,414	Carter, Jimmy*	324,644	454,131 R	51.5%	40.9%	55.7%	44.3%
1976	4,111,873	2,000,505	Ford, Gerald R.*	2,011,621	Carter, Jimmy	99,747	11,116 D	48.7%	48.9%	49.9%	50.1%
1972	4,094,787	2,441,827	Nixon, Richard M.*	1,558,889	McGovern, George S.	94,071	882,938 R	59.6%	38.1%	61.0%	39.0%
1968**	3,959,698	1,791,014	Nixon, Richard M.	1,700,586	Humphrey, Hubert Horatio Jr.	468,098	90,428 R	45.2%	42.9%	51.3%	48.7%
1964	3,969,196	1,470,865	Goldwater, Barry M. Sr.	2,498,331	Johnson, Lyndon B.*		1,027,466 D	37.1%	62.9%	37.1%	62.9%
1960	4,161,859	2,217,611	Nixon, Richard M.	1,944,248	Kennedy, John F.		273,363 R	53.3%	46.7%	53.3%	46.7%
1956	3,702,265	2,262,610	Eisenhower, Dwight D.*	1,439,655	Stevenson, Adlai E. II		822,955 R	61.1%	38.9%	61.1%	38.9%
1952	3,700,758	2,100,391	Eisenhower, Dwight D.	1,600,367	Stevenson, Adlai E. II		500,024 R	56.8%	43.2%	56.8%	43.2%
1948	2,936,071	1,445,684	Dewey, Thomas E.	1,452,791	Truman, Harry S.*	37,596	7,107 D	49.2%	49.5%	49.9%	50.1%

Note: An asterisk (*) denotes incumbent. **In past elections, the other vote included: 2000 - 117,799 Green (Ralph Nader); 1996 - 483,207 Reform (Ross Perot); 1992 - 1,036,426 Independent (Perot); 1980 - 254,472 Independent (John Anderson); 1968 - 467,495 American Independent (George Wallace).

OHIO

POSTWAR VOTE FOR GOVERNOR

Year	Total Vote	Republican Vote	Candidate	Democratic Vote	Candidate	Other Vote	Rep.-Dem. Plurality	Total Vote Rep.	Total Vote Dem.	Major Vote Rep.	Major Vote Dem.
2014	3,055,913	1,944,848	Kasich, John*	1,009,359	FitzGerald, Edward	101,706	935,489 R	63.6%	33.0%	65.8%	34.2%
2010	3,852,469	1,889,186	Kasich, John	1,812,059	Strickland, Ted*	151,224	77,127 R	49.0%	47.0%	51.0%	49.0%
2006	4,022,754	1,474,285	Blackwell, J. Kenneth	2,435,384	Strickland, Ted	113,085	961,099 D	36.6%	60.5%	37.7%	62.3%
2002	3,228,992	1,865,007	Taft, Robert Alphonso*	1,236,924	Hagan, Timothy	127,061	628,083 R	57.8%	38.3%	60.1%	39.9%
1998	3,354,213	1,678,721	Taft, Robert Alphonso	1,498,956	Fisher, Lee	176,536	179,765 R	50.0%	44.7%	52.8%	47.2%
1994	3,346,238	2,401,572	Voinovich, George*	835,849	Burch, Robert L.	108,817	1,565,723 R	71.8%	25.0%	74.2%	25.8%
1990	3,482,650	1,938,103	Voinovich, George	1,544,416	Celebrezze, Anthony J.	131	393,687 R	55.7%	44.3%	55.7%	44.3%
1986	3,066,611	1,207,264	Rhodes, James A.	1,858,372	Celeste, Richard F.*	975	651,108 D	39.4%	60.6%	39.4%	60.6%
1982	3,356,791	1,303,962	Brown, Clarence J. Jr.	1,981,952	Celeste, Richard F.	70,877	677,990 D	38.8%	59.0%	39.7%	60.3%
1978	2,843,351	1,402,167	Rhodes, James A.*	1,354,631	Celeste, Richard F.	86,553	47,536 R	49.3%	47.6%	50.9%	49.1%
1974	3,072,010	1,493,679	Rhodes, James A.	1,482,191	Gilligan, John J.*	96,140	11,488 R	48.6%	48.2%	50.2%	49.8%
1970	3,184,131	1,382,657	Cloud, Roger	1,725,560	Gilligan, John J.	75,914	342,903 D	43.4%	54.2%	44.5%	55.5%
1966	2,887,331	1,795,277	Rhodes, James A.*	1,092,054	Reams, Henry Frazier "Frazier" Jr.		703,223 R	62.2%	37.8%	62.2%	37.8%
1962	3,116,953	1,836,432	Rhodes, James A.	1,280,521	Disalle, Michael V.*		555,911 R	58.9%	41.1%	58.9%	41.1%
1958**	3,284,134	1,414,874	O'Neill, C. William*	1,869,260	Disalle, Michael V.		454,386 D	43.1%	56.9%	43.1%	56.9%
1956	3,542,091	1,984,988	O'Neill, C. William	1,557,103	Disalle, Michael V.		427,885 R	56.0%	44.0%	56.0%	44.0%
1954	2,597,790	1,192,528	Rhodes, James A.	1,405,262	Lausche, Frank J.*		212,734 D	45.9%	54.1%	45.9%	54.1%
1952	3,605,168	1,590,058	Taft, Charles P.	2,015,110	Lausche, Frank J.*		425,052 D	44.1%	55.9%	44.1%	55.9%
1950	2,892,819	1,370,570	Ebright, Don H.	1,522,249	Lausche, Frank J.*		151,679 D	47.4%	52.6%	47.4%	52.6%
1948	3,018,289	1,398,514	Herbert, Thomas J.*	1,619,775	Lausche, Frank J.		221,261 D	46.3%	53.7%	46.3%	53.7%
1946	2,303,750	1,166,550	Herbert, Thomas J.	1,125,997	Lausche, Frank J.*	11,203	40,553 R	50.6%	48.9%	50.9%	49.1%

Note: An asterisk (*) denotes incumbent. **The term of office of Ohio's governor was increased from two to four years effective with the 1958 election.

POSTWAR VOTE FOR SENATOR

Year	Total Vote	Republican Vote	Candidate	Democratic Vote	Candidate	Other Vote	Rep.-Dem. Plurality	Total Vote Rep.	Total Vote Dem.	Major Vote Rep.	Major Vote Dem.
2012	5,449,114	2,435,740	Mandel, Josh	2,762,757	Brown, Sherrod*	250,617	327,017 D	44.7%	50.7%	46.9%	53.1%
2010	3,815,098	2,168,742	Portman, Rob	1,503,297	Fisher, Lee	143,059	665,445 R	56.8%	39.4%	59.1%	40.9%
2006	4,019,236	1,761,037	DeWine, Michael "Mike"*	2,257,369	Brown, Sherrod	830	496,332 D	43.8%	56.2%	43.8%	56.2%
2004	5,426,196	3,464,651	Voinovich, George*	1,961,249	Fingerhut, Eric D.	296	1,503,402 R	63.9%	36.1%	63.9%	36.1%
2000	4,448,801	2,665,512	DeWine, Michael "Mike"*	1,595,066	Celeste, Theodore S.	188,223	1,070,446 R	59.9%	35.9%	62.6%	37.4%
1998	3,404,351	1,922,087	Voinovich, George	1,482,054	Boyle, Mary O.	210	440,033 R	56.5%	43.5%	56.5%	43.5%
1994	3,436,884	1,836,556	DeWine, Michael "Mike"	1,348,213	Hyatt, Joel	252,115	488,343 R	53.4%	39.2%	57.7%	42.3%
1992	4,793,953	2,028,300	DeWine, Michael "Mike"	2,444,419	Glenn, John H.*	321,234	416,119 D	42.3%	51.0%	45.3%	54.7%
1988	4,352,905	1,872,716	Voinovich, George	2,480,038	Metzenbaum, Howard M.*	151	607,322 D	43.0%	57.0%	43.0%	57.0%
1986	3,121,188	1,171,893	Kindness, Thomas N.	1,949,208	Glenn, John H.*	87	777,315 D	37.5%	62.5%	37.5%	62.5%
1982	3,395,463	1,396,790	Pfeifer, Paul E.	1,923,767	Metzenbaum, Howard M.*	74,906	526,977 D	41.1%	56.7%	42.1%	57.9%
1980	4,027,303	1,137,695	Betts, James E.	2,770,786	Glenn, John H.*	118,822	1,633,091 D	28.2%	68.8%	29.1%	70.9%
1976	3,920,613	1,823,774	Taft, Robert Alphonso*	1,941,113	Metzenbaum, Howard M.	155,726	117,339 D	46.5%	49.5%	48.4%	51.6%
1974	2,987,951	918,133	Perk, Ralph J.	1,930,670	Glenn, John H.	139,148	1,012,537 D	30.7%	64.6%	32.2%	67.8%
1970	3,151,274	1,565,682	Taft, Robert Alphonso	1,495,262	Metzenbaum, Howard M.	90,330	70,420 R	49.7%	47.4%	51.2%	48.8%
1968	3,743,121	1,928,964	Saxbe, William B.	1,814,152	Gilligan, John J.	5	114,812 R	51.5%	48.5%	51.5%	48.5%
1964	3,830,389	1,906,781	Taft, Robert Alphonso	1,923,608	Young, Stephen M.*		16,827 D	49.8%	50.2%	49.8%	50.2%
1962	2,995,105	1,151,292	Briley, John Marshall	1,843,813	Lausche, Frank J.*		692,521 D	38.4%	61.6%	38.4%	61.6%
1958	3,149,410	1,497,199	Bricker, John W.*	1,652,211	Young, Stephen M.		155,012 D	47.5%	52.5%	47.5%	52.5%
1956	3,525,499	1,660,910	Bender, George H.*	1,864,589	Lausche, Frank J.		203,679 D	47.1%	52.9%	47.1%	52.9%
1954S	2,512,773	1,257,874	Bender, George H.	1,254,899	Burke, Thomas A.		2,975 R	50.1%	49.9%	50.1%	49.9%
1952	3,442,291	1,878,961	Bricker, John W.*	1,563,330	Disalle, Michael V.		315,631 R	54.6%	45.4%	54.6%	45.4%
1950	2,860,102	1,645,643	Taft, Robert Alphonso*	1,214,459	Ferguson, Joseph T.		431,184 R	57.5%	42.5%	57.5%	42.5%
1946	2,237,269	1,275,774	Bricker, John W.	947,610	Huffman, James W.	13,885	328,164 R	57.0%	42.4%	57.4%	42.6%
1946S	2,123,526	1,193,942	Taft, Kingsley A.	929,584	Webber, Henry P.		264,358 R	56.2%	43.8%	56.2%	43.8%

Note: An asterisk (*) denotes incumbent. **One of the 1946 elections and the 1954 election were for short terms to fill a vacancy.

OHIO

GOVERNOR 2014

2010 Census Population	County	Total Vote	Republican (Kasich)	Democratic (FitzGerald)	Other	Rep.-Dem. Plurality	Percentage			
							Total Vote		Major Vote	
							Rep.	Dem.	Rep.	Dem.
28,550	ADAMS	6,100	4,499	1,462	139	3,037 R	73.8%	24.0%	75.5%	24.5%
106,331	ALLEN	27,259	19,587	7,091	581	12,496 R	71.9%	26.0%	73.4%	26.6%
53,139	ASHLAND	14,849	11,267	3,177	405	8,090 R	75.9%	21.4%	78.0%	22.0%
101,497	ASHTABULA	26,436	15,390	10,082	964	5,308 R	58.2%	38.1%	60.4%	39.6%
64,757	ATHENS	14,408	5,589	7,855	964	2,266 D	38.8%	54.5%	41.6%	58.4%
45,949	AUGLAIZE	13,597	11,031	2,287	279	8,744 R	81.1%	16.8%	82.8%	17.2%
70,400	BELMONT	19,144	10,205	8,410	529	1,795 R	53.3%	43.9%	54.8%	45.2%
44,846	BROWN	11,547	8,550	2,731	266	5,819 R	74.0%	23.7%	75.8%	24.2%
368,130	BUTLER	86,106	62,438	21,551	2,117	40,887 R	72.5%	25.0%	74.3%	25.7%
28,836	CARROLL	7,803	5,401	2,137	265	3,264 R	69.2%	27.4%	71.7%	28.3%
40,097	CHAMPAIGN	11,436	8,522	2,575	339	5,947 R	74.5%	22.5%	76.8%	23.2%
138,333	CLARK	38,514	25,640	11,957	917	13,683 R	66.6%	31.0%	68.2%	31.8%
197,363	CLERMONT	50,556	39,395	9,647	1,514	29,748 R	77.9%	19.1%	80.3%	19.7%
42,040	CLINTON	9,576	7,573	1,752	251	5,821 R	79.1%	18.3%	81.2%	18.8%
107,841	COLUMBIANA	26,925	18,895	7,217	813	11,678 R	70.2%	26.8%	72.4%	27.6%
36,901	COSHOCTON	9,087	6,365	2,489	233	3,876 R	70.0%	27.4%	71.9%	28.1%
43,784	CRAWFORD	11,900	8,870	2,778	252	6,092 R	74.5%	23.3%	76.2%	23.8%
1,280,122	CUYAHOGA	336,769	172,319	149,986	14,464	22,333 R	51.2%	44.5%	53.5%	46.5%
52,959	DARKE	14,679	12,213	2,220	246	9,993 R	83.2%	15.1%	84.6%	15.4%
39,037	DEFIANCE	10,853	7,747	2,831	275	4,916 R	71.4%	26.1%	73.2%	26.8%
174,214	DELAWARE	58,716	44,685	12,355	1,676	32,330 R	76.1%	21.0%	78.3%	21.7%
77,079	ERIE	23,137	13,944	8,512	681	5,432 R	60.3%	36.8%	62.1%	37.9%
146,156	FAIRFIELD	40,554	28,614	10,851	1,089	17,763 R	70.6%	26.8%	72.5%	27.5%
29,030	FAYETTE	6,304	4,821	1,339	144	3,482 R	76.5%	21.2%	78.3%	21.7%
1,163,414	FRANKLIN	290,863	161,747	115,871	13,245	45,876 R	55.6%	39.8%	58.3%	41.7%
42,698	FULTON	10,838	7,845	2,718	275	5,127 R	72.4%	25.1%	74.3%	25.7%
30,934	GALLIA	7,345	5,047	2,088	210	2,959 R	68.7%	28.4%	70.7%	29.3%
93,389	GEAUGA	30,716	23,072	6,579	1,065	16,493 R	75.1%	21.4%	77.8%	22.2%
161,573	GREENE	48,899	35,734	11,811	1,354	23,923 R	73.1%	24.2%	75.2%	24.8%
40,087	GUERNSEY	10,191	6,794	3,111	286	3,683 R	66.7%	30.5%	68.6%	31.4%
802,374	HAMILTON	236,285	142,066	85,535	8,684	56,531 R	60.1%	36.2%	62.4%	37.6%
74,782	HANCOCK	19,683	15,743	3,451	489	12,292 R	80.0%	17.5%	82.0%	18.0%
32,058	HARDIN	6,501	4,806	1,544	151	3,262 R	73.9%	23.8%	75.7%	24.3%
15,864	HARRISON	4,638	2,875	1,599	164	1,276 R	62.0%	34.5%	64.3%	35.7%
28,215	HENRY	7,860	5,948	1,717	195	4,231 R	75.7%	21.8%	77.6%	22.4%
43,589	HIGHLAND	10,004	7,718	2,078	208	5,640 R	77.1%	20.8%	78.8%	21.2%
29,380	HOCKING	7,554	4,894	2,418	242	2,476 R	64.8%	32.0%	66.9%	33.1%
42,366	HOLMES	6,513	5,398	943	172	4,455 R	82.9%	14.5%	85.1%	14.9%
59,626	HURON	14,021	9,776	3,838	407	5,938 R	69.7%	27.4%	71.8%	28.2%
33,225	JACKSON	7,020	4,579	2,217	224	2,362 R	65.2%	31.6%	67.4%	32.6%
69,709	JEFFERSON	18,952	10,974	7,342	636	3,632 R	57.9%	38.7%	59.9%	40.1%
60,921	KNOX	17,161	12,747	3,840	574	8,907 R	74.3%	22.4%	76.8%	23.2%
230,041	LAKE	67,970	46,189	19,698	2,083	26,491 R	68.0%	29.0%	70.1%	29.9%
62,450	LAWRENCE	14,346	9,120	4,817	409	4,303 R	63.6%	33.6%	65.4%	34.6%
166,492	LICKING	47,135	33,620	11,999	1,516	21,621 R	71.3%	25.5%	73.7%	26.3%
45,858	LOGAN	12,789	10,118	2,343	328	7,775 R	79.1%	18.3%	81.2%	18.8%
301,356	LORAIN	77,820	47,256	27,859	2,705	19,397 R	60.7%	35.8%	62.9%	37.1%
441,815	LUCAS	106,016	53,808	48,179	4,029	5,629 R	50.8%	45.4%	52.8%	47.2%
43,435	MADISON	10,162	7,492	2,348	322	5,144 R	73.7%	23.1%	76.1%	23.9%
238,823	MAHONING	66,276	35,578	28,376	2,322	7,202 R	53.7%	42.8%	55.6%	44.4%
66,501	MARION	15,798	11,129	4,147	522	6,982 R	70.4%	26.3%	72.9%	27.1%
172,332	MEDINA	48,137	34,541	12,117	1,479	22,424 R	71.8%	25.2%	74.0%	26.0%
23,770	MEIGS	5,666	3,612	1,811	243	1,801 R	63.7%	32.0%	66.6%	33.4%
40,814	MERCER	12,253	10,155	1,914	184	8,241 R	82.9%	15.6%	84.1%	15.9%
102,506	MIAMI	31,074	24,735	5,693	646	19,042 R	79.6%	18.3%	81.3%	18.7%
14,642	MONROE	4,965	2,197	2,577	191	380 D	44.2%	51.9%	46.0%	54.0%
535,153	MONTGOMERY	145,830	90,683	51,664	3,483	39,019 R	62.2%	35.4%	63.7%	36.3%
15,054	MORGAN	3,891	2,579	1,189	123	1,390 R	66.3%	30.6%	68.4%	31.6%
34,827	MORROW	9,747	7,168	2,270	309	4,898 R	73.5%	23.3%	75.9%	24.1%
86,074	MUSKINGUM	20,768	14,658	5,482	628	9,176 R	70.6%	26.4%	72.8%	27.2%

OHIO

GOVERNOR 2014

2010 Census Population	County	Total Vote	Republican (Kasich)	Democratic (FitzGerald)	Other	Rep.-Dem. Plurality	Percentage			
							Total Vote		Major Vote	
							Rep.	Dem.	Rep.	Dem.
14,645	NOBLE	3,783	2,331	1,319	133	1,012 R	61.6%	34.9%	63.9%	36.1%
41,428	OTTAWA	14,867	9,432	4,938	497	4,494 R	63.4%	33.2%	65.6%	34.4%
19,614	PAULDING	5,675	3,850	1,638	187	2,212 R	67.8%	28.9%	70.2%	29.8%
36,058	PERRY	8,899	5,840	2,788	271	3,052 R	65.6%	31.3%	67.7%	32.3%
55,698	PICKAWAY	13,343	9,964	3,058	321	6,906 R	74.7%	22.9%	76.5%	23.5%
28,709	PIKE	7,178	4,367	2,649	162	1,718 R	60.8%	36.9%	62.2%	37.8%
161,419	PORTAGE	40,783	25,432	13,545	1,806	11,887 R	62.4%	33.2%	65.2%	34.8%
42,270	PREBLE	11,473	9,056	2,155	262	6,901 R	78.9%	18.8%	80.8%	19.2%
34,499	PUTNAM	11,007	8,808	2,009	190	6,799 R	80.0%	18.3%	81.4%	18.6%
124,475	RICHLAND	32,890	23,122	9,039	729	14,083 R	70.3%	27.5%	71.9%	28.1%
78,064	ROSS	16,591	10,855	5,248	488	5,607 R	65.4%	31.6%	67.4%	32.6%
60,944	SANDUSKY	16,520	11,027	4,933	560	6,094 R	66.7%	29.9%	69.1%	30.9%
79,499	SCIOTO	18,034	9,864	7,617	553	2,247 R	54.7%	42.2%	56.4%	43.6%
56,745	SENECA	13,778	9,662	3,722	394	5,940 R	70.1%	27.0%	72.2%	27.8%
49,423	SHELBY	13,911	11,200	2,420	291	8,780 R	80.5%	17.4%	82.2%	17.8%
375,586	STARK	101,432	67,948	30,705	2,779	37,243 R	67.0%	30.3%	68.9%	31.1%
541,781	SUMMIT	134,694	79,004	50,865	4,825	28,139 R	58.7%	37.8%	60.8%	39.2%
210,312	TRUMBULL	56,936	31,382	23,536	2,018	7,846 R	55.1%	41.3%	57.1%	42.9%
92,582	TUSCARAWAS	23,621	15,361	7,618	642	7,743 R	65.0%	32.3%	66.8%	33.2%
52,300	UNION	14,030	10,987	2,598	445	8,389 R	78.3%	18.5%	80.9%	19.1%
28,744	VAN WERT	7,033	5,353	1,512	168	3,841 R	76.1%	21.5%	78.0%	22.0%
13,435	VINTON	3,195	1,993	1,079	123	914 R	62.4%	33.8%	64.9%	35.1%
212,693	WARREN	58,873	46,167	11,427	1,279	34,740 R	78.4%	19.4%	80.2%	19.8%
61,778	WASHINGTON	18,336	12,152	5,659	525	6,493 R	66.3%	30.9%	68.2%	31.8%
114,520	WAYNE	26,741	19,962	5,951	828	14,011 R	74.6%	22.3%	77.0%	23.0%
37,642	WILLIAMS	9,615	7,066	2,245	304	4,821 R	73.5%	23.3%	75.9%	24.1%
125,488	WOOD	35,042	22,296	11,482	1,264	10,814 R	63.6%	32.8%	66.0%	34.0%
22,615	WYANDOT	5,691	4,406	1,129	156	3,277 R	77.4%	19.8%	79.6%	20.4%
11,536,504	TOTAL	3,055,913	1,944,848	1,009,359	101,706	935,489 R	63.6%	33.0%	65.8%	34.2%

OHIO

HOUSE OF REPRESENTATIVES

CD	Year	Total Vote	Republican		Democratic		Other Vote	Rep.-Dem. Plurality	Percentage			
			Vote	Candidate	Vote	Candidate			Total Vote		Major Vote	
									Rep.	Dem.	Rep.	Dem.
1	2014	197,383	124,779	CHABOT, STEVE*	72,604	KUNDRATA, FRED		52,175 R	63.2%	36.8%	63.2%	36.8%
1	2012	349,716	201,907	CHABOT, STEVE*	131,490	SINNARD, JEFF	16,319	70,417 R	57.7%	37.6%	60.6%	39.4%
2	2014	201,111	132,658	WENSTRUP, BRAD R.*	68,453	TYSZKIEWICZ, MAREK		64,205 R	66.0%	34.0%	66.0%	34.0%
2	2012	331,381	194,299	WENSTRUP, BRAD R.	137,082	SMITH, WILLIAM		57,217 R	58.6%	41.4%	58.6%	41.4%
3	2014	143,261	51,475	ADAMS, JOHN	91,769	BEATTY, JOYCE*	17	40,294 D	35.9%	64.1%	35.9%	64.1%
3	2012	295,938	77,903	LONG, CHRIS	201,921	BEATTY, JOYCE	16,114	124,018 D	26.3%	68.2%	27.8%	72.2%
4	2014	186,072	125,907	JORDAN, JIM*	60,165	GARRETT, JANET		65,742 R	67.7%	32.3%	67.7%	32.3%
4	2012	312,998	182,643	JORDAN, JIM*	114,214	SLONE, JIM	16,141	68,429 R	58.4%	36.5%	61.5%	38.5%
5	2014	202,300	134,449	LATTA, ROBERT E.*	58,507	FRY, ROBERT	9,344	75,942 R	66.5%	28.9%	69.7%	30.3%
5	2012	351,878	201,514	LATTA, ROBERT E.*	137,806	ZIMMANN, ANGELA	12,558	63,708 R	57.3%	39.2%	59.4%	40.6%
6	2014	190,652	111,026	JOHNSON, BILL*	73,561	GARRISON, JENNIFER	6,065	37,465 R	58.2%	38.6%	60.1%	39.9%
6	2012	308,980	164,536	JOHNSON, BILL*	144,444	WILSON, CHARLES A. JR.		20,092 R	53.3%	46.7%	53.3%	46.7%
7	2014	143,959	143,959	GIBBS, BOB*				143,959 R	100.0%		100.0%	
7	2012	315,812	178,104	GIBBS, BOB*	137,708	HEALY-ABRAMS, JOYCE		40,396 R	56.4%	43.6%	56.4%	43.6%
8	2014	188,330	126,539	BOEHNER, JOHN A.*	51,534	POETTER, TOM	10,257	75,005 R	67.2%	27.4%	71.1%	28.9%
8	2012	246,442	246,380	BOEHNER, JOHN A.*			62	246,380 R	100.0%		100.0%	

OHIO

HOUSE OF REPRESENTATIVES

CD	Year	Total Vote	Republican		Democratic		Other Vote	Rep.-Dem. Plurality	Percentage			
									Total Vote		Major Vote	
			Vote	Candidate	Vote	Candidate			Rep.	Dem.	Rep.	Dem.
9	2014	160,715	51,704	MAY, RICHARD	108,870	KAPTUR, MARCY*	141	57,166 D	32.2%	67.7%	32.2%	67.8%
9	2012	298,166	68,666	WURZELBACHER, SAMUEL	217,775	KAPTUR, MARCY*	11,725	149,109 D	23.0%	73.0%	24.0%	76.0%
10	2014	200,606	130,752	TURNER, MICHAEL R.*	63,249	KLEPINGER, ROBERT	6,605	67,503 R	65.2%	31.5%	67.4%	32.6%
10	2012	349,671	208,201	TURNER, MICHAEL R.*	131,097	NEUHARDT, SHAREN SWARTZ	10,373	77,104 R	59.5%	37.5%	61.4%	38.6%
11	2014	172,566	35,461	ZETZER, MARK	137,105	FUDGE, MARCIA L.*		101,644 D	20.5%	79.5%	20.5%	79.5%
11	2012	258,378			258,378	FUDGE, MARCIA L.*		258,378 D		100.0%		100.0%
12	2014	221,081	150,573	TIBERI, PATRICK J.*	61,360	TIBBS, DAVID ARTHUR	9,148	89,213 R	68.1%	27.8%	71.0%	29.0%
12	2012	368,488	233,874	TIBERI, PATRICK J.*	134,614	REESE, JIM		99,260 R	63.5%	36.5%	63.5%	36.5%
13	2014	175,549	55,233	PEKAREK, THOMAS	120,230	RYAN, TIM*	86	64,997 D	31.5%	68.5%	31.5%	68.5%
13	2012	323,612	88,120	AGANA, MARISHA	235,492	RYAN, TIM*		147,372 D	27.2%	72.8%	27.2%	72.8%
14	2014	214,580	135,736	JOYCE, DAVID P.*	70,856	WAGER, MICHAEL	7,988	64,880 R	63.3%	33.0%	65.7%	34.3%
14	2012	339,884	183,660	JOYCE, DAVID P.	131,638	BLANCHARD, DALE VIRGIL	24,586	52,022 R	54.0%	38.7%	58.2%	41.8%
15	2014	194,621	128,496	STIVERS, STEVE*	66,125	WHARTON, SCOTT		62,371 R	66.0%	34.0%	66.0%	34.0%
15	2012	333,465	205,277	STIVERS, STEVE*	128,188	LANG, PAT		77,089 R	61.6%	38.4%	61.6%	38.4%
16	2014	207,375	132,176	RENACCI, JAMES B.*	75,199	CROSSLAND, PETE		56,977 R	63.7%	36.3%	63.7%	36.3%
16	2012	355,771	185,167	RENACCI, JAMES B.*	170,604	SUTTON, BETTY		14,563 R	52.0%	48.0%	52.0%	48.0%
TOTAL	2014	3,000,161	1,770,923		1,179,587		49,651	591,336 R	59.0%	39.3%	60.0%	40.0%
TOTAL	2012	5,140,580	2,620,251		2,412,451		107,878	207,800 R	51.0%	46.9%	52.1%	47.9%

Note: An asterisk (*) denotes incumbent.

OHIO

GENERAL AND PRIMARY ELECTIONS

2014 GENERAL ELECTIONS: OTHER VOTES

Governor   Other vote was 101,706 Green (Anita Rios)

House   Other vote was:

CD 3   17 Write-in (Ralph A. Applegate)
CD 5   9,344 Libertarian (Eric Eberly)
CD 6   6,065 Green (Dennis Lambert)
CD 8   10,257 Constitution (Jim Condit)
CD 9   112 Write-in (Cory Hoffman), 29 Write-in (George A. Skalsky)
CD 10   6,605 Libertarian (David Harlow)
CD 12   9,148 Green (Robert M. "Bob" Hart)
CD 13   86 Write-in (David Allen Pastorius)
CD 14   7,988 Libertarian (David Macko)

2014 PRIMARY ELECTIONS: SUPPLEMENTARY INFORMATION

Primary   May 6, 2014   **Registration** (as of May 6, 2014)   7,715,103   No Party Registration

Primary Type   Open—Any registered voter could participate in the primary of either party. However, records are kept of voter participation in recent primaries, and voters who cast a ballot in one party's primary could be challenged if they attempted to participate in the other party's primary. They could be asked to sign an affidavit affirming the fact that they were voting in the opposing party's primary and would become identified with that party because of their primary ballot cast.

OHIO

GENERAL AND PRIMARY ELECTIONS

	REPUBLICAN PRIMARIES			DEMOCRATIC PRIMARIES		
Governor	Kasich, John*	559,671	100.0%	FitzGerald, Ed	366,056	83.1%
				Ealy, Larry	74,197	16.9%
	TOTAL	559,671		TOTAL	440,253	
Congressional District 1	Chabot, Steve*	31,953	100.0%	Kundrata, Fred	7,369	55.9%
				Prues, Jim	5,814	44.1%
	TOTAL	31,953		TOTAL	13,183	
Congressional District 2	Wenstrup, Brad R.*	37,134	100.0%	Tyszkiewicz, Marek	4,812	29.7%
				Richards, Ronny	3,995	24.7%
				Smith, William	3,974	24.5%
				Sheil, John Arthur	3,416	21.1%
	TOTAL	37,134		TOTAL	16,197	
Congressional District 3	Adams, John	10,045	58.8%	Beatty, Joyce*	25,151	100.0%
	Vennon, Eric T.	7,032	41.2%			
	TOTAL	17,077		TOTAL	25,151	
Congressional District 4	Jordan, Jim*	47,967	100.0%	Garrett, Janet	1,471	100.0%
	TOTAL	47,967		TOTAL	1,471	
Congressional District 5	Latta, Robert E.*	42,288	100.0%	Fry, Robert	16,460	100.0%
	TOTAL	42,288		TOTAL	16,460	
Congressional District 6	Johnson, Bill*	30,799	100.0%	Garrison, Jennifer	22,359	72.9%
				Howard, Gregory D.	8,292	27.1%
	TOTAL	30,799		TOTAL	30,651	
Congressional District 7	Gibbs, Bob*	32,839	100.0%			
	TOTAL	32,839				
Congressional District 8	Boehner, John A.*	47,261	71.5%	Poetter, Tom	8,911	54.6%
	Winteregg, J.D.	15,030	22.7%	Guyette, Matthew J.	7,399	45.4%
	Gurr, Eric Robert	3,812	5.8%			
	TOTAL	66,103		TOTAL	16,310	
Congressional District 9	May, Richard	9,587	72.2%	Kaptur, Marcy*	32,464	100.0%
	Horrocks Jr., Robert C.	3,686	27.8%			
	TOTAL	13,273		TOTAL	32,464	
Congressional District 10	Turner, Michael R.*	32,550	79.8%	Klepinger, Robert	9,645	55.8%
	Anderson, John	8,214	20.2%	Conner, Bill	7,655	44.2%
	TOTAL	40,764		TOTAL	17,300	
Congressional District 11	Zetzer, Mark	8,839	100.0%	Fudge, Marcia L.*	55,088	100.0%
	TOTAL	8,839		TOTAL	55,088	
Congressional District 12	Tiberi, Patrick J.*	46,186	100.0%	Tibbs, David Arthur	18,259	100.0%
	TOTAL	46,186		TOTAL	18,259	
Congressional District 13	Pekarek, Thomas	351	100.0%	Ryan, Tim*	45,585	85.0%
				Luchansky, John Stephen	8,016	15.0%
	TOTAL	351		TOTAL	53,601	

OHIO

GENERAL AND PRIMARY ELECTIONS

	REPUBLICAN PRIMARIES			DEMOCRATIC PRIMARIES		
Congressional District 14	Joyce, David P.*	27,547	55.0%	Wager, Michael	23,533	100.0%
	Lynch, Matt	22,546	45.0%			
	TOTAL	50,093		TOTAL	23,533	
Congressional District 15	Stivers, Steve*	36,569	90.1%	Wharton, Scott	18,336	100.0%
	Chope, Charles	3,999	9.9%			
	TOTAL	40,568		TOTAL	18,336	
Congressional District 16	Renacci, James B.*	37,040	100.0%	Crossland, Pete	14,635	58.1%
				Donenwirth, James	10,575	41.9%
	TOTAL	37,040		TOTAL	25,210	

Note: An asterisk (*) denotes incumbent.

OKLAHOMA

Congressional districts first established for elections held in 2012

5 members

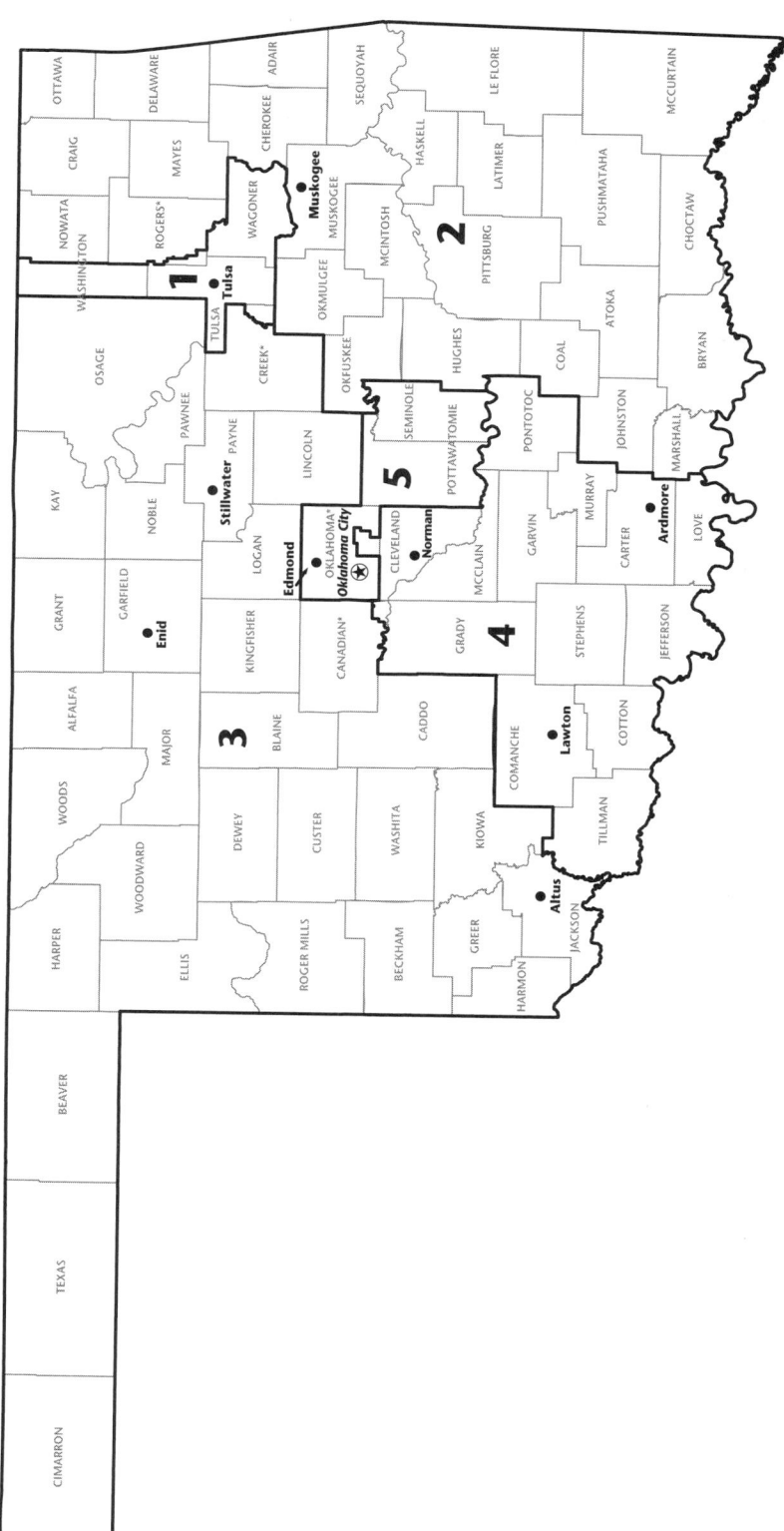

OKLAHOMA

GOVERNOR
Mary Fallin (R). Re-elected 2014 to a four-year term. Previously elected 2010.

SENATORS (2 Republicans)
James M. Inhofe (R). Re-elected 2014 to a six-year term. Previously elected 2008, 2002, 1996, and 1994 to fill out the remaining two years of the term vacated when David L. Boren (D) resigned in November 1994 to become president of the University of Oklahoma.

James Lankford (R). Elected 2014 to the final two years of the term vacated by Tom Coburn (R), who resigned January 3, 2015, after the recurrence of prostate cancer.

REPRESENTATIVES (5 Republicans)
1. Jim Bridenstine (R)
2. Markwayne Mullin (R)
3. Frank D. Lucas (R)
4. Tom Cole (R)
5. Steve Russell (R)

POSTWAR VOTE FOR PRESIDENT

Year	Total Vote	Republican		Democratic		Other Vote	Rep.-Dem. Plurality	Percentage			
		Vote	Candidate	Vote	Candidate			Total Vote		Major Vote	
								Rep.	Dem.	Rep.	Dem.
2012	1,334,872	891,325	Romney, W. Mitt	443,547	Obama, Barack H.*		447,778 R	66.8%	33.2%	66.8%	33.2%
2008	1,462,661	960,165	McCain, John S. III	502,496	Obama, Barack H.		457,669 R	65.6%	34.4%	65.6%	34.4%
2004	1,463,758	959,792	Bush, George W.*	503,966	Kerry, John F.		455,826 R	65.6%	34.4%	65.6%	34.4%
2000**	1,234,229	744,337	Bush, George W.	474,276	Gore, Albert Jr.	15,616	270,061 R	60.3%	38.4%	61.1%	38.9%
1996**	1,206,713	582,315	Dole, Robert "Bob"	488,105	Clinton, Bill*	136,293	94,210 R	48.3%	40.4%	54.4%	45.6%
1992**	1,390,359	592,929	Bush, George H.*	473,066	Clinton, Bill	324,364	119,863 R	42.6%	34.0%	55.6%	44.4%
1988	1,171,036	678,367	Bush, George H.	483,423	Dukakis, Michael S.	9,246	194,944 R	57.9%	41.3%	58.4%	41.6%
1984	1,255,676	861,530	Reagan, Ronald*	385,080	Mondale, Walter F.	9,066	476,450 R	68.6%	30.7%	69.1%	30.9%
1980**	1,149,708	695,570	Reagan, Ronald	402,026	Carter, Jimmy*	52,112	293,544 R	60.5%	35.0%	63.4%	36.6%
1976	1,092,251	545,708	Ford, Gerald R.*	532,442	Carter, Jimmy	14,101	13,266 R	50.0%	48.7%	50.6%	49.4%
1972	1,029,900	759,025	Nixon, Richard M.*	247,147	McGovern, George S.	23,728	511,878 R	73.7%	24.0%	75.4%	24.6%
1968**	943,086	449,697	Nixon, Richard M.	301,658	Humphrey, Hubert Horatio Jr.	191,731	148,039 R	47.7%	32.0%	59.9%	40.1%
1964	932,499	412,665	Goldwater, Barry M. Sr.	519,834	Johnson, Lyndon B.*		107,169 D	44.3%	55.7%	44.3%	55.7%
1960	903,150	533,039	Nixon, Richard M.	370,111	Kennedy, John F.		162,928 R	59.0%	41.0%	59.0%	41.0%
1956	859,350	473,769	Eisenhower, Dwight D.*	385,581	Stevenson, Adlai E. II		88,188 R	55.1%	44.9%	55.1%	44.9%
1952	948,984	518,045	Eisenhower, Dwight D.	430,939	Stevenson, Adlai E. II		87,106 R	54.6%	45.4%	54.6%	45.4%
1948	721,599	268,817	Dewey, Thomas E.	452,782	Truman, Harry S.*		183,965 D	37.3%	62.7%	37.3%	62.7%

Note: An asterisk (*) denotes incumbent. **In past elections, the other vote included: 1996 - 130,788 Reform (Ross Perot); 1992 - 319,878 Independent (Perot); 1980 - 38,284 Independent (John Anderson); 1968 - 191,731 American Independent (George Wallace).

OKLAHOMA

POSTWAR VOTE FOR GOVERNOR

Year	Total Vote	Republican		Democratic		Other Vote	Rep.-Dem. Plurality	Percentage			
		Vote	Candidate	Vote	Candidate			Total Vote		Major Vote	
								Rep.	Dem.	Rep.	Dem.
2014	824,831	460,298	Fallin, Mary*	338,239	Dorman, Joe	26,294	122,059 R	55.8%	41.0%	57.6%	42.4%
2010	1,034,767	625,506	Fallin, Mary	409,261	Askins, Jari		216,245 R	60.4%	39.6%	60.4%	39.6%
2006	926,462	310,327	Istook, Ernest J.	616,135	Henry, Brad*		305,808 D	33.5%	66.5%	33.5%	66.5%
2002**	1,035,620	441,277	Largent, Steve	448,143	Henry, Brad	146,200	6,866 D	42.6%	43.3%	49.6%	50.4%
1998	873,585	505,498	Keating, Frank*	357,552	Boyd, Laura	10,535	147,946 R	57.9%	40.9%	58.6%	41.4%
1994**	995,012	466,740	Keating, Frank	294,936	Mildren, Jack	233,336	171,804 R	46.9%	29.6%	61.3%	38.7%
1990	911,314	297,584	Price, Bill	523,196	Walters, David	90,534	225,612 D	32.7%	57.4%	36.3%	63.7%
1986	909,925	431,762	Bellmon, Henry Louis	405,295	Walters, David	72,868	26,467 R	47.5%	44.5%	51.6%	48.4%
1982	883,130	332,207	Daxon, Tom	548,159	Nigh, George*	2,764	215,952 D	37.6%	62.1%	37.7%	62.3%
1978	777,414	367,055	Shotts, Ron	402,240	Nigh, George	8,119	35,185 D	47.2%	51.7%	47.7%	52.3%
1974	804,842	290,459	Inhofe, James M.	514,383	Boren, David L.		223,924 D	36.1%	63.9%	36.1%	63.9%
1970	698,790	336,157	Bartlett, Dewey F.*	338,338	Hall, David	24,295	2,181 D	48.1%	48.4%	49.8%	50.2%
1966	677,258	377,078	Bartlett, Dewey F.	296,328	Moore, Preston J.	3,852	80,750 R	55.7%	43.8%	56.0%	44.0%
1962	709,763	392,316	Bellmon, Henry Louis	315,357	Atkinson, W. P.	2,090	76,959 R	55.3%	44.4%	55.4%	44.6%
1958	538,839	107,495	Ferguson, Phil	399,504	Edmondson, J. Howard	31,840	292,009 D	19.9%	74.1%	21.2%	78.8%
1954	609,194	251,808	Sparks, Reuben K.	357,386	Gary, Raymond		105,578 D	41.3%	58.7%	41.3%	58.7%
1950	644,276	313,205	Ferguson, Jo O.	329,308	Murray, Johnston	1,763	16,103 D	48.6%	51.1%	48.7%	51.3%
1946	494,599	227,426	Flynn, Olney F.	259,491	Turner, Roy J.	7,682	32,065 D	46.0%	52.5%	46.7%	53.3%

Note: An asterisk (*) denotes incumbent. **In past elections, the other vote included: 2002 - 146,200 Independent (Gary L. Richardson); 1994 - 233,336 Independent (Wes Watkins).

POSTWAR VOTE FOR SENATOR

Year	Total Vote	Republican		Democratic		Other Vote	Rep.-Dem. Plurality	Percentage			
		Vote	Candidate	Vote	Candidate			Total Vote		Major Vote	
								Rep.	Dem.	Rep.	Dem.
2014	820,733	558,166	Inhofe, James M.*	234,307	Silverstein, Matt	28,260	323,859 R	68.0%	28.5%	70.4%	29.6%
2014S	820,890	557,002	Lankford, James	237,923	Johnson, Connie	25,965	319,079 R	67.9%	29.0%	70.1%	29.9%
2010	1,017,151	718,482	Coburn, Tom*	265,814	Rogers, Jim	32,855	452,668 R	70.6%	26.1%	73.0%	27.0%
2008	1,346,819	763,375	Inhofe, James M.*	527,736	Rice, Andrew	55,708	235,639 R	56.7%	39.2%	59.1%	40.9%
2004	1,446,846	763,433	Coburn, Tom	596,750	Carson, Brad	86,663	166,683 R	52.8%	41.2%	56.1%	43.9%
2002	1,018,424	583,579	Inhofe, James M.*	369,789	Walters, David	65,056	213,790 R	57.3%	36.3%	61.2%	38.8%
1998	859,713	570,682	Nickles, Don*	268,898	Carroll, Don E.	20,133	301,784 R	66.4%	31.3%	68.0%	32.0%
1996	1,183,150	670,610	Inhofe, James M.*	474,162	Boren, Jim	38,378	196,448 R	56.7%	40.1%	58.6%	41.4%
1994S	982,430	542,390	Inhofe, James M.	392,488	McCurdy, Dave	47,552	149,902 R	55.2%	40.0%	58.0%	42.0%
1992	1,294,423	757,876	Nickles, Don*	494,350	Lewis, Steve	42,197	263,526 R	58.5%	38.2%	60.5%	39.5%
1990	884,498	148,814	Jones, Stephen	735,684	Boren, David L.*		586,870 D	16.8%	83.2%	16.8%	83.2%
1986	893,666	493,436	Nickles, Don*	400,230	Jones, James R.		93,206 R	55.2%	44.8%	55.2%	44.8%
1984	1,197,937	280,638	Crozier, Will E. Bill	906,131	Boren, David L.*	11,168	625,493 D	23.4%	75.6%	23.6%	76.4%
1980	1,098,294	587,252	Nickles, Don	478,283	Coats, Andrew	32,759	108,969 R	53.5%	43.5%	55.1%	44.9%
1978	754,264	247,857	Kamm, Robert B.	493,953	Boren, David L.	12,454	246,096 D	32.9%	65.5%	33.4%	66.6%
1974	791,809	390,997	Bellmon, Henry Louis*	387,162	Edmondson, Ed	13,650	3,835 R	49.4%	48.9%	50.2%	49.8%
1972	1,005,148	516,934	Bartlett, Dewey F.	478,212	Edmondson, Ed	10,002	38,722 R	51.4%	47.6%	51.9%	48.1%
1968	909,119	470,120	Bellmon, Henry Louis	419,658	Monroney, Almer Stillwell Mike*	19,341	50,462 R	51.7%	46.2%	52.8%	47.2%
1966	638,742	295,585	Patterson, Pat J.	343,157	Harris, Fred R.*		47,572 D	46.3%	53.7%	46.3%	53.7%
1964S	912,174	445,392	Wilkinson, Bud	466,782	Harris, Fred R.		21,390 D	48.8%	51.2%	48.8%	51.2%
1962	664,712	307,966	Crawford, B. Hayden	353,890	Monroney, Almer Stillwell Mike*	2,856	45,924 D	46.3%	53.2%	46.5%	53.5%
1960	864,475	385,646	Crawford, B. Hayden	474,116	Kerr, Robert Samuel Sr.*	4,713	88,470 D	44.6%	54.8%	44.9%	55.1%
1956	831,142	371,146	McKeever, Douglas	459,996	Monroney, Almer Stillwell Mike*		88,850 D	44.7%	55.3%	44.7%	55.3%
1954	600,120	262,013	Mock, Fred M.	335,127	Kerr, Robert Samuel Sr.*	2,980	73,114 D	43.7%	55.8%	43.9%	56.1%
1950	631,177	285,224	Alexander, W. H.	345,953	Monroney, Almer Stillwell Mike		60,729 D	45.2%	54.8%	45.2%	54.8%
1948	708,931	265,169	Rizley, Ross	441,654	Kerr, Robert Samuel Sr.	2,108	176,485 D	37.4%	62.3%	37.5%	62.5%

Note: An asterisk (*) denotes incumbent. **The 1964 and 1994 elections were for short terms to fill vacancies.

OKLAHOMA
GOVERNOR 2014

2010 Census Population	County	Total Vote	Republican (Fallin)	Democratic (Dorman)	Other	Rep.-Dem. Plurality	Percentage Total Vote Rep.	Dem.	Major Vote Rep.	Dem.
22,683	ADAIR	4,149	2,238	1,737	174	501 R	53.9%	41.9%	56.3%	43.7%
5,642	ALFALFA	1,548	972	530	46	442 R	62.8%	34.2%	64.7%	35.3%
14,182	ATOKA	3,487	1,825	1,527	135	298 R	52.3%	43.8%	54.4%	45.6%
5,636	BEAVER	1,516	1,110	343	63	767 R	73.2%	22.6%	76.4%	23.6%
22,119	BECKHAM	4,652	2,785	1,701	166	1,084 R	59.9%	36.6%	62.1%	37.9%
11,943	BLAINE	2,643	1,589	970	84	619 R	60.1%	36.7%	62.1%	37.9%
42,416	BRYAN	8,758	4,337	4,122	299	215 R	49.5%	47.1%	51.3%	48.7%
29,600	CADDO	5,819	2,625	3,082	112	457 D	45.1%	53.0%	46.0%	54.0%
115,541	CANADIAN	28,014	18,456	8,708	850	9,748 R	65.9%	31.1%	67.9%	32.1%
47,557	CARTER	10,725	5,990	4,241	494	1,749 R	55.9%	39.5%	58.5%	41.5%
46,987	CHEROKEE	9,085	4,093	4,655	337	562 D	45.1%	51.2%	46.8%	53.2%
15,205	CHOCTAW	3,129	1,743	1,282	104	461 R	55.7%	41.0%	57.6%	42.4%
2,475	CIMARRON	765	576	137	52	439 R	75.3%	17.9%	80.8%	19.2%
255,755	CLEVELAND	60,227	30,989	27,247	1,991	3,742 R	51.5%	45.2%	53.2%	46.8%
5,925	COAL	1,751	749	937	65	188 D	42.8%	53.5%	44.4%	55.6%
124,098	COMANCHE	20,000	10,091	9,299	610	792 R	50.5%	46.5%	52.0%	48.0%
6,193	COTTON	1,684	902	730	52	172 R	53.6%	43.3%	55.3%	44.7%
15,029	CRAIG	3,564	1,958	1,491	115	467 R	54.9%	41.8%	56.8%	43.2%
69,967	CREEK	15,337	9,618	5,210	509	4,408 R	62.7%	34.0%	64.9%	35.1%
27,469	CUSTER	6,518	4,210	2,124	184	2,086 R	64.6%	32.6%	66.5%	33.5%
41,487	DELAWARE	8,990	5,614	3,126	250	2,488 R	62.4%	34.8%	64.2%	35.8%
4,810	DEWEY	1,496	996	454	46	542 R	66.6%	30.3%	68.7%	31.3%
4,151	ELLIS	1,247	888	316	43	572 R	71.2%	25.3%	73.8%	26.2%
60,580	GARFIELD	12,683	7,247	4,906	530	2,341 R	57.1%	38.7%	59.6%	40.4%
27,576	GARVIN	6,034	3,417	2,428	189	989 R	56.6%	40.2%	58.5%	41.5%
52,431	GRADY	12,912	7,027	5,568	317	1,459 R	54.4%	43.1%	55.8%	44.2%
4,527	GRANT	1,598	979	558	61	421 R	61.3%	34.9%	63.7%	36.3%
6,239	GREER	1,488	820	616	52	204 R	55.1%	41.4%	57.1%	42.9%
2,922	HARMON	686	404	269	13	135 R	58.9%	39.2%	60.0%	40.0%
3,685	HARPER	1,077	750	289	38	461 R	69.6%	26.8%	72.2%	27.8%
12,769	HASKELL	2,487	1,254	1,176	57	78 R	50.4%	47.3%	51.6%	48.4%
14,003	HUGHES	2,922	1,555	1,262	105	293 R	53.2%	43.2%	55.2%	44.8%
26,446	JACKSON	4,207	3,071	1,018	118	2,053 R	73.0%	24.2%	75.1%	24.9%
6,472	JEFFERSON	1,240	640	555	45	85 R	51.6%	44.8%	53.6%	46.4%
10,957	JOHNSTON	2,356	1,133	1,119	104	14 R	48.1%	47.5%	50.3%	49.7%
46,562	KAY	9,989	6,131	3,551	307	2,580 R	61.4%	35.5%	63.3%	36.7%
15,034	KINGFISHER	3,706	2,662	948	96	1,714 R	71.8%	25.6%	73.7%	26.3%
9,446	KIOWA	2,458	1,305	1,090	63	215 R	53.1%	44.3%	54.5%	45.5%
11,154	LATIMER	2,360	1,016	1,266	78	250 D	43.1%	53.6%	44.5%	55.5%
50,384	LE FLORE	9,820	5,281	4,074	465	1,207 R	53.8%	41.5%	56.5%	43.5%
34,273	LINCOLN	8,715	5,377	3,001	337	2,376 R	61.7%	34.4%	64.2%	35.8%
41,848	LOGAN	10,689	6,864	3,462	363	3,402 R	64.2%	32.4%	66.5%	33.5%
9,423	LOVE	2,147	1,177	877	93	300 R	54.8%	40.8%	57.3%	42.7%
7,527	MAJOR	2,200	1,417	693	90	724 R	64.4%	31.5%	67.2%	32.8%
15,840	MARSHALL	3,419	1,792	1,494	133	298 R	52.4%	43.7%	54.5%	45.5%
41,259	MAYES	9,511	5,158	4,016	337	1,142 R	54.2%	42.2%	56.2%	43.8%
34,506	MCCLAIN	9,063	5,593	3,210	260	2,383 R	61.7%	35.4%	63.5%	36.5%
33,151	MCCURTAIN	6,723	3,445	2,917	361	528 R	51.2%	43.4%	54.1%	45.9%
20,252	MCINTOSH	4,609	2,361	2,098	150	263 R	51.2%	45.5%	52.9%	47.1%
13,488	MURRAY	2,952	1,606	1,251	95	355 R	54.4%	42.4%	56.2%	43.8%
70,990	MUSKOGEE	14,330	6,822	7,039	469	217 D	47.6%	49.1%	49.2%	50.8%
11,561	NOBLE	2,918	1,901	927	90	974 R	65.1%	31.8%	67.2%	32.8%
10,536	NOWATA	2,705	1,656	953	96	703 R	61.2%	35.2%	63.5%	36.5%
12,191	OKFUSKEE	2,635	1,290	1,254	91	36 R	49.0%	47.6%	50.7%	49.3%
718,633	OKLAHOMA	155,640	79,853	71,431	4,356	8,422 R	51.3%	45.9%	52.8%	47.2%
40,069	OKMULGEE	8,201	4,165	3,780	256	385 R	50.8%	46.1%	52.4%	47.6%
47,472	OSAGE	11,253	5,861	5,009	383	852 R	52.1%	44.5%	53.9%	46.1%
31,848	OTTAWA	5,218	2,950	2,066	202	884 R	56.5%	39.6%	58.8%	41.2%
16,577	PAWNEE	3,673	2,191	1,346	136	845 R	59.7%	36.6%	61.9%	38.1%
77,350	PAYNE	15,480	7,954	7,088	438	866 R	51.4%	45.8%	52.9%	47.1%

OKLAHOMA

GOVERNOR 2014

2010 Census Population	County	Total Vote	Republican (Fallin)	Democratic (Dorman)	Other	Rep.-Dem. Plurality	Total Vote Rep.	Dem.	Major Vote Rep.	Dem.
45,837	PITTSBURG	10,170	5,163	4,599	408	564 R	50.8%	45.2%	52.9%	47.1%
37,492	PONTOTOC	7,972	3,664	4,051	257	387 D	46.0%	50.8%	47.5%	52.5%
69,442	POTTAWATOMIE	14,621	8,909	5,237	475	3,672 R	60.9%	35.8%	63.0%	37.0%
11,572	PUSHMATAHA	2,575	1,319	1,136	120	183 R	51.2%	44.1%	53.7%	46.3%
3,647	ROGER MILLS	1,219	778	409	32	369 R	63.8%	33.6%	65.5%	34.5%
86,905	ROGERS	21,945	14,048	7,167	730	6,881 R	64.0%	32.7%	66.2%	33.8%
25,482	SEMINOLE	4,769	2,663	1,955	151	708 R	55.8%	41.0%	57.7%	42.3%
42,391	SEQUOYAH	8,640	4,676	3,649	315	1,027 R	54.1%	42.2%	56.2%	43.8%
45,048	STEPHENS	11,368	6,393	4,613	362	1,780 R	56.2%	40.6%	58.1%	41.9%
20,640	TEXAS	3,228	2,466	639	123	1,827 R	76.4%	19.8%	79.4%	20.6%
7,992	TILLMAN	1,693	991	644	58	347 R	58.5%	38.0%	60.6%	39.4%
603,403	TULSA	131,649	74,867	53,073	3,709	21,794 R	56.9%	40.3%	58.5%	41.5%
73,085	WAGONER	16,741	10,675	5,500	566	5,175 R	63.8%	32.9%	66.0%	34.0%
50,976	WASHINGTON	13,235	8,795	3,912	528	4,883 R	66.5%	29.6%	69.2%	30.8%
11,629	WASHITA	3,064	1,943	1,039	82	904 R	63.4%	33.9%	65.2%	34.8%
8,878	WOODS	2,454	1,440	916	98	524 R	58.7%	37.3%	61.1%	38.9%
20,081	WOODWARD	4,280	3,029	1,126	125	1,903 R	70.8%	26.3%	72.9%	27.1%
3,751,351	TOTAL	824,831	460,298	338,239	26,294	122,059 R	55.8%	41.0%	57.6%	42.4%

OKLAHOMA

SENATOR 2014

2010 Census Population	County	Total Vote	Republican (Inhofe)	Democratic (Silverstein)	Other	Rep.-Dem. Plurality	Total Vote Rep.	Dem.	Major Vote Rep.	Dem.
22,683	ADAIR	4,145	2,946	1,063	136	1,883 R	71.1%	25.6%	73.5%	26.5%
5,642	ALFALFA	1,544	1,307	181	56	1,126 R	84.7%	11.7%	87.8%	12.2%
14,182	ATOKA	3,472	2,441	912	119	1,529 R	70.3%	26.3%	72.8%	27.2%
5,636	BEAVER	4,606	3,673	795	138	2,878 R	79.7%	17.3%	82.2%	17.8%
22,119	BECKHAM	1,512	1,310	127	75	1,183 R	86.6%	8.4%	91.2%	8.8%
11,943	BLAINE	2,627	2,104	429	94	1,675 R	80.1%	16.3%	83.1%	16.9%
42,416	BRYAN	8,730	6,122	2,312	296	3,810 R	70.1%	26.5%	72.6%	27.4%
29,600	CADDO	5,785	4,014	1,608	163	2,406 R	69.4%	27.8%	71.4%	28.6%
115,541	CANADIAN	27,877	21,666	5,274	937	16,392 R	77.7%	18.9%	80.4%	19.6%
47,557	CARTER	10,687	7,800	2,492	395	5,308 R	73.0%	23.3%	75.8%	24.2%
46,987	CHEROKEE	9,057	5,257	3,491	309	1,766 R	58.0%	38.5%	60.1%	39.9%
15,205	CHOCTAW	3,122	2,198	821	103	1,377 R	70.4%	26.3%	72.8%	27.2%
2,475	CIMARRON	767	695	43	29	652 R	90.6%	5.6%	94.2%	5.8%
255,755	CLEVELAND	59,906	37,784	19,843	2,279	17,941 R	63.1%	33.1%	65.6%	34.4%
5,925	COAL	1,719	1,118	515	86	603 R	65.0%	30.0%	68.5%	31.5%
124,098	COMANCHE	19,902	13,172	5,925	805	7,247 R	66.2%	29.8%	69.0%	31.0%
6,193	COTTON	1,680	1,266	364	50	902 R	75.4%	21.7%	77.7%	22.3%
15,029	CRAIG	3,549	2,377	1,040	132	1,337 R	67.0%	29.3%	69.6%	30.4%
69,967	CREEK	15,286	11,167	3,652	467	7,515 R	73.1%	23.9%	75.4%	24.6%
27,469	CUSTER	6,501	5,185	1,120	196	4,065 R	79.8%	17.2%	82.2%	17.8%
41,487	DELAWARE	8,958	6,458	2,204	296	4,254 R	72.1%	24.6%	74.6%	25.4%
4,810	DEWEY	1,489	1,256	187	46	1,069 R	84.4%	12.6%	87.0%	13.0%
4,151	ELLIS	1,239	1,085	117	37	968 R	87.6%	9.4%	90.3%	9.7%
60,580	GARFIELD	12,682	9,890	2,304	488	7,586 R	78.0%	18.2%	81.1%	18.9%
27,576	GARVIN	6,003	4,441	1,373	189	3,068 R	74.0%	22.9%	76.4%	23.6%

OKLAHOMA

SENATOR 2014

2010 Census Population	County	Total Vote	Republican (Inhofe)	Democratic (Silverstein)	Other	Rep.-Dem. Plurality	Percentage			
							Total Vote		Major Vote	
							Rep.	Dem.	Rep.	Dem.
52,431	GRADY	12,823	9,666	2,735	422	6,931 R	75.4%	21.3%	77.9%	22.1%
4,527	GRANT	1,583	1,302	227	54	1,075 R	82.2%	14.3%	85.2%	14.8%
6,239	GREER	1,482	1,085	342	55	743 R	73.2%	23.1%	76.0%	24.0%
2,922	HARMON	680	538	128	14	410 R	79.1%	18.8%	80.8%	19.2%
3,685	HARPER	1,081	942	98	41	844 R	87.1%	9.1%	90.6%	9.4%
12,769	HASKELL	2,473	1,681	722	70	959 R	68.0%	29.2%	70.0%	30.0%
14,003	HUGHES	2,896	1,987	790	119	1,197 R	68.6%	27.3%	71.6%	28.4%
26,446	JACKSON	4,198	3,455	640	103	2,815 R	82.3%	15.2%	84.4%	15.6%
6,472	JEFFERSON	1,228	886	284	58	602 R	72.1%	23.1%	75.7%	24.3%
10,957	JOHNSTON	2,350	1,633	613	104	1,020 R	69.5%	26.1%	72.7%	27.3%
46,562	KAY	9,930	7,369	2,183	378	5,186 R	74.2%	22.0%	77.1%	22.9%
15,034	KINGFISHER	3,696	3,220	392	84	2,828 R	87.1%	10.6%	89.1%	10.9%
9,446	KIOWA	2,450	1,856	540	54	1,316 R	75.8%	22.0%	77.5%	22.5%
11,154	LATIMER	2,345	1,489	776	80	713 R	63.5%	33.1%	65.7%	34.3%
50,384	LE FLORE	9,742	6,507	2,757	478	3,750 R	66.8%	28.3%	70.2%	29.8%
34,273	LINCOLN	8,661	6,602	1,763	296	4,839 R	76.2%	20.4%	78.9%	21.1%
41,848	LOGAN	10,665	8,040	2,256	369	5,784 R	75.4%	21.2%	78.1%	21.9%
9,423	LOVE	2,136	1,534	520	82	1,014 R	71.8%	24.3%	74.7%	25.3%
7,527	MAJOR	2,207	1,806	203	198	1,603 R	81.8%	9.2%	89.9%	10.1%
15,840	MARSHALL	3,399	2,521	758	120	1,763 R	74.2%	22.3%	76.9%	23.1%
41,259	MAYES	9,466	6,356	2,735	375	3,621 R	67.1%	28.9%	69.9%	30.1%
34,506	MCCLAIN	9,018	6,982	1,735	301	5,247 R	77.4%	19.2%	80.1%	19.9%
33,151	MCCURTAIN	6,664	4,745	1,618	301	3,127 R	71.2%	24.3%	74.6%	25.4%
20,252	MCINTOSH	4,602	2,915	1,547	140	1,368 R	63.3%	33.6%	65.3%	34.7%
13,488	MURRAY	2,931	2,109	717	105	1,392 R	72.0%	24.5%	74.6%	25.4%
70,990	MUSKOGEE	14,279	8,616	5,148	515	3,468 R	60.3%	36.1%	62.6%	37.4%
11,561	NOBLE	2,907	2,316	516	75	1,800 R	79.7%	17.8%	81.8%	18.2%
10,536	NOWATA	2,700	1,961	642	97	1,319 R	72.6%	23.8%	75.3%	24.7%
12,191	OKFUSKEE	2,612	1,734	797	81	937 R	66.4%	30.5%	68.5%	31.5%
718,633	OKLAHOMA	154,477	93,410	55,715	5,352	37,695 R	60.5%	36.1%	62.6%	37.4%
40,069	OKMULGEE	8,178	4,986	2,945	247	2,041 R	61.0%	36.0%	62.9%	37.1%
47,472	OSAGE	11,213	7,078	3,757	378	3,321 R	63.1%	33.5%	65.3%	34.7%
31,848	OTTAWA	5,199	3,411	1,542	246	1,869 R	65.6%	29.7%	68.9%	31.1%
16,577	PAWNEE	3,663	2,602	937	124	1,665 R	71.0%	25.6%	73.5%	26.5%
77,350	PAYNE	15,382	9,923	4,899	560	5,024 R	64.5%	31.8%	66.9%	33.1%
45,837	PITTSBURG	10,139	7,029	2,811	299	4,218 R	69.3%	27.7%	71.4%	28.6%
37,492	PONTOTOC	7,937	5,591	2,069	277	3,522 R	70.4%	26.1%	73.0%	27.0%
69,442	POTTAWATOMIE	14,533	10,564	3,420	549	7,144 R	72.7%	23.5%	75.5%	24.5%
11,572	PUSHMATAHA	2,567	1,825	648	94	1,177 R	71.1%	25.2%	73.8%	26.2%
3,647	ROGER MILLS	1,209	1,030	147	32	883 R	85.2%	12.2%	87.5%	12.5%
86,905	ROGERS	21,877	16,173	4,873	831	11,300 R	73.9%	22.3%	76.8%	23.2%
25,482	SEMINOLE	4,735	3,327	1,262	146	2,065 R	70.3%	26.7%	72.5%	27.5%
42,391	SEQUOYAH	8,567	5,496	2,676	395	2,820 R	64.2%	31.2%	67.3%	32.7%
45,048	STEPHENS	11,310	8,606	2,270	434	6,336 R	76.1%	20.1%	79.1%	20.9%
20,640	TEXAS	3,230	2,777	326	127	2,451 R	86.0%	10.1%	89.5%	10.5%
7,992	TILLMAN	1,684	1,271	367	46	904 R	75.5%	21.8%	77.6%	22.4%
603,403	TULSA	131,143	84,435	42,907	3,801	41,528 R	64.4%	32.7%	66.3%	33.7%
73,085	WAGONER	16,686	12,139	4,033	514	8,106 R	72.7%	24.2%	75.1%	24.9%
50,976	WASHINGTON	13,208	9,817	2,935	456	6,882 R	74.3%	22.2%	77.0%	23.0%
11,629	WASHITA	3,042	2,499	473	70	2,026 R	82.1%	15.5%	84.1%	15.9%
8,878	WOODS	2,442	1,963	400	79	1,563 R	80.4%	16.4%	83.1%	16.9%
20,081	WOODWARD	4,263	3,629	521	113	3,108 R	85.1%	12.2%	87.4%	12.6%
3,751,351	TOTAL	820,733	558,166	234,307	28,260	323,859 R	68.0%	28.5%	70.4%	29.6%

OKLAHOMA
SENATOR SPECIAL 2014

2010 Census Population	County	Total Vote	Republican (Lankford)	Democratic (Johnson)	Other	Rep.-Dem. Plurality	Total Vote Rep.	Total Vote Dem.	Major Vote Rep.	Major Vote Dem.
22,683	ADAIR	4,110	2,758	1,187	165	1,571 R	67.1%	28.9%	69.9%	30.1%
5,642	ALFALFA	1,550	1,326	176	48	1,150 R	85.5%	11.4%	88.3%	11.7%
14,182	ATOKA	3,420	2,241	1,022	157	1,219 R	65.5%	29.9%	68.7%	31.3%
5,636	BEAVER	1,508	1,312	123	73	1,189 R	87.0%	8.2%	91.4%	8.6%
22,119	BECKHAM	4,628	3,680	847	101	2,833 R	79.5%	18.3%	81.3%	18.7%
11,943	BLAINE	2,627	2,032	500	95	1,532 R	77.4%	19.0%	80.3%	19.7%
42,416	BRYAN	8,631	5,696	2,543	392	3,153 R	66.0%	29.5%	69.1%	30.9%
29,600	CADDO	5,792	4,068	1,589	135	2,479 R	70.2%	27.4%	71.9%	28.1%
115,541	CANADIAN	27,998	21,909	5,320	769	16,589 R	78.3%	19.0%	80.5%	19.5%
47,557	CARTER	10,628	7,259	2,899	470	4,360 R	68.3%	27.3%	71.5%	28.5%
46,987	CHEROKEE	9,034	5,237	3,441	356	1,796 R	58.0%	38.1%	60.3%	39.7%
15,205	CHOCTAW	3,102	2,102	880	120	1,222 R	67.8%	28.4%	70.5%	29.5%
2,475	CIMARRON	756	660	64	32	596 R	87.3%	8.5%	91.2%	8.8%
255,755	CLEVELAND	60,082	38,040	20,145	1,897	17,895 R	63.3%	33.5%	65.4%	34.6%
5,925	COAL	1,690	946	646	98	300 R	56.0%	38.2%	59.4%	40.6%
124,098	COMANCHE	19,832	12,218	6,866	748	5,352 R	61.6%	34.6%	64.0%	36.0%
6,193	COTTON	1,674	1,240	379	55	861 R	74.1%	22.6%	76.6%	23.4%
15,029	CRAIG	3,526	2,341	1,082	103	1,259 R	66.4%	30.7%	68.4%	31.6%
69,967	CREEK	15,287	11,221	3,529	537	7,692 R	73.4%	23.1%	76.1%	23.9%
27,469	CUSTER	6,514	5,192	1,171	151	4,021 R	79.7%	18.0%	81.6%	18.4%
41,487	DELAWARE	8,906	6,352	2,228	326	4,124 R	71.3%	25.0%	74.0%	26.0%
4,810	DEWEY	1,479	1,253	184	42	1,069 R	84.7%	12.4%	87.2%	12.8%
4,151	ELLIS	1,246	1,090	129	27	961 R	87.5%	10.4%	89.4%	10.6%
60,580	GARFIELD	12,702	9,947	2,405	350	7,542 R	78.3%	18.9%	80.5%	19.5%
27,576	GARVIN	6,017	4,387	1,450	180	2,937 R	72.9%	24.1%	75.2%	24.8%
52,431	GRADY	12,871	9,649	2,722	500	6,927 R	75.0%	21.1%	78.0%	22.0%
4,527	GRANT	1,591	1,276	265	50	1,011 R	80.2%	16.7%	82.8%	17.2%
6,239	GREER	1,466	1,056	360	50	696 R	72.0%	24.6%	74.6%	25.4%
2,922	HARMON	683	521	143	19	378 R	76.3%	20.9%	78.5%	21.5%
3,685	HARPER	1,076	924	107	45	817 R	85.9%	9.9%	89.6%	10.4%
12,769	HASKELL	2,461	1,658	726	77	932 R	67.4%	29.5%	69.5%	30.5%
14,003	HUGHES	2,899	1,974	835	90	1,139 R	68.1%	28.8%	70.3%	29.7%
26,446	JACKSON	4,200	3,429	668	103	2,761 R	81.6%	15.9%	83.7%	16.3%
6,472	JEFFERSON	1,219	836	327	56	509 R	68.6%	26.8%	71.9%	28.1%
10,957	JOHNSTON	2,320	1,495	702	123	793 R	64.4%	30.3%	68.0%	32.0%
46,562	KAY	9,949	7,332	2,269	348	5,063 R	73.7%	22.8%	76.4%	23.6%
15,034	KINGFISHER	3,702	3,182	439	81	2,743 R	86.0%	11.9%	87.9%	12.1%
9,446	KIOWA	2,445	1,815	575	55	1,240 R	74.2%	23.5%	75.9%	24.1%
11,154	LATIMER	2,351	1,396	849	106	547 R	59.4%	36.1%	62.2%	37.8%
50,384	LE FLORE	9,670	6,182	2,985	503	3,197 R	63.9%	30.9%	67.4%	32.6%
34,273	LINCOLN	8,693	6,643	1,767	283	4,876 R	76.4%	20.3%	79.0%	21.0%
41,848	LOGAN	10,669	8,066	2,289	314	5,777 R	75.6%	21.5%	77.9%	22.1%
9,423	LOVE	2,096	1,355	645	96	710 R	64.6%	30.8%	67.8%	32.2%
7,527	MAJOR	2,204	1,904	240	60	1,664 R	86.4%	10.9%	88.8%	11.2%
15,840	MARSHALL	3,361	2,318	901	142	1,417 R	69.0%	26.8%	72.0%	28.0%
41,259	MAYES	9,433	6,390	2,715	328	3,675 R	67.7%	28.8%	70.2%	29.8%
34,506	MCCLAIN	9,049	7,033	1,761	255	5,272 R	77.7%	19.5%	80.0%	20.0%
33,151	MCCURTAIN	6,588	4,419	1,820	349	2,599 R	67.1%	27.6%	70.8%	29.2%
20,252	MCINTOSH	4,586	2,869	1,570	147	1,299 R	62.6%	34.2%	64.6%	35.4%
13,488	MURRAY	2,925	2,130	717	78	1,413 R	72.8%	24.5%	74.8%	25.2%
70,990	MUSKOGEE	14,200	8,503	5,183	514	3,320 R	59.9%	36.5%	62.1%	37.9%
11,561	NOBLE	2,905	2,327	493	85	1,834 R	80.1%	17.0%	82.5%	17.5%
10,536	NOWATA	2,687	1,877	684	126	1,193 R	69.9%	25.5%	73.3%	26.7%
12,191	OKFUSKEE	2,608	1,714	817	77	897 R	65.7%	31.3%	67.7%	32.3%
718,633	OKLAHOMA	155,429	94,249	57,305	3,875	36,944 R	60.6%	36.9%	62.2%	37.8%
40,069	OKMULGEE	8,176	4,931	2,975	270	1,956 R	60.3%	36.4%	62.4%	37.6%
47,472	OSAGE	11,191	6,999	3,788	404	3,211 R	62.5%	33.8%	64.9%	35.1%
31,848	OTTAWA	5,184	3,336	1,588	260	1,748 R	64.4%	30.6%	67.7%	32.3%
16,577	PAWNEE	3,656	2,587	930	139	1,657 R	70.8%	25.4%	73.6%	26.4%
77,350	PAYNE	15,402	10,041	4,908	453	5,133 R	65.2%	31.9%	67.2%	32.8%

OKLAHOMA

SENATOR SPECIAL 2014

2010 Census Population	County	Total Vote	Republican (Lankford)	Democratic (Johnson)	Other	Rep.-Dem. Plurality	Percentage Total Vote Rep.	Dem.	Major Vote Rep.	Dem.
45,837	PITTSBURG	10,090	6,488	3,196	406	3,292 R	64.3%	31.7%	67.0%	33.0%
37,492	PONTOTOC	7,932	5,447	2,178	307	3,269 R	68.7%	27.5%	71.4%	28.6%
69,442	POTTAWATOMIE	14,608	10,835	3,361	412	7,474 R	74.2%	23.0%	76.3%	23.7%
11,572	PUSHMATAHA	2,536	1,687	729	120	958 R	66.5%	28.7%	69.8%	30.2%
3,647	ROGER MILLS	1,222	1,006	194	22	812 R	82.3%	15.9%	83.8%	16.2%
86,905	ROGERS	21,869	16,661	4,503	705	12,158 R	76.2%	20.6%	78.7%	21.3%
25,482	SEMINOLE	4,751	3,384	1,248	119	2,136 R	71.2%	26.3%	73.1%	26.9%
42,391	SEQUOYAH	8,498	5,327	2,762	409	2,565 R	62.7%	32.5%	65.9%	34.1%
45,048	STEPHENS	11,290	8,383	2,525	382	5,858 R	74.3%	22.4%	76.9%	23.1%
20,640	TEXAS	3,222	2,740	348	134	2,392 R	85.0%	10.8%	88.7%	11.3%
7,992	TILLMAN	1,678	1,219	423	36	796 R	72.6%	25.2%	74.2%	25.8%
603,403	TULSA	130,887	86,569	40,533	3,785	46,036 R	66.1%	31.0%	68.1%	31.9%
73,085	WAGONER	16,666	12,288	3,847	531	8,441 R	73.7%	23.1%	76.2%	23.8%
50,976	WASHINGTON	13,192	10,013	2,705	474	7,308 R	75.9%	20.5%	78.7%	21.3%
11,629	WASHITA	3,050	2,474	509	67	1,965 R	81.1%	16.7%	82.9%	17.1%
8,878	WOODS	2,444	1,947	425	72	1,522 R	79.7%	17.4%	82.1%	17.9%
20,081	WOODWARD	4,271	3,611	564	96	3,047 R	84.5%	13.2%	86.5%	13.5%
3,751,351	TOTAL	820,890	557,002	237,923	25,965	319,079 R	67.9%	29.0%	70.1%	29.9%

OKLAHOMA

HOUSE OF REPRESENTATIVES

CD	Year	Total Vote	Republican Vote	Candidate	Democratic Vote	Candidate	Other Vote	Rep.-Dem. Plurality	Percentage Total Vote Rep.	Dem.	Major Vote Rep.	Dem.
1	2014			BRIDENSTINE, JIM*				R				
1	2012	285,312	181,084	BRIDENSTINE, JIM	91,421	OLSON, JOHN	12,807	89,663 R	63.5%	32.0%	66.5%	33.5%
2	2014	158,407	110,925	MULLIN, MARKWAYNE*	38,964	EVERETT, EARL E.	8,518	71,961 R	70.0%	24.6%	74.0%	26.0%
2	2012	250,612	143,701	MULLIN, MARKWAYNE	96,081	WALLACE, ROB	10,830	47,620 R	57.3%	38.3%	59.9%	40.1%
3	2014	169,605	133,335	LUCAS, FRANK D.*	36,270	ROBBINS, FRANKIE		97,065 R	78.6%	21.4%	78.6%	21.4%
3	2012	268,003	201,744	LUCAS, FRANK D.*	53,472	MURRAY, TIMOTHY RAY	12,787	148,272 R	75.3%	20.0%	79.0%	21.0%
4	2014	166,268	117,721	COLE, TOM*	40,998	SMITH, BERT	7,549	76,723 R	70.8%	24.7%	74.2%	25.8%
4	2012	260,331	176,740	COLE, TOM*	71,846	BEBO, DONNA MARIE	11,745	104,894 R	67.9%	27.6%	71.1%	28.9%
5	2014	159,133	95,632	RUSSELL, STEVE	57,790	MCAFFREY, AL	5,711	37,842 R	60.1%	36.3%	62.3%	37.7%
5	2012	261,677	153,603	LANKFORD, JAMES*	97,504	GUILD, TOM	10,570	56,099 R	58.7%	37.3%	61.2%	38.8%
TOTAL	2014	653,413	457,613		174,022		21,778	283,591 R	70.0%	26.6%	72.4%	27.6%
TOTAL	2012	1,325,935	856,872		410,324		58,739	446,548 R	64.6%	30.9%	67.6%	32.4%

Note: An asterisk (*) denotes incumbent.

OKLAHOMA

GENERAL AND PRIMARY ELECTIONS

2014 GENERAL ELECTIONS: OTHER VOTES

Governor	Other vote was 17,169 Independent (Kimberly Willis), 9,125 Independent (Richard Prawdzienski)
Senate (Full Term)	Other vote was 10,554 Independent (Joan Farr), 9,913 Independent (Ray Woods), 7,793 Independent (Aaron DeLozier)
Senate (Short Term)	Other vote was 25,965 Independent (Mark T. Beard)
House	Other vote was:
CD 2	8,518 Independent (Jon Douthitt)
CD 4	7,549 Independent (Dennis Johnson)
CD 5	2,176 Independent (Robert T. Murphy), 2,065 Independent (Tom Boggs), 1,470 Independent (Buddy Ray)

2014 PRIMARY ELECTIONS: SUPPLEMENTARY INFORMATION

Primary	June 24, 2014	**Registration** (as of January 15, 2014)	1,978,812	Democratic	885,609
				Republican	854,329
				Americans Elect	4
				Independent	238,870

Primary Runoff August 26, 2014

Primary Type Closed—Only registered Democrats and Republicans could vote in their party's primary.

REPUBLICAN PRIMARIES				DEMOCRATIC PRIMARIES		
Senator (Full Term)	Inhofe, James M.*	231,291	87.7%	Silverstein, Matt	Unopposed	
	Rogers, Evelyn L.	11,960	4.5%			
	Wyatt, Erick Paul	11,713	4.4%			
	Moye, Rob	4,846	1.8%			
	McBride-Samuels, D. Jean	3,965	1.5%			
	TOTAL	263,775				
Senator (Short Term)	James Lankford	152,749	57.2%	Cannie Johnson	71,462	43.8%
	T. W. Shannon	91,854	34.4%	Jim Rogers	57,598	35.3%
	Randy Brogdon	12,934	4.8%	Patrick Michael Hayes	33,943	20.8%
	Kevin Crow	2,828	1.1%	TOTAL	163,003	
	Andy Craig	2,427	0.9%			
	Eric C. McCray	2,272	0.9%			
	Jason Weger	1,794	0.7%			
	TOTAL	266,858				
				PRIMARY RUNOFF		
				Johnson, Connie	54,762	58.0%
				Rogers, Jim	39,664	42.0%
				TOTAL	94,426	
Governor	Fallin, Mary*	200,035	75.5%	Dorman, Joe	Unopposed	
	Moody, Chad	40,839	15.4%			
	Ewbank, Dax	24,020	9.1%			
	TOTAL	264,894				

OKLAHOMA

GENERAL AND PRIMARY ELECTIONS

REPUBLICAN PRIMARIES			DEMOCRATIC PRIMARIES		
Congressional District 1	Bridenstine, Jim*	Unopposed			
Congressional District 2	Mullin, Markwayne*	26,245	79.7%	Everett, Earl E.	33,119	62.6%
	Robertson, Darrel	6,673	20.3%	Harris-Till, Joshua	19,813	37.4%
	TOTAL	32,918		TOTAL	52,932	
Congressional District 3	Lucas, Frank D.*	54,847	82.8%	Robbins, Frankie	Unopposed	
	Hubbard, Robert	7,925	12.0%			
	Murray, Timothy Ray	3,449	5.2%			
	TOTAL	66,221				
Congressional District 4	Cole, Tom*	40,790	84.4%	Smith, Bert	24,268	81.6%
	Flatt, Anna	7,511	15.6%	Si, Tae	5,485	18.4%
	TOTAL	48,301		TOTAL	29,753	
Congressional District 5	Russell, Steve	14,604	26.6%	Guild, Tom	11,603	42.1%
	Douglas, Patrice	13,445	24.5%	McAffrey, Al	8,507	30.9%
	Jolley, Clark	9,232	16.8%	Leonard, Leona	7,431	27.0%
	Turner, Mike J.	7,760	14.1%			
	Jett, Shane	7,022	12.8%			
	Sparks, Harvey	2,898	5.3%			
	TOTAL	54,961		TOTAL	27,541	
	PRIMARY RUNOFF			**PRIMARY RUNOFF**		
	Russell, Steve	19,374	59.3%	McAffrey, Al	10,417	54.2%
	Douglas, Patrice	13,319	40.7%	Guild, Tom	8,793	45.8%
	TOTAL	32,693		TOTAL	19,210	

Note: An asterisk (*) denotes incumbent.

OREGON

Congressional districts first established for elections held in 2012
5 members

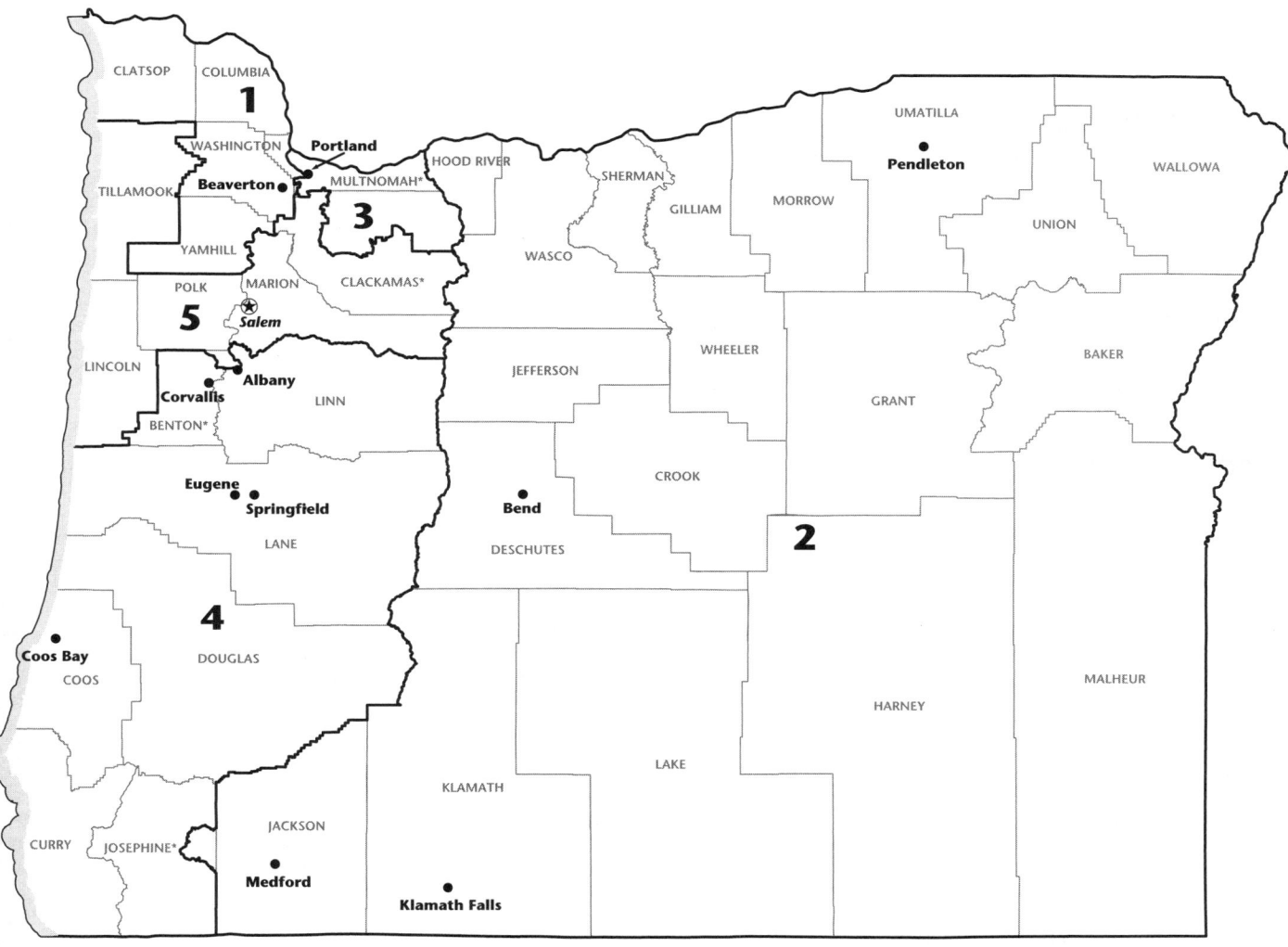

* Asterisk indicates a county whose boundaries include parts of two or more congressional districts.

OREGON

GOVERNOR

Kate Brown (D). Assumed governorship upon the resignation February 18, 2015, of John Kitzhaber (D), who left office under an ethics cloud involving conflict of interest charges spawned by his fiancée.

SENATORS (2 Democrats)

Jeff Merkley (D). Reelected 2014 to a six-year term. Previously elected 2008.

Ron Wyden (D). Reelected 2010 to a six-year term. Previously elected 2004, 1998, and in a special election January 30, 1996, to serve the remaining three years of the term vacated when Senator Robert W. Packwood (R) resigned in October 1995.

REPRESENTATIVES (1 Republican, 4 Democrats)

1. Suzanne Bonamici (D)
2. Greg Walden (R)
3. Earl Blumenauer (D)
4. Peter A. DeFazio (D)
5. Kurt Schrader (D)

POSTWAR VOTE FOR PRESIDENT

| Year | Total Vote | Republican | | Democratic | | Other Vote | Rep.-Dem. Plurality | Percentage | | | |
| | | Vote | Candidate | Vote | Candidate | | | Total Vote | | Major Vote | |
								Rep.	Dem.	Rep.	Dem.
2012	1,789,270	754,175	Romney, W. Mitt	970,488	Obama, Barack H.*	64,607	216,313 D	42.1%	54.2%	43.7%	56.3%
2008	1,827,864	738,475	McCain, John S. III	1,037,291	Obama, Barack H.	52,098	298,816 D	40.4%	56.7%	41.6%	58.4%
2004	1,836,782	866,831	Bush, George W.*	943,163	Kerry, John F.	26,788	76,332 D	47.2%	51.3%	47.9%	52.1%
2000**	1,533,968	713,577	Bush, George W.	720,342	Gore, Albert Jr.	100,049	6,765 D	46.5%	47.0%	49.8%	50.2%
1996**	1,377,760	538,152	Dole, Robert "Bob"	649,641	Clinton, Bill*	189,967	111,489 D	39.1%	47.2%	45.3%	54.7%
1992**	1,462,643	475,757	Bush, George H.*	621,314	Clinton, Bill	365,572	145,557 D	32.5%	42.5%	43.4%	56.6%
1988	1,201,694	560,126	Bush, George H.	616,206	Dukakis, Michael S.	25,362	56,080 D	46.6%	51.3%	47.6%	52.4%
1984	1,226,527	685,700	Reagan, Ronald*	536,479	Mondale, Walter F.	4,348	149,221 R	55.9%	43.7%	56.1%	43.9%
1980**	1,181,516	571,044	Reagan, Ronald	456,890	Carter, Jimmy*	153,582	114,154 R	48.3%	38.7%	55.6%	44.4%
1976	1,029,876	492,120	Ford, Gerald R.*	490,407	Carter, Jimmy	47,349	1,713 R	47.8%	47.6%	50.1%	49.9%
1972	927,946	486,686	Nixon, Richard M.*	392,760	McGovern, George S.	48,500	93,926 R	52.4%	42.3%	55.3%	44.7%
1968**	819,622	408,433	Nixon, Richard M.	358,866	Humphrey, Hubert Horatio Jr.	52,323	49,567 R	49.8%	43.8%	53.2%	46.8%
1964	786,305	282,779	Goldwater, Barry M. Sr.	501,017	Johnson, Lyndon B.*	2,509	218,238 D	36.0%	63.7%	36.1%	63.9%
1960	776,421	408,060	Nixon, Richard M.	367,402	Kennedy, John F.	959	40,658 R	52.6%	47.3%	52.6%	47.4%
1956	736,132	406,393	Eisenhower, Dwight D.*	329,204	Stevenson, Adlai E. II	535	77,189 R	55.2%	44.7%	55.2%	44.8%
1952	695,059	420,815	Eisenhower, Dwight D.	270,579	Stevenson, Adlai E. II	3,665	150,236 R	60.5%	38.9%	60.9%	39.1%
1948	524,080	260,904	Dewey, Thomas E.	243,147	Truman, Harry S.*	20,029	17,757 R	49.8%	46.4%	51.8%	48.2%

Note: An asterisk (*) denotes incumbent. **In past elections, the other vote included: 2000 - 77,357 Green (Ralph Nader); 1996 - 121,221 Reform (Ross Perot); 1992 - 354,091 Independent (Perot); 1980 - 112,389 Independent (John Anderson); 1968 - 49,683 American Independent (George Wallace).

OREGON

POSTWAR VOTE FOR GOVERNOR

Year	Total Vote	Republican Vote	Republican Candidate	Democratic Vote	Democratic Candidate	Other Vote	Rep.-Dem. Plurality	Total Vote Rep.	Total Vote Dem.	Major Vote Rep.	Major Vote Dem.
2014	1,469,717	648,542	Richardson, Dennis	733,230	Kitzhaber, John*	87,945	84,688 D	44.1%	49.9%	46.9%	53.1%
2010	1,453,548	694,287	Dudley, Chris	716,525	Kitzhaber, John	42,736	22,238 D	47.8%	49.3%	49.2%	50.8%
2006	1,379,475	589,748	Saxton, Ron	699,786	Kulongoski, Ted*	89,941	110,038 D	42.8%	50.7%	45.7%	54.3%
2002	1,260,497	581,785	Mannix, Kevin L.	618,004	Kulongoski, Ted	60,708	36,219 D	46.2%	49.0%	48.5%	51.5%
1998	1,113,098	334,001	Sizemore, Bill	717,061	Kitzhaber, John*	62,036	383,060 D	30.0%	64.4%	31.8%	68.2%
1994	1,221,010	517,874	Smith, Denny	622,083	Kitzhaber, John	81,053	104,209 D	42.4%	50.9%	45.4%	54.6%
1990**	1,112,847	444,646	Frohnmayer, Dave	508,749	Roberts, Barbara	159,452	64,103 D	40.0%	45.7%	46.6%	53.4%
1986	1,059,630	506,986	Paulus, Norma	549,456	Goldschmidt, Neil	3,188	42,470 D	47.8%	51.9%	48.0%	52.0%
1982	1,042,009	639,841	Atiyeh, Victor*	374,316	Kulongoski, Ted	27,852	265,525 R	61.4%	35.9%	63.1%	36.9%
1978	911,143	498,452	Atiyeh, Victor	409,411	Straub, Robert W.*	3,280	89,041 R	54.7%	44.9%	54.9%	45.1%
1974	770,574	324,751	Atiyeh, Victor	444,812	Straub, Robert W.	1,011	120,061 D	42.1%	57.7%	42.2%	57.8%
1970	666,394	369,964	McCall, Tom*	293,892	Straub, Robert W.	2,538	76,072 R	55.5%	44.1%	55.7%	44.3%
1966	682,862	377,346	McCall, Tom	305,008	Straub, Robert W.	508	72,338 R	55.3%	44.7%	55.3%	44.7%
1962	637,407	345,497	Hatfield, Mark O.*	265,359	Thornton, Robert Y.	26,551	80,138 R	54.2%	41.6%	56.6%	43.4%
1958	599,994	331,900	Hatfield, Mark O.	267,934	Holmes, Robert D.*	160	63,966 R	55.3%	44.7%	55.3%	44.7%
1956S	731,279	361,840	Smith, Elmo E.	369,439	Holmes, Robert D.		7,599 D	49.5%	50.5%	49.5%	50.5%
1954	566,701	322,522	Patterson, Paul	244,179	Carson, Joseph K. Jr.		78,343 R	56.9%	43.1%	56.9%	43.1%
1950	505,910	334,160	McKay, Douglas*	171,750	Flegal, Austin F.		162,410 R	66.1%	33.9%	66.1%	33.9%
1948S	509,624	271,295	McKay, Douglas	226,949	Wallace, Lew	11,380	44,346 R	53.2%	44.5%	54.5%	45.5%
1946	344,155	237,681	Snell, Earl*	106,474	Donaugh, Carl C.		131,207 R	69.1%	30.9%	69.1%	30.9%

Note: An asterisk (*) denotes incumbent. **In past elections, the other vote included: 1990 - 144,062 Independent (Al Mobley). The 1948 and 1956 elections were for short terms to fill a vacany.

POSTWAR VOTE FOR SENATOR

Year	Total Vote	Republican Vote	Republican Candidate	Democratic Vote	Democratic Candidate	Other Vote	Rep.-Dem. Plurality	Total Vote Rep.	Total Vote Dem.	Major Vote Rep.	Major Vote Dem.
2014	1,461,618	538,847	Wehby, Monica	814,537	Merkley, Jeff*	108,234	275,690 D	36.9%	55.7%	39.8%	60.2%
2010	1,442,588	566,199	Huffman, Jim	825,507	Wyden, Ron*	50,882	259,308 D	39.2%	57.2%	40.7%	59.3%
2008	1,767,504	805,159	Smith, Gordon H.*	864,392	Merkley, Jeff	97,953	59,233 D	45.6%	48.9%	48.2%	51.8%
2004	1,780,550	565,254	King, Al	1,128,728	Wyden, Ron*	86,568	563,474 D	31.7%	63.4%	33.4%	66.6%
2002	1,267,221	712,287	Smith, Gordon H.*	501,898	Bradbury, Bill	53,036	210,389 R	56.2%	39.6%	58.7%	41.3%
1998	1,117,747	377,739	Lim, John	682,425	Wyden, Ron*	57,583	304,686 D	33.8%	61.1%	35.6%	64.4%
1996	1,360,230	677,336	Smith, Gordon H.*	624,370	Bruggere, Tom	58,524	52,966 R	49.8%	45.9%	52.0%	48.0%
1996S	1,196,608	553,519	Smith, Gordon H.	571,739	Wyden, Ron	71,350	18,220 D	46.3%	47.8%	49.2%	50.8%
1992	1,376,033	717,455	Packwood, Robert W.*	639,851	Aucoin, Les	18,727	77,604 R	52.1%	46.5%	52.9%	47.1%
1990	1,099,255	590,095	Hatfield, Mark O.*	507,743	Lonsdale, Harry	1,417	82,352 R	53.7%	46.2%	53.8%	46.2%
1986	1,042,555	656,317	Packwood, Robert W.*	375,735	Bauman, Rick	10,503	280,582 R	63.0%	36.0%	63.6%	36.4%
1984	1,214,735	808,152	Hatfield, Mark O.*	406,122	Hendriksen, Margie	461	402,030 R	66.5%	33.4%	66.6%	33.4%
1980	1,140,494	594,290	Packwood, Robert W.*	501,963	Kulongoski, Ted	44,241	92,327 R	52.1%	44.0%	54.2%	45.8%
1978	892,518	550,165	Hatfield, Mark O.*	341,616	Cook, Vernon	737	208,549 R	61.6%	38.3%	61.7%	38.3%
1974	766,414	420,984	Packwood, Robert W.*	338,591	Roberts, Betty	6,839	82,393 R	54.9%	44.2%	55.4%	44.6%
1972	920,833	494,671	Hatfield, Mark O.*	425,036	Morse, Wayne L.	1,126	69,635 R	53.7%	46.2%	53.8%	46.2%
1968	814,176	408,646	Packwood, Robert W.	405,353	Morse, Wayne L.*	177	3,293 R	50.2%	49.8%	50.2%	49.8%
1966	685,067	354,391	Hatfield, Mark O.	330,374	Duncan, Robert B.	302	24,017 R	51.7%	48.2%	51.8%	48.2%
1962	636,558	291,587	Unander, Sig	344,716	Morse, Wayne L.*	255	53,129 D	45.8%	54.2%	45.8%	54.2%
1960	755,875	343,009	Smith, Elmo E.	412,757	Neuberger, Maurine B.*	109	69,748 D	45.4%	54.6%	45.4%	54.6%
1956	732,254	335,405	McKay, Douglas	396,849	Morse, Wayne L.*		61,444 D	45.8%	54.2%	45.8%	54.2%
1954	569,088	283,313	Cordon, Guy*	285,775	Neuberger, Richard L.		2,462 D	49.8%	50.2%	49.8%	50.2%
1950	503,455	376,510	Morse, Wayne L.*	116,780	Latourette, Howard	10,165	259,730 R	74.8%	23.2%	76.3%	23.7%
1948	498,570	299,295	Cordon, Guy*	199,275	Wilson, Manley J.		100,020 R	60.0%	40.0%	60.0%	40.0%

Note: An asterisk (*) denotes incumbent. **The January 1996 election was for a short term to fill a vacancy.

OREGON

GOVERNOR 2014

2010 Census Population	County	Total Vote	Republican (Richardson)	Democratic (Kitzhaber)	Other	Rep.-Dem. Plurality	Percentage Total Vote Rep.	Total Vote Dem.	Major Vote Rep.	Major Vote Dem.
16,134	BAKER	7,116	4,842	1,951	323	2,891 R	68.0%	27.4%	71.3%	28.7%
85,579	BENTON	37,099	13,245	21,694	2,160	8,449 D	35.7%	58.5%	37.9%	62.1%
375,992	CLACKAMAS	154,997	77,059	70,071	7,867	6,988 R	49.7%	45.2%	52.4%	47.6%
37,039	CLATSOP	14,137	6,550	6,449	1,138	101 R	46.3%	45.6%	50.4%	49.6%
49,351	COLUMBIA	19,835	9,887	8,477	1,471	1,410 R	49.8%	42.7%	53.8%	46.2%
63,043	COOS	23,926	12,260	10,120	1,546	2,140 R	51.2%	42.3%	54.8%	45.2%
20,978	CROOK	8,862	5,753	2,601	508	3,152 R	64.9%	29.4%	68.9%	31.1%
22,364	CURRY	9,692	5,211	3,946	535	1,265 R	53.8%	40.7%	56.9%	43.1%
157,733	DESCHUTES	69,063	34,104	31,518	3,441	2,586 R	49.4%	45.6%	52.0%	48.0%
107,667	DOUGLAS	41,281	24,553	13,829	2,899	10,724 R	59.5%	33.5%	64.0%	36.0%
1,871	GILLIAM	878	546	284	48	262 R	62.2%	32.3%	65.8%	34.2%
7,445	GRANT	3,269	2,294	834	141	1,460 R	70.2%	25.5%	73.3%	26.7%
7,422	HARNEY	2,958	2,083	724	151	1,359 R	70.4%	24.5%	74.2%	25.8%
22,346	HOOD RIVER	8,289	2,988	4,875	426	1,887 D	36.0%	58.8%	38.0%	62.0%
203,206	JACKSON	82,588	43,498	35,235	3,855	8,263 R	52.7%	42.7%	55.2%	44.8%
21,720	JEFFERSON	6,813	4,048	2,333	432	1,715 R	59.4%	34.2%	63.4%	36.6%
82,713	JOSEPHINE	33,960	19,926	12,032	2,002	7,894 R	58.7%	35.4%	62.4%	37.6%
66,380	KLAMATH	22,836	15,155	6,416	1,265	8,739 R	66.4%	28.1%	70.3%	29.7%
7,895	LAKE	3,191	2,310	736	145	1,574 R	72.4%	23.1%	75.8%	24.2%
351,715	LANE	143,823	53,156	82,132	8,535	28,976 D	37.0%	57.1%	39.3%	60.7%
46,034	LINCOLN	19,367	7,609	10,469	1,289	2,860 D	39.3%	54.1%	42.1%	57.9%
116,672	LINN	43,184	25,463	14,890	2,831	10,573 R	59.0%	34.5%	63.1%	36.9%
31,313	MALHEUR	7,548	5,226	1,904	418	3,322 R	69.2%	25.2%	73.3%	26.7%
315,335	MARION	101,256	53,377	41,858	6,021	11,519 R	52.7%	41.3%	56.0%	44.0%
11,173	MORROW	3,133	2,065	870	198	1,195 R	65.9%	27.8%	70.4%	29.6%
735,334	MULTNOMAH	289,670	66,780	202,617	20,273	135,837 D	23.1%	69.9%	24.8%	75.2%
75,403	POLK	29,870	15,809	12,375	1,686	3,434 R	52.9%	41.4%	56.1%	43.9%
1,765	SHERMAN	891	596	252	43	344 R	66.9%	28.3%	70.3%	29.7%
25,250	TILLAMOOK	10,508	4,895	4,907	706	12 D	46.6%	46.7%	49.9%	50.1%
75,889	UMATILLA	18,848	12,337	5,517	994	6,820 R	65.5%	29.3%	69.1%	30.9%
25,748	UNION	10,149	6,526	3,087	536	3,439 R	64.3%	30.4%	67.9%	32.1%
7,008	WALLOWA	3,611	2,474	1,008	129	1,466 R	68.5%	27.9%	71.1%	28.9%
25,213	WASCO	9,145	4,557	3,959	629	598 R	49.8%	43.3%	53.5%	46.5%
529,710	WASHINGTON	190,872	81,484	98,203	11,185	16,719 D	42.7%	51.4%	45.3%	54.7%
1,441	WHEELER	685	440	203	42	237 R	64.2%	29.6%	68.4%	31.6%
99,193	YAMHILL	36,367	19,436	14,854	2,077	4,582 R	53.4%	40.8%	56.7%	43.3%
3,831,074	TOTAL	1,469,717	648,542	733,230	87,945	84,688 D	44.1%	49.9%	46.9%	53.1%

OREGON

SENATOR 2014

2010 Census Population	County	Total Vote	Republican (Wehby)	Democratic (Merkley)	Other	Rep.-Dem. Plurality	Percentage Total Vote Rep.	Total Vote Dem.	Major Vote Rep.	Major Vote Dem.
16,134	BAKER	7,063	4,238	2,334	491	1,904 R	60.0%	33.0%	64.5%	35.5%
85,579	BENTON	36,993	11,452	23,073	2,468	11,621 D	31.0%	62.4%	33.2%	66.8%
375,992	CLACKAMAS	154,205	64,447	79,219	10,539	14,772 D	41.8%	51.4%	44.9%	55.1%
37,039	CLATSOP	14,338	5,143	8,148	1,047	3,005 D	35.9%	56.8%	38.7%	61.3%
49,351	COLUMBIA	19,789	7,879	9,957	1,953	2,078 D	39.8%	50.3%	44.2%	55.8%

OREGON

SENATOR 2014

2010 Census Population	County	Total Vote	Republican (Wehby)	Democratic (Merkley)	Other	Rep.-Dem. Plurality	Percentage Total Vote Rep.	Total Vote Dem.	Major Vote Rep.	Major Vote Dem.
63,043	COOS	23,735	10,294	11,521	1,920	1,227 D	43.4%	48.5%	47.2%	52.8%
20,978	CROOK	8,823	4,874	3,233	716	1,641 R	55.2%	36.6%	60.1%	39.9%
22,364	CURRY	9,583	4,470	4,371	742	99 R	46.6%	45.6%	50.6%	49.4%
157,733	DESCHUTES	68,573	29,114	34,680	4,779	5,566 D	42.5%	50.6%	45.6%	54.4%
107,667	DOUGLAS	40,856	21,112	16,401	3,343	4,711 R	51.7%	40.1%	56.3%	43.7%
1,871	GILLIAM	872	440	366	66	74 R	50.5%	42.0%	54.6%	45.4%
7,445	GRANT	3,207	1,943	1,051	213	892 R	60.6%	32.8%	64.9%	35.1%
7,422	HARNEY	2,925	1,784	911	230	873 R	61.0%	31.1%	66.2%	33.8%
22,346	HOOD RIVER	8,189	2,540	5,139	510	2,599 D	31.0%	62.8%	33.1%	66.9%
203,206	JACKSON	81,399	34,619	40,740	6,040	6,121 D	42.5%	50.0%	45.9%	54.1%
21,720	JEFFERSON	6,767	3,440	2,809	518	631 R	50.8%	41.5%	55.0%	45.0%
82,713	JOSEPHINE	33,392	15,722	14,218	3,452	1,504 R	47.1%	42.6%	52.5%	47.5%
66,380	KLAMATH	22,570	12,522	8,150	1,898	4,372 R	55.5%	36.1%	60.6%	39.4%
7,895	LAKE	3,142	1,930	966	246	964 R	61.4%	30.7%	66.6%	33.4%
351,715	LANE	143,595	44,815	89,269	9,511	44,454 D	31.2%	62.2%	33.4%	66.6%
46,034	LINCOLN	19,367	6,360	11,484	1,523	5,124 D	32.8%	59.3%	35.6%	64.4%
116,672	LINN	42,637	20,664	18,050	3,923	2,614 R	48.5%	42.3%	53.4%	46.6%
31,313	MALHEUR	7,420	4,755	2,051	614	2,704 R	64.1%	27.6%	69.9%	30.1%
315,335	MARION	100,041	43,917	48,581	7,543	4,664 D	43.9%	48.6%	47.5%	52.5%
11,173	MORROW	3,114	1,722	1,119	273	603 R	55.3%	35.9%	60.6%	39.4%
735,334	MULTNOMAH	290,344	53,035	216,613	20,696	163,578 D	18.3%	74.6%	19.7%	80.3%
75,403	POLK	29,576	13,118	14,356	2,102	1,238 D	44.4%	48.5%	47.7%	52.3%
1,765	SHERMAN	855	523	283	49	240 R	61.2%	33.1%	64.9%	35.1%
25,250	TILLAMOOK	10,481	4,187	5,463	831	1,276 D	39.9%	52.1%	43.4%	56.6%
75,889	UMATILLA	18,698	10,676	6,655	1,367	4,021 R	57.1%	35.6%	61.6%	38.4%
25,748	UNION	10,046	5,498	3,816	732	1,682 R	54.7%	38.0%	59.0%	41.0%
7,008	WALLOWA	3,548	2,140	1,215	193	925 R	60.3%	34.2%	63.8%	36.2%
25,213	WASCO	9,091	3,787	4,563	741	776 D	41.7%	50.2%	45.4%	54.6%
529,710	WASHINGTON	189,971	69,406	106,769	13,796	37,363 D	36.5%	56.2%	39.4%	60.6%
1,441	WHEELER	679	344	275	60	69 R	50.7%	40.5%	55.6%	44.4%
99,193	YAMHILL	35,734	15,937	16,688	3,109	751 D	44.6%	46.7%	48.8%	51.2%
3,831,074	TOTAL	1,461,618	538,847	814,537	108,234	275,690 D	36.9%	55.7%	39.8%	60.2%

OREGON

HOUSE OF REPRESENTATIVES

CD	Year	Total Vote	Republican Vote	Republican Candidate	Democratic Vote	Democratic Candidate	Other Vote	Rep.-Dem. Plurality	Percentage Total Vote Rep.	Total Vote Dem.	Major Vote Rep.	Major Vote Dem.
1	2014	279,253	96,245	YATES, JASON	160,038	BONAMICI, SUZANNE*	22,970	63,793 D	34.5%	57.3%	37.6%	62.4%
1	2012	331,980	109,699	MORGAN, DELINDA	197,845	BONAMICI, SUZANNE*	24,436	88,146 D	33.0%	59.6%	35.7%	64.3%
2	2014	287,425	202,374	WALDEN, GREG*	73,785	CHRISTOFFERSON, AELEA	11,266	128,589 R	70.4%	25.7%	73.3%	26.7%
2	2012	332,255	228,043	WALDEN, GREG*	96,741	SEGERS, JOYCE B.	7,471	131,302 R	68.6%	29.1%	70.2%	29.8%
3	2014	292,757	57,424	BUCHAL, JAMES	211,748	BLUMENAUER, EARL*	23,585	154,324 D	19.6%	72.3%	21.3%	78.7%
3	2012	355,875	70,325	GREEN, RONALD	264,979	BLUMENAUER, EARL*	20,571	194,654 D	19.8%	74.5%	21.0%	79.0%
4	2014	310,179	116,534	ROBINSON, ART	181,624	DEFAZIO, PETER A.*	12,021	65,090 D	37.6%	58.6%	39.1%	60.9%
4	2012	360,088	140,549	ROBINSON, ART	212,866	DEFAZIO, PETER A.*	6,673	72,317 D	39.0%	59.1%	39.8%	60.2%
5	2014	281,088	110,332	SMITH, TOOTIE	150,944	SCHRADER, KURT*	19,812	40,612 D	39.3%	53.7%	42.2%	57.8%
5	2012	327,970	139,223	THOMPSON, FRED	177,229	SCHRADER, KURT*	11,518	38,006 D	42.4%	54.0%	44.0%	56.0%
TOTAL	2014	1,450,702	582,909		778,139		89,654	195,230 D	40.2%	53.6%	42.8%	57.2%
TOTAL	2012	1,708,168	687,839		949,660		70,669	261,821 D	40.3%	55.6%	42.0%	58.0%

Note: An asterisk (*) denotes incumbent.

OREGON

GENERAL AND PRIMARY ELECTIONS

2014 GENERAL ELECTIONS: OTHER VOTES

Governor Other vote was 29,561 Pacific Green (Jason Levin), 21,903 Libertarian (Paul Grad), 15,929 Constitution (Aaron Auer), 13,898 Progressive (Chris Henry), 6,654 scattered write-in

Senate Other vote was 44,916 Libertarian (Mike Montchalin), 32,434 Pacific Green (Christina Jean Lugo), 24,212 Constitution (James E. Leuenberger), 6,672 scattered write-in

House Other vote was:

CD 1 11,213 Libertarian (James Foster), 11,163 Pacific Green (Steven Cody Reynolds), 594 scattered write-in
CD 2 10,491 Libertarian (Sharon Durbin), 775 scattered write-in
CD 3 12,106 Pacific Green (Michael Meo), 6,381 Libertarian (Jeffrey J. Langan), 4,009 Nonaffiliated (David Walker), 1,089 scattered write-in
CD 4 6,863 Pacific Green (Michael Allan Beilstein), 4,676 Libertarian (David L. Chester), 482 scattered write-in
CD 5 7,674 Independent (Marvin Sannes), 6,208 Constitution (Raymond Baldwin), 5,198 Libertarian (Daniel K. Souza), 732 scattered write-in

2014 PRIMARY ELECTIONS: SUPPLEMENTARY INFORMATION

Primary May 20, 2014 **Registration** (as of April 30, 2015) 2,160,095

Democratic	833,812
Republican	658,792
Independent Party	101,421
Libertarian	16,385
Working Families	10,885
Pacific Green	10,253
Constitution	3,467
Progressive	1,963
American Elect	197
Other	21,041
Non Affiliated	501,879

Primary Type Closed—Only registered Democrats and Republicans could vote in their party's primary.

	REPUBLICAN PRIMARIES			DEMOCRATIC PRIMARIES		
Senator	Wehby, Monica	134,627	50.0%	Merkley, Jeff*	277,120	92.0%
	Conger, Jason	101,401	37.6%	Bryk, William	11,330	3.8%
	Callahan, Mark	18,220	6.8%	Goberman, Pavel	8,436	2.8%
	Perkins, Jo Rae	7,602	2.8%	Write-In	4,194	1.4%
	Crawley, Timothy	6,566	2.4%			
	Write-In	1,027	0.4%			
	TOTAL	*269,443*		*TOTAL*	*301,080*	
Governor	Richardson, Dennis	163,695	65.9%	Kitzhaber, John*	268,654	89.0%
	Challstrom, Gordon	24,693	9.9%	Diru, Ifeanyichukwu C.	27,833	9.2%
	Cuff, Bruce A.	23,912	9.6%	Write-In	5,388	1.8%
	Rafferty, Mae	16,920	6.8%			
	Carr, Tim	14,847	6.0%			
	Karr, Darren	2,474	1.0%			
	Write-In	2,011	0.8%			
	TOTAL	*248,552*		*TOTAL*	*301,875*	

OREGON

GENERAL AND PRIMARY ELECTIONS

	REPUBLICAN PRIMARIES			DEMOCRATIC PRIMARIES		
Congressional District 1	Yates, Jason	16,466	42.3%	Bonamici, Suzanne*	50,903	98.8%
	Delgado Morgan, Delinda	15,521	39.9%	Write-In	601	1.2%
	Niemeyer, Bob	6,637	17.0%			
	Write-In	312	0.8%			
	TOTAL	38,936		TOTAL	51,504	
Congressional District 2	Walden, Greg*	64,603	75.5%	Christofferson, Aelea	24,407	61.8%
	Linthicum, Dennis Bradley	20,745	24.3%	Spera, Bernard "Barney"	7,996	20.2%
	Write-In	185	0.2%	Vulliet, C F "Frank"	6,103	15.4%
				Write-In	1,007	2.5%
	TOTAL	85,533		TOTAL	39,513	
Congressional District 3	Buchal, James	15,083	97.8%	Blumenauer, Earl*	69,753	98.6%
	Write-In	338	2.2%	Write-In	969	1.4%
	TOTAL	15,421		TOTAL	70,722	
Congressional District 4	Robinson, Art	45,391	97.3%	DeFazio, Peter A.*	57,970	98.3%
	Write-In	1,255	2.7%	Write-In	1,016	1.7%
	TOTAL	46,646		TOTAL	58,986	
Congressional District 5	Smith, Tootie	31,883	62.8%	Schrader, Kurt*	42,041	83.1%
	Pollock, Ben	18,595	36.6%	Brown, Anita	8,106	16.0%
	Write-In	268	0.5%	Write-In	445	0.9%
	TOTAL	50,746		TOTAL	50,592	

Note: An asterisk (*) denotes incumbent.

PENNSYLVANIA

Congressional districts first established for elections held in 2012

18 members

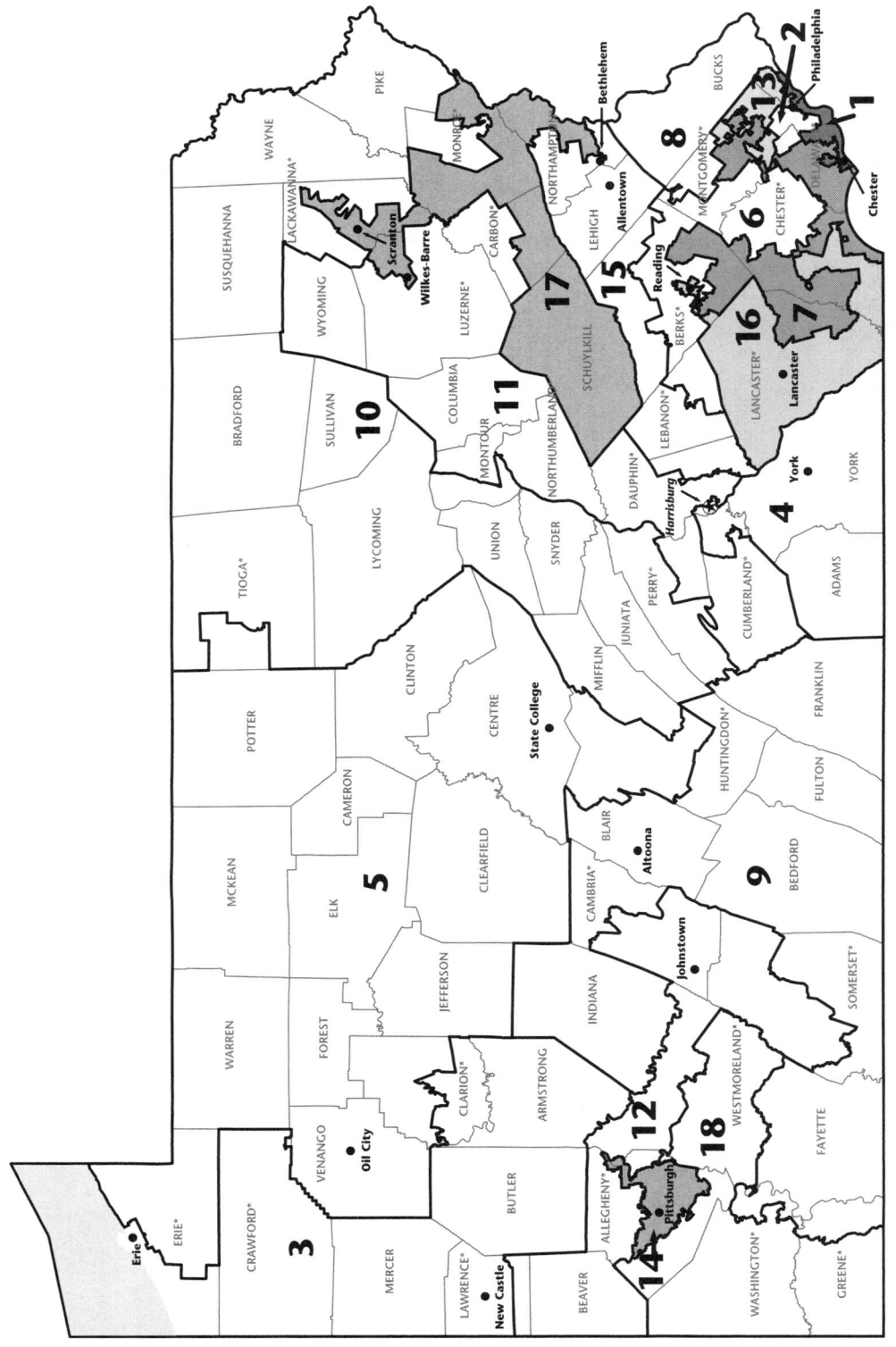

The city of Philadelphia is coextensive with the county of Philadelphia.

* Asterisk indicates a county whose boundaries include parts of two or more congressional districts.

PENNSYLVANIA
Greater Pittsburgh Area

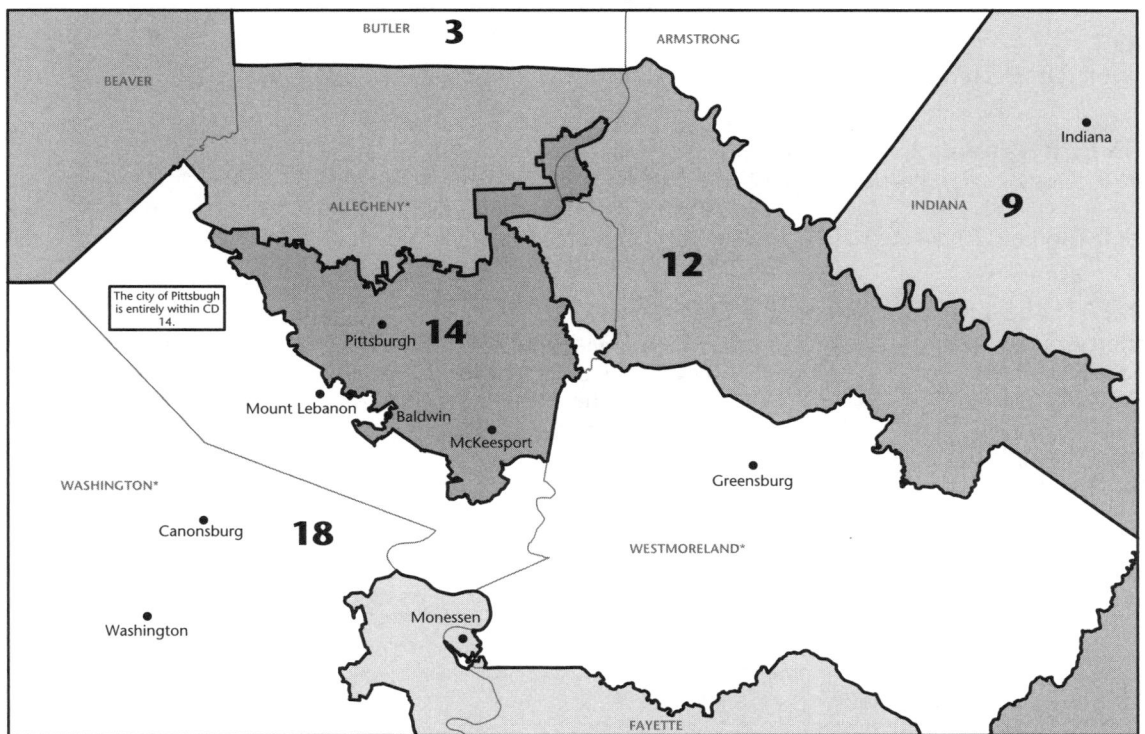

Greater Philadelphia Area

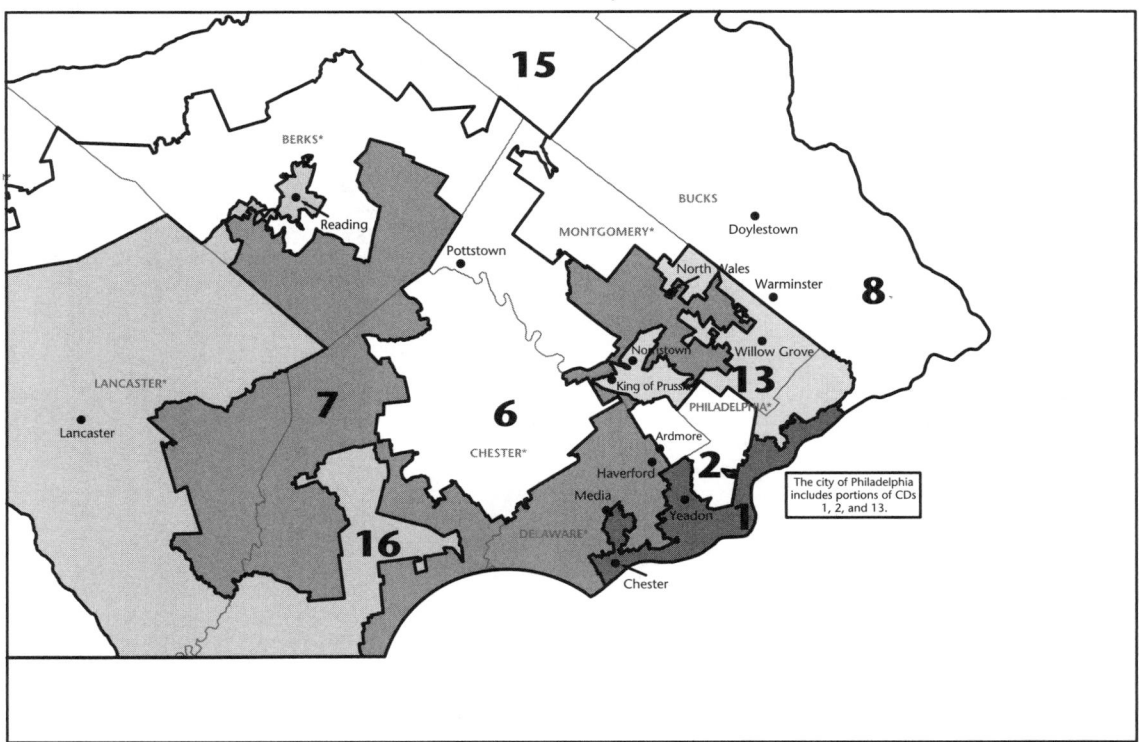

* Asterisk indicates a county whose boundaries include parts of two or more congressional districts.

PENNSYLVANIA

GOVERNOR
Tom Wolf (D). Elected 2014 to a four-year term.

SENATORS (1 Republican, 1 Democrat)
Robert P. Casey Jr. (D). Re-elected 2012 to a six-year term. Previously elected 2006.

Patrick J. Toomey (R). Elected 2010 to a six-year term.

REPRESENTATIVES (13 Republicans, 5 Democrats)

1. Robert A. Brady (D)	7. Patrick Meehan (R)	13. Brendan F. Boyle (D)
2. Chaka Fattah (D)	8. Michael G. Fitzpatrick (R)	14. Michael F. Doyle (D)
3. Mike Kelly (R)	9. Bill Shuster (R)	15. Charles W. Dent (R)
4. Scott Perry (R)	10. Tom Marino (R)	16. Joseph R. Pitts (R)
5. Glenn Thompson (R)	11. Lou Barletta (R)	17. Matt Cartwright (D)
6. Ryan A. Costello (R)	12. Keith J. Rothfus (R)	18. Tim Murphy (R)

POSTWAR VOTE FOR PRESIDENT

Year	Total Vote	Republican		Democratic		Other Vote	Rep.-Dem. Plurality	Total Vote		Major Vote	
		Vote	Candidate	Vote	Candidate			Rep.	Dem.	Rep.	Dem.
2012	5,753,670	2,680,434	Romney, W. Mitt	2,990,274	Obama, Barack H.*	82,962	309,840 D	46.6%	52.0%	47.3%	52.7%
2008	6,013,272	2,655,885	McCain, John S. III	3,276,363	Obama, Barack H.	81,024	620,478 D	44.2%	54.5%	44.8%	55.2%
2004	5,769,590	2,793,847	Bush, George W.*	2,938,095	Kerry, John F.	37,648	144,248 D	48.4%	50.9%	48.7%	51.3%
2000**	4,913,119	2,281,127	Bush, George W.	2,485,967	Gore, Albert Jr.	146,025	204,840 D	46.4%	50.6%	47.9%	52.1%
1996**	4,506,118	1,801,169	Dole, Robert "Bob"	2,215,819	Clinton, Bill*	489,130	414,650 D	40.0%	49.2%	44.8%	55.2%
1992**	4,959,810	1,791,841	Bush, George H.*	2,239,164	Clinton, Bill	928,805	447,323 D	36.1%	45.1%	44.5%	55.5%
1988	4,536,251	2,300,087	Bush, George H.	2,194,944	Dukakis, Michael S.	41,220	105,143 R	50.7%	48.4%	51.2%	48.8%
1984	4,844,903	2,584,323	Reagan, Ronald*	2,228,131	Mondale, Walter F.	32,449	356,192 R	53.3%	46.0%	53.7%	46.3%
1980**	4,561,501	2,261,872	Reagan, Ronald	1,937,540	Carter, Jimmy*	362,089	324,332 R	49.6%	42.5%	53.9%	46.1%
1976	4,620,787	2,205,604	Ford, Gerald R.*	2,328,677	Carter, Jimmy	86,506	123,073 D	47.7%	50.4%	48.6%	51.4%
1972	4,592,106	2,714,521	Nixon, Richard M.*	1,796,951	McGovern, George S.	80,634	917,570 R	59.1%	39.1%	60.2%	39.8%
1968**	4,747,928	2,090,017	Nixon, Richard M.	2,259,405	Humphrey, Hubert Horatio Jr.	398,506	169,388 D	44.0%	47.6%	48.1%	51.9%
1964	4,822,690	1,673,657	Goldwater, Barry M. Sr.	3,130,954	Johnson, Lyndon B.*	18,079	1,457,297 D	34.7%	64.9%	34.8%	65.2%
1960	5,006,541	2,439,956	Nixon, Richard M.	2,556,282	Kennedy, John F.	10,303	116,326 D	48.7%	51.1%	48.8%	51.2%
1956	4,576,503	2,585,252	Eisenhower, Dwight D.*	1,981,769	Stevenson, Adlai E. II	9,482	603,483 R	56.5%	43.3%	56.6%	43.4%
1952	4,580,969	2,415,789	Eisenhower, Dwight D.	2,146,269	Stevenson, Adlai E. II	18,911	269,520 R	52.7%	46.9%	53.0%	47.0%
1948	3,735,348	1,902,197	Dewey, Thomas E.	1,752,426	Truman, Harry S.*	80,725	149,771 R	50.9%	46.9%	52.0%	48.0%

Note: An asterisk (*) denotes incumbent. **In past elections, the other vote included: 2000 - 103,392 Green (Ralph Nader); 1996 - 430,984 Reform (Ross Perot); 1992 - 902,667 Independent (Perot); 1980 - 292,921 Independent (John Anderson); 1968 - 378,582 American Independent (George Wallace).

PENNSYLVANIA

POSTWAR VOTE FOR GOVERNOR

Year	Total Vote	Republican		Democratic		Other Vote	Rep.-Dem. Plurality	Percentage			
		Vote	Candidate	Vote	Candidate			Total Vote		Major Vote	
								Rep.	Dem.	Rep.	Dem.
2014	3,495,866	1,575,511	Corbett, Tom*	1,920,355	Wolf, Tom		344,844 D	45.1%	54.9%	45.1%	54.9%
2010	3,989,102	2,172,763	Corbett, Tom	1,814,788	Onorato, Dan	1,551	357,975 R	54.5%	45.5%	54.5%	45.5%
2006	4,096,077	1,622,135	Swann, Lynn	2,470,517	Rendell, Edward G.*	3,425	848,382 D	39.6%	60.3%	39.6%	60.4%
2002	3,583,179	1,589,408	Fisher, Mike	1,913,235	Rendell, Edward G.	80,536	323,827 D	44.4%	53.4%	45.4%	54.6%
1998**	3,025,152	1,736,844	Ridge, Thomas J.*	938,745	Itkin, Ivan	349,563	798,099 R	57.4%	31.0%	64.9%	35.1%
1994**	3,588,526	1,627,976	Ridge, Thomas J.	1,433,099	Singel, Mark S.	527,451	194,877 R	45.4%	39.9%	53.2%	46.8%
1990	3,052,760	987,516	Hafer, Barbara	2,065,244	Casey, Robert*		1,077,728 D	32.3%	67.7%	32.3%	67.7%
1986	3,388,275	1,638,268	Scranton, William W.	1,717,484	Casey, Robert	32,523	79,216 D	48.4%	50.7%	48.8%	51.2%
1982	3,683,985	1,872,784	Thornburgh, Richard*	1,772,353	Ertel, Allen E.	38,848	100,431 R	50.8%	48.1%	51.4%	48.6%
1978	3,741,969	1,966,042	Thornburgh, Richard	1,737,888	Flaherty, Peter	38,039	228,154 R	52.5%	46.4%	53.1%	46.9%
1974	3,491,234	1,578,917	Lewis, Andrew L.	1,878,252	Shapp, Milton J.*	34,065	299,335 D	45.2%	53.8%	45.7%	54.3%
1970	3,700,060	1,542,854	Broderick, Raymond	2,043,029	Shapp, Milton J.*	114,177	500,175 D	41.7%	55.2%	43.0%	57.0%
1966	4,050,668	2,110,349	Shafer, Raymond P.	1,868,719	Shapp, Milton J.	71,600	241,630 R	52.1%	46.1%	53.0%	47.0%
1962	4,378,042	2,424,918	Scranton, William W.	1,938,627	Dilworth, Richardson	14,497	486,291 R	55.4%	44.3%	55.6%	44.4%
1958	3,986,918	1,948,769	McGonigle, Arthur T.	2,024,852	Lawrence, David L.	13,297	76,083 D	48.9%	50.8%	49.0%	51.0%
1954	3,720,457	1,717,070	Wood, Lloyd H.	1,996,266	Leader, George M.	7,121	279,196 D	46.2%	53.7%	46.2%	53.8%
1950	3,540,059	1,796,119	Fine, John S.	1,710,355	Dilworth, Richardson	33,585	85,764 R	50.7%	48.3%	51.2%	48.8%
1946	3,123,994	1,828,462	Duff, James H.	1,270,947	Rice, John S.	24,585	557,515 R	58.5%	40.7%	59.0%	41.0%

Note: An asterisk (*) denotes incumbent. **In past elections, the other vote included: 1998 - 315,761 Constitutional (Peg Luksik); 1994 - 460,269 Constitutional (Luksik).

POSTWAR VOTE FOR SENATOR

Year	Total Vote	Republican		Democratic		Other Vote	Rep.-Dem. Plurality	Percentage			
		Vote	Candidate	Vote	Candidate			Total Vote		Major Vote	
								Rep.	Dem.	Rep.	Dem.
2012	5,629,491	2,509,132	Smith, Tom	3,021,364	Casey, Robert P. Jr.*	98,995	512,232 D	44.6%	53.7%	45.4%	54.6%
2010	3,977,661	2,028,945	Toomey, Patrick J.	1,948,716	Sestak, Joe		80,229 R	51.0%	49.0%	51.0%	49.0%
2006	4,081,043	1,684,778	Santorum, Rick*	2,392,984	Casey, Robert P. Jr.	3,281	708,206 D	41.3%	58.6%	41.3%	58.7%
2004	5,559,105	2,925,080	Specter, Arlen*	2,334,126	Hoeffel, Joseph M.	299,899	590,954 R	52.6%	42.0%	55.6%	44.4%
2000	4,735,504	2,481,962	Santorum, Rick*	2,154,908	Klink, Ron	98,634	327,054 R	52.4%	45.5%	53.5%	46.5%
1998	2,957,772	1,814,180	Specter, Arlen*	1,028,839	Lloyd, Bill	114,753	785,341 R	61.3%	34.8%	63.8%	36.2%
1994	3,513,361	1,735,691	Santorum, Rick	1,648,481	Wofford, Harris*	129,189	87,210 R	49.4%	46.9%	51.3%	48.7%
1992	4,802,410	2,358,125	Specter, Arlen*	2,224,966	Yeakel, Lynn	219,319	133,159 R	49.1%	46.3%	51.5%	48.5%
1991S	3,382,746	1,521,986	Thornburgh, Richard	1,860,760	Wofford, Harris*		338,774 D	45.0%	55.0%	45.0%	55.0%
1988	4,366,598	2,901,715	Heinz, Henry John III*	1,416,764	Vignola, Joseph C.	48,119	1,484,951 R	66.5%	32.4%	67.2%	32.8%
1986	3,378,226	1,906,537	Specter, Arlen*	1,448,219	Edgar, Robert W.	23,470	458,318 R	56.4%	42.9%	56.8%	43.2%
1982	3,604,108	2,136,418	Heinz, Henry John III*	1,412,965	Wecht, Cyril H.	54,725	723,453 R	59.3%	39.2%	60.2%	39.8%
1980	4,418,042	2,230,404	Specter, Arlen	2,122,391	Flaherty, Peter	65,247	108,013 R	50.5%	48.0%	51.2%	48.8%
1976	4,546,353	2,381,891	Heinz, Henry John III	2,126,977	Green, William J. III	37,485	254,914 R	52.4%	46.8%	52.8%	47.2%
1974	3,477,812	1,843,317	Schweiker, Richard S.*	1,596,121	Flaherty, Peter	38,374	247,196 R	53.0%	45.9%	53.6%	46.4%
1970	3,644,305	1,874,106	Scott, Hugh*	1,653,774	Sesler, William G.	116,425	220,332 R	51.4%	45.4%	53.1%	46.9%
1968	4,624,218	2,399,762	Schweiker, Richard S.	2,117,662	Clark, Joseph S.*	106,794	282,100 R	51.9%	45.8%	53.1%	46.9%
1964	4,803,835	2,429,858	Scott, Hugh*	2,359,223	Blatt, Genevieve	14,754	70,635 R	50.6%	49.1%	50.7%	49.3%
1962	4,383,475	2,134,649	Van Zandt, James E.	2,238,383	Clark, Joseph S.*	10,443	103,734 D	48.7%	51.1%	48.8%	51.2%
1958	3,988,622	2,042,586	Scott, Hugh	1,929,821	Leader, George M.	16,215	112,765 R	51.2%	48.4%	51.4%	48.6%
1956	4,529,874	2,250,671	Duff, James H.*	2,268,641	Clark, Joseph S.	10,562	17,970 D	49.7%	50.1%	49.8%	50.2%
1952	4,519,761	2,331,034	Martin, Edward*	2,168,546	Bard, Guy Kurtz	20,181	162,488 R	51.6%	48.0%	51.8%	48.2%
1950	3,548,703	1,820,400	Duff, James H.	1,694,076	Myers, Francis J.*	34,227	126,324 R	51.3%	47.7%	51.8%	48.2%
1946	3,127,860	1,853,458	Martin, Edward	1,245,338	Guffey, Joseph F.*	29,064	608,120 R	59.3%	39.8%	59.8%	40.2%

Note: An asterisk (*) denotes incumbent. **The 1991 election was for a short term to fill a vacancy.

PENNSYLVANIA

GOVERNOR 2014

2010 Census Population	County	Total Vote	Republican (Corbett)	Democratic (Wolf)	Other	Rep.-Dem. Plurality	Percentage Total Vote Rep.	Dem.	Major Vote Rep.	Dem.
101,407	ADAMS	27,920	16,790	11,130		5,660 R	60.1%	39.9%	60.1%	39.9%
1,223,348	ALLEGHENY	355,074	148,057	207,017		58,960 D	41.7%	58.3%	41.7%	58.3%
68,941	ARMSTRONG	18,715	11,520	7,195		4,325 R	61.6%	38.4%	61.6%	38.4%
170,539	BEAVER	47,758	23,302	24,456		1,154 D	48.8%	51.2%	48.8%	51.2%
49,762	BEDFORD	13,836	9,050	4,786		4,264 R	65.4%	34.6%	65.4%	34.6%
411,442	BERKS	101,845	50,005	51,840		1,835 D	49.1%	50.9%	49.1%	50.9%
127,089	BLAIR	30,518	17,718	12,800		4,918 R	58.1%	41.9%	58.1%	41.9%
62,622	BRADFORD	14,987	9,905	5,082		4,823 R	66.1%	33.9%	66.1%	33.9%
625,249	BUCKS	198,396	94,584	103,812		9,228 D	47.7%	52.3%	47.7%	52.3%
183,862	BUTLER	55,989	35,818	20,171		15,647 R	64.0%	36.0%	64.0%	36.0%
143,679	CAMBRIA	40,346	18,325	22,021		3,696 D	45.4%	54.6%	45.4%	54.6%
5,085	CAMERON	1,388	779	609		170 R	56.1%	43.9%	56.1%	43.9%
65,249	CARBON	17,027	7,864	9,163		1,299 D	46.2%	53.8%	46.2%	53.8%
153,990	CENTRE	38,882	16,489	22,393		5,904 D	42.4%	57.6%	42.4%	57.6%
498,886	CHESTER	155,798	75,097	80,701		5,604 D	48.2%	51.8%	48.2%	51.8%
39,988	CLARION	10,789	6,418	4,371		2,047 R	59.5%	40.5%	59.5%	40.5%
81,642	CLEARFIELD	20,843	11,161	9,682		1,479 R	53.5%	46.5%	53.5%	46.5%
39,238	CLINTON	8,512	3,929	4,583		654 D	46.2%	53.8%	46.2%	53.8%
67,295	COLUMBIA	15,157	8,585	6,572		2,013 R	56.6%	43.4%	56.6%	43.4%
88,765	CRAWFORD	23,213	13,219	9,994		3,225 R	56.9%	43.1%	56.9%	43.1%
235,406	CUMBERLAND	74,936	43,625	31,311		12,314 R	58.2%	41.8%	58.2%	41.8%
268,100	DAUPHIN	79,487	39,111	40,376		1,265 D	49.2%	50.8%	49.2%	50.8%
558,979	DELAWARE	182,114	71,180	110,934		39,754 D	39.1%	60.9%	39.1%	60.9%
31,946	ELK	8,809	4,536	4,273		263 R	51.5%	48.5%	51.5%	48.5%
280,566	ERIE	72,504	30,389	42,115		11,726 D	41.9%	58.1%	41.9%	58.1%
136,606	FAYETTE	31,231	13,129	18,102		4,973 D	42.0%	58.0%	42.0%	58.0%
7,716	FOREST	1,635	820	815		5 R	50.2%	49.8%	50.2%	49.8%
149,618	FRANKLIN	38,374	25,913	12,461		13,452 R	67.5%	32.5%	67.5%	32.5%
14,845	FULTON	3,761	2,650	1,111		1,539 R	70.5%	29.5%	70.5%	29.5%
38,686	GREENE	9,310	4,080	5,230		1,150 D	43.8%	56.2%	43.8%	56.2%
45,913	HUNTINGDON	12,747	7,247	5,500		1,747 R	56.9%	43.1%	56.9%	43.1%
88,880	INDIANA	22,422	12,199	10,223		1,976 R	54.4%	45.6%	54.4%	45.6%
45,200	JEFFERSON	11,833	7,458	4,375		3,083 R	63.0%	37.0%	63.0%	37.0%
24,636	JUNIATA	6,603	4,431	2,172		2,259 R	67.1%	32.9%	67.1%	32.9%
214,437	LACKAWANNA	59,761	18,081	41,680		23,599 D	30.3%	69.7%	30.3%	69.7%
519,445	LANCASTER	140,773	83,179	57,594		25,585 R	59.1%	40.9%	59.1%	40.9%
91,108	LAWRENCE	23,162	11,166	11,996		830 D	48.2%	51.8%	48.2%	51.8%
133,568	LEBANON	36,367	22,738	13,629		9,109 R	62.5%	37.5%	62.5%	37.5%
349,497	LEHIGH	81,552	36,894	44,658		7,764 D	45.2%	54.8%	45.2%	54.8%
320,918	LUZERNE	74,214	32,605	41,609		9,004 D	43.9%	56.1%	43.9%	56.1%
116,111	LYCOMING	31,103	20,106	10,997		9,109 R	64.6%	35.4%	64.6%	35.4%
43,450	MCKEAN	8,256	5,311	2,945		2,366 R	64.3%	35.7%	64.3%	35.7%
116,638	MERCER	29,863	15,397	14,466		931 R	51.6%	48.4%	51.6%	48.4%
46,682	MIFFLIN	10,810	7,318	3,492		3,826 R	67.7%	32.3%	67.7%	32.3%
169,842	MONROE	34,910	15,046	19,864		4,818 D	43.1%	56.9%	43.1%	56.9%
799,874	MONTGOMERY	260,926	104,726	156,200		51,474 D	40.1%	59.9%	40.1%	59.9%
18,267	MONTOUR	5,023	2,900	2,123		777 R	57.7%	42.3%	57.7%	42.3%
297,735	NORTHAMPTON	74,107	33,354	40,753		7,399 D	45.0%	55.0%	45.0%	55.0%
94,528	NORTHUMBERLAND	21,518	10,666	10,852		186 D	49.6%	50.4%	49.6%	50.4%
45,969	PERRY	13,023	8,679	4,344		4,335 R	66.6%	33.4%	66.6%	33.4%
1,526,006	PHILADELPHIA	378,807	45,268	333,539		288,271 D	12.0%	88.0%	12.0%	88.0%
57,369	PIKE	12,918	7,553	5,365		2,188 R	58.5%	41.5%	58.5%	41.5%
17,457	POTTER	4,664	3,140	1,524		1,616 R	67.3%	32.7%	67.3%	32.7%
148,289	SCHUYLKILL	37,712	17,168	20,544		3,376 D	45.5%	54.5%	45.5%	54.5%
39,702	SNYDER	9,754	5,772	3,982		1,790 R	59.2%	40.8%	59.2%	40.8%
77,742	SOMERSET	22,749	13,150	9,599		3,551 R	57.8%	42.2%	57.8%	42.2%
6,428	SULLIVAN	2,103	1,325	778		547 R	63.0%	37.0%	63.0%	37.0%
43,356	SUSQUEHANNA	12,105	7,805	4,300		3,505 R	64.5%	35.5%	64.5%	35.5%
41,981	TIOGA	11,470	7,929	3,541		4,388 R	69.1%	30.9%	69.1%	30.9%
44,947	UNION	10,146	5,362	4,784		578 R	52.8%	47.2%	52.8%	47.2%

PENNSYLVANIA

GOVERNOR 2014

2010 Census Population	County	Total Vote	Republican (Corbett)	Democratic (Wolf)	Other	Rep.-Dem. Plurality	Percentage Total Vote Rep.	Dem.	Major Vote Rep.	Dem.
54,984	VENANGO	14,104	7,771	6,333		1,438 R	55.1%	44.9%	55.1%	44.9%
41,815	WARREN	11,159	6,194	4,965		1,229 R	55.5%	44.5%	55.5%	44.5%
207,820	WASHINGTON	60,261	31,203	29,058		2,145 R	51.8%	48.2%	51.8%	48.2%
52,822	WAYNE	13,708	7,621	6,087		1,534 R	55.6%	44.4%	55.6%	44.4%
365,169	WESTMORELAND	106,217	60,716	45,501		15,215 R	57.2%	42.8%	57.2%	42.8%
28,276	WYOMING	7,872	4,381	3,491		890 R	55.7%	44.3%	55.7%	44.3%
434,972	YORK	121,990	69,604	52,386		17,218 R	57.1%	42.9%	57.1%	42.9%
12,702,379	TOTAL	3,495,866	1,575,511	1,920,355		344,844 D	45.1%	54.9%	45.1%	54.9%

PENNSYLVANIA

HOUSE OF REPRESENTATIVES

CD	Year	Total Vote	Republican Vote	Republican Candidate	Democratic Vote	Democratic Candidate	Other Vote	Rep.-Dem. Plurality	Total Vote Rep.	Dem.	Major Vote Rep.	Dem.
1	2014	158,441	27,193	RATH, MEGAN ANN	131,248	BRADY, ROBERT A.*		104,055 D	17.2%	82.8%	17.2%	82.8%
1	2012	277,102	41,708	FEATHERMAN, JOHN J.	235,394	BRADY, ROBERT A.*		193,686 D	15.1%	84.9%	15.1%	84.9%
2	2014	206,538	25,397	JAMES, ARMOND	181,141	FATTAH, CHAKA*		155,744 D	12.3%	87.7%	12.3%	87.7%
2	2012	356,386	33,381	MANSFIELD, ROBERT	318,176	FATTAH, CHAKA*	4,829	284,795 D	9.4%	89.3%	9.5%	90.5%
3	2014	187,790	113,859	KELLY, MIKE*	73,931	LAVALLEE, DANIEL		39,928 R	60.6%	39.4%	60.6%	39.4%
3	2012	302,514	165,826	KELLY, MIKE*	123,933	EATON, MISSA	12,755	41,893 R	54.8%	41.0%	57.2%	42.8%
4	2014	197,340	147,090	PERRY, SCOTT*	50,250	THOMPSON, LINDA DELIAH		96,840 R	74.5%	25.5%	74.5%	25.5%
4	2012	303,980	181,603	PERRY, SCOTT	104,643	PERKINSON, HARRY	17,734	76,960 R	59.7%	34.4%	63.4%	36.6%
5	2014	180,857	115,018	THOMPSON, GLENN*	65,839	TAYLOR, KERITH STRANO		49,179 R	63.6%	36.4%	63.6%	36.4%
5	2012	282,465	177,740	THOMPSON, GLENN*	104,725	DUMAS, CHARLES		73,015 R	62.9%	37.1%	62.9%	37.1%
6	2014	212,544	119,643	COSTELLO, RYAN A.	92,901	TRIVEDI, MANAN		26,742 R	56.3%	43.7%	56.3%	43.7%
6	2012	335,528	191,725	GERLACH, JAMES W.*	143,803	TRIVEDI, MANAN		47,922 R	57.1%	42.9%	57.1%	42.9%
7	2014	235,125	145,869	MEEHAN, PATRICK*	89,256	BALCHUNIS, MARY ELLEN		56,613 R	62.0%	38.0%	62.0%	38.0%
7	2012	353,451	209,942	MEEHAN, PATRICK*	143,509	BADEY, GEORGE		66,433 R	59.4%	40.6%	59.4%	40.6%
8	2014	222,498	137,731	FITZPATRICK, MICHAEL G.*	84,767	STROUSE, KEVIN		52,964 R	61.9%	38.1%	61.9%	38.1%
8	2012	352,238	199,379	FITZPATRICK, MICHAEL G.*	152,859	BOOCKVAR, KATHY		46,520 R	56.6%	43.4%	56.6%	43.4%
9	2014	173,317	110,094	SHUSTER, BILL*	63,223	HARTZOK, ALANNA K.		46,871 R	63.5%	36.5%	63.5%	36.5%
9	2012	274,305	169,177	SHUSTER, BILL*	105,128	RAMSBURG, KAREN		64,049 R	61.7%	38.3%	61.7%	38.3%
10	2014	180,322	112,851	MARINO, TOM*	44,737	BRION, SCOTT F.	22,734	68,114 R	62.6%	24.8%	71.6%	28.4%
10	2012	273,790	179,563	MARINO, TOM*	94,227	SCOLLO, PHILLIP		85,336 R	65.6%	34.4%	65.6%	34.4%
11	2014	184,692	122,464	BARLETTA, LOU*	62,228	OSTROWSKI, ANDY J.		60,236 R	66.3%	33.7%	66.3%	33.7%
11	2012	285,198	166,967	BARLETTA, LOU*	118,231	STILP, GENE		48,736 R	58.5%	41.5%	58.5%	41.5%
12	2014	215,921	127,993	ROTHFUS, KEITH J.*	87,928	MCCLELLAND, ERIN		40,065 R	59.3%	40.7%	59.3%	40.7%
12	2012	338,941	175,352	ROTHFUS, KEITH J.	163,589	CRITZ, MARK S.*		11,763 R	51.7%	48.3%	51.7%	48.3%
13	2014	184,150	60,549	ADCOCK, CARSON DEE	123,601	BOYLE, BRENDAN F.		63,052 D	32.9%	67.1%	32.9%	67.1%
13	2012	303,819	93,918	ROONEY, JOE	209,901	SCHWARTZ, ALLYSON Y.*		115,983 D	30.9%	69.1%	30.9%	69.1%
14	2014	148,351			148,351	DOYLE, MICHAEL F.*		148,351 D		100.0%		100.0%
14	2012	327,634	75,702	LESSMANN, HANS	251,932	DOYLE, MICHAEL F.*		176,230 D	23.1%	76.9%	23.1%	76.9%
15	2014	128,285	128,285	DENT, CHARLES W.*				128,285 R	100.0%		100.0%	
15	2012	297,724	168,960	DENT, CHARLES W.*	128,764	DAUGHERTY, RICK		40,196 R	56.8%	43.2%	56.8%	43.2%
16	2014	176,235	101,722	PITTS, JOSEPH R.*	74,513	HOUGHTON, THOMAS D.		27,209 R	57.7%	42.3%	57.7%	42.3%
16	2012	284,781	156,192	PITTS, JOSEPH R.*	111,185	STRADER, ARYANNA	17,404	45,007 R	54.8%	39.0%	58.4%	41.6%
17	2014	165,051	71,371	MOYLAN III, DAVID J.	93,680	CARTWRIGHT, MATT*		22,309 D	43.2%	56.8%	43.2%	56.8%
17	2012	267,601	106,208	CUMMINGS, LAUREEN	161,393	CARTWRIGHT, MATT		55,185 D	39.7%	60.3%	39.7%	60.3%

PENNSYLVANIA

HOUSE OF REPRESENTATIVES

CD	Year	Total Vote	Republican		Democratic		Other Vote	Rep.-Dem. Plurality	Percentage			
									Total Vote		Major Vote	
			Vote	Candidate	Vote	Candidate			Rep.	Dem.	Rep.	Dem.
18	2014	166,076	166,076	MURPHY, TIM*				166,076 R	100.0%		100.0%	
18	2012	338,873	216,727	MURPHY, TIM*	122,146	MAGGI, LARRY		94,581 R	64.0%	36.0%	64.0%	36.0%
TOTAL	2014	3,323,533	1,833,205		1,467,594		22,734	365,611 R	55.2%	44.2%	55.5%	44.5%
TOTAL	2012	5,556,330	2,710,070		2,793,538		52,722	83,468 D	48.8%	50.3%	49.2%	50.8%

Note: An asterisk (*) denotes incumbent.

PENNSYLVANIA

GENERAL AND PRIMARY ELECTIONS

2014 GENERAL ELECTIONS: OTHER VOTES

House   Other vote was:

CD 10   22,734 Independent (Nick Troiano)

2014 PRIMARY ELECTIONS: SUPPLEMENTARY INFORMATION

Primary   May 20, 2014   **Registration**   8,229,118   Democratic   4,091,989
                                   (as of May 20, 2014)   Republican   3,028,846
                                                                        Libertarian   45,735
                                                                        Other   1,062,548

Primary Type   Closed—Only registered Democrats and Republicans could vote in their party's primary.

	REPUBLICAN PRIMARIES			DEMOCRATIC PRIMARIES		
Governor	Corbett, Tom*	373,465	100.0%	Wolf, Tom	488,917	57.9%
				Schwartz, Allyson Y.	149,027	17.6%
				McCord, Robert M.	142,311	16.8%
				McGinty, Katie A.	64,754	7.7%
	TOTAL	373,465		TOTAL	845,009	
Congressional District 1	Rath, Megan Ann	6,995	100.0%	Brady, Robert A.*	47,565	100.0%
	TOTAL	6,995		TOTAL	47,565	
Congressional District 2	James, Armond	3,117	100.0%	Fattah, Chaka*	82,167	100.0%
	TOTAL	3,117		TOTAL	82,167	
Congressional District 3	Kelly, Mike*	33,475	100.0%	Lavallee, Daniel	30,153	100.0%
	TOTAL	33,475		TOTAL	30,153	
Congressional District 4	Perry, Scott*	35,020	100.0%	Thompson, Linda Deliah	24,312	100.0%
	TOTAL	35,020		TOTAL	24,312	

PENNSYLVANIA

GENERAL AND PRIMARY ELECTIONS

	REPUBLICAN PRIMARIES			DEMOCRATIC PRIMARIES		
Congressional District 5	Thompson, Glenn*	37,564	100.0%	Taylor, Kerith Strano	18,172	53.8%
				Tarantella, Thomas E.	15,603	46.2%
	TOTAL	37,564		TOTAL	33,775	
Congressional District 6	Costello, Ryan A.	24,313	100.0%	Trivedi, Manan	27,359	100.0%
	TOTAL	24,313		TOTAL	27,359	
Congressional District 7	Meehan, Patrick*	31,020	100.0%	Balchunis, Mary Ellen	29,444	100.0%
	TOTAL	31,020		TOTAL	29,444	
Congressional District 8	Fitzpatrick, Michael G.*	22,170	100.0%	Strouse, Kevin	18,440	51.1%
				Naughton, Shaughnessy	17,623	48.9%
	TOTAL	22,170		TOTAL	36,063	
Congressional District 9	Shuster, Bill*	24,465	52.8%	Hartzok, Alanna K.	30,938	100.0%
	Halvorson, Arthur L. "Art"	16,021	34.5%			
	Schooley, Travis	5,885	12.7%			
	TOTAL	46,371		TOTAL	30,938	
Congressional District 10	Marino, Tom*	32,538	100.0%	Brion, Scott F.	22,860	100.0%
	TOTAL	32,538		TOTAL	22,860	
Congressional District 11	Barletta, Lou*	29,772	100.0%	Ostrowski, Andy J.	28,567	100.0%
	TOTAL	29,772		TOTAL	28,567	
Congressional District 12	Rothfus, Keith J.*	23,291	100.0%	McClelland, Erin R.	32,971	68.0%
				Hugya, John	15,547	32.0%
	TOTAL	23,291		TOTAL	48,518	
Congressional District 13	Adcock, Carson Dee	10,211	65.8%	Boyle, Brendan F.	24,775	40.6%
	Plosa-Bowser, Beverly	5,312	34.2%	Margolies, Marjorie	16,723	27.4%
				Leach, Daylin	10,130	16.6%
				Arkoosh, Valerie	9,386	15.4%
	TOTAL	15,523		TOTAL	61,014	
Congressional District 14				Doyle, Michael F.*	57,039	84.1%
				Brooks, Janis C.	10,806	15.9%
				TOTAL	67,845	
Congressional District 15	Dent, Charles W.*	20,700	100.0%			
	TOTAL	20,700				
Congressional District 16	Pitts, Joseph R.*	25,611	100.0%	Houghton, Thomas D.	14,386	62.7%
				Kittappa, Raja	8,541	37.3%
	TOTAL	25,611		TOTAL	22,927	
Congressional District 17	Moylan III, David J.	9,227	44.6%	Cartwright, Matt*	47,992	100.0%
	Connolly, Matthew Donald "Matt"	7,000	33.8%			
	Dietz, Matthew H.	4,465	21.6%			
	TOTAL	20,692		TOTAL	47,992	
Congressional District 18	Murphy, Tim*	19,575	100.0%			
	TOTAL	19,575				

Note: An asterisk (*) denotes incumbent.

RHODE ISLAND

Congressional districts first established for elections held in 2012

2 members

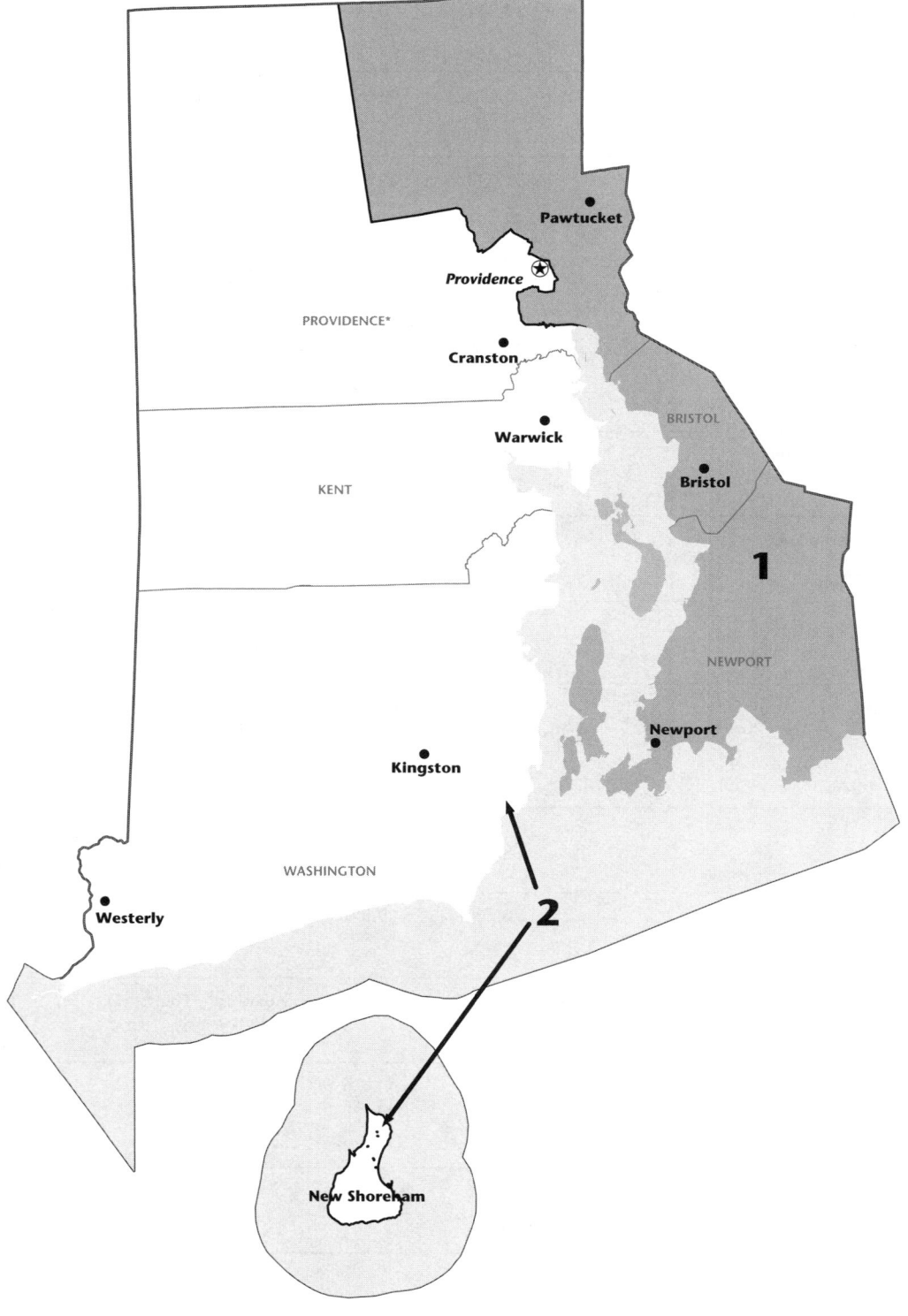

* Asterisk indicates a county whose boundaries include parts of two or more congressional districts.

RHODE ISLAND

GOVERNOR

Gina Raimondo (D). Elected 2014 to a four-year term.

SENATORS (2 Democrats)

Jack Reed (D). Reelected 2014 to a six-year term. Previously elected 2008, 2002, 1996.

Sheldon Whitehouse (D). Reelected 2012 to a six-year term. Previously elected 2006.

REPRESENTATIVES (2 Democrats)

1. David N. Cicilline (D)   2. James R. Langevin (D)

POSTWAR VOTE FOR PRESIDENT

| | | Republican | | Democratic | | | | Percentage | | | |
| | | | | | | | | Total Vote | | Major Vote | |
Year	Total Vote	Vote	Candidate	Vote	Candidate	Other Vote	Rep.-Dem. Plurality	Rep.	Dem.	Rep.	Dem.
2012	446,049	157,204	Romney, W. Mitt	279,677	Obama, Barack H.*	9,168	122,473 D	35.2%	62.7%	36.0%	64.0%
2008	471,766	165,391	McCain, John S. III	296,571	Obama, Barack H.	9,804	131,180 D	35.1%	62.9%	35.8%	64.2%
2004	437,134	169,046	Bush, George W.*	259,760	Kerry, John F.	8,328	90,714 D	38.7%	59.4%	39.4%	60.6%
2000**	409,047	130,555	Bush, George W.	249,508	Gore, Albert Jr.	28,984	118,953 D	31.9%	61.0%	34.4%	65.6%
1996**	390,284	104,683	Dole, Robert "Bob"	233,050	Clinton, Bill*	52,551	128,367 D	26.8%	59.7%	31.0%	69.0%
1992**	453,477	131,601	Bush, George H.*	213,299	Clinton, Bill	108,577	81,698 D	29.0%	47.0%	38.2%	61.8%
1988	404,620	177,761	Bush, George H.	225,123	Dukakis, Michael S.	1,736	47,362 D	43.9%	55.6%	44.1%	55.9%
1984	410,492	212,080	Reagan, Ronald*	197,106	Mondale, Walter F.	1,306	14,974 R	51.7%	48.0%	51.8%	48.2%
1980**	416,072	154,793	Reagan, Ronald	198,342	Carter, Jimmy*	62,937	43,549 D	37.2%	47.7%	43.8%	56.2%
1976	411,170	181,249	Ford, Gerald R.*	227,636	Carter, Jimmy	2,285	46,387 D	44.1%	55.4%	44.3%	55.7%
1972	415,808	220,383	Nixon, Richard M.*	194,645	McGovern, George S.	780	25,738 R	53.0%	46.8%	53.1%	46.9%
1968**	385,000	122,359	Nixon, Richard M.	246,518	Humphrey, Hubert Horatio Jr.	16,123	124,159 D	31.8%	64.0%	33.2%	66.8%
1964	390,091	74,615	Goldwater, Barry M. Sr.	315,463	Johnson, Lyndon B.*	13	240,848 D	19.1%	80.9%	19.1%	80.9%
1960	405,535	147,502	Nixon, Richard M.	258,032	Kennedy, John F.	1	110,530 D	36.4%	63.6%	36.4%	63.6%
1956	387,609	225,819	Eisenhower, Dwight D.*	161,790	Stevenson, Adlai E. II		64,029 R	58.3%	41.7%	58.3%	41.7%
1952	414,498	210,935	Eisenhower, Dwight D.	203,293	Stevenson, Adlai E. II	270	7,642 R	50.9%	49.0%	50.9%	49.1%
1948	327,702	135,787	Dewey, Thomas E.	188,736	Truman, Harry S.*	3,179	52,949 D	41.4%	57.6%	41.8%	58.2%

Note: An asterisk (*) denotes incumbent. **In past elections, the other vote included: 2000 - 25,052 Green (Ralph Nader); 1996 - 43,723 Reform (Ross Perot); 1992 - 105,045 Independent (Perot); 1980 - 59,819 Independent (John Anderson); 1968 - 15,678 American Independent (George Wallace).

RHODE ISLAND

POSTWAR VOTE FOR GOVERNOR

Year	Total Vote	Republican		Democratic		Other Vote	Rep.-Dem. Plurality	Percentage			
								Total Vote		Major Vote	
		Vote	Candidate	Vote	Candidate			Rep.	Dem.	Rep.	Dem.
2014	324,055	117,428	Fung, Allan	131,899	Raimondo, Gina	74,728	14,471 D	36.2%	40.7%	47.1%	52.9%
2010**	342,545	114,911	Robitaille, John F.	78,896	Caprio, Frank T.	148,738	36,015 R**	33.5%	23.0%	59.3%	40.7%
2006	387,010	197,366	Carcieri, Donald L.*	189,562	Fogarty, Charles J.	82	7,804 R	51.0%	49.0%	51.0%	49.0%
2002	332,655	181,827	Carcieri, Donald L.	150,229	York, Myrth	599	31,598 R	54.7%	45.2%	54.8%	45.2%
1998	306,383	156,180	Almond, Lincoln C.*	129,105	York, Myrth	21,098	27,075 R	51.0%	42.1%	54.7%	45.3%
1994**	361,377	171,194	Almond, Lincoln C.	157,361	York, Myrth	32,822	13,833 R	47.4%	43.5%	52.1%	47.9%
1992	424,818	145,590	Leonard, Elizabeth Ann	261,484	Sundlun, Bruce G.*	17,744	115,894 D	34.3%	61.6%	35.8%	64.2%
1990	356,672	92,177	Diprete, Edward*	264,411	Sundlun, Bruce G.	84	172,234 D	25.8%	74.1%	25.8%	74.2%
1988	400,516	203,550	Diprete, Edward*	196,936	Sundlun, Bruce G.	30	6,614 R	50.8%	49.2%	50.8%	49.2%
1986	322,724	208,822	Diprete, Edward*	104,508	Sundlun, Bruce G.	9,394	104,314 R	64.7%	32.4%	66.6%	33.4%
1984	408,375	245,059	Diprete, Edward	163,311	Solomon, Anthony J.	5	81,748 R	60.0%	40.0%	60.0%	40.0%
1982	337,259	79,602	Marzullo, Vincent	247,208	Garrahy, J. Joseph*	10,449	167,606 D	23.6%	73.3%	24.4%	75.6%
1980	405,916	106,729	Cianci, Vincent A.	299,174	Garrahy, J. Joseph*	13	192,445 D	26.3%	73.7%	26.3%	73.7%
1978	314,363	96,596	Almond, Lincoln C.	197,386	Garrahy, J. Joseph*	20,381	100,790 D	30.7%	62.8%	32.9%	67.1%
1976	398,683	178,254	Taft, James L.	218,561	Garrahy, J. Joseph	1,868	40,307 D	44.7%	54.8%	44.9%	55.1%
1974	321,660	69,224	Nugent, James W.	252,436	Noel, Philip W.*		183,212 D	21.5%	78.5%	21.5%	78.5%
1972	412,866	194,315	DeSimone, Herbert F.	216,953	Noel, Philip W.	1,598	22,638 D	47.1%	52.5%	47.2%	52.8%
1970	346,342	171,549	DeSimone, Herbert F.	173,420	Licht, Frank*	1,373	1,871 D	49.5%	50.1%	49.7%	50.3%
1968	383,725	187,958	Chafee, John H.*	195,766	Licht, Frank	1	7,808 D	49.0%	51.0%	49.0%	51.0%
1966	332,064	210,202	Chafee, John H.*	121,862	Hobbs, Horace E.		88,340 R	63.3%	36.7%	63.3%	36.7%
1964	391,668	239,501	Chafee, John H.*	152,165	Gallogly, Edward P.	2	87,336 R	61.1%	38.9%	61.1%	38.9%
1962	327,506	163,952	Chafee, John H.	163,554	Notte, John A. Jr.*		398 R	50.1%	49.9%	50.1%	49.9%
1960	401,362	174,044	Del Sesto, Christopher*	227,318	Notte, John A. Jr.		53,274 D	43.4%	56.6%	43.4%	56.6%
1958	346,780	176,505	Del Sesto, Christopher	170,275	Roberts, Dennis J.*		6,230 R	50.9%	49.1%	50.9%	49.1%
1956	383,919	191,604	Del Sesto, Christopher	192,315	Roberts, Dennis J.*		711 D	49.9%	50.1%	49.9%	50.1%
1954	328,670	137,131	Lewis, Dean J.	189,595	Roberts, Dennis J.*	1,944	52,464 D	41.7%	57.7%	42.0%	58.0%
1952	409,689	194,102	Archambault, Raoul	215,587	Roberts, Dennis J.*		21,485 D	47.4%	52.6%	47.4%	52.6%
1950	296,808	120,683	Lachapelle, Eugene J.	176,125	Roberts, Dennis J.		55,442 D	40.7%	59.3%	40.7%	59.3%
1948	323,863	124,441	Ruerat, Albert P.	198,056	Pastore, John O.*	1,366	73,615 D	38.4%	61.2%	38.6%	61.4%
1946	275,341	126,456	Murphy, John G.	148,885	Pastore, John O.*		22,429 D	45.9%	54.1%	45.9%	54.1%

Note: An asterisk (*) denotes incumbent. A pound sign (#) indicates that the winner was an independent candidate. **In past elections, the other vote included: 2014 - 69,278 Moderate (Robert J. Healey Jr.); 2010 - 123,571 Independent (Lincoln Chafee), who was elected with 36.1 percent of the total vote. The term of office of Rhode Island's governor was increased from two to four years effective with the 1994 election.

RHODE ISLAND

POSTWAR VOTE FOR SENATOR

Year	Total Vote	Republican Vote	Republican Candidate	Democratic Vote	Democratic Candidate	Other Vote	Rep.-Dem. Plurality	Total Vote Rep.	Total Vote Dem.	Major Vote Rep.	Major Vote Dem.
2014	316,898	92,684	Zaccaria, Mark S.	223,675	Reed, Jack*	539	130,991 D	29.2%	70.6%	29.3%	70.7%
2012	418,189	146,222	Hinckley, Barry	271,034	Whitehouse, Sheldon*	933	124,812 D	35.0%	64.8%	35.0%	65.0%
2008	438,812	116,174	Tingle, Robert G.	320,644	Reed, Jack*	1,994	204,470 D	26.5%	73.1%	26.6%	73.4%
2006	385,451	179,001	Chafee, Lincoln D.*	206,110	Whitehouse, Sheldon	340	27,109 D	46.4%	53.5%	46.5%	53.5%
2002	323,912	69,881	Tingle, Robert G.	253,922	Reed, Jack*	109	184,041 D	21.6%	78.4%	21.6%	78.4%
2000	391,537	222,588	Chafee, Lincoln D.*	161,023	Weygand, Robert A.	7,926	61,565 R	56.8%	41.1%	58.0%	42.0%
1996	363,371	127,368	Mayer, Nancy J.	230,676	Reed, Jack	5,327	103,308 D	35.1%	63.5%	35.6%	64.4%
1994	345,388	222,856	Chafee, John H.*	122,532	Kushner, Linda J.		100,324 R	64.5%	35.5%	64.5%	35.5%
1990	364,062	138,947	Schneider, Claudine	225,105	Pell, Claiborne*	10	86,158 D	38.2%	61.8%	38.2%	61.8%
1988	397,996	217,273	Chafee, John H.*	180,717	Licht, Richard A.	6	36,556 R	54.6%	45.4%	54.6%	45.4%
1984	395,285	108,492	Leonard, Barbara	286,780	Pell, Claiborne*	13	178,288 D	27.4%	72.6%	27.4%	72.6%
1982	342,779	175,495	Chafee, John H.*	167,283	Michaelson, Julius C.	1	8,212 R	51.2%	48.8%	51.2%	48.8%
1978	305,618	76,061	Reynolds, James G.	229,557	Pell, Claiborne*		153,496 D	24.9%	75.1%	24.9%	75.1%
1976	398,906	230,329	Chafee, John H.*	167,665	Lorber, Richard P.	912	62,664 R	57.7%	42.0%	57.9%	42.1%
1972	413,432	188,990	Chafee, John H.	221,942	Pell, Claiborne*	2,500	32,952 D	45.7%	53.7%	46.0%	54.0%
1970	341,222	107,351	McLaughlin, John	230,469	Pastore, John O.*	3,402	123,118 D	31.5%	67.5%	31.8%	68.2%
1966	324,173	104,838	Briggs, Ruth M.	219,331	Pell, Claiborne*	4	114,493 D	32.3%	67.7%	32.3%	67.7%
1964	386,322	66,715	Lagueux, Ronald R.	319,607	Pastore, John O.*		252,892 D	17.3%	82.7%	17.3%	82.7%
1960	399,983	124,408	Archambault, Raoul	275,575	Pell, Claiborne		151,167 D	31.1%	68.9%	31.1%	68.9%
1958	344,519	122,353	Ewing, Bayard	222,166	Pastore, John O.*		99,813 D	35.5%	64.5%	35.5%	64.5%
1954	326,624	132,970	Sundlun, Walter I.	193,654	Green, Theodore Francis*		60,684 D	40.7%	59.3%	40.7%	59.3%
1952	410,978	185,850	Ewing, Bayard	225,128	Pastore, John O.*		39,278 D	45.2%	54.8%	45.2%	54.8%
1950S	299,410	114,890	Levy, Austin T.	184,520	Pastore, John O.		69,630 D	38.4%	61.6%	38.4%	61.6%
1948	320,952	130,668	Hazard, Thomas P.	190,284	Green, Theodore Francis*		59,616 D	40.7%	59.3%	40.7%	59.3%
1946	273,528	122,780	Dyer, W. Gurnee	150,748	McGrath, J. Howard		27,968 D	44.9%	55.1%	44.9%	55.1%

Note: An asterisk (*) denotes incumbent. **The 1950 election was for a short term to fill a vacancy.

RHODE ISLAND

GOVERNOR 2014

2010 Census Population	County	Total Vote	Republican (Fung)	Democratic (Raimondo)	Moderate (Healey)	Other	Rep.-Dem. Plurality	Percentage Total Vote		
								Rep.	Dem.	Mod.
49,875	BRISTOL	18,336	4,806	7,312	6,060	158	2,506 D	26.2%	39.9%	33.0%
166,158	KENT	59,015	23,009	20,176	14,937	893	2,833 R	39.0%	34.2%	25.3%
82,888	NEWPORT	29,520	10,122	12,888	5,898	612	2,766 D	34.3%	43.7%	20.0%
626,667	PROVIDENCE	169,698	61,519	73,262	32,086	2,831	11,743 D	36.3%	43.2%	18.9%
126,979	WASHINGTON	47,486	17,972	18,261	10,297	956	289 D	37.8%	38.5%	21.7%
1,052,567	TOTAL	324,055	117,428	131,899	69,278	5,450	14,471 D	36.2%	40.7%	21.4%

2010 Census Population	City/Town	Total Vote	Republican (Fung)	Democratic (Raimondo)	Moderate (Healey)	Other	Rep.-Dem. Plurality	Percentage Total Vote		
								Rep.	Dem.	Mod.
16,310	BARRINGTON	7,192	2,022	3,566	1,554	50	1,544 D	28.1%	49.6%	21.6%
22,954	BRISTOL TOWN	7,371	1,959	2,628	2,709	75	669 D#	26.6%	35.7%	36.8%
15,955	BURRILLVILLE	4,670	1,861	1,334	1,371	104	490 R	39.9%	28.6%	29.4%
19,376	CENTRAL FALLS	2,047	358	1,359	280	50	1,001 D	17.5%	66.4%	13.7%
7,827	CHARLESTOWN	3,101	1,137	1,177	728	59	40 D	36.7%	38.0%	23.5%
35,014	COVENTRY	12,634	4,979	3,812	3,610	233	1,167 R	39.4%	30.2%	28.6%
80,387	CRANSTON	27,006	14,853	8,159	3,716	278	6,694 R	55.0%	30.2%	13.8%
33,506	CUMBERLAND	11,684	4,325	4,661	2,478	220	336 D	37.0%	39.9%	21.2%
13,146	EAST GREENWICH	5,592	2,315	2,364	848	65	49 D	41.4%	42.3%	15.2%
47,037	EAST PROVIDENCE	13,705	3,718	5,958	3,804	225	2,154 D	27.1%	43.5%	27.8%
6,425	EXETER	2,713	1,147	771	742	53	376 R	42.3%	28.4%	27.3%
4,606	FOSTER	1,910	732	534	604	40	128 R	38.3%	28.0%	31.6%
9,746	GLOCESTER	3,540	1,503	963	1,019	55	484 R	42.5%	27.2%	28.8%
8,188	HOPKINTON	2,707	1,080	836	723	68	244 R	39.9%	30.9%	26.7%
5,405	JAMESTOWN	2,869	901	1,325	590	53	424 D	31.4%	46.2%	20.6%
28,769	JOHNSTON	10,032	4,502	3,270	2,126	134	1,232 R	44.9%	32.6%	21.2%
21,105	LINCOLN	8,212	3,249	2,974	1,870	119	275 R	39.6%	36.2%	22.8%
3,492	LITTLE COMPTON	1,634	648	674	288	24	26 D	39.7%	41.2%	17.6%
16,150	MIDDLETOWN	5,352	1,902	2,241	1,090	119	339 D	35.5%	41.9%	20.4%
15,868	NARRAGANSETT	6,087	2,410	2,395	1,198	84	15 R	39.6%	39.3%	19.7%
1,051	NEW SHOREHAM	726	174	365	173	14	191 D	24.0%	50.3%	23.8%
24,672	NEWPORT CITY	7,554	2,312	3,734	1,331	177	1,422 D	30.6%	49.4%	17.6%
26,486	NORTH KINGSTOWN	11,088	4,305	4,166	2,422	195	139 R	38.8%	37.6%	21.8%
32,078	NORTH PROVIDENCE	11,102	4,505	4,013	2,414	170	492 R	40.6%	36.1%	21.7%
11,967	NORTH SMITHFIELD	4,380	1,870	1,456	986	68	414 R	42.7%	33.2%	22.5%
71,148	PAWTUCKET	13,779	3,391	7,144	2,960	284	3,753 D	24.6%	51.8%	21.5%
17,389	PORTSMOUTH	6,863	2,477	2,824	1,426	136	347 D	36.1%	41.1%	20.8%
178,042	PROVIDENCE CITY	37,943	8,445	24,662	4,116	720	16,217 D	22.3%	65.0%	10.8%
7,708	RICHMOND	2,882	1,153	851	825	53	302 R	40.0%	29.5%	28.6%
10,329	SCITUATE	4,582	2,203	1,170	1,146	63	1,033 R	48.1%	25.5%	25.0%
21,430	SMITHFIELD	7,672	3,241	2,587	1,725	119	654 R	42.2%	33.7%	22.5%
30,639	SOUTH KINGSTOWN	10,692	3,562	4,606	2,291	233	1,044 D	33.3%	43.1%	21.4%
15,780	TIVERTON	5,248	1,882	2,090	1,173	103	208 D	35.9%	39.8%	22.4%
10,611	WARREN	3,773	825	1,118	1,797	33	293 D#	21.9%	29.6%	47.6%
82,672	WARWICK	30,165	11,383	10,559	7,795	428	824 R	37.7%	35.0%	25.8%
6,135	WEST GREENWICH	2,419	1,097	605	684	33	413 R	45.3%	25.0%	28.3%
29,191	WEST WARWICK	8,205	3,235	2,836	2,000	134	399 R	39.4%	34.6%	24.4%
22,787	WESTERLY	7,490	3,004	3,094	1,195	197	90 D	40.1%	41.3%	16.0%
41,186	WOONSOCKET	7,434	2,763	3,018	1,471	182	255 D	37.2%	40.6%	19.8%
1,052,567	TOTAL	324,055	117,428	131,899	69,278	5,450	14,471 D	36.2%	40.7%	21.4%

Note: A pound sign (#) indicates that the winner was the Moderate candidate.

RHODE ISLAND

SENATOR 2014

2010 Census Population	County	Total Vote	Republican (Zaccaria)	Democratic (Reed)	Other	Rep.-Dem. Plurality	Percentage Total Vote Rep.	Dem.	Major Vote Rep.	Dem.
49,875	BRISTOL	17,825	4,940	12,856	29	7,916 D	27.7%	72.1%	27.8%	72.2%
166,158	KENT	58,063	19,663	38,320	80	18,657 D	33.9%	66.0%	33.9%	66.1%
82,888	NEWPORT	29,037	8,472	20,532	33	12,060 D	29.2%	70.7%	29.2%	70.8%
626,667	PROVIDENCE	165,294	43,866	121,097	331	77,231 D	26.5%	73.3%	26.6%	73.4%
126,979	WASHINGTON	46,657	15,742	30,849	66	15,107 D	33.7%	66.1%	33.8%	66.2%
	Votes Not Reported by County	22	1	21		20 D	4.5%	95.5%	4.5%	95.5%
1,052,567	TOTAL	316,898	92,684	223,675	539	130,991 D	29.2%	70.6%	29.3%	70.7%

2010 Census Population	City/Town	Total Vote	Republican (Zaccaria)	Democratic (Reed)	Other	Rep.-Dem. Plurality	Percentage Total Vote Rep.	Dem.	Major Vote Rep.	Dem.
16,310	BARRINGTON	7,068	2,012	5,047	9	3,035 D	28.5%	71.4%	28.5%	71.5%
22,954	BRISTOL TOWN	7,145	1,947	5,183	15	3,236 D	27.2%	72.5%	27.3%	72.7%
15,955	BURRILLVILLE	4,602	1,672	2,924	6	1,252 D	36.3%	63.5%	36.4%	63.6%
19,376	CENTRAL FALLS	1,987	257	1,725	5	1,468 D	12.9%	86.8%	13.0%	87.0%
7,827	CHARLESTOWN	3,047	1,044	2,002	1	958 D	34.3%	65.7%	34.3%	65.7%
35,014	COVENTRY	12,436	4,563	7,861	12	3,298 D	36.7%	63.2%	36.7%	63.3%
80,387	CRANSTON	26,296	8,360	17,895	41	9,535 D	31.8%	68.1%	31.8%	68.2%
33,506	CUMBERLAND	11,422	3,605	7,799	18	4,194 D	31.6%	68.3%	31.6%	68.4%
13,146	EAST GREENWICH	5,483	2,152	3,326	5	1,174 D	39.2%	60.7%	39.3%	60.7%
47,037	EAST PROVIDENCE	13,382	3,259	10,095	28	6,836 D	24.4%	75.4%	24.4%	75.6%
6,425	EXETER	2,662	1,124	1,535	3	411 D	42.2%	57.7%	42.3%	57.7%
4,606	FOSTER	1,882	780	1,099	3	319 D	41.4%	58.4%	41.5%	58.5%
9,746	GLOCESTER	3,478	1,386	2,087	5	701 D	39.9%	60.0%	39.9%	60.1%
8,188	HOPKINTON	2,659	1,000	1,654	5	654 D	37.6%	62.2%	37.7%	62.3%
5,405	JAMESTOWN	2,820	750	2,070		1,320 D	26.6%	73.4%	26.6%	73.4%
28,769	JOHNSTON	9,764	3,172	6,572	20	3,400 D	32.5%	67.3%	32.6%	67.4%
21,105	LINCOLN	8,077	2,662	5,404	11	2,742 D	33.0%	66.9%	33.0%	67.0%
3,492	LITTLE COMPTON	1,614	590	1,020	4	430 D	36.6%	63.2%	36.6%	63.4%
16,150	MIDDLETOWN	5,288	1,474	3,806	8	2,332 D	27.9%	72.0%	27.9%	72.1%
15,868	NARRAGANSETT	5,988	1,935	4,041	12	2,106 D	32.3%	67.5%	32.4%	67.6%
1,051	NEW SHOREHAM	717	138	578	1	440 D	19.2%	80.6%	19.3%	80.7%
24,672	NEWPORT CITY	7,402	1,676	5,716	10	4,040 D	22.6%	77.2%	22.7%	77.3%
26,486	NORTH KINGSTOWN	10,907	4,047	6,843	17	2,796 D	37.1%	62.7%	37.2%	62.8%
32,078	NORTH PROVIDENCE	10,844	3,066	7,760	18	4,694 D	28.3%	71.6%	28.3%	71.7%
11,967	NORTH SMITHFIELD	4,284	1,529	2,753	2	1,224 D	35.7%	64.3%	35.7%	64.3%
71,148	PAWTUCKET	13,466	2,710	10,728	28	8,018 D	20.1%	79.7%	20.2%	79.8%
17,389	PORTSMOUTH	6,780	2,255	4,517	8	2,262 D	33.3%	66.6%	33.3%	66.7%
178,042	PROVIDENCE CITY	36,558	4,848	31,593	117	26,745 D	13.3%	86.4%	13.3%	86.7%
7,708	RICHMOND	2,840	1,127	1,704	9	577 D	39.7%	60.0%	39.8%	60.2%
10,329	SCITUATE	4,454	1,901	2,544	9	643 D	42.7%	57.1%	42.8%	57.2%
21,430	SMITHFIELD	7,546	2,660	4,883	3	2,223 D	35.3%	64.7%	35.3%	64.7%
30,639	SOUTH KINGSTOWN	10,503	3,037	7,454	12	4,417 D	28.9%	71.0%	28.9%	71.1%
15,780	TIVERTON	5,133	1,727	3,403	3	1,676 D	33.6%	66.3%	33.7%	66.3%
10,611	WARREN	3,612	981	2,626	5	1,645 D	27.2%	72.7%	27.2%	72.8%
82,672	WARWICK	29,695	9,249	20,395	51	11,146 D	31.1%	68.7%	31.2%	68.8%
6,135	WEST GREENWICH	2,375	1,081	1,291	3	210 D	45.5%	54.4%	45.6%	54.4%
29,191	WEST WARWICK	8,074	2,618	5,447	9	2,829 D	32.4%	67.5%	32.5%	67.5%
22,787	WESTERLY	7,334	2,290	5,038	6	2,748 D	31.2%	68.7%	31.2%	68.8%
41,186	WOONSOCKET	7,252	1,999	5,236	17	3,237 D	27.6%	72.2%	27.6%	72.4%

RHODE ISLAND

HOUSE OF REPRESENTATIVES

| | | | Republican | | Democratic | | Other | Rep.-Dem. | Percentage | | | |
| | | | | | | | | | Total Vote | | Major Vote | |
CD	Year	Total Vote	Vote	Candidate	Vote	Candidate	Vote	Plurality	Rep.	Dem.	Rep.	Dem.
1	2014	146,353	58,877	LYNCH, CORMICK	87,060	CICILLINE, DAVID N.*	416	28,183 D	40.2%	59.5%	40.3%	59.7%
1	2012	205,115	83,737	DOHERTY, BRENDAN P.	108,612	CICILLINE, DAVID N.*	12,766	24,875 D	40.8%	53.0%	43.5%	56.5%
2	2014	169,904	63,844	REIS, RHUE	105,716	LANGEVIN, JAMES R.*	344	41,872 D	37.6%	62.2%	37.7%	62.3%
2	2012	222,660	78,189	RILEY, MICHAEL G.	124,067	LANGEVIN, JAMES R.*	20,404	45,878 D	35.1%	55.7%	38.7%	61.3%
TOTAL	2014	316,257	122,721		192,776		760	70,055 D	38.8%	61.0%	38.9%	61.1%
TOTAL	2012	427,775	161,926		232,679		33,170	70,753 D	37.9%	54.4%	41.0%	59.0%

Note: An asterisk (*) denotes incumbent.

RHODE ISLAND

GENERAL AND PRIMARY ELECTIONS

2014 GENERAL ELECTIONS: OTHER VOTE

Governor Other vote was 69,278 Moderate (Robert J. Healey Jr.), 3,483 Independent (Kate Fletcher), 1,228 Independent (Leon M. Kayarian), 739 scattered write-in

Senate Other vote was 539 scattered write-in

House Other vote was:

CD 1 416 scattered write-in
CD 2 344 scattered write-in

2014 PRIMARY ELECTIONS: SUPPLEMENTARY INFORMATION

Primary September 9, 2014 **Registration** 750,135 Democratic 292,511
(as of August 10, 2014) Republican 75,338
Moderate 1,945
Unaffiliated 380,341

Primary Type Semi-open—Registered Democrats and Republicans could vote only in their party's primary. Unaffiliated voters could participate in either party's primary.

	REPUBLICAN PRIMARIES			DEMOCRATIC PRIMARIES		
Senator	Zaccaria, Mark S.	23,780	100.0%	Reed, Jack*	98,610	100.0%
	TOTAL	23,780		TOTAL	98,610	
Governor	Fung, Allan	17,530	54.9%	Raimondo, Gina	53,990	42.1%
	Block, Kenneth J.	14,399	45.1%	Taveras, Angel	37,326	29.1%
				Pell, Herbert Claiborne "Clay" IV	34,515	26.9%
				Giroux, Todd	2,264	1.8%
	TOTAL	31,929		TOTAL	128,095	
Congressional District 1	Lynch, Cormick	6,527	72.4%	Cicilline, David N.*	38,186	63.0%
	Tran, Stanford "Stan"	2,483	27.6%	Fecteau, Matthew J.	22,447	37.0%
	TOTAL	9,010		TOTAL	60,633	
Congressional District 2	Reis, Rhue	14,143	100.0%	Langevin, James R.*	44,512	100.0%
	TOTAL	14,143		TOTAL	44,512	

Note: An asterisk (*) denotes incumbent.

SOUTH CAROLINA

Congressional districts first established for elections held in 2012

7 members

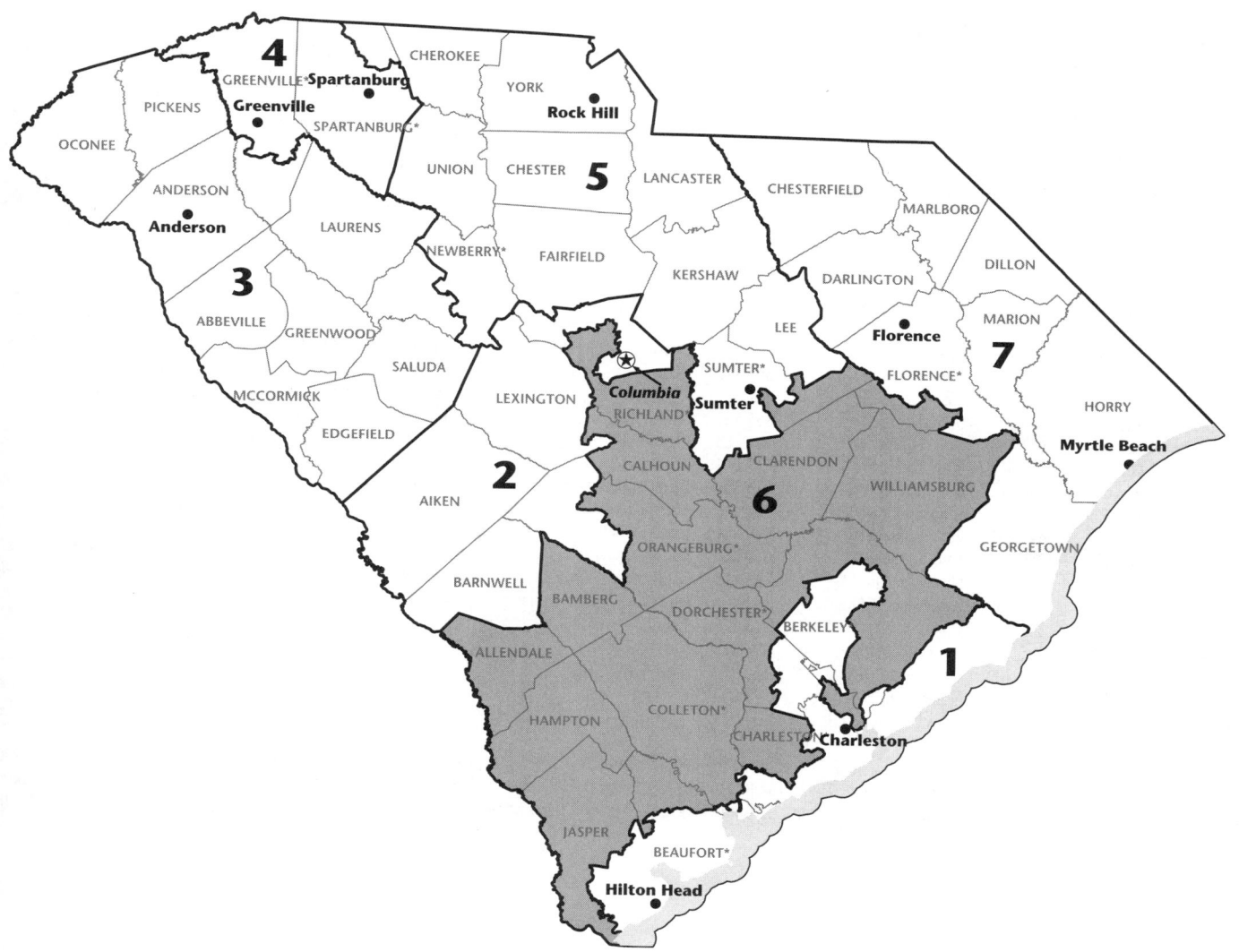

* Asterisk indicates a county whose boundaries include parts of two or more congressional districts.

SOUTH CAROLINA

GOVERNOR
Nikki R. Haley (R). Re-elected 2014 to a four-year term. Previously elected 2010.

SENATORS (2 Republicans)
Lindsey Graham (R). Re-elected 2014 to a six-year term. Previously elected 2008, 2002.

Tim Scott (R). Elected 2014 to a six-year term. Initially sworn in on January 3, 2013, to fill the vacancy created by the resignation of Jim DeMint (R), who resigned two days eariler to become president of the Heritage Foundation.

REPRESENTATIVES (6 Republicans, 1 Democrat)
1. Mark Sanford (R)
2. Joe Wilson (R)
3. Jeff Duncan (R)
4. Trey Gowdy (R)
5. Mick Mulvaney (R)
6. James E. Clyburn (D)
7. Tom Rice (R)

POSTWAR VOTE FOR PRESIDENT

		Republican		Democratic		Other	Rep.-Dem.	Total Vote		Major Vote	
Year	Total Vote	Vote	Candidate	Vote	Candidate	Vote	Plurality	Rep.	Dem.	Rep.	Dem.
2012	1,964,118	1,071,645	Romney, W. Mitt	865,941	Obama, Barack H.*	26,532	205,704 R	54.6%	44.1%	55.3%	44.7%
2008	1,920,969	1,034,896	McCain, John S. III	862,449	Obama, Barack H.	23,624	172,447 R	53.9%	44.9%	54.5%	45.5%
2004	1,617,730	937,974	Bush, George W.*	661,699	Kerry, John F.	18,057	276,275 R	58.0%	40.9%	58.6%	41.4%
2000**	1,382,717	785,937	Bush, George W.	565,561	Gore, Albert Jr.	31,219	220,376 R	56.8%	40.9%	58.2%	41.8%
1996**	1,151,689	573,458	Dole, Robert "Bob"	506,283	Clinton, Bill*	71,948	67,175 R	49.8%	44.0%	53.1%	46.9%
1992**	1,202,527	577,507	Bush, George H.*	479,514	Clinton, Bill	145,506	97,993 R	48.0%	39.9%	54.6%	45.4%
1988	986,009	606,443	Bush, George H.	370,554	Dukakis, Michael S.	9,012	235,889 R	61.5%	37.6%	62.1%	37.9%
1984	968,529	615,539	Reagan, Ronald*	344,459	Mondale, Walter F.	8,531	271,080 R	63.6%	35.6%	64.1%	35.9%
1980**	894,071	441,841	Reagan, Ronald	430,385	Carter, Jimmy*	21,845	11,456 R	49.4%	48.1%	50.7%	49.3%
1976	802,583	346,149	Ford, Gerald R.*	450,807	Carter, Jimmy	5,627	104,658 D	43.1%	56.2%	43.4%	56.6%
1972	673,960	477,044	Nixon, Richard M.*	186,824	McGovern, George S.	10,092	290,220 R	70.8%	27.7%	71.9%	28.1%
1968**	666,978	254,062	Nixon, Richard M.	197,486	Humphrey, Hubert Horatio Jr.	215,430	56,576 R	38.1%	29.6%	56.3%	43.7%
1964	524,779	309,048	Goldwater, Barry M. Sr.	215,723	Johnson, Lyndon B.*	8	93,325 R	58.9%	41.1%	58.9%	41.1%
1960	386,688	188,558	Nixon, Richard M.	198,129	Kennedy, John F.	1	9,571 D	48.8%	51.2%	48.8%	51.2%
1956**	300,583	75,700	Eisenhower, Dwight D.*	136,372	Stevenson, Adlai E. II	88,511	60,672 D	25.2%	45.4%	35.7%	64.3%
1952	341,087	168,082	Eisenhower, Dwight D.	173,004	Stevenson, Adlai E. II	1	4,922 D	49.3%	50.7%	49.3%	50.7%
1948**	142,571	5,386	Dewey, Thomas E.	34,423	Truman, Harry S.*	102,762	29,037 D#	3.8%	24.1%	13.5%	86.5%

Note: An asterisk (*) denotes incumbent. A pound sign (#) indicates that the state was carried by a third party candidate. **In past elections, the other vote included: 2000 - 20,200 Green (Ralph Nader); 1996 - 64,386 Reform (Ross Perot); 1992 - 138,872 Independent (Perot); 1980 - 14,153 Independent (John Anderson); 1968 - 215,430 American Independent (George Wallace), who finished second; 1956 - 88,509 Uncommitted States' Rights electors, which placed second; 1948 - 102,607 States' Rights (Strom Thurmond), who won South Carolina with 72.0 percent of the total vote.

SOUTH CAROLINA

POSTWAR VOTE FOR GOVERNOR

Year	Total Vote	Republican		Democratic		Other Vote	Rep.-Dem. Plurality	Percentage			
								Total Vote		Major Vote	
		Vote	Candidate	Vote	Candidate			Rep.	Dem.	Rep.	Dem.
2014	1,246,301	696,645	Haley, Nikki R.*	516,166	Sheheen, Vincent A.	33,490	180,479 R	55.9%	41.4%	57.4%	42.6%
2010	1,344,198	690,525	Haley, Nikki R.	630,534	Sheheen, Vincent A.	23,139	59,991 R	51.4%	46.9%	52.3%	47.7%
2006	1,091,952	601,868	Sanford, Mark*	489,076	Moore, Tommy	1,008	112,792 R	55.1%	44.8%	55.2%	44.8%
2002	1,107,725	585,422	Sanford, Mark	521,140	Hodges, James H.*	1,163	64,282 R	52.8%	47.0%	52.9%	47.1%
1998	1,070,869	484,088	Beasley, David*	570,070	Hodges, James H.	16,711	85,982 D	45.2%	53.2%	45.9%	54.1%
1994	933,850	470,756	Beasley, David	447,002	Theodore, Nick A.	16,092	23,754 R	50.4%	47.9%	51.3%	48.7%
1990	760,965	528,831	Campbell, Carroll*	212,034	Mitchell, Theo	20,100	316,797 R	69.5%	27.9%	71.4%	28.6%
1986	753,751	384,565	Campbell, Carroll	361,325	Daniel, Mike	7,861	23,240 R	51.0%	47.9%	51.6%	48.4%
1982	671,625	202,806	Workman, W. D. III	468,819	Riley, Richard W.*		266,013 D	30.2%	69.8%	30.2%	69.8%
1978	627,182	236,946	Young, Edward L.	384,898	Riley, Richard W.	5,338	147,952 D	37.8%	61.4%	38.1%	61.9%
1974	523,199	266,109	Edwards, James B.	248,938	Dorn, W. J. Bryan	8,152	17,171 R	50.9%	47.6%	51.7%	48.3%
1970	484,257	221,233	Watson, Albert W.	249,951	West, John C.	13,073	28,718 D	45.7%	51.6%	47.0%	53.0%
1966	439,942	184,088	Rogers, Joseph O. Jr.	255,854	McNair, Robert E.*		71,766 D	41.8%	58.2%	41.8%	58.2%
1962	253,721			253,704	Russell, Donald S.	17	253,704 D		100.0%		100.0%
1958	77,740			77,714	Hollings, Ernest F.	26	77,714 D		100.0%		100.0%
1954	214,212			214,204	Timmerman, George Bell	8	214,204 D		100.0%		100.0%
1950	50,642			50,633	Byrnes, James F.	9	50,633 D		100.0%		100.0%
1946	26,520			26,520	Thurmond, James Strom		26,520 D		100.0%		100.0%

Note: An asterisk (*) denotes incumbent. **The Republican Party did not run a candidate in the gubernatorial elections of 1946, 1950, 1954, 1958, and 1962.

POSTWAR VOTE FOR SENATOR

Year	Total Vote	Republican		Democratic		Other Vote	Rep.-Dem. Plurality	Percentage			
								Total Vote		Major Vote	
		Vote	Candidate	Vote	Candidate			Rep.	Dem.	Rep.	Dem.
2014	1,240,075	672,941	Graham, Lindsey*	480,933	Hutto, C. Bradley "Brad"	86,201	192,008 R	54.3%	38.8%	58.3%	41.7%
2014S	1,238,982	757,215	Scott, Tim*	459,583	Dickerson, Joyce	22,184	297,632 R	61.1%	37.1%	62.2%	37.8%
2010	1,318,794	810,771	DeMint, James W. "Jim"*	364,598	Greene, Alvin M.	143,425	446,173 R	61.5%	27.6%	69.0%	31.0%
2008	1,871,431	1,076,534	Graham, Lindsey*	790,621	Conley, Bob	4,276	285,913 R	57.5%	42.2%	57.7%	42.3%
2004	1,597,221	857,167	DeMint, James W. "Jim"	704,384	Tenenbaum, Inez M.	35,670	152,783 R	53.7%	44.1%	54.9%	45.1%
2002	1,102,948	600,010	Graham, Lindsey	487,359	Sanders, Alex	15,579	112,651 R	54.4%	44.2%	55.2%	44.8%
1998	1,068,367	488,132	Inglis, Robert D.	562,791	Hollings, Ernest F.*	17,444	74,659 D	45.7%	52.7%	46.4%	53.6%
1996	1,161,372	619,859	Thurmond, James Strom*	510,951	Close, Elliott	30,562	108,908 R	53.4%	44.0%	54.8%	45.2%
1992	1,180,438	554,175	Hartnett, Thomas F.	591,030	Hollings, Ernest F.*	35,233	36,855 D	46.9%	50.1%	48.4%	51.6%
1990	750,716	482,032	Thurmond, James Strom*	244,112	Cunningham, Bob	24,572	237,920 R	64.2%	32.5%	66.4%	33.6%
1986	737,962	262,886	McMaster, Henry D.	465,500	Hollings, Ernest F.*	9,576	202,614 D	35.6%	63.1%	36.1%	63.9%
1984	965,130	644,815	Thurmond, James Strom*	306,982	Purvis, Melvin	13,333	337,833 R	66.8%	31.8%	67.7%	32.3%
1980	870,594	257,946	Mays, Marshall T.	612,554	Hollings, Ernest F.*	94	354,608 D	29.6%	70.4%	29.6%	70.4%
1978	632,852	351,733	Thurmond, James Strom*	281,119	Ravenel, Charles D.		70,614 R	55.6%	44.4%	55.6%	44.4%
1974	512,397	146,645	Bush, Gwenfred	356,126	Hollings, Ernest F.*	9,626	209,481 D	28.6%	69.5%	29.2%	70.8%
1972	672,246	426,601	Thurmond, James Strom*	245,457	Zeigler, Eugene N.	188	181,144 R	63.5%	36.5%	63.5%	36.5%
1968	652,855	248,780	Parker, Marshall	404,060	Hollings, Ernest F.*	15	155,280 D	38.1%	61.9%	38.1%	61.9%
1966	436,252	271,297	Thurmond, James Strom*	164,955	Morrah, Bradley		106,342 R	62.2%	37.8%	62.2%	37.8%
1966S	435,822	212,032	Parker, Marshall	223,790	Hollings, Ernest F.		11,758 D	48.7%	51.3%	48.7%	51.3%
1962	312,647	133,930	Workman, W. D. III	178,712	Johnston, Olin D.*	5	44,782 D	42.8%	57.2%	42.8%	57.2%
1960	330,266			330,164	Thurmond, James Strom*	102	330,164 D		100.0%		100.0%
1956	279,845	49,695	Crawford, L. P.	230,150	Johnston, Olin D.*		180,455 D	17.8%	82.2%	17.8%	82.2%
1956S	245,371			245,371	Thurmond, James Strom		245,371 D		100.0%		100.0%
1954**	226,967			83,525	Brown, Edgar A.	143,442	83,525 D**		36.8%		100.0%
1950	50,277			50,240	Johnston, Olin D.*	37	50,240 D		99.9%		100.0%
1948	135,998			135,998	Maybank, Burnet R.*		135,998 D		100.0%		100.0%

Note: An asterisk (*) denotes incumbent. A pound sign (#) indicates that the election was won by a write-in candidate. **In past elections, the other vote included: 1954 - 143,442 Independent Democratic (Strom Thurmond). Thurmond ran as a write-in candidate and won with 63.1 percent of the total vote. One each of the 1956 and 1966 elections was for a short term to fill a vacancy. The Republican Party did not run a Senate candidate in 1948, 1950, 1954, 1956 (for the short term), and 1960.

SOUTH CAROLINA

GOVERNOR 2014

2010 Census Population	County	Total Vote	Republican (Haley)	Democratic (Sheheen)	Other	Rep.-Dem. Plurality	Percentage			
							Total Vote		Major Vote	
							Rep.	Dem.	Rep.	Dem.
25,417	ABBEVILLE	7,202	4,256	2,756	190	1,500 R	59.1%	38.3%	60.7%	39.3%
160,099	AIKEN	45,518	30,491	14,126	901	16,365 R	67.0%	31.0%	68.3%	31.7%
10,419	ALLENDALE	2,305	581	1,671	53	1,090 D	25.2%	72.5%	25.8%	74.2%
187,126	ANDERSON	45,240	31,855	12,051	1,334	19,804 R	70.4%	26.6%	72.6%	27.4%
15,987	BAMBERG	4,906	1,700	3,133	73	1,433 D	34.7%	63.9%	35.2%	64.8%
22,621	BARNWELL	6,162	3,114	2,940	108	174 R	50.5%	47.7%	51.4%	48.6%
162,233	BEAUFORT	47,805	30,241	16,849	715	13,392 R	63.3%	35.2%	64.2%	35.8%
177,843	BERKELEY	43,183	24,639	17,008	1,536	7,631 R	57.1%	39.4%	59.2%	40.8%
15,175	CALHOUN	5,217	2,335	2,773	109	438 D	44.8%	53.2%	45.7%	54.3%
350,209	CHARLESTON	99,822	47,735	48,447	3,640	712 D	47.8%	48.5%	49.6%	50.4%
55,342	CHEROKEE	12,348	8,377	3,603	368	4,774 R	67.8%	29.2%	69.9%	30.1%
33,140	CHESTER	8,024	4,058	3,695	271	363 R	50.6%	46.0%	52.3%	47.7%
46,734	CHESTERFIELD	10,305	5,159	4,942	204	217 R	50.1%	48.0%	51.1%	48.9%
34,971	CLARENDON	10,365	4,526	5,691	148	1,165 D	43.7%	54.9%	44.3%	55.7%
38,892	COLLETON	10,802	5,507	5,044	251	463 R	51.0%	46.7%	52.2%	47.8%
68,681	DARLINGTON	18,665	8,772	9,477	416	705 D	47.0%	50.8%	48.1%	51.9%
32,062	DILLON	6,419	3,001	3,232	186	231 D	46.8%	50.4%	48.1%	51.9%
136,555	DORCHESTER	34,413	20,027	13,193	1,193	6,834 R	58.2%	38.3%	60.3%	39.7%
26,985	EDGEFIELD	7,028	4,190	2,722	116	1,468 R	59.6%	38.7%	60.6%	39.4%
23,956	FAIRFIELD	8,196	2,896	5,057	243	2,161 D	35.3%	61.7%	36.4%	63.6%
136,885	FLORENCE	36,446	18,027	17,538	881	489 R	49.5%	48.1%	50.7%	49.3%
60,158	GEORGETOWN	20,530	11,445	8,619	466	2,826 R	55.7%	42.0%	57.0%	43.0%
451,225	GREENVILLE	125,445	83,784	38,414	3,247	45,370 R	66.8%	30.6%	68.6%	31.4%
69,661	GREENWOOD	17,785	10,852	6,578	355	4,274 R	61.0%	37.0%	62.3%	37.7%
21,090	HAMPTON	5,894	2,124	3,657	113	1,533 D	36.0%	62.0%	36.7%	63.3%
269,291	HORRY	68,577	47,302	19,252	2,023	28,050 R	69.0%	28.1%	71.1%	28.9%
24,777	JASPER	6,702	3,027	3,519	156	492 D	45.2%	52.5%	46.2%	53.8%
61,697	KERSHAW	19,577	9,744	9,430	403	314 R	49.8%	48.2%	50.8%	49.2%
76,652	LANCASTER	20,158	12,103	7,695	360	4,408 R	60.0%	38.2%	61.1%	38.9%
66,537	LAURENS	15,176	9,665	5,169	342	4,496 R	63.7%	34.1%	65.2%	34.8%
19,220	LEE	5,797	1,718	4,008	71	2,290 D	29.6%	69.1%	30.0%	70.0%
262,391	LEXINGTON	76,012	48,453	24,179	3,380	24,274 R	63.7%	31.8%	66.7%	33.3%
33,062	MARION	8,742	2,985	5,589	168	2,604 D	34.1%	63.9%	34.8%	65.2%
28,933	MARLBORO	6,249	2,244	3,826	179	1,582 D	35.9%	61.2%	37.0%	63.0%
10,233	MCCORMICK	3,619	1,985	1,578	56	407 R	54.8%	43.6%	55.7%	44.3%
37,508	NEWBERRY	10,969	6,247	4,346	376	1,901 R	57.0%	39.6%	59.0%	41.0%
74,273	OCONEE	20,424	14,819	4,999	606	9,820 R	72.6%	24.5%	74.8%	25.2%
92,501	ORANGEBURG	28,068	7,630	20,111	327	12,481 D	27.2%	71.7%	27.5%	72.5%
119,224	PICKENS	27,399	20,822	5,849	728	14,973 R	76.0%	21.3%	78.1%	21.9%
384,504	RICHLAND	111,690	34,902	73,904	2,884	39,002 D	31.2%	66.2%	32.1%	67.9%
19,875	SALUDA	5,651	3,496	2,020	135	1,476 R	61.9%	35.7%	63.4%	36.6%
284,307	SPARTANBURG	65,053	42,447	20,906	1,700	21,541 R	65.2%	32.1%	67.0%	33.0%
107,456	SUMTER	30,024	12,822	16,674	528	3,852 D	42.7%	55.5%	43.5%	56.5%
28,961	UNION	7,909	4,506	3,156	247	1,350 R	57.0%	39.9%	58.8%	41.2%
34,423	WILLIAMSBURG	10,789	3,278	7,307	204	4,029 D	30.4%	67.7%	31.0%	69.0%
226,073	YORK	57,691	36,758	19,433	1,500	17,325 R	63.7%	33.7%	65.4%	34.6%
4,625,364	TOTAL	1,246,301	696,645	516,166	33,490	180,479 R	55.9%	41.4%	57.4%	42.6%

SOUTH CAROLINA
SENATOR 2014

2010 Census Population	County	Total Vote	Republican (Graham)	Democratic (Hutto)	Other	Rep.-Dem. Plurality	Percentage Total Vote Rep.	Total Vote Dem.	Major Vote Rep.	Major Vote Dem.
25,417	ABBEVILLE	7,182	4,057	2,623	502	1,434 R	56.5%	36.5%	60.7%	39.3%
160,099	AIKEN	45,431	28,344	14,254	2,833	14,090 R	62.4%	31.4%	66.5%	33.5%
10,419	ALLENDALE	2,305	533	1,727	45	1,194 D	23.1%	74.9%	23.6%	76.4%
187,126	ANDERSON	45,015	30,056	10,618	4,341	19,438 R	66.8%	23.6%	73.9%	26.1%
15,987	BAMBERG	4,922	1,474	3,338	110	1,864 D	29.9%	67.8%	30.6%	69.4%
22,621	BARNWELL	6,170	2,847	3,162	161	315 D	46.1%	51.2%	47.4%	52.6%
162,233	BEAUFORT	47,682	29,732	15,837	2,113	13,895 R	62.4%	33.2%	65.2%	34.8%
177,843	BERKELEY	43,043	23,133	16,502	3,408	6,631 R	53.7%	38.3%	58.4%	41.6%
15,175	CALHOUN	5,222	2,194	2,842	186	648 D	42.0%	54.4%	43.6%	56.4%
350,209	CHARLESTON	99,184	48,265	44,119	6,800	4,146 R	48.7%	44.5%	52.2%	47.8%
55,342	CHEROKEE	12,325	7,803	3,353	1,169	4,450 R	63.3%	27.2%	69.9%	30.1%
33,140	CHESTER	8,009	3,836	3,722	451	114 R	47.9%	46.5%	50.8%	49.2%
46,734	CHESTERFIELD	10,270	5,447	4,379	444	1,068 R	53.0%	42.6%	55.4%	44.6%
34,971	CLARENDON	10,295	4,396	5,564	335	1,168 D	42.7%	54.0%	44.1%	55.9%
38,892	COLLETON	10,841	5,358	4,906	577	452 R	49.4%	45.3%	52.2%	47.8%
68,681	DARLINGTON	18,617	8,648	9,217	752	569 D	46.5%	49.5%	48.4%	51.6%
32,062	DILLON	6,415	2,957	3,196	262	239 D	46.1%	49.8%	48.1%	51.9%
136,555	DORCHESTER	34,175	18,437	12,951	2,787	5,486 R	53.9%	37.9%	58.7%	41.3%
26,985	EDGEFIELD	6,985	3,812	2,773	400	1,039 R	54.6%	39.7%	57.9%	42.1%
23,956	FAIRFIELD	8,135	2,943	4,837	355	1,894 D	36.2%	59.5%	37.8%	62.2%
136,885	FLORENCE	36,354	17,727	16,787	1,840	940 R	48.8%	46.2%	51.4%	48.6%
60,158	GEORGETOWN	20,487	11,190	8,332	965	2,858 R	54.6%	40.7%	57.3%	42.7%
451,225	GREENVILLE	123,664	74,628	34,060	14,976	40,568 R	60.3%	27.5%	68.7%	31.3%
69,661	GREENWOOD	17,751	10,594	6,156	1,001	4,438 R	59.7%	34.7%	63.2%	36.8%
21,090	HAMPTON	5,872	1,952	3,750	170	1,798 D	33.2%	63.9%	34.2%	65.8%
269,291	HORRY	68,443	44,978	19,457	4,008	25,521 R	65.7%	28.4%	69.8%	30.2%
24,777	JASPER	6,660	2,893	3,518	249	625 D	43.4%	52.8%	45.1%	54.9%
61,697	KERSHAW	19,470	11,200	7,241	1,029	3,959 R	57.5%	37.2%	60.7%	39.3%
76,652	LANCASTER	20,158	12,272	6,930	956	5,342 R	60.9%	34.4%	63.9%	36.1%
66,537	LAURENS	15,127	8,684	4,788	1,655	3,896 R	57.4%	31.7%	64.5%	35.5%
19,220	LEE	5,784	1,750	3,881	153	2,131 D	30.3%	67.1%	31.1%	68.9%
262,391	LEXINGTON	75,792	50,001	19,866	5,925	30,135 R	66.0%	26.2%	71.6%	28.4%
33,062	MARION	8,760	3,054	5,454	252	2,400 D	34.9%	62.3%	35.9%	64.1%
28,933	MARLBORO	6,236	2,354	3,673	209	1,319 D	37.7%	58.9%	39.1%	60.9%
10,233	MCCORMICK	3,599	1,881	1,614	104	267 R	52.3%	44.8%	53.8%	46.2%
37,508	NEWBERRY	10,990	6,580	3,792	618	2,788 R	59.9%	34.5%	63.4%	36.6%
74,273	OCONEE	20,366	14,909	3,902	1,555	11,007 R	73.2%	19.2%	79.3%	20.7%
92,501	ORANGEBURG	28,078	7,116	20,537	425	13,421 D	25.3%	73.1%	25.7%	74.3%
119,224	PICKENS	27,291	19,208	5,079	3,004	14,129 R	70.4%	18.6%	79.1%	20.9%
384,504	RICHLAND	110,750	39,692	66,231	4,827	26,539 D	35.8%	59.8%	37.5%	62.5%
19,875	SALUDA	5,663	3,493	1,902	268	1,591 R	61.7%	33.6%	64.7%	35.3%
284,307	SPARTANBURG	64,574	38,016	18,989	7,569	19,027 R	58.9%	29.4%	66.7%	33.3%
107,456	SUMTER	29,942	12,487	16,307	1,148	3,820 D	41.7%	54.5%	43.4%	56.6%
28,961	UNION	7,874	4,081	3,040	753	1,041 R	51.8%	38.6%	57.3%	42.7%
34,423	WILLIAMSBURG	10,744	3,344	7,123	277	3,779 D	31.1%	66.3%	31.9%	68.1%
226,073	YORK	57,423	34,585	18,604	4,234	15,981 R	60.2%	32.4%	65.0%	35.0%
4,625,364	TOTAL	1,240,075	672,941	480,933	86,201	192,008 R	54.3%	38.8%	58.3%	41.7%

SOUTH CAROLINA
SENATOR SPECIAL 2014

2010 Census Population		Total Vote	Republican (Scott)	Democratic (Dickerson)	Other	Rep.-Dem. Plurality	Percentage			
							Total Vote		Major Vote	
							Rep.	Dem.	Rep.	Dem.
25,417	ABBEVILLE	7,157	4,472	2,577	108	1,895 R	62.5%	36.0%	63.4%	36.6%
160,099	AIKEN	45,388	31,063	13,557	768	17,506 R	68.4%	29.9%	69.6%	30.4%
10,419	ALLENDALE	2,267	596	1,647	24	1,051 D	26.3%	72.7%	26.6%	73.4%
187,126	ANDERSON	44,947	34,160	9,927	860	24,233 R	76.0%	22.1%	77.5%	22.5%
15,987	BAMBERG	4,866	1,668	3,147	51	1,479 D	34.3%	64.7%	34.6%	65.4%
22,621	BARNWELL	6,132	3,166	2,874	92	292 R	51.6%	46.9%	52.4%	47.6%
162,233	BEAUFORT	47,731	31,283	15,685	763	15,598 R	65.5%	32.9%	66.6%	33.4%
177,843	BERKELEY	43,159	27,573	14,970	616	12,603 R	63.9%	34.7%	64.8%	35.2%
15,175	CALHOUN	5,200	2,501	2,629	70	128 D	48.1%	50.6%	48.8%	51.2%
350,209	CHARLESTON	99,157	55,747	41,687	1,723	14,060 R	56.2%	42.0%	57.2%	42.8%
55,342	CHEROKEE	12,301	8,857	3,183	261	5,674 R	72.0%	25.9%	73.6%	26.4%
33,140	CHESTER	7,939	3,935	3,773	231	162 R	49.6%	47.5%	51.1%	48.9%
46,734	CHESTERFIELD	10,208	5,697	4,352	159	1,345 R	55.8%	42.6%	56.7%	43.3%
34,971	CLARENDON	10,261	4,741	5,413	107	672 D	46.2%	52.8%	46.7%	53.3%
38,892	COLLETON	10,817	6,006	4,655	156	1,351 R	55.5%	43.0%	56.3%	43.7%
68,681	DARLINGTON	18,586	9,365	9,029	192	336 R	50.4%	48.6%	50.9%	49.1%
32,062	DILLON	6,385	3,170	3,131	84	39 R	49.6%	49.0%	50.3%	49.7%
136,555	DORCHESTER	34,341	22,234	11,593	514	10,641 R	64.7%	33.8%	65.7%	34.3%
26,985	EDGEFIELD	6,991	4,261	2,643	87	1,618 R	60.9%	37.8%	61.7%	38.3%
23,956	FAIRFIELD	8,083	3,151	4,777	155	1,626 D	39.0%	59.1%	39.7%	60.3%
136,885	FLORENCE	36,316	19,659	16,243	414	3,416 R	54.1%	44.7%	54.8%	45.2%
60,158	GEORGETOWN	20,481	12,229	7,974	278	4,255 R	59.7%	38.9%	60.5%	39.5%
451,225	GREENVILLE	124,419	90,248	31,926	2,245	58,322 R	72.5%	25.7%	73.9%	26.1%
69,661	GREENWOOD	17,699	11,496	5,949	254	5,547 R	65.0%	33.6%	65.9%	34.1%
21,090	HAMPTON	5,786	2,080	3,622	84	1,542 D	35.9%	62.6%	36.5%	63.5%
269,291	HORRY	68,384	49,390	17,743	1,251	31,647 R	72.2%	25.9%	73.6%	26.4%
24,777	JASPER	6,642	3,084	3,463	95	379 D	46.4%	52.1%	47.1%	52.9%
61,697	KERSHAW	19,335	12,098	6,820	417	5,278 R	62.6%	35.3%	63.9%	36.1%
76,652	LANCASTER	20,021	12,671	6,938	412	5,733 R	63.3%	34.7%	64.6%	35.4%
66,537	LAURENS	15,148	10,339	4,522	287	5,817 R	68.3%	29.9%	69.6%	30.4%
19,220	LEE	5,757	1,863	3,841	53	1,978 D	32.4%	66.7%	32.7%	67.3%
262,391	LEXINGTON	75,524	55,615	17,992	1,917	37,623 R	73.6%	23.8%	75.6%	24.4%
33,062	MARION	8,729	3,302	5,344	83	2,042 D	37.8%	61.2%	38.2%	61.8%
28,933	MARLBORO	6,203	2,474	3,637	92	1,163 D	39.9%	58.6%	40.5%	59.5%
10,233	MCCORMICK	3,588	1,960	1,580	48	380 R	54.6%	44.0%	55.4%	44.6%
37,508	NEWBERRY	10,920	6,907	3,777	236	3,130 R	63.3%	34.6%	64.6%	35.4%
74,273	OCONEE	20,314	15,919	3,927	468	11,992 R	78.4%	19.3%	80.2%	19.8%
92,501	ORANGEBURG	27,976	8,137	19,625	214	11,488 D	29.1%	70.1%	29.3%	70.7%
119,224	PICKENS	27,339	22,249	4,551	539	17,698 R	81.4%	16.6%	83.0%	17.0%
384,504	RICHLAND	110,452	43,453	64,867	2,132	21,414 D	39.3%	58.7%	40.1%	59.9%
19,875	SALUDA	5,650	3,748	1,804	98	1,944 R	66.3%	31.9%	67.5%	32.5%
284,307	SPARTANBURG	64,797	45,981	17,570	1,246	28,411 R	71.0%	27.1%	72.4%	27.6%
107,456	SUMTER	29,841	13,573	15,891	377	2,318 D	45.5%	53.3%	46.1%	53.9%
28,961	UNION	7,859	4,591	3,070	198	1,521 R	58.4%	39.1%	59.9%	40.1%
34,423	WILLIAMSBURG	10,746	3,536	7,125	85	3,589 D	32.9%	66.3%	33.2%	66.8%
226,073	YORK	57,140	36,967	18,533	1,640	18,434 R	64.7%	32.4%	66.6%	33.4%
4,625,364	TOTAL	1,238,982	757,215	459,583	22,184	297,632 R	61.1%	37.1%	62.2%	37.8%

SOUTH CAROLINA

HOUSE OF REPRESENTATIVES

CD	Year	Total Vote	Republican		Democratic		Other Vote	Rep.-Dem. Plurality	Percentage			
									Total Vote		Major Vote	
			Vote	Candidate	Vote	Candidate			Rep.	Dem.	Rep.	Dem.
1	2014	127,815	119,392	SANFORD, MARK*			8,423	119,392 R	93.4%		100.0%	
1	2012	290,013	179,908	SCOTT, TIM*	103,557	ROSE, BOBBIE G.	6,548	76,351 R	62.0%	35.7%	63.5%	36.5%
2	2014	194,808	121,649	WILSON, JOE*	68,719	BLACK, PHIL	4,440	52,930 R	62.4%	35.3%	63.9%	36.1%
2	2012	203,718	196,116	WILSON, JOE*			7,602	196,116 R	96.3%		100.0%	
3	2014	164,009	116,741	DUNCAN, JEFF*	47,181	MULLIS, BARBARA JO	87	69,560 R	71.2%	28.8%	71.2%	28.8%
3	2012	254,763	169,512	DUNCAN, JEFF*	84,735	DOYLE, BRIAN RYAN B.	516	84,777 R	66.5%	33.3%	66.7%	33.3%
4	2014	149,049	126,452	GOWDY, TREY*			22,597	126,452 R	84.8%		100.0%	
4	2012	266,884	173,201	GOWDY, TREY*	89,964	MORROW, DEB	3,719	83,237 R	64.9%	33.7%	65.8%	34.2%
5	2014	175,145	103,078	MULVANEY, MICK*	71,985	ADAMS, TOM A.	82	31,093 R	58.9%	41.1%	58.9%	41.1%
5	2012	278,003	154,324	MULVANEY, MICK*	123,443	KNOTT, JOYCE	236	30,881 R	55.5%	44.4%	55.6%	44.4%
6	2014	173,432	44,311	CULLER, ANTHONY	125,747	CLYBURN, JAMES E.*	3,374	81,436 D	25.5%	72.5%	26.1%	73.9%
6	2012	233,615			218,717	CLYBURN, JAMES E.*	14,898	218,717 D		93.6%		100.0%
7	2014	171,524	102,833	RICE, TOM*	68,576	TINUBU, GLORIA BROMELL	115	34,257 R	60.0%	40.0%	60.0%	40.0%
7	2012	275,738	153,068	RICE, TOM	122,389	TINUBU, GLORIA BROMELL	281	30,679 R	55.5%	44.4%	55.6%	44.4%
TOTAL	2014	1,155,782	734,456		382,208		39,118	352,248 R	63.5%	33.1%	65.8%	34.2%
TOTAL	2012	1,802,734	1,026,129		742,805		33,800	283,324 R	56.9%	41.2%	58.0%	42.0%

Note: An asterisk (*) denotes incumbent.

SOUTH CAROLINA

GENERAL AND PRIMARY ELECTIONS

2014 GENERAL ELECTIONS: OTHER VOTES

Governor — Other vote was 15,438 Libertarian (Steve French), 11,496 Independent (Tom J. Ervin), 5,622 United Citizen (Morgan B. Reeves), 934 Scattered write-in

Senate (Full Term) — Other vote was 47,588 Independent (Thomas Ravenel), 33,839 Libertarian (Victor Kocher), 4,774 Scattered write-in

Senate (Short Term) — Other vote was 21,652 American (Jill Boss), 532 Scattered write-in

House — Other vote was:

CD 1 8,423 Scattered write-in
CD 2 4,158 Labor (Harold Geddings), 282 Scattered write-in
CD 3 87 Scattered write-in
CD 4 21,969 Libertarian (Curtis E. Mclaughlin), 628 Scattered write-in
CD 5 82 Scattered write-in
CD 6 3,176 Libertarian (Kevin R. Umbaugh), 198 Scattered write-in
CD 7 115 Scattered write-in

2014 PRIMARY ELECTIONS: SUPPLEMENTARY INFORMATION

Primary	June 10, 2014	**Registration**	2,836,470	No Party Registration
Primary Runoff	June 24, 2014	(as of June 10, 2014)		

Primary Type — Open—Any registered voter could participate in either the Democratic or Republican primary, although any voter who participated in one party's primary could not vote in a primary runoff of the other party.

SOUTH CAROLINA

GENERAL AND PRIMARY ELECTIONS

	REPUBLICAN PRIMARIES			DEMOCRATIC PRIMARIES		
Senator	Graham, Lindsey*	178,833	56.4%	Hutto, C. Bradley "Brad"	87,552	76.6%
(Full Term)	Bright, Lee	48,904	15.4%	Stamper, Jeremy Michael "Jay"	26,678	23.4%
	Cash, Richard	26,325	8.3%			
	Bowers Jr., Franklin DeTrevelle "Det"	23,172	7.3%			
	Mace, Nancy	19,634	6.2%			
	Connor, Bill	16,912	5.3%			
	Dunn, Benjamin	3,209	1.0%			
	TOTAL	316,989		TOTAL	114,230	
Senator	Tim Scott*	276,147	90.0%	Joyce Dickerson	72,874	65.4%
(Short Term)	Randall Young	30,741	10.0%	Sidney Moore	26,310	23.6%
				Harry Pavilack	12,253	11.0%
	TOTAL	306,888		TOTAL	111,437	
Governor	Haley, Nikki R.*	Unopposed		Sheheen, Vincent A.	Unopposed	
Congressional District 1	Sanford, Mark*	Unopposed				
Congressional District 2	Wilson, Joe*	43,687	81.6%	Black, Phil	6,699	54.2%
	McCain Jr., George Edward "Eddie"	9,842	18.4%	Greenleaf II, Harry Edloe "Ed"	5,663	45.8%
	TOTAL	53,529		TOTAL	12,362	
Congressional District 3	Duncan, Jeff*	Unopposed		Mullis, Barbara Jo	4,989	66.6%
				Cleveland, Hosea	2,501	33.4%
				TOTAL	7,490	
Congressional District 4	Gowdy, Trey*	Unopposed				
Congressional District 5	Mulvaney, Mick*	Unopposed		Adams, Tom A.	Unopposed	
Congressional District 6	Culler, Anthony	10,377	66.5%	Clyburn, James E.*	37,429	86.0%
	Winn, Leon	5,231	33.5%	Smith, Karen	6,101	14.0%
	TOTAL	15,608		TOTAL	43,530	
Congressional District 7	Rice, Tom*	Unopposed		Tinubu, Gloria Bromell	Unopposed	

Note: An asterisk (*) denotes incumbent.

SOUTH DAKOTA

One member At Large

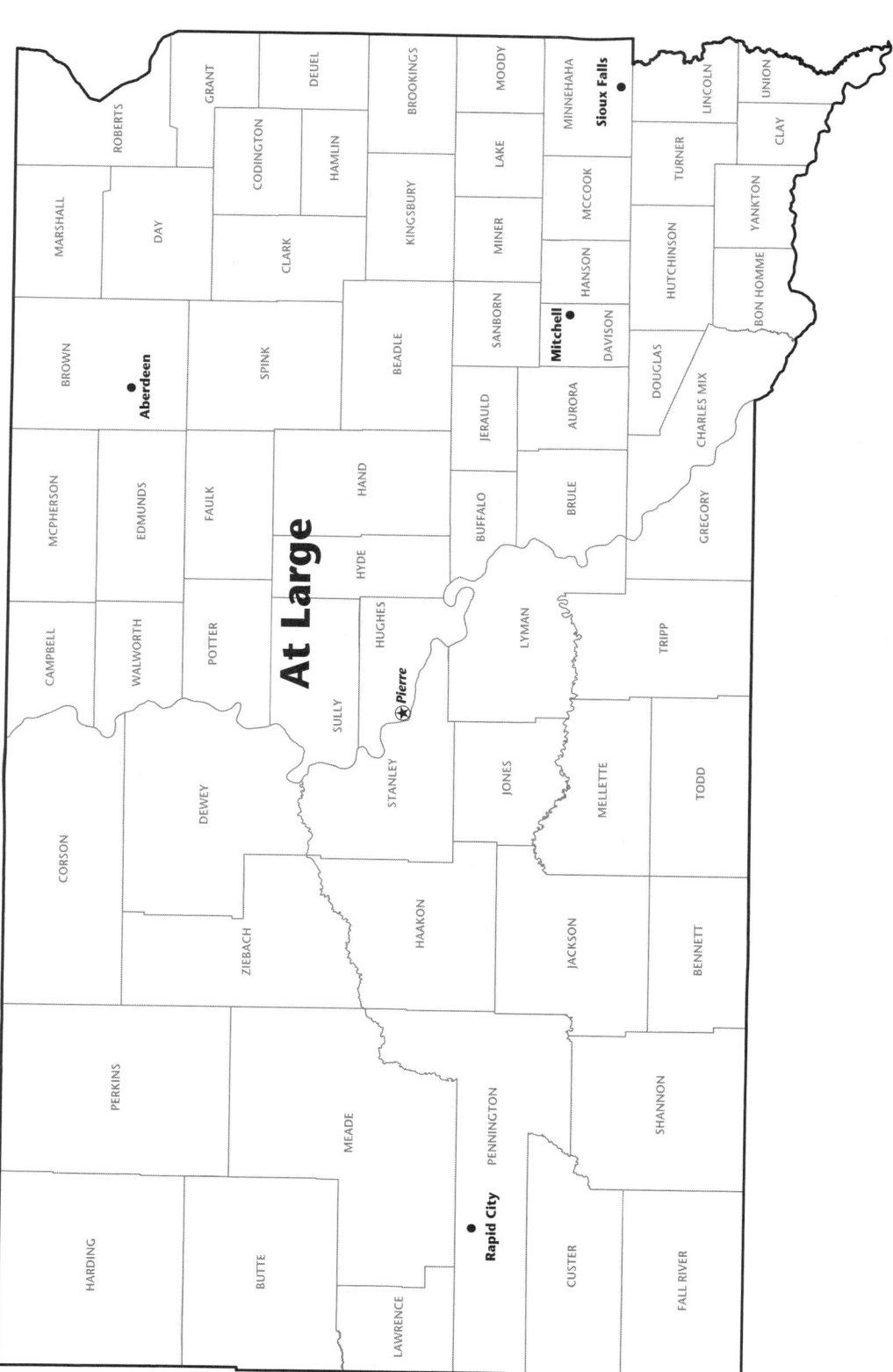

SOUTH DAKOTA

GOVERNOR
Dennis Daugaard (R). Reelected 2014 to a four-year term. Previously elected 2010.

SENATORS (2 Republicans)
Mike Rounds (R). Elected 2014 to a six-year term.

John Thune (R). Reelected 2010 to a six-year term. Previously elected 2004.

REPRESENTATIVE (1 Republican)
At Large. Kristi L. Noem (R)

POSTWAR VOTE FOR PRESIDENT

		Republican		Democratic		Other Vote	Rep.-Dem. Plurality	Total Vote		Major Vote	
Year	Total Vote	Vote	Candidate	Vote	Candidate			Rep.	Dem.	Rep.	Dem.
2012	363,815	210,610	Romney, W. Mitt	145,039	Obama, Barack H.*	8,166	65,571 R	57.9%	39.9%	59.2%	40.8%
2008	381,975	203,054	McCain, John S. III	170,924	Obama, Barack H.	7,997	32,130 R	53.2%	44.7%	54.3%	45.7%
2004	388,215	232,584	Bush, George W.*	149,244	Kerry, John F.	6,387	83,340 R	59.9%	38.4%	60.9%	39.1%
2000**	316,269	190,700	Bush, George W.	118,804	Gore, Albert Jr.	6,765	71,896 R	60.3%	37.6%	61.6%	38.4%
1996**	323,826	150,543	Dole, Robert "Bob"	139,333	Clinton, Bill*	33,950	11,210 R	46.5%	43.0%	51.9%	48.1%
1992**	336,254	136,718	Bush, George H.*	124,888	Clinton, Bill	74,648	11,830 R	40.7%	37.1%	52.3%	47.7%
1988	312,991	165,415	Bush, George H.	145,560	Dukakis, Michael S.	2,016	19,855 R	52.8%	46.5%	53.2%	46.8%
1984	317,867	200,267	Reagan, Ronald*	116,113	Mondale, Walter F.	1,487	84,154 R	63.0%	36.5%	63.3%	36.7%
1980**	327,703	198,343	Reagan, Ronald	103,855	Carter, Jimmy*	25,505	94,488 R	60.5%	31.7%	65.6%	34.4%
1976	300,678	151,505	Ford, Gerald R.*	147,068	Carter, Jimmy	2,105	4,437 R	50.4%	48.9%	50.7%	49.3%
1972	307,415	166,476	Nixon, Richard M.*	139,945	McGovern, George S.	994	26,531 R	54.2%	45.5%	54.3%	45.7%
1968**	281,264	149,841	Nixon, Richard M.	118,023	Humphrey, Hubert Horatio Jr.	13,400	31,818 R	53.3%	42.0%	55.9%	44.1%
1964	293,118	130,108	Goldwater, Barry M. Sr.	163,010	Johnson, Lyndon B.*		32,902 D	44.4%	55.6%	44.4%	55.6%
1960	306,487	178,417	Nixon, Richard M.	128,070	Kennedy, John F.		50,347 R	58.2%	41.8%	58.2%	41.8%
1956	293,857	171,569	Eisenhower, Dwight D.*	122,288	Stevenson, Adlai E. II		49,281 R	58.4%	41.6%	58.4%	41.6%
1952	294,283	203,857	Eisenhower, Dwight D.	90,426	Stevenson, Adlai E. II		113,431 R	69.3%	30.7%	69.3%	30.7%
1948	250,105	129,651	Dewey, Thomas E.	117,653	Truman, Harry S.*	2,801	11,998 R	51.8%	47.0%	52.4%	47.6%

Note: An asterisk (*) denotes incumbent. **In past elections, the other vote included: 1996 - 31,250 Reform (Ross Perot); 1992 - 73,295 Independent (Perot); 1980 - 21,431 Independent (John Anderson); 1968 - 13,400 American Independent (George Wallace).

SOUTH DAKOTA

POSTWAR VOTE FOR GOVERNOR

Year	Total Vote	Republican Vote	Candidate	Democratic Vote	Candidate	Other Vote	Rep.-Dem. Plurality	Percentage Total Vote Rep.	Dem.	Major Vote Rep.	Dem.
2014	277,403	195,477	Daugaard, Dennis*	70,549	Wismer, Susan	11,377	124,928 R	70.5%	25.4%	73.5%	26.5%
2010	317,083	195,046	Daugaard, Dennis	122,037	Heidepriem, Scott		73,009 R	61.5%	38.5%	61.5%	38.5%
2006	335,508	206,990	Rounds, Mike*	121,226	Billion, Jack	7,292	85,764 R	61.7%	36.1%	63.1%	36.9%
2002	334,559	189,920	Rounds, Mike	140,263	Abbott, Jim	4,376	49,657 R	56.8%	41.9%	57.5%	42.5%
1998	260,187	166,621	Janklow, William J.*	85,473	Hunhoff, Bernie	8,093	81,148 R	64.0%	32.9%	66.1%	33.9%
1994	311,613	172,515	Janklow, William J.	126,273	Beddow, Jim	12,825	46,242 R	55.4%	40.5%	57.7%	42.3%
1990	256,723	151,198	Mickelson, George S.*	105,525	Samuelson, Bob L.		45,673 R	58.9%	41.1%	58.9%	41.1%
1986	294,441	152,543	Mickelson, George S.	141,898	Herseth, R. Lars		10,645 R	51.8%	48.2%	51.8%	48.2%
1982	278,565	197,429	Janklow, William J.*	81,136	O'Connor, Michael J.		116,293 R	70.9%	29.1%	70.9%	29.1%
1978	259,795	147,116	Janklow, William J.	112,679	McKellips, Roger		34,437 R	56.6%	43.4%	56.6%	43.4%
1974**	278,228	129,077	Olson, John E.	149,151	Kneip, Richard F.*		20,074 D	46.4%	53.6%	46.4%	53.6%
1972	308,177	123,165	Thompson, Carveth	185,012	Kneip, Richard F.*		61,847 D	40.0%	60.0%	40.0%	60.0%
1970	239,963	108,347	Farrar, Frank*	131,616	Kneip, Richard F.		23,269 D	45.2%	54.8%	45.2%	54.8%
1968	276,906	159,646	Farrar, Frank	117,260	Chamerlin, Robert		42,386 R	57.7%	42.3%	57.7%	42.3%
1966	228,214	131,710	Boe, Nils A.*	96,504	Chamerlin, Robert		35,206 R	57.7%	42.3%	57.7%	42.3%
1964	290,570	150,151	Boe, Nils A.	140,419	Lindley, John F.		9,732 R	51.7%	48.3%	51.7%	48.3%
1962	256,120	143,682	Gubbrud, Archie M.*	112,438	Herseth, Ralph		31,244 R	56.1%	43.9%	56.1%	43.9%
1960	304,625	154,530	Gubbrud, Archie M.	150,095	Herseth, Ralph*		4,435 R	50.7%	49.3%	50.7%	49.3%
1958	258,281	125,520	Saunders, Phil	132,761	Herseth, Ralph		7,241 D	48.6%	51.4%	48.6%	51.4%
1956	292,017	158,819	Foss, Joe*	133,198	Herseth, Ralph		25,621 R	54.4%	45.6%	54.4%	45.6%
1954	236,255	133,878	Foss, Joe	102,377	Martin, Ed C.		31,501 R	56.7%	43.3%	56.7%	43.3%
1952	289,514	203,102	Anderson, Sigurd*	86,412	Iverson, Sherman A.		116,690 R	70.2%	29.8%	70.2%	29.8%
1950	253,316	154,254	Anderson, Sigurd	99,062	Robbie, Joe		55,192 R	60.9%	39.1%	60.9%	39.1%
1948	245,372	149,883	Mickelson, George T.*	95,489	Volz, Harold J.		54,394 R	61.1%	38.9%	61.1%	38.9%
1946	162,292	108,998	Mickelson, George T.	53,294	Haeder, Richard		55,704 R	67.2%	32.8%	67.2%	32.8%

Note: An asterisk (*) denotes incumbent. **The term of office of South Dakota's governor was increased from two to four years effective with the 1974 election.

POSTWAR VOTE FOR SENATOR

Year	Total Vote	Republican Vote	Candidate	Democratic Vote	Candidate	Other Vote	Rep.-Dem. Plurality	Percentage Total Vote Rep.	Dem.	Major Vote Rep.	Dem.
2014	279,412	140,741	Rounds, Mike	82,456	Weiland, Rick	56,215	58,285 R	50.4%	29.5%	63.1%	36.9%
2010	227,947	227,947	Thune, John*				227,947 R	100.0%		100.0%	
2008	380,673	142,784	Dykstra, Joel	237,889	Johnson, Timothy P.*		95,105 D	37.5%	62.5%	37.5%	62.5%
2004	391,188	197,848	Thune, John	193,340	Daschle, Thomas A.*		4,508 R	50.6%	49.4%	50.6%	49.4%
2002	337,508	166,957	Thune, John	167,481	Johnson, Timothy P.*	3,070	524 D	49.5%	49.6%	49.9%	50.1%
1998	262,111	95,431	Schmidt, Ron	162,884	Daschle, Thomas A.*	3,796	67,453 D	36.4%	62.1%	36.9%	63.1%
1996	324,487	157,954	Pressler, Larry*	166,533	Johnson, Timothy P.		8,579 D	48.7%	51.3%	48.7%	51.3%
1992	334,495	108,733	Haar, Charlene	217,095	Daschle, Thomas A.*	8,667	108,362 D	32.5%	64.9%	33.4%	66.6%
1990	258,976	135,682	Pressler, Larry*	116,727	Muenster, Ted	6,567	18,955 R	52.4%	45.1%	53.8%	46.2%
1986	295,830	143,173	Abdnor, James*	152,657	Daschle, Thomas A.		9,484 D	48.4%	51.6%	48.4%	51.6%
1984	315,713	235,176	Pressler, Larry*	80,537	Cunningham, George V.		154,639 R	74.5%	25.5%	74.5%	25.5%
1980	327,478	190,594	Abdnor, James	129,018	McGovern, George S.*	7,866	61,576 R	58.2%	39.4%	59.6%	40.4%
1978	255,599	170,832	Pressler, Larry	84,767	Barnett, Don		86,065 R	66.8%	33.2%	66.8%	33.2%
1974	278,884	130,955	Thorsness, Leo K.	147,929	McGovern, George S.*		16,974 D	47.0%	53.0%	47.0%	53.0%
1972	306,386	131,613	Hirsch, Robert W.	174,773	Abourezk, James George*		43,160 D	43.0%	57.0%	43.0%	57.0%
1968	279,912	120,951	Gubbrud, Archie M.	158,961	McGovern, George S.*		38,010 D	43.2%	56.8%	43.2%	56.8%
1966	227,080	150,517	Mundt, Karl E.*	76,563	Wright, Donn H.		73,954 R	66.3%	33.7%	66.3%	33.7%
1962	254,319	126,861	Bottum, Joe*	127,458	McGovern, George S.		597 D	49.9%	50.1%	49.9%	50.1%
1960	305,442	160,181	Mundt, Karl E.*	145,261	McGovern, George S.		14,920 R	52.4%	47.6%	52.4%	47.6%
1956	290,622	147,621	Case, Francis*	143,001	Holum, Kenneth		4,620 R	50.8%	49.2%	50.8%	49.2%
1954	235,745	135,071	Mundt, Karl E.*	100,674	Holum, Kenneth		34,397 R	57.3%	42.7%	57.3%	42.7%
1950	251,362	160,670	Case, Francis	90,692	Engel, John A.		69,978 R	63.9%	36.1%	63.9%	36.1%
1948	242,833	144,084	Mundt, Karl E.	98,749	Engel, John A.		45,335 R	59.3%	40.7%	59.3%	40.7%

Note: An asterisk (*) denotes incumbent. **The Democratic Party did not run a Senate candidate in the 2010 election.

SOUTH DAKOTA
GOVERNOR 2014

2010 Census Population	County	Total Vote	Republican (Daugaard)	Democratic (Wismer)	Other	Rep.-Dem. Plurality		Percentage			
								Total Vote		Major Vote	
								Rep.	Dem.	Rep.	Dem.
2,710	AURORA	1,139	776	312	51	464	R	68.1%	27.4%	71.3%	28.7%
17,398	BEADLE	5,604	3,974	1,433	197	2,541	R	70.9%	25.6%	73.5%	26.5%
3,431	BENNETT	920	606	276	38	330	R	65.9%	30.0%	68.7%	31.3%
7,070	BON HOMME	2,398	1,718	577	103	1,141	R	71.6%	24.1%	74.9%	25.1%
31,965	BROOKINGS	9,224	6,105	2,792	327	3,313	R	66.2%	30.3%	68.6%	31.4%
36,531	BROWN	12,019	7,801	3,864	354	3,937	R	64.9%	32.1%	66.9%	33.1%
5,255	BRULE	1,765	1,323	388	54	935	R	75.0%	22.0%	77.3%	22.7%
1,912	BUFFALO	455	188	244	23	56	D	41.3%	53.6%	43.5%	56.5%
10,110	BUTTE	3,204	2,484	513	207	1,971	R	77.5%	16.0%	82.9%	17.1%
1,466	CAMPBELL	622	516	82	24	434	R	83.0%	13.2%	86.3%	13.7%
9,129	CHARLES MIX	3,179	2,172	893	114	1,279	R	68.3%	28.1%	70.9%	29.1%
3,691	CLARK	1,531	1,140	324	67	816	R	74.5%	21.2%	77.9%	22.1%
13,864	CLAY	3,756	2,124	1,372	260	752	R	56.5%	36.5%	60.8%	39.2%
27,227	CODINGTON	9,109	6,656	2,158	295	4,498	R	73.1%	23.7%	75.5%	24.5%
4,050	CORSON	910	491	363	56	128	R	54.0%	39.9%	57.5%	42.5%
8,216	CUSTER	3,710	2,735	780	195	1,955	R	73.7%	21.0%	77.8%	22.2%
19,504	DAVISON	6,048	4,590	1,255	203	3,335	R	75.9%	20.8%	78.5%	21.5%
5,710	DAY	2,404	1,256	1,065	83	191	R	52.2%	44.3%	54.1%	45.9%
4,364	DEUEL	1,762	1,203	484	75	719	R	68.3%	27.5%	71.3%	28.7%
5,301	DEWEY	1,456	721	666	69	55	R	49.5%	45.7%	52.0%	48.0%
3,002	DOUGLAS	1,322	1,121	171	30	950	R	84.8%	12.9%	86.8%	13.2%
4,071	EDMUNDS	1,714	1,288	380	46	908	R	75.1%	22.2%	77.2%	22.8%
7,094	FALL RIVER	2,913	2,125	609	179	1,516	R	72.9%	20.9%	77.7%	22.3%
2,364	FAULK	892	712	157	23	555	R	79.8%	17.6%	81.9%	18.1%
7,356	GRANT	2,895	1,981	827	87	1,154	R	68.4%	28.6%	70.5%	29.5%
4,271	GREGORY	1,807	1,369	366	72	1,003	R	75.8%	20.3%	78.9%	21.1%
1,937	HAAKON	866	774	72	20	702	R	89.4%	8.3%	91.5%	8.5%
5,903	HAMLIN	2,232	1,670	472	90	1,198	R	74.8%	21.1%	78.0%	22.0%
3,431	HAND	1,494	1,172	290	32	882	R	78.4%	19.4%	80.2%	19.8%
3,331	HANSON	1,339	1,005	280	54	725	R	75.1%	20.9%	78.2%	21.8%
1,255	HARDING	610	517	47	46	470	R	84.8%	7.7%	91.7%	8.3%
17,022	HUGHES	6,957	5,688	1,113	156	4,575	R	81.8%	16.0%	83.6%	16.4%
7,343	HUTCHINSON	2,767	2,215	466	86	1,749	R	80.1%	16.8%	82.6%	17.4%
1,420	HYDE	603	479	111	13	368	R	79.4%	18.4%	81.2%	18.8%
3,031	JACKSON	906	616	233	57	383	R	68.0%	25.7%	72.6%	27.4%
2,071	JERAULD	840	627	197	16	430	R	74.6%	23.5%	76.1%	23.9%
1,006	JONES	463	390	60	13	330	R	84.2%	13.0%	86.7%	13.3%
5,148	KINGSBURY	2,113	1,480	568	65	912	R	70.0%	26.9%	72.3%	27.7%
11,200	LAKE	4,870	3,493	1,205	172	2,288	R	71.7%	24.7%	74.4%	25.6%
24,097	LAWRENCE	8,896	6,434	2,000	462	4,434	R	72.3%	22.5%	76.3%	23.7%
44,828	LINCOLN	16,870	12,768	3,513	589	9,255	R	75.7%	20.8%	78.4%	21.6%
3,755	LYMAN	1,237	863	318	56	545	R	69.8%	25.7%	73.1%	26.9%
4,656	MARSHALL	1,763	760	970	33	210	D	43.1%	55.0%	43.9%	56.1%
5,618	MCCOOK	2,057	1,522	462	73	1,060	R	74.0%	22.5%	76.7%	23.3%
2,459	MCPHERSON	1,028	848	160	20	688	R	82.5%	15.6%	84.1%	15.9%
25,434	MEADE	8,308	6,503	1,373	432	5,130	R	78.3%	16.5%	82.6%	17.4%
2,048	MELLETTE	681	424	224	33	200	R	62.3%	32.9%	65.4%	34.6%
2,389	MINER	876	621	224	31	397	R	70.9%	25.6%	73.5%	26.5%
169,468	MINNEHAHA	54,264	37,228	14,716	2,320	22,512	R	68.6%	27.1%	71.7%	28.3%
6,486	MOODY	2,393	1,658	638	97	1,020	R	69.3%	26.7%	72.2%	27.8%
100,948	PENNINGTON	33,455	24,340	7,551	1,564	16,789	R	72.8%	22.6%	76.3%	23.7%
2,982	PERKINS	1,327	1,066	184	77	882	R	80.3%	13.9%	85.3%	14.7%
2,329	POTTER	1,166	973	170	23	803	R	83.4%	14.6%	85.1%	14.9%
10,149	ROBERTS	3,219	1,787	1,346	86	441	R	55.5%	41.8%	57.0%	43.0%
2,355	SANBORN	865	634	203	28	431	R	73.3%	23.5%	75.7%	24.3%
13,586	SHANNON	2,671	590	1,875	206	1,285	D	22.1%	70.2%	23.9%	76.1%
6,415	SPINK	2,534	1,812	650	72	1,162	R	71.5%	25.7%	73.6%	26.4%
2,966	STANLEY	1,292	1,042	208	42	834	R	80.7%	16.1%	83.4%	16.6%

SOUTH DAKOTA
GOVERNOR 2014

2010 Census Population	County	Total Vote	Republican (Daugaard)	Democratic (Wismer)	Other	Rep.-Dem. Plurality	Rep.	Dem.	Rep.	Dem.
1,373	SULLY	681	565	96	20	469 R	83.0%	14.1%	85.5%	14.5%
9,612	TODD	2,144	658	1,354	132	696 D	30.7%	63.2%	32.7%	67.3%
5,644	TRIPP	2,193	1,793	348	52	1,445 R	81.8%	15.9%	83.7%	16.3%
8,347	TURNER	3,297	2,373	713	211	1,660 R	72.0%	21.6%	76.9%	23.1%
14,399	UNION	5,101	3,754	1,092	255	2,662 R	73.6%	21.4%	77.5%	22.5%
5,438	WALWORTH	1,915	1,493	370	52	1,123 R	78.0%	19.3%	80.1%	19.9%
22,438	YANKTON	7,724	5,310	2,088	326	3,222 R	68.7%	27.0%	71.8%	28.2%
2,801	ZIEBACH	628	357	238	33	119 R	56.8%	37.9%	60.0%	40.0%
814,180	TOTAL	277,403	195,477	70,549	11,377	124,928 R	70.5%	25.4%	73.5%	26.5%

SOUTH DAKOTA
SENATOR 2014

2010 Census Population	County	Total Vote	Republican (Rounds)	Democratic (Weiland)	Independent (Pressler)	Other	Rep.-Dem. Plurality	Rep.	Dem.	Ind.
2,710	AURORA	1,154	480	355	259	60	125 R	41.6%	30.8%	22.4%
17,398	BEADLE	5,653	3,018	1,622	810	203	1,396 R	53.4%	28.7%	14.3%
3,431	BENNETT	930	445	341	110	34	104 R	47.8%	36.7%	11.8%
7,070	BON HOMME	2,432	1,157	785	408	82	372 R	47.6%	32.3%	16.8%
31,965	BROOKINGS	9,296	4,226	3,195	1,662	213	1,031 R	45.5%	34.4%	17.9%
36,531	BROWN	12,062	5,382	4,023	2,417	240	1,359 R	44.6%	33.4%	20.0%
5,255	BRULE	1,767	889	451	346	81	438 R	50.3%	25.5%	19.6%
1,912	BUFFALO	465	105	292	56	12	187 D	22.6%	62.8%	12.0%
10,110	BUTTE	3,213	1,910	539	572	192	1,371 R	59.4%	16.8%	17.8%
1,466	CAMPBELL	631	414	115	79	23	299 R	65.6%	18.2%	12.5%
9,129	CHARLES MIX	3,204	1,511	1,111	498	84	400 R	47.2%	34.7%	15.5%
3,691	CLARK	1,550	737	394	361	58	343 R	47.5%	25.4%	23.3%
13,864	CLAY	3,795	1,433	1,689	615	58	256 D	37.8%	44.5%	16.2%
27,227	CODINGTON	9,167	4,605	2,572	1,771	219	2,033 R	50.2%	28.1%	19.3%
4,050	CORSON	926	399	368	109	50	31 R	43.1%	39.7%	11.8%
8,216	CUSTER	3,733	2,107	859	616	151	1,248 R	56.4%	23.0%	16.5%
19,504	DAVISON	6,080	3,097	1,582	1,227	174	1,515 R	50.9%	26.0%	20.2%
5,710	DAY	2,414	868	989	493	64	121 D	36.0%	41.0%	20.4%
4,364	DEUEL	1,788	847	530	341	70	317 R	47.4%	29.6%	19.1%
5,301	DEWEY	1,486	457	788	208	33	331 D	30.8%	53.0%	14.0%
3,002	DOUGLAS	1,329	877	205	187	60	672 R	66.0%	15.4%	14.1%
4,071	EDMUNDS	1,738	947	422	326	43	525 R	54.5%	24.3%	18.8%
7,094	FALL RIVER	2,938	1,587	674	510	167	913 R	54.0%	22.9%	17.4%
2,364	FAULK	892	508	180	175	29	328 R	57.0%	20.2%	19.6%
7,356	GRANT	2,913	1,405	887	534	87	518 R	48.2%	30.4%	18.3%
4,271	GREGORY	1,828	996	483	284	65	513 R	54.5%	26.4%	15.5%
1,937	HAAKON	863	563	96	151	53	467 R	65.2%	11.1%	17.5%
5,903	HAMLIN	2,244	1,191	551	391	111	640 R	53.1%	24.6%	17.4%
3,431	HAND	1,499	864	341	240	54	523 R	57.6%	22.7%	16.0%
3,331	HANSON	1,349	752	365	165	67	387 R	55.7%	27.1%	12.2%
1,255	HARDING	598	371	46	121	60	325 R	62.0%	7.7%	20.2%
17,022	HUGHES	6,950	4,197	1,573	1,058	122	2,624 R	60.4%	22.6%	15.2%
7,343	HUTCHINSON	2,784	1,640	575	494	75	1,065 R	58.9%	20.7%	17.7%
1,420	HYDE	605	384	128	72	21	256 R	63.5%	21.2%	11.9%
3,031	JACKSON	919	472	269	133	45	203 R	51.4%	29.3%	14.5%

SOUTH DAKOTA

SENATOR 2014

2010 Census Population	County	Total Vote	Republican (Rounds)	Democratic (Weiland)	Independent (Pressler)	Other	Rep.-Dem. Plurality	Rep.	Dem.	Ind.
2,071	JERAULD	846	361	292	167	26	69 R	42.7%	34.5%	19.7%
1,006	JONES	463	292	66	72	33	226 R	63.1%	14.3%	15.6%
5,148	KINGSBURY	2,132	1,026	669	376	61	357 R	48.1%	31.4%	17.6%
11,200	LAKE	4,899	2,283	1,862	637	117	421 R	46.6%	38.0%	13.0%
24,097	LAWRENCE	8,959	4,793	2,262	1,582	322	2,531 R	53.5%	25.2%	17.7%
44,828	LINCOLN	16,985	9,353	4,218	3,005	409	5,135 R	55.1%	24.8%	17.7%
3,755	LYMAN	1,241	630	361	194	56	269 R	50.8%	29.1%	15.6%
4,656	MARSHALL	1,754	684	693	360	17	9 D	39.0%	39.5%	20.5%
5,618	MCCOOK	2,063	998	561	418	86	437 R	48.4%	27.2%	20.3%
2,459	MCPHERSON	1,031	677	173	154	27	504 R	65.7%	16.8%	14.9%
25,434	MEADE	8,376	4,910	1,565	1,456	445	3,345 R	58.6%	18.7%	17.4%
2,048	MELLETTE	686	252	305	98	31	53 D	36.7%	44.5%	14.3%
2,389	MINER	884	405	296	151	32	109 R	45.8%	33.5%	17.1%
169,468	MINNEHAHA	54,662	25,771	17,739	9,886	1,266	8,032 R	47.1%	32.5%	18.1%
6,486	MOODY	2,417	1,062	833	447	75	229 R	43.9%	34.5%	18.5%
100,948	PENNINGTON	33,718	18,812	8,244	5,439	1,223	10,568 R	55.8%	24.4%	16.1%
2,982	PERKINS	1,343	792	242	208	101	550 R	59.0%	18.0%	15.5%
2,329	POTTER	1,165	758	211	174	22	547 R	65.1%	18.1%	14.9%
10,149	ROBERTS	3,241	1,326	1,377	464	74	51 D	40.9%	42.5%	14.3%
2,355	SANBORN	872	407	211	213	41	196 R	46.7%	24.2%	24.4%
13,586	SHANNON	2,795	226	2,277	252	40	2,051 D	8.1%	81.5%	9.0%
6,415	SPINK	2,543	1,151	833	491	68	318 R	45.3%	32.8%	19.3%
2,966	STANLEY	1,295	803	289	177	26	514 R	62.0%	22.3%	13.7%
1,373	SULLY	685	446	115	102	22	331 R	65.1%	16.8%	14.9%
9,612	TODD	2,216	407	1,529	238	42	1,122 D	18.4%	69.0%	10.7%
5,644	TRIPP	2,201	1,328	506	300	67	822 R	60.3%	23.0%	13.6%
8,347	TURNER	3,307	1,701	854	617	135	847 R	51.4%	25.8%	18.7%
14,399	UNION	5,135	3,150	1,268	584	133	1,882 R	61.3%	24.7%	11.4%
5,438	WALWORTH	1,933	1,213	420	251	49	793 R	62.8%	21.7%	13.0%
22,438	YANKTON	7,738	3,663	2,497	1,339	239	1,166 R	47.3%	32.3%	17.3
2,801	ZIEBACH	632	220	293	90	29	73 D	34.8%	46.4%	14.2
814,180	TOTAL	279,412	140,741	82,456	47,741	8,474	58,285 R	50.4%	29.5%	17.1

SOUTH DAKOTA

HOUSE OF REPRESENTATIVES

CD	Year	Total Vote	Republican Vote	Candidate	Democratic Vote	Candidate	Other Vote	Rep.-Dem. Plurality	Rep.	Dem.	Rep.	Dem
At Large	2014	276,319	183,834	NOEM, KRISTI L.*	92,485	ROBINSON, CORINNA		91,349 R	66.5%	33.5%	66.5%	33.5
At Large	2012	361,429	207,640	NOEM, KRISTI L.*	153,789	VARILEK, MATT	19,134	53,851 R	57.4%	42.6%	57.4%	42.6
At Large	2010	319,426	153,703	NOEM, KRISTI L.	146,589	SANDLIN, STEPHANIE HERSETH*	19,134	7,114 R	48.1%	45.9%	51.2%	48.8
At Large	2008	379,007	122,966	LIEN, CHRIS	256,041	SANDLIN, STEPHANIE HERSETH*		133,075 D	32.4%	67.6%	32.4%	67.6
At Large	2006	333,562	97,864	WHALEN, BRUCE W.	230,468	SANDLIN, STEPHANIE HERSETH*	5,230	132,604 D	29.3%	69.1%	29.8%	70.2
At Large	2004	389,468	178,823	DIEDRICH, LARRY W.	207,837	SANDLIN, STEPHANIE HERSETH*	2,808	29,014 D	45.9%	53.4%	46.2%	53.8
At Large	2002	336,807	180,023	JANKLOW, WILLIAM J.	153,656	SANDLIN, STEPHANIE HERSETH	3,128	26,367 R	53.4%	45.6%	54.0%	46.0
At Large	2000	314,761	231,083	THUNE, JOHN*	78,321	HOHN, CURT	5,357	152,762 R	73.4%	24.9%	74.7%	25.
At Large	1998	258,590	194,157	THUNE, JOHN*	64,433	MOSER, JEFF		129,724 R	75.1%	24.9%	75.1%	24.
At Large	1996	323,203	186,393	THUNE, JOHN	119,547	WEILAND, RICK	17,263	66,846 R	57.7%	37.0%	60.9%	39.
At Large	1994	305,922	112,054	BERKHOUT, JAN	183,036	JOHNSON, TIMOTHY P.*	10,832	70,982 D	36.6%	59.8%	38.0%	62.
At Large	1992	332,902	89,375	TIMMER, JOHN	230,070	JOHNSON, TIMOTHY P.*	13,457	140,695 D	26.8%	69.1%	28.0%	72.
At Large	1990	257,298	83,484	FRANKENFELD, DON	173,814	JOHNSON, TIMOTHY P.*		90,330 D	32.4%	67.6%	32.4%	67.
At Large	1988	311,916	88,157	VOLK, DAVID	223,759	JOHNSON, TIMOTHY P.*		135,602 D	28.3%	71.7%	28.3%	71.
At Large	1986	289,723	118,261	BELL, DALE	171,462	JOHNSON, TIMOTHY P.		53,201 D	40.8%	59.2%	40.8%	59.
At Large	1984	316,222	134,821	BELL, DALE	181,401	DASCHLE, THOMAS A.*		46,580 D	42.6%	57.4%	42.6%	57.
At Large	1982	275,652	133,530	ROBERTS, CLINT*	142,122	DASCHLE, THOMAS A.*		8,592 D	48.4%	51.6%	48.4%	51.

Note: An asterisk (*) denotes incumbent.

SOUTH DAKOTA

GENERAL AND PRIMARY ELECTIONS

2014 GENERAL ELECTIONS: OTHER VOTES

Governor   Other vote was 11,377 Independent (Michael J. Myers)

Senate   Other vote was 47,741 Independent (Larry Pressler), 8,474 Independent (Gordon Howie)

2014 PRIMARY ELECTIONS: SUPPLEMENTARY INFORMATION

Primary	June 3, 2014	**Registration** (as of June 3, 2014 – excluding 44,737 inactive registrants)	509,533	Republican Democratic Libertarian Constitution Americans Elect No Party Affiliation/ Independent	235,770 175,454 1,277 599 6 96,427

Primary Type   Republicans held a "closed" primary, with only registered Republicans allowed to vote in it. Democrats held a "semi-open" primary, with registered Democrats, independents, and other voters not affiliated with a recognized political party eligible to cast a Democratic primary ballot.

	REPUBLICAN PRIMARIES			DEMOCRATIC PRIMARIES		
Senator	Rounds, Mike Rhoden, Larry Nelson, Stace Bosworth, Annette Ravnsborg, Jason *TOTAL*	41,377 13,593 13,179 4,283 2,066 *74,498*	55.5% 18.2% 17.7% 5.7% 2.8%	Weiland, Rick	Unopposed	
Governor	Daugaard, Dennis* Hubbel, Lora *TOTAL*	60,017 14,196 *74,213*	80.9% 19.1%	Wismer, Susan Lowe, Joe *TOTAL*	15,311 12,283 *27,594*	55.5% 44.5%
Congressional At Large	Noem, Kristi L.*	Unopposed		Robinson, Corinna	Unopposed	

Note: An asterisk (*) denotes incumbent.

TENNESSEE

Congressional districts first established for elections held in 2012

9 members

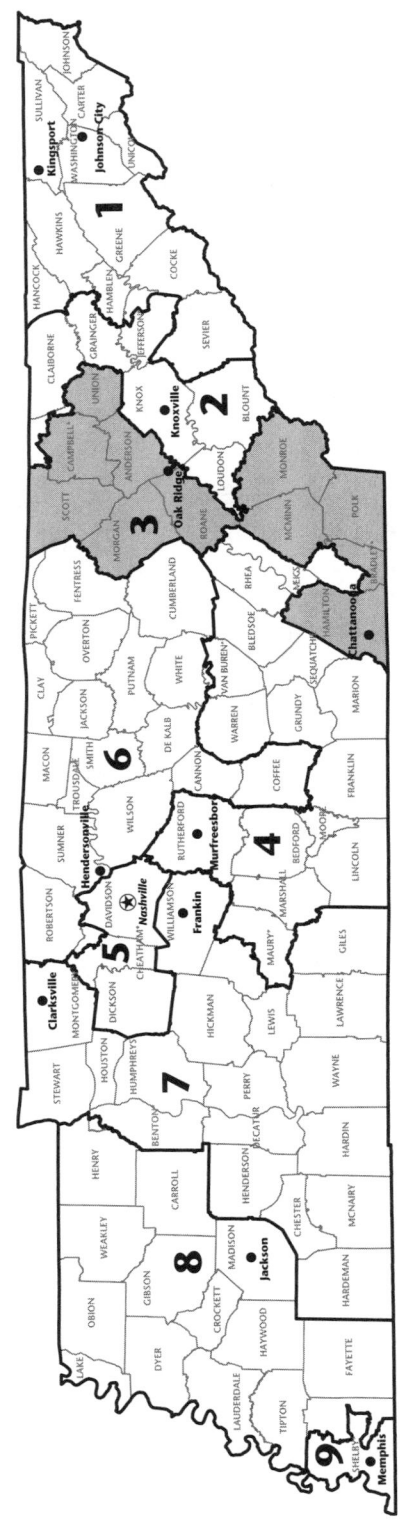

* Asterisk indicates a county whose boundaries include parts of two or more congressional districts.

TENNESSEE

GOVERNOR
Bill Haslam (R). Reelected 2014 to a four-year term. Previously elected 2010.

SENATORS (2 Republicans)
Lamar Alexander (R). Reelected 2014 to a six-year term. Previously elected 2008, 2002.

Bob Corker (R). Reelected 2012 to a six-year term. Previously elected 2006.

REPRESENTATIVES (7 Republicans, 2 Democrats)
1. Phil Roe (R)
2. John J. Duncan Jr. (R)
3. Charles J. "Chuck" Fleischmann (R)
4. Scott DesJarlais (R)
5. Jim Cooper (D)
6. Diane Black (R)
7. Marsha Blackburn (R)
8. Stephen Lee Fincher (R)
9. Steve Cohen (D)

POSTWAR VOTE FOR PRESIDENT

| | | Republican | | Democratic | | | | Percentage | | | |
| | | | | | | | | Total Vote | | Major Vote | |
Year	Total Vote	Vote	Candidate	Vote	Candidate	Other Vote	Rep.-Dem. Plurality	Rep.	Dem.	Rep.	Dem.
2012	2,458,577	1,462,330	Romney, W. Mitt	960,709	Obama, Barack H.*	35,538	501,621 R	59.5%	39.1%	60.4%	39.6%
2008	2,599,749	1,479,178	McCain, John S. III	1,087,437	Obama, Barack H.	33,134	391,741 R	56.9%	41.8%	57.6%	42.4%
2004	2,437,319	1,384,375	Bush, George W.*	1,036,477	Kerry, John F.	16,467	347,898 R	56.8%	42.5%	57.2%	42.8%
2000**	2,076,181	1,061,949	Bush, George W.	981,720	Gore, Albert Jr.	32,512	80,229 R	51.1%	47.3%	52.0%	48.0%
1996**	1,894,105	863,530	Dole, Robert "Bob"	909,146	Clinton, Bill*	121,429	45,616 D	45.6%	48.0%	48.7%	51.3%
1992**	1,982,638	841,300	Bush, George H.*	933,521	Clinton, Bill	207,817	92,221 D	42.4%	47.1%	47.4%	52.6%
1988	1,636,250	947,233	Bush, George H.	679,794	Dukakis, Michael S.	9,223	267,439 R	57.9%	41.5%	58.2%	41.8%
1984	1,711,994	990,212	Reagan, Ronald*	711,714	Mondale, Walter F.	10,068	278,498 R	57.8%	41.6%	58.2%	41.8%
1980**	1,617,616	787,761	Reagan, Ronald	783,051	Carter, Jimmy*	46,804	4,710 R	48.7%	48.4%	50.1%	49.9%
1976	1,476,345	633,969	Ford, Gerald R.*	825,879	Carter, Jimmy	16,497	191,910 D	42.9%	55.9%	43.4%	56.6%
1972	1,201,182	813,147	Nixon, Richard M.*	357,293	McGovern, George S.	30,742	455,854 R	67.7%	29.7%	69.5%	30.5%
1968**	1,248,617	472,592	Nixon, Richard M.	351,233	Humphrey, Hubert Horatio Jr.	424,792	121,359 R	37.8%	28.1%	57.4%	42.6%
1964	1,143,946	508,965	Goldwater, Barry M. Sr.	634,947	Johnson, Lyndon B.*	34	125,982 D	44.5%	55.5%	44.5%	55.5%
1960	1,051,792	556,577	Nixon, Richard M.	481,453	Kennedy, John F.	13,762	75,124 R	52.9%	45.8%	53.6%	46.4%
1956	939,404	462,288	Eisenhower, Dwight D.*	456,507	Stevenson, Adlai E. II	20,609	5,781 R	49.2%	48.6%	50.3%	49.7%
1952	892,553	446,147	Eisenhower, Dwight D.	443,710	Stevenson, Adlai E. II	2,696	2,437 R	50.0%	49.7%	50.1%	49.9%
1948**	550,283	202,914	Dewey, Thomas E.	270,402	Truman, Harry S.*	76,967	67,488 D	36.9%	49.1%	42.9%	57.1%

Note: An asterisk (*) denotes incumbent. **In past elections, the other vote included: 2000 - 19,781 Green (Ralph Nader); 1996 - 105,918 Reform (Ross Perot); 1992 - 199,968 Independent (Perot); 1980 - 35,991 Independent (John Anderson); 1968 - 424,792 American Independent (George Wallace), who finished second; 1948 - 73,815 States' Rights (Strom Thurmond).

TENNESSEE

POSTWAR VOTE FOR GOVERNOR

Year	Total Vote	Republican Vote	Republican Candidate	Democratic Vote	Democratic Candidate	Other Vote	Rep.-Dem. Plurality		Total Vote Rep.	Total Vote Dem.	Major Vote Rep.	Major Vote Dem.
2014	1,353,728	951,796	Haslam, Bill*	309,237	Brown, Charles V. "Charlie"	92,695	642,559	R	70.3%	22.8%	75.5%	24.5%
2010	1,601,549	1,041,545	Haslam, Bill	529,851	McWherter, Mike	30,153	511,694	R	65.0%	33.1%	66.3%	33.7%
2006	1,818,549	540,853	Bryson, Jim	1,247,491	Bredesen, Phil*	30,205	706,638	D	29.7%	68.6%	30.2%	69.8%
2002	1,653,167	786,803	Hilleary, Van	837,284	Bredesen, Phil	29,080	50,481	D	47.6%	50.6%	48.4%	51.6%
1998	976,236	669,973	Sundquist, Don*	287,750	Hooker, John Jay Jr.	18,513	382,223	R	68.6%	29.5%	70.0%	30.0%
1994	1,487,124	807,107	Sundquist, Don	664,243	Bredesen, Phil	15,774	142,864	R	54.3%	44.7%	54.9%	45.1%
1990	790,441	289,348	Henry, Dwight	480,885	McWherter, Ned*	20,208	191,537	D	36.6%	60.8%	37.6%	62.4%
1986	1,210,339	553,449	Dunn, Winfield	656,602	McWherter, Ned	288	103,153	D	45.7%	54.2%	45.7%	54.3%
1982	1,238,927	737,963	Alexander, Lamar*	500,937	Tyree, Randy	27	237,026	R	59.6%	40.4%	59.6%	40.4%
1978	1,189,695	661,959	Alexander, Lamar	523,495	Butcher, Jake	4,241	138,464	R	55.6%	44.0%	55.8%	44.2%
1974	1,040,714	455,467	Alexander, Lamar	576,833	Blanton, L. Ray	8,414	121,366	D	43.8%	55.4%	44.1%	55.9%
1970	1,108,247	575,777	Dunn, Winfield	509,521	Hooker, John Jay Jr.	22,949	66,256	R	52.0%	46.0%	53.1%	46.9%
1966	656,566			532,998	Ellington, Buford	123,568	532,998	D		81.2%		100.0%
1962**	620,758	99,884	Patty, Hubert D.	315,648	Clement, Frank G.	205,226	215,764	D	16.1%	50.8%	24.0%	76.0%
1958**	432,545	35,938	Wall, Thomas P.	248,874	Ellington, Buford	147,733	212,936	D	8.3%	57.5%	12.6%	87.4%
1954**	322,586			281,291	Clement, Frank G.*	41,295	281,291	D		87.2%		100.0%
1952	806,771	166,377	Witt, R. Beecher	640,290	Clement, Frank G.	104	473,913	D	20.6%	79.4%	20.6%	79.4%
1950**	236,194			184,437	Browning, Gordon*	51,757	184,437	D		78.1%		100.0%
1948	543,881	179,957	Acuff, Roy	363,903	Browning, Gordon	21	183,946	D	33.1%	66.9%	33.1%	66.9%
1946	229,456	73,222	Lowe, W. O.	149,937	McCord, James N.*	6,297	76,715	D	31.9%	65.3%	32.8%	67.2%

Note: An asterisk (*) denotes incumbent. **In past elections, the other vote included: 1962 - 203,765 Independent (William R. Anderson), who finished second; 1958 - 136,399 Independent (Jim Nance McCord), who finished second; 1954 - 39,574 Independent (John R. Neal), who finished second; 1950 - 51,757 Independent (Neal), who finished second. The Republican Party did not run a gubernatorial candidate in 1950, 1954, and 1966. The term of office of Tennessee's governor was increased from two to four years effective with the 1954 election.

POSTWAR VOTE FOR SENATOR

Year	Total Vote	Republican Vote	Republican Candidate	Democratic Vote	Democratic Candidate	Other Vote	Rep.-Dem. Plurality		Total Vote Rep.	Total Vote Dem.	Major Vote Rep.	Major Vote Dem.
2014	1,366,628	850,087	Alexander, Lamar*	437,848	Ball, Gordon	78,693	412,239	R	62.2%	32.0%	66.0%	34.0%
2012	2,321,477	1,506,443	Corker, Bob*	705,882	Clayton, Mark E.	109,152	800,561	R	64.9%	30.4%	68.1%	31.9%
2008	2,424,585	1,579,477	Alexander, Lamar*	767,236	Tuke, Robert D.	77,872	812,241	R	65.1%	31.6%	67.3%	32.7%
2006	1,833,695	929,911	Corker, Bob	879,976	Ford, Harold E. Jr.	23,808	49,935	R	50.7%	48.0%	51.4%	48.6%
2002	1,642,421	891,420	Alexander, Lamar	728,295	Clement, Robert Nelson	22,706	163,125	R	54.3%	44.3%	55.0%	45.0%
2000	1,928,613	1,255,444	Frist, William H.*	621,152	Clark, Jeff	52,017	634,292	R	65.1%	32.2%	66.9%	33.1%
1996	1,778,664	1,091,554	Thompson, Fred*	654,937	Houston, Gordon J.	32,173	436,617	R	61.4%	36.8%	62.5%	37.5%
1994	1,480,391	834,226	Frist, William H.	623,164	Sasser, James R.*	23,001	211,062	R	56.4%	42.1%	57.2%	42.8%
1994S	1,465,862	885,998	Thompson, Fred	565,930	Cooper, Jim	13,934	320,068	R	60.4%	38.6%	61.0%	39.0%
1990	783,922	233,703	Hawkins, William R.	530,898	Gore, Albert Jr.*	19,321	297,195	D	29.8%	67.7%	30.6%	69.4%
1988	1,567,181	541,033	Anderson, Bill	1,020,061	Sasser, James R.*	6,087	479,028	D	34.5%	65.1%	34.7%	65.3%
1984	1,648,036	557,016	Ashe, Victor	1,000,607	Gore, Albert Jr.	90,413	443,591	D	33.8%	60.7%	35.8%	64.2%
1982	1,259,785	479,642	Beard, Robin L.	780,113	Sasser, James R.*	30	300,471	D	38.1%	61.9%	38.1%	61.9%
1978	1,157,094	642,644	Baker, Howard H. Jr.*	466,228	Eskind, Jane	48,222	176,416	R	55.5%	40.3%	58.0%	42.0%
1976	1,432,046	673,231	Brock, William E.*	751,180	Sasser, James R.	7,635	77,949	D	47.0%	52.5%	47.3%	52.7%
1972	1,164,195	716,539	Baker, Howard H. Jr.*	440,599	Blanton, L. Ray	7,057	275,940	R	61.5%	37.8%	61.9%	38.1%
1970	1,097,041	562,645	Brock, William E.	519,858	Gore, Albert Sr.*	14,538	42,787	R	51.3%	47.4%	52.0%	48.0%
1966	866,961	483,063	Baker, Howard H. Jr.	383,843	Clement, Frank G.	55	99,220	R	55.7%	44.3%	55.7%	44.3%
1964	1,064,018	493,475	Kuykendall, Daniel H.	570,542	Gore, Albert Sr.*	1	77,067	D	46.4%	53.6%	46.4%	53.6%
1964S	1,091,093	517,330	Baker, Howard H. Jr.	568,905	Bass, Ross	4,858	51,575	D	47.4%	52.1%	47.6%	52.4%
1960	828,519	234,053	Frazier, A. Bradley	594,460	Kefauver, Estes*	6	360,407	D	28.2%	71.7%	28.2%	71.8%
1958	401,666	76,371	Atkins, Hobart F.	317,324	Gore, Albert Sr.*	7,971	240,953	D	19.0%	79.0%	19.4%	80.6%
1954	356,094	106,971	Wall, Tom	249,121	Kefauver, Estes*	2	142,150	D	30.0%	70.0%	30.0%	70.0%
1952	735,219	153,479	Atkins, Hobart F.	545,432	Gore, Albert Sr.	36,308	391,953	D	20.9%	74.2%	22.0%	78.0%
1948	499,138	166,947	Reece, B. Carroll	326,062	Kefauver, Estes	6,129	159,115	D	33.4%	65.3%	33.9%	66.1%
1946	218,713	57,237	Ladd, W. B.	145,654	McKellar, Kenneth D.*	15,822	88,417	D	26.2%	66.6%	28.2%	71.8%

Note: An asterisk (*) denotes incumbent. **One each of the 1964 and 1994 elections was for a short term to fill a vacancy.

TENNESSEE
GOVERNOR 2014

2010 Census Population	County	Total Vote	Republican (Haslam)	Democratic (Brown)	Other	Rep.-Dem. Plurality	Percentage			
							Total Vote		Major Vote	
							Rep.	Dem.	Rep.	Dem.
75,129	ANDERSON	17,758	13,367	3,171	1,220	10,196 R	75.3%	17.9%	80.8%	19.2%
45,058	BEDFORD	7,440	5,653	1,227	560	4,426 R	76.0%	16.5%	82.2%	17.8%
16,489	BENTON	3,731	2,415	991	325	1,424 R	64.7%	26.6%	70.9%	29.1%
12,876	BLEDSOE	2,573	1,786	620	167	1,166 R	69.4%	24.1%	74.2%	25.8%
123,010	BLOUNT	29,660	23,653	4,171	1,836	19,482 R	79.7%	14.1%	85.0%	15.0%
98,963	BRADLEY	20,085	16,709	2,528	848	14,181 R	83.2%	12.6%	86.9%	13.1%
40,716	CAMPBELL	6,434	4,981	1,145	308	3,836 R	77.4%	17.8%	81.3%	18.7%
13,801	CANNON	2,770	1,977	546	247	1,431 R	71.4%	19.7%	78.4%	21.6%
28,522	CARROLL	6,202	4,313	1,430	459	2,883 R	69.5%	23.1%	75.1%	24.9%
57,424	CARTER	10,777	8,376	1,530	871	6,846 R	77.7%	14.2%	84.6%	15.4%
39,105	CHEATHAM	8,524	6,191	1,535	798	4,656 R	72.6%	18.0%	80.1%	19.9%
17,131	CHESTER	3,384	2,659	510	215	2,149 R	78.6%	15.1%	83.9%	16.1%
32,213	CLAIBORNE	5,269	4,015	948	306	3,067 R	76.2%	18.0%	80.9%	19.1%
7,861	CLAY	1,445	963	378	104	585 R	66.6%	26.2%	71.8%	28.2%
35,662	COCKE	7,171	5,615	1,032	524	4,583 R	78.3%	14.4%	84.5%	15.5%
52,796	COFFEE	10,923	7,986	2,008	929	5,978 R	73.1%	18.4%	79.9%	20.1%
14,586	CROCKETT	2,930	2,222	558	150	1,664 R	75.8%	19.0%	79.9%	20.1%
56,053	CUMBERLAND	16,426	12,978	2,543	905	10,435 R	79.0%	15.5%	83.6%	16.4%
626,681	DAVIDSON	133,953	71,661	47,438	14,854	24,223 R	53.5%	35.4%	60.2%	39.8%
11,757	DECATUR	2,292	1,634	510	148	1,124 R	71.3%	22.3%	76.2%	23.8%
18,723	DEKALB	3,571	2,423	834	314	1,589 R	67.9%	23.4%	74.4%	25.6%
49,666	DICKSON	9,885	6,830	2,297	758	4,533 R	69.1%	23.2%	74.8%	25.2%
38,335	DYER	7,344	5,710	1,162	472	4,548 R	77.8%	15.8%	83.1%	16.9%
38,413	FAYETTE	10,554	8,141	1,976	437	6,165 R	77.1%	18.7%	80.5%	19.5%
17,959	FENTRESS	3,239	2,371	617	251	1,754 R	73.2%	19.0%	79.4%	20.6%
41,052	FRANKLIN	9,290	6,595	2,022	673	4,573 R	71.0%	21.8%	76.5%	23.5%
49,683	GIBSON	11,120	7,819	2,300	1,001	5,519 R	70.3%	20.7%	77.3%	22.7%
29,485	GILES	5,529	3,922	1,229	378	2,693 R	70.9%	22.2%	76.1%	23.9%
22,657	GRAINGER	4,148	3,274	635	239	2,639 R	78.9%	15.3%	83.8%	16.2%
68,831	GREENE	13,302	10,146	2,118	1,038	8,028 R	76.3%	15.9%	82.7%	17.3%
13,703	GRUNDY	2,400	1,556	645	199	911 R	64.8%	26.9%	70.7%	29.3%
62,544	HAMBLEN	11,087	8,978	1,515	594	7,463 R	81.0%	13.7%	85.6%	14.4%
336,463	HAMILTON	79,641	56,750	19,462	3,429	37,288 R	71.3%	24.4%	74.5%	25.5%
6,819	HANCOCK	920	676	166	78	510 R	73.5%	18.0%	80.3%	19.7%
27,253	HARDEMAN	4,888	2,891	1,809	188	1,082 R	59.1%	37.0%	61.5%	38.5%
26,026	HARDIN	5,050	4,046	764	240	3,282 R	80.1%	15.1%	84.1%	15.9%
56,833	HAWKINS	10,944	8,730	1,575	639	7,155 R	79.8%	14.4%	84.7%	15.3%
18,787	HAYWOOD	3,373	1,940	1,341	92	599 R	57.5%	39.8%	59.1%	40.9%
27,769	HENDERSON	4,978	3,836	790	352	3,046 R	77.1%	15.9%	82.9%	17.1%
32,330	HENRY	7,289	5,297	1,533	459	3,764 R	72.7%	21.0%	77.6%	22.4%
24,690	HICKMAN	4,273	2,956	976	341	1,980 R	69.2%	22.8%	75.2%	24.8%
8,426	HOUSTON	1,791	1,005	634	152	371 R	56.1%	35.4%	61.3%	38.7%
18,538	HUMPHREYS	4,174	2,512	1,201	461	1,311 R	60.2%	28.8%	67.7%	32.3%
11,638	JACKSON	2,276	1,451	611	214	840 R	63.8%	26.8%	70.4%	29.6%
51,407	JEFFERSON	10,438	8,423	1,370	645	7,053 R	80.7%	13.1%	86.0%	14.0%
18,244	JOHNSON	3,253	2,547	484	222	2,063 R	78.3%	14.9%	84.0%	16.0%
432,226	KNOX	101,976	78,571	15,986	7,419	62,585 R	77.0%	15.7%	83.1%	16.9%
7,832	LAKE	1,163	629	409	125	220 R	54.1%	35.2%	60.6%	39.4%
27,815	LAUDERDALE	4,083	2,652	1,201	230	1,451 R	65.0%	29.4%	68.8%	31.2%
41,869	LAWRENCE	8,531	6,264	1,681	586	4,583 R	73.4%	19.7%	78.8%	21.2%
12,161	LEWIS	2,613	1,857	531	225	1,326 R	71.1%	20.3%	77.8%	22.2%
33,361	LINCOLN	6,235	4,720	1,077	438	3,643 R	75.7%	17.3%	81.4%	18.6%
48,556	LOUDON	14,359	12,015	1,610	734	10,405 R	83.7%	11.2%	88.2%	11.8%
22,248	MACON	3,163	2,436	483	244	1,953 R	77.0%	15.3%	83.5%	16.5%
98,294	MADISON	22,531	14,563	6,640	1,328	7,923 R	64.6%	29.5%	68.7%	31.3%
28,237	MARION	6,204	4,233	1,685	286	2,548 R	68.2%	27.2%	71.5%	28.5%
30,617	MARSHALL	5,938	4,279	1,224	435	3,055 R	72.1%	20.6%	77.8%	22.2%
80,956	MAURY	18,466	12,790	4,145	1,531	8,645 R	69.3%	22.4%	75.5%	24.5%
52,266	MCMINN	10,270	8,120	1,654	496	6,466 R	79.1%	16.1%	83.1%	16.9%
26,075	MCNAIRY	5,349	4,019	1,032	298	2,987 R	75.1%	19.3%	79.6%	20.4%

TENNESSEE

GOVERNOR 2014

2010 Census Population	County	Total Vote	Republican (Haslam)	Democratic (Brown)	Other	Rep.-Dem. Plurality	Percentage — Total Vote Rep.	Dem.	Percentage — Major Vote Rep.	Dem.
11,753	MEIGS	2,260	1,683	439	138	1,244 R	74.5%	19.4%	79.3%	20.7%
44,519	MONROE	9,815	7,567	1,788	460	5,779 R	77.1%	18.2%	80.9%	19.1%
172,331	MONTGOMERY	29,063	20,185	7,073	1,805	13,112 R	69.5%	24.3%	74.1%	25.9%
6,362	MOORE	1,565	1,145	306	114	839 R	73.2%	19.6%	78.9%	21.1%
21,987	MORGAN	3,609	2,453	962	194	1,491 R	68.0%	26.7%	71.8%	28.2%
31,807	OBION	6,606	4,428	1,369	809	3,059 R	67.0%	20.7%	76.4%	23.6%
22,083	OVERTON	3,975	2,613	1,025	337	1,588 R	65.7%	25.8%	71.8%	28.2%
7,915	PERRY	1,406	945	327	134	618 R	67.2%	23.3%	74.3%	25.7%
5,077	PICKETT	1,611	1,154	328	129	826 R	71.6%	20.4%	77.9%	22.1%
16,825	POLK	3,511	2,505	829	177	1,676 R	71.3%	23.6%	75.1%	24.9%
72,321	PUTNAM	14,333	10,425	2,727	1,181	7,698 R	72.7%	19.0%	79.3%	20.7%
31,809	RHEA	5,916	4,792	873	251	3,919 R	81.0%	14.8%	84.6%	15.4%
54,181	ROANE	13,405	10,310	2,178	917	8,132 R	76.9%	16.2%	82.6%	17.4%
66,283	ROBERTSON	13,789	10,177	2,501	1,111	7,676 R	73.8%	18.1%	80.3%	19.7%
262,604	RUTHERFORD	51,994	36,467	11,323	4,204	25,144 R	70.1%	21.8%	76.3%	23.7%
22,228	SCOTT	3,087	2,318	630	139	1,688 R	75.1%	20.4%	78.6%	21.4%
14,112	SEQUATCHIE	3,106	2,418	549	139	1,869 R	77.8%	17.7%	81.5%	18.5%
89,889	SEVIER	18,689	15,400	2,205	1,084	13,195 R	82.4%	11.8%	87.5%	12.5%
927,644	SHELBY	185,263	107,089	69,193	8,981	37,896 R	57.8%	37.3%	60.7%	39.3%
19,166	SMITH	4,126	2,720	1,048	358	1,672 R	65.9%	25.4%	72.2%	27.8%
13,324	STEWART	2,982	1,999	760	223	1,239 R	67.0%	25.5%	72.5%	27.5%
156,823	SULLIVAN	33,112	26,837	4,399	1,876	22,438 R	81.0%	13.3%	85.9%	14.1%
160,645	SUMNER	36,602	28,090	6,121	2,391	21,969 R	76.7%	16.7%	82.1%	17.9%
61,081	TIPTON	12,368	9,636	2,104	628	7,532 R	77.9%	17.0%	82.1%	17.9%
7,870	TROUSDALE	1,476	965	392	119	573 R	65.4%	26.6%	71.1%	28.9%
18,313	UNICOI	3,930	2,999	596	335	2,403 R	76.3%	15.2%	83.4%	16.6%
19,109	UNION	3,004	2,311	520	173	1,791 R	76.9%	17.3%	81.6%	18.4%
5,548	VAN BUREN	1,512	903	483	126	420 R	59.7%	31.9%	65.2%	34.8%
39,839	WARREN	7,543	5,285	1,648	610	3,637 R	70.1%	21.8%	76.2%	23.8%
122,979	WASHINGTON	26,296	19,707	4,485	2,104	15,222 R	74.9%	17.1%	81.5%	18.5%
17,021	WAYNE	2,732	2,122	423	187	1,699 R	77.7%	15.5%	83.4%	16.6%
35,021	WEAKLEY	7,365	5,082	1,600	683	3,482 R	69.0%	21.7%	76.1%	23.9%
25,841	WHITE	5,701	4,030	1,214	457	2,816 R	70.7%	21.3%	76.8%	23.2%
183,182	WILLIAMSON	56,860	45,329	7,501	4,030	37,828 R	79.7%	13.2%	85.8%	14.2%
113,993	WILSON	29,731	22,580	5,075	2,076	17,505 R	75.9%	17.1%	81.6%	18.4%
6,346,105	TOTAL	1,353,728	951,796	309,237	92,695	642,559 R	70.3%	22.8%	75.5%	24.5%

TENNESSEE

SENATOR 2014

2010 Census Population	County	Total Vote	Republican (Alexander)	Democratic (Ball)	Other	Rep.-Dem. Plurality	Percentage — Total Vote Rep.	Dem.	Percentage — Major Vote Rep.	Dem.
75,129	ANDERSON	17,892	11,612	5,262	1,018	6,350 R	64.9%	29.4%	68.8%	31.2%
45,058	BEDFORD	7,506	5,044	1,995	467	3,049 R	67.2%	26.6%	71.7%	28.3%
16,489	BENTON	3,717	2,202	1,293	222	909 R	59.2%	34.8%	63.0%	37.0%
12,876	BLEDSOE	2,593	1,812	635	146	1,177 R	69.9%	24.5%	74.0%	26.0%
123,010	BLOUNT	29,703	20,560	7,160	1,983	13,400 R	69.2%	24.1%	74.2%	25.8%

TENNESSEE
SENATOR 2014

2010 Census Population	County	Total Vote	Republican (Alexander)	Democratic (Ball)	Other	Rep.-Dem. Plurality	Percentage			
							Total Vote		Major Vote	
							Rep.	Dem.	Rep.	Dem.
98,963	BRADLEY	20,355	16,137	3,277	941	12,860 R	79.3%	16.1%	83.1%	16.9%
40,716	CAMPBELL	6,379	4,522	1,549	308	2,973 R	70.9%	24.3%	74.5%	25.5%
13,801	CANNON	2,816	1,771	826	219	945 R	62.9%	29.3%	68.2%	31.8%
28,522	CARROLL	6,201	4,091	1,677	433	2,414 R	66.0%	27.0%	70.9%	29.1%
57,424	CARTER	10,773	7,983	2,053	737	5,930 R	74.1%	19.1%	79.5%	20.5%
39,105	CHEATHAM	8,557	5,542	2,366	649	3,176 R	64.8%	27.6%	70.1%	29.9%
17,131	CHESTER	3,379	2,408	646	325	1,762 R	71.3%	19.1%	78.8%	21.2%
32,213	CLAIBORNE	5,289	3,695	1,326	268	2,369 R	69.9%	25.1%	73.6%	26.4%
7,861	CLAY	1,461	905	468	88	437 R	61.9%	32.0%	65.9%	34.1%
35,662	COCKE	7,267	4,391	2,499	377	1,892 R	60.4%	34.4%	63.7%	36.3%
52,796	COFFEE	11,238	7,414	3,037	787	4,377 R	66.0%	27.0%	70.9%	29.1%
14,586	CROCKETT	2,893	1,980	737	176	1,243 R	68.4%	25.5%	72.9%	27.1%
56,053	CUMBERLAND	16,304	11,439	3,737	1,128	7,702 R	70.2%	22.9%	75.4%	24.6%
626,681	DAVIDSON	136,413	59,972	69,665	6,776	9,693 D	44.0%	51.1%	46.3%	53.7%
11,757	DECATUR	2,273	1,450	693	130	757 R	63.8%	30.5%	67.7%	32.3%
18,723	DEKALB	3,611	2,165	1,191	255	974 R	60.0%	33.0%	64.5%	35.5%
49,666	DICKSON	10,169	6,282	3,175	712	3,107 R	61.8%	31.2%	66.4%	33.6%
38,335	DYER	7,274	5,093	1,574	607	3,519 R	70.0%	21.6%	76.4%	23.6%
38,413	FAYETTE	10,473	7,402	2,517	554	4,885 R	70.7%	24.0%	74.6%	25.4%
17,959	FENTRESS	3,239	2,250	744	245	1,506 R	69.5%	23.0%	75.2%	24.8%
41,052	FRANKLIN	9,423	5,889	2,998	536	2,891 R	62.5%	31.8%	66.3%	33.7%
49,683	GIBSON	11,108	7,235	2,825	1,048	4,410 R	65.1%	25.4%	71.9%	28.1%
29,485	GILES	5,548	3,474	1,710	364	1,764 R	62.6%	30.8%	67.0%	33.0%
22,657	GRAINGER	4,155	2,950	987	218	1,963 R	71.0%	23.8%	74.9%	25.1%
68,831	GREENE	13,456	9,688	2,775	993	6,913 R	72.0%	20.6%	77.7%	22.3%
13,703	GRUNDY	2,355	1,372	817	166	555 R	58.3%	34.7%	62.7%	37.3%
62,544	HAMBLEN	11,198	8,157	2,484	557	5,673 R	72.8%	22.2%	76.7%	23.3%
336,463	HAMILTON	79,663	51,347	25,373	2,943	25,974 R	64.5%	31.9%	66.9%	33.1%
6,819	HANCOCK	931	650	231	50	419 R	69.8%	24.8%	73.8%	26.2%
27,253	HARDEMAN	4,813	2,623	1,993	197	630 R	54.5%	41.4%	56.8%	43.2%
26,026	HARDIN	5,101	3,803	1,057	241	2,746 R	74.6%	20.7%	78.3%	21.7%
56,833	HAWKINS	10,991	8,037	2,288	666	5,749 R	73.1%	20.8%	77.8%	22.2%
18,787	HAYWOOD	3,385	1,727	1,544	114	183 R	51.0%	45.6%	52.8%	47.2%
27,769	HENDERSON	4,954	3,576	962	416	2,614 R	72.2%	19.4%	78.8%	21.2%
32,330	HENRY	7,167	4,816	1,968	383	2,848 R	67.2%	27.5%	71.0%	29.0%
24,690	HICKMAN	4,327	2,584	1,387	356	1,197 R	59.7%	32.1%	65.1%	34.9%
8,426	HOUSTON	1,778	947	735	96	212 R	53.3%	41.3%	56.3%	43.7%
18,538	HUMPHREYS	4,150	2,227	1,561	362	666 R	53.7%	37.6%	58.8%	41.2%
11,638	JACKSON	2,415	1,326	838	251	488 R	54.9%	34.7%	61.3%	38.7%
51,407	JEFFERSON	10,496	7,429	2,448	619	4,981 R	70.8%	23.3%	75.2%	24.8%
18,244	JOHNSON	3,226	2,400	595	231	1,805 R	74.4%	18.4%	80.1%	19.9%
432,226	KNOX	103,081	66,093	30,802	6,186	35,291 R	64.1%	29.9%	68.2%	31.8%
7,832	LAKE	1,145	619	418	108	201 R	54.1%	36.5%	59.7%	40.3%
27,815	LAUDERDALE	4,005	2,411	1,393	201	1,018 R	60.2%	34.8%	63.4%	36.6%
41,869	LAWRENCE	8,646	5,888	2,306	452	3,582 R	68.1%	26.7%	71.9%	28.1%
12,161	LEWIS	2,650	1,655	736	259	919 R	62.5%	27.8%	69.2%	30.8%
33,361	LINCOLN	6,271	4,569	1,239	463	3,330 R	72.9%	19.8%	78.7%	21.3%
48,556	LOUDON	14,543	10,751	3,031	761	7,720 R	73.9%	20.8%	78.0%	22.0%
22,248	MACON	3,255	2,312	725	218	1,587 R	71.0%	22.3%	76.1%	23.9%
98,294	MADISON	22,768	13,377	7,871	1,520	5,506 R	58.8%	34.6%	63.0%	37.0%
28,237	MARION	6,187	3,963	1,968	256	1,995 R	64.1%	31.8%	66.8%	33.2%
30,617	MARSHALL	5,914	3,650	1,898	366	1,752 R	61.7%	32.1%	65.8%	34.2%
80,956	MAURY	18,667	11,489	5,831	1,347	5,658 R	61.5%	31.2%	66.3%	33.7%
52,266	MCMINN	10,484	7,717	2,177	590	5,540 R	73.6%	20.8%	78.0%	22.0%
26,075	MCNAIRY	5,327	3,696	1,343	288	2,353 R	69.4%	25.2%	73.3%	26.7%
11,753	MEIGS	2,248	1,579	550	119	1,029 R	70.2%	24.5%	74.2%	25.8%
44,519	MONROE	9,859	6,838	2,516	505	4,322 R	69.4%	25.5%	73.1%	26.9%
172,331	MONTGOMERY	28,982	17,561	9,721	1,700	7,840 R	60.6%	33.5%	64.4%	35.6%
6,362	MOORE	1,690	1,152	445	93	707 R	68.2%	26.3%	72.1%	27.9%
21,987	MORGAN	3,624	2,426	982	216	1,444 R	66.9%	27.1%	71.2%	28.8%

TENNESSEE

SENATOR 2014

2010 Census Population	County	Total Vote	Republican (Alexander)	Democratic (Ball)	Other	Rep.-Dem. Plurality	Percentage Total Vote Rep.	Dem.	Major Vote Rep.	Dem.
31,807	OBION	6,714	4,631	1,500	583	3,131 R	69.0%	22.3%	75.5%	24.5%
22,083	OVERTON	3,978	2,334	1,321	323	1,013 R	58.7%	33.2%	63.9%	36.1%
7,915	PERRY	1,397	838	447	112	391 R	60.0%	32.0%	65.2%	34.8%
5,077	PICKETT	1,624	1,105	426	93	679 R	68.0%	26.2%	72.2%	27.8%
16,825	POLK	3,539	2,411	958	170	1,453 R	68.1%	27.1%	71.6%	28.4%
72,321	PUTNAM	14,788	9,127	3,892	1,769	5,235 R	61.7%	26.3%	70.1%	29.9%
31,809	RHEA	5,935	4,601	1,071	263	3,530 R	77.5%	18.0%	81.1%	18.9%
54,181	ROANE	13,420	9,194	3,477	749	5,717 R	68.5%	25.9%	72.6%	27.4%
66,283	ROBERTSON	13,870	9,028	3,751	1,091	5,277 R	65.1%	27.0%	70.6%	29.4%
262,604	RUTHERFORD	54,132	33,612	16,761	3,759	16,851 R	62.1%	31.0%	66.7%	33.3%
22,228	SCOTT	3,045	2,143	755	147	1,388 R	70.4%	24.8%	73.9%	26.1%
14,112	SEQUATCHIE	3,074	2,258	652	164	1,606 R	73.5%	21.2%	77.6%	22.4%
89,889	SEVIER	18,794	14,073	3,627	1,094	10,446 R	74.9%	19.3%	79.5%	20.5%
927,644	SHELBY	186,010	90,415	88,921	6,674	1,494 R	48.6%	47.8%	50.4%	49.6%
19,166	SMITH	4,271	2,559	1,427	285	1,132 R	59.9%	33.4%	64.2%	35.8%
13,324	STEWART	2,969	1,815	968	186	847 R	61.1%	32.6%	65.2%	34.8%
156,823	SULLIVAN	32,888	24,425	6,243	2,220	18,182 R	74.3%	19.0%	79.6%	20.4%
160,645	SUMNER	37,274	25,615	9,292	2,367	16,323 R	68.7%	24.9%	73.4%	26.6%
61,081	TIPTON	12,170	8,550	2,825	795	5,725 R	70.3%	23.2%	75.2%	24.8%
7,870	TROUSDALE	1,518	856	554	108	302 R	56.4%	36.5%	60.7%	39.3%
18,313	UNICOI	3,924	2,876	759	289	2,117 R	73.3%	19.3%	79.1%	20.9%
19,109	UNION	2,992	2,016	794	182	1,222 R	67.4%	26.5%	71.7%	28.3%
5,548	VAN BUREN	1,518	888	531	99	357 R	58.5%	35.0%	62.6%	37.4%
39,839	WARREN	7,559	4,761	2,352	446	2,409 R	63.0%	31.1%	66.9%	33.1%
122,979	WASHINGTON	26,430	18,265	6,286	1,879	11,979 R	69.1%	23.8%	74.4%	25.6%
17,021	WAYNE	2,703	2,017	535	151	1,482 R	74.6%	19.8%	79.0%	21.0%
35,021	WEAKLEY	7,454	5,067	1,852	535	3,215 R	68.0%	24.8%	73.2%	26.8%
25,841	WHITE	5,908	3,721	1,678	509	2,043 R	63.0%	28.4%	68.9%	31.1%
183,182	WILLIAMSON	58,773	42,501	12,660	3,612	29,841 R	72.3%	21.5%	77.0%	23.0%
113,993	WILSON	30,196	20,260	7,903	2,033	12,357 R	67.1%	26.2%	71.9%	28.1%
6,346,105	TOTAL	1,366,628	850,087	437,848	78,693	412,239 R	62.2%	32.0%	66.0%	34.0%

TENNESSEE

HOUSE OF REPRESENTATIVES

CD	Year	Total Vote	Republican Vote	Candidate	Democratic Vote	Candidate	Other Vote	Rep.-Dem. Plurality	Percentage Total Vote Rep.	Dem.	Major Vote Rep.	Dem.
1	2014	139,470	115,533	ROE, PHIL*			23,937	115,533 R	82.8%		100.0%	
1	2012	239,672	182,252	ROE, PHIL*	47,663	WOODRUFF, ALAN	9,757	134,589 R	76.0%	19.9%	79.3%	20.7%
2	2014	166,751	120,883	DUNCAN, JOHN J. JR.*	37,612	SCOTT, BOB	8,256	83,271 R	72.5%	22.6%	76.3%	23.7%
2	2012	264,505	196,894	DUNCAN, JOHN J. JR.*	54,522	GOODALE, TROY	13,089	142,372 R	74.4%	20.6%	78.3%	21.7%
3	2014	156,097	97,344	FLEISCHMANN, CHARLES J. CHUCK*	53,983	HEADRICK, MARY M.	4,770	43,361 R	62.4%	34.6%	64.3%	35.7%
3	2012	256,909	157,830	FLEISCHMANN, CHARLES J. CHUCK*	91,094	HEADRICK, MARY M.	7,985	66,736 R	61.4%	35.5%	63.4%	36.6%
4	2014	145,418	84,815	DESJARLAIS, SCOTT*	51,357	SHERRELL, LENDA	9,246	33,458 R	58.3%	35.3%	62.3%	37.7%
4	2012	230,590	128,568	DESJARLAIS, SCOTT*	102,022	STEWART, ERIC		26,546 R	55.8%	44.2%	55.8%	44.2%
5	2014	154,276	55,078	RIES, BOB	96,148	COOPER, JIM*	3,050	41,070 D	35.7%	62.3%	36.4%	63.6%
5	2012	263,095	86,240	STAATS, BRAD	171,621	COOPER, JIM*	5,234	85,381 D	32.8%	65.2%	33.4%	66.6%
6	2014	162,097	115,231	BLACK, DIANE*	37,232	POWERS, AMOS SCOTT	9,634	77,999 R	71.1%	23.0%	75.6%	24.4%
6	2012	241,241	184,383	BLACK, DIANE*			56,858	184,383 R	76.4%		100.0%	
7	2014	157,907	110,534	BLACKBURN, MARSHA*	42,280	CRAMER, DANIEL N.	5,093	68,254 R	70.0%	26.8%	72.3%	27.7%
7	2012	257,306	182,730	BLACKBURN, MARSHA*	61,679	AMOUZOUVIK, CREDO	12,897	121,051 R	71.0%	24.0%	74.8%	25.2%

TENNESSEE

HOUSE OF REPRESENTATIVES

| CD | Year | Total Vote | Republican | | Democratic | | Other Vote | Rep.-Dem. Plurality | Percentage | | | |
| | | | Vote | Candidate | Vote | Candidate | | | Total Vote | | Major Vote | |
									Rep.	Dem.	Rep.	Dem.
8	2014	172,595	122,255	FINCHER, STEPHEN LEE*	42,433	BRADLEY, WES	7,907	79,822 R	70.8%	24.6%	74.2%	25.8%
8	2012	279,422	190,923	FINCHER, STEPHEN LEE*	79,490	DIXON, TIMOTHY	9,009	111,433 R	68.3%	28.4%	70.6%	29.4%
9	2014	116,550	27,173	BERGMANN, CHARLOTTE	87,376	COHEN, STEVE*	2,001	60,203 D	23.3%	75.0%	23.7%	76.3%
9	2012	250,987	59,742	FLINN, GEORGE S. "JR."	188,422	COHEN, STEVE*	2,823	128,680 D	23.8%	75.1%	24.1%	75.9%
TOTAL	2014	1,371,161	848,846		448,421		73,894	400,425 R	61.9%	32.7%	65.4%	34.6%
TOTAL	2012	2,283,727	1,369,562		796,513		117,652	573,049 R	60.0%	34.9%	63.2%	36.8%

Note: An asterisk (*) denotes incumbent.

TENNESSEE

GENERAL AND PRIMARY ELECTIONS

2014 GENERAL ELECTIONS: OTHER VOTES

Governor   Other vote was 30,579 Independent (John J. Hooker), 26,580 Constitution (Shaun Crowell), 18,570 Green (Isa Infante), 8,612 Independent (Steve Coburn), 8,321 Independent (Daniel Lewis), 33 Scattered write-in

Senate   Other vote was 36,088 Constitution (Joe Wilmoth), 12,570 Green (Martin Pleasant), 11,157 Independent (Tom Emerson), 7,713 Independent (Danny Page), 5,678 Independent (Joshua James), 2,386 Independent (Bartholomew J. Phillips), 2,314 Independent (Ed Gauthier), 787 Independent (C. Salekin)

House   Other vote was:

CD 1   9,906 Independent (Robert D. Franklin), 9,869 Green (Robert N. Smith), 4,148 Independent (Michael D. Salyer), 14 Write-in (Scott Kudialis)

CD 2   4,223 Independent (Casey Adam Gouge), 4,033 Green (Norris Dryer)

CD 3   4,770 Independent (Cassandra J. Mitchell)

CD 4   9,246 Independent (Robert Rankin Doggart)

CD 5   3,050 Independent (Paul Deakin)

CD 6   9,634 Independent (Mike Winton)

CD 7   5,093 Independent (Leonard D. Ladner)

CD 8   4,451 Constitution (Mark J. Rawles), 3,452 Independent (James L. Hart), 4 Write-in (Dana Matheny)

CD 9   766 Independent (Floyd Wayne Alberson), 752 Independent (Paul Cook), 483 Independent (Herbert A. Bass)

2014 PRIMARY ELECTIONS: SUPPLEMENTARY INFORMATION

Primary   August 7, 2014   **Registration** (as of June 1, 2014 – includes 523,678 inactive registrants)   3,932,124   No Party Registration

Primary Type   Open—Any registered voter could participate in either the Democratic or Republican primary, although state party rules can spell out the grounds for a challenge to primary voters who were not party "members."

TENNESSEE

GENERAL AND PRIMARY ELECTIONS

	REPUBLICAN PRIMARIES			DEMOCRATIC PRIMARIES		
Senator	Alexander, Lamar*	331,705	49.7%	Ball, Gordon	87,829	36.5%
	Carr, Joe	271,324	40.6%	Adams Jr., Terry Glen	85,794	35.6%
	Flinn, George S. "Jr."	34,668	5.2%	Davis, Gary G.	42,549	17.7%
	Agnew, F. Christian	11,320	1.7%	Crim, Larry	24,777	10.3%
	Lenard, Brenda S.	7,908	1.2%			
	King, John D.	7,748	1.2%			
	Magee, Erin Kent	3,366	0.5%			
	TOTAL	668,039		TOTAL	240,949	
Governor	Haslam, Bill*	570,997	87.7%	Brown, Charles V. "Charlie"	95,114	41.7%
	Brown, Mark "Connrippy"	44,165	6.8%	Mckamey, W. H. "John"	59,200	26.0%
	McFolin, Donald Ray	22,968	3.5%	Johnson, Kennedy Spellman	55,718	24.4%
	Marceaux, Basil	13,117	2.0%	Noonan, Ron	17,993	7.9%
	TOTAL	651,247		TOTAL	228,025	
Congressional District 1	Roe, Phil*	73,212	83.7%			
	Hartley, Daniel J.	7,582	8.7%			
	Rader, John Paul	6,663	7.6%			
	TOTAL	87,457				
Congressional District 2	Duncan, John J. Jr.*	50,532	60.5%	Scott, Bob	12,715	100.0%
	Zachary, Jason	33,054	39.5%			
	TOTAL	83,586		TOTAL	12,715	
Congressional District 3	Fleischmann, Charles J. "Chuck"*	46,556	50.8%	Headrick, Mary M.	23,646	100.0%
	Wamp, Weston	45,082	49.2%			
	Lane, Harry	2				
	TOTAL	91,640		TOTAL	23,646	
Congressional District 4	DesJarlais, Scott*	34,793	44.9%	Sherrell, Lenda	22,859	100.0%
	Tracy, Jim	34,755	44.8%			
	Anderson, John	4,592	5.9%			
	Lane, Steve P.	1,483	1.9%			
	Tate, David R.	938	1.2%			
	Warden, Michael S.	659	0.9%			
	Faparusi Sr., Oluyomi "Fapas"	284	0.4%			
	TOTAL	77,504		TOTAL	22,859	
Congressional District 5	Ries, Bob	11,415	37.8%	Cooper, Jim*	40,831	100.0%
	Carter, Chris	9,004	29.8%			
	Smith, John "Big John"	5,330	17.7%			
	Holden, Ronnie	4,434	14.7%			
	TOTAL	30,183		TOTAL	40,831	
Congressional District 6	Black, Diane*	67,907	76.7%	Powers, Amos Scott	22,347	100.0%
	Lowery, Jerry	20,664	23.3%			
	TOTAL	88,571		TOTAL	22,347	
Congressional District 7	Blackburn, Marsha*	64,984	84.2%	Cramer, Daniel N.	20,266	81.0%
	Brimm, Jacob	12,202	15.8%	Amouzouvik, Credo	4,751	19.0%
	TOTAL	77,186		TOTAL	25,017	
Congressional District 8	Fincher, Stephen Lee*	68,472	79.0%	Bradley, Wes	9,400	34.7%
	Matheny, Dana	11,823	13.6%	Hobson, Rickey	9,014	33.3%
	Mills, John	6,339	7.3%	Reasons, Tom	5,547	20.5%
	Pegues, Nicholas	1		Pivnick, Lawrence A.	3,105	11.5%
	TOTAL	86,635		TOTAL	27,066	
Congressional District 9	Bergmann, Charlotte	18,579	100.0%	Cohen, Steve*	45,423	66.2%
				Wilkins, Ricky E.	22,336	32.5%
				Richmond, Isaac	876	1.3%
	TOTAL	18,579		TOTAL	68,635	

Note: An asterisk (*) denotes incumbent.

TEXAS

Congressional districts first established for elections held in 2012

36 members

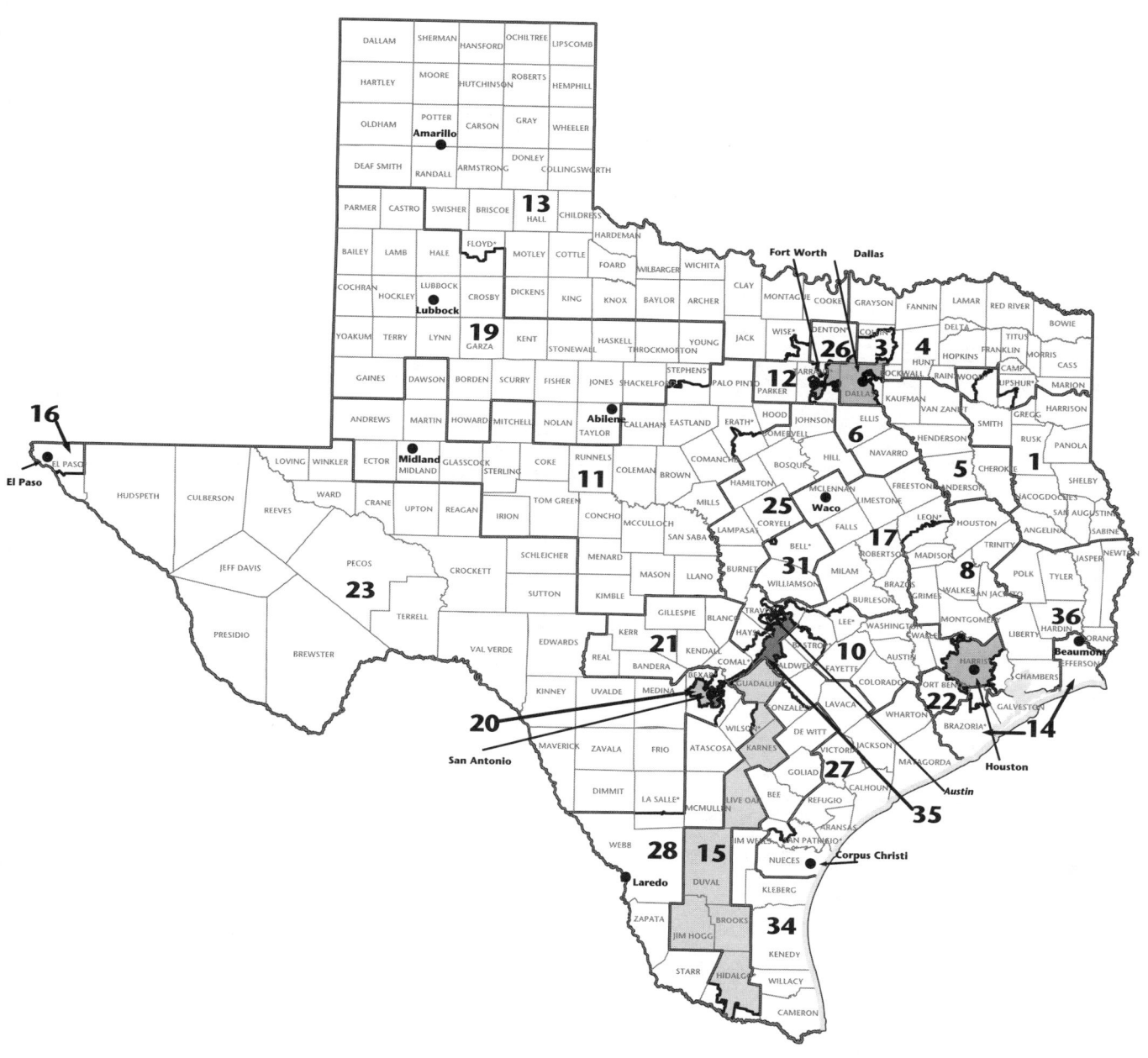

* Asterisk indicates a county whose boundaries include parts of two or more congressional districts.

TEXAS
Greater Dallas–Fort Worth Area

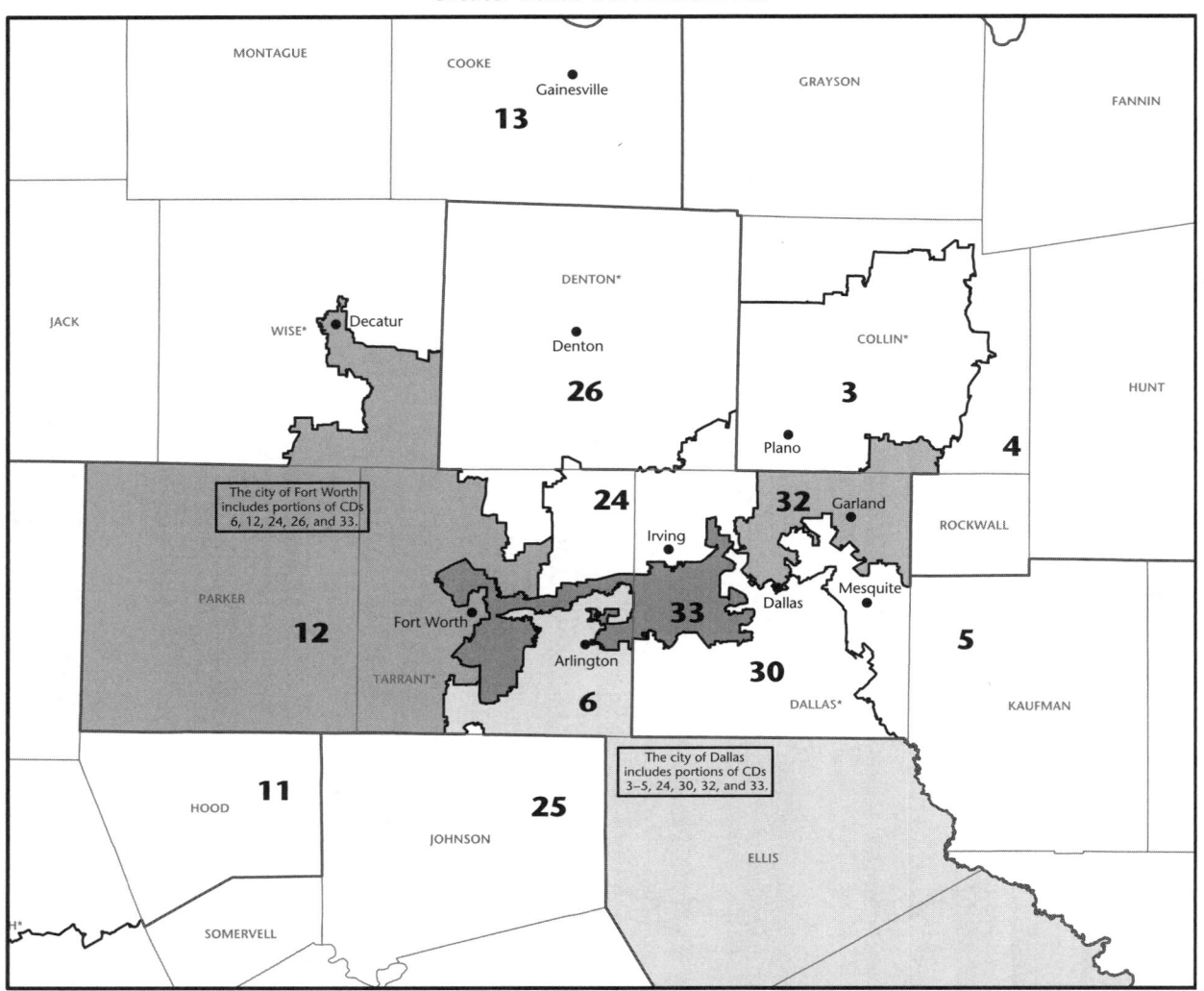

* Asterisk indicates a county whose boundaries include parts of two or more congressional districts.

TEXAS

Greater Houston Area

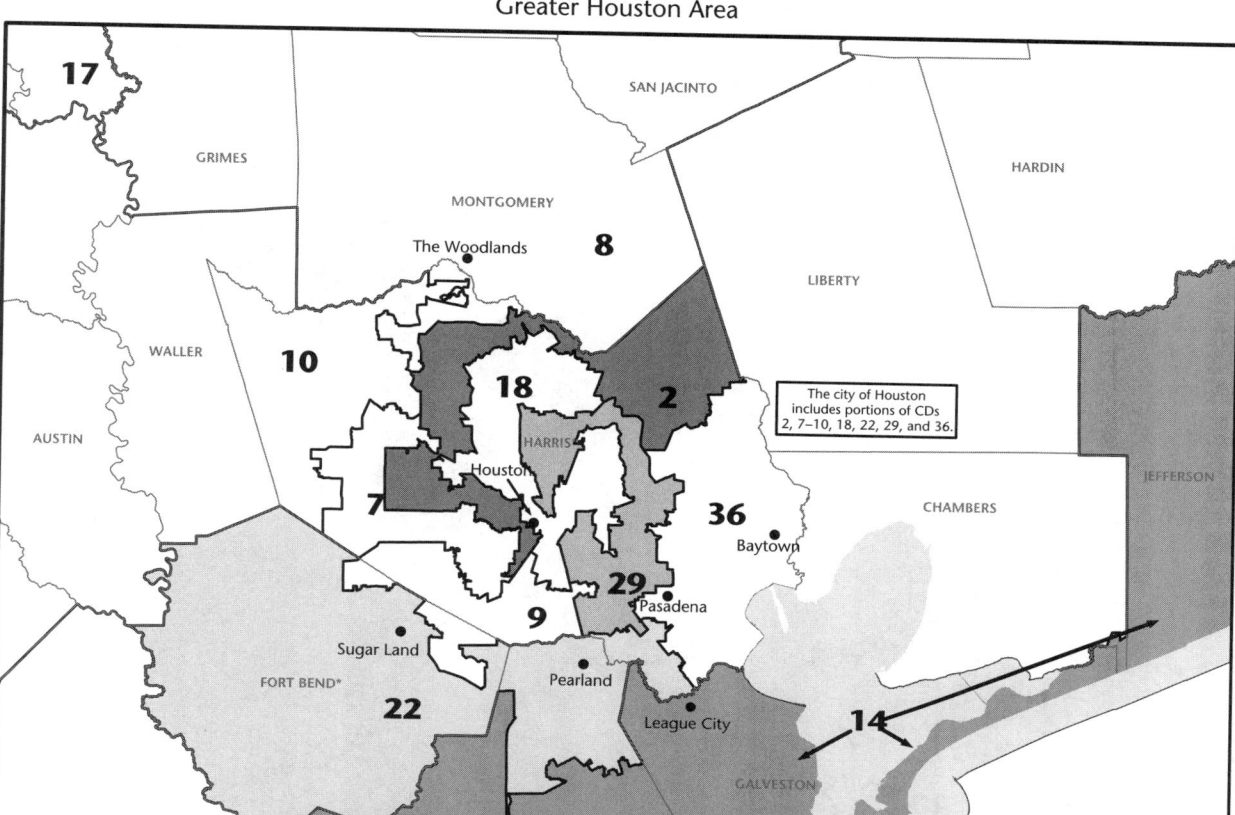

The city of Houston includes portions of CDs 2, 7–10, 18, 22, 29, and 36.

* Asterisk indicates a county whose boundaries include parts of two or more congressional districts.

TEXAS

Greater San Antonio, Austin Areas

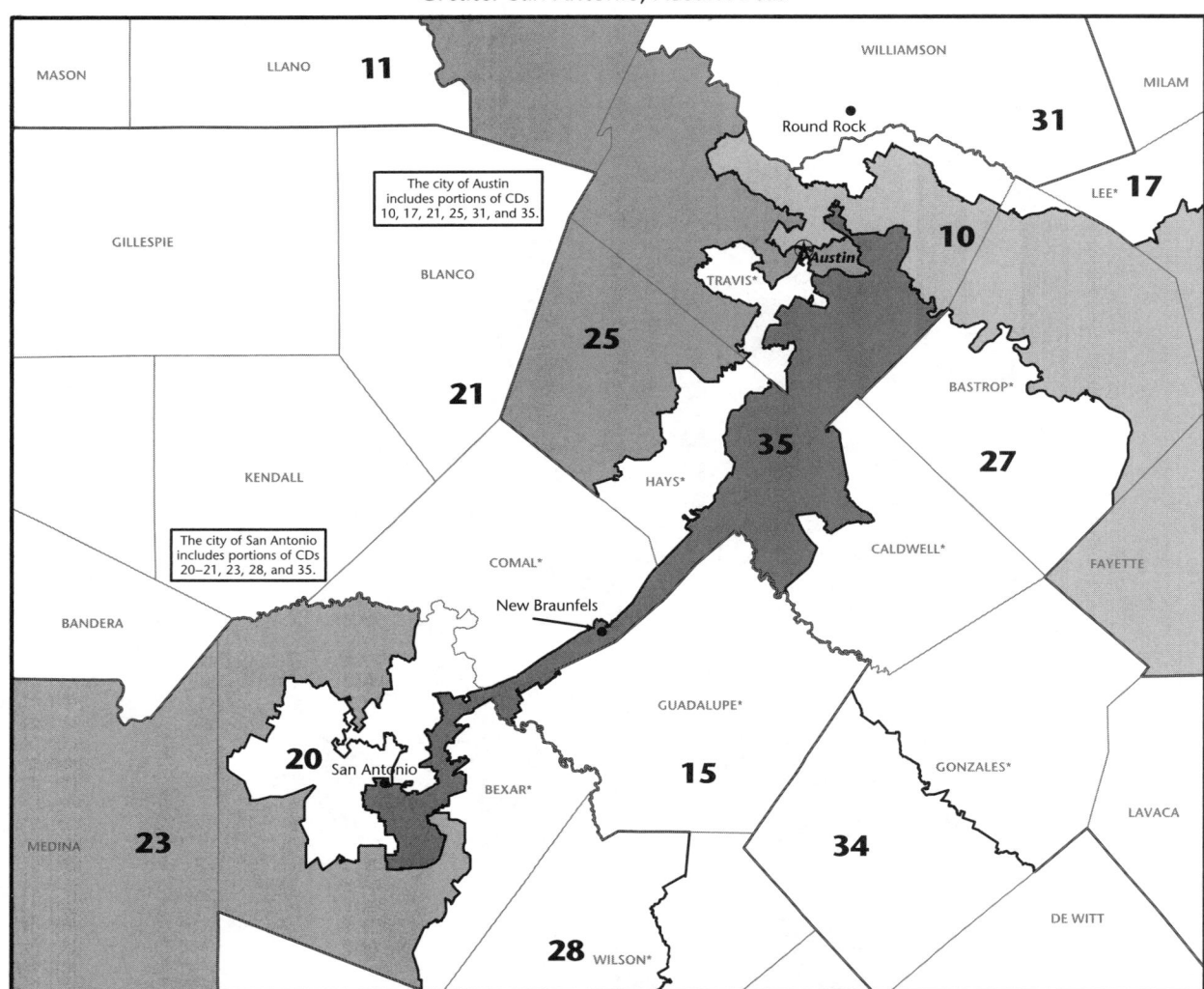

The city of Austin includes portions of CDs 10, 17, 21, 25, 31, and 35.

The city of San Antonio includes portions of CDs 20–21, 23, 28, and 35.

* Asterisk indicates a county whose boundaries include parts of two or more congressional districts.

TEXAS

GOVERNOR

Greg Abbott (R). Elected 2014 to a four-year term.

SENATORS (2 Republicans)

John Cornyn (R). Reelected 2014 to a six-year term. Previously elected 2008, 2002.

Ted Cruz (R). Elected 2012 to a six-year term.

REPRESENTATIVES (25 Republicans, 11 Democrats)

1. Louie Gohmert (R)
2. Ted Poe (R)
3. Sam Johnson (R)
4. John Ratcliffe (R)
5. Jeb Hensarling (R)
6. Joe Barton (R)
7. John Culberson (R)
8. Kevin Brady (R)
9. Al Green (D)
10. Michael T. McCaul (R)
11. K. Michael Conaway (R)
12. Kay Granger (R)
13. Mac Thornberry (R)
14. Randy K. Weber (R)
15. Rubén Hinojosa (D)
16. Beto O'Rourke (D)
17. Bill Flores (R)
18. Sheila Jackson Lee (D)
19. Randy Neugebauer (R)
20. Joaquin Castro (D)
21. Lamar Smith (R)
22. Pete Olson (R)
23. Will Hurd (R)
24. Kenny Marchant (R)
25. Roger Williams (R)
26. Michael C. Burgess (R)
27. Blake Farenthold (R)
28. Henry Cuellar (D)
29. Gene Green (D)
30. Eddie Bernice Johnson (D)
31. John R. Carter (R)
32. Pete Sessions (R)
33. Marc A. Veasey (D)
34. Filemon Vela (D)
35. Lloyd Doggett (D)
36. Brian Babin (R)

POSTWAR VOTE FOR PRESIDENT

Year	Total Vote	Republican Vote	Republican Candidate	Democratic Vote	Democratic Candidate	Other Vote	Rep.-Dem. Plurality	Total Vote Rep.	Total Vote Dem.	Major Vote Rep.	Major Vote Dem.
2012	7,993,851	4,569,843	Romney, W. Mitt	3,308,124	Obama, Barack H.*	115,884	1,261,719 R	57.2%	41.4%	58.0%	42.0%
2008	8,077,795	4,479,328	McCain, John S. III	3,528,633	Obama, Barack H.	69,834	950,695 R	55.5%	43.7%	55.9%	44.1%
2004	7,410,765	4,526,917	Bush, George W.*	2,832,704	Kerry, John F.	51,144	1,694,213 R	61.1%	38.2%	61.5%	38.5%
2000**	6,407,637	3,799,639	Bush, George W.	2,433,746	Gore, Albert Jr.	174,252	1,365,893 R	59.3%	38.0%	61.0%	39.0%
1996**	5,611,644	2,736,167	Dole, Robert "Bob"	2,459,683	Clinton, Bill*	415,794	276,484 R	48.8%	43.8%	52.7%	47.3%
1992**	6,154,018	2,496,071	Bush, George H.*	2,281,815	Clinton, Bill	1,376,132	214,256 R	40.6%	37.1%	52.2%	47.8%
1988	5,427,410	3,036,829	Bush, George H.	2,352,748	Dukakis, Michael S.	37,833	684,081 R	56.0%	43.3%	56.3%	43.7%
1984	5,397,571	3,433,428	Reagan, Ronald*	1,949,276	Mondale, Walter F.	14,867	1,484,152 R	63.6%	36.1%	63.8%	36.2%
1980**	4,541,636	2,510,705	Reagan, Ronald	1,881,147	Carter, Jimmy*	149,784	629,558 R	55.3%	41.4%	57.2%	42.8%
1976	4,071,884	1,953,300	Ford, Gerald R.*	2,082,319	Carter, Jimmy	36,265	129,019 D	48.0%	51.1%	48.4%	51.6%
1972	3,471,285	2,298,896	Nixon, Richard M.*	1,154,293	McGovern, George S.	18,096	1,144,603 R	66.2%	33.3%	66.6%	33.4%
1968**	3,079,216	1,227,844	Nixon, Richard M.	1,266,804	Humphrey, Hubert Horatio Jr.	584,568	38,960 D	39.9%	41.1%	49.2%	50.8%
1964	2,626,811	958,566	Goldwater, Barry M. Sr.	1,663,185	Johnson, Lyndon B.*	5,060	704,619 D	36.5%	63.3%	36.6%	63.4%
1960	2,311,084	1,121,310	Nixon, Richard M.	1,167,567	Kennedy, John F.	22,207	46,257 D	48.5%	50.5%	49.0%	51.0%
1956	1,955,168	1,080,619	Eisenhower, Dwight D.*	859,958	Stevenson, Adlai E. II	14,591	220,661 R	55.3%	44.0%	55.7%	44.3%
1952	2,075,946	1,102,878	Eisenhower, Dwight D.	969,228	Stevenson, Adlai E. II	3,840	133,650 R	53.1%	46.7%	53.2%	46.8%
1948**	1,249,577	303,467	Dewey, Thomas E.	824,235	Truman, Harry S.*	121,875	520,768 D	24.3%	66.0%	26.9%	73.1%

Note: An asterisk (*) denotes incumbent. **In past elections, the other vote included: 2000 - 137,994 Green (Ralph Nader); 1996 - 378,537 Reform (Ross Perot); 1992 - 1,354,781 Independent (Perot); 1980 - 111,613 Independent (John Anderson); 1968 - 584,269 American Independent (George Wallace); 1948 - 113,920 States' Rights (Strom Thurmond).

TEXAS

POSTWAR VOTE FOR GOVERNOR

Year	Total Vote	Republican		Democratic		Other Vote	Rep.-Dem. Plurality	Percentage			
								Total Vote		Major Vote	
		Vote	Candidate	Vote	Candidate			Rep.	Dem.	Rep.	Dem.
2014	4,718,268	2,796,547	Abbott, Greg	1,835,596	Davis, Wendy R.	86,125	960,951 R	59.3%	38.9%	60.4%	39.6%
2010	4,979,870	2,737,481	Perry, Rick*	2,106,395	White, Bill	135,994	631,086 R	55.0%	42.3%	56.5%	43.5%
2006**	4,399,116	1,716,792	Perry, Rick*	1,310,337	Bell, Chris	1,371,987	406,455 R	39.0%	29.8%	56.7%	43.3%
2002	4,553,987	2,632,591	Perry, Rick*	1,819,798	Sanchez, Tony	101,598	812,793 R	57.8%	40.0%	59.1%	40.9%
1998	3,738,483	2,551,454	Bush, George W.*	1,165,444	Mauro, Garry	21,585	1,386,010 R	68.2%	31.2%	68.6%	31.4%
1994	4,396,242	2,350,994	Bush, George W.	2,016,928	Richards, Ann*	28,320	334,066 R	53.5%	45.9%	53.8%	46.2%
1990	3,892,487	1,826,231	Williams, Clayton	1,925,670	Richards, Ann	140,586	99,439 D	46.9%	49.5%	48.7%	51.3%
1986	3,441,460	1,813,779	Clements, William P.	1,584,515	White, Mark*	43,166	229,264 R	52.7%	46.0%	53.4%	46.6%
1982	3,191,091	1,465,937	Clements, William P.*	1,697,870	White, Mark	27,284	231,933 D	45.9%	53.2%	46.3%	53.7%
1978	2,369,764	1,183,839	Clements, William P.	1,166,979	Hill, John	18,946	16,860 R	50.0%	49.2%	50.4%	49.6%
1974**	1,654,957	514,725	Granberry, Jim	1,016,334	Briscoe, Dolph*	123,898	501,609 D	31.1%	61.4%	33.6%	66.4%
1972	3,410,071	1,534,060	Grover, Henry C.	1,633,913	Briscoe, Dolph	242,098	99,853 D	45.0%	47.9%	48.4%	51.6%
1970	2,235,855	1,037,723	Eggers, Paul W.	1,197,736	Smith, Preston*	396	160,013 D	46.4%	53.6%	46.4%	53.6%
1968	2,916,508	1,254,331	Eggers, Paul W.	1,662,019	Smith, Preston	158	407,688 D	43.0%	57.0%	43.0%	57.0%
1966	1,425,861	368,025	Kennerly, T. E.	1,037,517	Connally, John B.*	20,319	669,492 D	25.8%	72.8%	26.2%	73.8%
1964	2,544,753	661,675	Crichton, Jack	1,877,793	Connally, John B.*	5,285	1,216,118 D	26.0%	73.8%	26.1%	73.9%
1962	1,569,181	715,025	Cox, Jack	847,036	Connally, John B.	7,120	132,011 D	45.6%	54.0%	45.8%	54.2%
1960	2,250,718	612,963	Steger, William	1,637,755	Daniel, Price*		1,024,792 D	27.2%	72.8%	27.2%	72.8%
1958	789,133	94,098	Mayer, Edwin S.	695,035	Daniel, Price*		600,937 D	11.9%	88.1%	11.9%	88.1%
1956	1,826,242	271,088	Bryant, William R.	1,433,051	Daniel, Price	122,103	1,161,963 D	14.8%	78.5%	15.9%	84.1%
1954	636,892	66,154	Adams, Tod R.	569,533	Shivers, Allan*	1,205	503,379 D	10.4%	89.4%	10.4%	89.6%
1952	1,890,535			1,853,863	Shivers, Allan*	36,672	1,853,863 D		98.1%		100.0%
1950	407,138	39,793	Currie, Ralph W.	367,345	Shivers, Allan*		327,552 D	9.8%	90.2%	9.8%	90.2%
1948	1,208,860	177,399	Lane, Alvin H.	1,024,160	Jester, Beauford H.*	7,301	846,761 D	14.7%	84.7%	14.8%	85.2%
1946	378,784	33,277	Nolte, Eugene Jr.	345,507	Jester, Beauford H.		312,230 D	8.8%	91.2%	8.8%	91.2%

Note: An asterisk (*) denotes incumbent. **In past elections, the other vote included: 2006 - 796,851 Independent (Carole Keeton Strayhorn); 547,674 Independent (Richard "Kinky" Friedman). The term of office of Texas's governor was increased from two to four years effective with the 1974 election. The Republican Party did not run a candidate in the 1952 gubernatorial election.

TEXAS

POSTWAR VOTE FOR SENATOR

Year	Total Vote	Republican Vote	Candidate	Democratic Vote	Candidate	Other Vote	Rep.-Dem. Plurality	Total Vote Rep.	Total Vote Dem.	Major Vote Rep.	Major Vote Dem.
2014	4,648,358	2,861,531	Cornyn, John*	1,597,387	Alameel, David	189,440	1,264,144 R	61.6%	34.4%	64.2%	35.8%
2012	7,864,822	4,440,137	Cruz, Ted	3,194,927	Sadler, Paul	229,758	1,245,210 R	56.5%	40.6%	58.2%	41.8%
2008	7,912,075	4,337,469	Cornyn, John*	3,389,365	Noriega, Richard J. "Rick"	185,241	948,104 R	54.8%	42.8%	56.1%	43.9%
2006	4,314,663	2,661,789	Hutchison, Kay Bailey*	1,555,202	Radnofsky, Barbara Ann	97,672	1,106,587 R	61.7%	36.0%	63.1%	36.9%
2002	4,514,012	2,496,243	Cornyn, John	1,955,758	Kirk, Ron	62,011	540,485 R	55.3%	43.3%	56.1%	43.9%
2000	6,276,652	4,082,091	Hutchison, Kay Bailey*	2,030,315	Kelly, Gene	164,246	2,051,776 R	65.0%	32.3%	66.8%	33.2%
1996	5,527,441	3,027,680	Gramm, W. Phil*	2,428,776	Morales, Victor M.	70,985	598,904 R	54.8%	43.9%	55.5%	44.5%
1994	4,279,940	2,604,218	Hutchison, Kay Bailey*	1,639,615	Mattox, Jim	36,107	964,603 R	60.8%	38.3%	61.4%	38.6%
1993S	1,765,254	1,188,716	Hutchison, Kay Bailey	576,538	Krueger, Robert*		612,178 R	67.3%	32.7%	67.3%	32.7%
1990	3,822,157	2,302,357	Gramm, W. Phil*	1,429,986	Parmer, Hugh	89,814	872,371 R	60.2%	37.4%	61.7%	38.3%
1988	5,323,606	2,129,228	Boulter, E. Beau	3,149,806	Bentsen, Lloyd M. Jr.*	44,572	1,020,578 D	40.0%	59.2%	40.3%	59.7%
1984	5,319,178	3,116,348	Gramm, W. Phil	2,202,557	Doggett, Lloyd	273	913,791 R	58.6%	41.4%	58.6%	41.4%
1982	3,103,167	1,256,759	Collins, James M.	1,818,223	Bentsen, Lloyd M. Jr.*	28,185	561,464 D	40.5%	58.6%	40.9%	59.1%
1978	2,312,540	1,151,376	Tower, John G.*	1,139,149	Krueger, Robert	22,015	12,227 R	49.8%	49.3%	50.3%	49.7%
1976	3,874,516	1,636,370	Steelman, Alan	2,199,956	Bentsen, Lloyd M. Jr.*	38,190	563,586 D	42.2%	56.8%	42.7%	57.3%
1972	3,413,918	1,822,877	Tower, John G.*	1,511,985	Sanders, Barefoot	79,056	310,892 R	53.4%	44.3%	54.7%	45.3%
1970	2,231,671	1,035,794	Bush, George H.	1,194,069	Bentsen, Lloyd M. Jr.	1,808	158,275 D	46.4%	53.5%	46.5%	53.5%
1966	1,493,182	842,501	Tower, John G.*	643,855	Carr, Waggoner	6,826	198,646 R	56.4%	43.1%	56.7%	43.3%
1964	2,603,856	1,134,337	Bush, George H.	1,463,958	Yarborough, Ralph*	5,561	329,621 D	43.6%	56.2%	43.7%	56.3%
1961S	886,091	448,217	Tower, John G.	437,874	Blakley, William A.*		10,343 R	50.6%	49.4%	50.6%	49.4%
1960	2,253,764	926,653	Tower, John G.	1,306,605	Johnson, Lyndon B.*	20,506	379,952 D	41.1%	58.0%	41.5%	58.5%
1958	787,128	185,926	Whittenburg, Roy	587,030	Yarborough, Ralph*	14,172	401,104 D	23.6%	74.6%	24.1%	75.9%
1957S	957,298				Ralph, Yarborough	875,338	D				
1954	636,475	94,131	Watson, Carlos G.	539,319	Johnson, Lyndon B.*	3,025	445,188 D	14.8%	84.7%	14.9%	85.1%
1952	1,894,671			1,894,671	Daniel, Price		1,894,671 D		100.0%		100.0%
1948	1,061,363	349,665	Porter, Jack	702,785	Johnson, Lyndon B.	8,913	353,120 D	32.9%	66.2%	33.2%	66.8%
1946	380,550	43,619	Sells, Murray C.	336,931	Connally, Tom T.*		293,312 D	11.5%	88.5%	11.5%	88.5%

Note: An asterisk (*) denotes incumbent. **The June 1993 election was for a short term to fill a vacancy; the vote above was for the special election runoff. The April 1957 and May 1961 elections were also for short terms to fill vacancies. Although neither vote was held with official party designations, the 1961 vote above reflected the result of a runoff between unofficial party candidates. In 1957 there was a single ballot without a runoff and Democrat Ralph Yarborough polled 364,605 votes (38.1 percent of the total vote) and won the election with a 73,802-vote plurality over Democrat Martin Dies. The Republican Party did not run a candidate in the 1952 Senate election.

TEXAS

GOVERNOR 2014

2010 Census Population	County	Total Vote	Republican (Abbott)	Democratic (Davis)	Other	Rep.-Dem. Plurality	Total Vote Rep.	Total Vote Dem.	Major Vote Rep.	Major Vote Dem.
58,458	ANDERSON	10,213	7,732	2,286	195	5,446 R	75.7%	22.4%	77.2%	22.8%
14,786	ANDREWS	2,221	1,988	203	30	1,785 R	89.5%	9.1%	90.7%	9.3%
86,771	ANGELINA	16,802	12,940	3,686	176	9,254 R	77.0%	21.9%	77.8%	22.2%
23,158	ARANSAS	6,070	4,460	1,480	130	2,980 R	73.5%	24.4%	75.1%	24.9%
9,054	ARCHER	2,636	2,297	302	37	1,995 R	87.1%	11.5%	88.4%	11.6%
1,901	ARMSTRONG	571	502	59	10	443 R	87.9%	10.3%	89.5%	10.5%
44,911	ATASCOSA	7,465	4,760	2,589	116	2,171 R	63.8%	34.7%	64.8%	35.2%
28,417	AUSTIN	7,182	5,813	1,252	117	4,561 R	80.9%	17.4%	82.3%	17.7%
7,165	BAILEY	1,004	868	130	6	738 R	86.5%	12.9%	87.0%	13.0%
20,485	BANDERA	6,346	4,911	1,257	178	3,654 R	77.4%	19.8%	79.6%	20.4%
74,171	BASTROP	16,961	9,803	6,566	592	3,237 R	57.8%	38.7%	59.9%	40.1%
3,726	BAYLOR	844	700	134	10	566 R	82.9%	15.9%	83.9%	16.1%
31,861	BEE	5,226	2,972	2,128	126	844 R	56.9%	40.7%	58.3%	41.7%
310,235	BELL	43,983	28,778	14,412	793	14,366 R	65.4%	32.8%	66.6%	33.4%
1,714,773	BEXAR	300,950	149,697	145,711	5,542	3,986 R	49.7%	48.4%	50.7%	49.3%
10,497	BLANCO	3,608	2,622	874	112	1,748 R	72.7%	24.2%	75.0%	25.0%
641	BORDEN	260	240	18	2	222 R	92.3%	6.9%	93.0%	7.0%
18,212	BOSQUE	4,908	3,881	933	94	2,948 R	79.1%	19.0%	80.6%	19.4%
92,565	BOWIE	21,532	15,583	5,564	385	10,019 R	72.4%	25.8%	73.7%	26.3%
313,166	BRAZORIA	62,280	41,373	19,703	1,204	21,670 R	66.4%	31.6%	67.7%	32.3%
194,851	BRAZOS	31,608	21,859	9,125	624	12,734 R	69.2%	28.9%	70.5%	29.5%
9,232	BREWSTER	2,908	1,499	1,311	98	188 R	51.5%	45.1%	53.3%	46.7%
1,637	BRISCOE	510	431	75	4	356 R	84.5%	14.7%	85.2%	14.8%
7,223	BROOKS	2,146	588	1,478	80	890 D	27.4%	68.9%	28.5%	71.5%
38,106	BROWN	8,201	7,176	901	124	6,275 R	87.5%	11.0%	88.8%	11.2%
17,187	BURLESON	4,208	3,199	959	50	2,240 R	76.0%	22.8%	76.9%	23.1%
42,750	BURNET	11,883	8,995	2,571	317	6,424 R	75.7%	21.6%	77.8%	22.2%
38,066	CALDWELL	8,906	5,037	3,578	291	1,459 R	56.6%	40.2%	58.5%	41.5%
21,381	CALHOUN	4,155	2,737	1,326	92	1,411 R	65.9%	31.9%	67.4%	32.6%
13,544	CALLAHAN	2,969	2,636	285	48	2,351 R	88.8%	9.6%	90.2%	9.8%
406,220	CAMERON	39,407	16,556	21,859	992	5,303 D	42.0%	55.5%	43.1%	56.9%
12,401	CAMP	2,613	1,862	718	33	1,144 R	71.3%	27.5%	72.2%	27.8%
6,182	CARSON	1,857	1,634	193	30	1,441 R	88.0%	10.4%	89.4%	10.6%
30,464	CASS	6,947	5,185	1,687	75	3,498 R	74.6%	24.3%	75.5%	24.5%
8,062	CASTRO	1,152	917	217	18	700 R	79.6%	18.8%	80.9%	19.1%
35,096	CHAMBERS	8,415	6,778	1,490	147	5,288 R	80.5%	17.7%	82.0%	18.0%
50,845	CHEROKEE	9,688	7,709	1,862	117	5,847 R	79.6%	19.2%	80.5%	19.5%
7,041	CHILDRESS	1,095	944	134	17	810 R	86.2%	12.2%	87.6%	12.4%
10,752	CLAY	2,842	2,436	363	43	2,073 R	85.7%	12.8%	87.0%	13.0%
3,127	COCHRAN	495	423	65	7	358 R	85.5%	13.1%	86.7%	13.3%
3,320	COKE	770	696	67	7	629 R	90.4%	8.7%	91.2%	8.8%
8,895	COLEMAN	2,240	1,974	234	32	1,740 R	88.1%	10.4%	89.4%	10.6%
782,341	COLLIN	177,131	116,365	57,757	3,009	58,608 R	65.7%	32.6%	66.8%	33.2%
3,057	COLLINGSWORTH	802	651	132	19	519 R	81.2%	16.5%	83.1%	16.9%
20,874	COLORADO	5,157	3,881	1,192	84	2,689 R	75.3%	23.1%	76.5%	23.5%
108,472	COMAL	34,720	26,642	7,428	650	19,214 R	76.7%	21.4%	78.2%	21.8%
13,974	COMANCHE	3,069	2,447	544	78	1,903 R	79.7%	17.7%	81.8%	18.2%
4,087	CONCHO	598	511	77	10	434 R	85.5%	12.9%	86.9%	13.1%
38,437	COOKE	8,819	7,402	1,273	144	6,129 R	83.9%	14.4%	85.3%	14.7%
75,388	CORYELL	8,685	6,465	2,017	203	4,448 R	74.4%	23.2%	76.2%	23.8%
1,505	COTTLE	362	310	48	4	262 R	85.6%	13.3%	86.6%	13.4%
4,375	CRANE	851	713	127	11	586 R	83.8%	14.9%	84.9%	15.1%
3,719	CROCKETT	835	624	203	8	421 R	74.7%	24.3%	75.5%	24.5%
6,059	CROSBY	1,072	813	239	20	574 R	75.8%	22.3%	77.3%	22.7%
2,398	CULBERSON	328	172	146	10	26 R	52.4%	44.5%	54.1%	45.9%
6,703	DALLAM	844	727	100	17	627 R	86.1%	11.8%	87.9%	12.1%
2,368,139	DALLAS	407,260	178,273	223,136	5,851	44,863 D	43.8%	54.8%	44.4%	55.6%
13,833	DAWSON	2,044	1,687	335	22	1,352 R	82.5%	16.4%	83.4%	16.6%
20,097	DE WITT	4,018	3,269	695	54	2,574 R	81.4%	17.3%	82.5%	17.5%
19,372	DEAF SMITH	2,728	2,182	503	43	1,679 R	80.0%	18.4%	81.3%	18.7%

TEXAS

GOVERNOR 2014

2010 Census Population	County	Total Vote	Republican (Abbott)	Democratic (Davis)	Other	Rep.-Dem. Plurality		Percentage			
								Total Vote		Major Vote	
								Rep.	Dem.	Rep.	Dem.
5,231	DELTA	1,378	984	351	43	633	R	71.4%	25.5%	73.7%	26.3%
662,614	DENTON	144,010	93,683	47,238	3,089	46,445	R	65.1%	32.8%	66.5%	33.5%
2,444	DICKENS	517	452	60	5	392	R	87.4%	11.6%	88.3%	11.7%
9,996	DIMMIT	1,877	599	1,245	33	646	D	31.9%	66.3%	32.5%	67.5%
3,677	DONLEY	943	803	120	20	683	R	85.2%	12.7%	87.0%	13.0%
11,782	DUVAL	3,084	750	2,251	83	1,501	D	24.3%	73.0%	25.0%	75.0%
18,583	EASTLAND	3,931	3,503	372	56	3,131	R	89.1%	9.5%	90.4%	9.6%
137,130	ECTOR	14,827	12,139	2,478	210	9,661	R	81.9%	16.7%	83.0%	17.0%
2,002	EDWARDS	786	540	222	24	318	R	68.7%	28.2%	70.9%	29.1%
800,647	EL PASO	80,408	29,953	48,506	1,949	18,553	D	37.3%	60.3%	38.2%	61.8%
149,610	ELLIS	32,175	23,604	7,963	608	15,641	R	73.4%	24.7%	74.8%	25.2%
37,890	ERATH	7,393	5,953	1,301	139	4,652	R	80.5%	17.6%	82.1%	17.9%
17,866	FALLS	3,064	2,147	877	40	1,270	R	70.1%	28.6%	71.0%	29.0%
33,915	FANNIN	6,490	4,897	1,449	144	3,448	R	75.5%	22.3%	77.2%	22.8%
24,554	FAYETTE	7,540	5,885	1,547	108	4,338	R	78.1%	20.5%	79.2%	20.8%
3,974	FISHER	1,245	891	334	20	557	R	71.6%	26.8%	72.7%	27.3%
6,446	FLOYD	1,095	955	133	7	822	R	87.2%	12.1%	87.8%	12.2%
1,336	FOARD	310	205	102	3	103	R	66.1%	32.9%	66.8%	33.2%
585,375	FORT BEND	132,468	73,749	56,825	1,894	16,924	R	55.7%	42.9%	56.5%	43.5%
10,605	FRANKLIN	2,594	2,197	353	44	1,844	R	84.7%	13.6%	86.2%	13.8%
19,816	FREESTONE	4,450	3,473	902	75	2,571	R	78.0%	20.3%	79.4%	20.6%
17,217	FRIO	1,843	863	953	27	90	D	46.8%	51.7%	47.5%	52.5%
17,526	GAINES	2,512	2,235	235	42	2,000	R	89.0%	9.4%	90.5%	9.5%
291,309	GALVESTON	64,854	40,422	23,201	1,231	17,221	R	62.3%	35.8%	63.5%	36.5%
6,461	GARZA	840	752	80	8	672	R	89.5%	9.5%	90.4%	9.6%
24,837	GILLESPIE	8,848	7,168	1,502	178	5,666	R	81.0%	17.0%	82.7%	17.3%
1,226	GLASSCOCK	400	377	15	8	362	R	94.2%	3.8%	96.2%	3.8%
7,210	GOLIAD	2,788	1,873	873	42	1,000	R	67.2%	31.3%	68.2%	31.8%
19,807	GONZALES	3,712	2,789	840	83	1,949	R	75.1%	22.6%	76.9%	23.1%
22,535	GRAY	3,725	3,358	302	65	3,056	R	90.1%	8.1%	91.7%	8.3%
120,877	GRAYSON	23,509	18,103	5,067	339	13,036	R	77.0%	21.6%	78.1%	21.9%
121,730	GREGG	23,240	17,210	5,808	222	11,402	R	74.1%	25.0%	74.8%	25.2%
26,604	GRIMES	4,955	3,716	1,125	114	2,591	R	75.0%	22.7%	76.8%	23.2%
131,533	GUADALUPE	30,579	21,235	8,788	556	12,447	R	69.4%	28.7%	70.7%	29.3%
36,273	HALE	4,320	3,703	567	50	3,136	R	85.7%	13.1%	86.7%	13.3%
3,353	HALL	570	485	74	11	411	R	85.1%	13.0%	86.8%	13.2%
8,517	HAMILTON	2,430	1,891	491	48	1,400	R	77.8%	20.2%	79.4%	20.6%
5,613	HANSFORD	1,176	1,105	55	16	1,050	R	94.0%	4.7%	95.3%	4.7%
4,139	HARDEMAN	666	523	130	13	393	R	78.5%	19.5%	80.1%	19.9%
54,635	HARDIN	11,576	9,923	1,494	159	8,429	R	85.7%	12.9%	86.9%	13.1%
4,092,459	HARRIS	680,076	349,639	320,160	10,277	29,479	R	51.4%	47.1%	52.2%	47.8%
65,631	HARRISON	14,660	10,384	4,086	190	6,298	R	70.8%	27.9%	71.8%	28.2%
6,062	HARTLEY	1,108	1,006	87	15	919	R	90.8%	7.9%	92.0%	8.0%
5,899	HASKELL	1,065	821	230	14	591	R	77.1%	21.6%	78.1%	21.9%
157,107	HAYS	39,331	21,002	17,300	1,029	3,702	R	53.4%	44.0%	54.8%	45.2%
3,807	HEMPHILL	830	715	100	15	615	R	86.1%	12.0%	87.7%	12.3%
78,532	HENDERSON	17,125	13,118	3,689	318	9,429	R	76.6%	21.5%	78.1%	21.9%
774,769	HIDALGO	80,219	27,909	50,303	2,007	22,394	D	34.8%	62.7%	35.7%	64.3%
35,089	HILL	8,919	6,855	1,887	177	4,968	R	76.9%	21.2%	78.4%	21.6%
22,935	HOCKLEY	3,697	3,222	425	50	2,797	R	87.2%	11.5%	88.3%	11.7%
51,182	HOOD	13,639	10,784	2,577	278	8,207	R	79.1%	18.9%	80.7%	19.3%
35,161	HOPKINS	7,637	5,745	1,759	133	3,986	R	75.2%	23.0%	76.6%	23.4%
23,732	HOUSTON	4,650	3,696	901	53	2,795	R	79.5%	19.4%	80.4%	19.6%
35,012	HOWARD	4,279	3,492	664	123	2,828	R	81.6%	15.5%	84.0%	16.0%
3,476	HUDSPETH	437	267	151	19	116	R	61.1%	34.6%	63.9%	36.1%
86,129	HUNT	16,324	12,294	3,688	342	8,606	R	75.3%	22.6%	76.9%	23.1%
22,150	HUTCHINSON	4,494	3,956	462	76	3,494	R	88.0%	10.3%	89.5%	10.5%
1,599	IRION	435	383	43	9	340	R	88.0%	9.9%	89.9%	10.1%
9,044	JACK	1,727	1,473	225	29	1,248	R	85.3%	13.0%	86.7%	13.3%
14,075	JACKSON	2,945	2,420	488	37	1,932	R	82.2%	16.6%	83.2%	16.8%

TEXAS

GOVERNOR 2014

2010 Census Population	County	Total Vote	Republican (Abbott)	Democratic (Davis)	Other	Rep.-Dem. Plurality	Percentage Total Vote Rep.	Dem.	Major Vote Rep.	Dem.
35,710	JASPER	7,135	5,644	1,415	76	4,229 R	79.1%	19.8%	80.0%	20.0%
2,342	JEFF DAVIS	1,029	623	366	40	257 R	60.5%	35.6%	63.0%	37.0%
252,273	JEFFERSON	53,215	26,876	25,799	540	1,077 R	50.5%	48.5%	51.0%	49.0%
5,300	JIM HOGG	720	190	521	9	331 D	26.4%	72.4%	26.7%	73.3%
40,838	JIM WELLS	5,711	2,589	3,016	106	427 D	45.3%	52.8%	46.2%	53.8%
150,934	JOHNSON	29,272	22,715	5,978	579	16,737 R	77.6%	20.4%	79.2%	20.8%
20,202	JONES	3,341	2,745	534	62	2,211 R	82.2%	16.0%	83.7%	16.3%
14,824	KARNES	2,521	1,770	715	36	1,055 R	70.2%	28.4%	71.2%	28.8%
103,350	KAUFMAN	20,353	14,590	5,449	314	9,141 R	71.7%	26.8%	72.8%	27.2%
33,410	KENDALL	11,875	9,713	1,989	173	7,724 R	81.8%	16.7%	83.0%	17.0%
416	KENEDY	125	64	59	2	5 R	51.2%	47.2%	52.0%	48.0%
808	KENT	310	251	49	10	202 R	81.0%	15.8%	83.7%	16.3%
49,625	KERR	14,933	11,740	2,901	292	8,839 R	78.6%	19.4%	80.2%	19.8%
4,607	KIMBLE	1,224	1,096	113	15	983 R	89.5%	9.2%	90.7%	9.3%
286	KING	93	90	1	2	89 R	96.8%	1.1%	98.9%	1.1%
3,598	KINNEY	1,148	747	375	26	372 R	65.1%	32.7%	66.6%	33.4%
32,061	KLEBERG	5,759	2,836	2,804	119	32 R	49.2%	48.7%	50.3%	49.7%
3,719	KNOX	899	726	159	14	567 R	80.8%	17.7%	82.0%	18.0%
6,886	LA SALLE	865	434	422	9	12 R	50.2%	48.8%	50.7%	49.3%
49,793	LAMAR	10,899	7,785	2,869	245	4,916 R	71.4%	26.3%	73.1%	26.9%
13,977	LAMB	2,112	1,841	251	20	1,590 R	87.2%	11.9%	88.0%	12.0%
19,677	LAMPASAS	4,628	3,745	787	96	2,958 R	80.9%	17.0%	82.6%	17.4%
19,263	LAVACA	5,026	4,180	784	62	3,396 R	83.2%	15.6%	84.2%	15.8%
16,612	LEE	4,284	3,199	963	122	2,236 R	74.7%	22.5%	76.9%	23.1%
16,801	LEON	4,251	3,694	511	46	3,183 R	86.9%	12.0%	87.8%	12.2%
75,643	LIBERTY	12,502	9,576	2,681	245	6,895 R	76.6%	21.4%	78.1%	21.9%
23,384	LIMESTONE	4,306	3,278	979	49	2,299 R	76.1%	22.7%	77.0%	23.0%
3,302	LIPSCOMB	853	740	93	20	647 R	86.8%	10.9%	88.8%	11.2%
11,531	LIVE OAK	2,455	2,007	400	48	1,607 R	81.8%	16.3%	83.4%	16.6%
19,301	LLANO	7,053	5,552	1,363	138	4,189 R	78.7%	19.3%	80.3%	19.7%
82	LOVING	41	35	4	2	31 R	85.4%	9.8%	89.7%	10.3%
278,831	LUBBOCK	47,193	36,038	10,438	717	25,600 R	76.4%	22.1%	77.5%	22.5%
5,915	LYNN	1,209	1,013	180	16	833 R	83.8%	14.9%	84.9%	15.1%
13,664	MADISON	2,429	1,941	462	26	1,479 R	79.9%	19.0%	80.8%	19.2%
10,546	MARION	2,213	1,480	705	28	775 R	66.9%	31.9%	67.7%	32.3%
4,799	MARTIN	1,155	1,016	116	23	900 R	88.0%	10.0%	89.8%	10.2%
4,012	MASON	1,371	1,104	243	24	861 R	80.5%	17.7%	82.0%	18.0%
36,702	MATAGORDA	6,952	4,691	2,115	146	2,576 R	67.5%	30.4%	68.9%	31.1%
54,258	MAVERICK	5,298	1,392	3,723	183	2,331 D	26.3%	70.3%	27.2%	72.8%
8,283	MCCULLOCH	1,748	1,456	258	34	1,198 R	83.3%	14.8%	84.9%	15.1%
234,906	MCLENNAN	44,298	30,507	13,092	699	17,415 R	68.9%	29.6%	70.0%	30.0%
707	MCMULLEN	263	222	34	7	188 R	84.4%	12.9%	86.7%	13.3%
46,006	MEDINA	9,853	7,194	2,506	153	4,688 R	73.0%	25.4%	74.2%	25.8%
2,242	MENARD	482	411	65	6	346 R	85.3%	13.5%	86.3%	13.7%
136,872	MIDLAND	23,577	20,204	3,012	361	17,192 R	85.7%	12.8%	87.0%	13.0%
24,757	MILAM	4,964	3,576	1,293	95	2,283 R	72.0%	26.0%	73.4%	26.6%
4,936	MILLS	1,353	1,194	134	25	1,060 R	88.2%	9.9%	89.9%	10.1%
9,403	MITCHELL	1,211	1,020	176	15	844 R	84.2%	14.5%	85.3%	14.7%
19,719	MONTAGUE	6,743	5,691	916	136	4,775 R	84.4%	13.6%	86.1%	13.9%
455,746	MONTGOMERY	104,895	83,938	19,179	1,778	64,759 R	80.0%	18.3%	81.4%	18.6%
21,904	MOORE	2,766	2,421	301	44	2,120 R	87.5%	10.9%	88.9%	11.1%
12,934	MORRIS	3,108	2,033	1,031	44	1,002 R	65.4%	33.2%	66.4%	33.6%
1,210	MOTLEY	372	344	20	8	324 R	92.5%	5.4%	94.5%	5.5%
64,524	NACOGDOCHES	12,042	9,021	2,845	176	6,176 R	74.9%	23.6%	76.0%	24.0%
47,735	NAVARRO	9,532	6,983	2,376	173	4,607 R	73.3%	24.9%	74.6%	25.4%
14,445	NEWTON	2,905	2,161	703	41	1,458 R	74.4%	24.2%	75.5%	24.5%
15,216	NOLAN	2,645	2,117	474	54	1,643 R	80.0%	17.9%	81.7%	18.3%
340,223	NUECES	57,005	30,854	24,746	1,405	6,108 R	54.1%	43.4%	55.5%	44.5%
10,223	OCHILTREE	1,590	1,500	70	20	1,430 R	94.3%	4.4%	95.5%	4.5%
2,052	OLDHAM	559	519	33	7	486 R	92.8%	5.9%	94.0%	6.0%

TEXAS
GOVERNOR 2014

2010 Census Population	County	Total Vote	Republican (Abbott)	Democratic (Davis)	Other	Rep.-Dem. Plurality	Percentage Total Vote Rep.	Dem.	Major Vote Rep.	Dem.
81,837	ORANGE	17,266	13,400	3,600	266	9,800 R	77.6%	20.9%	78.8%	21.2%
28,111	PALO PINTO	5,671	4,410	1,141	120	3,269 R	77.8%	20.1%	79.4%	20.6%
23,796	PANOLA	5,752	4,614	1,069	69	3,545 R	80.2%	18.6%	81.2%	18.8%
116,927	PARKER	31,859	25,683	5,540	636	20,143 R	80.6%	17.4%	82.3%	17.7%
10,269	PARMER	1,400	1,234	153	13	1,081 R	88.1%	10.9%	89.0%	11.0%
15,507	PECOS	3,031	2,146	817	68	1,329 R	70.8%	27.0%	72.4%	27.6%
45,413	POLK	10,496	7,858	2,410	228	5,448 R	74.9%	23.0%	76.5%	23.5%
121,073	POTTER	13,755	10,584	2,925	246	7,659 R	76.9%	21.3%	78.3%	21.7%
7,818	PRESIDIO	1,004	364	613	27	249 D	36.3%	61.1%	37.3%	62.7%
10,914	RAINS	2,451	1,976	440	35	1,536 R	80.6%	18.0%	81.8%	18.2%
120,725	RANDALL	28,217	24,134	3,650	433	20,484 R	85.5%	12.9%	86.9%	13.1%
3,367	REAGAN	506	425	68	13	357 R	84.0%	13.4%	86.2%	13.8%
3,309	REAL	1,055	862	175	18	687 R	81.7%	16.6%	83.1%	16.9%
12,860	RED RIVER	2,768	1,993	730	45	1,263 R	72.0%	26.4%	73.2%	26.8%
13,783	REEVES	1,222	695	510	17	185 R	56.9%	41.7%	57.7%	42.3%
7,383	REFUGIO	2,040	1,238	750	52	488 R	60.7%	36.8%	62.3%	37.7%
929	ROBERTS	345	324	15	6	309 R	93.9%	4.3%	95.6%	4.4%
16,622	ROBERTSON	5,105	3,270	1,768	67	1,502 R	64.1%	34.6%	64.9%	35.1%
78,337	ROCKWALL	21,086	16,100	4,670	316	11,430 R	76.4%	22.1%	77.5%	22.5%
10,501	RUNNELS	2,312	2,057	230	25	1,827 R	89.0%	9.9%	89.9%	10.1%
53,330	RUSK	10,528	8,517	1,906	105	6,611 R	80.9%	18.1%	81.7%	18.3%
10,834	SABINE	2,762	2,372	355	35	2,017 R	85.9%	12.9%	87.0%	13.0%
8,865	SAN AUGUSTINE	2,724	1,920	756	48	1,164 R	70.5%	27.8%	71.7%	28.3%
26,384	SAN JACINTO	6,434	4,641	1,632	161	3,009 R	72.1%	25.4%	74.0%	26.0%
64,804	SAN PATRICIO	11,531	7,202	4,071	258	3,131 R	62.5%	35.3%	63.9%	36.1%
6,131	SAN SABA	1,445	1,280	145	20	1,135 R	88.6%	10.0%	89.8%	10.2%
3,461	SCHLEICHER	859	635	213	11	422 R	73.9%	24.8%	74.9%	25.1%
16,921	SCURRY	2,862	2,518	298	46	2,220 R	88.0%	10.4%	89.4%	10.6%
3,378	SHACKELFORD	810	751	50	9	701 R	92.7%	6.2%	93.8%	6.2%
25,448	SHELBY	5,504	4,330	1,116	58	3,214 R	78.7%	20.3%	79.5%	20.5%
3,034	SHERMAN	600	538	52	10	486 R	89.7%	8.7%	91.2%	8.8%
209,714	SMITH	48,834	37,360	10,846	628	26,514 R	76.5%	22.2%	77.5%	22.5%
8,490	SOMERVELL	2,245	1,796	405	44	1,391 R	80.0%	18.0%	81.6%	18.4%
60,968	STARR	5,185	1,104	4,008	73	2,904 D	21.3%	77.3%	21.6%	78.4%
9,630	STEPHENS	1,935	1,737	169	29	1,568 R	89.8%	8.7%	91.1%	8.9%
1,143	STERLING	470	429	33	8	396 R	91.3%	7.0%	92.9%	7.1%
1,490	STONEWALL	381	297	76	8	221 R	78.0%	19.9%	79.6%	20.4%
4,128	SUTTON	743	619	113	11	506 R	83.3%	15.2%	84.6%	15.4%
7,854	SWISHER	1,424	1,029	362	33	667 R	72.3%	25.4%	74.0%	26.0%
1,809,034	TARRANT	372,973	213,120	153,214	6,639	59,906 R	57.1%	41.1%	58.2%	41.8%
131,506	TAYLOR	23,401	19,100	3,876	425	15,224 R	81.6%	16.6%	83.1%	16.9%
984	TERRELL	398	273	108	17	165 R	68.6%	27.1%	71.7%	28.3%
12,651	TERRY	2,293	1,896	366	31	1,530 R	82.7%	16.0%	83.8%	16.2%
1,641	THROCKMORTON	535	456	66	13	390 R	85.2%	12.3%	87.4%	12.6%
32,334	TITUS	5,162	3,802	1,288	72	2,514 R	73.7%	25.0%	74.7%	25.3%
110,224	TOM GREEN	18,533	14,670	3,559	304	11,111 R	79.2%	19.2%	80.5%	19.5%
1,024,266	TRAVIS	267,795	91,301	169,141	7,353	77,840 D	34.1%	63.2%	35.1%	64.9%
14,585	TRINITY	3,930	2,837	996	97	1,841 R	72.2%	25.3%	74.0%	26.0%
21,766	TYLER	4,769	3,788	885	96	2,903 R	79.4%	18.6%	81.1%	18.9%
39,309	UPSHUR	8,848	7,294	1,426	128	5,868 R	82.4%	16.1%	83.6%	16.4%
3,355	UPTON	670	555	106	9	449 R	82.8%	15.8%	84.0%	16.0%
26,405	UVALDE	5,143	2,967	2,101	75	866 R	57.7%	40.9%	58.5%	41.5%
48,879	VAL VERDE	7,082	3,306	3,608	168	302 D	46.7%	50.9%	47.8%	52.2%
52,579	VAN ZANDT	11,921	9,751	1,938	232	7,813 R	81.8%	16.3%	83.4%	16.6%
86,793	VICTORIA	17,148	12,657	4,233	258	8,424 R	73.8%	24.7%	74.9%	25.1%
67,861	WALKER	11,387	7,669	3,476	242	4,193 R	67.3%	30.5%	68.8%	31.2%
43,205	WALLER	9,195	6,329	2,741	125	3,588 R	68.8%	29.8%	69.8%	30.2%
10,658	WARD	1,980	1,535	411	34	1,124 R	77.5%	20.8%	78.9%	21.1%
33,718	WASHINGTON	8,991	6,886	1,952	153	4,934 R	76.6%	21.7%	77.9%	22.1%
250,304	WEBB	26,404	7,622	17,963	819	10,341 D	28.9%	68.0%	29.8%	70.2%

TEXAS

GOVERNOR 2014

2010 Census Population	County	Total Vote	Republican (Abbott)	Democratic (Davis)	Other	Rep.-Dem. Plurality		Percentage			
								Total Vote		Major Vote	
								Rep.	Dem.	Rep.	Dem
41,280	WHARTON	8,399	6,215	2,075	109	4,140	R	74.0%	24.7%	75.0%	25.0%
5,410	WHEELER	1,322	1,185	120	17	1,065	R	89.6%	9.1%	90.8%	9.2%
131,500	WICHITA	21,256	16,130	4,822	304	11,308	R	75.9%	22.7%	77.0%	23.0%
13,535	WILBARGER	2,751	2,141	574	36	1,567	R	77.8%	20.9%	78.9%	21.1%
22,134	WILLACY	2,185	854	1,274	57	420	D	39.1%	58.3%	40.1%	59.9%
422,679	WILLIAMSON	103,910	61,496	39,516	2,898	21,980	R	59.2%	38.0%	60.9%	39.1%
42,918	WILSON	10,429	7,506	2,707	216	4,799	R	72.0%	26.0%	73.5%	26.5%
7,110	WINKLER	985	829	136	20	693	R	84.2%	13.8%	85.9%	14.1%
59,127	WISE	12,639	10,181	2,178	280	8,003	R	80.6%	17.2%	82.4%	17.6%
41,964	WOOD	11,310	9,778	1,403	129	8,375	R	86.5%	12.4%	87.5%	12.5%
7,879	YOAKUM	1,149	1,046	93	10	953	R	91.0%	8.1%	91.8%	8.2%
18,550	YOUNG	5,303	4,497	679	127	3,818	R	84.8%	12.8%	86.9%	13.1%
14,018	ZAPATA	1,177	372	788	17	416	D	31.6%	66.9%	32.1%	67.9%
11,677	ZAVALA	1,484	350	1,110	24	760	D	23.6%	74.8%	24.0%	76.0%
25,145,561	TOTAL	4,718,268	2,796,547	1,835,596	86,125	960,951	R	59.3%	38.9%	60.4%	39.6%

TEXAS

SENATOR 2014

2010 Census Population	County	Total Vote	Republican (Cornyn)	Democratic (Alameel)	Other	Rep.-Dem. Plurality		Percentage			
								Total Vote		Major Vote	
								Rep.	Dem.	Rep.	Dem
58,458	ANDERSON	10,134	7,791	2,017	326	5,774	R	76.9%	19.9%	79.4%	20.6%
14,786	ANDREWS	2,193	1,943	178	72	1,765	R	88.6%	8.1%	91.6%	8.4%
86,771	ANGELINA	16,656	12,867	3,414	375	9,453	R	77.3%	20.5%	79.0%	21.0%
23,158	ARANSAS	5,889	4,512	1,165	212	3,347	R	76.6%	19.8%	79.5%	20.5%
9,054	ARCHER	2,521	2,202	252	67	1,950	R	87.3%	10.0%	89.7%	10.3%
1,901	ARMSTRONG	563	497	44	22	453	R	88.3%	7.8%	91.9%	8.1%
44,911	ATASCOSA	7,239	4,834	2,103	302	2,731	R	66.8%	29.1%	69.7%	30.3%
28,417	AUSTIN	7,138	5,919	995	224	4,924	R	82.9%	13.9%	85.6%	14.4%
7,165	BAILEY	987	853	115	19	738	R	86.4%	11.7%	88.1%	11.9%
20,485	BANDERA	6,278	4,994	920	364	4,074	R	79.5%	14.7%	84.4%	15.6%
74,171	BASTROP	16,763	10,027	5,580	1,156	4,447	R	59.8%	33.3%	64.2%	35.8%
3,726	BAYLOR	818	688	107	23	581	R	84.1%	13.1%	86.5%	13.5%
31,861	BEE	5,004	2,981	1,827	196	1,154	R	59.6%	36.5%	62.0%	38.0%
310,235	BELL	43,591	28,838	13,124	1,629	15,714	R	66.2%	30.1%	68.7%	31.3%
1,714,773	BEXAR	297,160	160,577	124,030	12,553	36,547	R	54.0%	41.7%	56.4%	43.6%
10,497	BLANCO	3,581	2,671	699	211	1,972	R	74.6%	19.5%	79.3%	20.7%
641	BORDEN	253	236	12	5	224	R	93.3%	4.7%	95.2%	4.8%
18,212	BOSQUE	4,836	3,908	734	194	3,174	R	80.8%	15.2%	84.2%	15.8%
92,565	BOWIE	21,229	15,687	4,801	741	10,886	R	73.9%	22.6%	76.6%	23.4%
313,166	BRAZORIA	61,210	41,752	16,853	2,605	24,899	R	68.2%	27.5%	71.2%	28.8%
194,851	BRAZOS	31,068	22,174	7,438	1,456	14,736	R	71.4%	23.9%	74.9%	25.1%
9,232	BREWSTER	2,838	1,437	1,169	232	268	R	50.6%	41.2%	55.1%	44.9%
1,637	BRISCOE	501	432	59	10	373	R	86.2%	11.8%	88.0%	12.0%
7,223	BROOKS	1,980	455	1,319	206	864	D	23.0%	66.6%	25.6%	74.4%
38,106	BROWN	8,124	7,079	788	257	6,291	R	87.1%	9.7%	90.0%	10.0%
17,187	BURLESON	4,090	3,121	858	111	2,263	R	76.3%	21.0%	78.4%	21.6%
42,750	BURNET	11,730	9,263	1,980	487	7,283	R	79.0%	16.9%	82.4%	17.6%
38,066	CALDWELL	8,782	5,171	3,076	535	2,095	R	58.9%	35.0%	62.7%	37.3%
21,381	CALHOUN	4,068	2,750	1,130	188	1,620	R	67.6%	27.8%	70.9%	29.1%
13,544	CALLAHAN	2,919	2,579	244	96	2,335	R	88.4%	8.4%	91.4%	8.6%

TEXAS

SENATOR 2014

2010 Census Population	County	Total Vote	Republican (Cornyn)	Democratic (Alameel)	Other	Rep.-Dem. Plurality	Percentage			
							Total Vote		Major Vote	
							Rep.	Dem.	Rep.	Dem.
406,220	CAMERON	38,462	16,747	19,188	2,527	2,441 D	43.5%	49.9%	46.6%	53.4%
12,401	CAMP	2,588	1,818	693	77	1,125 R	70.2%	26.8%	72.4%	27.6%
6,182	CARSON	1,834	1,627	163	44	1,464 R	88.7%	8.9%	90.9%	9.1%
30,464	CASS	6,840	5,082	1,538	220	3,544 R	74.3%	22.5%	76.8%	23.2%
8,062	CASTRO	1,143	903	200	40	703 R	79.0%	17.5%	81.9%	18.1%
35,096	CHAMBERS	8,345	6,818	1,227	300	5,591 R	81.7%	14.7%	84.7%	15.3%
50,845	CHEROKEE	9,419	7,440	1,724	255	5,716 R	79.0%	18.3%	81.2%	18.8%
7,041	CHILDRESS	1,085	959	107	19	852 R	88.4%	9.9%	90.0%	10.0%
10,752	CLAY	2,793	2,375	319	99	2,056 R	85.0%	11.4%	88.2%	11.8%
3,127	COCHRAN	485	411	57	17	354 R	84.7%	11.8%	87.8%	12.2%
3,320	COKE	752	675	53	24	622 R	89.8%	7.0%	92.7%	7.3%
8,895	COLEMAN	2,208	1,934	200	74	1,734 R	87.6%	9.1%	90.6%	9.4%
782,341	COLLIN	175,617	120,164	49,145	6,308	71,019 R	68.4%	28.0%	71.0%	29.0%
3,057	COLLINGSWORTH	780	649	101	30	548 R	83.2%	12.9%	86.5%	13.5%
20,874	COLORADO	5,074	3,978	952	144	3,026 R	78.4%	18.8%	80.7%	19.3%
108,472	COMAL	34,521	27,211	5,936	1,374	21,275 R	78.8%	17.2%	82.1%	17.9%
13,974	COMANCHE	2,997	2,453	425	119	2,028 R	81.8%	14.2%	85.2%	14.8%
4,087	CONCHO	588	500	65	23	435 R	85.0%	11.1%	88.5%	11.5%
38,437	COOKE	8,744	7,460	990	294	6,470 R	85.3%	11.3%	88.3%	11.7%
75,388	CORYELL	8,558	6,445	1,779	334	4,666 R	75.3%	20.8%	78.4%	21.6%
1,505	COTTLE	352	295	45	12	250 R	83.8%	12.8%	86.8%	13.2%
4,375	CRANE	822	664	120	38	544 R	80.8%	14.6%	84.7%	15.3%
3,719	CROCKETT	816	600	167	49	433 R	73.5%	20.5%	78.2%	21.8%
6,059	CROSBY	1,045	802	198	45	604 R	76.7%	18.9%	80.2%	19.8%
2,398	CULBERSON	290	158	113	19	45 R	54.5%	39.0%	58.3%	41.7%
6,703	DALLAM	834	718	77	39	641 R	86.1%	9.2%	90.3%	9.7%
2,368,139	DALLAS	400,903	187,981	199,021	13,901	11,040 D	46.9%	49.6%	48.6%	51.4%
13,833	DAWSON	1,986	1,626	290	70	1,336 R	81.9%	14.6%	84.9%	15.1%
20,097	DE WITT	3,910	3,270	517	123	2,753 R	83.6%	13.2%	86.3%	13.7%
19,372	DEAF SMITH	2,684	2,161	412	111	1,749 R	80.5%	15.4%	84.0%	16.0%
5,231	DELTA	1,331	1,030	248	53	782 R	77.4%	18.6%	80.6%	19.4%
662,614	DENTON	142,683	96,561	39,488	6,634	57,073 R	67.7%	27.7%	71.0%	29.0%
2,444	DICKENS	499	434	49	16	385 R	87.0%	9.8%	89.9%	10.1%
9,996	DIMMIT	1,797	595	1,120	82	525 D	33.1%	62.3%	34.7%	65.3%
3,677	DONLEY	927	801	94	32	707 R	86.4%	10.1%	89.5%	10.5%
11,782	DUVAL	2,925	578	2,183	164	1,605 D	19.8%	74.6%	20.9%	79.1%
18,583	EASTLAND	3,861	3,402	338	121	3,064 R	88.1%	8.8%	91.0%	9.0%
137,130	ECTOR	14,675	11,929	2,234	512	9,695 R	81.3%	15.2%	84.2%	15.8%
2,002	EDWARDS	730	523	154	53	369 R	71.6%	21.1%	77.3%	22.7%
800,647	EL PASO	79,689	31,744	43,038	4,907	11,294 D	39.8%	54.0%	42.4%	57.6%
149,610	ELLIS	31,919	24,106	6,703	1,110	17,403 R	75.5%	21.0%	78.2%	21.8%
37,890	ERATH	7,254	6,053	961	240	5,092 R	83.4%	13.2%	86.3%	13.7%
17,866	FALLS	2,970	2,125	770	75	1,355 R	71.5%	25.9%	73.4%	26.6%
33,915	FANNIN	6,352	4,991	1,128	233	3,863 R	78.6%	17.8%	81.6%	18.4%
24,554	FAYETTE	7,427	6,017	1,184	226	4,833 R	81.0%	15.9%	83.6%	16.4%
3,974	FISHER	1,203	808	359	36	449 R	67.2%	29.8%	69.2%	30.8%
6,446	FLOYD	1,081	947	110	24	837 R	87.6%	10.2%	89.6%	10.4%
1,336	FOARD	295	196	90	9	106 R	66.4%	30.5%	68.5%	31.5%
585,375	FORT BEND	131,061	76,027	51,162	3,872	24,865 R	58.0%	39.0%	59.8%	40.2%
10,605	FRANKLIN	2,556	2,189	295	72	1,894 R	85.6%	11.5%	88.1%	11.9%
19,816	FREESTONE	4,393	3,519	775	99	2,744 R	80.1%	17.6%	82.0%	18.0%
17,217	FRIO	1,818	880	883	55	3 D	48.4%	48.6%	49.9%	50.1%
17,526	GAINES	2,440	2,137	224	79	1,913 R	87.6%	9.2%	90.5%	9.5%
291,309	GALVESTON	64,057	41,407	19,857	2,793	21,550 R	64.6%	31.0%	67.6%	32.4%
6,461	GARZA	826	742	66	18	676 R	89.8%	8.0%	91.8%	8.2%
24,837	GILLESPIE	8,770	7,217	1,153	400	6,064 R	82.3%	13.1%	86.2%	13.8%
1,226	GLASSCOCK	394	372	10	12	362 R	94.4%	2.5%	97.4%	2.6%
7,210	GOLIAD	2,698	1,865	741	92	1,124 R	69.1%	27.5%	71.6%	28.4%
19,807	GONZALES	3,658	2,840	689	129	2,151 R	77.6%	18.8%	80.5%	19.5%
22,535	GRAY	3,650	3,314	243	93	3,071 R	90.8%	6.7%	93.2%	6.8%

TEXAS

SENATOR 2014

2010 Census Population	County	Total Vote	Republican (Cornyn)	Democratic (Alameel)	Other	Rep.-Dem. Plurality	Percentage			
							Total Vote		Major Vote	
							Rep.	Dem.	Rep.	Dem.
120,877	GRAYSON	23,349	18,146	4,522	681	13,624 R	77.7%	19.4%	80.1%	19.9%
121,730	GREGG	22,746	16,939	5,275	532	11,664 R	74.5%	23.2%	76.3%	23.7%
26,604	GRIMES	4,850	3,698	958	194	2,740 R	76.2%	19.8%	79.4%	20.6%
131,533	GUADALUPE	30,331	21,885	7,267	1,179	14,618 R	72.2%	24.0%	75.1%	24.9%
36,273	HALE	4,277	3,675	492	110	3,183 R	85.9%	11.5%	88.2%	11.8%
3,353	HALL	565	486	70	9	416 R	86.0%	12.4%	87.4%	12.6%
8,517	HAMILTON	2,377	1,933	356	88	1,577 R	81.3%	15.0%	84.4%	15.6%
5,613	HANSFORD	1,204	1,124	42	38	1,082 R	93.4%	3.5%	96.4%	3.6%
4,139	HARDEMAN	665	536	112	17	424 R	80.6%	16.8%	82.7%	17.3%
54,635	HARDIN	11,213	9,610	1,304	299	8,306 R	85.7%	11.6%	88.1%	11.9%
4,092,459	HARRIS	668,462	362,887	281,407	24,168	81,480 R	54.3%	42.1%	56.3%	43.7%
65,631	HARRISON	14,545	10,473	3,714	358	6,759 R	72.0%	25.5%	73.8%	26.2%
6,062	HARTLEY	1,105	1,004	75	26	929 R	90.9%	6.8%	93.0%	7.0%
5,899	HASKELL	1,044	787	234	23	553 R	75.4%	22.4%	77.1%	22.9%
157,107	HAYS	38,770	21,633	14,567	2,570	7,066 R	55.8%	37.6%	59.8%	40.2%
3,807	HEMPHILL	822	717	70	35	647 R	87.2%	8.5%	91.1%	8.9%
78,532	HENDERSON	16,776	13,264	3,027	485	10,237 R	79.1%	18.0%	81.4%	18.6%
774,769	HIDALGO	77,932	27,303	46,112	4,517	18,809 D	35.0%	59.2%	37.2%	62.8%
35,089	HILL	8,840	7,023	1,533	284	5,490 R	79.4%	17.3%	82.1%	17.9%
22,935	HOCKLEY	3,673	3,194	370	109	2,824 R	87.0%	10.1%	89.6%	10.4%
51,182	HOOD	13,547	11,090	2,007	450	9,083 R	81.9%	14.8%	84.7%	15.3%
35,161	HOPKINS	7,296	5,728	1,384	184	4,344 R	78.5%	19.0%	80.5%	19.5%
23,732	HOUSTON	4,615	3,646	851	118	2,795 R	79.0%	18.4%	81.1%	18.9%
35,012	HOWARD	4,234	3,433	644	157	2,789 R	81.1%	15.2%	84.2%	15.8%
3,476	HUDSPETH	480	265	170	45	95 R	55.2%	35.4%	60.9%	39.1%
86,129	HUNT	16,103	12,635	2,879	589	9,756 R	78.5%	17.9%	81.4%	18.6%
22,150	HUTCHINSON	4,476	3,978	376	122	3,602 R	88.9%	8.4%	91.4%	8.6%
1,599	IRION	427	375	37	15	338 R	87.8%	8.7%	91.0%	9.0%
9,044	JACK	1,702	1,493	170	39	1,323 R	87.7%	10.0%	89.8%	10.2%
14,075	JACKSON	2,887	2,411	405	71	2,006 R	83.5%	14.0%	85.6%	14.4%
35,710	JASPER	7,046	5,522	1,349	175	4,173 R	78.4%	19.1%	80.4%	19.6%
2,342	JEFF DAVIS	986	571	328	87	243 R	57.9%	33.3%	63.5%	36.5%
252,273	JEFFERSON	52,297	26,687	24,553	1,057	2,134 R	51.0%	46.9%	52.1%	47.9%
5,300	JIM HOGG	698	160	514	24	354 D	22.9%	73.6%	23.7%	76.3%
40,838	JIM WELLS	5,466	2,481	2,762	223	281 D	45.4%	50.5%	47.3%	52.7%
150,934	JOHNSON	29,057	23,153	4,784	1,120	18,369 R	79.7%	16.5%	82.9%	17.1%
20,202	JONES	3,271	2,644	491	136	2,153 R	80.8%	15.0%	84.3%	15.7%
14,824	KARNES	2,465	1,832	559	74	1,273 R	74.3%	22.7%	76.6%	23.4%
103,350	KAUFMAN	20,152	14,930	4,619	603	10,311 R	74.1%	22.9%	76.4%	23.6%
33,410	KENDALL	11,755	9,854	1,477	424	8,377 R	83.8%	12.6%	87.0%	13.0%
416	KENEDY	116	59	52	5	7 R	50.9%	44.8%	53.2%	46.8%
808	KENT	303	250	42	11	208 R	82.5%	13.9%	85.6%	14.4%
49,625	KERR	14,790	11,866	2,242	682	9,624 R	80.2%	15.2%	84.1%	15.9%
4,607	KIMBLE	1,188	1,071	87	30	984 R	90.2%	7.3%	92.5%	7.5%
286	KING	90	87	1	2	86 R	96.7%	1.1%	98.9%	1.1%
3,598	KINNEY	1,114	738	299	77	439 R	66.2%	26.8%	71.2%	28.8%
32,061	KLEBERG	5,606	2,805	2,463	338	342 R	50.0%	43.9%	53.2%	46.8%
3,719	KNOX	867	703	141	23	562 R	81.1%	16.3%	83.3%	16.7%
6,886	LA SALLE	813	400	369	44	31 R	49.2%	45.4%	52.0%	48.0%
49,793	LAMAR	10,680	8,062	2,274	344	5,788 R	75.5%	21.3%	78.0%	22.0%
13,977	LAMB	2,082	1,785	244	53	1,541 R	85.7%	11.7%	88.0%	12.0%
19,677	LAMPASAS	4,546	3,714	689	143	3,025 R	81.7%	15.2%	84.4%	15.6%
19,263	LAVACA	4,956	4,242	595	119	3,647 R	85.6%	12.0%	87.7%	12.3%
16,612	LEE	4,197	3,212	797	188	2,415 R	76.5%	19.0%	80.1%	19.9%
16,801	LEON	4,207	3,688	432	87	3,256 R	87.7%	10.3%	89.5%	10.5%
75,643	LIBERTY	12,071	9,493	2,161	417	7,332 R	78.6%	17.9%	81.5%	18.5%
23,384	LIMESTONE	4,257	3,257	903	97	2,354 R	76.5%	21.2%	78.3%	21.7%
3,302	LIPSCOMB	842	743	73	26	670 R	88.2%	8.7%	91.1%	8.9%
11,531	LIVE OAK	2,431	2,030	313	88	1,717 R	83.5%	12.9%	86.6%	13.4%
19,301	LLANO	6,962	5,662	1,057	243	4,605 R	81.3%	15.2%	84.3%	15.7%

TEXAS

SENATOR 2014

2010 Census Population	County	Total Vote	Republican (Cornyn)	Democratic (Alameel)	Other	Rep.-Dem. Plurality	Percentage			
							Total Vote		Major Vote	
							Rep.	Dem.	Rep.	Dem.
82	LOVING	38	34	3	1	31 R	89.5%	7.9%	91.9%	8.1%
278,831	LUBBOCK	46,719	35,927	8,956	1,836	26,971 R	76.9%	19.2%	80.0%	20.0%
5,915	LYNN	1,179	979	164	36	815 R	83.0%	13.9%	85.7%	14.3%
13,664	MADISON	2,373	1,923	402	48	1,521 R	81.0%	16.9%	82.7%	17.3%
10,546	MARION	2,172	1,461	657	54	804 R	67.3%	30.2%	69.0%	31.0%
4,799	MARTIN	1,120	959	111	50	848 R	85.6%	9.9%	89.6%	10.4%
4,012	MASON	1,361	1,100	201	60	899 R	80.8%	14.8%	84.6%	15.4%
36,702	MATAGORDA	6,888	4,820	1,793	275	3,027 R	70.0%	26.0%	72.9%	27.1%
54,258	MAVERICK	5,186	1,284	3,479	423	2,195 D	24.8%	67.1%	27.0%	73.0%
8,283	MCCULLOCH	1,725	1,446	206	73	1,240 R	83.8%	11.9%	87.5%	12.5%
234,906	MCLENNAN	43,787	31,117	11,276	1,394	19,841 R	71.1%	25.8%	73.4%	26.6%
707	MCMULLEN	249	216	17	16	199 R	86.7%	6.8%	92.7%	7.3%
46,006	MEDINA	9,764	7,405	2,024	335	5,381 R	75.8%	20.7%	78.5%	21.5%
2,242	MENARD	465	408	43	14	365 R	87.7%	9.2%	90.5%	9.5%
136,872	MIDLAND	23,403	19,939	2,624	840	17,315 R	85.2%	11.2%	88.4%	11.6%
24,757	MILAM	4,851	3,584	1,098	169	2,486 R	73.9%	22.6%	76.5%	23.5%
4,936	MILLS	1,323	1,186	105	32	1,081 R	89.6%	7.9%	91.9%	8.1%
9,403	MITCHELL	1,178	964	166	48	798 R	81.8%	14.1%	85.3%	14.7%
19,719	MONTAGUE	6,648	5,700	716	232	4,984 R	85.7%	10.8%	88.8%	11.2%
455,746	MONTGOMERY	103,538	84,512	15,338	3,688	69,174 R	81.6%	14.8%	84.6%	15.4%
21,904	MOORE	2,748	2,414	249	85	2,165 R	87.8%	9.1%	90.6%	9.4%
12,934	MORRIS	3,045	1,990	978	77	1,012 R	65.4%	32.1%	67.0%	33.0%
1,210	MOTLEY	363	346	12	5	334 R	95.3%	3.3%	96.6%	3.4%
64,524	NACOGDOCHES	11,735	8,867	2,497	371	6,370 R	75.6%	21.3%	78.0%	22.0%
47,735	NAVARRO	9,376	7,129	1,960	287	5,169 R	76.0%	20.9%	78.4%	21.6%
14,445	NEWTON	2,855	2,073	680	102	1,393 R	72.6%	23.8%	75.3%	24.7%
15,216	NOLAN	2,595	2,072	419	104	1,653 R	79.8%	16.1%	83.2%	16.8%
340,223	NUECES	55,758	31,828	21,239	2,691	10,589 R	57.1%	38.1%	60.0%	40.0%
10,223	OCHILTREE	1,581	1,483	53	45	1,430 R	93.8%	3.4%	96.5%	3.5%
2,052	OLDHAM	557	518	24	15	494 R	93.0%	4.3%	95.6%	4.4%
81,837	ORANGE	17,065	13,192	3,378	495	9,814 R	77.3%	19.8%	79.6%	20.4%
28,111	PALO PINTO	5,610	4,529	900	181	3,629 R	80.7%	16.0%	83.4%	16.6%
23,796	PANOLA	5,726	4,615	986	125	3,629 R	80.6%	17.2%	82.4%	17.6%
116,927	PARKER	31,278	25,880	4,218	1,180	21,662 R	82.7%	13.5%	86.0%	14.0%
10,269	PARMER	1,395	1,242	121	32	1,121 R	89.0%	8.7%	91.1%	8.9%
15,507	PECOS	2,925	1,857	855	213	1,002 R	63.5%	29.2%	68.5%	31.5%
45,413	POLK	10,323	8,019	1,932	372	6,087 R	77.7%	18.7%	80.6%	19.4%
121,073	POTTER	13,659	10,592	2,497	570	8,095 R	77.5%	18.3%	80.9%	19.1%
7,818	PRESIDIO	922	318	533	71	215 D	34.5%	57.8%	37.4%	62.6%
10,914	RAINS	2,387	1,966	347	74	1,619 R	82.4%	14.5%	85.0%	15.0%
120,725	RANDALL	27,838	23,990	2,885	963	21,105 R	86.2%	10.4%	89.3%	10.7%
3,367	REAGAN	494	421	51	22	370 R	85.2%	10.3%	89.2%	10.8%
3,309	REAL	1,035	868	127	40	741 R	83.9%	12.3%	87.2%	12.8%
12,860	RED RIVER	2,615	1,953	597	65	1,356 R	74.7%	22.8%	76.6%	23.4%
13,783	REEVES	1,188	599	519	70	80 R	50.4%	43.7%	53.6%	46.4%
7,383	REFUGIO	1,966	1,228	653	85	575 R	62.5%	33.2%	65.3%	34.7%
929	ROBERTS	338	318	12	8	306 R	94.1%	3.6%	96.4%	3.6%
16,622	ROBERTSON	4,959	3,165	1,643	151	1,522 R	63.8%	33.1%	65.8%	34.2%
78,337	ROCKWALL	20,916	16,510	3,793	613	12,717 R	78.9%	18.1%	81.3%	18.7%
10,501	RUNNELS	2,261	2,000	198	63	1,802 R	88.5%	8.8%	91.0%	9.0%
53,330	RUSK	10,429	8,437	1,759	233	6,678 R	80.9%	16.9%	82.7%	17.3%
10,834	SABINE	2,718	2,307	348	63	1,959 R	84.9%	12.8%	86.9%	13.1%
8,865	SAN AUGUSTINE	2,625	1,805	740	80	1,065 R	68.8%	28.2%	70.9%	29.1%
26,384	SAN JACINTO	6,283	4,671	1,342	270	3,329 R	74.3%	21.4%	77.7%	22.3%
64,804	SAN PATRICIO	11,133	7,159	3,487	487	3,672 R	64.3%	31.3%	67.2%	32.8%
6,131	SAN SABA	1,430	1,262	125	43	1,137 R	88.3%	8.7%	91.0%	9.0%
3,461	SCHLEICHER	843	610	181	52	429 R	72.4%	21.5%	77.1%	22.9%
16,921	SCURRY	2,824	2,471	278	75	2,193 R	87.5%	9.8%	89.9%	10.1%
3,378	SHACKELFORD	798	735	45	18	690 R	92.1%	5.6%	94.2%	5.8%
25,448	SHELBY	5,418	4,293	997	128	3,296 R	79.2%	18.4%	81.2%	18.8%

TEXAS

SENATOR 2014

2010 Census Population	County	Total Vote	Republican (Cornyn)	Democratic (Alameel)	Other	Rep.-Dem. Plurality	Percentage Total Vote Rep.	Dem.	Percentage Major Vote Rep.	Dem.
3,034	SHERMAN	592	545	30	17	515 R	92.1%	5.1%	94.8%	5.2%
209,714	SMITH	48,409	36,935	10,110	1,364	26,825 R	76.3%	20.9%	78.5%	21.5%
8,490	SOMERVELL	2,215	1,841	302	72	1,539 R	83.1%	13.6%	85.9%	14.1%
60,968	STARR	4,968	961	3,795	212	2,834 D	19.3%	76.4%	20.2%	79.8%
9,630	STEPHENS	1,915	1,725	159	31	1,566 R	90.1%	8.3%	91.6%	8.4%
1,143	STERLING	465	433	20	12	413 R	93.1%	4.3%	95.6%	4.4%
1,490	STONEWALL	369	284	72	13	212 R	77.0%	19.5%	79.8%	20.2%
4,128	SUTTON	733	626	91	16	535 R	85.4%	12.4%	87.3%	12.7%
7,854	SWISHER	1,377	1,033	288	56	745 R	75.0%	20.9%	78.2%	21.8%
1,809,034	TARRANT	367,270	220,424	132,713	14,133	87,711 R	60.0%	36.1%	62.4%	37.6%
131,506	TAYLOR	23,156	18,916	3,376	864	15,540 R	81.7%	14.6%	84.9%	15.1%
984	TERRELL	383	240	118	25	122 R	62.7%	30.8%	67.0%	33.0%
12,651	TERRY	2,224	1,818	307	99	1,511 R	81.7%	13.8%	85.6%	14.4%
1,641	THROCKMORTON	521	445	53	23	392 R	85.4%	10.2%	89.4%	10.6%
32,334	TITUS	5,090	3,812	1,146	132	2,666 R	74.9%	22.5%	76.9%	23.1%
110,224	TOM GREEN	18,286	14,631	2,961	694	11,670 R	80.0%	16.2%	83.2%	16.8%
1,024,266	TRAVIS	264,076	98,018	147,783	18,275	49,765 D	37.1%	56.0%	39.9%	60.1%
14,585	TRINITY	3,829	2,878	827	124	2,051 R	75.2%	21.6%	77.7%	22.3%
21,766	TYLER	4,638	3,652	814	172	2,838 R	78.7%	17.6%	81.8%	18.2%
39,309	UPSHUR	8,561	6,979	1,271	311	5,708 R	81.5%	14.8%	84.6%	15.4%
3,355	UPTON	627	505	92	30	413 R	80.5%	14.7%	84.6%	15.4%
26,405	UVALDE	5,019	2,979	1,856	184	1,123 R	59.4%	37.0%	61.6%	38.4%
48,879	VAL VERDE	6,985	3,333	3,237	415	96 R	47.7%	46.3%	50.7%	49.3%
52,579	VAN ZANDT	11,785	9,864	1,547	374	8,317 R	83.7%	13.1%	86.4%	13.6%
86,793	VICTORIA	16,971	12,706	3,701	564	9,005 R	74.9%	21.8%	77.4%	22.6%
67,861	WALKER	11,219	7,926	2,785	508	5,141 R	70.6%	24.8%	74.0%	26.0%
43,205	WALLER	9,070	6,426	2,352	292	4,074 R	70.8%	25.9%	73.2%	26.8%
10,658	WARD	1,949	1,447	416	86	1,031 R	74.2%	21.3%	77.7%	22.3%
33,718	WASHINGTON	8,921	7,052	1,582	287	5,470 R	79.0%	17.7%	81.7%	18.3%
250,304	WEBB	25,714	7,488	15,223	3,003	7,735 D	29.1%	59.2%	33.0%	67.0%
41,280	WHARTON	8,284	6,315	1,749	220	4,566 R	76.2%	21.1%	78.3%	21.7%
5,410	WHEELER	1,297	1,168	97	32	1,071 R	90.1%	7.5%	92.3%	7.7%
131,500	WICHITA	20,857	16,039	4,133	685	11,906 R	76.9%	19.8%	79.5%	20.5%
13,535	WILBARGER	2,651	2,098	481	72	1,617 R	79.1%	18.1%	81.3%	18.7%
22,134	WILLACY	2,042	804	1,093	145	289 D	39.4%	53.5%	42.4%	57.6%
422,679	WILLIAMSON	103,070	63,387	33,857	5,826	29,530 R	61.5%	32.8%	65.2%	34.8%
42,918	WILSON	10,339	7,755	2,182	402	5,573 R	75.0%	21.1%	78.0%	22.0%
7,110	WINKLER	959	787	129	43	658 R	82.1%	13.5%	85.9%	14.1%
59,127	WISE	12,485	10,330	1,670	485	8,660 R	82.7%	13.4%	86.1%	13.9%
41,964	WOOD	11,059	9,564	1,249	246	8,315 R	86.5%	11.3%	88.4%	11.6%
7,879	YOAKUM	1,124	1,017	75	32	942 R	90.5%	6.7%	93.1%	6.9%
18,550	YOUNG	5,147	4,431	524	192	3,907 R	86.1%	10.2%	89.4%	10.6%
14,018	ZAPATA	1,122	313	745	64	432 D	27.9%	66.4%	29.6%	70.4%
11,677	ZAVALA	1,423	322	1,037	64	715 D	22.6%	72.9%	23.7%	76.3%
25,145,561	*TOTAL*	4,648,358	2,861,531	1,597,387	189,440	1,264,144 R	61.6%	34.4%	64.2%	35.8%

TEXAS

HOUSE OF REPRESENTATIVES

CD	Year	Total Vote	Republican Vote	Republican Candidate	Democratic Vote	Democratic Candidate	Other Vote	Rep.-Dem. Plurality	Total Vote Rep.	Total Vote Dem.	Major Vote Rep.	Major Vote Dem.
1	2014	148,560	115,084	GOHMERT, LOUIE*	33,476	MCKELLAR, SHIRLEY J.		81,608 R	77.5%	22.5%	77.5%	22.5%
1	2012	249,658	178,322	GOHMERT, LOUIE*	67,222	MCKELLAR, SHIRLEY J.	4,114	111,100 R	71.4%	26.9%	72.6%	27.4%
2	2014	150,026	101,936	POE, TED*	44,462	LETSOS, NIKO	3,628	57,474 R	67.9%	29.6%	69.6%	30.4%
2	2012	246,328	159,664	POE, TED*	80,512	DOUGHERTY, JIM	6,152	79,152 R	64.8%	32.7%	66.5%	33.5%
3	2014	138,280	113,404	JOHNSON, SAM*			24,876	113,404 R	82.0%		100.0%	
3	2012	187,180	187,180	JOHNSON, SAM*				187,180 R	100.0%		100.0%	
4	2014	115,085	115,085	RATCLIFFE, JOHN				115,085 R	100.0%		100.0%	
4	2012	250,343	182,679	HALL, RALPH M.*	60,214	HATHCOX, VALINDA	7,450	122,465 R	73.0%	24.1%	75.2%	24.8%
5	2014	104,262	88,998	HENSARLING, JEB*			15,264	88,498 R	85.4%		100.0%	
5	2012	208,230	134,091	HENSARLING, JEB*	69,178	MROSKO, LINDA S.	4,961	64,913 R	64.4%	33.2%	66.0%	34.0%
6	2014	150,996	92,334	BARTON, JOE*	55,027	COZAD, DAVID E.	3,635	37,307 R	61.1%	36.4%	62.7%	37.3%
6	2012	249,936	145,019	BARTON, JOE*	98,053	SANDERS, KENNETH	6,864	46,966 R	58.0%	39.2%	59.7%	40.3%
7	2014	143,219	90,606	CULBERSON, JOHN*	49,478	CARGAS, JAMES	3,135	41,128 R	63.3%	34.5%	64.7%	35.3%
7	2012	234,837	142,793	CULBERSON, JOHN*	85,553	CARGAS, JAMES	6,491	57,240 R	60.8%	36.4%	62.5%	37.5%
8	2014	140,013	125,066	BRADY, KEVIN*			14,947	125,066 R	89.3%		100.0%	
8	2012	251,052	194,043	BRADY, KEVIN*	51,051	BURNS, NEIL	5,958	142,992 R	77.3%	20.3%	79.2%	20.8%
9	2014	86,003			78,109	GREEN, AL*	7,894	78,109 D		90.8%		100.0%
9	2012	183,566	36,139	MUELLER, STEVE	144,075	GREEN, AL*	3,352	107,936 D	19.7%	78.5%	20.1%	79.9%
10	2014	176,460	109,726	MCCAUL, MICHAEL T.*	60,243	CADIEN, TAWANA W.	6,491	49,483 R	62.2%	34.1%	64.6%	35.4%
10	2012	264,019	159,783	MCCAUL, MICHAEL T.*	95,710	CADIEN, TAWANA W.	8,526	64,073 R	60.5%	36.3%	62.5%	37.5%
11	2014	119,574	107,939	CONAWAY, K. MICHAEL*			11,635	107,939 R	90.3%		100.0%	
11	2012	226,023	177,742	CONAWAY, K. MICHAEL*	41,970	RILEY, JIM	6,311	135,772 R	78.6%	18.6%	80.9%	19.1%
12	2014	158,730	113,186	GRANGER, KAY*	41,757	GREENE, MARK	3,787	71,429 R	71.3%	26.3%	73.1%	26.9%
12	2012	247,712	175,649	GRANGER, KAY*	66,080	ROBINSON, DAVE	5,983	109,569 R	70.9%	26.7%	72.7%	27.3%
13	2014	131,451	110,842	THORNBERRY, MAC*	16,822	MINTER, MIKE G.	3,787	94,020 R	84.3%	12.8%	86.8%	13.2%
13	2012	206,388	187,775	THORNBERRY, MAC*			18,613	187,775 R	91.0%		100.0%	
14	2014	145,698	90,116	WEBER, RANDY K.*	52,545	BROWN, DONALD G.	3,037	37,571 R	61.9%	36.1%	63.2%	36.8%
14	2012	245,839	131,460	WEBER, RANDY K.	109,697	LAMPSON, NICK	4,682	21,763 R	53.5%	44.6%	54.5%	45.5%
15	2014	90,184	39,016	ZAMORA, EDDIE	48,708	HINOJOSA, RUBÉN*	2,460	9,692 D	43.3%	54.0%	44.5%	55.5%
15	2012	146,661	54,056	BRUEGGEMANN, DALE A.	89,296	HINOJOSA, RUBÉN*	3,309	35,240 D	36.9%	60.9%	37.7%	62.3%
16	2014	73,105	21,324	ROEN, COREY DEAN	49,338	O'ROURKE, BETO*	2,443	28,014 D	29.2%	67.5%	30.2%	69.8%
16	2012	155,005	51,043	CARRASCO, BARBARA	101,403	O'ROURKE, BETO	2,559	50,360 D	32.9%	65.4%	33.5%	66.5%
17	2014	132,865	85,807	FLORES, BILL*	43,049	HAYNES, NICK	4,009	42,758 R	64.6%	32.4%	66.6%	33.4%
17	2012	179,262	143,284	FLORES, BILL*			35,978	143,284 R	79.9%		100.0%	
18	2014	106,010	26,249	SEIBERT, SEAN	76,097	JACKSON LEE, SHEILA*	3,664	49,848 D	24.8%	71.8%	25.6%	74.4%
18	2012	194,932	44,015	SEIBERT, SEAN	146,223	JACKSON LEE, SHEILA*	4,694	102,208 D	22.6%	75.0%	23.1%	76.9%
19	2014	116,818	90,160	NEUGEBAUER, RANDY*	21,458	MARCHBANKS, JAMES NEAL	5,200	68,702 R	77.2%	18.4%	80.8%	19.2%
19	2012	192,063	163,239	NEUGEBAUER, RANDY*			28,824	163,239 R	85.0%		100.0%	
20	2014	87,964			66,554	CASTRO, JOAQUIN*	21,410	66,554 D		75.7%		100.0%
20	2012	186,177	62,376	ROSA, DAVID	119,032	CASTRO, JOAQUIN	4,769	56,656 D	33.5%	63.9%	34.4%	65.6%
21	2014	188,996	135,660	SMITH, LAMAR*			53,336	135,660 R	71.8%		100.0%	
21	2012	308,865	187,015	SMITH, LAMAR*	109,326	DUVAL, CANDACE E.	12,524	77,689 R	60.5%	35.4%	63.1%	36.9%
22	2014	151,566	100,861	OLSON, PETE*	47,844	BRISCOE, FRANK	2,861	53,017 R	66.5%	31.6%	67.8%	32.2%
22	2012	250,911	160,668	OLSON, PETE*	80,203	ROGERS, KESHA	10,040	80,465 R	64.0%	32.0%	66.7%	33.3%
23	2014	115,429	57,459	HURD, WILL	55,037	GALLEGO, PETE P.*	2,933	2,422 R	49.8%	47.7%	51.1%	48.9%
23	2012	192,169	87,547	CANSECO, FRANCISCO "QUICO"*	96,676	GALLEGO, PETE P.	7,946	9,129 D	45.6%	50.3%	47.5%	52.5%
24	2014	144,073	93,712	MARCHANT, KENNY*	46,548	MCGEHEARTY, PATRICK	3,813	47,164 R	65.0%	32.3%	66.8%	33.2%
24	2012	243,489	148,586	MARCHANT, KENNY*	87,645	RUSK, TIM	7,258	60,941 R	61.0%	36.0%	62.9%	37.1%
25	2014	177,883	107,120	WILLIAMS, ROGER*	64,463	MONTOYA, MARCO	6,300	42,657 R	60.2%	36.2%	62.4%	37.6%
25	2012	263,932	154,245	WILLIAMS, ROGER	98,827	HENDERSON, ELAINE M.	10,860	55,418 R	58.4%	37.4%	60.9%	39.1%
26	2014	141,470	116,944	BURGESS, MICHAEL C.*			24,526	116,944 R	82.7%		100.0%	
26	2012	258,723	176,642	BURGESS, MICHAEL C.*	74,237	SANCHEZ, DAVID	7,844	102,405 R	68.3%	28.7%	70.4%	29.6%
27	2014	131,047	83,342	FARENTHOLD, BLAKE*	44,152	REED, WESLEY C.	3,553	39,190 R	63.6%	33.7%	65.4%	34.6%
27	2012	212,651	120,684	FARENTHOLD, BLAKE*	83,395	HARRISON, ROSE MEZA	8,572	37,289 R	56.8%	39.2%	59.1%	40.9%
28	2014	76,136			62,508	CUELLAR, HENRY*	13,628	62,508 D		82.1%		100.0%
28	2012	165,645	49,309	HAYWARD, WILLIAM R.	112,456	CUELLAR, HENRY*	3,880	63,147 D	29.8%	67.9%	30.5%	69.5%
29	2014	46,143			41,321	GREEN, GENE*	4,822	41,321 D		89.5%		100.0%
29	2012	95,611			86,053	GREEN, GENE*	9,558	86,053 D		90.0%		100.0%

TEXAS
HOUSE OF REPRESENTATIVES

CD	Year	Total Vote	Republican Vote	Republican Candidate	Democratic Vote	Democratic Candidate	Other Vote	Rep.-Dem. Plurality	Total Vote Rep.	Total Vote Dem.	Major Vote Rep.	Major Vote Dem.
30	2014	105,793			93,041	JOHNSON, EDDIE BERNICE*	12,752	93,041 D		87.9%		100.0%
30	2012	217,014	41,222	WASHINGTON, TRAVIS	171,059	JOHNSON, EDDIE BERNICE*	4,733	129,837 D	19.0%	78.8%	19.4%	80.6%
31	2014	143,028	91,607	CARTER, JOHN R.*	45,715	MINOR, LOUIE	5,706	45,892 R	64.0%	32.0%	66.7%	33.3%
31	2012	237,187	145,348	CARTER, JOHN R.*	82,977	WYMAN, STEPHEN M.	8,862	62,371 R	61.3%	35.0%	63.7%	36.3%
32	2014	156,096	96,495	SESSIONS, PETE*	55,325	PEREZ, FRANK	4,276	41,170 R	61.8%	35.4%	63.6%	36.4%
32	2012	251,636	146,653	SESSIONS, PETE*	99,288	MCGOVERN, KATHERINE SAVERS	5,695	47,365 R	58.3%	39.5%	59.6%	40.4%
33	2014	50,592			43,769	VEASEY, MARC A.*	6,823	43,769 D		86.5%		100.0%
33	2012	117,375	30,252	BRADLEY, CHUCK	85,114	VEASEY, MARC A.	2,009	54,862 D	25.8%	72.5%	26.2%	73.8%
34	2014	79,877	30,811	SMITH, LARRY S.	47,503	VELA, FILEMON*	1,563	16,692 D	38.6%	59.5%	39.3%	60.7%
34	2012	144,778	52,448	BRADSHAW, JESSICA PUENTE	89,606	VELA, FILEMON	2,724	37,158 D	36.2%	61.9%	36.9%	63.1%
35	2014	96,225	32,040	NARVAIZ, SUSAN	60,124	DOGGETT, LLOYD*	4,061	28,084 D	33.3%	62.5%	34.8%	65.2%
35	2012	165,179	52,894	NARVAIZ, SUSAN	105,626	DOGGETT, LLOYD*	6,659	52,732 D	32.0%	63.9%	33.4%	66.6%
36	2014	133,842	101,663	BABIN, BRIAN	29,543	COLE, MICHAEL K.	2,636	72,120 R	76.0%	22.1%	77.5%	22.5%
36	2012	233,832	165,405	STOCKMAN, STEVE	62,143	MARTIN, MAX	6,284	103,262 R	70.7%	26.6%	72.7%	27.3%
TOTAL	2014	4,453,499	2,684,592		1,474,016		294,891	1,210,576 R	60.3%	33.1%	64.6%	35.4%
TOTAL	2012	7,664,208	4,429,270		2,949,900		285,038	1,479,370 R	57.8%	38.5%	60.0%	40.0%

Note: An asterisk (*) denotes incumbent.

TEXAS
GENERAL AND PRIMARY ELECTIONS

2014 GENERAL ELECTIONS: OTHER VOTES

Governor   Other vote was 66,543 Libertarian (Kathie Glass), 18,520 Green (Brandon Parmer), 1,062 Write-in (Sarah M. Pavitt)

Senate   Other vote was 133,751 Libertarian (Rebecca Paddock), 54,701 Green (Emily Marie "Spicybrown" Sanchez), 988 Write-in (Mohammed Abbajebel Tahiro)

House   Other vote was:

CD 2   2,316 Libertarian (James B. Veasaw), 1,312 Green (Mark A. Roberts)
CD 3   24,876 Green (Paul Blair)
CD 5   15,264 Libertarian (Ken Ashby)
CD 6   3,635 Libertarian (Hugh Chauvin)
CD 7   3,135 Libertarian (Gerald Fowler)
CD 8   14,947 Libertarian (Ken Petty)
CD 9   7,894 Libertarian (Johnny Johnson)
CD 10   6,491 Libertarian (Bill Kelsey)
CD 11   11,635 Libertarian (Ryan T. Lange)
CD 12   3,787 Libertarian (Ed Colliver)
CD 13   2,863 Libertarian (Emily Pivoda), 924 Green (Don Cook)
CD 14   3,037 Libertarian (John Wieder)
CD 15   2,460 Libertarian (Johnny Partain)
CD 16   2,443 Libertarian (Jaime O. Perez)
CD 17   4,009 Libertarian (Shawn Michael Hamilton)
CD 18   2,362 Independent (Vince Duncan), 1,302 Green (Remington Alessi)
CD 19   5,146 Libertarian (Richard "Chip" Peterson), 54 Write-in (Donald L. Vance)
CD 20   21,410 Libertarian (Jeffrey C. Blunt)
CD 21   27,831 Green (Antonio Diaz), 25,505 Libertarian (Ryan Shields)

TEXAS

GENERAL AND PRIMARY ELECTIONS

CD 22   2,861 Libertarian (Rob Lapham)
CD 23   2,933 Libertarian (Ruben Corvalan)
CD 24   3,813 Libertarian (Mike Kolls)
CD 25   6,300 Libertarian (John Betz)
CD 26   24,526 Libertarian (Mark Boler)
CD 27   3,553 Libertarian (Roxanne Simonson)
CD 28   10,153 Libertarian (William Aikens), 3,475 Green (Michael D. Cary)
CD 29   4,822 Libertarian (James Stanczak)
CD 30   7,154 Libertarian (Max Koch), 5,598 Independent (Eric LeMonte Williams)
CD 31   5,706 Libertarian (Scott J. Ballard)
CD 32   4,276 Libertarian (Ed Rankin)
CD 33   6,823 Libertarian (Jason Reeves)
CD 34   1,563 Libertarian (Ryan Edward Rowley)
CD 35   2,767 Libertarian (Cory W. Bruner), 1,294 Green (Kat Swift)
CD 36   1,951 Libertarian (Rodney Veach), 685 Green (Hal Ridley)

2014 PRIMARY ELECTIONS: SUPPLEMENTARY INFORMATION

Primary	March 4, 2014	**Registration**	13,601,324	No Party Registration
Primary Runoff	May 27, 2014	(as of March 4, 2014)		

Primary Type   Open—Any registered voter could participate in the Democratic or Republican primary, although if he or she voted in the primary of one party, he or she could not vote in the runoff of the other party.

	REPUBLICAN PRIMARIES			DEMOCRATIC PRIMARIES		
Senator	Cornyn, John*	781,259	59.4%	Alameel, David#	239,914	47.0%
	Stockman, Steve	251,577	19.1%	Rogers, Kesha#	110,146	21.6%
	Stovall, Dwayne	140,794	10.7%	Scherr, Maxey Marie	90,359	17.7%
	Vega, Linda	50,057	3.8%	Kim, Harry	45,207	8.9%
	Cope, Ken	34,409	2.6%	Fjetland, Michael "Fjet"	24,383	4.8%
	Mapp, Chris	23,535	1.8%			
	Reasor, Reid	20,600	1.6%			
	Cleaver, Curt	12,325	0.9%	*TOTAL*	*510,009*	
	TOTAL	*1,314,556*				
				PRIMARY RUNOFF		
				Alameel, David	145,227	72.2%
				Rogers, Kesha	56,056	27.8%
				TOTAL	*201,283*	
Governor	Abbott, Greg	1,224,014	91.5%	Davis, Wendy R.	432,595	78.1%
	Fritsch, Lisa	59,221	4.4%	Madrigal, Reynaldo "Ray"	121,419	21.9%
	Martinez, Miriam	35,585	2.7%			
	Kilgore, SECEDE	19,055	1.4%			
	TOTAL	*1,337,875*		*TOTAL*	*554,014*	
Congressional District 1	Gohmert, Louie*	57,830	100.0%	McKellar, Shirley J.	7,240	100.0%
	TOTAL	*57,830*		*TOTAL*	*7,240*	
Congressional District 2	Poe, Ted*	34,863	100.0%	Letsos, Niko	5,906	100.0%
	TOTAL	*34,863*		*TOTAL*	*5,906*	
Congressional District 3	Johnson, Sam*	31,178	80.6%			
	Pierce, Harry	3,004	7.8%			
	Dean, Cami	2,435	6.3%			
	Loveless, Joshua	2,086	5.4%			
	TOTAL	*38,703*				

TEXAS

GENERAL AND PRIMARY ELECTIONS

	REPUBLICAN PRIMARIES			DEMOCRATIC PRIMARIES		
Congressional District 4	Hall, Ralph M.*	29,848	45.4%			
	Ratcliffe, John	18,917	28.8%			
	Gigliotti, Lou	10,601	16.1%			
	Stacy, John	2,812	4.3%			
	Lawson, Brent	2,290	3.5%			
	Arterburn, Tony	1,252	1.9%			
	TOTAL	65,720				
	PRIMARY RUNOFF					
	Ratcliffe, John	22,271	52.8%			
	Hall, Ralph M.*	19,899	47.2%			
	TOTAL	42,170				
Congressional District 5	Hensarling, Jeb*	41,634	100.0%			
	TOTAL	41,634				
Congressional District 6	Barton, Joe*	32,618	72.7%	Cozad, David E.	11,727	100.0%
	Kuchar, Frank C.	12,272	27.3%			
	TOTAL	44,890		TOTAL	11,727	
Congressional District 7	Culberson, John*	31,065	100.0%	Cargas, James	4,098	62.2%
				Squiers, Lissa	2,491	37.8%
	TOTAL	31,065		TOTAL	6,589	
Congressional District 8	Brady, Kevin*	42,368	68.3%			
	McMichael, Craig	19,687	31.7%			
	TOTAL	62,055				
Congressional District 9				Green, Al*	13,442	100.0%
				TOTAL	13,442	
Congressional District 10	McCaul, Michael T.*	38,406	100.0%	Cadien, Tawana W.	13,915	100.0%
	TOTAL	38,406		TOTAL	13,915	
Congressional District 11	Conaway, K. Michael*	53,272	73.7%			
	Brown, Wade	19,010	26.3%			
	TOTAL	72,282				
Congressional District 12	Granger, Kay*	39,907	100.0%	Greene, Mark	9,700	100.0%
	TOTAL	39,907		TOTAL	9,700	
Congressional District 13	Thornberry, Mac*	45,168	68.2%	Minter, Mike G.	4,842	100.0%
	Hays, Elaine	12,330	18.6%			
	Barlow, Pamela Lee	8,723	13.2%			
	TOTAL	66,221		TOTAL	4,842	
Congressional District 14	Weber, Randy K.*	34,131	100.0%	Brown, Donald G.	9,780	68.2%
				Willis, Frank Buchanan "Buck"	3,699	25.8%
				Panjhazari, Gagan	853	6.0%
	TOTAL	34,131		TOTAL	14,332	
Congressional District 15	Zamora, Eddie	7,810	54.9%	Hinojosa, Rubén*	29,916	100.0%
	Carlile, Doug	6,407	45.1%			
	TOTAL	14,217		TOTAL	29,916	
Congressional District 16	Roen, Corey Dean	6,239	100.0%	O'Rourke, Beto*	24,728	100.0%
	TOTAL	6,239		TOTAL	24,728	

TEXAS

GENERAL AND PRIMARY ELECTIONS

	REPUBLICAN PRIMARIES			DEMOCRATIC PRIMARIES		
Congressional District 17	Flores, Bill*	32,770	100.0%	Haynes, Nick	10,141	100.0%
	TOTAL	32,770		TOTAL	10,141	
Congressional District 18	Seibert, Sean	6,527	100.0%	Jackson Lee, Sheila*	14,373	100.0%
	TOTAL	6,527		TOTAL	14,373	
Congressional District 19	Neugebauer, Randy*	39,611	64.4%	Marchbanks, James Neal	6,476	100.0%
	May, Donald R.	14,498	23.6%			
	Winn, Chris	7,429	12.1%			
	TOTAL	61,538		TOTAL	6,476	
Congressional District 20				Castro, Joaquin*	16,275	100.0%
				TOTAL	16,275	
Congressional District 21	Smith, Lamar*	40,441	60.4%			
	McCall, Matt	22,681	33.9%			
	Smith, Michael J.	3,796	5.7%			
	TOTAL	66,918				
Congressional District 22	Olson, Pete*	33,167	100.0%	Briscoe, Frank	3,378	53.2%
				Gibson, Mark	2,973	46.8%
	TOTAL	33,167		TOTAL	6,351	
Congressional District 23	Hurd, Will#	10,496	41.0%	Gallego, Pete P.*	26,484	100.0%
	Canseco, Francisco "Quico"#	10,332	40.3%			
	Lowry, Robert "Doc"	4,796	18.7%			
	TOTAL	25,624		TOTAL	26,484	
	PRIMARY RUNOFF					
	Hurd, Will	8,699	59.5%			
	Canseco, Francisco "Quico"	5,930	40.5%			
	TOTAL	14,629				
Congressional District 24	Marchant, Kenny*	34,265	100.0%	McGehearty, Patrick	8,247	100.0%
	TOTAL	34,265		TOTAL	8,247	
Congressional District 25	Williams, Roger*	43,030	100.0%	Montoya, Marco	11,691	75.2%
				Gourd, Stuart	3,863	24.8%
	TOTAL	43,030		TOTAL	15,554	
Congressional District 26	Burgess, Michael C.*	33,909	82.6%			
	Krause, Joel A.	6,433	15.7%			
	Watrous, Divenchy	698	1.7%			
	TOTAL	41,040				
Congressional District 27	Farenthold, Blake*	31,727	100.0%	Reed, Wesley C.	11,585	100.0%
	TOTAL	31,727		TOTAL	11,585	
Congressional District 28				Cuellar, Henry*	36,821	100.0%
				TOTAL	36,821	
Congressional District 29				Green, Gene*	6,244	100.0%
				TOTAL	6,244	
Congressional District 30				Johnson, Eddie Bernice*	23,756	69.9%
				Caraway, Barbara Mallory	10,216	30.1%
				TOTAL	33,972	

TEXAS

GENERAL AND PRIMARY ELECTIONS

	REPUBLICAN PRIMARIES			DEMOCRATIC PRIMARIES		
Congressional District 31	Carter, John R.*	30,011	100.0%	Minor, Louie	8,036	100.0%
	TOTAL	30,011		TOTAL	8,036	
Congressional District 32	Sessions, Pete*	28,981	63.6%	Perez, Frank	10,681	100.0%
	Pierson, Katrina	16,574	36.4%			
	TOTAL	45,555		TOTAL	10,681	
Congressional District 33				Veasey, Marc A.*	13,292	73.5%
				Sanchez, Tom	4,798	26.5%
				TOTAL	18,090	
Congressional District 34	Smith, Larry S.	7,427	100.0%	Vela, Filemon*	26,237	100.0%
	TOTAL	7,427		TOTAL	26,237	
Congressional District 35	Narvaiz, Susan	9,717	100.0%	Doggett, Lloyd*	15,399	100.0%
	TOTAL	9,717		TOTAL	15,399	
Congressional District 36	Babin, Brian#	17,194	33.4%	Cole, Michael K.	6,507	100.0%
	Streusand, Ben#	12,024	23.3%			
	Manlove, John	3,556	6.9%			
	Centilli, Doug	3,506	6.8%			
	Fitzgerald, John Philip "Phil"	3,388	6.6%			
	Riley, Robin	2,648	5.1%			
	Norman, Dave	2,325	4.5%			
	Meyer, Charles B. "Chuck"	1,574	3.1%			
	Amdur, John	1,470	2.9%			
	Morrell, Kim	1,444	2.8%			
	Engstrand, Jim	1,288	2.5%			
	Kasprzak, Patricia "Pat"	1,116	2.2%			
	TOTAL	51,533		TOTAL	6,507	
	PRIMARY RUNOFF					
	Babin, Brian	19,301	57.8%			
	Streusand, Ben	14,069	42.2%			
	TOTAL	33,370				

Note: An asterisk (*) denotes incumbent. A pound sign (#) indicates the two primary candidates who qualified for a runoff states.

UTAH

Congressional districts first established for elections held in 2012

4 members

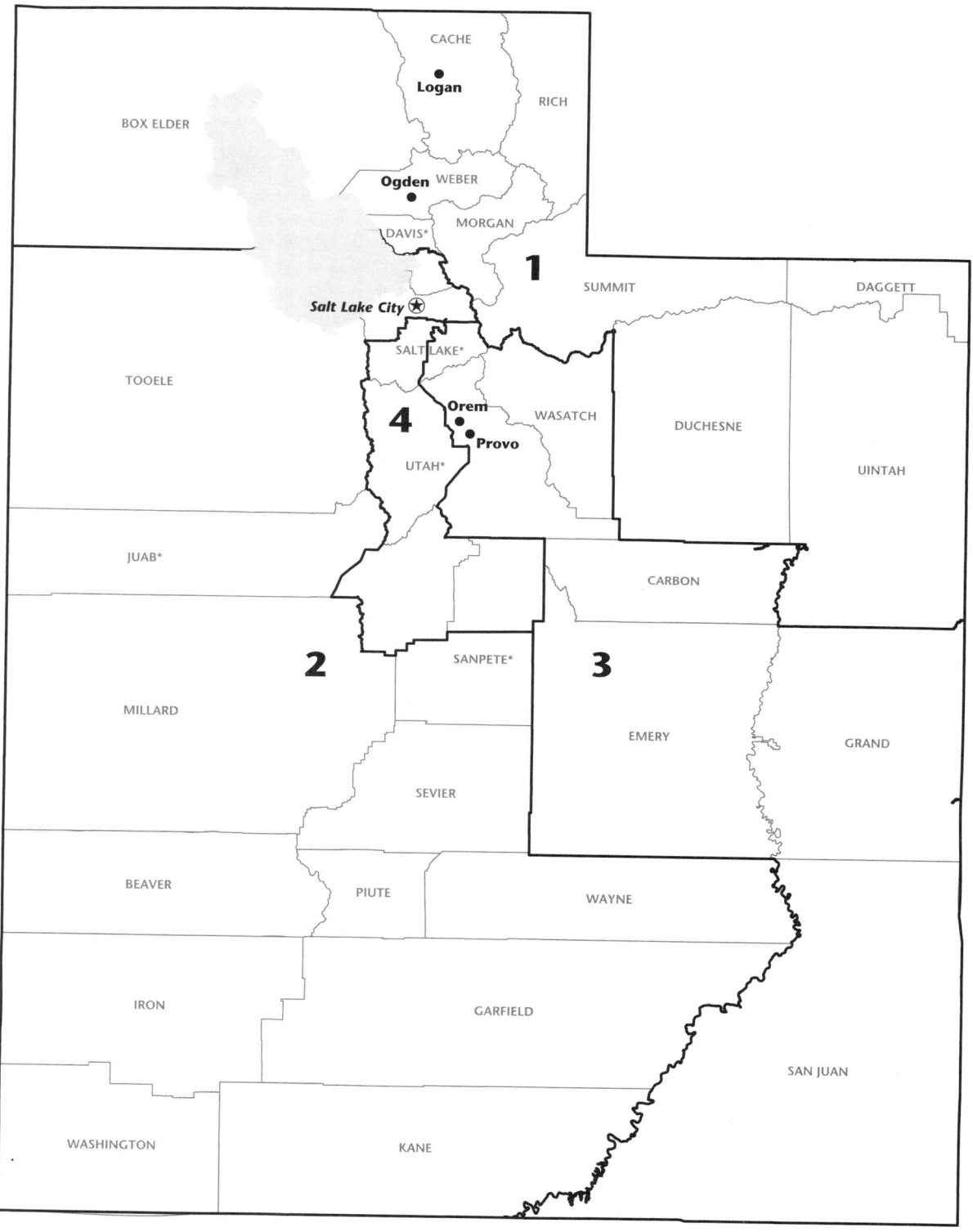

* Asterisk indicates a county whose boundaries include parts of two or more congressional districts.

UTAH

GOVERNOR

Gary R. Herbert (R). Reelected 2012 to a four-year term. Previously elected 2010 to remaining two years of term vacated by resignation of Jon Huntsman Jr. (R) to become ambassador to China. Herbert sworn in as governor August 11, 2009.

SENATORS (2 Republicans)

Orrin G. Hatch (R). Reelected 2012 to a six-year term. Previously elected 2006, 2000, 1994, 1988, 1982, 1976.

Mike Lee (R). Elected 2010 to a six-year term.

REPRESENTATIVES (4 Republicans)

1. Rob Bishop (R)
2. Chris Stewart (R)
3. Jason Chaffetz (R)
4. Mia B. Love (R)

POSTWAR VOTE FOR PRESIDENT

| Year | Total Vote | Republican | | Democratic | | Other Vote | Rep.-Dem. Plurality | Percentage | | | |
| | | Vote | Candidate | Vote | Candidate | | | Total Vote | | Major Vote | |
								Rep.	Dem.	Rep.	Dem.
2012	1,017,440	740,600	Romney, W. Mitt	251,813	Obama, Barack H.*	25,027	488,787 R	72.8%	24.7%	74.6%	25.4%
2008	952,370	596,030	McCain, John S. III	327,670	Obama, Barack H.	28,670	268,360 R	62.6%	34.4%	64.5%	35.5%
2004	927,844	663,742	Bush, George W.*	241,199	Kerry, John F.	22,903	422,543 R	71.5%	26.0%	73.3%	26.7%
2000**	770,754	515,096	Bush, George W.	203,053	Gore, Albert Jr.	52,605	312,043 R	66.8%	26.3%	71.7%	28.3%
1996**	665,629	361,911	Dole, Robert "Bob"	221,633	Clinton, Bill*	82,085	140,278 R	54.4%	33.3%	62.0%	38.0%
1992**	743,999	322,632	Bush, George H.*	183,429	Clinton, Bill	237,938	139,203 R	43.4%	24.7%	63.8%	36.2%
1988	647,008	428,442	Bush, George H.	207,343	Dukakis, Michael S.	11,223	221,099 R	66.2%	32.0%	67.4%	32.6%
1984	629,656	469,105	Reagan, Ronald*	155,369	Mondale, Walter F.	5,182	313,736 R	74.5%	24.7%	75.1%	24.9%
1980**	604,222	439,687	Reagan, Ronald	124,266	Carter, Jimmy*	40,269	315,421 R	72.8%	20.6%	78.0%	22.0%
1976	541,198	337,908	Ford, Gerald R.*	182,110	Carter, Jimmy	21,180	155,798 R	62.4%	33.6%	65.0%	35.0%
1972	478,476	323,643	Nixon, Richard M.*	126,284	McGovern, George S.	28,549	197,359 R	67.6%	26.4%	71.9%	28.1%
1968**	422,568	238,728	Nixon, Richard M.	156,665	Humphrey, Hubert Horatio Jr.	27,175	82,063 R	56.5%	37.1%	60.4%	39.6%
1964	401,413	181,785	Goldwater, Barry M. Sr.	219,628	Johnson, Lyndon B.*		37,843 D	45.3%	54.7%	45.3%	54.7%
1960	374,709	205,361	Nixon, Richard M.	169,248	Kennedy, John F.	100	36,113 R	54.8%	45.2%	54.8%	45.2%
1956	333,995	215,631	Eisenhower, Dwight D.*	118,364	Stevenson, Adlai E. II		97,267 R	64.6%	35.4%	64.6%	35.4%
1952	329,554	194,190	Eisenhower, Dwight D.	135,364	Stevenson, Adlai E. II		58,826 R	58.9%	41.1%	58.9%	41.1%
1948	276,306	124,402	Dewey, Thomas E.	149,151	Truman, Harry S.*	2,753	24,749 D	45.0%	54.0%	45.5%	54.5%

Note: An asterisk (*) denotes incumbent. **In past elections, the other vote included: 2000 - 35,850 Green (Ralph Nader); 1996 - 66,461 Reform (Ross Perot); 1992 - 203,400 Independent (Perot), who finished second; 1980 - 30,284 Independent (John Anderson); 1968 - 26,906 American Independent (George Wallace).

UTAH

POSTWAR VOTE FOR GOVERNOR

Year	Total Vote	Republican		Democratic		Other Vote	Rep.-Dem. Plurality	Percentage			
		Vote	Candidate	Vote	Candidate			Total Vote		Major Vote	
								Rep.	Dem.	Rep.	Dem.
2012	1,006,524	688,592	Herbert, Gary R.*	277,622	Cooke, Peter S.	40,310	410,970 R	68.4%	27.6%	71.3%	28.7%
2010S	643,307	412,151	Herbert, Gary R.*	205,246	Corroon, Peter	25,910	206,905 R	64.1%	31.9%	66.8%	33.2%
2008	945,525	734,049	Huntsman, Jon Jr.*	186,503	Springmeyer, Bob	24,973	547,546 R	77.6%	19.7%	79.7%	20.3%
2004	919,960	531,190	Huntsman, Jon Jr.	380,359	Matheson, Scot Jr.	8,411	150,831 R	57.7%	41.3%	58.3%	41.7%
2000	761,806	424,837	Leavitt, Mike O.*	321,979	Orton, Bill	14,990	102,858 R	55.8%	42.3%	56.9%	43.1%
1996	671,879	503,693	Leavitt, Mike O.*	156,616	Bradley, Jim	11,570	347,077 R	75.0%	23.3%	76.3%	23.7%
1992**	762,549	321,713	Leavitt, Mike O.	177,181	Hanson, Stewart	263,655	144,532 R	42.2%	23.2%	64.5%	35.5%
1988**	649,114	260,462	Bangerter, Norman H.*	249,321	Wilson, Ted	139,331	11,141 R	40.1%	38.4%	51.1%	48.9%
1984	629,619	351,792	Bangerter, Norman H.	275,669	Owens, Wayne	2,158	76,123 R	55.9%	43.8%	56.1%	43.9%
1980	600,019	266,578	Wright, Bob	330,974	Matheson, Scott M.*	2,467	64,396 D	44.4%	55.2%	44.6%	55.4%
1976	539,649	248,027	Romney, Vernon B.	280,706	Matheson, Scott M.	10,916	32,679 D	46.0%	52.0%	46.9%	53.1%
1972	476,447	144,449	Strike, Nicholas L.	331,998	Rampton, Calvin L.*		187,549 D	30.3%	69.7%	30.3%	69.7%
1968	421,012	131,729	Buehner, Carl W.	289,283	Rampton, Calvin L.*		157,554 D	31.3%	68.7%	31.3%	68.7%
1964	398,256	171,300	Melich, Mitchell	226,956	Rampton, Calvin L.		55,656 D	43.0%	57.0%	43.0%	57.0%
1960	371,489	195,634	Clyde, George Dewey*	175,855	Barlocker, William A.		19,779 R	52.7%	47.3%	52.7%	47.3%
1956**	332,889	127,164	Clyde, George Dewey	111,297	Romney, L. C.	94,428	15,867 R	38.2%	33.4%	53.3%	46.7%
1952	327,704	180,516	Lee, J. Bracken*	147,188	Glade, Earl J.		33,328 R	55.1%	44.9%	55.1%	44.9%
1948	275,067	151,253	Lee, J. Bracken	123,814	Maw, Herbert B.*		27,439 R	55.0%	45.0%	55.0%	45.0%

Note: An asterisk (*) denotes incumbent. **In past elections, the other vote included: 1992 - 255,753 Independent (Merrill Cook), who finished second; 1988 - 136,651 Independent Cook); 1956 - 94,428 Independent (J. Bracken Lee). The 2010 election was for a short term to fill a vacancy.

POSTWAR VOTE FOR SENATOR

Year	Total Vote	Republican		Democratic		Other Vote	Rep.-Dem. Plurality	Percentage			
		Vote	Candidate	Vote	Candidate			Total Vote		Major Vote	
								Rep.	Dem.	Rep.	Dem.
2012	1,006,901	657,608	Hatch, Orrin G.*	301,873	Howell, Scott N.	47,420	355,735 R	65.3%	30.0%	68.5%	31.5%
2010	633,829	390,179	Lee, Mike	207,685	Granato, Sam	35,965	182,494 R	61.6%	32.8%	65.3%	34.7%
2006	571,252	356,238	Hatch, Orrin G.*	177,459	Ashdown, Pete	37,555	178,779 R	62.4%	31.1%	66.7%	33.3%
2004	911,726	626,640	Bennett, Robert F.*	258,955	Van Dam, R. Paul	26,131	367,685 R	68.7%	28.4%	70.8%	29.2%
2000	769,704	504,803	Hatch, Orrin G.*	242,569	Howell, Scott N.	22,332	262,234 R	65.6%	31.5%	67.5%	32.5%
1998	494,909	316,652	Bennett, Robert F.*	163,172	Leckman, Scott	15,085	153,480 R	64.0%	33.0%	66.0%	34.0%
1994	519,323	357,297	Hatch, Orrin G.*	146,938	Shea, Patrick A.	15,088	210,359 R	68.8%	28.3%	70.9%	29.1%
1992	758,479	420,069	Bennett, Robert F.	301,228	Owens, Wayne	37,182	118,841 R	55.4%	39.7%	58.2%	41.8%
1988	640,702	430,089	Hatch, Orrin G.*	203,364	Moss, Brian	7,249	226,725 R	67.1%	31.7%	67.9%	32.1%
1986	435,111	314,608	Garn, E. J.*	115,523	Oliver, Craig	4,980	199,085 R	72.3%	26.6%	73.1%	26.9%
1982	530,802	309,332	Hatch, Orrin G.*	219,482	Wilson, Ted	1,988	89,850 R	58.3%	41.3%	58.5%	41.5%
1980	594,298	437,675	Garn, E. J.*	151,454	Berman, Dan	5,169	286,221 R	73.6%	25.5%	74.3%	25.7%
1976	540,108	290,221	Hatch, Orrin G.	241,948	Moss, Frank E.*	7,939	48,273 R	53.7%	44.8%	54.5%	45.5%
1974	420,642	210,299	Garn, E. J.	185,377	Owens, Wayne	24,966	24,922 R	50.0%	44.1%	53.1%	46.9%
1970	374,303	159,004	Burton, Laurence J.	210,207	Moss, Frank E.*	5,092	51,203 D	42.5%	56.2%	43.1%	56.9%
1968	419,262	225,075	Bennett, Wallace F.*	192,168	Weilenmann, Milton	2,019	32,907 R	53.7%	45.8%	53.9%	46.1%
1964	397,384	169,562	Wilkinson, Ernest L.	227,822	Moss, Frank E.*		58,260 D	42.7%	57.3%	42.7%	57.3%
1962	318,411	166,755	Bennett, Wallace F.*	151,656	King, David S.		15,099 R	52.4%	47.6%	52.4%	47.6%
1958**	291,311	101,471	Watkins, Arthur V.*	112,827	Moss, Frank E.	77,013	11,356 D	34.8%	38.7%	47.4%	52.6%
1956	330,381	178,261	Bennett, Wallace F.*	152,120	Hopkin, Alonzo F.		26,141 R	54.0%	46.0%	54.0%	46.0%
1952	327,033	177,435	Watkins, Arthur V.*	149,598	Granger, Walter K.		27,837 R	54.3%	45.7%	54.3%	45.7%
1950	264,440	142,427	Bennett, Wallace F.	121,198	Thomas, Elbert D.*	815	21,229 R	53.9%	45.8%	54.0%	46.0%
1946	197,399	101,142	Watkins, Arthur V.	96,257	Murdock, Abe*		4,885 R	51.2%	48.8%	51.2%	48.8%

Note: An asterisk (*) denotes incumbent. **In past elections, the other vote included: 1958 - 77,013 Independent (J. Bracken Lee).

UTAH

HOUSE OF REPRESENTATIVES

CD	Year	Total Vote	Republican Vote	Republican Candidate	Democratic Vote	Democratic Candidate	Other Vote	Rep.-Dem. Plurality	Total Vote Rep.	Total Vote Dem.	Major Vote Rep.	Major Vote Dem.
1	2014	130,034	84,231	BISHOP, ROB*	36,422	MCALEER, DONNA M.	9,381	47,809 R	64.8%	28.0%	69.8%	30.2
1	2012	245,528	175,487	BISHOP, ROB*	60,611	MCALEER, DONNA M.	9,430	114,876 R	71.5%	24.7%	74.3%	25.7
2	2014	146,188	88,915	STEWART, CHRIS*	47,585	ROBLES, LUZ	9,688	41,330 R	60.8%	32.6%	65.1%	34.9
2	2012	248,545	154,523	STEWART, CHRIS	83,176	SEEGMILLER, JAY	10,846	71,347 R	62.2%	33.5%	65.0%	35.0
3	2014	142,580	102,952	CHAFFETZ, JASON*	32,059	WONNACOTT, BRIAN	7,569	70,893 R	72.2%	22.5%	76.3%	23.7
3	2012	259,547	198,828	CHAFFETZ, JASON*	60,719	SIMONSEN, SOREN D.		138,109 R	76.6%	23.4%	76.6%	23.4
4	2014	147,168	74,936	LOVE, MIA B.	67,425	OWENS, DOUG	4,807	7,511 R	50.9%	45.8%	52.6%	47.4
4	2012	245,277	119,035	LOVE, MIA B.	119,803	MATHESON, JIM*	6,439	768 D	48.5%	48.8%	49.8%	50.2
TOTAL	2014	565,970	351,034		183,491		31,445	167,543 R	62.0%	32.4%	65.7%	34.3
TOTAL	2012	998,897	647,873		324,309		26,715	323,564 R	64.9%	32.5%	66.6%	33.4

Note: An asterisk (*) denotes incumbent.

UTAH

GENERAL AND PRIMARY ELECTIONS

2014 GENERAL ELECTIONS: OTHER VOTES

House — Other vote was:

CD 1 4,847 Libertarian (Craig R. Bowden), 4,534 American Independent (Dwayne A. Vance)

CD 2 4,509 Constitution (Shaun McCausland), 3,328 Independent American (Wayne L. Hill), 1,734 Unaffiliated (Bill Barron), 117 Write-in (Warren Rogers)

CD 3 3,192 Independent American (Zack Strong), 2,584 Unaffiliated (Stephen Tryon), 1,513 Unaffiliated (Ben Mates), 280 Write-in (David A. Else)

CD 4 2,032 Independent American (Tim Aalders), 1,424 Constitution (Collin Robert Simonsen), 1,351 Libertarian (Jim L. Vein)

2014 PRIMARY ELECTIONS: SUPPLEMENTARY INFORMATION

Primary June 24, 2014 **Registration** (as of June 20, 2014) 1,474,151

Republican	659,196
Democratic	139,549
Libertarian	8,137
Independent American	4,948
Constitution	4,142
Unaffiliated	658,179

Primary Type Any registered voter could participate in the Democratic primary. Registered Republicans and unaffiliated voters who chose to change their registration to Republican on primary day could vote in the Republican primary.

UTAH

GENERAL AND PRIMARY ELECTIONS

	REPUBLICAN PRIMARIES		DEMOCRATIC PRIMARIES	
Congressional District 1	Bishop, Rob*	Nominated by Convention	McAleer, Donna M.	Nominated by Convention
Congressional District 2	Stewart, Chris*	Nominated by Convention	Robles, Luz	Nominated by Convention
Congressional District 3	Chaffetz, Jason*	Nominated by Convention	Wonnacott, Brian	Nominated by Convention
Congressional District 4	Love, Mia B.	Nominated by Convention	Owens, Doug	Nominated by Convention

Note: An asterisk (*) denotes incumbent.

VERMONT

One member At Large

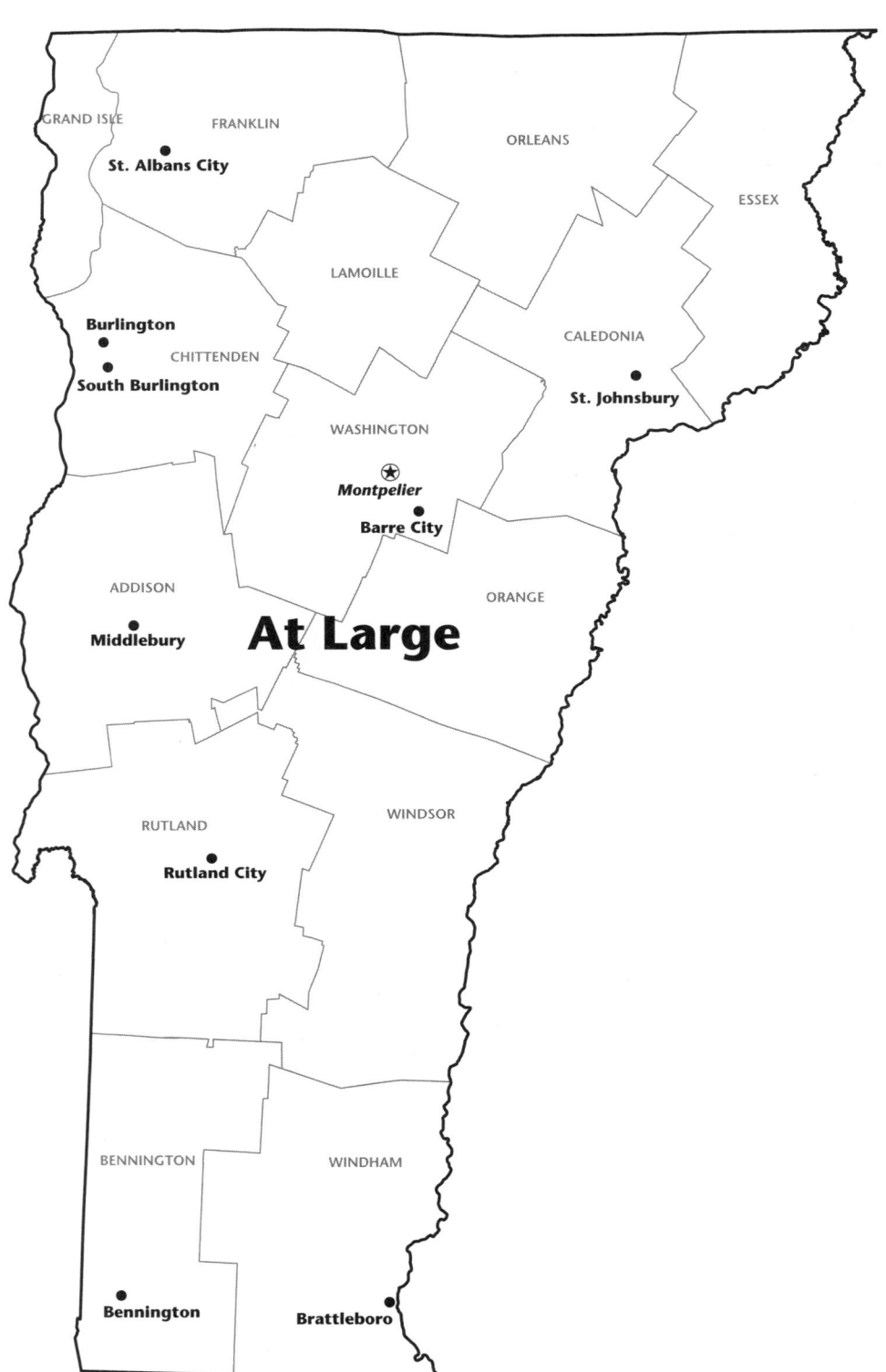

GRAND ISLE

FRANKLIN

ORLEANS

ESSEX

● St. Albans City

LAMOILLE

CALEDONIA

Burlington
●

CHITTENDEN

St. Johnsbury
●

South Burlington
●

WASHINGTON

Montpelier
✪
●
Barre City

ADDISON

ORANGE

At Large

Middlebury
●

WINDSOR

RUTLAND

Rutland City
●

BENNINGTON

WINDHAM

Bennington
●

Brattleboro
●

VERMONT

GOVERNOR

Peter Shumlin (D). Reelected by the state legislature in January 2015 to a two-year term. Previously elected 2012 and January 2011 by the state legislature. Shumlin had finished first in the 2010 and 2014 general election but failed to win a majority of the vote as required by Vermont law.

SENATORS (1 Democrat, 1 Independent)

Patrick J. Leahy (D). Reelected 2010 to a six-year term. Previously elected 2004, 1998, 1992, 1986, 1980, 1974.

Bernard Sanders (Ind.). Reelected 2012 to a six-year term. Previously elected 2006.

REPRESENTATIVE (1 Democrat)

At Large. Peter Welch (D)

POSTWAR VOTE FOR PRESIDENT

| | | Republican | | Democratic | | | | Percentage | | | |
| | | | | | | Other Vote | Rep.-Dem. Plurality | Total Vote | | Major Vote | |
Year	Total Vote	Vote	Candidate	Vote	Candidate			Rep.	Dem.	Rep.	Dem.
2012	299,290	92,698	Romney, W. Mitt	199,239	Obama, Barack H.*	7,353	106,541 D	31.0%	66.6%	31.8%	68.2%
2008	325,046	98,974	McCain, John S. III	219,262	Obama, Barack H.	6,810	120,288 D	30.4%	67.5%	31.1%	68.9%
2004	312,309	121,180	Bush, George W.*	184,067	Kerry, John F.	7,062	62,887 D	38.8%	58.9%	39.7%	60.3%
2000**	294,308	119,775	Bush, George W.	149,022	Gore, Albert Jr.	25,511	29,247 D	40.7%	50.6%	44.6%	55.4%
1996**	258,449	80,352	Dole, Robert "Bob"	137,894	Clinton, Bill*	40,203	57,542 D	31.1%	53.4%	36.8%	63.2%
1992**	289,701	88,122	Bush, George H.*	133,592	Clinton, Bill	67,987	45,470 D	30.4%	46.1%	39.7%	60.3%
1988	243,328	124,331	Bush, George H.	115,776	Dukakis, Michael S.	3,221	8,555 R	51.1%	47.6%	51.8%	48.2%
1984	234,561	135,865	Reagan, Ronald*	95,730	Mondale, Walter F.	2,966	40,135 R	57.9%	40.8%	58.7%	41.3%
1980**	213,299	94,628	Reagan, Ronald	81,952	Carter, Jimmy*	36,719	12,676 R	44.4%	38.4%	53.6%	46.4%
1976	187,765	102,085	Ford, Gerald R.*	80,954	Carter, Jimmy	4,726	21,131 R	54.4%	43.1%	55.8%	44.2%
1972	186,947	117,149	Nixon, Richard M.*	68,174	McGovern, George S.	1,624	48,975 R	62.7%	36.5%	63.2%	36.8%
1968**	161,404	85,142	Nixon, Richard M.	70,255	Humphrey, Hubert Horatio Jr.	6,007	14,887 R	52.8%	43.5%	54.8%	45.2%
1964	163,089	54,942	Goldwater, Barry M. Sr.	108,127	Johnson, Lyndon B.*	20	53,185 D	33.7%	66.3%	33.7%	66.3%
1960	167,324	98,131	Nixon, Richard M.	69,186	Kennedy, John F.	7	28,945 R	58.6%	41.3%	58.6%	41.4%
1956	152,978	110,390	Eisenhower, Dwight D.*	42,549	Stevenson, Adlai E. II	39	67,841 R	72.2%	27.8%	72.2%	27.8%
1952	153,557	109,717	Eisenhower, Dwight D.	43,355	Stevenson, Adlai E. II	485	66,362 R	71.5%	28.2%	71.7%	28.3%
1948	123,382	75,926	Dewey, Thomas E.	45,557	Truman, Harry S.*	1,899	30,369 R	61.5%	36.9%	62.5%	37.5%

Note: An asterisk (*) denotes incumbent. **In past elections, the other vote included: 2000 - 20,374 Green (Ralph Nader); 1996 - 31,024 Reform (Ross Perot); 1992 - 65,991 Independent (Perot); 1980 - 31,761 Independent (John Anderson); 1968 - 5,104 American Independent (George Wallace).

VERMONT

POSTWAR VOTE FOR GOVERNOR

Year	Total Vote	Republican		Democratic		Other Vote	Rep.-Dem. Plurality	Percentage			
		Vote	Candidate	Vote	Candidate			Total Vote		Major Vote	
								Rep.	Dem.	Rep.	Dem.
2014**	193,087	87,075	Milne, Scott	89,509	Shumlin, Peter*	16,503	2,434 D	45.1%	46.4%	49.3%	50.7%
2012	295,261	110,940	Brock, Randy	170,598	Shumlin, Peter*	13,723	59,658 D	37.6%	57.8%	39.4%	60.6%
2010**	241,605	115,212	Dubie, Brian E.	119,543	Shumlin, Peter	6,850	4,331 D	47.7%	49.5%	49.1%	50.9%
2008**	319,085	170,492	Douglas, Jim*	69,534	Symington, Gaye	79,059	100,958 R	53.4%	21.8%	71.0%	29.0%
2006	262,524	148,014	Douglas, Jim*	108,090	Parker, Scudder	6,420	39,924 R	56.4%	41.2%	57.8%	42.2%
2004	309,285	181,540	Douglas, Jim*	117,327	Clavell, Peter	10,418	64,213 R	58.7%	37.9%	60.7%	39.3%
2002**	230,161	103,436	Douglas, Jim	97,565	Racine, Doug	29,160	5,871 R	44.9%	42.4%	51.5%	48.5%
2000	293,473	111,359	Dwyer, Ruth	148,059	Dean, Howard B.*	34,055	36,700 D	37.9%	50.5%	42.9%	57.1%
1998	218,120	89,726	Dwyer, Ruth	121,425	Dean, Howard B.*	6,969	31,699 D	41.1%	55.7%	42.5%	57.5%
1996	254,648	57,161	Gropper, John L.	179,544	Dean, Howard B.*	17,943	122,383 D	22.4%	70.5%	24.1%	75.9%
1994	212,046	40,292	Kelley, David F.	145,661	Dean, Howard B.*	26,093	105,369 D	19.0%	68.7%	21.7%	78.3%
1992	285,728	65,837	McClaughry, John	213,523	Dean, Howard B.*	6,368	147,686 D	23.0%	74.7%	23.6%	76.4%
1990	211,422	109,540	Snelling, Richard A.	97,321	Welch, Peter	4,561	12,219 R	51.8%	46.0%	53.0%	47.0%
1988	242,879	105,191	Bernhardt, Michael	134,438	Kunin, Madeline*	3,250	29,247 D	43.3%	55.4%	43.9%	56.1%
1986**	196,716	75,162	Smith, Peter	92,379	Kunin, Madeline*	29,175	17,217 D	38.2%	47.0%	44.9%	55.1%
1984	233,753	113,264	Easton, John J.	116,938	Kunin, Madeline	3,551	3,674 D	48.5%	50.0%	49.2%	50.8%
1982	169,251	93,111	Snelling, Richard A.*	74,394	Kunin, Madeline	1,746	18,717 R	55.0%	44.0%	55.6%	44.4%
1980	210,381	123,229	Snelling, Richard A.*	77,363	Diamond, M. Jerome	9,789	45,866 R	58.6%	36.8%	61.4%	38.6%
1978	124,482	78,181	Snelling, Richard A.*	42,482	Granai, Edwin C.	3,819	35,699 R	62.8%	34.1%	64.8%	35.2%
1976	185,929	99,268	Snelling, Richard A.	75,262	Hackel, Stella B.	11,399	24,006 R	53.4%	40.5%	56.9%	43.1%
1974	141,156	53,672	Kennedy, Walter L.	79,842	Salmon, Thomas P.*	7,642	26,170 D	38.0%	56.6%	40.2%	59.8%
1972	189,237	82,491	Hackett, Luther F.	104,533	Salmon, Thomas P.	2,213	22,042 D	43.6%	55.2%	44.1%	55.9%
1970	153,528	87,458	Davis, Deane C.*	66,028	O'Brien, Leo	42	21,430 R	57.0%	43.0%	57.0%	43.0%
1968	161,089	89,387	Davis, Deane C.	71,656	Daley, John J.	46	17,731 R	55.5%	44.5%	55.5%	44.5%
1966	136,262	57,577	Snelling, Richard A.	78,669	Hoff, Philip H.*	16	21,092 D	42.3%	57.7%	42.3%	57.7%
1964	164,199	57,576	Foote, Ralph A.	106,611	Hoff, Philip H.*	12	49,035 D	35.1%	64.9%	35.1%	64.9%
1962	121,422	60,035	Keyser, F. Ray Jr.*	61,383	Hoff, Philip H.	4	1,348 D	49.4%	50.6%	49.4%	50.6%
1960	164,632	92,861	Keyser, F. Ray Jr.	71,755	Niquette, Russell F.	16	21,106 R	56.4%	43.6%	56.4%	43.6%
1958	123,728	62,222	Stafford, Robert T.	61,503	Leddy, Bernard J.	3	719 R	50.3%	49.7%	50.3%	49.7%
1956	153,809	88,379	Johnson, Joseph B.*	65,420	Branon, E. Frank	10	22,959 R	57.5%	42.5%	57.5%	42.5%
1954	114,360	59,778	Johnson, Joseph B.	54,554	Branon, E. Frank	28	5,224 R	52.3%	47.7%	52.3%	47.7%
1952	150,836	78,338	Emerson, Lee Earl*	60,051	Larrow, Robert W.	12,447	18,287 R	51.9%	39.8%	56.6%	43.4%
1950	87,155	64,915	Emerson, Lee Earl	22,227	Moran, J. Edward	13	42,688 R	74.5%	25.5%	74.5%	25.5%
1948	120,183	86,394	Gibson, Ernest Willard Jr.*	33,588	Ryan, Charles F.	201	52,806 R	71.9%	27.9%	72.0%	28.0%
1946	72,044	57,849	Gibson, Ernest Willard Jr.	14,096	Coburn, Berthold C.	99	43,753 R	80.3%	19.6%	80.4%	19.6%

Note: An asterisk (*) denotes incumbent. **In past elections, the other vote included: 2008 - 69,791 Independent (Anthony Pollina), who finished second; 1986 - 28,430 Independent (Bernard Sanders). After the 1986, 2002, 2010, and 2014 elections in the absence of a majority of the total vote for any candidate, the state legislature elected the governor — Democrat Madeleine M. Kunin in January 1987, Republican Jim Douglas in January 2003, and Democrat Peter Shumlin in January 2011 and January 2015.

VERMONT

POSTWAR VOTE FOR SENATOR

		Republican		Democratic				Percentage			
								Total Vote		Major Vote	
Year	Total Vote	Vote	Candidate	Vote	Candidate	Other Vote	Rep.-Dem. Plurality	Rep.	Dem.	Rep.	Dem.
2012**	294,267	73,198	MacGovern, John			221,069	73,198 R#	24.9%		100.0%	
2010	235,178	72,699	Britton, Len	151,281	Leahy, Patrick J.*	11,198	78,582 D	30.9%	64.3%	32.5%	67.5%
2006**	262,419	84,924	Tarrant, Richard			177,495	84,924 R#	32.4%		100.0%	
2004	307,208	75,398	McMullen, Jack	216,972	Leahy, Patrick J.*	14,838	141,574 D	24.5%	70.6%	25.8%	74.2%
2000	288,500	189,133	Jeffords, James M.*	73,352	Flanagan, Ed	26,015	115,781 R	65.6%	25.4%	72.1%	27.9%
1998	214,036	48,051	Tuttle, Fred	154,567	Leahy, Patrick J.*	11,418	106,516 D	22.4%	72.2%	23.7%	76.3%
1994	211,672	106,505	Jeffords, James M.*	85,868	Backus, Jan	19,299	20,637 R	50.3%	40.6%	55.4%	44.6%
1992	285,739	123,854	Douglas, Jim	154,762	Leahy, Patrick J.*	7,123	30,908 D	43.3%	54.2%	44.5%	55.5%
1988	240,108	163,183	Jeffords, James M.	71,460	Gray, William	5,465	91,723 R	68.0%	29.8%	69.5%	30.5%
1986	196,532	67,798	Snelling, Richard A.	124,123	Leahy, Patrick J.*	4,611	56,325 D	34.5%	63.2%	35.3%	64.7%
1982	168,003	84,450	Stafford, Robert T.*	79,340	Guest, James A.	4,213	5,110 R	50.3%	47.2%	51.6%	48.4%
1980	209,124	101,421	Ledbetter, Stewart M.	104,176	Leahy, Patrick J.*	3,527	2,755 D	48.5%	49.8%	49.3%	50.7%
1976	189,046	94,481	Stafford, Robert T.*	85,682	Salmon, Thomas P.	8,883	8,799 R	50.0%	45.3%	52.4%	47.6%
1974	142,772	66,223	Mallary, Richard W.	70,629	Leahy, Patrick J.	5,920	4,406 D	46.4%	49.5%	48.4%	51.6%
1972S	71,348	45,888	Stafford, Robert T.*	23,842	Major, Randolph T.	1,618	22,046 R	64.3%	33.4%	65.8%	34.2%
1970	154,899	91,198	Prouty, Winston L.*	62,271	Hoff, Philip H.	1,430	28,927 R	58.9%	40.2%	59.4%	40.6%
1968**	157,375	157,154	Aiken, George David*			221	157,154 R	99.9%		100.0%	
1964	164,350	87,879	Prouty, Winston L.*	76,457	Fayette, Frederick J.	14	11,422 R	53.5%	46.5%	53.5%	46.5%
1962	121,571	81,241	Aiken, George David*	40,134	Johnson, W. Robert	196	41,107 R	66.8%	33.0%	66.9%	33.1%
1958	124,442	64,900	Prouty, Winston L.	59,536	Fayette, Frederick J.	6	5,364 R	52.2%	47.8%	52.2%	47.8%
1956	155,289	103,101	Aiken, George David*	52,184	O'Shea, Bernard G.	4	50,917 R	66.4%	33.6%	66.4%	33.6%
1952	154,052	111,406	Flanders, Ralph E.*	42,630	Johnston, Allan R.	16	68,776 R	72.3%	27.7%	72.3%	27.7%
1950	89,171	69,543	Aiken, George David*	19,608	Bigelow, James E.	20	49,935 R	78.0%	22.0%	78.0%	22.0%
1946	73,340	54,729	Flanders, Ralph E.	18,594	McDevitt, Charles P.	17	36,135 R	74.6%	25.4%	74.6%	25.4%

Note: An asterisk (*) denotes incumbent. A pound sign (#) indicates that the winner was an independent. **In past elections, the other vote included: 2012 - 209,053 Independent (Bernard Sanders), who received 71.0 percent of the total vote and was re-elected; 2006 - 171,638 Independent (Bernard Sanders), who received 65.4 percent of the total vote and was elected. Sanders also won the Democratic primary in 2006 and 2012, but declined the nomination each time in order to run as an independent. The Democratic Party did not run a candidate in the 2006 or 2012 Senate election. The January 1972 election was for a short term to fill a vacancy. In 1968 the Republican candidate (George D. Aiken) won both major party nominations.

VERMONT

GOVERNOR 2014

2010 Census Population	County	Total Vote	Republican (Milne)	Democratic (Shumlin)	Other	Rep.-Dem. Plurality	Percentage			
							Total Vote		Major Vote	
							Rep.	Dem.	Rep.	Dem.
36,821	ADDISON	12,920	5,765	6,025	1,130	260 D	44.6%	46.6%	48.9%	51.1%
37,125	BENNINGTON	11,188	4,180	6,207	801	2,027 D	37.4%	55.5%	40.2%	59.8%
31,227	CALEDONIA	8,929	4,962	3,137	830	1,825 R	55.6%	35.1%	61.3%	38.7%
156,545	CHITTENDEN	47,124	18,988	23,753	4,383	4,765 D	40.3%	50.4%	44.4%	55.6%
6,306	ESSEX	1,643	967	524	152	443 R	58.9%	31.9%	64.9%	35.1%
47,746	FRANKLIN	13,411	7,353	4,850	1,208	2,503 R	54.8%	36.2%	60.3%	39.7%
6,970	GRAND ISLE	2,953	1,490	1,196	267	294 R	50.5%	40.5%	55.5%	44.5%
24,475	LAMOILLE	7,730	3,810	3,207	713	603 R	49.3%	41.5%	54.3%	45.7%
28,936	ORANGE	9,481	4,532	4,329	620	203 R	47.8%	45.7%	51.1%	48.9%
27,231	ORLEANS	7,846	4,521	2,448	877	2,073 R	57.6%	31.2%	64.9%	35.1%
61,642	RUTLAND	19,055	10,289	7,210	1,556	3,079 R	54.0%	37.8%	58.8%	41.2%
59,534	WASHINGTON	20,405	9,290	9,190	1,925	100 R	45.5%	45.0%	50.3%	49.7%
44,513	WINDHAM	12,603	3,776	7,829	998	4,053 D	30.0%	62.1%	32.5%	67.5%
56,670	WINDSOR	17,799	7,152	9,604	1,043	2,452 D	40.2%	54.0%	42.7%	57.3%
625,741	TOTAL	193,087	87,075	89,509	16,503	2,434 D	45.1%	46.4%	49.3%	50.7%

Note: * We're winning the VT 600 vote by city/town.

VERMONT

GUBERNATORIAL ELECTION 2014 (CITY/TOWN)

Total Pop (2010 Census)	City/Town	Total Vote	Republican (Milne)	Democratic (Shumlin)	Other	Rep.-Dem. Plurality	Percentage Total Vote Rep.	Dem.	Major Vote Rep.	Dem
9,052	Barre City	2,118	1,174	769	175	405 R	55.4	36.3	60.4	39.(
7,924	Barre Town	2,890	1,980	771	139	1,209 R	68.5	26.7	72.0	28.(
15,764	Bennington	3,826	1,148	2,393	285	1,245 D	30.0	62.5	32.4	67.(
12,046	Brattleboro	3,062	624	2,220	218	1,596 D	20.4	72.5	21.9	78.:
42,417	Burlington	9,604	2,276	6,401	927	4,125 D	23.7	66.6	26.2	73.:
17,067	Colchester	4,521	2,262	1,836	423	426 R	50.0	40.6	55.2	44.:
4,621	Derby	1,426	884	454	88	430 R	62.0	31.8	66.1	33.:
19,587	Essex	6,334	2,963	2,615	756	348 R	46.8	41.3	53.1	46.:
9,952	Hartford	4,038	1,502	2,359	177	857 D	37.2	58.4	38.9	61.:
5,009	Jericho	2,210	988	1,025	197	37 D	44.7	46.4	49.1	50.:
5,981	Lyndon	1,230	759	357	114	402 R	61.7	29.0	68.0	32.(
4,391	Manchester	1,557	757	723	77	34 R	48.6	46.4	51.1	48.:
8,496	Middlebury	2,213	733	1,341	139	608 D	33.1	60.6	35.3	64.:
10,352	Milton	2,787	1,656	857	274	799 R	59.4	30.7	65.9	34.:
7,855	Montpelier	3,029	758	1,918	353	1,160 D	25.0	63.3	28.3	71.:
5,227	Morristown	1,651	813	682	156	131 R	49.2	41.3	54.4	45.(
6,207	Northfield	1,373	790	491	92	299 R	57.5	35.8	61.7	38.:
4,778	Randolph	1,529	721	707	101	14 R	47.2	46.2	50.5	49.:
4,081	Richmond	1,664	621	878	165	257 D	37.3	52.8	41.4	58.(
5,282	Rockingham	1,182	339	730	113	391 D	28.7	61.8	31.7	68.:
16,495	Rutland City	4,451	2,322	1,787	342	535 R	52.2	40.1	56.5	43.:
4,054	Rutland Town	1,646	987	547	112	440 R	60.0	33.2	64.3	35.:
7,144	Shelburne	2,950	1,224	1,542	184	318 D	41.5	52.3	44.3	55.:
17,904	South Burlington	5,674	2,276	2,935	463	659 D	40.1	51.7	43.7	56.:
9,373	Springfield	2,096	981	967	148	14 R	46.8	46.1	50.4	49.(
6,918	St. Albans City	1,614	713	740	161	27 D	44.2	45.8	49.1	50.:
5,999	St. Albans Town	1,889	1,081	656	152	425 R	57.2	34.7	62.2	37.:
7,603	St. Johnsbury	1,932	1,059	728	145	331 R	54.8	37.7	59.3	40.:
4,314	Stowe	1,482	731	641	110	90 R	49.3	43.3	53.3	46.:
6,427	Swanton	1,589	955	518	116	437 R	60.1	32.6	64.8	35.:
5,064	Waterbury	1,768	756	828	184	72 D	42.8	46.8	47.7	52.:
8,698	Williston	3,131	1,494	1,404	233	90 R	47.7	44.8	51.6	48.:
7,267	Winooski	1,475	508	827	140	319 D	34.4	56.1	38.1	61.:
3,048	Woodstock	1,211	461	708	42	247 D	38.1	58.5	39.4	60.(

VERMONT

HOUSE OF REPRESENTATIVES

CD	Year	Total Vote	Republican Vote	Republican Candidate	Democratic Vote	Democratic Candidate	Other Vote	Rep.-Dem. Plurality	Percentage Total Vote Rep.	Dem.	Major Vote Rep.	Dem.
At Large	2014	191,504	59,432	DONKA, MARK	123,349	WELCH, PETER*	8,723	63,917 D	31.0%	64.4%	32.5%	67.5%
At Large	2012	289,931	67,543	DONKA, MARK	208,600	WELCH, PETER*	13,788	141,057 D	23.3%	71.9%	24.5%	75.5%
At Large	2010	238,521	76,403	BEAUDRY, PAUL D.	154,006	WELCH, PETER*	8,112	77,603 D	32.0%	64.6%	33.2%	66.8%
At Large	2008	298,151			248,203	WELCH, PETER*	49,948	248,203 D		83.2%		100.0%
At Large	2006	262,726	117,023	RAINVILLE, MARTHA	139,815	WELCH, PETER	5,888	22,792 D	44.5%	53.2%	45.6%	54.4%
At Large	2004	305,008	74,271	PARKE, GREG	21,684	DROWN, LARRY	209,053	52,587 R	24.4%	7.1%	77.4%	22.6%
At Large	2002	225,476	72,813	MEUB, WILLIAM			152,663	72,813 R#	32.3%		100.0%	
At Large	2000	283,366	51,977	KERIN, KAREN ANN	14,918	DIAMONDSTONE, PETE	216,471	37,059 R#	18.3%	5.3%	77.7%	22.3%
At Large	1998	215,133	70,740	CANDON, MARK			144,393	70,740 R#	32.9%		100.0%	
At Large	1996	254,706	83,021	SWEETSER, SUSAN W.	23,830	LONG, JACK	147,855	59,191 R#	32.6%	9.4%	77.7%	22.3%
At Large	1994	211,449	98,523	CARROLL, JOHN			112,926	98,523 R#	46.6%		100.0%	
At Large	1992	281,626	86,901	PHILBIN, TIMOTHY	22,279	YOUNG, LEWIS E.	172,446	64,622 R#	30.9%	7.9%	79.6%	20.4%
At Large	1990	209,856	82,938	SMITH, PETER*	6,315	SANDOVAL, DOLORES	120,603	76,623 R#	39.5%	3.0%	92.9%	7.1%
At Large	1988	240,131	98,937	SMITH, PETER	45,330	POIRIER, PAUL N.	95,864	53,607 R	41.2%	18.9%	68.6%	31.4%
At Large	1986	188,954	168,403	JEFFORDS, JAMES M.*			20,551	168,403 R	89.1%		100.0%	
At Large	1984	226,297	148,025	JEFFORDS, JAMES M.*	60,360	POLLINA, ANTHONY	17,912	87,665 R	65.4%	26.7%	71.0%	29.0%
At Large	1982	164,951	114,191	JEFFORDS, JAMES M.*	38,296	KAPLAN, MARK A.	12,464	75,895 R	69.2%	23.2%	74.9%	25.1%
At Large	1980	194,697	154,274	JEFFORDS, JAMES M.*			40,423	154,274 R	79.2%		100.0%	
At Large	1978	120,502	90,688	JEFFORDS, JAMES M.*	23,228	DIETZ, S. MARIE	6,586	67,460 R	75.3%	19.3%	79.6%	20.4%

VERMONT

HOUSE OF REPRESENTATIVES

			Republican		Democratic				Percentage			
									Total Vote		Major Vote	
CD	Year	Total Vote	Vote	Candidate	Vote	Candidate	Other Vote	Rep.-Dem. Plurality	Rep.	Dem.	Rep.	Dem.
At Large	1976	184,783	124,458	JEFFORDS, JAMES M.*	60,202	BURGESS, JOHN A.	123	64,256 R	67.4%	32.6%	67.4%	32.6%
At Large	1974	140,899	74,561	JEFFORDS, JAMES M.	56,342	CAIN, FRANCIS J.	9,996	18,219 R	52.9%	40.0%	57.0%	43.0%
At Large	1972	186,028	120,924	MALLARY, RICHARD W.	65,062	MEYER, WILLIAM H.	42	55,862 R	65.0%	35.0%	65.0%	35.0%
At Large	1970	152,557	103,806	STAFFORD, ROBERT T.*	44,415	O'SHEA, BERNARD G.	4,336	59,391 R	68.0%	29.1%	70.0%	30.0%
At Large	1968	157,133	156,956	STAFFORD, ROBERT T.*			177	156,956 R	99.9%		100.0%	
At Large	1966	135,748	89,097	STAFFORD, ROBERT T.*	46,643	RYAN, WILLIAM J.	8	42,454 R	65.6%	34.4%	65.6%	34.4%
At Large	1964	163,452	92,252	STAFFORD, ROBERT T.*	71,193	O'SHEA, BERNARD G.	7	21,059 R	56.4%	43.6%	56.4%	43.6%
At Large	1962	121,381	68,822	STAFFORD, ROBERT T.*	52,535	REYNOLDS, HAROLD	24	16,287 R	56.7%	43.3%	56.7%	43.3%
At Large	1960	166,035	94,905	STAFFORD, ROBERT T.	71,111	MEYER, WILLIAM H.*	19	23,794 R	57.2%	42.8%	57.2%	42.8%
At Large	1958	122,702	59,536	ARTHUR, HAROLD J.	63,131	MEYER, WILLIAM H.	35	3,595 D	48.5%	51.5%	48.5%	51.5%
At Large	1956	154,536	103,736	PROUTY, WINSTON L.*	50,797	ST. AMOUR, CAMILLE	3	52,939 R	67.1%	32.9%	67.1%	32.9%
At Large	1954	114,289	70,143	PROUTY, WINSTON L.*	44,141	BOYLAN, JOHN J.	5	26,002 R	61.4%	38.6%	61.4%	38.6%
At Large	1952	153,060	109,871	PROUTY, WINSTON L.*	43,187	COMINGS, HERBERT B.	2	66,684 R	71.8%	28.2%	71.8%	28.2%
At Large	1950	88,851	65,248	PROUTY, WINSTON L.	22,709	COMINGS, HERBERT B.	894	42,539 R	73.4%	25.6%	74.2%	25.8%
At Large	1948	121,968	74,076	PLUMLEY, CHARLES A.*	47,767	READY, ROBERT W.	125	26,309 R	60.7%	39.2%	60.8%	39.2%
At Large	1946	73,066	46,985	PLUMLEY, CHARLES A.*	26,056	CALDBECK, MATTHEW J.	25	20,929 R	64.3%	35.7%	64.3%	35.7%

Note: An asterisk (*) denotes incumbent. A pound sign (#) indicates that the winner was an independent candidate (Bernard Sanders).

VERMONT

GENERAL AND PRIMARY ELECTIONS

2014 GENERAL ELECTIONS: OTHER VOTES

Governor

Other vote was 8,428 Libertarian (Dan Feliciano), 3,157 Independent (Emily Peyton), 1,673 Liberty Union (Pete Diamondstone), 1,434 Independent (Bernard Peters), 1,089 Independent (Cris Ericson), 722 scattered write-in

House

CD At Large

2,750 Independent (Cris Ericson), 2,071 Liberty Union (Matthew Andrews), 2,024 Independent (Jerry Trudell), 1,685 Independent (Randall Meyer), 193 scattered write-in

2014 PRIMARY ELECTIONS: SUPPLEMENTARY INFORMATION

Primary August 26, 2014   **Registration** (as of August 26, 2014)   440,194   No Party Registration

Primary Type Open—Any registered voter could participate in the primary of any recognized party.

	REPUBLICAN PRIMARIES			DEMOCRATIC PRIMARIES		
Governor	Milne, Scott	11,486	71.7%	Shumlin, Peter*	15,260	77.0%
	write-in	2,358	14.7%	Paige, H. Brooke	3,199	16.1%
	Berry, Steve	1,106	6.9%	write-in	1,369	6.9%
	Peyton, Emily	1,060	6.6%			
	TOTAL	16,010		TOTAL	19,828	
Congressional At Large	Donka, Mark	4,340	33.7%	Welch, Peter*	19,284	98.9%
	Russell, Don	4,026	31.2%	write-in	224	1.1%
	Nolte, Donald Walter	3,803	29.5%			
	write-in	719	5.6%			
	TOTAL	12,888		TOTAL	19,508	

Note: An asterisk (*) denotes incumbent.

VIRGINIA

Congressional districts first established for elections held in 2012

11 members

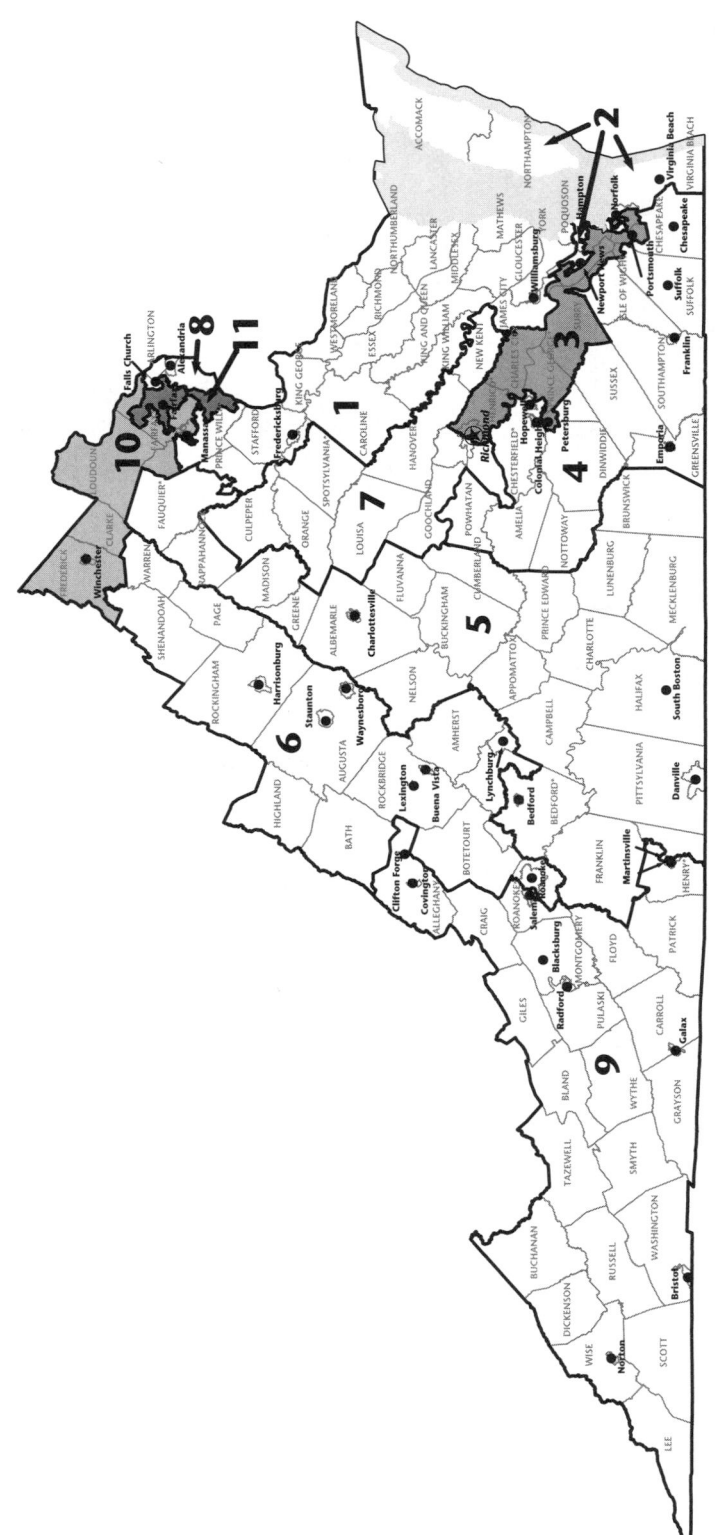

Independent cities are treated as county equivalents; in most cases, labels are included for the cities.

* Asterisk indicates a county whose boundaries include parts of two or more congressional districts.

VIRGINIA

Northern Virginia Area

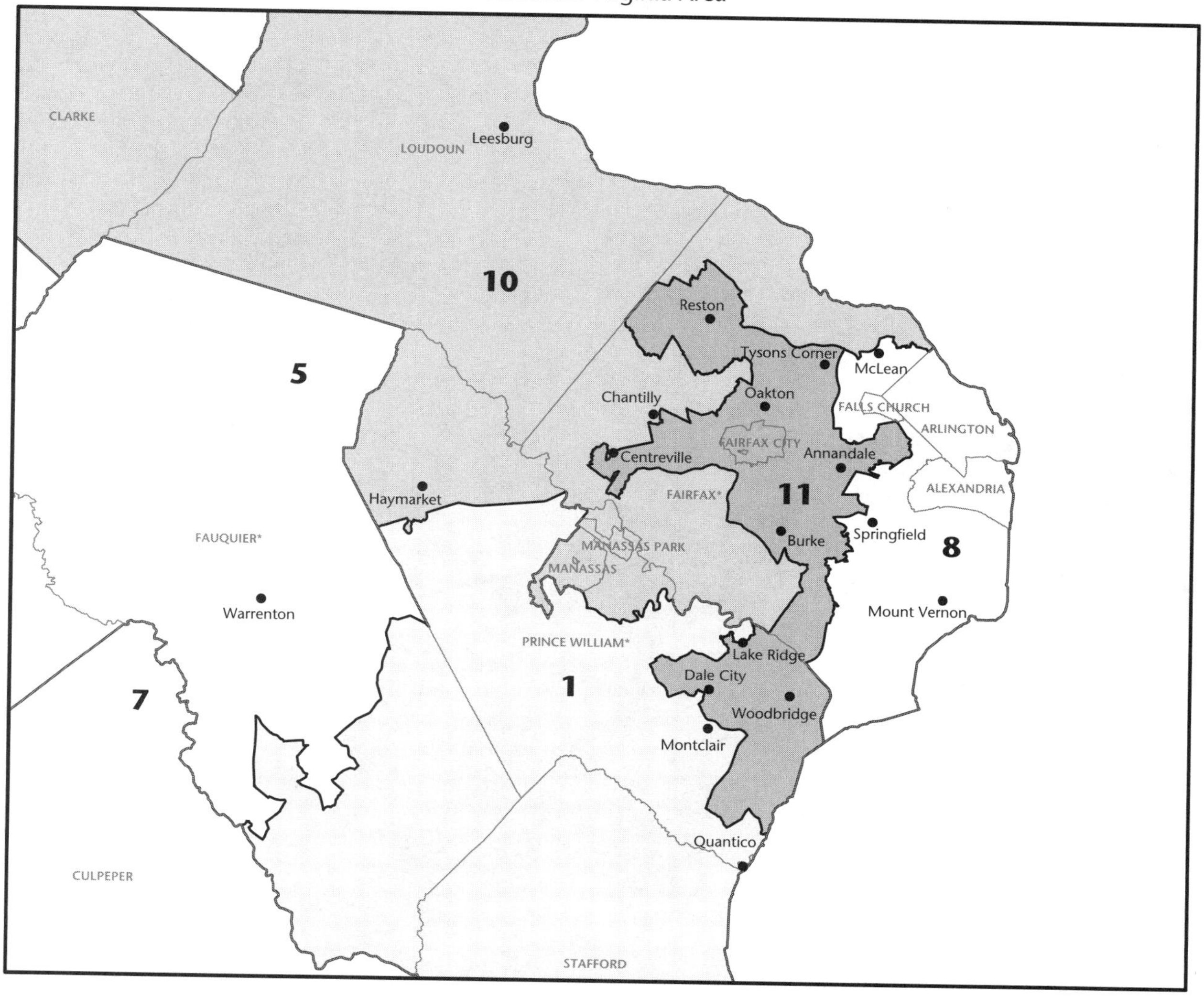

CLARKE

LOUDOUN   Leesburg

10

5

Reston

Tysons Corner
McLean
Chantilly   Oakton
FALLS CHURCH
ARLINGTON
FAIRFAX CITY
Centreville   Annandale
ALEXANDRIA
FAIRFAX*
11
Haymarket
Burke   Springfield
8

FAUQUIER*
MANASSAS PARK
MANASSAS
Mount Vernon
Warrenton

PRINCE WILLIAM*
Lake Ridge
7   Dale City
1   Woodbridge
Montclair

Quantico

CULPEPER

STAFFORD

* Asterisk indicates a county whose boundaries include parts of two or more congressional districts.

VIRGINIA

Hampton Roads, Virginia Beach Areas

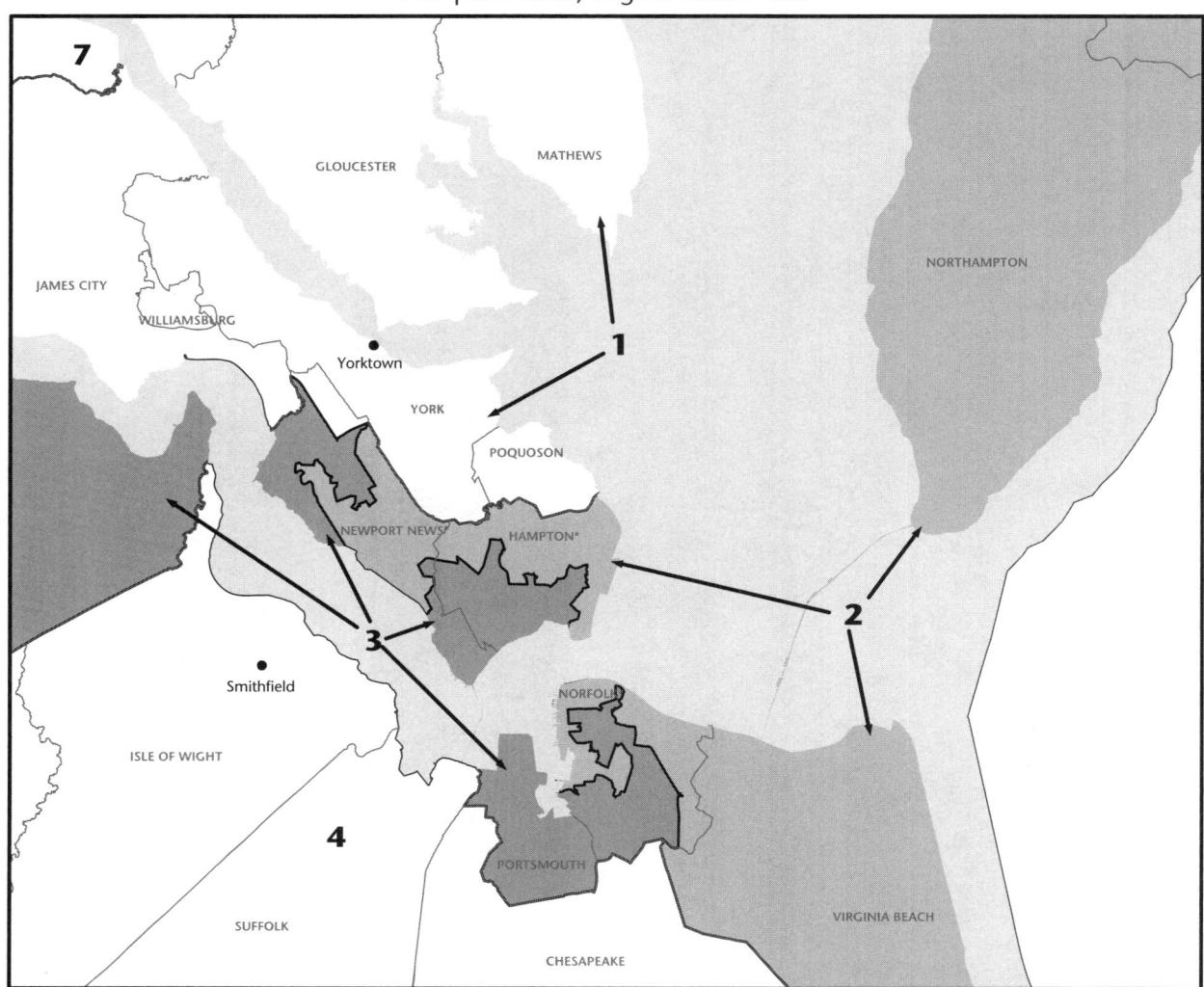

* Asterisk indicates a county whose boundaries include parts of two or more congressional districts.

VIRGINIA

GOVERNOR
Terry McAuliffe (D). Elected 2013 to a four-year term.

SENATORS (2 Democrats)
Tim Kaine (D). Elected 2012 to a six-year term.

Mark R. Warner (D). Reelected 2014 to a six-year term. Previously elected 2008.

REPRESENTATIVES (8 Republicans, 3 Democrats)
1. Robert J. Wittman (R)
2. E. Scott Rigell (R)
3. Robert C. Bobby Scott (D)
4. J. Randy Forbes (R)
5. Robert Hurt (R)
6. Bob Goodlatte (R)
7. Dave Brat (R)
8. Donald S. Beyer Jr. (D)
9. H. Morgan Griffith (R)
10. Barbara Comstock (R)
11. Gerald E. "Gerry" Connolly (D)

POSTWAR VOTE FOR PRESIDENT

| | | Republican | | Democratic | | | | Percentage | | | |
| | | | | | | | | Total Vote | | Major Vote | |
Year	Total Vote	Vote	Candidate	Vote	Candidate	Other Vote	Rep.-Dem. Plurality	Rep.	Dem.	Rep.	Dem.
2012	3,854,489	1,822,522	Romney, W. Mitt	1,971,820	Obama, Barack H.*	60,147	149,298 D	47.3%	51.2%	48.0%	52.0%
2008	3,723,260	1,725,005	McCain, John S. III	1,959,532	Obama, Barack H.	38,723	234,527 D	46.3%	52.6%	46.8%	53.2%
2004	3,198,367	1,716,959	Bush, George W.*	1,454,742	Kerry, John F.	26,666	262,217 R	53.7%	45.5%	54.1%	45.9%
2000**	2,739,447	1,437,490	Bush, George W.	1,217,290	Gore, Albert Jr.	84,667	220,200 R	52.5%	44.4%	54.1%	45.9%
1996**	2,416,642	1,138,350	Dole, Robert "Bob"	1,091,060	Clinton, Bill*	187,232	47,290 R	47.1%	45.1%	51.1%	48.9%
1992**	2,558,665	1,150,517	Bush, George H.*	1,038,650	Clinton, Bill	369,498	111,867 R	45.0%	40.6%	52.6%	47.4%
1988	2,191,609	1,309,162	Bush, George H.	859,799	Dukakis, Michael S.	22,648	449,363 R	59.7%	39.2%	60.4%	39.6%
1984	2,146,635	1,337,078	Reagan, Ronald*	796,250	Mondale, Walter F.	13,307	540,828 R	62.3%	37.1%	62.7%	37.3%
1980**	1,866,032	989,609	Reagan, Ronald	752,174	Carter, Jimmy*	124,249	237,435 R	53.0%	40.3%	56.8%	43.2%
1976	1,697,094	836,554	Ford, Gerald R.*	813,896	Carter, Jimmy	46,644	22,658 R	49.3%	48.0%	50.7%	49.3%
1972	1,457,019	988,493	Nixon, Richard M.*	438,887	McGovern, George S.	29,639	549,606 R	67.8%	30.1%	69.3%	30.7%
1968**	1,361,491	590,319	Nixon, Richard M.	442,387	Humphrey, Hubert Horatio Jr.	328,785	147,932 R	43.4%	32.5%	57.2%	42.8%
1964	1,042,267	481,334	Goldwater, Barry M. Sr.	558,038	Johnson, Lyndon B.*	2,895	76,704 D	46.2%	53.5%	46.3%	53.7%
1960	771,449	404,521	Nixon, Richard M.	362,327	Kennedy, John F.	4,601	42,194 R	52.4%	47.0%	52.8%	47.2%
1956	697,978	386,459	Eisenhower, Dwight D.*	267,760	Stevenson, Adlai E. II	43,759	118,699 R	55.4%	38.4%	59.1%	40.9%
1952	619,689	349,037	Eisenhower, Dwight D.	268,677	Stevenson, Adlai E. II	1,975	80,360 R	56.3%	43.4%	56.5%	43.5%
1948**	419,256	172,070	Dewey, Thomas E.	200,786	Truman, Harry S.*	46,400	28,716 D	41.0%	47.9%	46.1%	53.9%

Note: An asterisk (*) denotes incumbent. **In past elections, the other vote included: 2000 - 59,398 Green (Ralph Nader); 1996 - 159,861 Reform (Ross Perot); 1992 - 348,639 Independent (Perot); 1980 - 95,418 Independent (John Anderson); 1968 - 321,833 American Independent (George Wallace); 1948 - 43,393 States' Rights (Strom Thurmond).

VIRGINIA

POSTWAR VOTE FOR GOVERNOR

Year	Total Vote	Republican Vote	Republican Candidate	Democratic Vote	Democratic Candidate	Other Vote	Rep.-Dem. Plurality	Percentage Total Vote Rep.	Dem.	Major Vote Rep.	Dem.
2013	2,241,071	1,013,354	Cuccinelli, Ken	1,069,789	McAuliffe, Terry	157,928	56,435 D	45.2%	47.7%	48.6%	51.4%
2009	1,985,103	1,163,651	McDonnell, Robert F.	818,950	Deeds, R. Creigh	2,502	344,701 R	58.6%	41.3%	58.7%	41.3%
2005	1,983,778	912,327	Kilgore, Jerry W.	1,025,942	Kaine, Tim	45,509	113,615 D	46.0%	51.7%	47.1%	52.9%
2001	1,886,721	887,234	Earley, Mark	984,177	Warner, Mark R.	15,310	96,943 D	47.0%	52.2%	47.4%	52.6%
1997	1,736,314	969,062	Gilmore, James S. III	738,971	Beyer, Donald S. Jr.	28,281	230,091 R	55.8%	42.6%	56.7%	43.3%
1993	1,793,916	1,045,319	Allen, George F.	733,527	Terry, Mary Sue	15,070	311,792 R	58.3%	40.9%	58.8%	41.2%
1989	1,789,078	890,195	Coleman, J. Marshall	896,936	Wilder, L. Douglas	1,947	6,741 D	49.8%	50.1%	49.8%	50.2%
1985	1,343,240	601,649	Durrette, Wyatt B.	741,438	Baliles, Gerald L.	153	139,789 D	44.8%	55.2%	44.8%	55.2%
1981	1,420,638	659,398	Coleman, J. Marshall	760,384	Robb, Charles S.	856	100,986 D	46.4%	53.5%	46.4%	53.6%
1977	1,250,940	699,302	Dalton, John N.	541,319	Howell, Henry	10,319	157,983 R	55.9%	43.3%	56.4%	43.6%
1973**	1,035,495	525,075	Godwin, Mills E. Jr.			510,420	525,075 R	50.7%		100.0%	
1969	915,764	480,869	Holton, Linwood	415,695	Battle, William C.	19,200	65,174 R	52.5%	45.4%	53.6%	46.4%
1965**	562,789	212,207	Holton, Linwood	269,526	Godwin, Mills E. Jr.	81,056	57,319 D	37.7%	47.9%	44.1%	55.9%
1961	394,490	142,567	Pearson, H. Clyde	251,861	Harrison, Albertis S. Jr.	62	109,294 D	36.1%	63.8%	36.1%	63.9%
1957	517,655	188,628	Dalton, Ted	326,921	Almond, J. Lindsay Jr.	2,106	138,293 D	36.4%	63.2%	36.6%	63.4%
1953	414,025	183,328	Dalton, Ted	226,998	Stanley, Thomas B.	3,699	43,670 D	44.3%	54.8%	44.7%	55.3%
1949	262,350	71,991	Johnson, Walter	184,772	Battle, John S.	5,587	112,781 D	27.4%	70.4%	28.0%	72.0%
1945	164,741	52,386	Landreth, S. Lloyd	112,355	Tuck, William M.		59,969 D	31.8%	68.2%	31.8%	68.2%

Note: An asterisk (*) denotes incumbent. **In past elections, the other vote included: 1973 - 510,103 Independent (Henry Howell); 1965 - 75,307 Conservative (William J. Story Jr.). The Democratic Party did not run a candidate in the 1973 gubernatorial election.

POSTWAR VOTE FOR SENATOR

Year	Total Vote	Republican Vote	Republican Candidate	Democratic Vote	Democratic Candidate	Other Vote	Rep.-Dem. Plurality	Percentage Total Vote Rep.	Dem.	Major Vote Rep.	Dem.
2014	2,184,473	1,055,940	Gillespie, Edward W. "Ed"	1,073,667	Warner, Mark R.*	54,866	17,727 D	48.3%	49.1%	49.6%	50.4%
2012	3,802,196	1,785,542	Allen, George F.	2,010,067	Kaine, Tim	6,587	224,525 D	47.0%	52.9%	47.0%	53.0%
2008	3,643,294	1,228,830	Gilmore, James S. III	2,369,327	Warner, Mark R.	45,137	1,140,497 D	33.7%	65.0%	34.2%	65.8%
2006	2,370,445	1,166,277	Allen, George F.*	1,175,606	Webb, Jim H. Jr.	28,562	9,329 D	49.2%	49.6%	49.8%	50.2%
2002	1,489,422	1,229,894	Warner, John W.*			259,528	1,229,894 R	82.6%		100.0%	
2000	2,718,301	1,420,460	Allen, George F.	1,296,093	Robb, Charles S.*	1,748	124,367 R	52.3%	47.7%	52.3%	47.7%
1996	2,354,715	1,235,744	Warner, John W.*	1,115,982	Warner, Mark R.	2,989	119,762 R	52.5%	47.4%	52.5%	47.5%
1994**	2,057,463	882,213	North, Oliver L.	938,376	Robb, Charles S.*	236,874	56,163 D	42.9%	45.6%	48.5%	51.5%
1990**	1,083,660	876,782	Warner, John W.*			206,878	876,782 R	80.9%		100.0%	
1988	2,068,897	593,652	Dawkins, Maurice A.	1,474,086	Robb, Charles S.	1,159	880,434 D	28.7%	71.2%	28.7%	71.3%
1984	2,007,487	1,406,194	Warner, John W.*	601,142	Harrison, Edythe C.	151	805,052 R	70.0%	29.9%	70.1%	29.9%
1982	1,415,622	724,571	Trible, Paul	690,839	Davis, Richard	212	33,732 R	51.2%	48.8%	51.2%	48.8%
1978	1,222,256	613,232	Warner, John W.	608,511	Miller, Andrew P.	513	4,721 R	50.2%	49.8%	50.2%	49.8%
1976**	1,557,500			596,009	Zumwalt, Elmo R.	961,491	596,009 D#		38.3%		100.0%
1972	1,396,268	718,337	Scott, William L.	643,963	Spong, William B.*	33,968	74,374 R	51.4%	46.1%	52.7%	47.3%
1970**	946,751	145,031	Garland, Ray L.	295,057	Rawlings, George C.	506,663	150,026 D#	15.3%	31.2%	33.0%	67.0%
1966	733,879	245,681	Ould, James P. Jr.	429,855	Spong, William B.	58,343	184,174 D	33.5%	58.6%	36.4%	63.6%
1966S	729,839	272,804	Traylor, Lawrence M.	389,028	Byrd, Harry Flood Jr.*	68,007	116,224 D	37.4%	53.3%	41.2%	58.8%
1964**	928,363	176,624	May, Richard A.	592,260	Byrd, Harry F.*	159,479	415,636 D	19.0%	63.8%	23.0%	77.0%
1960**	622,820			506,169	Robertson, A. Willis*	116,651	506,169 D		81.3%		100.0%
1958**	457,640			317,221	Byrd, Harry F.*	140,419	317,221 D		69.3%		100.0%
1954**	306,447			244,844	Robertson, A. Willis*	61,603	244,844 D		79.9%		100.0%
1952**	543,516			398,677	Byrd, Harry F.*	144,839	398,677 D		73.4%		100.0%
1948	386,998	119,366	Woods, Robert H.	253,865	Robertson, A. Willis*	13,767	134,499 D	30.8%	65.6%	32.0%	68.0%
1946	252,863	77,005	Parsons, Lester S.	163,960	Byrd, Harry F.*	11,898	86,955 D	30.5%	64.8%	32.0%	68.0%
1946S	248,962	72,253	Woods, Robert H.	169,680	Robertson, A. Willis	7,029	97,427 D	29.0%	68.2%	29.9%	70.1%

Note: An asterisk (*) denotes incumbent. A pound sign (#) indicates that the winner was an independent. **In past elections, the other vote included: 1994 - 235,324 Independent (J. Marshall Coleman); 1990 - 196,755 Independent (Nancy Spannaus), who finished second; 1976 - 890,778 Independent (Harry Flood Byrd Jr.), who won the election with 57.2 percent of the total vote; 1970 - 506,633 Independent (Harry Flood Byrd Jr.), who won the election with 53.5 percent of the total vote; 1964 - 95,526 Independent (James W. Respess); 1960 - 88,718 Independent Democrat (Stuart D. Baker), who finished second; 1958 - 120,224 Independent (Louis Wensel), who finished second; 1954 - 32,681 Independent Democrat (Charles William Lewis Jr.), who finished second; 1952 - 69,133 Independent Democrat (H. M. Vise Sr.), who finished second; 67,281 Social Democrat (Clarke T. Robb). On each of the 1946 and 1966 elections was for a short term to fill a vacancy. The Democratic Party did not run a candidate in the Senate elections of 1990 and 2002. The Republican Party did not run a candidate in the Senate elections of 1952, 1954, 1958, 1960, and 1976.

VIRGINIA
GOVERNOR 2013

2010 Census Population	County	Total Vote	Republican (Cuccinelli)	Democratic (McAuliffe)	Other	Rep.-Dem. Plurality	Percentage Total Vote Rep.	Dem.	Percentage Major Vote Rep.	Dem.
33,164	ACCOMACK	9,086	4,879	3,806	401	1,073 R	53.7%	41.9%	56.2%	43.8%
98,970	ALBEMARLE	35,088	12,408	19,039	3,641	6,631 D	35.4%	54.3%	39.5%	60.5%
16,250	ALLEGHANY	4,136	1,993	1,628	515	365 R	48.2%	39.4%	55.0%	45.0%
12,690	AMELIA	4,257	2,613	1,338	306	1,275 R	61.4%	31.4%	66.1%	33.9%
32,353	AMHERST	9,039	5,466	2,993	580	2,473 R	60.5%	33.1%	64.6%	35.4%
14,973	APPOMATTOX	5,084	3,475	1,241	368	2,234 R	68.4%	24.4%	73.7%	26.3%
207,627	ARLINGTON	67,539	14,978	48,346	4,215	33,368 D	22.2%	71.6%	23.7%	76.3%
73,750	AUGUSTA	20,409	13,817	5,100	1,492	8,717 R	67.7%	25.0%	73.0%	27.0%
4,731	BATH	1,213	686	392	135	294 R	56.6%	32.3%	63.6%	36.4%
68,676	BEDFORD	25,020	17,330	5,802	1,888	11,528 R	69.3%	23.2%	74.9%	25.1%
6,824	BLAND	1,849	1,300	388	161	912 R	70.3%	21.0%	77.0%	23.0%
33,148	BOTETOURT	11,313	7,366	2,924	1,023	4,442 R	65.1%	25.8%	71.6%	28.4%
17,434	BRUNSWICK	4,523	1,618	2,704	201	1,086 D	35.8%	59.8%	37.4%	62.6%
24,098	BUCHANAN	4,849	3,275	1,461	113	1,814 R	67.5%	30.1%	69.2%	30.8%
17,146	BUCKINGHAM	4,163	2,053	1,804	306	249 R	49.3%	43.3%	53.2%	46.8%
54,842	CAMPBELL	15,867	11,133	3,712	1,022	7,421 R	70.2%	23.4%	75.0%	25.0%
28,545	CAROLINE	7,785	3,380	3,794	611	414 D	43.4%	48.7%	47.1%	52.9%
30,042	CARROLL	7,878	5,061	2,182	635	2,879 R	64.2%	27.7%	69.9%	30.1%
7,256	CHARLES CITY	2,542	828	1,558	156	730 D	32.6%	61.3%	34.7%	65.3%
12,586	CHARLOTTE	3,732	2,104	1,358	270	746 R	56.4%	36.4%	60.8%	39.2%
316,236	CHESTERFIELD	104,992	51,114	42,865	11,013	8,249 R	48.7%	40.8%	54.4%	45.6%
14,034	CLARKE	4,907	2,596	2,002	309	594 R	52.9%	40.8%	56.5%	43.5%
5,190	CRAIG	1,632	1,063	396	173	667 R	65.1%	24.3%	72.9%	27.1%
46,689	CULPEPER	11,940	7,272	3,923	745	3,349 R	60.9%	32.9%	65.0%	35.0%
10,052	CUMBERLAND	2,908	1,456	1,190	262	266 R	50.1%	40.9%	55.0%	45.0%
15,903	DICKENSON	3,433	2,125	1,184	124	941 R	61.9%	34.5%	64.2%	35.8%
28,001	DINWIDDIE	7,458	3,507	3,380	571	127 R	47.0%	45.3%	50.9%	49.1%
11,151	ESSEX	3,115	1,487	1,381	247	106 R	47.7%	44.3%	51.8%	48.2%
1,081,726	FAIRFAX	306,430	110,681	178,746	17,003	68,065 D	36.1%	58.3%	38.2%	61.8%
65,203	FAUQUIER	20,992	12,565	7,376	1,051	5,189 R	59.9%	35.1%	63.0%	37.0%
15,279	FLOYD	4,580	2,636	1,488	456	1,148 R	57.6%	32.5%	63.9%	36.1%
25,691	FLUVANNA	7,910	3,774	3,348	788	426 R	47.7%	42.3%	53.0%	47.0%
56,159	FRANKLIN	16,324	10,011	4,756	1,557	5,255 R	61.3%	29.1%	67.8%	32.2%
78,305	FREDERICK	20,605	13,148	6,339	1,118	6,809 R	63.8%	30.8%	67.5%	32.5%
17,286	GILES	4,997	2,944	1,541	512	1,403 R	58.9%	30.8%	65.6%	34.4%
36,858	GLOUCESTER	11,204	6,688	3,633	883	3,055 R	59.7%	32.4%	64.8%	35.2%
21,717	GOOCHLAND	9,198	5,155	3,077	966	2,078 R	56.0%	33.5%	62.6%	37.4%
15,533	GRAYSON	4,853	3,094	1,400	359	1,694 R	63.8%	28.8%	68.8%	31.2%
18,403	GREENE	5,352	3,069	1,719	564	1,350 R	57.3%	32.1%	64.1%	35.9%
12,243	GREENSVILLE	2,870	1,012	1,724	134	712 D	35.3%	60.1%	37.0%	63.0%
36,241	HALIFAX	10,022	5,432	3,909	681	1,523 R	54.2%	39.0%	58.2%	41.8%
99,863	HANOVER	38,820	23,415	10,862	4,543	12,553 R	60.3%	28.0%	68.3%	31.7%
306,935	HENRICO	103,689	39,400	53,132	11,157	13,732 D	38.0%	51.2%	42.6%	57.4%
54,151	HENRY	13,533	8,024	4,558	951	3,466 R	59.3%	33.7%	63.8%	36.2%
2,321	HIGHLAND	903	557	279	67	278 R	61.7%	30.9%	66.6%	33.4%
35,270	ISLE OF WIGHT	12,162	6,547	4,843	772	1,704 R	53.8%	39.8%	57.5%	42.5%
67,009	JAMES CITY	26,916	13,756	11,344	1,816	2,412 R	51.1%	42.1%	54.8%	45.2%
6,945	KING AND QUEEN	2,197	1,051	968	178	83 R	47.8%	44.1%	52.1%	47.9%
23,584	KING GEORGE	6,668	3,985	2,289	394	1,696 R	59.8%	34.3%	63.5%	36.5%
15,935	KING WILLIAM	5,238	2,976	1,671	591	1,305 R	56.8%	31.9%	64.0%	36.0%
11,391	LANCASTER	4,537	2,367	1,786	384	581 R	52.2%	39.4%	57.0%	43.0%
25,587	LEE	4,796	3,507	1,180	109	2,327 R	73.1%	24.6%	74.8%	25.2%
312,311	LOUDOUN	89,540	40,464	44,369	4,707	3,905 D	45.2%	49.6%	47.7%	52.3%
33,153	LOUISA	9,953	5,381	3,546	1,026	1,835 R	54.1%	35.6%	60.3%	39.7%
12,914	LUNENBURG	3,347	1,705	1,397	245	308 R	50.9%	41.7%	55.0%	45.0%
13,308	MADISON	4,522	2,510	1,575	437	935 R	55.5%	34.8%	61.4%	38.6%
8,978	MATHEWS	3,487	2,044	1,194	249	850 R	58.6%	34.2%	63.1%	36.9%
32,727	MECKLENBURG	7,554	4,226	3,038	290	1,188 R	55.9%	40.2%	58.2%	41.8%
10,959	MIDDLESEX	3,918	2,131	1,375	412	756 R	54.4%	35.1%	60.8%	39.2%
94,392	MONTGOMERY	23,349	10,133	10,689	2,527	556 D	43.4%	45.8%	48.7%	51.3%

VIRGINIA

GOVERNOR 2013

2010 Census Population	County	Total Vote	Republican (Cuccinelli)	Democratic (McAuliffe)	Other	Rep.-Dem. Plurality	Percentage			
							Total Vote		Major Vote	
							Rep.	Dem.	Rep.	Dem.
15,020	NELSON	5,369	2,314	2,523	532	209 D	43.1%	47.0%	47.8%	52.2%
18,429	NEW KENT	7,321	4,365	2,120	836	2,245 R	59.6%	29.0%	67.3%	32.7%
12,389	NORTHAMPTON	3,950	1,589	2,048	313	459 D	40.2%	51.8%	43.7%	56.3%
12,330	NORTHUMBERLAND	5,231	2,823	1,961	447	862 R	54.0%	37.5%	59.0%	41.0%
15,853	NOTTOWAY	4,001	1,899	1,756	346	143 R	47.5%	43.9%	52.0%	48.0%
33,481	ORANGE	9,995	5,561	3,629	805	1,932 R	55.6%	36.3%	60.5%	39.5%
24,042	PAGE	6,089	3,754	2,001	334	1,753 R	61.7%	32.9%	65.2%	34.8%
18,490	PATRICK	5,124	3,553	1,373	198	2,180 R	69.3%	26.8%	72.1%	27.9%
63,506	PITTSYLVANIA	18,255	11,682	5,419	1,154	6,263 R	64.0%	29.7%	68.3%	31.7%
28,046	POWHATAN	10,197	6,748	2,327	1,122	4,421 R	66.2%	22.8%	74.4%	25.6%
23,368	PRINCE EDWARD	5,338	2,252	2,674	412	422 D	42.2%	50.1%	45.7%	54.3%
35,725	PRINCE GEORGE	9,316	5,011	3,580	725	1,431 R	53.8%	38.4%	58.3%	41.7%
402,002	PRINCE WILLIAM	97,116	42,431	50,441	4,244	8,010 D	43.7%	51.9%	45.7%	54.3%
34,872	PULASKI	8,062	4,720	2,581	761	2,139 R	58.5%	32.0%	64.6%	35.4%
7,373	RAPPAHANNOCK	2,920	1,499	1,290	131	209 R	51.3%	44.2%	53.7%	46.3%
9,254	RICHMOND	2,301	1,295	836	170	459 R	56.3%	36.3%	60.8%	39.2%
92,376	ROANOKE	30,973	18,040	9,844	3,089	8,196 R	58.2%	31.8%	64.7%	35.3%
22,307	ROCKBRIDGE	6,720	3,640	2,431	649	1,209 R	54.2%	36.2%	60.0%	40.0%
76,314	ROCKINGHAM	22,128	14,968	5,725	1,435	9,243 R	67.6%	25.9%	72.3%	27.7%
28,897	RUSSELL	6,051	3,920	1,914	217	2,006 R	64.8%	31.6%	67.2%	32.8%
23,177	SCOTT	5,293	4,001	1,158	134	2,843 R	75.6%	21.9%	77.6%	22.4%
41,993	SHENANDOAH	11,603	7,345	3,565	693	3,780 R	63.3%	30.7%	67.3%	32.7%
32,208	SMYTH	7,532	4,880	2,307	345	2,573 R	64.8%	30.6%	67.9%	32.1%
18,570	SOUTHAMPTON	5,129	2,578	2,295	256	283 R	50.3%	44.7%	52.9%	47.1%
122,397	SPOTSYLVANIA	31,730	17,755	12,220	1,755	5,535 R	56.0%	38.5%	59.2%	40.8%
128,961	STAFFORD	34,121	18,595	13,657	1,869	4,938 R	54.5%	40.0%	57.7%	42.3%
7,058	SURRY	2,678	977	1,576	125	599 D	36.5%	58.8%	38.3%	61.7%
12,087	SUSSEX	3,246	1,259	1,834	153	575 D	38.8%	56.5%	40.7%	59.3%
45,078	TAZEWELL	10,135	7,490	2,358	287	5,132 R	73.9%	23.3%	76.1%	23.9%
37,575	WARREN	9,702	5,873	3,392	437	2,481 R	60.5%	35.0%	63.4%	36.6%
54,876	WASHINGTON	14,485	9,989	3,936	560	6,053 R	69.0%	27.2%	71.7%	28.3%
17,454	WESTMORELAND	4,465	2,116	2,115	234	1 R	47.4%	47.4%	50.0%	50.0%
41,452	WISE	8,324	5,830	2,196	298	3,634 R	70.0%	26.4%	72.6%	27.4%
29,235	WYTHE	7,712	4,967	2,049	696	2,918 R	64.4%	26.6%	70.8%	29.2%
65,464	YORK	21,129	11,923	7,745	1,461	4,178 R	56.4%	36.7%	60.6%	39.4%

2010 Census Population	City	Total Vote	Republican (Cuccinelli)	Democratic (McAuliffe)	Other	Rep.-Dem. Plurality	Percentage			
							Total Vote		Major Vote	
							Rep.	Dem.	Rep.	Dem.
139,966	ALEXANDRIA	41,218	9,405	29,584	2,229	20,179 D	22.8%	71.8%	24.1%	75.9%
17,835	BRISTOL	3,996	2,536	1,305	155	1,231 R	63.5%	32.7%	66.0%	34.0%
6,650	BUENA VISTA	1,245	721	422	102	299 R	57.9%	33.9%	63.1%	36.9%
43,475	CHARLOTTESVILLE	12,508	1,922	9,440	1,146	7,518 D	15.4%	75.5%	16.9%	83.1%
222,209	CHESAPEAKE	63,277	28,855	30,838	3,584	1,983 D	45.6%	48.7%	48.3%	51.7%
17,411	COLONIAL HEIGHTS	5,060	3,319	1,131	610	2,188 R	65.6%	22.4%	74.6%	25.4%
5,961	COVINGTON	1,275	513	590	172	77 D	40.2%	46.3%	46.5%	53.5%
43,055	DANVILLE	10,836	4,824	5,389	623	565 D	44.5%	49.7%	47.2%	52.8%
5,927	EMPORIA	1,655	569	987	99	418 D	34.4%	59.6%	36.6%	63.4%
22,565	FAIRFAX CITY	7,196	2,777	3,987	432	1,210 D	38.6%	55.4%	41.1%	58.9%
12,332	FALLS CHURCH	4,942	1,142	3,523	277	2,381 D	23.1%	71.3%	24.5%	75.5%
8,582	FRANKLIN CITY	2,303	833	1,362	108	529 D	36.2%	59.1%	37.9%	62.1%
24,286	FREDERICKSBURG	6,072	2,154	3,488	430	1,334 D	35.5%	57.4%	38.2%	61.8%
7,042	GALAX	1,285	728	455	102	273 R	56.7%	35.4%	61.5%	38.5%
137,436	HAMPTON	36,971	10,384	24,631	1,956	14,247 D	28.1%	66.6%	29.7%	70.3%

VIRGINIA

GOVERNOR 2013

2010 Census Population	County	Total Vote	Republican (Cuccinelli)	Democratic (McAuliffe)	Other	Rep.-Dem. Plurality	Percentage			
							Total Vote		Major Vote	
							Rep.	Dem.	Rep.	Dem.
48,914	HARRISONBURG	8,037	3,236	4,190	611	954 D	40.3%	52.1%	43.6%	56.4%
22,591	HOPEWELL	5,429	2,446	2,499	484	53 D	45.1%	46.0%	49.5%	50.5%
7,042	LEXINGTON	1,519	499	936	84	437 D	32.9%	61.6%	34.8%	65.2%
75,568	LYNCHBURG	19,852	10,632	7,923	1,297	2,709 R	53.6%	39.9%	57.3%	42.7%
37,821	MANASSAS	8,241	3,828	4,013	400	185 D	46.5%	48.7%	48.8%	51.2%
14,273	MANASSAS PARK	2,126	888	1,142	96	254 D	41.8%	53.7%	43.7%	56.3%
13,821	MARTINSVILLE	3,392	1,411	1,723	258	312 D	41.6%	50.8%	45.0%	55.0%
180,719	NEWPORT NEWS	42,419	14,803	25,085	2,531	10,282 D	34.9%	59.1%	37.1%	62.9%
242,803	NORFOLK	46,260	11,654	31,708	2,898	20,054 D	25.2%	68.5%	26.9%	73.1%
3,958	NORTON	871	482	346	43	136 R	55.3%	39.7%	58.2%	41.8%
32,420	PETERSBURG	8,300	798	7,260	242	6,462 D	9.6%	87.5%	9.9%	90.1%
12,150	POQUOSON	4,415	2,987	1,040	388	1,947 R	67.7%	23.6%	74.2%	25.8%
95,535	PORTSMOUTH	25,953	6,776	17,671	1,506	10,895 D	26.1%	68.1%	27.7%	72.3%
16,408	RADFORD	2,924	1,254	1,364	306	110 D	42.9%	46.6%	47.9%	52.1%
204,214	RICHMOND CITY	58,554	9,854	42,957	5,743	33,103 D	16.8%	73.4%	18.7%	81.3%
97,032	ROANOKE CITY	21,781	7,786	11,714	2,281	3,928 D	35.7%	53.8%	39.9%	60.1%
24,802	SALEM	7,176	4,019	2,324	833	1,695 R	56.0%	32.4%	63.4%	36.6%
23,746	STAUNTON	6,472	2,869	3,058	545	189 D	44.3%	47.2%	48.4%	51.6%
84,585	SUFFOLK	24,240	9,906	13,132	1,202	3,226 D	40.9%	54.2%	43.0%	57.0%
437,994	VIRGINIA BEACH	108,253	51,494	49,357	7,402	2,137 R	47.6%	45.6%	51.1%	48.9%
21,006	WAYNESBORO	5,006	2,598	1,918	490	680 R	51.9%	38.3%	57.5%	42.5%
14,068	WILLIAMSBURG	4,364	1,337	2,748	279	1,411 D	30.6%	63.0%	32.7%	67.3%
26,203	WINCHESTER	5,684	2,702	2,631	351	71 R	47.5%	46.3%	50.7%	49.3%
7,994,802	TOTAL	2,241,071	1,013,354	1,069,789	157,928	56,435 D	45.2%	47.7%	48.6%	51.4%

VIRGINIA

SENATOR 2014

2010 Census Population	County	Total Vote	Republican (Gillespie)	Democratic (Warner)	Other	Rep.-Dem. Plurality	Percentage			
							Total Vote		Major Vote	
							Rep.	Dem.	Rep.	Dem.
33,164	ACCOMACK	9,658	5,259	4,137	262	1,122 R	54.5%	42.8%	56.0%	44.0%
98,970	ALBEMARLE	33,040	13,930	17,924	1,186	3,994 D	42.2%	54.2%	43.7%	56.3%
16,250	ALLEGHANY	4,155	1,835	2,211	109	376 D	44.2%	53.2%	45.4%	54.6%
12,690	AMELIA	4,068	2,588	1,377	103	1,211 R	63.6%	33.8%	65.3%	34.7%
32,353	AMHERST	8,798	5,370	3,243	185	2,127 R	61.0%	36.9%	62.3%	37.7%
14,973	APPOMATTOX	4,736	3,234	1,399	103	1,835 R	68.3%	29.5%	69.8%	30.2%
207,627	ARLINGTON	67,683	18,239	47,709	1,735	29,470 D	26.9%	70.5%	27.7%	72.3%
73,750	AUGUSTA	19,733	14,011	5,153	569	8,858 R	71.0%	26.1%	73.1%	26.9%
4,731	BATH	1,171	638	489	44	149 R	54.5%	41.8%	56.6%	43.4%
68,676	BEDFORD	24,711	17,280	6,855	576	10,425 R	69.9%	27.7%	71.6%	28.4%
6,824	BLAND	1,820	1,266	514	40	752 R	69.6%	28.2%	71.1%	28.9%
33,148	BOTETOURT	11,077	7,296	3,488	293	3,808 R	65.9%	31.5%	67.7%	32.3%
17,434	BRUNSWICK	4,415	1,692	2,675	48	983 D	38.3%	60.6%	38.7%	61.3%
24,098	BUCHANAN	4,635	2,794	1,794	47	1,000 R	60.3%	38.7%	60.9%	39.1%
17,146	BUCKINGHAM	3,910	2,015	1,785	110	230 R	51.5%	45.7%	53.0%	47.0%
54,842	CAMPBELL	15,494	10,761	4,428	305	6,333 R	69.5%	28.6%	70.8%	29.2%
28,545	CAROLINE	7,576	3,517	3,879	180	362 D	46.4%	51.2%	47.6%	52.4%
30,042	CARROLL	7,054	4,587	2,265	202	2,322 R	65.0%	32.1%	66.9%	33.1%
7,256	CHARLES CITY	2,478	834	1,593	51	759 D	33.7%	64.3%	34.4%	65.6%
12,586	CHARLOTTE	3,574	2,062	1,462	50	600 R	57.7%	40.9%	58.5%	41.5%

VIRGINIA
SENATOR 2014

2010 Census Population	County	Total Vote	Republican (Gillespie)	Democratic (Warner)	Other	Rep.-Dem. Plurality	Percentage			
							Total Vote		Major Vote	
							Rep.	Dem.	Rep.	Dem.
316,236	CHESTERFIELD	101,132	53,306	44,491	3,335	8,815 R	52.7%	44.0%	54.5%	45.5%
14,034	CLARKE	4,993	2,893	1,954	146	939 R	57.9%	39.1%	59.7%	40.3%
5,190	CRAIG	1,621	1,011	559	51	452 R	62.4%	34.5%	64.4%	35.6%
46,689	CULPEPER	11,621	7,487	3,823	311	3,664 R	64.4%	32.9%	66.2%	33.8%
10,052	CUMBERLAND	2,776	1,451	1,228	97	223 R	52.3%	44.2%	54.2%	45.8%
15,903	DICKENSON	3,376	1,897	1,416	63	481 R	56.2%	41.9%	57.3%	42.7%
28,001	DINWIDDIE	7,323	3,694	3,467	162	227 R	50.4%	47.3%	51.6%	48.4%
11,151	ESSEX	3,022	1,545	1,419	58	126 R	51.1%	47.0%	52.1%	47.9%
1,081,726	FAIRFAX	305,869	122,857	176,418	6,594	53,561 D	40.2%	57.7%	41.1%	58.9%
65,203	FAUQUIER	20,615	13,219	6,985	411	6,234 R	64.1%	33.9%	65.4%	34.6%
15,279	FLOYD	4,621	2,558	1,889	174	669 R	55.4%	40.9%	57.5%	42.5%
25,691	FLUVANNA	8,325	4,480	3,563	282	917 R	53.8%	42.8%	55.7%	44.3%
56,159	FRANKLIN	15,729	9,664	5,650	415	4,014 R	61.4%	35.9%	63.1%	36.9%
78,305	FREDERICK	21,953	14,693	6,659	601	8,034 R	66.9%	30.3%	68.8%	31.2%
17,286	GILES	4,760	2,856	1,760	144	1,096 R	60.0%	37.0%	61.9%	38.1%
36,858	GLOUCESTER	10,996	6,988	3,729	279	3,259 R	63.6%	33.9%	65.2%	34.8%
21,717	GOOCHLAND	9,356	5,735	3,381	240	2,354 R	61.3%	36.1%	62.9%	37.1%
15,533	GRAYSON	4,146	2,585	1,441	120	1,144 R	62.3%	34.8%	64.2%	35.8%
18,403	GREENE	5,072	3,223	1,655	194	1,568 R	63.5%	32.6%	66.1%	33.9%
12,243	GREENSVILLE	2,760	984	1,738	38	754 D	35.7%	63.0%	36.1%	63.9%
36,241	HALIFAX	9,599	5,005	4,435	159	570 R	52.1%	46.2%	53.0%	47.0%
99,863	HANOVER	38,705	24,995	12,437	1,273	12,558 R	64.6%	32.1%	66.8%	33.2%
306,935	HENRICO	98,133	41,171	54,049	2,913	12,878 D	42.0%	55.1%	43.2%	56.8%
54,151	HENRY	13,488	7,549	5,695	244	1,854 R	56.0%	42.2%	57.0%	43.0%
2,321	HIGHLAND	919	564	318	37	246 R	61.4%	34.6%	63.9%	36.1%
35,270	ISLE OF WIGHT	11,935	6,714	4,979	242	1,735 R	56.3%	41.7%	57.4%	42.6%
67,009	JAMES CITY	26,482	14,403	11,577	502	2,826 R	54.4%	43.7%	55.4%	44.6%
6,945	KING AND QUEEN	2,138	1,067	1,012	59	55 R	49.9%	47.3%	51.3%	48.7%
23,584	KING GEORGE	6,783	4,148	2,460	175	1,688 R	61.2%	36.3%	62.8%	37.2%
15,935	KING WILLIAM	5,150	3,168	1,797	185	1,371 R	61.5%	34.9%	63.8%	36.2%
11,391	LANCASTER	4,593	2,573	1,924	96	649 R	56.0%	41.9%	57.2%	42.8%
25,587	LEE	5,812	3,690	2,030	92	1,660 R	63.5%	34.9%	64.5%	35.5%
312,311	LOUDOUN	92,698	45,500	45,042	2,156	458 R	49.1%	48.6%	50.3%	49.7%
33,153	LOUISA	10,075	5,802	3,936	337	1,866 R	57.6%	39.1%	59.6%	40.4%
12,914	LUNENBURG	3,285	1,736	1,481	68	255 R	52.8%	45.1%	54.0%	46.0%
13,308	MADISON	4,083	2,560	1,418	105	1,142 R	62.7%	34.7%	64.4%	35.6%
8,978	MATHEWS	3,401	2,141	1,208	52	933 R	63.0%	35.5%	63.9%	36.1%
32,727	MECKLENBURG	7,769	4,375	3,266	128	1,109 R	56.3%	42.0%	57.3%	42.7%
10,959	MIDDLESEX	3,823	2,304	1,427	92	877 R	60.3%	37.3%	61.8%	38.2%
94,392	MONTGOMERY	21,766	9,776	11,110	880	1,334 D	44.9%	51.0%	46.8%	53.2%
15,020	NELSON	5,076	2,288	2,496	292	208 D	45.1%	49.2%	47.8%	52.2%
18,429	NEW KENT	7,176	4,668	2,303	205	2,365 R	65.1%	32.1%	67.0%	33.0%
12,389	NORTHAMPTON	3,571	1,553	1,890	128	337 D	43.5%	52.9%	45.1%	54.9%
12,330	NORTHUMBERLAND	5,128	2,939	2,089	100	850 R	57.3%	40.7%	58.5%	41.5%
15,853	NOTTOWAY	3,820	1,942	1,796	82	146 R	50.8%	47.0%	52.0%	48.0%
33,481	ORANGE	9,699	5,814	3,629	256	2,185 R	59.9%	37.4%	61.6%	38.4%
24,042	PAGE	5,640	3,883	1,654	103	2,229 R	68.8%	29.3%	70.1%	29.9%
18,490	PATRICK	4,885	3,228	1,538	119	1,690 R	66.1%	31.5%	67.7%	32.3%
63,506	PITTSYLVANIA	18,095	11,278	6,558	259	4,720 R	62.3%	36.2%	63.2%	36.8%
28,046	POWHATAN	9,686	6,785	2,525	376	4,260 R	70.0%	26.1%	72.9%	27.1%
23,368	PRINCE EDWARD	4,867	2,194	2,550	123	356 D	45.1%	52.4%	46.2%	53.8%
35,725	PRINCE GEORGE	9,081	5,132	3,700	249	1,432 R	56.5%	40.7%	58.1%	41.9%
402,002	PRINCE WILLIAM	95,528	45,366	48,140	2,022	2,774 D	47.5%	50.4%	48.5%	51.5%
34,872	PULASKI	8,303	4,796	3,301	206	1,495 R	57.8%	39.8%	59.2%	40.8%
7,373	RAPPAHANNOCK	2,801	1,531	1,213	57	318 R	54.7%	43.3%	55.8%	44.2%
9,254	RICHMOND	2,076	1,194	844	38	350 R	57.5%	40.7%	58.6%	41.4%
92,376	ROANOKE	30,614	18,166	11,605	843	6,561 R	59.3%	37.9%	61.0%	39.0%
22,307	ROCKBRIDGE	6,563	3,696	2,713	154	983 R	56.3%	41.3%	57.7%	42.3%
76,314	ROCKINGHAM	20,626	14,744	5,323	559	9,421 R	71.5%	25.8%	73.5%	26.5%
28,897	RUSSELL	6,501	3,947	2,442	112	1,505 R	60.7%	37.6%	61.8%	38.2%

VIRGINIA
SENATOR 2014

2010 Census Population	County	Total Vote	Republican (Gillespie)	Democratic (Warner)	Other	Rep.-Dem. Plurality	Total Vote Rep.	Total Vote Dem.	Major Vote Rep.	Major Vote Dem.
23,177	SCOTT	5,179	3,699	1,406	74	2,293 R	71.4%	27.1%	72.5%	27.5%
41,993	SHENANDOAH	11,092	7,624	3,219	249	4,405 R	68.7%	29.0%	70.3%	29.7%
32,208	SMYTH	6,855	4,296	2,405	154	1,891 R	62.7%	35.1%	64.1%	35.9%
18,570	SOUTHAMPTON	5,062	2,594	2,377	91	217 R	51.2%	47.0%	52.2%	47.8%
122,397	SPOTSYLVANIA	32,584	19,445	12,381	758	7,064 R	59.7%	38.0%	61.1%	38.9%
128,961	STAFFORD	33,989	19,790	13,436	763	6,354 R	58.2%	39.5%	59.6%	40.4%
7,058	SURRY	2,569	963	1,545	61	582 D	37.5%	60.1%	38.4%	61.6%
12,087	SUSSEX	2,987	1,241	1,710	36	469 D	41.5%	57.2%	42.1%	57.9%
45,078	TAZEWELL	9,673	6,972	2,574	127	4,398 R	72.1%	26.6%	73.0%	27.0%
37,575	WARREN	9,237	5,933	3,048	256	2,885 R	64.2%	33.0%	66.1%	33.9%
54,876	WASHINGTON	14,015	9,361	4,402	252	4,959 R	66.8%	31.4%	68.0%	32.0%
17,454	WESTMORELAND	4,654	2,338	2,217	99	121 R	50.2%	47.6%	51.3%	48.7%
41,452	WISE	7,723	5,414	2,181	128	3,233 R	70.1%	28.2%	71.3%	28.7%
29,235	WYTHE	7,142	4,562	2,393	187	2,169 R	63.9%	33.5%	65.6%	34.4%
65,464	YORK	20,625	12,141	7,974	510	4,167 R	58.9%	38.7%	60.4%	39.6%

2010 Census Population	City	Total Vote	Republican (Gillespie)	Democratic (Warner)	Other	Rep.-Dem. Plurality	Total Vote Rep.	Total Vote Dem.	Major Vote Rep.	Major Vote Dem.
139,966	ALEXANDRIA	41,431	11,480	29,047	904	17,567 D	27.7%	70.1%	28.3%	71.7%
17,835	BRISTOL	3,806	2,445	1,294	67	1,151 R	64.2%	34.0%	65.4%	34.6%
6,650	BUENA VISTA	1,206	692	475	39	217 R	57.4%	39.4%	59.3%	40.7%
43,475	CHARLOTTESVILLE	10,719	2,054	8,241	424	6,187 D	19.2%	76.9%	20.0%	80.0%
222,209	CHESAPEAKE	60,763	29,899	29,602	1,262	297 R	49.2%	48.7%	50.2%	49.8%
17,411	COLONIAL HEIGHTS	4,679	3,351	1,187	141	2,164 R	71.6%	25.4%	73.8%	26.2%
5,961	COVINGTON	1,213	457	731	25	274 D	37.7%	60.3%	38.5%	61.5%
43,055	DANVILLE	10,812	4,436	6,259	117	1,823 D	41.0%	57.9%	41.5%	58.5%
5,927	EMPORIA	1,373	501	855	17	354 D	36.5%	62.3%	36.9%	63.1%
22,565	FAIRFAX CITY	6,993	3,018	3,812	163	794 D	43.2%	54.5%	44.2%	55.8%
12,332	FALLS CHURCH	5,034	1,309	3,599	126	2,290 D	26.0%	71.5%	26.7%	73.3%
8,582	FRANKLIN CITY	2,175	818	1,328	29	510 D	37.6%	61.1%	38.1%	61.9%
24,286	FREDERICKSBURG	5,721	2,211	3,341	169	1,130 D	38.6%	58.4%	39.8%	60.2%
7,042	GALAX	1,340	743	564	33	179 R	55.4%	42.1%	56.8%	43.2%
137,436	HAMPTON	34,329	10,149	23,483	697	13,334 D	29.6%	68.4%	30.2%	69.8%
48,914	HARRISONBURG	7,539	3,332	3,865	342	533 D	44.2%	51.3%	46.3%	53.7%
22,591	HOPEWELL	4,748	2,197	2,412	139	215 D	46.3%	50.8%	47.7%	52.3%
7,042	LEXINGTON	1,518	501	981	36	480 D	33.0%	64.6%	33.8%	66.2%
75,568	LYNCHBURG	19,395	10,627	8,284	484	2,343 R	54.8%	42.7%	56.2%	43.8%
37,821	MANASSAS	8,141	3,891	4,004	246	113 D	47.8%	49.2%	49.3%	50.7%
14,273	MANASSAS PARK	2,097	924	1,107	66	183 D	44.1%	52.8%	45.5%	54.5%
13,821	MARTINSVILLE	3,544	1,317	2,146	81	829 D	37.2%	60.6%	38.0%	62.0%
180,719	NEWPORT NEWS	38,770	14,548	23,405	817	8,857 D	37.5%	60.4%	38.3%	61.7%
242,803	NORFOLK CITY	42,543	12,252	29,210	1,081	16,958 D	28.8%	68.7%	29.5%	70.5%
3,958	NORTON	782	462	294	26	168 R	59.1%	37.6%	61.1%	38.9%
32,420	PETERSBURG	7,748	843	6,800	105	5,957 D	10.9%	87.8%	11.0%	89.0%
12,150	POQUOSON	4,305	3,128	1,077	100	2,051 R	72.7%	25.0%	74.4%	25.6%
95,535	PORTSMOUTH	24,452	6,760	17,101	591	10,341 D	27.6%	69.9%	28.3%	71.7%
16,408	RADFORD	2,791	1,256	1,446	89	190 D	45.0%	51.8%	46.5%	53.5%
204,214	RICHMOND CITY	51,437	10,750	38,963	1,724	28,213 D	20.9%	75.7%	21.6%	78.4%
97,032	ROANOKE CITY	20,764	7,714	12,311	739	4,597 D	37.2%	59.3%	38.5%	61.5%
24,802	SALEM	6,876	3,914	2,750	212	1,164 R	56.9%	40.0%	58.7%	41.3%
23,746	STAUNTON	6,237	3,045	3,010	182	35 R	48.8%	48.3%	50.3%	49.7%
84,585	SUFFOLK	24,187	10,202	13,533	452	3,331 D	42.2%	56.0%	43.0%	57.0%
437,994	VIRGINIA BEACH	106,744	54,602	49,218	2,924	5,384 R	51.2%	46.1%	52.6%	47.4%
21,006	WAYNESBORO	4,812	2,675	1,951	186	724 R	55.6%	40.5%	57.8%	42.2%
14,068	WILLIAMSBURG	3,917	1,360	2,466	91	1,106 D	34.7%	63.0%	35.5%	64.5%
26,203	WINCHESTER	5,921	2,985	2,732	204	253 R	50.4%	46.1%	52.2%	47.8%
7,994,802	TOTAL	2,184,473	1,055,940	1,073,667	54,866	17,727 D	48.3%	49.1%	49.6%	50.4%

VIRGINIA

HOUSE OF REPRESENTATIVES

CD	Year	Total Vote	Republican Vote	Republican Candidate	Democratic Vote	Democratic Candidate	Other Vote	Rep.-Dem. Plurality	Percentage Total Vote Rep.	Total Vote Dem.	Major Vote Rep.	Major Vote Dem.
1	2014	209,621	131,861	WITTMAN, ROBERT J.*	72,059	MOSHER, NORMAN	5,701	59,802 R	62.9%	34.4%	64.7%	35.3%
1	2012	356,806	200,845	WITTMAN, ROBERT J.*	147,036	COOK, ADAM M.	8,925	53,809 R	56.3%	41.2%	57.7%	42.3%
2	2014	173,060	101,558	RIGELL, E. SCOTT*	71,178	PATRICK, SUZANNE	324	30,380 R	58.7%	41.1%	58.8%	41.2%
2	2012	309,222	166,231	RIGELL, E. SCOTT*	142,548	HIRSCHBIEL, PAUL O. JR.	443	23,683 R	53.8%	46.1%	53.8%	46.2%
3	2014	147,402			139,197	SCOTT, ROBERT C. "BOBBY"*	8,205	139,197 D		94.4%		100.0%
3	2012	318,936	58,931	LONGO, DEAN J.	259,199	SCOTT, ROBERT C. "BOBBY"*	806	200,268 D	18.5%	81.3%	18.5%	81.5%
4	2014	200,638	120,684	FORBES, J. RANDY*	75,270	FAUSZ, ELLIOTT	4,684	45,414 R	60.2%	37.5%	61.6%	38.4%
4	2012	350,046	199,292	FORBES, J. RANDY*	150,190	WARD, ELLA P.	564	49,102 R	56.9%	42.9%	57.0%	43.0%
5	2014	204,945	124,735	HURT, ROBERT*	73,482	GAUGHAN, WALTER LAWRENCE	6,728	51,253 R	60.9%	35.9%	62.9%	37.1%
5	2012	348,111	193,009	HURT, ROBERT*	149,214	DOUGLASS, JOHN WADE	5,888	43,795 R	55.4%	42.9%	56.4%	43.6%
6	2014	179,708	133,898	GOODLATTE, BOB*			45,810	133,898 R	74.5%		100.0%	
6	2012	323,893	211,278	GOODLATTE, BOB*	111,949	SCHMOOKLER, ANDY	666	99,329 R	65.2%	34.6%	65.4%	34.6%
7	2014	243,351	148,026	BRAT, DAVE	89,914	TRAMMELL, JOHN K. "JACK"	5,411	58,112 R	60.8%	36.9%	62.2%	37.8%
7	2012	381,909	222,983	CANTOR, ERIC I.*	158,012	POWELL, E. WAYNE	914	64,971 R	58.4%	41.4%	58.5%	41.5%
8	2014	203,076	63,810	EDMOND, MICAH	128,102	BEYER, DONALD S. JR.	11,164	64,292 D	31.4%	63.1%	33.2%	66.8%
8	2012	351,187	107,370	MURRAY, J. PATRICK	226,847	MORAN, JAMES P. JR.*	16,970	119,477 D	30.6%	64.6%	32.1%	67.9%
9	2014	162,815	117,465	GRIFFITH, H. MORGAN*			45,350	117,465 R	72.1%		100.0%	
9	2012	301,658	184,882	GRIFFITH, H. MORGAN*	116,400	FLACCAVENTO, ANTHONY J.	376	68,482 R	61.3%	38.6%	61.4%	38.6%
10	2014	222,910	125,914	COMSTOCK, BARBARA	89,957	FOUST, JOHN	7,039	35,957 R	56.5%	40.4%	58.3%	41.7%
10	2012	366,444	214,038	WOLF, FRANK R.*	142,024	CABRAL, KRISTIN A.	10,382	72,014 R	58.4%	38.8%	60.1%	39.9%
11	2014	187,787	75,796	SCHOLTE, SUZANNE	106,780	CONNOLLY, GERALD E. "GERRY"*	5,211	30,984 D	40.4%	56.9%	41.5%	58.5%
11	2012	332,243	117,902	PERKINS, CHRIS S.	202,606	CONNOLLY, GERALD E. "GERRY"*	11,735	84,704 D	35.5%	61.0%	36.8%	63.2%
TOTAL	2014	2,135,313	1,143,747		845,939		145,627	297,808 R	53.6%	39.6%	57.5%	42.5%
TOTAL	2012	3,740,455	1,876,761		1,806,025		57,669	70,736 R	50.2%	48.3%	51.0%	49.0%

Note: An asterisk (*) denotes incumbent.

VIRGINIA

GENERAL AND PRIMARY ELECTIONS

2014 GENERAL ELECTIONS: OTHER VOTES

Governor (2013) Other vote was 146,084 Libertarian (Robert C. Sarvis), 11,844 scattered write-in

Senate Other vote was 53,102 Libertarian (Robert Christopher Sarvis), 1,764 scattered write-in

House Other vote was:

CD 1   5,097 Green (G. Gail Parker), 604 scattered write-in

CD 2   324 scattered write-in

CD 3   8,205 scattered write-in

CD 4   4,427 Libertarian (Bo C. Brown), 257 scattered write-in

CD 5   4,298 Libertarian (Paul Francis Jones), 2,209 Green (Kenneth J. Hildebrandt), 221 scattered write-in

CD 6   22,161 Libertarian (Will M. Hammer), 21,447 Green (Elaine B. Hildebrandt), 2,202 scattered write-in

CD 7   5,086 Libertarian (James A. Carr), 325 scattered write-in

CD 8   5,420 Independent (Gwendolyn Beck), 4,409 Libertarian (Jeffrey S. Carson), 963 Green (Gerrard C. "Gerry" Blais), 372 scattered write-in

CD 9   39,412 Independent (William R. Carr), 5,938 scattered write-in

CD 10   3,393 Libertarian (William B. Redpath), 2,442 Independent (Brad A. Eickholt), 946 Green (Dianne L. Blais), 258 scattered write-in

CD 11   3,246 Libertarian (Marc M. Harrold), 1,739 Green (Joe F. Galdo), 226 scattered write-in

VIRGINIA

GENERAL AND PRIMARY ELECTIONS

2014 PRIMARY ELECTIONS: SUPPLEMENTARY INFORMATION

Primary   June 10, 2014   **Registration**   5,272,079   No Party Registration
(as of June 1, 2014
– includes 411,883
inactive registrants)

Primary Type   Open—Any registered voter could participate in the primary of either party.

REPUBLICAN PRIMARIES			DEMOCRATIC PRIMARIES		
Senator	Gillespie, Edward W. "Ed"	Nominated by convention	Warner, Mark R.*	Unopposed	
Governor (2013)	Cuccinelli, Ken	Nominated by convention	McAuliffe, Terry	Unopposed	
Congressional District 1	Wittman, Robert J. "Rob"* Riedel, Anthony TOTAL	13,292 76.2% 4,159 23.8% 17,451	Mosher, Norman	Unopposed	
Congressional District 2	Rigell, E. Scott*	Unopposed	Patrick, Suzanne	Unopposed	
Congressional District 3			Scott, Robert C. "Bobby"*	Unopposed	
Congressional District 4	Forbes, J. Randy*	Unopposed	Fausz, Elliott	Unopposed	
Congressional District 5	Hurt, Robert*	Unopposed	Gaughan, Walter Lawrence	Nominated by convention	
Congressional District 6	Goodlatte, Bob*	Unopposed			
Congressional District 7	Brat, Dave Cantor, Eric I.* TOTAL	36,105 55.5% 28,912 44.5% 65,017	Trammell, John K. "Jack"	Unopposed	
Congressional District 8	Edmond, Micah		Beyer, Donald S. Jr. Hope, Patrick Ebbin, Adam Euille, Bill Levine, Mark H. Chatman, Lavern Hyra, Derek Herring, Charniele Lerhonda Shuttleworth, Bruce B. Korpe, Satish W. TOTAL	17,783 45.8% 7,095 18.3% 5,262 13.5% 3,264 8.4% 2,613 6.7% 2,117 5.4% 479 1.2% 126 0.3% 83 0.2% 42 0.1% 38,864	
Congressional District 9	Griffith, H. Morgan*	Unopposed			
Congressional District 10	Comstock, Barbara Marshall, R. G. "Bob" Lind, Howard Rhodes "Howie" Hollingshead, Stephen B. Wasinger, Rob Savitt, Marc TOTAL	7,337 53.9% 3,829 28.1% 1,108 8.1% 816 6.0% 301 2.2% 218 1.6% 13,609	Foust, John	Unopposed	
Congressional District 11	Scholte, Suzanne	Unopposed	Connolly, Gerald E. "Gerry"*	Unopposed	

Note: An asterisk (*) denotes incumbent.

WASHINGTON
Congressional districts first established for elections held in 2012
10 members

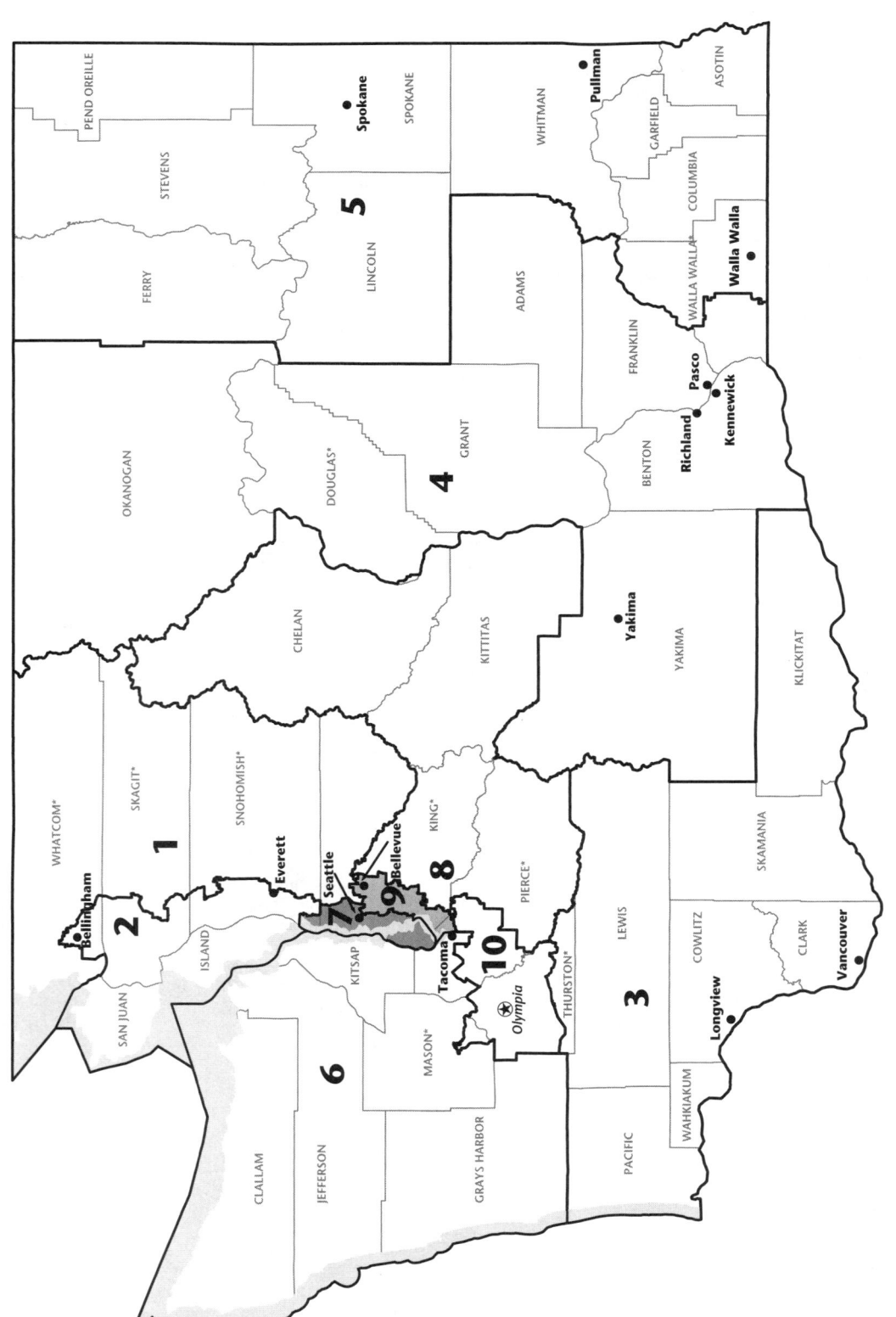

WASHINGTON

Seattle Area

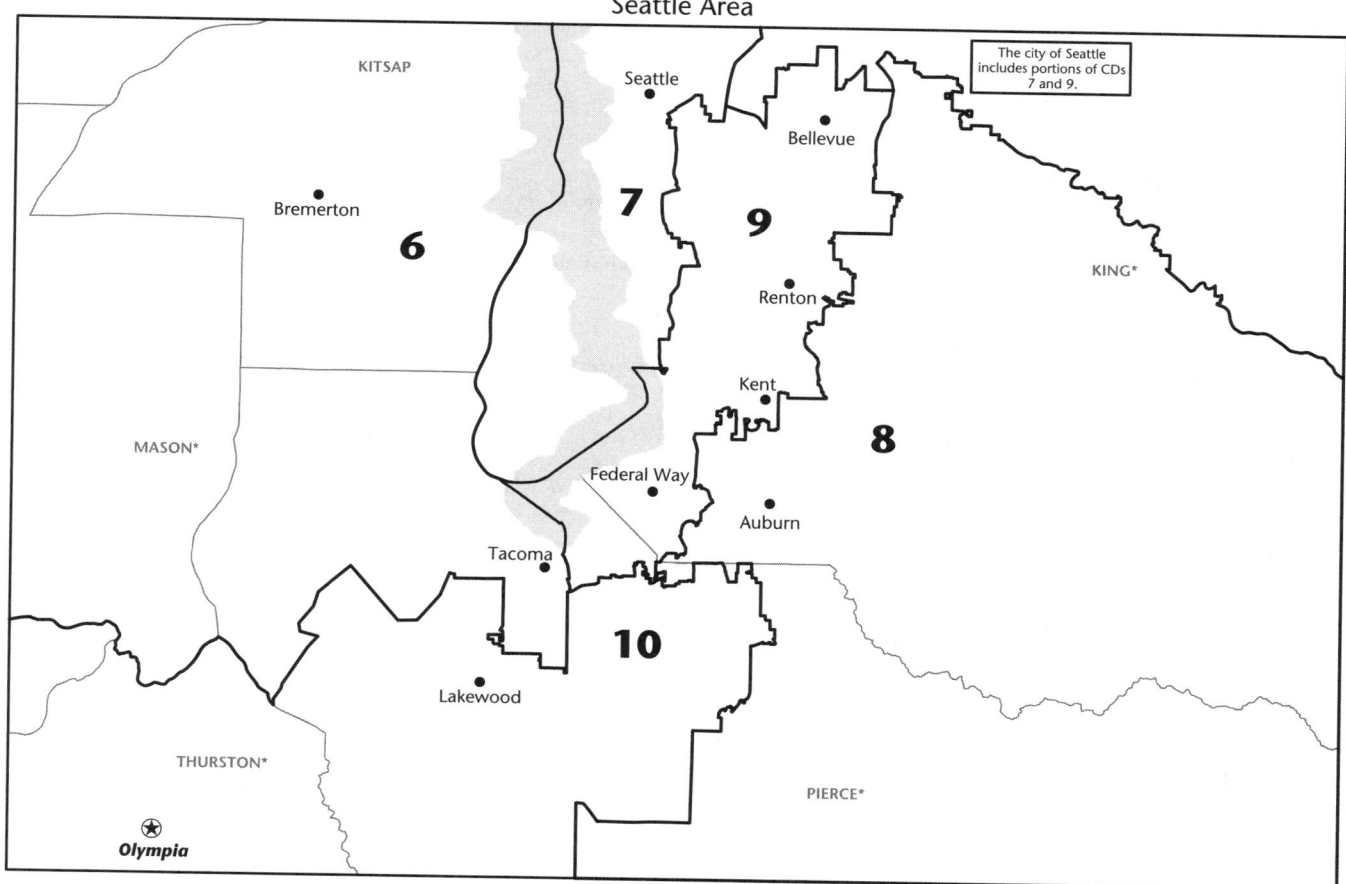

The city of Seattle includes portions of CDs 7 and 9.

* Asterisk indicates a county whose boundaries include parts of two or more congressional districts.

WASHINGTON

GOVERNOR

Jay Inslee (D). Elected 2012 to a four-year term.

SENATORS (2 Democrats)

Maria Cantwell (D). Reelected 2012 to a six-year term. Previously elected 2006, 2000.

Patty Murray (D). Reelected 2010 to a six-year term. Previously elected 2004, 1998, 1992.

REPRESENTATIVES (4 Republicans, 6 Democrats)

1. Suzan K. DelBene (D)
2. Rick Larsen (D)
3. Jaime Herrera Beutler (R)
4. Dan Newhouse (R)
5. Cathy McMorris Rodgers (R)
6. Derek Kilmer (D)
7. Jim McDermott (D)
8. David G. Reichert (R)
9. Adam Smith (D)
10. Denny Heck (D)

POSTWAR VOTE FOR PRESIDENT

| | | Republican | | Democratic | | Other Vote | Rep.-Dem. Plurality | Percentage | | | |
| | | | | | | | | Total Vote | | Major Vote | |
Year	Total Vote	Vote	Candidate	Vote	Candidate			Rep.	Dem.	Rep.	Dem.
2012	3,125,516	1,290,670	Romney, W. Mitt	1,755,396	Obama, Barack H.*	79,450	464,726 D	41.3%	56.2%	42.4%	57.6%
2008	3,036,878	1,229,216	McCain, John S. III	1,750,848	Obama, Barack H.	56,814	521,632 D	40.5%	57.7%	41.2%	58.8%
2004	2,859,084	1,304,894	Bush, George W.*	1,510,201	Kerry, John F.	43,989	205,307 D	45.6%	52.8%	46.4%	53.6%
2000**	2,487,433	1,108,864	Bush, George W.	1,247,652	Gore, Albert Jr.	130,917	138,788 D	44.6%	50.2%	47.1%	52.9%
1996**	2,253,837	840,712	Dole, Robert "Bob"	1,123,323	Clinton, Bill*	289,802	282,611 D	37.3%	49.8%	42.8%	57.2%
1992**	2,288,230	731,234	Bush, George H.*	993,037	Clinton, Bill	563,959	261,803 D	32.0%	43.4%	42.4%	57.6%
1988	1,865,253	903,835	Bush, George H.	933,516	Dukakis, Michael S.	27,902	29,681 D	48.5%	50.0%	49.2%	50.8%
1984	1,883,910	1,051,670	Reagan, Ronald*	807,352	Mondale, Walter F.	24,888	244,318 R	55.8%	42.9%	56.6%	43.4%
1980**	1,742,394	865,244	Reagan, Ronald	650,193	Carter, Jimmy*	226,957	215,051 R	49.7%	37.3%	57.1%	42.9%
1976	1,555,534	777,732	Ford, Gerald R.*	717,323	Carter, Jimmy	60,479	60,409 R	50.0%	46.1%	52.0%	48.0%
1972	1,470,847	837,135	Nixon, Richard M.*	568,334	McGovern, George S.	65,378	268,801 R	56.9%	38.6%	59.6%	40.4%
1968**	1,304,281	588,510	Nixon, Richard M.	616,037	Humphrey, Hubert Horatio Jr.	99,734	27,527 D	45.1%	47.2%	48.9%	51.1%
1964	1,258,556	470,366	Goldwater, Barry M. Sr.	779,881	Johnson, Lyndon B.*	8,309	309,515 D	37.4%	62.0%	37.6%	62.4%
1960	1,241,572	629,273	Nixon, Richard M.	599,298	Kennedy, John F.	13,001	29,975 R	50.7%	48.3%	51.2%	48.8%
1956	1,150,889	620,430	Eisenhower, Dwight D.*	523,002	Stevenson, Adlai E. II	7,457	97,428 R	53.9%	45.4%	54.3%	45.7%
1952	1,102,708	599,107	Eisenhower, Dwight D.	492,845	Stevenson, Adlai E. II	10,756	106,262 R	54.3%	44.7%	54.9%	45.1%
1948	905,058	386,314	Dewey, Thomas E.	476,165	Truman, Harry S.*	42,579	89,851 D	42.7%	52.6%	44.8%	55.2%

Note: An asterisk (*) denotes incumbent. **In past elections, the other vote included: 2000 - 103,002 Green (Ralph Nader); 1996 - 201,003 Reform (Ross Perot); 1992 - 541,780 Independent (Perot); 1980 - 185,073 Independent (John Anderson); 1968 - 96,990 American Independent (George Wallace).

WASHINGTON

POSTWAR VOTE FOR GOVERNOR

Year	Total Vote	Republican		Democratic		Other Vote	Rep.-Dem. Plurality	Percentage			
								Total Vote		Major Vote	
		Vote	Candidate	Vote	Candidate			Rep.	Dem.	Rep.	Dem.
2012	3,071,047	1,488,245	McKenna, Rob	1,582,802	Inslee, Jay		94,557 D	48.5%	51.5%	48.5%	51.5%
2008	3,002,862	1,404,124	Rossi, Dino	1,598,738	Gregoire, Christine*		194,614 D	46.8%	53.2%	46.8%	53.2%
2004**	2,810,058	1,373,232	Rossi, Dino	1,373,361	Gregoire, Christine	63,465	129 D	48.9%	48.9%	50.0%	50.0%
2000	2,469,852	980,060	Carlson, John	1,441,973	Locke, Gary*	47,819	461,913 D	39.7%	58.4%	40.5%	59.5%
1996	2,237,030	940,538	Craswell, Ellen	1,296,492	Locke, Gary		355,954 D	42.0%	58.0%	42.0%	58.0%
1992	2,270,826	1,086,216	Eikenberry, Ken	1,184,315	Lowry, Mike	295	98,099 D	47.8%	52.2%	47.8%	52.2%
1988	1,874,929	708,481	Williams, Bob	1,166,448	Gardner, Booth*		457,967 D	37.8%	62.2%	37.8%	62.2%
1984	1,888,987	881,994	Spellman, John D.*	1,006,993	Gardner, Booth		124,999 D	46.7%	53.3%	46.7%	53.3%
1980	1,730,896	981,083	Spellman, John D.	749,813	McDermott, James A.		231,270 R	56.7%	43.3%	56.7%	43.3%
1976	1,546,380	687,039	Spellman, John D.	821,797	Ray, Dixy Lee	37,544	134,758 D	44.4%	53.1%	45.5%	54.5%
1972	1,472,542	747,825	Evans, Daniel J.*	630,613	Rosellini, Albert D.	94,104	117,212 R	50.8%	42.8%	54.3%	45.7%
1968	1,265,354	692,377	Evans, Daniel J.*	560,262	O'Connell, John J.	12,715	132,115 R	54.7%	44.3%	55.3%	44.7%
1964	1,250,274	697,256	Evans, Daniel J.	548,692	Rosellini, Albert D.*	4,326	148,564 R	55.8%	43.9%	56.0%	44.0%
1960	1,215,748	594,122	Andrews, Lloyd J.	611,987	Rosellini, Albert D.*	9,639	17,865 D	48.9%	50.3%	49.3%	50.7%
1956	1,128,977	508,041	Anderson, Emmett T.	616,773	Rosellini, Albert D.	4,163	108,732 D	45.0%	54.6%	45.2%	54.8%
1952	1,078,497	567,822	Langlie, Arthur B.*	510,675	Mitchell, Hugh B.		57,147 R	52.6%	47.4%	52.6%	47.4%
1948	883,141	445,958	Langlie, Arthur B.	417,035	Wallgren, Monrad C.*	20,148	28,923 R	50.5%	47.2%	51.7%	48.3%

Note: An asterisk (*) denotes incumbent. **In 2004, the initial official vote count put Republican Dino Rossi ahead by 261 votes. A machine recount reduced Rossi's margin to 42 votes. A subsequent manual recount gave Democrat Christine Gregoire the election by a margin of 129 votes (see above), and she was inaugurated governor.

POSTWAR VOTE FOR SENATOR

Year	Total Vote	Republican		Democratic		Other Vote	Rep.-Dem. Plurality	Percentage			
								Total Vote		Major Vote	
		Vote	Candidate	Vote	Candidate			Rep.	Dem.	Rep.	Dem.
2012	3,069,417	1,213,924	Baumgartner, Michael	1,855,493	Cantwell, Maria*		641,569 D	39.5%	60.5%	39.5%	60.5%
2010	2,511,094	1,196,164	Rossi, Dino	1,314,930	Murray, Patty*		118,766 D	47.6%	52.4%	47.6%	52.4%
2006	2,083,734	832,106	McGavick, Mike	1,184,659	Cantwell, Maria*	66,969	352,553 D	39.9%	56.9%	41.3%	58.7%
2004	2,818,651	1,204,584	Nethercutt, George R.	1,549,708	Murray, Patty*	64,359	345,124 D	42.7%	55.0%	43.7%	56.3%
2000	2,461,379	1,197,208	Gorton, Slade*	1,199,437	Cantwell, Maria	64,734	2,229 D	48.6%	48.7%	50.0%	50.0%
1998	1,888,561	785,377	Smith, Linda	1,103,184	Murray, Patty*		317,807 D	41.6%	58.4%	41.6%	58.4%
1994	1,700,173	947,821	Gorton, Slade*	752,352	Sims, Ron		195,469 R	55.7%	44.3%	55.7%	44.3%
1992	2,219,162	1,020,829	Chandler, Rod	1,197,973	Murray, Patty	360	177,144 D	46.0%	54.0%	46.0%	54.0%
1988	1,848,542	944,359	Gorton, Slade	904,183	Lowry, Mike		40,176 R	51.1%	48.9%	51.1%	48.9%
1983S	1,213,307	672,326	Evans, Daniel J.*	540,981	Lowry, Mike		131,345 R	55.4%	44.6%	55.4%	44.6%
1982	1,368,476	332,273	Jewett, Doug	943,655	Jackson, Henry M.*	92,548	611,382 D	24.3%	69.0%	26.0%	74.0%
1980	1,728,369	936,317	Gorton, Slade	792,052	Magnuson, Warren G.*		144,265 R	54.2%	45.8%	54.2%	45.8%
1976	1,491,111	361,546	Brown, George M.	1,071,219	Jackson, Henry M.*	58,346	709,673 D	24.2%	71.8%	25.2%	74.8%
1974	1,007,847	363,626	Metcalf, Jack	611,811	Magnuson, Warren G.*	32,410	248,185 D	36.1%	60.7%	37.3%	62.7%
1970	1,066,807	170,790	Elicker, Charles W.	879,385	Jackson, Henry M.*	16,632	708,595 D	16.0%	82.4%	16.3%	83.7%
1968	1,236,063	435,894	Metcalf, Jack	796,183	Magnuson, Warren G.*	3,986	360,289 D	35.3%	64.4%	35.4%	64.6%
1964	1,213,088	337,138	Andrews, Lloyd J.	875,950	Jackson, Henry M.*		538,812 D	27.8%	72.2%	27.8%	72.2%
1962	943,229	446,204	Christensen, Richard G.	491,365	Magnuson, Warren G.*	5,660	45,161 D	47.3%	52.1%	47.6%	52.4%
1958	886,822	278,271	Bantz, William B.	597,040	Jackson, Henry M.*	11,511	318,769 D	31.4%	67.3%	31.8%	68.2%
1956	1,122,217	436,652	Langlie, Arthur B.	685,565	Magnuson, Warren G.*		248,913 D	38.9%	61.1%	38.9%	61.1%
1952	1,058,735	460,884	Cain, Harry P.*	595,288	Jackson, Henry M.	2,563	134,404 D	43.5%	56.2%	43.6%	56.4%
1950	744,783	342,464	Williams, Walter	397,719	Magnuson, Warren G.*	4,600	55,255 D	46.0%	53.4%	46.3%	53.7%
1946	660,342	358,847	Cain, Harry P.	298,683	Mitchell, Hugh B.	2,812	60,164 R	54.3%	45.2%	54.6%	45.4%

Note: An asterisk (*) denotes incumbent. **The 1983 election was for a short term to fill a vacancy.

WASHINGTON

HOUSE OF REPRESENTATIVES

CD	Year	Total Vote	Republican		Democratic		Other Vote	Rep.-Dem. Plurality	Percentage			
									Total Vote		Major Vote	
			Vote	Candidate	Vote	Candidate			Rep.	Dem.	Rep.	Dem.
1	2014	225,579	101,428	CELIS, PEDRO	124,151	DELBENE, SUZAN K.*		22,723 D	45.0%	55.0%	45.0%	55.0%
1	2012	328,212	151,187	KOSTER, JOHN	177,025	DELBENE, SUZAN K.*		25,838 D	46.1%	53.9%	46.1%	53.9%
2	2014	201,691	79,518	GUILLOT, B. J.	122,173	LARSEN, RICK*		42,655 D	39.4%	60.6%	39.4%	60.6%
2	2012	302,291	117,465	MATTHEWS, DAN	184,826	LARSEN, RICK*		67,361 D	38.9%	61.1%	38.9%	61.1%
3	2014	202,814	124,796	BEUTLER, JAIME HERRERA*	78,018	DINGETHAL, BOB		46,778 R	61.5%	38.5%	61.5%	38.5%
3	2012	293,884	177,446	BEUTLER, JAIME HERRERA*	116,438	HAUGEN, JON T.		61,008 R	60.4%	39.6%	60.4%	39.6%
4	2014	153,079	77,772	NEWHOUSE, DAN			75,307#	77,772 R	50.8%		100.0%	
4	2012	233,689	154,749	HASTINGS, DOC*	78,940	BAECHLER, MARY		75,809 R	66.2%	33.8%	66.2%	33.8%
5	2014	223,242	135,470	RODGERS, CATHY MCMORRIS*	87,772	PAKOOTAS, JOSEPH		47,698 R	60.7%	39.3%	60.7%	39.3%
5	2012	308,578	191,066	RODGERS, CATHY MCMORRIS*	117,512	COWAN, RICH		73,554 R	61.9%	38.1%	61.9%	38.1%
6	2014	224,290	83,025	MCCLENDON, MARTIN "MARTY"	141,265	KILMER, DEREK*		58,240 D	37.0%	63.0%	37.0%	63.0%
6	2012	316,386	129,725	DRISCOLL, BILL	186,661	KILMER, DEREK		56,936 D	41.0%	59.0%	41.0%	59.0%
7	2014	251,875	47,921	KELLER, CRAIG	203,954	MCDERMOTT, JIM*		156,033 D	19.0%	81.0%	19.0%	81.0%
7	2012	374,580	76,212	BEMIS, RON	298,368	MCDERMOTT, JIM*		222,156 D	20.3%	79.7%	20.3%	79.7%
8	2014	198,744	125,741	REICHERT, DAVID Gr.*	73,003	RITCHIE, JASON		52,738 R	63.3%	36.7%	63.3%	36.7%
8	2012	302,090	180,204	REICHERT, DAVID Gr.*	121,886	PORTERFIELD, KAREN		58,318 R	59.7%	40.3%	59.7%	40.3%
9	2014	166,794	48,662	BASLER, DOUG	118,132	SMITH, ADAM*		69,470 D	29.2%	70.8%	29.2%	70.8%
9	2012	268,139	76,105	POSTMA, JAMES	192,034	SMITH, ADAM*		115,929 D	28.4%	71.6%	28.4%	71.6%
10	2014	181,492	82,213	MCDONALD, JOYCE	99,279	HECK, DENNY*		17,066 D	45.3%	54.7%	45.3%	54.7%
10	2012	278,417	115,381	MURI, RICHARD	163,036	HECK, DENNY		47,655 D	41.4%	58.6%	41.4%	58.6%
TOTAL	2014	2,029,600	906,546		1,047,747		75,307	141,201 D	44.7%	51.6%	46.4%	53.6%
TOTAL	2012	3,006,266	1,369,540		1,636,726			267,186 D	45.6%	54.4%	45.6%	54.4%

Note: An asterisk (*) denotes incumbent. A pound sign (#) indicates that 75,307 votes were cast for Republican Clint Didier, which are included above in the Other Vote column.

WASHINGTON

GENERAL AND PRIMARY ELECTIONS

2014 PRIMARY ELECTIONS: SUPPLEMENTARY INFORMATION

Primary   August 5, 2014   **Registration** (as of August 5, 2014)   3,925,663   No Party Registration

Primary Type   Open—Any registered voter could participate in the primary, in which candidates of all parties ran together on the same ballot. The top two vote-getters advanced to the November general election.

ALL-PARTY PRIMARIES

Congressional District 1

DelBene, Suzan K.* (Democrat)#	59,798	50.7%
Celis, Pedro (Republican)#	19,407	16.4%
Sutherland, Robert (Republican)	18,424	15.6%
Orlinski, John (Republican)	11,891	10.1%
Moats, Edwin "Ed" (Republican)	5,252	4.5%
Todd, Richard J. (No Party Affiliation)	2,044	1.7%
Mike The Mover, (National Union)	1,192	1.0%
TOTAL	118,008	

Congressional District 2

Larsen, Rick* (Democrat)#	61,150	55.6%
Guillot, B.J. (Republican)#	36,002	32.7%
Lapointe, Mike (Independent)	12,844	11.7%
TOTAL	109,996	

WASHINGTON

GENERAL AND PRIMARY ELECTIONS

ALL-PARTY PRIMARIES

Congressional District 3	Beutler, Jaime Herrera* (Republican)#	58,913	48.8%
	Dingethal, Bob (Democrat)#	45,788	37.9%
	Delavar, Michael (Republican)	15,959	13.2%
	TOTAL	*120,660*	
Congressional District 4	Didier, Clint (Republican)#	33,965	31.8%
	Newhouse, Dan (Republican)#	27,326	25.6%
	Beltran, Estakio (Democrat)	13,062	12.2%
	Newbry, Janéa Holmquist (Republican)	11,061	10.4%
	Cicotte, George (Republican)	6,863	6.4%
	Sandoval, Tony (Democrat)	6,744	6.3%
	Wright, Richard (Independent)	3,270	3.1%
	Seim, Gavin (Republican)	2,107	2.0%
	Ramirez, Josh (Independent)	1,496	1.4%
	Stockwell, Glen R. "Stocky" (Republican)	547	0.5%
	Pross, Gordon Allen (Republican)	178	0.2%
	Midbust, Kevin (Republican)	161	0.2%
	TOTAL	*106,780*	
Congressional District 5	Rodgers, Cathy McMorris* (Republican)#	74,416	51.7%
	Pakootas, Joseph (Democrat)#	41,203	28.7%
	Wilson, Dave (Independent)	16,382	11.4%
	Horne, Tom (Republican)	11,811	8.2%
	TOTAL	*143,812*	
Congressional District 6	Kilmer, Derek* (Democrat)#	82,552	58.7%
	McClendon, Martin "Marty" (Republican)#	48,268	34.3%
	Milholland, Douglas (Green)	4,918	3.5%
	Mcpherson, W. "Greybeard" (No Party Affiliation)	4,890	3.5%
	TOTAL	*140,628*	
Congressional District 7	McDermott, Jim* (Democrat)#	114,039	76.9%
	Keller, Craig (Republican)#	13,586	9.2%
	Sutherland, Scott (Republican)	9,707	6.5%
	Mcquaid, Doug (Independent)	9,371	6.3%
	Goodspaceguy (Work and Wealth)	1,665	1.1%
	TOTAL	*148,368*	
Congressional District 8	Reichert, David G.* (Republican)#	66,715	62.5%
	Ritchie, Jason (Democrat)#	30,759	28.8%
	Arnold, Keith (Democrat)	9,273	8.7%
	TOTAL	*106,747*	
Congressional District 9	Smith, Adam* (Democrat)#	59,489	64.0%
	Basler, Doug (Republican)#	25,290	27.2%
	Rivers, Donovan (Democrat)	5,434	5.8%
	Greene, Mark (Citzens)	2,737	2.9%
	TOTAL	*92,950*	
Congressional District 10	Heck, Denny* (Democrat)#	51,738	51.6%
	McDonald, Joyce (Republican)#	41,416	41.3%
	Ferguson, Jennifer (Independent)	4,811	4.8%
	Wright, Sam (Human Rights)	2,342	2.3%
	TOTAL	*100,307*	

Note: An asterisk (*) denotes incumbent. A pound sign (#) indicates the top two vote getters, who qualified for the general election ballot.

WEST VIRGINIA

Congressional districts first established for elections held in 2012

3 members

WEST VIRGINIA

GOVERNOR

Earl Ray Tomblin (D). Reelected 2012 to a four-year term. Previously elected 2011 to fill the final year of the term vacated by Joe Manchin (D), who was elected senator in 2010. Tomblin sworn in as acting governor November 15, 2010.

SENATORS (1 Republican, 1 Democrat)

Shelley Moore Capito (R). Elected 2014 to a six-year term.

Joe Manchin III (D). Reelected 2012 to a six-year term. Previously elected 2010 to fill the remaining two years of the term vacated by the death of Robert C. Byrd (D) in June 2010. Carte Goodwin (D) was appointed to fill the vacancy until the special election could be held in November 2010.

REPRESENTATIVES (3 Republicans)

1. David B. McKinley (R)   2. Alexander X. Mooney (R)   3. Evan H. Jenkins (R)

POSTWAR VOTE FOR PRESIDENT

| Year | Total Vote | Republican | | Democratic | | Other Vote | Rep.-Dem. Plurality | Percentage | | | |
| | | Vote | Candidate | Vote | Candidate | | | Total Vote | | Major Vote | |
								Rep.	Dem.	Rep.	Dem.
2012	670,438	417,655	Romney, W. Mitt	238,269	Obama, Barack H.*	14,514	179,386 R	62.3%	35.5%	63.7%	36.3%
2008	713,451	397,466	McCain, John S. III	303,857	Obama, Barack H.	12,128	93,609 R	55.7%	42.6%	56.7%	43.3%
2004	755,887	423,778	Bush, George W.*	326,541	Kerry, John F.	5,568	97,237 R	56.1%	43.2%	56.5%	43.5%
2000**	648,124	336,475	Bush, George W.	295,497	Gore, Albert Jr.	16,152	40,978 R	51.9%	45.6%	53.2%	46.8%
1996**	636,459	233,946	Dole, Robert "Bob"	327,812	Clinton, Bill*	74,701	93,866 D	36.8%	51.5%	41.6%	58.4%
1992**	683,762	241,974	Bush, George H.*	331,001	Clinton, Bill	110,787	89,027 D	35.4%	48.4%	42.2%	57.8%
1988	653,311	310,065	Bush, George H.	341,016	Dukakis, Michael S.	2,230	30,951 D	47.5%	52.2%	47.6%	52.4%
1984	735,742	405,483	Reagan, Ronald*	328,125	Mondale, Walter F.	2,134	77,358 R	55.1%	44.6%	55.3%	44.7%
1980**	737,715	334,206	Reagan, Ronald	367,462	Carter, Jimmy*	36,047	33,256 D	45.3%	49.8%	47.6%	52.4%
1976	750,964	314,760	Ford, Gerald R.*	435,914	Carter, Jimmy	290	121,154 D	41.9%	58.0%	41.9%	58.1%
1972	762,399	484,964	Nixon, Richard M.*	277,435	McGovern, George S.		207,529 R	63.6%	36.4%	63.6%	36.4%
1968**	754,206	307,555	Nixon, Richard M.	374,091	Humphrey, Hubert Horatio Jr.	72,560	66,536 D	40.8%	49.6%	45.1%	54.9%
1964	792,040	253,953	Goldwater, Barry M. Sr.	538,087	Johnson, Lyndon B.*		284,134 D	32.1%	67.9%	32.1%	67.9%
1960	837,781	395,995	Nixon, Richard M.	441,786	Kennedy, John F.		45,791 D	47.3%	52.7%	47.3%	52.7%
1956	830,831	449,297	Eisenhower, Dwight D.*	381,534	Stevenson, Adlai E. II		67,763 R	54.1%	45.9%	54.1%	45.9%
1952	873,548	419,970	Eisenhower, Dwight D.	453,578	Stevenson, Adlai E. II		33,608 D	48.1%	51.9%	48.1%	51.9%
1948	748,750	316,251	Dewey, Thomas E.	429,188	Truman, Harry S.*	3,311	112,937 D	42.2%	57.3%	42.4%	57.6%

Note: An asterisk (*) denotes incumbent. **In past elections, the other vote included: 2000 - 10,680 Green (Ralph Nader); 1996 - 71,639 Reform (Ross Perot); 1992 - 108,829 Independent (Perot); 1980 - 31,691 Independent (John Anderson); 1968 - 72,560 American Independent (George Wallace).

WEST VIRGINIA

POSTWAR VOTE FOR GOVERNOR

Year	Total Vote	Republican		Democratic		Other Vote	Rep.-Dem. Plurality	Percentage			
		Vote	Candidate	Vote	Candidate			Total Vote		Major Vote	
								Rep.	Dem.	Rep.	Dem.
2012	664,455	303,291	Maloney, Bill	335,468	Tomblin, Earl Ray*	25,696	32,177 D	45.6%	50.5%	47.5%	52.5%
2011S**	301,084	141,656	Maloney, Bill	149,202	Tomblin, Earl Ray*	10,226	7,546 D	47.0%	49.6%	48.7%	51.3%
2008	706,046	181,612	Weeks, Russ	492,697	Manchin, Joe III*	31,737	311,085 D	25.7%	69.8%	26.9%	73.1%
2004	744,433	253,131	Warner, Monty	472,758	Manchin, Joe III	18,544	219,627 D	34.0%	63.5%	34.9%	65.1%
2000	648,047	305,926	Underwood, Cecil H.*	324,822	Wise, Robert Ellsworth	17,299	18,896 D	47.2%	50.1%	48.5%	51.5%
1996	628,559	324,518	Underwood, Cecil H.	287,870	Pritt, Charlotte	16,171	36,648 R	51.6%	45.8%	53.0%	47.0%
1992	657,193	240,390	Benedict, Cleveland K.	368,302	Caperton, Gaston*	48,501	127,912 D	36.6%	56.0%	39.5%	60.5%
1988	649,593	267,172	Moore, Arch A. Jr.*	382,421	Caperton, Gaston		115,249 D	41.1%	58.9%	41.1%	58.9%
1984	741,502	394,937	Moore, Arch A. Jr.	346,565	See, Clyde M.		48,372 R	53.3%	46.7%	53.3%	46.7%
1980	742,150	337,240	Moore, Arch A. Jr.	401,863	Rockefeller, John D. IV*	3,047	64,623 D	45.4%	54.1%	45.6%	54.4%
1976	749,270	253,420	Underwood, Cecil H.	495,661	Rockefeller, John D. IV	189	242,241 D	33.8%	66.2%	33.8%	66.2%
1972	774,279	423,817	Moore, Arch A. Jr.*	350,462	Rockefeller, John D. IV		73,355 R	54.7%	45.3%	54.7%	45.3%
1968	743,845	378,315	Moore, Arch A. Jr.	365,530	Sprouse, James M.		12,785 R	50.9%	49.1%	50.9%	49.1%
1964	788,582	355,559	Underwood, Cecil H.	433,023	Smith, Hulett		77,464 D	45.1%	54.9%	45.1%	54.9%
1960	827,420	380,665	Neely, Harold E.	446,755	Barron, W. W.		66,090 D	46.0%	54.0%	46.0%	54.0%
1956	817,623	440,502	Underwood, Cecil H.	377,121	Mollohan, Robert H.		63,381 R	53.9%	46.1%	53.9%	46.1%
1952	882,527	427,629	Holt, Rush D.	454,898	Marland, William C.		27,269 D	48.5%	51.5%	48.5%	51.5%
1948	768,061	329,309	Boreman, Herbert S.	438,752	Patteson, Okey L.		109,443 D	42.9%	57.1%	42.9%	57.1%

Note: An asterisk (*) denotes incumbent. **The 2011 election was for a short term to fill a vacancy.

POSTWAR VOTE FOR SENATOR

Year	Total Vote	Republican		Democratic		Other Vote	Rep.-Dem. Plurality	Percentage			
		Vote	Candidate	Vote	Candidate			Total Vote		Major Vote	
								Rep.	Dem.	Rep.	Dem.
2014	453,659	281,820	Capito, Shelley Moore	156,360	Tennant, Natalie E.	15,479	125,460 R	62.1%	34.5%	64.3%	35.7%
2012	660,212	240,787	Raese, John R.	399,908	Manchin, Joe III*	19,517	159,121 D	36.5%	60.6%	37.6%	62.4%
2010S	529,948	230,013	Raese, John R.	283,358	Manchin, Joe III	16,577	53,345 D	43.4%	53.5%	44.8%	55.2%
2008	702,308	254,629	Wolfe, Jay	447,560	Rockefeller, John D. IV*	119	192,931 D	36.3%	63.7%	36.3%	63.7%
2006	459,884	155,043	Raese, John R.	296,276	Byrd, Robert C.*	8,565	141,233 D	33.7%	64.4%	34.4%	65.6%
2002	436,183	160,902	Wolfe, M. Jay	275,281	Rockefeller, John D. IV*		114,379 D	36.9%	63.1%	36.9%	63.1%
2000	603,477	121,635	Gallaher, David T.	469,215	Byrd, Robert C.*	12,627	347,580 D	20.2%	77.8%	20.6%	79.4%
1996	595,614	139,088	Burks, Betty A.	456,526	Rockefeller, John D. IV*		317,438 D	23.4%	76.6%	23.4%	76.6%
1994	420,936	130,441	Klos, Stan	290,495	Byrd, Robert C.*		160,054 D	31.0%	69.0%	31.0%	69.0%
1990	404,305	128,071	Yoder, John	276,234	Rockefeller, John D. IV*		148,163 D	31.7%	68.3%	31.7%	68.3%
1988	634,547	223,564	Wolfe, M. Jay	410,983	Byrd, Robert C.*		187,419 D	35.2%	64.8%	35.2%	64.8%
1984	722,212	344,680	Raese, John R.	374,233	Rockefeller, John D. IV	3,299	29,553 D	47.7%	51.8%	47.9%	52.1%
1982	565,314	173,910	Benedict, Cleveland K.	387,170	Byrd, Robert C.*	4,234	213,260 D	30.8%	68.5%	31.0%	69.0%
1978	493,351	244,317	Moore, Arch A. Jr.	249,034	Randolph, Jennings*		4,717 D	49.5%	50.5%	49.5%	50.5%
1976	566,790			566,423	Byrd, Robert C.*	367	566,423 D		99.9%		100.0%
1972	731,841	245,531	Leonard, Louise	486,310	Randolph, Jennings*		240,779 D	33.5%	66.5%	33.5%	66.5%
1970	445,623	99,658	Dodson, Elmer H.	345,965	Byrd, Robert C.*		246,307 D	22.4%	77.6%	22.4%	77.6%
1966	491,216	198,891	Love, Francis J.	292,325	Randolph, Jennings*		93,434 D	40.5%	59.5%	40.5%	59.5%
1964	761,087	246,072	Benedict, Cooper P.	515,015	Byrd, Robert C.*		268,943 D	32.3%	67.7%	32.3%	67.7%
1960	828,292	369,935	Underwood, Cecil H.	458,355	Randolph, Jennings*	2	88,420 D	44.7%	55.3%	44.7%	55.3%
1958	644,917	263,172	Revercomb, Chapman*	381,745	Byrd, Robert C.		118,573 D	40.8%	59.2%	40.8%	59.2%
1958S	630,677	256,510	Hoblitzell, John D. Jr.*	374,167	Randolph, Jennings		117,657 D	40.7%	59.3%	40.7%	59.3%
1956S	805,174	432,123	Revercomb, Chapman	373,051	Marland, William C.		59,072 R	53.7%	46.3%	53.7%	46.3%
1954	593,329	268,066	Sweeney, Thomas	325,263	Neely, Matthew M.*		57,197 D	45.2%	54.8%	45.2%	54.8%
1952	876,573	406,554	Revercomb, Chapman	470,019	Kilgore, Harley M.*		63,465 D	46.4%	53.6%	46.4%	53.6%
1948	763,888	328,534	Revercomb, Chapman*	435,354	Neely, Matthew M.		106,820 D	43.0%	57.0%	43.0%	57.0%
1946	542,768	269,617	Sweeney, Thomas	273,151	Kilgore, Harley M.*		3,534 D	49.7%	50.3%	49.7%	50.3%

Note: An asterisk (*) denotes incumbent. **The 1956 election, one of the 1958 elections, and the 2010 election were for short terms to fill a vacancy. The Republican Party did not run a candidate in the 1976 Senate election.

WEST VIRGINIA

SENATOR 2014

2010 Census Population	County	Total Vote	Republican (Capito)	Democratic (Tennant)	Other	Rep.-Dem. Plurality	Percentage Total Vote Rep.	Dem.	Major Vote Rep.	Dem.
16,589	BARBOUR	4,216	2,772	1,265	179	1,507 R	65.7%	30.0%	68.7%	31.3%
104,169	BERKELEY	21,508	14,446	6,396	666	8,050 R	67.2%	29.7%	69.3%	30.7%
24,629	BOONE	6,461	3,478	2,798	185	680 R	53.8%	43.3%	55.4%	44.6%
14,523	BRAXTON	3,674	2,050	1,509	115	541 R	55.8%	41.1%	57.6%	42.4%
24,069	BROOKE	6,362	3,606	2,453	303	1,153 R	56.7%	38.6%	59.5%	40.5%
96,319	CABELL	21,225	12,687	7,955	583	4,732 R	59.8%	37.5%	61.5%	38.5%
7,627	CALHOUN	1,781	1,104	605	72	499 R	62.0%	34.0%	64.6%	35.4%
9,386	CLAY	2,283	1,464	747	72	717 R	64.1%	32.7%	66.2%	33.8%
8,202	DODDRIDGE	1,680	1,262	339	79	923 R	75.1%	20.2%	78.8%	21.2%
46,039	FAYETTE	10,226	5,473	4,354	399	1,119 R	53.5%	42.6%	55.7%	44.3%
8,693	GILMER	1,687	989	572	126	417 R	58.6%	33.9%	63.4%	36.6%
11,937	GRANT	2,714	2,265	354	95	1,911 R	83.5%	13.0%	86.5%	13.5%
35,480	GREENBRIER	9,555	5,515	3,663	377	1,852 R	57.7%	38.3%	60.1%	39.9%
23,964	HAMPSHIRE	5,264	3,795	1,259	210	2,536 R	72.1%	23.9%	75.1%	24.9%
30,676	HANCOCK	7,657	4,729	2,528	400	2,201 R	61.8%	33.0%	65.2%	34.8%
14,025	HARDY	3,387	2,335	894	158	1,441 R	68.9%	26.4%	72.3%	27.7%
69,099	HARRISON	17,951	10,375	6,910	666	3,465 R	57.8%	38.5%	60.0%	40.0%
29,211	JACKSON	8,390	5,474	2,697	219	2,777 R	65.2%	32.1%	67.0%	33.0%
53,498	JEFFERSON	13,753	7,943	5,356	454	2,587 R	57.8%	38.9%	59.7%	40.3%
193,063	KANAWHA	53,235	30,746	21,036	1,453	9,710 R	57.8%	39.5%	59.4%	40.6%
16,372	LEWIS	4,651	3,054	1,412	185	1,642 R	65.7%	30.4%	68.4%	31.6%
21,720	LINCOLN	4,452	2,709	1,599	144	1,110 R	60.8%	35.9%	62.9%	37.1%
36,743	LOGAN	7,639	4,700	2,780	159	1,920 R	61.5%	36.4%	62.8%	37.2%
56,418	MARION	14,402	7,329	6,575	498	754 R	50.9%	45.7%	52.7%	47.3%
33,107	MARSHALL	8,432	5,590	2,607	235	2,983 R	66.3%	30.9%	68.2%	31.8%
27,324	MASON	7,010	4,448	2,371	191	2,077 R	63.5%	33.8%	65.2%	34.8%
22,113	MCDOWELL	3,612	1,909	1,615	88	294 R	52.9%	44.7%	54.2%	45.8%
62,264	MERCER	14,476	9,668	4,356	452	5,312 R	66.8%	30.1%	68.9%	31.1%
28,212	MINERAL	6,591	4,735	1,538	318	3,197 R	71.8%	23.3%	75.5%	24.5%
26,839	MINGO	6,107	3,789	2,180	138	1,609 R	62.0%	35.7%	63.5%	36.5%
96,189	MONONGALIA	19,369	10,515	8,063	791	2,452 R	54.3%	41.6%	56.6%	43.4%
13,502	MONROE	3,598	2,257	1,220	121	1,037 R	62.7%	33.9%	64.9%	35.1%
17,541	MORGAN	5,053	3,452	1,396	205	2,056 R	68.3%	27.6%	71.2%	28.8%
26,233	NICHOLAS	6,800	4,295	2,173	332	2,122 R	63.2%	32.0%	66.4%	33.6%
44,443	OHIO	11,878	7,656	3,889	333	3,767 R	64.5%	32.7%	66.3%	33.7%
7,695	PENDLETON	2,114	1,557	515	42	1,042 R	73.7%	24.4%	75.1%	24.9%
7,605	PLEASANTS	1,729	1,150	507	72	643 R	66.5%	29.3%	69.4%	30.6%
8,719	POCAHONTAS	2,510	1,426	894	190	532 R	56.8%	35.6%	61.5%	38.5%
33,520	PRESTON	7,209	4,857	2,023	329	2,834 R	67.4%	28.1%	70.6%	29.4%
55,486	PUTNAM	16,038	11,103	4,543	392	6,560 R	69.2%	28.3%	71.0%	29.0%
78,859	RALEIGH	20,558	13,558	6,388	612	7,170 R	65.9%	31.1%	68.0%	32.0%
29,405	RANDOLPH	6,970	4,499	2,116	355	2,383 R	64.5%	30.4%	68.0%	32.0%
10,449	RITCHIE	2,805	2,118	555	132	1,563 R	75.5%	19.8%	79.2%	20.8%
14,926	ROANE	3,967	2,418	1,408	141	1,010 R	61.0%	35.5%	63.2%	36.8%
13,927	SUMMERS	3,227	1,806	1,281	140	525 R	56.0%	39.7%	58.5%	41.5%
16,895	TAYLOR	4,331	2,667	1,521	143	1,146 R	61.6%	35.1%	63.7%	36.3%
7,141	TUCKER	2,700	1,741	815	144	926 R	64.5%	30.2%	68.1%	31.9%
9,208	TYLER	2,121	1,518	499	104	1,019 R	71.6%	23.5%	75.3%	24.7%
24,254	UPSHUR	6,153	4,356	1,576	221	2,780 R	70.8%	25.6%	73.4%	26.6%
42,481	WAYNE	9,968	6,028	3,649	291	2,379 R	60.5%	36.6%	62.3%	37.7%
9,154	WEBSTER	1,995	1,105	795	95	310 R	55.4%	39.8%	58.2%	41.8%
16,583	WETZEL	4,072	2,423	1,491	158	932 R	59.5%	36.6%	61.9%	38.1%
5,717	WIRT	1,448	1,001	382	65	619 R	69.1%	26.4%	72.4%	27.6%
86,956	WOOD	21,665	14,723	6,226	716	8,497 R	68.0%	28.7%	70.3%	29.7%
23,796	WYOMING	5,000	3,152	1,712	136	1,440 R	63.0%	34.2%	64.8%	35.2%
1,852,994	TOTAL	453,659	281,820	156,360	15,479	125,460 R	62.1%	34.5%	64.3%	35.7%

WEST VIRGINIA

HOUSE OF REPRESENTATIVES

			Republican		Democratic		Other	Rep.-Dem.	Percentage			
									Total Vote		Major Vote	
CD	Year	Total Vote	Vote	Candidate	Vote	Candidate	Vote	Plurality	Rep.	Dem.	Rep.	Dem.
1	2014	144,600	92,491	MCKINLEY, DAVID B.*	52,109	GAINER, GLEN B. III		40,382 R	64.0%	36.0%	64.0%	36.0%
1	2012	214,151	133,809	MCKINLEY, DAVID B.*	80,342	THORN, SUE		53,467 R	62.5%	37.5%	62.5%	37.5%
2	2014	154,238	72,619	MOONEY, ALEXANDER X.	67,687	CASEY, NICK	13,932	4,932 R	47.1%	43.9%	51.8%	48.2%
2	2012	226,766	158,206	CAPITO, SHELLEY MOORE*	68,560	SWINT, HOWARD		89,646 R	69.8%	30.2%	69.8%	30.2%
3	2014	140,401	77,713	JENKINS, EVAN H.	62,688	RAHALL, NICK J. II*		15,025 R	55.4%	44.6%	55.4%	44.6%
3	2012	200,437	92,238	SNUFFER, RICK	108,199	RAHALL, NICK J. II*		15,961 D	46.0%	54.0%	46.0%	54.0%
TOTAL	2014	439,239	242,823		182,484		13,932	60,339 R	55.3%	41.5%	57.1%	42.9%
TOTAL	2012	641,354	384,253		257,101			127,152 R	59.9%	40.1%	59.9%	40.1%

Note: An asterisk (*) denotes incumbent.

WEST VIRGINIA

GENERAL AND PRIMARY ELECTIONS

2014 GENERAL ELECTIONS: OTHER VOTES

Senate Other vote was 7,409 Libertarian (John S. Buckley), 5,504 Mountain (Bob Henry Baber), 2,566 Constitution (Phil Hudok)

House Other vote was:

CD 2 7,682 Libertarian (Davy Jones), 6,250 Independent (Edward "Ed" Rabel)

2014 PRIMARY ELECTIONS: SUPPLEMENTARY INFORMATION

Primary	May 13, 2014	**Registration** (as of April 22, 2014)	1,225,844	Democratic	613,518
				Republican	352,858
				Libertarian	1,606
				Mountain	1,487
				Other	24,768
				No Party	231,607

Primary Type Semi-Open—Registered Democrats and registered Republicans could vote only in their party's primary. Those voters registered with no party could participate in either the Democratic or Republican primary.

	REPUBLICAN PRIMARIES			DEMOCRATIC PRIMARIES		
Senator	Capito, Shelley Moore	74,655	87.5%	Tennant, Natalie E.	104,598	77.9%
	Dodrill, Matthew	7,072	8.3%	Melton, Dennis	15,817	11.8%
	Butcher, Larry Eugene	3,595	4.2%	Wamsley, David B.	13,773	10.3%
	TOTAL	85,322		TOTAL	134,188	
Congressional District 1	McKinley, David B.*	27,589	100.0%	Gainer, Glen B. III	34,764	100.0%
	TOTAL	27,589		TOTAL	34,764	

WEST VIRGINIA

GENERAL AND PRIMARY ELECTIONS

	REPUBLICAN PRIMARIES			DEMOCRATIC PRIMARIES		
Congressional District 2	Mooney, Alexander X.	12,678	36.0%	Casey, Nick	21,646	60.6%
	Reed, Ken	7,848	22.3%	Poore, Meshea L.	14,061	39.4%
	Lane, Charlotte	6,358	18.1%			
	Harrison, Steve	3,885	11.0%			
	Walters, Ron Jr.	2,125	6.0%			
	Moss, Jim	1,684	4.8%			
	Fluharty, Robert Lawrence	621	1.8%			
	TOTAL	35,199		TOTAL	35,707	
Congressional District 3	Jenkins, Evan H.	14,374	100.0%	Rahall, Nick J. II*	37,176	66.5%
				Ojeda, Richard II	18,767	33.5%
	TOTAL	14,374		TOTAL	55,943	

Note: An asterisk (*) denotes incumbent.

WISCONSIN

Congressional districts first established for elections held in 2012

8 members

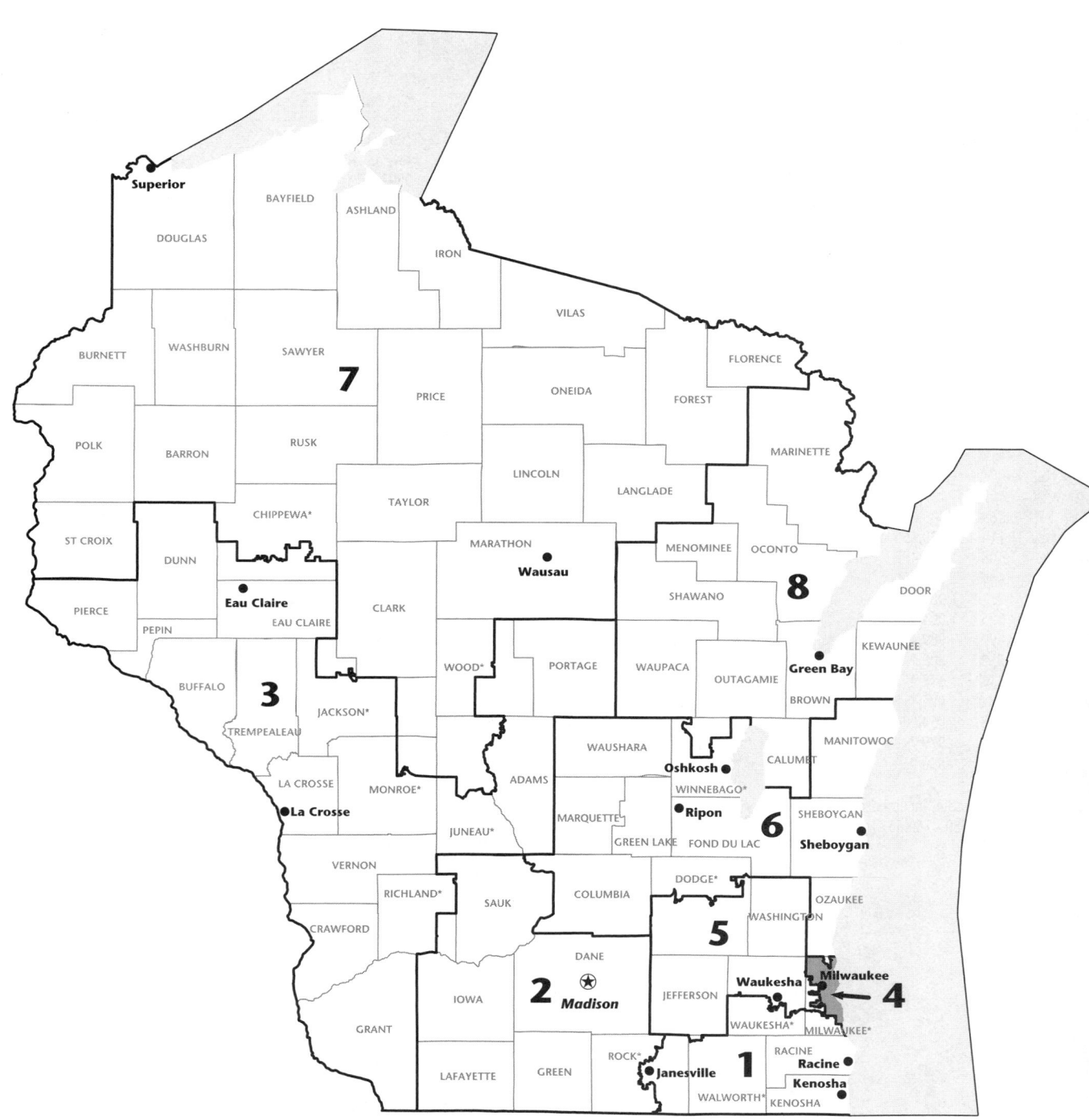

DOUGLAS
Superior
BAYFIELD
ASHLAND
IRON
BURNETT
WASHBURN
SAWYER
VILAS
PRICE
FLORENCE
7
ONEIDA
FOREST
POLK
BARRON
RUSK
LINCOLN
MARINETTE
ST CROIX
CHIPPEWA*
TAYLOR
MARATHON
LANGLADE
MENOMINEE
OCONTO
DUNN
Wausau
DOOR
PIERCE
Eau Claire
EAU CLAIRE
CLARK
SHAWANO
8
KEWAUNEE
PEPIN
BUFFALO
3
WOOD*
PORTAGE
WAUPACA
OUTAGAMIE
Green Bay
BROWN
JACKSON*
TREMPEALEAU
WAUSHARA
MANITOWOC
LA CROSSE
MONROE*
ADAMS
Oshkosh
CALUMET
La Crosse
WINNEBAGO*
SHEBOYGAN
JUNEAU*
MARQUETTE
Ripon
6
Sheboygan
VERNON
GREEN LAKE
FOND DU LAC
DODGE*
OZAUKEE
RICHLAND*
SAUK
COLUMBIA
WASHINGTON
CRAWFORD
5
DANE
Madison
Waukesha
Milwaukee
2
JEFFERSON
4
IOWA
WAUKESHA*
MILWAUKEE*
GRANT
Janesville
1
RACINE
Racine
LAFAYETTE
GREEN
ROCK*
Kenosha
WALWORTH*
KENOSHA

* Asterisk indicates a county whose boundaries include parts of two or more congressional districts.

WISCONSIN

GOVERNOR

Scott Walker (R). Reelected 2014 to a four-year term. Previously elected 2010. Won special recall election June 5, 2012, to remain in office.

SENATORS (1 Republican, 1 Democrat)

Tammy Baldwin (D). Elected 2012 to a six-year term.

Ron Johnson (R). Elected 2010 to a six-year term.

REPRESENTATIVES (5 Republicans, 3 Democrats)

1. Paul Ryan (R)
2. Mark Pocan (D)
3. Ron Kind (D)
4. Gwen Moore (D)
5. F. James Sensenbrenner Jr. (R)
6. Glenn Grothman (R)
7. Sean P. Duffy (R)
8. Reid J. Ribble (R)

POSTWAR VOTE FOR PRESIDENT

| Year | Total Vote | Republican | | Democratic | | Other Vote | Rep.-Dem. Plurality | Percentage | | | |
| | | Vote | Candidate | Vote | Candidate | | | Total Vote | | Major Vote | |
								Rep.	Dem.	Rep.	Dem.
2012	3,068,434	1,407,966	Romney, W. Mitt	1,620,985	Obama, Barack H.*	39,483	213,019 D	45.9%	52.8%	46.5%	53.5%
2008	2,983,417	1,262,393	McCain, John S. III	1,677,211	Obama, Barack H.	43,813	414,818 D	42.3%	56.2%	42.9%	57.1%
2004	2,997,007	1,478,120	Bush, George W.*	1,489,504	Kerry, John F.	29,383	11,384 D	49.3%	49.7%	49.8%	50.2%
2000**	2,598,607	1,237,279	Bush, George W.	1,242,987	Gore, Albert Jr.	118,341	5,708 D	47.6%	47.8%	49.9%	50.1%
1996**	2,196,169	845,029	Dole, Robert "Bob"	1,071,971	Clinton, Bill*	279,169	226,942 D	38.5%	48.8%	44.1%	55.9%
1992**	2,531,114	930,855	Bush, George H.*	1,041,066	Clinton, Bill	559,193	110,211 D	36.8%	41.1%	47.2%	52.8%
1988	2,191,608	1,047,499	Bush, George H.	1,126,794	Dukakis, Michael S.	17,315	79,295 D	47.8%	51.4%	48.2%	51.8%
1984	2,211,689	1,198,584	Reagan, Ronald*	995,740	Mondale, Walter F.	17,365	202,844 R	54.2%	45.0%	54.6%	45.4%
1980**	2,273,221	1,088,845	Reagan, Ronald	981,584	Carter, Jimmy*	202,792	107,261 R	47.9%	43.2%	52.6%	47.4%
1976	2,104,175	1,004,987	Ford, Gerald R.*	1,040,232	Carter, Jimmy	58,956	35,245 D	47.8%	49.4%	49.1%	50.9%
1972	1,852,890	989,430	Nixon, Richard M.*	810,174	McGovern, George S.	53,286	179,256 R	53.4%	43.7%	55.0%	45.0%
1968**	1,691,538	809,997	Nixon, Richard M.	748,804	Humphrey, Hubert Horatio Jr.	132,737	61,193 R	47.9%	44.3%	52.0%	48.0%
1964	1,691,815	638,495	Goldwater, Barry M. Sr.	1,050,424	Johnson, Lyndon B.*	2,896	411,929 D	37.7%	62.1%	37.8%	62.2%
1960	1,729,082	895,175	Nixon, Richard M.	830,805	Kennedy, John F.	3,102	64,370 R	51.8%	48.0%	51.9%	48.1%
1956	1,550,558	954,844	Eisenhower, Dwight D.*	586,768	Stevenson, Adlai E. II	8,946	368,076 R	61.6%	37.8%	61.9%	38.1%
1952	1,607,370	979,744	Eisenhower, Dwight D.	622,175	Stevenson, Adlai E. II	5,451	357,569 R	61.0%	38.7%	61.2%	38.8%
1948	1,276,800	590,959	Dewey, Thomas E.	647,310	Truman, Harry S.*	38,531	56,351 D	46.3%	50.7%	47.7%	52.3%

Note: An asterisk (*) denotes incumbent. **In past elections, the other vote included: 2000 - 94,070 Green (Ralph Nader); 1996 - 227,339 Reform (Ross Perot); 1992 - 544,479 Independent (Perot); 1980 - 160,657 Independent (John Anderson); 1968 - 127,835 American Independent (George Wallace).

WISCONSIN

POSTWAR VOTE FOR GOVERNOR

Year	Total Vote	Republican		Democratic		Other Vote	Rep.-Dem. Plurality	Percentage			
								Total Vote		Major Vote	
		Vote	Candidate	Vote	Candidate			Rep.	Dem.	Rep.	Dem
2014	2,410,314	1,259,706	Walker, Scott*	1,122,913	Burke, Mary	27,695	136,793 R	52.3%	46.6%	52.9%	47.1%
2012S**	2,516,065	1,335,585	Walker, Scott*	1,164,480	Barrett, Thomas M.	16,000	171,105 R	53.1%	46.3%	53.4%	46.6%
2010	2,160,832	1,128,941	Walker, Scott	1,004,303	Barrett, Thomas M.	27,588	124,638 R	52.2%	46.5%	52.9%	47.1%
2006	2,161,700	979,427	Green, Mark	1,139,115	Doyle, James E.*	43,158	159,688 D	45.3%	52.7%	46.2%	53.8%
2002**	1,775,349	734,779	McCallum, Scott*	800,515	Doyle, James E.	240,055	65,736 D	41.4%	45.1%	47.9%	52.1%
1998	1,756,014	1,047,716	Thompson, Tommy G.*	679,553	Garvey, Ed	28,745	368,163 R	59.7%	38.7%	60.7%	39.3%
1994	1,563,835	1,051,326	Thompson, Tommy G.*	482,850	Chvala, Chuck	29,659	568,476 R	67.2%	30.9%	68.5%	31.5%
1990	1,379,727	802,321	Thompson, Tommy G.*	576,280	Loftus, Thomas	1,126	226,041 R	58.2%	41.8%	58.2%	41.8%
1986	1,526,960	805,090	Thompson, Tommy G.	705,578	Earl, Anthony S.*	16,292	99,512 R	52.7%	46.2%	53.3%	46.7%
1982	1,580,344	662,838	Kohler, Terry J.	896,812	Earl, Anthony S.	20,694	233,974 D	41.9%	56.7%	42.5%	57.5%
1978	1,500,996	816,056	Dreyfus, Lee S.	673,813	Schreiber, Martin J.*	11,127	142,243 R	54.4%	44.9%	54.8%	45.2%
1974	1,181,976	497,195	Dyke, William D.	628,639	Lucey, Patrick J.*	56,142	131,444 D	42.1%	53.2%	44.2%	55.8%
1970**	1,343,160	602,617	Olson, Jack B.	728,403	Lucey, Patrick J.	12,140	125,786 D	44.9%	54.2%	45.3%	54.7%
1968	1,689,738	893,463	Knowles, Warren P.*	791,100	Lafollette, Bronson C.	5,175	102,363 R	52.9%	46.8%	53.0%	47.0%
1966	1,170,173	626,041	Knowles, Warren P.*	539,258	Lucey, Patrick J.	4,874	86,783 R	53.5%	46.1%	53.7%	46.3%
1964	1,694,887	856,779	Knowles, Warren P.	837,901	Reynolds, John W.*	207	18,878 R	50.6%	49.4%	50.6%	49.4%
1962	1,265,900	625,536	Kuehn, Philip G.	637,491	Reynolds, John W.	2,873	11,955 D	49.4%	50.4%	49.5%	50.5%
1960	1,728,009	837,123	Kuehn, Philip G.	890,868	Nelson, Gaylord Anton*	18	53,745 D	48.4%	51.6%	48.4%	51.6%
1958	1,202,219	556,391	Thomson, Vernon W.*	644,296	Nelson, Gaylord Anton	1,532	87,905 D	46.3%	53.6%	46.3%	53.7%
1956	1,557,788	808,273	Thomson, Vernon W.	749,421	Proxmire, William	94	58,852 R	51.9%	48.1%	51.9%	48.1%
1954	1,158,666	596,158	Kohler, Walter J. Jr.*	560,747	Proxmire, William	1,761	35,411 R	51.5%	48.4%	51.5%	48.5%
1952	1,615,214	1,009,171	Kohler, Walter J. Jr.*	601,844	Proxmire, William	4,199	407,327 R	62.5%	37.3%	62.6%	37.4%
1950	1,138,148	605,649	Kohler, Walter J. Jr.	525,319	Thompson, Carl W.	7,180	80,330 R	53.2%	46.2%	53.6%	46.4%
1948	1,266,139	684,839	Rennebohm, Oscar*	558,497	Thompson, Carl W.	22,803	126,342 R	54.1%	44.1%	55.1%	44.9%
1946	1,040,444	621,970	Goodland, Walter S.*	406,499	Hoan, Daniel W.	11,975	215,471 R	59.8%	39.1%	60.5%	39.5%

Note: An asterisk (*) denotes incumbent. **The 2012 Wisconsin gubernatorial contest was a special recall election held in June 2012. Governor Scott Walker retained his office. In past elections, the other vote included: 2002 - 185,455 Libertarian (Ed Thompson). The term of office of Wisconsin's governor was increased from two to four years effective with the 1970 election.

POSTWAR VOTE FOR SENATOR

Year	Total Vote	Republican		Democratic		Other Vote	Rep.-Dem. Plurality	Percentage			
								Total Vote		Major Vote	
		Vote	Candidate	Vote	Candidate			Rep.	Dem.	Rep.	Dem
2012	3,009,411	1,380,126	Thompson, Tommy G.	1,547,104	Baldwin, Tammy	82,181	166,978 D	45.9%	51.4%	47.1%	52.9%
2010	2,171,331	1,125,999	Johnson, Ron	1,020,958	Feingold, Russell D.*	24,374	105,041 R	51.9%	47.0%	52.4%	47.6%
2006	2,138,297	630,299	Lorge, Robert Gerald	1,439,214	Kohl, Herbert H.*	68,784	808,915 D	29.5%	67.3%	30.5%	69.5%
2004	2,949,743	1,301,183	Michels, Tim	1,632,697	Feingold, Russell D.*	15,863	331,514 D	44.1%	55.4%	44.4%	55.6%
2000	2,540,083	940,744	Gillespie, John	1,563,238	Kohl, Herbert H.*	36,101	622,494 D	37.0%	61.5%	37.6%	62.4%
1998	1,760,836	852,272	Neumann, Mark W.	890,059	Feingold, Russell D.*	18,505	37,787 D	48.4%	50.5%	48.9%	51.1%
1994	1,565,628	636,989	Welch, Robert T.	912,662	Kohl, Herbert H.*	15,977	275,673 D	40.7%	58.3%	41.1%	58.9%
1992	2,455,124	1,129,599	Kasten, Robert W.*	1,290,662	Feingold, Russell D.	34,863	161,063 D	46.0%	52.6%	46.7%	53.3%
1988	2,168,190	1,030,440	Engeleiter, Susan	1,128,625	Kohl, Herbert H.	9,125	98,185 D	47.5%	52.1%	47.7%	52.3%
1986	1,483,174	754,573	Kasten, Robert W.*	702,963	Garvey, Ed	25,638	51,610 R	50.9%	47.4%	51.8%	48.2%
1982	1,544,981	527,355	McCallum, Scott	983,311	Proxmire, William*	34,315	455,956 D	34.1%	63.6%	34.9%	65.1%
1980	2,204,202	1,106,311	Kasten, Robert W.	1,065,487	Nelson, Gaylord Anton*	32,404	40,824 R	50.2%	48.3%	50.9%	49.1%
1976	1,935,183	521,902	York, Stanley	1,396,970	Proxmire, William*	16,311	875,068 D	27.0%	72.2%	27.2%	72.8%
1974	1,199,495	429,327	Petri, Thomas E.	740,700	Nelson, Gaylord Anton*	29,468	311,373 D	35.8%	61.8%	36.7%	63.3%
1970	1,338,967	381,297	Erickson, John E.	948,445	Proxmire, William*	9,225	567,148 D	28.5%	70.8%	28.7%	71.3%
1968	1,654,861	633,910	Leonard, Jerris	1,020,931	Nelson, Gaylord Anton*	20	387,021 D	38.3%	61.7%	38.3%	61.7%
1964	1,673,776	780,116	Renk, Wilbur N.	892,013	Proxmire, William*	1,647	111,897 D	46.6%	53.3%	46.7%	53.3%
1962	1,260,168	594,846	Wiley, Alexander*	662,342	Nelson, Gaylord Anton	2,980	67,496 D	47.2%	52.6%	47.3%	52.7%
1958	1,194,678	510,398	Steinle, Roland J.	682,440	Proxmire, William*	1,840	172,042 D	42.7%	57.1%	42.8%	57.2%
1957S	772,620	312,931	Kohler, Walter J. Jr.	435,985	Proxmire, William	23,704	123,054 D	40.5%	56.4%	41.8%	58.2%
1956	1,523,356	892,473	Wiley, Alexander*	627,903	Maier, Henry W.	2,980	264,570 R	58.6%	41.2%	58.7%	41.3%
1952	1,605,228	870,444	McCarthy, Joseph R.*	731,402	Fairchild, Thomas E.	3,382	139,042 R	54.2%	45.6%	54.3%	45.7%
1950	1,116,135	595,283	Wiley, Alexander*	515,539	Fairchild, Thomas E.	5,313	79,744 R	53.3%	46.2%	53.6%	46.4%
1946	1,014,594	620,430	McCarthy, Joseph R.	378,772	McMurray, Howard J.	15,392	241,658 R	61.2%	37.3%	62.1%	37.9%

Note: An asterisk (*) denotes incumbent. **The August 1957 election was for a short term to fill a vacancy.

WISCONSIN
GOVERNOR 2014

2010 Census Population	County	Total Vote	Republican (Walker)	Democratic (Burke)	Other	Rep.-Dem. Plurality	Percentage Total Vote Rep.	Percentage Total Vote Dem.	Percentage Major Vote Rep.	Percentage Major Vote Dem.
20,875	ADAMS	8,185	4,297	3,762	126	535 R	52.5%	46.0%	53.3%	46.7%
16,157	ASHLAND	6,566	2,333	4,150	83	1,817 D	35.5%	63.2%	36.0%	64.0%
45,870	BARRON	16,749	9,696	6,832	221	2,864 R	57.9%	40.8%	58.7%	41.3%
15,014	BAYFIELD	8,023	3,075	4,888	60	1,813 D	38.3%	60.9%	38.6%	61.4%
248,007	BROWN	100,291	58,408	40,751	1,132	17,657 R	58.2%	40.6%	58.9%	41.1%
13,587	BUFFALO	5,504	3,169	2,267	68	902 R	57.6%	41.2%	58.3%	41.7%
15,457	BURNETT	6,537	3,868	2,615	54	1,253 R	59.2%	40.0%	59.7%	40.3%
48,971	CALUMET	21,614	14,086	7,285	243	6,801 R	65.2%	33.7%	65.9%	34.1%
62,415	CHIPPEWA	24,506	13,765	10,402	339	3,363 R	56.2%	42.4%	57.0%	43.0%
34,690	CLARK	11,391	7,409	3,848	134	3,561 R	65.0%	33.8%	65.8%	34.2%
56,833	COLUMBIA	24,700	11,837	12,527	336	690 D	47.9%	50.7%	48.6%	51.4%
16,644	CRAWFORD	6,273	2,974	3,225	74	251 D	47.4%	51.4%	48.0%	52.0%
488,073	DANE	252,469	73,676	175,937	2,856	102,261 D	29.2%	69.7%	29.5%	70.5%
88,759	DODGE	36,838	23,715	12,732	391	10,983 R	64.4%	34.6%	65.1%	34.9%
27,785	DOOR	15,170	8,160	6,842	168	1,318 R	53.8%	45.1%	54.4%	45.6%
44,159	DOUGLAS	15,745	6,001	9,590	154	3,589 D	38.1%	60.9%	38.5%	61.5%
43,857	DUNN	15,520	8,229	7,066	225	1,163 R	53.0%	45.5%	53.8%	46.2%
98,736	EAU CLAIRE	42,105	20,304	21,239	562	935 D	48.2%	50.4%	48.9%	51.1%
4,423	FLORENCE	2,001	1,349	629	23	720 R	67.4%	31.4%	68.2%	31.8%
101,633	FOND DU LAC	42,929	27,485	15,014	430	12,471 R	64.0%	35.0%	64.7%	35.3%
9,304	FOREST	3,592	2,032	1,511	49	521 R	56.6%	42.1%	57.4%	42.6%
51,208	GRANT	18,166	9,149	8,704	313	445 R	50.4%	47.9%	51.2%	48.8%
36,842	GREEN	15,338	7,193	7,948	197	755 D	46.9%	51.8%	47.5%	52.5%
19,051	GREEN LAKE	7,874	5,336	2,464	74	2,872 R	67.8%	31.3%	68.4%	31.6%
23,687	IOWA	10,580	4,480	5,937	163	1,457 D	42.3%	56.1%	43.0%	57.0%
5,916	IRON	2,874	1,755	1,085	34	670 R	61.1%	37.8%	61.8%	38.2%
20,449	JACKSON	7,545	3,812	3,631	102	181 R	50.5%	48.1%	51.2%	48.8%
83,686	JEFFERSON	35,762	21,443	13,876	443	7,567 R	60.0%	38.8%	60.7%	39.3%
26,664	JUNEAU	9,032	4,817	4,080	135	737 R	53.3%	45.2%	54.1%	45.9%
166,426	KENOSHA	56,482	28,398	27,367	717	1,031 R	50.3%	48.5%	50.9%	49.1%
20,574	KEWAUNEE	9,134	5,676	3,379	79	2,297 R	62.1%	37.0%	62.7%	37.3%
114,638	LA CROSSE	48,422	22,321	25,429	672	3,108 D	46.1%	52.5%	46.7%	53.3%
16,836	LAFAYETTE	6,251	3,191	2,982	78	209 R	51.0%	47.7%	51.7%	48.3%
19,977	LANGLADE	8,478	5,476	2,921	81	2,555 R	64.6%	34.5%	65.2%	34.8%
28,743	LINCOLN	12,148	6,866	5,104	178	1,762 R	56.5%	42.0%	57.4%	42.6%
81,442	MANITOWOC	34,033	21,044	12,563	426	8,481 R	61.8%	36.9%	62.6%	37.4%
134,063	MARATHON	56,513	34,583	21,305	625	13,278 R	61.2%	37.7%	61.9%	38.1%
41,749	MARINETTE	15,788	9,610	6,023	155	3,587 R	60.9%	38.1%	61.5%	38.5%
15,404	MARQUETTE	6,326	3,611	2,629	86	982 R	57.1%	41.6%	57.9%	42.1%
4,232	MENOMINEE	999	215	753	31	538 D	21.5%	75.4%	22.2%	77.8%
947,735	MILWAUKEE	368,093	132,706	231,316	4,071	98,610 D	36.1%	62.8%	36.5%	63.5%
44,673	MONROE	15,088	8,446	6,399	243	2,047 R	56.0%	42.4%	56.9%	43.1%
37,660	OCONTO	16,135	10,300	5,657	178	4,643 R	63.8%	35.1%	64.5%	35.5%
35,998	ONEIDA	17,314	9,852	7,190	272	2,662 R	56.9%	41.5%	57.8%	42.2%
176,695	OUTAGAMIE	74,945	44,543	29,503	899	15,040 R	59.4%	39.4%	60.2%	39.8%
86,395	OZAUKEE	46,741	32,696	13,696	349	19,000 R	70.0%	29.3%	70.5%	29.5%
7,469	PEPIN	3,163	1,791	1,333	39	458 R	56.6%	42.1%	57.3%	42.7%
41,019	PIERCE	14,637	7,760	6,666	211	1,094 R	53.0%	45.5%	53.8%	46.2%
44,205	POLK	16,068	9,345	6,516	207	2,829 R	58.2%	40.6%	58.9%	41.1%
70,019	PORTAGE	30,358	14,650	15,283	425	633 D	48.3%	50.3%	48.9%	51.1%
14,159	PRICE	6,502	3,725	2,700	77	1,025 R	57.3%	41.5%	58.0%	42.0%
195,408	RACINE	79,581	42,944	35,769	868	7,175 R	54.0%	44.9%	54.6%	45.4%
18,021	RICHLAND	6,836	3,435	3,315	86	120 R	50.2%	48.5%	50.9%	49.1%
160,331	ROCK	58,448	24,993	32,523	932	7,530 D	42.8%	55.6%	43.5%	56.5%
14,755	RUSK	5,888	3,502	2,286	100	1,216 R	59.5%	38.8%	60.5%	39.5%
61,976	SAUK	25,609	12,222	13,041	346	819 D	47.7%	50.9%	48.4%	51.6%
16,557	SAWYER	6,826	3,721	3,029	76	692 R	54.5%	44.4%	55.1%	44.9%
41,949	SHAWANO	16,838	10,937	5,730	171	5,207 R	65.0%	34.0%	65.6%	34.4%
115,507	SHEBOYGAN	50,232	31,728	17,955	549	13,773 R	63.2%	35.7%	63.9%	36.1%
84,345	ST. CROIX	33,760	20,066	13,231	463	6,835 R	59.4%	39.2%	60.3%	39.7%
20,689	TAYLOR	7,744	5,406	2,248	90	3,158 R	69.8%	29.0%	70.6%	29.4%
29,773	TREMPEALEAU	10,731	5,617	4,974	140	643 R	52.3%	46.4%	53.0%	47.0%
29,773	VERNON	11,771	5,687	5,932	152	245 D	48.3%	50.4%	48.9%	51.1%
21,430	VILAS	11,317	6,942	4,240	135	2,702 R	61.3%	37.5%	62.1%	37.9%
102,228	WALWORTH	39,712	25,415	13,809	488	11,606 R	64.0%	34.8%	64.8%	35.2%

WISCONSIN

GOVERNOR 2014

2010 Census Population	County	Total Vote	Republican (Walker)	Democratic (Burke)	Other	Rep.-Dem. Plurality	Total Vote Rep.	Total Vote Dem.	Major Vote Rep.	Major Vote Dem
15,911	WASHBURN	7,092	3,945	3,074	73	871 R	55.6%	43.3%	56.2%	43.8
131,887	WASHINGTON	66,263	50,278	15,507	478	34,771 R	75.9%	23.4%	76.4%	23.6
389,891	WAUKESHA	203,248	147,266	54,500	1,482	92,766 R	72.5%	26.8%	73.0%	27.0
52,410	WAUPACA	20,798	13,130	7,471	197	5,659 R	63.1%	35.9%	63.7%	36.3
24,496	WAUSHARA	9,809	6,100	3,609	100	2,491 R	62.2%	36.8%	62.8%	37.2
166,994	WINNEBAGO	69,213	37,894	30,258	1,061	7,636 R	54.7%	43.7%	55.6%	44.4
74,749	WOOD	31,101	17,820	12,861	420	4,959 R	57.3%	41.4%	58.1%	41.9
5,686,986	TOTAL	2,410,314	1,259,706	1,122,913	27,695	136,793 R	52.3%	46.6%	52.9%	47.1

WISCONSIN

HOUSE OF REPRESENTATIVES

CD	Year	Total Vote	Republican Vote	Republican Candidate	Democratic Vote	Democratic Candidate	Other Vote	Rep.-Dem. Plurality	Total Vote Rep.	Total Vote Dem.	Major Vote Rep.	Major Vote Dem
1	2014	288,170	182,316	RYAN, PAUL*	105,552	ZERBAN, ROB	302	76,764 R	63.3%	36.6%	63.3%	36.7
1	2012	365,058	200,423	RYAN, PAUL*	158,414	ZEBRAN, ROB	6,221	42,009 R	54.9%	43.4%	55.9%	44.1
2	2014	328,847	103,619	THERON, PETER	224,920	POCAN, MARK*	308	121,301 D	31.5%	68.4%	31.5%	68.5
2	2012	390,898	124,683	LEE, CHAD	265,422	POCAN, MARK	793	140,739 D	31.9%	67.9%	32.0%	68.0
3	2014	275,161	119,540	KURTZ, TONY	155,368	KIND, RON*	253	35,828 D	43.4%	56.5%	43.5%	56.5
3	2012	339,764	121,713	BOLAND, RAY	217,712	KIND, RON*	339	95,999 D	35.8%	64.1%	35.9%	64.1
4	2014	254,892	68,490	SEBRING, DAN	179,045	MOORE, GWEN*	7,357	110,555 D	26.9%	70.2%	27.7%	72.3
4	2012	325,788	80,787	SEBRING, DAN	235,257	MOORE, GWEN	9,744	154,470 D	24.8%	72.2%	25.6%	74.4
5	2014	332,826	231,160	SENSENBRENNER, F. JAMES JR.*	101,190	ROCKWOOD, CHRIS B.	476	129,970 R	69.5%	30.4%	69.6%	30.4
5	2012	369,664	250,335	SENSENBRENNER, F. JAMES JR.*	118,478	HEASTER, DAVE	851	131,857 R	67.7%	32.1%	67.9%	32.1
6	2014	299,033	169,767	GROTHMAN, GLENN	122,212	HARRIS, MARK L.	7,054	47,555 R	56.8%	40.9%	58.1%	41.9
6	2012	359,745	223,460	PETRI, THOMAS E.*	135,921	KALLAS, JOSEPH C.	364	87,539 R	62.1%	37.8%	62.2%	37.8
7	2014	286,603	169,891	DUFFY, SEAN P.*	112,949	WESTLUND, KELLY	3,763	56,942 R	59.3%	39.4%	60.1%	39.9
7	2012	359,669	201,720	DUFFY, SEAN P.*	157,524	KREITLOW, PAT	425	44,196 R	56.1%	43.8%	56.2%	43.8
8	2014	290,048	188,553	RIBBLE, REID J.*	101,345	GRUETT, RON	150	87,208 R	65.0%	34.9%	65.0%	35.0
8	2012	355,464	198,874	RIBBLE, REID J.*	156,287	WALL, JAMIE	303	42,587 R	55.9%	44.0%	56.0%	44.0
TOTAL	2014	2,355,580	1,233,336		1,102,581		19,663	130,755 R	52.4%	46.8%	52.8%	47.2
TOTAL	2012	2,866,050	1,401,995		1,445,015		19,040	43,020 D	48.9%	50.4%	49.2%	50.8

Note: An asterisk (*) denotes incumbent.

WISCONSIN

GENERAL AND PRIMARY ELECTIONS

2014 GENERAL ELECTIONS: OTHER VOTES

Governor   Other vote was 18,720 Libertarian (Robert Burke), 7,530 People's Party (Dennis Fehr), 1,248 (scattered write-in), 108 write-in (Mary Jo Walters), 52 write-in (Brett D. Hulsey), 15 write-in (Jumoka A. Johnson) 9 write-in (Steve R. Evans), 8 write-in (Susan P. Resch), 5 write-in (Jessica Nicole Perry)

WISCONSIN

GENERAL AND PRIMARY ELECTIONS

House	Other vote was:
CD 1	273 scattered write-in, 29 write-in (Kerth R. Deschler)
CD 2	308 scattered write-in
CD 3	128 Write-in (Ken Van Doren), 125 scattered write-in
CD 4	7,002 Independent (Robert R. Raymond), 355 scattered write-in
CD 5	476 scattered write-in
CD 6	6,865 Independent (Gus Fahrendorf), 189 scattered write-in
CD 7	3,686 Independent (Lawrence Dale), 42 scattered write-in, 30 write-in (Rob Taylor), 5 write-in (John Schiess)
CD 8	150 scattered write-in

2014 PRIMARY ELECTIONS: SUPPLEMENTARY INFORMATION

Primary	August 12, 2014	**Registration** (as of August 12, 2014)	3,453,356	No Party Registration

Primary Type   Open—Any registered voter could participate in the party primary of his or her choice.

	REPUBLICAN PRIMARIES			DEMOCRATIC PRIMARIES		
Governor	Walker, Scott*	238,715	99.4%	Burke, Mary	259,926	83.3%
	Evans, Steve R.	1,293	0.5%	Hulsey, Brett	51,830	16.6%
	write-in	94		write-in	350	0.1%
	TOTAL	240,102		TOTAL	312,106	
Congressional District 1	Ryan, Paul*	40,813	94.3%	Zerban, Rob	25,627	77.6%
	Ryan, Jeremy	2,450	5.7%	Kaleka, Amar	7,318	22.2%
	write-in	30	0.1%	write-in	71	0.2%
	TOTAL	43,293		TOTAL	33,016	
Congressional District 2	Theron, Peter	12,464	99.8%	Pocan, Mark*	52,517	99.6%
	write-in	20	0.2%	write-in	216	0.4%
	TOTAL	12,484		TOTAL	52,733	
Congressional District 3	Kurtz, Tony	13,552	56.7%	Kind, Ron*	28,783	99.8%
	Mueller, Karen L.	5,630	23.6%	write-in	70	0.2%
	Van Doren, Ken	4,704	19.7%			
	write-in	17	0.1%			
	TOTAL	23,903		TOTAL	28,853	
Congressional District 4	Sebring, Dan	3,386	79.7%	Moore, Gwen*	52,413	70.9%
	King, David D.	855	20.1%	George, Gary R.	21,242	28.7%
	write-in	9	0.2%	write-in	257	0.3%
	TOTAL	4,250		TOTAL	73,912	
Congressional District 5	Sensenbrenner, F. James Jr.*	43,266	99.8%	Rockwood, Chris B.	21,715	99.4%
	write-in	82	0.2%	write-in	141	0.6%
	TOTAL	43,348		TOTAL	21,856	
Congressional District 6	Grothman, Glenn	23,247	36.2%	Harris, Mark L.	19,714	99.8%
	Leibham, Joe	23,028	35.8%	write-in	49	0.2%
	Stroebel, Duane S. "Duey"	15,837	24.6%			
	Denow, Tom	2,117	3.3%			
	write-in	30				
	TOTAL	64,259		TOTAL	19,763	
Congressional District 7	Duffy, Sean P.*	25,707	87.6%	Westlund, Kelly	18,631	77.9%
	Raihala, Don	3,607	12.3%	Krsiean, Mike	5,256	22.0%
	write-in	20	0.1%	write-in	24	0.1%
	Schiess, John	2				
	TOTAL	29,336		TOTAL	23,911	
Congressional District 8	Ribble, Reid J.*	33,330	99.7%	Gruett, Ron	18,030	99.8%
	write-in	85	0.3%	write-in	34	0.2%
	TOTAL	33,415		TOTAL	18,064	

Note: An asterisk (*) denotes incumbent.

WYOMING

One member At Large

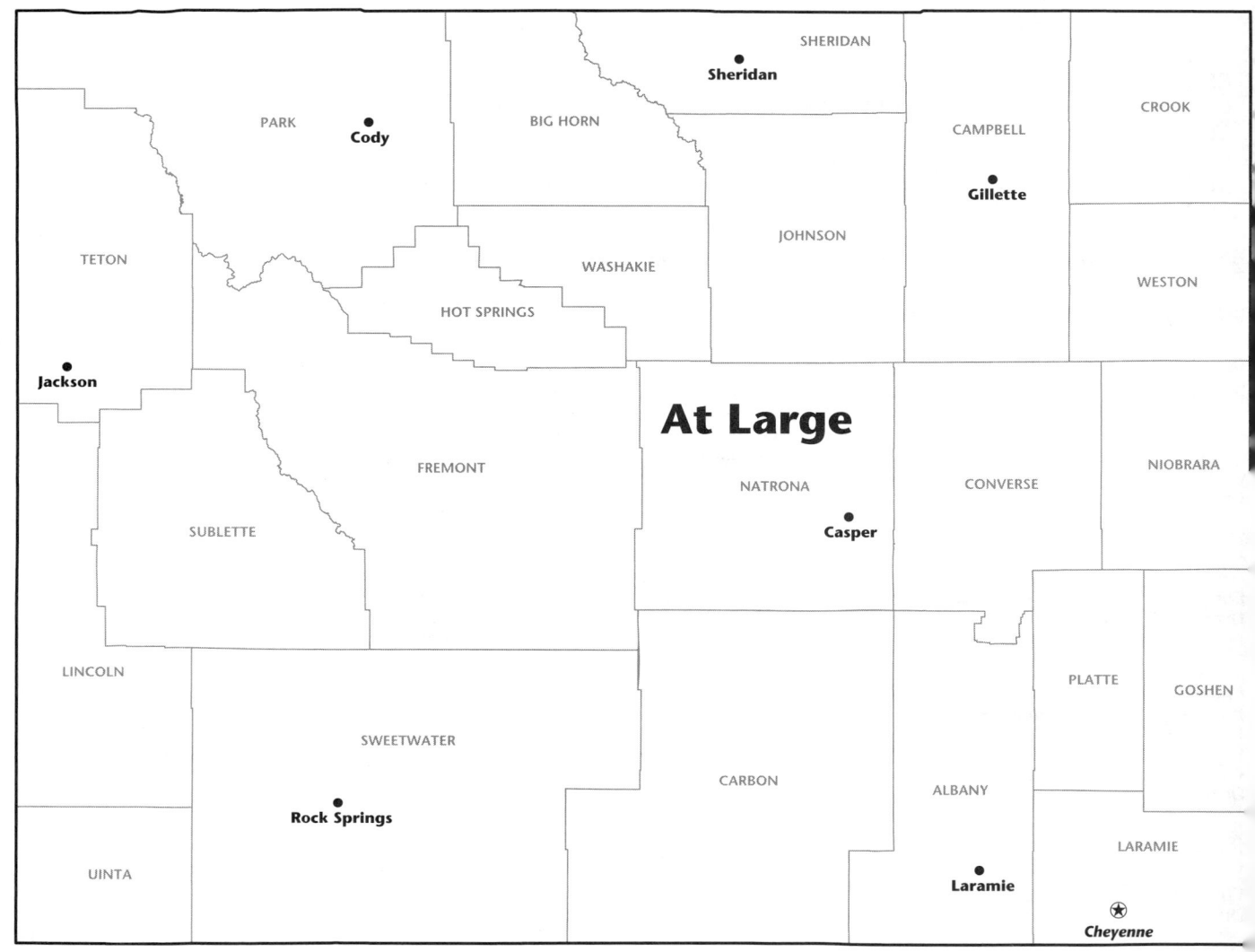

WYOMING

GOVERNOR
Matt Mead (R). Reelected 2014 to a four-year term. Previously elected 2010.

SENATORS (2 Republicans)
John Barrasso (R). Reelected 2012. Previously elected 2008 to fill out the remaining four years of the term vacated by the June 2007 death of Senator Craig Thomas (R); sworn in as Thomas's successor June 25, 2007.

Michael B. Enzi (R). Reelected 2014 to a six-year term. Previously elected 2008, 2002, 1996.

REPRESENTATIVE (1 Republican)
At Large. Cynthia M. Lummis (R)

POSTWAR VOTE FOR PRESIDENT

		Republican		Democratic		Other	Rep.-Dem.	Total Vote		Major Vote	
Year	Total Vote	Vote	Candidate	Vote	Candidate	Vote	Plurality	Rep.	Dem.	Rep.	Dem.
2012	249,061	170,962	Romney, W. Mitt	69,286	Obama, Barack H.*	8,813	101,676 R	68.6%	27.8%	71.2%	28.8%
2008	254,658	164,958	McCain, John S. III	82,868	Obama, Barack H.	6,832	82,090 R	64.8%	32.5%	66.6%	33.4%
2004	243,428	167,629	Bush, George W.*	70,776	Kerry, John F.	5,023	96,853 R	68.9%	29.1%	70.3%	29.7%
2000**	218,351	147,947	Bush, George W.	60,481	Gore, Albert Jr.	9,923	87,466 R	67.8%	27.7%	71.0%	29.0%
1996**	211,571	105,388	Dole, Robert "Bob"	77,934	Clinton, Bill*	28,249	27,454 R	49.8%	36.8%	57.5%	42.5%
1992**	200,598	79,347	Bush, George H.*	68,160	Clinton, Bill	53,091	11,187 R	39.6%	34.0%	53.8%	46.2%
1988	176,551	106,867	Bush, George H.	67,113	Dukakis, Michael S.	2,571	39,754 R	60.5%	38.0%	61.4%	38.6%
1984	188,968	133,241	Reagan, Ronald*	53,370	Mondale, Walter F.	2,357	79,871 R	70.5%	28.2%	71.4%	28.6%
1980**	176,713	110,700	Reagan, Ronald	49,427	Carter, Jimmy*	16,586	61,273 R	62.6%	28.0%	69.1%	30.9%
1976	156,343	92,717	Ford, Gerald R.*	62,239	Carter, Jimmy	1,387	30,478 R	59.3%	39.8%	59.8%	40.2%
1972	145,570	100,464	Nixon, Richard M.*	44,358	McGovern, George S.	748	56,106 R	69.0%	30.5%	69.4%	30.6%
1968**	127,205	70,927	Nixon, Richard M.	45,173	Humphrey, Hubert Horatio Jr.	11,105	25,754 R	55.8%	35.5%	61.1%	38.9%
1964	142,716	61,998	Goldwater, Barry M. Sr.	80,718	Johnson, Lyndon B.*		18,720 D	43.4%	56.6%	43.4%	56.6%
1960	140,782	77,451	Nixon, Richard M.	63,331	Kennedy, John F.		14,120 R	55.0%	45.0%	55.0%	45.0%
1956	124,127	74,573	Eisenhower, Dwight D.*	49,554	Stevenson, Adlai E. II		25,019 R	60.1%	39.9%	60.1%	39.9%
1952	129,253	81,049	Eisenhower, Dwight D.	47,934	Stevenson, Adlai E. II	270	33,115 R	62.7%	37.1%	62.8%	37.2%
1948	101,425	47,947	Dewey, Thomas E.	52,354	Truman, Harry S.*	1,124	4,407 D	47.3%	51.6%	47.8%	52.2%

Note: An asterisk (*) denotes incumbent. **In past elections, the other vote included: 2000 - 4,625 Green (Ralph Nader); 1996 - 25,928 Reform (Ross Perot); 1992 - 51,263 Independent (Perot); 1980 - 12,072 Independent (John Anderson); 1968 - 11,105 American Independent (George Wallace).

WYOMING

POSTWAR VOTE FOR GOVERNOR

Year	Total Vote	Republican Vote	Candidate	Democratic Vote	Candidate	Other Vote	Rep.-Dem. Plurality	Percentage Total Vote Rep.	Dem.	Major Vote Rep.	Dem.
2014	167,877	99,700	Mead, Matt*	45,752	Gosar, Peter	22,425	53,948 R	59.4%	27.3%	68.5%	31.5
2010	188,463	123,780	Mead, Matt	43,240	Petersen, Leslie	21,443	80,540 R	65.7%	22.9%	74.1%	25.9
2006	193,892	58,100	Hunkins, Ray	135,516	Freudenthal, Dave*	276	77,416 D	30.0%	69.9%	30.0%	70.0
2002	185,459	88,873	Bebout, Eli	92,662	Freudenthal, Dave	3,924	3,789 D	47.9%	50.0%	49.0%	51.0
1998	174,888	97,235	Geringer, Jim*	70,754	Vinich, John P.	6,899	26,481 R	55.6%	40.5%	57.9%	42.1
1994	200,990	118,016	Geringer, Jim	80,747	Karpan, Kathy	2,227	37,269 R	58.7%	40.2%	59.4%	40.6
1990	160,109	55,471	Mead, Mary	104,638	Sullivan, Mike*		49,167 D	34.6%	65.4%	34.6%	65.4
1986	164,720	75,841	Simpson, Peter	88,879	Sullivan, Mike		13,038 D	46.0%	54.0%	46.0%	54.0
1982	168,555	62,128	Morton, Warren A.	106,427	Herschler, Ed*		44,299 D	36.9%	63.1%	36.9%	63.1
1978	137,567	67,595	Ostlund, John C.	69,972	Herschler, Ed*		2,377 D	49.1%	50.9%	49.1%	50.9
1974	128,386	56,645	Jones, Dick	71,741	Herschler, Ed		15,096 D	44.1%	55.9%	44.1%	55.9
1970	118,257	74,249	Hathaway, Stanley K.*	44,008	Rooney, John J.		30,241 R	62.8%	37.2%	62.8%	37.2
1966	120,873	65,624	Hathaway, Stanley K.	55,249	Wilkerson, Ernest		10,375 R	54.3%	45.7%	54.3%	45.7
1962	119,268	64,970	Hansen, Clifford P.	54,298	Gage, Jack R.*		10,672 R	54.5%	45.5%	54.5%	45.5
1958	112,537	52,488	Simpson, Milward L.*	55,070	Hickey, John J.	4,979	2,582 D	46.6%	48.9%	48.8%	51.2
1954	111,438	56,275	Simpson, Milward L.	55,163	Jack, William		1,112 R	50.5%	49.5%	50.5%	49.5
1950	96,959	54,441	Barrett, Frank A.	42,518	McIntyre, John J.		11,923 R	56.1%	43.9%	56.1%	43.9
1946	81,353	38,333	Wright, Earl	43,020	Hunt, Lester C.*		4,687 D	47.1%	52.9%	47.1%	52.9

Note: An asterisk (*) denotes incumbent.

POSTWAR VOTE FOR SENATOR

Year	Total Vote	Republican Vote	Candidate	Democratic Vote	Candidate	Other Vote	Rep.-Dem. Plurality	Percentage Total Vote Rep.	Dem.	Major Vote Rep.	Dem.
2014	168,390	121,554	Enzi, Michael B.*	29,377	Hardy, Charles E. "Charlie"	17,459	92,177 R	72.2%	17.4%	80.5%	19.5
2012	244,862	185,250	Barrasso, John*	53,019	Chestnut, Tim	6,593	132,231 R	75.7%	21.7%	77.7%	22.3
2008	249,946	189,046	Enzi, Michael B.*	60,631	Rothfuss, Chris	269	128,415 R	75.6%	24.3%	75.7%	24.3
2008S	249,558	183,063	Barrasso, John*	66,202	Carter, Nick	293	116,861 R	73.4%	26.5%	73.4%	26.6
2006	193,136	135,174	Thomas, Craig*	57,671	Groutage, Dale	291	77,503 R	70.0%	29.9%	70.1%	29.9
2002	183,280	133,710	Enzi, Michael B.*	49,570	Corcoran, Joyce Jansa		84,140 R	73.0%	27.0%	73.0%	27.0
2000	213,659	157,622	Thomas, Craig*	47,087	Logan, Mel	8,950	110,535 R	73.8%	22.0%	77.0%	23.0
1996	211,077	114,116	Enzi, Michael B.	89,103	Karpan, Kathy	7,858	25,013 R	54.1%	42.2%	56.2%	43.8
1994	201,710	118,754	Thomas, Craig	79,287	Sullivan, Mike	3,669	39,467 R	58.9%	39.3%	60.0%	40.0
1990	157,632	100,784	Simpson, Alan K.*	56,848	Helling, Kathy		43,936 R	63.9%	36.1%	63.9%	36.1
1988	180,964	91,143	Wallop, Malcolm*	89,821	Vinich, John P.		1,322 R	50.4%	49.6%	50.4%	49.6
1984	186,898	146,373	Simpson, Alan K.*	40,525	Ryan, Victor A.		105,848 R	78.3%	21.7%	78.3%	21.7
1982	167,191	94,725	Wallop, Malcolm*	72,466	McDaniel, Rodger		22,259 R	56.7%	43.3%	56.7%	43.3
1978	133,364	82,908	Simpson, Alan K.	50,456	Whitaker, Raymond B.		32,452 R	62.2%	37.8%	62.2%	37.8
1976	155,368	84,810	Wallop, Malcolm	70,558	McGee, Gale*		14,252 R	54.6%	45.4%	54.6%	45.4
1972	142,067	101,314	Hansen, Clifford P.*	40,753	Vinich, Mike		60,561 R	71.3%	28.7%	71.3%	28.7
1970	120,486	53,279	Wold, John S.	67,207	McGee, Gale*		13,928 D	44.2%	55.8%	44.2%	55.8
1966	122,689	63,548	Hansen, Clifford P.	59,141	Roncalio, Teno		4,407 R	51.8%	48.2%	51.8%	48.2
1964	141,670	65,185	Wold, John S.	76,485	McGee, Gale*		11,300 D	46.0%	54.0%	46.0%	54.0
1962S	119,372	69,043	Simpson, Milward L.	50,329	Hickey, John J.*		18,714 R	57.8%	42.2%	57.8%	42.2
1960	138,550	78,103	Thomson, E. Keith	60,447	Whitaker, Raymond B.		17,656 R	56.4%	43.6%	56.4%	43.6
1958	114,157	56,122	Barrett, Frank A.*	58,035	McGee, Gale		1,913 D	49.2%	50.8%	49.2%	50.8
1954	112,252	54,407	Harrison, William Henry	57,845	O'Mahoney, Joseph C.*		3,438 D	48.5%	51.5%	48.5%	51.5
1952	130,097	67,176	Barrett, Frank A.	62,921	O'Mahoney, Joseph C.*		4,255 R	51.6%	48.4%	51.6%	48.4
1948	101,480	43,527	Robertson, Edward V.*	57,953	Hunt, Lester C.		14,426 D	42.9%	57.1%	42.9%	57.1
1946	81,557	35,714	Henderson, Harry B.	45,843	O'Mahoney, Joseph C.*		10,129 D	43.8%	56.2%	43.8%	56.2

Note: An asterisk (*) denotes incumbent. **The 1962 election and one of the 2008 elections were for short terms to fill a vacancy.

WYOMING

GOVERNOR 2014

2010 Census Population	County	Total Vote	Republican (Mead)	Democratic (Gosar)	Other	Rep.-Dem. Plurality	Total Vote Rep.	Total Vote Dem.	Major Vote Rep.	Major Vote Dem.
36,299	ALBANY	10,331	4,520	4,885	926	365 D	43.8%	47.3%	48.1%	51.9%
11,668	BIG HORN	4,093	2,717	545	831	2,172 R	66.4%	13.3%	83.3%	16.7%
46,133	CAMPBELL	10,592	7,667	1,267	1,658	6,400 R	72.4%	12.0%	85.8%	14.2%
15,885	CARBON	4,539	2,948	1,164	427	1,784 R	64.9%	25.6%	71.7%	28.3%
13,833	CONVERSE	4,200	2,572	823	805	1,749 R	61.2%	19.6%	75.8%	24.2%
7,083	CROOK	2,755	1,970	304	481	1,666 R	71.5%	11.0%	86.6%	13.4%
40,123	FREMONT	12,212	6,655	4,126	1,431	2,529 R	54.5%	33.8%	61.7%	38.3%
13,249	GOSHEN	4,252	2,494	1,066	692	1,428 R	58.7%	25.1%	70.1%	29.9%
4,812	HOT SPRINGS	2,008	1,155	536	317	619 R	57.5%	26.7%	68.3%	31.7%
8,569	JOHNSON	3,288	2,179	812	297	1,367 R	66.3%	24.7%	72.9%	27.1%
91,738	LARAMIE	25,803	14,270	7,780	3,753	6,490 R	55.3%	30.2%	64.7%	35.3%
18,106	LINCOLN	5,767	4,045	867	855	3,178 R	70.1%	15.0%	82.3%	17.7%
75,450	NATRONA	21,070	12,454	5,796	2,820	6,658 R	59.1%	27.5%	68.2%	31.8%
2,484	NIOBRARA	1,036	579	167	290	412 R	55.9%	16.1%	77.6%	22.4%
28,205	PARK	9,461	6,163	1,518	1,780	4,645 R	65.1%	16.0%	80.2%	19.8%
8,667	PLATTE	3,524	1,857	915	752	942 R	52.7%	26.0%	67.0%	33.0%
29,116	SHERIDAN	9,529	6,400	2,311	818	4,089 R	67.2%	24.3%	73.5%	26.5%
10,247	SUBLETTE	3,209	1,757	968	484	789 R	54.8%	30.2%	64.5%	35.5%
43,806	SWEETWATER	11,277	6,431	3,857	989	2,574 R	57.0%	34.2%	62.5%	37.5%
21,294	TETON	7,938	3,998	3,573	367	425 R	50.4%	45.0%	52.8%	47.2%
21,118	UINTA	5,693	3,251	1,620	822	1,631 R	57.1%	28.5%	66.7%	33.3%
8,533	WASHAKIE	2,843	2,041	500	302	1,541 R	71.8%	17.6%	80.3%	19.7%
7,208	WESTON	2,457	1,577	352	528	1,225 R	64.2%	14.3%	81.8%	18.2%
563,626	TOTAL	167,877	99,700	45,752	22,425	53,948 R	59.4%	27.3%	68.5%	31.5%

WYOMING

SENATOR 2014

2010 Census Population	County	Total Vote	Republican (Enzi)	Democratic (Hardy)	Other	Rep.-Dem. Plurality	Total Vote Rep.	Total Vote Dem.	Major Vote Rep.	Major Vote Dem.
36,299	ALBANY	10,263	5,672	3,276	1,315	2,396 R	55.3%	31.9%	63.4%	36.6%
11,668	BIG HORN	4,151	3,398	351	402	3,047 R	81.9%	8.5%	90.6%	9.4%
46,133	CAMPBELL	10,651	8,903	716	1,032	8,187 R	83.6%	6.7%	92.6%	7.4%
15,885	CARBON	4,569	3,356	820	393	2,536 R	73.5%	17.9%	80.4%	19.6%
13,833	CONVERSE	4,237	3,255	384	598	2,871 R	76.8%	9.1%	89.4%	10.6%
7,083	CROOK	2,790	2,369	196	225	2,173 R	84.9%	7.0%	92.4%	7.6%
40,123	FREMONT	12,332	8,629	2,331	1,372	6,298 R	70.0%	18.9%	78.7%	21.3%
13,249	GOSHEN	4,317	3,302	511	504	2,791 R	76.5%	11.8%	86.6%	13.4%
4,812	HOT SPRINGS	2,035	1,529	190	316	1,339 R	75.1%	9.3%	88.9%	11.1%
8,569	JOHNSON	3,283	2,735	320	228	2,415 R	83.3%	9.7%	89.5%	10.5%
91,738	LARAMIE	25,863	17,647	5,560	2,656	12,087 R	68.2%	21.5%	76.0%	24.0%
18,106	LINCOLN	5,800	4,758	580	462	4,178 R	82.0%	10.0%	89.1%	10.9%
75,450	NATRONA	21,075	14,361	3,387	3,327	10,974 R	68.1%	16.1%	80.9%	19.1%
2,484	NIOBRARA	1,051	875	84	92	791 R	83.3%	8.0%	91.2%	8.8%
28,205	PARK	9,550	7,695	1,066	789	6,629 R	80.6%	11.2%	87.8%	12.2%
8,667	PLATTE	3,549	2,625	552	372	2,073 R	74.0%	15.6%	82.6%	17.4%
29,116	SHERIDAN	9,551	7,307	1,474	770	5,833 R	76.5%	15.4%	83.2%	16.8%
10,247	SUBLETTE	3,185	2,546	416	223	2,130 R	79.9%	13.1%	86.0%	14.0%
43,806	SWEETWATER	11,257	7,656	2,711	890	4,945 R	68.0%	24.1%	73.8%	26.2%
21,294	TETON	7,827	4,261	3,103	463	1,158 R	54.4%	39.6%	57.9%	42.1%

WYOMING

SENATOR 2014

2010 Census Population	County	Total Vote	Republican (Enzi)	Democratic (Hardy)	Other	Rep.-Dem. Plurality	Percentage Total Vote Rep.	Dem.	Major Vote Rep.	Dem
21,118	UINTA	5,716	4,368	892	456	3,476 R	76.4%	15.6%	83.0%	17.0
8,533	WASHAKIE	2,853	2,280	263	310	2,017 R	79.9%	9.2%	89.7%	10.
7,208	WESTON	2,485	2,027	194	264	1,833 R	81.6%	7.8%	91.3%	8.
563,626	TOTAL	168,390	121,554	29,377	17,459	92,177 R	72.2%	17.4%	80.5%	19.

WYOMING

HOUSE OF REPRESENTATIVES

CD	Year	Total Vote	Republican Vote	Republican Candidate	Democratic Vote	Democratic Candidate	Other Vote	Rep.-Dem. Plurality	Total Vote Rep.	Dem.	Major Vote Rep.	Dem
At Large	2014	165,100	113,038	LUMMIS, CYNTHIA M.*	37,803	GRAYSON, RICHARD	14,259	75,235 R	68.5%	22.9%	74.9%	25.1
At Large	2012	241,621	166,452	LUMMIS, CYNTHIA M.*	57,573	HENRICHSEN, CHRIS	17,596	108,879 R	68.9%	23.8%	74.3%	25.7
At Large	2010	186,969	131,661	LUMMIS, CYNTHIA M.*	45,768	WENDT, DAVID	9,540	85,893 R	70.4%	24.5%	74.2%	25.8
At Large	2008	249,395	131,244	LUMMIS, CYNTHIA M.	106,758	TRAUNER, GARY	11,393	24,486 R	52.6%	42.8%	55.1%	44.9
At Large	2006	193,369	93,336	CUBIN, BARBARA*	92,324	TRAUNER, GARY	7,709	1,012 R	48.3%	47.7%	50.3%	49.7
At Large	2004	239,034	132,107	CUBIN, BARBARA*	99,989	LADD, TED	6,938	32,118 R	55.3%	41.8%	56.9%	43.1
At Large	2002	182,152	110,229	CUBIN, BARBARA*	65,961	AKIN, RON	5,962	44,268 R	60.5%	36.2%	62.6%	37.4
At Large	2000	212,312	141,848	CUBIN, BARBARA*	60,638	GREEN, MICHAEL ALLEN	9,826	81,210 R	66.8%	28.6%	70.1%	29.9
At Large	1998	174,219	100,687	CUBIN, BARBARA*	67,399	FARRIS, SCOTT	6,133	33,288 R	57.8%	38.7%	59.9%	40.1
At Large	1996	209,983	116,004	CUBIN, BARBARA*	85,724	MAXFIELD, PETE	8,255	30,280 R	55.2%	40.8%	57.5%	42.5
At Large	1994	196,197	104,426	CUBIN, BARBARA	81,022	SCHUSTER, BOB	10,749	23,404 R	53.2%	41.3%	56.3%	43.7
At Large	1992	196,977	113,882	THOMAS, CRAIG*	77,418	HERSCHLER, JON	5,677	36,464 R	57.8%	39.3%	59.5%	40.5
At Large	1990	158,055	87,078	THOMAS, CRAIG	70,977	MAXFIELD, PETE		16,101 R	55.1%	44.9%	55.1%	44.9
At Large	1988	177,651	118,350	CHENEY, RICHARD*	56,527	SHARRATT, BRYAN	2,774	61,823 R	66.6%	31.8%	67.7%	32.3
At Large	1986	159,787	111,007	CHENEY, RICHARD*	48,780	GILMORE, RICK		62,227 R	69.5%	30.5%	69.5%	30.5
At Large	1984	187,904	138,234	CHENEY, RICHARD*	45,857	MCFADDEN, HUGH B.	3,813	92,377 R	73.6%	24.4%	75.1%	24.9
At Large	1982	159,277	113,236	CHENEY, RICHARD*	46,041	HOMMEL, THEODORE H.		67,195 R	71.1%	28.9%	71.1%	28.9
At Large	1980	169,699	116,361	CHENEY, RICHARD*	53,338	ROGERS, JIM		63,023 R	68.6%	31.4%	68.6%	31.4
At Large	1978	129,377	75,855	CHENEY, RICHARD	53,522	BAGLEY, BILL		22,333 R	58.6%	41.4%	58.6%	41.4
At Large	1976	151,868	66,147	HART, LARRY	85,721	RONCALIO, TENO*		19,574 D	43.6%	56.4%	43.6%	56.4
At Large	1974	126,933	57,499	STROOCK, TOM	69,434	RONCALIO, TENO*		11,935 D	45.3%	54.7%	45.3%	54.7
At Large	1972	146,299	70,667	KIDD, WILLIAM	75,632	RONCALIO, TENO*		4,965 D	48.3%	51.7%	48.3%	51.7
At Large	1970	116,304	57,848	ROBERTS, HARRY	58,456	RONCALIO, TENO*		608 D	49.7%	50.3%	49.7%	50.3
At Large	1968	123,313	77,363	WOLD, JOHN S.	45,950	LINFORD, VELMA		31,413 R	62.7%	37.3%	62.7%	37.3
At Large	1966	120,426	62,984	HARRISON, WILLIAM HENRY	57,442	CHRISTIAN, AL		5,542 R	52.3%	47.7%	52.3%	47.7
At Large	1964	139,175	68,482	HARRISON, WILLIAM HENRY	70,693	RONCALIO, TENO*		2,211 D	49.2%	50.8%	49.2%	50.8
At Large	1962	116,474	71,489	HARRISON, WILLIAM HENRY*	44,985	MANKUS, LOUIS A.		26,504 R	61.4%	38.6%	61.4%	38.6
At Large	1960	134,331	70,241	HARRISON, WILLIAM HENRY	64,090	ARMSTRONG, HEPBURN T.		6,151 R	52.3%	47.7%	52.3%	47.7
At Large	1958	111,780	59,894	THOMSON, E. KEITH*	51,886	WHITAKER, RAYMOND B.		8,008 R	53.6%	46.4%	53.6%	46.4
At Large	1956	120,128	69,903	THOMSON, E. KEITH*	50,225	O'CALLAGHAN, JERRY A.		19,678 R	58.2%	41.8%	58.2%	41.8
At Large	1954	108,771	61,111	THOMSON, E. KEITH	47,660	TULLY, SAM		13,451 R	56.2%	43.8%	56.2%	43.8
At Large	1952	126,720	76,161	HARRISON, WILLIAM HENRY*	50,559	ROSS, ROBERT R. JR.		25,602 R	60.1%	39.9%	60.1%	39.9
At Large	1950	93,348	50,865	HARRISON, WILLIAM HENRY	42,483	CLARK, JOHN B.		8,382 R	54.5%	45.5%	54.5%	45.5
At Large	1948	97,464	50,218	BARRETT, FRANK A.*	47,246	FLANNERY, L. G.		2,972 R	51.5%	48.5%	51.5%	48.5
At Large	1946	79,438	44,482	BARRETT, FRANK A.*	34,956	MCINTYRE, JOHN J.		9,526 R	56.0%	44.0%	56.0%	44.0

Note: An asterisk (*) denotes incumbent.

WYOMING

GENERAL AND PRIMARY ELECTIONS

2014 GENERAL ELECTIONS: OTHER VOTES

Governor	Other vote was 9,895 Independent (Don Wills), 8,490 scattered write-in, 4,040 Libertarian (Dee Cozzens)
Senate	Other vote was 13,311 Independent (Curt Gottshall), 3,677 Libertarian (Joseph S. "Joe" Porambo), 471 scattered write-in
House	Other vote was:
CD At Large	7,112 Libertarian (Richard Brubaker), 6,749 Constitution (Daniel Clyde Cummings), 398 scattered write-in

2014 PRIMARY ELECTIONS: SUPPLEMENTARY INFORMATION

Primary	August 19, 2014	**Registration** (as of August 19, 2014)	259,113	Republican	168,957
				Democratic	52,681
				Libertatian	1,939
				Constitution	322
				Other	111
				Unaffiliated	35,103

Primary Type   Semi-Open—Only registered Democrats and Republicans could vote in their party's primary, although on primary day any new voter could register with the party of his or her choice and any previously registered voter could participate in another party's primary by changing his or her registration to that party.

	REPUBLICAN PRIMARIES			DEMOCRATIC PRIMARIES		
Senator	Enzi, Michael B.*	77,965	81.8%	Hardy, Charles E. "Charlie"	7,200	47.7%
	Miller, Bryan E.	9,330	9.8%	Wilde, Rex	3,012	20.0%
	Gregory, James "Coaltrain"	3,740	3.9%	Hamburg, Al	2,988	19.8%
	Bleming, Thomas	2,504	2.6%	Bryk, William	1,670	11.1%
	Clifton, Arthur Bruce	1,403	1.5%	Write-In	216	1.4%
	Write-In	346	0.4%			
	TOTAL	*95,288*		*TOTAL*	*15,086*	
Governor	Mead, Matt*	53,673	54.8%	Gosar, Peter	15,289	96.8%
	Haynes, Taylor H.	31,532	32.2%	Write-In	510	3.2%
	Hill, Cindy	12,464	12.7%			
	Write-In	215	0.2%			
	TOTAL	*97,884*		*TOTAL*	*15,799*	
Congressional At Large	Lummis, Cynthia M.*	70,918	75.9%	Grayson, Richard	14,209	98.7%
	Senteney, Jason Adam	22,251	23.8%	Write-In	190	1.3%
	Write-In	274	0.3%			
	TOTAL	*93,443*		*TOTAL*	*14,399*	

Note: An asterisk (*) denotes incumbent.

CQ Press, an imprint of SAGE, is the leading publisher of books, periodicals, and electronic products on American government and international affairs. CQ Press consistently ranks among the top commercial publishers in terms of quality, as evidenced by the numerous awards its products have won over the years. CQ Press owes its existence to Nelson Poynter, former publisher of the St. Petersburg Times, and his wife Henrietta, with whom he founded Congressional Quarterly in 1945. Poynter established CQ with the mission of promoting democracy through education and in 1975 founded the Modern Media Institute, renamed The Poynter Institute for Media Studies after his death. The Poynter Institute (www.poynter.org) is a nonprofit organization dedicated to training journalists and media leaders.

In 2008, CQ Press was acquired by SAGE, a leading international publisher of journals, books, and electronic media for academic, educational, and professional markets. Since 1965, SAGE has helped inform and educate a global community of scholars, practitioners, researchers, and students spanning a wide range of subject areas, including business, humanities, social sciences, and science, technology, and medicine. A privately owned corporation, SAGE has offices in Los Angeles, London, New Delhi, and Singapore, in addition to the Washington DC office of CQ Press.